Colossus Reborn

Colossus Reborn

The Red Army at War, 1941–1943

David M. Glantz

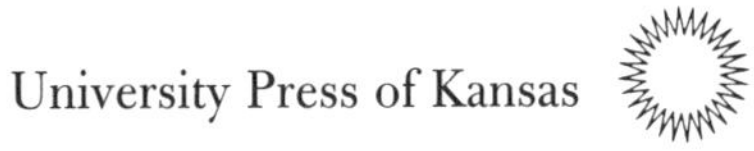

Published by the University Press of Kansas (Lawrence, Kansas 66049), which was organized by the Kansas Board of Regents and is operated and funded by Emporia State University, Fort Hays State University, Kansas State University, Pittsburg State University, the University of Kansas, and Wichita State University

Library of Congress Cataloging-in-Publication Data

Glantz, David M.
Colossus reborn : the Red Army at war : 1941–1943 / David M. Glantz.
p. cm.—(Modern war studies)
Includes bibliographical references and index.
ISBN 0-7006-1353-6 (cloth : alk. paper)
1. Soviet Union. Raboche-Krest' ëiianskëaiia Krasnëaiia Armiëiia—History—World War, 1939–1945. 2. World War, 1939–1945—Campaigns—Eastern Front. 3. Soviet Union—History, Military. I. Title. II. Series.
D764.G5558 2005
940.54'1247—dc22 2004013594

British Library Cataloguing-in-Publication Data is available.

Printed in the United States of America

10 9 8 7 6 5 4 3 2 1

The paper used in this publication meets the minimum requirements of the American National Standard for Permanence of Paper for Printed Library Materials Z39.48-1984.

Contents

List of Maps, Tables, and Illustrations ix

Introduction xv

PART I. THE RED ARMY AT WAR, 1941–1943

1. The First Period of the War, 22 June 1941 to 18 November 1942 3

   The Summer–Fall Campaign, 22 June to 5 December 1941 5
   The Winter Campaign, December 1941 to April 1942 17
   The Summer–Fall Campaign, May–November 1942 25

2. The Second Period of the War, 1943 37

   The Winter Campaign, November 1942 to April 1943 37
   The Summer–Fall Campaign, June–December 1943 48
   The Impact of War, 1941–1943 59

3. Soviet Military Art 63

   Military Strategy 63
   Strategic Defensive Operations 69
   Strategic Offensive Operations 82
   Strategic Reserves 96
   Operational Art 100
   Tactics 114
   Conclusions 120

PART II. THE FORCE

4. Strength and Major Components 135

   The Armed Forces 135
   The Field Forces 139
   PVO Strany (National Air Defense Forces) 147
   The *Stavka* Reserve 149
   Military Districts and Nonoperating Fronts 152

5. The Shadow Army: NKVD Forces 157

   Missions and Size 157
   Structure in 1941 158
   Wartime Evolution 164

6. Rifle and Airborne Forces 178

Rifle Forces 179
Airborne Forces 186
Operating Strengths 189
Infantry (Rifle) Weaponry 191

7. Tank, Mechanized, and Cavalry Forces 216

Tank and Mechanized Forces 218
Cavalry Forces 237
Operating Strengths 241
Armored Vehicles and Trucks 246

8. Artillery and Air Forces 285

Artillery 285
Air Forces 311
Artillery and Aircraft 319

9. Engineer, Signal, Chemical, Railroad, Auto-Transport and Road, and Construction Forces 333

Engineer (Sapper) Forces 333
Signal Forces 343
Chemical Forces 348
Railroad Forces 351
Auto-Transport and Road Construction and Repair Forces 353
Construction Troops 356
Engineer, Signal, and Chemical Weapons 360

PART III. THE LEADERS AND THE LED

10. Strategic Leadership and Control Organs 369

Strategic Leadership 369
Control Organs 378
Personalities 385

11. Central Military Administration 403

People's Commissariat of Defense (NKO) 403
Internal Security Forces (NKVD) 446
Red Army General Staff (GShKA) 449

12. The Officer Corps and Command Cadre 466

From Crisis to Recovery 466
Command Cadre 476

13. The Red Army Soldier 536

Conscription 536
Ethnicity (Non-Slavic Soldiers) 547
Women in the Red Army 551

The Soldier's Life 554
Order and Discipline 564
Motivation and Morale 582
Conclusions 588

14. Conclusions 609

The Course of War 609
The Forgotten War 611
The Force 614
The Leaders 615
The Led 619
The Costs of War 621

Notes *631*

Selected Bibliography *731*

Index *755*

Maps, Tables, and Illustrations

Maps

The Summer–Fall Campaign, 22 June to 30 September 1941 8
The Summer–Fall Campaign, 1 October to 5 December 1941 9
The Winter Campaign, December 1941 to April 1942 19
The Summer–Fall Campaign, May–October 1942 28
The Winter Campaign, November 1942 to April 1943 39
The Summer–Fall Campaign, June–December 1943 52

Tables

Red Army Strategic Defensive Operations during 1941 125
Red Army Strategic Defensive Operations during 1942 125
Red Army Strategic Defensive Operations during 1943 126
Comparison of the Strategic Defensive Operations the *Stavka* Conducted at Moscow, Stalingrad, and Kursk 126
Red Army Defense Lines, 1941 127
Red Army Strategic Offensive (Counteroffensive) Operations during the Summer–Fall Campaign of 1941 and the Winter Campaign of 1941–42 127
Red Army Strategic Offensive (Counteroffensive) Operations during the Winter Campaign of 1942–43 and the Summer–Fall Campaign of 1943 128
Comparative Scale of Red Army Strategic Offensive (Counteroffensive) Operations, 1941–1942 130
Comparative Scale of Red Army Strategic Offensive (Counteroffensive) Operations, 1942–1943 131
Red Army Field Strength (in Personnel), 1941–1943 155
Red Army Field Strength (in Formations and Units), 1941–1943 156
NKVD Border Guards Forces, 22 June 1941 171
NKVD Operational Forces, 22 June 1941 174
Subordination of NKVD Operational Forces to Red Army *Fronts*, 23 June 1941 175

NKVD Security Forces, 22 June 1941 176
NKVD Convoy Security Forces, August 1942 176
Planned NKVD Deployment of NKVD Rear Area Security Forces, June 1941 177
Composition of the Separate NKVD Army (Later the 70th Army) 177
Composition of the Red Army Rifle Corps, June 1941 to June 1944 194
Relative Strength of Red Army Rifle Divisions, 5 April 1941 to 18 December 1944 195
Relative Strength of Various Types of Red Army Rifle Brigades, October 1941 to July 1943 197
Formation of Red Army Infantry Brigades, 1940–1942 198
Formation of Red Army Naval Rifle Brigades, 1941 and 1942 199
Relative Strength of Red Army Machine Gun–Artillery Battalions, 1942–1943 200
Personnel Strength of Selected Red Army Field Armies, Rifle Corps, Rifle Divisions, and Rifle Brigades, 22 June 1941 to 1 January 1944 201
Relative Strength of Red Army Tank Brigades, 1941–1943 252
Relative Strength of Red Army Motorized Rifle Brigades, 1942–1943 253
Composition and Strength of Red Army Tank Regiments, September 1942 to 31 December 1943 253
Relative Strength of Red Army Tank Corps, April 1942 to 1 January 1944 254
Initial Formation of Red Army Tank Corps, March–December 1942 256
Formation and Composition of Red Army Mechanized Corps, September–December 1942 256
Composition and Relative Strength of Red Army Mechanized Corps, September 1942 to 1 January 1944 257
Composition and Relative Strength of Red Army Mechanized Brigades, September 1942 to 1 January 1944 258
Formation of Red Army Tank Armies, May–September 1942 259
Formation or Reorganization of Red Army Tank Armies, January–July 1943 260
Quantity of Tank and Mechanized Corps Assigned to Red Army Tank Armies during Offensive Operations, 1 January 1943 to May 1945 261
Minimum and Maximum Personnel and Weapons Strength of Red Army Tank Armies during Offensive Operations, 1943–1945 261
Average Strength of Red Army Tank Armies, 1943–1945 261
Relative Strength of Red Army Cavalry Corps, 22 June 1941 to 1943 262
Relative Strength of Red Army Cavalry Divisions, 1941–1943 263
Relative Strength of Red Army Mechanized Corps, 22 June 1941 264

Distribution of Modern Tanks in Red Army Mechanized Corps, 22 June 1941 264
Tank Strength of Selected Red Army Tank Armies, Tank and Mechanized Corps, Tank Divisions, Separate Tank and Mechanized Brigades, and Separate Tank Regiments, 22 June 1941 to 1 January 1944 265
Personnel Strength of Selected Red Army Cavalry Corps and Divisions, 22 June 1941 to 31 December 1943 283
Quantity and Authorized Strength of RGK Artillery Regiments and Separate Battalions, 22 June 1941 324
Quantity and Location of RVGK Antitank Artillery Regiments Formed in 1941 325
Quantity and Distribution of RVGK Tank Destroyer Artillery Regiments, 15 November 1942 (by Strategic Axis and Type) 326
Distribution of RVGK Separate Tank Destroyer Artillery Regiments, 1 January 1943 (by Type) 328
Distribution of RVGK Tank Destroyer Artillery Brigades and Separate Tank Destroyer Artillery Regiments and Battalions, 31 December 1943 (by Type) 329
Composition and Subordination of Red Army Air Armies Formed from May to November 1942 331
Formation, Composition, Missions, and Ultimate Disposition of Sapper Armies, 1941–1942 366
Deputy Supreme Commander and Wartime Red Army Branch Chiefs 462
Organization of the Red Army General Staff, 22 June 1941 to 1 January 1944 463
Organization of the General Staff's Main Intelligence Directorate (GRU), 20 February 1942 464
Structure of the General Staff's Intelligence Directorate (RU) and Subordinate Intelligence Departments (ROs), 1 May 1943 464
Red Army Officers Killed or Missing in Action, 1941–1945 535
Expansion of the Red Army, 1939–1941 590
Age (Year Group) of Serving Soldiers and Ethnic Composition of Selected Red Army Divisions, 1941–1945 591
Red Army National Military Formation Strength, 1 January 1938 598
Red Army National Military Formation Strength, 22 June 1941 to 1943 600
Red Army National Military Formation Strength, 1941–1945 603
The Wartime Red Army's Ethnic Composition and Death Rate (by Nationality) 604

The Red Army Soldier's Authorized Daily Food Ration, 22 September 1941 605
Identified Red Army Penal Subunits and Their Subordination, 1942–1945 607
Red Army and Navy Personnel Losses, 1941–1943 624
German High Command (OKW) Records of Red Army Soldiers in Captivity, 1942–1944 625
Red Army Weapons Losses in Combat, 1941–1943 626

ILLUSTRATIONS

Following page 62:
Red Army troops assembling in Red Square (1941)
Red Army propaganda poster, "Under the Banner of Lenin, Forward to Victory!" (1941)
Red Army propaganda poster, "Pincers in pincers" (Moscow, 1941)
Red Army propaganda poster, "We defend the Motherland Moscow" (1941)
Tanks on the attack (1941)
Tanks and infantry in the assault
Infantry in the assault
Regimental artillery deploying for action
Planning an attack
The carnage at Prokhorovka

Following page 332:
Infantry wielding PPSh submachine guns
PTRD 14.5mm antitank rifles
PM-1910 7.62mm heavy machine gun
45mm antitank gun
T-26 light tank
T-35 heavy tank
T-60 light tank
T-70 light tank
T-34 medium tank (1943)
KV-1S heavy tank
KV-2 heavy tank with T-34 medium tank (1940) on right
British Churchill Lend-Lease tank
American M-3 Grant Lend-Lease tank
SU-76 self-propelled gun
SU-152 self-propelled gun
76mm field guns
152mm ML-20 howitzers

37mm antiaircraft guns
Katiusha multiple-rocket launchers
I-16 *Rata* fighter
LaGG-3 fighter
Il-2 *Sturmovik* assault
MiG-3 fighters
Pe-2 bomber
Pe-8 (TB-7) bomber

Following page 402:
I. V. Stalin
G. K. Zhukov
A. M. Vasilevsky
B. M. Shaposhnikov
A. I. Antonov
A. A. Novikov
N. N. Voronov (center)
L. A. Govorov
N. G. Kuznetsov
L. Z. Mekhlis

Following page 608:
S. M. Budenny
K. E. Voroshilov
S. K. Timoshenko
F. I. Kuznetsov
D. G. Pavlov
M. P. Kirponis
M. M. Popov
A. I. Eremenko
I. S. Konev (right)
K. K. Rokossovsky
N. F. Vatutin
R. Ia. Malinovsky
I. Kh. Bagramian
V. D. Sokolovsky
I. V. Tiulenev
F. I. Tolbukhin
I. E. Petrov (far left)
F. I. Golikov
M. A. Purkaev
P. A. Kurochkin

K. A. Meretskov
V. A. Frolov
P. S. Rybalko
M. E. Katukov
S. I. Bogdanov
P. A. Rotmistrov (center)

Introduction

Suddenly and without warning, over 3 million Axis forces lunged across the Soviet state border early on the morning of 22 June 1941, commencing Hitler's infamous Operation Barbarossa. Spearheaded by four powerful panzer groups and protected by an impenetrable curtain of air support, the seemingly invincible *Wehrmacht* advanced from the Soviet Union's western borders to the immediate outskirts of Leningrad, Moscow, and Rostov in the shockingly brief period of less than six months. Faced with this sudden, deep, and relentless German advance, the Red Army and Soviet state were forced to fight desperately for their very survival.

The ensuing struggle, which encompassed a region totaling roughly 600,000 square miles, lasted for almost four years before the Red Army triumphantly raised the Soviet flag over the ruins of Hitler's Reich's Chancellery in Berlin in late April 1945. The Soviet Union's self-proclaimed "Great Patriotic War" was one of unprecedented brutality. It was a veritable *"Kulturkampf,"* a war to the death between two cultures, which killed as many as 35 million Russian soldiers and civilians, almost 4 million German soldiers, and countless German civilians and inflicted unimaginable damage and destruction upon the population and institutional infrastructure of most of Central and Eastern Europe.

By the time this deadly conflict ended on 9 May 1945, the Soviet Union and its Red Army had occupied and dominated the bulk of Central and Eastern Europe. Within three years after victory, an Iron Curtain had descended across Europe, dividing the continent into opposing camps for over 40 years. More important still, the searing effect of this terrible war on the Russian soul endured for generations, shaping the development of the postwar Soviet Union and contributing to its demise in 1991.

Ironically, despite its massive scale, scope, cost, and global impact, the Soviet Union's Great Patriotic War remains in large part obscure and imperfectly understood by Westerners and Russians alike. Worse still, this obscurity and misunderstanding has perverted the history of World War II overall by masking the Red Army's and Soviet state's contributions to ultimate Allied victory.

Those in the West who understand anything at all about the Soviet-German war regard it as a mysterious and brutal four-year struggle between Europe's bitterest political enemies and its largest and most formidable armies. During this struggle the *Wehrmacht* and Red Army waged war over territory whose sheer size, physical complexity, and severe climatic conditions made the conflict appear to consist of a series of seamless offensives punctuated by months of stagnant combat and periodic dramatic battles of immense scale, such as the Battles of Moscow, Stalingrad, Kursk, Belorussia, and Berlin. The paucity of detailed information in English about the Soviet-German war has reinforced the natural American (and Western) penchant for viewing it as a mere backdrop for more dramatic and significant battles in western theaters, such as El Alamein, Salerno, Anzio, Normandy, and the Bulge.

This distorted layman's view of the war so prevalent in the West is understandable since most histories of the conflict have been based largely on German sources, which routinely describe the war as a struggle against a faceless and formless enemy whose chief attributes were its army's immense size and limitless supply of expendable human resources. Against this pale mosaic of four years of combat, only truly sensational events stand out.

Even those better informed share in these common misperceptions. Although they know about the Battles of Moscow, Stalingrad, and Kursk, von Manstein's counterstroke in the Donbas and at Khar'kov, the fights in the Cherkassy Pocket and at Kamenets-Podolsk, the collapse of Army Group Center, and Soviet perfidy at the gates of Warsaw, the very terms they use to describe these struggles, as well as their persistent reference to "the War on the Eastern Front," indicate that their understanding is based primarily on German sources. This lack of sufficient knowledge and understanding of the Soviet-German war precludes an adequate understanding of the war's importance and regional and global significance within the context of World War II as a whole.

Who, then, is at fault for promoting this unbalanced view of the war? Certainly Western historians share in the blame, although most had no choice but to rely on German sources, the only credible sources available. Ethnocentrism, which conditions a people to appreciate only what they have themselves experienced, has also helped produce this unbalanced view of the war on both sides. More important still, however, is the collective failure of Soviet and, more recently, Russian historians to provide Western (and Russian) readers and scholars with a credible account of the war. In this case, ideology, political motivations, and persistent shibboleths born of the Cold War have combined to inhibit the work and to warp the perceptions of many Soviet and Russian historians.

Although Soviet and Russian historians have written many detailed, scholarly, and surprisingly accurate studies of the war and wartime battles and operations, too often government censors have forced them to either skirt or ignore facts and events considered embarrassing to the state, its army, or its most famous generals. General works on the war most accessible to Western audiences tend to be the most biased, the most highly politicized, and the least accurate, and until quite recently official state organs routinely vetted even the most scholarly of these books for political and ideological reasons. Even now, over ten years after the fall of the Soviet Union, political pressure and limited archival access prevent Russian historians from researching or revealing many events subject to censorship in the past.

These sad realities have undercut the credibility of Soviet and Russian historical works, permitting German-based histories and interpretation to prevail and, coincidentally, undermining the credibility of those few Western writers who have incorporated Soviet historical materials into their accounts of the war. These stark realities explain why, even today, sensational, unfair, and wildly inaccurate accounts of certain aspects of the war so attract the Western reading public and why debates still rage concerning the war's direction, course, and significance.

The trilogy of books on the Red Army at war, of which this volume is a part, is designed to help set the record straight. The first volume in this series, *Stumbling Colossus: The Red Army on the Eve of World War* (1998), examined the Red Army on the threshold of the world war and concluded that, although colossal in size and ambition, as the subsequent course of war indicated, in June 1941 the Red Army was a colossus with feet of clay. Yet, despite the unprecedented and catastrophic defeats it suffered during 1941 and 1942, the Red Army rose like a phoenix from the ashes to inflict equally unprecedented defeats on the vaunted *Wehrmacht* at Stalingrad during November 1942 and at Kursk during July and August 1943. After the Battle of Kursk, the Red Army then embarked on a victorious march that ultimately propelled it to victory over Nazi Germany at Berlin during April and May 1945.

Colossus Reborn: The Red Army at War, 1941–1943, the second volume in this trilogy, investigates in detail the vitally important and mutually related issues of the "forgotten war" and the wartime Red Army from an institutional perspective. Its first part, "The Red Army at War," surveys the course of the war operationally to reveal the war's "forgotten battles," that is, roughly 40 percent of the war's battles and operations, which, for various reasons, Soviet and Russian historians have downplayed, ignored, or covered up in order to preserve reputations and national pride. This part also identifies and draws fresh conclusions regarding many of the major controversies associated with the first 30 months of the war.

The book's second and third parts examine in detail the Red Army as an evolving institution led and manned by flesh and blood human beings. Exploiting a wealth of newly released Soviet (Russian) archival materials, the second part, "The Force," exposes the multifaceted Red Army in terms of its size and strength and the configuration of its massive and complex force structure. Within this context, it also describes the army's evolving combat techniques, its immensely complex command, control, and administrative structure, and its educational and training system and methods.

The third part, "The Leaders and the Led," exploits an expanding wealth of recently released memoirs and archival materials concerning the men who led the Red Army from 1941 through 1943 and managed its transformation from a stumbling colossus into a formidable and ultimately victorious fighting force. Finally, and no less important, this part presents the perspectives of the Red Army's soldiers, Slav and non-Slav, men and women alike, who fought in the army's ranks and either perished or survived in a war whose ferocity and brutality knew few bounds.

While lifting the veil on the Red Army's "forgotten battles," *Colossus Reborn* also exposes a wide variety of Soviet military forces never before examined. These include the Soviet Union's "shadow army," its formidable NKVD forces, and the Red Army's vital but hitherto totally obscure engineer (sapper), railroad, auto-transport, and construction forces, the approximately 1 million women who served in Red Army uniforms during wartime, and the Soviet High Command's ubiquitous and dreaded penal units and blocking detachments, which ensured draconian discipline within the army's ranks during the war. In addition, the book offers a detailed and unprecedented assessment of the evolution of the Red Army's most important command and political cadre during wartime.

While placing a human face on the Red Army's command and political cadre, this book paints a unique and equally unprecedented picture of the stark realities of the soldiers' lives in the Red Army based on both recently released archival documents and the personal testimony of individual soldiers. This picture includes a detailed description of the Red Army's pervasive political control mechanisms and the severe disciplinary and punitive regime under which the soldier existed, the austere living conditions the soldiers endured while at the front and in the rear, and the forces that motivated the soldiers to fight and, in some cases, survive and prevail.

The book's selected bibliography complements the book's exhaustive textual notes, identifying the most important formerly classified source materials the Russian government has yet released, "classic" works about the wartime Red Army, recently released collections of Soviet archival materials on Red Army institutions, specific military operations, and other topics associated with the war as a whole, and newly published memoir materials.

Finally, those who would like a richer and much more complete documentary and statistical foundation for the presentation in this book are encouraged to secure a copy of *Companion to Colossus Reborn,* which provides key documents relating to the everyday lives of the army's soldiers, a full roster of the Red Army's senior command cadre during wartime, a description of the army's weaponry and equipment during the war, and an exhaustive listing of the Red Army's and NKVD's order of battle at six crucial points during the period from 22 June 1941 through 31 December 1943.

In addition to expressing my thanks to the current Russian government for releasing and publishing a steady and growing stream of vital archival materials concerning the war, I reserve my special thanks for those Red Army veterans of the war who are now sharing their candid but often painful recollections of a struggle they were indeed fortunate to survive.

PART I

THE RED ARMY AT WAR, 1941–1943

CHAPTER 1

The First Period of the War, 22 June 1941 to 18 November 1942

The Soviet-German war, commonly referred to as the War on the German Eastern Front, lasted from 22 June 1941 through 9 May 1945, slightly less than four years. For the purpose of studying and analyzing the war, Soviet and Russian military theorists and historians have since war's end subdivided the prolonged conflict into three distinct periods, according to the overall fortunes of war and the strategic nature of military operations.[1] In turn, these theorists and historians have subdivided each wartime period into several distinct campaigns, each of which occurred during one or more seasons of the year.

According to this construct, the first period of the war lasted from Hitler's initiation of German Operation Barbarossa, on 22 June 1941, through 18 November 1942, the precise date that German Operation *Blau* (Blue), the *Wehrmacht's* advance to Stalingrad, ended. This period, which lasted just short of 18 months, encompassed Hitler's two most famous and spectacular strategic offensives, Operation Barbarossa in 1941 and Operation *Blau* in 1942. Even though the Red Army was able to halt the *Wehrmacht's* advance on Leningrad, Moscow, and Rostov in December 1941, albeit with tremendous exertions and at staggering human and materiel cost, and was able to organize a strategic offensive of its own in the winter of 1941–42, throughout the first period of the war the strategic initiative remained predominantly in German hands. The *Wehrmacht's* tactical and operational military skills far exceeded those of the Red Army, and the rigors of incessant combat, the vastness of the theater of military operations, and the harshness of the climate had not yet significantly dulled the cutting edge of German military power.

During the first period of the war, the virtual destruction of its prewar army and military force structure forced the Soviet military leadership to create a simpler and more fragile force structure for its Red Army while it educated its military leaders and developed a more mature force structure that could compete effectively with its more experienced foe. Despite the Red Army's travails, it produced one of the first turning points of the war at Moscow in the winter of 1941–42. In short, the Red Army's Moscow counteroffensive in December 1941 and its subsequent winter offensive in January and February 1942 defeated Operation Barbarossa and ensured that Germany could no longer win the war on the terms initially articulated by Hitler.

The second period of the war lasted from the commencement of the Red Army's Stalingrad counteroffensive, on 19 November 1942, to the Red Army's successful penetration of German defenses along the Dnepr River and its invasion of Belorussia and the Ukraine from October through the end of December 1943. This transitional period, during which the strategic initiative shifted inexorably and irrevocably into the Red Army's hands, was the most important of the war in terms of the struggle's ultimate outcome. During this period, and in near constant combat, the Red Army restructured itself into a modern army that could more effectively engage and, ultimately, defeat *Wehrmacht* forces.

The Red Army's winter campaign of 1942–43 began with massive multi-*front* offensives in the Rzhev (Operation Mars) and Stalingrad (Operation Uranus) regions in mid-November 1942. It ended with the surrender of the German Sixth Army at Stalingrad in early February 1943 and subsequent massive Red Army offensives during February and March 1943 along virtually the entire German Eastern Front from the Baltic to the Black Sea. Although the Red Army fell short of fulfilling Stalin's ambitious objectives, its winter campaign of 1942–43 represented the second and most decisive turning point in the war. After the defeat at Stalingrad, it was abundantly clear that Germany would lose the war. Only the scope and terms of that defeat remained to be determined.

The Red Army's offensives during the ensuing summer–fall campaign of 1943 produced the third major turning point of the war: Soviet victory in the Battle of Kursk. After the Red Army's momentous victory at Kursk, it was clear that German defeat would be both inexorable and total; only the time and costs it would entail remained undetermined. After its Kursk victory, the Red Army orchestrated a successful strategic offensive by multiple *fronts* attacking simultaneously across a broad front from Vitebsk to the Black Sea. By late December 1943, this offensive had propelled Red Army forces to and across the Dnepr River and into Belorussia and the Ukraine.

During the third period of the war, which lasted from 1 January 1944 through May 1945, the Soviet Union maintained the strategic initiative nearly constantly. The military campaigns comprising this period encompassed nearly continuous Red Army strategic offensive operations, punctuated only by brief pauses while the Soviet war machine replenished the men and weaponry necessary to continue its advance. This period was characterized by an inexorable and unalterable decline in German military strength and fortunes and the final maturation of the Red Army in terms of leadership, force structure, and operational and tactical combat techniques. After Kursk the strength and combat effectiveness of the German armies in the East entered a period of near constant decline. Although periodic influxes of new conscripts and equipment accorded the defending Germans the means to conduct local counterattacks and counterstrokes, these counteractions were steadily more feeble and less effective, due to both the growing sophistication of Soviet troop training and experience and the steady decay in German troop training and combat effectiveness.

During this period of the war, the Red Army's strategic offensive capabilities matured to an unprecedented level of sophistication as it undertook both simultaneous and consecutive offensives across the entire combat front from the Barents Sea to the Black Sea. During the winter campaign of 1944, the Red Army conducted simultaneous and successive offensives in the Leningrad region, Belorussia, the Ukraine, and the Crimea. Although the Belorussian offensive faltered short of its goals, Red Army forces cleared German defenders from most of the southern Leningrad region, the Ukraine westward to the Polish and Romanian borders, and the Crimean peninsula.

In the summer–fall campaign of 1944, the Red Army conducted successive and dramatically successful strategic offensives against German army groups defending Belorussia, southern Poland, Romania, the Baltic region, and later Hungary and the Balkan region. By early December 1944, these offensives had engulfed the entire combat front from the Baltic Sea to Budapest and Belgrade and had propelled Red Army forces into East Prussia and Poland and deep into the Danube basin. During the ensuing winter campaign of 1945, Red Army forces smashed German army groups in East Prussia, Poland, western Hungary, and eastern Austria, reaching the Oder River only 36 miles from Berlin and the Danube River at Vienna. The Red Army capped its successes during this third and final period of war in April and May 1945 by mounting its twin Berlin and Prague offensives, climactic struggles that ended Hitler's thousand-year Third Reich in just short of four years of war.

As dénouement to its victory over Nazi Germany, at the United States' request, during the summer of 1945 the Red Army regrouped almost 1 million men to the Far East and, in a brief but violent offensive in August and September 1945, destroyed the Japanese Kwantung Army in Manchuria, helping hasten the end of the war in the Pacific.

THE SUMMER–FALL CAMPAIGN, 22 JUNE TO 5 DECEMBER 1941

In late June 1941, Hitler's *Wehrmacht* invaded the Soviet Union with a force of over 3 million men, crushed Red Army forces in the frontier region, and raced inexorably toward Leningrad, Moscow, and Kiev, leaving a shattered Red Army in its wake and forcing Stalin to evacuate the bulk of the Soviet government to Kuibyshev in October. The United States was at peace, and in October Congress renewed the draft by a single vote. U.S. Army strength reached 1.5 million men. The 5.5 million–man Red Army had lost at least 2.8 million men by 1 October and 1.6 million more by 31 December. During this period the Red Army raised 821 division equivalents (483 rifle, 73 tank, 31 mechanized, and 101 cavalry divisions and 266 rifle, tank, and ski brigades) and lost a total of 229 division equivalents. In November, the *Wehrmacht* began its final advance on Moscow, the United States extended $1 billion in Lend-Lease credit to the Soviet Union, and the British won the initial phase of the Battle of Britain in the air and conducted a limited offensive in North Africa.

Context

War is not fought in a vacuum, and in this regard the Soviet-German war was no exception. When Germany invaded the Soviet Union on 22 June 1941, war had already ravaged the remainder of Europe for almost two years. After June 1940, when its armies were expelled from continental Europe by Hitler's *Wehrmacht*, Great Britain struggled on against the onslaught of Hitler's *Luftwaffe* and under near-constant threat of ground invasion for almost two years, protected by its formidable moat, the English Channel. Conflict raged on, too, along the periphery of Europe, from the icy fiords of Norway to the endless sands of northern Africa as the pitiful remnants of democratic Europe struggled to hold back the tide of Nazi totalitarianism. In the wings stood the United States, protected by vast ocean expanses and wedded to its time-honored but perceptively weakening faith in the safety and security of splendid isolation.

After 22 June 1941 and until 7 December of the same year, the Soviet Union fought on with only weakened England as a feeble strategic military partner. During this period, the Red Army faced the bulk of Hitler's *Wehrmacht*, and the Soviet Union suffered the awful devastation produced in the German Army's immense wake. Only on 7 December did the rash Japanese surprise attack on Pearl Harbor wake the sleeping American giant from its isolationist slumber. Thereafter, what came to be known as the Grand Alliance began to evolve, slowly at first, as a reluctant marriage of convenience between Hitler's mortal enemies, and only later as a vibrant and active wartime alliance dedicated to the destruction first of Nazi Germany and ultimately of Imperial Japan.

Whether based on German or Soviet sources, while they ignore differences over the importance or cost of particular battles and operations, most histories of the Soviet-German war have agreed upon a common chronology of military operations.[2] This chronology is based on the relatively accessible military records of the *Wehrmacht*, the writings of *Wehrmacht* veterans, and the accounts written since war's end by Soviet and Russian military historians and memoir writers. Although this understanding of the war has endured for over 50 years, it is woefully complete. For a wide variety of political and military reasons, Soviet (and Russian) historiography has permitted immense gaps in the public record of the war. These gaps exist either to protect the reputations of more recent political or military leaders or to satisfy the penchant for secrecy, particularly regarding the protection of unique and invaluable military experiences, which many Russians and Soviets before them considered as national treasures warranting careful protection. Hence, the conventional view of the war ignores as much as 40 percent of the Red Army's wartime military experiences. Any investigation of the Red Army during wartime must begin by highlighting the conventional and forgotten aspects of the war, at least in terms of military operations

The Conventional View

History portrays the *Wehrmacht's* advance during Operation Barbarossa as a veritable juggernaut: four successive offensives that culminated in late November and early December 1941 with German Army Group Center's dramatic but ill-fated attempt to capture Moscow (see Maps 1.1 and 1.2). These successive offensives (stages) included the border (frontier) battles in late June and early July 1941, the battles for Luga, Smolensk, and Uman' in July and August 1941, the battles for Leningrad and Kiev in September 1941, and the German advance to Tikhvin, Moscow, and Rostov from October through early December 1941.

After smashing the Red Army's frontier defenses in late June and early July during the first stage of Operation Barbarossa, the *Wehrmacht* advanced rapidly along the northwestern, western, and southwestern strategic axes, forcing the Red Army to conduct a prolonged strategic defense. German Army Groups North and Center overcame the forward defenses of the Red Army's Northwestern and Western Fronts, encircled the bulk of the 3rd, 4th, and 10th Armies west of Minsk, and thrust eastward across the Western Dvina and Dnepr rivers, the Red Army's second strategic defense line.[3] Once across those two key river barriers, the two army groups lunged toward Leningrad and the key city of Smolensk. To the south, Army Group South advanced inexorably eastward toward Kiev against stouter resistance offered by the Red Army's Southwestern Front, while other German and Romanian forces invaded Moldavia, penetrated the Southern Front's defenses, and threatened the Soviet Black Sea port of Odessa.

During Operation Barbarossa's second stage, which unfolded in July and August, Army Group North captured Riga and Pskov and advanced northward toward Luga and Novgorod, brushing aside the Red Army's Northwestern Front and forcing the Northern Front to erect hasty defenses on the

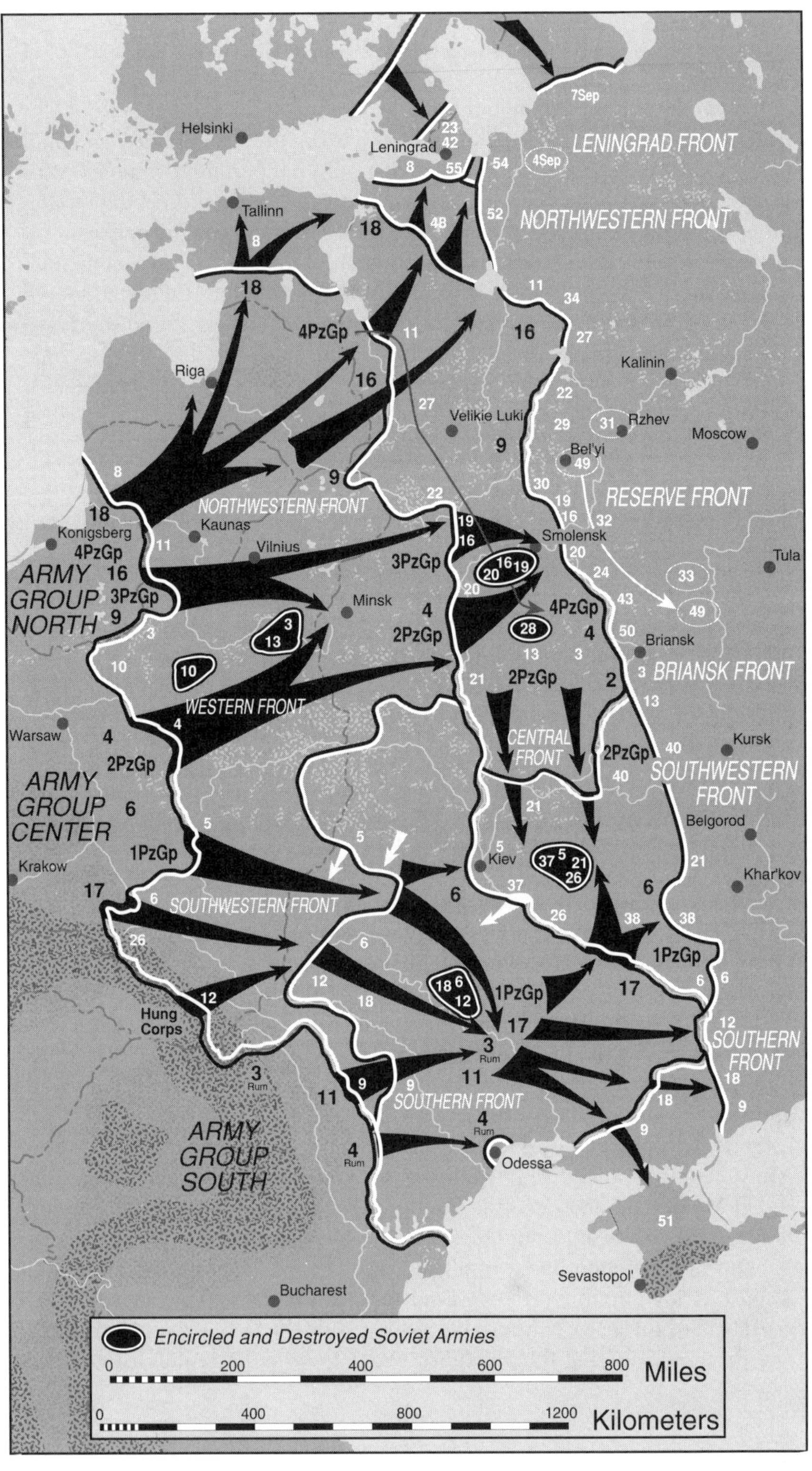

Map 1.1. The Summer–Fall Campaign, 22 June to 30 September 1941

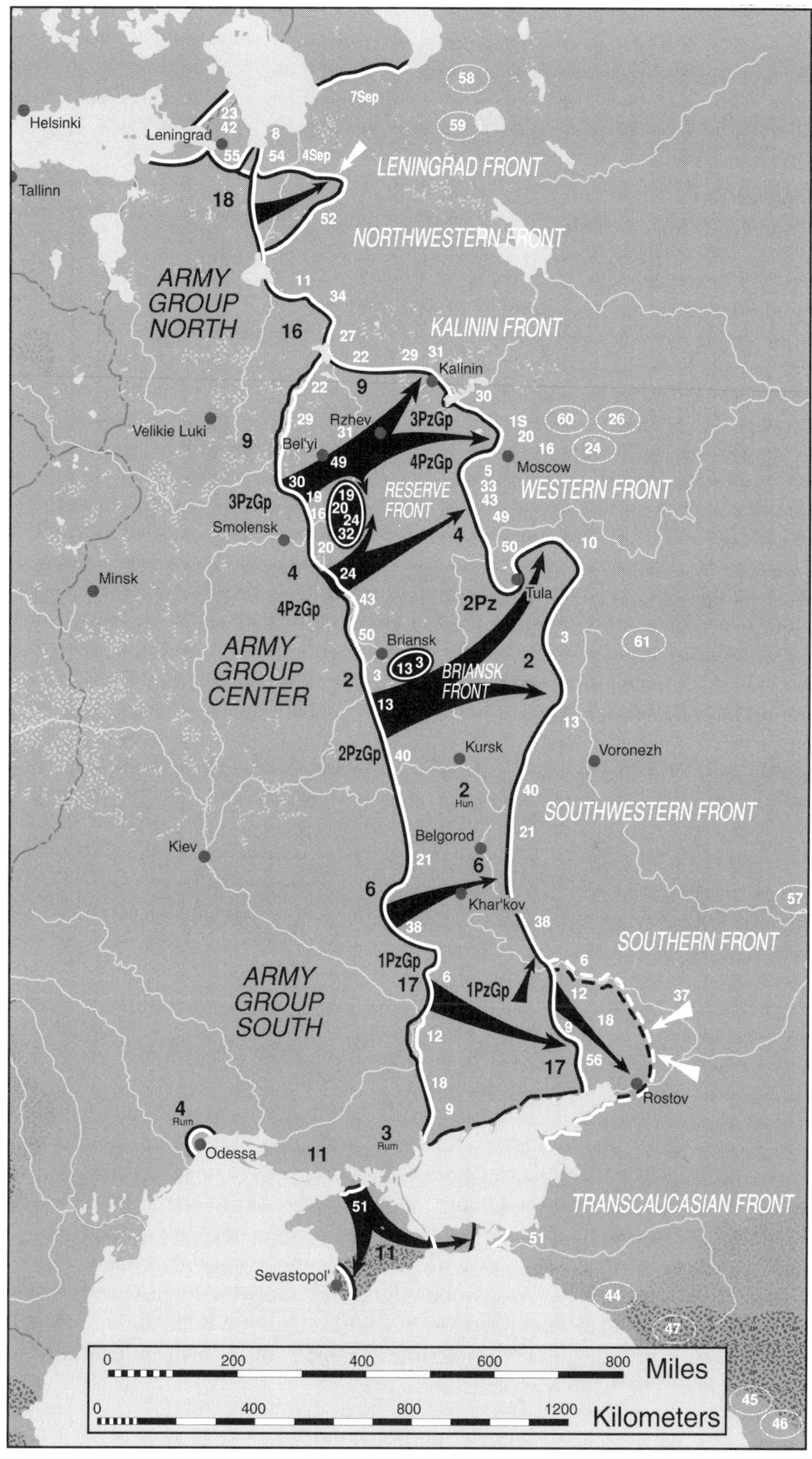

Map 1.2. The Summer–Fall Campaign, 1 October to 5 December 1941

southern approaches to Leningrad. At the same time, Army Group Center began a month-long struggle for the city of Smolensk, in the process partially encircling the Western Front's 16th, 19th, and 20th Armies in the Smolensk region and fending off increasingly strong and desperate Red Army counterattacks to relieve their forces isolated around the city. To the south, Army Group South drove eastward toward Kiev, encircled and destroyed the Southwestern Front's 6th and 12th Armies in the Uman' region, and blockaded Soviet forces in Odessa. The second stage of this determined German advance ended in late August, when Hitler decided to halt his direct thrusts on Leningrad and Moscow temporarily and, instead, attack to eliminate Soviet forces stubbornly defending Kiev and the central Ukraine.

In Barbarossa's third stage, which unfolded in late August and September, Army Group North besieged but failed to capture Leningrad, while Army Groups Center and South jointly attacked and encircled the bulk of the Red Army's Southwestern Front, which was defending in the Kiev region. In the process, *Wehrmacht* forces encircled and destroyed the Southwestern Front's 5th, 21st, 26th, and 37th Armies at and east of Kiev, bringing the total "bag" of Soviet forces eliminated in the Ukraine to the awesome figure of over 1 million men.

The *Wehrmacht* began the fourth stage of Operation Barbarossa, its culminating offensive on Moscow (Operation Typhoon), in early October. While Army Groups North and South continued their advances toward Leningrad in the north and Khar'kov and the Donets Basin (Donbas) in the south, Army Group Center, whose advance was spearheaded by three of the *Wehrmacht's* four panzer groups, mounted a concerted offensive to capture Moscow. The attacking German forces tore through Red Army defenses, routed the Red Army's Western, Reserve, and Briansk Fronts, and quickly encircled and destroyed the 16th, 19th, 20th, 24th, and 32nd Armies around Viaz'ma and the 50th, 3rd, and 13th Armies north and south of Briansk. After a short delay prompted by deteriorating weather and sharply increasing Red Army resistance, Operation Typhoon culminated in mid-November when Army Group Center attempted to envelop Red Army forces defending Moscow by dramatic armored thrusts from the north and south.

In early December 1941, however, the cumulative debilitating effects of time, space, attrition, desperate Red Army resistance, and sheer fate denied the *Wehrmacht* a triumphant climax to its six months of near constant victories. Weakened by months of heavy combat in a theater of war it never really understood, the vaunted *Wehrmacht* finally succumbed to the multiple foes of harsh weather, alien terrain, and a fiercely resisting enemy. Amassing its reserve armies, in early December the *Stavka* (Soviet High Command) halted the German drive toward Moscow within sight of the Kremlin's spires and unexpectedly unleashed a counteroffensive of its own that inflicted unprecedented defeat on Hitler's *Wehrmacht*. Simultaneously, other Red Army forces struck back at their German tormentors in the north and to the south. Red Army offensives at Tikhvin, east of Leningrad, and at Rostov in the south drove German forces back, denying Hitler victory along any of the three principal strategic axes into the depth of the Soviet Union.

As articulated above, this conventional view of military operations during the summer–fall campaign of 1941 includes the following major operations:

- the Border (Frontier) Battles (22 June to early July 1941)
- the German advance on Leningrad (July–September 1941)
- the Battle of Smolensk (July–September)
- the Uman' and Kiev encirclements (August–September 1941)
- German Operation Typhoon and the Viaz'ma and Briansk encirclements (30 September to 5 November 1941)
- the German advance on Moscow (7 November to 4 December 1941)
- the German Tikhvin offensive (16 October to 18 November 1941)
- the German advance on Khar'kov, the Crimea, and Rostov (18 October to 16 November 1941)
- the Soviet Rostov counterstroke (17 November to 2 December 1941)
- the Soviet Tikhvin counterstroke (November–December 1941)

The Forgotten War

Newly released archival materials now indicate that, from the very day that Operation Barbarossa began, Stalin and the *Stavka* consistently and repeatedly attempted to halt and even drive back the German juggernaut.[4] Beginning in late June and extending into July, August, and September, they ordered the Red Army to conduct a series of operations in the form of counterattacks, counterstrokes, and, in one case, a full-fledged counteroffensive, all of which represented concerted, albeit clumsy, attempts to implement the Red Army's 1941 State Defense Plan. However, the extremely fluid combat situation and the rapid German advance made these offensive operations seem uncoordinated and prevented the Germans from recognizing them for what they actually were. Close examination of newly released documents, including *Stavka* and *front* orders, clearly indicates that the *Stavka* attempted to coordinate these operations in regard to their timing, conduct, and initial and ultimate military objectives.[5]

The "forgotten battles" or partially obscured military operations during the summer–fall campaign of 1941 include the following:

- Soviet counterstrokes at Kelme, Raseinai, Grodno, and Dubno (late June 1941)

- Soviet counterstrokes at Sol'tsy, Lepel', Bobruisk, and Kiev (July 1941)
- Soviet counterstrokes at Staraia Russa, Smolensk, and Kiev (August 1941)
- the Soviet offensive at Smolensk, El'nia, and Roslavl' (September 1941)
- the Soviet counterstroke at Kalinin (October 1941)

The initial counterattacks and counterstrokes the Red Army launched in the frontier region in late June 1941 were poorly coordinated and usually futile attempts by the commanders of the Red Army's three operating *fronts* to implement their standing war plans, which required them to react vigorously and offensively to any prospective enemy advance. In Lithuania the Northwestern Front's 3rd and 12th Mechanized Corps struck back at Army Group North at Kelme and Raseinai, in Belorussia the Western Front's 6th, 11th, and 14th Mechanized Corps counterattacked against Army Group Center near Grodno and Brest, and in the Ukraine the Southwestern Front's 6th, 8th, 9th, 15th, 19th, and 22nd Mechanized Corps launched massive counterstrokes against Army Group South near Brody and Dubno. Poorly coordinated and supported, these assaults proved utterly futile and often suicidal and ultimately resulted in the destruction of most of the Red Army's tank and mechanized forces and over 10,000 tanks. Only the massive assaults in the south, personally supervised by Army General G. K. Zhukov, chief of the Red Army General Staff, had any appreciable effect on the precipitous German advance.[6]

In July, the Red Army launched yet another series of heavy counterstrokes in three critical regions, all of which were timed to coincide. First, in the north, two Northwestern Front shock groups struck the 8th Panzer Division, the vanguard of Army Group North's LVI Motorized Corps, near Sol'tsy southwest of Lake Il'men' on 14 July, delaying the German advance toward Leningrad by about one week.[7] In the center, beginning on 6 July, the Western and Central Fronts launched multiple unsuccessful counterstrokes to contain Army Group Center's forces along the Dnepr River. These futile struggles included the spectacular defeat of the Western Front's 5th and 7th Mechanized Corps near Lepel', the notorious but pathetically weak "Timoshenko offensive" against Guderian's Second Panzer Group along the Sozh River, and a failed counterstroke near Bobruisk, all of which failed to halt Army Group Center's advance toward Smolensk.[8] In the south multiple counterattacks by the Southwestern Front near Korosten' slowed but failed to halt Army Group South's advance toward Kiev.[9]

Undeterred by its July failures, the Red Army continued striking back against the advancing Germans in August. In the north the Northern 48th and Northwestern Front's 11th, 34th, and 27th Armies ferociously assaulted Army Group North's X Army Corps near Staraia Russa on 12 August, again delaying the German advance on Leningrad for a week.[10] In the center beginning on 20 July, the Western Front assaulted Army Group Center east of Smolensk with five ad hoc shock groups to rescue its forces encircled around this city.[11] Finally, smaller-scale Red Army counterattacks west of Kiev failed quickly without achieving any positive results.[12] Although all of these Red Army attacks ended in failure, their ferocity persuaded Hitler to delay his advance on Moscow and instead engage "softer" and more lucrative targets around Kiev.

In late August the Western, Reserve, and Briansk Fronts launched a massive counteroffensive in the Smolensk, El'nia, and Roslavl' regions to prevent Army Group Center from continuing its advance on Moscow and Kiev. Despite the Reserve Front's local victory at El'nia, the Western and Briansk Fronts' efforts were a bloody failure.[13] This failure so weakened the Red Army's defenses along the Moscow axis that it contributed directly to its disastrous defeats at Viaz'ma and Briansk in early October, and led to the *Wehrmacht's* spectacular advance on Moscow during Operation Typhoon. Finally, during the initial stage of Operation Typhoon in late October, the Northwestern Front employed a special operational group (headed by N. F. Vatutin, the Northwestern Front's chief of staff) near the city of Kalinin to halt the German Ninth Army's advance to the vital Leningrad–Moscow railroad line and ultimately prevent that army from participating in the final *Wehrmacht* drive on Moscow.[14]

While demonstrating that the Red Army's strategic defense in 1941 was not as haphazard, improvised, and passive as previously described, and the *Wehrmacht's* offensive not as seamless and inexorable as previously described, these "forgotten battles" also explain why the *Wehrmacht* ultimately suffered defeat at the gates of Moscow in early December.

Reflections

The Soviet military and political leadership and Red Army suffered defeats of staggering proportions along the Soviet Union's western borders in June and July 1941, subsequent catastrophic defeats in the Ukraine and at Kiev in August and September, and equally devastating disasters at Viaz'ma and Briansk in October. By November, triumphant German forces were approaching Leningrad, Moscow, and Rostov proper along a vast expanse of front stretching from the Baltic to the Black Sea. Faced with these frightening realities, the Soviet leadership could either learn how to wage war successfully against the more experienced *Wehrmacht* or simply perish. In this case, necessity, that is, the very survival of the Red Army and Soviet state, became the mother of invention.

Since Stalin and his fledgling *Stavka* well understood the scope of the catastrophe befalling them and sensed the mortal danger Hitler's Operation

Barbarossa posed to the Soviet Union's survival, both acted forcefully to stave off disaster from the very first days of the war. Despite immense obstacles, they ordered the Red Army to act offensively, and they strove to coordinate these offensive actions in terms of timing, location, and objective. However, they also seriously overestimated the Red Army's combat capabilities and congenitally underestimated those of the *Wehrmacht*. Consequently, the *Stavka* assigned utterly unrealistic missions to its forces–with predictably disastrous results.

Complicating this situation, the Red Army's command cadre, particularly its senior officers but also its junior officers, noncommissioned officers (NCOs), and enlisted soldiers, lacked the experience necessary to contend with the better-led and more tactically and operationally proficient *Wehrmacht*. The *Stavka's* failure to understand this reality until late 1942 led inevitably to repeated Red Army defensive and offensive frustration and failures, even during its partially successful Moscow offensive in the winter of 1941–42, when it failed to fulfill the *Stavka's* overly ambitious objective of destroying Army Group Center at the gates of Moscow. Making matters worse, the Red Army's logistical support infrastructure proved totally inadequate to meet the requirements of modern, highly mobile war throughout the first six months of the war and would remain inadequate throughout much of 1942.

Historical Debates

The summer–fall campaign of 1941 is replete with debate and controversy regarding the rationale for and efficacy and consequences of the key strategic and operational decisions Hitler, Stalin, and their key military advisers reached at the most crucial times during the campaign. These debates include both the "what ifs" of history and diverging interpretations regarding what actually did occur and why.

The "what ifs" include "What if Hitler had launched Operation Barbarossa in May 1941 instead of late June?" "What if Hitler had ordered the *Wehrmacht* to continue its advance on Moscow in late August or early September 1941 instead of October 1941?" and "What if Stalin had ordered the Red Army to fall back before the Germans' Barbarossa onslaught?" Since, by their very nature, these "what ifs" are mere suppositions, inferences, flights of fancy regarding what might have happened had Hitler or Stalin reached different decisions, they defy resolution and remain outside the parameters of real history.

On the other hand, diverging interpretations reflect genuine and legitimate debate over the validity or efficacy of specific decisions regarding certain real events. These include such issues as "Did the Soviet Union intend to conduct a preventive war against Germany in the summer of 1941?" "Did Stalin order an assault on Berlin in February 1945?" and "If not, why?" Since these debates concern actual historical events, their resolution depends directly on the weight of historical evidence. Even though the personal motives of the key persons who reached these decisions is often difficult if not impossible to ascertain, the issues themselves remain an essential parts of the history of the war.

Like the remainder of the war, the summer–fall campaign of 1941 has generated prolonged debates over a wide range of important issues, including those that follow.

The Myth of Stalin's Preventive War. On 15 May 1941, G. K. Zhukov, chief of the Red Army General Staff, dispatched a proposal to his superiors regarding a possible preemptive offensive against *Wehrmacht* forces, which were then concentrating in eastern Poland. Although the Soviet Union's commissar of defense, Marshal of the Soviet Union S. K. Timoshenko, initialed the proposal, no evidence exists that Stalin either read or acted upon it. Nonetheless, the mere existence of this proposal and other fragmentary evidence has provided the basis for recent claims that Stalin indeed intended to conduct a preventive war against Germany beginning in early July 1941, but was prevented from doing so when Hitler struck first.[15]

All existing archival sources refute this contentious assertion.[16] As this evidence and subsequent events indicate, the Red Army was in no condition to wage war in the summer of 1941 either offensively or, as the actual course of combat indicated, defensively. Furthermore, although genuine, Zhukov's proposal reflected normal contingency planning, a routine function of the General Staff. Finally, while Zhukov's original proposal bears Timoshenko's initials, it lacks Stalin initials or usual marginalia, indicating that Stalin probably never saw it.

The Timing of Operation Barbarossa. Hitler commenced Operation Barbarossa on 22 June 1941, after delaying his invasion of the Soviet Union for roughly two months so that the *Wehrmacht* could conquer Yugoslavia and Greece. Many historians claim that this delay proved fatal for Operation Barbarossa. Had Germany invaded the Soviet Union in April rather than June, they argue, Moscow and Leningrad would have fallen, and Hitler would have achieved his Barbarossa objectives, particularly the capture of Moscow and Leningrad.

This assertion is also incorrect.[17] Hitler embarked on his Balkan diversion at a time of year when the *rasputitsa* ("time of rain-clogged roads") prevented extensive military operations on any scale, particularly mobile panzer operations, in the western Soviet Union. Furthermore, the force Hitler committed in the Balkans was but a small portion of his overall Barbarossa invasion force, and it returned from the Balkans in good condition, in time to fulfill its role in Barbarossa.

A corollary to this issue is the thesis that the *Wehrmacht* would have performed better had Hitler postponed Barbarossa until the summer of 1942. This too is quite unlikely, since Stalin's program to reform, reorganize, and reequip the Red Army, which was woefully incomplete when the Germans struck in June 1941, would have been fully completed by the summer of 1942. Although the *Wehrmacht* would still have been more tactically and operationally proficient than the Red Army in 1942, the latter would have possessed a larger and more formidable mechanized force equipped with armor superior to that of the Germans. Furthermore, by this time, a decision by Hitler to invade the Soviet Union would have saddled Germany with the onerous task of waging a two-front war against the United States (and Britain) and the Soviet Union.

Guderian's Southward Turn (The Kiev Encirclement). Red Army resistance to the *Wehrmacht* stiffened east of Smolensk in August 1941, and in September Hitler temporarily abandoned his direct thrust on Moscow by turning one-half of Army Group Center's panzer forces (Guderian's Second Panzer Group) to the south to envelop and destroy the Soviet Southwestern Front, which was defending Kiev. By virtue of Guderian's southward turn, the *Wehrmacht* destroyed the entire Southwestern Front east of Kiev during September, inflicting 600,000 losses on the Red Army, while the forces of the Soviet Western, Reserve, and Briansk Fronts, deployed west of Moscow, conducted a futile and costly offensive against German forces around Smolensk. After conducting this Kiev diversion, Hitler launched Operation Typhoon in early October, only to see his offensive falter at the gates of Moscow in early December. Some historians claim that had Hitler launched Operation Typhoon in early September rather than early October, the *Wehrmacht* would have avoided the terrible weather conditions and reached and captured Moscow before the onset of winter.

This argument too does not hold up under close examination.[18] Had Hitler launched Operation Typhoon in early September, Army Group Center would have had to penetrate deep Soviet defenses manned by a force that had not squandered its strength in fruitless offensives against German defenses east of Smolensk. Furthermore, Army Group Center would have launched its Moscow offensive while a force of more than 600,000 men was threatening its ever-extended right flank and, in the best reckoning, would have reached the gates of Moscow after mid-October, just as the fall rainy season was beginning.

Finally, the *Stavka* saved Moscow by raising, fielding, and employing ten reserve armies, which took part in the November defense of the city, the December counterstrokes, and the January 1942 counteroffensive. These armies would have gone into action regardless of when Hitler launched Operation Typhoon. Although they ultimately halted and drove back the *Wehrmacht* offensive short of Moscow in December, without major assistance from forces on the Germans' flanks, they would also have been available to do the same had the Germans attacked Moscow a month earlier, this time assisted by the 600,000–plus force deployed along Army Group Center's overextended right flank.

"What If" Moscow Had Fallen in the Fall of 1941. The argument that Hitler would have won the war if the *Wehrmacht* had been able to capture Moscow, a corollary to the arguments described above, is also subject to serious question. If Hitler's legions had actually reached and tried to capture Moscow, Stalin would probably have assigned one or more of his reserve armies to fight and die in its defense.[19] Although the Germans might well have seized the bulk of the city, they would then found themselves facing the same lamentable dilemma that the Sixth Army faced at Stalingrad a year later. More ominous still, had it captured Moscow, the *Wehrmacht* would have faced the daunting task of trying to winter in Moscow, with the inherent danger of emulating the fate of Napoleon's army in 1812.

THE WINTER CAMPAIGN, DECEMBER 1941 TO APRIL 1942

On 7 December 1941, the United States lost the bulk of its Pacific Fleet at Pearl Harbor to a surprise attack by Japan and declared war on the Empire of Japan (8 December), and Germany declared war on the United States (11 December). U.S. Army strength reached 1,643,477 men in four armies and 37 divisions (including five armored and two cavalry). After just six months of war, the Soviet Union had lost almost 5 million men, virtually its entire prewar army, and territory equivalent in U.S. terms to the entire region from the Atlantic coast to Springfield, Illinois, but survived and, during the Battle for Moscow, inflicted the first defeat that Hitler's *Wehrmacht* had ever experienced. Red Army strength reached 4.2 million men in 43 armies.

In January 1942, the German *Afrika Korps* began its advance toward Egypt with three German and seven Italian divisions against seven British divisions. In January and February 1942, nine Red Army *fronts* (army groups) with 37 armies and over 350 divisions smashed German defenses on a front of 600 miles (Staraia Russa to Belgorod) and drove German forces back 80–120 miles before the Germans stabilized their defensive front in March.

Context

The dramatic events of December 1941, particularly the sudden attack by the Japanese empire on U.S. and British interests in the Pacific Ocean region, fundamentally altered the face of war. These savage surprise attacks wakened a sleeping giant, and the ensuing waves of declarations of war transformed the war in Europe into a genuine global war. Despite the wholesale expansion of the conflict, however, the conflict's Soviet-German war remained the center of gravity in terms of committed ground forces, the scope and ferocity of the fighting, and the human and materiel cost of combat. While the U.S. military fended off determined Japanese efforts to spread its military power across the Pacific and Great Britain clung precariously to its shrinking territories in North Africa, the Red Army waged near constant battle against over 80 percent of the *Wehrmacht's* fighting power along the German Eastern Front.

The Conventional View of the War

While the *Wehrmacht* was conducting Operation Typhoon, the *Stavka* was frantically raising and deploying fresh reserves to counter the German onslaught.[20] Straining every available resource, it fielded ten additional field armies during November and December 1941, six of which it committed to combat in or adjacent to the Moscow region (the 10th, 26th, 39th, 1st Shock, 60th, and 61st) during its November defense, December counterstroke, and January 1942 counteroffensives. Even though these fresh armies were only pale reflections of what Soviet military theory required them to be, their presence proved the adage that quantity has a quality of its own. These hastily assembled reserves were especially valuable given the attrition that afflicted the *Wehrmacht* during its final thrust toward Moscow. By 1 November it had lost fully 20 percent of its committed strength (686,000 men), up to two-thirds of its 1.5 million motor vehicles, and 65 percent of its tanks. The German Army High Command (OKH) rated its 136 divisions as equivalent to 83 full-strength divisions. Logistics were strained to the breaking point, and, as the success of the Red Army's counteroffensive indicated, the Germans were clearly not prepared for combat in winter conditions.

At this juncture, to the Germans' surprise, on 5 December the Red Army struck back with the first in what became a long series of counterstrokes, which ultimately grew into a full-fledged counteroffensive (see Map 1.3). In reality, the December 1941 counteroffensive, which ended in early January 1942, consisted of a series of consecutive and then simultaneous multi-army operations whose cumulative effect was to drive German forces back from the immediate approaches to Moscow.

During the initial phase of this counteroffensive, the right wing and center of Zhukov's Western Front, spearheaded by the new 1st Shock Army and a cavalry corps commanded by Major General L. M. Dovator, drove Army Group Center's Third and Fourth Panzer Groups westward from the northern

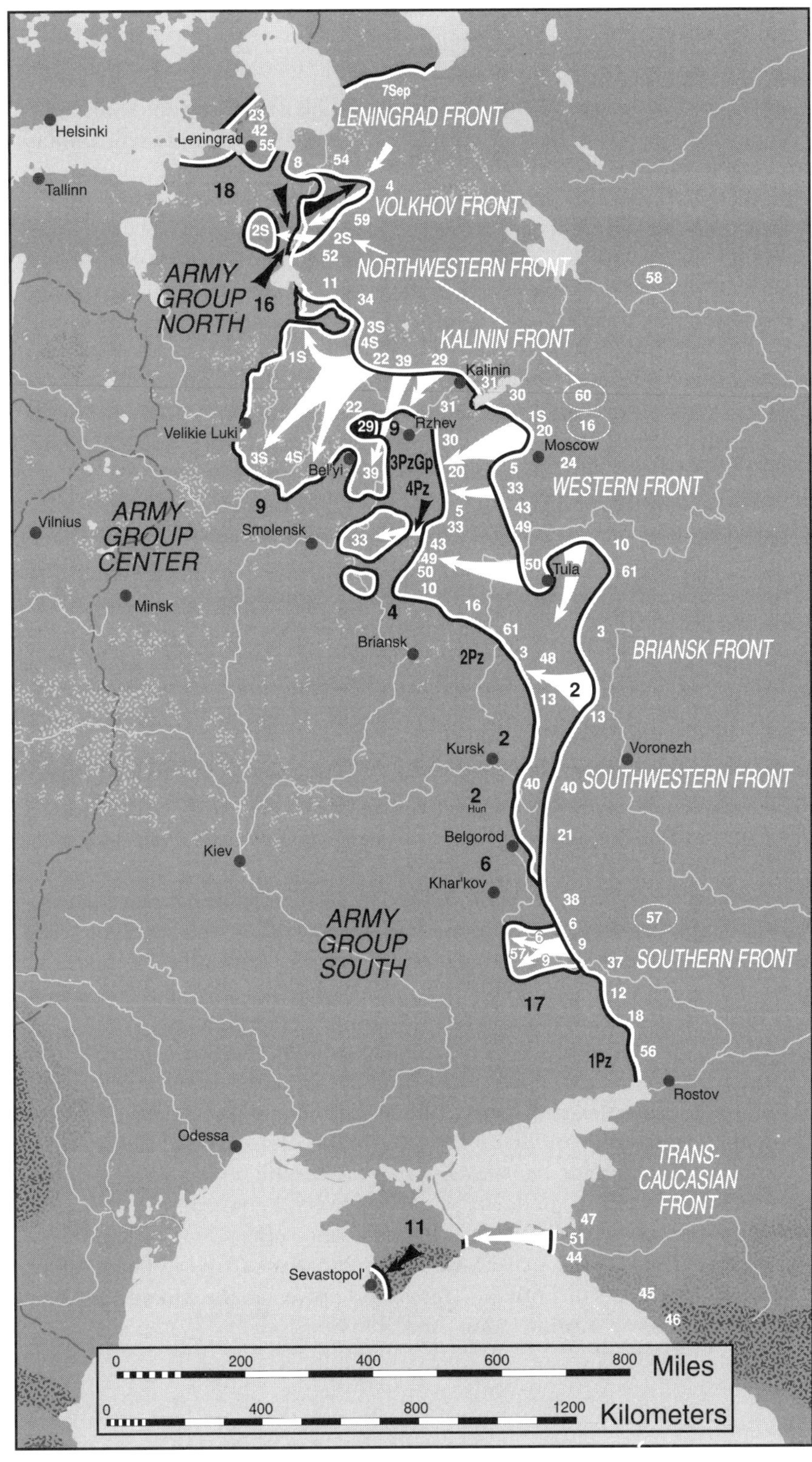

Map 1.3. The Winter Campaign, December 1941 to April 1942

outskirts of Moscow through Klin to the Volokolamsk region. Soon after, Colonel General I. S. Konev's Kalinin Front added insult to German injury by seizing Kalinin and advancing to the northern outskirts of Rzhev. To the south, the Western Front's left wing, which included the new 10th Army and a cavalry group commanded by Major General P. A. Belov, sent Guderian's Second Panzer Army reeling westward in disorder from Tula. Subsequently, the Western and Southwestern Fronts, which included the new 61st Army, nearly encircled major elements of Army Group Center's Fourth Army near Kaluga, split this army away from Second Panzer Army by a deep thrust past Mosal'sk and Sukhinichi, and drove German Second Army's forces southward toward Orel. The ferocity and relentlessness of the Red Army's assaults sorely tested the *Wehrmacht's* staying power and prompted Hitler to issue his "stand fast" order, which likely forestalled complete German rout.

Swept away by a burst of optimism born of his army's sudden and unexpected success, in early January 1942 Stalin ordered the Red Army to commence a general offensive along the entire front from the Leningrad region to the Black Sea. The second stage of the Red Army's Moscow counteroffensive, which began on 8 January, consisted of several distinct *front* offensive operations whose overall aim was the complete destruction of German Army Group Center. The almost frenzied Soviet counteroffensives in the Moscow region placed enormous pressure on defending German forces as they sought to regain their equilibrium. The counteroffensive also resulted in immense losses among Soviet forces, which by late February had lost much of their offensive punch. By this time Red Army forces had reached the approaches to Vitebsk, Smolensk, Viaz'ma, Briansk, and Orel and had carved huge gaps in the *Wehrmacht's* defenses west of Moscow.

While the Red Army's Kalinin and Western Fronts were savaging the Army Group Center west of Moscow, other Red Army *fronts* were conducting major offensives southeast of Leningrad and south of Khar'kov in the Ukraine, and they managed to penetrate the *Wehrmacht's* defenses and lunge deep into its rear area. However, even though the advancing Soviet forces seized huge swathes of open countryside across the entire front, the Germans held firm to the cities, towns, and major roads. By late February the front was a patchwork quilt of overlapping Soviet and German forces, and neither side was able to overcome the other. In fact, the Soviet offensive had stalled, and, despite his exhortations, entreaties, and threats, Stalin could not rekindle the offensive flame. Although the local counterstrokes in the immediate vicinity of Moscow had grown into a full-fledged counteroffensive and then into a general strategic offensive that formed the centerpiece of a full-fledged Red Army winter campaign, both the Moscow offensive and the winter campaign expired in utter exhaustion in late April 1942.

Thus, the conventional view of the winter campaign of 1941–42 includes the following major operations:

- the Soviet Moscow counteroffensive (5 December 1941 to 7 January 1942)
- the Soviet Moscow offensive (the Battle for Moscow) (8 January to 20 April 1942)
- the Soviet Tikhvin offensive (10 November to 30 December 1941)
- the Soviet Demiansk offensive (7 January to 25 February 1942)
- the Soviet Toropets-Kholm offensive (9 January to 6 February 1942)
- the Soviet Barvenkovo-Lozovaia offensive (18–31 January 1942)
- the Soviet Kerch-Feodosiia offensive (25 December 1941 to 2 January 1942)

The Forgotten War

Glaring gaps exist in the historical record of the Red Army's winter campaign of 1941–42, the gravest of them being the near-total absence of substantial accounts of the intense combat that took place along the extreme northern and southern flanks of the Red Army's Moscow counteroffensive and in the regions southeast of Leningrad and in the Crimea. These operations, which Soviet and German historians alike have overlooked, include three major failed Red Army offensives along the southern flank of the Battle for Moscow, two partially successful Soviet offensives farther north, and another failed Red Army offensive in the Crimea. The "forgotten battles" or partially neglected operations during the winter campaign of 1941–42 include the following:

- the Soviet Leningrad-Novgorod (Liuban') offensive (7 January to 30 April 1942)
- the Soviet Demiansk offensive (1 March to 30 April 1942)
- the Soviet Rzhev-Viaz'ma offensive (15 February to 1 March 1942)
- the Soviet Orel-Bolkhov offensive (7 January to 18 February 1942)
- the Soviet Bolkhov offensive (24 March to 3 April 1942)
- the Soviet Oboian'-Kursk offensive (3–26 January 1942)
- the Soviet Crimean offensive (27 February to 15 April 1942)

Although much has been written about the Red Army's offensive at Moscow in January 1942, deafening silence surrounds several major offensive operations the Red Army conducted along the flanks of the Moscow offensive. In early January 1942, for example, the 10th Army and Cavalry Group Belov, which were operating on the left flank of Zhukov's Western Front, penetrated westward to the approaches to the city of Kirov, in the process forming an enormous gap between the defenses of Army Group Center's Fourth and Second Panzer Armies. At the same time, on the Western Front's right flank, the 4th Shock, 29th, and 39th Armies of Konev's Kalinin Front advanced southward from Rzhev toward Viaz'ma into Army Group Center's deep rear. These twin Soviet advances threatened to envelop, surround, and destroy all of Army Group Center's forces operating east of Smolensk.

In early February 1942, Stalin quickly seized the opportunity to cap his Moscow victories with one grand encirclement operation against Army Group Center by ordering Belov's cavalry and the 50th Army to swing northward toward Viaz'ma to link up with the Kalinin Front's forces advancing from the north and airborne forces parachuted into the Viaz'ma region. Simultaneously, he ordered the 10th Army to sever communications between the German Fourth and Second Panzer Armies. Although the Red Army's two attacking pincers failed to link up at Viaz'ma and months of fruitless seesaw struggle resulted, the 10th Army's progress created yet another new offensive opportunity.

The 10th Army's advance toward Kirov isolated Army Group Center's Second Panzer and Second Armies in a huge salient formed around the cities of Belev and Bolkhov, which blocked any subsequent Red Army advance to Kursk and Belgorod. Understanding that the reduction of this salient was vital to the ultimate success of the Moscow offensive, the *Stavka* ordered the Briansk and Southwestern Fronts to conduct twin operations aimed at eradicating the pesky German bulge. However, the so-called Oboian'-Kursk and Bolkhov offensives failed to achieve their ends and have since literally disappeared from the annals of the war.[21]

During the same period, Stalin ordered the Leningrad and Volkhov Fronts to raise the siege of Leningrad by conducting concentric assaults across the Neva and Volkhov rivers against Army Group North's Eighteenth Army. Although the Volkhov Front's 2nd Shock Army and 13th Cavalry Corps managed to penetrate German defenses, they were soon isolated deep in the German rear, only to be destroyed by German counterstrokes between May and July 1942.[22] This operation, too, languished in obscurity for over 40 years, primarily because it was an embarrassing failure but also because the 2nd Shock Army's last commander was the infamous Lieutenant General A. A. Vlasov, who surrendered in disgust to the Germans and later created the Russian Liberation Army (ROA), which sought to fight alongside German forces until war's end.

Similarly, an unsuccessful Red Army offensive during the winter of 1941–42 against Army Group North's forces in the Demiansk region and an offensive by the Crimean Front designed to rescue Red Army forces besieged in the city of Sevastopol' also ended in failure and disappeared from the pages of history.[23]

Reflections

Even though the Red Army's striking and unprecedented victories over the overextended *Wehrmacht* around Moscow, at Tikhvin, Barvenkovo, and Rostov, and in the Crimea during the winter of 1941–42 proved heady and inspiring, they were also fleeting. The OKH successfully halted the Soviet counteroffensive and then resumed a massive and ambitious offensive operation, Operation *Blau*, in the summer of 1942. Nevertheless, the Red Army's victory at Moscow did revitalize Soviet fortunes, and the morale of the Soviet population soared. On the other hand, the victory also fueled excessive optimism on the part of the *Stavka* that, in turn, ultimately contributed to Soviet military failures and frustrations in the future. Not only did the Soviets fail to achieve their strategic aims (principally the destruction of German Army Group Center) in the winter of 1941–42, but they also dramatically "overreached" themselves in the spring.

It is now abundantly clear that the Red Army's offensives planned by Stalin, Zhukov, and other *Stavka* members during the winter campaign of 1941–42 were nothing less than a comprehensive and coordinated attempt to collapse the *Wehrmacht's* defenses across the entire span of the Soviet-German front. It is also clear that, in comparison with the Red Army's actual capabilities, these strategic offensives were excessively ambitious. As is so often the case in the initial period of any war, few if any of the Soviet players understood the real capabilities of their forces or, even more telling, those of the enemy.

During the first stage of the Soviet counteroffensive in early December 1941, memories of the Red Army's disastrous experiences in the summer limited both Stalin's and the *Stavka's* strategic horizons. For example, in December 1941 Stalin sought to achieve success only at Tikhvin, Rostov, and in the immediate vicinity of Moscow, where the German threat was most acute. By mid-December, however, the spectacular success the Red Army had achieved in these regions prompted the *Stavka* to expand its offensive with utter and ruthless abandon. Urged on by Stalin, as early as 17 December, it ordered ambitious attacks along virtually the entire Soviet-German front, employing all of the Red Army's strategic and operational reserves. Nor did considerations of the human cost of these efforts dampen the offensive ardor of the Red Army's senior leadership. Predictably, however, the offensives fell well short of achieving their strategic ends. Once they had recovered from the shock of the initial setbacks, the German Army High Command coolly parried the *Stavka's* blows and, by the end of April 1942 halted Stalin's ambitious offensive, inflicting massive and grievous casualties on the Red Army in the process.

Historical Debates

The winter campaign of 1941–42 also left a legacy of bitter historical controversy, including debates over Stalin's military strategy and the degree to which the Battle of Moscow represented a turning point in the ultimate course of the war.

Stalin's "Broad Front" Strategy. Postwar Soviet and Russian critiques of Stalin's direction of the Battle of Moscow, including those written by his closest colleagues, harshly criticize the dictator's employment of a "broad front" strategy to defeat the *Wehrmacht*. This strategy, they claim, dissipated the Red Army's limited strength by requiring it to conduct offensive operations along multiple axes and ensured that no single offensive could achieve its ultimate aims. The same critics, in particular Zhukov, argue that Stalin finally began heeding his advisers' advice after the spring of 1942 and discarded the "broad front" strategy in favor of a more selective approach. Thereafter, they claim, Stalin and the *Stavka* carefully selected key offensive axes, concentrated the Red Army along these axes, and tailored the attacking forces to match their assigned missions.

Recently, however, newly revealed archival materials and more detailed examination of the nature of wartime military operations clearly refute this claim in two respects. First, although Stalin did indeed adopt a "broad front" offensive strategy in the winter of 1941–42, his key advisers (including Zhukov) acquiesced in and encouraged that strategy, agreeing with Stalin that the best way to collapse German defenses in any specific sector of the front was to apply maximum pressure in as many sectors as possible. Second, rather than abandoning that strategy after the spring of 1942, Stalin and the *Stavka* adhered to it in 1942, 1943, and early 1944 for the same reasons they had in 1941.[24] Only in the summer of 1944 did they adopt the policy of conducting staggered and successive offensive operations. As late as January 1945, the Red Army once again employed the "broad front" strategy, albeit on a smaller scale, in its strategic offensive into East Prussia, central Poland, and, later, western Hungary and Austria.

The Battle of Moscow as a Turning Point. Debates have raged for years among historians over turning points in the Soviet-German war, specifically, regarding precisely when the fortunes of war turned in the Red Army's favor and why. These debates have surfaced three leading candidates for the honor of being designated "turning points": the Battles of Moscow, Stalingrad, and Kursk and, more recently, a fourth, Guderian's southward turn to Kiev. Two of these battles occurred during the first period of the war, throughout which the *Wehrmacht* maintained the strategic initiative, with the exception of the five-month period from December 1941 through April 1942, when the Red Army conducted its winter offensive. By definition, therefore, Russian historians have tended to identify the Battle of Stalingrad as the most important turning point in the war since that battle irrevocably deprived the Germans of the strategic initiative.

In retrospect, the Battle of Moscow represents but one of three turning points in the war, but by no means was it the most decisive. At Moscow the Red Army inflicted an unprecedented defeat on the *Wehrmacht* and prevented Hitler from achieving the objectives of Operation Barbarossa. In short, after the Battle of Moscow, Germany could no longer defeat the Soviet Union or win the war on the terms originally set forth by Hitler.[25]

Finally, Guderian's southward turn and the ensuing delay in Hitler's offensive to capture Moscow cannot qualify as a crucial "turning point." In fact, it may have improved the *Wehrmacht's* chances for victory over the Red Army at Moscow by eliminating the Red Army's massive Southwestern Front as a key player in the fall portion of the campaign and by setting up the Western, Reserve, and Briansk Fronts for their equally decisive October defeats. Furthermore, at the time, few if any figures in the *Wehrmacht's* senior strategic leadership either opposed Guderian's "turn" or anticipated the subsequent German defeat at Moscow.[26]

THE SUMMER–FALL CAMPAIGN, MAY–NOVEMBER 1942

In June 1942, the British Army was still in full retreat in North Africa, the Battle of the Atlantic was raging, and the United States had turned back the Japanese advance in the Pacific at Midway. The U.S. Army had 520,000 men deployed overseas (60 percent in the Pacific, and 40 percent in the Caribbean). On 28 June 1942, Hitler launched Operation *Blau* with roughly 2 million troops toward Stalingrad and the Caucasus, smashing the defenses of about 1.8 million Red Army troops in southern Russia.

In September 1942, British forces halted the German advance in North Africa and prepared a counteroffensive with ten divisions. U.S. strength in Europe reached 170,000 men. By September 1942, German forces had advanced to a depth equivalent in U.S. terms to the entire region from the Atlantic coast to Topeka, Kansas, reaching Stalingrad and the foothills of the Caucasus Mountains, and halted their advance in late October to destroy Soviet forces in Stalingrad.

Context

World War II took on more of a global nature in the second half of 1942, primarily due to improving U.S. fortunes in the Pacific region, the slow revival of U.S. and British power in North Africa, particularly in October 1942, and the tumultuous and critical battle for control of vital sea lanes in the Atlantic. Nonetheless, the bulk of Hitler's *Wehrmacht* remained decisively engaged on Germany's Eastern Front in a struggle that all Allied and Axis leaders alike realized was crucial to the ultimate outcome of the war. Even in the Pacific, the bulk of the Japanese Army concentrated on occupying the vast area of mainland China, while the still powerful Kwantung Army in Manchuria kept a wary eye on Red Army forces in the Far East.

While Hitler's legions were unleashing their second major strategic offensive of the war, Operation *Blau* toward Stalingrad, British forces clung to their tenuous positions in Egypt against the panzers of Erwin Rommel's vaunted *Afrika Korps*, and the United States struggled to halt the Japanese juggernaut in the Pacific region. With the Battle of the Atlantic raging and Britain's tenuous logistical umbilical cord to the U.S. arsenal of democracy mortally threatened, Nazi Germany was at the high-water mark of its military fortunes, and the Western Allies' hope of a return to the continent of Europe remained but a dream. By fall the best the Western Allies could achieve was the insertion of an American army on the coast of northern Africa.

The Conventional View of the War

After the Red Army's first winter offensive collapsed in late April 1942, a period of relative calm descended over the Soviet-German front during which both sides reorganized and refitted their forces and sought ways to regain the strategic initiative.[27] Eager to seize objectives that had eluded him during the previous winter, Stalin demanded the Red Army resume its general offensive in the late spring or early summer of 1942. After prolonged debate, however, other *Stavka* members persuaded the dictator that Hitler was sure to renew his offensive to capture Moscow during the summer to accomplish Operation Barbarossa's most important aim. Although Stalin ultimately authorized the Red Army to begin its summer campaign with a deliberate strategic defense along the Moscow axis, he also ordered it to conduct two offensives in the spring, the first in the Khar'kov region and the second in the Crimea, both aimed at "spoiling" the expected German offensive toward Moscow and, if possible, regaining the strategic initiative.[28]

Nor was Hitler chastened by the *Wehrmacht's* winter setbacks. Confident that his forces could still achieve many of Operation Barbarossa's original aims, Hitler and his OKH planned an ambitious new offensive designed to erase sad memories and fulfill the Third Reich's most ambitious strategic aims. Hitler issued Fuehrer Directive No. 41, dated 5 April 1942, ordering the *Wehrmacht* to conduct Operation *Blau*, a massive offensive aimed at capturing Stalingrad and the oil-rich Caucasus region and later Leningrad, in midsummer 1942. Ultimately, the *Wehrmacht* commenced *Blau* on 28 June, but only after it had foiled Stalin's twin offensives in southern Russia.

Stalin's first "spoiling" offensive began on 12 May 1942, when Marshal S. K. Timoshenko's Southwestern Front struck Army Group South's defenses north and south of Khar'kov (see Map 1.4). Predictably, however, Timoshenko's offensive faltered after only limited gains, and less than a week later German panzer forces assembled to conduct Operation *Blau* counterattacked and crushed Timoshenko's assault force, killing or capturing over 270,000 Red Army troops.[29] Days before, German General Erich von Manstein's Eleventh Army, which was deployed in the Crimea, added insult to Soviet injury by defeating a feeble offensive launched by the inept Crimean Front and then drove its remnants into the sea, killing or capturing another 150,000 Red Army soldiers. Although Stalin's twin offensive disasters delayed the launch of Operation *Blau*, they also severely weakened the Red Army in southern Russia and conditioned it for even greater defeat when *Blau* finally began.

On 28 June, the massed forces of German Fourth Panzer, Second, and Sixth Armies, and Hungarian Second Army, deployed as Army Group Weichs on Army Group South's left wing, struck and shattered the Briansk and Southwestern Fronts' defenses along a 280–mile front from the Kursk region to the Northern Donets River. Thrusting rapidly eastward toward Voronezh on the Don River, Group Weichs then swung southward along the south bank of the Don. German First Panzer and Seventeenth Armies and Romanian Third and Fourth Armies, on Army Group South's right wing, joined the offensive on 7 July, advancing eastward along a 170–mile front and then wheeling southward across the open steppes toward Rostov. Within two weeks, the *Wehrmacht's* offensive had completely demolished the Red Army's defenses in southern Russia, forcing an increasingly frantic *Stavka* to try to repair the damage and slow the German juggernaut. In order to control its forces more effectively in so vast a theater, in early July the OKH reorganized Army Group South into Army Groups "A" and "B."

Finally acknowledging that the German summer offensive was actually taking place in southern Russia, Stalin altered his strategy a week after Operation *Blau* began. He ordered his Southwestern and Southern Fronts to withdraw their decimated forces eastward toward the Don River, Stalingrad, and Rostov and then directed the *Stavka* to field ten new reserve armies and organize counterstrokes and counteroffensives at times and places of its own choosing to slow and contain the Axis advance.

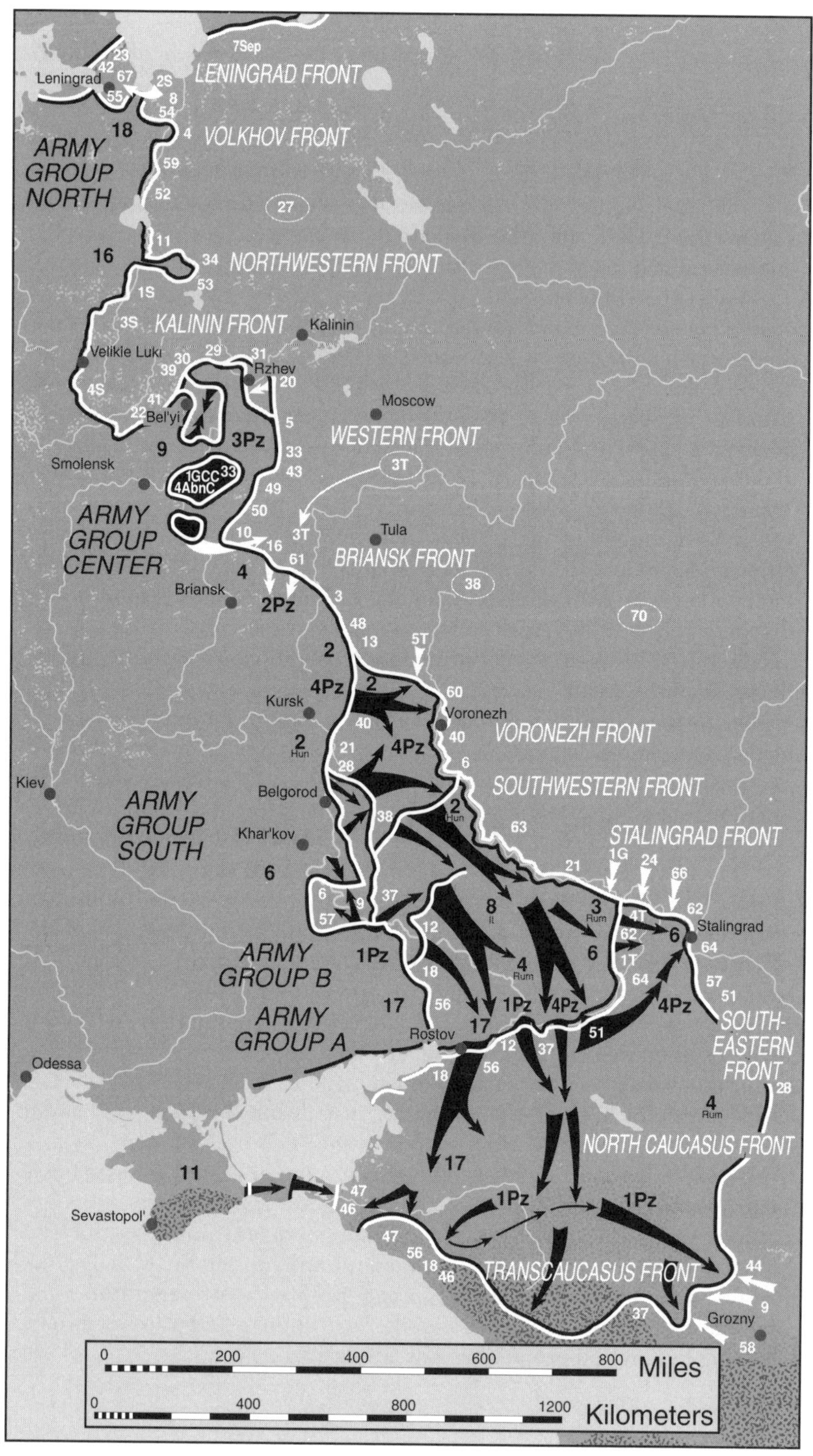

Map 1.4. The Summer–Fall Campaign, May–October 1942

Army Groups "A" and "B" continued their dramatic eastward advance toward and across the Don River to Stalingrad and through Rostov into the Caucasus region during July and August. After capturing Voronezh on 6 July, Army Group "B's" Second Army dug in along the Don River, and its Fourth Panzer and Sixth Armies swung southeastward through Millerovo toward Kalach on the Don, encircling and decimating the Soviet 9th, 28th, and 38th Armies in the process. Further south, Army Group "A's" First Panzer and Seventeenth Armies cleared Red Army forces from the Voroshilovgrad region and wheeled southward toward Rostov on the Don against light resistance. Army Group "B's" spearheads reached Kalach on the Don River, less than 50 miles west of Stalingrad, on 24 July, and Army Group "A's" forces captured Rostov and prepared to cross the Don River and advance into the Caucasus region.

Hitler then altered his offensive plan to capitalize on his forces' remarkable success. Instead of attacking Stalingrad with Army Group "B's" Sixth and Fourth Panzer Armies, he ordered the latter to shift its advance axis southward toward the Don River east of Rostov to cut off Red Army forces before they could withdraw across the river. This left the Sixth Army with the arduous task of forcing the Don River and advancing on Stalingrad alone. Deprived of its support, the Sixth Army's advance slowed significantly in late July and early August against determined Red Army resistance and incessant counterattacks.

Impatient over the Sixth Army's slow progress, in mid-August Hitler altered his plan once again by ordering the Fourth Panzer Army to reverse course and advance on Stalingrad from the southwest. As the two German armies approached Stalin's city, Red Army resistance stiffened significantly, sapping the German armies' strength as they fought their way into the city's suburbs. On 23 August, the Sixth Army's XIV Panzer Corps finally carved a narrow corridor to the Volga River north of Stalingrad. Three days later the Fourth Panzer Army's forces came within artillery range of the Volga south of Stalingrad, marking the beginning of two months of desperate and intense fighting for possession of Stalingrad proper, during which German forces fought to the point of utter exhaustion against fanatical Red Army resistance.

While German forces were beginning the dramatic battle for Stalingrad, Army Group "A" advanced deep into the Caucasus region, leaving only the Romanian Third and Fourth and the Italian Eighth Armies in Army Group "B's" reserve. Because both the Sixth and Fourth Panzer Armies were decisively engaged in the heavy fighting in Stalingrad, Army Group "B" was forced to commit the three Allied armies to protect its flanks north and south of Stalingrad during late August and September.

While Axis forces were advancing toward Stalingrad, Stalin deliberately ordered the Red Army to withdraw eastward, delay the advancing Germans, and buy time to assemble fresh strategic reserves capable of mounting a counteroffensive. Accordingly, the Briansk and Southwestern Fronts withdrew to defenses from west of Voronezh southward along the Don River, and the Southern Front withdrew through Rostov to the northern Caucasus region, where it became the North Caucasus Front and received the mission of protecting the rich Caucasian oilfields. The *Stavka* then formed the Voronezh, Stalingrad, and Southeastern Fronts to defend the Voronezh sector and the northern and southern approaches to Stalingrad. During the fierce fighting in the rubble of Stalingrad city and its famous factory district, Stalin committed just enough forces to keep the conflagration raging and tie down German forces while the *Stavka* prepared its decisive counteroffensive.

As the Red Army withdrew hastily toward the Don and Volga rivers and Stalingrad and the Caucasus, the *Stavka* organized limited counterattacks to wear down advancing *Wehrmacht* forces and "shape" the German strategic penetration. These counterattacks occurred near Voronezh in early July, along the Don River near Kalach in late July, and, thereafter, along the approaches to Stalingrad and within the city proper. All the while, Stalin employed the first of his ten reserve armies in July and August to halt the German advance along the Don River but retained control over the remainder for use in his future counteroffensive.

While Operation *Blau* was under way in the south, from early July through September, the *Stavka* ordered Red Army forces in the Leningrad region and west of Moscow to conduct limited-objective offensives at Siniavino and Rzhev to pin down German forces and prevent the OKH from shifting reinforcements to the south.

According to this construct, the summer–fall campaign includes the following major military operations:

- the Soviet Khar'kov offensive (12–29 May 1942)
- the Soviet Crimean debacle (8–19 May 1942)
- German Operation *Blau*: the advance to Stalingrad and the Caucasus (28 June to 3 September 1942)
- the Soviet Siniavino offensive (19 August to 10 October 1942)
- the Soviet Rzhev-Sychevka offensive (30 July to 23 August 1942)
- the Battle of Stalingrad (3 September to 18 November 1942)

The Forgotten War

Existing descriptions of military operations during the summer and fall campaign of 1942 are woefully incomplete in several important respects. First, the Red Army reacted far more offensively than previously thought while the *Wehrmacht* was conducting Operation *Blau*. Rather than abandoning the strategic initiative to the Germans, the Red Army began operations in May 1942 by conducting major offensives at Khar'kov and in the Crimea. Even after these offensives failed and the Germans began Operation *Blau*, the Red Army struck back fiercely at the *Wehrmacht* as it advanced toward Stalingrad.

Second, the Red Army that the *Stavka* employed in the spring and summer of 1942 was far more capable than its threadbare predecessor of the previous year. By this time the Red Army had achieved notable victories of its own and was in the midst of a major reorganization and reconstruction program designed to enable it to engage *Wehrmacht* forces successfully in both the summer and the winter. After besting the *Wehrmacht* around Moscow and in several other regions only six months before, in 1942 Stalin was reluctant to abandon the field to the Germans and then wait months for the proper moment to launch a major counteroffensive. Therefore, Stalin began the campaign with major offensives of his own, and when they failed, he insisted the Red Army contest the *Wehrmacht's* advance wherever and whenever possible. Consequently, the fighting on the road to Stalingrad and elsewhere along the front during the summer and early fall was far more severe than history has recorded.

During July and August 1942, Red Army conducted numerous counterattacks and counterstrokes against *Wehrmacht* forces advancing toward Stalingrad and against German defenses elsewhere along the front. Masked by the dramatic German advance, these "forgotten battles" include three major offensives near Voronezh, one in concert with a major counterstroke west of Stalingrad, and other offensives near Siniavino, Demiansk, Rzhev, Zhizdra, and Bolkhov in the northwestern and central sectors of the front. Existing Russian accounts, however, have addressed only two of these operations, the Leningrad and Volkhov Fronts' Siniavino offensive in August and September 1942 against Army Group North and the Western and Kalinin Fronts' Rzhev-Sychevka offensive against Army Group Center's defenses in the Rzhev salient during July and August 1942.

The "forgotten battles" or partially neglected operations during the summer–fall campaign of 1942 include the following:

- German destruction of Soviet 2nd Shock Army at Miasnoi Bor (13 May to 10 July 1942)
- German reduction of encircled Group Belov (Operation Hannover) (24 May to 21 June 1942)
- German destruction of Soviet 39th Army southwest of Rzhev (2–27 July 1942)
- the Soviet defense of the Donbas region (7–24 July 1942)
- the Soviet Voronezh-Don counteroffensive (4–26 July 1942)
- the Soviet Zhizdra-Bolkhov counterstroke (5–14 July 1942)

- the Soviet Demiansk offensive (17–24 July 1942)
- the Soviet 1st Rzhev-Sychevka offensive (30 July to 23 August 1942)
- the Soviet 2nd Siniavino offensive (19 August to 15 October 1942)
- the Soviet Demiansk offensive (10–21 August 1942)
- the Soviet Bolkhov offensive (23–29 August 1942)
- the Soviet Voronezh counterstroke (12–15 August 1942)
- the Soviet Voronezh counterstroke 15–28 September 1942)
- the Soviet Demiansk offensive (15–16 September 1942)

Existing Russian accounts of the Red Army's fighting withdrawal from the Donbas region remain inadequate. Contrary to Russian assertions, German forces managed to encircle and decimate the bulk of five of the withdrawing Soviet armies (the 28th, 38th, 57th, 9th, and 24th).[30] In addition, although it receives brief mention in the most thorough Soviet histories, the Red Army's defense along the Stalingrad axis, particularly the counterstrokes by the 1st and 4th Tank Armies, requires more detailed analysis, especially since these tank armies attacked in apparent close coordination with the 5th Tank Army's July counterstroke near Voronezh. Finally, the series of almost set-piece penetration operations by the Sixth Army in its advance from the Don to the Volga rivers also requires more detailed analysis.

The Red Army conducted its largest-scale counterstrokes to defeat Operation *Blau* during July, August, and September in the Voronezh region.[31] Although Russian sources have briefly described the ill-fated offensive by the Briansk Front's new 5th Tank Army west of Voronezh in early July, these sources understate the strength, duration, and ambitious intent of the offensive. Ultimately, these counterstrokes lasted several weeks and involved as many as seven tank corps equipped with up to 1,500 tanks. Moreover, the *Stavka* coordinated the 5th Tank Army's assault west of Voronezh with major counterstrokes by the Stalingrad Front's 1st and 4th Tank Armies along the approaches to the Don River west of Stalingrad.

The Red Army also timed its offensives in the Demiansk, Rzhev, Zhizdra, and Bolkhov regions to coincide with operations near Voronezh and Stalingrad.[32] For example, the Western and Briansk Fronts employed several tank corps and, later, the new 3rd Tank Army in their July and August offensives near Zhizdra and Bolkhov. On the other hand, the Western and Kalinin Fronts' offensive in August and September near Rzhev, which was orchestrated by Zhukov and achieved moderate success, became a virtual dress rehearsal for an even larger counteroffensive in the same region later in the year (Operation Mars).

Although the Leningrad and Volkhov Fronts' second offensive at Siniavino in August and September 1942 failed disastrously, it prevented German forces from capturing Leningrad and tied down the German Eleventh Army, which could have been put to better use elsewhere on the Soviet-German Front.[33] As a result, the 2nd Shock Army, which the Germans had destroyed at Miasnoi Bor by early July, was destroyed once again in September near Siniavino.

Reflections

The summer–fall campaign of 1942 was momentous for the Red Army in general and for the *Stavka* in particular. In April and May 1942, Stalin and his *Stavka* optimistically concluded that they could capitalize on the Red Army's winter victories by conducting offensives to preempt renewed German offensive operations. The *Stavka's* hopes were dashed, however, when anticipated success quickly turned into the twin debacles at Khar'kov and in the Crimea. These disasters were clearly of the *Stavka's* own making; although it had amassed almost a full year of combat experiences, it failed to comprehend either its own capabilities or those of the *Wehrmacht*.

Even in the wake of these disasters and throughout Operation *Blau*, as evidenced by the heavy fighting around Voronezh, Zhizdra, and Bolkhov, the *Stavka* remained convinced that Red Army forces could either blunt or repel the German advance. When these counterstrokes failed, assuming that the OKH must have reduced its strength elsewhere along the front in order to assemble so massive a force in southern Russia, the *Stavka* stubbornly insisted the Red Army launch fresh coordinated counterstrokes along the entire front. The Red Army's numerical superiority in these offensives was indicative of the *Stavka's* expectations for success. Only in late August did Stalin completely understand the stark reality that the Red Army would emerge victorious only after it was capable of organizing massive strategic counteroffensives in the most critical sectors of the Soviet-German front.

Quite naturally, since they have been attracted to the dramatic fighting at Stalingrad like a moth to light, historians have focused their attention primarily on the most spectacular operations during the summer–fall campaign, specifically, the Red Army's spectacular defeats in May 1942, the equally heady (although, in retrospect, impulsive and rash) *Wehrmacht* drive to Stalingrad and into the Caucasus, and the fierce and relentless fighting in Stalingrad proper. All else seemed simply peripheral. As is so often the case, however, the seemingly peripheral was indeed significant. In short, the thousands of cuts that these and associated "forgotten battles" inflicted on the *Wehrmacht* literally "set the German Army up" for the devastating defeat it would suffer at Stalingrad later in the year.

The twin disasters the Red Army experienced at Khar'kov and in the Crimea in May 1942 and the Red Army's subsequent defeats in the early stages of Operation *Blau* had a sobering effect on Stalin and his *Stavka*. At the very least, these setbacks indicated that the Red Army's military education was far from complete, its forces structure was still inadequate to contest successfully with the *Wehrmacht*, and more innovative planning was necessary. As the Red Army's defenses collapsed under the hammer bows of advancing German panzer spearheads, Stalin began accepting the advice of his *Stavka* advisers and accelerated his program to convert the Red Army into a modern mobile fighting force. This reform program accelerated as German forces advanced to the Don River at Voronezh and then sped, in succession, into the Stalingrad and Caucasus regions. In addition to testing new types of combat formations, including new tank and mechanized corps and fledgling tank armies, as the fighting progressed, the *Stavka* and General Staff honed their forces' operational and tactical skills, all the while marshaling reserves necessary to conduct a new wave of counterstrokes and counteroffensives in the fall.

When these counteroffensives finally materialized in November 1942, the Red Army demonstrated to the world and the *Wehrmacht* that the Red Army had indeed become better educated in the conduct of modern mobile war. Nevertheless, the pain the Red Army endured in 1942 and even during the counteroffensives at year's end also clearly indicated that the education was far from complete. In short, further innovation would be required before the Red Army could achieve victory.

Historical Debates

The high drama associated with Operation *Blau* and the ensuing carnage at Stalingrad generated considerable controversy on both sides. Among the most heatedly debated questions associated with this campaign relate to responsibility for the Red Army's disasters at Khar'kov and in the Crimea, the wisdom of Hitler's strategy for Operation *Blau*, and the impact of the German diversion of Manstein's Eleventh Army to the Leningrad region on the outcome of the Battle of Stalingrad.

Responsibility for the Red Army's May 1942 Military Debacles? Since the war's end, Russian historians have struggled to assess responsibility for the Red Army disasters at Khar'kov and in the Crimea, which caused such disastrous Red Army losses and paved the way for Hitler's successful launch of Operation *Blau*.[34] During the spring of 1942, Stalin and his chief military advisers debated what strategic posture the Red Army should adopt throughout the summer. Although Stalin argued that the Red Army should go on the offensive, Zhukov, Vasilevsky, and others, citing the Red Army's limited capabilities and experience, particularly with regard to the conduct of offensive operations during the summer, urged Stalin to adopt a strategic defense along the Moscow axis, where they expected the *Wehrmacht* to conduct its summer offensive. Only after the Red Army defeated the German thrust, they argued, could the Red Army resume successful offensive operations.

Stalin accepted his advisers' recommendations, but with reservations. As a sop to his own wishes and those of his commanders in southern Russia, he ordered the Red Army to conduct the two unsuccessful spoiling offensives. Hence, primary responsibility for the Red Army's May defeats rests primarily with Stalin and Timoshenko, the commander of the Southwestern Direction Command, who planned and conducted the failed offensives. In addition, Nikita Khrushchev and General I. Kh. Bagramian, Timoshenko's commissar and chief of staff, and General R. Ia. Malinovsky, the commander of the Southern Front, and his chief of staff, General A. I. Antonov, also share blame for the Khar'kov fiasco.

Hitler's Strategy in Operation Blau. Given the disastrous results of Operation *Blau* and the devastating effect it had on the German war effort, historians have long debated Hitler's wisdom in conducting Operation *Blau*, especially his decision to seize Stalingrad and advance into the Caucasus region simultaneously. Some have argued that Hitler should have ordered the *Wehrmacht* to resume its offensive to seize Moscow in 1942 instead of advancing toward Stalingrad and into the Caucasus.[35]

This criticism of Hitler's strategic decisionmaking is entirely valid. As he had done in 1941, in 1942 he assigned the *Wehrmacht* missions far beyond its capabilities. Hitler's appetite for economic gain, specifically, his desire to conquer the oil-rich Caucasus region, prompted him to overextend his forces by committing a single army group (Army Group South), which, by definition, was capable of operating effectively along one strategic axis, into a region encompassing two distinct strategic axes (the Stalingrad and Caucasus axes). Although he artificially split Army Group South into Army Groups "B" an "A" to maintain the fiction that there were adequate forces operating along both axes, neither army group was capable of fulfilling its mission, and both were ultimately defeated. Inevitably, Hitler had no choice but to assign the inadequately trained and poorly equipped Romanian Third and Fourth, Italian Eighth, and Hungarian Second Armies to frontline combat sectors, where all became vulnerable targets for subsequent destruction by the Red Army.

The argument that Hitler's *Wehrmacht* could have seized Moscow in the summer and fall of 1942 is equally ludicrous for a variety of reasons. First, had it attacked Moscow, the *Wehrmacht* would have been advancing into the teeth of Red Army defenses where the *Stavka* expected the offensive to occur. The Red Army defended the Moscow axis in depth, manning heavy fortified lines backed up by the bulk of its strategic and operational reserves. Furthermore, by mounting an offensive against Moscow, the *Wehrmacht* would have had to thin out its forces in other sectors of the front, thereby improving the

Red Army's chances for offensive success in southern Russia and elsewhere.[36] Simply stated, a *Wehrmacht* advance on Moscow in 1942 would likely have replicated its sad experiences of 1941.

The Impact of the Leningrad Diversion. After capturing Stalingrad in late summer 1942, Hitler planned to employ von Manstein's Eleventh Army, which was engaged in destroying Red Army forces besieged in Sevastopol' and capturing the Crimean peninsula, to capture Leningrad. Some historians assert that Hitler's decision to employ the Eleventh Army at Leningrad deprived *Wehrmacht* forces in southern Russia of a large reserve when it most needed it, while others argue that Manstein should be faulted for failing to capture Leningrad.[37]

Although the first assertion is indeed valid, the second is wholly unfounded. In fairness to Hitler, he dispatched Manstein's army to the Leningrad region only after he was convinced German forces would reach and capture Stalingrad. With Stalingrad and most of the Caucasus in German hands, he assumed the time was ripe to seize Leningrad. This assumption proved incorrect largely because German intelligence significantly underestimated Soviet resistance at Stalingrad and the size of *Stavka* strategic reserves.

With regard to the second assertion, the Germans failed to capture Leningrad because the *Stavka* unleashed an offensive of its own in the region to preempt the Germans' attack. The massive offensive the Leningrad and Volkhov Fronts conducted in August 1942 against Army Group North's defenses at Siniavino caught the Germans by surprise and almost lifted the blockade of the city.[38] Army Group North was able to defeat the Red Army's 2nd Siniavino offensive and destroy the 2nd Shock Army for the second time in a single year only by committing the fresh forces of Manstein's Eleventh Army. The battle so decimated Manstein's army that it was incapable of mounting a subsequent assault to capture Leningrad.

The first period of the war ended in November 1942 with the *Wehrmacht's* once formidable Sixth Army suffering from severe attrition and sitting utterly exhausted in the rubble of Stalin's namesake city. Operation *Blau* and, with it, the high expectations of Hitler and his OKH for achieving decisive victory in 1942 also collapsed in shambles along the banks of the Volga River. Exploiting apparent Axis weaknesses and painstakingly marshaling its strategic reserves, the *Stavka* carefully prepared for two new Red Army offensives of unprecedented power and magnitude. Those offensives, which it unleashed near Rzhev west of Moscow and north and south of Stalingrad, quickly and violently shifted the strategic initiative into Red Army hands and signaled the beginning of a distinctly new period of the war.

CHAPTER 2

The Second Period of the War, 1943

THE WINTER CAMPAIGN, NOVEMBER 1942 TO APRIL 1943

From October through December 1942, 10 British divisions, including three armored divisions with 480 tanks, defeated nine German and Italian divisions (including two panzer divisions) in the Battle of El Alamein, inflicting 60,000 casualties on the Germans, and four to five Allied divisions (107,000 men) landed in Morocco and Algeria in Operation Torch. During the same period, seven Soviet armies with 83 divisions, 817,000 men and 2,352 tanks attacked 23 divisions of the German's Ninth Army at Rzhev (Operation Mars), suffering almost 250,000 casualties, including almost 100,000 dead, and losing roughly 1,700 tanks in the failed offensive.

From November 1942 through early February 1943 at Stalingrad and along the Don River, 17 Soviet armies with 1,143,000 men, over 160 divisions, and 3,500 tanks destroyed or badly damaged five Axis armies, including two German armies totaling more than 50 divisions, and killed or captured more than 600,000 Axis troops. On 1 January 1943, U.S. Army strength reached 5.4 million men in 73 divisions, with 1 million men and nine divisions in Europe.

From January through March 1943 in North Africa, 20 Allied divisions with almost 300,000 men drove 15 German and Italian divisions with about 275,000 men into Tunisia, while 11 Red Army *fronts,* including 44 armies, over 4.5 million men, and over 250 divisions, conducted massive offensives along a 1,000–mile front before being halted by German counterstrokes.

Context

From the perspective of the global armed struggle, Allied fortunes in the vast Pacific theater of war, southeastern Asia and China, the Mediterranean theater, and the Atlantic Ocean took a turn for the better in late 1942. American forces in the Pacific began the arduous and prolonged task of island-hopping their way through the bastion of island defenses Japan had erected in 1942 to protect its Asian co-prosperity sphere. Allied defenses solidified in the soft underbelly of southeastern Asia, and conflict in continental China slowly degenerated into virtual stalemate. The scales tipped to the Allies' favor in

North Africa when British forces smashed Field Marshal Erwin Rommel's *Afrika Korps* at El Alamein in the Egyptian desert and American and other British forces fought their way into Tunisia. In the Atlantic theater, too, Allied forces broke the German stranglehold over Allied shipping lanes, permitting freer flow of vital Lend-Lease equipment and supplies from the American arsenal of democracy to its beleaguered Allies.

Despite these Allied successes, however, the Red Army still bore the brunt of the ground fighting as it surrounded and destroyed *Wehrmacht* forces at Stalingrad and began the long and arduous process of expelling Axis forces from the Soviet Union.

The Conventional View of the War

The Red Army's counteroffensive at Stalingrad and the ensuing winter campaign of 1942–43 proved to be crucial moments in the Soviet-German war. At Stalingrad, for the second time in the war, the Red Army succeeded in halting a major Axis offensive and mounted a successful counteroffensive of its own. For the first time in the war, the Red Army's larger and more formidable tank and mechanized force was able to exploit deep into the enemy's rear area, encircle, and, subsequently, destroy whole enemy armies. For this reason, Stalingrad became one of three turning points in the war. The year before, the German defeat at Moscow had meant that Operation Barbarossa had failed and Germany could no longer hope to win the war on Hitler's initial terms. The Red Army's victory at Stalingrad in 1942 proved that Germany could not win the war on any terms. Later still, in the summer of 1943, the immense Battle of Kursk would confirm that Germany would indeed lose the war. The only issues remaining to be resolved after Kursk were how long it would take to achieve victory and how costly that victory would be.

The Red Army's fall counteroffensive and ensuing winter campaign spanned the period from mid-November 1942 to late March 1943 (see Map 2.1). It commenced Operation Uranus, the Stalingrad counteroffensive, on 19 November 1942, at a time when the bulk of Army Group "B's" Sixth and Fourth Panzer Armies were still locked in a struggle for the city of Stalingrad.[1] Within days, the Southwestern, Don, and Stalingrad Fronts' mobile forces had routed the Romanian Third and Fourth Armies, defending north and south of the city, exploited into the depth, and linked up west of Stalingrad, encircling 300,000 German and Romanian forces in the infamous Stalingrad pocket.

While the Don and Stalingrad Fronts prepared to reduce the encircled Sixth Army, Hitler appointed von Manstein to command Army Group "B" (soon renamed Army Group Don) and ordered him to restore the situation in southern Russia, specifically, to relieve German forces encircled at Stalingrad while the

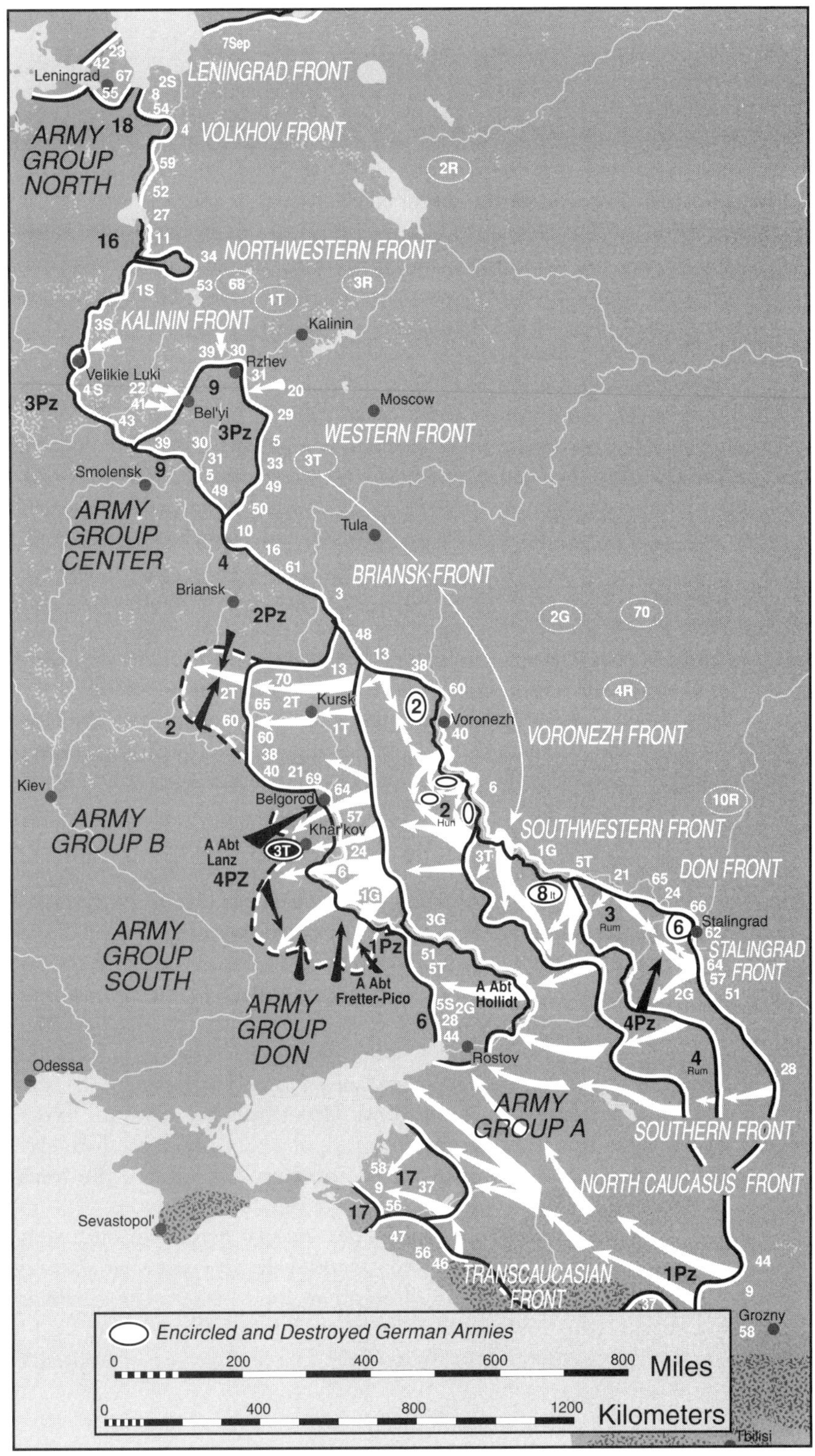

Map 2.1. The Winter Campaign, November 1942 to April 1943

OKH withdrew Army Group "A's" overextended forces from the Caucasus region. Manstein planned to conduct two relief operations in mid-December to rescue the encircled Stalingrad force: the first, a thrust by the LVII Panzer Corps northeastward from the Kotel'nikovsky region and, the second, an advance by the XXXXVIII Panzer Corps eastward from the Chir River. However, the former faltered in heavy and frustrating winter fighting and a Red Army offensive along the Chir preempted the latter. After a prolonged and terrible siege, the remnants of the German Sixth Army surrendered in Stalingrad on 2 February 1943.

Most histories of the Battle of Stalingrad claim Manstein's relief efforts failed for two reasons. First, the Southwestern Front and Voronezh Front's left wing launched a massive offensive, code-named Operation Little Saturn, across the Don River in mid-December against the Italian Eighth Army, which destroyed that army and preempted the XXXXVIII Panzer Corps' relief effort. Second, a tenacious Red Army defense and counterstroke in mid-December spearheaded by the powerful 2nd Guards Army first halted and then drove back the LVII Panzer Corps' relief effort after the panzer corps closed to within 35 miles of its objective. Some historians argue that Sixth Army's refusal to break out condemned the rescue effort to failure; others assert that the severe winter conditions simply made relief impossible.

Once the two German relief efforts failed, in early January 1943 the Don Front besieged the German Sixth Army in Stalingrad and the Southwestern and Stalingrad Fronts drove German forces from the Don River bend toward Millerovo and Rostov. Simultaneously, on 13 January 1943, the Southwestern and Voronezh Fronts began their Ostrogozhsk-Rossosh' offensive against the Hungarian Second Army and Italian Alpine Corps, which were defending farther north along the Don River, encircled and defeated the two Axis armies, tore an immense gap in Axis defenses, and threatened the flank of the German Second Army defending the Voronezh region. Before the Germans could restore the collapsed front, on 24 January 1943, the Briansk and Voronezh Fronts began their Voronezh-Kastornoe offensive, which defeated and nearly encircled Army Group "B's" Second Army west of Voronezh and forced the army to withdraw westward in disorder toward Kursk and Belgorod. Meanwhile, the Southwestern Front drove German forces westward to the Northern Donets River and Voroshilovgrad, and the Southern (formerly Stalingrad) Front captured Rostov on 14 February and reached the Mius River by 18 February.[2]

Exploiting its successes, in late January the *Stavka* ordered the Southwestern and Voronezh Fronts to mount two new offensives toward Khar'kov and Kursk and into the Donbas region.[3] After forcing the Northern Donets River in early February, the Southwestern Front captured Voroshilovgrad on 14 February and approached Zaporozh'e on the Dnepr River by 18 February (the Donbas operation). Simultaneously, the Voronezh Front captured Kursk and Belgorod on 8 and 9 February and Khar'kov on 16 February. Swept away by unbridled optimism and convinced that the Germans were about to abandon the Donbas region, the *Stavka* assigned its forces ever deeper objectives, even though Red Army forces were clearly becoming ragged and overextended and were outrunning their logistical support.

Beset by ever expanding Red Army offensives, Manstein orchestrated a miraculous feat that preserved German fortunes in the region. On 20 February, employing units withdrawn from the Caucasus and fresh units from the West, he struck the flanks of the Southwestern Front's exploiting forces as they neared the Dnepr River. Within days, the entire Red Army's offensive had collapsed and recoiled back to the Northern Donets River in disorder. Virtually without pause, Manstein's forces continued their advance in early March, striking and defeating the overextended Voronezh Front, recapturing Khar'kov and Belgorod on 16 and 18 March, and threatening the coherence of Soviet forward positions in the Kursk region.

By thwarting the Red Army's ambitious winter offensive, Manstein's counterstroke produced utter consternation within the *Stavka*. To forestall further defeat, Stalin and the *Stavka* transferred fresh forces to the Kursk and Belgorod regions, which, together with deteriorating spring weather, forced Manstein's forces to postpone further offensive action. During this period the Germans also abandoned their precarious and vulnerable salients in the Demiansk and Rzhev regions to create a straighter and more defensible front. The legacy of the intense combat during this campaign was the infamous Kursk Bulge, which protruded westward into German defenses in the central sector of the Soviet-German front.

As described above, the conventional view of the winter campaign of 1942–43 includes the following major operations:

- the Soviet Stalingrad offensive, Operation Uranus (19 November 1942 to 2 February 1943)
- the Soviet Kotel'nikovsky defense and offensive (12–30 December 1942)
- Soviet Operation Little Saturn (16–30 December 1942)
- the Soviet Rostov offensive (1 January to 18 February 1943)
- the Soviet Krasnodar-Novorossiisk offensive (11 January to 24 May 1943)
- the Soviet 3rd Siniavino offensive, Operation Spark (12–30 January 1943)
- the Soviet Ostrogozhsk-Rossosh' offensive (13–27 January 1943)
- the Soviet Voronezh-Kastornoe offensive (24 January to 5 February 1943)

- the Soviet Donbas (Voroshilovgrad) offensive (29 January to 19 February 1943)
- the Soviet Khar'kov offensive (2–23 February 1943)
- Manstein's Donbas counterstroke (20 February to 6 March 1943)
- Manstein's Khar'kov counterstroke (5–23 March 1943)
- the Demiansk offensive (15 February to 1 March 1943)
- the Rzhev-Viaz'ma offensive (2 March to 1 April 1943)

The Forgotten War

Existing accounts of military operations during the winter campaign of 1942–43 totally overlook three major Red Army strategic offensives, severely understate the scope of a fourth offensive, overemphasize the Red Army's achievements in the Demiansk and Rzhev regions, and distort both Stalin's and the *Stavka's* strategic intent in the late winter of 1943.

As directed by Stalin, the Red Army struck back at the Germans along virtually every major strategic axis along the Soviet-German front in mid-November 1942. In addition to conducting Operation Uranus at Stalingrad along the southern axis, under Zhukov's overall supervision, the Red Army's Kalinin and Western Fronts launched Operation Mars against Army Group Center's defenses in the Rzhev-Viaz'ma salient astride the equally vital western axis, in close coordination with offensives by neighboring *fronts*. The Kalinin Front's 3rd Shock Army began the offensive on 24 November by attacking the defenses of Army Group Center's Third Panzer Army at Velikie Luki, and, the next day, the Kalinin and Western Fronts' 41st, 22nd, 39th, 31st, 20th, and 29th Armies assaulted Ninth Army's defenses around the entire periphery of Rzhev salient, which both Germans and Russians perceived as "a dagger aimed at Moscow." Completing this array of offensive actions, on 28 November the Northwestern Front assaulted the defenses of Army Group North's Sixteenth Army around the infamous Demiansk salient.

After Zhukov's offensive along the western axis failed in mid-December, the *Stavka* shifted its attention to the south, where it sought to exploit the Red Army's Stalingrad success. Encouraged by the army's offensive progress during late December and early January south of the Don River and east of Rostov, in late January and early February, the *Stavka* ordered the Red Army to undertake additional offensive operations simultaneously along the northwestern, western, and southwestern central axes, specifically, Operation Polar Star, the Orel-Briansk-Smolensk operation, and the Donbas-Melitopol' operation.

The *Stavka's* decision to conduct these three massive offensives indicated that it sought nothing less than the complete defeat of all three German army groups by early spring and a Red Army advance along a broad front to the eastern borders of the Baltic region and Belorussia and the Dnepr River to the Black Sea. Directly or indirectly, these three strategic offensives involved forces from virtually every Red Army *front* operating between the Baltic and the Black Sea.

The "forgotten battles" or partially neglected operations during the winter campaign of 1942–43 include the following major operations:

- Operation Mars: The Soviet 2nd Rzhev-Sychevka Offensive (25 November to 20 December 1942)
- the Soviet 1st Donbas (Voroshilovgrad and Mariupol') offensive (29 January to 23 February 1943)
- the Soviet Orel-Briansk-Smolensk offensive (5 February to 28 March 1943)
- Soviet Operation Polar Star (15 February to 19 March 1943)

All four of these offensives were massive in scope and ambitious in aim. The 2nd Rzhev-Sychevka offensive, code-named Operation Mars, was the *Stavka's* companion piece to its counteroffensive at Stalingrad, Operation Uranus. The Western and Kalinin Fronts conducted the offensive under Zhukov's personal direction from 25 November through 20 December 1942, in close cooperation with operations by the Northwestern and Kalinin Fronts against *Wehrmacht* forces at Demiansk and Velikie Luki. The offensive's strategic objective was to destroy the Germans' Ninth Army, seize the Rzhev-Viaz'ma salient, and, if possible, defeat Army Group Center and capture Smolensk in a follow-on operation likely code-named Jupiter or Neptune. If the offensive failed, the *Stavka* hoped it would at least prevent the *Wehrmacht* from transferring forces to the south. Although Operation Mars failed after three weeks of intense fighting, it did tie down German Army Group Center's reserves and, in the process, seriously weakened the Ninth Army to the extent that Hitler authorized Army Group Center to abandon the Rzhev salient several months later.[4] History had almost completely forgotten this offensive, primarily to preserve Zhukov's high reputation.[5]

The Briansk, Western, and newly formed Central Front conducted the Orel-Briansk-Smolensk offensive in February and March 1943 in an attempt to collapse German defenses in central Russia and drive *Wehrmacht* forces back across the Dnepr River.[6] Even though Rokossovsky's Central Front penetrated westward as far as the Desna River, the offensive faltered in early March 1943, when the three *fronts* failed to crack powerful German defenses around Orel. This massive offensive failed largely because of hasty but tardy regrouping of requisite forces northward to the region west of Kursk, inadequate logistical support, poor coordination, deteriorating weather conditions, and the success of Manstein's Donbas and Khar'kov counterstrokes, which forced the *Stavka* to divert critical strategic reserves southward to contain Manstein's assault. When this offensive faltered, the Red Army's new front lines formed the northern and western perimeter of the infamous Kursk Bulge.

The Northwestern, Leningrad, and Volkhov Fronts conducted Operation Polar Star in February 1943 to lift the blockade of Leningrad and liberate the entire southern Leningrad region and perhaps to begin liberating the Baltic region. Also planned and directed by Zhukov as a continuation of Operation Spark, his January offensive that pierced the Leningrad blockade, Operation Polar Star sought to penetrate Army Group North's defenses in the Staraia Russa region, liquidate the Germans' Demiansk salient, and exploit with a full tank army to Narva and Pskov to encircle and destroy Army Group North's forces south of Leningrad.[7] While the Northwestern Front launched Zhukov's main attack from the Staraia Russa region to avoid further costly operations in the immediate vicinity of Leningrad, both the Leningrad and Volkhov Fronts supported the Northwestern Front by conducting smaller offensives of their own in the Leningrad region.

Operation Polar Star failed because the Germans abandoned the Demiansk salient on the eve of the offensive and, more importantly, because the *Stavka* deprived Zhukov of his 1st Tank Army, which it dispatched south to counter Manstein's threatening counterstrokes. Despite Zhukov's failure, Operation Polar Star became a dress rehearsal for the *Stavka's* January 1944 offensive, which ultimately liberated Leningrad.

In addition to these three major "forgotten" offensive operations, certain critical aspects of a fourth relatively familiar offensive remain neglected or entirely forgotten. History has recorded that the Southwestern Front alone conducted the ill-fated Donbas offensive operation in February 1943. In reality, however, the Southern Front also took part in the offensive, in the process spectacularly losing up to two mobile corps, which penetrated deep into the German rear area only to be decimated before they could escape.[8] Finally, the fighting associated with the German withdrawal from the Demiansk and Rzhev salients, whose ferocity Russian historians have exaggerated, also requires further detailed study and analysis.[9]

Reflections

In terms of its ultimate impact on the outcome of the war, the winter campaign of 1942–43, with the Red Army's spectacular victory at Stalingrad as its centerpiece, was one of the most decisive campaigns of the war. The German defeat and loss of its Sixth Army at Stalingrad, coupled with the destruction of three other Allied armies, proved to be the most decisive turning point in the war. In short, after Stalingrad, Hitler could not hope to win the war on any terms. In addition to proving that Germans could no longer win the war, after Stalingrad the Red Army began its inexorable westward march that ended at the Reichstag in April 1945. Less tangibly, the *Wehrmacht's* defeat at Stalingrad had an immensely negative effect on German morale by challenging the innate German sense of moral if not ethnic superiority over their Slavic opponents. Although German officers and troops soldiered on stoically and effectively, they were increasingly plagued by a feeling of impending doom.

The Red Army's wildly changing fortunes during its ensuing winter offensive demonstrated once again that the *Stavka* and many of its *front* commands still misunderstood the relative military capabilities of the Red Army and *Wehrmacht*. This explains why the Red Army's heady advance into the Donbas and toward the Dnepr and Desna rivers ended with ignominious and costly retreats that deprived the Soviets of about one-third of their offensive gains. As Manstein's counteroffensive clearly demonstrated, the *Wehrmacht* remained a deadly and effective enemy even when severely wounded.

Finally, during the winter campaign of 1942–43, Stalin and his *Stavka* began displaying strategic and operational habits that would endure to war's end, the most important of which was their tendency to test the Red Army's operational limits during virtually every strategic offensive operation. After the Red Army's victory at Stalingrad, throughout the remainder of 1943, and into 1944, the *Stavka* routinely and often deliberately assigned the Red Army strategic tasks that were clearly beyond its capability. It did so, first, to test the staying power of the *Wehrmacht* and, second, to determine what the Red Army was actually capable of achieving offensively with specific forces in a specific region. Although this practice resulted in inordinately high Red Army losses in men and weapons, it did enable the *Stavka* to establish more realistic objectives in future large-scale offensive operations.

The *Stavka* first evidenced this habit in February 1943, when it sought to defeat or destroy all three German army groups operating in the East by conducting simultaneously the Donbas, Khar'kov, and Orel-Briansk-Smolensk offensives and Operation Polar Star. Furthermore, this *Stavka* consistently pursued the same strategic aim in the summer and fall of 1943 and the winter of 1944, when it required the Red Army to conduct simultaneous offensive operations along multiple strategic axes, offensives that tested the endurance of the Red Army and *Wehrmacht* alike.

Historical Debates

The staggering proportions of the German defeat at Stalingrad and its influence on the subsequent course of the war generated heated controversy among those seeking to understand the war's nature from the German point of view. Likewise, the Red Army's unprecedented victory at Stalingrad contrasted to the collapse of the *Stavka's* ambitious winter offensive in February and March 1943 produced similar controversy on the Russian side. The most vexing issues associated with the winter campaign of 1942–43 are Stalin's strategic intent when planning the Red Army's November counteroffensive, the inevitability of German Sixth Army's destruction in Stalingrad, the real scope of the *Stavka's* winter offensive, the importance of Manstein's military response to the Red Army's winter offensive, and the degree to which the Battle of Stalingrad represented a turning point in the fortunes of war.

Stalin's Strategy. Stalin's and the *Stavka's* strategy during the winter of 1942–43 has generated considerable debate. First, most historians argue that, beginning in November 1942, Stalin and his key military advisers abandoned the "broad front" military strategy they had employed in the winter of 1942–43 and instead began carefully concentrating the Red Army's offensive efforts along the southwestern axis throughout the duration of the campaign. Therefore, they classify all other Red Army offensive actions as being simply diversionary in nature.[10]

Second, historians disagree over Stalin's strategic intent in the winter of 1942–43. Some argue that the expansion of the Stalingrad offensive was unpremeditated and simply took advantage of the deteriorating German situation in the south, while others claim that, from the very start, the *Stavka* intended to project Red Army's forces forward to the Dnepr River line from the Kremenchug region southward to the Black Sea.

Although the first claim regarding Stalin's "broad front strategy" is incorrect, neither of the interpretations regarding Stalin's strategy does justice to his full intent during the winter campaign. Archival evidence proves that, from November 1942 to the summer of 1944, Stalin's pursued a military strategy of conducting simultaneous large-scale offensives against *Wehrmacht* forces defending along multiple strategic axes. Hence, in November 1942, the Red Army launched Operations Mars and Uranus along the western and southwestern axis, and in February 1943 the Red Army conducted Operation Polar Star and the Orel-Briansk-Smolensk, Khar'kov, Donbas, Rostov, and Krasnodar offensives along the northwestern, western, southwestern, and southern axis, that is, across virtually the entire breadth of the Soviet-German front. Collectively, these offensives sought to drive *Wehrmacht* forces back to Narva, Pskov, Vitebsk, the Dnepr River, and the Black Sea by the end of the winter campaign.

This pattern endured in the fall of 1943, when Stalin ordered the Red Army to conduct simultaneous strategic offensives in Belorussia and the Ukraine, as well as in the winter of 1944, when he ordered the Red Army to launch strategic offensives in the Leningrad region, the Ukraine, and northern Romania, while other Red Army *fronts* launched heavy assaults against German defenses in eastern Belorussia.[11] This pattern persisted until the summer of 1944, when Stalin began staggering his strategic offensives by conducting them successively along different strategic axes, although, even in these cases, each offensive commenced while the previous offensive was still under way.[12]

The Rescue of German Sixth Army. The tragic loss of the German Sixth Army at Stalingrad has generated prolonged and heated debate regarding, in particular, the feasibility and relative significance of German attempts to rescue their encircled Sixth and Fourth Panzer Armies. Many historians argue that the encircled Germans could have been saved had Hitler permitted General Paulus, the Sixth Army commander, to withdraw from Stalingrad or had Paulus decided to break out of encirclement on his own volition before his army was destroyed. Both assertions are incorrect.

After assigning Manstein command of the new Army Group Don, Hitler ordered him to rescue Paulus's army by mounting two relief efforts, the first by the XXXXVIII Panzer Corps from the west and the second by LVII Panzer Corps from the southwest. However, anticipating these relief efforts, the *Stavka* ordered its Southwestern and Voronezh Fronts to conduct offensives against German and Italian forces defending along the Chir and Don rivers in mid-December.[13]

After initiating unsuccessful offensive operations along the Chir River in early December, the two Red Army *fronts* launched Operation Little Saturn across the Don River in mid-December. The offensive destroyed the Italian Eighth Army, diverted the German XXXXVIII Panzer Corps from its relief attempt, and utterly smashed Axis defenses along the Don River northwest of Stalingrad. Soon after, the *Stavka* employed its powerful 2nd Guards Army to defeat the second German LVII Panzer Corps along the Aksai River southwest of Stalingrad. Coupled with the inherent weakness of Paulus's encircled Sixth Army, the commitment of this powerful reserve force in the so-called Kotel'nikovsky offensive ensured defeat of the second German relief attempt and led to the subsequent dramatic Red Army advance toward Rostov-on-the-Don.

The Impact of von Manstein's February Counterstroke. Historians have been justly fascinated by the success and unrealized potential of Manstein's counterstrokes in the Donbas and at Khar'kov in February and March 1943. While agreeing that this counterstroke reversed German fortunes in southern Russia and restored stability to the German Eastern Front at a time when the catastrophic defeat at Stalingrad could have caused the *Wehrmacht* to collapse, some assert that had Hitler permitted Manstein to continue his counterstroke into March and April, the Germans would not have been defeated at Kursk in July 1943. Although these historians have significantly underestimated the scope and importance of Manstein's victory, this assertion is seriously flawed.

In addition to ending the Red Army's hopes of victory in southern Russia during the winter of 1942–43, together with skillful German actions elsewhere along the front, Manstein's counterstrokes, also seriously disrupted the Red Army's ambitious strategic offensives along the northwestern and western strategic axes. In short, his successful counterstrokes prevented the entire German Eastern Front from collapsing by drawing significant Red Army forces from other critical axes. Therefore, in terms of their scope, impact, and significance, Manstein's counterstrokes had an effect equivalent to a full-fledged successful strategic offensive.[14] It would take another major campaign and six months of heavy fighting for the Red Army to fulfill the missions the *Stavka* had assigned it in February 1943.

Manstein's counteroffensive also achieved its full potential. In light of the deteriorating weather conditions associated with the spring *razputitsa* (rainy season), the powerful reinforcements the *Stavka* dispatched to the Kursk region from other strategic axes made further German offensive action risky if not futile. In short, subsequent German offensive operations would likely have resulted in fresh defeats, negating some if not all of what Manstein had accomplished in his successful February and March counteroffensive.

The Battle of Stalingrad as a Turning Point. The Battle of Stalingrad was indeed the most important turning point in the Soviet-German war because the Red Army's successful counteroffensive and subsequent winter offensive clearly indicated that Germany could no longer win the war on any terms.

This fact was underscored by the grim reality that, at Stalingrad and during its subsequent offensives, the Red Army accomplished the unprecedented feat of encircling and destroying the bulk of the German Sixth and Fourth Panzer Armies and destroying or severely damaging the German Second, the Romanian Third and Fourth, the Italian Eighth, and the Hungarian Second Armies. In the future, the Axis could neither replace these armies nor conduct successful offensives without them.

THE SUMMER–FALL CAMPAIGN, JUNE–DECEMBER 1943

In July and August 1943, 160,000 U.S. and British forces invaded Sicily, defeated 60,000 German defenders, and advanced into southern Italy. At the same time, 2.5 million Red Army troops defeated over 1 million German troops at Kursk and over 6 million Red Army soldiers launched subsequent offensives against 2.5 million Germans along a front of over 1,500 miles and advanced toward the Dnepr River.

In October and November 1943, 11 Allied divisions drove nine German divisions back 16–39 miles from the Volturno River to Cassino in Italy, while six Red Army *fronts* with 37 armies, over 4 million men, and over 300 divisions assaulted German defenses in a 770-mile sector in Belorussia, at Kiev, and along the lower Dnepr River, piercing the German Eastern Wall in four sectors. By 31 December 1943, the U.S. Army was fielding 1.4 million men and 17 divisions in Europe, and the Red Army 6.2 million men and more than 500 divisions.

Context

Even though Stalin's Western Allies failed to establish a genuine second front on Europe's western coast in 1943, Hitler's *Wehrmacht* had to cope with the Allied seizure of Sicily and invasion of southern Italy, as well as perceived threats to the Balkans and France's coastal defenses. For the first time in the war, the *Wehrmacht* had to divert forces from its Eastern Front during the summer and fall of 1943 to deal with threats looming in the West. Worse still, the fall of Mussolini in 1943 resulted in the withdrawal of Italy from the Rome-Berlin axis.

In the Pacific region, American forces had seized control of the seas and were penetrating the Japanese defensive island cordon. With the Battle of the Atlantic won, the flow of critical equipment and supplies from the United States to its European allies was expanding into a veritable flood, exceeding the productive capabilities of the German armaments industry. Nevertheless, at year's end the German Eastern Front remained the decisive combat theater, and in light of the Red Army's continuing offensive successes, the German High Command was once again transferring vital strategic reserves to this theater.

The Conventional View of the War

For both the *Wehrmacht* and the Red Army, the summer of 1943 was one of the most pivotal periods in the Soviet-German war. Prior to this time, operations on the Soviet-German front involved a clear seasonal pattern of alternating strategic successes, with the *Wehrmacht* routinely victorious in the summer and the Red Army successful only in the winter. Although the *Wehrmacht* demonstrated its offensive prowess in Operations Barbarossa and *Blau* during the summers of 1941 and 1942, it faltered at the culminating point of each of these offensives after it encountered unanticipated Red Army resistance, the rigors of Russian weather, attrition of its forces, and deterioration of its logistical support.

Likewise, during the winter of 1941–42 and 1942–43, the Red Army managed to halt both *Wehrmacht* offensives short of their objectives, mount effective counteroffensives of their own, and then expand these counteroffensives into massive winter campaigns that stretched German strategic defenses to the breaking point. In both cases, however, even though the *Wehrmacht's* defenses bent, they did not break. As a result, the Germans were able to frustrate the *Stavka's* strategic aims, largely by exploiting the *Stavka's* carelessness, the skill and tenacity of their own forces, and the vexing spring thaw.

By the summer of 1943, two years of war experience seemed to indicate that the *Wehrmacht* "owned" the summers and the Red Army the winters. Even though this prescription for continued stalemate frustrated both sides, it was of greater concern to the Germans since they were waging war globally in an ever increasing number of continental and oceanic theaters. In addition to being bogged down in Russia's vastness, Germany was also waging a losing U-boat war in the Atlantic, facing an Allied air offensive over its homeland, fighting an unsuccessful ground war in North Africa, and defending the French and Norwegian coasts against the imminent threat of a "second front."

In short, by the summer of 1943, the *Wehrmacht's* success in the war, as well as the fate of Hitler's *Reich*, depended on the achievement of some sort of victory in the East, at the least, a victory that would exhaust the Red Army and force Stalin to negotiate a separate peace on whatever terms possible. Hitler decided to achieve this victory by launching his third major strategic offensive of the war, Operation Citadel, against Red Army forces concentrated in the so-called Kursk Bulge.[15]

Stalin and his *Stavka* also faced serious, but less daunting challenges in the summer of 1943. Although the Red Army had inflicted unprecedented defeats on Axis forces the previous winter, the *Wehrmacht* had managed to stabilize the front. Therefore, the *Stavka* could not defeat the *Wehrmacht* and expel it from Russian soil unless the Red Army could defeat it in the summer as well as the winter.

The *Stavka* decided to begin its summer–fall campaign by conducting a deliberate defense in the Kursk Bulge, where it knew the *Wehrmacht* was likely to focus its offensive. After parrying this offensive, the *Stavka* planned to unleash the Red Army in a series of counteroffensives of its own, first in the Kursk region and, subsequently, along the distant flanks of the Kursk Bulge. As was the case in its offensive the previous February, the *Stavka* ultimately sought to project Red Army forces forward to the Dnepr River and, if possible, into Belorussia and the Ukraine.[16]

The summer–fall campaign developed in three distinct stages: the Battle of Kursk proper; the Red Army's offensives on the distant flanks of the Kursk Bulge and subsequent advance (race) to the Dnepr River; and the Red Army's struggle to seize bridgeheads across the Dnepr River (see Map 2.2).

During the first stage, which began on 5 July, the Red Army's Central, Voronezh, and Steppe Fronts thwarted Operation Citadel by defeating the offensive by Army Groups Center's Ninth Army and Army Group South's Fourth Panzer Army and Army Detachment Kempf against the flanks of the Kursk salient. On 12 July, even before Citadel ended, the Western, Briansk, and Central Fronts launched Operation Kutuzov, attacking and defeating Army Group Center's Second Panzer Army in the Orel salient. About two weeks later and before the fighting subsided around Orel, on 3 August, the Voronezh and Steppe Fronts commenced Operation Rumiantsev, attacking and defeating Army Group South's Fourth Panzer Army and Army Detachment Kempf south of the Kursk Bulge and capturing Belgorod and Khar'kov by 23 August.[17]

On the distant flanks of the Kursk Bulge, the Kalinin and Western Fronts launched Operation Suvorov on 7 August, driving Army Group Center's Third Panzer and Fourth Armies westward, liberating Spas-Demensk, El'nia, Roslavl', and Smolensk, and reaching the eastern border of Belorussia by 2 October. To the south, the Briansk Front began its offensive on 17 August, defeating Army Group Center's Ninth Army and driving it from Briansk, and farther south the Southwestern and Southern Fronts attacked on 13 August, defeating Army Group South, driving its forces from the Donbas region and advancing to the outskirts of Zaporozh'e and Melitopol' by 22 September. At the front's southern extremity, the North Caucasus Front drove German troops from the Krasnodar region in the north Caucasus into the Taman' peninsula.

Once the Red Army accomplished all of its offensive aims in the Kursk, Orel, and Smolensk regions, during the second stage of the campaign, the *Stavka* ordered the Red Army to exploit its offensive southwestward and southward along the Kursk-Kiev and Kursk-Kremenchug axes to the Dnepr River. On 26 August, the Central, Voronezh, and Steppe Fronts began multiple offensives, known collectively as the Chernigov-Poltava operation, which by 30 September had driven Army Group South's Second, Fourth Panzer, and Eighth Armies back to the Dnepr River along a broad front from north of Kiev southward to the outskirts of Dnepropetrovsk. Soon after, Red Army forces seized small but vital bridgeheads over the Dnepr River south of Gomel' in eastern Belorussia, near Chernobyl' and Liutezh north of Kiev, at Bukrin south of Kiev, and south of Kremenchug in the central Ukraine.

During the second half of October, the Belorussian (formerly Central) and 1st Ukrainian (formerly Voronezh) Fronts consolidated their footholds over the

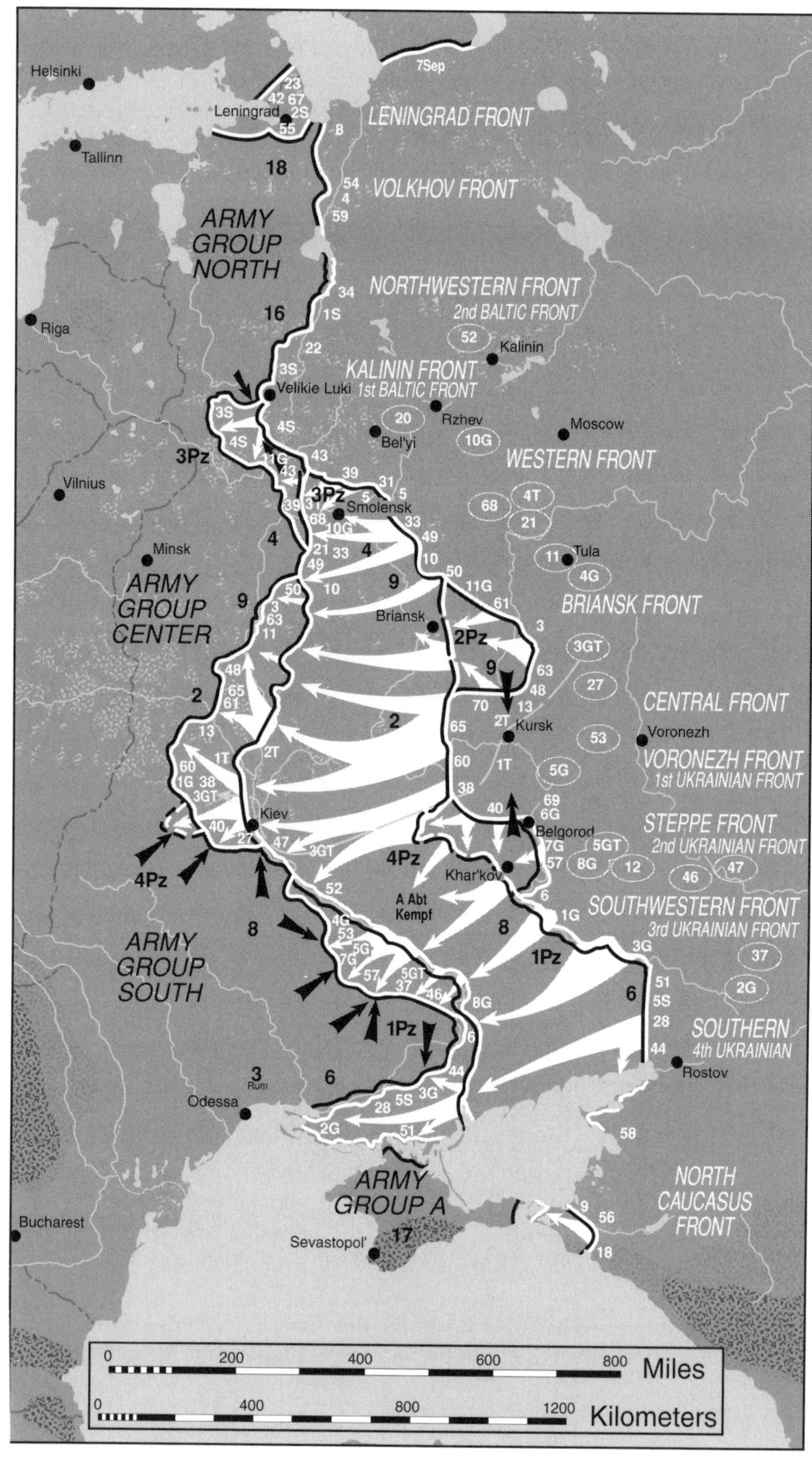

Map 2.2. The Summer–Fall Campaign, June to December 1943

Dnepr south of Gomel' and north and south of Kiev, and the 2nd and 3rd Ukrainian (formerly Steppe and Southwestern) Fronts cleared *Wehrmacht* forces from the eastern bank of the Dnepr, captured Dnepropetrovsk and Zaporozh'e, and established bridgeheads on the river's southern bank. Simultaneously, the 4th Ukrainian (formerly Southern) Front seized Melitopol' and the territory between the Dnepr River and the approaches to the Crimea, herded German forces into a bridgehead on the east bank of the Dnepr opposite Nikopol', and isolated the German Seventeenth Army in the Crimea.

The third stage of the campaign commenced in early November, when the 1st, 2nd, and 3rd Ukrainian Fronts attacked from their bridgeheads across the Dnepr. The 1st Ukrainian Front struck from the Liutezh bridgehead north of Kiev on 3 November, captured Kiev, Fastov, and Zhitomir from Army Group South's Fourth Panzer Army, and seized a strategic-size bridgehead west of the Ukrainian capital. From 13 November through 23 December, the *front* defended this bridgehead against fierce German counterstrokes orchestrated by Manstein.

During the same period, the 2nd and 3rd Ukrainian Fronts assaulted across the Dnepr River south of Kremenchug and at Dnepropetrovsk but failed to capture their objective of Krivoi Rog from Army Group South's defending Eighth and First Panzer Armies. For the next two months, the two *fronts* managed to expand their bridgehead, primarily to the west, while the 4th Ukrainian Front besieged elements of the new German Sixth Army in the Nikopol' bridgehead east of the Dnepr River. Finally, in late December, the reinforced 1st Ukrainian Front seized Zhitomir and attacked toward Berdichev and Vinnitsa in an offensive against Army Group South's Fourth Panzer Army that continued well into the new year.

Most accounts of the war assert that the *Stavka* accorded priority to the 1st, 2nd, and 3rd Ukrainian Fronts' operations in the Ukraine throughout the entire fall of 1943 rather than dissipating the Red Army's strength in numerous offensives along multiple strategic axes as it had in previous campaigns. These accounts relegate all Red Army operations along other axes, including offensives near Nevel' and Gomel' in October, near Nevel' and Rechitsa in November, and near Gorodok and west of Rechitsa in December, to secondary and supporting status.[18]

Thus, the conventional view of the summer–fall campaign of 1943 includes the following major military operations:

- German Operation Citadel (Battle of Kursk) (5–23 July 1943)
- the Soviet Orel offensive (Operation Kutuzov) (12 July to 18 August 1943)
- the Soviet Belgorod-Khar'kov offensive (Operation Rumiantsev) (3–23 August 1943)

- the Soviet Smolensk offensive (Operation Suvorov) (7 August to 2 October 1943)
- the Soviet Briansk offensive (1 September to 3 October 1943)
- the Soviet Chernigov-Poltava offensive (Red Army advance to the Dnepr River) (26 August to 30 September 1943)
- the Soviet Donbas offensive (13 August to 22 September)
- the Soviet Melitopol' offensive (26 September to 5 November 1943)
- the Soviet Novorossiisk-Taman' offensive (10 September to 9 October 1943)
- the Soviet Nevel'-Gorodok offensive (6 October to 31 December 1943)
- the Soviet Gomel-Rechitsa offensive (10–30 November 1943)
- the Soviet Kiev offensive (3–13 November 1943)
- the Soviet Lower Dnepr offensive (26 September to 20 December 1943)
- Manstein's counterstrokes at Kiev (13 November to 22 December 1943)
- The Soviet Zhitomir-Berdichev offensive (24 December 1943 to 14 January 1944)

The Forgotten War

Existing accounts of the summer–fall campaign of 1943 cover the Battle of Kursk and the Battle for the Dnepr River in exhaustive detail, yet leave yawning gaps in the historical record. Although these larger and more famous battles overshadow all other action during this period, the Red Army did conduct major operations of great potential significance elsewhere along the front. Nonetheless, Russian historians routinely and deliberately minimized the significance of these operations or utterly overlooked them for either political or military reasons, and their German counterparts ignored them, blinded by their staggering defeats elsewhere along the front.

Once again, most of these forgotten battles occurred when the *Stavka* tested the Red Army's operational limits at the end of successful offensive operations. After operating *fronts* fulfilled their initial strategic missions, the *Stavka* routinely assigned them new offensive missions to test or collapse German new defenses. In retrospect, most of these missions were overly ambitious and beyond the *fronts'* capability. In fairness to the *Stavka*, though, the excessive optimism it displayed when formulating these fresh missions was indicative of its entirely valid if not obligatory practice of attempting to exploit every Red Army strategic success to the maximum extent possible.

Contrary to persistent postwar assertions by Soviet historians that Stalin and his *Stavka* focused the Red Army's efforts along the southwestern axis into the

Ukraine, in reality, they once again demanded the Red Army conduct strategic offensives along multiple axes and across a broad front. Therefore, the Red Army launched major offensives along the western, southwestern, and southern axes during each stage of the campaign and operations of lesser significance along the northwestern and Caucasus axes.

The "forgotten battles" or partially neglected operations during the summer–fall campaign include the following:

- the Soviet Taman' offensives (4 April to 10 May and 26 May to 22 August 1943)
- the Soviet 2nd Donbas offensive (Izium-Barvenkovo and Mius River) (17 July to 2 August 1943)
- the Soviet 6th Siniavino offensive (15–18 September 1943)
- the Soviet 1st Belorussian offensive (Vitebsk, Orsha, Gomel', and Bobruisk) (3 October to 31 December 1943)
- the Soviet 1st Kiev offensive (Chernobyl', Gornostaipol', Liutezh, and Bukrin) (1–24 October 1943)
- the Soviet Krivoi Rog–Nikopol' offensive (Krivoi Rog, Aleksandriia-Znamenka, Apostolovo, and Nikopol') (14 November to 31 December 1943)

The first three of these "forgotten battles" were either constituent parts or continuations of larger and well-known Red Army offensive operations. The North Caucasus Front's Taman' offensive, for example, was a continuation of the better-known Krasnodar offensive operation, which took place from 9 February to 24 May 1943 and was designed to clear German forces from the northern Caucasus region. Directed by Zhukov for a time, the Taman' offensive, which lasted from early April to August 1943, included a prolonged series of unsuccessful assaults against German Seventeenth Army's fortified defenses around the towns of Krymskaia and Moldavanskoe, which anchored Hitler's last foothold in the Taman' region.[19]

The 2nd Donbas offensive occurred within the context of the Battle of Kursk, when the Southwestern and Southern Fronts jointly attacked German Army Group South's defenses along the Northern Donets and Mius rivers. Although the motives for this offensive remain unclear, it was probably designed to collapse German defenses in the Donbas and draw German attention and vital panzer reserves away from the Kursk region. Russian historians have studiously ignored these operations, preferring instead to cover the August 1943 versions of these operations in detail.[20] Finally, the Leningrad Front's 6th Siniavino offensive in mid-September was a furious, bloody, but ultimately successful attempt to overcome Army Group North's defenses on

Siniavino Heights, a target that had eluded Soviet capture for over two years. Although the assaulting forces seized the heights, Russian historians have studiously ignored this costly battle as they have many of the earlier attempts to seize the heights.[21]

The most dramatic "forgotten battles" during this campaign began in early October, when the Kalinin (1st Baltic), Western, Briansk, and Central (Belorussian) Fronts attacked into eastern Belorussia to capture Minsk, the Voronezh (1st Ukrainian) Front began operations to expand or seize new bridgeheads over the Dnepr River north and south of Kiev, and the Steppe (2nd Ukrainian), Southwestern (3rd), and Southern (4th Ukrainian) Fronts struggled to clear German forces from the Dnepr River bend from Kremenchug to Nikopol'.

During the 1st Belorussian offensive, which began in early October and continued unabated through year's end, the Kalinin (1st Baltic), Western, Briansk, and Central (Belorussian) Fronts sought to penetrate Army Group Center's defenses in eastern Belorussia and capture Nevel', Vitebsk, Orsha, Bobruisk, and Minsk. During the three months of intense and costly fighting, the Kalinin Front captured Nevel', driving a wedge between Army Groups North and South, the Kalinin and Western Fronts reached the approaches to Vitebsk and Orsha, and the Central Front captured Gomel' and Rechitsa in southern Belorussia.[22] However, none of the *fronts* could advance farther. Existing histories describe small fragments of this massive offensive, such as the Nevel' and Gomel-Rechitsa operations, but they studiously ignore the offensive's full scope and ambitious intentions.

The same accounts also routinely ignore the Central and Voronezh (1st Ukrainian) Front's bitter struggle in October 1943 to seize strategic bridgeheads across the Dnepr River north and south of Kiev. During three weeks of bloody but futile fighting, the Voronezh Front's 38th, 60th, 40th, 3rd Guards Tank, 27th, and 47th Armies, in conjunction with the Central Front's 13th and 60th Armies, failed to dislodge forces from Army Group South's Fourth Panzer and Eighth Armies, which contained Red Army bridgeheads in the Chernobyl', Gornostaipol', Liutezh, and Velikii Bukrin regions.[23] In this instance, the Voronezh Front's spectacular victory at Kiev in November erased these failed offensives from both memory and history.

Finally, in November and December 1943, the 2nd, 3rd, and 4th Ukrainian Fronts conducted the equally frustrating Krivoi Rog-Nikopol' offensive aimed at clearing the forces of army Group South's First Panzer and Seventeenth Armies from the lower Don River region. Although the three *fronts* tried repeatedly to revive their offensives and, in the process, seriously dented German defenses in several sectors, the defenses held, and both Krivoi Rog and Nikopol' remained in German hands until early 1944.[24]

Reflections

The Red Army's momentous victory at Kursk and its subsequent westward march to the Dnepr River validated its earlier triumph at Stalingrad and ended any German illusions regarding the outcome of the war. After Kursk, Germany could not even pretend to hold the strategic initiative in the East, and, as if to prove this point, the Red Army remained on the offensive throughout the rest of the war. If Stalingrad ordained that Germany would lose the war, Kursk proved to the world that the war would end with the Third Reich's total destruction. Only the matters of time and cost were left to be resolved.

Like the winter campaign of 1942–43, the climactic struggle along the Soviet-German front during the summer and fall campaign was far more complex than history has indicated. In short, beginning in mid-summer 1943, virtually every major Red Army victory was preceded, accompanied, or followed by a significant battlefield failure. Because these "forgotten battles" occurred within the context of spectacular Red Army victories, it was relatively easy for the Russians to conceal these battles and for the Germans to overlook them.

Just as Operation Uranus masked failed Operation Mars in November 1942, in July 1943 the Red Army's victory at Kursk obscured defeat in the Donbas and Taman' region, and in the fall the Red Army November victory at Kiev concealed its failure at Kiev in October and its defeats at Krivoi Rog and Nikopol' in November and December. In the same fashion, the Red Army's dramatic victories along the Dnepr in the fall of 1943, and in Operation Bagration in the summer of 1944, masked the army's unsuccessful offensive against Army Group Center in Belorussia during the fall of 1943 and, later, during the winter of 1944. In fact, this pattern would endure throughout 1944 and to war's end in 1945.[25]

Throughout the summer and fall of 1943 and the first half of 1944, the *Stavka* organized and conducted major offensives along virtually every strategic axis, thereby bringing immense pressure to bear on the *Wehrmacht* along the entire front. From early August through December 1943, every Red Army *front* from the Velikie Luki region to the Black Sea was on the attack, and the Leningrad and Volkhov Fronts joined the offensive in January 1944. Although this incessant offensive action failed to defeat and destroy complete Axis armies as it had at Stalingrad in late 1942 and early 1943, the "thousand cuts" seriously weakened *Wehrmacht* forces, conditioning them for the catastrophic defeats they would suffer in 1944.

During the summer–fall campaign, the Red Army finally completed the long, harsh, and costly education in modern war that it had begun in June 1941 and emerged as a modern mobile fighting force. Although its education would continue in 1944 and 1945, at Kursk it proved itself capable of contending successfully with Europe's most accomplished army.

Politically, too, the summer–fall campaign was of immense import. Demonstrating as it did that the Soviet Union would defeat Hitler's Germany, if necessary, by itself, the Red Army victory at Kursk had profound political impact. By increasing the importance of the Soviet Union within the Allied camp, it also accorded the Soviet Union a key role in defining the future political organization of postwar Europe and no doubt hastened the Allies' decision to open a second front in Western Europe. Not coincidentally, shortly after the summer–fall campaign ended, Stalin shifted the strategic focus of Red Army offensive operations into the Ukraine, and, after conquering this region, attempted to invade Romania and the Balkans in April and May 1944.

Historical Debates

The German defeat at Kursk and the Red Army advance to the Dnepr River in the summer–fall campaign of 1943 left a legacy of major historical controversies, the most contentious of which regard the wisdom of Hitler's decision to launch Operation Citadel, Stalin's strategy, and the degree to which the Battle of Kursk represented a turning point in the war.

The Timing, Wisdom, and Feasibility of Hitler's Operation Citadel. Many historians have questioned the wisdom of Hitler's decision to conduct Operation Citadel in the first place. Others have argued that he should have begun the offensive on the heels of Manstein's counteroffensive in March, and still others have criticized his decision to terminate the offensive before it achieved its full potential.[26]

First, in retrospect, the imposing strength of Red Army field forces and strategic reserves in the summer of 1943, its powerful defenses in the Kursk Bulge, and the predictability of a German offensive against the Kursk Bulge seemed to ensure Red Army victory at Kursk. Within the context of Operations Barbarossa and *Blau*, however, Hitler and his generals had every reason to expect success at Kursk because the *Wehrmacht* had always "owned" the summer and the Red Army had never before contained a concerted *Wehrmacht* offensive before it reached the strategic, much less the operational, depths. This grim reality explains why Stalin and the *Stavka* began the Battle of Kursk with a premeditated defense.

Second, it would have been foolhardy for Hitler to begin Operation Citadel in March or April 1943 because the *Wehrmacht* required considerable time to repair the damage inflicted on it during the Red Army's winter offensive and concentrate the forces and weaponry necessary to achieve victory in Citadel. Furthermore, the *Stavka* concentrated an imposing array of its strategic reserves in the Kursk and Voronezh regions in March and April 1943, including a total of nine fresh armies, which could have spelled doom for a renewed German offensive.[27]

Third, Hitler had no choice but to terminate Operation Citadel on 14 July. By this time, the *Wehrmacht's* assaulting forces had been severely weakened in two weeks of intense fighting, and vastly superior Red Army forces were smashing German defenses at Orel and along the Northern Donets and Mius rivers. While these two Red Army offensives threatened to collapse German defenses on the flanks of the Kursk Bulge, they were also drawing critical German forces away from the focal point of the Kursk fighting. Worse still for the Germans, at the very moment Manstein's panzer spearheads were struggling with the Voronezh Front's 5th Guards and 5th Guards Tank Armies on the infamous Prokhorovka battlefield, unbeknownst to the Germans, the Red Army's fresh 27th and 53rd Armies and 4th Guards Tank and 1st Mechanized Corps were poised to join the battle.[28]

Stalin's "Broad Front" Strategy. As in the winter campaign of 1942–43, claims that Stalin adhered to a "broad front" rather than a "narrow front" strategy are manifestly false. After the Battle of Kursk and particularly during the Red Army's subsequent advance to the Dnepr River, the *Stavka* applied relentless pressure against *Wehrmacht* defenses along the entire front from the Velikie Luki region to the Black Sea. By the time the campaign ended, nine Red Army *fronts* totaling almost 6 million soldiers were conducting active offensive operations along this front. However, during this campaign the *Stavka* often staggered the start dates for these offensives to keep the Germans off balance and frustrate their ability to shift operational reserves from one sector to another in a timely fashion.[29]

Kursk as a Turning Point. Although the Battle of Stalingrad was the most significant turning point in the war, the Battle of Kursk was also a turning point in several important respects. First, the battle presented the *Wehrmacht* with its final opportunity to achieve any sort of strategic success. Second, the battle's outcome proved conclusively that the war would end in Germany's total defeat.[30] After Kursk, a Red Army victory was inevitable.

THE IMPACT OF WAR, 1941–1943

The first two and one half years of war subjected the Soviet Union's political and military leadership and the Red Army's command cadre and soldiers alike to a harrowing, costly, but ultimately beneficial education in the conduct of modern war. This education encompassed virtually every aspect of war and military operations, including the war's strategic direction, the organization of operations at the operational and tactical levels, the structuring of combat forces so that they could fight, survive, and win in mobile warfare, and the organization of logistics to support and sustain high-intensity combat operations.

Despite the appalling chaos and confusion produced by cascading catastrophic defeats, within days after hostilities began Stalin regained his balance and began fashioning a strategic command and control structure organ, the *Stavka*, which in time proved capable of managing the war effort efficiently. At the same time, the inability of Red Army *front* commanders to plan and direct strategic operations efficiently prompted the *Stavka* to designate senior officers to coordinate the actions of multiple *fronts* operating along specific strategic directions (axes). However, lacking adequate staffs, requisite authority, and talented commanders, these new headquarters also proved ineffective. As a result, in 1942 the *Stavka* began employing its own representatives to coordinate major defensive and offensive operations, a practice it continued with ever greater effectiveness to war's end.

In addition to serving as a veritable "wrecking ball," which demolished the Red Army's force structure during the initial period of the war, Hitler's Operation Barbarossa also demonstrated how ill prepared the Red Army was to conduct modern mobile war. Within weeks after war began, the *Wehrmacht* had turned the Red Army's cumbersome rifle armies and rifle corps, unwieldy mechanized corps and tank and mechanized divisions, anachronistic heavy cavalry corps, and heavy antitank brigades into mere burnt out shells. Six months later, these forces were simply memories.

In short, the advancing *Wehrmacht* either killed or captured the bulk of the Red Army's initial wartime force during the first six months of war. By year's end in 1941, combat attrition and *Stavka* edict had transformed the once powerful Red Army into an assemblage of small rifle armies composed of austere rifle divisions and brigades, pathetically weak tank brigades, and fragile cavalry divisions. Because they were more effective in combat than their cumbersome predecessors and more easily controlled by inexperienced commanders, these new forces served to educate a new generation of Red Army combat commanders, but at immense cost in terms of human lives.

By savaging the Red Army's force structure during the first few weeks on war, the *Wehrmacht* also vividly exposed the Red Army's numerous shortcomings, leaving the *Stavka* no choice but to reform its army amid the heat of battle, lest it perish. Unwittingly, therefore, the Red Army's wholesale defeat in Barbarossa forced the *Stavka* and its General Staff to innovate on a grand scale in the mutually related realms of conducting military operations and structuring forces necessary to conduct those operations successfully.

Since they understood that reform was necessary if the Soviet Union and its Red Army were to survive, the *Stavka* and General Staff had no choice but to remedy the havoc wrought by *Wehrmacht* forces. In the spring of 1942, equipped with experiences gleaned from its first two wartime campaigns, the *Stavka* began forging a new Red Army that was more capable of contending successfully with the *Wehrmacht*.

The *Stavka* began reforming the Red Army's force structure in April 1942 by forming 15 new tank corps of panzer-division size to serve *front* and army commanders by conducting operational maneuvers and exploiting tactical into operational success. Although employed disastrously at Khar'kov in May 1942 and during the ensuing summer, the new tank corps proved effective enough for the *Stavka* to field eight new mechanized corps in late summer 1942 to serve as "test beds" for the conduct of mobile warfare.

After the *Wehrmacht* began Operation *Blau* in summer 1942, the *Stavka* fielded four new tank armies to contest with the Germans' vaunted motorized (panzer) corps. A curious mixture of track (tank), hoof (cavalry), and foot (infantry) forces that possessed little in the way of fire or logistical support, these first-generation tank armies served nonetheless as test beds for larger and more effective armored and mechanized forces in the future. The *Stavka* employed these armies extensively in 1942, first in late July and August against *Wehrmacht* forces at Zhizdra, Voronezh, and on the approaches to Stalingrad and later and more effectively in its counteroffensive at Stalingrad in November and its failed Orel-Briansk-Smolensk offensive in February and March 1943.

The Red Army's force structure matured in other ways during 1942 and 1943 as well. For example, in late 1942 the *Stavka* began forming new rifle corps within its field armies and expanding the structure of its field armies' fire and logistical support. In addition to fielding entirely new or larger artillery, antitank, and self-propelled artillery formations (corps and divisions) and units (brigades and regiments), the Red Army's operating *fronts* and its own reserve, the *Stavka* formed a more mature repair, reconstruction, and logistical structure within its vital tank and mechanized formations, and, in late 1942, air armies to support its operating *fronts*. In short, during the heat of battle and at immense cost, the *Stavka* had by the summer of 1943 forged and fielded a new Red Army, tried and tested in actual combat.

Nor did the *Stavka* and General Staff neglect the development of the vital implements of war. Despite the ravages of the prewar purges on Soviet military designers and design bureaus, after the war's outbreak the People's Commissariat of Defense exploited its prewar prowess in weapons development to produce an imposing array of new weaponry in vast quantities. These weapons included new series medium T-34 and heavy KV tanks, antitank weapons, artillery and *Katiusha* multiple rocket launchers, and advanced combat aircraft.

More importantly from the standpoint of combat operations, during the first two and a half years of war, the *Stavka* and General Staff had to identify, educate, and train Red Army commanders who could contend more effectively with their more experienced and skilled *Wehrmacht* counterparts, not only in terms of the war's strategic direction but also in terms of its conduct operationally and tactically. Strategically, at least, the Germans' congenital habit of overreaching clearly eased the *Stavka*'s task in 1941 and 1942. During Operation Barbarossa, for example, Hitler's attempt to accomplish too much with far too few forces and his pursuit of poorly defined strategic aims largely negated the adverse effects of the Red Army's dismal strategic leadership and the appalling operational and tactical ineptitude of its commanders and conditioned German defeat at Moscow. During Operation *Blau* the following year, the *Wehrmacht's* defeat proved even costlier since the German leadership displayed the same faults as it had in 1941, while the Red Army's leadership at the strategic and operational levels improved markedly. The result was the Battle of Stalingrad and the Axis's subsequent loss of five armies.

The challenge the *Stavka* faced in 1943 was quite different from what it had confronted during the two previous years. By this time, the Stavka realized the Red Army would have to wage war more effectively at all levels if it was to achieve final victory over the *Wehrmacht*. The Red Army would have to perform the unprecedented feat of containing a *Wehrmacht* offensive short of the strategic depths and then defeat the Germans with offensives of its own during the height of summer. The Red Army finally accomplished these tasks at Kursk in mid-summer 1943.

The Red Army was able to transform itself into a modern fighting force primarily because it was able to learn from its experiences. Throughout the trials of the first 18 months of war, the Red Army General Staff established a formal structure at *front* and later higher command levels to collect, process, and analyze every aspect of combat experience. It then formalized this entire process in November 1942 by forming the Section for the Exploitation of War Experience within its Military-Historical Directorate, and, later still, elevated the war experience section to the status of a full directorate.

In conjunction with the Voroshilov General Staff and Frunze academies, these war experience organs spearheaded the process of innovation by issuing collections of combat documents, candid appraisals, case studies, and, in time, comprehensive studies of all aspects of past military operations, all of which became grist for preparing specific directives, orders, and instructions to remedy the Red Army's many shortcoming.[31] By mid-1943 Germans and Russians alike realized that the Red Army's battlefield performance was validating the General Staff's war experience effort. Despite the appalling defeats it suffered in 1941 and 1942, in late 1942 and 1943 the Red Army graduated from this harrowing education to defeat the most professional and competent army in the world at Stalingrad and Kursk. By mid-1943, with the Red Army's victories at Moscow, Stalingrad, and Kursk behind them, few in the Soviet leadership doubted the war's ultimate outcome. Victory was ensured, but no one could say how long it would take or what price the Red Army would have to pay.

Red Army troops assembling in Red Square (1941)

Red Army propaganda poster, "Under the Banner of Lenin, Forward to Victory!" (1941)

Red Army propaganda poster, “Pincers in pincers” (Moscow, 1941)

Red Army propaganda poster, “We defend the Motherland Moscow” (1941)

Tanks on the attack (1941)

Tanks and infantry in the assault

Infantry in the assault

Regimental artillery deploying for action

Planning an attack

The carnage at Prokhorovka

CHAPTER 3

Soviet Military Art

MILITARY STRATEGY

The immense scale, prolonged duration, and dizzying complexity of military operations on the Soviet-German front, combined with the unprecedented ferocity and sheer brutality of the fighting, stretched the limits of Soviet military art and strategy. It also severely tested the Soviet Union's strategic leadership, especially the State Defense Committee (GKO) and *Stavka* (High Command), both of which were dominated by the Soviet dictator, I. S. Stalin. Fighting for the survival of his state and its Red Army against a surprise invasion by Europe's most formidable military power, Stalin made it his first priority during the 18 months of the war to mobilize the state's resources to repel the onslaught of Hitler's *Wehrmacht*. At the same time, he also worked to forge an international alliance against Nazi Germany, particularly after the entry of the United States into the war in December 1941, and, thereafter, persistently pressed his Allies to open a second front on the European continent.

After driving the *Wehrmacht* back from the gates of Moscow in December 1941 and defeating it at Stalingrad in November 1942, Stalin's Red Army attacked with abandon over the next three months to ensure that the fortunes of war remained tipped in the Red Army's favor. Although the *Wehrmacht* was able to contain the Red Army's offensive in the winter of 1942–43 and even orchestrate one more strategic offensive of its own in the summer of 1943, the Red Army's victory at Kursk in July 1943 spelled certain doom for the *Wehrmacht* and, ultimately, Nazi Germany. As his Red Army unleashed massive new offensives in the second half of 1943, Stalin coordinated these operations more closely with those conducted by Allied forces operating in the Western European and Mediterranean theaters of war, all the while urging them to establish a second front on the European continent. By this time, however, Stalin was convinced that the Red Army could defeat Nazi Germany with or without further Allied assistance.

By Soviet definition, military strategy encompassed a wide range of tasks. Before wartime, for example, it included planning the mobilization, formation, and strategic deployment of the armed forces, organizing the country's air defenses, and preparing theaters of military operations. Once war began, military strategy governed the strategic employment of forces and weapons, planning and conducting military campaigns and strategic operations during wartime, providing strategic leadership for the armed forces, creating strategic force shock groupings, raising, training, and employing strategic reserves, determining the most effective means and forms for conducting warfare according to the situation, organizing strategic cooperation military forces, and effectively exploiting the state's military and economic capabilities to achieve victory over the enemy.[1]

Of necessity, after Hitler unleashed Operation Barbarossa, Stalin's military strategy during the ensuing 18 months of war was inherently defensive and aimed solely at stripping the strategic initiative from the *Wehrmacht's* hands:

> When the enemy held the strategic initiative during the first period of the war, military strategy focused on creating an active strategic defense, primarily by employing the tactics of determined resistance along existing, created, or natural positions to exhaust the enemy, by using determined counterstrokes to frustrate the enemy's plans, and by conducting separate offensive operations (army and *front*). In the process, as a rule, the strategic defense we conducted in 1941 was forced on us by the course of active enemy offensive operations, we prepared our [strategic] defense in 1942 in advance, and we conducted [our strategic defense] in 1943 deliberately to exhaust the enemy and launch a counteroffensive. . . . The execution of a strategic counteroffensive by Soviet forces near Moscow and their expansion of it into a general offensive in the winter of 1941–42 were important achievements of Soviet military strategy.[2]
>
> Thereafter, however, Stalin's strategy remained offensive in nature until war's end, "The Soviet Army seized the strategic initiative during the second period of the war and secured it once and for all. All subsequent development of Soviet military strategy was related to the main type of strategic operations–the strategic offensive."[3]

Strategic Command and Control

The immense and daunting challenges the Soviet Union faced when war began forced Stalin to centralize strategic direction of the war in a finite number of command and control organs, the most important of which were the State Defense Committee, the *Stavka*, the People's Commissariat of Defense, and the Red Army General Staff, and a few less visible control organs (see Chapter 10). The most formidable task these organs faced was to create a military command and control system capable of effectively coordinating multiple Red Army *fronts* in strategic defensive operations. Although prewar Soviet military theory had envisioned single *fronts* conducting defensive and offensive operations along a single strategic axis, Operation Barbarossa proved they could not do so.

Therefore, immediately after war began, the *Stavka* began experimenting with new command structures capable of coordinating the actions of multiple *fronts*, in defensive operations in the summer and fall of 1941 and in offensive operations during the winter of 1941–42. When these commands proved ineffective, beginning in the fall of 1942, the *Stavka* began employing its own personal "representatives" to control operations by groups of operating *fronts*, a system of strategic control that endured to war's end.

Within the parameters of this command and control system, the *Stavka* conveyed its strategic decisions to operating *fronts* and fleets by means of directives specifying which commands would conduct operations, when, where, how, and with what forces.[4] The General Staff's and NKO's directorates and Red Army service (VVS) and branch chiefs (armored, artillery, engineer, etc.) also routinely provided input for these directives, and, prior to each operation, *front* and even army commanders could question decisions and suggest alternative courses of action. After the *Stavka* issued final operational directives and while operations were under way, it issued fragmentary and warning orders assigning additional missions to operating *fronts* as the situation required.[5]

During the first period of the war, the *Stavka* usually issued operational directives personally to its main commands, *fronts*, and sometimes even armies by summoning their commanders to Moscow. During the second period of war, however, to an ever-increasing degree, it issued these directives through representatives that it assigned to groups of *fronts* to coordinate the planning and conduct of major offensive or defensive operations. Although the *Stavka* initiated most of these directives on its own, usually after conferring with its representatives and *front* commanders, *front* commanders themselves could prepare proposals for future operations. In these instances, *front* commanders submitted written proposals to the *Stavka* after conferring with their military councils (the commander and his chief of staff and commissar) and their *Stavka* representatives, if they were assigned. The *Stavka* then studied, corrected, and either approved or disapproved the proposal, and, if it approved, issued its operational directive.

Strategic Planning

Prior to the fall of 1942, the *Stavka* planned only specific operations, most of which were defensive or counteroffensive in nature, and did not prepare plans for multiple successive operations or campaigns.[6] However, in the fall of 1942, for the first time in the war, it prepared a single unified campaign plan that included broad and well-defined strategic objectives and required its participating *fronts* to conduct virtually simultaneous offensives in the Velikie Luki, Rzhev, and Stalingrad regions, subsequent offensives toward Viaz'ma and Rostov, and at least the first stages of a subsequent winter campaign.[7] After the Red Army's offensives in the Stalingrad region succeeded, the *Stavka* developed in stages an even more elaborate campaign plan during January and early February 1943. This plan required the Red Army's *fronts* to conduct offensives along multiple axes encompassing two-thirds of the Soviet-German front and reach objectives extending from the eastern border of the Baltic region along the Dnepr River to the Black Sea by the end of March. However, during the latter stages of this campaign, the *Stavka* permitted its attacking forces to become overextended, and the campaign failed in the face of skillful German resistance. On the positive side, the failures it experienced during this campaign prompted the *Stavka* to adopt a far more realistic and prudent approach in its strategic planning in the spring and summer of 1943.

Although inherently offensive in nature, the *Stavka's* campaign plan governing Red Army operations during the summer and fall of 1943 required its operating *fronts* to begin the campaign on the defense, primarily in the Kursk region, where the *Stavka* expected the *Wehrmacht* to attack. In addition to planning this defense in detail, the *Stavka* also planned subsequent offensive operations in and adjacent to the Kursk region and along an even broader front once its initial offensives succeeded. This required its participating *fronts* to reach the Vitebsk region and cross the Sozh and Dnepr rivers. However, when Red Army forces reached their campaign objectives in early October, the *Stavka* once again overreached itself by ordering them to capture Minsk and Vinnitsa. Although these subsequent offensives failed, in this instance the *Stavka's* campaign planning demonstrated a justifiable intent to exploit the Red Army's successes to the fullest possible extent, a practice it would continue to pursue until war's end.

Strategic Cooperation

When planning and conducting operations during 1941 and 1942, the *Stavka* learned that organizing effective strategic cooperation *(vzaimodeistvie)* among its operating *fronts*, strategic reserves, and other supporting forces was a perquisite to achieving success in strategic defensive or offensive operations and campaigns:

> The *Stavka* and General Staff organized strategic cooperation between groups of Soviet Armed Forces operating along various strategic axes on the basis of mission, axis, and variant of action, and the main commands of strategic directions and representative of the *Stavka* VGK organized

> operational-strategic cooperation between elements of operational-strategic formations and large formations of [various] types of armed forces within the limits of a single strategic defensive operation.[8]

In 1941 and 1942, the *Stavka* was unable to organize effective strategic cooperation during the initial stages of Operations Barbarossa and *Blau* because the *Wehrmacht* achieved surprise and seized the strategic initiative in both offensives. Subsequently, however, it was able to undertake some cooperative actions to disrupt German implementation of their offensive plans. For example, immediately after these offensives began, the *Stavka* conducted offensives against the flanks of the advancing Germans with forces positioned along their flanks to distract the Germans and prevent them from reinforcing their main efforts.[9] It also organized counterattacks, counterstrokes, and, in some instances, even counteroffensive to defeat, disrupt, or simply weaken the advancing *Wehrmacht* forces.[10] In addition, while shifting aviation forces from secondary sectors to weight the defense along critical strategic axes, during its defense of Leningrad, Moscow, Odessa, and Sevastopol', the *Stavka* integrated local air defense forces (MPVO) and naval forces into ground defenses by requiring them to engage ground targets.

Although the *Stavka* failed to organize effective strategic cooperation between its operating *fronts* during the strategic offensives it orchestrated during the winter campaign of 1941–42, it did so to a far greater extent during its partially successful winter campaign of 1942–43. For example, during this campaign the *Stavka* coordinated offensives by five *fronts* in November 1942, eight *fronts* in January 1943, and 11 *fronts* in February and March 1943, in offensives that ultimately engulfed the entire Soviet-German front.[11]

During the initial stages of its summer–fall campaign of 1943, for the first time in the war, the *Stavka* organized cooperation among its operating *fronts* by employing them in "groups of *fronts*," first, to conduct defensive operations and, later, to conduct offensive operations along multiple strategic axes.[12] In addition, prior to and during these operations, for the first time in the war, the *Stavka* conducted large-scale air operations with long-range and *front* aviation in conjunction with ground operations to disrupt German transport and communications and weaken the already flagging strength of the German *Luftwaffe*.[13] The *Stavka* also conducted large-scale partisan operations in the *Wehrmacht's* rear area to disrupt communication and inhibit the free movement of its reserves.[14]

Finally, during the latter stages of its summer–fall campaign of 1943, the *Stavka* arranged cooperation among three groups of *fronts* tasked with advancing to and beyond the Dnepr River, specifically, three *fronts* advancing into Belorussia, two more into the Ukraine in the Kiev and Vinnitsa regions, and three others into the Krivoi Rog region in the eastern Ukraine.[15] While these massive air-ground operations coordinated by the *Stavka* resulted in important strategic gains, more importantly they paved the way for even larger and better-coordinated strategic operations in 1944 and 1945.

The Role of Personality

Although many of the problems the *Stavka* experienced in controlling and coordinating its forces effectively during the first two periods of the war resulted from the *Wehrmacht's* achievement of surprise, the immense complexity of military operations, the inexperience and lack of training of many officers and soldiers, and shortages of necessary weaponry, they also reflected the influence of Stalin's personality on strategic decisionmaking and the inexperience of other *Stavka* members.[16]

Prior to the war, Stalin had purged the Red Army's most experienced and imaginative commanders, thereby disrupting continuity in Soviet military theory, obliterating its most positive aspects, and perverting its military strategy on the eve of war. Once war began, Stalin personally dominated all strategic decisionmaking during the entire first period of the war. Based on whim and prejudice, Stalin's judgments frequently masked objective realities. Although Stalin's involvement provided a certain unity to strategic planning on the one hand, on the other it intimidated the General Staff and senior military leaders.

Stalin's demands that the Red Army cling to untenable positions and his meddling in strategic and operational decisionmaking were directly responsible for its disasters at Uman', Kiev, Viaz'ma, and elsewhere in 1941. His influence deprived the *Stavka* of its initiative and limited its strategic horizons, forcing it to plan reactively to the single imperative of restoring stability to the front, but his single-minded insistence on marshaling reserves and his ruthless, but often stingy, allocation of these reserves ultimately strengthened the Red Army strategically. As a result, the Red Army's stubborn resistance during the battles for Leningrad, Moscow, and Rostov and the energy, sacrifice, and determination it displayed during the ensuing winter campaign reflected Stalin's iron will. Stalin's strategic blunders notwithstanding, in December 1941 the threadbare Red Army fought with a ferocity and desperation that mirrored its leader's determination and ruthlessness.

Stalin's misjudgments also contributed to the Red Army disasters at Khar'kov and the Crimea in May 1942 and the cascading series of defeats it experienced on the road to Stalingrad in the summer and early fall of 1942: "The chief reason for the failure of the summer campaign of 1942 was the High Command's erroneous decision 'to affix' numerous separate offensive operations on all fronts to the strategic defensive operation. This dispersal of strength and premature expenditure of strategic reserves certainly doomed Stalin's plan to failure."[17]

At Stalingrad in the fall of 1942, however, Stalin replicated his positive performance of the previous year–but only because he began to heed the advice of his most trusted key military advisers, such as Zhukov, Vasilevsky, Antonov, and Voronov. Thereafter, Stalin continued following his advisers' counsel throughout the remainder of 1942 and all of 1943, though not without retaining tight control over all of his political and military subordinates. As he had earlier in the war, when he deemed it necessary, he treated those he suspected of disloyalty with harsh disciplinary measures, and he often confused combat failures or perceived ineptitude on the part of field commanders with outright disloyalty.[18]

To ensure that his commanders remained politically reliable, Stalin employed the onerous commissar system he had created early in the war to maintain discipline and reliability throughout the army and often punctuated his strategic guidance with outright intimidation. Although he abolished this commissar system in late 1942, for the remainder of the war Stalin continued to require members of the military council (in reality, commissars) at higher command levels to validate their commanders' orders, maintained political deputies at all other levels of command to monitor commanders' reliability, and resorted to investigation, arbitrary arrest, and even execution of those commanders and other senior officers who failed to carry out his orders.

Stalin did indeed led the Red Army to victory, but in the final analysis his ruthless determination also contributed to its immense human losses.

STRATEGIC DEFENSIVE OPERATIONS

Strategically, the most crucial and difficult challenge the *Stavka* and Red Army faced during the first 30 months of the war was the need to organize and conduct effective strategic defensive operations to slow, halt, and ultimately repel *Wehrmacht* forces conducting Operations Barbarossa, *Blau*, and Citadel during the summers of 1941, 1942, and 1943. In addition to planning and coordinating these operations, the *Stavka* had to arrange for the construction of strategic defense lines forward of and around such key cities as Kiev, Leningrad, and Moscow and, later, Stalingrad, and Kursk, raise and field strategic reserves, and plan and coordinate counterstrokes and counteroffensives to restore the strategic initiative to the Red Army. Worse still, during the first two years of the war, it had to conduct these defenses over immense distance against seemingly irresistible *Wehrmacht* forces after the Soviet Union and Red Army suffered catastrophic losses of territory, industrial facilities, agricultural lands, manpower, weaponry, and other material.

In 1941 the Red Army conducted its strategic defense during Operation Barbarossa across a more than 2,500–kilometer front extending from the

Barents Sea to the Black Sea and to depths of 50–950 kilometers from the Soviet Union's western frontiers to the approaches to Murmansk, Leningrad, Moscow, and Rostov. The most intense of these operations took place in the almost 1,200-kilometer-wide sector between the Baltic and Black Seas. It began its defense with a force of 20 mechanized corps and 103 divisions in its operating *fronts* and armies, 5 mechanized corps and 42 divisions in its own reserves (the RGK), and more than 17,000 tanks. During over five months of defense, the *Stavka* reinforced its defending forces with 291 divisions and 94 separate brigades, discounting losses, increasing the strength of defending forces to 274 divisions in its operating *fronts* and armies and 57 in its reserves (now called the RVGK) on 1 December 1941 (see Appendix 1 in the companion volume).

Before halting the German juggernaut in early December 1941, the *Stavka* organized and coordinated, albeit often quite poorly, from one to three separate, distinct, and successive strategic defensive operations, punctuated by short-lived counterattacks, counterstrokes, or counteroffensives along each of the three main strategic axes stretching across the Soviet Union's heartland. Within this vast space, during 1941 the Red Army conducted 11 distinct strategic defensive operations along frontages of 300–1,100 kilometers to depths of 50–600 kilometers over periods of 20–100 days (see Table 3.1).[19]

In 1942 the Red Army conducted its strategic defense during Operation *Blau* across a 600–2,100 kilometer front extending initially from northeast of Kursk to Taganrog and ultimately from the Voronezh region through Stalingrad to the Caucasus Mountains and to a depth of from 150 to almost 800 kilometers. It began its defense with a force of 11 tank corps, 111 divisions, and 62 tank brigades in its operating *fronts*, 38 divisions in the RVGK, and about 5,000 tanks. During almost five months of defense, the *Stavka* reinforced its defending *fronts* with 11 tank and mechanized corps, two cavalry corps, 72 rifle divisions, and 38 tank brigades, discounting losses, increasing the strength of its defending forces to nine tank, three mechanized, and six cavalry corps, 203 rifle divisions, and 60 tank brigades in its operating *fronts*, and four tank and two mechanized corps, eight rifle divisions, and one tank brigade in its RVGK on 1 December 1942.[20]

Before halting the *Wehrmacht's* offensive in mid-November 1942, the *Stavka* conducted both positional and maneuver defenses, first along the Voronezh and Stalingrad strategic axes and, later, along the Caucasus axis as well, while defending or conducting local counterattacks or full-scale counterstrokes along the remainder of the Soviet-German front. The *Stavka's* strategic defense included three distinct defensive operations, conducted on frontages of 250–1,000 kilometers and to depths of 150–800 kilometers over periods of 50–125 days (see Table 3.2).

In contrast to 1941 and 1942, the *Stavka* required the Red Army to conduct strategic defensive operations only twice during 1943, first in February and March, when a *Wehrmacht* counteroffensive forced it to do so, and second in July, when the defensive operation contributed materially to the achievement of its overall strategic offensive aims. The *Stavka* conducted the first of these strategic defensive operations across a 500-kilometer front and to depths of 50–210 kilometers in the Donbas, Khar'kov, Sevsk, and Kursk regions during February and March 1943 to preserve the gains the Red Army achieved during its winter offensive of 1942–43 against a concerted *Wehrmacht* counteroffensive. It conducted its second in July across a 550-kilometer front and to depths of 10–35 kilometers in the Kursk region as a premeditated strategic defense designed to blunt an expected German offensive prior to the conduct of a general strategic offensive of its own.

The *Stavka's* strategic defense in February and March 1943 included three *front*-level defensive operations conducted across frontages ranging from 200 to 300 kilometers to depths of 50–210 kilometers during periods of 10–22 days. The *Stavka's* strategic defense in July included only a single strategic defensive operation (at Kursk) conducted by two *fronts* and a portion of a third (see Table 3.3).[21] Thus, the strategic defensive operations the *Stavka* conducted in 1942 and 1943 were far more elaborate and, hence, far more effective than those it conducted in 1941 (see Table 3.4).

During the strategic defenses the *Stavka* orchestrated in 1941, 1942, and 1943, the Red Army employed a combination of positional and maneuver defensive techniques, successive battles along predetermined defense lines echeloned in depth, and, wherever possible, numerous counterattacks, counterstrokes, and in a few instances, full-fledged counteroffensives.[22]

Largely because of the *Wehrmacht's* diminishing offensive power, while the strength, durability, and effectiveness of its strategic defenses improved during the first 30 months of the war, the spatial dimensions of these defenses decreased significantly. For example, during the initial stages of Operation Barbarossa, the *Wehrmacht's* advance encompassed virtually the entire front but registered its greatest gains along the vital northwestern, western, and southern axes, which led ultimately to Leningrad, Moscow, and Rostov. Although the *Stavka* initially conducted its strategic defense along these axes with its Northwestern, Western, and Southwestern Fronts and, later, its Southern Front, it had deployed its Central, Reserve, and Briansk Fronts along these axes from July through October and a total of eight operating *fronts* (Leningrad, Northwestern, Kalinin, Western, Briansk, Southwestern, Southern, and Trans-Caucasus) by early December.

When the *Wehrmacht* commenced Operation *Blau* in late June and July 1942, it initially confined its offensive operations to what it presumed was the single southern axis. In reality, however, by July its forces were operating along two strategic axes, the first extending to Voronezh and the second to Stalingrad, and by November a third strategic axis reaching deep into the Caucasus region. Initially, the *Stavka* countered the *Wehrmacht's* advance with its Briansk, Southwestern, and Southern Fronts, but as the offensive developed, it reshuffled and renamed several of its *fronts* in the late summer and early fall, by mid-November employing six *fronts* (Briansk, Voronezh, Stalingrad [Southwestern], Stalingrad, Southern, and North Caucasus) to defend the Voronezh, Stalingrad, and Caucasus axes.

When *Wehrmacht* forces mounted what amounted to a full counteroffensive during February and March 1943 to halt the Red Army's winter offensive along the central, southwestern, and southern axes, the *Stavka* conducted a strategic defense along the central and southwestern axes with a total of five *fronts* (the Briansk, Central, Voronezh, and Southwestern).

Finally, when the *Wehrmacht* launched Operation Citadel in July 1943 along the central (Kursk-Voronezh) axis, the *Stavka* conducted its strategic defense with the Central and Voronezh Fronts backed up by the Steppe Military District (Front) and later conducted an initial counteroffensive along the same axis with four *fronts* (Briansk, Central Voronezh, and Steppe) and portions of two additional *fronts* (Western and Southwestern).

Force Configuration (Echelonment)

True to Soviet prewar military theory, the *Stavka* and General Staff sought to conduct their strategic defenses during the summers of 1941, 1942, and 1943 with their forces deeply echeloned and protected by extensive fortified defense lines constructed in great depth and backed up by powerful strategic reserves. In 1941, for example, the General Staff's Defense Plan (DP-41) envisioned Red Army forces conducting an active defense to "prevent both enemy ground and air invasion of the district's territory" and, in the event of an enemy incursion, to "be prepared, if conditions are favorable, to deliver decisive blows against the enemy in accordance with the High Command's (future *Stavka*'s) orders."[23]

As a result, in June 1941 the Red Army defended with its Northern, Northwestern, Western, Southwestern, and Southern Fronts in first strategic echelon within the border military districts backed up by a Front of Reserve Armies deployed along the Dnepr River in second strategic echelon and a strategic reserve made up of additional mobilized armies defending in the strategic depths. Two defense lines consisting of fortified regions, the first constructed along the 1941 border and the second along the 1939 borders in the depths, protected the forward deployed *fronts,* and powerful mechanized forces within the forward *fronts* and armies were prepared to conduct counterattacks and counterstrokes. Partially mobilized before war began, the second-echelon Front of Reserve Armies, which also fielded powerful mechanized forces, was to prevent enemy forces from penetrating across the Dnepr River and cooperate with the forward *fronts* in delivering powerful counterstrokes to repel any invading enemy force.

However, the *Wehrmacht's* sudden offensive caught the Red Army by surprise and totally confounded the Red Army General Staff's defense plans. Advancing more rapidly than anticipated, during the initial stages of Operation Barbarossa *Wehrmacht* forces prevented the Red Army's forward *fronts* from manning their defensive positions, overran their prepared defenses, forced their poorly trained, prepared, and equipped mechanized forces to counterattack prematurely and decimated them when they did, and totally disrupted subsequent Red Army mobilization. As a result, the powerful offensive shattered the Red Army's first strategic echelon and its powerful mechanized forces within the astonishingly short period of 7–10 days, engaged and defeated its second strategic echelon armies within a period of 15–20 days, and, thereafter, forced the *Stavka* to rely frantically on ad hoc defenses manned by hastily mobilized armies deployed in only partially prepared defenses far to the rear.

Subsequently, the *Stavka* attempted to conduct a strategic defense in depth from mid-July through September with a first strategic echelon made up of seven *fronts* (Northern [Leningrad], Northwestern, Western, Briansk, Central, Southwestern, and Southern) backed up by a second strategic echelon consisting of a Reserve Front and numerous small understrength armies made up largely of poorly trained reservists and conscripts, which it deployed in rows one after another in weak field defenses astride the vital Leningrad, Moscow, and Kiev axes.

However, as the *Wehrmacht* lunged eastward in July and August, it penetrated the Red Army's first-echelon *fronts* and the successive ranks of armies in the Red Army's second strategic echelon with relative ease, in the process encircling immense numbers of Red Army soldiers at Smolensk and Uman'. As it continued its advance in late August and September, the *Wehrmacht* shattered the Red Army's defenses forward of Leningrad and Kiev, reached and besieged the former, and encircled and destroyed the entire Southwestern Front near the latter.

The heady German advance toward Leningrad and Kiev in September and toward Moscow and Rostov in November totally disrupted the stability of the *Stavka's* strategic defenses, forcing it, simultaneously, to re-create coherent and viable first strategic echelon forces, erect new strategic defense lines forward of and around these vital cities, and raise new strategic reserves to halt the German advance and conduct essential counterattacks and counterstrokes. During this period the *Stavka* tried to recreate viable strategic defenses by resting and refitting a portion of its forces despite ongoing military operations, regrouping sizable forces within and between its operating *fronts*, dispatching well-trained divisions from the Far East, and raising fresh reserve armies in its internal military districts.[24]

For example, after losing Smolensk and Kiev, in late September the *Stavka* tried to defend Moscow with the armies of its Western and Briansk Fronts in first strategic echelon and those of its Reserve Front in second echelon, backed up by newly mobilized forces manning its partially constructed Mozhaisk Defense Line. Despite the fiction of a deep two-echelon defensive configuration, however, the *Stavka's* defenses west of Moscow were less than 80 kilometers deep. What ultimately saved the day for the *Stavka* at Moscow and elsewhere along the Soviet-German front was its ability to raise and field strategic reserves, in this case the total of 11 reserve armies it was able to raise and field from October through December 1941. In combination with the attrition in the *Wehrmacht's* ranks and the severe winter weather, these reserves enabled the *Stavka* to defend Moscow and Rostov and even mount successful counteroffensives of its own at Moscow and elsewhere in December 1941.

The *Stavka* also attempted to construct a deeply echeloned strategic defense in 1942, despite its mistaken assessment that the *Wehrmacht* would resume offensive operations toward Moscow in the summer. This defense, which encompassed the entire front, consisted of a first strategic echelon made up of nine forward deployed *fronts* (Leningrad, Volkhov, Northwestern, Kalinin, Western, Briansk, Southwestern, Southern, and Caucasus), extensive defense lines protecting Leningrad, Moscow, and the approaches to Voronezh, Stalingrad, and Rostov, and an imposing array of ten reserve armies and at least one tank army, which it formed in May and June 1942 to constitute both a second strategic echelon and potential *Stavka* reserve.

As in 1941, though, the rapid and surprise *Wehrmacht* advance during Operation *Blau* preempted the *Stavka's* strategic defenses before they were complete, savaged the armies in its first-echelon Southwestern and Southern Fronts, overcame its partially prepared defense lines, and forced it to create an entirely new strategic defensive configuration for its forces defending along the Voronezh, Stalingrad, and Caucasus axes. Ultimately, the *Stavka* formed a new first strategic echelon along the Don and Volga rivers and deep into the Caucasus region, which consisted of six *fronts* (Briansk, Voronezh, Southwestern, Stalingrad, Southeastern, and North Caucasus) and which, with some alterations later in the fall, conducted the strategic defense and, in mid-November, the Stalingrad counteroffensive.

When a *Wehrmacht* counteroffensive forced the *Stavka* to go over to the defense in the Sevsk, Khar'kov, and Donbas regions in February and March 1943, the *Stavka* had no choice but to defend with its Central, Voronezh, and Southwestern Fronts deployed in a single-echelon strategic formation. While striking back, the counterattacking German forces had destroyed many of the Voronezh and Southwestern Fronts' exploiting forces and had driven the remainder back in disorder. However, in March and April, the *Stavka* reinforced these *fronts* with fresh reserve armies, such as the 21st, 62nd, 64th Armies and the 1st Tank Army, which it regrouped from other sectors of the front. At the same time, however, the *Stavka* created what amounted to a new second strategic echelon by deploying the 63rd, 24th, and 66th Armies into deeper defensive positions along the upper reaches of the Don River. Subsequently, in late March and April, it formed a new deeply echeloned strategic defense with its Briansk (Orel), Central, Kursk (for a brief period), and Voronezh Fronts in first strategic echelon, and, ultimately, a new Reserve Front in second strategic echelon.[25]

After amassing two years of experience in conducting strategic defenses, the *Stavka* began conducting strategic defensive operations in the summer of 1943 employing well-coordinated groups of *fronts* operating within the parameters of an overall defensive plan: "[A strategic defensive operation] is an aggregate of interrelated defensive operations by large formations subordinate to *fronts* and operations and combat actions by large formations and formations subordinate to long-range aviation, PVO Strany, and fleets conducted in accordance with a single concept to achieve strategic aims."[26]

Even though Red Army forces were already numerically superior to *Wehrmacht* forces in the summer of 1943 and were capable of seizing the strategic initiative at any time, the *Stavka* prudently decided to begin its summer campaign by conducting a deliberate strategic defense before conducting a strategic offensive of its own. In addition to erecting formidable and deeply echeloned defenses in the Kursk region, where it expected Hitler to launch his next offensive, the *Stavka* also did so along its entire front from Moscow to the Black Sea.

The *Stavka* began its strategic defense in July 1943 with 12 *fronts* (Northern, Leningrad, Volkhov, Northwestern, Kalinin, Western, Briansk, Central, Voronezh, Southwestern, Southern, and North Caucasus) deployed in its first strategic echelon across the entire Soviet-German front. In addition, it deployed the Steppe Military District's six armies in second strategic echelon along the Kursk and Voronezh axes and retained four more armies in its strategic reserve. The *Stavka* ordered the *fronts* constituting its first strategic echelon to prepare elaborate and defenses echeloned in depth, construct deep and elaborate defenses, form their own reserve armies, and defend their respective sectors resolutely. In addition, the *Stavka* formed two echelons of *fronts* in the threatened Kursk region and prepared multiple defense belts and lines extending in depth from the forward edge eastward to the Don River.

Finally, after its first-echelon *fronts* defeated the expected *Wehrmacht* offensive, the *Stavka* planned to employ the powerful Steppe Military District, now functioning as a *front* in its own right, and the reserve armies of its other first-echelon *fronts*, to mount multiple strategic counteroffensive and offensives, first in the Kursk region, and later along the entire front.

For the first time in the war, the *Stavka's* defense in the Kursk region developed as planned. About one week after the *Wehrmacht* began Operation Citadel, the *Stavka* was able first to blunt and then to halt the *Wehrmacht's* offensive. In short order, first on 12 July and then on 5 August, the *Stavka* was able to dispense with its strategic defense and commence a strategic offensive of its own. Within a matter of weeks, the *Stavka* had transformed its initial strategic defense into the most mighty strategic offensive it had yet to conduct during the war.

Defensive Techniques

The specific defensive techniques the *Stavka's* operating *fronts* employed, individually and collectively, also improved significantly as the scope and scale of Red Army strategic defensive operations increased during the first 30 months of the war and the *Stavka's* planning, coordination, and control of these operations became more effective. These improvements were most evident in the durability of the Red Army's strategic defenses and the dynamism (offensiveness) its operating *fronts* or groups of *fronts* displayed when conducting their defensive operations.

The durability of the *Stavka's* strategic defenses depended primarily on the effectiveness of its operating *fronts'* operational formation and how well they organized themselves for combat, the strength of defense lines and positions the *Stavka* erected and the positional defenses its operating *fronts* conducted, and, given the *Wehrmacht's* formidable panzer forces, the degree to which the defending forces could counter the deadly panzer threat.

Defensive Operational Formations. In general, shortages of both forces and weaponry during the first six months of the war forced the Red Army's operating *fronts* to defend in single-echelon operational formation with only negligible reserves. As the NKO raised and fielded fresh forces in late 1941, however, its *fronts* were able to create second echelons consisting of single armies, although they usually employed these armies only offensively. In the summer of 1942, its operating *fronts* once again defended in a single echelon of armies, this time because the *Stavka* had squandered its available reserves conducting unsuccessful offensive operations during May. In addition, the rapid *Wehrmacht* advance in late June and July denied the *Stavka* time to assign any of its ten reserve armies to its forward operating *fronts* to employ as second echelons in their defensive operations.

This situation changed dramatically in the summer of 1943, when larger reserves became available. Therefore, during the strategic defense at Kursk and elsewhere along the front in July 1943, depending on the circumstances, the Red Army's operating *fronts* were able to organize defensively into operational formations of either one or two echelons of armies. In addition, these *fronts* were able to field more numerous and powerful tank and antitank reserves and form more powerful groupings of artillery to support their defenses. In fact, even though the *Wehrmacht* seldom forced the Red Army to resort to a prepared defense after the Battle of Kursk, when it did so, its *fronts* routinely prepared elaborate, deeply echeloned defensive formations anchored on well-prepared defensive positions with strong *front* reserves.[27]

Strategic Defense Lines and Positional Defenses. The durability of the Red Army's strategic defenses during the first 30 months of the war also depended directly on the strength, utility, and effectiveness of strategic defense lines erected by the *Stavka* or its operating *fronts* and the positional defenses its operating *fronts* conducted. In general, defensive construction improved markedly during 1941 and early 1942 largely because the NKO increased the strength of engineer and sapper support it assigned to its operating *fronts* and armies and because it formed and fielded sapper armies to construct rear defense lines for operational and strategic reserves to occupy before and during each defensive operation.

Even during the first few weeks of war, the *Wehrmacht's* offensive tempo slowed appreciably when it encountered the Southwestern Front's fortified regions at Rava-Russkaia, Peremyshl', Novgorod-Volynskii, and Korosten'. As a result, during the next four months, the *Stavka* ordered the construction of five major and several lesser defense lines protecting the approaches to Leningrad, Moscow, Stalingrad, and Rostov (see Table 3.5).[28]

After *Wehrmacht* forces shattered Red Army forward defenses in late June, the *Stavka* ordered the construction of a new strategic defense line 200 kilometers east of the frontiers to block the German advance along the northwestern and western axes and the erection of other defense lines along the southwestern axis to protect the cities of Kiev and Odessa, the approaches to the Crimea and Donbas region, the city of Stalingrad, and, later, the approaches into the Caucasus region (see Chapter 9).[29] Ultimately, with the assistance of civilian labor, the *Stavka* built elaborate rear defensive lines and field fortifications extending to depths of 200–400 kilometers in late 1941.

Despite the Red Army's victory at Moscow in late 1941, in early 1942 the *Stavka* continued to construct new defense lines. The new system, which sapper armies and civilian labor built in early 1942, reinforced the defenses protecting Moscow and protected the approaches to the Don River, Stalingrad, and the Caucasus region.[30] Overall, the *Stavka* erected defense lines and fortifications to a depth of up 600 kilometers inside the Soviet Union's western borders in 1942.

Despite its successes, this immense construction effort was also plagued by problems: first, the acute shortage of experienced engineer personnel, equipment, and materials necessary to erect them in timely fashion; second, the absence of forces to man them; and third, the *Wehrmacht's* tendency to overrun them before they were completed. For example, "Out of the 291 rifle divisions and 66 rifle brigades the *Stavka* VGK dispatched to its operating armies in the summer of 1941, only 66 divisions (22.6 percent) and 4 brigades (6 percent) were used to occupy rear defense lines in timely fashion."[31]

In addition to constructing and employing strategic defense lines and positions, when they were conducting strategic defensive operations, the *Stavka* also required its operating *fronts* to conduct deliberate positional defenses, both in the open field and in defense of key cities such as Smolensk, Leningrad, Kiev, Moscow, and Rostov in 1941 and Stalingrad in 1942. Although the capabilities of these operating *fronts* to conduct positional defenses improved measurably during the first 30 months of the war, Stalin's frequent insistence that they defend untenable positions caused strategic disasters and unnecessary and indefensible losses during both Operation Barbarossa and Operation *Blau*.

During Operation Barbarossa, for example, this occurred during the defense of Mogilev and the Dnepr River line in early July, during the defense of Smolensk in late July, and during the defense of Kiev in September. During Operation *Blau* this occurred once again in July 1942, when Red Army forces were attempting to withdraw from the path of the *Wehrmacht's* juggernaut toward Stalingrad. Often these catastrophic failures of positional defenses resulted in the encirclement and destruction of massive pockets of Red Army forces. Although the liquidation of these pockets delayed or otherwise temporarily disrupted the *Wehrmacht's* subsequent advances, it also seriously weakened the *Stavka's* capability for conducting these strategic defenses.[32]

Antitank Defense. The immense damage the *Wehrmacht's* panzer divisions, panzer (motorized) corps, and panzer groups (armies) inflicted on the Red Army's strategic defenses during the summer and fall of 1941 underscored the vital importance of antitank defense to the durability of the *Stavka's* strategic defenses and those of its operating *fronts* during the subsequent summers of 1942 and 1943. The NKO had recognized the importance of strategic antitank defense even prior to the war and, for this reason, formed large antitank brigades to cooperate with its formidable mechanized corps both defensively and offensively during wartime.

After the *Wehrmacht* destroyed the Red Army's antitank brigades during the first several weeks of the war, the *Stavka* and its *front* commanders worked feverishly to improve their antitank defenses. However, shortages of antitank weapons, the tendency of field commanders to employ them in dispersed fashion, and the ineffectiveness of heavy caliber artillery and aircraft against German tanks forced the operating *fronts* to rely increasingly on their own armor to defeat *Wehrmacht* panzers. Even during 1942 and early 1943, despite numerous NKO entreaties that the Red Army's force of tank and mechanized forces were to be used primarily against enemy infantry, *front* commanders tended to rely on them for antitank defense.

At the same time, however, beginning first at the tactical and later at the operational level, the Red Army's operating *fronts* slowly began employing both their antitank and other artillery as antitank weapons in their own right and to configure these weapons in combination with infantry to create an ever more elaborate and effective antitank defense. If, on average, the number of antitank guns available to *front* commanders during the first six months of the war was limited to fewer than five per kilometer of front—certainly not enough to permit army much less *front* commanders to integrate them into their combat schemes—this situation changed for the better in 1942.

By the summer of 1942, a drastic increase in the number of available antitank weapons finally permitted army commanders to begin forming antitank strong points and regions echeloned in depth along axes of advance that *Wehrmacht* panzers were likely to employ. Further increases in the fielding of antitank guns later in 1942 also made it feasible for army commanders to form and employ antitank reserves within their subordinate rifle corps and rifle divisions and so increased the density, mobility, and effectiveness of their antitank defenses.

Finally, based on their experiences in 1941 and 1942, the Red Army's operating *fronts* were finally able in the summer of 1943 to establish imposing antitank defenses, which extended throughout the entire depth of their *fronts'* first defensive belts. Consisting of a dense and complex network of mutually supporting company antitank strong points and battalion antitank regions, which were protected by infantry and dense curtains of massed artillery fires, these antitank defenses became operational and strategic weapons in the Red Army' arsenal of defensive techniques during 1943 and the remainder of the war.

Dynamism. Finally, to a significant extent, the effectiveness of Red Army strategic defensive operations throughout the entire war depended directly on the degree to which the *Stavka* and its defending *fronts* displayed what Russians called *aktivnost'*, a term best defined as "dynamism." This term refers specifically to the degree to which the *Stavka* and its operating *fronts* integrated vigorous offensive actions such as counterattacks, counterstrokes, and counteroffensives into their strategic defensive operations. Although history records that the *Stavka* concluded its strategic defenses in 1941, 1942, and 1943 with successful counteroffensives at Moscow, Stalingrad, and Kursk, it has generally ignored the Red Army's dynamic resistance to the *Wehrmacht's* advances during Operations Barbarossa and *Blau*, primarily because this resistance was frequently poorly organized, futile, and costly in terms of human losses.[33] However, the cumulative effects of these numerous offensive "pinpricks" in the Germans' hide ultimately eroded the *Wehrmacht's* offensive strength and contributed significantly to the defeats it ultimately suffered at Leningrad in September 1941, at Moscow and Rostov in December 1941, and at Stalingrad in November 1942.

For example, the Red Army's operating *fronts*, as well as the *Stavka*, once it was formed, reacted dynamically against invading *Wehrmacht* forces during the very first days of Operation Barbarossa and continued to resist dynamically throughout the duration of the offensive. However, history has ignored the significance of this resistance, in part because it was poorly organized, coordinated, and controlled, and also because it usually failed and resulted in heavy Red Army losses.

As called for in the General Staff's strategic defense plan, the Red Army's operating *fronts* conducted numerous counterattacks, counterstrokes, and, in at least one case, a full-fledged counteroffensive while the *Wehrmacht* was conducting Operation Barbarossa. In addition, more often than not, the *Stavka* ordered these operations be conducted and attempted to coordinate them with regard to their location and timing. The most important of these actions included counterstrokes near Kelme, Raseinai, Grodno, Dubno, Brody in late June, at Sol'tsy, Lepel', Bobruisk, and Korosten' in early July, at Staraia Russa in August, and at Kalinin in October, and counteroffensives at Smolensk in late July and early August and at Smolensk, El'nia, and west of Briansk in late August and early September (see Chapter 1).[34]

Although all of these counterstrokes and counteroffensives failed, many had a significant effect on the course and outcome of Operation Barbarossa. For example, the Southwestern Front's mechanized counterstroke in the Dubno and Brody region in late June significantly slowed the advance of German Army Group South toward Kiev. Likewise, the Northwestern Front's counterstrokes at Sol'tsy in July and at Staraia Russa in August delayed Army Group North's advance on Leningrad by about two weeks. Later, the Western, Reserve, and Briansk Front's counteroffensives at Smolensk in July and August contributed to Hitler's decision to delay his advance on Moscow by conducting an offensive to capture Kiev, a decision that contributed significantly to the *Wehrmacht's* subsequent defeat at the gates of Moscow:

> For the first time in World War II, [at Smolensk] the German-Fascist forces were forced to cease their offensive along the main axis and go over to the defense. An important result of the Smolensk operation was the winning of time for the strengthening of the restored strategic defensive front along the Moscow axis, for preparing the capital's defenses, and for subsequently defeating the Hitlerites in front of Moscow.[35]

The *Stavka* and its operating *fronts* also reacted dynamically to resist advancing *Wehrmacht* forces for the entire duration of Operation *Blau*. In this case the *Stavka* and its operating *fronts* organized and conducted a major counterstroke against the advancing Germans about one week after they commenced their offensive and continued conducting counterstrokes, some on the scale of counteroffensives, throughout the entire German offensive. Furthermore, in 1942 the *Stavka* organized, controlled, and coordinated these operations far more effectively than it had in 1941. The most important of these actions along the Stalingrad axis included major armored counterstrokes at Voronezh and along the Don River in July, one of which resembled in scale and intent a full-fledged counteroffensive, at Voronezh in August and September, along the Don River at Serafimovich and Kletskaia in July and August, and in the Stalingrad region proper during August, September, and October (see Chapter 2).[36]

In addition, as Operation *Blau* unfolded, the *Stavka* organized offensives elsewhere along the Soviet-German front to distract German attention and reserves from the Stalingrad and Caucasus axes. These included offensives at Demiansk, Zhizdra, and Bolkhov in July, at Siniavino, Demiansk, Rzhev, Sychevka, Gzhatsk, Viaz'ma, and Bolkhov in August, and at Demiansk in September.

Although all of the counterstrokes and counteroffensives the *Stavka* organized along the Stalingrad axis either failed or achieved only limited gains, both these and the offensives it organized along other axes contributed significantly to the course and outcome of Operation *Blau*. For example, taken collectively, the many counterstrokes the *Stavka* organized along the Stalingrad axis from July through October sapped the German Sixth Army's strength and undermined its efforts to capture Stalingrad proper. In addition, the Red Army's successful seizure of bridgeheads across the Don River in August, which the Germans were not able to recapture, provided it with ideal launching points for its subsequent November offensive. Finally, the numerous offensives the *Stavka* organized in other sectors of the Soviet-German front prevented the Germans from reinforcing their forces at Stalingrad at a time when those reinforcements were vitally necessary.

The most dynamic and effective strategic defense the *Stavka* organized and coordinated and its operating *fronts* conducted during the first 30 months of the war was in July 1943, during its defense against *Wehrmacht* forces conducting Operation Citadel. Although the limited spatial dimensions of this defense precluded the necessity of conducting prolonged defensive operations over large spaces in extended periods of time, the Kursk defense was dynamic in several important regards. First and foremost, for the first time in the war, the *Stavka* planned its defense only as a prelude to a major strategic offensive of its own. Therefore, even while it planned its initial defense, the *Stavka* assigned its defending *fronts* missions regarding their roles in the subsequent offensive.

In addition, during the defensive stage of the Kursk operation, the *Stavka* ordered its defending *fronts* to maneuver their tactical and operational reserves and conduct counterattacks and counterstrokes to make their defenses more dynamic, while at the same time the *Stavka* itself maneuvered its strategic reserves to increase the effectiveness of the defense. The most important of these actions included tactical counterattacks along the Red Army's entire defensive front during the *Wehrmacht's* initial thrust, coordinated counterstrokes at the point or along the flanks of the German offensive as it was developing, and a major counterstroke at Prokhorovka by large *Stavka* reserves during the culminating phase of the defense. Finally, during the climactic fighting at Prokhorovka, the *Stavka* unleashed a general counteroffensive by two full *fronts* against *Wehrmacht* forces defending the Orel salient.[37]

In short, after two years of harsh and often costly experience in organizing and conducting strategic defenses and strategic defensive operations, by the summer of 1943, the *Stavka* and its operating *fronts* had developed dynamic defensive techniques that it would employ successfully to war's end.

STRATEGIC OFFENSIVE OPERATIONS

As defined by postwar Soviet military theorists, a strategic offensive operation consists of "a system of offensive operations unified by a single *Stavka* concept and conducted to achieve the military-political aims of a campaign."[38] However, even though Soviet military theory generally ascribed to this definition before 1941, it would take over 18 months of near constant combat before the *Stavka* and its operating *fronts* could conduct successful strategic offensive operations suited to this definition. Although they finally conducted strategic offensives that matched this definition at Moscow in December 1941 and at Rzhev and Stalingrad in November 1942, in both cases they did so only after halting strong and determined *Wehrmacht* strategic offensives.

Finally, after conducting only partially successful strategic offensives and full-fledged offensive campaigns in the wake of its victories at Moscow and

Stalingrad, in July 1943 the *Stavka* and its operating *fronts* orchestrated a strategic offensive at Kursk, which, after it expanded to embrace most of the Soviet-German front, became a virtual model for subsequent Red Army strategic offensive operations throughout the remainder of the war.

Lost amid this extensive chronology of successful Red Army strategic offensives are others the *Stavka* tried to conduct during both Operations Barbarossa and *Blau* and during its summer–fall campaign of 1943. During the first period of the war, for example, these include its failed strategic offensive in the Smolensk region during July and August 1941, its unsuccessful offensive at Voronezh and along the approaches to Stalingrad in July 1942, and, finally, the strategic companion piece to its Stalingrad offensive, its unsuccessful 2nd Rzhev-Sychevka offensive of November 1942. Finally, during the second period of the war, these include the abortive Operation Polar Star in February 1943, the spectacular but unsuccessful Orel-Briansk-Smolensk offensive in February and March 1943, the forgotten offensive in Belorussia from October through December 1943, the failed offensive to capture Kiev in October 1943, and repeated unsuccessful offensives to capture the Taman' peninsula region from April through June 1943.

During Operation Barbarossa and the ensuing winter campaign of 1941–42, the *Stavka* conducted or attempted to conduct seven distinct strategic offensive operations, many of which began as counterstrokes. It conducted these offensives in sectors ranging in width from 50 to 550 kilometers, and, during these offensives, Red Army forces advanced to depths of 50–250 kilometers into the German rear area before the offensives collapsed (see Table 3.6).

After unsuccessfully conducting its first two strategic offensives in the Smolensk region during July and August 1941, during late 1941 and early 1942, the *Stavka* conducted five offensive operations, first, successively at Tikhvin, Rostov, and Moscow with three *fronts* (Leningrad, Southern, and Western), and, later, simultaneously across roughly 50 percent of the Soviet-German front with a total of nine *fronts* (Leningrad, Volkhov, Northwestern, Kalinin, Western, Briansk, Southwestern, Southern, and Crimean). Ultimately, these strategic offensives engulfed roughly 2,000 kilometers, about half of the 4,000-kilometer-wide Soviet-German front.

All of these offensives failed to meet the *Stavka's* expectations, in part because it was overly ambitious and assigned its operating *fronts* unrealistic missions and, in part, because its operating *fronts* lacked adequate forces and supporting air, tank, artillery, and other support. The course and outcome of these strategic offensives made it abundantly clear to the *Stavka* that it still had much to learn about the art of the possible.

As was the case with its strategic defensive operations, during late 1942 and 1943, the strategic offensive operations the *Stavka* planned and coordinated and its operating *fronts* conducted increased drastically in terms of their scope, scale, and complexity. As a result, they also achieved far greater success. During this period the *Stavka* conducted a total of 20 strategic offensive operations, eight during the winter campaign of 1942–43 and 12 more during the summer–fall campaign of 1943. During the winter campaign, it conducted its offensives in sectors ranging in width from 45 to 850 kilometers to depths of 5–600 kilometers and, during the summer–fall campaign, in sectors ranging in width from 200 to 400 kilometers and to depths of 4–300 kilometers (see Table 3.7).

The *Stavka* conducted the first two strategic offensive operations during its winter campaign of 1942–43 at Rzhev and Stalingrad in November 1942 with five *fronts* (Kalinin, Western, Southwestern, Don, and Stalingrad) and 18 armies attacking across a total front of about 1,200 kilometers to depths ranging from 10 to 200 kilometers. Thereafter, from January through early March 1943, the *Stavka* orchestrated six more strategic offensive operations with a total of 11 *fronts* (Leningrad, Volkhov, Northwestern, Kalinin, Western Briansk, Central, Voronezh, Southwestern, Southern, and North Caucasus) and over 60 armies operating across roughly 3,000 kilometers, or about 50 percent of the Soviet-German front, to depths of 5–600 kilometers.

The *Stavka* began offensive operations during its summer campaign of 1943 by conducting two strategic offensive operations along the flank of the Kursk bulge with four full *fronts* (Briansk, Central, Voronezh, and Steppe) and portions of two other *fronts* (Western and Southwestern) and 24 armies attacking across a total front of 700–800 kilometers to depths of 140–150 kilometers. Thereafter, it conducted two more strategic offensive operations throughout the remainder of the summer and the fall, which ultimately included ten *fronts* (Kalinin [1st Baltic], Western, Briansk, Central [Belorussian], Voronezh [1st Ukrainian], Steppe [2nd Ukrainian], Southwestern [3rd Ukrainian], Southern [4th Ukrainian], and North Caucasus) and 40 armies and five tank armies operating along a 1,800-kilometer front to a depth of 150–300 kilometers.

Although the Red Army fell well short of fulfilling the ambitious missions the *Stavka* assigned to it during the winter campaign of 1942–43, it did achieve most of its assigned missions during the summer–fall campaign of 1943.

The *Stavka's* strategic offensive operations also became increasingly more successful during the first 30 months of the war, in part because *Stavka* planned and coordinated these offensives more effectively because the Red Army's strength steadily increased and because the Red Army's command cadre and soldiers gained experience in the conduct of high-intensity maneuver war (see Tables 3.8 and 3.9).

Objectives and Axes

Although the scope and scale of the Red Army's strategic offensive operations increased steadily during the first 30 months of the war, with the exception of the offensives it launched during Operation Barbarossa, the *Stavka's* strategic objectives in these operations remained strikingly consistent and, at least until the summer of 1943, overly ambitious. When planning its strategic offensive operations, the *Stavka* routinely targeted *Wehrmacht* force groupings whose destruction would lead to "a fundamental change in the military-political conditions in the theater of military operations, along a strategic axis, or along the entire strategic front" as the focal point for its strategic efforts.[39]

During Operation Barbarossa, for example, the *Stavka* conducted its counteroffensives in the Smolensk region during July and August to defeat and destroy a significant portion of *Wehrmacht* forces operating along the western strategic axis, to halt its advance toward Moscow, and to compel it to halt its general offensive. The *Stavka's* offensive at Moscow during December, which began as a modest counterstroke, ultimately sought to drive German forces from the immediate approaches to Moscow.

After thwarting Operation Barbarossa with its Moscow counteroffensive, the *Stavka* sought to inflict maximum damage on *Wehrmacht* forces in every strategic offensive it planned and conducted and, in the process, collapse a major portion of its defenses along one or more strategic axes. For example, the *Stavka's* strategic objectives during its Rzhev-Viaz'ma offensive and ensuing winter campaign of 1941–42 were, first and foremost, to destroy German Army Group Center and recapture Smolensk, and, secondarily, to raise the siege of Leningrad and force Army Group South to withdraw its forces from the Donbas, Khar'kov, and Crimean regions to the Dnepr River line.

Likewise, during the waning stages of Operation *Blau* in late November 1942, the *Stavka's* initial strategic objectives in its 2nd Rzhev-Sychevka and Stalingrad offensives were to defeat and destroy major portions of Army Groups Center, "A," and "B," which were operating along the Western, Stalingrad, and Caucasus axes, expel their forces from the Moscow, Stalingrad, and Caucasus regions, and capture Smolensk and Rostov. After its Stalingrad offensive succeeded, the *Stavka* dramatically expanded its strategic aims during its subsequent winter campaign. First, in January 1943 it sought to defeat Army Groups "B," Don, and "A" in southern Russia and drive their forces back to the Dnepr River and, simultaneously, to raise the siege of Leningrad. Then, in February it expanded its offensives to include virtually all of its operating *fronts* as it attempted to collapse *Wehrmacht* defenses along the northwestern, western, and southwestern axes and drive its forces back to the eastern borders of the Baltic and Belorussian regions and the Dnepr River line.

During its strategic offensive in the summer of 1943, the *Stavka* conducted an imposing series of successive and simultaneous strategic operations to achieve the objectives that had eluded it in February and March 1943. After conducting a strategic defensive operation to defend the Kursk bulge, it conducted strategic offensive operations against *Wehrmacht* forces defending the flanks of the Kursk bulge to capture Orel and Khar'kov. Then in August and September the *Stavka* expanded its operations to encompass the entire region from Velikie Luki to the Black Sea by conducting multiple strategic offensives aimed at collapsing the defenses of Army Groups Center and South, expelling their forces from the entire region east of the Dnepr River, capturing Vitebsk, Mogilev, and the Dnepr River line, and seizing bridgeheads over the Dnepr River. After these operations succeeded, in late September and early October, the *Stavka* ordered its attacking *fronts* to invade eastern Belorussia and the central and eastern Ukraine and capture Minsk, Kiev, Vinnitsa, and Krivoi Rog, missions that its operating *fronts* only partially attained.

Thus, the objectives the *Stavka* assigned to its operating *fronts* during all of the strategic offensive operations it planned and conducted from January 1942 through July 1943 were remarkably consistent, since, in every instance, they included the capture of the Smolensk region and the expulsion of *Wehrmacht* forces from territories east of the Dnepr River. However, while consistent, during much of this period, these objectives were also unrealistic. Simply stated, the *Stavka* did not achieve the objectives it assigned to its operating *fronts* in January 1942 until September 1943 for two fundamental reasons. First, before that time, it had not been capable of planning such complex and demanding operations; and second, its operating *fronts* were not strong enough to conduct them successfully.

During the final stages of its summer–fall campaign of 1943, and thereafter, during the winter of 1943–44, the *Stavka* continued assigning its operating *fronts* strategic objectives that were clearly beyond their capabilities. However, by this time, it was simply testing the limits of *Wehrmacht* resistance based on the premise that, at some point, the *Wehrmacht's* defenses might utterly collapse under such unrelenting pressure.

Offensive Planning

During the first 30 months of the war and thereafter, the success of strategic offensive operations conducted by the Red Army depended directly on how effectively the *Stavka* and its operating *fronts* and groups of *fronts* planned these offensives. This planning included such vital matters as creating favorable conditions for conducting the offensives, correctly calculating the correlation of opposing forces, selecting appropriate main attack axes, regrouping, concentrating, and employing attacking forces and strategic reserves in timely fashion, determining the most effective strategic offensive formations, selecting the most advantageous timing for the offensive, ensuring secrecy, and, when possible, achieving surprise. As the results of its strategic offensives indicated, during this period, *Stavka* and *front* planning steadily became more effective in all of these respects.

Timing and Location. Throughout the first 30 months of the war, German actions, specifically, the nature and course of *Wehrmacht* offensive operations, dictated precisely when and where, and to a lesser extent how and with what forces, the *Stavka* conducted its strategic offensives. For example, the *Stavka* conducted its hastily organized offensives at Smolensk in July and August 1941 out of sheer desperation and with ad hoc forces in a futile attempt to halt the *Wehrmacht's* advance toward Moscow. It did the same in November 1941, when it organized and conducted more successful but also hastily planned offensives at Tikhvin and Rostov to protect Leningrad and the approaches to Stalingrad. Finally, the *Stavka* began its offensive at Moscow only as an equally desperate counterstroke to fend off German encirclement of the city. When the counterstroke succeeded, the *Stavka* exploited the Germans' discomfiture, first by expanding the counterstroke into an offensive and subsequently by expanding the offensive into a full-fledged winter campaign.

Likewise, at least in part, *Wehrmacht* offensive activity also dictated where and when the *Stavka* conducted its strategic offensives in late 1942. Since the *Wehrmacht* conducted Operation *Blau* along only the Stalingrad and Caucasus axes and still manned positions menacing Moscow, the *Stavka* organized two strategic offensives to defeat Axis forces in both regions. Ultimately, however, the situation in and around Stalingrad determined the timing of both offensives. In contrast to 1941, though, during the fall of 1942, the *Stavka* had time to plan its offensives more thoroughly and to regroup, concentrate, and deploy its attacking forces and also plan follow-on offensives and, at least in outline, a subsequent winter campaign. However, as the winter campaign developed and the *Stavka* became more ambitious and overconfident, it planned its subsequent offensive operations in far more hasty and careless fashion. To a considerable extent, this explains why the Germans were able to contain these offensives in February and March 1943.

The strategic offensive operations the *Stavka* conducted during the summer–fall campaign of 1943 differed fundamentally from those it had conducted during the previous two years. First, it was able to exploit the operational lull across the Soviet-German front that existed from April through June to plan its offensives far more carefully than before. In addition, the Red Army was much stronger in 1943 than it had been in 1941 and 1942, and improved Soviet intelligence permitted the *Stavka* to determine when and where the *Wehrmacht's* Operation Citadel would occur well in advance of when it actually did. As a result, even though the *Stavka* planned its offensives based on the expected timing of the German offensive, it planned its initial offensives in considerable detail and multiple subsequent offensives in outline form. In addition, it was able to regroup its forces strategically and concentrate and deploy many of them into offensive positions before the *Wehrmacht* began its summer offensive. As a result, it transformed its strategic defense virtually seamlessly into, first, a strategic offensive, and later, an offensive campaign.

In short, after its victory at Kursk, the *Stavka* was able to mount multiple strategic offensives of its own at times and places of its own choosing, virtually until war's end.

Force Configuration and Coordination. When the *Wehrmacht* seized and maintained the strategic initiative during Operation Barbarossa, the threadbare Red Army lacked the forces and weaponry necessary to conduct strategic offensive operations on a scale recommended by prewar military theory. Therefore, when it organized its offensives at Smolensk in July and August, the *Stavka* deployed its three attacking *fronts* (Western, Reserve, and Briansk) into a shallow single-echelon operational formation of armies and their subordinate divisions with no second echelon and only a negligible reserve. While this attack configuration maximized the initial force of the assault, it provided no capability for strengthening the offensive while it was under way. Worse still, cooperation within and between the attacking *fronts* was weak at best and the only maneuver force available to the *fronts* was a small cavalry group, which the Western Front employed to conduct a deep raid in the German rear area to disrupt communications.[40]

Nor was the situation significantly different during the *Stavka's* Moscow offensive. At Moscow the deteriorating situation compelled it to begin its operation by conducting multiple limited counterattacks north of Moscow with a small portion of its strategic reserves (1st Shock Army). After these initial counterattacks proved successful, the *Stavka* expanded them, first, into multiple counterstrokes by the Western Front north and south of Moscow, and, finally, full offensives by the Kalinin, Western, and Southwestern Fronts along an even broader front. Ultimately, it ordered all of its operating *fronts* to join in what turned out to be a full-fledged winter offensive campaign engulfing more than half of the entire Soviet-German front.

The development of the winter campaign from local counterattacks into a general offensive was so haphazard that the *Stavka* was never able to coordinate its attacking forces effectively. All of its *fronts* attacked in single-echelon formation of armies and divisions with only limited reserves as had been the case at Smolensk, and the *Stavka* also employed reinforced cavalry corps to exploit deep into the German rear area, this time in conjunction with large-scale parachute drops by airborne corps and brigades. However, the attacking *fronts* could not sustain deep offensive operations, and in every case the offensives collapsed in exhaustion by late February and could not be revived.

The Red Army's increased size and strength and more adequate planning time enabled the *Stavka* to plan and coordinate more elaborate and effective strategic offensive operations in November 1942 and the ensuing winter campaign of 1942–43. It coordinated the offensives in the Rzhev and Stalingrad regions during November and December, and its representatives coordinated the actions within the groups of *fronts* conducting the offensives in each region.[41] Although these representatives still configured the attacking *fronts* into single-echelon formation, they also established more powerful reserves and employed numerous mobile groups *(podvizhnye gruppy)*, consisting primarily of tank, mechanized, and cavalry corps operating singly or in combination, to conduct operational maneuvers into the depths of the German defenses.[42]

For the remainder of the winter campaign of 1942–43, however, increasingly severe time constraints forced the *Stavka* to plan and conduct its subsequent strategic offensives in hastier fashion and with less effective coordination. The Voronezh, Southwestern, and Stalingrad Fronts began these offensives in single-echelon formation with small reserves, but during January the *Stavka* reinforced them with its 3rd Tank Army and with the Briansk Front, which began a fresh offensive on their right flank. In addition, during January the *Stavka's* Leningrad and Volkhov Fronts conducted an offensive to crack the Germans' iron grip on Leningrad. Then, during February, the *Stavka* ordered its Western and Briansk Fronts to join the offensive by attacking German defenses in the Orel salient and, for the first time in the war, formed a new *front,* the Central Front, and directed it to conduct an offensive toward Briansk and Smolensk. At the same time, it ordered its Leningrad, Volkhov, and Northwestern Fronts to conduct Operation Polar Star to raise the siege of Leningrad and advance to the eastern border of the Baltic region.[43]

Although the *Stavka* hastily planned its expanded February offensive and continued to configure its attacking *fronts* in single-echelon formations, for the first time in the war, it was able to form far stronger second echelons or mobile groups within its attacking *fronts*.[44] However, poor intelligence and coordination, severe force attrition, and skillful and determined German resistance thwarted all of these ambitious offensives.

By every measure, the strategic offensives the *Stavka* and its representatives planned, coordinated, and conducted during the summer–fall campaign of 1943 were far better planned, organized, and conducted and, hence, considerably more successful than any of its previous offensives. Although it continued configuring its attacking *fronts* in single-echelon formation, after launching offensives by groups of *fronts* against *Wehrmacht* forces defending Orel and Khar'kov it unleashed new offensives by other groups of *fronts* against *Wehrmacht* forces defending Smolensk while the previous offensives were still under way. Ultimately, by late August and early September, all of its operating *fronts* from the Vitebsk region to the Black Sea were participating in a general offensive. Although *Stavka* representatives planned and coordinated groups of *fronts* throughout all of these offensives, they also routinely employed single or multiple tank armies and tank, mechanized, and cavalry corps to conduct deep exploitation operations and larger second echelons and reserves consisting of multiple armies to strengthen the offensives while they were under way. As a result, these offensives were far more successful and became virtual models for those the *Stavka* would conduct later in the war.[45]

Strategic Surprise and Deception. The *Wehrmacht* achieved strategic surprise and seized and maintained the strategic initiative during both Operations Barbarossa and *Blau*, thereby paralyzing and decimating the Red Army early in each campaign and shaping the course and nature of most of the ensuing campaigns. On occasion, however, the Red Army was also able to benefit from the element of surprise during both campaigns, albeit usually by accident during Operation Barbarossa but increasingly by design during Operation *Blau*.

For example, during the disasters it suffered during Operation Barbarossa, the Red Army surprised the *Wehrmacht* by the ferocity of its armored counterstrokes in the Ukraine during late June, by its stout resistance and the strong counterstrokes and counteroffensives it launched in the Baltic region and at Smolensk in July and August, and by its counteroffensives in the Tikhvin and Rostov regions and its determined defense along the approaches to Moscow in late October and November 1941. In many instances these surprises were significant enough to prompt Hitler to alter his offensive plans significantly. Finally, the *Stavka's* offensive at Moscow, which occurred at a time when German intelligence estimated the Red Army was down to "its last few battalions," caught the *Wehrmacht* by surprise and forced it to retreat in near panic.[46]

Throughout Operation *Blau* as well, the Red Army's strong resistance surprised the *Wehrmacht* on numerous occasions. These included, for example, the Red Army's counterstrokes in July at Voronezh and along the Don River, its seizure of bridgeheads on the southern bank of the Don River in August, its stout defense in Stalingrad proper, and its repeated counterstrokes in the Stalingrad region during September and October. Although many of these Red Army operations failed, the surprise they achieved frequently forced Hitler to alter his offensive plans. Finally, at Stalingrad and to a lesser extent at Rzhev in November 1942, the *Stavka* was able to achieve strategic surprise in major offensives of its own and, by doing so, inflict paralysis and major damage on *Wehrmacht* and other Axis forces.

Most significantly, the *Stavka* achieved strategic surprise during both Operations Barbarossa and *Blau* by raising massive strategic reserves, which German intelligence never detected, and by employing these reserves to reinforce their strategic defenses and conduct their strategic offensives before the Germans learned of their existence.

Finally, during late 1942 and 1943, the *Stavka* employed increasingly effective strategic deception to create more favorable conditions for its strategic offensive operations, as it did prior to its November 1942 offensive at Stalingrad by covertly regrouping and concentrating its attacking forces and concealing most of its offensive preparations. It also did so effectively before its July and August offensives during the Battle of Kursk by covertly regrouping and assembling massive strategic reserves and by deceiving the *Wehrmacht* regarding the timing, location, and strength of its numerous strategic offensives, in part by concealing its forces and in part by conducting diversionary operations and simulations. In this way, the *Stavka* and Red Army achieved a significant degree of surprise during both the Stalingrad and Kursk strategic offensives.[47] Thereafter, the *Stavka* employed deception to achieve surprise on several occasions during its expanded offensive in the fall of 1943, most notably in November 1943, when it seized a strategic bridgehead across the Dnepr River at Kiev.

Offensive Techniques

As was the case with its strategic defensive operations, the techniques the *Stavka* and its operating *fronts* employed to conduct strategic offensive operations also matured significantly as the war progressed and became increasingly effective and deadly throughout the first 30 months of the war. The most important changes in this regard involved how the *Stavka* organized its operating *fronts* to conduct these offensives, how it timed and sequenced the offensives, and how it employed its *fronts* and groups of *fronts* to conduct the offensives.

Organization. During most of Operation Barbarossa, prewar theory and the Red Army's general weakness compelled the *Stavka* to conduct strategic offensive operations with single *fronts* operating in relative isolation, even when they were attacking along adjacent axes, as they did during the offensives in the Smolensk region during July and August, at Tikhvin and Rostov in November, and at Moscow in December. The *Stavka's* experience in these offensives convinced it to conduct future strategic offensives with multiple *fronts* operating in close cooperation because "during campaigns, large-scale military-political aims were resolved by the forces of several *fronts* in cooperation with other types of armed forces."[48] Thereafter, the

Stavka employed multiple *fronts* to conduct all of its strategic offensive operations and, to an increasing degree, appointed *Stavka* representatives to coordinate their operations.

For example, the *Stavka* conducted its strategic offensives in the Rzhev and Stalingrad regions in November and December 1942 with two groups of *fronts* operating under the supervision of its representatives and continued this process throughout the ensuing winter campaign. However, this coordination began to flag and became less effective during February and March, when Red Army forces tired and became more overextended, and, as a result, the strategic offensive ultimately faltered short of its intended goals.

The strategic offensive operations the *Stavka* orchestrated during the summer–fall campaign of 1943 were even more effective than those it conducted in previous campaigns, at least in part because it relied entirely on groups of *fronts* supervised by its representatives to coordinate these offensives. With few exceptions, during the remainder of 1943 and until the war's end, the *Stavka* employed closely coordinated groups of *fronts* to conduct all of its strategic offensive operations.

Timing and Sequencing. Throughout the summer stage of Operation Barbarossa, the Red Army's reduced strength prevented the *Stavka* from conducting more than one strategic offensive at a time. Thereafter, during the subsequent stages of Operation Barbarossa, the first time the *Stavka* was able to orchestrate multiple strategic offensives was at Tikhvin and Rostov in November. In these instances, however, it was motivated to do so more by strategic necessity and the presence of modest strategic reserves rather than any overarching strategic design.

Later still, during January and February 1942, the *Stavka* was finally able to plan and conduct strategic offensives simultaneously along multiple strategic axes, although in these cases it also did so on the basis of necessity and was unable to develop these offensives successively by conducting follow-on offensives to achieve even greater strategic aims.

The first time in the war the *Stavka* was able to plan and conduct both simultaneous and successive strategic operations was in the fall of 1942, when it planned its November offensives in the Rzhev and Stalingrad regions. In this case, in addition to the two initial simultaneous offensives code-named Operations Mars and Uranus, it also planned two successive strategic offensives in considerable detail and successive campaigns in only outline form.

Although Operation Mars failed, the successful offensives in the Stalingrad region permitted the *Stavka*, first, to plan and conduct successive offensives along the southwestern and southern axes to exploit its victory at Stalingrad and, later, to plan and conduct simultaneous strategic offensives along the northwestern and western strategic axes that ultimately engulfed most of the Soviet-German front. However, together with unanticipated German resistance, the *Stavka*'s inability to coordinate and reinforce its attacking *fronts* to compensate for the losses they suffered during these offensives prevented the *Stavka* from sustaining its winter offensive and achieving its intended aims.

During the summer of 1943, for the first time in the war, the *Stavka* proved capable of conducting and sustaining both simultaneous and successive strategic operations. It began its strategic offensive in mid-July and early August 1943 with successive and ultimately simultaneous strategic offensives by its *fronts* operating in the Orel and Khar'kov regions and expanded these offensives in early and late August by conducting new offensives by its *fronts* operating in the Smolensk and Donbas regions. Finally, in early and late September, it ordered all of its *fronts* operating in the sector from the Smolensk region to the Black Sea coast, first, to conduct simultaneous pursuit operations to reach the eastern border of Belorussia and the Dnepr River and, later, successive offensives to seize strategic bridgeheads in Belorussia and across the Dnepr River.

Although the Red Army's advance faltered during the later stages of these offensives, collectively these offensives cleared German forces of the region east of Belorussia and the Dnepr River and secured vital bridgeheads for further offensives in the winter of 1943 and 1944. More important still, they paved the way for the *Stavka* to conduct even more devastating simultaneous and successive offensives during the remainder of the war.

Forms and Methods. The form of the *Stavka's* strategic offensives, that is, the manner in which its *fronts* conducted them, remained remarkably uniform throughout the first 30 months of the war, but the methods it used to conduct these offensives changed significantly, particularly regarding the concentration of its attacking forces and its employment of maneuver during the penetration and exploitation phases of these operations. In general, with some exceptions, the *Stavka* conducted its offensives in as simple a fashion as possible, relying on frontal attacks with increasingly concentrated forces to penetrate German defenses and simple maneuver along specific direct axes by its mobile forces to exploit these penetrations into the operational depths. In particular, except at Stalingrad in November 1942, it avoided conducting elaborate envelopment or encirclement operations, which required its mobile forces to conduct complex and coordinated operational maneuver to great depths.

During Operation Barbarossa, for example, the *Stavka* lacked the time and forces necessary to create proper shock groups to conduct penetration operations, and its mobile forces were too weak to conduct sustained maneuver to any appreciable depth. Therefore, it usually organized its attacking *fronts* in linear formation with only minimal force concentration, and it employed shock groups formed on an ad hoc basis or multiple rifle divisions or brigades, sometimes supported by separate understrength tank divisions, brigades, or battalions, to conduct its *fronts'* main attacks. Finally, it employed weak and fragile cavalry divisions, cavalry groups, or reinforced cavalry corps to either support the penetration operations or to exploit the penetrations.[49]

During the strategic offensive operations they conducted in November and December 1942 and their ensuing winter campaign of 1942–43, the *Stavka's* attacking *fronts* concentrated their forces more effectively during penetration operations and conducted more extensive exploitation operations. In addition to employing tank armies in first echelon to lead their main attacks, *fronts* conducted their penetration operations with shock groups consisting of multiple rifle divisions and brigades reinforced by infantry support tank brigades and sometimes the lead tank or mechanized brigades from their tank armies or other supporting mobile corps, and concentrated these shock groups in increasingly narrow main attack sectors. In addition, they employed single or, in some cases, multiple separate tank, mechanized, or cavalry corps and, in some instances, full tank armies both to complete their penetration operations and to spearhead their subsequent exploitation operations.

Although the *Stavka* deliberately planned and conducted envelopment operations at Stalingrad in November 1942 and during its subsequent offensives along the Middle Don, Chir, and Aksai rivers in December, during these offensives its attacking *fronts* encountered difficulties in coordinating and sustaining deep maneuver with multiple tank, mechanized, and cavalry corps exploiting along multiple separate axes. Therefore, in January 1943 the *Stavka* ceased conducting envelopment operations and instead reverted to more linear forms of attack. At the same time, it began combining its mobile corps into distinct groups (such as Group Popov) to improve their ability to conduct and sustain deep operations. Despite these improvements, however, the *Stavka* continued to employ its tank armies to lead its *fronts'* main attacks and its groups of mobile corps to conduct its *fronts'* exploitations. The losses these tank armies suffered during penetration operations and the attrition these tank armies and mobile groups or corps experienced during exploitation operations, though, sapped their strength, limited the depth to which they could sustain deep operations, and exposed them to defeat in detail by counterattacking German forces.[50]

Despite the Red Army's dramatically increased numerical strength and its more elaborate forces structure, which included a much more formidable mobile force of five powerful tank armies and numerous tank, mechanized, and cavalry corps, when conducting its strategic offensives during the summer–fall campaign of 1943, the *Stavka* avoided large-scale and complex envelopment or encirclement operations. Instead, it continued organizing simple and linear frontal penetration operations and essentially linear and direct, although deeper, exploitation operations.

The most common form of offensive operations the *Stavka's* attacking *fronts* employed during the summer and fall of 1943 was the so-called deep cutting blow *(glubokii rassekaiushchii udar)*. This offensive form involved the use of rifle divisions and supporting tank and sapper forces concentrated in increasingly narrow main attack sectors and usually under rifle corps control to penetrate the *Wehrmacht's* tactical defenses by means of well-organized and highly intricate frontal attacks supported by increasingly massive artillery fire and air strikes. Thereafter, the *fronts* and their subordinate armies were supposed to employ tank armies, separate tank and mechanized corps, or separate tank, mechanized, and cavalry corps organized into cavalry mechanized groups to exploit successful tactical penetrations into the operational depths of the defense.[51]

However, even though the *Stavka* required its attacking *fronts* to employ its valuable tank armies and separate tank and mechanized corps intact and only to conduct exploitation operations, more often than not the increased durability of *Wehrmacht* defenses forced the attacking *fronts* to employ the lead brigades of their tank armies and separate mobile corps to complete the penetration operations. Although this premature employment of their tank forces usually guaranteed successful penetration, it also significantly limited the scale and success of the subsequent exploitation operations. Characteristic of this form of offensive action was the *Stavka's* attacking *fronts'* failure to encircle any sizable *Wehrmacht* forces during the summer and fall of 1943, and, in most of its strategic offensives, regrouped *Wehrmacht* operational reserves managed to contain exploiting Red Army mobile forces before they penetrated significantly into the operational depths.

Furthermore, this offensive form proved far less effective during strategic offensives conducted by groups of *fronts* that lacked supporting tank armies, for example, during operations such as the Kalinin and Western Front's Smolensk offensive in August and the Kalinin (1st Baltic), Western, and Central (Belorussian) Fronts' offensive in Belorussia from October through December 1943. In these instances, the offensives developed in distinct stages lasting weeks and even months and resulted in far less dramatic advances.[52]

By conducting powerful attacks with groups of *fronts* along multiple strategic axes across so broad a front during the strategic offensive operations it conducted in the late summer and fall of 1943, the *Stavka* was able to apply maximum pressure against the *Wehrmacht's* already sagging defenses, effect multiple penetrations, and fragment these defenses. By conducting numerous exploitations along parallel or diverging axes into the operational depths of the *Wehrmacht's* defenses, the *Stavka's* attacking *fronts* isolated separate defending groups from one another and forced the entire German force to conduct a strategic withdrawal along successive lines to the Sozh and Dnepr rivers. Although this strategic offensive was indeed both spectacular and successful, ultimately the Red Army's offensive momentum ebbed in early October. Thereafter, it would take a full month for the *Stavka* to concentrate sufficient forces to seize strategic scale bridgeheads on the western banks of these rivers.

STRATEGIC RESERVES

The most important factor contributing to the *Stavka's* successful conduct of both strategic defensive and offensive operations during the first 30 months of the war was its ability to raise, field, and employ strategic reserves effectively. Just as these reserves played a vital role in the strategic defensive operations it conducted to first blunt and then halt the *Wehrmacht's* advances during Operations Barbarossa, *Blau*, and Citadel, they also proved vital when the *Stavka* orchestrated its strategic offensives during the winters of 1941–42 and 1942–43, and the summer and fall of 1943. The reserves performed such vital functions as reinforcing defending *fronts*, establishing new defense lines, eliminating *Wehrmacht* penetrations, and providing much of the force with which the *Stavka* and its operating *fronts* conducted their counterstrokes, counteroffensives, and offensives.

The size of the Reserve of the Headquarters of the Main Command (RGK), as it was called when war began, and the Reserve of the Headquarters of the Supreme High Command, or simply RVGK, as it was renamed in August 1941, varied on a daily basis. At any given time, it consisted of up to eight armies, up to 47 rifle divisions, and up to seven rifle brigades, and, during the first six months of the war, it ranged in strength from highs of seven armies and 47 rifle divisions on 1 July and eight armies, 44 rifle divisions, and seven rifle brigades on 1 December to lows of no armies or rifle divisions on 1 August and no armies and four to five rifle divisions in September and October.[53] During this period the *Stavka* allocated a total of 291 rifle divisions and 94 rifle brigades from its strategic reserves to its operating *fronts*, including 150 rifle divisions and 44 rifle brigades to *fronts* operating along the western axis and 141 rifle divisions and 50 rifle brigades to those operating along the northwestern and southwestern axes.[54] Of these divisions and brigades, 85 percent were new, hastily organized, and frequently severely understrength formations possessing only limited combat capabilities, raised in the strategic rear area, and 15 percent were formations withdrawn from operating *fronts* for reorganization and refitting.

The *Stavka* employed its strategic reserves in 1941 to slow the *Wehrmacht's* Barbarossa onslaught during the period from July through November and to conduct its offensives at Tikhvin, Rostov, and Moscow in November and December and during its subsequent winter campaign. Although it used the bulk of these reserves to bolster the defensive and offensive capabilities of *fronts* operating along the most critical strategic axes, it also employed some along lower-priority axes, where they participated in more than 40 local offensives or counterattacks to tie down *Wehrmacht* forces and prevent them from shifting reinforcements to more critical axes.

For example, in late June and July, the *Stavka* employed its first 14 reserve armies with roughly 60 rifle divisions to reinforce the Western and Northern Fronts and help form the Reserve and Trans-Caucasus Fronts.[55] Most of these armies took part in the *Stavka's* offensive in the Smolensk region during August and early September. After its offensive at Smolensk failed, the *Stavka* formed 12 more armies in its strategic reserve from September through December and parceled them out to its operating *fronts*, first to halt the *Wehrmacht's* offensive in November and then to conduct offensives of its own in the Leningrad, Moscow, and Rostov regions during November and December and across the entire front during the ensuing winter campaign.[56] By doing so skillfully, the *Stavka* almost doubled the Western Front's strength from 30 rifle divisions, one rifle brigade, three tank brigades, and three cavalry divisions on 1 October to 50 rifle divisions, 16 rifle brigades, 22 tank brigades, and 16 cavalry divisions on 5 December.[57]

After reducing the size of its strategic reserves significantly during the winter campaign of 1941–42, the *Stavka* expanded them dramatically from May through July 1942 in order to bolster its strategic defenses and create new forces it could employ in future strategic offensive operations.[58] At any given time throughout the next six months, its reserve consisted of 2–11 armies, 2–11 tank, mechanized, or cavalry corps, 8–65 rifle or cavalry divisions, and 2–28 rifle, motorized rifle, tank, or airborne brigades. During this period, its reserves ranged in strength from a high of 11 armies, six tank or cavalry corps, 65 rifle or cavalry divisions, and 28 brigades of various types on 1 July to a low of four armies, three tank corps, 18 rifle divisions, and 24 brigades on 1 September. These included ten reserve armies (the 1st through the 10th), seven formed by 1 June and three more by 1 July, and one tank army (the 3rd). In general, the reserve formations the *Stavka* raised in 1942 were far better organized, trained, and equipped than those it had raised and fielded in 1941.

As was the case in 1941, the *Stavka* employed these reserves to help conduct its unsuccessful offensives at Khar'kov and in the Crimea during May 1942, to bolster its strategic defenses and conduct counterattacks and counterstrokes against advancing *Wehrmacht* forces during Operation *Blau* in the late summer and early fall, and, finally, to participate in the strategic offensives it conducted in the Rzhev and Stalingrad regions during November and December and during the ensuing winter campaign. For example, the RVGK included a total of 189 rifle divisions, 30 tank or mechanized corps, 78 rifle brigades, and 159 separate tank brigades during the summer and fall of 1942. Of this total, it allocated 72 rifle divisions, 11 tank and mechanized corps, two cavalry corps, 38 tank brigades, plus 100 artillery and ten aviation regiments to reinforce its *fronts* operating along the Stalingrad axis and about the same size force to reinforce its *fronts* operating along the northwestern and western axes. In turn, its *fronts* operating in the Stalingrad region used 25 of these rifle divisions, three tank corps, and three mechanized corps to reinforce their main shock groups spearheading the Stalingrad offensive.[59]

Thus, the strategic reserves the *Stavka* assigned to its operating *fronts* during the first period of the war not only increased the strength and depth of the Red Army's strategic defenses but ultimately also provided the numerical superiority necessary for it to effect its successful transition to the offensive both in December 1941 and in November 1942:

> The timely and skillful commitment of the *Stavka* VGK's strategic reserves to combat during the summer–fall campaigns of 1941 and 1942 was one of the most important factors in the achievement of the aims of strategic defense during the first period of war. During both campaigns, the strategic reserves not only exhausted and bled enemy shock groups white and halted their offensive but also guaranteed that Soviet forces could successfully make the transition to the counteroffensive and develop a general offensive.[60]

Although the RVGK played a vital role in the *Stavka's* strategic defensive at Kursk in July 1943, it played an even more important role in the strategic offensives it conducted earlier in the year and after its victory at Kursk. For example, while preparing to conduct its winter campaign of 1942–43, the *Stavka* withdrew one tank army (the 5th), ten tank corps, and 71 rifle divisions from its operating *fronts* for refitting and began forming five other new armies, and, by the time the campaign began, it had five field armies, one tank army (the 3rd), eight tank, and two mechanized corps in its reserve.[61] Later still, while preparing for its summer–fall campaign, the *Stavka* expanded the RVGK by early July to include eight combined-arms armies (the 4th and 5th Guards, 11th, 27th, 47th, 52nd, 53rd, and 68th), two tank armies (the 3rd and 5th Guards), and one air army (the 5th). It used five of these combined-arms armies and the tank and air armies, plus six tank and mechanized corps and three cavalry corps, to form its new Reserve Front, which became the Steppe Military District under its direct control in April and the Steppe Front on 9 July.[62]

Throughout the year, the *Stavka* formed anew five armies, six corps, 64 rifle or cavalry divisions, and 55 separate brigades of various types in its strategic reserves and reorganized and refitted another 31 armies, 44 corps, 204 divisions, and 50 separate brigades after withdrawing them from its operating *fronts*.[63] At any given time during this period, the RVGK consisted of 2–12 combined-arms, tank, or air armies, 2–26 rifle, tank, mechanized, or cavalry corps, 12–78 rifle and cavalry divisions or fortified regions, and 9–30 rifle, motorized rifle, tank, or airborne brigades. During this period its reserves ranged in strength from a high of 12 armies, 25–26 rifle, tank or cavalry corps, 78 rifle and cavalry divisions or fortified regions, and 10–22 brigades of various types on 1 July to a low of two armies, two tank corps, 18 rifle divisions, and nine brigades on 1 January.[64]

In contrast to 1941 and 1942, when the *Stavka* raised the bulk of its strategic reserves from scratch in the rear area before employing them in its strategic offensives, the Red Army's numerical superiority over the *Wehrmacht* in 1943 and its seizure of the strategic initiative at Stalingrad and Kursk permitted the *Stavka* to withdraw large numbers of formations from its operating *fronts* while they were conducting offensive operations, assemble them in the RVGK for rest and refitting, and then reassign them to its operating *fronts* to conduct subsequent offensive operations. As a result, 70 percent of the *Stavka's* strategic reserves during this period consisted of formations withdrawn from its operating *fronts*, and only 30 percent of newly formed forces. Since most of these formations retained their former organizational structure and included a nucleus of trained and combat-experienced veteran soldiers (3,000 on average per rifle division), they proved far more effective when committed to combat.[65] This, in turn, reduced the preparation time necessary to mount new strategic offensives and permitted the *Stavka* to reinforce Red Army offensives already in progress.

More significant still, in comparison with 1941 and 1942, the quantity of strategic reserve formations under the *Stavka's* direct control during 1943, in particular, mobile ground and air formations, almost doubled in size. For the most part, the *Stavka* employed these reserves either to conduct strategic defensive or offensive operations on an ever-larger scale or to strengthen strategic offensives already under way. For example, during its strategic defense at Kursk, the *Stavka* employed RVGK formations to create its deeply echeloned strategic defenses, to reinforce its defending *fronts* during the *Wehrmacht's* offensive, and to create shock groups with which to conduct its own counteroffensives and offensives. Subsequently, during the fall it employed its reserve primarily to strengthen its *fronts* attacking toward and across the Dnepr River.[66] In short, the striking defensive success the Red Army achieved at Kursk in July 1943 and the equally dramatic offensive successes it recorded during the late summer and fall of 1943, when it conducted sustained offensives to ever-increasing depths, resulted directly from the *Stavka's* skillful employment of its expanded force of strategic reserves.

OPERATIONAL ART

Soviet military theorists considered the operational level of war as the essential link between tactics and strategy; therefore, they also believed that successful practice of "operational art" was the only way its *front* and army commanders could transform tactical successes into strategic victories. Within the parameters of this definition, the Red Army's ability to defend successfully during Operations Barbarossa, *Blau*, and Citadel and to conduct strategic offensives of its own once it did so depended directly on the ability of its operating *fronts* and armies to conduct effective defensive and offensive operations at the operational level.[67] The best of many ways to analyze the effectiveness of Red Army *front* and army operations is to examine their scope and scale and the operational formations and techniques *front* and army commanders employed when conducting them, in particular, their employment of operational maneuver. In all of these regards, it is clear that *front* and army commander did indeed undergo a harsh education in conducting both defensive and offensive operations during 1941 and 1942, though ultimately they exploited this education to operate far more effectively in 1943.

Scope and Scale

Defensive Operations. During the summer–fall campaigns of 1941 and 1942, the Red Army's operating *fronts* conducted defensive operations against *Wehrmacht* forces conducting Operations Barbarossa and *Blau* under *Stavka* or main direction command control, while its armies did so either under *front* or *Stavka* control. Since all of these operations were "forced" in the sense that they represented reactions to *Wehrmacht* offensives, and since they all formed an integral part of *Stavka*-directed strategic defenses, their scope and scale tended to blend seamlessly into overarching strategic defensive operations. In fact, the only operations Red Army *front* and army commanders organized independently during these periods were essentially offensive in nature.[68]

In general, although they were weak during the initial months of the war and remained so for much of 1941, the defenses conducted by *fronts* and armies strengthened in several important respects in 1942. For example, *fronts* and armies generally conducted defensive operations on frontages of 300–500 kilometers and 70–120 kilometers, respectively, during the summer and fall of 1941. The depths of these operations varied depending on the *Wehrmacht's* advance during each operation and generally extended to the depth of the overall strategic defensive operation or to the depth at which the respective *front* or army was destroyed.[69] On the other hand, reflecting the increased size and strength of the Red Army, *fronts* and armies conducted defensive operations on slightly diminished frontages of 250–450 kilometers and 50–90 kilometers, respectively, during the summer of 1942. Once again in 1942, the depths of these defensive operations extended to the overall strategic defenses depth or until the depth at which the respective army was destroyed, although fewer armies met that grim fate.[70]

As the Red Army became stronger still in 1943, when they were able to plan strategic defensive operations, *fronts* and armies could better concentrate their forces in increasingly narrower defensive sectors and, by doing so, increase the strength and resilience of their defenses. However, the defense conducted by the Central, Voronezh, and Southwestern Fronts in February and March 1943 was a clear exception to this rule because, in this instance, the three attacking *fronts* were forced on the defense by a sudden and devastating *Wehrmacht* counteroffensive in the Donbas and other counterstrokes west of Kursk. Therefore, the three *fronts* conducting these defensive operations did so in broad sectors as others had done in 1941 and 1942 and conducted their defense with forces at hand or reinforcements provided by the *Stavka*.

At Kursk in July 1943, however, increased planning time enabled the operating *fronts* and armies participating in the strategic defense to conduct well-prepared defensive operations in far narrower sectors than before. During the Kursk defenses, *fronts* and armies defended sectors of 250–300 kilometers and 40–70 kilometers, respectively, and conducted their defense in a matter of only days to far more limited depths. Thereafter, the Red Army's defense at Kursk served as a model for subsequent defensive operations conducted by *fronts* and armies later in the war.

Offensive Operations. Throughout 1941 and most of 1942, Red Army *fronts* and armies conducted offensive operations either within the context of multi-*front or* single-*front* strategic offensive operations organized by the *Stavka*, such as the Smolensk offensive of August and Moscow offensive of January–April 1942, or separately as directed by the *Stavka*, such as the Northern Front's offensive at Sol'tsy in August, the Volkhov Front's offensive at Liuban' in January 1942, and the Southern Front's Barvenkovo-Lozovaia offensive in January 1942. Most of the *front* and army offensives conducted in the summer and fall of 1941 were haphazard affairs, but they became far more elaborate and effective over time as the Red Army increased in strength and its *front* and army commanders gained greater combat experience.

During the few offensives the Red Army conducted during the summer of 1941, its *fronts* and armies advanced in frontages ranging from 90 to 250 kilometers and 20 to 50 kilometers, respectively, and advanced up to 50 kilometers.[71] During its largest-scale offensive, the Moscow offensive during December 1941 and January–April 1942, attacking *fronts* and armies advanced on frontages of 300–400 kilometers and 20–80 kilometers, respectively, against objectives 120–250 kilometers deep for *fronts* and 30–35 kilometers deep for armies, which they were to attain within six to eight days.[72] Although they failed to attain these objectives, they did record unprecedented advances before the Germans brought the offensive to a halt.[73]

Since *front* and army commanders tended to disperse their attacking forces over a wide front during the winter campaign, diluting the strength and impact of their assaults, in early January the *Stavka* ordered commanders at all levels to mass their forces in narrower main attack sectors by forming shock groups.[74] Henceforth, *fronts* were to conduct their main attacks in 30-kilometer-wide penetration sectors and armies in 15-kilometer-wide penetration sectors. This increased the operational density of artillery in *front* and army main attack sectors from seven to 12 guns and mortars per kilometer of front in 1941 to 45–65 guns and mortars per kilometer of front in 1942.[75]

During the Red Army's offensive in late 1942 and the winter campaign of 1942–43, *fronts* and armies attacked on frontages of 250–350 kilometers and 50–80 kilometers, respectively, from army penetration sectors of 12–14 kilometers to secure army and *front* immediate objectives 20–28 and 100–140 kilometers deep, respectively. However, the Red Army's mixed experiences during the winter campaign prompted the *Stavka* to concentrate its forces to a far greater extent during its summer offensives of 1943. Consequently, during its offensives in mid- and late 1943, *fronts* and armies attacked frontages of 150–200 kilometers and 20–35 kilometers, respectively, and organized penetration sectors ranging in width from 25 to 30 kilometers for *fronts* and 6 to 12 kilometers for armies. As a result, rifle divisions' penetration sectors shrank to a width of 2.5–3 kilometers, and the operational densities of artillery and armor supporting *front* and army penetration (main attack) sectors increased to 150–80 guns and mortars and 30–40 tanks per kilometer of front.[76] So configured, the *Stavka* expected armies to accomplish their immediate missions at depths of 12–15 kilometers and their parent *fronts'* immediate missions at depths of 80–100 kilometers into the *Wehrmacht's* defenses. However, few *fronts* and armies fulfilled these ambitious missions until mid-1944.

Operational Formations

Defensive Operations. When conducting offensive operations during the summer and fall of 1941 and 1942, operating *fronts* (with four to six armies) and armies (with four to five rifle divisions) defended in shallow, single-echelon operational formations with only small reserves.[77] For example, *fronts* usually defended with three to five armies in first echelon with one or two rifle divisions in reserve in sectors 300–500 kilometers wide and 30–35 kilometers deep, and armies defended with three to four rifle divisions in first echelon with up to one rifle division in reserve in sectors 70–120 kilometers wide and 13–24 kilometers deep. These defenses were often fragmentary, defending formations frequently fought in isolation from one another, and reserves seldom maneuvered along the front and in the depths.

However, increased availability of forces enabled *fronts* and armies to form stronger and deeper defensive operational formations during the summer of 1942. For example, *fronts* (with four to six armies, one or two tank or mechanized corps, and one or two cavalry corps) deployed in two-echelon formations, with three to five armies in first echelon and one army and several mobile corps in second echelon or reserve. At the same time, the width of *fronts'* defensive formations decreased to 250–450 kilometers and the depth of their defenses increased to up to 50–150 kilometers.

Within *fronts*, armies (with four to six rifle divisions or brigades and one or two tank brigades) defended sectors 50–90 kilometers wide in two echelons with three to four divisions and brigades in first echelon and one or two divisions or brigades in second echelon to depths of roughly 15–25 kilometers. In addition, for the first time, armies were able to create artillery and antiaircraft artillery support groups and sizable artillery and antitank reserves. As a result, the operational densities of artillery within defending armies increased to 15–25 guns and mortars per kilometers of front.

As the Red Army strengthened its defenses during the late fall of 1942, its *fronts* increased the depth of their defenses to 40–50 kilometers and, in some instances, up to 75–150 kilometers when they were able to construct a rear defense line. At the same time, armies deployed in a single-echelon main defensive belt manned defenses 12–15 kilometers deep and defenses up to 25 kilometers deep if they were able to organize a second defensive belt. At the same time, they improved the resilience of their first defensive belts by forming an increasing number of battalion defensive regions within them.[78] Depending on whether they defended along primary or secondary axes, the operational densities of artillery and armor within these armies increased to 15–27 guns and mortars and six to seven tanks per kilometer of front.

As the Red Army refined its defensive techniques during 1943, it decreased the defensive sectors of its *fronts* and armies further and increased the depth of their defenses, thereby drastically increasing the operational densities of men and weaponry in the defense and its overall resiliency. During the summer of 1943, *fronts* (with four to nine armies, up to one tank army, and up to five tank or mechanized corps) defended sectors ranging 250–300 kilometers in width to depths of 120–150 kilometers, with three to six armies in first echelon and one to three armies, its tank army, and several mobile corps in second echelon, and a rifle corps and several mobile corps in reserve. Within these *fronts*, armies (with one to three rifle corps, 3–12 rifle divisions or brigades, and up to seven tank or self-propelled artillery brigades or regiments) defended sectors ranging in width from 40 to 70 kilometers to depths of 30–40 kilometers, with two rifle corps and three to six rifle divisions or brigades and several tank brigades or regiments in first echelon defending two defensive belts, and one rifle corps and three to six rifle divisions or brigades in second echelon, and one to two rifle divisions and several tank or self-propelled artillery brigades or regiments in reserve in the armies' third (rear) defensive belt.

The Central and Voronezh Fronts' elaborate defense at Kursk in July 1943 stands as a model of both effective strategic and operational defense and remained the standard for *front* and army defensive operations for the remainder of the war.[79] Finally, from the standpoint of the durability of these defenses, by the summer of 1943 *front* defensive zones were three to six times deeper and army defensive zones twice as deep as during 1941 and 1942. This produced operational densities of artillery and tanks and self-propelled guns of 30–80 guns and mortars and 7–27 tanks and self-propelled guns per kilometer of defensive front.[80]

When conducting their defenses, *front* commanders normally employed their second-echelon tank armies and reserve tank or mechanized corps to halt and repel German panzer penetrations. In addition, armies and rifle corps formed and employed a wide variety of artillery and antiaircraft artillery groups, antitank reserves to defeat tactical penetrations, and mobile obstacle detachments to inhibit enemy maneuver on the battlefield. Finally, when organizing a hasty defense during the waning stages of a prolonged offensive operation, *front* commanders normally deployed their rifle and tank armies in single-echelon formations, with the tank armies defending along the main axis of advance.[81]

Offensive Operations. When conducting offensive operations during 1941, *fronts* and armies launched their main attacks in excessively broad and imprecise penetration sectors and relied on rifle forces or fragile cavalry divisions, groups, or, later, reinforced cavalry corps, to conduct exploitation operations. *Fronts* (with three to six armies, but with nine to ten armies in the Western Front in December 1941 and January 1942) normally deployed most or all of their attacking armies in a single-echelon operational formation, with two to three rifle divisions and one to two tank divisions or brigades in reserve across frontages of 300–400 kilometers to depths of 30–40 kilometers. During the same period, armies (with 3–10 rifle divisions or brigades, one cavalry corps, and up to eight tank divisions or brigades) deployed most of their forces in single echelon across frontages of 50–80 kilometers to depths of 12–16 kilometers with small reserves and a cavalry corps to conduct exploitation operations from second echelon. These armies concentrated their attacks in one or two main attack sectors up to 15–20 kilometers wide.

As the Red Army increased in strength during the spring and summer of 1942, *fronts* and armies continued attacking in single-echelon formation but increased the size of their reserves, created various types of artillery groups and antitank, tank, and engineer reserves to support their penetration operations. In addition, during the spring, *fronts* began employing mobile groups *(podvizhnye gruppy)*, which consisted of one or more tank corps formed in their second echelons, to conduct operational exploitations and, during the summer and fall, began employing tank armies to spearhead their assaults by attacking in their first echelons.[82] As a result, the width of *front* and army offensive sectors decreased 250–350 kilometers and 50–80 kilometers, respectively, and the depth increased to 30–40 kilometers and 15–20 kilometers, respectively.[83]

As the *Stavka* organized an ever-increasing number of offensive operations across an ever-expanding front beginning in November 1942 and continuing throughout 1943, Red Army *fronts* and armies employed more deeply echeloned offensive formations consisting of tailored shock groups supported by massive artillery and armor forces to penetrate *Wehrmacht* forward defenses and mobile groups made up of highly maneuverable tank or mechanized corps at army level and one or two tank armies and sometimes a cavalry corps at *front* level to exploit into the operational depths of *Wehrmacht* defenses. Consequently, the scale, complexity, advance tempo, and depth of Red Army offensive operations increased steadily during this period as the offensive skills of Red Army *front* and army commanders improved.

For example, during offensive operations they conducted during the winter of 1942–43, *fronts* normally deployed in stronger single-echelon formations, often with a tank army conducting their main attacks, with one or two rifle divisions in reserve, and with one or two tank, mechanized corps, or cavalry corps in reserve to conduct exploitation operations either singly or in combination as cavalry-mechanized groups.[84] Within these *fronts*, attacking rifle armies normally deployed in two-echelon formations of rifle corps or divisions supported by army mobile groups, normally consisting of one separate tank, mechanized, or cavalry corps.

As the *Wehrmacht* improved its operational defenses in the summer of 1943 by making them deeper and stronger, *fronts* and armies adjusted their operational formations accordingly by routinely deploying their forces in two echelons of armies in the case of *fronts* or rifle corps and rifle divisions in the case of armies, supported by mobile groups deployed in second echelon or reserve. *Fronts* deployed their attacking forces in sectors ranging in width from 150 to 250 kilometers to a depth of 20–25 kilometers and their subordinate armies in sectors 40–55 kilometers wide to a depth of 25 kilometers. Mobile groups consisting of one tank army assigned to each *front* and one tank and mechanized corps assigned to each army advanced in the wake of first-echelon forces conducting the penetrations in the *fronts'* and armies' main attack axes usually employed their lead brigades to assist in the penetration operations and then conducted operational exploitations into the depth of the *Wehrmacht's* defenses. In addition, armies employed a variety of artillery and antiaircraft artillery groups, mobile obstacle detachments, and combined-arms, antitank, and tank reserves.[85]

Operational Techniques

Among the many operational techniques the Red Army depended upon to conduct offensive and defensive operations successfully, the most important involved its capability for employing operational maneuver, its development and use of antitank, artillery, and air forces, and its employment of operational deception to achieve surprise, particularly in its offensive operations.

Operational Maneuver. Just as the strategic victory could only be achieved by conducting effective operations, operational success depended on the effective employment of operational maneuver by mobile formations, in particular, large tank, mechanized, and cavalry forces. Although the Germans did not call it operational maneuver, the *Wehrmacht's* conduct of mobile deep operations with panzer groups and armies and panzer (motorized) corps produced its most dramatic successes during Operations Barbarossa and *Blau*. Although the Red Army was not able to match the *Wehrmacht's* mobile capabilities by conducting effective operational maneuver of its own during 1941 and early 1942, it did begin an intensive program to construct mobile forces that could do so in the spring and summer of 1942. After conducting operational maneuver with only marginal success during the summer and fall of 1942, it achieved its first major victory employing mobile forces at Stalingrad in November 1942. After the Battle of Stalingrad and to war's end, strategically and operationally, all of the Red Army's offensive victories resulted in large measure from the ability of its mobile forces to conduct effective operational maneuver in offensive as well as defensive operations. In short, it became axiomatic that, where its tank armies went, the Red Army followed, and when they faltered, the Red Army faltered.

Defensive operational maneuver primarily involved the regrouping and maneuver of large mobile forces, particularly reserves, prior to and during defensive operations so that they could block *Wehrmacht* panzer attacks and conduct counterattacks and counterstrokes of their own. For the most part, Red Army *fronts* and armies conducted defensive operational maneuver poorly during 1941 and 1942.

For example, during the first week of Operation Barbarossa, all three Red Army defending *fronts* attempted to employ operational maneuver with their mechanized corps to halt and drive back the *Wehrmacht*'s advance. In all of these cases, however, inept command and control and paralyzing logistical deficiencies combined to produce near instant defeat and the utter destruction of these mechanized corps.[86] The destruction of the Red Army's mechanized corps during the first few weeks of the war and the absence of large mobile forces in its force structures prevented its *fronts* and armies from conducting any defensive operational maneuver throughout the remainder of Operation Barbarossa.

After forming a nucleus of a new mobile force in the spring and early summer of 1942, the Red Army once again attempted to employ defensive operational maneuver to defeat *Wehrmacht* forces during the first few weeks of Operation *Blau*. As was the case in late June 1941, in early July 1942, the Red Army's *fronts* defending in southern Russia attempted to employ their new tank armies and tank corps in concerted counteroffensives against advancing *Wehrmacht* forces. Once again, though, poor command and control confounded effective operational maneuver and ended in the defeat, destruction, or decimation of the mobile forces.[87]

The first and only time the Red Army employed defensive operational maneuver effectively during the first 30 months of the war was while it was conducting its strategic defense at Kursk in July 1943. In this case, the *fronts* conducting the Kursk defense effectively maneuvered their armies and separate tank corps to shape, blunt, and ultimately block the *Wehrmacht's* panzer penetrations, first, by conducting essentially positional defenses with their tank armies and, second, by extensively and repeatedly maneuvering their separate tank corps to strike the flanks of the developing penetrations. Finally, at the height of the defense, the *Stavka* maneuvered a reinforced tank army to strike the nose of the most dangerous penetration (at Prokhorovka) and halt it in its tracks.[88]

Finally, during the late fall of 1943, *fronts* and armies often employed effective defensive operational maneuver by tank armies and tank and mechanized corps to contain *Wehrmacht* forces conducting counterattacks and counterstrokes in the wake of successful Red Army offensives. This occurred in the regions north of Krivoi Rog in October 1943 and in the region west of Kiev in November and December 1943.[89]

Based on their successful employment of defensive operational maneuver in mid- and late 1943, thereafter *fronts* and armies routinely incorporated planned maneuver by mobile forces in all of their defensive operations and unplanned maneuver during defenses they conducted in the wake of successful offensive operations.

After its mechanized corps were destroyed by the *Wehrmacht* during the initial stage of Operation Barbarossa, the Red Army possessed virtually no capability whatsoever for conducting offensive operational maneuver, even during its Moscow offensive and ensuing winter campaign. During this period, *fronts* and armies routinely employed cavalry corps and divisions and airborne corps and brigades, reinforced at times with tank brigades, to spearhead their pursuit operations and conduct deep exploitations. However, the limited firepower of these forces and their threadbare logistical support made resupply difficult if not impossible, and they could not sustain these operations to any appreciable depth. In addition, since the *Stavka* and its operating *fronts* could not coordinate these deep operations with follow-on infantry, they inevitably failed.

In sharp contrast to 1941, the new mixed-composition tank armies and separate tank and mechanized corps the NKO formed and fielded during the spring and summer of 1942 were far more capable of conducting offensive operational maneuver than their predecessors had been. Therefore, at the *Stavka's* direction, in the spring of 1942, *fronts* and armies began using them to form mobile groups tasked with exploiting penetration operations into the operational depths of the *Wehrmacht's* defenses. Initially, however, the composition of these fledgling tank forces was unbalanced and inadequate because tank corps lacked adequate accompanying mechanized infantry, and tank armies consisted of a strange mixture of foot (infantry), hoof (cavalry), and tracked (tank) forces and were difficult to coordinate with other types of forces and extremely vulnerable when fighting in isolation from their supporting infantry and artillery. Worse still, as the defeats at Khar'kov in May, at Voronezh and along the Don River in July, and at Zhizdra in August indicated, the commanders of these mobile forces did not know how to employ them properly.[90]

On 16 October, after analyzing the causes of these and other mobile force debacles during the summer, the NKO issued Order No. 325, which analyzed mobile group failures during the spring and summer of 1942 and directed tank and mechanized corps commanders to employ their corps singly and intact in "powerful attacks or counterattacks" and prohibited the "fragmented use of those valuable operational formations."[91]

As a result of this and other orders, the so-called mobile group *(podvizhnaia gruppa)* became the most important component in the operational formations of *fronts* and armies during the second period of the war in terms of both the frequency of their employment and their operational effectiveness. These groups' primary missions were to conduct operational maneuver to facilitate penetration operations, to conduct exploitations deep into the *Wehrmacht's* rear area once penetration operations had succeeded, and to conduct deep pursuit operations.[92] Beginning at Stalingrad in November 1942 and through the remainder of the war, *fronts* and armies routinely employed tank armies and single or multiple tank or mechanized corps as their mobile groups to expand the scale, scope, and duration of their offensive operations.

The most important forces serving as mobile groups at *front* level during late 1942 and 1943 were the mixed-composition tank armies the NKO fielded in the summer of 1942 and experimented with from November 1942 through the winter of 1942–43 and the new model tank armies it fielded in early and mid-1943. During the same period, armies employed separate tank and mechanized corps as their mobile groups. *Fronts* and armies experimented extensively with these tank armies and various combinations of separate tank and mechanized corps from November 1942 through March 1943 as they sought to develop a capability for conducting uninterrupted exploitation operations deep into the *Wehrmacht's* operational rear.

For example, during their offensives at Stalingrad, the Southwestern Front employed the 5th Tank Army as its mobile group and deployed it in first echelon to penetrate Romanian defenses north of the city and conduct its subsequent deep exploitation. During the same offensive, the Stalingrad Front employed several tank and mechanized corps as its mobile groups to penetrate Romanian defenses south of the city and exploit to link up with the 5th Tank Army. In this instance, however, even though the mobile groups corps successfully encircled German Sixth Army, the heavy losses they suffered prevented them from developing their offensives further.

During the ensuing winter campaign of 1942–43, while some attacking *fronts* continued employing their tank armies as mobile groups operating in first echelon, other *fronts* and armies used their separate tank and mechanized corps either singly or in combination as mobile groups to conduct exploitation operations from second echelon.[93] However, ineffective command and control of these mobile forces and logistical problems combined with bad weather and effective German resistance to lessen the effectiveness of operation maneuver and thwarted these offensives before they achieved their intended ends.

Although the Red Army's employment of operational maneuver during the winter of 1942–43 yielded only limited and often fleeting successes, the experience the *Stavka* and its *fronts* and armies garnered during this campaign provided a sound basis for conducting operational maneuver during the summer and fall of 1943. In short, by July 1943 the NKO was fielding forces more capable of conducting sustained operational maneuver, and *fronts* and armies had developed far more effective operational and tactical techniques for its conduct. Thereafter, at both *front* and army level, offensive operational maneuver by mobile groups became the most useful, if not vital, tool for the conduct of successful offensive operations.

In virtually every major offensive operation they conducted after July 1943, *fronts* and armies concentrated their mobile groups (tank armies in the case of *fronts* and separate tank or mechanized corps in the case of armies) in jumping-off positions for their attacks only hours before their offensives began and committed their mobile groups into combat late on the first day of their offensives either to complete their tactical penetrations or to exploit the penetrations into the operational depths.[94]

Mobile groups serving *fronts*, armies, and, in some cases, even rifle corps employed operational maneuver with even greater effectiveness during the late summer and fall of 1943. In addition to conducting ever-deeper operations, during exploitations they frequently regrouped their subordinate formations and units from one axis to another to shift their direction of advance to more favorable axes or to defeat *Wehrmacht* counterattacks or counterstrokes. To an increasing extent, they were also able to conceal these maneuvers from the prying eyes of German intelligence.

The most important and effective combat technique *fronts* and armies developed to conduct successful operational and tactical maneuver during 1943 was the fielding and use of forward detachments *(peredovye otriady)* to spearhead advances by both their mobile groups and their first-echelon rifle corps. Beginning in July 1943, *front* and army mobile groups and the first-echelon rifle corps of attacking combined-arm armies formed and employed forward detachments to increase the tempo of their penetration, exploitation, and pursuit operations. Usually formed around the nucleus of separate tank brigades and specifically tailored with appropriate reinforcements, forward detachments led their parent forces' advance in semi-independent fashion to disrupt *Wehrmacht* defenses, capture key terrain features such as river crossings and road junctions, facilitate the overall offensive, and exploit the offensive as deeply as possible.[95]

Although the independent nature of forward detachment operations often made them vulnerable to *Wehrmacht* counterattacks and counterstrokes and sometimes led to their outright destruction, they ultimately proved an indispensable tool in the conduct of effective offensive operational maneuver.

Antitank Operations. The *Stavka*, NKO, and General Staff also improved the Red Army's antitank capabilities throughout the entire war, but particularly in 1943, if only because they had to if its *fronts* and armies were to defeat the *Wehrmacht's* imposing panzer forces. These defenses proved wholly ineffective during 1941 and early 1942, largely because of the destruction of the Red Army's antitank brigades during the initial weeks of the war, the general shortage of antitank weapons, and the tendency of commanders to employ what antitank weapons they possessed scattered evenly across their fronts. Driven by necessity, beginning in the fall of 1941, commanders also began employing field and antiaircraft artillery, often in a direct fire role, to engage German panzer forces and reinforce their antitank defenses.[96]

Although antitank artillery remained in scarce supply until mid-1942, permitting *fronts* and armies to field fewer than two to five guns per kilometer of front, in late 1941 and the first half of 1942, they began forming antitank strong points and regions echeloned in depth along likely German tank axes of advance. In addition, during the summer and fall of 1942, *fronts* and armies were able to increase the density and mobility of their antitank defenses by assigning antitank units to lower-echelon commands so that they could create their own antitank reserves.

As a result of these negative experiences with antitank defense during Operations Barbarossa and *Blau*, the nature of *front* and army antitank defenses changed dramatically after November 1942, principally regarding the increased availability of antitank weapons, their improved integration into *front* and army operational formations, and more skillful employment of them by commanders at all levels. For example, although continuing low densities of antitank units and weapons within *fronts* and armies during the winter campaign of 1942–43 permitted the *Wehrmacht* to halt the Red Army's offensives and compel them to retreat from July 1943 to year's end, the general proliferation of antitank forces and weapons within operating *fronts* and armies enabled them to establish far more durable defenses in the face of *Wehrmacht* panzer attacks and improved the sustainability of their offensive operations.[97]

In short, to an increasing extent, during mid- and late 1943, defending *fronts* and armies were able to improve the durability of their defensive formations and make them far more difficult to penetrate by significantly increasing the number of antitank strong points and regions in the defensive belts of their first-echelon armies and rifle corps and also to increase the number of antitank reserves and mobile obstacle detachments. As a result, the operational density of antitank weapons in *front* and army main defensive sectors increased to 20–25 antitank guns per kilometer of front, a four- to tenfold increase over mid-1942.[98] In addition, extensive and more sophisticated employment of antiaircraft (85mm) and artillery weapons (even *Katiusha* multiple-rocket launchers) in antitank defenses, expanded use of engineer antitank obstacles, and more flexible maneuvering of antitank forces also increased the resilience and effectiveness of Red Army antitank defenses.

Finally, offensively, the integration of more numerous and larger antitank regiments and brigades into the *fronts* and armies improved their antitank capabilities while they conducted offensive operations. Significantly, from mid-1943 through war's end, these antitank weapons exacted a heavier toll on *Wehrmacht* panzers than did the Red Army's expanding tank force.

Artillery and Air Support. Largely because the *Wehrmacht* had decimated the Red Army's artillery and air forces during the early stages of Operation Barbarossa, artillery and air support of *fronts* and armies was disjointed at best and essentially ineffective throughout the summer and fall of 1941. For example, during offensive operations the operational densities of supporting artillery in main attacks sectors amounted to 20–80 guns and mortars per kilometer of front. Worse still, the relatively immobile artillery could not keep up with advancing tanks and even infantry, forcing the latter to conduct subsequent operations without fire support.

The *Stavka* began improving this situation in January 1942, when it issued a directive establishing the concept of the artillery offensive. According to this concept, *fronts* and armies were supposed to mass all of their artillery resources to support their main attacks and to provide continuous artillery support throughout the duration of their offensives.[99] While providing for centrally planned and controlled and on-call fires by all artillery available within *fronts* throughout the entire duration of their offensives, this concept also divided existing inflexible and unresponsive army artillery groups into a variety of more flexible and far more responsive functional artillery groups to support advancing forces during all phases of operations.

As the Red Army implemented this concept over time, massed *front*, army, corps, and division artillery conducted well-coordinated and time-phased supporting fire, such as barrages and single or multiple concentrations to precede and accompany attacking infantry and tanks as they penetrated tactical defenses and, to a lesser degree, in support of their subsequent exploitation into the operational depths. As a result of these and other measures, the operational density of supporting artillery rose precipitously to exceed more than several hundred guns and mortars per kilometer of front in 1943. At the same time, the duration of artillery preparations and the depths of their devastating effects increased from 80–90 minutes and 2.5–5 kilometers in 1941 and 1942 to 140–175 minutes and 10–15 kilometers in mid-1943.[100] Finally, during 1943 the NKO added self-propelled artillery, truck-towed antitank artillery, *Katiusha* multiple-rocket launchers, and antiaircraft artillery units and subunits to its tank armies and tank, mechanized, and cavalry corps to provide them artillery support during exploitation operations.

During the first year of the war, the Red Army Air Force (VVS) employed as much as 60 percent of its aviation forces decentralized under army command. In light of the VVS's immense losses during the initial period of the war, *fronts* and armies concentrated its aviation forces only "episodically" and in relatively dispersed fashion across the entire front to support specific operations as they occurred. Obviously, this led to inadequate air support in most major operations, both defense and offensive.

To remedy this problem, in the fall of 1942, the *Stavka* introduced the concept of the "air offensive" to supplement the NKO's recent formation of new air armies under *front* control. First employed in the November offensives at Rzhev and Stalingrad, the air offensive called for the centralized and concentrated employment of all aircraft under operating *fronts*. As with the artillery offensive, the air offensive mandated time-phased air support for attacking ground forces by the conduct of increasingly elaborate air preparations and continuous air support for ground forces as they conducted penetration and exploitation operations. To assist in coordinating air support with deep operational advances, by the end of 1943, the *fronts'* air armies were also allocating specific aviation formations to support specific tank armies and cavalry-mechanized groups during deep exploitation operations.

Collectively, these changes in the operational employment of artillery and air forces transformed the former into the most effective and fearsome force during offensive operations and a means by which *fronts* and armies steadily increased the operational "reach" of their offensive operations.

Operational Deception and Surprise. The *Stavka* and the Red Army *fronts* also attempted to conduct operational deception *(maskirovka)* to achieve surprise in many of the offensive operations they conducted during 1941 and 1942; however, with notable exceptions most of these efforts proved unsuccessful.[101] After this poor beginning, achieving operational surprise through active and passive deception became far more important because *fronts* and armies had to penetrate stronger and deeper *Wehrmacht* defenses.

Beginning with their offensives at Rzhev and Stalingrad in November, *fronts* and armies conducted their operational planning within a cloak of draconian secrecy, used feints and demonstrations more extensively and effectively, and routinely employed both active and passive deception to achieve surprise regarding the time, location, and form of their attacks. Combined with a more thorough Soviet understanding of German operational methods, these measures enabled *fronts* and armies to overcome *Wehrmacht* defenses more quickly, reduced their casualties while doing so, and, over time, helped the advancing *fronts* forestall or parry anticipated and usually inevitable *Wehrmacht* counterattacks and counterstrokes.

The best examples of successful Soviet use of operational deception to achieve surprise occurred prior to the Voronezh and Steppe Fronts' Belgorod-Khar'kov offensive in August 1943 and the 1st Ukrainian Front's Kiev offensive in November 1943. In addition, on several occasions the *Stavka* and its operating *fronts* conducted deliberate full-fledged offensives of a diversionary nature to distract the *Wehrmacht's* attention and its operational reserves and other forces from their real offensive targets.[102]

TACTICS

By Soviet definition, "tactics makes the steps from which operational leaps are assembled; strategy points out the path."[103] This relationship between strategy, operational art, and tactics asserts that, offensively or defensively, success in *front* and army operations depended on the effectiveness of the tactics employed by their subordinate corps, divisions, brigades, and regiments.

Defensive Tactics

When war began, the Red Army's tactics suffered from many of the same problems as its operational art. As was the case at *front* and army level, some first-line corps and divisions were at or near full strength in personnel, but most had between 7,000 and 11,000 of their required 14,000 men, and others, particularly second-line divisions, had only 5,000–6,000 men. All the corps and divisions suffered from manpower shortages in many vital military specialties, many of their officers and soldiers were poorly trained, and modern heavy weaponry was in short supply. Worse still, second-line and mobilization divisions suffered from more severe shortages of weapons and trained personnel. The chaotic mobilization after war began only exacerbated these problems.

When conducting combat operations, rifle corps and divisions deployed in inflexible linear battle formations and tended to operate stereotypically with little maneuver or improvisation. Defensively, rifle corps formed for battle in single-echelon configurations across frontages of 25 kilometers in theory but 20–60 kilometers in practice to depths of 15–20 kilometers in theory but 20–40 kilometers in practice, with two to three divisions in first-echelon and regimental-size reserves. Theoretically, rifle divisions were supposed to deploy for combat in two echelons of regiments across frontages of 8–12 kilometers to depths of 5–8 kilometers. In practice, however, they formed single-echelon battle formations with three rifle regiments deployed abreast on frontages 14–20 kilometers wide to depths of only 3–5 kilometers and retained only small battalion-size reserves. In addition to being small, corps and division reserves were not mobile enough to conduct effective counterattacks, and infantry support artillery groups within the corps and divisions, if they existed at all, were too weak to provide adequate artillery support.

As a result, tactical densities of both infantrymen and supporting weapons, which, on average, amounted to roughly one-half to two-thirds of a rifle battalion and three guns and mortars deployed per kilometer of defensive front, were inadequate to conduct an effective defense. Worse still, rifle divisions' defenses normally consisted of noncontiguous battalion defense regions with only feeble antitank and engineer support.[104]

The increasing strength of the Red Army in late 1941 and 1942 improved the defensive capabilities of rifle divisions. For example, by late 1941 increased engineer support permitted rifle division commanders to construct trench lines and construct more elaborate first defensive positions containing a greater number of interconnected battalion defensive regions. Further increases in manpower and weaponry during early 1942 permitted rifle divisions to increase the density of battalion defensive regions in their first-echelon regiments, create new battalion defensive regions in their forward regiments' second echelons, and, in some instances, even form second echelons, small tank and antitank reserves, and stronger artillery groups. By late 1942 they were able to form complete second and third defensive positions.

Despite these improvements, however, rifle divisions' defensive battle formations remained relatively shallow for most of 1942. Normally, divisions defended in two echelons across frontages of 12–14 kilometers to depths of 4–6 kilometers, with two regiments in first echelon and one in second echelon and with their training battalions in reserve. Deployed in this configuration, the tactical densities in infantrymen and supporting weapons within defending rifle divisions rose during 1942 to one rifle battalion and 20 guns and mortars per kilometer of front, which was clearly inadequate to mount an effective defense.[105] Thus, even though these defenses contained up to three defensive positions organized into one rudimentary defensive belt, the divisions' artillery and antitank support remained quite weak, as the success of *Wehrmacht* offensives indicated.

The durability of rifle divisions' defenses continued to improve throughout the winter campaign of 1942–43. While the rifle division's defensive frontages expanded somewhat to roughly 16–20 kilometers, the depth of their defenses increased to 5–7 kilometers, and the divisions began fielding greater numbers of antitank strong points in their first-echelon regiments, stronger regimental and division reserves, and division long-range artillery groups to supplemented existing infantry support artillery groups supporting their first-echelon rifle regiments.

The most important improvements in the Red Army's tactical defenses occurred during the summer of 1943, on the one hand, because of the widespread introduction of rifle corps into its force structure and, on the other, because of increases in manpower and weaponry. In short, during the summer of 1943, rifle corps and rifle divisions transformed their defenses from a noncontiguous series of often disconnected trenches and battalion and antitank strong points into dense and deeply echeloned defenses anchored on elaborate trench systems and interconnected strong points providing far greater protection for defending infantry and more concealed maneuver by forces and weapons along the front and in the depths. As a result, although the widths of rifle corps and rifle divisions defensive sectors decreased, the strength, depth, and durability of their defensive zones increased significantly.

During the Battle of Kursk, in the summer and fall of 1943, rifle corps defended in a two-echelon battle formation across frontages of 15–30 kilometers to depths of 14–20 kilometers, with two rifle divisions in first echelon manning their first defensive belts and one in second echelon deployed in their second defensive belts. Rifle divisions within these corps defended sectors ranging in width from 8 to 15 kilometers in most threatened sectors and to up to 25 kilometers in secondary sectors to depths of from 5–6 kilometers at Kursk to 6–8 kilometers elsewhere. Divisions routinely formed into one- or two-echelon battle formations, either with three regiments on line or with two rifle regiments in first echelon and one in second. Within the divisions, rifle regiments normally defended in a two-echelon battle formation of rifle battalions. In addition, rifle corps and divisions routinely formed various types of artillery groups, antitank strong points or complete antitank regions, artillery antitank reserves, and mobile obstacle detachments to support their defending forces.[106]

More important still, rifle corps and divisions improved the strength, durability, and effectiveness of their defenses by employing their antitank and tank resources more effectively. For example, in addition to integrating a greater number of increasingly formidable antitank strong points and regions throughout the entire depth of their defenses, they formed tank reserves from their separate tank brigades and regiments and self-propelled gun regiments to reinforce their first-echelon divisions and regiments, sometimes by deploying them as fixed or mobile firing points, or to conduct counterattacks or counterstrokes.

Therefore, the Red Army's tactical defenses became far more durable and mobile during the second half of 1943. By this time, commanders had learned how to integrate all types of forces and weapons into their defenses and to make their defenses more active by using both rifle and mobile forces to conduct more frequent counterattacks and counterstrokes in support of their forward defending corps, divisions, and regiments. As a result, whereas rifle corps and divisions on the defense in 1941 and 1942 could not halt attacking *Wehrmacht* forces short of the operational and even strategic depths, in the summer of 1943 they often contained these attacks in the tactical depths.

Offensive Tactics

Offensively, the harsh combat realities rifle corps and divisions faced in 1941 forced them to deviate sharply from offensive techniques called for in prewar tactical regulations. At least in theory, those regulations had required rifle corps designated to conduct army main attacks to deploy in single-echelon battle formations of rifle divisions across frontages of 8–12 kilometers and advance to depths of up to 20 kilometers. Rifle divisions were to conduct their attacks in two-echelon battle formation across frontages of 3.5–4.5 kilometers, with two regiments in first echelon and one in second, and advance to depths of up to 8 kilometers.

Throughout 1941 and most of 1942, however, after the *Wehrmacht's* Barbarossa offensive savaged defending Red Army forces, forcing it to disband its rifle corps, rifle divisions tried to operate offensively in a two-echelon battle formation. For example, during the winter campaign of 1941–42, rifle divisions formed in two-echelon offensive battle formations in sectors 5–6 kilometers wide (in some instances as much as 10 kilometers wide), with two regiments forward and one to the rear, and were expected to advance to a depth of 5–12 kilometers (and, in isolated instances, as much as 20 kilometers). As *Wehrmacht* defenses strengthened in early 1942, rifle divisions narrowed their attack sectors to 3–4 kilometers and sought to advance 5–7 kilometers in several days. As a result, offensive tactical densities of forces and weapons increased from one to two rifle battalions, 20–30 guns and mortars, and two to three tanks per kilometer of front during the winter campaign of 1941–42 to two to four battalions, 30–40 guns and mortars, and 10–14 tanks per kilometer of front in the summer of 1942.[107]

Artillery support for attacking rifle divisions also improved during this period since they were able to form an increasing number of infantry support (*podderzhka pekhoty*, or PP) artillery groups and, in some instances, also long-range (*dal'nye deistviia*, or DD) artillery groups. By this time, divisional artillery normally participated in centralized artillery preparations planned by armies and, thereafter, decentralized their artillery support by allocating single artillery batteries to support each of their attacking rifle battalions.

However, since these divisions were still generally attacking with two regiments forward and one to the rear and their regiments were also attacking with two rifle battalions in their first echelons and one in their second, only eight of the divisions' 27 rifle companies participated directly in these attacks. Given the weakness of most rifle divisions, these battle formations proved utterly futile and particularly vulnerable to *Wehrmacht* artillery and air strikes.

Worse still, armor support for attacking rifle divisions, rifle regiments, and rifle battalions remained quite weak and poorly coordinated and, as a result, often resulted in heavy tank losses. For this reason, offensive operations conducted by rifle divisions prior to the fall of 1942 were generally unsuccessful.

The NKO finally began remedying this situation in October 1942 by issuing orders altering tactical offensive battle formations and the employment of tanks during offensive operations. First, on 8 October, NKO Order No. 306 required commanders at all levels of command from rifle companies through rifle divisions to deploy their forces in single-echelon battle formations and create and employ tactical reserves comprising one-ninth of the overall force during offensive operations.[108] In effect, this order required divisions to employ 80 percent of their combat power well forward to facilitate the achievement of tactical penetrations. Second, on 16 October, NKO Order No. 325 required army, corps, and division commanders to employ their separate tank brigades, regiments, and battalions as complete entities rather than in fragmented fashion in support of attacking rifle forces, but only after proper reconnaissance and in close coordination with appropriate infantry, artillery, and aviation commanders.[109]

Under the provisions of Order No. 306, which were in effect when the Red Army conducted its offensives at Rzhev and Stalingrad in November 1942, rifle divisions conducted their attacks in single-echelon attack formations in sectors 4–5 kilometers wide with three rifle regiments abreast. Within the divisions, rifle regiments also attacked in single echelons in sectors 1.5–2 kilometers wide with three rifle battalions abreast, and rifle battalions attacked in sectors 500–700 meters wide. This attack configuration brought 16 or more of the rifle divisions' 27 rifle companies to bear on the enemy instead of the previous eight. Thus, although these offensive sectors were 1.5 times wider than at the beginning of the war, the single-echelon attack formations permitted divisions to concentrate almost all rather than only two-thirds of their combat power in their attacks.[110]

Field regulations issued by the NKO in 1942 required rifle divisions, supported by artillery and reinforced by infantry support tanks from attached separate tank brigades or regiments, to advance to depths of 4–5 kilometers to accomplish their immediate missions and up to 10–12 kilometers to accomplish their subsequent missions (their so-called missions of the day). This meant that rifle divisions were supposed to penetrate the entire tactical depth of the enemy's defense in the course of a single day. However, since these assigned missions proved utterly unrealistic, particularly for divisions deployed in such shallow attack formations, few rifle divisions achieved their assigned missions in actual combat during the winter of 1942–43.

During the spring and summer of 1943, when the *Wehrmacht's* defenses became stronger and deeper, the *Stavka* and General Staff acted decisively to correct the deficiencies it noted in the Red Army's offensive tactics, first, by truncating the missions it assigned to its corps and divisions to make them more realistic and, second, by deepening their offensive battle formation to better sustain offensive operations. In July, for example, they decreased the missions of rifle divisions by requiring them to penetrate to a depth of 3–4 kilometers to accomplish their immediate missions and 12–15 kilometers to accomplish their missions of the day. At the same time, they ordered rifle corps, rifle divisions, and rifle regiments to attack in two-echelon battle formations with two rifle divisions, regiments, and battalions in first echelon and with one division, regiment, and battalion in second echelon, respectively. Although the width of rifle corps and rifle division attack sectors decreased to 4–10 kilometers and 2–3 kilometers respectively, the depth of their battle formations increased to 4–5 kilometers and 6–10 kilometers, respectively. Quite naturally, this new combat formation also drastically increased the tactical densities of attacking troops and supporting weapons.[111]

Beginning in July 1943 and for the remainder of the year, rifle corps and divisions employed systematic reconnaissances-in-force *(razvedka boem)* prior to offensive operations. In addition, during their offensives, they employed tactical maneuver, particularly with forward detachments, more effectively, and exploited their artillery and tanks more efficiently than earlier in the war. For example, several days prior to every offensive, first-echelon rifle divisions routinely conducted tactical reconnaissances-in-force with so-called advanced battalions, which were reinforced rifle battalions from each of their first-echelon rifle regiments, to determine precise troop dispositions and weapons concentrations in the Germans' first defensive position and to evaluate whether or not the Germans intended to hold on to these defenses so as to avoid wasting an artillery preparation against weakly defended or abandoned positions. In addition, rifle corps and even rifle divisions began employing small forward detachments consisting of reinforced rifle battalions mounted in trucks to lead their advances, particularly during pursuit operations.

Rifle corps and divisions also employed their organic and attached artillery, tanks, and self-propelled artillery in far more sophisticated fashion than before. Although rifle corps still used long-range artillery groups to deliver long-range artillery fire and rifle divisions still employed infantry support artillery groups to support their first-echelon rifle regiments, in late 1943 divisions began subordinating infantry support artillery groups directly to their regimental commanders. In the summer, armies, rifle corps, and rifle divisions began allocating more tanks and self-propelled guns to support first-echelon rifle regiments leading the advance along their main attack axes.[112] Similarly, the NKO doubled engineer and sapper support within rifle divisions in 1943, improving the rifle divisions' jumping-off positions and facilitating the clearance of obstacles, mines, and minefields forward of and within the Germans' defenses.

The NKO also improved the command and control of this expanding array of tactical forces by allocating more radios, some vehicle-mounted, to commanders at every level so that they could outfit stationary, mobile, and even aerial command posts to control their forces. In addition, tank, mechanized, and cavalry corps, which were operating independently at great distances from their parent *fronts*, armies, or tank armies, employed operational groups of staff officers equipped with radios to control the tempo of their mobile operations and to maintain communications with their parent forces. Finally, prior to offensive operations, most commanders from *front* down to regimental level routinely assembled their subordinate force commanders participating in specific operations at a single command post so that they could effect final coordination and force cooperation.

Improved command and control, increased fire support, and more effective tactical techniques enabled rifle corps and divisions to overcome the *Wehrmacht's* first two defensive positions on their own. However, continuing shortages of infantry support tanks and the reduced effectiveness of artillery fire at greater ranges tended to leave the enemy's third defensive positions intact. Therefore, corps and divisions had to continue relying on the separate tank, mechanized, and sometimes cavalry corps that constituted the armies' mobile groups to penetrate the third defensive position in the Germans' first defensive belt and the entire second defensive belt. Thus, further tactical improvements at rifle corps and rifle division level were necessary after 1943.

CONCLUSIONS

Hitler's hitherto invincible *Wehrmacht* inflicted severe damage on the Soviet state and catastrophic defeats on its Red Army during the first 18 months of war, advancing into the Soviet Union to a depth equivalent to the distance between the Atlantic coast and the Mississippi River in North America. German military forces conquered about 30 percent of the European Soviet Union, with its large population and rich industrial and agricultural base, and inflicted almost 12 million casualties, including over 6 million dead, missing, and captured, on the Red Army. After losing more than 3 million men—roughly two-thirds of its peacetime strength and one-third of its total mobilized strength—during Operation Barbarossa in 1941, the Red Army and Navy lost another 3.2 million men, or about one-third of their strength when 1942 began, during Operation *Blau*.

During 1941 and 1942, the Red Army had to perform the prodigious feat of defeating two powerful *Wehrmacht* offensives, both spearheaded by large, well-trained, experienced, blooded, and as yet undefeated panzer and motorized forces. Worse still, it had to do so with a mass force, which, although large and often numerically superior to its foe, was, for the most part, poorly led, trained, and equipped and lacked effective armored or mechanized forces of its own. This imposing challenge forced the *Stavka*, NKO, and General Staff to build an entirely new force structure for the Red Army from scratch, to raise, train, and equip forces to man this force structure, and to train a command cadre capable of leading the army effectively, all in the midst of a fearsome struggle for its very existence. Understandably, it took considerable time and blood to accomplish these formidable feats.

The dismal combat performance of the Red Army and its command cadre during 1941 and most of 1942 vividly demonstrated what changes had to occur if the Red Army was to vanquish the *Wehrmacht*. As cruel and costly as they were, the numerous strategic, operational, and tactical defeats the Red Army suffered during 1941 and 1942 were necessary prerequisites for the ultimate transformation of the Red Army into an effective modern fighting force in two significant respects. First, they tested, educated, and culled the army's command cadre to make it more effective; and second, they prompted the structural and doctrinal reforms necessary for the army to defeat the *Wehrmacht* tactically, operationally, and strategically. The *front*, army, corps, and division commanders who led the Red Army to victory during the last 30 months of the war were those who survived the maelstroms of the first 18 months of war, which taught them the military techniques necessary to achieve victory.

While the Red Army was receiving its education in the conduct of modern war during the first 18 months of war, the *Stavka*, NKO, and General Staff were exploiting its many military disasters to reform its command and control organs, revitalize its force structure, and formulate and implement new operational and tactical techniques necessary for it to operate more effectively at all levels of command. At the same time, mobilized to a full war footing, weapons design bureaus and Soviet industry strained every sinew to provide the army with modern weapons in sufficient quantities so that it could operate more successfully against the smaller but far better led, trained, and equipped *Wehrmacht*.

As a result, beginning in early 1942 and continuing through the first half of 1943, operating collectively and in stages, the *Stavka*, NKO, and General Staff managed to create and field a new and far more capable Red Army led by a command cadre educated and culled in the heat of battle and equipped with ever-increasing quantities of modern weapons whose effectiveness matched and sometimes even exceeded those which German industry provided to the

Wehrmacht. In this regard, Allied delivery of essential military supplies under the Lend-Lease program proved particularly important. Emerging from its stupor of 1941 with a reinvigorated command cadre, better-trained soldiers, and great quantities of modern weapons, this new Red Army recorded signal victories at Stalingrad and Kursk and tipped the scales of war in the Soviet Union's favor effort.

The year 1943 proved to be decisive for the Soviet war effort. Seizing the strategic initiative at Stalingrad and Kursk, the Red Army would never again lose it. Nor did Stalin, the *Stavka*, or the General Staff ever waver in their oft-stated goal of achieving total victory over Nazi Germany. Guided by a more focused military policy and strategy and possessing a thoroughly reformed, reconstructed, and reinvigorated Red Army led by an increasingly competent command cadre, by the summer of 1943 ultimate Soviet victory was inevitable, as many factors indicated.

First, the Red Army's successful premeditated defense at Kursk and the equally successful massive strategic offensives it conducted throughout the summer and fall of 1943 proved that its command cadre at all levels from *front* down to division knew how to operate effectively both on the defense and on the offensive in both static and mobile operations. The Red Army's victories during the second half of 1943 ensured that, with few exceptions, it would remain on the offensive until war's end.

Second, although these sometimes failed to achieve all of their intended aims, the simultaneous and successive strategic offensive operations the *Stavka* insisted the Red Army conduct during late 1942 and all of 1943 set the stage for even larger-scale Red Army strategic offensives in 1944 and 1945. Also conducted both simultaneously and successively, these strategic offensives proved increasingly more effective and lethal to the *Wehrmacht*. Third, throughout late 1942 and 1943, the *Stavka* and General Staff developed and the Red Army's operating *fronts*, armies, corps, and divisions tested and implemented an imposing array of new operational and tactical techniques necessary for the Red Army to conduct those increasingly successful strategic offensive operations during 1943, 1944, and 1945. If the Red Army experienced its primary, secondary, and university education at the hands of the *Wehrmacht* in 1941, 1942, and 1943, it conducted war at the graduate level in 1944 and 1945.

Although the Red Army's combat performance improved steadily and sometimes dramatically through the summer and fall of 1943 and would continue to improve thereafter, though, it was also plagued by certain problems that persisted to war's end. The most severe of these problems related to certain "bad habits" developed by some senior command cadre during the first period of the war that they were not able to rid themselves of prior to war's end.

The worst of these bad habits was the propensity of some commanders, particularly *Stavka* representatives and *front* and army commanders, to squander valuable manpower and equipment needlessly, particularly by planning and conducting costly frontal assaults during penetration operations, sometimes repeatedly, after it was apparent the penetration could not succeed, when other less costly methods of penetrating defenses might have succeeded. Spoiled by their perception that the Soviet Union could continue to produce seemingly endless ranks of fresh manpower, as it had during the first period of the war, many senior commanders displayed a callous disregard for combat losses.

Even though the *Stavka* frequently ordered its operating *fronts* to reduce their losses, their casualties remained high to war's end, at least in part because Stalin, the *Stavka's* other members, and many *front* commanders often treated combat failures and failed commanders with contempt or even worse.[113] Nor was this phenomenon limited to the highest command levels. For example, when queried about the losses his rifle regiment suffered during penetration operations he conducted from 1941 through 1945, a former Red Army regimental commander answered, "We lost almost 50 percent of our men, regardless of the period of war."[114] In short, the lofty reputations many senior Red Army commanders earned by virtue of successful operations they conducted during the first and second periods of the war and the prominent positions many of them occupied in the postwar Soviet Union protected them against criticism for their heavy losses. Therefore, it is not surprising that many Russians today still categorize some Red Army marshals and generals as "bloody" and others as "human."[115]

Although somewhat easier to explain, another problem the Red Army displayed to war's end was the apparent lack of flexibility and initiative on the part of its command cadre at army level and particularly at corps level and below. This problem, however, was a direct consequence of how *fronts* and armies organized penetration operations. To succeed, penetration operations required attacking forces at each level of command to fulfill their missions and orders precisely and strictly according to plan, like single cogs in a giant mechanical device. Any deviation from the plan by a single corps, division, regiment, or even rifle battalion could disrupt the entire operation. Therefore, *front* and army commanders discouraged "excessive" initiative by their subordinates lest they disrupt the overall offensive. As a result, throughout the war, the rifle forces and their supporting arms assigned to its operating *fronts* and armies, which constituted over 80 percent of the Red Army, resembled a massive streamroller shoving its way through the *Wehrmacht's* defenses regardless of human cost. Casualties were highest when this steamroller faltered, but they also were high when it accomplished its deadly mission.

Although this stereotypical perception of the nature of the wartime Red Army is partially correct, it overlooks a wholly different part of the army that began to emerge after May 1942 and became its most important element during and after the summer of 1943: its mobile force. This new element, which included tank armies, tank, mechanized, and cavalry corps, and separate tank brigades comprising about 20 percent of the Red Army's force structure by mid-1943 and which contributed most to the Red Army's successful conduct of offensive operations from July 1943 through war's end, varied sharply from this enduring stereotype. To achieve its operational and strategic victories, the Red Army needed these mobile forces to use their offensive power flexibly to complete and exploit penetrations and conduct deep exploitation and pursuit operations. Mobile force commanders had to—and, as the Red Army's impressive victories in 1944 and 1945 indicated, did—display a high degree of flexibility and personal initiative while conducting these complex operations.

Another serious problem that plagued the Red Army to war's end was the maintenance of political reliability and good order and discipline among its officers and soldiers (see Chapters 12 and 13). Although the GKO ostensibly abolished the commissar system in 1943, it maintained stringent political control over the military by continuing its infamous prewar purges of the officers corps during wartime, albeit more covertly and at a reduced level, by employing political deputies at all levels of command and by creating a harsh and often arbitrary and brutal security regime managed by the NKVD to detect any disloyalty on the part of officers and soldiers.

Coupled with this political control, the Red Army continued employing Draconian and often brutal techniques to ensure discipline in the ranks and reliable combat performance by its soldiers. These techniques included the formation and employment of penal units from platoon to even corps size, the use of blocking detachments to prevent desertion, and denunciations and investigations of officers and soldiers by the counterintelligence organ SMERSH (Death to Spies), which evoked terror in the hearts of Soviet commanders and soldiers alike.

Combined with Red Army soldiers' clear hatred of the invading Germans and appeals to latent Russian nationalism, the soldiers' traditional love of homeland *(rodina)*, and their hopes for a better postwar future, these measures helped ensure that Red Army soldiers fought on, regardless of casualties. At the same time, of course, these harsh disciplinary measures also increased the risk that, at some point, the Red Army might simply fall apart like its predecessor Tsarist Army had fallen apart in 1918, or that its threatened and intimidated command cadre would carry out a coup. The fact that neither collapse nor coup took place bore mute testimony to the ruthless effectiveness of Stalin's regime.

Table 3.1. Red Army Strategic Defensive Operations during 1941

Strategic Axis	Operations and Duration	Scale (km)	
		Width	Depth
Northern	Defensive operations in the Arctic region and Karelia, 29 June to 10 October	800	50–150
Northwestern (Leningrad)	Defensive operations in the Baltic region, 22 June to 9 July	350–450	400–450
	Leningrad defensive operation, 10 July to 30 September	450	270–300
	Tikhvin defensive operation, 10 October to 10 November	300–350	100–120
Western (Moscow)	Defensive operations in Belorussia, 22 June to 9 July	450–800	450–600
	Battle of Smolensk, 10 July to 10 September	600–650	200–250
	Moscow defensive operation, 30 September to 5 December	700–1,100	300–350
Southwestern (Kiev)	Defensive operations in the western Ukraine, 22 June to 6 July	600–700	300–350
	Kiev defensive operation, 7 July to 26 September	300	600
Southern	Donbas-Rostov defensive operation, 29 September to 16 November	400–670	150–300
	Siege of Sevastopol', 5 October 1941 to 4 July 1942	NA	NA

Source: "Itogi diskussii o strategicheskikh operatsiiakh Velikoi Otechestvennoi voiny 1941–1945 gg." [Results of the discussion on strategic operations of the Great Patriotic War 1941–1945], *Voenno-istoricheskii zhurnal* [Military-historical journal], no. 10 (October 1987); 14–16.

Table 3.2. Red Army Strategic Defensive Operations during 1942

Strategic Axis	Operations and Duration	Scale (km)	
		Width	Depth
Southwestern	Voronezh-Voroshilovgrad defensive operation, 28 June to 24 July	900	150–400
	Stalingrad (Volga) defensive operation, 17 July to 18 November	250–500	150
Southern	North Caucasus defensive operation, 25 July to 31 December	320–1,000	400–800

Source: "Itogi diskussii o strategicheskikh operatsiiakh Velikoi Otechestvennoi voiny 1941–1945 gg." [Results of the discussion on strategic operations of the Great Patriotic War 1941–1945], *Voenno-istoricheskii zhurnal* [Military-historical journal], no. 10 (October 1987); 17.

Table 3.3. Red Army Strategic Defensive Operations during 1943

Strategic Axis	Operations and Duration	Scale (km) Width	Depth
Southwestern and Central (Donbas, Khar'kov, Sevsk, Orel-Briansk)	Donbas, Khar'kov, and Sevsk-Kursk defensive operations, 21 February to 28 March*	500	50–200
	Kursk Defensive Operation, 5–27 July	550	10–35
Southwestern (Khar'kov-Kiev)	Donbas and Khar'kov Defensive Operation, 19 February to 25 March	300–350	100–150

*Soviet (Russian) sources do not consider the Donbas, Khar'kov, and Sevsk-Kursk defensive operations collectively to constitute a full-fledged strategic defensive operation planned by the *Stavka*.
Sources: "Itogi diskussii o strategicheskikh operatsiiakh Velikoi Otechestvennoi voiny 1941–1945 gg." [Results of the discussion on strategic operations of the Great Patriotic War 1941–1945], *Voenno-istoricheskii zhurnal* [Military-historical journal], no. 10 (October 1987); 17–20; David M. Glantz, *The Soviet-German War 1941–1945: Myths and Realities:A Survey Essay* (Carlisle, PA: Self-published, 2001); and David M. Glantz, *Forgotten Battles of the German-Soviet War (1941–1945), volume IV, The Winter Campaign (19 November 1942–21 March 1943)* (Carlisle, PA: Self-published, 1999).

Table 3.4. Comparison of the *Stavka's* Strategic Defensive Operations at Moscow, Stalingrad, and Kursk, 1941 and 1942–1943

Forces and Weaponry	Moscow Defense	Stalingrad Defense	Kursk Defense
Personnel	160,000	1,250,000	1,909,000
Guns and mortars	2,200	7,600	26,499
Tanks	400	990	4,995
Aircraft	454	677	2,172

Source: R. A. Savushkin, ed., *Razvitie Sovetskikh vooruzhennykh sil i voennogo iskusstva v Velikoi Otechestvennoi voine 1941–1945 gg.* [The development of the Soviet Armed Forces and military art in the Great Patriotic War 1941–1945] (Moscow: Lenin Political-Military Academy, 1988), 111.

Table 3.5. Red Army Defense Lines, 1941

Date of Stavka Order	Defensive Line	Mission
24 June	Luga defense line	Protect the approaches to Leningrad
25 June	Nevel'-Vitebsk-Mogilev-Kremenchug defense line	Protect the second strategic echelon
28 June	Viaz'ma defense line	Protect the distant approaches to Moscow
Mid-July	Mozhaisk defense line	Protect the close approaches to Moscow
12 October	Moscow defense lines	Protect the city of Moscow
October	Volga defense line (Iaroslavl'-Saratov-Stalingrad-Astrakhan)	Protect the strategic rear

Source: "Boevoi opyt ukreplennykh raionov (UR)" [Combat experiences of fortified regions], in *Sbornik materialov po izucheniiu opyta voiny, no. 3, noiabr'–dekabr 1942. g.* [Collection of materials for the study of war experience, no. 3, November–December 1942] (Moscow: Voenizdat, 1942), 122–32.

Table 3.6. Red Army Strategic Offensive (Counteroffensive) Operations during the Summer–Fall Campaign of 1941 and the Winter Campaign of 1941–1942

		Scale (km)	
Strategic Axis	Operations	Width	Depth
Northern	None	NA	NA
Northwestern	Tikhvin offensive operation, 10 November to 30 December 1941	300–350	100–120
Western	Smolensk offensive operation, 21 July to 7 August 1941	450–500	0
	Smolensk, El'nia, and Roslavl' offensive operation, 17 August to 12 September 1941	600–650	0–30
	Moscow offensive operation, 5 December 1941 to 7 January 1942	1,000	100–250
	Rzhev-Viaz'ma offensive operation, 8 January to 20 April 1942	650	80–250
Southwestern	None	NA	NA
Southern	Rostov offensive operation, 17 November to 2 December 1941	170	80
	Kerch-Feodosiia offensive operation, 25 December 1941 to 2 January 1942	250	100–110

Source: "Itogi diskussii o strategicheskikh operatsiiakh Velikoi Otechestvennoi voiny 1941–1945 gg." [Results of the discussion on strategic operations of the Great Patriotic War 1941–1945], *Voenno-istoricheskii zhurnal* [Military-historical journal], no. 10 (October 1987); 14–16.

Table 3.7. Red Army Strategic Offensive (Counteroffensive) Operations during the Winter Campaign of 1942–1943 and the Summer–Fall Campaign of 1943

Strategic Axis	Operations	Scale (km) Width	Scale (km) Depth
Northern	None	NA	NA
Northwestern	Operation to penetrate the Leningrad blockade (Operation Spark), 12–30 January 1943	45	60
	Staraia Russa-Pskov offensive operation (Operation Polar Star), 15–28 February and 4–19 March 1943	200	5–10
Western (Moscow-Smolensk-Vitebsk)	2nd Rzhev-Sychevka offensive operation (Operation Mars), 25 November to 20 December 1942)	350	10–35
	Smolensk offensive operation (Operation Suvorov), 7 August to 2 October 1943	400	200–250
	Belorussian offensive operation (Vitebsk, Orsha, Polotsk-Vitebsk, Gomel'-Rechitsa, Novyi-Bykhov-Propoisk, Gorodok, Kalinkovichi-Bobruisk), 3 October to 31 December 1943	500	40–25
Central (Kursk-Orel-Briansk)	Orel-Briansk-Smolensk offensive operation, 5 February to 28 March 1943	200–300	30–100
	Orel offensive operation (Operation Kutuzov), 12 July to 18 August 1943	400	150
Southwestern (Stalingrad-Khar'kov-Kiev)	Stalingrad offensive operation (Operations Uranus and Little Saturn), 19 November 1942 to 2 February 1943	850	150–200
	Voronezh-Khar'kov offensive operation (Ostrogozsk-Rossosh', Voronezh-Kastornoe, Khar'kov), 13 January to 3 March 1943	250–400	360–520
	Belgorod-Khar'kov offensive operation (Operation Rumiantsev), 3–23 August 1943	300–400	140
	Chernigov-Poltava offensive operation (Chernigov-Pripiat', Sumy-Priluki, Poltava), 26 August to 30 September 1943	600	250–300
	Kiev offensive operation (Chernobyl'-Radomysl', Gornostaipol', Liutezh, and Bukrin), 1–24 October and 3–13 November 1943	320–500	150
	Zhitomir-Berdichev offensive operation, 24 December 1943 to 14 January 1944	250–480	100–150

Table 3.7. (Continued)

Strategic Axis	Operations	Scale (km) Width	Depth
Southern	Donbas offensive operation, 31 January to 23 February 1943	300	10–120
	Donbas offensive operation, 13 August to 22 September 1943	450	250–300
	Lower Dnepr offensive operation (Krivoi-Rog, Aleksandriia-Znamenka, Apostolovo, Nikopol'), 26 September to 20 December 1943	750–800	100–300
Caucasus	North Caucasus offensive operation, 1 January to 4 February 1943	840	300–600
	Krasnodar-Novorossiisk offensive operation, 8 February to 16 March 1943	250	50–190
	Taman' offensive operation, 4–17 April, 29 April to 10 May, 26 May to 7 June 1943	250	4–12
	Novorossiisk-Taman' offensive operation, 10 September to 9 October 1943	80	150

Sources: "Itogi diskussii o strategicheskikh operatsiiakh Velikoi Otechestvennoi voiny 1941–1945 gg." [Results of the discussion on strategic operations of the Great Patriotic War 1941–1945], *Voenno-istoricheskii zhurnal* [Military-historical journal], no. 10 (October 1987); 17–20; David M. Glantz, *The Soviet-German War 1941–1945: Myths and Realities: A Survey Essay* (Carlisle, PA: Self-published, 2001); and David M. Glantz, *Forgotten Battles of the German-Soviet War (1941–1954), volume V: The Summer-Fall Campaign (1 July–31 December 1943)* (Carlisle, PA: Self-published, 2000).

Table 3.8. Comparative Scale of Red Army Strategic Offensive (Counteroffensive) Operations, 1941–1942

Strategic Offensives			
Forces	Smolensk [1]	Moscow	Stalingrad[2]
Fronts	3	3	3
Armies	11	15	10
Tank armies	0	0	1
Air armies	0	0	4
Divisions [3]			
Red Army	ca. 60	110	83
Axis forces	34	74	50
Separate tank and mechanized corps	9 (divisions)	0	9
Personnel			
Red Army	ca. 1,200,000	1,021,700 (388,000)[4]	1,103,000
Axis forces	ca. 900,000	1,708,000 (240,000)	1,011,000
Guns and mortars			
Red Army	unknown	7,652 (5,635)	15,501
Axis forces	unknown	13,500 (5,350)	10,290
Tanks and self-propelled guns			
Red Army	unknown	774 (500)	2,778
Axis forces	unknown	1,170 (600)	675
Combat aircraft			
Red Army	unknown	1,100	1,350
Axis forces	unknown	615	1,210

[1]This refers to the Smolensk offensive operation of August–September 1941 conducted by the Western, Reserve, and Briansk Fronts.
[2]Although it did not occur in the first period of the war, the Stalingrad strategic offensive is included for the sake of comparison.
[3] Includes cavalry divisions and rifle brigades calculated on the basis of two brigades equaling one division.
[4] Figures in parenthesis are from the formerly classified book, B. M. Shaposhnikov, ed., *Razgrom nemetskikh voisk pod Moskvoi chast' 1, 2, :3* [The defeat of German forces at Moscow parts 1, 2, and 3] (Moscow: Voenizdat, 1943). These figures show forces and weaponry available for combat use.
Sources: R. A. Savushkin, ed., *Razvitie Sovetskikh vooruzhennykh sil i voennogo iskusstva v Velikoi Otechestvennoi voine 1941–1945 gg.* [The development of the Soviet Armed Forces and military art in the Great Patriotic War 1941–1945] (Moscow: Lenin Politi cal-Military Academy, 1988), 65 and David M. Glantz, *The Battle for Smolensk, 7 July–September 1941* (Carlisle, PA; Self-published, 2001).

Table 3.9. Comparative Scale of Red Army Strategic Offensive (Counteroffensive) Operations, 1942–1943

Forces	Strategic Offensives		
	Stalingrad	Rzhev-Sychevka	Kursk
Fronts	3	2	5
Armies	10	9	19
Tank armies	1	1	5
Air armies	4	2	5
Divisions			
Red Army	65[1]	64[1]	134
Axis forces	36	24	55
Separate tank and mechanized corps	9	11	14
Personnel			
Red Army	1,103,000	631,770[2] (830,700)[1]	2,226,000
Axis forces[3]	1,011,000	ca. 250,000	900,000
Guns and mortars			
Red Army	15,510	18,000	33,000
Axis forces	10,290	unknown	10,000
Tanks and self-propelled guns			
Red Army	1,560[1]	2,352[1]	4,800
Axis forces	675	ca. 400	1,800
Aircraft			
Red Army	1,350	1,100	4,300
Axis forces	1,210	unknown	2,100

Sources: R. A. Savushkin, ed., *Razvitie Sovetskikh vooruzhennykh sil i voennogo iskusstva v Velikoi Otechestvennoi voine 1941–1945 gg.* [The development of the Soviet Armed Forces and military art in the Great Patriotic War 1941–1945] (Moscow: Lenin Political-Military Academy, 1988), 65; V. V. Gurkin, "Liudskie poteri Sovetskikh vooruzhennykh sil v 1941–1945: Novye aspekty" [Personnel losses of the Soviet armed forces 1941–1945: New aspects], *Voemo-istoricheskii zhurnal* [military-historical journal], no. 2 (March–April 1999); 6; and David M. Glantz, *Zhukov's Greatest Defeat: The Red Army's Epic Disaster in Operation Mars, 1942* (Lawrence: University Press of Kansas, 1999).

[1]Strengths shown are for the first stage of the offensive operation.

[2]Upper figure notes official strength figure for Operation Mars but does not include the related Velikie Luki offensive.

[3]Includes Romanian and Italian forces, of which roughly 600,000 were German troops.

PART II

THE FORCE

CHAPTER 4

Strength and Major Components

THE ARMED FORCES

Eighteen months of intense and often frustrating war had significantly altered the face of the Red Army by 1 January 1943. The catastrophic combat losses the Red Army suffered during this period consumed a large proportion of those who were serving in June 1941 and also a sizable proportion of the millions of replacements who subsequently joined the Red Army's ranks. The Red Army numbered roughly 5.5 million men on 22 June 1941, about 2.7 million of which were serving in the field forces stationed in the Western (border) military districts. At that time, the Soviet mobilization pool contained about 12 million men, which included many fully or partially trained reservists. This mobilization capability produced the forces necessary to replace those soldiers lost in 1941 and 1942 and even increased the Red Army's overall strength.

Consequently, despite losing 4,473,820 men in 1941 (3,137,673 of which were non-recoverable, meaning killed, captured, missing, or unfit for service due to wounds) and another 7,369,278 men in 1942 (3,258,216 of which were non-recoverable), the Red Army's field strength increased to 6,101,000 on 2 February 1943, 6,724,000 on 9 July 1943, and 6,165,000 on 31 December 1943 (see Table 4.1).[1] During the period from 1 July to 31 December 1943, the number of Red Army *fronts* (groups of armies), armies (tank armies), and divisional equivalents deployed for field duty or serving in the *Stavka's* reserve rose from 5, 23, and 281, respectively, to 11, 63, and 603 (see Table 4.2 and Appendix 5, Red Army Orders of Battle in the companion volume to this book, for the data on all Red Army force components).

These stark figures vividly capture the scope and scale of the Red Army's transformation in terms of size and overall configuration. In a less tangible sense, they also bear striking witness to the army's ability to endure combat of unprecedented ferocity and proportion, yet still emerge intact. These cold and hard impersonal numbers also provide clear evidence of the Red Army soldiers' seemingly limitless capability for surviving amid excruciating suffering. Hatred of the enemy born of nationalism or ideological fervor together with healthy doses of harsh discipline and official intimidation, to say nothing of traditional Russian fatalism, combined to sustain the Red Army in the field and to propel it intact through nearly ceaseless conflict.

These staggering figures, however, do not adequately reflect the scope of the internal transformation within the Red Army, which enabled it to compete with and ultimately defeat the vaunted German *Wehrmacht*. As large and imposing as the Red Army's force structure was on paper in 1941, war proved it to be a cumbersome and inept military force ill equipped to contest the more tried and tested *Wehrmacht*. Size alone could not compensate for shortsighted strategic leadership, clumsy mobilization, inflexible command and control at the operational and tactical levels, and ill-trained and ill-equipped soldiers in the field. Consequently, the *Wehrmacht* savaged the Red Army during the first six months of war, wrecking both its prewar concepts for waging war and its military forces. Faced with seemingly limitless cascading calamities, the Red Army recoiled, trading territory and soldiers' lives for time.

In the last analysis, a combination of factors permitted the Soviet Union and its Red Army to survive this terrible war. First, the German Army attempted to wage warfare in the immense expanse of Eurasia employing strategic and operational techniques better suited to the more limited confines of Western and Central Europe. Hence, it was woefully ill prepared to operate in and cope with the unique terrain and climatic conditions in the Soviet Union, much less its vast territorial expanse.

Second, excessive German ambition coupled with congenital overconfidence and a nearly constant inability on the part of the Armed Forces (OKW) and Army High Commands (OKH) to define precise and achievable strategic objectives confounded the abilities of the even most talented of German field commanders. Time and again, the *Wehrmacht's* reach exceeded its grasp.

Third, although the Soviet Union's mobilization system was slow and cumbersome, once set in motion it was inexorable, producing wave after wave of new armies, which, although often scarcely worthy of the name, repeatedly refilled the Red Army's depleted order of battle at times when the Germans were convinced the Soviets were down to their last battalions. The fact was that quantity did matter, both materially and psychologically. However weak the new Soviet armies were, their existence and surprise appearance disconcerted German commanders and indicated that quantity had a quality of its own.

The fourth and most important factor in the Red Army's ability to survive was the ability of the Soviet Union's political and military leadership to adjust to a wide variety of quite nasty realities. Despite its monumental initial failings, dire circumstances themselves impelled the Soviet strategic leadership, principally Stalin and the *Stavka* (Headquarters of the Supreme High Command), to recognize that wholesale changes were required in the way in which it planned for and waged war.

For the duration of what the Soviet Union calls its Great Patriotic War, the Soviet Armed Forces consisted of four major ground and air force elements subordinate to the People's Commissariat of Defense (*Narodnyi komissariat oborony*, or NKO). The first and most significant element was the ground element of the armed forces that took active part in the struggle with Nazi Germany and her Axis allies. This force was termed the operating army (*deistvuiushchaia armiia*)—in essence, the field forces, which consisted of the Red Army's operating *fronts* and separate armies or corps engaged in active combat against enemy forces.

The second combat element was the so-called Force for the Air Defense of the Country's Territory (*Voiska PVO territorii strany*), which were sometimes termed National Air Defense Forces or, more frequently, simply just PVO Strany. PVO Strany forces comprised air defense forces assigned to protect the field forces and defend major potential military objectives within the Soviet Union. The remainder of PVO forces, which formed an integral part of ground force formations and units in the field operating forces, were named simply PVO forces (*PVO voisk*).

No less vital to the war effort was the third element of the armed forces, the Reserve of the *Stavka* of the Supreme High Command (*Reserv Stavki verkhovnogo glavnokomandovaniia*), commonly known as the *Stavka* Reserve or the RVGK. This reserve encompassed all types of forces, ranging in size from separate *fronts* down to individual battalions that the *Stavka* retained under its control to influence the future course of combat. The strength of the *Stavka* Reserve varied considerably throughout the war but was normally largest during periods when the Red Army was on the defense but anticipating counteroffensive operations. RVGK forces were stationed in the frontal zone or in military districts in close proximity to that zone.

The fourth and final element of the armed forces comprised the military districts and nonoperating *fronts* (*voennye okruga i nedeistvuiushchie fronty*). This element consisted of forces assigned to military districts and separate *fronts* located outside the theater of war and frontal combat zone. Nonoperating *fronts*, which consisted of the same types of combat forces as other operating *fronts*, protected regions where there was some likelihood that future hostilities would erupt, such as the Far East and Central Asia. The military districts represented the mobilization base of the Soviet Armed Forces. As such, throughout the war they contained mobilizing forces (ranging in size from army down to separate brigade), forces that were resting and refitting, and, in some instances, reserve forces.

In addition to the ground and air forces under NKO control, other forces participated in or supported the war effort under the control of other commissariats. These included the Soviet Navy (VMF) under the People's Commissariat of the Navy (NKVMF), and a large but shadowy army of internal security forces operating under the People's Commissariat of Internal Affairs (NKVD) control. While the VMF cooperated closely with the NKO's forces under the *Stavka's* control, primarily in maritime or coastal theaters of war, the NKVD's forces performed a multitude of functions often ignored in combat histories of the war.

NKVD forces performed a wide variety of security missions, including protecting the borders (with border guards detachments), securing the extensive Soviet system of labor and punishment camps (the GULAG), and providing security for the *front* rear area, road and rail transport, and vital military and political objectives. NKVD forces also combated German diversionary actions on Soviet territory by employing a wide array of destruction battalions and regiments, and they performed counterintelligence tasks by rooting out German *Abwehr* (counterintelligence) agents and groups operating in the Soviet rear area. Finally, they supported field force operations by preventing Red Army soldiers and units from deserting (often by employing the infamous "blocking detachments"), helping enforce army discipline, and, at times, participating actively in combat operations as front-line forces.

The overall ration (present for duty) strength of the Red Army and its associated air forces on 2 February 1943 was 9,455,000 personnel with another 890,000 soldiers hospitalized throughout the Soviet Union. Of this total, 6,101,000 personnel manned the field forces (operating armies), 1,030,000 served in nonoperating *fronts*, and 2,324,000 were assigned to Soviet military districts. Of those hospitalized, 659,000 were located at field forces' installations, 6,000 were stationed with nonoperating *fronts*, and 325,000 were recuperating in military district facilities.

Above and beyond the Red Army, the Soviet Navy numbered 400,000 personnel plus a total of 16,000 personnel in hospitals. Outside the armed forces, the NKVD's shadowy field and security forces fielded a force of 516,000 men with another 4,600 personnel in hospitals. Finally, 720,900 personnel worked in other capacities within various central ministries, including the 672,000 in the People's Commissariats of Defense, 25,900 in the People's Commissariat of the Navy, and 25,900 in the People's Commissariat of Internal Affairs.[2]

By 9 July 1943, the Red Army and Air Forces' ration strength had risen to 10,300,000 personnel with another 819,000 recuperating in hospitals. Of the nonhospitalized soldiers, 6,724,000 were serving in the field forces, 1,398,000 were assigned to nonoperating *fronts*, and 2,178,000 were assigned to military districts. Of those hospitalized, 446,445 were in field force hospitals, 70,000 were resting in nonoperating *front* hospitals, and 302,555 were recuperating in military district health facilities. By this time the strength of the Soviet Navy had risen to 410,000 personnel, of which 16,600 were in hospitals. On the other hand, by July the strength of NKVD forces fell to 473,000 men with 6,000 in hospitals since the State Defense Committee (GKO) had converted many large NKVD formations into regular Red Army formations.

On 9 July 1943, another 801,600 personnel served in central administrative organs, including 712,600 in the NKO, 26,000 in the NKVMF, and 63,000 in the NKVD.[3]

After the completion of the Red Army's intense and prolonged summer–fall campaign, on 31 December 1943, the Red Army and Air Force's ration strength stood at roughly 10,200,000 personnel, of which almost 1 million were recuperating in hospitals. Of this number, 6,165,000 personnel were serving in operating *fronts* and armies, and almost 1 million personnel resided in *front* and army hospitals.

THE FIELD FORCES

Strength

The spearhead of the Soviet war effort was the over 6 million personnel assigned to the Red Army's field forces, which, in accordance with *Stavka* strategic priorities, were deployed unevenly across the entire German-Soviet front from the Barents Sea to the Black Sea. In February 1943, about 40 percent of this force was arrayed along the southwestern and southern axes from the city of Voronezh to the Black Sea coast, about 34 percent along the western axis from the town of Kholm to Voronezh, about 20 percent on the northwestern axis from Lake Ladoga to Kholm, and the remaining 6 percent in the Kola peninsula and Karelian region of the far north, defending the approaches to Murmansk and Arkhangel'sk.

During the course of the winter campaign, these forces steadily gravitated toward the Kursk and Orel regions at the confluence of the western and southwestern axis. By 1 July 1943, 54 percent of Red Army field forces were located along the southern and southwestern axes, 24 percent along the western axis, 17 percent along the northwestern axis, and 5 percent in the far north (Arctic region).[4] This change in field force disposition reflected the *Stavka's* deliberate regrouping and concentration of forces on the eve of the Battle of Kursk and the associated summer–fall campaign.

Composition

On 1 February 1943, the Red Army's field and PVO Strany forces consisted of 13 combined-arms *fronts*, one PVO (Air Defense) *front*, one separate army, and forces assigned to the Moscow Defense Zone. The field forces themselves were organized into 64 combined-arms armies, three tank armies, 13 air armies, two PVO armies, two operational groups, and one defense zone. This marked a steady growth in the Red Army from the nadir of its strength in the fall of 1941.

After completing its winter campaign of 1942–43, the Red Army's field forces decreased in size because the *Stavka* transferred large forces into its reserve in preparation for the anticipated summer–fall campaign. In addition, the *Stavka* reorganized its air defense forces to create more numerous larger formations. Thus, on 1 July 1943, field and PVO forces consisted of 12 combined-arms *fronts*, three PVO *fronts* (with two PVO armies and one PVO air army), four PVO zones, and one separate army. The field forces themselves were organized into 60 combined-arms armies, two tank armies, 12 air armies, and one operational group.

During the six months following the Battle of Kursk, the Red Army's compositions grew in size, complexity, and firepower, with a burgeoning in the quantity of rifle and artillery penetration corps and a wide variety of supporting formations, most of which the *Stavka* assigned to its operating *fronts*. By 1 December 1943, field and PVO forces consisted of 11 combined-arms *fronts*, two PVO *fronts* (with three PVO armies), four PVO zones, and one separate air army. The field forces themselves were organized into 57 combined-arms armies, three tank armies, and 12 air armies. Although the number of armies, tank armies, and separate tank and mechanized corps within the field force's operating *fronts* did not increase significantly by 1 July, these strength figures are deceptive in light of the vastly increased size and combat strength of the *Stavka* Reserve (see below).

Throughout the winter of 1942–43, the Red Army force structure was in the midst of wholesale transition from the truncated and often threadbare force that fought at Moscow in the winter of 1941–42 to the fully articulated force that emerged in the summer and fall of 1943. In general terms, this transformation involved an increase in the strength and firepower of each operational and tactical entity and an increase in the complexity of the force structure as a whole. At the same time, more effective combat support (artillery, air, engineer) and combat service support (logistics and maintenance) systems evolved that were essential for supporting sustained combat operations to ever greater depths. Throughout this process, the *Stavka* sought to field a force whose structure was flexible enough to meet its strategic priorities. This meant that forces had to be tailored carefully to be able to operate under the conditions and requirements of the many and diverse strategic axes comprising the vast theater of war. They also had to be standardized enough to engage successfully in heavy combat along the most critical axes with German forces that still possessed greater skill and combat experience.

Fronts

The Red Army's premier operational-strategic large formation *(ob"edenenie)* in 1943 was the *front*, which was roughly equivalent in size to a Western army group. On the eve of the Soviet-German war, the Soviet High Command expected the Red Army's wartime *fronts* to perform strategic (war-winning) missions by conducting decisive military operations along their respective strategic axes (northwestern, western, and southwestern). However, the sobering experiences of the initial period of war, when the more experienced *Wehrmacht* decimated the Red Army's operating *fronts*, convinced the *Stavka* that single *fronts* so poorly led, organized, and equipped were incapable of performing such vital missions.

Consequently, immediately after Operation Barbarossa commenced, the *Stavka* began experimenting with methods for grouping several *fronts* along each strategic axis, with each grouping tasked with performing operational-strategic—in essence, intermediate—missions. The first such experiment began on 10 July 1941, when the *Stavka* formed three theater-level strategic commands known as Main Commands of Directions' Forces (*Glavnye komandovaniia voisk napravleniia*) in order to control its operating *fronts*. These commands provided unity of control for all *fronts* and other forces operating along a single strategic axis. Originally, these included the Northwestern Direction, commanded by Marshal K. E. Voroshilov, the Western Direction, headed by Marshal S. K. Timoshenko, and the Southwestern Direction, commanded by Marshal S. M. Budenny. Subsequently, in April 1942, the *Stavka* created a fourth main direction command headquarters in the North Caucasus and assigned Marshal Budenny to command it.

However, as the course of combat in late 1941 and early 1942 indicated, these main direction command headquarters performed little better than the single *fronts* of 1941, in part, admittedly, because Stalin appointed his favorites to command them. Additionally, they lacked an adequate headquarters staff, had no logistical support, and proved too cumbersome to be effectively controlled had their commanders been experienced and well qualified. Consequently, the *Stavka* disbanded the Northwestern Direction headquarters on 27 August 1941, the Western Direction on 5 May 1942, the North Caucasus Direction on 19 May 1942, and the Southwestern Direction on 21 June 1942. Thereafter, the *Stavka* combined the forces of several *fronts* to accomplish strategic tasks and assigned its own trusted special representatives to coordinate major operations by these groups of *fronts*.

Since the *front* was the most important operational-strategic large formation in the Red Army, the *Stavka* normally assigned it a geographical name in accordance with the operational axis along which it operated. For example, the Western Front operated along the western (or Moscow) axis, the Leningrad Front along the Leningrad axis, and the Voronezh Front in the Voronezh region. To supplement its ground *fronts*, by July 1943 the *Stavka* had formed PVO *fronts* that organized national air defense on a regional basis (Western, Moscow, and Eastern). The *fronts* themselves had no standard table of organization and varied tremendously in strength and composition depending on the region and operational context in which they operated. In general, after being severely truncated in the later summer and fall of 1941, they became larger, stronger, and more sophisticated in terms of their composition during 1942 and 1943. Nevertheless, *fronts* operating along the more important strategic axes were assigned the strongest forces.[5]

On 1 February 1943, the largest Red Army *front* in terms of the number of armies assigned to it was the Western Front, which was operating along the vital Moscow axis. It consisted of 11 combined-arms armies, one air army, and three tank corps. However, the strength of its component armies varied from as few as four to as many as nine rifle divisions and brigades and from a battalion of tanks to over three full tank brigades. At the other extreme, the Karelian, Leningrad, North Caucasus, and Trans-Caucasus Fronts had four combined-arms armies and one air army each. Moreover, the Karelian Front had to cover a broad sector stretching from the Murmansk region in the far north to the northern shores of Lake Ladoga. Although it had three combined-arms armies, eight fewer than the Western Front, on 1 February the Southwestern Front fielded a tank army, a mobile group with three tank corps and six separate tank corps and one separate mechanized corps, that is, a total of 12 mobile corps, nine more than the Western Front.

The Red Army's *fronts* also varied widely in terms of armor, artillery, and other supporting arms assigned to them. For example, the Karelian, Leningrad, Volkhov, Northwestern, Don, North Caucasus, and Trans-Caucasus Fronts possessed no tank or mechanized forces larger than a brigade, and the Kalinin Front had only a single mechanized corps. On the other hand, armor support increased in accordance with the importance of each *front's* mission. Accordingly, in February the Western Front fielded three tank corps, the Briansk Front two tank corps, the Voronezh Front one tank army, one separate tank and one cavalry corps, the Southwestern Front one tank army, a mobile group with three tank corps, six separate tank corps and one mechanized corps, and the Southern Front one tank army, one separate tank corps, and four separate mechanized corps. Differences in artillery and engineer support were even more pronounced.

By July 1943 the relative strength of individual Red Army *fronts* had changed somewhat in light of the *Stavka's* concentration of forces in the Kursk region prior to the expected German offensive in that region. While the Western Front, which numbered nine armies, one air army, and two tank corps with a strength of 787,000 men, remained the largest *front*, the three *fronts* defending the Kursk salient and the vital Voronezh axis were almost as strong. The Central Front and Voronezh Fronts, each with six armies (including one tank), one air army, and two tank corps numbered 711,000 and 625,000, respectively.

Because of the strategic importance of the Kursk sector, the *Stavka* also deployed the Steppe Military District (Front) with five armies, one tank army, one air army, and six tank and mechanized corps manned by a total of over 570,000 personnel to back up the two *fronts* already defending that sector. In this case, the *Stavka's* decision to maintain a strong Western Front was indicative of its increased prudence. Unlike in the spring of 1942, in early summer 1943 the *Stavka* took care to defend the Moscow axis adequately lest its strategic assessment of German intentions prove incorrect.

Elsewhere along the front on 1 July 1943, the Southwestern Front, which defended the Khar'kov and Northern Donets River sector, fielded seven armies, one air army, and three tank or mechanized corps for a total of 700,000 men. At the other extreme, the Volkhov, Northwestern, and Kalinin Fronts, each of which consisted of three to four armies and one air army with almost 400,000 personnel, had no assigned mobile corps.[6]

During the Red Army's Kursk strategic offensive, the ensuing advance to the Dnepr River, and the struggle to penetrate the German defenses (the Eastern Wall) along the Dnepr and Sozh rivers and advance into eastern Belorussia and the central Ukraine, the Red Army's center of gravity shifted to the south somewhat. The Western Front shrank from nine armies and two tank corps to five armies and one tank corps, and on 10 October the *Stavka* incorporated most of the Briansk Front's forces into the Belorussian (former Central) Front, with the Briansk Front's headquarters forming the headquarters for the new Baltic (then 2nd Baltic) Front. Accordingly, the Belorussian (Central) Front grew in strength from five combined-arms armies, one tank army, one air army, and two tank corps on 1 July to seven combined-arms armies, one air army, and two tank and two cavalry corps on 1 November.

The strongest Red Army *fronts* throughout the fall of 1943 were the Belorussian (Central) and 1st and 2nd Ukrainian (Voronezh and Steppe) Fronts, followed closely by the 1st Baltic and Western Fronts.

Armies

The basic building block of the Red Army's ground force structure and its associated air force were the combined-arms and air armies, which were numerically identified, operational-level formations *(soedineniia)* designated to conduct military operations independently or in conjunction with other armies assigned to a wartime *front*.[7] The *Stavka* also assigned armies to its reserve (the RVGK), military districts, and nonoperating *fronts*.

Like *fronts*, armies had no standard table of organization, and they varied considerably by type and by size and strength, which depended on their assigned mission and operational sector. By 1943 they included combined-arms (field) armies, tank armies, air armies, and PVO (air defense) armies. Special reserve armies (for example, the ten reserve armies formed in 1942), which were subordinate to the *Stavka* Reserve, served as mobilization conduits for the Red Army as a whole. The *Stavka* fielded a fourth type of army, the sapper [engineer] army, in early 1942. However, these proved too inflexible and cumbersome to operate effectively, and the *Stavka* abolished them later in the year.

The *Stavka* also awarded the title "shock" to selected combined-arms armies and the honorific title "guards" to selected combined-arms and tank armies (as well as all other types of formations and units). The designation "shock" was a throwback to the 1930s, when Soviet military theorists envisioned employing shock armies to conduct penetration operations along key offensive axes. As its name indicated, the shock army was stronger than normal field armies in every respect, but especially in armor and artillery support. True to Soviet prewar military theory, in November and December 1941, the *Stavka* formed the 1st Shock Army and ordered it to spearhead the Red Army's December counteroffensive north of Moscow.

Subsequently, the *Stavka* formed three more shock armies, two of which (the 3rd and 4th Shock) led the Red Army's expanded offensive in the winter campaign of 1942–43. The last shock army formed, the 2nd Shock, conducted the ill-fated Liuban' operation south of Leningrad the same winter, only to earn everlasting fame because the army's commander, Lieutenant General A. A. Vlasov, surrendered his encircled army and later shifted his allegiance to the Germans. The *Stavka* added the 5th Shock Army to the Red Army's order of battle a year later during the Stalingrad counteroffensive. By early 1943, however, the title meant little and, other than in name, shock armies differed little from normal field armies.

In accordance with a practice begun in late 1941 and early 1942, when it had awarded the honorific title "guards" to many divisions, corps, brigades, and smaller units that distinguished themselves in combat, during early stages of the Battle for Stalingrad in August 1942, the *Stavka* began awarding the same honorific to armies, the first of which was the 1st Guards Army. By December it had also created the 2nd and 3rd Guards Army, both of which played key roles in the heavy fighting during various stages of the Stalingrad counteroffensive. Unlike the designation "shock" army, the "guards" title was awarded for distinction, and guards armies tended to have stronger tables of organization (establishments) than other armies and were often more effective.

The catastrophic results of fighting during the summer and fall of 1941 convinced the *Stavka* that the structure and composition of its prewar field armies did not meet the requirement of modern mobile warfare. Therefore, beginning with its mobilization of fresh armies in the summer of 1941 and throughout the fall, because of both this realization and the stark fact that the *Wehrmacht* had already demolished many armies, the *Stavka* formed smaller armies, which, while more numerous, could be more effectively controlled and employed than their predecessors. The obvious tradeoff, however, was the sad fact that, when facing a determined German assault, these armies lacked the strength to survive or sustain operations, whether defensive or offensive. For that reason, as soon as it was feasible to do so, the *Stavka* and General Staff strengthened these armies with more combat formations and units and newer and more effective weaponry, in particular, tanks, artillery, and antitank guns. In mid- and late 1942, the *Stavka* began reintroducing the rifle corps link back into these armies so that they could better control larger forces.

When ordering the Red Army to conduct offensive operations during the winter campaign of 1941–42 and the remainder of 1942, the *Stavka* tended to designate particular armies, normally its strongest and best led, to spearhead these offensive operations. For example, during the winter campaign, the 4th Army and later the 2nd Shock and 54th Armies led the Red Army's offensive operations at Tikhvin and Liuban' in the Leningrad region, and the 3rd and 4th Shock Armies spearheaded the advance toward Staraia Russa and Smolensk. In southern Russia, the 37th Army served as the shock force in the Rostov offensive, and, later, the 6th and 57th Armies led the assault at Barvenkovo south of Khar'kov. In the critical Moscow region, the 1st Shock and 16th Armies led the offensive, supported by the 5th, 20th, 30th, and 33rd Armies.

During the spring of 1942, the 28th and 6th Armies led the Red Army's offensive at Khar'kov; during the summer, the 30th, 20th and 16th Armies and the new 3rd Tank Army carried the brunt of the action along the western axis (the Rzhev-Sychevka and Zhizdra offensive operations). Later still, in November 1942, the 41st and 20th Armies spearheaded the *Stavka's* offensive west of Moscow (Operation Mars), while the 5th Tank and 65th, 21st, and 51st played the most critical role in the Red Army's offensive at Stalingrad (Operation Uranus). Finally, the Red Army's new guards armies (1st, 2nd, and 3rd) played a significant role in the expansion of the Stalingrad offensive into a full-fledged winter campaign.

By early 1943 most armies of all types were far stronger than their predecessors of 1941 and 1942. As was the case with *fronts*, however, the strength and composition of specific armies varied considerably depending on the nature and importance of the axis along which it operated. For example, by 1 February 1943, 16 of the Red Army's combined-arms armies (and all of the guards armies) contained at least one and as many as three rifle corps as intermediate links between the army and subordinate divisions and brigades, and all fielded a broader and more diverse array of both combat and combat support forces. The strength of combined-arms armies in February 1943 ranged from 50,000 to 100,000 men each, supported by up to 400 tanks and self-propelled guns, and up to 2,500 guns and mortars.

By July 1943 the distinction in size and strength between armies became even more pronounced as the number of corps headquarters and supporting arms increased dramatically in many armies. On the other hand, armies operating in secondary sectors remained small. By this time, 35 of the Red Army's combined-arms armies contained intermediate corps headquarters. The strength of combined-arms armies varied widely from 60,000 to 130,000 men supported by up to 450 tanks and self-propelled guns and 2,700 guns and mortars.

The *Stavka* continued varying the strength, configuration, and complexity of its operating armies through the end of 1943, tailoring them to meet the combat requirements of their missions and the terrain over which they operated. By December 1943 the difference in size and strength between armies became even more pronounced as the number of corps headquarters within armies increased to encompass 48 of the Red Army's 57 combined-arms armies. The strength of combined-arms armies varied widely from 50,000 to 130,000 men supported by up to 500 tanks and self-propelled guns and 3,000 guns and mortars.

These vast variations in army strength and composition existed along the entire front and applied to all types of armies throughout 1943. As a rule, armies occupying or supporting key offensive sectors were stronger than other armies, followed closely by those in secondary offensive sectors and those defending key sectors. By 1943 the *Stavka* well understood the combat principle of economy of force and deployed its weakest armies along secondary axes and in inactive *front* sectors, where, ironically, German forces often outnumbered their Soviet opponents.

Establishment Organizations

A vast panoply of military forces known by the generic terms "formation" *(soedinenie)*, "unit" *(chast')*, and "subunit" *(podrazdelenie)* were subordinate to the Red Army's operating *fronts* and field armies, as well as the *Stavka* Reserve, nonoperating *fronts*, and military districts. Formations were operational-tactical or tactical organizations and were formed either on a standard or temporary basis and included corps and divisions *(divizii)* of various types (such as rifle, tank, motorized, and cavalry). Units, which were the basic low-level tactical organization in the Red Army, included brigades and regiments of various types, and subunits included battalions and companies of all types. Most formations, units and subunits were organized in standard uniform fashion on the basis of *Stavka*-approved tables of organization *(shtat)*, which were equivalent to the table of organization and equipment (TO&E) in the United States Army and the establishment in the British Army.

These forces, which were found in all four elements of the Soviet Armed Forces and will be covered in more detail below, were also in a state of extreme transition during the first 30 months of the war. In general, after the forced truncation of the Red Army in 1941, like the Red Army's *fronts* and armies, these organizations became weaker and less complex and, hence, easier to control in combat but far less combat-capable. However, throughout 1942 and the first six months of 1943, numerous changes to establishments and the addition of new type of forces and weaponry increased the sophistication and combat capability of all formations and units. Much more was required, though, before these tactical forces could compete on the battlefield with their more experienced *Wehrmacht* counterparts.

PVO STRANY (NATIONAL AIR DEFENSE FORCES)

PVO Strany provided air defenses for the Red Army's field forces and for the country as a whole. Specifically, the air defense organization was the principal means for protecting the Soviet Union's large administrative, political, and economic centers, important military objectives, field force groupings, and vital communication from enemy air attack. Aviation elements assigned to PVO Strany also cooperated with the Red Army Air Force in the struggle to achieve air superiority and in all Red Army defensive and offensive operations.

The *Stavka* reorganized the structure of PVO Strany several times during the first 18 months of the war in an attempt to improve its defensive efficiency and responsiveness to the needs of the Red Army's operating *fronts*. In general, this process involved consolidating air defense assets (antiaircraft guns and fighter aviation) on a regional basis through the formation of, first, brigade and, later, division and corps regions and the fielding of PVO brigades and corps to provide air defense to the Red Army's operating *fronts*. Beginning in early 1943, this structure increased in sophistication and responsiveness with the formation of PVO armies and *fronts*.

Dispositions

PVO Strany forces were subdivided into three subelements in early 1943: PVO *fronts* and armies, PVO forces protecting objectives within the zone of action of the field forces, and PVO forces protecting vital political and economic objectives in the country as a whole. The first subelement consisted of a single PVO *front* and two PVO armies, which protected major centers of national importance. These included the Moscow PVO Front and the Leningrad and Baku PVO Armies, all of which had been created in April 1942, the former from the Moscow PVO Corps Region and the latter from the 2nd and 3rd

PVO Corps. Each formation contained antiaircraft artillery, antiaircraft machine gun, projector, VNOS (early warning), and aerostatic obstacle regiments and an air element in the form of fighter aviation regiments combined under fighter aviation corps.[8] The *front* differed from the armies only in that it had a greater number of forces assigned to it.

PVO forces supporting the Red Army in the field were organized into corps and divisional air defense regions that supported one or more individual *fronts* depending on the size and importance of each *front's* sector. On 1 February 1943, these forces totaled one corps and seven division regions. As was the case with the PVO *fronts* and armies, the corps and division regions were assigned a mixture of antiaircraft and supporting regiments and fighter aviation aircraft. Unlike the *fronts* and armies, each of which had one fighter aviation corps assigned, the regions had one or two fighter aviation divisions. PVO forces in each region were subordinate to the respective *front* commanders, and the Moscow PVO Front provided air defense for the Western Front.

The forces of PVO Strany located in the remainder of the country were organized within specific military districts and nonoperating *fronts* and were subordinate to the respective military district or *front* commander. These forces were organized into PVO corps, division, and brigade regions. In turn, the various PVO regions fielded a mixture of antiaircraft and support regiments and battalions in accordance with the threat, which in many cases was minimal. Each military district, *front*, or zone was also assigned a fighter aviation division, except for the Ural and Central Asian Military Districts, which had no need for air defense aircraft.

Beginning on 10 June 1943, the State Defense Committee (GKO) reorganized PVO Strany forces to improve command and control and system effectiveness. The reorganization abolished the position of Commander of PVO Forces and his associated directorate and placed all PVO Forces under the Commander of Red Army Artillery. At the same time, it abolished the existing PVO *fronts* and armies and replaced them with two new PVO *fronts* (the Western and Eastern), which protected all of the European Soviet Union. In addition, it assigned all other existing PVO armies and corps, division, and brigade regions to four new PVO zones, each subordinate to a military district commander. The reformed structure was in transition on 1 July 1943, with the Moscow PVO Front still in existence.

By 1 August 1943, the reorganization was complete. The Moscow PVO Front with its subordinate 1st Air Army was absorbed into the Western PVO Front as the Special Moscow PVO Army, and the *Stavka* adjusted the number and names of PVO regions subordinate to each *front* to correspond to the altered military situation and the configuration of active theaters of military operations. The Leningrad PVO Army, however, remained a separate entity through the entire reorganization. As before, PVO corps, division, and brigade regions were distinguished from one another by the quantity of anti-aircraft, air, and VNOS units and subunits assigned to each.

THE *STAVKA* RESERVE

The most vital element in the Red Army force structure other then the field forces was the *Stavka* Reserve. These forces, which were strategic reserves under direct *Stavka* control, were the primary means by which Stalin and the *Stavka* could influence the course and outcome of major military operations, particularly strategic defenses and strategic offensives. Throughout the war, this reserve consisted of freshly mobilized or reorganized forces and veteran formations withdrawn from the *front* for reorganization, rest and refitting.

During the summer and fall of 1941 and 1942, prior to and during the Battles for Moscow and Stalingrad, for example, the *Stavka* Reserve was quite large and served as the primary means by which the *Stavka* assembled sizable forces necessary to halt German strategic offensives and to conduct major counterstrokes or counteroffensives. On the other hand, when the Red Army was on the offensive during the winters of 1941–42 and 1942–43, the *Stavka* Reserve was relatively weaker.

Composition

In early 1943 the *Stavka* Reserve was quite small because the heavy fighting at Stalingrad and during the post-Stalingrad Red Army offensive had depleted its forces. For example, on 1 February the reserve contained 1 field army headquarters (the 24th), the 57th Army (with only token units), and the 2nd Reserve Army with 2 rifle divisions and a rifle brigade, which served as a mobilization conduit for the Red Army. In addition, at this time, the *Stavka* retained only two cavalry corps; 31 rifle, airborne, and cavalry divisions, 30 rifle, tank, and ski brigades; and a wide variety of supporting units in its reserve.

The most important force assigned to the *Stavka* Reserve on 1 February does not appear in key official Red Army documents because, at the time, it was in the process of being transferred from NKVD to Red Army control. This formation was a new NKVD Army, which was formed between October 1942 and February 1943 and consisted of NKVD internal security troops and border guards, primarily from the Trans-Baikal and Far East regions (see Chapter 4). The NKVD Army was transferred to *Stavka* control on 5 February, after which the *Stavka* designated it as the 70th Army (the highest number in the Red Army order of battle). The army's six rifle divisions assembled in early February near Elets, where it received its combat and combat service support elements. Since the *Stavka* considered the 70th Army to be an elite force, at least in terms of its soldiers' motivation and discipline since many were Party and Komsomol members, it accorded it an important role in the culminating phase of the winter offensive by assigning it to Rokossovsky's new Central Front.

Additionally, during the first week of February, the *Stavka* transferred its newly formed 2nd Tank Army from the Briansk Front to its reserve. This army had been formed in January and early February 1943 on the base of the Briansk Front's former 3rd Reserve Army with the veteran 11th and 16th Tank Corps as its nucleus. The *Stavka* assigned it to a vital role in forthcoming offensive operations as a part of Rokossovsky's *front*.

Despite the relatively small size of the *Stavka* Reserve in February 1943, the *Stavka* earmarked its most important elements for employment in its expanded winter offensive. Specifically, it assigned the 70th Army, 2nd Tank Army, and 2nd Guards Cavalry Corps to operate with the new Central Front, which it formed on 15 February, and it dispatched the bulk of its new guards airborne divisions to reinforce newly formed Group Khozin, which conducted the exploitation phase of the Northwestern Front's ambitious Operation Polar Star.

The *Stavka* expanded its reserve significantly during the period from the end of the Red Army's winter offensive in late March 1943 through late June. It did so for two purposes: first, to marshal the strategic reserves necessary to defend against the anticipated German summer offensive; and second, to create shock groups with which it could launch its own ambitious summer offensive operations, which it intended to conduct immediately after the Red Army halted the *Wehrmacht's* expected summer offensive.

The *Stavka* began forming its new strategic reserve on 11 March 1943, when it disbanded the Briansk Front effective the next day and assigned its 61st Army to the Western Front, its 3rd, 48th, and 13th Armies to the Central Front, and its headquarters to the *Stavka* Reserve. The *Stavka* was hedging its bets. On the one hand, it was attempting to reinvigorate the Central and Western Fronts' flagging offensive against German forces at Orel by improving the two *fronts'* command and control. On the other hand, it was creating the nucleus of a new strategic reserve lest the Red Army's offensive fail and the Germans resume offensive operations. Effective on 13 March, the *Stavka* then transformed the former Briansk Front's headquarters into a new Reserve Front, which was to consist of the 2nd Reserve, 24th, and 66th Armies plus three tank corps (4th Guards, 10th, and 3rd). However, the Reserve Front never received its new armies because the operational situation changed sharply in the Germans' favor.[9]

On 19 March, after the offensive by Rokossovsky's Central Front failed and German forces began counterstrokes of their own in concert with Manstein's counteroffensive toward Belgorod, the *Stavka* renamed the Reserve Front the Kursk Front effective 23 March, assigned it the 60th and 38th Armies, which were deployed on Central Front's left flank, and promised to assign it the 63rd and 66th Armies as soon as they were available. The new Kursk Front was responsible for defending along the Kursk-Voronezh axis, that is, against any German thrust against Kursk from the west, while the Voronezh Front protected the southern approaches to Kursk against Manstein's forces.[10]

Soon after, the situation changed once again. Manstein's offensive ended on 23 March, and Rokossovsky managed to stabilize the front west and northwest of Kursk. Therefore, the *Stavka* once again reshuffled its *fronts*, this time to erect sound defenses against any future attempt by the Germans to mount a new strategic offensive in the Kursk region. Accordingly, on 24 March the *Stavka* disbanded the Kursk Front effective three days later, returned its 60th and 38th armies to the Central and Voronezh Fronts, and established the new Orel Front, consisting of the Western Front's 61st Army, the Central Front's 3rd Army, and the 15th Air Army. The Orel Front's mission was to defend opposite the apex of the German salient east of Orel. Finally, on 28 March the *Stavka* completed this frenetic round of reorganizations by renaming the Orel Front the Briansk Front.[11]

On 6 April, with its forward defenses secured, the *Stavka* formed a new Reserve Front in the Voronezh region effective 30 April, this time consisting of the 2nd Reserve, 24th, 53rd, 66th, 47th, and 46th, Armies, the 5th Guards Tank Army, and eight mobile corps (1st, 3rd, and 4th Guards Tank, 3rd, 10th, and 18th Tank, and 1st and 5th Mechanized), supported later by the Trans-Caucasus Front's 5th Air Army. Most of these forces were regrouped primarily from the Northwestern and North Caucasus Fronts or already in the *Stavka* Reserve.[12] On 13 April, effective 15 April, the *Stavka* renamed this *front* the Steppe Military District and assigned it responsibility for all forces in the Voronezh, Kursk, Tambov and, Rostov districts.[13]

Headquartered in Voronezh, the Steppe Military District's mission was to construct a defensive line forward of the Don River from Livny southward to Millerovo, prevent German forces from penetrating defenses east of the Don, and if the enemy penetrated the defense, destroy him with counterstrokes and subsequently go over to the offensive.[14] By 1 May the Steppe Military District included the 24th, 27th, 46th, 47th, 53rd, and 66th Armies, the 5th Guards Tank Army, and the 5th Air Army. Thereafter, the *Stavka* assigned some of these forces to operating *fronts* and replaced them with forces from other sectors of the front.

The *Stavka* committed most of its strategic reserves, including the Steppe Military District (renamed the Steppe Front on 7 July), to combat during and after the Battle of Kursk. These reserves formed the nucleus of the force with which the Red Army conducted its counteroffensive and, in the fall, spearheaded the Red Army's advance to and across the Sozh and Dnepr rivers into Belorussia and the Ukraine. All the while, though, the *Stavka* was rebuilding a new strategic reserve consisting of tank armies depleted in the counteroffensive that would, after being rehabilitated, reinforce the Red Army's continuing offensive operations during the winter of 1943–44.

Thus, unlike the case during the previous two years, in late 1943 the *Stavka* managed to amass new strategic reserves while it was conducting prolonged offensive operations in the late summer and fall. Consequently, it was able to sustain those offensive operations through the ensuing winter and into the following spring.

MILITARY DISTRICTS AND NONOPERATING FRONTS

Military Districts

Supplementing the over 6 million troops in the Red Army's field forces in early 1943 were the over 3 million soldiers serving in its military districts and nonoperating *fronts*. On 2 February 1943, the Soviet Union's seven military districts, which encompassed Soviet territory outside the confines of real or potential theaters of war, fielded 2,324,000 soldiers.[15] By 1 July 1943, the number of military districts increased to eight, which, plus the new Moscow Defense Zone, numbered 2,178,000 military personnel.[16] Finally, by 1 December 1943, the number of military districts increased to ten, with an overall strength in excess of 2.4 million troops.

The military districts served primarily as the Red Army's mobilization base and, secondarily, as fitting-out areas for new types of formations, units, and subunits. As such, throughout the war they raised, equipped, trained, and sent to the front hundreds of corps, divisions, brigades, regiments, and battalions of all types of combat troops for both the Red Army and the Navy (between July and December 1941 alone, 291 divisions and 94 brigades).

The 16 military districts total that existed on 22 June 1941 decreased in number sharply after the outbreak of war. The western border districts were immediately converted into full wartime *fronts*, and, in time, other military districts in threatened border sectors also became nonoperating *fronts*. By late 1942, the seven remaining military districts ceased dispatching full formations and units to the front and instead focused on mobilizing personnel replacements for existing forces. In mid-1943 the number of military districts began expanding as the Red Army's forces liberated occupied Soviet territory.

The number of military districts and the composition of each varied widely throughout the war depending on the military situation and the strategic importance of each district during each period of the war. On 22 June 1941, the military districts with the most forces were those adjacent to the Soviet Union's three special military districts on the western borders, which became wartime *fronts*, and those along the country's southern and eastern borders. These districts fielded many of the rifle, mechanized, and airborne corps as well as other supporting units that were designated to reinforce deploying armies during prewar mobilization.

Thereafter, the Moscow Military District was the strongest military district throughout the entire war both because of its political and military significance and because of its close proximity to the front. It served as one of the most important staging areas for specialized and new types of formations such as sapper armies, airborne corps, and guards-mortar, self-propelled, antitank, and high-power and special-power artillery units. In early 1943 it was also the home base for the 1st Separate Women's Rifle Brigade, the parent unit for the training and fielding of snipers throughout the Red Army. The Volga, Stalingrad, and North Caucasus Military Districts were also particularly strong from July 1942 through February 1943, primarily because they provided a repository for forces committed to the Battles of Stalingrad and the Caucasus and the ensuing winter campaign.

As the Red Army advanced westward in late 1943, the *Stavka* carved new military districts, such as the Orel, Belorussian, and Khar'kov Military Districts, from territories liberated from German control and assigned them forces sufficient for their defense, such as air and engineers.

Nonoperating *Fronts*

In addition to its operating *fronts*, which were actively engaged in military operations against the *Wehrmacht* and other Axis forces, during wartime the *Stavka* transformed the military districts along the Soviet Union's most threatened borders, for example, opposite Turkey and Japanese-occupied Manchukuo (Manchuria) into nonoperating *fronts*. Even before the Germans began their Barbarossa invasion, in June 1938, the Soviet NKO had already transformed its Special Red Banner Far Eastern Army, which faced Japanese forces in Manchuria, into the Far Eastern Front.

After war began, in September 1941 the *Stavka* converted its Trans-Baikal Military District into the Trans-Baikal Front to help protect the Soviet border against a Japanese offensive from Inner Mongolia and western Manchuria. About a month before, in August 1941, the *Stavka* had also formed the Trans-Caucasus Front from the Trans-Caucasus Military District and assigned it the mission of protecting the approaches into the Caucasus from the Don region in the north and Turkey and Iran in the south. Renamed the Caucasus Front in December 1941, this *front* was unique in that it contained both operating and nonoperating forces. The former protected the Caucasus against any German invasion from the north, and the latter were stationed in the southern Caucasus region and occupied key Lend-Lease supply routes through Iran.

Throughout all of 1943, three nonoperating *fronts* protected the southern and eastern borders of the Soviet Union. The nonoperating portion of the Trans-Caucasus Front protected the southern flank of the Red Army's field forces with forces operating south of the Caucasus Mountains and in Iran, where they cooperated with forces from the Central Asian Military District. The Trans-Baikal and Far Eastern Fronts performed the same tasks in eastern Siberia and the Soviet Far East, protecting against Japanese forces in Manchuria, Korea, Sakhalin Island, and the Kuril Island chain, while still serving as a mobilization base for the Red Army as a whole. The strength of the nonoperating *fronts* rose from 1,030,000 personnel (with 6,000 in hospitals) on 2 February 1943 to 1,398,000 on 1 July (with 70,000 in hospitals) and roughly 1.4 million on 1 December 1943.[17] Like their counterparts in the West, the nonoperating *fronts* were organized into armies, corps, and separate formations and units.

These nonoperating *fronts* were fully combat-capable forces whose composition changed in accordance with strategic conditions. For example, Soviet forces in the Far East were particularly strong when war began because of the serious border engagements that had occurred between the Red Army and Japanese Kwantung Army at Lake Khasan and Khalkhin-Gol in 1938 and 1939. Stalin feared that the Japanese would seek revenge for their defeats in 1938 and 1939 by launching their own invasion of the Far East, perhaps in concert with their Axis ally Germany. However, when Stalin negotiated a neutrality pact with Japan in April 1941, the likelihood of hostilities in the Far East decreased significantly, permitting the *Stavka* to transfer sizable forces from the region to the Western theater to defend Moscow when the *Wehrmacht* threatened the Soviet capital in November and December 1941.

When the Germans began Operation Barbarossa, Red Army strength in the Far East stood at 32 division equivalents. Between July and November 1941, the *Stavka* recalled 12 divisions westward from the Far East and Trans-Baikal regions; nevertheless, the massive ongoing mobilization still kept Red Army strength in the Far East at a level of 39 division equivalents.[18] Despite transferring an additional 23 divisions and 19 brigades westward in 1942, the *Stavka* increased Red Army strength in the Far East to 46 division equivalents by 19 November 1942. The forces transferred westward from the Far East during 1941 and 1942 did contribute significantly to the Red Army's victories at Moscow and Stalingrad.

By the summer 1943, however, all transfer of forces westward ended abruptly. With the Red Army on the offensive in the West, thereafter, forces began flowing eastward, albeit at first very slowly. By 1 July 1943, the strength and combat capability of nonoperating *fronts* in the Far East had increased inexorably to 45.5 divisions. Nor did this trend change. By 1 January 1944, Red Army strength in the Far East and Trans-Baikal region, impelled in part by Allied attempts to enlist the Red Army's services in the Asian war, had reached 55 division equivalents.

Table 4.1. Red Army Field Strength (in Personnel), 1941–1943

	Date and Strengths (field/hospital/total)							
Force	1 Jul 41	11 Sep 41	5 May 42	5 July 42	7 Oct 42	2 Feb 43	9 Jul 43	31 Dec 43
Red Army	5,500,000	7,400,000	8,950,000/ 850,000/ 9,800,000	9,205,000/ 772,450/ 10,977,450	9,254,000/ 900,000/ 10,154,000	9,455,000/ 890,000/ 10,345,000	10,300,000/ 819,000/ 11,119,000	10,200,000/ 1,000,000/ 11,200,000
Operating *fronts*	2,700,000	3,463,000	5,449,898/ 414,400/ 5,864,298	5,647,000/ 298,480/ 5,945,480	5,912,000/ 476,670/ 6,388,670	6,101,000/ 659,000/ 6,760,000	6,724,000/ 446,445/ 7,170,445	6,165,000
Non-operating *fronts*	NA	NA	1,187,303/ 20,200/ 1,207,503	1,590,000/ 46,210/ 1,636,210	1,100,000/ 7,000/ 1,107,000	1,030,000 6,000/ 1,036,000	1,398,000/ 70,000/ 1,468,000	Unk
Military districts	2,800,000	3,426,000	3,312,799/ 515,400/ 3,828,199	1,968,000/ 427,760/ 2,395,760	2,242,000/ 416,330/ 2,658,330	2,324,000/ 325,000/ 2,649,000	2,178,000/ 302,555/ 2,480,555	Unk
Red Fleet	Unk	Unk	550,000	540,000/ 19,000/ 559,000	450,000/ 16,000/ 466,000	400,000/ 16,000/ 416,000	410,000/ 16,600/ 416,600	Unk
NKVD	171,900	Unk	510,000	519,000/ 4,300/ 523,300	506,000/ 6,000/ 512,000	516,000/ 4,600/ 520,600	473,000/ 6,000/ 479,000	Unk
Commissariats	Unk	511,000	Unk	688,783	620,150	720,900	801,600	Unk
NKO	Unk	Unk	NA	664,148	586,000	672,000	712,600	Unk
NKVMF	Unk	Unk	NA	24,635	24,650	25,900	26,000	Unk
NKVD	Unk	Unk	NA	Unk	9,500	23,000	63,000	Unk

Note: The strength of the Red Army on 22 June 1941 was approximately 5,164,600 men, including roughly 2,700,000 in the western military districts. See A. G. Lensky, *Sukhoputnye sily RKKA v predvoennye gody* [RKKA ground forces in the prewar years] (Saint Petersburg, n.p., 2000), 58.

Sources: The strength figures are from "GKO Decrees" dated as above in *TsPA UML* [Central Party Archives of the Institute of Marxism and Leninism], f. 644, op. 1, d. 9, l. 50; f. 644, op. 1, d. 33, ll. 48–50; f. 644, op. 1, d. 41, ll. 163–65; f. 644, op. 1, d. 61, ll. 88–91; f. 644, op. 1, d. 100, l. 95, and f. 644, op. 1, d. 125, ll. 35–36.

Table 4.2. Red Army Field Strength (in Formations and Units), 1941–1943

	1 July 1941			1 February 1943			1 December 1943		
Type Force	Field Forces	*Stavka* Reserve	Total	Field Forces	*Stavka* Reserve	Total	Field Forces	*Stavka* Reserve	Total
Fronts	5	0	5	13	0	13	11	0	11
Armies	16	7	23	64	3	67	57	6	63
Tank armies	0	0	0	3	0	3	3	2	5
Air armies	0	0	0	13	0	13	12	1	13
Division equivalents*	216	65	281	531	50	581	566	37	603

*This figure counts two rifle or airborne brigades (of varying types) as one division, three destroyer brigades as one division, each tank and mechanized corps as one division, and three separate tank brigades or four separate tank regiments as one division.

Sources: Boevoi sostav Sovetskoi armii, chast' 1 (iiun'–dekabr' 1941), chast' 3 (ianvar'–dekabr' 1942) [The combat composition of the Soviet Army, part 1 (June–December 1941), part 3 (January–December 1943)] (Moscow: Voroshilov Academy of the General Staff, 1963; and Voenizdat, 1966), prepared by the General Staff's Military-Scientific Directorate and classified secret.

CHAPTER 5

The Shadow Army: NKVD Forces

MISSIONS AND SIZE

Although the large and presumably powerful Red Army bore primary responsibility for the defense of the Soviet Union in 1941, it was not the only armed force tasked with the defense of the Soviet state. In addition to the Red Army, which was controlled by the People's Commissariat of Defense (NKO), the People's Commissariat of Internal Affairs, commonly referred to by its acronym, the NKVD, fielded an imposing structure of security forces termed NKVD forces *(voiska NKVD* or *vnutrennie voiska).*

Stalin and his Politburo began establishing these new security forces in early 1941 with the express intent of employing them to support the Red Army and provide security for the state in the event of war. This process began on 3 February, when the Presidium of the USSR's Supreme Soviet split the former People's Commissariat of Internal Affairs into the NKVD and a new People's Commissariat of State Security (*Narodnyi komissariat gosudarstvennoi bezopasnosti,* or NKGB). Several days later, on 8 February, the Presidium placed the NKVD's special departments *(osobye otdely),* which had been responsible for ensuring internal security within the Soviet Armed Forces, under the direct control of the People's Commissariat of Defense and the People's Commissariat of the Navy (NKVMF). The NKO and NKVMF then formed their own Third Directorates to perform this vital internal security function, and, in turn, created Third (Special) Departments in all of their subordinate military districts, armies, and other forces down to regimental level.[1]

During this February reorganization, the Council of People's Commissars authorized the NKVD's nine directorates—the border guards, convoy, security, railroad forces, military construction, airfield construction, main roads, military supply, and local air defense (MPVO) directorates—to retain control over the border guards and security forces they already fielded. Finally, on 28 February, the Council of People's Commissars directed the NKVD to organize a 10th Directorate, the Operational Directorate, and form new security forces in that directorate as well.

When war began on 22 June, the total strength of NKVD forces was 334,900 men, including 173,900 in the internal forces and 161,000 in the border guards forces. Thereafter, the size and capabilities of NKVD forces increased steadily throughout the war, reaching a total strength of 493,379 men on 7 March 1942, 516,000 men on 2 February 1943, and 540,000 men on 12 March 1944.[2]

The State Defense Committee (GKO) assigned the NKVD and its internal and border guards forces the wartime missions of protecting vital "state" objectives such as important government and Party officials, government and administrative centers, buildings, and facilities, transportation arteries and communications hubs, and key industrial and economic centers, and fulfilling "other non-specific service-related combat missions." These nonspecific tasks included protecting the Soviet Union's frontiers, securing and administering the Soviet Union's extensive system of labor and penal camps (the GULAG), combating enemy (German *Abwehr*) intelligence, counterintelligence, reconnaissance, and diversionary operations on Soviet territory, and conducting counterintelligence operations of their own. In addition, the NKVD's internal forces were responsible for preventing Red Army troops from deserting during combat, for enforcing troop discipline, for assisting the Red Army's "recruiting" efforts in territories it liberated, often by impressing civilians, and, if necessary, for engaging in active combat operations to assist regular Red Army field forces.

The GKO assigned the NKVD's forces additional rear area security missions in January 1942, including responsibility for garrisoning all cities and towns captured by Red Army forces and for assisting other NKVD internal security forces in rooting out and destroying stay-behind enemy agents and Nazi sympathizers.[3] Finally, during April 1942 the GKO established an even larger directorate responsible for security operations in the rear area of the Red Army's operating *fronts,* which was called the Directorate of NKVD Forces for the Security of the Soviet Field Armies and was elevated to an independent main directorate in May 1943. At the same time, the GKO assigned a new and expanded mission to the new directorate:

> In close cooperation with the forces of the field armies, the NKVD forces will maintain order in the immediate rear areas of the *fronts [prifrontovaia polosa],* combat enemy reconnaissance and diversionary groups, participate in the construction of defensive lines [positions], evacuate industrial enterprises, protect and defend important communications and objectives, and escort and protect military prisoners of war and also personnel convicted by military courts of grave crimes.[4]

STRUCTURE IN 1941

The NKVD's security force structure was both large and extremely complex when war began. Its main components included border guards forces, operational forces (renamed internal forces in January 1942), railroad security forces, installation security forces protecting important economic objectives, convoy security forces (which also secured camps in the GULAG), and forces manning the state's secure VCh (enciphered telegraphy) communications network. The strength of NKVD major force components on 1 June 1941 was as follows:

Border guard forces	167,582 (161,000 in other sources)
Operational forces	27,300 (less those in military schools)
Railroad security forces	63,700
Convoy security forces	38,300
Installation security forces	29,300
Other forces	44,600
Total	379,782[5]

Border Guards Forces

The border guards forces represented the NKVD's front-line shock troops. Organized in detachments deployed along the Soviet Union's western frontiers from the Barents to the Black Sea and in the Trans-Caucasus region, Central Asia, and the Far East, the 167,582 men assigned to these detachments in June 1941, which included 3,020 men in aviation units, consisted primarily of lightly armed security troops manning border guards posts in close cooperation with fortified regions (*ukreplennye raiony*, or FR) the Red Army deployed along the Soviet frontier.

These NKVD border guards forces were organized into 17 border guards districts *(okrugi)*, made up of a total of 96 ground and six naval border guards detachments, 18 separate border guards commands *(komendatury)*, one fighter aviation regiment, and six fighter aviation squadrons. In addition, the border guards districts fielded 52 specialized units and subunits, including naval detachments, boat battalions, aviation detachments, border control points, signal battalions and companies, sapper and construction companies, and officer and noncommissioned officer training schools and courses.[6]

The bulk of the NKVD's border guards forces, a total of 127,300 men, were deployed along the Soviet Union's western frontiers in June 1941. These forces manned eight border guards districts, 47 ground and six naval border guards detachments (the latter controlled by the People's Commissariat of the Navy), nine separate border guards commands, and 11 regiments of NKVD operational forces (see Table 5.1).

Although most of these borders guards forces were equipped with only light infantry weapons, antitank rifles, and 50mm mortars, those detachments deployed in the most threatened border regions also fielded tank, artillery, and cavalry subunits. This was particularly true of border guards forces in the Far East, southern Central Asia, and the Trans-Caucasus region, where few NKVD operational forces were available to back them up. For example, the 58th and 59th Border Guards Detachments, which were deployed along the eastern border of Manchuria, each fielded a tank company, the 43rd, 48th, and 54th Border Guards Detachments in Kazakhstan, Central Asia, and the Trans-Baikal Districts each had attached cavalry squadrons, and the 54th and 67th Border Guards Detachments in the Trans-Baikal region and Kazakhstan fielded one artillery battery each.[7]

In addition, 14 border guards detachments, the 86–88th, 90–95th, 97th, 98th, and 105–107th, which were deployed along the western frontier, formed special maneuver groups called operational reaction outposts (*zastavy operativnogo reagirovaniia*) to protect the border. As a result, many of these detachments fielded as many as 2,265 men each. Finally, the 97th, 105th, 106th, and 107th Border Guards Detachments, which manned 15 more 42-man border outposts than their counterparts, each fielded almost 3,000 men.[8]

Operational Forces

The NKVD's operational forces on the eve of war consisted of a single motorized rifle division, the F. E. Dzerzhinsky Separate Special Designation Motorized Rifle Division based in Moscow; 18 separate NKVD regiments, including 13 motorized rifle, one rifle, and four cavalry regiments, 11 of which were based in the western military districts; four separate rifle battalions, one of which was based in the western military districts; and a separate communications company (see Table 5.2). These forces were responsible for reinforcing regular Red Army forces in the event of an enemy incursion across the state frontiers. The overall strength of NKVD operational forces rose steadily from 27,840 men on 28 February 1941 to a total of 41,589 men on 22 June 1941.[9]

Formed as an infantry division in 1924 and reorganized as a motorized rifle division in September 1937, the F. E. Dzerzhinsky Special Designation Motorized Rifle Division fielded 6,725 men in February 1941. Initially, the division consisted of three motorized rifle regiments, a cavalry regiment, single tank and artillery battalions, and separate signal and sapper companies. However, before war began, the NKVD upgraded its tank and artillery battalions to full regiments.[10] After war began, in July 1941 the Dzerzhinsky Division also provided cadre to form the 2nd NKVD Motorized Rifle Division.

After organizing motorized rifle regiments in its operational force structure during the 1930s, the NKVD deployed these regiments, such as the 4th Kiev, 5th Rostov, and 13th Alma Ata Motorized Rifle Regiments, on a territorial basis near large cities from which they derived their designations. During the two years preceding the outbreak of war, however, the NKVD relocated most of these regiments to the West and assigned them new names. For example, the 5th Kiev Regiment became the 6th L'vov NKVD Motorized Rifle Regiment, and the 5th Rostov Regiment became the 1st Belostok NVKD Motorized Rifle Regiment.[11]

The precise organizational structure of each NKVD motorized rifle regiment depended on its assigned mission. For example, the 13th and 14th NKVD Motorized Rifle Regiments, which were formed and stationed in the Vyborg, Keksholm, and Sortavala regions in the Leningrad Border District during the spring of 1940, consisted of only two motorized rifle battalions, while the separate motorized rifle regiment deployed in Latvia in late 1940 consisted of four motorized rifle battalions, a tank company, and an artillery battalion, a structure that was roughly analogous to that of a regular Red Army rifle brigade. Often the NKVD reinforced these regiments with special weapons provided by the People's Commissariat of Defense, including extra mortars, BT-7 tanks, BA-10 armored cars, and artillery pieces up to 152mm caliber.[12] As a result, by June 1941 these regiments fielded a total of 167 BT-7 light tanks.

In early June 1941, the NKVD began reorganizing its 11 motorized rifle regiments located in the three western military districts into three full operational divisions, the 21st NKVD Motorized Rifle Division in the Baltic Special Military District, the 22nd in the Western Special Military District, and the 23rd in the Kiev Special Military District. However, this reorganization was still incomplete when war began. Since the strength of these regiments varied considerably, the strength of the new divisions also varied from 4,000 to 8,000 men each, and none were comparable in strength to regular Red Army rifle divisions.

Shortly after the German invasion began, on 23 June, the NKO transferred control of the three motorized division in the NKVD's operational forces from the NKVD to the chief of security for the Red Army's *fronts'* rear area (see Table 5.3).[13] At the same time, the NKO also subordinated many of the NKVD's security and railroad forces in the western border region to the Red Army's operating *fronts,* although the chaos surrounding the *Wehrmacht's* advance rendered this measure largely superfluous. At roughly the same time, the NKVD brought the Dzerzhinsky Motorized Rifle Division to full wartime strength by calling up reserves and conscripts.

By 5 July 1942, the strength of the NKVD's operational forces had reached 189,800 men assigned to an expanded force structure. By this time, however, the strength of the NKVD's border guards forces had fallen to 96,900 men, largely because the invading *Wehrmacht* had destroyed most of the of border guards units along the Soviet Union's western borders.[14]

Railroad Security Forces

On the eve of war, the NKVD maintained a large security force, which was responsible for protecting the country's vital communications network, particularly its railroads, securing the prisoner-of-war collection and transportation system, protecting key government facilities, and securing and administering the extensive Soviet penal camp system. The NKVD's security forces were organized into 13 divisions and 18 brigades in June 1941, including 7 divisions and 2 brigades in the western military districts (see Table 5.4).

The NKVD's railroad security forces were responsible for protecting 1,679 key objectives, primarily main and secondary railroad lines and key rail junctions and terminals. It did so with eight NKVD railroad security divisions and five separate railroad brigades manned by 63,700 railroad troops and equipped with a total of 50 NKVD armored train subunits fielding a total of 25 armored trains, 32 armored artillery railroad cars, 36 motorized armored railroad cars, and seven armored motor vehicles.[15] These armored train subunits consisted of subunits bearing the same number as their parent NKVD regiment, while the regiments themselves were a constituent part of the NKVD's railroad security divisions.

For example, armored train and motorized railroad car subunits assigned to the 2nd NKVD Railroad Security Division's regiments protected the Kirov, Oktiabr' (October), and Leningrad railroads in June 1941 with a force of 11,200 men. In the same fashion, the 15,000-man-strong 3rd and 9th NKVD Railroad Security Divisions protected the railroads in the Soviet Union's western regions, and the 4th and 10th NKVD Railroad Security Divisions secured the railroads in the country's southwestern region with roughly the same strength. The 3rd NKVD Railroad Security Division, whose organization was typical for such a division, fielded the 29th, 53rd, 58th, 76th, and 78th Armored Train Battalions. Finally, the 5th, 6th, and 7th NKVD Railroad Security Divisions secured Soviet railroad communications farther to the East.[16]

Despite the severe damage the *Wehrmacht* inflicted on the NKVD railroad security forces in 1941, the strength of these forces had increased to 120,000 men by 7 May 1942.[17]

Convoy Security Forces

In addition to its border guards, operational forces, and railroad security forces, on the eve of war the NKVD maintained a formidable force responsible for transporting and securing prisoners of war and convicts and securing and administering its elaborate system of penal labor camps run by the Main Directorate of Camps of the NKVD USSR—the infamous GULAG. The convoy security forces themselves were subordinate to the independent Main Directorate of Convoy Forces, which was organized in February 1939 and manned jointly by the Red Army and NKVD. This directorate's mission was to "convoy the condemned, military prisoners of war, and persons subject to deportation, and also to provide external security for prisoner-of-war camps, prisons, and some objectives in which the work of 'special contingents' was employed."[18]

In June 1941 the NKVD controlled two convoy forces' security divisions and seven brigades with a total strength of 38,311 men to perform these missions. These included the 13th NKVD Convoy Forces Security Division, which was stationed in the western Ukraine, the 14th NKVD Convoy Forces Security Division, which operated in the Moscow region, and six separate convoy brigades. These brigades included the 41st Convoy Forces Security Brigade deployed along the northwestern axis, the 42nd Brigade along the western axis, and the 43rd Brigade along the southwestern axis.

The NKVD increased the strength of its convoy security forces steadily throughout the war. In August 1942, for example, the NKVD fielded a total of four convoy forces' security divisions and five convoy forces' security brigades, and the total strength of its convoy forces rose from 38,300 men on 1 June 1941 to 44,800 men on 5 July 1943, and 151,200 men on 15 August 1945 (see Table 5.5).[19]

Installation Security Forces

While the number of NKVD forces assigned responsibility for the defense of vital political and economic objectives increased steadily during the war, the actual configuration of these forces varied widely depending on the size, importance, and vulnerability of the objective they were defending. In general, the NKVD structured these forces to supplement the regular Red Army forces, whose mission inherently included such defensive tasks, in accordance with an August 1941 GKO directive, which officially assigned the NKVD responsibility for the defense of specific key objectives.

After war began, the NKVD's 11th and 12th NKVD Special Installation Security Divisions defended installations in the Moscow region, and its 20th NKVD Special Installation Security Division defended similar facilities in Leningrad and its environs. Initially at least, the 20th NKVD Special Installation Security Division consisted of the 1st and 56th NKVD Special Installation Security Brigades, each organized into regiments. At the same time, the 57th and 71st NKVD Special Installation Security Brigades defended objectives in the Ukraine, and another unidentified brigade protected objectives in the Stalingrad region.[20]

Many of these security forces were subordinate to the NKVD's Main Directorate for Local Antiaircraft Defense (MPVO). Overall, during the initial period of the war, the NKVD's installation security forces defended 145 vital objectives with a force of 29,300 men. This force, too, expanded during wartime and numbered 66,200 men by 5 July 1942.[21]

WARTIME EVOLUTION

On the eve of Operation Barbarossa, the Communist Party's Politburo directed the NKO to strengthen the four *fronts* it planned to field in the event of war, specifically, the Northern, Northwestern, Western and Southwestern Fronts, create a fifth *front* designated the Southern, and form a separate command to control the so-called armies of the second line. This new command, which the *Stavka* designated the Group of Reserve Armies on 25 June, was headquartered in Briansk and was responsible for backing up the Red Army's forward defenses along the Soviet Union's western border.[22] The *Stavka* assigned Lieutenant General of NKVD Forces I. A. Bogdanov command of the new group on 29 June, with Commissar of State Security 3rd Rank S. N. Kruglov as his commissar.[23]

On the eve of war, the Politburo ordered the NKVD to form a new security force to protect the rear areas of the Red Army's forward operating *fronts*. According to this directive, the NKVD was to support each forward operating *front* with a tailored mixture of divisions, regiments, battalions, and detachments of border guards, operational, railroad security, and convoy security forces (see Table 5.6). Ultimately, on 29 June, the *Stavka* appointed five NKVD generals to command the rear area security forces in these *fronts* and in the "armies of the second line" and a sixth to command the Moscow Military District.[24]

Despite the enormous chaos produced by the *Wehrmacht's* precipitous advance after 22 June and the massive disruption it caused in the Red Army's mobilization, the NKVD tried valiantly to fulfill the Politburo's orders. Immediately after the invasion began, it completed forming the 21st, 22nd, and 23rd NKVD Motorized Rifle Divisions from its 11 operational regiments stationed in the Northern, Northwestern, and Southwestern Fronts and single motorized rifle regiment in the Western Front.

The ensuing mobilization added 41,500 men to the NKVD's force structure, 16,000 of these from the border military districts. Simultaneously, NKVD headquarters in the Soviet Union's internal military districts filled out and fielded additional NKVD formations in accordance with mobilization plans. Unexpectedly, however, because the Red Army suffered such catastrophic losses during the initial period of the war, the *Stavka* had no choice but to turn to the NKVD with requests for additional manpower, formations, and command cadre to reinforce the Red Army.[25]

On 29 June 1941, for example, the *Stavka* ordered the NKVD "to form 15 new divisions immediately, including ten rifle divisions and five motorized rifle divisions," and use 1,500 NKVD command cadre and personnel from NKVD border guards and operational forces as the nucleus of each new division.[26] People's Commissar of Internal Affairs L. P. Beriia was personally responsible for raising the new divisions. This represented the first increment of a total of 25 divisions the NKO required the NKVD to form by 17 July 1941. In response, the NKVD formed the 243rd, 244th, 246th, 247th, 249th, 250th, 251st, 252nd, 254th, and 256th Rifle Divisions for employment along the western strategic axis, the 257th, 259th, 262nd, 265th, and 268th Rifle Divisions for use along the northwestern axis, and the 12th, 15th, 16th, 17th, and 26th Mountain Rifle Divisions to reinforce the southern axis.[27]

During August and September 1941, when the *Wehrmacht* was threatening Leningrad with encirclement, the NKVD ordered the Leningrad Front to form three NKVD rifle divisions, a separate NKVD brigade, and several NKVD regiments from existing border guards and other internal security forces. These included the 1st, 20th, and 21st NKVD Rifle Division, which took active part in the defense of the beleaguered city in September and October 1941.[28]

In early December, after the *Wehrmacht's* forces captured Khar'kov and were threatening Rostov, the Southwestern Front combined the remnants of the 91st, 92nd, 94th, and 98th Border Guards Detachments with the 6th, 16th, and 28th NKVD Motorized Rifle Regiments to form the 8th NKVD Motorized Rifle Division. This new division took part in offensive operations near Belgorod in December 1941 and January 1942 under the control of the Southwestern Front's 21st Army before being transferred to the Red Army as the 63rd Rifle Division in July 1942.[29]

In the wake of the Red Army's disastrous defeats at Viaz'ma and Briansk in early October 1941, on 12 October 1941, the Main Directorate of NKVD Internal Forces formed five rifle and three motorized rifle divisions from operational, internal security, and border guards forces.[30] These divisions, which were designated the 5th and 6th NKVD Rifle, the 7th, 8th, and 9th NKVD Motorized Rifle, and the 10th, 11th, and 12th NKVD Rifle Divisions, were formed in Tikhvin, Kalinin, Tula, Voronezh, Rostov, Stalingrad, Krasnodar, and Saratov and were responsible for protecting Red Army and NKVD garrisons and combating enemy agents. However, deteriorating operational conditions forced the *Stavka* to convert the 10th and 11th NKVD Rifle and the 8th and 9th NKVD Motorized Rifle Divisions into regular Red Army divisions, the 181st Rifle, the 2nd Guards Rifle, and the 63rd and 41st Rifle Division, respectively, and employ them in active combat operations.[31]

While *Wehrmacht* forces were advancing toward Stalingrad and into the Caucasus region during Operation *Blau* in the summer of 1942, the GKO directed the NKVD to form yet another wave of rifle divisions whose principal mission was to protect key economic objectives and communications arteries in the threatened regions. These divisions included the 10th Stalingrad NKVD Rifle Division and the Ordzhonikidze Rifle Division of NKVD Internal Forces. It assigned the latter responsibility for the defense of its namesake city and the vital Georgian Military Road, which served as the vital umbilical between the Trans-Caucasus and North Caucasus regions. During the same period, the NKVD also formed the Groznyi, Sukhumi, and Makhachkala Rifle Divisions of NKVD Internal Forces to perform similar roles in other parts of the Caucasus region.

In its own force structure throughout the war, the NKVD fielded a total of 53 divisions, 20 brigades, several hundred regiments of various types of forces, either separate or assigned to Red Army *fronts* and armies, and hundreds of smaller units and subunits such as battalions, detachments, and 30 armored trains (see Appendix 2 in companion volume for all NKVD forces).[32] In addition, it transferred significant forces to the Red Army, including 103,000 troops in August 1941, 75,000 in 1942, three full NKVD divisions in late 1942, and, in early 1943, the Separate Army of NKVD Forces, which the GKO and *Stavka* had formed in October 1942.[33] Redesignated as the Red Army's 70th Army in February 1943, this force consisted of six NKVD rifle divisions made up of border guards troops from six eastern military districts (see Table 5.7).

The advancing German Army destroyed or decimated most of the NKVD's border guards detachments along the Soviet Union's western frontiers during the summer, rendering those that survived the onslaught utterly superfluous. As a result, the NKVD disbanded its remaining 13 detachments, 2 reserve regiments, and 4 separate border guards commands in mid-September and on 26 September established new border regiments numbering 1,394 men each, in their stead.[34] For example, in the Leningrad region, the 104th, 106th, 6th, and 99th NKVD Border Guards Regiments replaced the former 8th, 106th, 6th, and 99th Border Guards Detachments.[35]

Since these new regiments also proved too fragile to perform their security or combat missions effectively, the NKVD reinforced some of them with artillery, mortar, antitank rifle, and submachine gun subunits and converted others into full brigades or divisions. For example, the 6th NKVD Rifle Regiment fought both separately and under the control of the 21st NKVD Division.[36] When they were not engaged in active combat operations, these regiments protected the operating *fronts'* rear areas, combated German *Abwehr* (counterintelligence) agents and teams, and formed blocking detachments to prevent Red Army soldiers from deserting.

In early 1943 the Main Directorate of NKVD Forces reorganized its subordinate forces into four principal subdirectorates in accordance with their assigned missions. These included the Headquarters for Border Guard Troops (the Main Directorate for Border Guard Forces), the Headquarters for Internal Forces, including internal (formerly operational) forces, convoy security forces, and railroad security and construction forces, the Headquarters of Destruction Battalions, and the Directorate for Fire Brigades. In addition, the NKVD fielded a separate Directorate for Special Departments (*osobye otdely*, or OO), which controlled all of the Special Departments in operating *fronts* and armies and organized and controlled counterintelligence operations agent operations in the *Wehrmacht's* rear area.

At the same time, the NKVD reorganized its Border Guards Forces into commands, regiments, and detachments and assigned them responsibility for securing the Soviet Union's border regions. Border guards regiments, each consisting of three battalions with six or seven companies each, a reconnaissance company, and chemical, medical, and transport platoons, and numbering 800–1,000 men each, served as the basic building blocks of the NKVD's new Border Guards Forces. German intelligence estimated the NKVD was fielding from 100,000 to 160,000 men in its border guards forces by 1 January 1943.

The NKVD formed additional border guards regiments and detachments in late 1943 and 1944 to protect the Soviet Union's new frontiers and to provide internal security within the territories liberated from German control, particularly in the Baltic republics, Belorussia, and the Ukraine. For example, in August 1944 the 1st Belorussian Front was employing the 157th, 127th, and 18th Border Guards Regiments in eastern Poland against forces of the Polish National Liberation Committee, and the 1st Ukrainian Front was using the 2nd, 16th, and 83rd Border Guards Regiments in similar fashion to combat Ukrainian nationalist forces in the western Ukraine.[37] On the other hand, as the length of the combat front shrank during the last year of the war, the NKVD often truncated its force structure by merging its regiments.[38]

By mid-1943 the NKVD's Directorate for Internal Forces controlled the NKVD's most important forces, including its internal, convoy security, railroad security, and installation security forces. The directorate organized these forces into divisions, brigades, and regiments, the latter either assigned to divisions or operating separately. These NKVD divisions, brigades, and regiments were fully combat-capable forces deployed in support of Red Army *fronts* or separately under control of the Main Directorate of NKVD Forces.

The NKVD structured its rifle divisions (and their motorized rifle variants) flexibly, assigning up to eight regiments to each, including, on occasion, motorized or cavalry regiments and a variety of separate battalions. In addition, some divisions fielded an attached artillery battalion or full regiment, and all of the divisions contained smaller subunits including antitank and sapper battalions, each organized similarly to those in Red Army rifle divisions, and a separate reconnaissance or sniper company. The strength of these divisions ranged between 8,000 and 14,000 men.

During wartime, the NKVD's separate brigades consisted initially of regiments but later of a varying number of separate battalions and supporting subunits and numbered up to roughly 5,000 men each. On the other hand, each NKVD rifle regiment consisted of a headquarters element with reconnaissance, chemical reconnaissance, and sapper platoons, an intelligence company; three rifle battalions, an antitank battery with four 45mm guns, a mortar company with four 82mm and eight 50mm mortars, a motorized sapper company, and small service support elements. The average NKVD rifle regiment fielded a force of 1,651 men equipped with four 45mm antitank guns, four 82mm mortars, eight 50mm mortars, and 27 antitank rifles. At the lowest level of command, each of the rifle regiment's rifle battalions consisted of at least three but sometimes as many as nine rifle companies and a machine-gun platoon for a strength of at least 397 men.

In addition to its divisions, brigades, and regiments of internal forces and railroad, convoy, and installation security forces, the NKVD fielded several separate formations that performed important and highly specialized but far less visible missions throughout the war. The most important of these formations was the so-called Separate Special Designation Motorized Rifle Brigade (*Otdel'naia motostrelkovaia brigada osobogo naznacheniia,* or OMSBON NKVD SSSR)—OMSBON for short.

The OMSBON began its evolution on 27 June 1941, when the Politburo of the Communist Party's Central Committee and the NKO instructed the NKVD to establish a special group of detachments "designated chiefly to conduct reconnaissance and diversionary operations in the Fascist's rear area." Initially, this force consisted of two brigades, and sapper-demolition, autotransport, and signal companies. In October 1941, however, the NKVD reorganized these forces into a Separate Special Designation Motorized Rifle Brigade, the OMSBON, which consisted of two motorized rifle regiments, separate combat security, sapper, and signal companies, medical and parachute *desant* [assault] services, several schools, and an aviation element. In October 1943 the NKVD transformed the OMSBON into a Separate Detachment responsive to missions assigned by NKVD Central (the Main Directorate), the NKGB (People's Commissariat of State Security), and the 2nd NKVD Motorized Rifle Division (to which it had been subordinate from October through December 1941).[39]

When fully formed, the Special Detachment fielded detachments numbering 1,000–1,200 men each to support the Red Army's operating *fronts* and special detachments with 30–100 men each and small groups with 3–10 men each to conduct reconnaissance and diversionary operations in the enemy's deep rear area. The Special Detachment and its subordinate detachments and groups performed these missions in support of the *Stavka* and General Staff's Main Intelligence Directorate (GRU) across the entire front throughout the war. In addition, they performed the same missions in support of the Moscow Defense Zone from October through December 1941, the Western Front and the Western Front's 16th Army in 1941 and 1942, the Main Caucasus Mountains Defense Headquarters and the North Caucasus, Briansk, and Trans-Caucasus Fronts in 1942 and 1943, the Central Front in 1943, the 1st Belorussian Front in 1943 and 1944, and virtually all the Red Army's *fronts* in 1944 and 1945.[40]

NKVD Central required the OMSBON and its successor Special Detachment to perform a wide variety of missions throughout the war. The most common missions these forces performed included reconnaissance and combined-arms combat missions at the front, special missions such as constructing engineer-mine obstacles and creating combined systems employing new technology at the front, mining and mine-clearing around important state objectives, and combat-diversionary, reconnaissance, and airborne *descents* with subunits, small teams, and individuals into the enemy's deep rear area.[41]

The OMSBON and Separate Detachment trained and fielded an imposing array of reconnaissance and diversionary specialists, often termed SPETSNAZ (*Spetsial'naia naznachenie*—special designation), from late 1941 through 1944, including 84 mid-level commanders, 519 sergeants, 803 radiomen, 534 demolition instructors, 5,255 demolition specialists, 126 vehicle drivers, 107 mortar men, 350 snipers, and over 3,000 parachutists. In turn, this cadre of highly trained specialists formed, trained, and fielded 212 specialized detachments and groups totaling 7,316 men who performed a wide variety of missions at the front and in the enemy's rear area.

This cadre of SPETSNAZ troops also trained another 580 specialists in demolitions and diversionary techniques to serve in other specialized units operating under the *Stavka's* direct control and hundreds of specialists to support partisan forces.[42] For example, during February, March, and April 1943, special miner detachments subordinate to the OMSBON cleared mines from critical sites in newly liberated cities such as Khar'kov, while three groups totaling 500 men restored and repaired communications lines in the Voronezh, Kursk, and Orel regions.

In addition to the OMSBON and Special Detachments, other forces controlled by the Red Army Engineer Directorate conducted diversionary and sabotage work in the German rear area under NKVD supervision. These forces included the reconnaissance and diversionary forces of the 1st Guards Brigade of Miners, which was subordinate to the Moscow Military District, and separate guards-miner battalions subordinate to individual Red Army operating *fronts*. The *Stavka* formed the 1st Guards Brigade of Miners in August 1942 and assigned it to the Moscow Military District in September.

At the same time, it assigned its first two battalions of miners, the 13th and 15th, to the Voronezh and North Caucasus Fronts. By year's end in 1943, virtually every Red Army operating *front* had been assigned its own dedicated battalion of miners.

In addition to these reconnaissance and diversionary forces, early in the war, the *Stavka* also required the NKVD to create and field special paramilitary forces designed to assist the work of regular NKVD security forces. Specifically, during the summer of 1941, the *Stavka* ordered the NKVD to create special destruction *(istrebitel'nyi)* battalions and regiments under the control of its central and regional headquarters. Once formed, the special destruction forces were responsible primarily for "securing the rear area from the intrigues of enemy agents." In later directives, the NKVD also required these forces to operate in the German rear alongside partisan forces to perform the same types of missions as the OMSBON's detachments and groups.[43] Initially, each destruction battalion consisted of 100–200 men armed with small arms, grenades, and light infantry weapons. Ultimately, but primarily during the first year of the war, the NKVD formed hundreds of these battalions in each of its headquarters in the Soviet Union's republics and *oblasti* (regions).

Aside from the administrative and security tasks they performed in the GULAG system, the most onerous and infamous tasks the NKVD's forces performed during wartime involved ensuring discipline within the Red Army's operating *fronts* and armies, primarily by preventing desertion, and raising manpower for the Red Army's operating forces. Specifically, beginning as early as late 1941, but routinely by 1943, the *Stavka* required the NKVD to form and employ blocking detachments *(zagraditel'nye otriady),* whose specific function was to prevent Red Army troops from deserting and to impress military-age civilians in the region liberated by the Red Army into the Red Army's ranks, if necessary by force (see Chapter 13 for details).

It is indeed astonishing that, despite its imposing size and ubiquitous nature and the many vital missions it performed during wartime, the Soviet Union's NKVD forces have been utterly ignored by the historical record. Even though they played only a peripheral role in operational and tactical combat, these forces conducted extensive and significant reconnaissance and diversionary operations in the enemy's rear area and had an equally vital role in maintaining security in the rear area of the Red Army's operating *fronts* and the country as a whole. Furthermore, the draconian discipline these black-clad troopers enforced within the Red Army itself helped hold the Red Army together as a fighting force in times of peril and ultimately contributed materially to its achievement of final victory.

Table 5.1 NKVD Border Guards Forces, 22 June 1941

District (Headquarters)	Commander	Border Guard Detachments and Separate Commands	
		First Line (pre-1939 borders)	Second Line (Reserves) (post-1939 borders)
Murmansk (Murmansk)	Major Gen. K. E. Sinilov	82nd Restikent Det.	
		100th Ozerkov Det.	
		101st Kuoloiarsk Det.	
		1st Northern Naval Command	
		17th Sep. Command	
		20th Sep. Command	
Karelo-Finnish (Petrozavodsk)	Maj. Gen. V. N. Dolmatov	1st Ukhtinsk Det.	
		3rd Sortovala Det.	
		72nd Olan'sk Det.	
		73rd Rebol'sk Det.	
		80th Kipran-Miask Det.	
Leningrad (Leningrad)	Lt. Gen. G. A. Stepanov	5th Red Banner Enso Det.	7th Kingisepp Det.
		33rd Vyborg Det.	9th Pskov Det.
		99th Hango Naval Defense Command	11th Sebezh Det.
		1st Baltic Sea Det.	103rd Rempetta Det.
		102nd Elisenvaar Det.	
Baltic (Tallin)	Maj. Gen. K. I. Rakutin	6th Rakvere Det.	
		8th Haapsala Det.	
		10th Kurosaar Det.	
		12th Leipaia Det.	
		2nd Baltic Naval Det.	
		12th Sep. Aviation Sq. (10 SBs, 2 MBR-2s)	
Belorussian (Belostok)	Lt. Gen. I. A. Bogdanov	17th Red Banner Brest Det.	
		86th Augustov Det.	13th Berezina Det.
		87th Lomzha Det.	16th Dzerzhinsk Det.
		88th Shepetovka Det.	18th Zhitkovichi Det.
		105th Kretinga Det.	22nd Belostok Det.
		106th Taurage Det.	83rd Slobodka Det.
		107th Mariampol' Det.	4th Sep. Aviation Sq.

—*Continued*

Table 5.1 (continued)

District (Headquarters)	Commander	Border Guard Detachments and Separate Commands: First Line (pre-1939 borders)	Border Guard Detachments and Separate Commands: Second Line (Reserves) (post-1939 borders)
Ukrainian (L'vov)	Maj. Gen. V. L. Khomenko	90th Vladimir-Volynskii Det.	20th Smolensk Det.
		91st Rava-Russkaia Det.	89th Volochinsk Det.
		92nd Peremyshl' Det.	93rd Liskovsk Det.
		94th Skole' Det.	95th Nadvornaia Det.
		97th Chernovtsy Det.	96th Slavuta Det.
		98th Liuboml' Det.	5th Sep. Aviation Sq.
Moldavian (Kishinev)	Maj. Gen. N. A. Nikol'sky	2nd Kalarash Det.	2nd Sep. Command
		23rd Red Banner Lipkany Det.	3rd Sep. Command
		24th Bel'tsky Det.	4th Sep. Command
		25th Kagul Det.	5th Sep. Command
		79th Izmail Det.	6th Sep. Command
Black Sea (Simferopol')	Kombrig P. I. Kiselev	26th Odessa Det.	23rd Sep. Command
		32nd Crimean Det.	24th Sep. Command
		1st Black Sea Naval Det.	25th Sep. Command
		2nd Black Sea Naval Det.	6th Sep. Aviation Sq.
		4th Black Sea Naval Det.	7th Sep. Aviation Sq.
Georgian (Tbilisi)	Unk	27th Batumi Det.	
		28th Akhaltsikhe Det.	
		30th Sukhumi Det.	
		34th Mugaisk Det.	
		35th Dzebrail'sk Det.	
		3rd Black Sea Naval Det.	
Armenian (Erevan)	Col. Sidorov	36th Echmiadzin Det.	
		37th Beliasuvar Det.	
		38th Megrin Det.	
		39th Leninakan Det.	
Azerbaidzhani (Baku)	Col. Rasovsky	40th Oktemberiansk Det.	
		41st Nakhichevan (Bakhtinsk) Det.	
		42nd Gasan-Kuliisk Det.	
		1st Caspian Sea Det.	
Turkmen (Ashkhabad)	Maj. Gen. D. I. Badeinov	44th Takhta-Bazar Det.	
		45th Merv Det.	

		46th Ashkhabad Det.	
		47th Geok-Tepe Det.	
		49th Kyzyl-Atrek Det.	
		71st Bakharden Det.	
		1st Guarak Sep. Command	
Central Asian (Tashkent)	Maj. Gen. M. M. Ryndziunsky	4th Tashkent Det.	
		48th Pamir Det.	
		50th Kerki Det.	
		81st Kuliab Det.	
		26th Murgab Sep. Command	
Kazakh (Alma-Ata)	Unk	43rd Alai-Gul'chin Det.	
		67th Nakanchin Det.	
Trans-Baikal	Maj. Gen. P. V. Burmak	29th Minusin Det.	51st Kiakhta Cav. Command
		53rd Dauriia Det.	54th Nerchinsk Cav. Command
		55th Trotskoslav Det.	
		64th Dzhalinda Det.	
		68th Manguta Det.	
		74th Shilkin Det.	
Red Banner Khabarovsk	Maj. Gen. A. A. Nikiforov	52nd Order of Lenin Sakhalin Naval Command	
		56th Blagoveshchensk Det.	
		63rd Ussuriisk Det.	
		75th Birobidzhan Det.	
		76th Khingan Det.	
		77th Bikin Det.	
		78th Aleksandrovka Det.	
Coastal	Col. Zyrianov	55th Khanka Det.	
		57th Red Banner Iman Det.	
		58th Red Banner Grodekovo Det.	
		59th Red Banner Khasan Det.	
		61st Nagaev Det.	
		62nd Vladivostok Naval Defense Command	
		64th Order of Lenin Kamchatka Naval Defense Command	
		65th Nikolaevsk Det.	
		66th Nakhodka Det.	
Under Border Guards Central HQS		1st Border Guards Fighter Aviation Regiment	

Sources: K. A. Kalashnikov, V. I. Fes'kov, A. Iu. Chmykhalo, and V. I. Golikov, *Krasnaia Armiia v iiune 1941 goda* [The Red Army in June 1941] (Tomsk: Tomsk University Press, 2001), 161–62; A. G. Lensky, *Sukhoputnye sily RKKA v predvoennye gody* [RKKA ground forces in the prewar years] (Saint Petersburg: n.p., 2000), 186–87; and A. I. Chugunov, *Granitsy srazhaiutsia* [Border guards battle] (Moscow: Voenizdat, 1989), 1–284.

Table 5.2 NKVD Operational Forces, 22 June 1941

NKVD Border District	Operational Force
Murmansk	181st Separate NKVD Rifle Battalion
Leningrad	13th NKVD Motorized Rifle Regiment
	14th Red Banner NKVD Motorized Rifle Regiment
	15th NKVD Motorized Rifle Regiment
	35th NKVD Motorized Rifle Regiment
	8th NKVD Rifle Regiment
Baltic	1st NKVD Motorized Rifle Regiment
	3rd NKVD Motorized Rifle Regiment
	5th NKVD Motorized Rifle Regiment
	23rd NKVD Motorized Rifle Regiment
Belorussian	4th NKVD Motorized Rifle Regiment
	Unk. NKVD Motorized Rifle Regiment
Ukrainian	6th NKVD Motorized Rifle Regiment
	16th NKVD Motorized Rifle Regiment
	28th NKVD Motorized Rifle Regiment
	21st NKVD Cavalry Regiment
Moldavian	172nd Separate NKVD Rifle Battalion
Turkmen	10th NKVD Cavalry Regiment
Coastal	25th Separate NKVD Rifle Battalion
NKVD Central	1st Order of Lenin Dzerzhinsky Special Designation NKVD Motorized Rifle Division

Sources: K. A. Kalashnikov, V. I. Fes'kov, A. Iu. Chmykhalo, and V. I. Golikov, *Krasnaia Armiia v iiune 1941 goda* [The Red Army in June 1941] (Tomsk: Tomsk University Press, 2001), 161–62; A. G. Lensky, *Sukhoputnye sily RKKA v predvoennye gody* [RKKA ground forces in the prewar years] (Saint Petersburg: n.p., 2000), 186–87; and A. I. Chugunov, *Granitsy srazhaiutsia* [Border guards battle] (Moscow: Voenizdat, 1989), 1–284.

Table 5.3 Subordination of NKVD Operational Forces to Red Army *Fronts,* 23 June 1941

Front	NKVD Operational Forces
Northern	21st NKVD Motorized Rifle Division
	13th NKVD Motorized Rifle Regiment
	14th NKVD Motorized Rifle Regiment
	35th NKVD Motorized Rifle Regiment
	Strength: 5,915 men
Northwestern	22nd NKVD Motorized Rifle Division
	1st NKVD Motorized Rifle Regiment
	3rd NKVD Motorized Rifle Regiment
	5th NKVD Motorized Rifle Regiment
	Strength: 3,904 men
Western	4th NKVD Motorized Rifle Regiment
	Strength: 1,191 men
Southwestern	23rd NKVD Motorized Rifle Division
	6th NKVD Motorized Rifle Regiment
	16th NKVD Motorized Rifle Regiment
	28th NKVD Motorized Rifle Regiment
	Strength: 8,193 men
Southern	172nd Separate NKVD Rifle Battalion
	Strength: 30 men

Sources: K. A. Kalashnikov, V. I. Fes'kov, A. Iu. Chmykhalo, and V. I. Golikov, *Krasnaia Armiia v iiune 1941 goda* [The Red Army in June 1941] (Tomsk: Tomsk University Press, 2001), 21; A. G. Lensky, *Sukhoputnye sily RKKA v predvoennye gody* [RKKA ground forces in the prewar years] (Saint Petersburg: n.p., 2000), 187–88; and A. I. Chugunov, *Granitsy srazhaiutsia* [Border guards battle] (Moscow: Voenizdat, 1989), 1–284.

Table 5.4 NKVD Security Forces, 22 June 1941

Type Force	Configuration	Identified Forces
Railroad security	8 divisions	2nd NKVD Railroad Division (Leningrad region)
	5 brigades	3rd NKVD Railroad Division (western region)
		4th NKVD Railroad Division (southwestern region)
		5th NKVD Railroad Division (eastern region)
		6th NKVD Railroad Division (eastern region)
		7th NKVD Railroad Division (eastern region)
		9th NKVD Railroad Division (western region)
		10th NKVD Railroad Division (southwestern region)
Convoy (POW/Penal)	2 divisions	13th NKVD Convoy Division (western Ukraine)
	7 brigades	14th NKVD Convoy Division (Moscow region)
		41st NKVD Convoy Brigade (northwestern axis)
		42nd NKVD Convoy Brigade (western axis)
		43rd NKVD Convoy Brigade (southwestern axis)
		44th NKVD Convoy Brigade (Kuibyshev)
		45th NKVD Convoy Brigade (Sverdlovsk)
		46th NKVD Convoy Brigade (unknown)
		47th NKVD Convoy Brigade (Tashkent)
Installation security	3 divisions	11th NKVD Division (Moscow)
	6 brigades	12th NKVD Division (Moscow)
		20th NKVD Division (Leningrad)
		57th NKVD Brigade (Ukraine)
		71st NKVD Brigade (Ukraine)
		unk NKVD Brigade (Stalingrad)

Sources: K. A. Kalashnikov, V. I. Fes'kov, A. Iu. Chmykhalo, and V. I. Golikov, *Krasnaia Armiia v iiune 1941 goda* [The Red Army in June 1941] (Tomsk: Tomsk University Press, 2001), 21; A. G. Lensky, *Sukhoputnye sily RKKA v predvoennye gody* [RKKA ground forces in the prewar years] (Saint Petersburg: n.p., 2000), 188–91; and A. I. Chugunov, *Granitsy srazhaiutsia* [Border guards battle] (Moscow: Voenizdat, 1989), 1–284.

Table 5.5 NKVD Convoy Security Forces, August 1942

Force	Location
35th NKVD Convoy Division	Borisoglebsk (Voronezh)
36th NKVD Convoy Division	Minusinsk (Krasnoiarsk)
37th NKVD Convoy Division	Marfino (Volodarsk)
38th NKVD Convoy Division	Irkutsk
41st NKVD Convoy Brigade	Vologda
43rd NKVD Convoy Brigade	Piatigorsk (Stavropol')
44th NKVD Convoy Brigade	Kuibyshev
45th NKVD Convoy Brigade	Sverdlovsk
47th NKVD Convoy Brigade	Tashkent

Source: A. G. Lensky, *Sukhoputnye sily RKKA v predvoennye gody* [RKKA ground forces in the prewar years] (Saint Petersburg n.p., 2000), 188–91.

Table 5.6 Planned NKVD Deployment of NKVD Rear Area Security Forces, June 1941

Front (men)	NKVD Security Force (men)
Northern Front (50,735)	14 border guards detachments (17,082)
	1 reserve border guards regiment (2,153)
	2 reserve border guards battalions (1,322)
	1 motorized rifle division of operational forces (5,915)
	1 railroad security division (11,164)
	1 security division for economic objectives (9,490)
	1 convoy brigade (3,509)
Northwestern Front (10,073)	3 border guards detachments (3,580)
	1 motorized rifle division of operational forces (3,904)
	1 railroad security brigade (1,447)
	2 convoy battalions (1,142)
Western Front (19,177)	2 border guards detachments (1,577)
	1 reserve border guards regiment (2,153)
	1 motorized rifle regiment of operational forces (1,191)
	4 railroad security regiments (8,520)
	1 convoy brigade (5,736)
Southwestern Front (60,052)	9 border guards detachments (15,000)
	1 reserve border guards regiment (2,153)
	2 railroad security divisions (15,068)
	2 security brigades for economic objectives (10,676)
	4 convoy regiments (7,820)
	2 separate battalions (1,142)
Southern Front (14,227)	5 border guards detachments (8,800)
	1 reserve border guards regiment (2,153)
	1 battalion of operational forces (300)
	2 convoy regiments (2,974)
Special Group of Forces of the Red Army (in support of armies of the "second line") (9,124)	3 border guards detachments (2,076)
	2 railroad security regiments (4,931)
	1 reserve railroad security battalion (517)
	1 convoy regiment (1,600)

Source: A. G. Lensky, *Sukhoputnye sily RKKA v predvoennye gody* [RKKA ground forces in the prewar years] (Saint Petersburg: n.p., 2000), 191.

Table 5.7 Composition of the Separate NKVD Army (Later the 70th Army)

Original Designation	Location	Subsequent Designation
Far Eastern NKVD Rifle	Khabarovsk	102nd Rifle
Trans-Baikal NKVD Rifle	Chita	106th Rifle
Ural NKVD Rifle	Sverdlovsk	175th Rifle
Siberian NKVD Rifle	Novosibiirsk	140th Rifle
Stalingrad NKVD Rifle	Cheliabinsk	181st Rifle
Central Asian NKVD Rifle	Tashkent	162nd Rifle

Source: G. P. Sechkin, *Pogranichnye voiska v Velikoi Oechestvennoi voine* [Border guards forces in the Great Patriotic War] (Moscow: Order of Lenin Red Banner Higher Border Guards Command Courses of the KGB USSR, 1990), 91–92.

CHAPTER 6

Rifle and Airborne Forces

Throughout the war, the Red Army's operating *fronts* and armies were flexible organizations whose composition the *Stavka* carefully tailored to meet specific requirements corresponding to its military strategy, perceived threats, and terrain and weather conditions in the areas where they operated. The only exceptions to this general rule were the Red Army's tank armies, which the *Stavka* began forming in January 1943 to replace the four tank armies it formed and employed during the summer and fall of 1942, whose ad hoc mixture of subordinate tank corps, rifle divisions, and cavalry corps proved too cumbersome and unwieldy to be effective in modern mobile combat (see Chapter 7).

Subordinate to the Red Army's operating *fronts* and armies, military districts, and nonoperating *fronts* were a vast array of combat, combat support, and combat service support formations (corps and divisions), units (brigades and regiments), and subunits (battalions, squadrons, companies, and batteries), most of which were organized on the basis of fixed though ever-changing tables of organization and equipment (TO&Es, or establishments).

Although the Soviets routinely categorized these forces by type, such as rifle, tank and mechanized, cavalry, artillery, engineer, and air forces, each category included forces that seemed to violate this simple typology. For example, rifle forces included airborne divisions and brigades, naval infantry, naval rifle, ski, and other specialized brigades, destroyer divisions and brigades earmarked to enemy armor, and fortified regions made up of artillery and machine-gun battalions. Likewise, in addition to armored forces, Red Army tank and mechanized forces included the quaint and short-lived ski-mounted aerosleigh battalions, motorcycle forces, and armored trains, and its artillery forces included antitank and antiaircraft formations and units.

In the last analysis, therefore, the Red Army categorized its forces according to the missions they performed and the weapons they employed. Thus, the Red Army considered airborne forces as infantry because, even though aircraft delivered them to the battlefield, they engaged the enemy in close combat with only light infantry weaponry. Likewise, the Red Army classified its destroyer formations and units and its fortified regions as infantry because, although the former were designated to combat enemy tanks and the latter were equipped with machine guns and artillery, both forces fought in close combat in the front lines.

RIFLE FORCES

Rifle Corps

The only type of rifle force below army level that the Red Army did not organize on the basis of a completely fixed table of organization during the war was the rifle corps *(strelkovyi korpus)*. Although all the Red Army's field armies consisted of multiple rifle corps when war began, after six months of combat the *Stavka* abolished the rifle corps as an intermediate command level between armies and divisions because, although useful in theory, they proved ineffective in practice. When the Red Army began maturing in the wake of its victory at Moscow, however, during the summer of 1942, the *Stavka* began reintroducing rifle corps into its most combat-experienced armies.

Like their predecessors of 1941, the rifle corps the *Stavka* created in 1942 were the largest tactical formations in the Red Army. On the offense, the rifle corps were structured so that they could penetrate the entire depth of enemy tactical defenses. Conversely, on the defense, they were responsible for preventing enemy penetration through the tactical depth of the Red Army's defenses and facilitating the conduct of counterattacks by supporting tank, mechanized, cavalry, and rifle forces. As with other forces, the Red Army fielded both regular rifle corps and slightly stronger guards versions.

Although rifle corps varied considerably in strength throughout the war, most contained two or three rifle divisions, three to five rifle brigades, or a combination of the two, with fire and logistical support tailored to satisfy the missions assigned to them. Their supporting forces usually included an artillery regiment, separate signal and sapper battalions, and, in some cases, quite modest logistical support (see Table 6.1). A bit larger than regular rifle corps, guards corps were also usually stronger in terms of support.[1]

The Red Army fielded 62 rifle corps in June 1941, but only six remained in the Red Army force structure on 1 January 1942 (see Appendix 1 in the companion volume to this book for all rifle forces in the Red Army). After the *Stavka* began creating new rifle corps in early 1942, however, the total quantity of rifle corps rose dramatically to 19 on 1 July 1942, 34 on 1 February 1943, 82 on 1 July 1943, and 161 by year's end in 1943. However, although the increase in the quantity of rifle corps in the Red Army underscored the growing sophistication of its force structure, it was also indicative of the declining strength of the rifle division, which fell to roughly 6,000–8,000 men each in mid-1943. Therefore, with an average strength of two to three rifle divisions and 12,000–24,000 men, by mid-1943 the average rifle corps was roughly equivalent to a full-strength American or British infantry division.

Rifle Divisions

Throughout the war the rifle division *(strelkovaia diviziia)* was the Red Army's largest and most ubiquitous infantry formation *(soedenenie)* possessing a fixed organizational structure. As such, it served as the basic tactical building block of the Red Army's rifle corps and field (combined-arms) armies, although it sometimes operated in direct subordination to a *front*. When war began, rifle divisions consisted of three rifle regiments, two artillery regiments, and a wide variety of supporting battalions and companies, with a paper strength of over 14,000 men and 16 light tanks (see Table 6.2).

As was the case with the rest of the Red Army's force structure, however, these divisions proved too cumbersome for their inexperienced command cadre to control effectively in combat, and their logistical support was inadequate to satisfy the requirements of modern mobile warfare. As a result, in the late summer and fall of 1941, the People's Commissariat of Defense (NKO) truncated the organizational structure of its rifle divisions and began forming smaller rifle brigades, in reality, demi (light)-divisions, in their stead. Although their reduced size made them ideal vehicles for training Red Army command cadre in how to command and control forces at division-level and below, these weak rifle divisions lacked firepower and mobility sufficient to conduct or sustain high-intensity mobile defensive or offensive operations, and, as a result, they often suffered catastrophic losses at the hands of the more experienced and stronger *Wehrmacht*.

Therefore, in the spring of 1942, the NKO ceased forming rifle brigades, began converting rifle brigades into full divisions, and slowly but progressively increased the rifle divisions' firepower and logistical support by adding new weapons and supporting subunits to the rifle division's organizational structure.

As a result of this process, in February 1943 rifle divisions consisted of three rifle regiments, an artillery regiment, a training battalion, and smaller supporting subunits including antitank and sapper (engineer) battalions. Rifle regiments contained three rifle battalions, a single battery of four 76mm infantry field guns, an antitank battery of six 45mm antitank guns, a mortar battery with six 120mm mortars, and an automatic weapons company. In turn, rifle battalions consisted of three rifle companies, a machine-gun company, a mortar company with nine 82mm mortars, and a platoon of two 45mm antitank guns. Divisional artillery consisted of twenty 76mm and twelve 122mm guns organized into three battalions.

So organized, the rifle division's overall strength was 9,435 personnel, thirty-two 76mm and twelve 122mm guns, one-hundred sixty 82mm and

122mm (and sometimes 50mm) mortars, forty-eight 37mm or 45mm antitank guns, 212 antitank rifles, 6,474 rifles and carbines, 727 submachine guns, 494 light machine guns, 111 heavy machine guns, 123 vehicles, and 1,700 horses.[2] Throughout the first half of 1943, the NKO decreased the rifle division's personnel strength slightly but increased its firepower by increasing its submachine gun strength by 50 percent. Overall, the quantity of rifle divisions in the Red Army increased from 198 on 22 June 1941, to 489 on 31 December 1943 (see Appendix 1 in companion volume for all rifle forces in the Red Army).

To recognize rifle divisions that distinguished themselves in combat, during the summer of 1941 the NKO awarded the guards rifle division designation to three of its rifle divisions. Continuing this practice throughout the remainder of the year, by 31 December it had awarded the designation of 1st through 10th Guards Rifle Divisions to the former 100th, 127th, 153rd, 161st, 107th, 120th, 64th, 316th, 78th, and 52nd Rifle Divisions. With their 10,670 men and a 36-gun artillery regiment added to them in December 1942, the new guards rifle divisions were somewhat stronger than their standard counterpart. However, regardless of their designation, most Red Army rifle divisions fought at substantially reduced strength throughout the war, sometimes with as few as 1,500 men and with little artillery support. The quantity of guards rifle divisions in the Red Army continued to increase throughout 1943, reaching a total of 99 on 1 February, 96 on 1 July, and 97 on 31 December.

When war began, the Red Army fielded only three motorized rifle divisions, one of which, the famous 1st Moscow Motorized Rifle Division, was assigned to the 7th Mechanized Corps based at Moscow and two of which were based in the Far East. After the 1st Moscow Motorized Rifle Division was destroyed in combat at Orsha and Smolensk in early July 1941, the NKO reformed it as the 1st Tank Division in August 1941, a new 1st Motorized Rifle Division in September, and shortly thereafter, as the 1st Guards Motorized Division until mid-1943.

Although it was designated a motorized rifle division, the 82nd Motorized Rifle Division, which was assigned to the Trans-Baikal Military District when war began, was structured as a motorized division. After being transferred westward to Moscow in October 1941, the NKO reorganized this division into a standard rifle configuration. Finally, the NKO reorganized its 108th Tank Division into the 107th Motorized Rifle Division in late September 1941, but also converted it into a standard rifle division in mid-1942. The only other motorized rifle divisions in the Red Army in June 1941, the 36th and 57th Motorized Rifle Division, which were remnants of older 1940 vintage mechanized corps, remained in the Far East until war's end. Thus, by early 1943 the Red Army included only three motorized rifle divisions, the 1st Guards Moscow Motorized Rifle Division, which was a motorized version of a guards rifle division, and two motorized rifle divisions in the Far East.

In June 1941 the Red Army also fielded specialized mountain rifle divisions, whose structure was somewhat lighter than that of a standard rifle division and which were equipped to conduct operations in mountainous terrain. Nineteen of these divisions were situated in the Southwestern Front, the North Caucasus, Trans-Caucasus, Central Asian, and Far Eastern Military Districts, and the Separate 9th Army in the Crimea. These rifle divisions consisted of four mountain rifle regiments, two mountain artillery regiments, an antitank battery, a sapper battalion, and service support subunits. In place of the rifle division's normal weaponry, mountain divisions fielded twenty-five 122mm pack howitzers, sixteen 76mm mountain guns, sixty 50 mm mortars, sixteen 82mm mortars, twelve 107mm mountain mortars, eight 45mm antitank guns, and eight 37mm antiaircraft guns.[3] Although as strong in manpower as standard rifle divisions, mountain divisions were far more fragile than their line counterparts.

After the advancing *Wehrmacht* destroyed most of these mountain divisions during Operation Barbarossa, the NKO either disbanded or converted the remainder into standard rifle divisions, leaving only a handful in the mountainous Caucasus region. In addition, the Red Army also included a small number of mountain rifle brigades, regiments, and detachments. The quantity of mountain rifle divisions in the Red Army decreased from 19 on 22 June 1941 to 4 on 31 December 1943.

Rifle Brigades and Their Variants

The rifle brigade and its variant student *(kursantnaia brigada),* naval rifle *(brigada morskoi pekhoty),* naval infantry *(morskaia strelkovaia brigada),* and ski brigade *(lyzhnaia brigada),* was a demi-division consisting of three or four rifle battalions, two mortar (82mm and 120mm) battalions, single artillery, automatic weapons, and antitank battalions, an antitank rifle company, and various supporting subunits. The NKO formed vast quantities of these brigades from September 1941 through April 1942 in order economize on scarce weaponry and help resolve the Red Army's severe command and control problems but converted most of these brigades into full rifle divisions in the summer and fall of 1942 and early 1943. Depending on their type, these brigades ranged in strength from as few as 3,800 to as many at 5,100 men but had only roughly half the weaponry of a standard rifle division (see Table 6.3).

To exploit the manpower available to the Red Navy (*Voenno-morskoi flot,* or VMF), during the summer of 1941 the NKO required its individual fleets to form numerous naval infantry brigades and, later, naval rifle brigades, whose structure was quite similar to that of the standard rifle brigade. For example, the Baltic Fleet fielded the 1st through 7th Naval Infantry Brigades, plus a student brigade, in 1941 and added two more in 1942. The Black Sea Fleet produced four such brigades in 1941 and another three in 1942, and the Northern and Pacific Fleets formed three brigades each in 1941 and 1942 (see Table 6.4).

Initially, each naval infantry brigade consisted of four to six infantry battalions, one to two artillery battalions, two mortar battalions, and smaller service support subunits. Because they were hastily formed, these brigades varied widely in composition, strength, and combat capability. In the fall of 1941, however, the NKO converted all of these brigades to the organization of a standard rifle brigade. The Navy fielded a total of 21 naval infantry brigades and several naval infantry regiments during the war, all of which fought under Red Army control.[4]

In addition to these naval infantry brigades, on 18 October 1941, the NKO ordered the Navy to form naval rifle brigades, whose organization was nearly identical to the standard rifle brigade (see Table 6.5). Naval rifle brigades consisted of three rifle battalions with 715 men each, a separate artillery battalion with eight 76mm field guns, a separate antitank battalion with twelve 57mm guns, a separate mortar battalion with sixteen 82mm and eight 120mm mortars, reconnaissance, antitank rifle, and submachine gun companies, an antiaircraft platoon, a separate signal battalion, and sapper, auto-transport, and medical companies. So organized, the brigade's overall strength was 4,334 men, eight 76mm guns, twelve 57m guns, sixteen 82mm and eight 120mm mortars, 149 submachine guns, 48 heavy machine guns, 612 PPSh submachine guns, 48 antitank rifles, 178 vehicles, and 818 horses.[5]

Subsequently, the naval rifle brigade experienced the same organizational changes as normal rifle brigades, and several received guards designations for their accomplishments in combat. The NKO sharply reduced the number of naval brigades in the Red Army in late 1942 and early 1943, when it abolished many and reorganized the remainder into full rifle divisions. Overall, the NKO fielded a total of 38 naval rifle brigades during the war.[6]

To take advantage of the keen winter skills of most Red Army soldiers, in late 1941 the NKO began forming ski forces so that the Red Army could operate more effectively during the incoming winter months. After the NKO raised and fielded 84 ski battalions in December 1941 and another 77 in January 1942 to its operating *fronts,* in March and April 1942, several *fronts* and armies combined these ski battalions into ski brigades to improve their striking power. For example, during this period, the Western Front's 1st Shock Army formed the 1st and 2nd Ski Brigades with five battalions each, and the Karelian Front formed the 2nd through 8th Ski Brigades with three battalions each.

These ski brigades, which played an important and extensive role in combat during the winter campaign of 1941–42, consisted of three ski battalions, an antitank battalion, reconnaissance, submachine–gun, and mortar companies, an antiaircraft machine–gun platoon, and medical and supply companies. The average strength of a ski brigade was 3,800 personnel, and it fielded six 82mm mortars, nine 50mm mortars, twelve 45mm antitank guns, 45 antitank rifles, 18 light machine guns, and three heavy antiaircraft machine guns (DShK).

However, variations did exist in the ski brigades' structures. For example, the 3rd Ski Brigade fielded a mortar battalion in place of the normal mortar company, 82mm mortars instead of 50mm mortars in its ski battalions, 50mm mortars in its rifle companies, additional antitank rifles in its antitank battalion, and a signal company. Therefore, it fielded fifty-one 82mm mortars, twenty-seven 50mm mortars, and 54 antitank rifles.[7] In addition to these brigades, the NKO also fielded several separate ski battalions. After completing its winter campaign of 1942–43, the NKO converted most of these ski forces into other types of forces throughout the remainder of 1943. The total quantity of rifle and other types of brigades in the Red Army rose precipitously to 231 on 1 February 1943, but thereafter fell to 59 brigades on 31 December 1943.

Destroyer Forces

In addition to its standard rifle divisions and brigades and their numerous variants, the Red Army also fielded formations such as "destroyer" *(istrebitel'nye)* divisions and brigades, fortified regions, and airborne corps and brigades, which were responsible for performing more specialized combat missions in the front lines. Although categorized officially as rifle forces, destroyer divisions and brigades were combined-arms formations, which possessed stronger than normal antitank capability, whose mission was to combat enemy armor forces.

As originally configured, destroyer brigades consisted of: one antitank artillery regiment consisting of four batteries with four 76m guns each, three batteries with four 45mm guns each, and one battery with four 37mm antiaircraft guns; two antitank rifle battalions, each with of three companies fielding 24 antitank rifles each; one engineer-mine battalion with three companies; one tank battalion consisting of two medium companies with 10 T-34 tanks each and one light company with 11 T-40 or T-60 light tanks; and one mortar battalion consisting of two batteries with 4 82mm mortars each and one battery with four 120mm mortars.

So configured, the strength of the destroyer brigade was 1,791 men, and it fielded sixteen 76mm guns, twelve 45mm guns, four 37mm guns, four 120mm mortars, eight 82mm mortars, 144 antitank rifles, 21 medium tanks, 11 light tanks, 177 vehicles, and 20 motorcycles.[8]

Destroyer divisions consisted of two destroyer brigades, a separate signal company, a separate medical battalion, and a separate auto-transport company for an overall strength of almost 4,000 men, 56 antitank guns, eight antiaircraft guns, 24 mortars, and 64 tanks.

Although destroyer divisions and brigades were primarily responsible for combating enemy armor, they also performed a wide array of offensive missions, including protecting mobile exploitation echelons (mobile groups) while they were operating in the depth of the enemy defense, defending against counterattacking enemy tank formations, and protecting Red Army tank formations during meeting engagements.

After forming its first destroyer formations in April and May 1942, the NKO fielded a total of three destroyer divisions and 13 separate destroyer brigades throughout the remainder of the year. However, since these forces proved largely ineffective against enemy armor, the NKO abolished all of these divisions and brigades by the end of 1943.

Fortified Regions

In June 1941 the only force capable of erecting and manning fortified defensive positions in the Red Army was the fortified region (*ukreplennyi raion*, or UR). On the eve of war, the Red Army's extensive network of fortified regions was responsible for protecting the Soviet Union's frontiers and the wartime mobilization and deployment of the Red Army's main forces. The NKO formed its first 19 fortified regions during the period 1928–37 and created another eight in 1938 and 1939 to defend Leningrad, Kiev, and the Soviet Union's western and eastern frontiers.

After the Soviet Union seized eastern Poland and the Baltic states in 1939 and 1940, in 1940 and 1941 the NKO began creating additional fortified regions to protect its new frontier with Finland, the rump German state in Poland, and Romania, but failed to complete this construction by the time of the German invasion. By the time Germany unleashed its *Wehrmacht* in Operation Barbarossa, the Red Army fielded a total of 57 fortified regions, 41 in its operating *fronts* and armies in the West and 16 in its internal military districts and nonoperating *fronts* in the Caucasus and Far East

In June 1941 the Red Army's fortified regions were brigade- or regimental-size formations consisting of a varying number of separate machine-gun artillery battalions (usually three) with only minimal infantry and logistical support, which manned fixed concrete and earth fortifications. Since they were immobile, they were incapable of surviving in modern mobile warfare, so the advancing *Wehrmacht* destroyed most of the fortified regions deployed in their path during the summer of 1941.

In accordance with the *Stavka's* defense plans, the NKO *Stavka* began forming new fortified regions in the spring and summer of 1942 to man new defensive lines in the depth of the Soviet Union and serve as primarily economy-of-force formations to release regular Red Army forces for field duty. These new fortified regions, which were lighter than their predecessors in manpower but heavier in firepower, had an average strength of 4,100 men and consisted of an 85-man headquarters and a variable number (usually five to ten) of 667-man machine-gun artillery battalions with infantry, armor, and sapper support. An average-size fortified region consisted of six machine-gun rifle battalions fielding forty-eight 76mm guns, forty-eight 50mm and forty-eight 82mm mortars, forty-eight 45mm antitank guns, 168 antitank rifles, 78 submachine guns, and 192 light and 192 heavy machine guns.[9]

Machine-gun artillery battalions consisted of a headquarters section, a signals platoon, a sapper section, four machine-gun artillery companies, and support elements, while machine-gun artillery companies included a small headquarters, several machine-gun platoons, a mortar platoon with light 50mm and medium 82mm mortars, and an artillery battery with a 45mm antitank platoon and a 76mm field gun platoon.[10] To conserve on manpower, the battalions had only enough men to man its machine guns and field guns (see Table 6.6).

As the Red Army increased the size of its mobile forces in late 1942, the NKO began forming and fielding so-called field fortified regions. Slightly larger than the standard fortified region, these formations had more trucks assigned them to improve their mobility and enable them to participate more effectively in fluid offensive operations. The quantity of fortified regions in the Red Army's force structure decreased from 57 on 22 June 1941 to 19 on 1 January 1942, but thereafter increased to 48 by 31 December 1943.

AIRBORNE FORCES

As pioneers in the development of airborne forces, the Red Army fielded a substantial airborne force on the eve of war. This force, which was subordinate to the Red Army Air Force commander, consisted of the 1st through 5th Airborne Corps, which were subordinate to the Baltic Special, Western Special, Kiev Special, Khar'kov, and Odessa Military Districts in the western Soviet Union, and the 202nd Separate Airborne Brigade in the Far East.

Airborne corps consisted of three airborne brigades, an air-landed light tank battalion consisting of three companies equipped with 50 (but later 32) light tanks, a flight of control aircraft, a long-range radio platoon, and a motorcycle platoon with 15 vehicles. On paper at least, each corps was manned by 10,419 men and fielded 50 tanks, 18 field guns, and 18 mortars. Airborne brigades consisted of four parachute battalions, brigade artillery with six 76mm guns and twelve 45mm antitank guns, a reconnaissance company with 113 bicycles, a mortar company with six 82mm mortars, an antiaircraft company with six 12.7mm machine guns, and a signal company for a total strength of roughly 3,000 men.[11]

The chaos produced by the German invasion and the ensuing sudden and near total collapse of the Red Army's defenses left the *Stavka* no choice but to employ its valuable airborne forces as infantry in ground combat under the control of its operating *fronts*. As a result, the advancing *Wehrmacht* had destroyed or decimated most of the Red Army's airborne corps by late September 1941.

Amid this disaster, in late June the NKO withdrew its airborne forces from *front* control and subordinated them to its newly formed Directorate of Airborne Forces (UVDV). Later still, in September 1941 the NKO appointed a commander-in-chief for the airborne forces, reorganized the existing UVDV into a Directorate of the Commander of Airborne Forces, and subordinated all surviving airborne forces to the new VDV commander with strict instructions he use them only with the *Stavka's* specific approval. Soon after, the NKO also formed dedicated transport aviation forces designated to transport the airborne forces into combat.

In the early fall of 1941, the NKO refitted and reinforced the airborne brigades that had survived the bloodletting in the summer of 1941 and formed five new airborne corps from the remnants of its former corps, bringing the total to ten. The *Stavka* employed its new 4th, 5th, and 10th Airborne Corps to conduct air assault operations west of Moscow during its winter offensive of 1941–42, during which all three corps suffered heavy losses.[12] After the winter offensive ended in April 1942, the NKO reorganized its ten airborne corps into eight and created five new maneuver airborne brigades configured to conduct coordinated parachute and ground operations. Three of these maneuver brigades participated in the Northwestern Front's unsuccessful attempts to crush German forces encircled at Demiansk during March and April 1942 but also suffered heavy losses.[13]

In July 1942, after the *Wehrmacht* began its dramatic advance across southern Russia during Operation *Blau*, the NKO reorganized its airborne corps and maneuver airborne brigades into ten guards rifle divisions (the 32nd through 41st) and five rifle brigades (the 5th through 9th) and assigned them to their operating *fronts* fighting in the Stalingrad region. However, since the *Stavka* remained convinced that airborne forces could play a vital role in modern mobile war, in late August it ordered the NKO to form a new force of eight airborne corps and five maneuver airborne brigades in the Moscow Military District, using the same organization and force designations as the previous forces.[14]

However, when the Red Army began expanding its new winter offensive in late December 1942, the NKO responded to the *Stavka*'s requests for additional forces by converting its airborne forces into the 1st through 10th Guards Airborne Divisions and dispatching them, first, to the Northwestern Front and, later, to the Kursk region, where they once again fought as elite ground troops. Therefore, the only remaining airborne unit in the Red Army on 1 January 1943 was the 202nd Airborne Brigade deployed in the Far East.

During its preparations for the summer campaign of 1943, the *Stavka* ordered the NKO to form 20 new guards airborne brigades, including the 1st through the 7th in the *Stavka* Reserve in April and the 8th through the 20th also in the *Stavka* Reserve in June.[15] As the fighting intensified throughout the summer, in September the *Stavka* assigned the 1st, 3rd, and 5th Guards Airborne Brigades to the Voronezh Front and the 4th, 6th, and 7th Guards Airborne Brigades to the Southern Front, but retained the remaining 14 guards airborne brigades in its reserve.[16]

Later still, in October 1943, the *Stavka* assigned the 1st, 2nd, and 11th Guards Airborne Brigades to the 1st Baltic Front in October and used them to form a provisional airborne corps, designated the 8th Guards Airborne Corps, which it planned to insert into the rear of German forces defending Vitebsk and Polotsk during its November offensive into northern Belorussia in 1943. However, heavy German resistance and deteriorating weather conditions forced the *Stavka* to cancel the operation.[17]

Thereafter, the NKO retained 20 guards airborne brigades in the Red Army's force structure until December 1943, when it converted them into the 11th–16th Guards Rifle Divisions. By the end of 1943, the only airborne brigades in the Red Army's force structure were the 3rd and 8th Guards Airborne Brigades in the *Stavka* Reserve and the 202nd Airborne Brigade in the Far East.[18]

Slightly stronger than their 1941–42 predecessors, the 1943 airborne brigades consisted of four parachute battalions, an antitank battalion, an antiaircraft machine-gun company, and signal and reconnaissance companies for a total strength of 3,553 men. The brigade's parachute battalions consisted of three parachute companies, each armed with 9 light machine guns and three 50mm mortars, an antitank company with 27 antitank rifles, a machine-gun company with 12 Maxim machine guns, a sapper company, and signal and medical platoons, for a total strength of 715 men. To provide antitank and antiaircraft defense, the airborne brigade fielded an antitank battalion of two batteries with four 45mm guns each, and an antitank rifle company with 18 antitank rifles and an antiaircraft machine-gun company with 12 DShK machine guns. Finally, the brigade included a signal battalion with six backpack RB and two longer-range RSB model radios and a reconnaissance battalion with 91 bicycles.[19]

OPERATING STRENGTHS

As was the case with the Red Army as a whole, the actual personnel (field ration) strength of Red Army rifle formations and units in the field seldom if ever met the requirements of the forces' actual table of organization throughout the first 30 months of war. Although field armies, rifle corps, and rifle divisions and brigades sometimes fielded more than their authorized quantities of weaponry and equipment, manpower shortages were routine if not endemic. In fact, these manpower shortfalls persisted even after the NKO and General Staff refitted and replenished their *fronts* and armies prior to conducting major offensive or defensive operations. Worse still, manpower shortages became even more pronounced during prolonged offensive operations because Stalin, the *Stavka,* and most *front* and army commanders displayed little concern for personnel losses as they strove to fulfill their assigned missions. Instead of periodically withdrawing their depleted forces for rest and refitting, the *Stavka* required its *front* and army commanders to drive their forces on until they were utterly burned out, sometimes literally to the last battalion.

Despite the Soviets' congenital reticence to reveal the actual operating strengths of the Red Army's operating forces, fragmentary evidence documents the actual strength of the Red Army's rifle forces (see Table 6.7). When Operation Barbarossa began, for example, documents indicate that the average strength of rifle divisions subordinate to the Red Army's initial four operating *fronts* was 9,648 men, about 67 percent of their authorized 14,483 men.[20]

While the Red Army was mobilizing and defending in depth across the entire front in the summer and fall of 1941, the Red Army's rifle divisions seldom managed to assemble more than 30–35 percent of their authorized prewar strength or 50 percent of the 11,000 men they were authorized by their revised July 1941 table of organization. In addition, both existing and newly mobilized divisions experienced severe shortages of weapons and other combat equipment.[21]

During early spring of 1942, the NKO and General Staff managed to increase the strength of its rifle forces, particularly those taking part in major offensives and those deployed along key strategic axes, to roughly 70 percent of their authorized manpower and close to 100 percent of their weaponry. At the same time, however, its divisions and brigades operating along secondary axes remained at 50 percent or lower fill.

When the *Wehrmacht* resumed major offensive operations in late May and expanded their offensive in July and August, it once again decimated many of the Red Army's refitted rifle forces, this time primarily along the southwestern and southern axes. Despite the Red Army's immense losses in the summer and fall of 1942, the NKO and General Staff were able to raise and field many new reserve armies whose rifle divisions were often at or above 90 percent fill in personnel, even though they were still often deficient in weaponry and other equipment.

The heavy fighting that occurred during the summer phase of Operation *Blau,* and particularly in the rubble of Stalingrad during the fall, decimated many Red Army divisions and brigades. Often, rifle divisions that fielded over 12,000 men in early July lost 90 percent of their men in July and were filled out with replacements in August, only to lose 90 percent of their strength again in September and October. In sharp contrast, rifle divisions earmarked to spearhead the Red Army's November counteroffensives, such as those assigned to the 5th Tank, 65th Army, and 1st and 3rd Guards Armies, averaged 75–80 percent of their authorized strength.

Depending on the specific army, Red Army rifle forces operating along main offensive axes in the winter of 1942–43, which averaged between 55 and 95 percent of their authorized manpower strength, were far stronger than those that had participated in the Red Army's winter offensive of 1941–42, when most rifle divisions averaged less than 50 percent of their authorized strength. Once again, however, attrition exacted its awful toll, and in the heavy fighting many rifle formations eroded to a fraction of their previous strength, a fact that explains in large measure why Manstein was able to terminate the Red Army's winter juggernaut in February and March 1943.

In 1943, for the first time in the war, the Red Army was both willing and able to conduct successful offensive operations in the summer, at least in part because of the improved combat skills of its commanders and soldiers and the increased strength of its rifle forces. Most Red Army rifle divisions operating along main attack axes in July 1943 were at 75–80 percent (and in a few instances, over 90 percent) of their required personnel fill. Their improved strength enabled them to penetrate the *Wehrmacht* defenses, exploit into the enemy's tactical and operational depths, and sustain their offensive operations to unprecedented depths.

Even after the Red Army won the Battle of Kursk and initiated its many other successful but costly offensives in August and September, it had strength enough to sustain these offensive operations to the Dnepr River in the fall. This was because its rifle forces retained strengths of 30–60 percent and because the *Stavka* released fresh forces from its strategic reserves to reinforce its operating fronts when their forces exhausted themselves in incessant combat.

Thus, while the NKO steadily reduced the authorized personnel strength of Red Army rifle divisions from over 14,000 men on the eve of war to 9,380 men in December 1943, at least on a seasonal basis, the percent fill of those divisions steadily increased. At the same time, the division's firepower increased significantly in terms of the quantity and quality of authorized weaponry and actual weapons on hand. As a result, even though each Red Army rifle division remained far weaker than its German counterpart, the sheer quantity of rifle divisions the Red Army fielded in 1943 more than compensated for their individual weakness. Therefore, after July 1943 the *Wehrmacht* began experiencing the cascading series of defeats that would ultimately culminate in its utter destruction in May 1945.

INFANTRY (RIFLE) WEAPONRY

The tools of the Red Army's trade, its combat weaponry, improved significantly throughout the first 30 months of the war in terms of both quantity and quality. These improvement benefited rifleman, artilleryman, cavalryman, *tankist*, sapper (engineer), and signalman alike. Traditionally, Soviet design bureaus emphasized simplicity, ruggedness, and low production costs as they developed weapons for the Red Army. This approach satisfied the demands of a mass army for high quality, durable, and reliable weapons such as pistols, rifles, submachine guns, machine guns, and artillery, but it led to reduced reliability and frequent mechanical problems in larger and more complex weapons systems.

Pistols and Rifles

Red Army riflemen (infantry) entered the war equipped with more than adequate rifle weapons. However, production delays and the multiplicity of weapons models were key deficiencies at the outbreak of the war. These shortcomings, coupled with the catastrophic Red Army losses in 1941, produced frequent and severe, though only temporary, weapons shortages. By late 1942, however, Soviet industry had more than made up for these shortages by ruthlessly committing necessary resources to the arms production effort. In the realm of officers' and sergeants' side arms, the most ubiquitous weapons produced and employed were the 7.62mm Tokarev (TT2) Model 1933 automatic pistol and the heavier 7.62mm Nagant Model 1895 revolver. After providing the Red Army with 120,903 of the former and 118,453 of the latter in 1941, Soviet industry geared up production dramatically and manufactured 161,485 automatic pistols and 15,485 revolvers during 1942 and an even greater quantity in 1943 (see Appendix 3 in companion volume for the characteristics of these and other Red Army infantry weapons).[22]

The Red Army's standard infantry rifle was the magazine-fed, bolt-action 7.62mm Moisin Nagant Model 1891/1930, which was also available in a sniper version. Cavalrymen were armed with the 7.62mm Moisin Nagant Model 1938 carbine. Soviet infantry had to put up with this rather heavy and cumbersome standard rifle until a lighter carbine, the 7.62mm Moisin Nagant Model 1944, replaced it in early 1944.[23]

After extensive tests during the late 1930s, the NKO also fielded the semi-automatic 7.62mm Tokarev SVT-40 rifle, which was equipped with a 10-round magazine and had an effective range of 1,500 meters, in 1940 and a fully automatic version in the summer of 1942 as a substitute for the standard light machine gun. However, this weapon's complexity and perceived unreliability and inaccuracy prompted the NKO to curtain its production during the war and, instead, emphasize the development and fielding of submachine guns capable of high-volume fire.

Submachine Guns

After extensive experimentation with submachine guns in the late 1930s, the NKO developed and fielded, first, the Degtiarev PPD Model 1934/38 machine pistol, which ceased production in 1939 due to its many deficiencies, second, the Degtiarev PPD Model 1940 submachine gun, which was equipped with a disc magazine, and, finally, the most famous and ubiquitous Red Army infantry weapon, the 7.62mm pistol-machine gun Shpagin PPSh Model 1941 (PPSh-41), which was referred to commonly as simply the PPSh submachine gun. The Shpagin PPSh, which could deliver high volumes of fire and used inexpensive and readily available pistol ammunition in a disc magazine, supplemented the infantryman's standard Moisin rifle. At least in theory, the NKO equipped one rifle (submachine gun) company per rifle regiment with the PPSh, and, in addition, created a machine-gun platoon in the 1st, 4th, and 7th Rifle Companies in each Red Army rifle battalion.

The immense popularity of the PPSh submachine gun prompted Soviet industry to develop an even cheaper and more reliable substitute for it in 1943. After experimenting with the Sudaev Model 1942 PPS submachine gun in early 1943, during the summer Soviet industry developed and fielded the lighter, cheaper, and more effective Sudaev Model 1943 PPS submachine gun. As the war progressed, the production of submachine guns grew dramatically relative to the production of rifles and carbines. For example, Soviet industry produced 1,567,100 rifles and carbines and 89,700 submachine guns from July through December 1941, 4,049,000 rifle and carbines and 1,506,400 submachine guns in 1942, and 3,436,200 rifles and carbines and 2,2023,600 submachine guns in 1943. During the war as a whole, the Soviets produced 18,313,200 infantry weapons, 6,173,900 (34 percent) of which were submachine guns.[24] In addition, the United States provided the Red Army with 137,729 Thompson .45 caliber submachine guns within the auspices of its Lend-Lease program.

Machine Guns

The Red Army's standard infantry light machine gun throughout most of the war was the 7.62mm Degtarev DP machine gun, which was assigned to rifle platoons and squads. Called by the troops the "record player" because of its large drum magazine, it dominated this weapons genre through 1944, when the NKO replaced it with the modernized DPM Model 1944.

The most prevalent crew-served machine gun assigned to machine-gun subunits in Red Army rifle forces was the 7.62mm Maxim Model 1910 water-cooled machine gun, which was mounted on a variety of wheeled carriages. Since this weapon was both cumbersome and ancient, the NKO began replacing it with the simpler and lighter Goruniov SG-43 machine gun in May 1943. In addition, the NKO also fielded the 7.62mm heavy machine gun DS Model 1939.

The standard Soviet heavy machine gun was the 12.7mm Degtarev DShK, which, although originally designed for antiaircraft defense, was also occasionally employed on a wheeled mount in an infantry support role. To supplement this weaponry, Lend-Lease provided the Red Army with 2,487 Bren guns and 5,403 Browning .30 caliber light machine guns.

Antitank Weapons

One of the Red Army's most serious shortcomings at the outbreak of war was the absence of an effective antitank weapon within its rifle forces. After experiments with several types of infantry antitank weapons failed to produce satisfactory results, in August 1941 the NKO fielded the single-shot 14.5mm Degtarev PTRD antitank rifle and the magazine-fed Simonov PTRS antitank rifle, each of which was served by a two-man crew. Although these rifles had their limitations, by 31 December 1942, Soviet industry fielded 202,488 of the former, which was simpler and cheaper to mass-produce, and 63,385 of the latter. The actual number of antitank rifles in the Red Army weapons inventory rose from 8,116 rifles on 1 January 1942 to 118,563 rifles on 1 January 1943.[25]

These antitank rifles had to suffice during the first year of the war, but by 1943 advances in armor technology had rendered them largely ineffective against the frontal armor of most German tanks. Henceforth, in order to "kill" German tanks, Red Army riflemen had to employ these rifles at extremely close ranges and only against the most vulnerable surfaces on the tanks' sides and rear, which was an exceedingly risky task for even the most experienced riflemen. Despite the obvious shortcomings of these antitank rifles, Red Army riflemen relied heavily on them throughout the remainder of the war.

To supplement the antitank rifle, the Soviets also fielded the RPG-40 Model 1940 antitank grenade. However, this weapon also proved ineffective against most modern models of German tanks. Therefore, the Soviets improvised by employing so-called Molotov cocktails—bottled filled with petrol, which were either improvised in thousands of different versions or mass-produced as so-called KS bottles. For a short period during 1941 and 1942, the Red Army also experimented with a mortar-type weapon called an *ampulemet,* which fired ampules filled with an incendiary fuel mixture. However, the NKO ceased producing these strange weapons in late 1942 for a variety of technical reasons including the danger they presented to their own crews. In addition, the NKO also fielded and employed antitank dog units, which were equipped with explosive-laden dogs (ironically usually German shepherds), which were trained to approach and destroy German tanks.

Table 6.1 Composition of the Red Army Rifle Corps, June 1941 to June 1944

Subordinate Units	Jun 1941	Jun 1942	Dec 1943	Jun 1944
Rifle divisions	3	2–3 or 3–5 rifle brigades	3	3–4
Artillery brigades	0	0	0	1
Corps artillery regiments	2	0	1	0
Self-propelled artillery brigades	0	0	0	1
Guards-mortar regiments	0	0	0	1
Sep. antiaircraft battalions	1	0	0	1
Sapper battalions	1	0	1	1
Signal battalions	1	0	1	1

Source: Iu. P. Babich and A. G. Baier, *Razvitie vooruzheniia i organizatsii sovetskikh sukhoputnykh voisk v gody Velikoi Otechestvennoi voiny* [The development of the weaponry and organization of Soviet ground forces in the years of the Great Patriotic War] (Moscow: Izdanie Akademii, 1990), 35.
Note: The June column is added for comparison

Table 6.2 Relative Strength of Red Army Rifle Divisions, 5 April 1941 to 18 December 1944

Category	5 Apr 1941	29 Jul 1941	6 Dec 1941	18 Mar 1942	28 Jul 1942	10 Dec 1942	15 Jul 1943	18 Dec 1944
Rifle regiments	3	3	3	3	3	3	3	3
Artillery regiment	1	1	1	1	1	1	1	1
Howitzer regiment	1	0	0	0	0	0	0	0
Mortar battalion	0	0	1–2	0	0	0	0	0
Guards-mortar battalion	0	0	1	0	0	0	0	0
Machine-gun battalion	0	0	0	1	1	0	0	0
Reconnaissance battalion	1	0	0	0	0	0	0	0
Reconnaissance company	0	1	1	0	1	1	1	1
Antitank battalion	1	0	1	1	1	1	1	1
Antiaircraft battalion	1	1	0	0	0	1	0	0
Antiaircraft battery	0	0	1	1	1	0	0	0
AA machine-gun company	0	0	0	0	0	0	0	1
Sapper battalion	1	1	1	1	1	1	1	0
Signal battalion	1	1	1	1	0	0	1	1
Signal company	0	0	0	0	1	1	1	1
Auto-transport battalion	1	0	0	0	0	0	0	0
Auto-transport company	0	1	1	1	1	1	1	1
Chemical defense company	1	0	1	1	1	1	1	1
Chemical defense platoon	0	1	0	0	0	0	0	0
Medical battalion	0	1	1	1	1	1	1	1
Training battalion	0	0	0	0	1	1	1	1
Light tank battalion (optional)	1	0	0	0	0	0	0	0
Personnel	14,483	10,859	11,626	12,725	10,386	9,435	9,380	11,706
Total artillery and mortars	228	144	198	214	232	204	204	191
Artillery								
76mm guns	34	28	28	32	32	32	32	44
122mm guns	32	8	8	12	12	12	12	20
152mm howitzers	12	0	0	0	0	0	0	0

—Continued

Table 6.2 Continued

Category	5 Apr 1941	29 Jul 1941	6 Dec 1941	18 Mar 1942	28 Jul 1942	10 Dec 1942	15 Jul 1943	18 Dec 1944
Mortars								
50mm mortars	84	54	72	76	85	56	56	0
82mm mortars	54	18	72	76	85	83	83	89
120mm mortars	12	6	18	18	18	21	21	38
Quad AA machine guns	15	18	0	0	0	0	0	0
37mm antiaircraft guns	8	6	6	6	6	0	0	12
76mm antiaircraft guns	4	4	0	0	0	0	0	0
37mm, 45mm antitank guns	54	18	18	30	30	48	48	36
57mm antitank guns	0	0	12	0	0	0	0	18
Antitank rifles	0	0	89	279	228	212	212	107
Light tanks	16	0	0	0	0	0	0	0
Armored cars	13	0	0	0	0	0	0	0
Rifles and carbines	10,420	8,341	8,565	9,375	7,241	6,474	6,274	6,330
Submachine guns	1,204	171	582	655	711	727	1,048	3,594
Light machine guns	392	162	251	352	337	434	434	337
Medium machine guns	166	108	108	114	112	111	111	166
DShK machine guns	18	9	12	9	9	0	0	18
Vehicles (cars and trucks)	558	203	248	154	149	123	124	342
Tractors	99	5	0	15	15	15	15	0
Horses	3,039	2,478	2,410	1,804	1,804	1,719	1,700	1,700

Sources: Iu. P. Babich and A. G. Baier, *Razvitie vooruzheniia i organizatsii sovetskikh sukhoputnykh voisk v gody Velikoi Otechestvennoi voiny* [The development of the weaponry and organization of the Soviet ground forces in the years of the Great Patriotic War] (Moscow: Izdanie Akademii, 1990), 34; A. A. Radzievsky, ed., *Taktika v boevykh primerakh (diviziia)* [Tactics by combat example (The division)] (Moscow: Voenizdat, 1976), scheme 1; and Steven J. Zaloga and Leland S. Ness, *Red Army Handbook, 1939–1945* (Gloucestershire, UK: Sutton, 1998), 35.

Table 6.3 Relative Strength of Various Types of Red Army Rifle Brigades, October 1941 to July 1942

Subordinate Subunits	Oct 41	Dec 41	Apr 42	Jul 42
Rifle battalions	3	3	4	4
Reconnaissance company	1	0	1	1
Artillery battalion	1	1	1	1
Mortar battalion (82mm)	1	1	1	0
Mortar battalion (120mm)	1	1	1	1
Antitank battalion	1	1	1	1
Antitank rifle company	1	1	0	0
Submachine-gun company	1	1	1	1
Sapper company	1	1	1	1
Signal company	0	0	0	0
Signal battalion	0	0	1	1
Auto-transport company	1	1	1	1
Medical company	1	1	1	1
Personnel	4,356	4,480	5,200	5,125
76mm guns	12	12	12	12
50mm mortars	24	24	24	48
82mm mortars	24	24	24	24
120mm mortars	0	0	8	8
45mm antitank guns	12	12	12	12
Antitank rifles	48	at least 48	80	80
Submachine guns	397	100	598	621
Light machine guns	59	72	73	144
Medium machine guns	36	36	48	48
Heavy machine guns	3	0	3	3
Vehicles	90	163	91	???

Sources: Steven J. Zaloga and Leland S. Ness, *Red Army Handbook, 1939–1945* (Gloucestershire, UK: Sutton, 1998), 37–42; and Iu. P. Babich and A. G. Baier, *Razvitie vooruzheniia i organizatsii sovetskikh sukhoputnykh voisk v gody VelikoiOtechestvennoi voiny* [The development of the weaponry and organization of the Soviet ground forces during the Great Patriotic War] (Moscow: Izdanie Akademii, 1990), 36.

Table 6.4 Formation of Red Army Naval Infantry Brigades, 1940–1942

Brigade	Date Formed	Location	Known Composition
1st	June 1940	Baltic Fleet	NA
2nd	June 1941	Baltic Fleet	3 battalions, later 5
3rd	June 1941	Baltic Fleet	4 battalions with 5,205 men
4th	June 1941	Baltic Fleet	committed as a student detachment
5th	July 1941	Baltic Fleet	NA
6th	September 1941	Baltic Fleet	4,980 men
7th	September 1941	Baltic Fleet	NA
56th	1942	Baltic Fleet	NA
260th	1942	Baltic Fleet	NA
Student	June 1941	Baltic Fleet	NA
7th	August 1941	Black Sea Fleet	NA
8th	August 1941	Black Sea Fleet	NA
9th	November 1941	Black Sea Fleet	6 battalions (destroyed at Kerch)
9th (2d formation)	December 1941	Black Sea Fleet	4 battalions (destroyed at Kerch)
9th (3rd formation)	Spring 1942	Black Sea Fleet	destroyed at Sevastopol'
83rd	1942	Black Sea Fleet	NA
255th	1942	Black Sea Fleet	NA
12th	Fall 1941	Northern Fleet	NA
63rd	Fall 1941	Northern Fleet	NA
254th	Fall 1941	Northern Fleet	NA
13th	1941–42	Pacific Fleet	NA
14th	1941–42	Pacific Fleet	NA
15th	1941–42	Pacific Fleet	NA

Source: Kh. Kh. Kamalov, *Morskaia pekhota v boiakh za rodinu* [Naval infantry in battles for the homeland] (Moscow: Voenizdat, 1966), 7–19.

Table 6.5 Formation of Red Army Naval Rifle Brigades, 1941 and 1942

Brigade*	Date Formed	Where Formed	Source of Troops	Subordination
61st	October 1941	Ural MD	Pacific Fleet	Karelian Front
62nd	October 1941	Ural MD	Pacific Fleet	1 SA, Western Front
63rd	October 1941	Ural MD	Pacific Fleet	Arkhangel'sk MD
64th	October 1941	Ural MD	Pacific Fleet	20 A, Western Front
65th	October 1941	Ural MD	Pacific Fleet	Karelian Front
66th	October 1941	Volga MD	Pacific Fleet, Amur Flotilla	Karelian Front
67th (45th RD)	October 1941	Volga MD	Pacific Fleet	Karelian Front
68th	October 1941	N. Caucasus MD	Caspian Fleet, Central Directorate	56 A, Southern Front
69th	October 1941	Siberian MD	Pacific Fleet, Central Directorate	7 Sep. A
70th	October 1941	Siberian MD	Pacific Fleet naval schools	7 Sep. A
71st	October 1941	Siberian MD	Pacific Fleet naval schools	1 SA, Western Front
72nd	October 1941	Siberian MD	Pacific Fleet	Karelian Front
73rd	October 1941	Siberian MD	Pacific Fleet	7 Sep. A
74th	October 1941	Central Asian MD	Caspian and Pacific Fleets	Moscow Def. Zone
75th (3rd GRB, 27th GRD)	October 1941	Central Asian MD	Black Sea Fleet officer's course	Moscow Def. Zone
76th	October 1941	N. Caucasus MD	Caspian and Pacific Fleet naval schools	56 A, Southern Front
77th	October 1941	N. Caucasus MD	Black Sea Fleet naval schools	Karelian Front
78th	October 1941	N. Caucasus MD	Black Sea Fleet naval schools	56 A, Southern Front
79th	October 1941	N. Caucasus MD	Black Sea Fleet naval schools	Sevastopol'
80th (45th RD)	October 1941	N. Caucasus MD	Black Sea Fleet naval schools	Karelian Front
81st	October 1941	N. Caucasus MD	Black Sea Fleet naval schools	56 A, Southern Front
82nd	October 1941	N. Caucasus MD	Black Sea Fleet naval schools	Arkhangel'sk MD
83rd	October 1941	N. Caucasus MD	Black Sea Fleet naval schools	51 A, Crimean Front
84th	October 1941	N. Caucasus MD	Black Sea Fleet naval schools	1 SA, Western Front
85th	October 1941	N. Caucasus MD	Black Sea Fleet naval schools	Karelian Front

*Indicates successor rifle division

Source: V. Shlomin, "Dvadtsat' piat' morskikh strelkovykh" [25th Naval Infantry], *Voenno-istoricheskii zhurnal* [Military-historical journal], no. 7 (July 1970): 96–99.

Table 6.6 Relative Strength of Red Army Machine-Gun Artillery Battalions, 1942–1943

Category	Mar 1942	Mar–Nov 1943
Personnel	667	669
76mm guns	8	12
50mm mortars	8	8
82mm mortars	8	8
45mm antitank guns	8	8
Antitank rifles	28	28
Submachine guns	13	??
Light machine guns	32	32
Medium machine guns	32	32
Vehicles	7	7
Wagons	16	16

Source: "Die M.G.-Artillerie-Bataillone der Roten Armee," Obkdo der Heeresgruppe Mitte, Abt. Ic/A.O./Ausw., 27.4.1944, in *Kreigsgliederungen der Roten Armee, Abteilung Fremde Heere Ost (IIc),* Anl. 4. National Archives Microfilm (NAM) series T-78, Roll 549; and Steven J. Zaloga and Leland S. Ness, *Red Army Handbook, 1939–1945* (Gloucestershire, UK: Sutton, 1998), 56.

Table 6.7 Personnel Strength of Selected Red Army Field Armies, Rifle Corps, Rifle Divisions, and Rifle Brigades, 22 June 1941 to 1 January 1944

Force (Subordination)	Authorized	Actual	Notes (% of fill)
22 Jun 1941			
Leningrad MD rifle divisions	14,483	11,985	Average (83%)
Northwestern Front divisions	14,483	8,712	Average (60%)
8 A, NWF	105,508	82,010	5 RDs, 1 MC, 1 ATB (12,285, 85%)
10 RC	32,057	25,480	2 RDs (88%)
11 RC	32,507	23,661	2 RDs (82%)
Western Front divisions	14,483	9,327	Average (64%)
4 A, WF	NA	68,700	4 RDs, 1 FR, 1 MC (11,625, 80%)
6 RD, 4 A, WF	14,483	11,592	(80%)
42 RD, 4 A, WF	14,483	11,505	(79%)
49 RD, 4 A, WF	14,483	11,690	(81%)
75 RD, 4 A, WF	14,483	11,712	(81%)
Southwestern Front divisions	14,483	8,712	Average (60%)
5 A, SWF	NA	102,431	5 RDs, 3 FRs, 1 MC, 1 ATB (9,838, 68%)
45 RD, 5 A, SWF	14,483	10,010	(69%) 84 of 82 guns, 150 of 150 mortars, 16 of 16 tanks, 264 of 558 vehicles
62 RD, 5 A, SWF	14,483	9,973	(69%) 80 of 82 guns, 152 of 150 mortars, 0 of 16 tanks, 464 of 558 vehicles
87 RD, 5 A, SWF	14,483	9,872	(68%) 82 of 82 guns, 152 of 150 mortars, 18 of 16 tanks, 536 of 558 vehicles
124 RD, 5 A, SWF	14,483	9,426	(65%) 82 of 82 guns, 141 of 150 mortars, 11 of 16 tanks, 248 of 558 vehicles
135 RD, 5 A, SWF	14,483	9,911	(68%) 80 of 82 guns, 149 of 150 mortars, 0 of 16 tanks, 276 of 558 vehicles
41 RD, 6 A, SWF	14,483	9,912	(68%) 74 of 82 guns, 222 of 558 vehicles
173 RD, 26 A, SWF	14,483	7,177	(50%) 59 of 82 guns, 251 of 558 vehicles
60 Mtn. RD, 12 A, SWF	14,483	8,313	(57%) 56 of 57 guns (>37mm)
Jul–Sep 1941			
Leningrad axis			
168 RD, 7 A, NF (1 Jul)	14,483	14,233	(98%)
1 DNO, LMD (15 Jul)	14,926	12,102	(81%) 9,739 rifles, 197 of 570 machine guns, 9 of 72 guns, 0 of 150 mortars.

—Continued

Table 6.7 Continued

Force (Subordination)	Authorized	Actual	Notes (% of fill)
2 DNO, LMD (15 Jul) (85 RD)	11,739	8,721	(74%) 8,500 rifles, 248 of 537 machine guns, 7 of 70 guns, 138 of 147 mortars.
3 DNO, LMD (15 Jul)	12,154	10,094	(83%) 9,650 rifles, 219 of 546 machine guns, 25 of 70 guns, 108 of 150 mortars.
1 GDNO, LMD (1 Aug) (80 RD)	10,815	10,538	(97%) 2,577 of 5,741 rifles, 10 of 550 machine guns, 0 of 34 guns, 0 of 72 mortars.
2 GDNO, LMD (1 Aug)	10,836	11,489	(106%) 4,355 of 8,947 rifles, 10 of 183 machine guns, 6 of 28 guns, 38 of 72 mortars.
4 Lt. DNO (1 Aug) (86 RD)	NA	4,267	
3 GDNO (20 Aug) (44 RD)	10,800	10,334	(96%)
4 GDNO (20 Aug) (5 DNO to 13 RD)	9,961	8,924	(90%)
6 DNO (15 Sep) (189 RD)	10,800	8,189	(76%)
7 DNO (15 Sep) (56 RD)	10,800	8,454	(78%)
Northwestern axis			
34 A, NWF	10 Aug	54,912	5 RD, 2 CDs (5,883, 41%)
	26 Aug	22,043	5 RDs, 2 CDs (2,362, 16 %)
Smolensk-Briansk axis			
34 RC, 16 A, WF	18 Jul	1,400	2 RDs
20 A, WF divisions	1 Aug	4–6,500	Range of strength (28%–45%)
30 A, Res. F. divisions	1 Aug	4–5,000	Range of strength (28%–35%)
28 A, Res. F. divisions	1 Aug	4–5,000	Range of strength (28%–35%)
279 RD, 50 A, Orel MD (1 Sep)	14,483	11,454	(79%)
290 RD, 50 A, Orel MD (1 Sep)	14,483	10,902	(75%)
260 RD, 50 A, Orel MD (1 Sep)	14,483	10,479	(72%)
258 RD, 50 A, Orel MD (1 Sep)	14,483	11,354	(78%)
1 DNO, Moscow MD (MMD)	11,600	10,000	(86%) 2,000 rifles, 30 machine guns, 11 guns and mortars, 15 light tanks. 60 RD in Sep
2 DNO, MMD (15 Aug)	11,600	8,385	(72%) 2 RD in Sep
4 DNO, MMD (15 Aug)	11,600	11,775	(102%) 7,260 men, 6,625 rifles, 472 machine guns, 29 guns on 31 October. 110 RD in Sep
5 DNO, MMD (15 Aug)	11,600	11,700	(101%) 7,291 men, 6,961 rifles, 271 machine guns, 29 guns on 31 October. 113 RD in Sep

6 DNO, MMD (15 Aug)	11,600	9,000	(78%) 160 RD in Sep
7 DNO, MMD (30 Aug)	11,600	15,000	(>100%) 29 RD in Sep
8 DNO, MMD (30 Aug)	11,600	7,500	(65%) 8 RD in Sep
9 DNO, MMD (30 Aug)	11,600	10,500	(91%) 139 RD in Sep
13 DNO, MMD (15 Sep)	11,600	8,010	(69%) 140 RD in Sep
17 DNO, MMD (15 Sep)	11,600	10,000	(86%) 17 RD in Sep
18 DNO, MMD (30 Sep)	11,600	10,000	(86%) 18 RD in Sep
21 DNO, MMD (30 Sep)	11,600	7,660	(66%) 173 RD in Sep
Kiev axis			
135 RD, 31 RC, 5 A, SWF (9 Jul)	14,483	3,500	38 guns and mortars
193 RD, 5 A, 31 RC, SWF (9 Jul)	14,483	3,500	30–35 guns and mortars
87 RD, 15 RC, 5 A, SWF (9 Jul)	14,483	1,059	11 guns
195 RD, 31 RC, 5 A, SWF (18 Jul)	14,483	700–800	
195 RD, 31 RC, 5 A (22 Jul)	14,483	250–300	
135 RD, 31 RC, 5 A (22 Jul)	14,483	500	
15 RC, 5 A, SWF	22 Jul	5,000–6,000	Range of strength (45, 62 RD)
124 RD, 5 A (24 Jul)	14,483	1,600	
124 RD, 5 A (31 Jul)	14,483	2,800	including 1,500 replacements
228 RD, 5 A, SWF (14 Aug)	10,859	2,429	
31 RC, 5 A, SWF divisions	19 Aug	4,200–4,500	Range of strength (193, 195, 200 RD)
15 RC, 5 A, SWF divisions	19 Aug	4,000–4,500	Range of strength (45, 62, 135 RD)
124 RD, 5 A (19 Aug)	10,859	1,200	
228 RD, 5 A (19 Aug)	10,859	2,000	
15 RC, 5 A (28 Aug)	NA	15,312	62, 200 RD, 92 guns and mortars
135 RD, 1 Abn C, 1 ATB, 15 RC, 5 A	10 Sep	1,000	Survived encirclement
45, 62 RD, 15 RC, 5 A	10 Sep	500	Survived encirclement
31 RC, 5 A, SWF	10 Sep	2,000	100 guns and mortars, survived encirclement
193 RD, 31 RC, 5 A (10 Sep)	10,859	300	Survived encirclement
195 RD, 31 RC, 5 A (10 Sep)	10,859	300	Survived encirclement
200 RD, 31 RC, 5 A (10 Sep)	10,859	450	Survived encirclement
295 RD, 31 RC, 5 A (10 Sep)	10,859	300	Survived encirclement
228 RD, 31 RC, 5 A (10 Sep)	10,859	200	Survived encirclement
Odessa-Crimea axis			
Coastal Army (Odessa)	15 Jul	45,387	2 RDs, 1 CD (12,500, 86%)
95 RD, Coast. A (15 Jul)	14,483	14,373	(99%)

—Continued

Table 6.7 Continued

Force (Subordination)	Authorized	Actual	Notes (% of fill)
25 RD, Coast. A (15 Jul)	14,483	10,535	(73%)
51 A, Crimea	20 Aug	30,000	4 RDs (5,625, 39%)
Oct 1941 to Mar 1942			
Leningrad region			
42 A, LF	12 Oct 41	38,000	4 RDs, 1 ATB (7,125, 66%)
Northwestern axis			
3 SA, NWF	3 Jan 42	51,600	3 RDs, 6 RBs (6,450, 59%)
33 RD, 3 SA, NWF (3 Jan 42)	10,859	10,100	(93%)
3 SA, NWF divisions	15 Mar 42	4,100	Average (38%)
Viaz'ma-Briansk axis			
WF divisions	1 Oct 41	8,500	Average strength (78%)
30 A, WF	1 Oct 41	37,500	4 RDs
16 A, WF	15 Oct 41	56,590	4 RDs
112 RD, 16 A, WF (1 Oct)	10,859	10,091	(93%)
108 RD, 16 A, WF (1 Oct)	10,859	10,095	(93%)
38 RD, 16 A, WF (1 Oct)	10,859	9,836	(91%)
43 A, WF	1 Oct 41	51,100	4 RDs, 2 TBs
222 RD, 43 A, Res. F (1 Oct)	10,859	9,446	(87%)
211 RD, 43 A, Res. F (1 Oct)	10,859	9,673	(89%)
53 RD, 43 A, Res. F (1 Oct)	10,859	12,236	(113%)
217 RD, 50 A, BF (1 Oct)	10,859	11,953	(110%)
260 RD, 50 A. BF (1 Oct)	10,859	9,755	(90%)
279 RD, 50 A, BF (1 Oct)	10,859	7,964	(73%)
13 A, BF	15 Oct 41	28,460*	7 RDs
Moscow axis (Oct)			
Kalinin Front divisions	17 Oct 41	4,000–5,300	Range of strength (37%–49%)
252 RD, 31 A, KF (23 Oct)	10,859	7,000	(64%)
194 RD, 50 A, WF (24 Oct)	10,859	4,200	(39%)
290 RD, 50 A, WF (29 Oct)	10,859	2,119	(20%)
258 RD, 50 A, WF (29 Oct)	10,859	634	(6%)
154 RD, 50 A, WF (29 Oct)	10,859	1,930	(18%)

217 RD, 50 A, WF (29 Oct)	10,859	1,428	(13%)
260 RD, 50 A, WF (29 Oct)	10,859	674	(6%)
279 RD, 50 A, WF (29 Oct)	10,859	843	(8%)
299 RD, 50 A, WF (29 Oct)	10,859	825	(8%)
413 RD, 50 A, WF (30 Oct)	10,859	13,649	(125%)
316 RD, 16 A, WF (31 Oct)	10,859	8,249	(76%)
Moscow axis (Nov)			
22 A, KF divisions	11 Nov 41	3,000–4,000	Range of strength (28%–37%)
32 RD, 5 A, WF (1 Nov)	10,859	7,680	(71%)
3 Workers D, MMD (15 Nov)	NA	9,753	130 RD in Dec
4 Workers D, MMD (15 Nov)	NA	7,260	155 RD in Dec
5 Workers D, MMD (15 Nov)	NA	7,294	158 RD in Dec
30 A, WF	16 Nov 41	23,000	3 RDs, 1 CD, 2 TBs
16 A, WF	16 Nov 41	61,000	4 RDs, 4 CDs, 4 TBs, 1 TD
5 A, WF	16 Nov 41	31,000	4 RDs, 1 MRD, 3 TBs
144 RD, 5 A, WF (16 Nov)	10,859	7,601	(70%)
50 A, WF	16 Nov 41	28,000	6 RDs
10 A, WF	16 Nov 41	85,000	8 RDs, 3 CDs
239 RD, 3 A, SWF (17 Nov)	10,859	11,817	(109%)
299 RD, 50 A, WF (22 Nov)	10,859	230	(2%)
1 SA, WF	29 Nov 41	36,950	8 RBs, 12 Ski Bns
222 RD, 33 A, WF (30 Nov)	10,859	6,714	(62%)
113 RD, 33 A, WF (30 Nov)	10,859	4,025	(37%)
110 RD, 33 A, WF (30 Nov)	10,859	6,637	(61%)
Moscow axis (Dec)			
KF divisions	1 Dec 41	5,800	Average strength (53%)
31 A, KF divisions	6 Dec 41	4,344–9,230	Range of strength (40%–85%)
365 RD, 31 A, KF (6 Dec)	10,859	9,230	(85%)
30 A, WF	5 Dec 41	72,000	7 RDs, 4 CDs, 2 TBs
16 A, WF	5 Dec 41	55,000	5 RDs, 4 RBs, 4 TBs, 2 CDs
1 SA, WF	5 Dec 41	40,000 (28,000)*	1 RD, 1 CD, 8 RBs, 2 NRBs, 11 Ski Bns
5 A, WF	6 Dec 41	35,000	7 RDs, 1 MRD, 3 CDs
331 RD, 20 A, WF (6 Dec)	10,859	8,000	(74%)
50 A, WF divisions	6 Dec 41	4,760*	Average strength (44%)
50 A, WF	6 Dec 41	40,000	6 RDs, 1 CD, 1 TD, 3 TBs

—*Continued*

Table 6.7 Continued

Force (Subordination)	Authorized	Actual	Notes (% of fill)
10 A, WF	6 Dec 41	94,000	8 RDs, 3 CDs, 1 TB
10 A, WF, 7 rifle divisions	6 Dec 41	10,641	Average strength (98%)
239 RD, 10 A, WF (6 Dec)	10,859	5,538	(51%)
1 SA, WF	26 Dec 41	25,000	8 RBs, 3 NRBs, 2 CDs, 10 Ski Bns
	15 Mar 42	24,219	3 RDs, 3 RBs
29 RB, 1 SA, WF (26 Dec)	4,356	1,123	(26%)
55 RB, 1 SA, WF (26 Dec)	4,356	700	(16%)
340 RD, 50 A, WF (29 Dec)	10,859	2,300	(21%)
290 RD, 50 A, WF (29 Dec)	10,859	900	(8%)
154 RD, 50 A, WF (29 Dec)	10,859	440	(4%)
258 RD, 50 A, WF (29 Dec)	10,859	850	(8%)
Rzhev-Viaz'ma axis (Jan–Mar)			
39 A, KF	5 Jan 42	68,238	7 RDs
29 A, KF	5 Jan 42	27,879	4 RDs
50 A, WF	5 Jan 42	37,500*	6 RDs, 1 TD (TB), 1 CD
10 A, WF	5 Jan 42	48,250*	8 RDs
1 SA, WF	6 Jan 42	18,571 (13,000)*	6 RBs, 2 NRBs, 6 Ski Bns
32 RD, 5 A, WF (6 Jan)	11,626	5,000	(46%) 48 guns, 47 mortars, reinforced by 36 MtcR
173 RD, 50 A, WF (20 Jan)	10,859	3,578	(33%)
113, 160, 338 RD, 33 A, WF	2 Feb 42	2,500–3,000	Average strength
113, 160, 338 RD, 33 A, WF	5 Feb 42	8,500	
39 A, KF	28 Feb 42	24,643	7 RDs, 2 CDs
252 RD, 39 A, KF (28 Feb)	10,859	3,386	(31%)
256 RD, 39 A, KF (28 Feb)	10,859	5,013	(46%)
262 RD, 39 A, KF (28 Feb)	10,859	3,030	(28%)
361 RD, 39 A, KF (28 Feb)	10,859	4,189	(39%)
355 RD, 39 A, KF (28 Feb)	10,859	1,942	(18%)
357 RD, 39 A, KF (28 Feb)	10,859	2,466	(23%)
373 RD, 39 A, KF (28 Feb)	10,859	2,274	(21%)
50 A, WF	25 Mar 42	53,000*	9 RDs, 1 TB

Orel-Elets axis (Nov–Mar)			
3 A, BF	11 Nov 41	7,548*	(70%) 5,939 rifles, 74 machine guns, 119 guns in 4 RDs, 1 CD
13 A (Briansk Front)*	11 Nov 41	19,799	12,014 rifles, 158 machine guns, 140 guns in 6 RDs, 1 CD, 1 MtcR
13 A, BF	6 Dec 41	40,000	24,500 rifles, 1,102 machine guns, 156 guns, 89 mortars, 16 tanks in 7 RDs, 4 CDs, 1 MRB, 1 NKVD B
Southern axes			
63 Mtn RD, 9 RC, 44 A, Caus. F (28 Dec)	9,000	6,365	
6 A, SWF	18 Jan 42	43,601	27,395 rifles in 5 RDs, 1 CD
390 RD, 51 A, Crim. F (Feb 42)	10,859	10,738	Including 10,185 Armenians
Apr–May 1942			
Demiansk axis			
44 RB, 1 SA, NWF (30 Apr)	4,480	52	(1%)
41 RB, 1 SA, NWF (30 Apr)	4,480	50	(1%)
116 RB, 1 SA, NWF (30 Apr)	4,480	115	(3%)
27 RB, 1 SA, NWF (30 Apr)	4,480	150	(3%)
47 RB, 1 SA, NWF (30 Apr)	4,480	44	(1%)
Khar'kov axis			
SWF divisions (12 May)	12,725	8,000–10,000	Average strength (63%–79%)
28 A, SWF	12 May	62,470	6 RDs
6 A, SWF	12 May	101,000	8 RDs, 2 TC, 4 TBs
SF divisions (9, 57 A) (12 May)	12,725	5,000–7,000	Average strength (39%–55%)
Crimean axis			
47 A, Crim. F.	1 April	40,000	3 RDs, 1 CD
51 A, Crim. F.	1 April	95,000	6 RDs, 3 RBs, 4 TBs
Coastal Army, Crim. F.	1 April	93,000	7 RDs, 1 NRB, 2 NIB, 1 CD
Jun-Jul 1942			
Zhizdra-Bolkhov axis			
61 A, WF	5 July	103,000	7 RDs, 5 RBs, 1 TC, 2 TBs (7,607, 60%)
Stalingrad axis			
64 A, Stal. F.	23 July	61,600	6 RDs, 2 TBs (8,727, 69%)
62 A, Stal. F.	23 July	83,500	6 RDs, 2 TBs (12,260, 96%)
192 RD, 62 A, Stal. F. (23 Jul)	12,725	12,517	(98%)
33 GRD, 62 A, Stal. F. (23 Jul)	12,725	11,467	(90%)

—Continued

Table 6.7 Continued

Force (Subordination)	Authorized	Actual	Notes (% of fill)
181 RD, 62 A, Stal. F. (23 Jul)	12,725	12,699	(100%)
147 RD, 62 A, Stal. F. (23 Jul)	12,725	12,494	(98%)
196 RD, 62 A, Stal. F (23 Jul)	12,725	11,464	(90%)
184 RD, 62 A, Stal. F (23 Jul)	12,725	12.920	(102%)
Crimean axis			
79 NRB, Sevastopol' (7 Jul)	5,200	3,500	(67%)
Aug–Oct 1942			
Rzhev-Sychevka axis			
31 A (Western Front)	1 Aug	89,000	7 RDs, 4 TBs (9,539, 75%)
Stalingrad axis			
21 A, Stal. F. (7 rifle divisions)	1 Aug	5,180	Average strength (50%)
62 A, Stal. F.	1 Aug	53,965	6 RD, 1 TB
64 A, Stal. F.	1 Aug	61,603	6 RDs, 1 NRB, 2 TBs
51 A, SEF	16 Aug	3,342	2 RDs, 1 CD, 3 TBs (1,014, 10%)
62 A, Stal. F.	13 Sep	52,632	9 RDs, 6 RBs, 1 TC, 1 TB
62 A, Stal. F.	13 Sep	2,000–3,000	5 RDs (19%–28%)
62 A, Stal. F.	13 Sep	700–800	4 RDs (7%–8%)
64 A, Stal. F.	13 Sep	38,000	8 RDs, 2 RBs, 1 TC (2,450, 24%)
112 RD, 62 A (13 Sep)	10,386	7,000	(67%)
35 GRD, 62 A (13 Sep)	10,670	660	(6%)
39 GRD, 62 A (13 Sep)	10,670	3,900	(36%)
138 RD, 62 A (13 Sep.)	10,386	2,281	(22%)
13 GRD, 62 A (15–16 Sep)	10,670	10,600	(99%)
35 GRD, 62 A (21 Sep)	10,670	80	(1%)
193 RD, 62 A (27–28 Sep)	10,386	5,000	(48%)
95 RD, 62 A (27–28 Sep)	10,386	7,000	(67%)
112 RD, 62 A (29 Sep)	10,386	250	(2%)
37 GRD, 62 A (2–3 Oct)	10,670	7,000	(66%)
62 A, Stal. F.	9 Oct	55,000	9 RDs, 6 RBs, 1 FR
193 RD, 62 A (8 Oct)	10,386	350	(3%)
95 RD, 62 A (8 Oct)	10,386	3,075	(30%)

112 RD, 62 A (9 Oct)	10,386	2,300	(22%)
42 RB (62 A) (9 Oct)	5,200	937	(9%)
95 RD, 62 A (14 Oct)	10,386	500	(5%)
13 GRD, 62 A (15 Oct)	10,670	300	(3%)
37 GRD, 62 A (15 Oct)	10,670	250	(2%)
138 RD, 62 A 16 Oct)	10,386	9,000	(87%)
51 A, Stal. F.	21 Oct	13,765	2 RDs
91 RD, 51 A, Stal. F.	21 Oct	2,100	(20%)
302 RD, 51 A, Stal. F.	21 Oct	2,100	(20%)
Nov-Dec 1942			
Demiansk axis			
23 GRD, 1 SA, NWF (2 Nov)	10,670	9,651	(90%)
Velikie-Luki axis			
3 SA, NWF	23 Nov	95,608	7 RDs, 1 RB, 1 MC, 1 TB (8,394, 81%)
Rzhev-Sychevka axis			
20 A, WF	25 Nov	114,176	7 RDs, 3 RBs, 1 TC, 1 CC (8,453, 81%)
22 A, KF	25 Nov	80,000	4 RDs, 1 RB, 1 MC (10,000, 98%)
39 A, KF	25 Nov	90,000	6 RDs, 4 RBs (8,166, 78%)
41 A, KF	25 Nov	105,000	6 RDs, 4 RBs, 1 MC (8,166, 78%)
20 A, WF	11 Dec	112,411	10 RDs, 3 RBs, 2 TC, 1 CC (6,000, 58%)
Stalingrad axis			
1 GA, SWF divisions	19 Nov	8,200	Average strength (79%)
5 TA, SWF	19 Nov	103,627	6 RDs, 2 TCs, 1 CC, 1 TB (7,750, 75%)
5 TA, SWF divisions	19 Nov	7,750	Average strength (75%)
21 A, SWF divisions	19 Nov	7,850	Average strength (76%)
57 A, Stal. F.	19 Nov	36,200	2 RDs, 2 RBs, 1 FR, 1 MC, 1 TB
Middle Don axis			
6 A, VF	16 Dec	60,200	5 RDs, 1 TC (7,530, 73%)
1 GA, SWF	16 Dec	110,796	7 RDs, 3 TCs (8,442, 81%)
3 GA, SWF	16 Dec	110,000	7 RDs, 2 RBs, 1 MC (8,948, 86%)
Jan–Mar 1943			
Leningrad region			
67 A, LF	12 Jan	100,000	8 RDs, 5 R (Ski)Bs, 3 TBs (6,300, 67%)

—*Continued*

Table 6.7 Continued

Force (Subordination)	Authorized	Actual	Notes (% of fill)
Ostrogozhsk-Rossosh' axis			
291 RD, 18 RC, VF (12 Jan)	9,435	7,199	(76%)
270 RD, 18 RC, VF (12 Jan)	9,435	6,138	(65%)
161 RD, 18 RC, VF (12 Jan)	9,435	5,162	(55%)
309 RD, 18 RC, VF (12 Jan)	9,435	7,839	(83%)
129 RB, 18 RC, VF (12 Jan)	5,125	4,426	(86%)
Voronezh-Kastorne axis			
BF divisions	24 Jan	5,000–6,000	Range of strength (53%–64%)
BF brigades	24 Jan	3,000	Average strength (59%)
13 A, BF divisions	24 Jan	8,500–9,500	Average strength (90%–101%)
VF divisions	24 Jan	5,000–6,000	Range of strength (53%–64%)
VF brigades	24 Jan	3,000	Average strength (59%)
Khar'kov axis			
40 A, VF	31 Jan	90,000	8 RDs, 1 RB, 1 TC (6,500, 69%)
69 A, VF	31 Jan	40,000	4 RDs, 1 RB (6,300, 67%)
Donbas axis			
6 A, SWF	1 Feb	40,000	4 RDs, 1 RB (6,300, 67%)
1 GA, SWF	1 Feb	70,000	7 RDs (7,000, 70%)
3 GA, SWF	1 Feb	100,000	9 RDs, 3 TCs, 1 MC, 1 CC (3,889, 41%)
Belgorod-Kursk axis			
41 GRD, 6 A, SWF (21 Mar)	10,954	3,000	(27%)
350 RD, 3 TA, VF (22 Mar)	10,954	3,361	(31%)
350 RD, 3 TA, VF (17 Apr)	10,954	2,557	(23%)
Orel-Smolensk axis			
70 A, CF divisions	24 Feb	9,000–11,000	Range of strength (95%–117%)
37 GRD, 65 A, CF (24 Feb)	10,670	10,000	(94%)
69 RD, 65 A, CF (24 Feb)	9,435	7,600	(81%)
193 RD, 65 A, CF (24 Feb)	9,435	9,000	(95%)
149 RD, 65 A, CF (24 Feb)	9,435	6,800	(72%)
354 RD, 65 A, CF (24 Feb)	9,435	7,500	(79%)
121 RD, 60 A, VF (25 Mar)	9,435	7,025	(74%)
248 RB, 60 A, VF (25 Mar)	5,125	2,389	(47%)

Jul–Aug 1943			
Kursk axis			
CF divisions	5 Jul	7,000–7,500	Average strength range (70%–75%)
13 A, CF	5 Jul	114,000	12 RDs, 1 TB (6,650, 71%)
70 A, CF	5 Jul	96,000	8 RDs (8,400, 90%)
48 A, CF	5 Jul	84,000	7 RDs (8,400, 90%)
VF divisions	5 Jul	7,000–8,000	Average strength range (70%–80%)
6 GA, VF	5 Jul	79,700	7 RDs, 1 TB (7,970, 75%)
7 GA, VF	5 Jul	76,800	7 RDs, 2 TB (7,680, 72%)
78 GRD, 7 GA, VF (5 July)	10,670	7,854	(74%)
40 A, VF	5 Jul	69,000	(7 RDs) (7,079, 76%)
38 A, VF	5 Jul	60,000	6 RDs, 2 TBs (7,000, 75%)
1 GA, SWF	5 Jul	145,000	12 RDs, 2 TC, 4 TB (7,292, 68%)
Orel axis			
11 GA, WF	10 Jul	135,000	12 RDs, 2 TCs (6,708, 67%)
50 A, WF	10 Jul	54,062	7 RDs,1 TB (5,406, 57%)
Belgorod-Khar'kov axis			
VF divisions	3 Aug	7,180	Average
5 GA, VF	3 Aug	62,802	7 RDs, 1 TB (6,280, 59%)
St. F. divisions	3 Aug	6,070	Average
53 A, St. F.	3 Aug	77,000	7 RDs, 1 MC (6,500, 69%)
21 GRD, 57 A, SWF (25 Aug)	10,670	2,845	(30%)
Smolensk axis			
KF divisions	7 Aug	6,700	Average strength (71%)
3 SA, KF divisions	7 Aug	6,000–6,500	Range of strength (64%–69%)
4 SA, KF divisions	7 Aug	6,500–7,000	Range of strength (69%–75%)
43 A, KF divisions	7 Aug	7–7,200	Range of strength (75%–77%)
39 A, KF divisions	7 Aug	6,800–7,000	Range of strength (72%–75%)
KF brigades	7 Aug	4,243	Average strength (83%)
3 SA, KF brigades	7 Aug	3,800	Average strength (74%)
4 SA, KF brigades	7 Aug	4,430	Average strength (86%)
43 A, KF brigades	7 Aug	4,243	Average strength (83%)
39 A, KF brigades	7 Aug	5,140	Average strength (100%)
WF divisions	7 Aug	7,200	Average strength (77%)
31 A, WF divisions	7 Aug	6,500–7,000	Range of strength (69%–75%)

—*Continued*

Table 6.7 Continued

Force (Subordination)	Authorized	Actual	Notes (% of fill)
5 A, WF divisions	7 Aug	7,000–7,400	Range of strength (75%–79%)
10 GA, WF	1 Aug	75,000	6 RDs, 1 TB (8,250, 77%)
10 GA, WF	1 Aug	8,200–8,300	Range of strength (77%–78%)
10 GA, WF divisions	7 Aug	8,000–8,200	Range of strength (75%–77%)
33 A, WF divisions	7 Aug	7,000–7,400	Range of strength (75%–79%)
49 A, WF divisions	7 Aug	7,000–7,200	Range of strength (75%–77%)
10 A, WF divisions	7 Aug	6,900–7,100	Range of strength (74%–76%)
50 A, WF divisions	7 Aug	5,000–5,300	Range of strength (53%–57%)
68 A, WF divisions	7 Aug	7,000–7,400	Range of strength (75%–79%)
21 A, WF divisions	7 Aug	7,500–8,000	Range of strength (80%–85%)
10 GA, WF	20 Aug	38,400	7 RDs, 1 TB (3,840, 36%)
10 GA, WF	20 Aug	3,840	Average strength (36%)
29 GRD, 10 GA, WF (28 Aug)	10,670	8,000	(75%)
10 GA, WF	7 Sept	50,235	4 RDs, 1 TB (5,024, 47%)
56 GRD, 10 GA (7 Sep)	10,670	5,400	(51%)
22 GRD, 10 GA (7 Sep)	10,670	4,300	(40%)
65 GRD, 10 GA (7 Sep)	10,670	4,200	(39%)
29 GRD, 10 GA (7 Sep)	10,670	6,300	(59%)
85 GRD, 10 GA (7 Sep)	10,670	6,900	(65%)
30 GRD, 10 GA (7 Sep)	10,670	4,600	(43%)
208 RD, 7 GRC, 10 GA (7 Sep)	9,380	4,700	(50%)
Sep–Oct 1943			
Advance to the Dnepr			
28 RC, 13 A, CF	30 Sep	23,700	3 RDs
148 RD, 28 RC, 13 A (30 Sep)	9,380	6,200	(66%)
181 RD, 28 RC, 13 A (30 Sep)	9,380	7,300	(78%)
211 RD, 28 RC, 13 A (30 Sep)	9,380	7,500	(80%)
92 GRD, 37 A, St. F. (24 Sep)	10,670	8,472	(79%)
110 GRD, 37 A, St. F. (24 Sep)	10,670	8,818	(83%)
1 GAD, 37 A, St. F. (24 Sep)	10,670	8,256	(77%)
10 GAD, 37 A, St. F. (24 Sep)	10,670	7,818	(73%)

188 RD, 37 A, St. F. (24 Sep)	9,380	7,044	(75%)
89 GRD, 37 A, St. F. (24 Sep)	10,670	3,864	(36%)
72 GRD, 25 RC, 7 GA, St. F. (24 Sept)	10,670	3,152	(30%)
81 GRD, 25 RC, 7 GA, St. F. (24 Sept)	10,670	2,963	(28%)
Nevel' axis			
3 SA, KF divisions	30 Sep	3,000	Average strength (32%)
3 SA, KF divisions	6 Oct	6,000	Average strength (64%)
3 SA, KF brigades	6 Oct	3,500–4,000	Average strength (68%–78%)
Melitopol' axis			
54 RC, 51 A, SF	10 Oct	25,452	3 RDs (7,635, 81%)
91 RD, 54 RC, 51 A, SF (10 Oct)	9,380	7,511	(80%)
216 RD, 54 RC, 28 A, SF (10 Oct)	9,380	7,748	(83%)
315 RD, 54 RC, 28 A, SF (10 Oct)	9,380	7,648	(82%)
Nov–Dec 1943			
Gomel'-Rechitsa axis			
Belo. F.	15 Nov	485,293	(incl. 27,488 in *front* reserve)
3 A, Belo. F.	15 Nov	42,072	7 RDs (4,207, 49%)
11 A, Belo. F.	15 Nov	63,167	9 RDs (4,913, 52%)
48 A, Belo. F.	15 Nov	60,335	8 RDs (5,279, 56%)
50 A, Belo. F.	15 Nov	39,394	7 RDs (3,939, 42%)
61 A, Belo. F	15 Nov	50,049	7 RDs (5,004, 53%)
63 A, Belo. F.	15 Nov	60,587	8 RDs (5,310, 57%)
65 A, Belo. F.	15 Nov	142,201	10 RDs, 1 RB, 2 TC, 3 CCs (6,244, 67%)
Kiev axis			
38 A, 1 UF	3 Nov	137,000	11 RDs, 1 TC (8,082, 86%)
Krivoi Rog-Kirovograd axis			
52 A, 2 UF	13 Nov	26,327	3 RDs (6,143, 65%)
52 A, 2 UF divisions	13 Nov	6,000–6,300	Range of strength (64–67%)
Nikopol' axis			
49 GRD, 2 GA, 4 UF (16 Dec)	10,670	5,986	(56%)

*Denotes combat strength only.

1. Guns greater than 76mm except where indicated.

2. Line combat formations (divisions, corps, and brigades) normally made up 70–85 percent of an army's numerical strength and 90 percent of a rifle corps' strength, depending on the period of the war. Generally, the percentage was 75–85 from June 1941 through late 1942, but decreased to about 70 in 1943,

—*Continued*

Table 6.7 Continued

when the quantity of supporting arms within armies increased dramatically. Where shown, the average division strengths for armies are based on these rough figures. For the sake of calculations, the cavalry division is counted as a rifle division and post-spring 1942 tank and mechanized corps, as 10,000 and 15,000 men respectively.

Sources: B. M. Shaposhnikov, ed., *Razgrom Nemetskikh voisk pod Moskvoi, chast' 1, 2, and 3* [The defeat of German forces at Moscow, parts 1, 2, and 3] (Moscow: Voenizdat, 1943); A. A. Zabaluev, S. G. Goriachev, *Kalininskaia nastupatel'naia operatsiia* [The Kalinin offensive operation] (Moscow: Voroshilov Academy, 1942); *Eletskaia operatsiia (6–16 dekabria 1941 g.)* [The Elets operation (6–16 December 1941)] (Moscow: Voenizdat, 1943); *Barvenkovo-Lozovaia operatsiia (18–31 ianvaria 1942 g)* [The Barvenkovo-Lozovaia operation (18–31 January 1942)] (Moscow: Voenizdat, 1943; A. I. Radzievsky, ed., *Armeiskie operatsii* [Army operations] (Moscow: Voenizdat, 1977); K. V. Sychev and M. M. Malakhov, *Nastuplenie strelkovogo korpusa* [Rifle corps offensive] (Moscow: Voenizdat, 1958); R. M. Portugal'sky and P. Ia. Tsygankov, *Voennoe iskusstva Sovetskikh voisk v boiakh za Stalingrad* [Military art of Soviet forces in the battles for Stalingrad] (Moscow: Frunze Academy, 1983); R. M. Portugal'sky and L. A. Zaitsev, *Voennoe iskusstvo Sovietskikh voisk v bitve za Leningrad* [Military art of Soviet forces in the battle for Leningrad] (Moscow: Frunze Academy, 1989); B. I. Nevzorov, *Vozrastanie ustoichivosti oborony i osobennosti nastupleniia s khody v bitve pod Moskvoi (noiabr'–dekabr' 1941 g.)* [Growth in the durability of the defense and characteristics of the offensive from the march in the battle at Moscow] (Moscow: Frunze Academy, 1982); P. D. Alekseev and V. B. Makovsky, *Pervaia oboronitel'naia operatsiia 4-i armii v nachale Velikoi Otechestvennoi voiny* [The initial defensive operation of the 4th Army in the Great Patriotic War] (Moscow: Frunze Academy, 1992); O. N. Kudriashov and N. M. Ramanichev, *Boevye deistviia Sovetskikh voisk v nachal'nom periode Velikoi Otechestvennoi voiny* [Combat operations of Soviet forces in the initial period of the beginning of the Great Patriotic War] (Moscow: Frunze Academy, 1989); B. P. Frolov, *Forsirovanie rek Desny i Dnepra, osvobozhdenie Chernigov voiskami 13-i armii v Chernigovsko-Pripiatskoi operatsii (sentiabr' 1943 g)* [The forcing of the Dena and Dnepr rivers and the liberation of Chernigov by 13th Army forces in the Chernigov-Pripiat' operation] (Moscow: Frunze Academy, 1989); O. N. Kudriashov, *Proryv oborony protivnika i razvitie uspekha v operativnoi glubine soedineniami 5-i tankovoi armii. Sryv popytok protivnika deblokirovat' okruzhennuiu gruppirovku* [Penetration of enemy defense and development of success in operational depth by the formations of the 5th Tank Army. The disruption of enemy attempts to relieve the encircled grouping] (Moscow: Frunze Academy, 1987); E. K. Lukashev and V. I. Kuznetsov, *Podgotovka i vedenie nastupleniia 5-i gvardeiskoi armii vo vzaimodeistvii s podvizhnoi gruppoi fronta v kontrnastuplenii pod Kurskom* [The preparation and conduct of the offensive by the 5th Guards Army in cooperation with the front mobile group in the counteroffensive at Kursk] (Moscow: Frunze Academy, 1991); Iu. P. Babich, *Podgotovka oborony 62-i armii vne soprikosnoveniia s protivnikom i vedenie oboronitel'noi operatsii v usloviiakh prevoskhodstva protivnika v manevrennosti (po opytu Staloingradskoi bitvy)* [The preparation of the 62nd Army's defense outside contact with the enemy and the conduct of a defensive operation with a more maneuverable enemy (based on the experience of the Battle of Stalingrad)] (Moscow: Frunze Academy, 1991); Z. A. Shutov, *Puti dostizheniia ustoichivosti i aktivnosti oborony v gody Velikoi Otechestvennoi voiny* [The path to the achievement of durability and dynamism in the defense during the Great Patriotic War] (Moscow: Frunze Academy, 1990); *Sbornik voenno istoricheskikh materialov Velikoi Otechestvennoi voiny* [Collection of materials], no. 2] (Moscow: Voenizdat, 1949); *Sbornik voenno-istoricheskikh materialov Velikoi Otechestvennoi voiny* [Collection of materials], no. 7 (Moscow: Voenizdat, 1952); *Sbornik voenno-istoricheskikh materialov Velikoi Otechestvennoi voiny* [Collection of materials], no. 9 (Moscow: Voenizdat, 1953); *Sbornik voenno-istoricheskikh materialov Velikoi Otechestvennoi voiny* [Collection of materials], no. 12 (Moscow: Voenizdat, 1953); *Sbornik voenno-istoricheskikh materialov Velikoi Otechestvennoi voiny* [Collection of materials] no. 13 (Moscow: Voenizdat, 1954); *Sbornik voenno-istoricheskikh materialov Velikoi Otechestvennoi voiny* [Collection of materials] no. 14 (Moscow: Voenizdat, 1954); *Sbornik materialov po izucheniiu opyta voiny* [Collection of materials for the study of war experience], no. 5 (March 1943) (Moscow: Voenizdat, 1943); *Sbornik materialov po izucheniiu opyta voiny* [Collection of materials for the study of war experience], no. 10 (January–February 1943) (Moscow: Voenizdat, 1944); *Sbornik materialov po izucheniiu opyta voiny* [Collection of materials for the study of war experience], no. 14 (September–October 1944) (Moscow: Voenizdat, 1945); A. A. Volkov, *Kriticheskii prolog: Nezavershennye frontovye nastupatel'nye operatsii pervykh kampanii Velikoi Otechestvennoi voiny* [Critical prologue: Incompleted *front* offensive operations in the initial campaigns of the Great Patriotic War] (Moscow: Aviar, 1992); David M. Glantz, *Forgotten Battles of the German-Soviet War (1941–1945), volume V: The Summer–Fall Campaign (1 July–31 December 1943),* part 2 (Carlisle, PA: Self-published, 2000); G. I. Berdnikov, *Pervaia udarnaia* [First Shock (Army)] (Moscow: Voenizdat, 1985); F. D. Pankov, *Ognennye rubezhi: boevoi put' 50-i armii v Velikoi Otechestvennoi voine* [Fiery lines: The combat path of the 50th Army in the Great Patriotic War] (Moscow: Voenizdat, 1984); S. M. Sarkis'ian, *51-aia armiia* [51st Army] (Moscow: Voenizdat, 1983); G. G. Semonov, *Nastupaet udarnaia* [The shock (army) attacks] (Moscow: Voenizdat, 1988); P. K. Altukhov, ed., *Nezabyvaemye dorogy: Boevoi put' 10-i gvardeiskoi armii* [Unforgettable roads: The combat path of the 10th Guards Army] (Moscow: Voenizdat, 1974); D. Z. Muriev, *Proval operatsii 'Taifun'* [The defeat of Operation Typhoon] (Moscow: Voenizdat, 1966); *Voennoe isskustvo vo Vtoroi Mirovoi voine* [Military art in the Second World War] (Moscow: Voroshilov Academy, 1973); A. V. Vasil'ev, *Rzhevsko-Viazemskaia operatsiia Kalininskogo i Zapadnogo frontov (ianvar'–fevral' 1942 g.)* [The Kalinin and Western Fronts' Rzhev-Viaz'ma operation (January-February 1942] (Moscow: Voroshilov Academy, 1949); V. P. Istomin, *Smolenskaia nastupatel'naia operatsiia (1943 g.)* [The Smolensk offensive operation (1943)] (Moscow: Voenizdat, 1975); *Voenno-istoricheskii zhurnal,* no. 10 (October 1982) and A. V. Vladimirsky, *Na kievskom napravlenii* [On the Kiev axis] (Moscow: Voenizdat, 1989).

CHAPTER 7

Tank, Mechanized, and Cavalry Forces

The Soviet Union expended considerable time, resources, and energy during the late 1920s and most of the 1930s developing advanced theories, techniques, and forces necessary for the Red Army to conduct mobile warfare more effectively at the strategic, operational, and tactical levels. As a result, by 1938 the Red Army's force structure included an imposing array of mobile armored forces, including four powerful tank corps and numerous tank brigades, whose combat employment in wartime was governed by well-developed theories of "deep battle" and "deep operations."

Ironically, in November 1939, less than six months before Germany unleashed devastating blitzkrieg war in the West, the Soviet Union seemed to abandon its devotion to the theory of deep operations by abolishing the Red Army's fledgling but potentially powerful tank corps, ostensibly because Soviet-trained tank forces performed badly during the Spanish Civil War. In reality, however, it did so because Stalin had eliminated most of the Red Army's leading proponents of deep operational theory in his vicious purges of the late 1930s.

The spectacular successes the *Wehrmacht* and *Luftwaffe* achieved in the spring of 1940, when they employed blitzkrieg techniques to vanquish the British and French armies with unprecedented ease, both astonished and frightened the Soviet political and military leadership. Already disconcerted over the Red Army's dismal performance in its war with Finland during the winter of 1939–40, in the wake of the Germans' dramatic victory in the West, during 1940 and 1941, the NKO (People's Commissariat of Defense) frantically attempted to reform the Red Army's force structure by creating a large force of immense new mechanized corps to enable it to contend with the more experienced *Wehrmacht* should Hitler unleash it against the Soviet Union.

When Operation Barbarossa began on 22 June 1941, the NKO was in the midst of fielding 29 new mechanized corps, each consisting of two tank divisions and one motorized division, with a total strength of 36,000 men and 1,031 tanks. As imposing as these massive corps were on paper, though, none of them had their full complement of tanks and other vehicles, and in terms of command and control, personnel training, communications, and logistical support, none were suited to conduct, sustain, or survive in high-intensity combat operations.

Like a veritable wrecking ball, the *Wehrmacht* destroyed or decimated most of the Red Army's mechanized corps and over 10,000 of the Red Army's more than 23,000 tanks during the first month of Operation Barbarossa, leaving the few surviving corps as a pitiful reminder of the Red Army's once imposing mobile force structure. Acknowledging Operation Barbarossa's devastating effects, the *Stavka* abolished its surviving mechanized corps in August 1941, replacing them, first, with smaller tank divisions, and, later, with far smaller but more numerous tank brigades and tank battalions, on the assumption that their inexperienced commanders could more effectively command, control, and employ these smaller forces in combat.

Although correct, the *Stavka's* decision to abolish the Red Army's large tank formations also proved costly by significantly reducing Red Army's combat capabilities and increasing its casualties and materiel losses. After the Red Army struck back at the *Wehrmacht* with incessant but ultimately futile counterattacks, counterstrokes, and counteroffensives during the summer and fall of 1941 and in a more successful counteroffensive at Moscow during the winter of 1941–42, the *Stavka* realized the Red Army lacked a tank and mechanized force with sufficient power to defeat the *Wehrmacht's* motorized (panzer) forces and sustain operations into the strategic depths.

Simply stated, the cavalry, ski, and airborne forces the Red Army employed to conduct deep exploitations during its offensives around Moscow and elsewhere along the front during the winter campaign of 1941–42 vividly demonstrated to the *Wehrmacht* and *Stavka* alike how fragile these mobile forces were and convinced the *Stavka* of the necessity for fielding new tank and mechanized formations so that the Red Army could fulfill the strategic missions assigned to it in the future. Based on these experiences, in early 1942 the *Stavka* and NKO began creating a new mobile force structure within the Red Army that could prevail on the battlefield and sustain deep operations.

Prior to and during the Germans' second major offensive of the war, Operation *Blau*, the Red Army raised and fielded, in succession, new tank corps, tank armies, and mechanized corps designed to accord it a capability for conducting successful deep operations. After considerable experimentation and numerous operational failures, this new force structure proved its viability in the Battle of Stalingrad and the Red Army's winter offensive of 1942–43.

By 1 January 1943, the Red Army included a formidable force of 2 tank armies, 20 tank corps, and 8 mechanized corps designed specifically to conduct mobile operations at the operational level and an imposing array of tank and mechanized brigades and regiments capable of supporting its rifle forces at the tactical level. At the operational level, the Red Army's tank armies were its premier armored force. By definition, tank armies were operational large formations *(ob"edineniia)* roughly equivalent in size to German panzer corps but far less mobile, and tank and mechanized corps were operational-tactical formations *(soedineniia)* equivalent in size to German panzer and panzer grenadier divisions, but with significantly less motorized infantry.

Operating singly or in combination as mobile groups *(podvizhnye gruppy)* subordinate to the Red Army's operating *fronts*, by early 1943 the tank armies were responsible for conducting operational maneuver by exploiting tactical penetrations into the operational depths of the enemy's defenses and, thereafter, spearheading pursuit operations into the strategic depths. Operating either in groups of two or three subordinate to tank armies or singly within operating *fronts* and combined-arms armies, by this time the Red Army's tank and mechanized corps were responsible for converting tactical into operational success by exploiting tactical penetrations and initiating exploitation operations into the enemy's shallow operational depths.

The separate tank brigades, tank regiments, and tank battalions within the Red Army's field armies and rifle corps were responsible for providing direct armored support to strengthen the defenses of their parent rifle forces and to assist them when penetrating enemy defenses while on the offensive. In reality, however, the relative weakness of the Red Army's field armies in early 1943, as well as the imposing strength of the *Wehrmacht's* defenses, frequently forced Red Army *front* and army commanders to employ their tank armies and tank and mechanized corps prematurely to complete their penetration operations, usually at considerable cost in manpower and weaponry losses to these precious mobile forces. Over time, however, as the NKO increased the number and strength of the Red Army's tank armies, tank and mechanized corps, and infantry support tank regiments, it decreased sharply the number of separate tank brigades and battalions within the Red Army.

TANK AND MECHANIZED FORCES

Mechanized Corps

The nucleus of the Red Army's mobile armored and mechanized force on the eve of war were nine mechanized corps the NKO began forming on 6 July 1940 and another 20 it formed between March and June 1941.[1] The NKO formed these powerful corps in the wake of the *Wehrmacht's* victory in the Low Countries and France so that the Red Army would have an armored force capable of engaging and defeating German motorized (panzer) corps should war occur.

Significantly larger than the four tank corps the Red Army included in 1938, these mechanized corps consisted of two tank divisions, one motorized division, a motorcycle regiment, signal and motorized engineer battalions, an aviation troop, and small logistical elements for a strength on paper of 36,080 men, 1,031 tanks, including 126 KV and 420 T-34 tanks, 358 guns and mortars, 268 armored cars, 5,165 vehicles, and 352 tractors.[2]

The tank divisions subordinate to these corps consisted of two tank regiments, one motorized rifle regiment, and one artillery regiment, antitank, antiaircraft, signal, reconnaissance, and pontoon-bridge battalions, and small logistical elements for a strength of 11,343 men (reduced to 10,940 in 1941), 60 guns and mortars, and 375 tanks, including 63 KV and 270 T-34 models, and the motorized divisions fielded two motorized rifle regiments, one tank regiment, and one artillery regiment, and supporting subunits similar to those found in the tank division for a strength of 11,650 men, 98 guns and mortars, 275 light tanks, and 49 armored cars.

Although the NKO planned to complete fielding its new mechanized corps in the summer of 1942, the deteriorating international situation in May and June 1941 forced it to accelerate the formation process. As a result, when war began most of these corps were still seriously understrength in tanks, weaponry, and other equipment, and the officers and men who manned them were still largely untrained. Even the strongest of these corps, the first nine deployed in the western military districts, suffered from many of these problems, and, as war indicated, were not yet capable of conducting effective combat operations. Therefore, the *Wehrmacht* destroyed or decimated most of these mechanized corps on the field of battle during the first three weeks of Operation Barbarossa.

Separate Tank Divisions

On 19 July 1941, after the NKO had abolished the Red Army's surviving mechanized corps on 15 July, the NKO converted several of the tank divisions in mechanized corps that had survived the *Wehrmacht* onslaught into so-called 100-series tank divisions. Initially, these divisions included the 101st, 102nd, 104th, 105th, 108th, 109th, and 110th Tank Divisions and the 103rd and 106th Motorized Rifle Divisions, and the 111th and 112th Tank Divisions, which the NKO formed later in 1941.[3] Because they included tank platoons with three instead of five tanks, triangular rifle companies with three platoons of three squads each, and reduced quantities of weaponry, these tank divisions were far lighter than those fielded in the original mechanized corps.

These new model separate tank divisions consisted of a headquarters element, a reconnaissance battalion with ten T-40 light tanks, two tank regiments made up of one medium tank battalion and two light tank battalions with a total of 90 tanks each, one motorized rifle regiment, an artillery regiment, an antiaircraft battalion, and service support provided by transport, maintenance, and medical battalions for a strength on paper of 180 tanks.[4] The tank regiments within these divisions fielded medium tank battalions consisting of one heavy tank company with ten KV tanks and two medium tank companies with ten T-34 tanks each for a total of 30 tanks and light tank battalions consisting of three light tank companies with ten T-26 or BT tanks each for a total of 30 tanks.

In addition to their three rifle battalions, the tank divisions' motorized rifle regiments included an antitank battery with six 45mm guns, a mortar battery with four 120mm mortars, and a field gun battery with four 76mm regimental guns, and the tank divisions' artillery regiments consisted of three battalions, each fielding two batteries with four 76mm guns and one battery with four 122mm guns. Finally, the divisions' antiaircraft battalions consisted of three batteries with four 25mm or 37mm antiaircraft guns each.[5]

However, since continuing shortages of tanks and other combat weaponry prevented the NKO from maintaining these divisions at or even near full strength, by mid-August it had either disbanded most of these divisions or converted them into new and smaller tank brigades. Ten of these divisions were formed in 1941, but only three remained by October 1941, specifically, the 112th in the Western Front, which was converted into a tank brigade in early 1942, and the 61st and 111th, which remained in the Far East until war's end (see Appendix 1 in companion volume for all tank, mechanized, and cavalry forces in the Red Army).

Separate Tank and Motorized Rifle Brigades

On 12 August 1941, after the Red Army's prewar mechanized corps and wartime tank divisions failed to live up to its expectations, the NKO began forming the Red Army's first separate tank brigades to replace the destroyed or disbanded mechanized corps and to provide necessary support to the Red Army's beleaguered rifle forces. The original GKO (State Defense Committee) order upon which the NKO order was based required the NKO to form 120 tank brigades numbered one through 120 between August and December 1941, each consisting of 91 tanks, including seven KV, 20 T-34, and 64 T-60 tanks and a strength of 3,268 men.[6] Soon after, however, the NKO added two more T-34 tanks to this structure, presumably as command tanks, and reduced the brigades' manpower to more realistic levels.

Ultimately, these new tank brigades consisted of a single tank regiment with one composite battalion equipped with medium and heavy tanks and two battalions of light tanks, one motorized rifle and one antiaircraft battalion, and reconnaissance, maintenance, auto-transport, and medical companies, for a total strength of 1,943 men and 93 tanks, including seven KV heavy, 22 T-34 medium, and 64 T-40 light tanks (see Table 7.1 for the organization and strength of tank brigades from 1941 to 1943).[7]

However, since the regimental headquarters in these tank brigades unduly complicated command and control and the brigades proved clumsy and ineffective in combat, the NKO restructured them in September by eliminating the regimental headquarters and one of the brigade's light tank battalions. The new tank brigade consisted of two composite tank battalions with a mixture of light, medium, and heavy tanks; one motorized rifle battalion; and reconnaissance, maintenance, auto-transport, and medical companies, for a strength of 67 tanks, including seven KV heavy, 22 T-34 medium, and 39 T-40 light tanks.[8] The NKO raised and fielded 20 separate tank brigades through September 1941.

Dissatisfied by the performance of the separate tank brigades it had formed in August and September 1941, and after experimenting with new types of tank brigades suited to operate separately or in support of either rifle or cavalry forces, the NKO began fielding more streamlined tank brigades in December 1941. The new tank brigades consisted of two composite tank battalions and one motorized rifle battalion, supported by reconnaissance, maintenance, and auto-transport companies and a medical platoon. Their subordinate tank battalions contained one heavy tank company with two platoons and a total of five KV tanks, a medium company with three platoons and a total of ten T-34 tanks, and a light tank company with two platoons and a total of eight tanks. These tank battalions fielded 23 tanks, while their parent brigades had a strength of 1,471 men and 46 tanks, including ten KV tanks, 16 T-34 tanks, and 20 T-60 tanks. Even though they proved far more flexible and effective than their predecessor, their mixture of heavy, medium, and light tanks also limited their combat capabilities.

In addition to the numerous tank brigades it had formed by December 1941, in January 1942 the NKO attempted to form additional tank brigades uniquely structured to support rifle and cavalry divisions. Stripped of their motorized rifle battalion, these brigades consisted of two composite tank battalions, with ten KV, 16 T-34, and 20 T-60 tanks in the rifle version and 20 T-34 and 26 T-60 tanks in the cavalry version, with a strength of 372 men.[9] However, tank shortages prevented the NKO from fielding more than just a few of these tank brigades.

When the NKO began forming new tank corps during the spring of 1942, it also formed stronger, more streamlined, and better-organized tank brigades. When fully operational in July, these new tank brigades consisted of two tank battalions, the first equipped with medium tanks and the second with a mixture of medium and light models, a newly reorganized motorized rifle battalion, and an improved antitank capability in the form of a company of four 76mm antitank guns.

The new tank brigade's medium tank battalion, which had a strength of 151 men, consisted of two medium tank companies with three platoons fielding three T-34 tanks each, plus three T-34 company and battalion command tanks for a total of 21 T-34 tanks. The mixed tank battalion had three companies, one company with three platoons fielding three T-34 tanks each, and two companies with three platoons equipped with three T-70 tanks, plus three command tanks for a battalion total of ten T-34 and 21 T-70 tanks. Including the commander's tank, the tank brigade's total strength was 1,038 men and 53 tanks, including 32 T-34 and 21 T-70 tanks.[10]

During the same period, the NKO formed new separate motorized rifle brigades to provide motorized infantry support within the Red Army's tank corps and, in a few instances, to operate as separate entities. Initially, these motorized rifle brigades each consisted of three motorized rifle battalions, mortar, artillery, and antiaircraft artillery battalions, submachine-gun and antitank rifle companies, and service support subunits. The motorized rifle brigade's strength was 3,162 men, twelve 76mm guns, twelve 45mm guns, twelve 37mm guns, thirty 82mm mortars, four 120mm mortars, and 54 antitank rifles (see Table 7.2).[11]

The NKO exploited the Red Army's field combat experiences throughout the remainder of 1942 and into early 1943 in order to modify and rationalize the structure of the Red Army's tank and motorized rifle brigades to improve their effectiveness and survivability in field combat. The most important of these changes was the NKO's decision to equip the tank brigades' tank battalions with single types of either medium or light tanks. The NKO also adopted a uniform organizational structure for its motorized rifle brigades, which consisted of three motorized rifle battalions, one artillery, mortar, and antiaircraft battalion, and various rear service support subunits by the end of 1942. After fielding 20 separate tank brigades through September 1941, the NKO increased their number to 76 by 1 January 1942. Thereafter, while the NKO enlarged and strengthened the Red Army's tank force by forming new tank corps, it initially increased the number of separate tank brigades to 125 by 1 July 1942.

When the NKO increased the size and strength of the Red Army's mobile forces in 1943, it also increased the number and strength of its tank brigades. However, at the same time, it decreased the number of separate tank brigades and separate battalions in the Red Army and increased the number and variety of separate tank regiments as well as the range of missions these regiments performed. The decline in the number of separate tank brigades occurred principally because the NKO incorporated many of these units into its new tank armies and tank and mechanized corps. As a result, the number of separate tank brigades in the Red Army decreased from 125 on 1 July 1942 to 104 on 1 February 1943, to 101 on 1 July 1943, and to 83 on 31 December 1943, while the number of tank brigades assigned to tank armies and tank and mechanized corps increased from 69 on 2 February 1943 to 81 on 1 July and to 83 on 31 December.

Whether assigned to new tank and mechanized corps or operating separately, the NKO strengthened its tank brigades throughout 1943, primarily by replacing light tanks with medium models. The new tank brigade table of organization introduced by the NKO in November 1943 reorganized the brigades into a headquarters element with two T-34 tanks, three medium tank battalions with 21 T-34 tanks each, a motorized submachine-gun battalion, an antiaircraft machine-gun company, a trains company, and a medical platoon.

These new tank brigades included new medium tank battalions consisting of two tank companies equipped with ten T-34 tanks each and one command tank for a total of 21 T-34 tanks, and the submachine-gun battalion, which replaced the former motorized rifle battalion, consisted of three submachine-gun companies with three platoons each. These changes increased the strength of tank brigades to 1,354 men and 65 T-34 tanks and dramatically improved the brigades' firepower by replacing riflemen with submachine gunners.[12]

Separate Tank Battalions

Since the Red Army's operating *fronts* and armies experienced problems with supporting its relatively large tank brigades logistically during the initial period of the war, on 23 August 1941 the NKO also began fielding separate tank battalions to support its rifle forces. The first of these tank battalions consisted of a headquarters with two T-34 tanks, one medium tank company with two platoons and a total of seven T-34 tanks, and two light tank companies with three platoons each and a total of 20 T-40 or T-60s tanks, for a battalion strength of 130 personnel and 29 tanks.

However, although these battalions did prove capable of conducting effective defensive operations, the preponderance in them of light tanks made them too fragile to conduct successful offensive operations. Therefore, in November 1941 the NKO began fielding heavier separate tank battalions, each of which consisted of a headquarters company with one T-34 tank, a heavy tank company with two platoons and a total of five KV tanks, a medium tank company with two platoons and a total of ten T-34 tanks, and two light tank companies with a total of 20 T-40 or T-60 tanks. Manned by 202 men, the new tank battalion fielded 36 tanks, including five KV heavy, 11 T-34 medium, and 20 T-60 light tanks.[13] After the NKO fielded 52 separate tank battalion in September 1941 and raised this total to 100 by 1 January 1942, the total number of separate tank battalions in the Red Army thereafter shrank steadily to 80 on 1 July 1942.

In early 1943 separate tank battalions consisted of one heavy, one medium, and two light tank companies with a total of 36 tanks, including five KV, 11 T-34, and 20 T-70 tanks, manned by 198 officers and noncommissioned officers. However, as the NKO fielded new infantry support tank regiments in late 1942 and 1943, the utility of separate tank battalions decreased and the

NKO reduced their number to 63 on 1 February 1943, 45 on 1 July, and 26 on 31 December. Thereafter, it assigned these battalions primarily to areas such as Karelia, the Leningrad, Volkhov, and Caucasus regions, and the internal military districts, where heavier tank forces could not operate effectively.

Separate Tank Regiments

Another reason why the number of separate tank brigades in the Red Army decreased in 1943 was because the NKO replaced them with many new types of separate tank regiments specifically tailored to support rifle forces, particularly during penetration operations. Although the NKO formed several experimental separate tank regiments in early 1942, it did not begin doing so in earnest until September 1942. By this time, separate tank regiments were organized in the same fashion as those assigned to mechanized brigades and corps, that is, they consisted of two medium tank companies with 11 T-34 tanks each, one light tank company with 16 T-70 tanks, and a headquarters command tank for a strength of 339 men and 39 tanks, including 23 T-34 and 16 T-70 tanks (see Table 7.3 for the organization and strength of tank regiments from 1941 to 1943).

When it began strengthening the Red Army's tank and mechanized force structure in January 1943, the NKO also reorganized its tank regiments into a uniform structure. These new tank regiments consisted of a headquarters company with two T-34 tanks, three medium tank companies with ten T-34 tanks each, one light tank company with seven T-70 tanks, a 94-man submachine-gun company, and an antitank rifle platoon with 18 antitank rifles, for a regimental strength of 572 men, 39 tanks, including 32 T-34 and seven T-70 tanks, and three armored cars.[14]

As with its tank brigades, beginning in mid-1943, the NKO also began replacing the light tanks in its tank regiments with T-34 tanks, a process it finally completed in February 1944. By that time, tank regiments assigned to mechanized brigades and some separate tank regiment consisted of three tank companies and a total of 35 T-34 tanks and 401 men, while other separate tank regiments retained the 39-tank structure.[15]

In addition to its standard tank regiments, in late 1942 and 1943, the NKO also began fielding special types of tank regiments specifically tailored to perform such critical combat functions as destroying fortified enemy field positions and clearing minefields to facilitate the advance of Red Army mobile forces. For example, in October 1942, the NKO began removing heavy KV tanks from its tank brigades and separate tank battalion and consolidating them in new guards separate heavy tank penetration regiments. The NKO configured these new "bunker-busting" heavy tank regiments to support rifle forces during penetration operations through prepared enemy defenses in an attempt to avoid the catastrophic tank losses that normally occurred during these operations. These tank penetration regiments consisted of a headquarters element with one heavy command tank, four heavy tank companies equipped with five KV-1 or KV-2 tanks each, a maintenance company, and one armored car for the regimental commander and his staff with a regimental strength of 215 men, 21 KV tanks, and one light armored car.[16]

Later still, in June 1943 the NKO reconfigured some of its separate tank regiments as engineer tank regiments, which it tasked with clearing minefields and other manmade obstacles from Red Army main attack axes. These regiments were equipped with 22 T-34 tanks, 16 equipped with mine rollers, and 18 PT-3 amphibious tanks suited for crossing minor water obstacles. The NKO formed and fielded a total of 77 separate tank regiments from September through December 1942, including 15 heavy tank penetration versions. Thereafter, the number of tank regiments in the Red Army increased steadily to 94 on 1 February 1943, to 110 on 1 July, and to 115, including 34 heavy and several engineer tank versions, by 31 December.

Tank Corps

Shortly after completing its winter campaign of 1941–42, the *Stavka* directed the NKO to reorganize and enlarge the Red Army's tank and mechanized force during the spring and summer of 1942. This process took place in two stages, the first involving the formation of tank corps, primarily from March through July 1942, and the second involving the formation of mechanized corps, primarily from September through November 1942.

The NKO formed the Red Army's first four tank corps, numbered the 1st through the 4th, on 31 March 1942. These tank corps, which were simple combinations of existing tank and motorized rifle brigades without any additional fire or logistical support, consisted of two tank brigades and one motorized rifle brigade with a paper strength of 5,603 men and 100 tanks, including 20 KV, 40 T-34, and 40 T-70 tanks (see Table 7.4 for the organization and strength of Army tank corps in 1942 and 1943).

However, since the initial field tests indicated that these corps were too weak to accomplish their assigned tasks, in April the NKO added a third tank brigade to the corps and thereafter began supplementing each corps with additional fire and logistical support. As a result, by July 1942 the Red Army fielded several types of tank corps, ranging in strength from 146 to 180 tanks. Although one type included a tank brigade equipped primarily with KV heavy tanks, at least in theory, all of the corps included a reserve of 8 T-34 tanks. In addition, the NKO assigned a fuel supply company to tank corps in June and guards-mortar and reconnaissance battalions to each corps in July. Overall, the NKO formed 28 tank corps from early April through 31 December 1942, including four tank corps in March, nine more in April, six in May, four in June, three in July, and two in December (see Table 7.5). After the NKO converted several of these tank corps into mechanized corps in late 1942, the Red Army contained 20 tank corps on 1 January 1943.

In early 1943 the Red Army's tank corps consisted of a corps headquarters equipped with 3 T-34 tanks, three tank brigades, one motorized rifle brigade, reconnaissance and guards-mortar battalions, and sapper-mine, fuel transport, and two maintenance companies, the latter to service the artillery and tanks, for a strength of 7,853 men and 168 tanks, including 98 T-34 and 70 T-70 tanks, 38 guns, including twenty-four 76mm field, twelve 45mm antitank, and two 37mm antiaircraft guns, and 52 mortars, including forty-eight 82mm and four 120mm mortars, eight *Katiusha* multiple-rocket launchers, and, at least on paper, 20 armored cars. These tank corps were stronger then their predecessors, but they still lacked adequate artillery, antitank, antiaircraft, and engineer support.

The tank corps' component tank brigades consisted of a brigade headquarters and headquarters company equipped with one T-34 tank, one medium tank battalion with 31 T-34 tanks, one light tank battalion with 21 T-70 tanks, a motorized rifle battalion, an antitank battery with four 76mm antitank guns, a technical support detachment of company size, and a medical point (platoon), for a total of 1,038 men and 53 tanks, including 32 T-34 and 21 T-70 tanks.

The tank brigades' medium tank battalions consisted of a headquarters and headquarters platoon equipped with one T-34 tank, two medium tank companies with 10 T-34 tanks each, and a supply and trains group, for a strength of 151 men and 21 T-34 tanks, while the brigades' light tank battalions contained a headquarters and headquarters platoon with one T-70 tank, two companies of ten T-70 tanks, and a supply and trains (logistics) company, had a total strength of 146 personnel and 21 tanks. Finally, the tank brigades' motorized rifle battalions were organized into a headquarters and headquarters platoon, two rifle companies with 112 men each, a submachine-gun company, a mortar company with six 82mm mortars, and a medical platoon, for a total strength of 403 men.

The tank corps' motorized rifle brigades consisted of a headquarters section, three motorized rifle battalions, a battalion each of 82mm mortars, 76mm guns, and 37mm antiaircraft artillery, antitank rifle, automatic weapons, reconnaissance, engineer-mine, headquarters, and technical support companies (batteries), and a medical platoon. These brigades numbered 3,537 men and fielded twelve 76mm field guns, twelve 45mm antitank guns, twelve 37mm antiaircraft guns, thirty 82mm and four 120mm mortars, and 54 antitank rifles. Since these motorized rifle brigades lacked tracked armored transporters, their riflemen were forced to operate either on foot or riding on the hulls of the accompanying tanks.

The NKO labored feverishly throughout the first six months of 1943 to eliminate the tank corps' obvious shortcomings by strengthening their structure and the structure of their subordinate brigades. For example, on 10 January it ordered the addition of mortar and self-propelled artillery regiments and reserve tank detachments to each tank corps and antiaircraft batteries equipped with four 37mm guns and four DShK machine guns to each tank brigade. These new mortar regiments consisted of two 120mm mortar battalions with three batteries of six mortars each, for a total of 36 mortars, and the self-propelled artillery regiments consisted of six batteries fielding a total of 17 SU-76 or eight SU-122 self-propelled guns. Although the reserve tank detachments assigned to each tank corps were supposed to number 147 men and 40 replacement tanks each, including 33 T-34 and seven T-70 tanks, few of these detachments were at full strength. Finally, the NKO also improved the capabilities of the tank corps' fuel supply companies.

After analyzing the Red Army's experiences, in particular its mobile forces, during the Battle of Stalingrad and in its subsequent winter offensive, in February 1943 the NKO began altering the structure of its tank corps and brigades to enable them to operate more effectively deep in the enemy's rear area. It did so, incrementally, first by converting the corps' engineer-mine company into an engineer-sapper battalion in February and then, in March, by consolidating the brigades' antiaircraft batteries into a full corps antiaircraft artillery battalion equipped with sixteen 37mm guns and by replacing the corps' signal company with a battalion.

The NKO continued this process in April by adding an antitank artillery regiment with twenty 45mm antitank guns, an aviation liaison detachment with PO-2 aircraft, a field auto-bread bakery, and a medical platoon to its tank corps and in May by adding an antitank artillery battalion with twelve 76mm or 85mm antitank guns to the corps and by converting corps' mixed composition self-propelled artillery regiments into heavy self-propelled regiments, each armed with 12 SU-152 guns.[17]

In late August the NKO replaced the corps' towed antitank artillery regiments and battalions with two self-propelled artillery regiments, a light version fielding 21 SU-76 self-propelled guns and a medium version with 16 SU-122 self-propelled guns and one T-34 tank. Finally, in November the NKO improved the tank corps' reconnaissance capability by replacing their armored car battalions with motorcycle battalions, each consisting of two motorcycle, one tank, and one armored car company and an antitank artillery battery.[18]

The cumulative effect of these measures doubled the tank corps' personnel, tank, and self-propelled artillery strength, eased maintenance problems by reducing the number of tank models in the corps from four (KV, T-34, T-60, and T-70 tanks) to one (T-34–85 tanks), and, at the same time, increased the tanks' firepower and armored protection, measurably improving the corps' combat performance and sustainability. However, since this process went on incrementally, many tank corps fought on throughout 1943 without experiencing these structural improvements.

Mechanized Corps and Brigades

The poor combat performance of two of the Red Army's new tank corps at Khar'kov in May 1942 and as many as 14 others during the initial stages of Operation *Blau* in July and August 1942 demonstrated that these corps were not yet capable of conducting sustained offensive operations. Not only was the tank corps' motorized infantry, which totaled only 15 small rifle companies and lacked adequate transport, far too weak to protect the tank force adequately, but, worse still, the tank corps' artillery was also too weak and immobile to support its parent corps in either close combat or exploitation operations.

The NKO sought to remedy these problems in September 1942 when it began forming mechanized corps containing substantially more motorized infantry, artillery, and antitank support than the existing tank corps. The first two of these corps formed on 2 September and the NKO fielded six more by 31 December 1942. Since the new mechanized corps were formed from disparate sources and tailored to operate in vastly differing types of terrain, their composition varied substantially (see Table 7.6).

NKO fielded three distinctive types of mechanized corps by 31 December 1942, all of which formed around a nucleus of three mechanized brigades, antitank and antiaircraft artillery regiments, guards-mortar, reconnaissance (armored car), sapper, medical, and repair and reconstruction (maintenance) battalions, an engineer-mine company and a fuel supply company (called by some sources a field repair base), and a field bakery. In addition, each of the mechanized corps' mechanized brigades had its own organic tank regiment with 39 T-34 tanks.

In addition to this common nucleus, depending on its type, mechanized corps fielded either one or two tank brigades or two tank regiments. The first type of mechanized corps included one tank brigade with 53 tanks, for a corps' tank strength of 175 tanks, including 100 T-34 and 74 T-60 or T-70 tanks; the second type of corps included two tank brigades with 53 tanks each, for an overall strength of 224 tanks. The third type of mechanized corps fielded two separate tank regiments, for a strength of 204 tanks (see Table 7.7 for the organization and strength of mechanized corps in 1942 and 1943).[19] In addition to the first eight mechanized corps formed in 1942, in January 1943 the NKO formed the 4th Guards Mechanized Corps from the 13th Tank Corps, which had already been organized as a mechanized corps in October 1942, with three mechanized brigades, two separate tank regiments, and normal supporting units and subunits.[20]

The NKO also formed two types of mechanized brigades in September 1942, the first as a separate brigade and the second subordinate to the mechanized corps. All of these brigades consisted of three motorized rifle battalions, an optional tank regiment, and maintenance, auto-transport, and administrative platoons (see Table 7.8 for the organization and strength of mechanized brigades in 1942 and 1943). Unlike those assigned to the tank corps' motorized rifle brigade, motorized rifle battalions assigned to mechanized brigades included a machine-gun company and an expanded antitank rifle company. The NKO had initially included a tank regiment only in separate mechanized brigades, but subsequently it added the tank regiment to the mechanized brigades assigned to the mechanized corps.

Whether organic to mechanized brigades or separate, tank regiments consisted of two medium tank companies with three platoons and a total of 11 T-34 tanks, a light tank company with three platoons and a total of 16 T-70 tanks, an antitank artillery company, and reconnaissance, auto-transport, and service support platoons. Including a command tank in the regimental headquarters, the strength of this tank regiment was 339 men and 39 tanks, including 23 T-34 and 16 T-70 tanks.[21]

As it had with the tank corps, the NKO also implemented major structural changes to improve the combat capabilities of its mechanized corps and brigades during 1943. This process began in 1 January, when it made tank regiments a permanent element of the corps' mechanized brigade and increased the number of medium tanks in the regiments at the expense of the lighter models. These new tank regiments consisted of three medium tank companies with one command tank and three platoons with three T-34 tanks each for a total of ten T-34 tanks, one light tank company with one command tank and two platoons with three T-70 or T-60 tanks each for a total of seven T-70 or T-60 tanks, and two regimental command tanks, for a total of 339 men and 39 tanks in the regiment, including 30 T-34 and nine T-70 or T-60 tanks. The new organization also added a submachine-gun company and an antitank rifle platoon to the tank regiment. Later in January, the NKO added mortar regiments, mixed self-propelled artillery regiments equipped with 25 SU-76 or 17 SU-76 and eight SU-122 self-propelled guns, and reserve tank detachments to the corps.[22]

However, as had been the case with tank corps, since these changes took time to implement, many modified mechanized corps and tank regiments coexisted for months with the older variants. Furthermore, in February 1943 the Red Army's mechanized corps still varied significantly in their composition.

Although all consisted of three mechanized brigades, antiaircraft and antitank artillery regiments, guards-mortar, motorcycle or armored car, repair and reconstruction, and medical battalions, and engineer-mine and supply companies, some had one or two tank brigades and other fielded two separate tank regiments. Thus the corps' strength varied from 13,559 to 15,018 men and from 175 to 224 tanks depending on the variant, supported by 98 guns, 148 mortars, and eight "*Katiusha*" multiple-rocket launchers. The most numerous of this variant, the corps with 204 tanks, fielded 162 T-34 and 42 T-70 tanks.

In February the mechanized corps' mechanized brigades consisted of a headquarters and headquarters company, three motorized rifle battalions, one tank regiment with three tank companies, mortar and artillery battalions, reconnaissance, submachine-gun, antitank rifle, antiaircraft machine-gun, sapper-mine, and train companies and a medical platoon. As described above, the mechanized brigade's tank regiments fielded 39 tanks, raising the mechanized brigades' total strength to 3,558 men, 39 tanks, and 60 guns and mortars.

After February 1943 the NKO altered its mechanized corps and brigades in similar fashion to its tank corps and brigades. For example, in March it replaced the air defense regiments provided to the corps by PVO (Antiaircraft Defense) with corps' antiaircraft artillery regiments each of which fielded 16 37mm antiaircraft guns and 16 DShK antiaircraft machine guns, and it expanded the corps' signal companies into full battalions. After simply renaming the corps' antitank artillery regiments tank destroyer artillery regiments in April, in May the NKO added separate antitank battalions to the corps, and in August it replaced the corps' composite SU-76 and SU-122 self-propelled artillery regiments with three self-propelled artillery regiments, one armed with SU-76 guns, one with SU-85 guns, and the third with SU-152 guns. By year's end in 1943, all of these self-propelled artillery regiments fielded a standard number of 21 self-propelled guns.[23]

Tank Armies

By mid-1942 the tank army was the most important large armored formation *(ob"edinenie)* in the Red Army specifically structured to perform operational missions under the control of the Red Army's operating *fronts.* The NKO began forming these armies on 25 May 1942, at first on an experimental basis, in an attempt to create armored formations capable of engaging and defeating the *Wehrmacht's* formidable motorized (panzer) corps. The 3rd and 5th Tank Armies, which joined the *Stavka* Reserve in late June, and the 1st and 4th Tank Armies, which were assigned to the Stalingrad Front in early July, were ad hoc formations formed around the nucleus of existing field army headquarters. Lacking an official common table of organization, they usually consisted of two tank corps, one to two rifle divisions, and a wide variety of supporting units, sometimes even a cavalry corps (see Table 7.9).

The *Stavka* committed these four tank armies to combat in July 1942 to contain the *Wehrmacht's* advance toward the Don River and Stalingrad during the initial stage of Operation *Blau.* The 5th Tank Army spearheaded the Briansk Front's counterstroke west of Voronezh in early July 1942 but was unable to prevent the Germans from capturing the city. Then, in late July, the *Stavka* employed three of its new tanks armies, the 5th, 1st, and 4th, in concerted but spectacularly unsuccessful counterstrokes west of Voronezh and on the approaches to Stalingrad.[24] Later still, in August 1942, the *Stavka* employed its 3rd Tank Army's 12th and 15th Tank Corps, reinforced by the 3rd Tank Corps, to spearhead an unsuccessful offensive by the 16th and 61st Armies of Zhukov's Western Front along the Zhizdra River north of Orel.

All of the Red Army's new tank armies performed poorly in combat primarily because their commanders lacked experience in conducting large-scale armored operations and their strange mixture of tracked armor, foot-bound infantry, and sometimes horse-mounted cavalry made them exceedingly difficult to control and coordinate effectively in mobile combat. As a result, at the *Stavka's* direction, the NKO disbanded the 1st Tank Army in September, using its headquarters to form the new Southeastern Front, and converted the remnants of the 4th Tank Army into the new 65th Army in November.

Despite their defeats in July and August 1942, the *Stavka* employed the 3rd and 5th Tank Armies with far greater success later in the year and in early 1943. After being abolished in early August and recreated in September, the 5th Tank Army's 1st and 16th Tank Corps spearheaded the Southwestern Front's advance during the Stalingrad counteroffensive and was instrumental in encircling German Sixth Army at Stalingrad. After failing to penetrate German defenses along the Chir River in early December 1942, in late December 1942 the reorganized 5th Tank Army's 1st Guards Tank, 1st Tank, 5th Mechanized, and 8th Cavalry Corps led the Southwestern Front's advance to the Mius River.[25] After transferring its mobile corps to other forces, the *Stavka* converted the 5th Tank Army into the new 12th Army in mid-April 1943.[26]

After resting and refitting for several months following its August defeat, the 3rd Tank Army spearheaded the Southwestern Front's advance during in the Ostrogozhsk-Rossosh' offensive of January 1943 and the Voronezh Front's advance through Khar'kov in February. However, after the 3rd Tank Army was encircled and destroyed during Manstein's counteroffensive in March 1943, the *Stavka* converted its remnants into the new 57th Army.

The *Stavka* formed the 2nd Tank Army, its fifth and last old-style tank army, which consisted of the 11th and 16th Tank Corps, the 60th, 112th, and 194th Rifle Divisions, the 115th Rifle, 28th Ski, and 11th Guards Tank

Brigades, and support units, on 10 January 1943.[27] This tank army led the Central Front's unsuccessful Orel-Briansk-Smolensk offensive west of Kursk in February and March 1943.

The *Stavka* was not satisfied with the checkered combat performance of its first five ad hoc tank armies, primarily because their subordinate forces lacked uniform mobility and the armies as a whole lacked adequate fire and logistical support. Therefore, on 28 January 1943, as a result of the General Staff's study and analysis of tank army operations during the last six months of 1942, the GKO ordered the NKO to form new tank armies whose common organizational structure resolved these problems.

These armies were to consist of:

> combat formations and units, including one tank and one mechanized corps, motorcycle, antitank artillery, howitzer artillery, and guards-mortar regiments, one antiaircraft artillery battalion; supporting units, including signal and aviation liaison (PO-2) regiments and an engineer battalion; rear service units and subunits, including an auto-transport regiment, two repair and reconstruction (maintenance) battalions; detachments and units providing medical, food, supply transport, collection, assembly, and evacuation of vehicles; and field installations to supply fuel and lubricants, ammunition, and communications and chemical equipment.
>
> The tank army's authorized personnel strength was 46,000 men, and its tank strength from 648 to 654 tanks.[28]

However, as was so often the case during the first two years of the war, the *Stavka* lacked sufficient resources to form very many tank armies in accordance with its January directive. After ordering the NKO to form its first new model tank army, the 1st Tank Army (2nd formation), within the Northwestern Front on 30 January, thereafter it ordered the NKO to form five more tank armies by July 1943 but disbanded one, the 4th Guards, shortly after its formation in February and March (see Table 7.10). Therefore, the NKO formed new tank armies as conditions permitted and staffed them as close to the ideal as possible. During the remainder of the war, however, few of these armies ever achieved the ideal configuration envisioned by the GKO's January 1943 directive. The NKO fielded its sixth and final wartime tank army in January 1944.

The composition of the Red Army's five tank armies varied substantially after July 1943, particularly regarding the quantity and designation of tank and mechanized corps assigned to them, though their combat and logistical support elements remained fairly stable (see Table 7.11).

During the last six months of 1943, tank armies normally consisted of a nucleus of two or three tank or mechanized corps supported by a separate tank brigade or one to two tank regiments, one or more self-propelled artillery regiments, a motorcycle regiment, a guards-mortar regiment, one or two tank destroyer regiments, less frequently another type of artillery regiment, an antiaircraft artillery division, a motorized engineer battalion, a separate signal regiment, an aviation liaison regiment, and logistical support subunits.

The separate tank brigade and or regiments, usually guards units, served as the tank army commander's tank reserve and, during exploitation operations, helped exploit success, reinforce forward operating mobile corps, protect the army's vulnerable flanks, or lead the pursuit configured as an army forward detachment *(peredovoi otriad)*. The assigned motorcycle regiment and, less frequently, a motorcycle or armored car battalion, conducted reconnaissance for the tank army and its subordinate corps. Finally, the antiaircraft artillery division protected the tank army from air attack, and self-propelled artillery, guards-mortar, and tank destroyer regiments provided accompanying fire support during the tank army's march to contact and exploitation.

As with other Red Army forces, the NKO had significantly increased the fire support available to its tank armies by the end of 1943. In addition to strengthening its tank and mechanized corps and their component tank and mechanized brigades and tank regiments as mentioned above, in a 10 April 1943 directive the NKO added many new fire support units to the tank army to improve its sustainability in combat. These included two antitank artillery regiments with twenty 76mm guns each, two mortar regiments with thirty-six 120mm mortars each, two self-propelled artillery regiments with nine SU-76 and 12 SU-122 self-propelled guns each, at least two antiaircraft artillery regiments with sixteen 37mm antiaircraft guns and 16 DShK machine guns each, and, ultimately, a full division, and a guards-mortar regiment with 24 BM-13 multiple-rocket launchers. These forces increased the tank army's artillery support to over 700 guns and mortars.[29]

By in the end of 1943, combat experience had demonstrated that the single motorized engineer battalion assigned to the tank armies, which consisted of three companies and a technical platoon, was not capable of performing complex river crossings without additional support, so the NKO replaced these battalions with full separate engineer brigades in 1944.[30] The tank army's separate signal regiment, which provided the army with all of its communications, consisted of two separate cable companies and either one separate telegraph-construction company or one separate telegraph-exploitation company. In addition, tank armies also included an aviation liaison regiment equipped with light PO-2 reconnaissance aircraft to provide aerial communications between the army, its parent *front*, and its subordinate corps.[31]

Regardless of their armored strength, tank armies required considerable logistical support to operate effectively and sustain their operations, particularly in terms of motor transport, maintenance, supply of fuel, lubricants, and spare parts, and recovery, evacuation, and repair of damaged armored vehicles, trucks, and other equipment. To satisfy their transport and supply needs, by July 1943 tank armies included two to four auto-transport battalions and, later, a full auto-transport regiment and, depending on the number of subordinate corps, two to three fuel and lubricant (GSM) auto-transport companies to resupply them with critical fuel and lubricants. Nevertheless, because of the Red Army's chronic shortage of trucks and other transport vehicles, the tank armies and their subordinate corps had only 70–80 percent of their authorized vehicles, specifically 1,300–1,400 out of 1,849 authorized trucks and other vehicles in each tank army and 1,100–1,150 out of 1,456 authorized for their subordinate corps.[32] Since tractors were in even shorter supply, many of the tank armies' subordinate corps and brigades simply had to go without.

Prior to and during combat operations, tank armies required subunits that could control their movements along roads and supply them with fuel, lubricants, ammunition, and other vital materials necessary to sustain them in prolonged deep operations. Therefore, in January 1943 the NKO began adding armored, artillery, automotive, engineer, food, chemical, technical, medical, veterinary, clothing, trophy (captured material), and commandants (road service and guides) detachments, communications and fuel and lubricants installations, and army base (depot) elements to the tank armies' structure to perform these vital logistical functions.[33]

No less important was the task of recovering, evacuating, repairing, and salvaging damaged tanks, self-propelled guns, artillery, and trucks, particularly during combat. Also beginning in January 1943, the NKO assigned its tank armies two repair-reconstruction (maintenance) battalions, two to three evacuation companies equipped with heavy tractors, and one to two collection points for assembling and protecting damaged combat vehicles. During the second half of the year, these subunits accomplished 85 percent of all of the tank armies' necessary low- and mid-level field repairs.

Despite all of these improvements to the tank armies' force structure, the NKO implemented these changes slowly and unevenly. As a result, while the tank army's average strength increased each year from 450–500 tanks and roughly 46,000 men in 1943 to up to 700 tanks and 50,000 men in 1945, the strength of individual tank armies varied widely within any given year (see Tables 7.12 and 7.13).

Aerosleigh Battalions

One of the most curious forces in the Red Army's tank and mechanized force structure was the aerosleigh *(aerosanyi)* battalion, which the NKO began forming in January 1942 in an attempt to beef up its ski forces in terms of firepower and armor protection. The NKO had formed 18 aerosleigh battalions by January 1942 and a total of 49 by May.

Aerosleigh battalions consisted of a headquarters and supply company fielding 10 cargo sleighs and three combat companies equipped with ten combat aerosleighs each. The aerosleigh companies consisted of three aerosleigh platoons, each with three aerosleighs, and a tenth command sleigh. Thus, the overall strength of the aerosleigh battalion was about 100 men equipped with about 45 NKL-16 or NKL-26 aerosleighs. The NKL-16 aerosleigh consisted of an armor-plated turret with a 7.62mm machine gun mounted on four skis. It was propelled by a rear-mounted aircraft-type engine and propeller and could transport four or five men. The NKL-26 aerosleigh had the same armament but was more powerful and more heavily armored.

The Red Army's operating *fronts* and armies employed aerosleigh battalions to conduct winter raids, combat enemy ski troops, and transport supplies during operations across difficult terrain in snowy winter conditions, often in close cooperation with standard ski battalions and brigades.[34] After disbanding all of these brigades by 1 July 1942 because the warm weather had rendered them superfluous, the NKO once again formed aerosleigh battalions in the late fall of 1942. Thereafter, these battalions operated only during the winter in regions that were normally covered by forests and heavy snow. Although their organization and strength did not change, the number of aerosleigh battalions in the Red Army decreased from 62 on 1 February 1943 to 57 at year's end and none at all remained in the Red Army by June 1944.

Armored Car and Motorcycle Forces

On the eve of the war, the Red Army planned to employ armored car and motorcycle units and subunits to reinforce the reconnaissance efforts of regular rifle and cavalry reconnaissance forces subordinate to its wartime operating *fronts* and armies. Since Soviet industry failed to produce a reliable armored car before war began, the motorcycle was the vehicle of choice in most reconnaissance units. Nevertheless, after war began, the NKO used older and obsolete armored cars to form several armored car battalions in 1941. By relying on these older models, as well as captured German vehicles, the Red Army was able to field one armored car battalion on 1 January 1942, five on 1 July 1942, and 20 on 1 February 1943.

If armored cars were in short supply in the Red Army on the eve of war, motorcycles were not. When Operation Barbarossa began, the Red Army included a motorcycle regiment in each of its 29 mechanized corps, and, after the NKO disbanded its mechanized corps in August 1941, 12 motorcycle regiments remained in the *Stavka* Reserve. Thereafter, the Red Army included seven motorcycle regiments on 1 January 1942, five on 1 July 1942, and one on 1 January 1943.

By late 1942 the Red Army's motorcycle regiments consisted of three motorcycle rifle companies, a mortar company equipped with eighteen 50mm mortars, an antitank battery with four 45mm guns, an armored car company with four armored cars, and small service support subunits for a total strength of about 900 men. Each motorcycle rifle company contained three rifle platoons and one machine-gun platoon for a total of 180 men, 54 submachine guns, and nine light and four medium machine guns.

The NKO also formed separate motorcycle battalions in 1942 whose primary missions were to conduct reconnaissance and patrolling, effect liaison between mobile forces, and provide commandant's (traffic control) services. Each of these rather fragile battalions consisted of two to three rifle companies and an armored car company manned by 287 men.[35] The NKO raised 19 of these battalions between March and September 1942 but later assigned most of them to the Red Army's tank and mechanized corps. The quantity of motorcycle battalions in the Red Army increased from one on 1 January 1942 to 16 on 1 July 1942 and 1 February 1943.

Finally, the NKO also formed a motorcycle brigade in May 1942, the only one of its kind in the war, which it assigned to the Western Front. The NKO disbanded this brigade, which consisted of three motorcycle battalions and was an anomaly, in February 1943.[36]

Like the aerosleigh battalions, high-intensity warfare rendered the Red Army's small force of armored car battalions utterly superfluous. Although the Red Army still included 20 of these subunits on 1 February 1943, by year's end this figure had decreased to only eight. The NKO distributed most of the armored cars from these disbanded subunits to its new tank and mechanized corps.

Conversely, as the NKO strengthened its tank armies, tank and mechanized corps, separate tank, motorized rifle, and mechanized brigades, and separate tank regiments in 1943, it also strengthened its motorcycle forces. In March 1943, for example, the NKO began forming three new motorcycle regiments with a new organization. These regiments consisted of a motorcycle battalion with three motorcycle rifle companies, an antitank battalion with two batteries of four 45mm antitank guns and one battery of four 76mm antitank guns, a tank company with 16 T-70 light tanks and, later, ten T-34 medium tanks, a sapper company, and an armored personnel carrier company equipped with Lend-Lease M3A1 scout cars.[37] The number of these motorcycle regiments in the Red Army increased from five on 1 February 1943 to eight on 31 December.

The NKO also reorganized and strengthened its motorcycle battalions during the summer of 1943 by adding to them a tank company equipped with ten T-34 tanks and by replacing one of the battalion's motorcycle rifle companies with an armored personnel carrier company, raising the battalion's strength to 451 men.[38] Despite these measures, after increasing from 16 on 1 February 1943 to 19 on 1 July 1943, the number of motorcycle battalions in the Red Army decreased sharply to only four on 31 December 1943.

Armored Trains

In addition to tank and mechanized forces suited to combat employment in the field, the Red Army also employed a sizable number of separate armored train battalions and separate armored trains throughout the war. Although these battalions and separate trains seemed anachronistic in light of their extensive employment during the Russian Civil War years, the absence of an adequate road network in the Soviet Union more than justified their existence.

After war began, the NKO routinely assigned one or two of these battalions to its operating *fronts* and, occasionally, one to individual armies. While the Red Army included only seven armored train battalions in June 1941, the NKO had fielded another 33 battalions and three separate armored trains by year's end. Thereafter, the total number of armored train battalions increased dramatically to 64 on 1 July 1942, 62 on 1 February 1943, 66 on 1 July 1943, and 61 on 31 December 1943.

These armored train battalions consisted of one armored train made up of an armored locomotive, two or more armored railroad cars or armored gun platforms, and two or more armored command and control rail cars.[39] Each armored train usually carried one or two antiaircraft guns and four to eight heavy antiaircraft machine guns. Although they routinely provided general fire support to ground forces, the armored train battalions' primary mission was to protect important rail facilities and junctions against *Luftwaffe* air attack. In some instances, multiple-rocket launchers were mounted on the armor trains to provide ground forces with general area fire support.

CAVALRY FORCES

As anachronistic as they seemed, the Red Army relied heavily on horse cavalry forces, particularly in an offensive role, during the initial period of the war, when its tank forces were in disarray, and thereafter when they proved capable of operating effectively in difficult terrain. Hence, cavalry forces contributed significantly to the Red Army's victories at Moscow in the winter of 1941–42, at Stalingrad in November and December 1942, in the Ukraine during the winter of 1943–44, in Belorussia during the summer of 1944, and in Manchuria during August 1945.

At least in part, this phenomenon can be attributed to Stalin's infatuation with cavalry dating back to the Civil War years, when he served as political commissar in S. M. Budenny's famous 1st Cavalry Army. More important still, combat experience proved that, when skillfully led and reinforced by tanks, cavalry was a formidable offensive tool, particularly when cooperating with large tank or mechanized forces. Furthermore, the mobility of the cavalry enabled it to maneuver more effectively despite the Soviet Union's underdeveloped road network, particularly during winter and in rough terrain and inclement weather. Therefore, the Red Army retained a sizable cavalry force throughout the war and employed it effectively, particular in offensive operations in regions where it was not feasible to employ large tank and mechanized formations.

The Red Army's force structure on the eve of war included four cavalry corps and 13 cavalry divisions totaling 80,000 cavalrymen. Its 2nd, 5th, and 6th Cavalry Corps with six cavalry divisions were subordinate to its field forces in the West, its 4th Cavalry Corps with three cavalry divisions was stationed in the Central Asian Military District, and its remaining four cavalry divisions were subordinate to internal military districts or nonoperating *fronts*. Finally, four of these divisions were configured as mountain cavalry divisions.

Like the rest of the Red Army's force structure in June 1941, although imposing on paper, the cavalry corps and divisions were quite weak. The standard cavalry corps consisted of two cavalry divisions, a signal squadron, and very limited support for a total strength of 19,430 men and 16,020 horses, 128 BT-5 light tanks, 36–44 armored cars, sixty-four 76mm field guns, thirty-two 45mm or 76mm antitank guns, forty 37mm antiaircraft guns, one hundred twenty-eight 50mm and 82mm mortars, 1,270 vehicles, and 42 tractors (see Table 7.14 for the organization and strength of cavalry corps in the period 1941–43).[40]

Separate cavalry divisions and those subordinate to the cavalry corps consisted of four cavalry regiments with five cavalry and one machine-gun squadron each, one light tank regiment with three squadrons, cavalry artillery, antiaircraft artillery, antitank, and reconnaissance battalions, signal and sapper squadrons, and chemical, transport, and supply subunits and had a strength of 9,240 men and 7,910 horses, 64 BT-5 light tanks, 18 armored cars, thirty-two 76mm or 122mm field guns, sixteen 45mm antitank guns, twenty 37mm antiaircraft guns, and sixty-four 50mm or 82mm mortars (see Table 7.15 for the organization and strength of cavalry divisions in the period 1941–43).[41] Lighter than their regular counterparts, mountain cavalry divisions were organized into three cavalry regiments and a light tank squadron instead of a full tank regiment.

Within days after Operation Barbarossa began, the *Wehrmacht* destroyed the 6th Cavalry Corps east of Belostok and severely damaged the 5th Cavalry Corps in the Ukraine. In the wake of this carnage, on 6 July 1941 the NKO truncated the Red Army's cavalry force by reducing the size, strength, and quantity of cavalry corps and the size of cavalry divisions. Specifically, it stripped one cavalry regiment, the tank regiment, the antiaircraft battalion, and all noncombat support subunits from the cavalry divisions and reduced the division's artillery battalion and signal squadron by one-half.

The new cavalry divisions consisted of three cavalry regiments, one cavalry artillery battalion, and signal, sapper, ammunition, supply, chemical, and medical squadrons for an overall strength of about 4,200 men. The divisions' cavalry regiments consisted of four mounted saber squadrons, one machine-gun squadron, one battery of four 76mm field guns and four 45mm antitank guns, and antiaircraft, sapper, signal, transport, medical, and veterinary platoons, for a strength of about 900 men, and the divisions' cavalry artillery battalion fielded two 76mm gun batteries and two 120mm mortar batteries. Although separate cavalry divisions were supposed to field a tank squadron equipped with ten T-40 light tanks and armored cars, the critical shortage of tanks prevented their formation.

By 31 December 1941, the NKO had also formed new light cavalry divisions each with 3,447 men to economize on manpower and horses. These light cavalry divisions consisted of three cavalry regiments, an artillery battalion with one battery of four 76mm M-27 guns, one battery of four 76mm M-39 guns, and one battery of four 82mm mortars, a half-signal squadron, and limited logistical support. The divisions' light cavalry regiment consisted of four saber squadrons, one machine-gun squadron with 128 submachine guns, an artillery battery with four 76mm and two 45mm guns, an antitank platoon with seven antitank rifles, a sapper platoon, and medical and supply sections.[42]

The NKO created 82 new cavalry divisions between July and December 1941, six of which were of the light variety, and by year's end had combined many of these divisions into new cavalry corps. This brought the total number of cavalry corps in the Red Army to seven on 1 January 1942 and the quantity of cavalry divisions to 82. In addition, the NKO had formed 7 separate cavalry regiments by 1 January 1942, most of which operated in regions unsuited for operations by full cavalry corps and divisions. These cavalry corps and divisions proved invaluable during the fighting in late summer 1941 and, later, during the Battle of Moscow and the Red Army's winter offensive of 1941–42, when, in lieu of heavier mobile forces, they spearheaded offensive operations and conducted deep exploitation operations into the *Wehrmacht's* rear area.[43] The number of cavalry corps, divisions, and regiments in the Red Army reached its peak during the later stages of its winter offensive, in February 1942, when it fielded 17 cavalry corps, 87 cavalry divisions, and two separate cavalry regiments.

The NKO strengthened the structure of its cavalry corps and divisions throughout 1942. In June the average cavalry corps consisted of three cavalry divisions, a cavalry artillery battalion with twelve 76mm field guns, an antiaircraft artillery battalion with twelve 37mm antiaircraft guns, an antitank battalion with twelve 45mm antitank guns, a mortar regiment with twenty 120mm mortars, a signal battalion, and medical, veterinary, supply, and chemical platoons, plus a small training battalion with an overall strength of roughly 14,000 men. At the same time, cavalry divisions consisted of three cavalry regiments, a cavalry artillery battalion with twelve 76mm field guns, an antitank artillery battalion with twelve 45mm antitank guns, an antiaircraft battery with six 37mm guns, signal and sapper squadrons, and support elements, for a strength of 4,619 men.[44]

Based on its experiences in 1941 and 1942, the *Stavka* in 1943 routinely assigned its cavalry corps and their subordinate divisions the mission of conducting deep exploitation operations, often in tandem with exploiting tank and mechanized formations. According to new tables of organization issued by the NKO in February 1943, by May cavalry corps were to consist of a headquarters, three cavalry divisions, antitank, self-propelled artillery, and antiaircraft artillery regiments, two mortar battalions, a signal squadron, medical, chemical, and NKVD platoons, field and veterinary hospitals, a training battalion, and small service elements, for a paper strength of 21,000 men, 19,000 horses, and 117 tanks.[45]

The February table of organization also strengthened cavalry divisions. On paper at least, cavalry divisions consisted of a headquarters, three cavalry regiments, a tank regiment, an artillery-mortar regiment equipped with eight 76mm field guns, eighteen 120mm mortars, and ten DShK machine guns, an antiaircraft battalion with 18 DShK machine guns, reconnaissance, sapper, and signal squadrons (battalions), medical, chemical, veterinary platoons, and small logistical subunits, for a total strength of 6,000 men, 4,770 horses, 23 T-34 and 16 T-70 tanks, forty-four 76mm field guns, twelve 45mm antitank guns, eighteen 120mm mortars, thirty-six 82mm mortars, 28 DShK machine guns, and 112 antitank rifles.[46]

At the same time, cavalry regiments consisted of four saber squadrons, an artillery battery equipped with four 76mm field guns, an antitank battery with four 45mm antitank guns, a mortar battery with twelve 82mm mortars, and reconnaissance, sapper, signal, medical, chemical, and support platoons, for a total strength of 1,138 men. Tank regiments consisted of two medium tank companies with a total of 23 T-34 tanks and a light tank company with 16 T-70 tanks, for a regimental strength of 352 men.

In accordance with its February directive, the NKO strengthened its cavalry corps and divisions throughout 1943. For example, it added an antiaircraft regiment to the corps in April and May, a guards-mortar regiment in June, and a self-propelled artillery regiment in August. During the same period, it upgraded the corps' reconnaissance and signal elements to full battalions and added new rear service subunits and a mobile field hospital. As a result of these reinforcements, the strength of the average cavalry corps reached 21,000 men and 18,000 horses in late 1943.

Chronic shortages of horses and other equipment, however, prevented the NKO from implementing all these changes in timely fashion. As a result, many cavalry corps and divisions operated for months with their older organization. To compensate for their shortages of armor, the *Stavka* or parent *fronts* and armies often reinforced their cavalry corps with separate tank regiments or brigades. Beginning in the fall of 1943, these corps often operated with mechanized corps as cavalry-mechanized groups or with rifle divisions and brigade as cavalry-rifle groups, usually under command of the cavalry corps commander.

Because Red Army cavalry forces were so vulnerable to *Wehrmacht* artillery, tanks, and aircraft, and both horsemen and horses were increasingly in short supply, the NKO decreased its cavalry force structure to 12 cavalry corps, 46 cavalry divisions, and seven cavalry regiments on 1 July 1942; ten cavalry corps, 30 cavalry divisions, and three cavalry regiments on 1 February 1943; and eight cavalry corps and 26 cavalry divisions on 31 December 1943. Despite these reductions, cavalry forces would remain integral and valuable elements of the Red Army's mobile combined-arms team throughout the remainder of the war.

OPERATING STRENGTHS

Tank and Mechanized Forces

The Red Army's mobile forces, like its rifle forces, often operated with less than their full complement of weapons and other equipment during the first 30 months of war. Unlike the rifle forces, however, on the eve of Operation Barbarossa, most of the Red Army's 29 mechanized corps and four cavalry corps had their full complement of personnel and, in some instances, exceeded their authorized fill. However, with notable exceptions, all of the mechanized corps and their component tank and motorized division were deficient in terms of their authorized weaponry, particularly, tanks, trucks, tractors, and motor vehicles.

Apparently, the NKO allocated tanks and other equipment to its mechanized corps in accordance with their numerical designation and the strategic importance of each corps geographically (see Table 7.16). For example, mechanized corps bearing the lowest numerical designation, such as the 1st through 8th, tended to field a higher percentage of authorized tanks, while mechanized corps with higher numerical designations, such as the 17th, 20th, 21st, and 26th, were far weaker.[47] This correlation between the mechanized corps' numerical designation and tank strength applied as well within military districts.[48] The same general pattern also applied to the distribution of new model KV heavy and T-34 medium tanks, since mechanized corps with lower numerical designations appeared to receive priority distribution of new model tanks (see Table 7.17).[49]

In addition, despite their strength on paper, all of these mechanized corps lacked requisite logistical support and adequately trained personnel. Fuel and ammunition were in short supply, many tank guns were not bore-sighted and could not fire, and most of the mechanized corps' tank drivers had received minimal if any training. As a result, two days after war began, a battalion of KV tanks assigned to the 3rd Mechanized Corps' 2nd Tank Division went into combat against the German 6th Panzer Division near Raseinai, Lithuania, with orders to ram the enemy tanks, since its 30 KV tanks had not yet been bore-sighted and could not fire.[50] This division, as well as the whole 6th and 4th Mechanized Corps, which joined combat near Grodno in Belorussia and north of L'vov in the Ukraine, quickly ran out of both fuel and ammunition.[51] Elsewhere in the Ukraine, 31 KV tanks belonging to the 22nd Mechanized Corps' 41st Tank Division blundered into swampy terrain and perished, while the 8th Mechanized Corps' 12th Tank Division, which fielded 56 KV and 100 T-34 tanks, ran out of fuel and ammunition while attacking near Dubno.[52] In each instance, inexperienced commanders, poorly trained troops, and appallingly bad logistical support spelled doom for these mechanized corps.

The *Wehrmacht's* advancing panzers utterly savaged the Red Army's mobile forces during the first four weeks of war. The *Stavka's* August decision to disband its surviving mechanized corps simply responded to this sad reality. So severe was the destruction that the *Stavka* was unable to equip adequately even its new 100–series tank divisions and smaller tank brigades and tank battalions, which it fielded later in the summer. As a result, most of the Red Army's tank divisions, brigades, and battalions were operating well below 50 percent of their authorized strength by 1 October 1941 (see Table 7.18). The Red Army's subsequent disastrous defeats at Viaz'ma and Briansk in early October only exacerbated this situation, forcing the *Stavka* to defend Moscow with only handfuls of tank brigades and battalions averaging between 6 and 40 percent of their authorized strength.

It required immense efforts on the part of the *Stavka* to raise and field the small numbers of separate tank brigades and battalions with which the Red Army spearheaded its Moscow counteroffensive in December 1941. Although they were strong enough to support modest infantry advances, these small tank units, which averaged roughly 60 percent their authorized strength, were far too weak to sustain operations into the depths of the *Wehrmacht's* defenses. Therefore, during its winter offensive of 1941–42, the commanders of attacking Red Army *fronts* and armies relied primarily on fragile cavalry and airborne corps to conduct deep exploitation operations, only to learn that these corps too could not sustain deep operations for very long.

After the Red Army survived the winter campaign of 1941–42, the NKO began building a more formidable tank force within the Red Army. Even though it was able to field new tank corps and separate tank brigades and battalions at or near full personnel and tank strength during the spring of 1942, the Red Army's disastrous defeat at Khar'kov during May and during the opening stage of Operation *Blau* indicated that, while strong in armor, all of these forces were still woefully deficient in experienced commanders and trained soldiers.

As Operation *Blau* unfolded, the *Stavka* hurled its new tank armies and tank corps into the very teeth of the advancing *Wehrmacht*. For example, in July and early August, the Briansk Fronts' 2nd, 7th, and 11th Tank Corps, operating under the control of the new 5th Tank Army together with several other separate tank corps, conducted futile counterstrokes near Voronezh in conjunction with failed counterstrokes along the Don River west of Stalingrad by the 1st and 13th, 23rd, and 28th Tank Corps, which were subordinate to the Stalingrad Front's 1st and 4th Tank Armies. To the north, the Western Front's 3rd and 10th Separate Tank Corps and the 3rd Tank Army's 12th and 15th Tank Corps conducted counterstrokes near Zhizdra and Bolkhov in August, and the 6th and 8th Tank Corps spearheaded an offensive by the Western Front southeast of Rzhev. In all of these cases, inept command and control, inadequate troop training, and inadequate logistical support limited Red Army success, but resulted in heavy tank losses.

Although most of the tank armies and tank, mechanized, and cavalry corps participating in the Red Army's major counteroffensives near Rzhev and at Stalingrad in mid-November 1942 were at full strength, their strength quickly ebbed during the initial stages of these operations. For example, the 5th Tank Army's 1st Tank Corps, which spearheaded the Southwestern Front's offensive west of Stalingrad, fell in strength from 170 tanks on 19 November to 20 on 25 November, and, after being reinforced to a strength of about 100 tanks on 1 December, lost over half of these tanks in fighting along the Chir River during the first week of December. Likewise, the Voronezh and Southwestern Fronts' 17th, 18th, 24th, and 25th Tank and 1st Guards Mechanized Corps, which spearheaded the Red Army's offensive along the middle reaches of the Don River in December 1942, lost 90 percent of their tanks in two weeks of operations, primarily because of mechanical breakdown and logistical problems rather than German resistance.[53]

In mid-January 1943, the 3rd Tank Army, which led the Voronezh Front's Ostrogozhsk-Rossosh' offensive with a strength of 479 tanks, lost 314 tanks in two weeks of fighting, most to simple wear and tear. After resuming the offensive toward Khar'kov on 29 January with a force of 165 tanks (plus 122 in various states of disrepair), the same tank army dwindled to a strength of 27 tanks on 27 February and was annihilated in early March by a counterstroke conducted by Manstein's II SS Panzer Corps. During the same period, the Southwestern Front combined four understrength tank corps into Operational Group Popov (named after its commander), which began an offensive into the Donbas region on 28 January with a strength of 212 tanks. After it had dwindled in strength to 145 tanks on 16 February and 40 tanks on 19 February, counterattacking German panzer forces destroyed Popov's group in less than a week of heavy fighting.

Finally, during mid-February 1943, the newly formed 2nd Tank Army spearheaded the Central Front's Orel-Briansk-Smolensk offensive westward from the Kursk region. After beginning its offensive on 15 February with the full strength 11th and 16th Tank Corps and 408 tanks, difficult winter fighting against skillful German resistance reduced the tank army's strength to 182 tanks on 24 February and 162 tanks on 12 March, ultimately frustrating the offensive.

After analyzing its winter campaign and fielding newer and more powerful tank and mechanized forces, in July 1943 the Red Army began the summer–fall campaign with tank armies and tank and mechanized corps at or above full strength. Although the Red Army suffered immense tank losses during the ensuing Battle of Kursk, it also demonstrated a remarkable capability for reconstituting these forces quickly, often while combat was still under way, without reducing the forces' overall effectiveness. For example, the Voronezh Front's 1st Tank Army, which began its defense in the Kursk Bulge on 4 July with a strength of 563 tanks and self-propelled guns, lost 70 percent of these weapons by 15 July. Two weeks later, however, on 3 August, the refurbished 1st Tank Army led the Voronezh Front's offensive toward Khar'kov with a force of 542 tanks and self-propelled guns. After losing about 1,000 armored vehicles during the ensuing three weeks of heavy fighting, the army fielded 162 tanks and self-propelled guns on 25 August, when the *Stavka* withdrew it for rest and refitting.

Similarly, the Voronezh Front's 5th Guards Tank Army began its famous battle at Prokhorovka on 9 July with a force of 630 tanks and self-propelled guns, only to lose over half of its armored vehicles in a week of heavy fighting. Nonetheless, on 3 August the 5th Guards Tank Army led the Steppe Front's advance on Khar'kov with a force of 503 tanks and self-propelled guns. After hundreds of tanks had been lost, the *Stavka* withdrew this tank army's remaining 153 tanks and self-propelled guns into its reserve on 25 August. Albeit underscoring the high attrition in tank forces during offensive operations, these two examples also demonstrate the Red Army's capabilities for reinforcing their tank forces while they were on the offensive.[54]

After the Battle of Kursk and, in fact, until war's end, the Red Army's tank armies, tank, mechanized, and cavalry corps, and separate tank and mechanized brigades, regiments, and battalions began major operations equipped with all or nearly all of their required tanks and other major weapons systems, although shortages of trucks and other prime movers persisted. As in earlier campaigns, however, the tank strength of these forces eroded significantly during the course of each operation, although not as dramatically as before.

For example, the Voronezh (1st Ukrainian) Front's 3rd Guards Tank Army reached the Dnepr River on 19 September with a force of 686 tanks and self-propelled guns. Several weeks of heavy fighting in the Bukrin bridgehead across the Dnepr River reduced the tank army's strength to 514 armored vehicles on 3 October and 345 on 28 October. To the south along the Krivoi Rog axis, the Steppe (2nd Ukrainian) Front's 5th Guards Tank Army began offensive operations on 3 October with 300 tanks and self-propelled guns, increased in strength to 358 tanks and self-propelled guns on 11 November, and then decreased in strength to 295 armored vehicles on 3 December and 164 on 8 December.

Combat attrition within the Red Army's separate tank and mechanized corps and separate tank brigades and regiments was even higher because the *Stavka* often left its tank and mechanized corps at the front to support their parent armies and *fronts*. Thus, many remained in combat for weeks and even months, fighting as brigade or battalion groups with only a fraction of their original strength (see Table 7.9). The experiences of a single tank corps, the 10th, typify this phenomenon in the fall of 1943.

The 10th Tank Corps joined battle at Kursk on 12 July 1943, with a strength of 185 tanks and self-propelled guns, but fell in strength to 50 tanks during four days of heavy fighting near Prokhorovka. After being reinforced to 93 tanks and self-propelled guns on 19 July and 170 on 6 August, it lost 76 armored vehicles in ten days supporting the 40th Army's offensive toward Khar'kov. Despite these losses, the 10th Tank Corps led the army's advance toward the Dnepr River on 9 September with 72 tanks and self-propelled guns, but reached the river on 15 September with only 19 operational tanks. After being reinforced once again to a strength of 102 tanks and self-propelled guns on 11 October, the corps supported the Voronezh Front's bloody attempt to break out of the Bukrin bridgehead, in the process falling to a strength of only 41 tanks. Only then did the *Stavka* withdraw the corps for rest and refitting.

Cavalry Forces

Although far fewer in number than their tracked counterparts, the Red Army's cavalry corps and cavalry divisions often also fought at reduced strength, particularly during the initial stages of the war (see Table 7.19). Despite their weakness in manpower and firepower, cavalry forces exploited their unique mobility to conduct raid operations deep into the German rear area, in July 1941 in the Bobruisk region and in August 1941 north of Smolensk. Impressed with these efforts, the *Stavka* employed full cavalry corps, such as the 1st, 2nd, and 5th Guards, to spearhead its offensives in the Moscow region and south of Khar'kov during its subsequent winter campaign. Extremely mobile though they were, these corps were also fragile, however, and when they encountered determined resistance, they all suffered heavy losses and quickly lost their offensive punch.

Like the Red Army's tank and mechanized forces, most cavalry corps and divisions began offensive operations in the spring and summer of 1942 at full or nearly full strength but suffered heavy losses before being withdrawn for rest and refitting. Therefore, beginning in December 1941 and throughout 1942, *front* commanders routinely reinforced these horse cavalry corps with tanks and artillery to reduce their vulnerability. Rough terrain and logistical problems, however, usually separated the cavalry from the tanks.[55]

Throughout the remainder of 1942, the *Stavka* and *front* commanders routinely employed their cavalry corps either subordinate to or closely cooperating with tank forces to reduce their losses. For example, the 8th Cavalry Corps supported the 5th Tank Army's offensive near Voronezh in July and was subordinate to the same tank army during its offensive at Stalingrad in November, the 2nd Guards Cavalry Corps cooperated with the 6th Tank Corps in its offensive near Rzhev in November, the 2nd Guards Cavalry Corps, which included two full tank regiments, cooperated with the 2nd Tank Army's offensive west of Kursk in February and March 1943, and, during the same period, the 8th Cavalry Corps cooperated with two mechanized corps during the Red Army's offensive into the Donbas region.

Despite this cooperation, however, these cavalry corps often suffered heavy losses. As a result, by year's end in 1943, the *Stavka* began forming cavalry-mechanized groups consisting of cavalry and mechanized corps operating under the command of the cavalry corps commander. This close integration of tanks, motorized infantry, and artillery support finally reduced the losses suffered by the cavalry corps.

ARMORED VEHICLES AND TRUCKS

Tanks

Even though it fielded an imposing array of armored vehicles in 1941, the Red Army's inability to employ these vehicles effectively on the battlefield contributed to the series of spectacular and costly defeats it experienced during the summer of 1941 and the spring and summer of 1942. Thereafter, the successes the Red Army achieved in late 1942 and 1943 directly reflected the Soviet Union's increased capability to produce tanks and develop new tanks and the NKO's creation of tank and mechanized formations able to employ this new armored weaponry more effectively in field combat.

When war began on 22 June 1941, the bulk of the Red Army's tank park, roughly 2,060 of its total tank park's inventory of 23,767 tanks, were old and essentially obsolete models.[56] These older models included the light T-26 infantry tank, armed with a 45mm gun, the light BT-2 and BT-5 cavalry tanks, equipped with 37mm and 45mm guns, respectively, the medium T-28 tank armed with a 76mm gun, and the heavy T-35 tank, whose multiple turrets were armed with one 76mm and two 45mm guns. In addition, the Red Army employed light scouting tanks, the T-37 and T-38, which were equipped with machine guns and, in the case of the up-gunned version of the T-38, a 20mm gun (see Appendix 3 in companion volume for the characteristics of wartime Red Army and Lend-Lease tanks).

Given the obsolescence of these tanks, in 1940 the NKO began designing and fielding a new generation of tanks to replace the older models. These included T-40 light amphibious tanks to replace T-37 and T-38 tanks, T-50 infantry tanks to replace T-26 light tanks, T-34 medium tanks with 76mm guns to replace the BT-2 and BT-5 tanks, and the KV-1 and KV-2 heavy tanks, the former with 76mm guns and the latter with 152mm howitzers, to replace T-28 medium and T-35 heavy tanks.

Although over 2,000 of these new model tanks (excepting the light T-50 tanks) were present in the Red Army's tank park on 22 June 1941, the advancing *Wehrmacht* destroyed or captured most of them during the summer–fall campaign of 1941. Worse still for the Red Army, *Wehrmacht* forces overran or severely damaged many of the Soviet Union's principal tank production facilities, such as those at Khar'kov and Leningrad, during the first six months of the war, severely reducing Soviet tank production.

Soviet production of T-34 and KV tanks finally increased during early 1942 after tank factories either evacuated or constructed east of the Ural Mountains began operating. As the Soviet Union increased its production from 4,800 tanks in the last six months of 1941 and 11,200 during the first six months of 1942 to about 2,000 tanks per month after 1 January 1943, the overall strength of the Red Army's tank park rose from 1,731 tanks on 1 December 1941 to 3,160 on 1 May 1942, 3,088 in 1 November 1942, and 8,200 on 1 July 1943.[57]

Coupled with the Red Army's insatiable need for more tanks, the initial decline in Soviet tank production in 1941 forced the NKO to freeze its tank designs insofar as possible during 1942 in order to maximize tank production. Although the NKO modified the basic T-34 and KV models on several occasions in 1942, it carefully avoided developing and fielding entirely new tank model tanks. For example, the NKO incorporated a simplified hull design in its T-34 Model 1942 tanks and mounted more easily manufactured hexagonal cast turrets on its T-34 Model 1943 tanks. In addition, since T-50 light infantry tanks and T-40 light amphibious tanks proved almost as expensive to produce as T-34 tanks, the NKO replaced them with the cheaper, nonamphibious T-60 tanks, which were lightly armored and armed with 20mm guns.[58]

Despite these attempts to rationalize production, existing Soviet model tanks exhibited obvious deficiencies. For example, the cramped crew quarters in T-34 tanks required tank commanders also to serve as the tanks' gunners, the T-34 tanks lacked vision devices, and the T-34 tanks' poor hatch design prevented tank commanders from riding with their heads outside of the tanks. Finally, unlike many German tanks, most Red Army tanks lacked radios and hence were difficult to coordinate in complex combat situations. These problems often resulted in extraordinarily heavy Red Army tank losses and negated the Soviets' clear advantage in tank production.

However, increased Soviet tank production and the Red Army's continuing demands for more and better tanks prompted the NKO to permit its tank designers greater leeway in developing and fielding new tank models by early 1943. By this time the Red Army's heavy KV tanks had lost most of their battlefield advantages both because most German tanks now mounted a 75mm gun and because the KV tanks could not operate effectively with the more mobile T-34s. In addition, their crews perceived the lightly armored and undergunned T-60 tanks as nothing less than death traps. As a result, in early 1943 the NKO began removing KV heavy tanks from its tank brigades, assigning them instead to its separate infantry support tank regiments. At the same time, it developed KV-1S tanks, lighter and more mobile versions of the KV tanks, and T-70 light tanks, which were slightly larger than the older T-60 tanks and mounted more effective but still inadequate 45mm guns. In addition, in late 1942 Soviet designers added commanders' cupolas to T-34 tanks to improve their commanders' ability to view the battlefield. Finally, by early 1943 the NKO replaced most of the older Soviet tank models with even greater quantities of more effective model tanks.

The NKO continued improving its existing tanks and introducing more advanced tank models throughout 1943 and the remainder of the war. These new models included T-34-85 medium tanks mounting 85mm guns and three-man turrets, which it fielded in April 1944; KV-85 heavy tanks and KV-1S tanks armed with 85mm guns, which it fielded in the late summer 1943; IS-1 [Iosif Stalin] heavy tanks equipped with 85mm guns, which it developed in late 1943 but never fielded; and IS-2 heavy tanks armed with 122mm guns, which it fielded in April 1944.

In addition to these standard line tanks, the NKO also produced modified tanks to perform specialized tasks. The first of these modified models were

T-034 flamethrower tanks mounting Model AT-41 flamethrowers and improved versions of flamethrower tanks mounting ATO-42 flamethrowers, which it fielded in 1942. In addition, the NKO fielded KV-8 heavy flamethrower tanks mounting both ATO-42 flamethrowers and 45mm rather than 76mm guns in 1942 and T-034–85 tanks mounting ATO-42 flamethrowers in 1943. The weak firepower and reduced mobility of the former, however, prompted the NKO to discontinue its production in late 1942. The NKO also configured T-34 tanks to lay bridges and tow (recover) damaged tanks. For example, one version of the T-34 carried a 7.7-meter bridge and another mounted a mine-clearing device capable of clearing two 1.2-meter-paths through minefields.[59]

Finally, the Red Army also received and employed a vast array of tanks from its Western allies under the provisions of the of Lend-Lease program, a United States offer of military assistance, which the Soviet Union accepted on 6 September 1941.[60] Along with the 5,218 tanks provided by Great Britain and Canada, the 1,683 light and 5,488 medium tanks the United States shipped to the Soviet Union throughout the war amounted to roughly 16 percent of the 99,150 tanks Soviet industry produced during the war.[61]

British tank models provided to the Red Army included a few (20) Mk-VII Tetrarch light tanks armed with 2-pounder (40mm) guns; Mk-III, Mk-VIII, and Mk-XI Valentine light infantry tanks armed with 2-pounder (40mm), 6-pounder (57mm), and 75mm guns; Mk-III and Mk-IV Churchill heavy infantry tanks equipped with a 6-pounder (75mm) gun; and Mk-II Matilda heavy infantry tanks armed with a 2-pounder (40mm) gun. American models included M-3 Stuart light tanks armed with weak 37mm guns, which the Soviets considered classic cavalry tanks; M3 General Lee medium tanks armed with 75mm guns; M3A1 Stuart light tanks with 37mm guns; and, in 1943, more effective M4 A2 and A3 Sherman medium tanks mounting 75mm and 76mm guns, respectively.

The NKO mixed Lend-Lease tanks and Soviet models in its separate tank brigades and regiments in 1942, but it fielded entire regiments and brigades equipped with foreign models, particularly Sherman tanks, in late 1943. Early Lend-Lease models, however, often earned Soviet scorn. Red Army soldiers greeted Lend-Lease tanks with mixed reactions. For example, they nicknamed the General Lee tank the "grave for seven brothers" and criticized the Matilda and Stuart tanks for their weak armament.[62] On the other hand, they considered the Valentine tanks to be superb scout tanks and praised the Sherman tanks for their reliability and high mobility.

In addition to these tanks, the Red Army also received a smaller number of other model tanks, tank destroyers, training tanks, and tank recovery vehicles from the United States under the provisions of the Lend-Lease program. These included five newer M5 model Stuart tanks, two M24 Chaffee light tanks, one M26 General Pershing tank, 52 M10 tank destroyers (SAU) armed with 75mm guns mounted on Sherman tank chassis, and 115 M31 armored repair and evacuation vehicles mounted on M3 Lee hulls. The British also provided 25 bridge-layers mounted on Valentine tanks.[63]

Armored Personnel Carriers, Cars, and Trucks

One of the Red Army's most severe materiel deficiencies throughout the war was the absence in its force structure of effective armored cars and armored personnel carriers. When war began, the Red Army's equipment inventory included BA-10 and BA-20 model armored transporters, which, in reality, were armored cars. However, since neither model proved effective, the NKO ceased producing both models in late 1941. Although the NKO fielded a follow-on model BA-64 light armored car in 1942 and modernized BA-64B armored cars in 1943, both proved totally ineffective. As a result, until war's end, the Red Army employed only the limited number of armored transporters provided through Lend-Lease.

The Red Army's failure to develop and field armored troop transporters prevented it from creating the tank and infantry teams the *Wehrmacht* employed so effectively and, at least in part, explained why German tactical prowess endured to war's end. Deprived of armored personnel carriers, Red Army motorized riflemen either rode into battle on trucks or on the decks of accompanying tanks or supported the tanks on foot. Inevitably, this led to heavy losses in Red Army motorized rifle units, which found it difficult to keep pace with the advancing tanks they were supposed to defend and support.

The mobility of Red Army infantry, particularly motorized infantry assigned to its tank and mechanized corps, and the effectiveness of logistical support for all Red Army operating forces, but particularly its mobile forces, depended directly on the army's inventory of trucks and other transport vehicles. On the eve of war, the Red Army fielded two basic families of trucks, GAZ and ZIS vehicles. The former, which included twin-axle GAZ-AA and triple-axle GAZ-AAA light trucks, both produced under license from the American Ford Motor Company, constituted 85 percent of the Red Army's prewar truck park. The latter, which included twin-axle ZIS-5 and triple-axle ZIS-6 medium trucks, also produced under license from the American Autocar-2 series, made up the remaining 15 percent. Soviet industry produced more limited numbers of other models of trucks and vehicles, including the GAZ-61 staff car, which they also built under U.S. license.[64]

The advancing *Wehrmacht* wreaked havoc on the Red Army's vehicular park of 267,000 trucks and other vehicles during Operation Barbarossa, and the *Stavka* and NKO worsened the situation by concentrating on the production of armored vehicles at the expense of trucks. Although the Red Army made up for part of this 30 percent decrease in vehicular production by mobilizing civilian vehicles, mobilization fell far short of its wartime needs.

Subsequently, Soviet industry developed and produced vehicle series based on modified prewar designs, such as redesigned ZIS-5V trucks, substituting prefabricated wooden cabs for the metal cabs of the ZIS-5 and GAZ-55 trucks, which were close derivatives of GAZ-AA trucks. At the same time, they constructed a broad array of special-purpose vehicles such as ambulances and communications vans by exploiting a variety of existing models. GAZ-67B light trucks, which were equivalent to American jeeps, were one of the few uniquely produced Soviet models of military vehicles.[65]

The NKO's decision to accord priority to the production of combat weapons and armored vehicles at the expense of trucks forced the Red Army to rely on Lend-Lease deliveries for a major portion of its trucks and light vehicles. Although Soviet industry produced roughly 205,000 trucks and other vehicles during wartime, 150,400 of which it allocated to the Red Army, Lend-Lease provided another 401,000, including 77,972 Willies jeeps, 24,902 ¾-ton Dodge trucks, and 351,715 medium trucks, primarily ¼-ton Studebaker models.[66]

In general, Red Army soldiers appreciated these Lend-Lease vehicles and others such as the amphibious "Ducks" for their high quality, reliability, and durability, which far exceeded that of the Russian models. In the final analysis, Lend-Lease trucks played a vital role moving and supplying Red Army forces during their victorious westward advance from 1943 through 1945. For this reason, the words "Willies," "Studebaker," and "Duck" remained common words in the Russian vocabulary well after war's end.

If the Red Army considered its more numerous rifle forces the "queen" of battle and its artillery force "king," the Red Army's tank force deserved equal royal status, at least in terms of the conduct of modern high-intensity mobile mechanized warfare. Throughout the war as a whole, and particularly after late 1942, it became axiomatic that the Red Army's offensive success depended directly on the effectiveness of its tank and mechanized forces.

Based on the Red Army's combat experiences in 1941 and 1942, the *Stavka* and General Staff correctly concluded that the quantity and operational effectiveness of its tank, mechanized, and, to a lesser extent, cavalry forces were the most important factors contributing to success in modern offensive operations. Therefore, by the summer of 1943, after considerable testing in 1942 and early 1943, the NKO finally fielded a mobile force sufficiently large and effective to vanquish the *Wehrmacht's* vaunted panzers and ultimately win the war.

Table 7.1 Relative Strength of Red Army Tank Brigades, 1941–1943

Subordinate Units	Aug 1941	Sep 1941	Dec 1941	Jul 1942	Jan 1943	Nov 1943
Tank regiments	1	0	0	0	0	0
Tank battalions	1 med/hvy 2 light	1 med/hvy 1 light	2	2	2	3
Motorized rifle battalions	1	1	1	1	1	1
Reconnaissance company	1	1	0	0	0	0
Antitank artillery battery	1	0	0	1	1	0
Antiaircraft artillery battalions	1	0	0	0	0	0
Antiaircraft MG company	0	0	0	0	0	1
Antitank rifle company	0	0	0	0	0	1
Antiaircraft battery	0	0	1	0	1	1
Repair company	1	1	0	0	0	0
Motor transport company	1	1	0	0	0	0
Repair and transport company	0	0	0	1	1	1
Medical platoon	1	1	1	1	1	1
Personnel	1,943	1,471	1,471	1,038	1,058	1,354
Tanks and SP guns	93	67	46	53	53	65
Heavy	7	7	10	0	0	0
Medium	22	22	16	32	32	65
Light	64	38	20	21	21	0
Artillery and mortars	22	22	10	10	14	10
76mm antitank guns	0	0	0	4	4	0
82mm mortars	6	6	6	6	6	6
45mm antitank guns	8	8	0	0	0	4
37mm antiaircraft guns	8	8	4	0	4	0
DShK machine guns	0	0	0	0	4	9
Antitank rifles	0	0	6	6	6	18

Sources: O. A. Losik, ed., *Stroitel'stvo i boevoe primenenie Sovetskikh tankovykh voisk v gody Velikoi Otechestvennoi voiny* [The formation and combat use of Soviet tank forces in the years of the Great Patriotic War] (Moscow: Voenizdat, 1979), 47, 53, 65; I. M. Anan'ev, *Tankovye armii v nastuplenii* [Tank armies on the offensive] (Moscow: Voenizdat, 1988), 78–79; and Steven J. Zaloga and Leland S. Ness, *Red Army Handbook, 1939–1945* (Gloucestershire, UK: Sutton, 1998), 68–81.

Table 7.2 Relative Strength of Red Army Motorized Rifle Brigades, 1942–1943

	Apr 1942	Nov 1942	Jan 1943	Nov 1943
Motorized rifle battalions	3	3	3	3
Reconnaissance company	1	1	1	1
Submachine-gun company	1	1	1	1
Antitank rifle company	1	1	1	1
Mortar battalion	1	1	1	1
Artillery battalion	1	1	1	1
Antiaircraft battalion	1	1	1	0
Antiaircraft MG company	0	0	0	1
Transport company	1	1	1	1
Sapper platoon	1	1	1	0
Engineer-mine company	0	0	0	1
Medical platoon	1	1	1	1
Personnel	3,151	3,162	3,537	3,500 est.
Artillery and mortars	70	70	72	72
76mm guns	12	12	12	12
82mm mortars	30	30	30	30
120mm mortars	4	4	6	6
45mm antitank guns	12	12	12	12
37mm antiaircraft guns	12	12	12	0
DShK machine guns	0	0	0	9
Antitank rifles	504	54	54	54

Sources: I. M. Anan'ev, *Tankovye armii v nastuplenii* [Tank armies on the offensive] (Moscow: Voenizdat, 1988), 79; and Steven J. Zaloga and Leland S. Ness, *Red Army Handbook, 1939–1945* (Gloucestershire, UK: Sutton, 1998), 75–80.

Table 7.3 Composition and Strength of Red Army Tank Regiments, September 1942 to 31 December 1943

	Standard			*Heavy*		*Engineer*
	Sep 1942	Jan 1943	Jan 1944	Oct 1942	Feb 1943	Jun 1943
Heavy tank companies	0	0	0	4	4	0
Medium tank companies	2	3	3	0	0	3
Light tank companies	1	1	0	0	0	1
Antitank artillery company	1	1	1	0	0	1
Reconnaissance platoon	1	1	1	0	0	1
Sapper platoon	0	0	0	0	1	0
Submachine-gun company	0	1	1	0	1	1
AT rifle platoon	0	1	0	0	0	1
Auto-transport platoon	1	1	1	0	1	1
Maintenance company	0	0	0	1	0	0
Service support platoon	1	1	1	0	0	1
Personnel	339	572	401	215	374	572
Tanks	39	39	35	21	21	39
KV-1	0	0	0	21	21	0
T-34	23	32	35	0	0	32
T-60s, 70s	16	7	0	0	0	7
Mine-rollers	0	0	0	0	0	16
Antitank rifles	0	18	0	0	0	18

Sources: O. A. Losik, ed., *Stroitel'stvo i boevoe primenenie Sovetskikh tankovykh voisk v gody Velikoi Otechestvennoi voiny* [The formation and combat use of Soviet tank forces in the years of the Great Patriotic War] (Moscow: Voenizdat, 1979), 56–71; and Steven J. Zaloga and Leland S. Ness, *Red Army Handbook, 1939–1945* (Gloucestershire, UK: Sutton, 1998), 90–92.

Table 7.4 Relative Strength of Red Army Tank Corps, April 1942 to 1 January 1944

	31 Mar 1942	15 Apr 1942	31 Dec 1942	10 Jan 1943*	Nov 1943
Tank brigades	2	3	3	3	3
Motorized rifle brigades	1	1	1	1	1
SP artillery regiments	0	0	0	1	3
Mortar regiments	0	0	0	1	1
Antitank artillery regiments	0	0	0	1 (Apr–Aug)	0
Antitank artillery battalions	0	0	0	1 (May–Aug)	0
Antiaircraft artillery battalions	0	0	0	1	1
Antiaircraft artillery regiments	0	0	0	0	1
Sep. guards-mortar battalions	0	1 (Jul)	1	1	1
Reconnaissance battalions	0	1 (Jul)	1	1	1
Sapper battalion	0	0	0	0	1
Signal battalion	0	0	0	0	1
Engineer-mine company	0	1	1	1	0
Tank battalions	4	6	6	6	6
Motorized rifle (submachine-gun) battalions	5	6	6	6	6
Aviation detachment	0	0	0	0	1 (3-PO-2)
Maintenance company (auto)	0	0	1	1	1
Maintenance company (tank)	0	0	1	1	1
Fuel supply company	0	1 (Jun)	1	1	1
Chemical defense company	0	0	0	0	1
Medical platoon	0	0	0	0	1
Reserve tank detachment	8 (T-34)	8 (T-34)	8 (T-34)	33 T-34 7 T-70	

Personnel	5,603	7,200–7,600	7,853	7,800	10,977
Tanks and SP guns	100	146–180	170	202	257
			(162 + 8 res.)	(162 + 40 res.)	
Heavy	20	30–65	0	0	1 or 0
Medium	40	46–56	107	132	207 or 208
			(99 + 8 res.)	(99 + 33 res.)	
Light	40	60	63	70	0
		(63 + 7 res.)			
SU-76	0	0	0	0	21
SU-85	0	0	0	0	16
SU-122	0	0	0	0	0
SU-152	0	0	0	0	12
Artillery and mortars	98			108	160
76mm guns	20	20	24	24	12
82mm mortars	42	42	48	48	52
120mm mortars	4	6	4	4	42
57mm antitank guns	0	0	0	0	16
45mm antitank guns	12	12	0	12	12
				32 (Mar–Aug)	
85mm antitank guns	0	0	0	12 (May–Aug)	0
37mm AA guns	20	0	12	20	18
Multiple-rocket launchers	0	8 (Jul)	8	8	8
Armored cars	0	20 (Jul)	20		

*As mandated by 10 January 1943 NKO order and in transition through November. During 1942 the reconnaissance battalion was converted from an armored car to a motorcycle battalion. During 1943 the following units and subunits were first added and then deleted from the tank corps organization: a SU-76 and SU-122 regiment, a tank reserve detachment, an antitank regiment, and an antitank battalion.

Sources: P. A. Kurochkin, ed., *Obshchevoiskovaia armiia v nastuplenii* [The combined-arms army on the offensive] (Moscow: Voenizdat, 1966), 208; O. A. Losik, ed., *Stroitel'stvo i boevoe primenenie Sovetskikh tankovykh voisk v gody Velikoi Otechestvennoi voiny* [The formation and combat use of Soviet tank forces in the years of the Great Patriotic War] (Moscow: Voenizdat, 1979), 64–69; I. M. Anan'ev, *Tankovye armii v nastuplenii* [Tank armies on the offensive] (Moscow: Voenizdat, 1988), 81; and Steven J. Zaloga and Leland S. Ness, *Red Army Handbook, 1939–1945* (Gloucestershire, UK: Sutton, 1998), 75–82.

Table 7.5 Initial Formation of Red Army Tank Corps, March–December 1942

Month	Quantity of Corps	Corps Designations
Mar	4	1st–4th
Apr	9	5th–8th, 10th, 21st–24th
May	6	9th, 11th–15th
Jun	4	16th–18th, 27th
Jul	3	25th, 26th, 28th
Dec	2	19th–20th

Source: O. A. Losik, ed., *Stroitel'stvo i boevoe primenenie Sovetskikh tankovykh voisk v gody Velikoi Otechestvennoi voiny* [The formation and combat use of Soviet tank forces in the years of the Great Patriotic War] (Moscow: Voenizdat, 1979), 52.

Table 7.6 Formation and Composition of Red Army Mechanized Corps, September–December 1942

Corps	Date Formed	Base	Ultimate Composition
1st	Sep	27th Tank Corps	3 mechanized and 2 tank brigades
2nd	Sep		3 mechanized and 2 tank brigades
3rd	Sep–Oct	8th Tank Corps	3 mechanized and 2 tank brigades
4th	Nov	28th Tank Corps	3 mechanized brigades and 2 tank regiments
5th	Nov	22nd Tank Corps	3 mechanized brigades and 2 tank regiments
6th	Nov	14th Tank Corps	3 mechanized brigades and 2 tank regiments
1st Gds	Nov	1st Gds Rifle Division	3 mechanized brigades and 2 tank regiments
2nd Gds	Nov	22nd Gds. Rifle Division	3 mechanized brigades and 2 tank regiments

Source: Boevoi sostav Sovetskoi armii, chast' 2 (ianvar'–dekabr' 1942 g.) [The combat composition of the Soviet Army, part 2 (January–December 1942)] (Moscow: Voenizdat, 1968), 186–250.

Table 7.7 Composition and Relative Strength of Red Army Mechanized Corps, September 1942 to 1 January 1944

	8 Sep 1942	1 Jan* 1943	1 Jan 1944
Mechanized brigades	3	3	3
Tank brigades	1–2, tank brigades or 2 tank regiments	1†	1
Tank regiments	3–5	3	3
Self-propelled artillery regiments	0	1	3
Mortar regiments	0	1	1
Air defense (PVO) regiment	1	0	0
Antiaircraft artillery regiment	0	1	1
Antitank artillery regiment	1	1	1
Antitank artillery battalion	0	1 (May–Aug)	0
Separate guards-mortar battalions	1	1	1
Reconnaissance battalion	1	1	1
Sapper battalion	1	1	1
Engineer-mine company	1	1	1
Signal battalion	0	0	1
Signal company	1	1	0
Tank battalions	2–4	2	3
Motorized rifle (submachine-gun) battalions	10	10	10
Aviation detachment	0	0	1 (3 PO-2)
Maintenance battalion	1	0	1
Fuel supply company	1	0	1
Chemical defense company	0	0	1
Personnel	13,559	15,018	16,442
Tanks and SP guns	175 (204)	229	246
Heavy	0	0	0
Medium	100	162	183
Light	75	42	0
SU-76	0	17 or 25	21
SU-85	0	0	21
SU-122	0	0 or 8	0
SU-152	0	0	21
Artillery and mortars	266	246	252
76mm guns	40	36	36
82mm mortars	102	94	100
120mm mortars	48	54	54
57mm antitank guns	0	0	8
45mm antitank guns	36	36	36
37mm AA guns	40	26	18
DShK machine guns	0	16	16
Multiple-rocket launchers	8	8	8

*As mandated by 10 January 1943 NKO order and in transition through November. During 1942 the reconnaissance battalion was converted from an armored car to a motorcycle battalion. During 1943 the following units and subunits were first added and then deleted from the tank corps organization: a SU-76 and SU-152 regiment, a tank reserve detachment, an antitank regiment, and an antitank battalion.

†The conversion of tank regiments to a single tank brigade was a gradual process that, in some instances, was not completed until 1945.

Sources: O. A. Losik, ed., *Stroitel'stvo i boevoe primenenie Sovetskikh tankovykh voisk v gody Velikoi Otechestvennoi voiny* [The formation and combat use of Soviet tank forces in the years of the Great Patriotic War] (Moscow: Voenizdat, 1979), 70; I. M. Anan'ev, *Tankovye armii v nastuplenii* [Tank armies on the offensive] (Moscow: Voenizdat, 1988), 79–85; and Steven J. Zaloga and Leland S. Ness, *Red Army Handbook, 1939–1945* (Gloucestershire, UK: Sutton, 1998), 82–89.

Table 7.8 Composition and Relative Strength of Red Army Mechanized Brigades, September 1942 through 1 January 1944

	Sep 1942	Nov 1942	Feb 1943	Jan 1944
Motorized rifle battalions	3	3	3	3
Tank regiment	1	1	1	1
Mortar battalion	1	1	1	1
Artillery battalion	1	1	1	1
Antiaircraft battalion	1	1	0	0
Reconnaissance company	1	1	1	1
Submachine-gun company	1	1	1	1
Antitank rifle company	1	1	1	1
Antiaircraft MG company	0	0	1	1
Sapper-mine company	0	0	1	1
Repair and transport company	0	0	1	1
Medical platoon	1	1	1	1
Personnel	3,728	3,491	3,558	3,354
Tanks and SP guns	39	39	39	39
Heavy	0	0	0	0
Medium	23	23	32	39
Light	16	16	7	0
Artillery and Mortars	68	70	60	60
76mm antitank guns	12	24	12	12
82mm mortars	30	30	30	30
120mm mortars	6	4	6	6
45mm antitank guns	12	0	12	12
37mm antiaircraft guns	8	12	0	0
DShK machine guns	0	0	9	9
Antitank rifles	81		81	81

Sources: O. A. Losik, ed., *Stroitel'stvo i boevoe primenenie Sovetskikh tankovykh voisk v gody Velikoi Otechestvennoi voiny* [The formation and combat use of Soviet tank forces in the years of the Great Patriotic War] (Moscow: Voenizdat, 1979), 70; I. M. Anan'ev, *Tankovye armii v nastuplenii* [Tank armies on the offensive] (Moscow: Voenizdat, 1988), 79–80; and Steven J. Zaloga and Leland S. Ness, *Red Army Handbook, 1939–1945* (Gloucestershire, UK: Sutton, 1998), 82–89.

Table 7.9 Formation of Red Army Tank Armies, May–September 1942

Number (Date)	Nucleus	Subordination	Composition
3rd (May)	58th Army (HQ)	*Stavka* Reserve	12th and 15th Tank Corps, 154th and 264th Rifle Divisions, 179th Tank Brigade, 8th Motorcycle, 1172nd Antitank Artillery, 62nd Guards-Mortar, and 226th Antiaircraft Artillery Regiments, 54th Motorcycle, 182nd Motorized Engineer, 470th Antiaircraft Artillery, and 507th Signal Battalions, and other rear service subunits; 1st Guards Motorized Rifle Division added in Aug
5th (May)	NA	*Stavka* Reserve, Briansk Front	2nd and 11th Tank Corps, 340th Rifle Division, 19th Separate Tank Brigade, 611th Light Artillery and 66th Guards Mortar Regiment, 1382nd Separate Engineer Battalion, and other rear service subunits: 7th Tank Corps added in early Jul
1st (Jul)	38th Army (HQ)	Stalingrad Front	13th and 28th Tank Corps, 131st and 399th Rifle Divisions, 158th Separate Tank Brigade, 397th and 398th Antitank Artillery, 1261st and 1262nd Antiaircraft Regiments, 56th Separate Engineer and 516th Separate Sapper Battalions, and rear service subunits
4th (Jul)	28th Army (HQ)	Stalingrad Front	22nd and 23rd Tank Corps, 18th Rifle Division, 133rd Tank, 5th Separate Destroyer, and 1253rd Antitank Artillery Brigades, 223rd and 1264th Antiaircraft Artillery Regiments, 12th Separate Engineer and 1414th and 1570th Sapper Battalions, and rear service subunits
5th (Sep) (2nd formation)	NA	*Stavka* Reserve, Briansk Front	1st, 22nd, and 26th Tank Corps, 119th Rifle Division, 226th Antiaircraft Artillery Regiment, 17th and 19th Sapper Brigades, and rear service subunits: 8th Cavalry Corps added in Oct
5th (Dec) (3rd Formation)	NA	*Stavka* Reserve, Southwestern Front	1st Guards Tank, 1st Tank, 5th Mechanized, and 8th Cavalry Corps, 8th Guards Tank Brigade, 3rd Guards Motorcycle Regiment, 510th and 511th Tank and 56th Separate Motorcycle Battalions, 40th, 47th, and 54th Guards and 321st, 333rd, and 346th Rifle Divisions, 396th Army, 152nd Howitzer, 312th and 518th Gun Artillery Regiments, 33rd, 150th, 174th, 179th, 481st, and 534th Antitank Artillery Regiments, 107th Mortar Regiment, 35th and 75th Guards-Mortar Regiments, 307th Guards-Mortar Battalion, 3rd Antiaircraft Artillery Division, 247th and 586th Antiaircraft Artillery Regiments, 227th Separate Antiaircraft Artillery Battalion, 44th Special Designation Engineer Brigade, 181st and 269th Separate Engineer Battalions, 101st and 130th Pontoon-Bridge Battalions, and rear service subunits

Sources: Boevoi sostav Sovetskoi armii, part 2; I. M. Anan'ev, *Tankovye armii v nastuplenii* [Tank armies on the offensive] (Moscow: Voenizdat, 1988), 55–60; and A. M. Zvartsev, *3-ia gvardeiskaia tankovaia* [3d Guards Tank] (Moscow: Voenizdat, 1982), 6.

Table 7.10 Formation or Reorganization of Red Army Tank Armies, January–July 1943

Number (Date)	Nucleus	Subordination	Composition
1st (Jan–Feb)	29th Army (HQ)	Northwestern Front	6th Tank and 3rd Mechanized Corps, 112th Separate Tank Brigade, 7th, 62nd, 63rd, and 64th Separate Tank Regiments, 6th and 9th Guards Airborne Divisions, 14th, 15th, 20th, 21st, 22nd, and 23rd Ski Brigades, 79th and 316th Guards-Mortar, 395th and 989th Howitzer Artillery, 552nd, 1008th, and 1186th Antitank Artillery Regiments, 11th Antiaircraft Artillery Battalion, 59th Engineer-Sapper Brigade, 71st and 267th Motorized Engineer Battalions, 83rd Signal Regiment, and rear service subunits
2nd (Jan–Feb)	3rd Res. A (HQ)	Central Front	3rd and 16th Tank Corps, 11th Guards Tank Brigade, 6th Guards and 16th Rifle Divisions, 37th Guards-Mortar Regiment, 54th Separate Motorcycle Battalion, 357th Separate Motorized Engineer Battalion, and rear service subunits
2nd (Feb–Mar) (reorganization)		Central Front	11th and 16th Tank Corps, 11th Guards Tank Brigade, 60th, 112th, 194th Rifle Divisions, 115th Rifle Brigade, 28th Ski Brigade, 29th Guards Tank Regiment, 51st Separate Motorcycle Battalion, 563rd and 567th Antitank Artillery Regiments, 37th Guards-Mortar Regiment, 357th Separate Motorized Engineer Battalion, and rear service subunits
3rd (Feb–Mar)		Southwestern Front	12th and 15th Tank Corps, 179th and 39th Separate Armored Car Battalions, 25th, 48th, 62nd Guards, 111th, 160th, 184th Rifle Divisions, 8th Artillery Division, 481st, 1172nd, 1245th Antitank Artillery Regiments, 15th Separate Guards-Mortar Brigade, 62nd, 97th, 315th Guards-Mortar Regiments, 71st, 319th, 470th Antiaircraft Artillery Regiments, 15th Engineer-Mine Brigade, 182nd Separate Engineer Battalion, and rear service subunits
3rd Guards (May–Jun)		*Stavka* Reserve	12th and 15th Tank Corps, 91st Separate Tank Brigade, 50th Separate Motorcycle Regiment, 39th Separate Reconnaissance and 182nd Motorized Engineer Battalions, 138th Separate Signal Regiment, 372nd Separate Aviation Liaison Regiment (PO-2), and rear service subunits
4th Guards (Feb–Mar) (disbanded in Mar)		Southwestern Front	2nd Guards and 23rd Tank Corps and 1st Guards Mechanized Corps
4th (Jun) (2nd formation)		Moscow MD	11th and 30th Ural Volunteer Tank and 6th Guards Mechanized Corps, 1545th Heavy Self-Propelled Artillery and 51st Motorcycle Regiments, 51st Armored Car and 88th Motorized Engineer Battalions, 118th Signal Regiment, 593rd Aviation Squadron, and rear service subunits
5th Guards (Feb–Mar)		Southwestern Front	3rd Guards and 29th Tank Corps and 5th Guards Mechanized Corps
5th Guards (Mar) (reorganized)		*Stavka* Reserve	29th Tank and 5th Guards Mechanized Corps, 53rd Guards Separate Tank, 1st Guards Motorcycle, 678th Howitzer, 689th Antitank Artillery, and 76th Guards-Mortar Regiments, 6th Antiaircraft Artillery Division, 377th Motorized Engineer and 4th Signal Battalions, (later) 994th Aviation Liaison Regiment, and rear service subunits

Sources: I. M. Anan'ev, *Tankovye armii v nastuplenii* [Tank armies on the offensive] (Moscow: Voenizdat, 1988), 66–69; and *Boevoi sostav Sovetskoi armii, chast' 3 (ianvar'–dekabr' 1943 g.)* [The combat composition of the Soviet Army, part 3 (January–December 1943)] (Moscow, Voenizdat, 1972), 31–169. The latter is classified secret and prepared by the Military Scientific Directorate of the General Staff.

Table 7.11 Quantity of Tank and Mechanized Corps Assigned to Red Army Tank Armies during Offensive Operations, 1 January 1943 to May 1945

	Number of Operations		
Tank Army	Total	2 corps	3 corps
1st (1st Guards)	9	7	2
2nd (2nd Guards)	8	4	4
3rd Guards	12	0	12
4th (4th Guards)	11	7	4
5th Guards	12	5	7
6th (6th Guards)	12	9	3
Total	64	32	32

Source: I. M. Anan'ev, *Tankovye armii v nastuplenii* [Tank armies on the offensive] (Moscow: Voenizdat, 1988), 70.

Table 7.12 Minimum and Maximum Personnel and Weapons Strength of Red Army Tank Armies during Offensive Operations, 1943–1945

Tank Army	Personnel	Tanks and SP guns	Guns and Mortars	MRLs (M-8 and M-13)	Antiaircraft Guns
1st (1st Guards)	30,626–48,958	257–752	266–558	25–64	80–133
2nd (2nd Guards)	28,000–58,299	101–840	107–667	8–78	33–132
3rd (3rd Guards)	31,660–55,674	309–924	266–690	32–98	57–112
4th (4th Guards)	30,003–49,992	276–732	390–580	8–44	34–126
5th (5th Guards)	26,704–43,904	146–585	126–755	20–55	44–131
6th (6th Guards)	25,363–75,000	86–984	126–611	8–46	20–165

Source: I. M. Anan'ev, *Tankovye armii v nastuplenii* [Tank armies on the offensive] (Moscow: Voenizdat, 1988), 84.

Table 7.13 Average Strength of Red Army Tank Armies, 1943–1945

	1943	1944	1945
Personnel	46,000	48,000	50,000
Tanks	450–560	450–620	up to 700
Self-propelled guns	25	98–147	up to 250
Guns and mortars	500–600	650–750	up to 850
Gross tonnage	1,000–1,200	1,800–2,100	2,400–2,800

Source: A. I. Radzievsky, ed., *Tankovyi udar* [Tank attack] (Moscow: Voenizdat, 1977), figure 1.

Table 7.14 Relative Strength of Red Army Cavalry Corps, 22 June 1941–1943

	Jun 1941	Dec 1941	Jun 1942	Jul 1943
Cavalry divisions	2	2	3	3
Light cavalry division	0	1	0	0
Signal battalion	1	1	1	1
Artillery battalion	0	0	1	0
Antitank regiment	0	0	0	1
SP artillery regiment	0	0	0	1
Antitank battalion	0	0	1	0
Guards-mortar regiment	0	0	0	1
Antiaircraft regiment	0	0	1	1
Antiaircraft battalion	0	0	1	0
Mortar regiment	0	0	1	0
Mortar battalions	0	0	0	2
Medical platoon	0	0	1	1
Veterinary platoon	0	0	1	1
Chemical platoon	0	0	1	1
Supply platoon	0	0	1	1
Training battalion	0	0	1	1
Personnel	19,430	(12,000)	(14,000)	(21,000)
Tanks	128	0	0	117
BT-5	128	0	0	0
T-34	0	0	0	69
T-70	0	0	0	48
Armored cars	36	0	0	0
Self-propelled guns	0	0	0	12
Guns	136	90	126	200
Field (76mm, 122mm)	64	0	48	132
Antitank (45mm,76mm)	32	0	48	56
Antiaircraft (37mm)	40	0	30	12
Mortars	128	36	74	(78)
MRLs (BM-13)	0	0	0	24
DShK	0	0	0	(84)
Vehicles	1,270	NA	(1,200)	(1,400)
Tractors	42	NA	0	0
Horses	16,020	NA	16,937	18,000

Sources: Nachal'nyi period Velikoi Otechestvennoi voiny [The beginning period of the Great Patriotic War] (Moscow: Voroshilov Academy of the General Staff, 1989), 53; Iu. P. Babich and A. G. Baier, *Razvitie vooruzheniia i organizatsii sovetskikh sukhoputnykh voisk v gody Velikoi Otechestvennoi voiny* [The development of Soviet ground forces' weaponry and organization in the years of the Great Patriotic War] (Moscow: Izdanie Akademii, 1990), 61–63; and Steven J. Zaloga and Leland S. Ness, *Red Army Handbook, 1939–1945* (Gloucestershire, UK: Sutton, 1998), 107–16.

Table 7.15 Relative Strength of Red Army Cavalry Divisions, 1941–1943

	Jun 1941	Dec 1941*	Jun 1942	Jul 1943
Cavalry regiments	4	3	3	3
Tank regiment	1		0	1
Artillery-mortar regiment	0	0	0	1
Artillery battalion	1	0,1	1	0
Antiaircraft battalion	1	0	0	1
Antiaircraft battery	0	1	1	0
Reconnaissance battalion	1	0	0	1
Sapper squadron	1	1	1	1
Signal squadron	1	0,1	1	1
Chemical platoon	1	1	1	1
Transport platoon	1	0	1	1
Medical platoon	0	1	1	1
Supply platoon	1	1	1	1
Personnel	9,240	3,447–4,200	4,619	6,000
Tanks	64	0	0	39
BT-5	64	0	0	0
T-34	0	0	0	23
T-70	0	0	0	16
Armored cars	18	0	0	0
Guns	68	26–32	30	66
Field (76mm, 122mm)	32	20	12	44
Antitank (45mm)	16	6–12	12	12
Antiaircraft (37mm)	20	0	6	0
DShK	0	0	0	28
Mortars	64	16–20	18	18
Vehicles	555	118	332	0
Horses	7,940	4,242	4,770	4,770

*First number is for light cavalry divisions. One number applies to regular cavalry division.
Sources: Nachal'nyi period Velikoi Otechestvennoi voiny [The beginning period of the Great Patriotic War] (Moscow: Voroshilov Academy of the General Staff, 1989); 53; Iu. P. Babich and A. G. Baier, *Razvitie vooruzheniia i organizatsii sovetskikh sukhoputnykh voisk v gody Velikoi Otechestvennoi voiny* [The development of Soviet ground forces' weaponry and organization in the years of the Great Patriotic War] (Moscow: Izdanie Akademii, 1990); 61–63; and Steven J. Zaloga and Leland S. Ness, *Red Army Handbook, 1939–1945* (Gloucestershire, UK: Sutton, 1998), 107–16.

Table 7.16 Relative Strength of Red Army Mechanized Corps, 22 June 1941

Corps/Location	Percent Fill	Corps/Location	Percent Fill	Corps/Location	Percent Fill
1 MC, LMD	101	11 MC, WSMD	30	21 MC, MMD	10
2 MC, OMD	50	12 MC, BSMD	63	22 MC, KSMD	69
3 MC, BSMD	73	13 MC, WSMD	29	23 MC, Orel MD	40
4 MC, KSMD	91	14 MC, WSMD	46	24 MC, KSMD	22
5 MC, TBMD	93	15 MC, KSMD	63	25 MC, Khar MD	29
6 MC, WSMD	99	16 MC, KSMD	69	26 MC, NCMD	18
7 MC, MMD	93	17 MC, WSMD	7	27 MC, CAMD	35
8 MC, KSMD	94	18 MC, OMD	50	28 MC, TCMD	84
9 MC, KSMD	29	19 MC, KSMD	44	30 MC, FEMD	100
10 MC, LMD	45	20 MC, WSMD	9		

Sources: K. A. Kalashnikov, V. I. Fes'kov, A. Iu. Chmykhalo, and V. I. Golikov, *Krasnaia Armiia v iiune 1941 goda* [The Red Army in June 1941] (Tomsk: Tomsk University, 2002), 144; A. G. Lensky, *Sukhoputnye sily RKKA v predvoennye gody: Spravochnik* [RKKA ground forces in the prewar years: A handbook] (Saint-Petersburg: n.p., 2000); and David M. Glantz, *Stumbling Colossus: The Red Army on the Eve of World War* (Lawrence: University Press of Kansas, 1998), 156.

Table 7.17 Distribution of Modern Tanks in Red Army Mechanized Corps, 22 June 1941

Corps/Location	New Tanks	Corps/Location	New Tanks	Corps/Location	New Tanks
4 MC, KSMD	460	25 MC, Khar MD	20	17 MC, WSMD	0
6 MC, WSMD	352	1 MC, LMD	15	18 MC, OMD	0
8 MC, KSMD	229	7 MC, MMD	9	20 MC, SWMD	0
15 MC, KSMD	135	19 MC, KSMD	7	21 MC, MMD	0
3 MC, BSMD	109	5 MC, TBMD	0	24 MC, KSMD	0
16 MC, KSMD	76	9 MC, KSMD	0	26 MC, NCMD	0
2 MC, OMD	60	10 MC, LMD	0	27 MC, CAMD	0
11 MC, WSMD	44	12 MC, BSMD	0	28 MC, TCMD	0
22 MC, KSMD	31	13 MC, WSMD	0	30 MC, FEMD	0
23 MC, Orel MD	21	14 MC, WSMD	0	Total	1,568

Sources: K. A. Kalashnikov, V. I. Fes'kov, A. Iu. Chmykhalo, and V. I. Golikov, *Krasnaia Armiia v iiune 1941 goda* [The Red Army in June 1941] (Tomsk: Tomsk University, 2002), 144; A. G. Lensky, *Sukhoputnye sily RKKA v predvoennye gody: Spravochnik* [RKKA ground forces in the prewar years: A handbook] (Saint-Petersburg: n.p., 2000); and David M. Glantz, *Stumbling Colossus: The Red Army on the Eve of World War* (Lawrence: University Press of Kansas, 1998), 155.

Table 7.18 Tank Strength of Selected Red Army Tank Armies, Tank and Mechanized Corps, Tank Divisions, Separate Tank and Mechanized Brigades, and Separate Tank Battalions, 22 June 1941 to 1 January 1944

Force (Subordination)	Tank and SP Gun Strength		Composition (Percent Fill)
	Authorized	Actual	
22 Jun 1941			
1 MC, Leningrad MD	1,031	1,037	15 KV (101)
1 TD	375	370	(99)
3 TD	375	381	(101)
163 MD	275	275	(100)
10 MC, Leningrad MD	1,031	469	(45)
21 TD	375	200	(53)
24 TD	375	230	(61)
185 MD	275	39	(14)
3 MC, Baltic Special MD	1,031	749	77 KV, 32 T-34 (73)
2 TD	375	NA	30 KV
5 TD	375	NA	25 KV, 52 T-34
12 MC, Baltic Special MD	1,031	651	(63)
23 TD	375	333	(89)
28 TD	375	210	(56)
131 MD	275	108	(39)
6 MC, Western Special MD	1,031	1,021	114 KV, 238 T-34 (99)
4 TD	375	300	63 KV, 88 T-34 (80)
7 TD	375	368	51 KV, 150 T-34 (98)
11 MC, Western Special MD	1,031	305	10 KV, 34 T-34 (30)
29 TD	375	228	6 KV, 22 T-34 (61)
33 TD	375	37–47	4 KV, 12 T-34 (10–13)
204 MD	275	30–40	(11–15)
13 MC, Western Special MD	1,031	294	(29)
25 TD	375	200	(53)
31 TD	375	0	NA
14 MC, Western Special MD	1,031	478	(46)
22 TD	375	235	(63)
30 TD	375	189	(50)
205 MD	275	51	(19)
17 MC, Western Special MD	1,031	36	(3)
20 MC, Western Special MD	1,031	93	(9)
4 MC, Kiev Special MD	1,031	938	101 KV, 359 T-34 (91)
8 TD	375	325	50 KV, 124 T-34 (87)
32 TD	375	338	49 KV, 173 T-34 (90)
81 MD	275	275	(100)
8 MC, Kiev Special MD	1,031	969	119 KV, 100 T-34, 750 old (94)
12 TD	375	NA	56 KV, 100 T-34
34 TD	375	NA	NA
7 MD	275	NA	NA
9 MC, Kiev Special MD	1,031	300	(29)
20 TD	375	36	30 T-26, 3 BT, 3 Chem. (10)
35 TD	375	142	141 T-26, 1 Chem.(38)
131 MD	275	122	104 BT, 18 T-37 (44)
15 MC, Kiev Special MD	1,031	717	64 KV, 71 T-34, 582 old (70)
10 TD	375	365	63 KV, 38 T-34 (97)
37 TD	375	315	1 KV, 32 T-34 (81)
212 MD	275	37	(13)

—*Continued*

Force (Subordination)	*Tank and SP Gun Strength* Authorized	Actual	Composition (Percent Fill)
16 MC, Kiev Special MD	1,031	608	11 KV, 65 T-34 (50)
19 MC, Kiev Special MD	1,031	450	5 KV, 2 T-34, 443 old (44)
40 TD	375	158	19 T-26, 139 T-37 (42)
43 TD	375	237	5 KV, 2 T-34 230 T-26 (63)
213 MD	275	55	42 T-26, 13 T-37 (20)
22 MC, Kiev Special MD	1,031	707	31 KV (69)
19 TD	375	163	26 BT, 122 T-26, 7 Chem. (43)
41 TD	375	415	31 KV, 342 T-26, 41 Chem. (111)
215 MD	275	129	129 BT (47)
24 MC, Kiev Special MD	1,031	222	(22)
2 MC, Odessa MD	1,031	517	10 KV, 50 T-34 (50)
18 MC, Odessa MD	1,031	282	(27)
25 MC, Khar'kov MD	1,031	300	4 KV, 16 T-34 (29)
23 MC, Orel MD	1,031	413	8 KV, 13 T-34 (40)
7 MC, Moscow MD	1,031	959	4 KV, 5 T-34 (93)
21 MC, Moscow MD	1,031	98	(10)
26 MC, North Caucasus MD	1,031	184	(18)
28 MC, Trans-Caucasus MD	1,031	869	(84)
27 MC, Central Asian MD	1,031	356	(35)
5 MC, 16 A, Trans-Baikal, WF	1,400	1,300+	(>93)
13 TD	375	238	(63)
17 TD	375	255	(68)
57 TD	375	300+	(>80)
109 MD	275	300+	(>80)
30 MC (plus 59 TD, 69 MD)	1,675	2,969	(177)
Jun–Sep 1941			
Northwestern axis			
1 MC, NWF (11 Jul)	1,031	100	(10)
12 MC, NWF (11 Jul)	1,031	80	(8)
21 MC, NWF (11 Jul)	1,031	41	25 KV, 2 T-34 (4)
Smolensk-Briansk axis			
7 MC, WF (5 Jul)	1,031	715	(69)
17 TD, 20 A, WF (26 Jul)	375	29	(8)
13 TD, 20 A, WF (26 Jul)	375	29	(8)
57 TD, 20 A, WF (26 Jul)	375	7–8	(1)
48 TD, 22 A, WF (1 Aug)	375	113	(30)
50 TD, 13 A, BF (10 Aug)	375	30	(8)
102 TD, 24 A, Res. F. (28 Aug)	190	20	(11)
108 TD, 3 A, BF (28 Aug)	190	62	5 KV, 32 T-34 (33)
108 TD, 3 A, BF (6 Sep)	190	16	2 KV, 10 T-34 (8)
141 TB, 3 A, BF (6 Sep)	93	38	3 KV, 14 T-34 (41)
121 TB, Gp. Ermakov, BF (15 Sep)	93	20	(22)
150 TB, Gp. Ermakov, BF (15 Sep)	93	18	(19)
Kiev axis			
131 MD, 9 MC, SWF (26 Jun)	275	51	(19)
43 TD, 19 MC, SWF (26 Jun)	375	87	(23)
19 TD, 22 MC, SWF (24 Jun)	375	45	T-26 (12)

—Continued

Force (Subordination)	*Tank and SP Gun Strength* Authorized	Actual	Composition (Percent Fill)
19 TD, 22 MC, SWF (29 Jun)	375	16	T-26 (4)
9 MC, SWF (29 Jun)	1,031	32	(3)
9 MC, SWF (7 Jul)	1,031	164	(16)
9 MC, SWF (10 Jul)	1,031	66	25 T-26, 34 T-37, 7 BT-5 (6)
9 MC, SWF (15 Jul)	1,031	32	7 BT, 25 T-26 (3)
9 MC, SWF (17 Jul)	1,031	38	10 BT, 24 T-26, 4 T-40 (4)
9 MC, SWF (31 Jul)	1,031	40	(5)
9 MC, SWF (19 Aug)		0	
19 MC, SWF (7 Jul)	1,031	66	(6)
19 MC, SWF (10 Jul)	1,031	78	35 T-26, 13 T-26 chem, 30 T-34 (8)
19 MC SWF (15 Jul)	1,031	33	4 KV, 7 T-34, 22 T-26 (3)
19 MC, SWF (17 Jul)	1,031	77	31 T-34, 46 T-26 (7)
22 MC, SWF (29 Jun)	1,031	153	16 KV, 137 T-26 (15)
19 TC	375	16	16 T-26 (4)
41 TD	375	122	16 KV, 106 T-26 (30)
215 MD	275	15	15 T-26 (5)
22 MC, SWF (7 Jul)	1,031	340	(33)
22 MC, SWF (10 Jul)	1,031	33	33 T-26 (3)
22 MC, SWF (15 Jul)	1,031	30	2 BT, 28 T-26 (3)
22 MC, SWF (17 Jul)	1,031	40	(4)
22 MC, SWF (31 Jul)	1,031	40	(4)
22 MC, SWF (19 Aug)	NA	2	NA
15 MC, SWF (26 Jun)	1,031	325	(32)
10 TD	375	39	(10)
37 TD	375	219	(58)
212 MD	275	2	(1)
15 MC, SWF (6 Jul)	1,031	30	(3)
10 TD	375	20	(5)
37 TD	375	10	(3)
212 MD	275	0	(0)
15 MC, SWF (7 Jul)	1,031	66	(6)
15 MC, SWF (15 Jul)	1,031	6	(1)
15 MC, SWF (17 Jul)	1,031	10	1 T-34, 9 BT (1)
16 MC, SWF (15 Jul)	1,031	87	(8)
16 MC, SWF (17 Jul)	1,031	73	(7)
4 MC, SWF (7 Jul)	1,031	126	(12)
4 MC, SWF (15 Jul)	1,031	68	6 KV, 39 T-34, 23 BT (7)
4 MC, SWF (17 Jul)	1,031	100	10 KV, 49 T-34, 23 BT, 18 T-26 (10)
24 MC, SWF (5 Jul)	1,031	10	(1)
24 MC, SWF (7 Jul)	1,031	100	(10)
24 MC, SWF (17 Jul)	1,031	100	100 T-26 (10)
8 MC, SWF (7 Jul)	1,031	43	(4)
8 MC, SWF (17 Jul)	1,031	57	14 KV, 14 T-34, 16 BT, 13 T-26 (6)
14 TB, SWF (30 Sep)	67	25	(37)
Southern axis			
2 MC, SF (15 Jul)	1,031	468	(45)
18 MC. SF (15 Jul)	1,031	297	(29)

—Continued

Table 7.18 Continued

Force (Subordination)	Tank and SP Gun Strength: Authorized	Tank and SP Gun Strength: Actual	Composition (Percent Fill)
Oct 1941 to Mar 1942			
Leningrad region			
51 TBn, 42 A, LF (12 Oct)	29	27	(93)
Viaz'ma-Briansk axes (Oct)			
101 TD, WF (1 Oct)	190	35	(13)
107 TD, WF (1 Oct)	190	153	(56)
126, 127, 128, 143, ?? TB, WF (1 Oct)	268	256	mostly BT, T-26 (96)
126, 128 TB, WF (1 Oct)	134	115	(89)
TR, 1 MRD, WF (1 Oct)	NA	35	
145, 148 TB, 43 A, RF (1 Oct)	134	84	(63)
108 TD, 3 A, BF (6 Oct)	190	20	(14)
42 TB, 3 A, BF (8 Oct)	67	18	(27)
Moscow axis (Oct)			
8 TB, 30 A, KF (14 Oct)	67	61	7 KV, 22 T-34, 32 T-40 (91)
18, 19, 20 TB, 5 A, WF (15 Oct)	201	53	(26)
78 RD, 16 A, WF (17 Oct)	NA	23	23 T-26
28 TB, WF (22 Oct)	67	32	5 KV, 11 T-34, 16 T-60 (48)
58 TD, 30 A, KF (30 Oct)	190	78	(41)
32 TB, 50 A, WF (30 Oct)	67	31	(46)
Moscow axis (Nov)			
27, 28 TB, 16 A, WF (10 Nov)	134	52	(39)
1 G (8) TB, 16 A, WF (10 Nov)	67	23	(34)
32 TB, BF (10 Nov)	67	18	(27)
108 TD, 3 A, BF (10 Nov)	190	30	(16)
21 TB, 30 A, KF (11 Nov)	67	20	(30)
58 TD, 30 A, KF (18 Nov)	190	15	(8)
107 MRD, 30 A, KF. (23 Nov)	NA	15	
16 A, WF (16 Nov)	0	191	
58 TD, 17, 18, 20, 24 TB, WF res. (16 Nov)	458	125	to 16 A on 15 Nov as mobile group (27)
8 TB, 30 A, WF (16 Nov)	67	20	(30)
21 TB, 30 A, WF (16 Nov)	67	0	
1 GTB, 16 A, WF (14 Nov)	67	15	(22)
27 TB, 16 A, WF (15 Nov)	67	17	(25)
19 TB, 16 A, WF (16 Nov)	67	23	(34)
18, 20, 22 TB, 5 A, WF (16 Nov)	201	65	(32)
108 TD, 50 A, WF (16 Nov)	190	30	(16)
1 G, 23, 27, 28 TB, 16 A, WF (21 Nov)	268	15	(6)
107 MD, 30 A, WF (23 Nov)	??	15	
25 TB, 16 A, WF (23 Nov)	67	11	(16)
20 TB, 5 A, WF (24 Nov)	67	16	(24)
Moscow axis (Dec)			
18 RB, 33 A, WF (1 Dec)	NA	18	3 KV, 6 T-34, 9 BT
5 TB, 33 A, WF (1 Dec)	46	11	(24)
20 TB, 5 A, WF (1 Dec)	46	6	(13)
22 TB, 5 A, WF (1 Dec)	46	21	(46)
136, 140 TBn, 33 A, WF (2 Dec)	72	21	(29)
5 TB, 33 A, WF (3 Dec)	46	9	(20)

—Continued

Force (Subordination)	Tank and SP Gun Strength: Authorized	Actual	Composition (Percent Fill)
20 TB, 5 A, WF (3 Dec)	46	9	(20)
8, 21 TB, 30 A, WF (3 Dec)	92	35	(38)
24, 134 TB, 20 A, WF (3 Dec)	92	60	(65)
17, 33, 145, 146 TB, 16 A, WF (3 Dec)	184	125	(68)
123, 133 TBn, 1 SA, WF (3 Dec)	72	50	(69)
136, 140 TBn, 33 A, WF (3 Dec)	72	21	(29)
8, 21 TB, 107 MD, 30 A, WF (6 Dec)	NA	35	(21 in one source)
123, 133 TBn, 1 SA, WF (6 Dec)	72	50	(69)
24, 31 TB, 20 A, WF (6 Dec)	92	16	(17)
134 TBn, 20 A, WF (6 Dec)	36	16	(44)
135 TBn, 20 A, WF (6 Dec)	36	33	(92)
4 TBs, 16 A, WF (6 Dec)	184	125	(68)
5 TB, 33 A, WF (6 Dec)	46	50	(>100)
26 TB, 43 A, WF (6 Dec)	46	50	(>100)
33 TB, 16 A, WF (7 Dec)	46	9	(20)
22 TB, 2 GCC, 5 A, WF (11 Dec)	46	12	(26)
31 TB, 20 A, WF (12 Dec)	46	10	(22)
123, 149 TBn, 31 A, Kal. F (14 Dec)	72	34	(47)
26 TB, 43 A, WF (14 Dec)	46	30	14 T-34, 16 T-60 (65)
26 TB, 43 A, WF (18 Dec)	46	50	
112 TD, 50 A, WF (18 Dec)	190	17	(9)
131 TBn, 50 A, WF (18 Dec)	36	15	(42)
Orel-Elets axis (Dec–Mar)			
129 TB, 3 A, SWF (4 Dec)	46	16	Plus 24 in disrepair (35–87)
150 TB, 3 A, SWF (4 Dec)	46	0	
150 TB, 3 A, SWF (1 March)	46	38	2 KV, 19 BT, T-26, 17 T-60 (83)
Moscow axis (Jan–Mar)			
20 TB, 5 A, WF (1 Jan 42)	46	45	(98)
170 TBn, 3 SA, NWF (1 Jan)	36	35	(97)
1 G, 145, 31, 22 TB, 20 A, WF (6 Jan 42)	184	100	(54)
112 TB, 50 A, WF (6 Jan 42)	46	34	(74)
18, 26 TB, 43 A, WF (9 Jan 42)	92	40	(43)
2 GTB, Gp. Belov (1 GCC), WF (31 Jan)	46	8	8 T-60 (17)
18 TB, 43, WF (4 Feb)	46	9	1 KV, 3 T-34, 5 T-60 (18)
28 TB, 30 A, KF (21 Mar)	46	43	10 KV, 22 T-34, 11 T-37 (93)
Demiansk axis (Jan–Feb)			
8 TBn, NWF (3 Jan)	288	186	(65)
Rostov axis (Nov)			
6 TB, 56 A, N. Cauc. F. (20 Oct)	67	105	T-26 (>100)
2, 132 TB, 9 A, SF (5 Nov)	134	50	(37)
132 TB, 37 A, SF (15 Nov)	67	32	1 KV, 14 T-34, 15 BT, 2 T-26 (48)
3 TB, 37 A, SF (15 Nov)	67	30	(45)
2 TB, 37 A, SF (15 Nov)	67	30	23 T-34, 5 BT (45)
142 TB, 9 A, SF (15 Nov)	67	28	23 T-34, 5 BT (42)
6 TB, 57 A, SF (15 Nov)	67	105	4 KV, 10 T-34 (>100)

—Continued

Table 7.18 Continued

Force (Subordination)	Tank and SP Gun Strength Authorized	Actual	Composition (Percent Fill)
Barvenkovo axis (Jan)			
7, 13 TB, 6 A, SWF (28 Jan)	92	66	(72)
6, 12, 130 TB, 57 A, SF (28 Jan)	138	138	(100)
2, 3 TB, 37 A, SF (28 Jan)	92	92	(100)
54 TB, 12 A, SF (28 Jan)	46	48	(>100)
15, 132 TB, 1, 5 GCC, SF (28 Jan)	92	72	(78)
Crimean axis (Feb–Mar)			
39, 40, 55 TB, 229 TBn (KV), 51 A, Crim. F (1 Feb)	174	200	(>100)
124, 126 TBn, 44 A, Crim. F (1 Feb)	72	36	(50)
Apr–May 1942			
10 TC, *Stavka* Res. (Apr)	177	177	24 KV, 90 T-34, 63 T-60 (100)
178 TB, 10 TC, (Apr)	45	45	24 KV, 21 T-60 (100)
183 TB, 10 TC, (Apr)	65	65	44 T-34, 21 T-60 (100)
186 TB, 10 TC, (Apr)	65	65	44 T-34, 21 T-60 (100)
10 TC, *Stavka* Res. (15 May)	146	132	24 KV, 60 MK II, 48 T-70 (91)
Khar'kov axis			
21 TC, SWF (10 May)	146	134	destroyed by 25 May (92)
23 TC, SWF (10 May)	146	135	destroyed by 25 May (92)
13, 36, 133 TB, 38 A, SWF (10 May)	138	125	(91)
6 G, 57, 84, 90 TB, 28 A, SWF (10 May)	184	181	(98)
10 TB, 8 TBn, 21 A, SWF (10 May)	80	48	(60)
7 TB, Gp. Bobkin, SWF (10 May)	46	40	destroyed by 25 May (87)
5 G, 37, 38, 48 TB, 6 A, SWF (10 May)	184	166	destroyed by 25 May (90)
8, 7, 132 TBn, SWF (10 May)	108	96	(89)
15, 21 TB, 9 A, SF (16 May)	92	52	destroyed by 25 May (57)
39, 40, 55, 56 TB, 79, 229, 124, 126 TBn, Crim. Front (8 May)	328	213	(plus 70 in disrepair) (65); destroyed by 25 May
55 TB, Crim. Front (8 May)	46	47	(>100) destroyed by 25 May
Jun–Jul 1942			
157 TB, *Stavka* Res. (2 Jun)	53	53	32 T-34, 21 T-70 (100)
26 TC, *Stavka* Res. (5 Jun)	180	161	24 KV, 68 T-34, 69 T-70 (89)
17 TC, *Stavka* Res. (15 Jun)	180	180	23 KV, 91 T-34, 67 T-60 (100)
66 TB, 17 TC, (15 Jun)	53	50	23 KV, 27 T-60 (94)
67 TB, 17 TC, (15 Jun)	65	65	45 T-34, 20 T-60 (100)
174 TB, 17 TC, (15 Jun)	65	65	45 T-34, 20 T-60 (100)
12 TC, 3 TA, WF (30 Jun)	180	172	20 KV, 112 T-34, 10 T-70, 30 T-60 (96)
30 TB, 12 TC, 3 TA (30 Jun)	65	60	10 KV, 40 T-34, 10 T-70 (92)
86 TB, 12 TC, 3 TA (30 Jun)	53	55	5 KV, 35 T-34, 15 T-60 (>100)
97 TB, 12 TC, 3 TA (30 Jun)	53	55	5 KV, 35 T-34, 15 T-60 (>100)
106 TB, 12 TC, 3 TA, (31 Jul)	53	53	32 T-34, 21 T-70 (100)
195 TB, 15 TC, 3 TA (31 Jul)	53	53	32 T-34, 21 T-70 (100)

—*Continued*

Force (Subordination)	Tank and SP Gun Strength: Authorized	Actual	Composition (Percent Fill)
Zhizdra-Bolkhov axis			
10 TC, 16 A, WF (4 Jul)	180	152	85 KV, T-34, 25 MK-II, 20 T-60 (84)
94, 112, 146 TB, 16 A, WF (4 Jul)	159	131	75 KV, T-34, 56 light (82)
3 TC, 61 A, BF (4 Jul)	180	192	(>100)
68, 192 TB, 61 A, BF (4 Jul)	106	107	32 KV, T-34 (>100)
Voronezh axis			
13 TC, 21 A, BF (28 Jun)	180	180	(100)
2, 16, 17 TC, BF (28 Jun)	540	>500	(100)
5 TA, BF (4 Jul)	540	600	(>100)
2 TC, 5 TA, BF (4 Jul)	180	180	(100)
11 TC, 5 TA, BF (4 Jul)	180	180	(100)
7 TC, 5 TA, BF (4 Jul)	180	180	(100)
19 TB, 5 TA, BF (4 Jul)	65	60	(92)
67, 174 TB, 17 TC, 60 A, VF (7 Jul)	130	67	60 T-34, 7 T-70 (52)
14 TB, 40 A, VF (7 Jul)	46	35	(76)
25 TC, 60 A, VF (16 Jul)	168	166	103 T-34, 63 T-60, T-70 (99)
25 TC, VF (1 Sep)	168	53	45 T-34 (32)
1 TC, VF (12 Aug)	168	108	(64)
7 TC, VF (12 Aug)	180	173	(96)
11 TC, VF (12 Aug)	168	98	(58)
Stalingrad axis			
13, 28 TC, 1 TA, Sta. F (13 Jul)	336	250	(74)
13 TC, 62 A, Sta. F (13 Jul)	168	123	74 T-34, 49 T-60, 70 (73)
163 TB, 13 TC, 62 A (13 Jul)	53	41	(77)
166 TB, 13 TC, 62 A (13 Jul)	53	41	(77)
169 TB, 13 TC, 62 A (13 Jul)	53	41	(77)
28 TC, 62 A, Sta. F. (13 Jul)	168	125	(74)
13, 23, 28 TC, 62 A, Sta. F. (23 Jul)		322	20 KV, 161 T-34, 141 T-70
644, 645, 648, 649, 650, 651 TBn, 62 A, Sta. F (23 Jul)	216	168	(78)
40 TB, 138 TB, 62 A, Sta. F (23 Jul)	106	91	(86)
121, 137 TB, 64 A, Sta. F (23 Jul)	106	69	(65)
40 TB, 649 TBn, 62 A, Sta. F (22 Jul)	91	51	10 KV, 41 T-34 (56)
13 TC, 1 TA, Sta. F (21 Jul)	168	123	(73)
13 TC, 1 TA, Sta. F (24–25 Jul)	168	150	(89)
13 TC, 1 TA, Sta. F (27 Jul)	168	27	(16)
13 TC, 1 TA, Sta. F (30 Jul)	168	27	(16)
Aug–Oct 1942			
Demiansk axis			
103 TBn, 1 SA, NWF (27 Sep)	36	12	12 T-34 (33)
Rzhev-Sychevka axis			
28 TB, 30 A, KF (15 Aug)	53	14	9 T-34, 5 T-60 (26)
6 TC, 20 A, WF (1 Aug)	170	169	24 KV, 46 T-34, 30 T-70, 69 T-60 (99)

—Continued

Table 7.18 Continued

Force (Subordination)	Tank and SP Gun Strength: Authorized	Tank and SP Gun Strength: Actual	Composition (Percent Fill)
8 TC, 20 A, WF (1 Aug)	170	165	83 KV, T-34 (97)
11, 17, 20, 188, 213 TB, 20 A, WF (1 Aug)	265	255	(96)
17 TB, 20 A, WF (8 Aug)	53	20	(38)
28 TB, 30 A, KF (9 Sep)	53	15	15 T-34 (28)
Zhizdra-Bolkhov axis			
10 TC, 16 A, WF (12 Aug)	170	156	48 KV, 44 MK-II, 64 T-60 (92)
10 TC, 16 A, WF (13 Aug)	170	121	(71)
10 TC, 16 A, WF (29 Aug)	170	56	(33)
9 TC, 16 A, WF (12 Aug)	170	ca 150	(88)
9 TC, 16 A, WF (29 Aug)	170	50	(28)
3 TA, WF (21 Aug)		436	48 KV, 223 T-34, 162 T-60/70, 3 T-50
3 TC, 61 A, WF (12 Aug)	180	180	(100)
Stalingrad axis			
25 TC, 40 A, (1 Sep)	170	73	45 T-34 (20 in disrepair) (43)
13 TC, 64 A, SEF (6 Aug)	168	132	114 T-34, 18 T-60, 70 (79)
6 GTB, 13 TC, 64 A (6 Aug)	53	44	44 T-34 (83)
13 TB, 13 TC, 64 A (6 Aug)	53	44	44 T-34 (83)
254 TB, 13 TC, 64 A (6 Aug)	53	42	30 T-34, 12 T-60, 70 (79)
13 TC, 64 A, SEF (11 Aug)	168	76	(45)
56 TB, 13 TC, 64 A, SEF (2 Sep)	53	22	20 T-34, 2 T-60 (42)
13 TC, 64 A, SEF (12 Sep)	168	16	11 T-34, 5 T-60 (10)
56 TB, 13 TC, 64 A (12 Sep)	53	6	4 T-34, 2 T-60 (11)
13 TB, 13 TC, 64 A (12 Sep)	53	10	7 T-34, 2 T-60 (19)
13 TC, 64 A, SEF (27 Sep)	168	6	(4)
13 TC, 64 A, SEF (2 Oct)	168	16	(10)
Nov–Dec 1942			
Demiansk axis			
167 TR, 1 SA, NWF (1 Nov)	39	24	all T-34 tanks (62)
Velikie Luki axis			
2 MC, 3 SA, KF (20 Nov)	224	215	(96)
2 MC, 3 SA, KF (24 Nov)	224	161	(54 in disrepair) (72)
Rzhev-Sychevka axis			
1 MC, 41 A, KF (24 Nov)	224	224	10 KV, 119 T-34, 95 T-70 (100)
47th, 48th MB, 41 A, KF (24 Nov)	78	82	(>100)
3 MC, 22 A, KF (24 Nov)	224	232	(>100)
6 TC, 20 A, WF (24 Nov)	170	120	85 T-34 (71)
6 TC, 20 A, WF (27 Nov)	170	50	(29)
5 TC, WF (10 Dec)	170	131	(77)
6 TC, 20 A, WF (11 Dec)	170	100	7 KV, 64 T-34, 12 T-70, 17 T-60 (59)
10 TC, WF (20 Dec)	180	177	25 KV, 66 T-34, 9 MK II, 35 T-70, 42 T-60 (98)
Stalingrad axis			
4 MC, Sta. F (4 Nov)	204	220	(>100)
13 TC (MC), Sta. F (15 Nov)	204	205	(>100)
5 TA, SWF (19 Nov)		380	70 KV, 135 T-34, 175 T-70
5 TA, SWF (2 Dec)		182	

—*Continued*

Force (Subordination)	Tank and SP Gun Strength: Authorized	Actual	Composition (Percent Fill)
1 TC, 5 TA, SWF (19 Nov)	170	136	(80)
1 TC, 5 TA, SWF (25 Nov)	170	20	(12)
26 TC, 5 TA, SWF (19 Nov)	170	161	(95)
4 TC, 21 A, SWF (19 Nov)	170	143	29 KV, 57 T-43, 57 T-70 (84)
1, 2, 3 GTR, 21 A, SWF (19 Nov)	63	56	56 KV (89)
16 TC, 24 A, SWF (19 Nov)	170	103	(61)
4 MC, 254 TB, 51 A, Sta. F (20 Nov)	257	198	(77)
4 MC, 51 A, Sta. F (20 Nov)	204	109	(53)
13 TC, 57 A, Sta. F (19 Nov)	204	113	(55)
90 TB, 57 A, Sta. F (19 Nov)	53	53	(100)
4 TC, 21 A, Don F (19 Nov)	170	159	(94)
Middle Don axis			
17 TC, 115 TB, 82, 212 TR, 6 A, VF (15 Dec)	310	250	(83)
17 TC, 6 A, VF (15 Dec)	170	168	98 T-34, 70 T-70 (99)
115 TB, 6 A, VF (15 Dec)	53	41	(77)
1, 18, 24, 25 TC, 8, 15 GTB, 114, 119, 126, 141, 243 TR, 510, 511 TBn, 1, 3 GA, 5 TA, SWF (15 Dec)	1,053	920	(87)
18, 24, 25 TC, 126, 141 TR, 1 GA, SWF (15 Dec)	588	504	(86)
18 TC, 1 GA, SWF (15 Dec)	170	160	(94)
24 TC, 1 GA, SWF (15 Dec)	170	159	(94)
24 TC, 1 GA, SWF (24 Dec)	170	54	36 T-34, 18 T-70 (32)
24 TC, 1 GA, SWF (28 Dec)	170	58	39 T-34, 19 T-70 (34)
24 TC, 1 GA, SWF (29 Dec)	170	25	(15)
25 TC, 1 GA, SWF (15 Dec)	170	131	73 T-34 (77)
25 TC, 1 GA, SWF (28 Dec)	170	25	(15)
1 GMC, 114, 119, 243 TR, 3 GA, SWF (15 Dec)	321	234	(73)
1 GMC, 3 GA, SWF (12 Dec)	204	163	(80)
17 GTR, 1 GMC, SWF (12 Dec)	39	27	10 KV, 9 T-34, 8 T-70
1 TC, 8, 15 GTB, 510, 511 TBn, 5 TA, SWF (15 Dec)	348	182	(52)
1 TC, 5 TA, SWF (7 Dec)	170	72	(42)
5 MC, 5 TA, SWF (9 Dec)	204	193	(95) (not incl. in calculations above)
Kotel'nikovskii axis			
13 TC, 51 A, Sta. F (4 Dec)	204	49	in the 44, 163 TRs (24)
5 S, 51, 28 A, Stal. F (12 Dec)	NA	369	
7 TC, 4 MC, 5 SA, Stal. F (12 Dec)	374	252	
13 TC, 85, 235, 254 TB, 234 TR, 51 A, Stal. F (12 Dec)	402	77	
6 GTB, 565 TBn, 28 A, Stal. F (12 Dec)	89	40	
41, 139, 189, 198 TR, Stal. F (12 Dec)	156	147	

—Continued

Table 7.18 Continued

Force (Subordination)	Tank and SP Gun Strength: Authorized	Tank and SP Gun Strength: Actual	Composition (Percent Fill)
6 (2 G)MC, 2 GA, Sta. F (16 Dec)	204	195	117 T-34, 78 T-70 (96)
7 TC, 2 GA, Sta. F (16 Dec)	170	92	20 KV, 41 T-34, 31 T-70 (54)
4 (3 G)MC, 2 GA, Sta. F (12 Dec)	204	107	(52)
13 TC, 51 A, Sta. F (28 Dec)	204	14	(7)
Jan-Apr 1943			
Leningrad region			
61, 220, 152, TB, 119, 189 TBn, 67 A, LF (1 Jan)	231	222	(96)
16, 98, 122, 185 TB, 50, 501, 503, 507 TBn, 2 SA, Vol. F (1 Jan)	395	217	(55)
Ostrogozhsk-Rossosh' axis			
4 TC, VF (12 Jan)	202	219	(>100)
38, 60, 40 A, 3 TA, 18 RC, 7 CC, VF (12 Jan)		896	112 KV, 405 T-34, 87 MZS, 263 T-60/70, 29 MZL
86, 116, 150 TB, 40 A, VF (12 Jan)	159	133	(84)
150 TB, 38 A, VF (12 Jan)	53	29	(55)
14, 180 TB, 60 A, VF (12 Jan)	106	70	(66)
192 TB, 18 RC, VF (12 Jan)	53	51	51 MS-3 (96)
96 TB, 18 RC, VF (12 Jan)	53	49	49 T-34 (92)
262 TR, 18 RC, VF (12 Jan)	21	20	20 KV (95)
201 TB, 7 CC, VF (12 Jan)	53	65	(>100)
3 TA, VF (10 Jan)		479	
3 TA, VF (12 Jan)		371	plus 122 in disrepair
106 TB, 12 TC, 3 TA (15 Jan)	53	16	(30)
88 TB, 15 TC, 3 GTA (17 Jan)	53	20	(38)
113 TB, 12 TC, 3 TA (19 Jan)	53	8	(15)
195 TB, 12 TC, 3 TA (19 Jan)	53	10	(19)
183 TB, 10 TC, 1 GA, SWF (21 Jan)	53	40	(75)
Voronezh-Kastornoe axis			
13 A, BF, 38, 60, 40 A, VF (24 Jan)		640	
118, 129 TB, 42, 43, 193 TR, 13 A, BF (24 Jan)	223	251	(>100)
180 TB, 14, 150 TBn, 38 A, VF (24 Jan)	125	91	(73)
14, 86, 150 TB, 60 A, VF (24 Jan)	159	51	(32)
4 TC, 96, 192 TB, 40 A, VF (24 Jan)	308	247	(80)
10 TC, 1 GA, SWF (26 Jan)	170	41	more than 100 in disrepair (24)
186 TB, 10 TC, 1 GA (26 Jan)	53	7	(13)
Khar'kov axis			
3 TA, VF (29 Jan)	0	165	plus 140 in disrepair
12 TC, 3 TA, VF (1 Feb)	170	85	(50)

—Continued

Force (Subordination)	Tank and SP Gun Strength Authorized	Actual	Composition (Percent Fill)
15 TC, 3 TA, VF (1 Feb)	170	80	(47)
106 TB, 12 TC, 3 TA (8 Feb)	53	10	(19)
3 TA, VF (14 Feb)	0	100	
3 TA, VF (18 Feb)	0	110	
3 TA, VF (27 Feb)	0	39	
106 TB, 12 TC, 3 TA (28 Feb)	53	12	(23)
106 TB, 12 TC, 3 TA (3 Mar)	53	11	(21)
106 TB, 12 TC, 3 TA (5 Mar)	53	5	(9)
Donbas axis			
4 G, 3, 10, 18 TC, Gp. Popov, SWF (27 Jan)	680	212	(31)
10 TC, Gp. Popov (27 Jan)	170	101	(59)
4 GTC, Gp. Popov, SWF (27 Jan)	170	40	28 T-34, 12 T-70 (24)
4 GTC, Gp. Popov (4 Feb)	170	37	(22)
3 TC, Gp. Popov, SWF (4 Feb)	170	23	(14)
Gp. Popov, SWF (16 Feb)	680	145	(21)
4 GTC, Gp. Popov (18 Feb)	170	17	(10)
Gp. Popov (19 Feb)	680	40	(6)
4 GTC, Gp. Popov (24 Feb)	170	32	T-34 (19)
1 GTC, SWF (19 Feb)	170	150	(88)
25 TC, SWF (15 Feb)	170	156	90 T-34, 66 T-70 (92)
Belgorod-Kursk axis			
3 GTC, VF (1 Mar)	170	150	(88)
2 GTC, VF (1 Mar)	170	175	(>100)
Orel-Smolensk axis			
2 TA, CF (18 Feb)		408	
11 TC, 2 TA, CF (15 Feb)	202	192	(95)
16 TC, 2 TA, CF (15 Feb)	202	161	(80)
11 GTB, 2 TA, CF (15 Feb)	53	55	(>100)
2 TA, CF (24 Feb)	0	182	
11 TC, 2 TA, CF (24 Feb)	202	102	11 KV, 1 T-34, 41 T-60, T-70, 49 MK-II, III (50)
16 TC, 2 TA, CF (24 Feb)	202	47	33 T-34, 14 T-60, 70 (23)
11 GTB, 2 TA, CF (24 Feb)	53	40	25 T-34, 15 T-70 (75)
29 GTR, 2 TA, CF (24 Feb)	21	15	15 KV (71)
11 TC, 2 TA, CF (28 Feb)	202	135	(67) railhead
16 TC, 2 TA, CF (28 Feb)	202	70	(35) forward assembly area
11, 16 TC, 2 TA, CF (12 Mar)	404	162	100 operational (40) (25 op)
Rostov-Mius axis			
6 MC, 2 GA, SF (1 Jan)	204	150	(74)
4 GMC, 5 SA, SF (12 Feb)	204	76	76 T-34 (37)
4 GMC, 5 SA, SF (17 Feb)	204	20	(10)
1 GTC, Ste. F (24 April)	202	216	21 KV, 132 T-34, 63 T-70 (>100)
2 GTC, 4 GA, St F (24 April)	202	197	(98)
4 GMC, SF res. (30 April)	229	192	170 tanks, 22 SU-152 (94)
Jun–Aug 1943			
Kursk axis			
31 TC, 1 TA, Vor. F (15 Jun)	202	196	155 T-34, 41 T-60, 70 (97)
10 TC, 5 GA, St. F (15 Jun)	223	185	1 KV, 99 T-34, 64 T-70, 21 SP (83)

—Continued

Force (Subordination)	*Tank and SP Gun Strength* Authorized	Actual	Composition (Percent Fill)
87 TR, *Stavka* Res. (2 Jul)	39	39	12 T-34, 27 T-70 (100)
2 TA, CF (3 Jul)	0	456	435 T-34, 21 SP
1 TA, VF (3 Jul)	0	563	542 tanks, 21 SP
3 MC, 1 TA, VF (3 Jul)	229	211	(92)
6 TC, 1 TA, VF (3 Jul)	223	198	177 tanks, 21 SP (89)
6 TC, 1 TA, VF (18 Jul)	223	52	(23)
31 TC, 1 TA, VF (3 Jul)	202	154	113 T-34, 41 T-70 (76)
31 TC, 1 TA, VF (9 Jul)	202	68	(34)
242 TB, 31 TC, 1 TA (9 Jul)	53	20	(38)
100 TB, 31 TC, 1 TA (9 Jul)	53	27	(51)
237 TB, 31 TC, 1 TA (9 Jul)	53	19	(36)
100 TB, 31 TC, 1 TA (10 Jul)	53	6	(11)
59 TR, 31 TC, 1 TA (10 Jul)	39	10	8 T-34, 2 T-60 (26)
10 TC, 5 GA, St. F (7 Jul)	223	185	1 KV, 99 T-34, 64 T-70, 21 SP (83)
10 TC, VF (11 Jul)	223	50	(22)
10 TC, VF (13 Jul)	223	86	56 T-34, 30 T-70 (39)
10 TC, 6 GA, VF (16 Jul)	223	58	(26)
10 TC, 6 GA, VF (19 Jul)	223	93	(42)
5 GTC, VF (11 Jul)	241	50	(21)
2 TC, VF (12 Jul)	202	168	(83)
5 GTA, St. F (9 Jul)	0	630	593 tanks, 37 SP guns
18 TC, 5 GTA (9 Jul)	202	187	103 T-34, 63 T-70, 21 MK-IV (93)
29 TC, 5 GTA (9 Jul)	223	237	1 KV, 130 T-34, 85 T-70, 21 SP (>100)
5 GMC, 5 GTA (9 Jul)	229	228	212 tanks, 16 SP (100)
5 GTA, VF (11 Jul)	0	830	501 T-34, 261 T-70, 31 MK-IV, 37 SP (incl. 2 TC, 2 GTC)
Gp. Trufanov, 5 GTA (11 Jul)		100	71 T-34, 29 T-70
3 GTC, 4 GA, St. F (9 Jul)	223	178	(80)
4 GTC, St. F (15 Jul)	223	189	168 tanks, 21 SP (85)
1 MC, St. F (15 Jul)	229	204	(89)
5 GMC, 5 GTA, VF (20 Jul)	229	92	68 T-34, 24 T-70 (89)
Donbas axis (Jul)			
23 TC, 1 GA, SWF (16 Jul)	202	180	Most T-34, some MK-II (89)
1 GMC, 8 GA, SFW (16 Jul)	204	194	120 T-34 (95)
2 GMC, 2 GA, SF (16 Jul)	229	200	120 T-34 (87)
4 GMC, 2 GA, SF (16 Jul)	229	192	170 T-34, 22 SU-152 (84)
2 GMC, 2 GA, SF (5 Aug)	229	49	(21)
32 GTB, 5 SA, SF (16 Jul)	53	46	(87)
Orel axis (Jul–Aug)			
196 TB, 50 A, WF (12 Jul)	65	66	(100)
1 TC, WF (12 Jul)	218	184	168 tanks, 16 SP (84)
5 TC, WF (12 Jul)	218	184	168 tanks, 16 SP (84)
1 GTC, BF (12 Jul)	218	207	(95)
20 TC, 61 A, BF (13 Jul)	218	184	(84)
25 TC, 11 GA, WF (17 Jul)	202	196	(97)
3 GTA, BF (18 Jul)	0	730	473 T-34, 225 T-70, 32 SP
12 TC, 3 GTA (18 Jul)	218	225	209 tanks, 16 SP (>100)
15 TC, 3 GTA (18 Jul)	218	225	209 tanks, 16 SP (>100)

—*Continued*

Force (Subordination)	Tank and SP Gun Strength		Composition (Percent Fill)
	Authorized	Actual	
2 MC, 3 GTA, (18 Jul)	229	204	(89)
3 GTA, BF (4 Aug)	0	417	
4 TA, WF (18 Jul)	0	652	
6 GMC, 4 TA (18 Jul)	218	216	(99)
11 TC, 4 TA (18 Jul)	218	204	(94)
30 TC, 4 TA (18 Jul)	218	216	(99)
2 TA, CF (25 Aug)	0	265	
Belgorod-Khar'kov axis			
1 TA, VF (2 Aug)	0	542	417 T-43, 27 SP
6 TC, 1 TA (2 Aug)	223	200	(90)
31 TC, 1 TA (2 Aug)	202	142	98 T-34 (70)
3 MC, 1 TA (2 Aug)	229	185	(81)
1 TA, VF (11 Aug)	0	295	268 tanks, 27 SP
31 TC, 1 TA (11 Aug)	202	35	(17)
242 TB, 31 TC (11 Aug)	53	13	10 T-34, 3 T-70 (25)
100 TB, 31 TC (11 Aug)	53	15	(28)
237 TB, 31 TC (11 Aug)	53	5	(9)
31 TC, 1 TA (13 Aug)	202	27	(13)
237 TB, 31 TC, 1 TA (13 Aug)	53	15	(28)
242 TB, 31 TC, 1 TA (13 Aug)	53	9	(17)
100 TB, 31 TC, 1 TA (13 Aug)	53	1	(2)
1 TA, VF (18 Aug)	0	120	
3 MC, 1 TA (18 Aug)	229	88	59 T-34, 19 T-50, 4 T-60, 6 SP (38)
242 TB, 31 TC, 1 TA (19 Aug)	53	10	(19)
1 TA VF (25 Aug)	0	162	
5 GTA, St. F (3 Aug)	0	543	503 T-34, 40 SP
18 TC, 5 GTA, St. F (3 Aug)	202	180	(89)
18 TC, 5 GTA, St. F (18 Aug)	202	50	(25)
29 TC, 5 GTA, St. F (3 Aug)	223	180	(81)
29 TC, 5 GTA, St. F (18 Aug)	223	80	(36)
1 MC, 53 A, St. F (3 Aug)	229	212	(93)
10 TC, 27 A, VF (3 Aug)	223	93	60 T-34, 23 T-70, 5 SU-76, 5 SU-122 (42)
10 TC, 40 A, VF (6 Aug)	223	170	(76)
10 TC, 27 A, VF (16 Aug)	223	94	(42)
4 GTC, 27 A, VF (3 Aug)	223	180	(81)
4 GTC, 27 A, VF (9 Aug)	223	97	(43)
2 TC, 40 A, VF (3 Aug)	223	170	(76)
5 GTC, 6 GA, VF (3 Aug)	202	180	(89)
5 GTA, St. (11 Aug)	0	106	incl. SP
5 GMC, 5 GTA (11 Aug)	229	29	25 T-34, 4 T-70 (13)
5 GTA, St. F (24 Aug)	0	111	97 T-34, 14 T-70
5 GTA, St. F (25 Aug)	0	153	
93 TB, 5 GA, VF (1 Aug)	53	49	28 T-34, 21 T-70 (92)
28 GTR, 5 GA, VF (1 Aug)	21	19	19 KV (90)
57th GTR, 5 GA, VF (1 Aug)	21	21	21 KV (100)
3 GMC, 47 A, VF (12 Aug)	229	213	164 T-34, 49 T-70 (93)
Smolensk axis			
78 TB, 3 SA, KF (13 Aug)	53	52	incl. 2 unserviceable (100)
105 TR, 43 A, KF (13 Aug)	39	32	incl. 7 unserviceable (100)

—Continued

Force (Subordination)	Tank and SP Gun Strength: Authorized	Tank and SP Gun Strength: Actual	Composition (Percent Fill)
42 GTB, 31 A, WF (7 Aug)	53	48	7 KV, 22 T-34, 18 T-60, 4 T-70 (91)
42 GTB, 31 A, WF (10 Aug)	53	14	(26)
5 MC, 10 GA, WF (15 Aug)	229	193	182 foreign models (84)
2 GTC, WF (15 Aug)	202	201	131 T-34, 70 T-70 (100)
Donbas axis			
4 GMC, SF (13 Aug)	229	210	(92)
Sep–Oct 1943			
Advance to the Dnepr			
7 MC, Moscow MD (1 Sep)	229	238	(>100)
10 TC, VF (9 Sep)	223	72	30 T-34, 20 M-Zl, 10 T-70, 12 SP (32)
10 TC, 40 A, VF (22 Sep)	223	19	(9)
53 GTB, 6 GTC, 3 GTA, VF (8 Sep)	53	53	(100)
9 MC, 3 GTA, VF (15 Sep)	229	206	(90)
3 GTA, VF (19 Sep)		686	
Smolensk axis			
23, 248 TB, 21 A, WF (15 Sep)	106	15	(14)
2 GTC, 21 A, WF (15 Sep)	202	184	(91)
104, 193, 207 TR, 3 GCC, 21 A, WF (15 Sep)	117	117	(100)
2 GTC, 21 A, WF (16 Sep)	202	110	(54)
Kiev (Bukrin) axis			
5 GTC, 38 A, VF (11 Oct)	223	90	50 T-34, 15 MK-IV, 35 T-70 (40)
3 GTA, VF (3 Oct)		514	430 tanks, 84 SP
7 GTC, 3 GTA (6 Oct)	223	127	1 KV, 99 T-34, 19 SU-76, 8 SU-152 (57)
6 GTC, 3 GTA (6 Oct)	223	140	(63)
53 GTB, 6 GTC, 3 GTA (15 Oct)	53	25	(47)
8 GTC, 40 A, VF (10 Oct)	223	130	(58)
10 TC, 40 A, VF (10 Oct)	223	102	(46)
3 GMC, 47 A, VF (11 Oct)	229	150	(66)
10 TC, 40 A, VF (12 Oct)	223	41	(18)
6 GTC, 3 GTA, VF (13 Oct)	223	33	(15)
3 GTA, 1 UF (28 Oct)	0	345	
3 GTA, 1 UF (31 Oct)	0	400	
Vitebsk-Orsha axis			
2 GTC, 42 G, 153 TB, 119 TR, 31 A, 10 GA, WF (20 Oct)	347	172	(50)
Gomel'-Rechitsa axis			
129 TB, 13 A, CF (18 Sep)	53	16	(30)
1 GTC, Belo. F. (12 Oct)	283	269	218 T-34, 51 SP (95)
Krivoi Rog axis			
5 GTA, St. F (3 Oct)	0	300	
51 GTR, 10 GMB, 5 GMC, 5 GTA, St. F (19 Oct)	39	28	28 T-34 (72)
18 TC, 5 GTA, St. F (23 Oct)	223	49	(22)
29 TC, 5 GTA, St. F (23 Oct)	223	26	(12)
5 GMC, 7 GA, 2 UF (23 Oct)	229	75	(33)
1 GMC, 7 GA, 2 UF (23 Oct)	229	65	(28)
18 TC, 5 GTA, 2 UF (28 Oct)	223	23	(10)

—*Continued*

Table 7.18 Continued

Force (Subordination)	Tank and SP Gun Strength: Authorized	Actual	Composition (Percent Fill)
Melitopol' axis			
5 S, 44, 2 G, 28, 51 A, SF (26 Sep)	0	759	667 tanks, 92 SP in mobile corps
140, 238 TB, 5 SA, SF (26 Sep)	106	27	(25)
32 GTB, 62 GTR, 44 A, SF (26 Sep)	74	46	(62)
33 GTB, 1 GTR, 510 TBn, 2 GA, SF (26 Sep)	110	16	(15)
502 TBn, 28 A, SF (26 Sep)	36	7	(19)
51 A, SF (26 Sep)	0	3	
2, 4 GMC, 11, 19, 20 TC, 6 GTB, 22 GTR, SF (26 Sept)	1,201	678	586 tanks, 92 SP (56)
Nov–Dec 1943			
Vitebsk-Orsha axis			
1 TC, 11 GA, 1 Bal. F (13 Dec)	257	97	(38)
10 GTB, 11 GA (13 Dec)	65	46	(71)
2 GTR, 11 GA (13 Dec)	21	17	(81)
5 TC, 4 SA, 1 Bal. F (13 Dec)	257	91	(35)
34 GTB, 4 SA (13 Dec)	65	24	(37)
203 TR, 4 SA (13 Dec)	21	14	(67)
3 GTR, 3 GCC, 4 SA (13 Dec)	39	30	(77)
60 TB, 105 TR, TR, 46 MB, 43 A, 1 Bal. F (13 Dec)	142	60	(42)
28, 29 GTB, 47 MB, 39 A, 1 Bal. F (13 Dec)	169	100	(59)
2 GTC, 153, 256, 42 G, 23 GTB, 119, 63, 248, 63 G, 64 GTR, 10 G, 31, 5, 33 A, WF (14 Nov)	608	410	(67)
27, 29, 153, 42 GTB, 119, 248, 63 G, 64 GTR, 10 G, 31, 5, 33 A, WF (30 Nov)	332	284	(86)
1 TC, 11 GA, 1 Bal. F (13 Dec)	257	97	(38)
10 GTB, 11 GA, 1 Bal. F (13 Dec)	65	46	(71)
2 GTR, 11 GA, 1 Bal. F (13 Dec)	21	17	17 KV (81)
2 GTC, 2, 23 G, 213, 256 TB, 5 TRs, 33 A, WF (23 Dec)	644	147	(23)
Gomel'-Rechitsa axis			
3, 11, 48, 50, 61, 65 A, Belo. F (15 Nov)	0	493	
36 TR, 3 A, Belo. F (15 Nov)	39	10	(26)
42, 231, 253 TR, 11 A, Belo. F (15 Nov)	117	20	(17)
193 TR, 48 A, Belo. F (15 Nov)	39	10	(26)
233 TR, 50 A, Belo. F (15 Nov)	39	10	(26)
68 TB, 29 GTR, 61 A, Belo. F (15 Nov)	92	33	(36)

—*Continued*

Table 7.18 Continued

Force (Subordination)	Tank and SP Gun Strength: Authorized	Actual	Composition (Percent Fill)
26 GTR, 63 A, Belo. F (15 Nov)	21	10	(48)
9 TC, 45, 255 TR, 65 A, Belo. F (15 Nov)	303	200	(64)
1 GTC, Belo. F (15 Nov)	239	210	(88)
1 GTC, Belo. F (24 Nov)	239	177	(74)
Kiev-Vinnitsa axis			
3 GTA, 1 UF (2 Nov)	0	389	
3 GTA, 1 UF (3 Nov)	0	621	
87 TR, 7 GCD, 1 GCC, 1 UF (3 Nov)	39	20	(51)
6 GTC, 3 GTA, 1 UF (10 Nov)	257	21	(8)
3 GTA, 1 UF (24 Dec)	0	419	270 T-34, 45 T-70, 104 SP
1 GTA, 1 UF (24 Dec)	0	546	
4 GTC, 60 A, 1 UF (5 Dec)	257	210	150 tanks, 60 SP (82)
3 GTA, 1 UF (8 Jan 44)	0	85	59 tanks, 26 SP
Krivoi Rog-Kirovograd axis			
5 GTA, 2 UF (11 Nov)	0	358	253 T-34, 70 T-70, 35 SP
8 MC, 5 GA, 2 UF (20 Nov)	229	123	(54)
31 TB, 29 TC, 5 GTA (25 Nov)	65	13	(20)
31 TB, 29 TC, 5 GTA (28 Nov)	65	7	(11)
5 GTA, 2 UF (3 Dec)	0	295	
1 MC, 7 GA, 2 UF (5 Dec)	229	152	(66)
5 GTA, 2 UF (8 Dec)	0	164	
18 TC, 5 GTA, 2 UF (8 Dec)	257	37	(14)
29 TC, 5 GTA, 2 UF (8 Dec)	257	22	(9)
8 MC, 5 GTA, 2 UF (8 Dec)	229	52	(23)
5 GMC, 5 GTA, 2 UF (8 Dec)	229	53	(23)
181 TB, 29 TC, 5 GTA (9 Dec)	65	32	(49)
5 GMC, 5 GTA, 2 UF (15 Dec)	229	23	(10)
175 TB, 25 TC, 2 UF (23 Dec)	65	66	(100)
Apostolovo axis			
23 TC, 46 A, 3 UF (14 Nov)	223	100	(45)
23 TC, 8 GA, 3 UF (21 Nov)	223	25	14 T-34, 3 T-70, 8 SP (11)
5 G, 141 TR, 8 GA, (21 Nov)	61	23	(38)

Notes: Tank corps authorized strengths include 8 reserve tanks through January 1943 and 40 reserve tanks from January to November 1943. MK-II models are British Matilda tanks and MK-IV British Churchill tanks. MK-III are American Lee tanks. The nomenclature MZL probably refers to British Valentine light tanks, MZS to American Grant tanks, and MS-3 to British Churchill tanks.

Sources: A. G. Lensky, *Sukhoputnye sily RKKS v predvoennye gody* [RKKA ground forces in the prewar years] (Saint-Peterburg: n.p., 2000); David M. Glantz, *Stumbling Colossus: The Red Army on the Eve of War* (Lawrence: University Press of Kansas, 1998), 116–45, 209, 223–23; K. A. Kalashnikov, V. I. Fes'kov, A. Iu. Chmykhalo, and V. I. Golikov, *Krasnaia armiia v iiune 1941 goda* [The Red Army in June 1941] (Tomsk: Tomsk University, 2001); V. I. Gan'shin, *Tankovye voiska v moskovskoi operatsii* [Tank forces in the Moscow operation] (Moscow: Voroshilov Academy, 1948); B. M. Shaposhnikov, ed., *Razgrom nemetskikh voisk pod Moskvoi* [The Defeat of German forces at Moscow], parts 1–3 (Moscow: Voenizdat, 1943); D. Z. Muriev, *Proval operatsii 'Taifun'* [The defeat of Operation Typhoon] (Moscow: Voenizdat, 1966); *Barvenkovo-Lozovaia operatsiia (18–31 ianvaria 1942 g.)* [The Barvenkovo-Lozovaia operation (18–31 January 1942] (Moscow, Voenizdat, 1943); *Rostovskaia operatsiia, noiabr'–dekabr' 1941 g.* [The Rostov operation, November–December 1941] (Moscow: Voenizdat, 1943); David M. Glantz, *Kharkov 1942: Anatomy of a Military Disaster* (Rockville Center, NY: Sarpedon, 1998); David M. Glantz, *Forgotten*

—*Continued*

Battles of the German-Soviet War (1941–1945), volume II: The Winter Campaign (5 December 1941–April 1942) (Carlisle, PA: Self-published, 1999); David M. Glantz, *Forgotten Battles of the German-Soviet War (1941–1945), volume III: The Summer Campaign (12 May–18 November 1942)* (Carlisle, PA: Self-published, 1999); David M. Glantz, *Forgotten Battles of the German-Soviet War (1941–1945), volume IV: The Winter Campaign (19 November 1942–21 March 1943)* (Carlisle, PA: Self-published, 1999); David M. Glantz, *Deep Attack: The Soviet Conduct of Operational Maneuver* (Carlisle, PA: Self-published, 1998); David M. Glantz, *Zhukov's Greatest Defeat: The Red Army's Epic Defeat in Operation Mars, 1942* (Lawrence; University Press of Kansas, 1999); David M. Glantz, *From the Don to the Dnepr: Soviet Offensive Operations December 1942–August 1943* (London: Frank Cass, 1991); David M. Glantz and Jonathan M. House, *The Battle of Kursk* (Lawrence: University Press of Kansas, 1999); L. M. Sandalov, *Pogorelo-Gorodishchenskaia operatsiia* [Pogoreloe-Gorodishche operation] (Moscow: Voenizdat, 1960); P. D. Alekseev and V. B. Makovskii, *Pervaia oboronitel'naia operatsiia 4-i armii v nachale Velikoi Otechestvennoi voiny* [The initial defensive operation of the 4th Army in the beginning of the Great Patriotic War] (Moscow: Frunze Academy, 1992); O. N. Kudriashov and N. M. Ramanichev, *Boevye deistviia Sovetskikh voisk v nachal'nom periode Velikoi Otechestvennoi voiny* [Combat operations of Soviet forces in the initial period of the Great Patriotic War] (Moscow: Frunze Academy, 1989); O. N. Kudriashov, *Proryv oborony protivnika i razvitie uspekha v operativnoi glubine soedineniami 5-i tankovoi armii. Sryv popytok protivnika deblokirovat' okruzhennuiu gruppirovku* [Penetration of the enemy defense and development of success in operational depth by the formations of the 5th Tank Army. The disruption of the enemy attempt to relieve the encircled grouping] (Moscow: Frunze Academy, 1987); Iu. N. Sukhinin and Iu. N. Iarovenko, *Oborona 1-i Tankovoi armii pod Kurskom (6–11 iiulia 1943 g.)* [The 1st Tank Army's defense at Kursk (6–11 July 1943] (Moscow: Frunze Academy, 1989); E. K. Lukashev and V. I. Kuznetsov, *Podgotovka i vedenie nastupleniia 5-i gvardeiskoi armii vo vzaimodeistvii s podvizhnoi gruppoi fronta v kontrnastuplenii pod Kurskom* [The preparation and conduct of the offensive by the 5th Guards Army in cooperation with the front mobile group in the counteroffensive at Kursk] (Moscow: Frunze Academy, 1991); Iu. P. Babich, *Vstrechnye boi soedinenii 3–go mekhanizirovannogo korpusa v raione Akhtyrki 19–20 avgusta 1943 g. v kontrnastuplenii pod Kurskom* [Meeting engagements of the 3rd Mechanized Corps formations in the Akhtyrka region on 19–20 August 1943 in the Kursk counteroffensive] (Moscow: Frunze Academy, 1990); Iu. P. Babich, *Podgotovka oborony 62-i armii vne soprikosnoveniia s protivnikom i vedenie oboronitel'noi operatsii v usloviiakh prevoskhodstva protivnika v manevrennosti (po opytu Stalingradskoi bitvy)* [The preparation of the 62nd Army's defense in contact with the enemy and the conduct of a defensive operations with a more maneuverable enemy (based on the experience of the Battle of Stalingrad)] (Moscow: Frunze Academy, 1991); P. Ia. Egorov, I. V. Krivoborskii, I. K. Ivlev, A. I. Rogalevich, *Dorogami pobed: Boevoi put' 5–i gvardeiskoi tankovoi armii* [Roads to victory: The combat path of the 5th Guards Tank Army] (Moscow: Voenizdat, 1969); A. F. Smirov, K. S. Ogloblin, *Tanki za Vislou: Boevoi put' 31-go tankovogo korpusa* [Tanks beyond the Vistula: The combat path of the 31st Tank Corps] (Moscow: Voenizdat, 1991); V. A. Demin and R. M. Portugal'skii, *Tanki vkhodiat v proryv: Boevoi put' 25-go tankovogo korpusa* [Tanks enter the penetration: The combat path of the 25th Tank Corps] (Moscow: Voenizdat, 1988); N. G. Nersesian, *Kievsko-Berlinskii: Boevoi put' 6-go gvardeiskogo tankovogo korpusa* [Kiev-Berlin: The combat path of the 6th Guards Tank Corps] (Moscow: Voenizdat, 1974); A. M. Zvartsev, *3-ia gvardeiskaia tankovaia: Boevoi put' 3-i gvardeiskoi tankovoi armii* [3rd Guards Tank: The combat path of the 3rd Guards Tank Army] (Moscow: Voenizdat, 1982); A. P. Riazansky, *V ogne tankovykh srazhenii* [In the fire of tank battles] (Moscow: Nauka, 1975); S. A. Pogrebnoi, *Lavinoi stali i ognia: Boevoi put' 7–go mekhanizirovannogo Novoukrainsko-Khinganskogo ordena Lenina, Krasnoznamennogo, ordena Suvorova korpusa* [In an avalanche of steel and fire: The combat path of the 7th Novoukraine-Khingan Order of Lenin, Red Banner, Order of Suvorov Mechanized Corps] (Moscow: Voenizdat, 1980); K. A. Malygin, *V tsentre boevogo poriadka* [In the center of the combat formation] (Moscow: Voenizdat, 1986); M. F. Panov, Na napravlenii glavnogo udara [On the main attack axis] (Moscow: n.p., 1995); A. V. Kuz'min and I. I. Krasnov, *Kantemirovtsy: Boevoi put' 4–go gvardeiskogo tankovogo Kantemirovskogo ordena Lenina Krasnoznamennogo korpusa* [The men of Kantemirovka: The combat path of the 4th Guards Kantemirovka, Order of Lenin, Red Banner Tank Corps] (Moscow: Voenizdat, 1971); I. M. Kravchenko and V. V. Burkov, *Desiatyi tankovyi dneprovskii: Boevoi put' 10-go tankovogo Dneprovskogo ordena Suvorova korpusa* [The 10th Dnepr Tank: The combat path of the 10th Tank Dnepr, Order of Suvorov Corps] (Moscow: Voenizdat, 1986); V. F. Tolubko and N. I. Baryshev, *Na iuzhnom flange: Boevoi put' 4-go gvardeiskogo mekhanizirovannogo korpusa (1942–1945 gg.)* [On the southern flank: The combat path of the 4th Guards Mechanized Corps (1942–1945)] (Moscow: Nauka, 1973); A. M. Samsonov, *Ot Volgi do Baltiki: Ocherk istorii 3–go gvardeiskogo mekhanizirovannogo korpusa 1942–1945 gg.* [From the Volga to the Baltic: Studies in the history of the 3rd Guards Mechanized Corps 1942–1945] (Moscow: Nauka, 1973); *Sbornik voenno-istoricheskikh materialov Velikoi Otechestvennoi voiny* [Collection of military-historical materials of the Great Patriotic War], issue 1 (Moscow: Voenizdat, 1949); *Sbornik voenno-istoricheskikh materialov Velikoi Otechestvennoi voiny* [Collection of military-historical materials of the Great Patriotic

—Continued

War], issue 7 (Moscow: Voenizdat, 1952); *Sbornik voenno istoricheskikh materialov Velikoi Otechestvennoi voiny* [Collection of military-historical materials of the Great Patriotic War], issue 9 (Moscow: Voenizdat, 1953); *Sbornik voenno-istoricheskikh materialov Velikoi Otechestvennoi voiny* [Collection of military-historical materials of the Great Patriotic War], issue 13 (Moscow: Voenizdat, 1954); *Voenno-istoricheskii zhurnal* [Military-historical journal], no. 10 (October 1986) (hereafter cited as *VIZh*); *VIZh*, no. 11 (November 1976); *VIZh*, no. 12 (December 1962); *VIZh*, no. 1 (January 1991); *VIZh*, no. 12 (December 1971); *Voenno-istoricheskii arkhiv* [Military-historical archive], no. 1 (1997); V. P. Istomin, *Smolenskaia nastupatel'naia operatsiia (1943 g.)* [The Smolensk offensive operation (1943)] (Moscow: Voenizdat, 1975); *VIZh*, no. 8 (August 1992); O. A. Orekhov, "Maloizvestnye stranitsy Velikoi Otechestvennoi voiny: Velikolukskaia nastupatel'naia operatsiia [Little-known pages from the Great Patriotic War: The Velikie Luki offensive operation] (unpublished article, Moscow, n.d.); *VIZh*, no. 9 (September 1971); *VIZh*, no. 5 (May 1972); *VIZh*, no. 10 (October 1982); *VIZh*, no. 9 (September 1975); *VIZh*, no. 7 (July 1977); *VIZh*, no. 9 (September 1963); and David M. Glantz, *Forgotten Battles of the German-Soviet War (1941–1945), volume V, parts one and two; The Summer–Fall Campaign (1July–31 December 1943)* (Carlisle, PA: Self-published, 2000).

Table 7.19 Personnel Strength of Selected Red Army Cavalry Corps and Divisions, 22 June 1941 to 31 December 1943

Force (Subordination)	*Personnel Strength* Authorized	Actual	Composition (Percent Fill)
22 Jun 1941			
Red Army cavalry corps (22 Jun)	19,430	14,000	(72)
Red Army cavalry divisions (22 Jun)	9,240	6,000	Average strength (65)
5 CC, Gp. Kostenko, SWF (6 Dec)	12,000	5,796	(48)
32 CD, 5 CC, Gp. Kostenko (6 Dec)	4,200	2,390	(57)
1942			
11 CC, KF (5 Jan)	12,600	5,800	18, 24, 82 CD (46)
46 CD, 31 A, KF (5 Jan)	4,200	1,164	(28)
54 CD, 31 A, KF (5 Jan)	4,200	1,462	(35)
54 CD, 31 A, KF (18 Jan)	4,200	782	(19)
1 GCC, WF (27 Jan)	17,515	7,500	1, 2 G, 41, 57, 75 CD (43)
1 GCC, WF (20 Jan)	17,515	28,000	1, 2 G, 41, 57, 75 CDs, 325, 239 RDs, 5 Ski Bns, 1 TB (8 tanks) (86)
11 CC, KF (6 Feb)	12,600	4,937	18, 24, 82 CD (39)
18 CD, 11 CC (6 Feb)	4,200	3,186	(76)
24 CD, 11 CC (6 Feb)	4,200	891	(21)
82 CD, 11 CC (6 Feb)	4,200	860	(20)
11 CC, KF (1 Mar)	12,600	4,298	18, 24, 82 CD (34)
1 GCC, WF (13 Mar)	17,515	6,252	1, 2 G, 41, 57, 75 CD (36)
1, 5 CC, SF (17 Jan)	35,030	10,966	34, 60, 79, 35, 56, 68 CD, 2 TBs (90 tanks) (31)
6 CC, SWF (15 Jan)	17,515	8,550	26, 28, 49 CD, 5 GTB (6 T-34, 5 T-60) (49)
6 CC, SWF (12 Feb)	17,515	6,888	26, 28, 49 CD, 5 GTB (6 T-34, 5 T-60) (39)
2 GCC, 20 A, WF (24 Nov)	17,515	14,000	3, 4 G, 20 CD (80)
2 GCC, 20 A, WF (18 Dec)	17,515	7,283	3, 4 G, 20 CD (42)
3 GCC, 63 A, Sta. F (1 Nov)	22,488	22,526	5, 6 G, 32 CD (>100)
5 GCD, 3 GCC (1 Nov)	7,191	6,149	(86)
6 GCD, 3 GCC (1 Nov)	7,191	6,774	(94)
32 CD, 3 GCC (1 Nov)	4,951	6,310	(>100)
8 CC, 5 TA, SWF (7 Nov)	18,008	16,134	21, 55, 112 CD (90)
3 GCC, 21 A, DF (8 Nov)	22,488	22,512	5, 6 G, 32 CD (>100)
4 CC, Sta. F (7 Nov)	11,456	10,284	61, 81 CD (90)
3 GCC, 21 A, DF (10 Nov)	22,488	22,322	5, 6 G, 32 CD (99)
8 CC, 5 TA, SWF (2 Dec)	18,008	10,152	21, 55, 112 CD (56)
3 GCC, 5 TA, SWF (26 Nov)	22,488	13,204	5, 6 G, 32 CD (59)
4 CC, 51 A, Sta. F (18 Dec)	11,456	4,114	(36)
4 CC, 2 GA, Sta. F (31 Dec)	11,456	3,599	(31)
1943			
83 CD, 7 CC, VF (1 Jan)	4,951	4,702	8 T-70 tanks (95)
8 CC, 3 GA, SWF (7 Feb)	18,008	9,904	21, 55, 112 CD (55)
8 CC, 3 GA, SWF (10 Feb)	18,008	9,304	21, 55, 112 CD (52)
8 CC, 3 GA, SWF (23 Feb)	18,008	2,791	21, 55, 112 CD (15)
6 GCC, VF (1 Feb)	16,000	15,980	8, 13 GCD (100)
6 GCC, VF (15 Feb)	16,000	11,985	8, 13 GCD (75)
13 GCD, 6 GCC, VF (1 Mar)	6,000	2,500	(42)

—*Continued*

Table 7.19 Continued

Force (Subordination)	*Personnel Strength* Authorized	Actual	Composition (Percent Fill)
6 GCC, VF (13 Mar)	16,000	3,956	8, 13 GCD (25)
13 GCD, 6 GCC, VF (15 Mar)	6,000	1,387	(23)
20 CD, 2 GCC, 11 GA, WF (28 Jul)	6,000	5,906	39 T-34, T-70 (98)

Sources: Lieutenant General Kirpichnikov, *Osnovy boevykh deistvii krupnykh kavaleriiskikh soedinenii v tylu protivnika* [The bases of combat operations by large cavalry formations in the enemy rear] (Moscow: Voroshilov Academy, 1944); A. Vasil'ev, *Rzhevsko-Viazemskaia operatsiia Kalininskogo i Zapadnogo frontov (ianvar'–fevral' 1942 g.)* [The Kalinin and Western Fronts' Rzhev-Viaz'ma operation (January–February 1942)] (Moscow: Voroshilov Academy, 1949); *Barvenkovo-Lozovaia operatsiia (18–31 ianvaria 1942 g.)* [The Barvenkovo-Lozovaia operation (18–31 January 1942)] (Moscow: Voenizdat, 1943); *Sbornik materialov po izucheniiu opyta voiny, no. 6 (aprel'–mai 1943 g.)* [Collection of materials for the study of war experience, no. 6 (April–May 1943)] (Moscow: Voenizdat, 1943); *Sbornik materialov po izucheniiu opyta voiny, no. 7 (iiun'–iiul' 1943 g.)* [Collection of materials for the study of war experience, no. 7 (June–July 1943)] (Moscow: Voenizdat, 1943); A. N. Sekretov, *Gvardeiskaia postup'* [Guards gait] (Dushanbe: Donish, 1985); *TsAMO* [Central Archives of the Ministry of Defense], f. 3474, op. 1, d. 20, ll. 129–52, f. 3474, op. 1, d. 20, ll. 1–8; and *Eletskaia operatsiia (6–16 dekabria 1941 g.)* [The Elets operation (6–16 December 1941)] (Moscow: Voenizdat, 1943).

CHAPTER 8

Artillery and Air Forces

ARTILLERY

In June 1941, Red Army artillery was far from the formidable and dominant instrument of destruction it would become in 1943. On the eve of war, the NKO mistakenly abolished the post of chief of Red Army artillery and combined his directorate with its own Main Artillery Directorate, leaving Red Army artillery decentralized, poorly controlled, relatively immobile, without adequate logistical support, and largely ineffective when war began. The Germans exploited these weaknesses during Operation Barbarossa, relying on the superior mobility and flexibility of its artillery to demolish the Red Army's artillery force. Two years would pass before the NKO was able to restore artillery to its accustomed place as "king" of the battlefield.

The NKO began reforming its artillery on 19 July 1941 by reestablishing the post of chief of Red Army artillery to improve command and control over its decimated artillery. After the Red Army and its relatively feeble artillery force successfully weathered the first six months of war, the NKO began fielding larger, stronger, and more numerous artillery forces in early 1942, centralizing most of them under effective *Stavka* control and allocating them to the Red Army's operating *fronts* and armies only on the basis of demonstrated need. Underscoring the success of these reforms, by mid-1943 the *Stavka* and its operating *fronts* achieved artillery fire superiority over the *Wehrmacht* in virtually every operation they conducted. This superiority, which exceeded the Red Army's numerical advantage in other categories of combat power, increased from a factor of 5 to 1 in mid-1943 to as high as 10 to 1 in 1944 and 30 to 1 by war's end. Ultimately, at least in part, the *Wehrmacht* crumbled under the crushing weight of massive Red Army artillery fire.

The Red Army's artillery force included three distinct components subordinate to two separate NKO directorates when war began. The first two components, force artillery assigned to the Red Army's operating *fronts* and the artillery of the *Stavka* Reserve, were subordinate to the NKO's Artillery Directorate, while the third component, artillery for the air defense of the country *(artilleriia protivo-vozhdushnoi oborony strany)*, or National Air Defense (PVO Strany), was subordinate to the NKO's Main Directorate of PVO Strany of the Red Army, which controlled both artillery and air forces (see Chapter 11).

Force Artillery

Force *(voiskovaia)* artillery, which included all artillery units and subunits organic to battalions, regiments, divisions, and corps subordinate to operating *fronts* and armies, constituted the Red Army's strongest artillery force when war began. It included artillery regiments organic to rifle divisions and 94 corps artillery regiments, 52 assigned to operating *fronts*, 13 to the *Stavka* Reserve, and 29 to military districts and nonoperating *fronts*.

At the lowest levels of command, Red Army force artillery included an antitank platoon with two 45mm guns and a mortar company with two 82mm mortar in rifle battalions and antitank and field artillery batteries and a mortar company with six 45mm antitank guns, six 76mm field guns, and four 120mm mortars, respectively, in rifle regiments. A level higher, rifle divisions included a light artillery regiment fielding two battalions *(diviziony)* with eight 76mm field guns and four 122mm howitzers each for a total of 24 tubes, a howitzer artillery regiment fielding two light howitzer battalions with twelve 122mm howitzers each, and a medium howitzer battalion with twelve 152mm howitzers, for a total of 36 howitzers, an antitank battalion with eighteen 45mm guns, and an antiaircraft battalion with twelve 37mm antiaircraft guns for a total division strength of 294 guns and mortars (caliber 50mm or greater).[1]

At the highest level command within field armies, rifle corps included one or two corps artillery regiments, each fielding two to four artillery battalions armed with 107mm, 122mm, or 152mm guns, an artillery instrumental reconnaissance battalion, and a medium-caliber antiaircraft battalion. Since, contrary to its plans, the NKO was unable to support each rifle corps with two corps artillery regiments, it normally assigned an additional corps artillery regiment to support each field army.

Force artillery included three types of corps artillery regiments in June 1941. The first, formed by the NKO as standard in 1937 and 1938, consisted of two artillery battalions with twelve 107mm or 122mm guns each and a battalion of twelve 152mm howitzers or gun-howitzers for a total of 36 guns. The second, also formed in 1937 and 1938, included three battalions with twelve 152mm howitzer or gun-howitzers each for a total of 36 guns. The third, a revised standard type, which the NKO began forming during the Red Army's rapid expansion in 1939, after it realized there was not enough artillery to equip each rifle corps with two full regiments, consisted of two battalions of twelve 122mm guns and two battalions of twelve 152mm howitzers or gun-howitzers each for a total of 48 guns.[2]

Although force artillery constituted more than 90 percent of the Red Army's entire artillery park (inventory) when war began and most force artillery formations and units were at or near full strength in terms of their authorized manpower and weaponry, all suffered from acute shortages of trucks and tractors to tow the guns and carry cargo. General Staff mobilization plans required force artillery and the Red Army as a whole to obtain most of their required vehicles from the civilian sector, but the *Wehrmacht's* ensuing rapid and deep thrust disrupted these plans, leaving force artillery with little or no truck transport capability. For example, corps artillery regiments assigned to the Southwestern Front's 5th Army on 22 June 1941 had 82 percent of their required weaponry but few of their authorized trucks and tractors.[3]

The ensuing high-intensity mobile warfare during the first two months of Operation Barbarossa savaged the Red Army's force artillery, forcing the NKO to severely truncate its structure. On 24 July, for example, it abolished the bloated rifle divisions' howitzer artillery regiments and antitank artillery battalions, leaving each division with a single artillery regiment consisting of two artillery battalions with two 76mm field gun batteries, a 122mm howitzer battery, a small reconnaissance section, and survey, signal, and ammunition supply platoons, and a small logistical element each and reducing the number of artillery batteries in each division from 15 batteries to six. This measure reduced the rifle division's theoretical artillery strength from 294 guns and mortars, including thirty-four 76mm guns, thirty-two 122mm howitzers, and twelve 152mm howitzers, to 142 guns and mortars, including twenty-eight 76mm guns and eight 122mm howitzers.[4] Worse still from the standpoint of command and control, the reduction in the quantity of radios in artillery battalions from 12 to seven hindered the artillery's responsiveness to fire requests from the infantry it supported.[5]

In December 1941, before it made its next major change to the rifle divisions' structure in March 1942, the NKO added a rocket launcher battalion to its rifle divisions, at least on paper, concentrated the divisions' 82mm and 120mm mortars in new and larger mortar battalions at regimental and division level, and added an artillery headquarters to coordinate their artillery fire more effectively, raising the divisions' artillery strength from 142 guns and mortars to 234. Then, in a new divisional organization it introduced in March 1942, the NKO added a third battalion to the artillery regiment, a light version with only one gun and one howitzer battery, which increased the divisions' field artillery strength from 234, including twenty-eight 76mm guns and eight 122mm howitzers, to 250, including thirty-two 76mm guns and twelve 122mm howitzers.[6]

Even though the field artillery strength of rifle divisions remained essentially unchanged until December 1944, on 10 December 1942, the NKO beefed up the artillery strength of its increasing number of guards rifle divisions by adding a third 76mm artillery battery to the division's third battalion, increasing the strength of guards divisions' artillery strength to 268 guns and mortars, including thirty-six 76mm guns and twelve 122mm howitzers.[7]

Although force artillery's surviving corps artillery regiments reverted to the *Stavka's* reserve after the NKO abolished rifle corps in August 1941, it began forming new corps artillery regiments in early 1942 to provide requisite artillery support to its new rifle corps. After fielding 11 corps artillery regiments with sixteen 76mm guns and twelve 12mm howitzers each by July 1942, the NKO raised a total of 15, each consisting of one or two battalions of 122mm guns and one battalion of 152mm howitzers by 1 February 1943. Thereafter, throughout the remainder of 1943, the NKO transformed these regiments into battalions consisting of four batteries equipped with four 122mm guns or two 122mm guns and two 152mm howitzers.[8]

Thus, the strength of the Red Army's force artillery diminished sharply in 1941 and then increased modestly in 1942. During the same period, the strength and power of RVGK artillery present at all levels of command increased, first modestly in 1941 and early 1942 and then far more dramatically in 1943. The *Stavka* and NKO believed that artillery organic to forces with fixed tables of organization, such as rifle divisions and tank, mechanized, and cavalry corps, was more than adequate to support these forces when they were operating in static situations or when they were conducting local offensive or defensive operations; however, by late 1942, when the Red Army was conducting larger-scale offensive or defensive operations, the *Stavka* relied to an increasing extent on its reserve artillery to tip the scales in the Red Army's favor.

Artillery of the RGK-RVGK *(Stavka)* Reserve

Although far weaker than force artillery when war began, by late 1942 the most powerful artillery force in the Red Army was the artillery of the Supreme High Command Reserve (*Reserv Verkhovnogo Glavnokomandovaniia,* or RVGK), which began the war as the artillery of the High Command Reserve (*Reserv Glavnokomandovaniia,* or RGK). This force included all field artillery centralized under *Stavka's* direct control, which it allocated to the Red Army's operating *fronts,* military districts and nonoperating *fronts* or retained in its own reserve. It also included specialized types of mortar, antitank (tank destroyer), self-propelled, rocket, and antiaircraft artillery, which will be considered separately.

When war began, RGK field artillery consisted of 75 artillery regiments, including 14 gun and 61 howitzer regiments, ten antitank brigades formed only weeks before war began (see the antitank section below), and 13 artillery battalions, including 11 special-power *(osoboi moshnosti)* battalions equipped with 210mm guns, 203mm and 305mm howitzers, or 280mm mortars. Of this overall force, which was distributed relatively evenly throughout the Soviet Union, 35 artillery regiments, including nine gun and 26 howitzer, and seven battalions were assigned to the Red Army's operating *fronts;* four artillery regiments, including one gun and three howitzer, were in the RGK Reserve; and 36 artillery regiments, including three guns and 33 howitzer, and six battalions were allocated to military districts and nonoperating *fronts.* Therefore, on 22 June 1941, the Red Army's artillery force above division level consisted of 169 artillery regiments and 13 separate artillery battalions (see Appendix 1 in companion volume for field and other artillery in the Red Army).

The RGK included two types of gun artillery regiments: a standard version consisting of four battalions with twelve 122mm guns each for a total of 48 guns, and a heavier version with four battalions with six 152mm gun-howitzers each for a total of 24 guns. There were thirteen 122mm gun artillery regiments and one 152mm gun artillery regiment in the RGK force structure on 22 June 1941. In addition, the RGK included three types of howitzer artillery regiments, a standard version consisting of four battalions with twelve 152mm howitzers each for a strength of 48 guns and high-power and special-power versions with four battalions of six 203mm or six 305mm howitzers each for a total of 24 howitzers (see Table 8.1).[9] There were 29 howitzer artillery regiments, 31 high-power howitzer regiments, and one special-power howitzer regiment in the RGK force structure on 22 June 1941. However, the single special-power howitzer artillery regiment, the 281st, stationed in the Orel Military District, disbanded shortly after war began, and its component battalions (the 322nd, 328th, 330th, and 331st) became separate.

RGK artillery confronted severe problems on the eve of war. First, senior Red Army commanders underestimated the operational role of artillery, particularly the necessity for concentrating it in depth along key strategic and operational axes. Second, although most RGK artillery regiments and battalions were at or near full strength in personnel and weaponry, like force artillery they were unable to support flexible high-intensity mobile operations because they lacked as much as 80 percent of their trucks, tractors, and other authorized vehicles.[10] Worse still, artillery intelligence and target acquisition were weak, and communications were too unreliable to ensure coordinated fire control.

The *Wehrmacht* exploited these weaknesses, overwhelming and decimating Red Army forces and their supporting artillery in June and July 1941. In the wake of this disaster, when the NKO truncated the Red Army's force structure in August 1941, it allocated a small portion of its artillery forces to satisfy the minimal needs of its field commands but concentrated the remainder in the *Stavka's* reserves as RGK (later RVGK) artillery. Thereafter, it assigned most of its newly mobilized and trained artillery units to *Stavka* control for allocation to operating *fronts* as operational exigencies required.

After the NKO ruthlessly pruned the Red Army force structure in August, the amount of force artillery available to support rifle divisions and corps decreased sharply and proved inadequate to sustain either defensive or offensive operations during the late summer and fall. Nor was RVGK artillery able to compensate for this shortage of artillery because it too was subject to this same truncation process. In September 1941, for example, the NKO halved the strength of RVGK artillery regiments by decreasing the strength of their batteries from four to two guns.

At the same time, the NKO began forming two new types of RVGK artillery regiments with batteries of two guns, first, gun artillery regiments consisting of two battalions with three batteries each armed with 122mm guns and one battalion with three batteries of 152mm gun-howitzers, and, second, howitzer artillery regiments consisting of three battalions with three batteries each equipped with 152mm howitzers.[11] From July through December 1941, the NKO fielded a total of 12 gun artillery regiments, twenty-four 152mm army artillery regiments, and two 152mm howitzer artillery regiments, and redesignated many of its surviving corps artillery regiments as army artillery or gun artillery regiments. By 1 January 1942, the RVGK's force structure included 157 artillery regiments and 26 separate artillery battalions of various types.[12]

The NKO continued this reorganization process in early 1942 to conserve on manpower and make RVKG artillery regiments more responsive to the field forces' needs. Beginning on 19 April, it reorganized gun artillery regiments into two or three battalions consisting of three batteries of two guns each for a regimental strength of twelve to eighteen 107mm or 122mm guns or 152mm gun-howitzers. At the same time, it reduced the strength of howitzer artillery regiments from three battalions consisting of three batteries with four guns each to two battalions for a strength of twenty-four 152mm or 122mm howitzers, and it also fielded a smaller version with one less battery for a strength of twenty 122mm or 152mm howitzers. Finally, on 2 April it decreased the size of high-power artillery regiments from four battalions to two battalions, reducing the strength of these battalions to twelve 203mm howitzers while increasing the number of high-power artillery regiments.

As a result, the strength of RVGK artillery increased to a total of 323 artillery regiments and 26 separate artillery battalions of various types on 1 July 1942 and then decreased slightly to 301 artillery regiments and 23 separate artillery battalions by 1 February 1943.[13]

When Soviet weapons production increased dramatically in late 1942, permitting the fielding of increased quantities of RVGK artillery regiments and battalions, the NKO faced the challenge of creating new structures that would enable Red Army field commanders to command and control their artillery more effectively, particularly in the large-scale offensive operations the *Stavka* planned to conduct in November 1942. The NKO responded to this challenge on 31 October by combining many of the RVGK's separate regiments into 18 new artillery divisions and by forming 18 antiaircraft artillery divisions.

Initially these artillery divisions consisted of 8 artillery regiments, including three howitzer artillery regiments with three battalions and twenty 122mm howitzers each, two gun artillery regiments with two battalions and eighteen 152mm guns each, and three antitank artillery regiments with three battalions and twenty-four 76mm guns each, or instead of the antitank artillery regiments, two antiaircraft artillery regiments with twenty-four 85mm guns each, and a separate artillery reconnaissance (observation) battalion, for a division strength of 7,054 men and 168 guns in the antitank version and 144 guns in the antiaircraft version.[14]

These eight regiments proved difficult to command and control during the initial stages of the winter offensive, however, so on 14 December the NKO began forming new artillery divisions with four brigades instead of eight regiments. These divisions consisted of a light artillery (antitank) brigades with three regiments and a total of seventy-two 76mm guns, a howitzer artillery brigade with three regiments and a total of sixty 122mm or 152mm howitzers, a heavy gun artillery brigade with two regiments and a total of thirty-six 122mm guns or 152mm gun-howitzers, and a mortar brigade with four regiments and a total of eighty 120mm mortars, supported by an artillery reconnaissance battalion, an aviation squadron, and rear services for a division strength of 9,124 men, 168 guns and howitzers, and 80 mortars.[15] In addition, the NKO formed a heavy gun artillery division (the 19th), which consisted of five gun regiments, one high-power howitzer regiment, and one special-power artillery battalion.[16]

The *Stavka* and NKO continued strengthening the divisions, brigades, regiments, and battalions in RVGK artillery throughout 1943 to support and sustain the Red Army both on the defense and on the offensive and also began fielding full artillery corps. By marshaling this artillery under *Stavka* control, tailoring it to meet the needs of specific offensive or defensive situations, and parceling it out to operating *fronts* and armies in timely fashion, the *Stavka* provided increasingly flexible fire support for the Red Army as a whole and provided the Red Army with unprecedented artillery superiority over the *Wehrmacht* in virtually every major Red Army offensive.

The largest field artillery formations in the RVGK in early 1943 were the artillery divisions formed in October 1942 and modified in December 1942 and their subordinate artillery brigades. In addition, RVGK artillery included a few separate artillery brigades (152mm guns, for example) consisting of two or three regiments, fire control and signal battalions, and a transport subunit for ammunition resupply. By far the most ubiquitous artillery units in the Red Army in early 1943 were artillery regiments subordinate either to force artillery supporting field armies, rifle corps, and rifle divisions or to the RVGK.

In early 1943 the NKO fielded five versions of artillery regiments. These included gun artillery regiments consisting of three battalions with three batteries of two guns each for a strength of 1,120 men, nineteen 107mm or 122m guns or 152mm gun-howitzers, and 35 tractors; gun artillery regiments of two battalions with three batteries of two guns each for a strength of 758 men, twelve 107mm or 122mm guns, and 24 tractors; howitzer artillery regiments of two battalions with three batteries of four guns each for a strength of 947 men, twenty-four 122mm or 152mm howitzers, and 36 tractors; howitzer artillery regiments of one battalion with three batteries of four guns each and one battalion with two batteries of four guns each for a strength of 864 men, twenty 122mm or 152mm howitzers, and 30 tractors; and corps artillery regiments of one or two battalions with three to six 122mm guns each and one battalion with twelve 152mm gun-howitzers.[17]

The heaviest artillery in the RVGK in early 1943 were its "heavy" *(tiazhelyi)*, "high-power" *(bol'shoi moshnosti)*, and "special-power" *(osoboi moshnosti)* artillery regiments and battalions. "Heavy" regiments and battalions were equipped with 152mm BR-2 guns, "high-power" with 203mm B-4 howitzers, and "special-power" with 210mm and larger guns or 280mm and larger howitzers. High-power artillery regiments consisted of two firing battalions and a strength of 904 men, 12 B-4 howitzers, 26 tractors and 36 trucks, separate heavy artillery battalions fielded eight 152mm howitzers, separate high-power artillery battalions fielded six 203mm howitzers, and separate special-power artillery battalions had six heavy guns or howitzers.[18]

The NKO completed consolidating and expanding RVGK artillery on 13 April 1943, when it began forming five artillery penetration corps and artillery penetration divisions either separate or subordinate to artillery penetration corps. Artillery penetration corps consisted of two artillery penetration divisions, one multiple-rocket launcher division, and an artillery reconnaissance battalion for a strength of 712 guns and mortars ranging in caliber from 76mm to 203mm and 864 M-31 multiple-rocket launcher rails. Artillery penetration divisions consisted of six artillery brigades, including a light artillery brigade consisting of three gun artillery regiments with twenty-four 76mm guns each; a howitzer artillery brigade with three howitzer artillery regiments with twenty-eight 122mm guns each; a heavy gun artillery brigade with two gun regiments with eighteen 152mm guns each; a heavy howitzer artillery brigade with four howitzer battalions with eight 152mm howitzers each; a high-power howitzer artillery brigade with four howitzer battalions with six 203mm howitzers each; and a mortar brigade with three mortar regiments with thirty-six 120mm mortars each; and an artillery reconnaissance battalion. The artillery penetration divisions' strength was 10,869 men and 356 guns, howitzers, and mortars, including 72 of the 76mm guns, 84 of the 122mm howitzers, 32 of the 152mm howitzers, 36 of the 152mm guns, 24 of the 203mm howitzers, and 108 of the 120mm mortars.[19]

In addition, in June 1943 the NKO began creating experimental heavy gun artillery divisions to conduct counter-battery artillery fire. These divisions consisted of four brigades consisting of three battalions with four batteries of four gun-howitzers each for a total strength of 48 gun-howitzers in each brigade and 144 of the 152mm in each division. The NKO formed two divisions (the 4th and 6th Guards) of this type and a third (the 8th Guards) in October 1943, a gun artillery division, which was similar to the heavy type but included a battalion with four batteries of four 76mm guns in place of one of each gun brigade's 152mm battalions.[20]

The NKO formed 5 artillery penetration corps, 12 artillery penetration divisions, and 13 standard artillery divisions containing either three or four artillery brigades by 1 July 1943 and a total of 5 artillery penetration corps and 26 artillery divisions, including 17 artillery penetration divisions, six artillery divisions based on the December 1942 organization, and three counter-battery artillery divisions by 31 December.

As the Red Army's successful offensives in mid- and late 1943 indicated, the dramatic expansion in the size and power of RVGK artillery had a telling effect on the Red Army's ability to penetrate German tactical defenses. Specifically, from October 1942 through the end of 1943, the weight of artillery fire in preplanned Red Army offensive operations increased over fourfold and reached crushing proportions.[21]

Mortar Forces

Although less important operationally because of their limited range, the Red Army fielded a large force of mortars throughout the war, primarily to provide close support to rifle forces on the defense or during penetration operations. In addition to mortar forces organic to its field forces, the RGK began the war with a force of eight mortar battalions, two assigned to operating *fronts* and the other six to military districts or nonoperating *fronts*. These mortar battalions consisted of three batteries fielding twelve 120mm mortars each and a transport company, for a total strength of about 350 men, 36 mortars, and 36 five-ton trucks to transport the mortars and their crew. However, these battalions lacked their full complement of trucks when war began.[22]

Despite the heavy losses it suffered in the summer and fall of 1941, the NKO managed to increase the quantity of RVGK mortar battalions to 15, plus one ad hoc brigade in support of the 7th Separate Army by 1 January 1942. However, because these cumbersome forces were far too weak to have a positive impact on either defensive or offensive operations, the NKO began beefing up its mortar force in early 1942.

The NKO began this process in January 1942 by forming new mortar regiments consisting of one medium mortar battalion with four batteries and a total of sixteen 82mm mortars and one heavy mortar battalion with four batteries and sixteen 120mm mortars for a regimental strength of 800 men, 32 mortars, 273 horses, 116 wagons, and 14 motor vehicles. After these mortar forces performed inadequately during the Red Army's winter offensive of 1941–42, however, in April the NKO experimented with motorized and horse-drawn versions of a new mortar regiment, the former with three battalions of three batteries with four 120mm mortars each for a total strength of 848 men, 36 mortars, and 125 motor vehicles, and the latter with five batteries of four 120mm mortars each for a total strength of 477 men, of 20 mortars, 252 horses, 91 wagons, and seven motor vehicles.[23] Yet another variation of mortar regiment was the mountain mortar regiment, which consisted of five batteries each equipped with four 107mm mountain mortars for a total of 20 mortars. Since these units were relatively easy and inexpensive to form, the NKO fielded 75 RVGK mortar regiments by 1 July 1942 and increased their number significantly in early 1943.

In addition, to supplement the ad hoc brigade already in its force structure, in October 1942 the NKO began forming new mortar brigades, some separate but most subordinate to its new artillery divisions. When fielded in December 1942, these mortar brigades consisted of four motorized mortar regiments with twenty 120mm mortars each for total strength of 80 mortars. In April 1943 the NKO formed two more types of mortar brigades, the first subordinate to artillery penetration divisions and the second separate. The former consisted of three motorized mortar regiments with thirty-six 120mm mortars each for a total of 108 mortars and the latter of four mortar regiments of like composition with 144 mortars.[24]

By virtue of these measures, the strength of RVGK mortar forces increased from seven brigades and 102 separate regiments on 1 January 1943; to 12 brigades, 121 separate regiments, and 11 separate battalions on 1 February 1943; and to 11 brigades, 133 separate regiments, and four separate battalions on 1 July 1943; and then decreased to 11 brigades and 129 separate battalions on 31 December 1943.

Antitank (Tank Destroyer) Artillery

Since the Germans relied heavily on their panzer forces for success in Blitzkrieg war, the Red Army had to field a large and effective antitank (tank destroyer artillery) force if it hoped to vanquish the *Wehrmacht* and win the war. As Operations Barbarossa and *Blau* so vividly demonstrated, the Red Army lacked such a force in 1941 and 1942.

In addition to lighter antitank forces within its operating *fronts* and armies, when war began the Red Army's most important antitank forces at the operational level were its large but ineffective antitank brigades, ten of which the NKO formed in the RGK reserve in April 1941 and assigned to its border military districts shortly before war began. In addition, the NKO fielded an eleventh antitank brigade in late June and early July, but its existence was short-lived.[25] These antitank brigades consisted of two antitank regiments, an engineer-sapper battalion to lay mines, a motor transport battalion, and a small service element for a total strength of 5,309 men, 120 guns including forty-eight 76mm antitank guns, forty-eight 85mm antiaircraft guns, and, in theory, twenty-four 107mm antitank guns, sixteen 37mm antiaircraft guns, 12 DShK machine guns, 706 trucks and other vehicles, 10 motorcycles, 180 tractors (including 60 towing trailers), and two armored cars.[26]

The antitank regiments within these brigades consisted of five antitank battalions, the first and second armed with 76mm antitank guns, the third with 107mm guns, and the fourth and fifth with 85mm antiaircraft guns employed in an antitank role, and an antiaircraft battalion.[27] However, since the NKO never fielded these 107mm guns, the third battalion also fielded 76mm guns. These antitank battalions consisted of three batteries with four antitank guns each for a total of 12 guns each, and the brigades' antiaircraft battalion consisted of two batteries with four 37mm antiaircraft guns each and a heavy machine-gun company with 6 DShK 12.7mm heavy machine guns for a regimental strength of 60 antitank guns, including twenty-four 76mm, twenty-four 85mm, and twelve 107mm guns, eight 37mm antiaircraft guns, and six DShK machine guns.[28]

Though powerful on paper, in practice these brigades were plagued by problems, including their inability to conduct reconnaissance and acquire targets, their acute shortage of tractors and other vehicles, their excessive number of subordinate units, which made effective command and control impossible, and the ineffectiveness of their 85mm guns against German tanks. As a result, the advancing *Wehrmacht* savaged these brigades during the first few weeks of the war, destroying four outright during the border battles, and forced the NKO to reorganize their remnants into seven antitank artillery regiments.

After its initial debacle, the NKO slowly rebuilt the Red Army's antitank capability by adding antitank rifles and guns to its field forces and by forming numerous smaller antitank artillery regiments and battalions within the R(V)GK. It began this process in late June and July by fielding 20 antitank regiments organized in the same fashion as those assigned to the former antitank brigades. However, since these regiments performed as poorly as the original brigades, in mid-July the NKO formed 15 antitank regiments consisting of five batteries with four guns each for a total of 20 antitank guns, primarily older model 85mm guns since the 76mm models remained in short supply.[29] The NKO continued this unusual practice of subordinating batteries directly to regiments within its antitank forces until war's end.

Because these five-battery antitank regiments proved too weak to survive in combat against *Wehrmacht* panzer forces, in September 1941 the NKO began forming two new types of antitank regiments, one heavy and one light. Heavy regiments consisted of six batteries totaling twenty 76mm and four 25mm or 37mm antitank guns and light regiments fielded four batteries with eight 37mm or 45mm guns and eight 85mm guns.[30] The NKO fielded 37 of these regiments by year's end.

Underscoring the importance it attached to antitank forces, the 72 antitank regiments the NKO formed in 1941 included 2,396 antitank guns (including 960 of the 85mm antiaircraft guns), or 57 percent of the artillery added to the Red Army during the year (see Table 8.2).[31] By year's end, however, the *Wehrmacht* had destroyed 28 of these regiments, leaving a remnant of 57 antitank regiments, one antitank brigade, and one separate antitank battalion in the RVGK's force structure on 1 January 1942.[32] Despite the threefold increase in antitank artillery regiments, the number of antitank weapons in the Red Army decreased from 1,360 guns, or 17.5 percent of its total artillery weapons inventory on 22 June, to 1,188 guns, or 11 percent of the army's artillery weapons inventory on 31 December.[33] The *Stavka* rightfully considered this situation intolerable.

However, increased Soviet production of new ZIS-3 model 76mm antitank guns in late 1941 allowed the NKO to form new antitank artillery regiments equipped with this weapon, replace many of the regiments' largely effective 37mm and 85 mm antiaircraft guns, and allocate the replaced 85mm guns to strengthen its antiaircraft units. In December the NKO formed one new antitank regiment and reorganized nine others with the new ZIS-3 76mm gun to provide the Red Army with better antitank support during the Red Army's Moscow counteroffensive. These regiments consisted of six batteries with four guns each, five of the batteries armed with 76mm antitank guns and one with 25mm or 37mm antiaircraft guns for a total strength of 24 guns.

After the Red Army completed its winter campaign, the NKO standardized the organization of RVGK antitank forces in April and May 1942 by disbanding its last antitank brigade and converting all of its antitank regiments into five batteries equipped with four 76mm or 45mm antitank guns.[34] The NKO retained regiments equipped with 45mm guns because not enough 76mm guns were being produced to equip all antitank regiments with this weapon. However, in early July 1942 the NKO compensated for this deficiency by adding a sixth battery to each antitank regiment that distinguished itself in combat, increasing the total strength of some antitank regiments to 564 men and 24 guns.[35]

The NKO redesignated all of its antitank regiments as light artillery regiments in May 1942 to distinguish them from the destroyer regiments, brigades, and divisions it fielded in its rifle force structure during April and May 1942, which were also designed to combat enemy armor (see Chapter 6). This name change was short-lived, however, because the NKO designated all of its antitank and light artillery forces as destroyer antitank artillery *(istrebitel'no-protivotankovaia artilleriia)*, in short, tank destroyer artillery, on 1 July 1942.[36]

Despite the NKO's efforts to standardize the organization of antitank artillery regiments during 1942, the Red Army's operating *fronts* and the NKO itself formed regimental variants to satisfy local conditions or perform special tasks. For example, the Leningrad Front formed 11 RVGK antitank regiments consisting of four battalions fielding a total of thirty-six 76mm and eighteen 45mm guns.[37] On the other hand, the Trans-Caucasus Front formed two tank destroyer regiments in November 1942 consisting of four batteries fielding a total of twelve 45mm guns.[38] During the same period, the NKO formed two new types of specialized tank destroyer regiments. First, in June 1942 it fielded three new heavy RVGK tank destroyer regiments, specifically tailored to combat German heavy tanks, which consisted of five batteries with fifteen 107mm antitank guns, and in August 1942 it formed four antitank battalions consisting of three batteries and a total of twelve 76mm antitank guns to provide close-in antitank support to rifle forces.[39]

In spite of the NKO's vigorous program to revitalize RVGK antitank forces, the *Stavka* felt the Red Army needed a larger quantity of stronger and more effective tank destroyer forces to ensure success in the offensives it planned to conduct in November 1942. As a result, when the NKO began forming 18 new artillery divisions on 31 October, it included three tank destroyer regiments, each consisting of six batteries with a total of twenty-four 76mm guns, in each of these divisions.[40]

The NKO formed a total of 192 RVGK tank destroyer artillery regiments and four battalions during 1942, but incorporated the battalions into the regiments by year's end, increasing the strength of RVGK antitank artillery to a total of 249 regiments on 1 January 1943, including 171 separate regiments and 78 subordinate to artillery divisions. The NKO allocated 95 of these regiments to its operating *fronts*. During the same period, the NKO increased the Red Army's antitank strength over fivefold by adding 4,117 antitank guns to the RVGK's weapons inventory, 60 percent of the total increase in RVGK artillery, despite losing 31 tank destroyer regiments in combat.[41]

The quantity and distribution of RVGK tank destroyer artillery regiments among the Red Army 's operating *fronts* on 15 November 1942 indicated precisely where the *Stavka* planned to conduct its most important strategic offensives (counteroffensives) in the fall: along the Rzhev-Viaz'ma axis with its Kalinin and Western Fronts, backed up by the Moscow Defense Zone; and along the Stalingrad axis with its Southwestern, Don, and Stalingrad Fronts. At the same time, the *Stavka* also concentrated 55 of the 60 tank destroyer regiments in its reserve in the Moscow and Gor'kii Artillery Training Centers, in close proximity to the Western strategic axis (see Table 8.3).

In addition to strengthening its tank destroyer artillery forces, the NKO beefed up its antitank rifle force by forming 49 new separate antitank rifle battalions between 1 April and 30 September 1942. The first 33 of these battalions fielded three companies armed with 72 antitank rifles and the remaining battalions four companies with 108 antitank rifles, for a total deployment of 4,212 antitank rifles.[42]

The explosive expansion of antitank forces in the Red Army's force structure failed to prevent the *Wehrmacht* from achieving success during the initial stages of Operation *Blau;* however, it did help bring its advance to a halt in October and enabled the Red Army to conduct its successful Stalingrad offensive in November and its ensuing winter offensive. The collapse of the Red Army's offensive in March 1943, though, convinced the *Stavka* that stronger and more numerous tank destroyer forces were required if the Red Army was to conduct and sustain deeper offensive operations later in 1943.

The RVGK's tank destroyer artillery force on 1 January 1943 included 249 tank destroyer artillery regiments of six types, ranging in strength from four to six batteries with 15 to 54 antitank guns each, including 171 separate regiments and 78 regiments subordinate to 26 artillery divisions, which the *Stavka* allocated to its operating *fronts* in accordance with its strategic priorities and terrain conditions (see Table 8.4).[43] In addition, the RVGK fielded four tank destroyer artillery battalions with 12 antitank guns each and 53 antitank rifle battalions of two types, ranging in strength from three to four companies fielding 72 or 108 antitank rifles.[44] In addition to the RVGK's total inventory of 3,224 antitank guns, which included 45 of the 107mm, 2,276 of the 76mm, and 1,502 of the 45mm guns (60 percent of the RVGK's total weapons inventory) and 4,412 antitank rifles; the 83 antitank artillery regiments created in field armies on 1 January 1943 added another 1,992 guns to the Red Army's inventory of antitank weapons.[45]

The NKO worked feverishly to strengthen the Red Army's antitank forces throughout 1943 by adding separate tank destroyer artillery regiments to combined-arms and tank armies, by forming tank destroyer brigades and increasing the quantity of antitank guns in separate tank destroyer regiments in the RVGK, and by strengthening and improving the mobility of its tank destroyer artillery regiments.

The NKO began this process on 10 April 1943, when it added a new heavy type of tank destroyer artillery regiment to each combined-arms army and a lighter type to each tank army and also formed tank destroyer artillery brigades in the RVGK. The heavy regiments consisted of six batteries with a total of twenty-four 76mm guns each, and the light regiments included five batteries with twenty 45mm guns each. Eventually, the NKO converted all RVGK tank destroyer regiments equipped with 76mm guns to the former organization and those equipped with 45mm guns to the latter.[46]

Most important of all, the NKO's April order formed new tank destroyer artillery brigades within the RVGK. These brigades, the largest antitank formations the Red Army fielded during the war, consisted of three tank destroyer regiments with 20 guns each, a machine-gun platoon, a reconnaissance battalion, topographic-engineer and signal platoons, and a small transport element. Two of the brigades' tank destroyer regiments fielded five batteries with four 76mm guns and the third five batteries with four 45mm guns for a brigade strength of 1,297 men, forty 76mm and twenty 45mm antitank guns, 60 antitank rifles, 30 light machine guns, 115 trucks, and 75 tractors.[47]

The NKO continued refining the structure of these brigades and regiments throughout 1943. For example, in June it began replacing the weak 45mm guns in tank destroyer brigades with new ZIS-2 57mm antitank guns, which Soviet industry was producing in greater quantities, and it completed this process in September.[48] Soon after, it also replaced the 45mm guns in RVGK separate tank destroyer regiments with 57mm guns.

In June the NKO also began truncating the number of personnel and motor transport in many of its specialized and local variants of the RVGK's tank destroyer artillery regiments, and from June through September it disbanded the Red Army's remaining destroyer divisions and brigades in combined-arms armies, primarily because army and corps commanders were employing them as regular infantry formations, and converted 15 of these brigades into standard tank destroyer artillery brigades. During the same period, the NKO also abolished the RVGK's destroyer battalions and separate antitank rifle battalions, first, because they were ineffective against new German heavy tanks, and, second, because more effective antitank guns were now in plentiful supply.

Finally, since the Red Army's combat experiences during the second half of 1943 proved irrefutably that tank destroyer artillery brigades and regiments were the most effective instruments for combating the *Wehrmacht's* panzers, in December the NKO added a sixth battery to each regiment in some of its tank destroyer brigades, increasing the brigades' strength from 60 to 72 guns.[49]

As a result of these measures, the Red Army included 50 tank destroyer artillery brigades, 135 separate tank destroyer artillery regiments, and four separate tank destroyer artillery battalions within the RVGK on 31 December

1943 (see Table 8.5). By this time, the strength of the RVGK's antitank weapons inventory had risen to a total of 6,692 guns, including 30 of the 107mm, 5,228 of the 76mm, 1,132 of the 45mm, and 302 of the 45mm antitank guns, 37.8 percent of its entire weapons inventory. This represented a more than twofold increase over the 3,224 weapons in the RVGK's weapons' inventory on 1 January 1943 and a sixfold increase over its strength of 1,360 guns on 22 June 1941 and 1,188 on 1 January 1942.

Together with the expansion of the Red Army's tank and mechanized forces, this dramatic increase in the quantity, size, and effectiveness of the RVGK's antitank forces from January 1942 through 31 December 1943 transformed the Red Army into a potent offensive force and spelled certain doom for the *Wehrmacht*, its panzer forces, and blitzkrieg war.

Self-Propelled Artillery (Assault Guns)

During the first 18 months of the war, one of the Red Army force structure's most glaring weaknesses was its lack of mobile artillery capable of accompanying and supporting its tank, mechanized, and cavalry forces either on the defense or on the offense. Since tractor-towed and horse-drawn artillery could neither keep up with nor support these mobile forces with reliable direct or indirect fire, they were vulnerable to destruction by more mobile German artillery, assault guns, and the dreaded antitank guns, which the Germans called *Paks (Panzerabwehr Kanonen)*.

However, the NKO began remedying this situation in late 1942, when it developed and produced a new family of self-propelled artillery guns (assault guns) and units to employ them in combat. Because these new self-propelled guns exploited existing tank and gun technology by combining the chassis of existing tanks with existing gun systems, they incorporated the positive characteristics of tanks and artillery in terms of mobility, firepower, and minimal armor protection, being able to support tank, mechanized, and even cavalry forces exploiting into the depth of enemy defenses and being relatively inexpensive to produce. Armed with heavier guns, they were able to engage and destroy enemy tanks and assault fortified positions and hardened defenses.

On 7 December 1942, the GKO ordered the NKO to form a new Directorate for Mechanized Tractors and Self-Propelled Artillery within its Main Artillery Directorate and assigned the new directorate responsibility for developing, testing, and fielding new self-propelled artillery systems.[50] Less than three weeks later, on 27 December, the NKO ordered the formation of 30 new self-propelled artillery regiments in the RVGK. These regiments consisted of four batteries, two armed with four 76mm (SU-76) guns each and two with four 122mm (SU-122) howitzers each, and an SU-76 gun for the regimental commander for a regimental strength of 307 men, 17 SU-76 and eight SU-122 guns, 48 trucks, and 11 tractors.[51] The 76mm guns were mounted on the light turret of a T-70 tank chassis and the 122mm howitzer on the chassis of a T-34 tank.

After forming four regiments of this type at artillery training centers during January and February 1943, the NKO assigned two of them to the Volkhov Front in February for field testing and training and two more to the Western Front, where they entered combat for the first time during March. However, the NKO did not field these new regiments in significant numbers until April 1943.[52] In March, in the midst of this testing, the NKO ordered the formation of 16 heavy self-propelled gun regiments consisting of six batteries equipped with two 152mm (SU-152) Model 1937 gun-howitzers each, and a KV command tank for a total strength of 273 men, 12 SU-152 self-propelled guns, and one KV tank. The NKO developed the SU-152, which was mounted on the chassis of a KV-1c heavy tank, within a remarkably short period of 25 days in January 1943 and began serial production of the weapons in February.

Although these new self-propelled guns proved mobile enough to accompany and support mobile forces effectively, field experience in early 1943 indicated that the multiplicity of models made them difficult to supply logistically and maintain. To resolve these problems, on 23 April the NKO subordinated all of its self-propelled artillery forces to the commander of Red Army Armored and Mechanized Forces and his directorate and, more importantly, ordered the formation of two new types of self-propelled artillery regiments, one light and one medium, each equipped with one type of weapons system, to complement the existing heavy regiments.[53] Light self-propelled artillery regiment consisted of four batteries with five SU-76 guns each and a SU-76 command vehicle, for an overall strength of 259 men and 21 SU-76 self-propelled guns, and medium self-propelled artillery regiment consisted four batteries with four SU-122 guns each and a T-34 command tank, for a strength of 248 men, 16 SU-122 self-propelled guns, and one T-34 tank.

The NKO tested all of its guns during the summer of 1943 against German Tiger tanks captured at Leningrad during January and determined that the 85mm antiaircraft gun and the 122mm corps gun were far more effective against the new German tank than were the SU-76 gun and the SU-122 howitzer. Therefore, by August the NKO began fielding SU-85 self-propelled gun systems, which mounted 85mm guns on T-34 tank chassis, and ceased production of the SU-122 self-propelled guns. New medium SU-85 self-propelled artillery regiments consisted of four batteries with four guns apiece, for a total strength of 16 SU 85 self-propelled guns and one T-34 tank.[54]

The NKO continued strengthening its self-propelled artillery force during September by developing a new SU-152 self-propelled system to replace the 152mm gun-howitzers mounted on obsolete and highly vulnerable KV tank chassis. This new weapon, the ISU-152, which was armed with a 152mm

Model ML-20s gun-howitzer mounted on the chassis of a Joseph (Iosif) Stalin (IS) heavy tank, had far better armor protection, was more mobile than its predecessor, and also mounted a DShK machine gun to combat enemy aircraft. The NKO ceased production of the SU-152 when the ISU-152 went into service in December 1943.[55]

However, since Soviet industry failed to produce the necessary quantity of 152mm gun-howitzers, in addition to the ISU-152, the NKO began developing a new self-propelled gun—ISU-122 self-propelled guns equipped with 122mm A-19 model guns mounted on IS tank chassis and, later, 122mm D-25S guns mounted on the same chassis (ISU-122), each of which also mounted a DShK machine gun. The NKO began replacing SU-152 guns in its heavy self-propelled artillery regiments with these new weapons in December. Finally, after it decided to equip its T-34 tanks with 85mm guns in late December, the NKO began developing self-propelled guns (SU-100s) to match the T-34-85 tanks' power and range. However, the NKO did not begin fielding the T34-85 tanks and SU-100 self-propelled guns until April 1944.[56]

In addition to developing, testing, and fielding newer and more effective self-propelled artillery systems, the NKO also worked hard during 1943 to streamline its self-propelled artillery force structure. For example, in October it reorganized all self-propelled artillery regiments into four batteries, while maintaining their existing strength of 21 SU-76 guns in light regiments, 16 SU-122 or SU-85 guns and one T-34 tank in medium regiments, and 12 SU-152 or ISU-152 guns and one KV or IS-2 tank in heavy regiments.[57]

By 31 December 1943, the RVGK force structure included 41 separate self-propelled artillery regiments and Soviet industry had produced and fielded 1,200 self-propelled guns of various calibers.

Antiaircraft Artillery

When war began, antiaircraft companies and antiaircraft battalions organic to rifle battalions, rifle divisions, and rifle corps subordinate to the Red Army's field forces and separate antiaircraft battalions assigned to military districts were responsible for defending Red Army forces against air attack. In addition, a large and elaborate organization named PVO Strany was responsible for defending the homeland as a whole, including its key political, economic, and industrial centers and its vital communications centers and routes, against air attack (see Chapter 11).

Within the field forces, antiaircraft machine-gun companies assigned to rifle regiments consisted of two platoons, one heavy platoon with eight four-barreled 7.62mm antiaircraft machine guns and one light platoon with three heavy 12.7mm machine guns each, for a total of eight 7.62mm and three 12.7mm machine guns. Antiaircraft artillery battalions within rifle divisions consisted of two light batteries with four 37mm antiaircraft guns each and one heavy battery with four 76mm antiaircraft guns, for a total strength of 287 men, eight 37mm and four 76mm guns, 33 trucks, and one armored car. Although these battalions had two radios in their light batteries and four in their heavy batteries, the radios were unreliable, the radio operators were often poorly trained, and, worse still, these battalions lacked their full complement of antiaircraft guns.[58]

Separate antiaircraft artillery battalions, which provided rifle corps with air defense on the basis of one battalion per rifle corps, consisted of three firing batteries equipped with four 76mm or 85mm guns each, for a total of 12 antiaircraft guns. However, on 22 June 1941, only 40 of the Red Army's 61 rifle corps contained its requisite antiaircraft artillery battalion. Although a typical rifle corps consisting of three rifle divisions supported by a single separate antiaircraft artillery battalion was supposed to field 48 antiaircraft guns, 72 four-barreled 7.62mm antiaircraft machine guns, and 27 heavy 12.7mm machine guns, few possessed their full complement of antiaircraft weapons when war began.[59]

In addition to these antiaircraft artillery forces, the Red Army also included armored train battalions and separate armored trains, which were configured for employment as antiaircraft platforms throughout the war, primarily subordinate to PVO Strany (see Chapter 7).

As it had the Red Army as a whole, the advancing *Wehrmacht* utterly decimated the Red Army's antiaircraft forces during Operation Barbarossa:

> Because of our heavy aircraft losses and the impossibility of massing our aircraft, antiaircraft defense for our forces was carried out primarily by antiaircraft and artillery weaponry, which was adapted to fire on air targets. During these operations our antiaircraft forces suffered heavy equipment losses. Furthermore, a considerable quantity of our antiaircraft artillery weapons was employed to fill out our antitank units. Because of the evacuation of our industrial enterprises, which was just beginning, the production of antiaircraft artillery weapons was curtailed. All of this led to massive shortages of weapons in air defense units. For example, at the end of the second month of the war, the Southwestern Front had a total of 232 76.2mm and 176 37mm antiaircraft guns, which amounted to 70 and 40 percent of the *front's* authorized strength in those categories.[60]

When the NKO truncated the size of the Red Army's force structure during the terrible summer of 1941, in addition to abolishing rifle corps entirely, it also reduced the size of antiaircraft forces assigned to rifle regiments and divisions and shifted the responsibility for air defense to separate antiaircraft artillery battalions assigned to its field armies. For example, the NKO converted the rifle regiments' antiaircraft companies to platoons equipped with three heavy 12.7 mm antiaircraft machine guns and the rifle divisions' antiaircraft battalion to antiaircraft batteries armed six 37mm antiaircraft guns and nine trucks by December 1941.[61] The NKO completed this truncation process in late December by eliminating antiaircraft platoons from rifle regiments and antiaircraft batteries from rifle divisions, largely because the German air threat decreased and the 108 separate antiaircraft artillery battalions in the RVGK on 1 January 1942 seemed capable of protecting the Red Army's field forces until large RVGK antiaircraft forces could be fielded.

The NKO began expanding the RVGK's antiaircraft forces in early 1942 by forming small antiaircraft artillery regiments to protect its field armies. These regiments consisted of three batteries with four 37mm antiaircraft guns each and two antiaircraft machine-gun companies, one consisting of three platoons with four Maxim machine guns each and one containing two platoons with four DShK machine guns each, for a total strength of 326 men, twelve 37mm guns, twelve 7.92mm Maxim machine guns, and eight 12.7mm DShK machine guns.[62] The NKO assigned 35 of these regiments to its operating *fronts* in June 1942, including 18 to the Western Front, eight each to the Briansk and Southwestern Fronts, and one to the North Caucasus Front.[63] In addition, on 2 June the NKO streamlined command and control of air defense forces by subordinating all antiaircraft units, guns and machine guns, and all means of aerial observation, target identification, and communications within operating *fronts* and armies to the chief of Red Army artillery and newly designated deputy artillery commanders for air defense within its operating *fronts* and armies.[64]

To further strengthen its antiaircraft forces, the NKO formed two new types of antiaircraft artillery battalions in early and mid-August 1942, the first consisting of three batteries with four 76mm or 85m guns and one DShK machine gun each, and the second organized in the same fashion and with the same armament but with a strength of 514 men and a battery of six searchlights. Finally, the NKO formed a third and heavier type of antiaircraft regiment in late August consisting of two battalions with 12 guns apiece, but fielded only eight of these regiments by year's end.[65]

Despite these attempts to improve force antiaircraft defense, Red Army *front* and army commanders experienced difficulty massing enough antiaircraft weapons to protect their forces while they were conducting major operations. Consequently, on 22 October 1942, the NKO issued an order signed by Stalin requiring all *fronts* and armies to form antiaircraft artillery groups, which, in cooperation with *front* aviation, were to defend their forces during major operations:

1. Form antiaircraft groups from army antiaircraft artillery regiments and from antiaircraft batteries and antiaircraft machine-gun companies in rifle and other formations operating along secondary axes.

Employ from one-half to one-third of all of the *front's* (army's) force antiaircraft weaponry in the antiaircraft group.

Attach the antiaircraft group to the army's or *front's* shock group to protect it. [Stalin added this sentence to replace one reading, "All antiaircraft weapons in units making up the shock groups are included in the latter's overall antiaircraft defense system."]

2. Organize observation and identification services with special care while forces are in place or moving so that [the antiaircraft group] will have time to prepare itself to open fire on enemy aircraft [and create barrier fires] in timely fashion, and so that the forces will have time to undertake necessary measures to reduce losses from bombing and machine-gun fire from enemy aircraft.

3. The army commanders will entrust command of the attacking army's antiaircraft to the deputy chief of army artillery for air defense and place all necessary communications equipment at his disposal.

4. Command cadre in all force branches will provide necessary assistance and help to the antiaircraft group's antiaircraft batteries and machine-gun companies while they are moving behind the attacking forces. Let their march columns pass through junctions crossings, permit them to bypass force columns on the roads, and assist the antiaircraft units when they leave the roads and enter their firing positions.[66]

In response to Stalin's order, the NKO consolidated many of its antiaircraft artillery regiments into 18 new RVGK antiaircraft artillery divisions on 31 October 1942. These divisions consisted of a headquarters, four army-type antiaircraft artillery regiments with three 4-gun batteries each, and a small logistical subunit, for a total strength of 1,345 men, 48 of the 37mm antiaircraft guns, 48 Maxim machine guns, and 32 DShK antiaircraft machine guns.[67] As a result, the RVGK's force structure expanded during 1942 from 108 regiments on 1 January 1942 to 27 new antiaircraft artillery divisions, 123 separate antiaircraft artillery regiments, and 109 separate antiaircraft artillery battalions by 1 January 1943, and 30 divisions, 94 separate regiments, and 95 separate battalions on 1 February 1943.[68]

This expansion was possible only because the Soviet arms industry produced 3,499 of the 37mm antiaircraft guns and 2,761 of the 85mm antiaircraft guns in 1942 and another 5,472 of the 37mm guns and 3,713 of the 85mm guns in 1943. Despite this increased production, however, continuing shortages of medium 85mm antiaircraft guns prevented the Red Army's air defense forces from engaging aircraft flying higher than 3,000 meters.

The NKO significantly strengthened and streamlined its antiaircraft artillery forces in 1943. First, during the second half of February, it reorganized its antiaircraft artillery divisions by adding command and control batteries, disbanding one of the divisions' light regiments so that its guns could form a fourth battery in its remaining three light regiments, and adding a new fourth medium regiment equipped with 85mm antiaircraft guns to each division so that it could engage enemy aircraft flying above 3,000 meters. Once formed, these divisions consisted of three light regiments with four batteries equipped with four 37mm antiaircraft guns each for a total strength of 16 guns, one medium regiment organized into four 4-gun batteries with a total strength of sixteen 76mm or 85mm antiaircraft guns, and beefed up logistical support, for a total division strength of 64 antiaircraft guns.[69] In addition, the NKO completed eliminating antiaircraft artillery batteries from its rifle divisions, used the equipment to help fill out the new RVGK artillery divisions subordinate to the RVGK, and incorporated many antiaircraft artillery regiments and battalions into the new divisions.

Second, the NKO formed two new types of specialized antiaircraft artillery regiments during the same period. The first, which it began forming in February to protect airfields, fielded twelve 37mm guns, 12 Maxims, and eight DShK machine guns and were identical to the 1942 type regiment except that they lacked the earlier regiments transport vehicles and numbered 270 men. The second type, which the NKO began forming in April to protect field armies and were similar in structure to regiments in antiaircraft artillery divisions, had a strength of 420 men, twelve 37mm guns, 12 Maxim machine guns, and 12 DShK machine guns (organized into four rather than two platoons). The NKO formed 38 airfield defense regiments and 52 new separate antiaircraft artillery regiments in 1943, all but four of the latter on the basis of the older 12-gun regimental structure.[70]

Third, the NKO also formed new separate antiaircraft artillery battalions beginning on April 1943. These battalions consisted of three batteries with four 76mm or 85mm antiaircraft guns and one DShK machine gun each, for a total strength of about 380 men, twelve 76mm or 85mm antiaircraft guns, and three DShK machine guns. However, shortages of 76mm antiaircraft guns forced the NKO to form only two of these battalions, each consisting of two batteries with four 37mm guns and one battery with four 85mm guns.[71]

By dint of these reforms, the NKO was able to subordinate almost all of the Red Army's antiaircraft artillery force to RVGK control, with antiaircraft artillery regiments and divisions protecting the armies' and *fronts'* operating forces and medium-caliber antiaircraft artillery battalions protecting key rear area objectives. In addition, the Red Army also employed most of the Red Army's more than 60 armored trains for antiaircraft defense throughout 1943. For example, 35 armored trains supported Red Army forces during the Battle of Kursk.[72]

By virtue of its strenuous efforts, the NKO increased the strength of Red Army's antiaircraft artillery forces steadily to 48 divisions, 159 separate regiments, and 98 separate battalions by 1 July 1943, and 60 divisions, 157 separate regiments, and 96 separate battalions on 31 December 1943. As a result, the Red Army Air Force achieved overall air superiority over the *Luftwaffe* on the Soviet-German front by mid-1943, at least in part because Red Army antiaircraft forces could now help sweep German aircraft from the skies.

Rocket Artillery (Guards-Mortars)

The most novel and terrifying weapons in the Red Army artillery inventory were multiple-rocket launchers, officially "guards-mortars," but popularly referred to as *Katiushas*. First introduced as battalions of "secret" weapons in mid-July 1941, by early 1943 the Red Army included hundreds of guards-mortars organized into divisions, brigades, regiments, and separate battalions.[73] The NKO began fielding rocket artillery forces shortly after war began, beginning with three batteries of BM-13 rockets in July, five by early August, and two in late August, and eight regiments with either BM-8 or BM-13 launchers in August and September, all of which went into action immediately.[74] The NKO began combining separate rocket launcher batteries into separate battalions in late August, designating the first two as the 42nd and 43rd.

The first experimental rocket artillery batteries consisted of three firing platoons with seven truck-mounted BM-13 launcher systems and one 122mm howitzer for adjusting fire, a headquarters platoon, and small service and supply elements, plus 44 trucks capable of transporting 600 rockets, three refills of fuel and oil, and seven days of rations. Each battery could fire a single volley of 112 M-13 high-explosive rockets.[75] However, combat experience indicated that separate rocket launcher batteries with six to nine BM-13 launchers each were difficult to control in combat, the density of their fire did not inflict significant damage on the enemy, and the 122mm howitzer was essentially useless. Therefore, on 8 August the *Stavka* ordered the NKO to begin forming eight new rocket launcher regiments equipped with both BM-13 and lighter BM-8 launchers.[76]

These new multiple-rocket launcher regiments, which the NKO termed guards-mortars, consisted of three battalions of M-13 or M-8 launchers organized into three firing batteries with four launchers each, an antiaircraft battalion, and small support elements, for a total of 36 weapons. A full volley by a BM-8 regiment hurled 576 of the 82mm rockets containing 1.4 pounds of explosives each at the enemy, and the BM-13 regiment, 1,296 of the 132mm rockets carrying 10.8 pounds of explosives each. Although wildly inaccurate, these rocket launchers were ideally suited to saturate a wide area with massed, intense, though often inaccurate fire. When fired at night, their eerie sound and spectacular flash and the indiscriminate fire they rained down produced terror in the hearts of the enemy.[77]

The NKO fielded the new regiments quickly, dispatching a total of nine regiments to the front by the end of September.[78] The 1st Moscow Red Banner Artillery School and, later, the Moscow and Tatar Centers for the Formation of Guards-Mortar Units organized these regiments, and on 8 September the GKO created the position of commander of guards-mortar units (who was also a deputy commissar of defense) with a full staff and a Main Directorate for Guards-Mortar Units within the NKO to control guards-mortar forces.[79] Subsequently, the NKO fielded a total of 14 guards-mortar regiments and 19 separate battalions in October and November.

Front and army commanders employed their rocket dispersed in penny-parcel fashion during the chaotic and often desperate fighting between Smolensk and Moscow from September through November, largely negating their potential combat impact. As a result, the *Stavka* ordered its operating *fronts* to create operational groups of guards-mortars units to improve their combat performance in September and October and required all of its operating armies to do the same on 11 January 1942.[80] However, these measures still failed to solve the problem. Worse still, the NKO disbanded nine of the 14 regiments in November and December and formed 28 separate guards-mortar battalions with two batteries each in their stead, further reducing their combat effectiveness.[81] As a result, by year's end the Red Army's force structure included eight guards-mortar regiments and 73 separate guards-mortar battalions.

The NKO finally took action to concentrate its rocket forces more effectively on 14 January 1942, four days after the *Stavka* issued its famous 10 January directive, which sharply criticized the performance of the Red Army's artillery during the Moscow counteroffensive and required all of its operating *fronts* and armies to employ their artillery concentrated in "artillery offensives" in all future offensive operations.[82] It did so by forming 20 new BM-8 and BM-13 guards-mortar regiments, each capable of firing single volleys of 384 M-13 or 864 M-8 rockets. The regiments consisted of three battalions with two rocket batteries each for a total of 20 launchers.[83] In addition, on 25 February the GKO ordered the NKO to produce 1,215 launchers, including 405 BM-8 and 810 BM-13, and to equip 50 more regiments from March through May, and, soon after, ordered its weapons designers to begin work on two new rockets, the 132mm M-20 and 300mm M-30 models.[84]

These measures increased the number of guards-mortar regiments in the Red Army from 8 on 1 January 1942, to 70 on 1 July, and those supporting operating *fronts* to 57 by 26 June, an 11-fold increase since 1 January. During the same period, however, the quantity of battalions decreased from 74 to 42 because many of these battalions were assigned to new tank, mechanized, and cavalry corps.[85]

The NKO reorganized its guards-mortar forces again on 4 June so that they could support the Red Army more effectively during its summer–fall campaign. While upgrading the regiments' antiaircraft platoons into full batteries equipped with four 37mm guns each, it also fielded 20 new separate heavy guards-mortar battalions equipped with more powerful 300mm M-30 rocket launchers. These heavy battalions consisted of a headquarters and three firing batteries armed with a total of 32 rocket launchers with four rockets each. The new 300mm rocket projectiles each contained 64 pounds of explosives, and the new battalion could fire single volleys of 384 rockets to a range of 1.74 miles.[86] The Red Army guards-mortar force included 70 guards-mortar regiments and 52 separate guards-mortar battalions by 1 July, including several M-30 battalions.

In July, after the summer campaign began, the NKO formed 44 more separate M-30 guards-mortar battalions with two firing batteries of 24 launchers each, whose 48 launchers could fire volleys of 288 rockets.[87] It also began combining its new heavy guards-mortar battalions into heavy guards-mortar regiments, each consisting of four heavy guards-mortar battalions, and formed two such regiments by September 1942. On 1 October the Red Army fielded 79 M-8 and M-13 guards-mortar regiments, 77 separate M-30 battalions, and 36 separate M-8 and M-13 battalions, for a total of 350 battalions.[88]

After playing only a limited role in the defensive fighting during Operation *Blau*, the *Stavka* assigned its guards-mortar forces a more significant role in the offensives it conducted in the Rzhev and Stalingrad regions during November 1942. For example, it allocated 108 battalions, including 47 M-30 battalions, to its Western and Kalinin Fronts for employment in Operation Mars, and 130 battalions, including 20 M-30 battalions, to its Southwestern, Don, Stalingrad, and Trans-Caucasus Fronts for use in Operations Uranus and Saturn.[89]

On the eve of and during these new offensives, increased Soviet production of multiple-rocket systems permitted the fielding of guards-mortar brigades and divisions. First, before the offensives began, the headquarters of guards-mortar units and the headquarters of operational groups of guards-mortars within operating *fronts* formed ten heavy guards-mortar brigades, each consisting of five heavy M-30 regiments but with only limited logistical support.

After the November offensives began, pursuant to a *Stavka* directive, on 26 November, the NKO ordered its Directorate of Guards-Mortar Units to form three new heavy guards-mortar divisions, and later a fourth, numbered the 1st through the 4th, by 10 January 1943. These divisions consisted of a headquarters, two heavy M-30 guards-mortar brigades organized into six M-30 battalions, four M-13 regiments with M-20 or M-13 weapons, and a fire control element, and fielded 576 M-30 launcher rails and 96 BM-13 launcher systems capable of collectively delivering single volleys of 3,840 rockets (2,304 M-30 and 1,536 M-13) or 230 tons of explosives.[90] At the same time, the NKO reorganized its heavy M-30 guards-mortar brigades like those within the divisions.[91]

The NKO fielded a total of 11 new M-30 guards-mortar brigades and 47 new M-13 guards-mortar regiments in December 1942, raising the total strength of guards-mortar forces to four divisions, 11 brigades, 91 separate regiments, and 51 guards-mortar battalions by 1 January 1943. By this time, the NKO had also developed a new rocket launcher system for their guards-mortar forces, the M-31, which, while more powerful than the M-30, also increased its range to 4,325 meters and bursting diameter to 7–8 meters, and began producing in great quantities in early 1943.[92]

Nor did the NKO's efforts to increase the strength and quantity of its rocket flag in 1943. For example, in January and February, the NKO formed three more guards-mortar divisions, the 5th, 6th, and 7th. Stronger than their predecessors and more effectively controlled, these divisions consisted of three M-30 or M-31 heavy brigades organized into four battalions with three batteries apiece with a total of 864 launchers. While the brigades were capable of firing 1,152 rockets in single volleys, the divisions were able to fire devastating single volleys of 3,456 rockets (a decrease of 474 rockets) but with a total payload of 320 tons (a 90-ton increase) from a total of 864 rocket launcher systems.[93] At the same time, the NKO approved new uniform organizations for M-13 and M-8 guards-mortar regiments organic to tank armies, and tank, mechanized, and cavalry corps.

Based on the combat experiences of the winter campaign, on 29 April 1943, the GKO centralized artillery fire within the parameters of the concept of the "artillery offensive" by placing the commander of guards-mortar units and his directorate under the operational direction of the commander of Red Army artillery and designating the former as the latter's deputy. Likewise, the chiefs of each operating *front's* guards-mortar units became deputies to the *fronts'* artillery chiefs.[94]

The NKO subordinated many of its guards-mortar division to artillery penetration corps throughout the second half of 1943 but retained some as separate. For example, in July 1943, four of the RVGK's seven guards-mortar divisions were subordinate to artillery penetration corps (the 2nd to the 7th Corps, the 3rd to the 2nd Corps, the 5th to the 4th Corps, and the 7th to the 5th Corps), while three (the 1st, 4th, and 6th) remained separate or under direct RVGK control.[95]

Guards-mortar regiments and battalions still formed the basic building blocks of the RVGK's guards-mortar forces during this period. The former consisted of three battalions with two batteries of four launchers apiece, and the antiaircraft battalion remained the basic building block of the Red Army's guards-mortar force.[96] The latter consisted either of older and lighter M-8 and M-13 battalions made up of eight rocket launchers and minimal air defense and logistical support or heavier M-30 battalions fielding three batteries each with 32 four-rocket launching frames.[97]

By 31 December 1943, the Red Army's force structure included 7 guards-mortar divisions, 13 guards-mortar brigades, 108 guards-mortar regiments, and six separate guards-mortar battalions. By this time, when planning "artillery offensives" in support of major operations, *Stavka* representatives in the field and Red Army *front* commanders routinely incorporated massed guards-mortar fire directly into their offensive fire plans, in particular, into the artillery preparations that preceded all offensive operations. After the penetrations were complete, guards-mortar forces subordinate to exploiting tank armies, and tank, mechanized, and cavalry forces provided constant support to exploiting mobile forces throughout the duration of the offensive.

AIR FORCES

At the beginning of the war, the Red Army Air Force (*Voenno-vozdushnye sily,* or VVS) consisted of four main components, including Aviation of the High Command (*Aviatsiia Glavnogo komandovaniia,* or AGK) or, more simply, Long-Range Bomber Aviation (*Dal'nebombardirovochnaia aviatsiia,* or DBA), *Frontal* Aviation (*Frontovaia aviatsiia,* or FA), Army Aviation (*Armeiskaia aviatsiia,* or AA), and Force Aviation (*Voiskovaia aviatsiia,* or VA), which were all subordinate to the NKO's Main Directorate of the Air Force of the Red Army (*Glavnoe upravlenie Voenno-vozdushnykh sil Krasnoi Armii,* or GUVVSKA).[98] DBA consisted primarily of strategic bomber aircraft assigned to the High Command's Reserve (RGK), while aircraft subordinate to *Frontal,* Army, and Force Aviation were responsible for supporting the Red Army's operating *fronts,* armies, and corps.

A fifth air component, PVO Strany's aviation, which was subordinate to the NKO's Main Directorate for PVO Strany of the Red Army (*Glavnoe upravlenie protivovozdushnoi oborony strany Krasnoi Armii,* or GUPVO Strany KA), was responsible for the country's overall air defense (see Chapter 11).

Long-Range Bomber Aviation (BDA)

On the eve of war, BDA was a separate element of the Red Army's Air Force (VVS) whose forces were subordinate to the Long-Range Aviation headquarters of the High Command Reserve (RGK). This force consisted of five long-range bomber aviation corps, numbered the 1st through 5th, and the 18th, 26th, and 30th Separate Long-Range Bomber Aviation Divisions. While bomber aviation corps consisted of a headquarters, two bomber aviation divisions, and one fighter aviation division, bomber aviation divisions included a headquarters and two long-range bomber aviation regiments, and bomber aviation regiments consisted of five bomber squadrons equipped with three TB-7 bombers each and one squadron of ten IaK-1 or LaGG-3 fighters to protect the bombers. Bomber aviation regiments fielded 15 TB-7 bombers and ten fighters, bomber aviation divisions fielded 30 bombers and 20 fighters, and bomber aviation corps had a strength of 60 bombers and at least 40 fighters.[99]

In June 1941 DBA's force included 13 long-range bomber aviation divisions with 44 subordinate long-range bomber aviation regiments and five fighter aviation divisions; however, four of these fighter aviation divisions were still being formed. At this time, BDA deployed its long-range bomber aviation corps in the most strategically important military districts, with the 1st Long-Range Bomber Aviation Corps in the Leningrad Military District, the 2nd in the Khar'kov MD, the 3rd in the Western Special MD, the 4th in the Odessa MD, and the 5th, which was still forming, in the Far Eastern Front. The 18th Separate Long-Range Bomber Aviation Division was stationed in the Kiev Special Military District, the 26th was in the Trans-Caucasus Military District, and the 30th was in the Trans-Baikal Military District.

Even though the *Stavka* retained BDA forces in its reserve (RGK), the deteriorating combat situation during the initial period of the war forced it to employ these bombers in direct support of the Red Army's operating *fronts* instead of using them to fulfill their more important mission of attacking objectives deep in the enemy's rear area. As a result, DBA forces suffered heavy losses in close combat during the initial period of the war, and the *Stavka* was not able to replace these losses by transferring aircraft from the country's eastern regions.

Worse still, air combat during the first few months of war demonstrated that the entire VVS force was unwieldy and difficult to command and control, particularly in light of severe equipment shortages and the losses inflicted by the *Luftwaffe*. Therefore, when the *Stavka* reorganized the VVS as a whole in the worst of combat conditions during August 1941, it decreased the number of long-range bomber aviation corps in DBA from five to three. After the heavy combat during the fall, DBA had only 135 operational planes in its aircraft inventory on 31 December 1941.[100]

The GKO and *Stavka* began attempting to solve the command and control problems in the VVS and DBA in early 1942, all the while strengthening the DBA's forces by improving its long-range bombing capabilities. As a first step in this process, on 5 March 1942, the GKO changed the name DBA to Aviation of Long-Range Action (*Aviatsiia dal'nego deistviia*, or ADD), subordinated ADD directly to the *Stavka*, and assigned it the mission of attacking enemy operational and strategic objectives. After the NKO added new bomber aircraft to it, ADD forces increased in strength to 11 long-range aviation divisions and 1 long-range aviation regiment by 31 December 1942.[101] Finally, on 30 April 1943, the NKO reorganized most of its 11 separate long-range action aviation divisions into eight long-range action aviation corps, increasing the strength of AAD forces to a total of 700 combat aircraft.[102]

As a result of these reforms, by 1 July 1943, the ADD force structure consisted of eight aviation corps of long-range action with two aviation divisions each, 18 aviation divisions of long-range action with three long-range aviation regiments each (a fourth was added in 1944), and subordinate aviation regiments of long-range action with 32 Il-4 and Pe-8 aircraft each, supported by numerous field support battalions, forward aviation warehouses, and repair organs.

Despite the ADD's important strategic potential, the heavy ground fighting at the front forced the *Stavka* to employ virtually all of its ADD aircraft in attacks on operational and tactical rather than strategic targets, particularly during the first quarter of 1943. While ADD aircraft were able to begin engaging strategic targets in the enemy's deep rear area in full regimental, division, and corps strength in May 1943, this pattern of tactical and operational employment persisted until year's end.[103]

Front, Army, and Force Aviation

When war began, VVS *Frontal,* Army and Force Aviation were responsible for supporting Red Army field forces in peacetime and during wartime. *Frontal* aviation included specific fighter, bomber, and mixed aviation divisions, mixed aviation brigades, fighter, bomber, and mixed aviation regiments, and reconnaissance aviation regiments assigned to all military districts, including those which would become *fronts* in wartime. On 22 June *Frontal* Aviation fielded a total of 58 aviation divisions, including 19 fighter, 11 bomber, and 28 mixed aviation divisions; five mixed aviation brigades; five aviation regiments, including two fighter, one bomber, and two mixed regiments; and 11 reconnaissance aviation regiments.

Army Aviation, which the NKO had begun forming in the early summer of 1941, consisted of three mixed aviation divisions subordinate to armies stationed in the Leningrad Military District. Therefore, *Frontal* and Army Aviation fielded a total of 61 aviation divisions, five aviation brigades, and 16 aviation regiments of various types on 22 June. Force Aviation, the fourth component of the VVS, was in its infancy on 22 June. Although it was supposed to support rifle, mechanized, and cavalry corps with 95 separate reconnaissance and corrective aviation squadrons, only a fraction of its squadrons existed on 22 June.

The aviation divisions assigned to *Frontal* and Army Aviation, which were the VVS's basic tactical formations, consisted of four or five aviation regiments totaling 240–300 bomber, assault, fighter, and reconnaissance aircraft. Bomber, assault, fighter, and reconnaissance aviation regiments consisted of four or five squadrons of 12–15 aircraft each, plus one to three command aircraft for a total of 61–63 aircraft per regiment; mixed aviation regiments consisted of two bomber squadrons and one or two fighter squadrons, for a total of 25 bombers and up to 31 fighters; and separate aviation squadrons assigned to support rifle, mechanized, and cavalry corps consisted of ten reconnaissance and six communications aircraft.[104]

Therefore, the VVS as a whole consisted of 79 aviation divisions, five of which were in the process of forming, and five aviation brigades on 22 June. This force included 355 aviation regiments of various types either within divisions or separate, and 20,662 aircraft, including 15,559 combat aircraft, most of which were obsolete. The NKO rated 218 of these regiments as fully combat ready; another 50 had their full complement of aircraft and equipment but were still undergoing training; and the remainder had far less than their authorized aircraft, equipment, and personnel strength.[105]

The severe combat losses the VVS suffered during the initial period of the war and its continuing equipment shortages prompted the GKO to decrease the size of its aviation regiments to three squadrons with ten aircraft each plus two command aircraft, for a total of 32 aircraft per regiment in mid-July, and to reduce the number of aviation divisions in the VVS from 79, including 74 already fully formed, to 69 in August. On 20 August, when the VVS begin receiving a limited number of new model Il-2, Pe-2, and IaK-1 aircraft later in the summer, the NKO decreased the size of its aviation regiments equipped with the new models to two squadrons of nine aircraft each plus two command aircraft, for a total of 20 aircraft.[106]

The severe shortage of trained pilots and crews during late summer and fall also forced the NKO to assign women to some of its new regiments. For example, on 8 October it formed the 586th Fighter, 587th Close Bomber, and 588th Night Bomber Aviation Regiments, which were equipped with Il-2 fighters and Su-2 and U-2 bombers, respectively, and ordered, "The commander of the Red Army VVS will create these aviation regiments and man them with pilots and flight-technical crews from women cadres of the VVS, Red Army, Civil Air Fleet, and Osoaviakhim."[107]

In addition, after forming the experimental 81st, 82nd, 87th, 90th, 103rd, and 110th Aviation Divisions with two to four regiments each, the NKO reduced the number of regiments in each division to two in the late summer and on 28 September began forming 15 assault aviation divisions to supplement the fighter and bomber divisions already in the VVS force structure. Formed during October from existing assault aviation regiments, each of these divisions consisted of one assault aviation regiment equipped with Il-2 aircraft and two fighter regiments equipped with MiG-3, IaK-1, or LaGG-3 aircraft, many of the latter armed with aerial rockets.[108] Finally, because command and control still proved difficult, the NKO disbanded all aviation divisions assigned to *fronts* and armies in January and February 1942 and assigned their regiments to *front* VVS control.[109]

These reforms did resolve some problems, but they created others, the worst being the wholesale dispersal of air resources and the operating *fronts'* inability to concentrate their air power along decisive axes, particularly when on the offensive. The *Stavka* resorted to various temporary field expedients to solve these problems. For example, in light of the desperate shortages of reserve aircraft caused by heavy losses during the first few months of war, in August 1941, the *Stavka* ordered the NKO and VVS to form six reserve aviation groups (RAGs), resembling reinforced aviation divisions, consisting of five to eight aviation regiments of various types, for a strength of 80–100 aircraft each, to support its field forces. Later still, during the defense of Moscow in November, the *Stavka* created a special aviation operational group under the Red Army VVS commander to coordinate air operations by the Western and Kalinin Fronts, the Moscow Defense Zone, and additional reserve aviation groups under its direct control.

Because these groups proved less than fully effective, on 14 January 1942, the NKO established special aviation groups within the armies of operating *fronts* and, in addition, a special-designation aviation group at Moscow under *Stavka* control from Civil Aviation Fleet aircraft.[110] Although not fully effective, all of these temporary measures to centralize command and control of VVS and Civil Air Fleet aircraft became models for subsequent VVS reorganizations in 1942.

Efforts to expand the VVS force structure throughout 1941 and 1942 were assisted by an increase in Soviet aircraft production. For example, aircraft production increased from 693 aircraft in December 1941 to 976 in January 1942, 822 in February, 1,532 in March, and 1,432 in April, increasing the quantity of aircraft assigned to support the Red Army's field forces from 2,495 in December 1941 to 3,164 in May 1942. By this time, new model aircraft, including LaGG-3, IaK-1, IaK-76, Tu-2, and IaK-9 aircraft, made up 50 percent of the strength of VVS front-line forces.[111]

In early 1942 the NKO exploited this increased aircraft production and its experiences with employing ad hoc operational and reserve aviation groups to establish larger and more capable aviation formations. For example, between March and early May 1942, it formed ten mixed composition shock aviation groups (*udarnye aviatsionnye gruppy*, or UAG) consisting of two to eight aviation regiments each operating under direct RVGK control to reinforce *Frontal* Aviation during the Red Army's offensives in mid-May 1942.[112]

The *Stavka* ended its experimentation with operational, reserve, and shock aviation groups beginning on 5 May 1942, when, on the advice of the VVS chief, Lieutenant General A. A. Novikov, who had been appointed as deputy commissar of defense on 27 April 1942, it ordered the NKO to form new air armies from existing *Frontal* and Army Aviation forces to replace its vast array of operational, reserve, and experimental aviation shock groups.

The first air army the NKO formed, the Western Front's 1st Air Army, consisted of the 201st and 202nd Fighter Aviation Divisions, the 203rd and 204th Mixed Aviation Divisions, the 3rd Separate Training Aviation Regiment, one long-range aviation squadron with two wings totaling six aircraft, one communication squadron with ten U-2 aircraft, and one night bomber aviation squadron with 20 U-2 aircraft. The 1st Air Army's fighter aviation divisions consisted of four fighter regiments each, and the mixed aviation divisions, two fighter and two assault regiments and one bomber regiment each.[113] Ultimately, each of the 17 new air armies formed by November 1942 consisted of two or three fighter aviation divisions, one or two bomber aviation divisions, and one assault aviation division supported by a variety of separate aviation units with an average strength of 400 aircraft of all types (see Table 8.6).[114]

In addition, the NKO began forming two fighter aviation armies and one bomber aviation army consisting of three to five aviation divisions and 200–300 aircraft each on 1 July 1942, but ultimately formed only one of these armies, the 1st Fighter Aviation Army based at Elets. The *Stavka* employed this hastily formed army in early July during Operation *Blau* to support the counterstroke by its new 5th Tank Army near Voronezh in early July during Operation *Blau*. Because this fledgling air army proved clumsy and difficult to maneuver and control and lost 142 of its 213 aircraft during several weeks of intense fighting, the *Stavka* disbanded it in late July, incorporating its surviving aircraft into other air armies.[115]

While it was raising the new air armies, the NKO also formed uniform bomber, assault, and fighter aviation divisions consisting of two regiments each (a third regiment was added in the summer of 1944) whose single types of aircraft made them easier to form, employ, maintain, and supply. After fixing the composition of these regiments at 32 aircraft apiece by the fall of 1942, fighter and assault aviation regiments were able to employ 4 aircraft (flying in two pairs) in a single wing.[116]

The NKO took its final step in reorganizing the VVS on 26 August 1942, when it began combining aviation regiments into aviation corps, which served as a vital control link between the regiments and their parent air armies and consisted of two or more aviation divisions fielding 120–270 combat aircraft each. Although these corps were initially both single-type (fighter, assault, bomber) and mixed, the NKO later converted mixed aviation corps into single-type corps, endeavoring to equip them with new aircraft models. The NKO formed 13 aviation corps, including four fighter, three assault, three bomber, and three mixed types, by 31 December 1943, assigning nine, including two fighter, two assault, and two bomber, and three mixed corps to operating *fronts.*

As it was reforming the VVS during 1941 and 1942, the NKO also benefited from an increasing supply of aircraft provided to the Soviet Union by its Western allies under provisions of the Lend-Lease program, which the Soviet Union accepted on 6 September 1941. After arriving in driblets during late 1941, the flow of aircraft to the Soviet Union reached significant proportions in late 1942 and 1943. These shipments, most of which arrived through the Persian corridor or from Alaska, included Douglas transports, Boeing B-25 bombers, A-20 Boston bombers, and R-40E Kittyhawk and P-39 Airacobra fighters. Ultimately, the roughly 14,000 aircraft shipped to the Soviet Union under the Lend-Lease program amounted to approximately 11 percent of the roughly 100,000 aircraft the Soviet Union produced during the war.[117]

By mid-1943, VVS *Frontal* Aviation had absorbed Army and Force Aviation, and included bomber, fighter, assault (ground attack), mixed, and reconnaissance aviation forces organized into air armies and subordinate aviation corps, divisions, and regiments responsible for supporting the field forces. Normally allocated on the basis of one per *front,* air armies consisted of two to three fighter aviation divisions, one or two bomber or night bomber aviation divisions, one assault aviation division, a variety of separate fighter, assault, bomber, light bomber, mixed, transport, and reconnaissance aviation regiments, and, in many cases, corrective aviation squadrons.[118]

Although their composition varied considerably, air armies became stronger over time in direct proportion to increased Soviet aircraft production and the formation of additional aviation corps. For example, while the VVS's 6 air armies included a total of 13 aviation corps on 1 February 1943, by 1 July its eight air armies fielded a total of 22 aviation corps, and, during the same period, the average strength of all 17 VVS air armies increased from 400 to 500 aircraft. Reinforced by *Stavka* reserve aviation formations, single air armies fielded as many as 1,000 aircraft on 1 July.[119]

Bomber, fighter, and assault aviation corps subordinate to air armies usually consisted of a headquarters and two aviation divisions with a total of 132 combat aircraft, while mixed aviation corps included two to three mixed aviation divisions and a total of 132 to 198 aircraft. Bomber, light bomber, fighter, and assault aviation divisions subordinate to these corps consisted of a headquarters and two aviation regiments for a total of 66 combat aircraft. Mixed aviation divisions were stronger and included a headquarters, two fighter aviation regiments with 20 IaK-1 fighters each, one to two assault aviation regiments with 20 I-15 aircraft each or 32 Il-2 aircraft in guards regiments, and one to two bomber aviation regiments with 20 SB and Su-2 aircraft each or 32 Pe-2 aircraft in guards regiments, for a division strength of 80–144 aircraft.

Aviation regiments at the lowest level of command were the basic building blocks of the entire VVS force structure. Bomber, assault, and fighter aviation regiments consisted of a headquarters with two command aircraft and three aviation squadrons with ten aircraft each for a total of 32 aircraft. These aircraft including SB, Su-2 or Pe-2 bombers in regular bomber squadrons, SB, Il-4, R-5, and Po-2(U-2) bombers in night bomber squadrons, IaK-1, IaK-7, or La-5 fighters in fighter squadrons, and Il-2 *Shturmovik* assault aircraft in assault aviation regiments. Mixed aviation regiments fielded a headquarters and two to three squadrons with 24 to 32 aircraft of various types and reconnaissance regiments fielded three squadrons with 12 aircraft each.

Increased production and fielding of new model aircraft and radios had significantly improved the quality and effectiveness of VVS forces by mid-1943. For example, the average monthly production of new model aircraft rose from 2,100 in 1942 to 2,900 in 1943, permitting the VVS to replace most older-model aircraft. By this time, it equipped most of its fighter regiments with several variations of the new La-5fn and IaK-9 fighters, all of its assault aviation regiments with the Il-2 *Shturmovik* (primarily the two-seated version), and all of its bomber regiments except the night bomber varieties with Pe-2 bombers.[120] As a result, the only aviation regiments still largely with obsolete aircraft in mid-July were night bomber aviation regiments.[121]

More important still, beginning in the fall of 1942, air-ground communications and communications within VVS aviation units improved immeasurably as the NKO developed and fielded new model radios. For example, in October 1942 the GKO ordered radios be placed in half of the VVS's fighter aircraft. Thereafter, by the end of 1943, every VVS combat aircraft was equipped with a radio. More important still, air-ground communications also improved as the number of air-ground radio stations increased from 180 in 1942 to 420 in 1943, by which time virtually all *fronts* and armies and many mobile corps had nearly continuous radio contact with their supporting aviation forces.[122]

These and other qualitative changes within the VVS certainly made it more competitive with the *Luftwaffe*, but it was the VVS's quantitative growth that spelled doom for the *Luftwaffe*. For example, during the first 18 months of the war, the VVS's force structure expanded dramatically from five aviation corps, 74 divisions, five brigades, and 16 regiments to ten air armies, two aviation groups, ten corps, 107 divisions, and 235 separate regiments. This expansion enabled the VVS to weather the *Wehrmacht's* offensive onslaughts during the summers of 1941 and 1942 and effectively support the Red Army's successful and decisive counteroffensive in November 1942. In short, although the *Luftwaffe* managed to achieve air dominance over the VVS during the first few days of war and maintained air superiority throughout most of the first 18 months of war, slowly but inexorably it lost its superiority by November 1942 and faced a dominant VVS in the summer of 1943.

Although the fierce, relentless, and increasingly damaging Allied air attacks on the German homeland indeed helped erode *Luftwaffe* air dominance in the East, the VVS itself, which rose like a phoenix from the ashes of 1941, ultimately vanquished the *Luftwaffe* in the East.

ARTILLERY AND AIRCRAFT

Artillery Weaponry

The Red Army categorized its artillery force as field, antitank, antiaircraft, rocket, or self-propelled artillery. Considered correctly as the "King of Battle" because of its dominance on the battlefield, the quantity, sophistication, and effectiveness of Red Army artillery improved significantly throughout the first two years of war (see Appendix 3 in companion volume for the characteristics of all Red Army field, antitank, self-propelled, antiaircraft, and multiple-rocket launcher artillery and mortar systems).

Field artillery included all mortars, guns, howitzers, and gun-howitzers employed at regiment, division, corps, army, *front,* and RVGK level. Despite their relatively short range, mortars, since they were inexpensive to produce in great quantities, proved the most effective and, ultimately, the most ubiquitous infantry support weapon. When war began, the Red Army fielded 37mm and 50mm mortars at company level, 82mm mortars at battalion level, and 107mm and 120mm mortars at regiment and higher levels.

Since combat during 1941 had demonstrated that 37mm and 50mm Model 1940 mortars, which had constituted a sizable proportion of the army's weapon's inventory when war began, were too light to support rifle forces effectively, the NKO replaced many of them in 1942 but retained some in light cavalry, airborne, and partisan forces. On the other hand, combat during 1941 and early 1942 showed that 82mm, 107mm, and 120mm mortars were very effective artillery weapons. As a result, the NKO modernized the 82mm Model 1937 mortar in 1941 and once again in 1943 as the standard battalion mortar and retained the heavier 107mm and 120mm Model 1937 mortars at regiment level. The most ubiquitous of these weapons, the 120mm mortar, was also the weapon of choice in RVGK mortar brigades. Finally, in January 1944 the NKO also fielded the breech-loading 160mm MT-13 Model 1943 mortar at rifle corps and higher command levels.

The standard artillery piece fielded at rifle regiment level during the first two years of war was the short-barreled 76mm Model 1927 regimental gun, which the NKO had modernized in 1936 and 1939 and later fielded in several improved configurations. The NKO mounted this weapon on the same trail and frame as the 45mm antitank gun in 1943, creating the more maneuverable 76mm regimental Model 1943.

The standard artillery pieces fielded at the rifle division level were a variety of 76mm guns and 122mm and 152mm howitzers. In February 1942, the NKO replaced the 76mm Model 1927 gun with a new and lighter ZIS-3 gun, creating the 76mm Model 1942 gun, which, despite its reduced range, was more effective than its predecessor and could also be employed in an antitank role. The 122mm M-30 Model 1938 howitzer, which the NKO fielded on the eve of war, remained the mainstay of divisional artillery. In addition, the NKO fielded the 152mm M-10 Model 1938 howitzer, which, after it proved too expensive to produce and too heavy to employ, was replaced in 1943 with the 152mm D-1 Model 1943 howitzer mounted on the same carriage as the M-30s. At rifle corps level, in addition to 152mm D-1 Model 1943 howitzers, which were tasked with conducting counterbattery fire, the NKO fielded the 122mm A-19 1931 Model corps gun and the 152mm ML-20 Model 1937 gun-howitzer.

Field artillery pieces assigned to the RVGK included weapons of every caliber from 76mm to 280mm. In addition to those already mentioned, the NKO fielded five larger-caliber weapons, the first four mounted on similar tracked carriages. These included 203mm B-4 Model 1931 howitzers in high-power (BM) artillery units, 152mm BR-2 Model 1935 guns in heavy artillery units, and 210mm BR-17 Model 1939 guns and 280mm BR-5 Model 1939 mortars in special-power (OM) artillery units, and 305mm BR-18 Model 1939 howitzers in special railroad or coastal artillery units.

The standard Red Army antitank artillery weapon when war began was the 45mm Model 1937 antitank gun, a derivative of the German 37mm PaK 36, which Soviet industry had produced under German license since 1931. Inexpensive to produce, this relatively lightweight gun initially proved ideally suited to support infantry and deadly enough against early-model German tanks. However, after proving far less effective against new, more heavily armored German tanks in 1942, thereafter, Red Army forces used it primarily to support infantry rather than fight tanks. After experimenting extensively with 57mm, 85mm, and 107mm antitank guns, in April 1942 the NKO refitted its existing 45mm antitank guns with new projectiles, designating the new weapons as 45mm Model 1942 guns. Further modernized in 1943, this gun remained the Red Army's principal antitank weapon throughout the remainder of the war.

To deal more effectively with the increased German armor threat, the NKO also reconfigured 76mm divisional guns and 122mm guns to combat tanks by equipping them with antitank rounds. Finally, after the Battle of Kursk, it reconfigured 85mm antiaircraft guns for antitank defense in the same fashion as the famous German 88mm antiaircraft guns.[123]

When war began and for a considerable time thereafter, the Red Army was woefully deficient in antiaircraft guns, particularly at regiment and battalion level. Faced with a lack of effective air defenses, Red Army forces simply improvised by engaging German aircraft with rifles and machine guns, or such temporary systems as 7.62mm Tokorev Model 1931 machine guns, which mounted four Maxim Model 1910 machine guns on an ersatz mobile base such as a truck. However, the weight of this system limited its use to static defense.

At the division level, small-caliber antiaircraft artillery (MZA) weapons included 37mm 61–K Model 1939 antiaircraft guns, which were derived from the Swedish Bofor antiaircraft gun system, and lighter 25mm 72-K Model 1940 guns, which the NKO assigned to PVO forces and, occasionally, to units in field armies in lieu of 37mm guns. Mid-caliber antiaircraft artillery (SZA) guns included 76mm Model 1931 and 1938 antiaircraft guns, which the NKO assigned to rifle divisions on the basis of four each and to PVO units for higher altitude defense, and 85mm KS-12 Model 1939 antiaircraft guns, which it allocated to the PVO but also distributed to Red Army antitank units prior to the Battle of Kursk.[124] In addition to these models, the Soviet Union also received large quantities of British and American antiaircraft guns under the Lend-Lease program, including 5,511 British Bofors model guns and 251 U.S. 90mm antiaircraft guns.

The most unusual, fascinating, and famous artillery weapons the Red Army employed during the war were multiple-rocket launchers (MRLs). Christened officially as "Guards-mortars," Red Army soldiers called these awesome weapons *Katiushas* after a popular song of the period because of the wailing sound these weapons made when employed in volley fire. After developing it secretly before war began, the NKO fielded its first MRL system, the BM-13-16, which consisted of 16 rail-launched 132mm M-13 rockets mounted on a ZIS-6 truck, in July 1941, and soon after, the BM-8–36 system, which consisted of 36 rail-mounted 82mm M-8 rockets mounted on the same truck. After mounting these systems on a wide variety of truck chassis, by mid-1943 the NKO had mounted most on Lend-Lease trucks, particularly the American Studebaker. Both weapons, as well as a long-range version of the BM-13, were able to engage targets at ranges of 6–12 kilometers.

The NKO continually improved its guards-mortar systems and rocket warheads during the war. For example, in late 1942 it fielded heavier M-30 rockets fired from a towed wooden-frame transporter similar to the German *Nebelwerfer* engineer rocket-mortar. This system combined M-13 rocket engines with enlarged 300mm warheads and was capable of engaging targets to a range of 2.8 kilometers. Later still, the NKO fielded the BM 31–12 system, which combined the 300mm M-31 rocket with 12 launch cells that could be fired to a range of 4.3 kilometers from either a frame or a truck launcher.[125] Cheap to manufacture and superb as terror weapons, MRLs were capable of delivering devastating area-fire but were far less accurate against point targets.

Since combat experience indicated that infantry and tanks needed more mobile and flexible direct fire support while attacking or defending, in late 1942 the NKO began fielding self-propelled artillery systems (*samokhodno-artilleriiskie ustanovki,* SAU or SU). Modeled after the famous and effective German *StuG III Sturmgeschutz* (assault guns) and manned by tank troops, these self-propelled direct fire assault guns had lighter armor but heavier guns than tanks and were far less expensive to produce. After failed experiments early in the war with 57mm ZIS-30 Model 1938 self-propelled guns mounted on lightly armored tractors, the NKO finally began fielding effective self-propelled gun systems in late 1942.[126]

On 19 October 1942, the GKO ordered the NKO to field light self-propelled artillery regiments units equipped with 37mm and 76mm guns and medium regiments armed with 122mm guns. The first and most common light gun system, the SU-76M light assault gun, which was nicknamed *Suka* (bitch) by its unloving crews, weighed 10.5 tons and consisted of a 76mm ZIS-3 divisional gun in an open-topped lightly armored crew casement mounted to the rear of a T-70 light tank chassis.[127] The primary mission of this system was to accompany the infantry and provide it with direct fire support.

The medium gun system, which the NKO designated as the SU-122 and fielded in early 1943, weighed 30.3 tons and consisted of a 122mm M-30 howitzer mounted on a T-34 tank chassis. Although SU-122 guns were fully armored, the NKO never produced large quantities of this system. Later in the year, however, it fielded heavier 45.5-ton versions consisting of 122mm guns mounted on the chassis of KV-1S heavy tanks. Finally, in mid-1943 the NKO also fielded heavy self-propelled guns, 45.5-ton SU-152s, which consisted of massive 152mm howitzers mounted on the chassis of KV-1S heavy tanks. Because of their awesome power and lethality, these became the most popular self-propelled gun in the army's artillery weapons inventory. During the fighting at Kursk, these weapons earning the nickname *Zverboi* (animal hunters) because they were the only self-propelled guns capable of destroying new German Panther and Tiger tanks.[128]

Finally, to match the growing firepower of new-model German tanks, in late 1943 the NKO fielded medium 29.6-ton SU-85 self-propelled guns consisting of 85mm guns mounted on T-34 tank chassis and, in early 1944, medium 31.6-ton SU-100 guns with 100mm guns also mounted on T-34 tank chassis. In addition to protecting the infantry and "bunker busting," these weapons primarily served as tank destroyers.[129]

Aircraft

Although the NKO began producing and fielding a new generation of modern combat aircraft on the eve of war, including IaK-1, LaGG-2, and MiG-3 fighters, Pe-2 and Pe-8 bombers, and Il-2 assault aircraft, most of which were technically superior to their German counterparts, on 22 June 1941, 80 percent of the VVS's aircraft inventory were older, obsolete models. As was the case with the Red Army's tank fleet, the ferocity and destructiveness of the *Wehrmacht's* advance during Operation Barbarossa had decimated the VVS and severely disrupted Soviet aircraft production.

Through prodigious efforts, however, the GKO and NKO had reversed this situation by early 1942, sharply accelerating its aircraft production. Thereafter, Soviet industry produced 25,436 new aircraft of various types in 1942 and 34,884 more in 1943 (see Appendix 3 in the companion volume for the characteristics of all VVS and Lend-Lease aircraft).[130] In addition, the Allied Lend-Lease program contributed significantly to the VVS's wartime success. For example, from 22 June 1941 through 20 September 1945, the Lend-Lease program delivered a total of 14,589 aircraft to the Soviet Union, approximately 11 percent of total Soviet wartime aircraft production (see Table 8.6).

By early 1943 Soviet industry and the Lend-Lease program produced and fielded sufficient quantities of high-quality combat aircraft for the VVS to achieve at least air parity and sometimes air superiority in specific combat operations. By the summer of 1943, increased aircraft production had enabled the VVS to gain and maintain overall air superiority in most of its offensive operations.

Table 8.1 Quantity and Authorized Strength of RGK Artillery Regiments and Separate Battalions, 22 June 1941

	Quantity	Men	Tractors	Trucks	Weapons
Gun regiment	13	2,565	112	308	48 122mm guns
Heavy gun regiment	1	2,598	104	287	24 152mm gun-howitzers
Howitzer regiment	29	2,318	108	202	48 152mm howitzers
High-power howitzer regiment	31	2,304	112	252	24 203mm howitzers
Special-power howitzer regiment	1	2,304	112	252	24 305mm howitzers
Special-power artillery battalion	11	740–912	0–95	32–86	210mm guns, 203mm or 305mm howitzers

Sources: A. G. Lensky, *Sukhoputnye sily RKKA v predvoennye gody* [RKKA ground forces in the prewar years] (Saint Petersburg: n.p., 2000), 52; Steven J. Zaloga and Leland S. Ness, *Red Army Handbook 1939–1945* (Gloucestershire, UK: Sutton, 1998), 134–36; and *Boevoi sostav Sovetskoi armii, chast' 1 (iiun'–dekabr' 1941 g.)* [The combat composition of the Soviet Army, part 1 (June–December 1941)] (Moscow: Voroshilov Academy of the General Staff, 1963), 7–14.

Table 8.2 Quantity and Location of RVGK Antitank Artillery Regiments Formed in 1941

Front or MD	*Shtat* 08/55	*Shtat* 08/56	*Shtat* 08/70	*Shtat* 04/133	Total
Moscow	1	11	32	7	51
Kiev	0	0	0	8	8
Orel	0	1	4	3	8
Leningrad	0	1	0	0	1
Southwestern	0	0	0	1	1
Southern	0	0	0	1	1
Khar'kov	0	1	0	0	1
Northern Caucasus	0	1	0	0	1
Month formed					
Jun	0	0	0	5	5
Jul	0	14	0	15	29
Aug	0	1	8	0	9
Sep	0	0	4	0	4
Oct	1	0	24	0	25
Total	1	15	36	20	72

Source: A. N. Ianchinsky, *Boevoe ispol'zovanie istrebitel'no-protivotankovoi artillerii RVGK v Velikoi Otechestvennoi voine* [The combat employment of destroyer-antitank artillery of the RVGK in the Great Patriotic War] (Moscow: Voroshilov Academy, 1951), 13.

Table 8.3 Quantity and Distribution of RVGK Tank Destroyer Artillery Regiments, 15 November 1942 (by Strategic Axis and Type)

	Tables of Organization (Shtat)						
Front or army	08/107 (5-btry)	08/107 (6-btry)	135 (heavy)	08/100	08/166 (local)	08/84 (local)	Total
Western axis							
Western	9	15	0	1	0	0	25
Kalinin	14	5	0	4	0	0	23
Moscow Defense Zone	3	0	0	0	0	0	3
Total	26	20	0	5	0	0	51
Stalingrad axis							
Southwestern	7	6	0	10	0	0	23
Don	0	6	0	2	0	0	8
Stalingrad	12	0	0	7	0	0	19
Total	19	12	0	19	0	0	50
Voronezh-Kursk axis							
Briansk	4	4	0	3	0	0	11
Voronezh	6	7	0	2	0	0	15
Total	10	11	0	5	0	0	26
Caucasus axis							
Trans-Caucasus	10	0	0	12	2	0	24
Total	10	0	0	12	2	0	24

Leningrad axis							
Leningrad	2	0	0	0	0	11	13
Volkhov	1	3	0	0	0	0	4
Northwestern	7	0	0	0	0	0	7
Total	10	3	0	0	0	0	24
Karelian axis							
Karelian	4	0	0	0	0	0	4
7th Separate Army	2	0	0	0	0	0	2
Total	6	0	0	0	0	0	6
Stavka Reserve							
Gor'kii Training Center	0	24	0	4	0	0	28
Moscow Training Center	0	6	3	18	0	0	27
Stalingrad Training Center	0	3	0	0	0	0	3
Moscow MD	0	0	0	1	0	0	1
Volga MD	0	0	0	1	0	0	1
Total	0	33	3	24	0	0	60
Grand total	81	79	3	65	2	11	241

Source: A. N. Ianchinsky, *Boevoe ispol'zovanie istrebitel'no-protivotankovoi artillerii RVGK v Velikoi Otechestvennoi voine* [The combat employment of destroyer-antitank artillery of the RVGK in the Great Patriotic War] (Moscow: Voroshilov Academy, 1951), 27.

Table 8.4 Distribution of RVGK Separate Tank Destroyer Artillery Regiments, 1 January 1943 (by Type)

	Table of Organization (Shtat)					
Front, Army, or MD	08/84	08/107 (5-btry)	08/107 (6-btry)	08/100	08/166	Total
Western axis						
Kalinin	0	14	5	5	0	24
Western	0	10	8	2	0	20
Moscow Defense Zone	3	3	0	2	0	8
Total	3	27	13	9	0	52
Southwestern axis						
Southwestern	0	5	0	9	0	14
Don	0	10	0	5	0	15
Southern	0	5	0	7	0	12
Total	0	20	0	21	0	41
Caucasus axis						
Trans-Caucasus	0	10	0	12	2	24
Total	0	10	0	12	2	24
Voronezh-Kursk axis						
Briansk	0	3	1	4	0	8
Voronezh	0	6	1	2	0	9
Total	0	9	2	6	0	17
Northwestern axis						
Leningrad	11	1	0	0	0	12
Volkhov	0	1	0	0	0	1
Northwestern	0	1	0	0	0	1
Total	11	3	0	0	0	14
Karelian axis						
Karelian	0	4	0	0	0	4
7th Separate Army	0	2	0	0	0	2
Total	0	6	0	0	0	6
Far East	0	1	0	0	0	1
Total	0	1	0	0	0	1
Stavka Reserve						
Moscow Arty Center	0	0	0	12	0	12
Gor'kii Arty Center	0	0	0	4	0	4
Total	0	0	0	16	0	16
Grand total	14	76	15	64	2	171

Source: A. N. Ianchinsky, *Boevoe ispol'zovanie istrebitel'no-protivotankovoi artillerii RVGK v Velikoi Otechestvennoi voine* [The combat employment of destroyer-antitank artillery of the RVGK in the Great Patriotic War] (Moscow: Voroshilov Academy, 1951), 51–52.

Table 8.5 Distribution of RVGK Tank Destroyer Artillery Brigades and Separate Tank Destroyer Artillery Regiments and Battalions, 31 December 1943 (by Type)

	Table of Organization (Shtat)										
									Totals		
Front, Army, or MD	TDB 08/530	TDB 08/595*	TDR 08/547	TDR 08/586	TDR 08/548	TDR 08/549	TDR 08/868	TDBn 08/585	Bdes	Rgts	Bns
Northwestern axis											
Leningrad	0	0	0	1	0	9	2	0	0	12	0
2nd Baltic	2	0	0	0	0	0	6	0	2	6	0
Total	2	0	0	1	0	9	8	0	2	18	0
Belorussian axis											
1st Baltic	2	0	0	0	0	0	4	0	2	4	0
Western	4	0	0	0	0	0	6	0	4	6	0
Belorussian	7	0	0	1	0	0	8	0	7	9	0
Total	13	0	0	1	0	0	18	0	13	19	0
Southwestern axis											
1st Ukrainian	8	0	4	0	0	0	32	0	8	36	0
2nd Ukrainian	6	0	0	0	0	0	16	0	6	16	0
3rd Ukrainian	3	0	2	0	0	0	4	1	3	6	1
Total	17	0	6	0	0	0	52	1	17	58	1
Southern axis											
4th Ukrainian	4	0	3	0	0	0	8	0	4	11	0
Coastal Army	1	0	0	0	0	0	2	0	1	2	0
Total	5	0	3	0	0	0	10	0	5	13	0
Caucasus axis											
Transcaucasus	0	0	2	0	0	0	0	0	0	2	0
Total	0	0	2	0	0	0	0	0	0	2	0
Far East											
Far Eastern	0	0	0	0	0	0	13	0	0	13	0
Trans-Baikal	0	0	0	0	0	0	3	0	0	3	0
Total	0	0	0	0	0	0	16	0	0	16	0

—*Continued*

Table 8.5 Continued

	Table of Organization (*Shtat*)								Totals		
Front, Army, or MD	TDB 08/530	TDB 08/595*	TDR 08/547	TDR 08/586	TDR 08/548	TDR 08/549	TDR 08/868	TDBn 08/585	Bdes	Rgts	Bns
Karelian axis											
Karelian	0	0	0	0	0	0	1	0	0	1	0
7th Separate Army	0	0	0	0	0	0	2	0	0	2	0
Total	0	0	0	0	0	0	3	0	0	3	0
Stavka Reserve											
Khar'kov Arty Center	0	6	0	0	0	0	0	0	6	0	0
Gor'kii Arty Center	0	3	0	0	0	0	1	0	3	1	0
Kolomna Arty Center	0	3	0	0	0	0	0	3	3	0	3
Tambov Arty Center	0	0	0	0	0	0	3	0	0	3	0
Rybinsk Arty Center	0	1	0	0	0	0	0	0	1	0	0
Moscow MD	0	0	0	0	2	0	0	0	0	2	0
Total	0	13	0	0	2	0	4	3	13	6	3
Grand total	37	13	11	2	2	9	111	4	50	135	4

*Includes *shtats* 08/596–598.

Source: A. N. Ianchinsky, *Boevoe ispol'zovanie istrebitel'no-protivotankovoi artillerii RVGK v Velikoi Otechestvennoi voine* [The combat employment of destroyer-antitank artillery of the RVGK in the Great Patriotic War] (Moscow: Voroshilov Academy, 1951), 56.

Table 8.6 Composition and Subordination of Red Army Air Armies Formed May–November 1942

Air Army	Date Formed	Parent Front	Composition
1st	May 1942	Western	210th, 202nd, 203rd, 234th, 235th FADs, 214th, 224th, 231st, 232nd, 233rd AADs, 204th BAD, 213th NBAD, 215th MAD, 901st LBAR, 1st RAS
2nd	May 1942	Briansk	205th, 207th FADs, 225th, 227th BADs, 208th NBAD
3rd	May 1942	Kalinin	209th, 210th FADs, 211th, 212th MADs, 684th, 695th LBARs, 195th, 708th, 881st, 882nd, 883rd, 884th, 885th, 887th MARs, 3rd RAS
4th	May 1942	Southern	216th, 217th, 229th FADs, 230th AAD, 219th BAD, 218th NBAD, 192nd FAR, 889th LBAR
8th	May 1942	Southwestern	206th, 220th, 235th, 268th, 269th FADs, 226th, 228th AADs, 221st, 270th BADs, 271st, 272nd NBAD, 13th Gds. BAR, 43rd, 434th FARs, 8th RAR
5th	Jun 1942	North Caucasus	132nd BAD, 236th, 237th 265th FADs, 238th AAD, 742nd RAR, 763rd LBAR
6th	Jun 1942	Northwestern	239th, 240th FADs, 241st BAD, 242nd NBAD, 243rd AAD, 514th, 645th LBAR, 642nd, 644th, 649th, 677th MAR, 699th TAR, 6th RAS
14th	Jul 1942	Volkhov	278th, 279th FADs, 280th BAD, 281st AAD, 258th, 935th LBARs, 660th, 662nd, 689th, 691st, 696th MARs, 8th RAS, 33rd CAS
15th	Jul 1942	Briansk	225th AAD, 284th BAD, 286th FAD, 638th, 640th, 701st LBARs, 876th, 879th MARs
16th	Aug 1942	*Stavka* Reserve	291st AAD, 99th, 779th BARs, 714th LBAR, 929th FAR
12th	Aug 1942	Trans-Baikal	30th, 247th BADs, 245th, 246th FADs, 247th AAD, 12th RAR, 846th, 849th LBARs
9th	Aug 1942	Far Eastern	32nd, 249th, 250th FADs, 33rd, 34th BADs, 251st, 252nd AADs, 6th RAR
10th	Aug 1942	Far Eastern	29th FAD, 53rd, 83rd, 254th BADs, 253rd AAD, 7th RAR
11th	Aug 1942	Far Eastern	96th FAD, 82nd BAD, 296th MAD, 140th RAS
7th	Nov 1942	Karelian	258th, 259th FADs, 260th BAD, 261st AAD, 668th, 679th LBARs, 152nd, 839th FARs, 42nd, 118th RASs
13th	Nov 1942	Leningrad	275th FAD, 276th BAD, 277th AAD, 13th RAR, 12th CAS (forming: 196th, 286th FARs), 32nd Gds, 897th BARs
17th	Nov 1942	Southwestern	1st MAC (267th AAD, 288th FAD), 221st BAD, 262nd NBAD, 282nd FAD, 208th, 637th AARs, 282nd MAR, 371st LBAR, 10th RAS, 34th, 45th CASs
1st Fighter	Jul 1942	*Stavka* Reserve	287th, 288th FADs
2nd Fighter	Jul 1942	*Stavka* Reserve	274th, 282nd, 283d FADs, 291st, 292nd AADs
1st Bomber	Jul 1942	*Stavka* Reserve	221st, 222nd BADs

Source: Boevoi sostav Sovetskoi armii, chast' 2 (ianvar'–dekabr' 1942 g.) [The combat composition of the Soviet Army, part 2 (January–December 1942)] (Moscow: Voenizdat, 1966), 79–252. Classified secret and prepared by the Military-Scientific Directorate of the General Staff.

Infantry wielding PPSh submachine guns

PTRD 14.5mm antitank rifles

PM-1910 7.62mm heavy machine gun

45mm antitank gun

T-26 light tank

T-35 heavy tank

T-60 light tank

T-70 light tank

T-34 medium tank (1943)

KV-1S heavy tank

KV-2 heavy tank with T-34 medium tank (1940) on right

British Churchill Lend-Lease tank

American M-3 Grant Lend-Lease tank

SU-76 self-propelled gun

SU-152 self-propelled gun

76mm field guns

152mm ML-20 howitzers

37mm antiaircraft guns

Katiusha multiple-rocket launchers

I-16 *Rata* fighter

LaGG-3 fighter

Il-2 *Sturmovik* assault

MiG-3 fighters

Pe-2 Bomber

Pe-8 (TB-7) bomber

CHAPTER 9

Engineer, Signal, Chemical, Railroad, Auto-Transport and Road, and Construction Forces

ENGINEER (SAPPER) FORCES

Engineer and Sapper Regiments and Battalions

Throughout the war, Red Army engineer forces included force engineers organic to its operating *fronts* and engineers subordinate to RGK or RVGK control, which the *Stavka* intended to allocate to operating *fronts* and armies based on their wartime needs. Both forces were responsible for erecting and improving defenses and providing various types of engineer support during offensive and defensive operations.[1]

Force engineers within the Red Army's operating forces included sapper battalions or squadrons in rifle and cavalry corps, motorized engineer battalions in mechanized corps, separate sapper battalions or squadrons in rifle and cavalry divisions, N2P pontoon-bridge battalions in tank divisions, light engineer battalions in motorized divisions, sapper companies or platoons in rifle and cavalry regiments and tank and motorized rifle regiments and brigades, and sapper platoons in RGK and corps artillery regiments.[2]

Sapper battalions assigned to corps and divisions consisted of three sapper companies of three platoons, a technical company in battalions organic to rifle corps or a platoon in rifle divisions, bridging and secret weapons platoons, and small service elements for a total strength of 901 men in battalions assigned to rifle corps and 521 in those assigned to rifle divisions.[3] Depending on their parent division, these battalions were either foot-bound, motorized, or horse-drawn. On 22 June 1941, Red Army field forces included over 200 sapper battalions, all of which retained their prewar structure until December 1941, when the People's Commissariat of Defense (NKO) decreased their size to two companies largely because of the creation of larger and more effective engineer-sapper forces within the RVGK.

RGK engineer forces included 19 engineer and 15 pontoon-bridge regiments situated in the military districts, which the NKO had formed from 22 separate engineer battalions and 21 separate pontoon-bridge battalions during the first half of 1941. Of this number, ten engineer and eight pontoon-bridge regiments, seven engineer battalions, and two sapper battalions were assigned to operating *fronts*, two engineer and two sapper battalions were directly subordinate to the RGK, and the remainder were supporting military districts and nonoperating *fronts.*

RGK engineer regiments consisted of a headquarters, two engineer battalions (one motorized), a technical battalion with electro-technical, electro-obstacle, hydro-technical, and camouflage companies, a light pontoon-bridge park (NPL), and an officers school with specialized engineer equipment, 35 engineer vehicles, 48 trucks, and 21 tractors.[4] Pontoon-bridge regiments included a headquarters, three pontoon-bridge battalions (one only cadre), a technical company with road-position, bridge, woodcutting, electro-technical, and field water supply platoons, an N2P pontoon-bridge park, and an officers school equipped with pontoon bridges and technical equipment.[5]

On the eve of war, the General Staff's war plans required the NKO to support each of its field armies with at least one separate motorized engineer battalion, one motorized pontoon-bridge battalion, and separate field water supply, camouflage and deception *(maskirovka)* and electro-technical and hydro-technical support companies, a drilling detachment, and a separate reserve pontoon-bridge park equipped with N2P bridges. Additionally, it directed the NKO to assign each field army a reserve engineer regiment and a separate reserve special technical company to perform specialized engineer tasks. However, in addition to the overall shortage of engineer forces, on 22 June 1941 existing RGK engineer regiments and battalions lacked 35–60 percent of their authorized command cadre, 20–70 percent of their authorized noncommissioned officers, 35 percent of their enlisted strength, and roughly 50 percent of their authorized equipment.[6]

In addition to its force and RGK engineers, the NKO also fielded 25 military construction directorates on the eve of war, 23 of which were busy constructing fortified regions and field defenses in the western military districts along with most engineer and sapper forces organic to prospective wartime *fronts.* Therefore, when war began, most Red Army combat units lacked necessary engineer support.[7]

When *Wehrmacht* forces savaged the Red Army during Operation Barbarossa, they also decimated its already fragile engineer and sapper forces. The NKO reacted hurriedly by forming new sapper and engineer battalions from scratch, assigning them to the RGK and, later, to the RVGK for subsequent allocation to operating *fronts.* In July 1941, for example, the NKO disbanded all RGK engineer and pontoon-bridge regiments, used their remnants to form 100 small sapper battalions equipped with only rifles and other small arms, entrenching tools, explosives, and antitank mines, and assigned 25 of these battalion to rifle corps and another 75 to rifle divisions. As a result, the total number of engineer-sapper and pontoon-bridge battalions in the Red Army increased steadily from 20 on 1 July to 178 on 1 November, including 140 assigned to operating *fronts.*[8] During this same period, however, the engineer support for rifle divisions decreased markedly. On 29 July, for example, the NKO disbanded the technical, pontoon, and secret equipment platoons in its rifle division's sapper battalions, and in July 1942, after eliminating one the battalion's three sapper companies in December, it reduced the sapper battalions' strength by 60 men and many of their antitank and antipersonnel mines.[9]

However, the NKO began compensating for its shortages of force engineers beginning in early 1942 by assigning one or two separate new engineer or sapper battalions to its operating *fronts* and armies and new pontoon-bridge battalions to its *fronts*. The separate engineer battalions, which were either foot-bound or motorized, consisted of three engineer companies with three engineer or motorized platoons and one technical platoon with electric power station, woodcutting, and transport squads, for a total strength of 405 men. The separate sapper battalions fielded two or three sapper companies for a total strength of about 320 men. While the number of separate engineer and pontoon-bridge battalions in the Red Army increased from 82 and 46, respectively, on 1 January 1942 to 184 and 68, respectively, on 1 January 1944, during the same period, the quantity of separate sapper battalions decreased from 78 to three (see Appendix 1 in companion volume for all support forces in the Red Army).

Sapper Armies and Brigades

Although the NKO reduced the strength of the Red Army's force engineers and formed new separate RVGK engineer and sapper battalions during the initial stages of Operation Barbarossa, nevertheless the State Defense Committee (GKO) ordered the *Stavka* to erect new strategic defense lines and positions to slow the *Wehrmacht's* advance.[10] For example, on 24 June the GKO ordered the construction of a strategic defense line along the Luga River south of Leningrad, on 25 June a second line from Nevel', Vitebsk, and Gomel' and along the Dnepr River to Dnepropetrovsk, and on 28 June a third line from Ostashkov, Olenino, Dorogobuzh, and El'nia, and along the Desna River to Zhukovka, 50 kilometers west of Briansk.

As the *Wehrmacht's* advance accelerated, the GKO ordered the *Stavka* to erect two more major defense lines in mid-July, the first to protect Odessa, the Crimean peninsula, and Sevastopol', and the second to protect the approaches to Moscow. The Moscow Line, which blocked any *Wehrmacht* advance along the Volokolamsk, Mozhaisk, and Maloiaroslavets axes, consisted of the Rzhev-Viaz'ma Line, which extended from Rzhev to Viaz'ma, and the Kirov and Mozhaisk Line, which extended southward from the Moscow Reservoir along the Lama River and through Borodino and Kaluga to Tula.

The *Stavka* assigned responsibility for constructing these defense lines to the NKO's Main Military-Engineer Directorate (*Glavnoe voenno-inzhenernoe upravlenie*) and the NKVD's Main Directorate for Hydro-technical Work (*Glavgidrostroi*). The former was to employ military construction battalions assigned to *front* and army directorates for military-field construction to construct defense lines within their respective sectors; the latter was to use its construction forces to erect defense lines deeper in the rear area. When this arrangement proved ineffective, on 22 August the GKO reorganized the *Glavgidrostroi* into the NKVD's Main Directorate for Defensive Work (*Glavnoe upravlenie vozdushno-desantnykh voisk*, or GUOBR) and assigned it responsibility for coordinating the construction of rear defense lines.[11]

Despite the GKO's and *Stavka's* best efforts, the *Wehrmacht's* rapid advance decimated the Red Army's force engineers, preventing them from taking part in the construction effort, and preempted much of the *Stavka's* defensive construction effort. German forces overran the Red Army's Vitebsk and Gomel' and Luga Lines in August and September and penetrated its strategic defenses in the Viaz'ma and Briansk sectors in early October, encircling and destroying large forces. Alarmed by the prospects of a precipitous German advance on Moscow, on 12 October the *Stavka* formed the Moscow Defense Zone, which was to consist of a series of defensive rings around the city, the most important extending through Khlebnikovo, Skhodnia, Zvenigorod, Kubinka, and Naro-Fominsk and along the Pakhra and Moscow rivers.[12]

Since the Red Army lacked the engineer and construction forces necessary to construct these and other defense lines, on 13 October the GKO ordered the NKO to form six sapper armies made up of sapper brigades by 1 November 1941 and placed all Red Army engineer and construction forces within operating *fronts* and the rear area under GUOBR (NKVD) control. Numbered the 1st through the 6th, these armies were to form at Vologda, Gor'kii, Ul'ianovsk, Saratov, Stalingrad, and Armavir with an overall strength of 300,000 men.[13] The GKO assigned the GUOBR responsibility for constructing all rear defense lines and positions, particularly west of Moscow, by 10 December, and ordered it to train all personnel assigned to the new sapper armies and other Red Army engineer forces.[14]

The new sapper armies were to consist of five sapper brigades with roughly 50,000 men each, primarily reservists up to 45 years of age, engineer and construction personnel withdrawn from the zones of operating *fronts*, and other specialists already in the rear area; the sapper brigades were to contain 19 sapper battalions, one auto-tractor battalion, and one mechanized detachment each. The GKO also ordered the NKO to equip the sapper armies with 3,000 trucks, 90 light vehicles, 1,350 caterpillar tractors, and 2,350 tractor and vehicular trailers, 12,000 wagonloads of construction materials, and massive quantities of necessary construction tools and ordered the directorates of other commissariats and the civilian population to support the effort:[15]

> By order of the GKO, a mobilization of the local population was conducted for the construction of the defense lines. Basically, these were women, old men, schoolchildren and teenagers under draft age. On order of the military councils of *fronts* and military districts and regional and district party and administrative organs, workers battalions were formed from them [the mobilized], which were then subordinated to the sapper armies.[16]

Ultimately, the NKO formed nine sapper armies, numbered the 1st through the 9th, which consisted of 30 sapper brigades and a total of 570 sapper battalions, numbered the 1200th–1465th, 1467th–1541st, and 1543rd–1771st, with a total strength of 299,730 men by 1 November 1941, and a tenth, the 1st, by late December (see Table 9.1). However, severe shortages in engineer and construction forces limited the size and strength of these armies and brigades.[17]

Once formed, the first nine sapper armies consisted of a headquarters and two to four separate sapper brigades. The sapper brigades included a headquarters, 19 separate sapper battalions organized into three companies with four platoons for a strength of 497 men, a mechanized detachment with one road and one bridge platoon, a woodcutting platoon, a positional construction platoon, and an automobile tractor platoon with four squads.[18] Although the strength of each sapper brigade was supposed to be 9,979 men, most brigades remained well below full strength.[19] As a result, even though the sappers assigned to these armies, brigades, and battalions were supposed to spend 12 hours per day performing construction work and two hours in military training, in reality most spent 12–14 hours per day constructing defenses and did not train at all. The tenth sapper army, numbered the 1st, which completed its deployment to support the Western Front in January 1942, consisted of ten sapper brigades with eight sapper battalions each, for a grand total of 80 sapper battalions and 45,160 men.[20]

Initially, the sapper armies were subordinate to the NKVD's GUOBR but worked under the direct supervision of the NKO's Main Military Engineer Directorate. However, this command arrangement proved less than fully effective, and on 28 November the *Stavka* assigned the armies to the Red Army's Chief of Engineer Forces. In December 1942 the engineer chief assigned the nine sapper armies and 29 sapper brigades to military districts and nonoperating *fronts* and the three remaining brigades to operating *fronts* (two to the Western Front and one to the Karelian Front). By mid-January 1942, the Red Army's engineer force structure had expanded to include ten sapper armies, 40 sapper brigades, three engineer regiments, and 82 separate engineer, 78 sapper, and 46 pontoon-bridge battalions.

These sapper armies and brigades were primarily responsible for constructing strategic defense lines in the Red Army's deep rear area. The first of these lines, such as those located in the Moscow, Stalingrad, North Caucasus, and Volga Military Districts, were continuous in nature and consisted of an elaborate array of fortified battalion defensive regions and company strong points emplaced along probable German axes of advance and around major cities. However, on 27 December 1941, after the Red Army's victory at Moscow, the GKO ordered a halt to defensive work around Moscow so that more resources could be allocated for the transport of refugees, grain, and bread to needy populations and limited construction work on other strategic defense lines.[21]

In addition to their construction duties, the sapper armies also served as a training base for Red Army engineer forces as a whole. For example, during November and December 1941 the NKO designated two and later three battalions in each sapper brigade as training battalions and ultimately transferring over 90 of these battalions to the operating *fronts*. Trained as standard engineer, pontoon-bridge, or road-bridge battalions and manned by the most experienced personnel, battalions designated for transfer to the front immediately ceased all defensive work and engaged in intensive field training. After departing for the front, the sapper brigades formed new battalions to replace them in a cycle that steadily increased the strength of Red Army's engineer force. In addition, the sapper brigades also provided trained personnel for sapper battalions and companies assigned to new rifle and cavalry corps and divisions. However, the turbulence caused by this constant flow of personnel and units between the sapper armies and operating *fronts* had a negative effect on the former's performance.

Although the ten sapper armies proved their worth during the Red Army's winter offensive of 1941–42 by helping to maintain rear-area security and by bolstering the *fronts'* engineer and sapper capabilities, they proved clumsy, ineffective, and difficult to control, particularly during fluid combat situations. As a result, in February 1942 the GKO ordered the NKO to disband half of its sapper armies and brigades, assign others to operating *fronts*, and use the personnel from disbanded forces to help form new rifle divisions and brigades. During February and March, the NKO disbanded the 2nd, 4th, 5th, 9th, and 10th Sapper Armies and six sapper brigades, increased the strength of the Southwestern and Southern Fronts' 7th and 8th Sapper Armies to five and ten brigades respectively, and assigned four sapper armies, three separate sapper brigades, and many newly formed specialized engineer units to operating *fronts* and the Moscow Defense Zone.[22]

At the same time, the NKO's Main Directorate for the Formation and Manning of the Red Army withdrew command cadre from sapper armies and brigades for assignment to operating forces and reduced the number and size of sapper battalions within the sapper brigades.[23] The NKO took the second step during April by decreasing the strength of sapper battalions from 497 to 405 men, replacing auto-tractor battalions with auto-tractor companies with four automobile platoons and one tractor platoon each, and decreasing the size of sapper brigades to seven battalions plus one auto-tractor company for a total of 3,138 men.[24]

In late June, two months after completing this reorganization, the NKO faced the daunting task of blunting the *Wehrmacht's* new summer offensive, Operation *Blau.* In addition to providing engineer support for its defending *fronts,* the NKO's 1st, 3rd, 6th, 7th, and 8th Sapper Armies had to reinforce the defense lines west of Moscow, construct new lines to defend the approaches to Stalingrad and the Caucasus region, and generate manpower as replacements for depleted Red Army forces.

The five sapper armies worked strenuously to build these defenses, but on 26 July the GKO ordered the NKO to strip 400,000 men, including 60,000 sappers, from noncombat branches by 20 August for assignment to combat formations and streamline its remaining sapper armies and brigades, since they were "too large and immobile organizationally and could not effectively fulfill the missions of engineer support of our forces' combat operations, particularly in offensive operations."[25] The GKO's intent was to create more flexible and effective engineer forces that the *Stavka* could employ in defensive and offensive operations along the most critical axes in the late summer and fall of 1942. The NKO responded by deciding to abolish its remaining sapper armies and many of its sapper brigades and convert some of the brigades into specialized engineer brigades to support its operating *fronts.*

In an order dated 17 August, the NKO began reorganizing its five sapper armies and 27 sapper brigades into directorates for defensive construction (see Construction Troops section below), converted six sapper brigades into RVGK engineer brigades, which it subordinated to operating *fronts,* disbanded 8 other sapper brigades, and transferred 30,000 men from the former 1st, 7th, and 8th Sapper Armies to fill out newly formed rifle divisions.[26] Thereafter, it converted the 1st, 3rd, 6th, and 7th Sapper Armies into UOSs during September and the 8th Sapper Army into a UOS during October, and it reconfigured 12 brigades into engineer brigades to support operating *fronts* (see Table 9.1).[27] The 18 sapper brigades assigned to operating *fronts* on 15 October performed the dual functions of providing engineer support for the *fronts'* forces and serving as bases for the formation of new, more specialized engineer brigades and battalions.[28]

While they existed, the sapper armies and brigades contributed significantly to the Red Army's victories at Leningrad, Moscow, and Stalingrad by preparing defense lines, providing vital engineer support to the Red Army's operating *fronts,* and serving as a base for the formation of other more specialized engineer forces assigned to operating *fronts.* For example, in 1941 the 2nd–10th Sapper Armies organized, trained, and dispatched more than 150 specialized engineer battalions to the operating *fronts* in 1941, and in 1942 the sapper armies and brigades formed 27 specialized RVGK engineer brigades, 23 of which served until war's end and five of which still exist today.[29] Finally, sapper armies generated more than 150,000 replacements to fill out and form new rifle divisions.

Engineer Brigades

While it was disbanding its sapper armies during the spring of 1942, the NKO began fielding a wide variety of new engineer brigades and battalions in response to *front* commanders' requests that it form specialized and flexible engineer forces more responsive to their needs. For example, in response to a March request by the Western Front's chief of engineers, the NKO began forming special designation engineer brigades (SDEB) on 18 April. The first of these brigades, the Western Front's 33rd Special Designation Engineer Brigade, which was formed from the 1st Sapper Army's 33rd Sapper Brigade in May, consisted of six engineer obstacle battalions, two electro-technical battalions, one projector battalion, one electrification detachment, one electric generator train, one special technical engineer company, one auto-tractor company, and four electro-technical companies (attached) with an overall strength of 4,757 men.[30] Ultimately, the NKO formed six special designation engineer brigades by 1 July and another eight by 1 November, assigning them to the field forces on the basis of one per operating *front.*[31]

Although the structure of these special designation engineer brigades varied, most consisted of a headquarters, an auto-tractor company, five to eight engineer obstacle battalions, one of which was converted into a special mining battalion in October 1942, an electro-technical battalion, and an electrification detachment, for a strength of 3,097 men for a five-battalion brigade. Although the brigades' primary mission was to perform specialized missions such as laying and clearing minefields, emplacing command-detonated minefields, and constructing electrified and other types of obstacles, often they had to perform more dangerous combat tasks. For example, the Volkhov Front's 39th Special Designation Engineer Brigade employed its engineer obstacle battalions as assault detachments during the assault to pierce the Leningrad blockade during January 1943.[32]

In addition to these special designation engineer brigades, the NKO also formed separate engineer-mine battalions in April 1942 and assigned them to each of the Red Army's destroyer brigades with the mission of constructing antitank obstacles and destroying enemy tanks in conjunction with artillery forces.[33]

The NKO continued this process during the late summer of 1942, when it began forming and fielding guards battalions of miners, the most interesting and certainly the most secret of its specialized types of engineer forces. After deploying two guards-miner battalions to the Voronezh and North Caucasus Fronts during August, the NKO raised and deployed ten more to the field forces by 1 October, normally on the basis of one battalion per operating *front*.[34] Specifically formed to conduct diversionary operations and sabotage in the enemy's rear area, battalions formed and employed small diversionary and sabotage teams.

In addition to the guards-miner battalions, on 17 August the NKO formed a guards brigade of miners in the Moscow Military District under the *Stavka's* direct control. Formed from two sapper battalions of the 1st Sapper Army's 37th Sapper Brigade, the 1st Guards Brigade of Miners consisted of a headquarters element, a command and control company, and five guards battalions of miners for a total of 2,281 men.[35] Like the separate battalions, this brigade not only laid and cleared mines, it also formed and deployed small teams to conduct diversionary and sabotage operations, often in cooperation with partisans, against German lines of communications and other important rear-area objectives.

The NKO also formed a wide range of smaller specialized engineer subunits during the summer of 1942, including five separate *fugasse* (liquid fuel) flamethrower companies, several field water supply companies, and a deep drilling detachment to provide water for operating forces.

While preparing the Red Army for its major counteroffensives in November 1942 and its ensuing winter campaign, the *Stavka* ordered the NKO to form larger and more specialized engineer forces to support these offensives. In response, the NKO combined many of its existing engineer battalions into engineer-sapper brigades (ESB) during October, each of which consisted of four or five engineer-sapper battalions, a light NLP pontoon-bridge park, and a motorized engineer company for reconnaissance, and it configured several of these brigades into mountain engineer brigades organized with four mountain engineer-sapper battalions capable of operating effectively in mountainous terrain.[36]

On 12 November, in response to a 2 November request by Major General M. P. Vorob'ev, the chief of the Red Army's engineers, the NKO reorganized many sapper brigades into 15 engineer-mine brigades (EMB), numbered the 1st through the 15th, to provide more effective support to the operating *fronts*.[37] These brigades, which were responsible for constructing operational obstacles zones, consisted of a headquarters, headquarters company, and seven engineer-mine battalions for a total strength of 2,903 men.[38]

In addition, on 26 November the NKO ordered the conversion during November and December of the five sapper brigades in the Trans-Caucasus

Front into the 1st through the 5th RVGK Mountain Mine-Engineer Brigades.[39] Once formed, these mountain engineer-mine brigades (MEMB) consisted of five mountain miner-engineer battalions, whose companies and platoons were equipped with horses and donkeys rather than tractors, and a total strength of 2,344 men.[40]

The NKO also began forming larger and more effective pontoon-bridge units during the fall of 1942, primarily because the *Stavka* considered larger bridging units essential to achieve success in its expanded offensive operations. After reinforcing its operating *fronts* and armies with 11 RVGK separate pontoon-bridge parks during early fall, the NKO formed two pontoon-bridge brigades during November 1942 and assigned both to the Stalingrad Front for employment in the Stalingrad counteroffensive.[41] These brigades consisted of a headquarters company; three to seven (typically four) motorized N2P pontoon-bridge battalions; one DMP-42 pontoon-bridge battalion, with a load-bearing capacity of 50 tons; and several detachments to perform underwater work. As the offensive developed, the NKO assigned a third pontoon-bridge brigade to the Leningrad Front in January 1943, and reinforced these brigades with four new heavy pontoon-bridge regiments, each consisting of two battalions equipped with new 100-ton capacity TMP pontoon bridges, by February.[42]

In addition to forming and fielding this imposing array of new engineer brigades and battalions during 1942, the NKO also reinforced its force engineers by including engineer forces in new formations added to its operating *fronts* throughout the year. For example, it included sapper battalions in each of its new guards rifle and mechanized corps and engineer-mine companies in its new tank corps.[43] Thus, by 1 February 1943 the Red Army's engineer force structure had expanded to include 13 special designation engineer brigades, one sapper brigade, 17 engineer-sapper brigades (including five mountain), 15 engineer-mine brigades, 185 separate engineer battalions, ten separate sapper battalions, 16 mine-sapper battalions, one guards brigade of miners, 11 guards battalions of miners, three pontoon-bridge brigades, four pontoon-bridge regiments, and 78 pontoon-bridge battalions.

The NKO deliberately tailored its special designation, engineer-sapper, engineer-mine, pontoon-bridge, and guards-miner brigades, pontoon-bridge regiments, and mine-sapper, guards-miner, and pontoon-bridge battalions to accomplish their assigned missions either in support of operating *fronts* and armies or independently throughout the duration of specific offensive operations.

Rather than resting on its laurels, the NKO continued expanding and improving its engineer force structure during 1943. In February, for example, it began forming five rear-area obstacle brigades consisting of five to seven engineer battalions each, whose mission was to clear mines and obstacles from territory captured from the *Wehrmacht*.[44] After a lengthy formation process, in December 1943 the *Stavka* allocated one of these brigades to the Moscow Military District, two to the newly formed Khar'kov Military District, and one each to the North Caucasus and Ural Military Districts.

More important still, given the growing ferocity of the ground struggle and the increased durability of the *Wehrmacht's* defenses, the NKO began forming assault engineer-sapper brigades on 30 May. Converted from existing engineer-sapper brigades, these new brigades consisted of a headquarters, five assault engineer-sapper battalions, one motorized engineer reconnaissance company, a light river-crossing park, a mine-clearing company equipped with armor-protected mine-sniffing dogs, and light service support elements.[45] These new brigades were responsible for assisting infantry and tank forces in overcoming well-prepared enemy defensive lines and fortified positions.

When the Red Army expanded its offensive operations during late summer and early fall 1943, mine clearing became far more important than mine laying. Therefore, the NKO began replacing RVGK engineer-mine brigades with RVGK engineer-sapper brigades and reorganized both new and existing engineer-sapper brigades to improve their effectiveness.[46] As a result, while the number of engineer-mine brigades in the force structure fell from 15 on 1 February to 12 on 1 July and disappeared entirely by 31 December, the number of engineer-sapper brigades increased from 12 on 1 February to 13 on 1 July, and finally to 22 on 31 December. In addition, the NKO fielded 15 new assault engineer-sapper brigades by 1 July and a total of 20 by 31 December.

Finally, although they were not formally a part of the engineer force structure, in June 1943 the NKO began fielding new tank regiments equipped with 22 T-34 tanks and 18 PT-3 mine-clearing plows to clear paths through the numerous minefields the Germans emplaced throughout their defenses.[47]

Due to the NKO's efforts, the Red Army's engineer force structure grew dramatically in size and variety from a total of 32 sapper brigades, three engineer regiments, and 206 battalions of various types on 1 January 1942, to 68 brigades of various types, six pontoon-bridge regiments, and 270 engineer and pontoon bridge battalions on 31 December 1943. When the Red Army began operations in 1944, its massive engineer force structure certainly more than satisfied its dramatically expanding operational needs.

SIGNAL FORCES

Because they were poorly equipped, severely undermanned, and incapable of performing their primary wartime missions, the Red Army' signal forces were the weakest portion of the army's entire force structure on the eve of

Operation Barbarossa. Before war began, the army's signal forces consisted primarily of signal regiments and battalions assigned to it, which the NKO maintained at a peacetime strength of 40–45 percent, and signal units responsible for communications between the General Staff and field forces, which the NKO planned to mobilize in the event of war.

Communications studies the GKO conducted prior to the war indicated extensive radio communications were vital to ensuring reliable and effective command and control of Red Army forces and force coordination during wartime. However, Red Army forces at every level were desperately short of radios on the eve of war. The General Staff and prospective wartime *fronts* lacked 65 percent of their authorized radios, field armies and corps were short 89 percent of their radios, and divisions, regiments, and battalions lacked 38, 23, and 42 percent of their radios, respectively. Worse still, 75 percent of the radios within the *front* commands were obsolete, as were 22, 89, and 63 percent of the radios within field armies, divisions, and regiments. When these commands relied heavily on vehicle couriers and the postal service to communicate, they found vehicles and motorcycles also in short supply and the postal service far too untimely.

Theoretically, each wartime *front* was supposed to field one signal regiment, one radio battalion, five or six line (wire) signal battalions, three telegraph-construction companies, three telegraph-exploitation companies, three cable companies, one special designation radio battalion, one military carrier pigeon station, and warehouses and workshops. Each army was to field one signal regiment, one line signal battalion, two telegraph-signal, one telegraph-exploitation, and four cable companies, one carrier pigeon station, and warehouses and workshops. However, each military district and field army possessed only one signal regiment and, in many cases, only a battalion when war began.[48]

Within the field armies, all corps and divisions (except cavalry) included one signal battalion, all regiments (except cavalry) included a signal company, and battalions fielded a signal platoon. Finally, cavalry divisions and regiments fielded one signal squadron and half-squadron, respectively, and fortified regions included a signal battalion or companies. Overall, on 22 June 1941, the Red Army contained 19 signal regiments, 14 of which supported military districts and five specific armies, 25 separate line (wire) signal battalions, 16 separate radio battalions, including special designation radio battalions (OSNZ3), which served the General Staff and NKO, and four separate signal companies.[49]

At least on paper, *front* and army signal regiments consisted of a headquarters and support group, one radio and one telephone-telegraph battalion, one motorized cable-telegraph company, and a company equipped with mobile communications equipment. The regiments' telephone-telegraph battalions fielded two companies with three platoons each and telephone and telegraph stations, and their radio battalions were organized into two companies. In turn, cable-telegraph companies consisted of three cable-telegraph platoons and one telegraph-construction platoon, and mobile communications companies included a field courier platoon, a PSS platoon, whose function remains unclear, and a VNOS (early warning post). Finally, corps- and division-level signal battalions consisted of a headquarters, a headquarters company with radio, telephone, and mobile platoons, two telephone companies, and small support elements.[50]

Since the Red Army's signal forces were so weak in June 1941, the General Staff and its wartime *fronts* had no choice but to supplement its own meager communications means with the state communications networks. The NKO's Signal Directorate simply leased its circuits and communications lines from this network, which was owned and run by the People's Commissariat of Communications (*Narodnyi komissariat sviazi,* or NKS).

Active combat soon vividly underscored the many deficiencies in the Red Army's communications. The *Wehrmacht's* rapid advance during Operation Barbarossa preempted the mobilization of additional signal forces from existing separate signal battalions by decimating the latter, and neither the *Stavka* nor its *fronts* and armies were able to communicate effectively in fluid maneuver war. Obsolete immobile radio stations manned by inadequately trained radio operators paralyzed command and control, and wire communications broke down both because commanders frequently moved their command posts and the *Luftwaffe* and *Wehrmacht* diversionary forces targeted and destroyed communications lines and centers. The immense losses of communications equipment only exacerbated these problems, producing immediate and lasting chaos in command and control.

The GKO attempted to resolve these problems on 23 July 1941, by appointing Colonel General I. T. Peresypkin, then the people's commissar of communications, as chief of Red Army Signal Forces and by ordering the NKO to issue new instructions to improve army radio procedures.[51] The ensuing NKO order candidly described the problem:

> To a considerable degree, war experience indicates that unsatisfactory command and control of forces results from poor organization of communications work and, first and foremost, from ignoring radio communications as the most effective means of communications. Command and control of forces based primarily on the telephone is fragile and unreliable since it is interrupted for prolonged periods when telephone lines are damaged.
>
> This underestimation of radio communications as the most reliable communications means and the primary means for command and control is a result of stagnation within our headquarters and their misunderstanding

of the importance of radio communications in mobile forms of modern combat.

Violating every rule of telephone communications, we have conducted operational conversations openly naming units, formations, their missions and dispositions, and the names and ranks of commanders. In the process, top secret information has fallen into enemy hands.[52]

Castigating all headquarters for malfeasance, the NKO order demanded they employ radio communications effectively and use codebooks (SOIs) to encipher operational messages within strict time limits, and directed Peresypkin to establish secure BODO (teletype) communications at *front* and army level and immediately create special schools to train radio operators.[53] However, all of this was easier said than done. Despite NKO exhortations and threats, many of these communications problems endured well into the future.

To ensure that its field headquarters devoted necessary attention to effective communications, the NKO created the Red Army's Main Signal Directorate (*Glavnoe upravlenie sviazi Krasnoi armii,* or GUSKA) on 28 July and assigned it responsibility for establishing and monitoring communications between the *Stavka*, its operating *fronts* and armies, and force services and branches.[54] The new directorate used signal force personnel from disbanded rifle and mechanized corps to form new signal units and subunits within divisions, armies, and *fronts*. Further indicating the depth of the crisis in army radio communications, on 23 August, at a time when separate signal regiments assigned to *fronts* were at 60–70 percent strength and army signal battalions were at 80–90 percent strength, the NKO ordered the army to exploit all available civilian radio communications equipment for military purposes, particularly, radios belonging to local political and governmental organs.[55]

The NKO and NKS successfully beefed up the Red Army's signal forces during the fall of 1941. The former fielded numerous separate repair-reconstruction, telegraph-telephone, line (wire), and radio battalions, and telegraph-exploitation companies, line signal battalions, and separate cable companies by 1 December 1941, and the latter formed 6 reconstruction-exploitation battalions and communications trains, 37 telegraph-telephone and 35 telegraph-exploitation companies, eight construction columns, six detachments, and 135 military-operational signal centers during the same period. The NKO used these forces primarily to created reserve communications centers at the *Stavka, front,* and army level, to complete city and regional communications networks, and to improve national, General Staff, and *front-* and army-level communications.[56]

Despite the expanded communications force and network, communications within and between operating *fronts* remained threadbare and often chaotic during December 1941 and early 1942, particularly since the abolition of rifle corps during the summer meant that army commanders had to control as many as 12–15 subordinate formations, which was an impossible task. The armies also lacked sufficient communications equipment to establish auxiliary command posts to control these forces. Nor was the situation any better at division level. Although smaller restructured rifle divisions required only 12 instead of 63 radios, 100 instead of 473 kilometers of telephone cable, and 100 rather than 32 telephone sets, the NKO used most excess and new communications equipment to outfit new rifle divisions and brigades.[57]

While fielding new signal units and subunits, the NKO also worked diligently to increase the number of trained communications personnel. Since combat forces absorbed all available manpower, on 14 April 1942 the NKO authorized the mobilization of 30,000 women for training as signalmen and subsequent assignment to signal forces both at the front and in the rear. This mobilization took place in three stages and was completed by 1 September 1942.[58]

The Red Army's offensives during the winters of 1941–42 and 1942–43 once again stretched the army's communications to the breaking point and convinced the NKO that the army required a two- to threefold expansion in the quantity of *front*, army, and corps mobile radio stations if it hoped to sustain deep operations. After beginning the process of reinforcing the army's signal capabilities during 1942, the NKO finally achieved this goal by October 1943. For example, when it reestablished rifle corps within its armies during late 1942 and early 1943, the NKO assigned each rifle corps a separate signal battalion, although this was at the expense of shrinking the rifle divisions' signal battalion to a single signal company.[59] During June 1943 the NKO assigned its *fronts* nine separate radio battalions and five separate radio companies, and, during the fall, a separate rear-area signal company and an aviation signal regiment equipped with 32 communications aircraft.[60]

Below *front* level, during 1943 the NKO added a signal battalion to each of its combined-arms armies, a full signal regiment, an aviation signal regiment, two cable companies, and a telegraph-exploitation company to each tank army, a telegraph-construction company and a cable company to each rifle corps, and a signal company to the army signal chief's reserve. At the same time, it increased the number of tactical radios in rifle divisions and rifle regiments two- to threefold, permitting rifle battalions and artillery batteries in most divisions to communicate directly with their division headquarters by radio.

Overall, the NKO formed and fielded 464 signal units and subunits during 1943, including 11 separate signal regiments and 175 separate signal battalions, and ultimately formed and fielded more than 300 signal regiments and 1,000 signal battalions between July 1941 and May 1945.[61]

CHEMICAL FORCES

The Red Army's chemical corps, which was the army's smallest force branch on the eve of war, worked under the supervision of the NKO's Directorate of Military-Chemical Defense (*Upravlenie voenno-khimicheskoi zashchity*, or UVKhZ). Its forces consisted of chemical subunits assigned to the field forces and RGK units and subunits under the central directorate's direct control. Many of the latter were operationally subordinate to prospective wartime *fronts*, and all chemical forces were seriously understrength and poorly equipped when war began.

Chemical units and subunits assigned to the field forces included flame-thrower tank battalions, descendants of three flame tank regiments in the Red Army's force structure during early 1940, whose battalions the NKO parceled out to new tank divisions by early 1941, and small chemical defense companies and platoons assigned to rifle corps, divisions, and regiments. All of these forces were controlled by chemical departments in military districts and field armies whose chiefs were responsible for chemical training and supplying their forces with all necessary chemical equipment.

Rifle corps subordinate to field armies or military districts fielded chemical defense companies consisting of two platoons of detection and decontamination vehicles and a terrain decontamination platoon, and all rifle divisions included decontamination companies with a chemical reconnaissance and observation platoon, a terrain decontamination platoon, and an equipment decontamination platoon. Below division level, rifle regiments included chemical defense platoons consisting of chemical reconnaissance squads and decontamination equipment, and special flamethrower commands with two squads equipped with ten backpack ROKS-2 model flamethrowers each, and rifle battalions included an assigned chemical instructor.

Finally, tank divisions fielded flamethrower tank battalions of two types, older versions armed with 30–45 flamethrower tanks and new flamethrower tank battalions consisting of two companies with ten KV tanks each and two companies with 16 T-34 tanks each, for a total of 52 flamethrower tanks per battalion, many of which were equipped with the automatic tank flamethrower model AT-41. In addition, separate tank brigades included flamethrower companies responsible for flamethrowing, laying smokescreens, and decontaminating equipment and terrain.

RGK forces subordinate to the central chemical directorate included separate decontamination and chemical defense battalions, which performed general-purpose tasks, and chemical tank battalions, chemical armored car battalions, chemical mortar battalions, and flamethrower battalions, which performed more specialized tasks.[62] Decontamination battalions, which were responsible for decontaminating local terrain, weapons, and clothing, consisted of three companies equipped with 15 decontamination, administrative, and supply vehicles, and chemical defense battalions, which were responsible for decontaminating local terrain, laying smokescreens, releasing gas, and contaminating regions, fielded three companies equipped with chemical vehicles.

The more specialized chemical tank battalions, which were organized into three companies with 15 chemical tanks each, and chemical armored car battalions, which consisted of three companies with 15 cars each, were responsible for flamethrowing, creating smokescreens, and decontaminating terrain. Finally, chemical mortar battalions, which consisted of three 12-mortar companies, were responsible for destroying enemy troops and laying smokescreens.

Overall, the Red Army fielded 50 separate RGK chemical battalions of various types on 22 June 1941. Some of these were called decontamination battalions, others were called antichemical defense (*protivo-khimicheskaia oborona,* or PKhO) or chemical repulse (*khimicheskaia otpora,* or KhO) battalions.[63]

The Red Army's chemical forces suffered huge losses during the initial stages of Operation Barbarossa, primarily because commanders often employed them as infantry. As a result, the NKO issued three orders on 13 August emphasizing the dangers of chemical war and thoroughly reorganizing its chemical forces.[64] The first order redesignated all chemical defense battalions (PKhO) as chemical repulse battalions (KhO), removed them from *front* and army control, and centralized them in the RVGK under the direct control of the NKO's Main Military-Chemical Directorate (*Glavnoe voenno-khimicheskoe upravlenie,* or GVKhU). In addition, it reassigned the flamethrower platoons in the rifle divisions' chemical companies to the divisions' rifle regiments where they would be of greater utility.

The second NKO order transformed the Red Army's Directorate of Military-Chemical Defense into a Main Military-Chemical Directorate with subdirectorates for chemical repulse, chemical defense [*sic*], chemical supply, and chemical equipment, and appointed Major General of Technical Forces P. G. Mel'nikov as main directorate chief. The new main directorate was responsible for training chemical cadre and raising and fielding necessary chemical forces.

The third and most important NKO order reorganized the entire chemical force structure, created new chemical units, and strengthened chemical defenses at division and regimental level. In addition to converting the decontamination battalions into chemical defense battalions, one of which it allocated to each operating army, it also formed 10 new RGK chemical defense battalions subordinate to the Main Military-Chemical Directorate, whose future assignment was to be determined by the General Staff. These new RVGK separate chemical defense battalions, 39 of which the NKO had formed by 1 September 1941, consisted of a headquarters platoon, three decontamination companies, a combat support company, and a reconnaissance platoon.

The third order also converted all chemical companies in rifle and cavalry divisions and antichemical defense platoons in rifle regiments into chemical defense companies and platoons and reinforced them with observation and reconnaissance squads. Finally, the order categorically forbade commanders at all levels from employing chemical defense forces in any unauthorized role (for example, as infantry). This basic chemical defense force structure remained virtually unchanged throughout the first 30 months of the war.

In addition to reorganizing its basic chemical defense force structure, the NKO also reorganized and strengthened its separate man-pack and tank-mounted flamethrower forces during the first 18 months of war. First, during 1941 it reorganized its separate flamethrower tank battalions into new battalions and regiments under RVGK control.[65] Later, in consonance with its other force structure reforms, it created new and stronger flamethrower tank battalions and brigades during the summer of 1942. These flamethrower tank battalions consisted of two heavy flame tank companies equipped with five KV tanks each and one medium flame tank company equipped with 11 T-34 tanks, for a total of 21 tanks; the separate flamethrower tank brigades were organized into three battalions with a total of 59 tanks. Both units were responsible for engaging and defeating enemy tanks and destroying enemy pillboxes and other lighter fortifications.[66]

While reorganizing its flamethrower tank forces, the NKO also formed 50 separate explosive flamethrower companies during August 1941, each of which consisted of three platoons with three squads equipped with 20 FOG-1 flamethrowers each, for a company strength of 180 flamethrowers, and assigned them to its operating *fronts*. After these companies achieving notable success during the Battle for Moscow, the NKO formed 93 more by April 1942.[67] Later, the NKO added 11 even heavier separate backpack flamethrower companies to the chemical force structure during the summer of 1942. These heavy companies consisted of three platoons armed with 40 ROKS-2 model flamethrowers each, for a company total of 120 flamethrowers.[68] In addition, the NKO also added flamethrower companies equipped with 300 FOG-1 flamethrowers each to its new fortified regions.

Finally, during late 1941 and early 1942, the NKO also fielded curious and unique ampule-throwing *(ampulemet)* companies, which were armed with carriage-mounted breech-loading mortars that fired flammable shells. However, the NKO ceased fielding these companies in July 1942 because of weapons production problems and the dangers the strange and often unreliable weapons posed to their crews.[69]

Since the Red Army's counteroffensives at Rzhev and Stalingrad in November and December 1942 and ensuing winter campaign of 1942–43 indicated that none of the flamethrower-explosive companies in its chemical force structure were mobile enough to keep pace with its attacking tank and mechanized forces, in April 1943 the NKO created five separate motorized antitank flamethrower battalions. These battalions consisted of three motorized flamethrower companies and an auto-transport company with a total strength of 540 FOG-1 flamethrowers. At the same time, the NKO also formed separate horse-drawn flamethrower battalions consisting initially of three flamethrower companies equipped with a total of 648 FOG-1 model flamethrowers to accompany advancing cavalry corps and divisions.[70]

When the tide of battle turned decisively in the Red Army's favor during the summer of 1943, the *Stavka* feared the *Wehrmacht* might resort to employing chemical weapons. As a result, on 1 July it ordered the NKO to increase the quantity of chemical defense battalions in the army to 77 and to strengthen chemical reconnaissance in all chemical units and subunits. The NKO did so by reducing the size of chemical defense subunits while improving the effectiveness of their chemical equipment and by adding chemical defense subunits to tank and engineer forces. It also subordinated all flamethrower units and subunits directly to the RVGK, which allocated them to operating *fronts* and armies on the basis of specific *Stavka* guidance.

Satisfied by the improvements it instituted in 1942 and early 1943, the NKO made few changes to the Red Army's chemical force structure after late summer of 1943.[71] By 31 December 1943, the Red Army's force structure included 28 separate flamethrower battalions and 19 separate backpack flamethrower companies, including three battalions in the RVGK.

RAILROAD FORCES

On the eve of war, specialized forces of railroad troops whose mission, depending on the situation, was to maintain, construct, restore, obstruct, or protect railroad lines, supported the Red Army's field forces. However, the command and control of these forces was confused since they were subordinate to different masters. For example, the NKO's Military Communications Service (*Sluzhba voennykh soobshchenii,* or VOSO), which had no directorate of its own, fielded separate railroad regiments and battalions, and the People's Commissariat of Communications Routes (*Narodnyi komissariat putei soobshcheniia,* or NKPS) controlled the operations of a Special Corps of Railroad Forces, which consisted of five railroad brigades formed on 1 January 1939 (see Chapter 11). In addition, the NKVD's Main Directorate for the Protection of Railroad Facilities included railroad security forces (divisions) responsible for providing railroad security and performing local railroad reconstruction tasks on behalf of wartime *front* commanders.

Compounding this confusion, the General Staff's Directorate for Military Communications (*Upravlenie voennykh soobshchenii,* or UVS), whose first wartime chief was Lieutenant General of Technical Forces N. I. Trubetskoi, who was replaced in July 1941 by Military Engineer 1st Rank I. V. Kovalev, was also responsible for supervising portions of the railroad network subject to military use.

Nor did this confusion end after war began. For example, on 1 August the GKO created a Main Directorate of the Red Army's Rear within the NKO with its own chief, renamed the UVS the Directorate for Military Communications (*Upravlenie voennykh soobshchenii,* or UP VOSO), and subordinated VOSO to the new main directorate.[72] The GKO finally created order out of this confusion on 3 January 1943, when it assigned all railroad forces to the People's Commissariat of Communications Routes (NKPS).[73]

On the eve of war, the NKO was combining its separate railroad regiments and battalions into full railroad brigades, a process it had begun in February 1941. Subsequently, it fielded 13 new railroad brigades by June, each consisting of three railroad route battalions, a railroad bridge battalion, and a separate railroad exploitation company.[74] When Operation Barbarossa began, 10 of these brigades were supporting movement into and within the western military districts.[75]

During wartime these brigades were responsible for protecting the concentration and deployment of the Red Army's first strategic echelon forces during and after mobilization, evacuating its mobile equipment and most vital installations, blocking, obstructing, or interdicting enemy use of all railroad lines, and repairing and reconstructing railroads in support of the army's offensive operations. Although their heavy workload kept these brigades at a high state of combat readiness, all suffered from severe shortages of trucks and other vehicles. Worse still, in all frontier sectors the rail capacity on the Soviet side of the border was far more limited than on the German, Finnish, and Romanian sides.[76]

In addition to destroying many Soviet railroad lines and bridges, the *Wehrmacht's* rapid advance during Operation Barbarossa severely damaged forward deployed Red Army railroad brigades, forced the surviving railroad troops to fight as infantry, and disrupted the mobilization of additional railroad forces. To restore order to its remaining railroads in the wake of this disaster, during September the GKO ordered the NKPS to establish a central Military Reconstruction Directorate and form new military-reconstruction services to handle repair and reconstruction work in the rear areas of all operating *fronts* and armies. The NKPS formed 19 of these organs, which controlled reconstruction forces within their jurisdiction.[77]

The GKO further rationalized all railroad construction, reconstruction, and repair work on 3 January 1942 by assigning the NKPS responsibility for all of this work in both the operational zones and the rear areas of operating *fronts.* It required the NKPS to appoint representatives to all *fronts,* and they became formal members of the *fronts'* military councils. Together with their respective *front* commanders, these representatives were responsible for supervising all railroad work within the *fronts.* In addition, the GKO required the NKO's Main Directorate for the Formation and Manning of Red Army Forces to form five railroad brigades, 20 railroad battalions, five bridge battalions, six separate mechanization battalions, 11 separate exploitation companies, and two separate reserve railroad regiments, and turn them over to the NKPS.[78]

Later still, during early 1943, the NKPS reorganized all of its railroad forces into brigades consisting of a headquarters, four track battalions, each of which included special teams to reconnoiter railroad lines, one bridge and one mechanized battalion, and a service support company, for a total brigade strength of about 2,500 men. At the NKPS's request, the NKO reinforced these brigades throughout the remainder of 1943 with a communications reconstruction company, which it later strengthened into a full battalion, a water company, and, finally, a bridge reconstruction element and separate carpentry and heavy lift company. These reinforcements increased the strength of each brigade to about 3,000 men. Ultimately, the NKPS formed a total of 35 railroad brigades during the remainder of the war.

AUTO-TRANSPORT AND ROAD CONSTRUCTION AND REPAIR FORCES

Because the Soviet Union's road network was woefully underdeveloped on the eve of war, road transport played a far less significant role in the strategic and operational movement and deployment of forces, weaponry, and other bulky equipment than did rail transport. Nevertheless, road transport, particularly along the few existing main macadamized highways, which the Russians termed *shosse* and the Germans *rollbahn,* and along all other roads from the immediate rear to the front lines, which were usually only dirt tracks, remained significant for the tactical movement of men and equipment.

As was the case with railroad forces, no central directorate was responsible for constructing, repairing, and protecting roads or training and controlling road forces. Instead, the Road Department in the General Staff's Directorate for the Rear and Supply and Red Army's Motor-Armored Directorate shared responsibility for repairing and supplying automotive equipment, the NKO trained road construction troops, and the NKVD trained troops responsible for road security.

The Red Army's road forces on the eve of war included both auto-transport forces and road construction and repair forces. The former consisted of 19 automobile regiments, 38 separate automobile battalions (including four training battalions), and two separate automobile companies, and nine of these regiments and 14 of these battalions were stationed in the western military districts.[79] Since the NKO maintained these forces at cadre strength in peacetime and had yet to determine their precise wartime organization, they possessed only roughly 41 percent of their required wartime equipment and wildly varying quantities and types of vehicles and other equipment. For example, regiments fielded 180–1,090 vehicles each, battalions 113–610 vehicles, and companies roughly 62 vehicles. In addition, the Motor-Armored Directorate controlled 65 automobile depots, which were to form new automobile battalions once mobilization began.

At the same time, the army's road construction and repair forces consisted of 43 road exploitation regiments and eight road exploitation training regiments, 23 of which were stationed in the western military districts. The NKO maintained these regiments at cadre strength during peacetime, and each fielded only one operational battalion. During mobilization for war, these regiments were supposed to form new road units such as road exploitation regiments, road and bridge construction battalions, and forward road bases for assignment to the NKO and the NKVD's Main Directorate of Main Highways.[80] Once mobilized, these regiments, battalions, and bases were responsible for constructing, repairing, and maintaining militarily important roads. However, the NKO also failed to determine the precise wartime organization of these forces when war began, and none of them fielded their necessary equipment.[81]

The partial mobilization of the Red Army the GKO ordered prior to 22 June and the *Wehrmacht's* ensuing rapid advance during Operation Barbarossa produced utter havoc in the Red Army's motor-transport and road construction forces, decimating many of its units and forcing the remainder to fight as infantry.

In an attempt to rectify this situation, on 16 July the GKO reorganized command and control over its auto-transport and road forces and ordered the formation of a wide variety of new auto-transport and road units and subunits.[82] While creating a new Automobile-Road Directorate (*Avtomobil'no-dorozhnoe upravlenie,* or GADU) within the General Staff and appointing Major General Z. I. Kondrat'ev as its chief, the GKO also formed new automobile-road departments under Kondrat'ev's general supervision within the Red Army's operating *fronts.* Additionally, the GKO organized six military-automobile roads (*voenno-avtomobil'nye dorogi,* or VAD) along key operational axes and ordered the NKO to form 35 automobile battalions, eight road exploitation regiments, and 11 military road and bridge battalions by 25 July, as well as four automobile repair bases to repair tractors and other vehicles assigned to the other new forces.[83] Finally, it assigned Kondrat'ev responsibility for raising and fielding the new forces. Later still, on 1 August, the GKO subordinated the GADU to the chief of the Red Army's Rear and, soon after, elevated the GADU to the status of a main *(glavnoe)* directorate.[84]

Once established, the GADU mobilized civilian vehicles and created 120 auto-transport and road construction regiments, battalions, and companies throughout the summer of 1941, using many of them to form new brigades.[85] It also created new military roads (VADs) to supplement those formed in July and new numbered military-road directorates (*voenno-dorozhnie upravlenie,* or VDU), which were responsible for maintaining these roads and regulating the traffic along them. Thereafter, the GADU and its subordinate VDUs worked painstakingly with directorates from other commissariats to create an intricate network of *Stavka, front*, and army VADs to serve all of the army's operating *fronts* more effectively.[86] To tie this entire military road system together, the GADU also created a central VAD in the depths of the Soviet Union that linked the country's most important economic regions directly with the active theaters of military operations.

To establish order within this vast military road transport system, during late 1941 and 1942 the GADU subdivided the VADs into separate and distinct road commandant sectors, each of which consisted of a specific but varying number of separate road commandant companies whose mission was to operate and control traffic along these military roads. These road commandant companies employed traffic control service personnel and traffic control teams from the GADU's road service (exploitation) regiments to control two-way traffic flow, primarily by deploying traffic control points.[87]

The GKO improved the efficiency of its auto-transport and road-building and maintenance forces on 8 May 1942, when it ordered the NKO to establish a new Main Directorate of Auto-Transport and Road Services of the Red Army (*Glavnoe upravlenie avtotransportnoi i dorozhnoi sluzhby Krasnoi Armii,* or GUADSKA) and corresponding directorates and departments for auto-transport, road services, and road repair bases within the operating *fronts* and armies to manage all auto-transport and road service forces and missions. Once established on 12 May, the GUADSKA included the existing GADU and its associated directorates and departments in *fronts* and armies, as well as selected NKVD directorates for road service and bases.[88] As a result of this reorganization, the GUADSKA managed to field from three to six separate automobile transport battalions to each of its operating *fronts* and one to two to each army during 1942 and 1943.

Building on these reforms, in early January 1943, the NKO assigned GUADSKA responsibility for supervising the reconstruction and maintenance of all military roads, and GUADSKA's upgraded Main Auto-Road Directorate upgraded many of its automobile transport battalions to full regiments and attached a training battalion to each.

The GKO capped its road service reform efforts on 9 June 1943, when it ordered the NKO to subordinate GUADSKA to the chief of the Red Army's Rear (Services) and create corresponding road directorates and departments within *fronts* and armies. The NKO's 17 July order split GUADSKA into two parts, the Main Automobile Directorate of the Red Army and the Main Road Directorate of the Red Army (see Chapter 11). Although they performed distinctly differing functions, both main directorates cooperated closely throughout the remainder of the war.

As an integral part of this June reconstruction, the NKO began forming additional automobile brigades, assigning one to each operating *front*. These brigades consisted of three regiments with up to six battalions each and, on occasion, several separate automobile battalions. At the same time, the NKO upgraded automobile training battalions assigned to its *front* to training regiments with three battalions each and assigned a separate auto repair battalion to each operating *front* and army. By this time each field army included two to three auto-transport battalions.[89]

The NKO also improved its military road system further in 1943, first by requiring VADs to deploy separate numbered detachments *(otriady)* to carry out road work in specific road sectors, and, in June, by replacing many of the older and more cumbersome road service exploitation regiments with larger numbers of new and more streamlined road service battalions. This way, the NKO was able to create a far more extensive and effective automobile and road construction and maintenance force structure by 31 December 1943. To a considerable extent, the wholesale expansion of the Red Army's road service in 1943 and throughout the remainder of the war was made possible by an increasingly generous supply of trucks provided to the Soviet Union by its allies under the auspices of the Lend-Lease program (see below).[90]

CONSTRUCTION TROOPS

The Red Army included specialized construction forces (more properly, labor troops) on the eve of war that were responsible for building and repairing military buildings and facilities and civilian military-support installations. Subordinate to the NKO's Main Directorate for Defensive Construction (*Glavnoe upravlenie oboronitel'nogo stroitel'stva,* or GUOS), these military construction units and their facilities were under the operational control of 23 directorates of the chiefs of construction (*upravlenie nachal'nika stroitel'stva,* or UNS) assigned to the Red Army's military districts and armies on 22 June 1941. In turn, these UNSs were subdivided into 138 separate construction sectors, 110 of which were deployed in the western military districts, each of which fielded several military construction and sapper battalions and technical support specialists.[91] In addition, on the eve of war, two UNSs and three separate military construction sectors directly supported the USSR's Council of People's Commissars.

In addition to this official structure of construction troops, prior to and during the war, the Red Army fielded and employed a wide variety of ad hoc and often hastily formed construction battalions, "columns," and detachments, which it employed to construct major defense lines as well as a variety of more routine and mundane construction tasks. Usually created on a temporary basis, these subunits consisted primarily of personnel conscripted from non-Slavic ethnic and religious minorities, which the GKO and NKO considered too politically unreliable to perform even the simplest of combat tasks. These special construction troops included both men and women, many either under or well over normal draft age. More than 330 of these units participated in defensive construction throughout the war, including over 100 in the army, 60 in the navy, and 100 in the air force.

While the Red Army's engineer or construction services usually provided administrative and technical cadre for the separate construction battalions and detachments, construction "columns" consisted only of workers who were usually levied on the spot. Army automobile detachments, automobile "columns," heavy mechanized detachments and civilian automobile "columns" and detachments provided these special construction forces with transport and other mechanized equipment.

When the war began, most of the Red Army's organic construction forces were assisting its engineers in the construction of new fortified regions in the western military districts. The German invasion literally obliterated these forces within a matter of days, forcing the NKO to form new construction units virtually from scratch to build additional defense lines to the rear. During late June and early July, the NKO converted its Main Directorate of Defensive Construction into a Directorate for Military Field Construction (*Upravlenie voenno-polevogo stroitel'stva,* or UVPS) and reorganized most of its 16 surviving construction directorates (UNS) in its military districts and armies into either *front* or army directorates for military-field construction (*upravleniia voenno-polevogo stroitel'stva,* or UVPSs).[92] At the same time, it transformed the relatively inflexible construction sectors in its former UNSs, first, into military construction detachments, and, later, into military construction battalions.

On 1 September 1941, the Red Army's construction forces consisted of 59 UVPSs, including 13 *front* UVPSs allocated on the basis of one to two per *front,* 46 army UVPSs allocated on the basis of one to seven per *front,* and 66 construction battalions.[93] In addition, the NKVD's Main Directorate for Hydro-Technical Construction *(Glavgidrostroi)* fielded an additional 13 UVPSs responsible for constructing defenses around key political and economic objectives.

After penetrating the Red Army's frontier defenses at breakneck speed, the *Wehrmacht's* rapid advance forced the *Stavka* to hastily erect new defense lines protecting the approaches to Leningrad, Moscow, Kiev, and other vital objectives deeper into the Soviet Union. At this time, the severe shortage of Red Army construction troops forced the NKO to rely extensively on mobilized civilian labor formed into workers' and peasants' "brigades" and detachments to perform much of this construction work. However, because much of the NKO's construction efforts during the first few months of the war were haphazard and often inefficient, it had no choice but to reorganize its construction forces.

To correct this situation, in early October 1941 the GKO established a Main Directorate for Defensive Work (GUOBR) under the control of the NKVD and assigned it the responsibility for constructing rear defense lines and positions within guidance provided by the Red Army's Engineer Directorate. Although the new GUOBR absorbed and replaced the existing Northern, Northwestern, Western, Southwestern, and Southern Directorates for Defensive Work, it supplemented rather than replaced the UVPSs within the operating *fronts* and armies. However, the *Wehrmacht's* sudden advance toward Moscow in late October forced the GKO once again to try to centralize and rationalize construction efforts under the General Staff and its operating *fronts* so that they could better support the General Staff's defense plan.

In late October the GKO ordered the NKVD to establish a new Main Directorate for Defensive Construction (GUOS) and the NKO to form ten sapper armies. The GKO required these sapper armies not only to form engineer units and train engineer personnel but also to coordinate and conduct all defensive construction work under the supervision of the NKVD's GUOS. However, since this arrangement also did not function efficiently enough and the sapper armies failed to live up to expectations, in late November the GKO subordinated them to the chief of Red Army Engineers and, beginning in early 1942, began abolishing them and assigning their functions and forces to its operating *fronts* (see above).[94]

Since the experiment with sapper armies did not satisfy the *Stavka's* massive defensive construction requirements, beginning in early 1942 the GKO ordered the NKO to form new defensive construction directorates (UOSs) subordinate to the *Stavka* reserve, which were to replace the UVPSs at *front* and army level but perform the same basic functions. Subsequently, the NKO formed seven UOSs by April 1942 by incorporating the resources of the NKVD's former Main Directorate for Defensive Work (GUOBR), the seven UVPSs within the operating *fronts*, and the 22 UVPSs within the field armies. The new UOSs consisted of three to seven UVPSs for a total of 35 UVPSs, and the new UVPSs consisted of four sectors of military-construction work (*uchastka voenno-stroitel'nykh rabot*, or UVSR) each, for a total of 140 UVSRs. When fully organized, each UOS consisted of 8–20 construction columns with roughly 1,000 men each, and the total construction force consisted of roughly 100 columns with an overall strength of about 100,000 men.[95]

The seven UOSs formed prior to April 1942 were subordinate to the NKO's Directorate for Defensive Construction, which became a main directorate in 1943 and worked under the supervision of the chief of the Red Army's Engineers. Once assigned to operating *fronts* and armies, the UOSs were responsible for employing both military construction forces and civilian labor to construct fortified lines and positions in the *fronts'* and armies' rear areas. By April 1942 the NKO had assigned 2 UOSs to operating *fronts* and another 27 UOSs to field armies. In addition, the *Stavka* frequently reinforced these UOSs with obstacle construction detachments from its own reserve.

Although the GKO's and NKO's reorganization of the Red Army's construction forces during late 1941 and early 1942 satisfied the army's defensive needs, it did not provide the army adequate support when it resumed large-scale offensive operations in late 1942 and 1943. In short, more active and flexible construction work, such as mine clearing, protecting the flanks of and junctions between operating forces, and quickly establishing defenses along threatened operational axes became far more important than more passive tasks such as constructing prepared defenses, defense lines, and strong points. This made it necessary for the NKO to field more mobile, active, and flexible construction forces to support operating *fronts* and armies.

In response to this need, during early and mid-1943, the NKO ordered its operating *fronts* and armies to use their own organic engineer forces to form and employ more numerous mobile obstacle construction detachments. In addition, it reorganized and expanded its construction forces structure during July 1943 by forming additional UOSs, each consisting of four military construction detachments, within its operating *fronts*. At the same time, it reorganized its UOSs into RVGK directorates for defensive construction with two or three subordinate UVPSs, and it assigned each new UVPS its own sector and its own construction columns, including three main military-construction detachments with 700 men each, an automobile column, and a cargo transport detachment. The new formation, which combined both a labor force and technical supervision, was far more mobile, flexible, capable, and independent than the previous sector organizations.[96]

With only minor structural changes, these new RVGK UOSs continued to provide increasingly effective defensive and offensive construction support to the Red Army's operating *fronts* throughout the remainder of the war.

ENGINEER, SIGNAL, AND CHEMICAL WEAPONS

Engineer Equipment

Although the Red Army possessed a superb theoretical basis for conducting engineer operations on the eve of war, its engineer forces lacked the experience and equipment necessary to do so. By early 1943, however, the Red Army's harsh education at the hands of the *Wehrmacht* had taught the Soviet military leadership what was required to conduct effective engineer operations. By this time, the NKO had defined the nature and quantities of engineer equipment required, and Soviet industry was producing massive enough of that equipment to meet the requirements of modern mobile warfare.

First and foremost, the nature of German blitzkrieg convinced the *Stavka* and NKO of the need to develop and produce large quantities of effective mines, particularly antitank mines. The first antitank mines the NKO fielded during wartime were wooden IaM-5 antitank mines with five-kilogram explosive charges and metal TM-41 antitank mines with four-kilogram charges. Developed during August 1941, the latter were detonated by new MB-5 pressure sensitive fuses (see Appendix 3 in companion volume for the characteristics of Red Army engineer, signal, and chemical weapons and equipment). After developing and fielding TMB mines, also with five-kilogram explosive charges but with bodies fashioned from inexpensive paper castings, in 1942, the following year, the NKO fielded TMD model antitank mines, which it issued to Red Army forces en masse, and in early 1944 it fielded an improved version of TMD mines, TMD-44 mines with five-kilogram explosive charges.

Despite its preoccupation with producing antitank mines, the NKO also developed improved antipersonnel mines, including PMD-6, PMD-7, and PMD-7ts wooden antipersonnel mines, the latter with MUV igniters, which had 0.2-, 0.07-, and 0.07-kilogram explosive charges, respectively. In addition, it fielded model POMZ-2 tension-action antipersonnel fragmentation-obstacle mines and model OZM fragmentation-obstacle mines, both of which were engineered for delivery by artillery shell.

The Red Army's renewed emphasis on offensive operations during the fall of 1942 prompted the NKO to develop a new generation of mine-clearing equipment, which included mass-produced model VIM-203, VIM-203m, VIM-625, VIM-625m, and VIM-625v mine detectors. The VIM-203 models could operate continuously for up to 35 hours and the VIM-625 models up to 70 hours, and both were able to detect mines implanted to a depth of up to 60 centimeters. Finally, in early 1944 the NKO fielded model DIM-186 mine detectors able to detect mines to a depth of 75 centimeters. Overall, Soviet industry produced and fielded 246,112 mine detectors of various types throughout the war.[97]

By war's end Red Army engineer forces were also employing model UZ-1 standard explosive charges, similar in design to U.S. Bangalore torpedoes, to blast lanes through barbed wire and other obstacles. Finally, in 1942 the Red Army adopted its T-34 tanks to clear mines by adding model PT-3 minesweeper rollers to their chassis. Equipped with this roller, a single T-34 mine-clearing tank was capable of clearing two 1.2-meter lanes through enemy minefields, and minesweeping tanks equipped with these rollers were able to clear minefields at a rate of 25 kilometers per hour along roads and 10–12 kilometers per hour off the roads.[98]

Because the terrain throughout the vast expanse of European Russia was crisscrossed by numerous rivers, streams, and other water obstacles, the Red Army had to field effective bridging and river-crossing equipment if it was to conduct military operations successfully. Unfortunately, since the army lacked this equipment in 1941 and early 1942, it was forced to improvise and cross water obstacles *po ruchnoi,* meaning by any means at hand. Gradually, however, Soviet design bureaus managed over time to develop what became an imposing array of largely inexpensive engineer bridges and collective bridge parks.

The NKO fielded its first wartime bridges, model DMP-41 wooden prefabricated bridge parks, in October 1941 and began issuing them to its engineer forces in the spring of 1942. These heavy pontoon-bridge park kits consisted of 20 wooden ferryboats (actually rafts) that could be used either to ferry material across rivers or to erect bridges 64–129 meters long with load capacities of 16–30 tons. These ferries were able to transport 30 tons of material across rivers of average width in 35 minutes or form complete bridges in a somewhat longer period. By the end of 1942, the NKO modernized its DMP-41 bridge park kits into model DMP-42 kits with load-carrying capacities of up to 50 tons each. The new kits could emplace bridges up to 620 meters long in four hours and shorter bridges even more quickly.[99]

The NKO fielded two other bridge kits during 1942 as well. Unlike previous wooden bridges, the first kits, model MdPA-3 heavy pontoon-bridge parks, used some metal parts to increase their strength. These bridge kits could be used to erect 46-, 90-, and 111-meter bridges with load capacities ranging of up to 14 tons in about 70 minutes. The second kit, the model UVS-A-3 bridge park, consisted of ten inflatable pontoon boats and could assemble either ferries or 114-meter bridges with load-carrying capacities of up to 14 tons within a relatively short time.

The NKO continued these improvements to its bridging during 1943, when it fielded the model DLP light wooden bridge park, which was lighter and more effective and durable than its predecessors, particularly the MdPA-3 and the UVS-A-3 models. The new DLP model, which could carry 48 men on each of its 20 pontoons, was ideally suited for conducting assault river crossings. It could also conduct ferry crossings or erect complete 160-meter bridges with load-carrying capacities of up to 34 tons within two hours.

In addition to fielding this new bridging equipment, the NKO also began modernizing its older 1941 vintage Model N2P heavy pontoon-bridge parks during December 1941 and January 1942 by converting them into model N2P-41 pontoon bridges. The components of the new pontoon bridges were able to support assault crossings, ferry troops and material across rivers, and form 75-meter bridges with load capacities of up to 60 tons. Later still, the NKO fielded the largest of its pontoon-bridge parks, model TMP pontoon bridges, during the late summer of 1942 and employed them for the first time to cross the Volga River at Stalingrad during September 1942. These new pontoon-bridge parks could erect 450-meter pontoon bridges with load capacities of up to 80 tons across rivers as broad as the Volga within three to five hours.

Despite the NKO's intense efforts to develop and field bridges and pontoon bridges, it failed to provide the Red Army with any motorized assault crossing equipment throughout the war. Instead, it fielded a wide variety of boats and river craft of more limited use in the conduct of assault river crossings.

Finally, the NKO developed and fielded a vast array of specialized equipment, including camouflage netting, artificial terrain-masking materials, mockup and dummy tanks, artillery, and other large weapons, and other deceptive devices, to conceal and otherwise camouflage its units, men, weapons, and other equipment. It allocated much of these materials to deception *(maskirovka)* companies, which it then assigned to the Red Army's operating *fronts* on the basis of their specific operational needs.

Signal Equipment

The Red Army faced a critical shortage of reliable communications equipment, particularly radios, during the first year of war. Although the NKO had developed and tested an imposing array of new series radios and other types of communications equipment on the eve of war, it failed to field sufficient quantities of this equipment to satisfy the Red Army's tactical and operational needs. Therefore, the Red Army's forces lacked adequate communications of any type during the most critical periods of Operation Barbarossa, in particular, mobile communications necessary to ensure effective command and control over forces during mobile and fluid military operations.

The NKO attempted to resolve the Red Army's higher-level communications problems by developing and fielding Almaz model radio-teletype sets during 1942 and Karbid model radio-teletype sets during 1944. However, since both of these sets were difficult to redeploy, neither was suited for use in mobile combat situations.

At the strategic and operational levels, during 1941 and early 1942, the *Stavka* and General Staff employed RAT model radio sets, whose effective operating range was up to 2,000 kilometers, to communicate with their subordinate *fronts* and armies, and armies employed RAF model and RSB model radio sets, whose effective operating ranges were up to 600 kilometers and up to 60 kilometers, respectively, to communicate with their subordinate corps, divisions, and brigades.

The NKO managed to improve strategic and operational radio communications somewhat during the summer and fall of 1942 and early 1943 by fielding BODO model secure teletype systems for use between the *Stavka* and its operating *fronts,* medium-power RAF-KV radios and the low power Sever radios for use at *front* and army level, CT-35 telegraphs at army level, and 12 RP and 13R radios at corps and division level.[100]

Subsequently, the NKO was able to field newer model radios to the Red Army's field forces in ever greater quantities throughout 1943. For example, Soviet industry produced 192 RAT radio sets, 188 RB sets, and 320 BDO teletype sets and increased its production of field telephones by 130 percent during 1943.

After war began, some Red Army divisions employed portable RB and 6PK radios, whose effective range was up to 10 kilometers, for tactical communications, although these radios remained in short supply. The Red Army's most effective tactical radios were the portable RBM radio stations, which the NKO began fielding during 1942 and which soon became the standard tactical radio employed by the Red Army. These radios, the personal radios for most Red Army division, corps, and army commanders, had an effective range of up to 30 kilometers.[101]

In addition, the NKO fielded other tactical radio sets during late 1943, including prototypes of new A-7 model radios, which were designated for employment by rifle and artillery battalions, and numerous 12PT radio stations, which served operating tanks and functioned at distances of 5–20 kilometers in static situations and 3–14 kilometers while on the march.[102]

Once fielded, these new systems increased the number of radios in *fronts* and armies threefold and at the tactical level two- to threefold, and permitted commanders at all levels to echelon their radio nets in far greater depth than had been the case during 1942. As a result, the NKO was able to equip virtually every Red Army tank army, tank and mechanized corps and every major element of the RVGK with adequate radio communications by the end of 1943.[103]

As regards landline cable and wire communications, the Red Army relied extensively on model TAI-43 magneto telephone apparatuses and model PK-30 and PK-10 switchboards after war began. Of course, these communications were of very limited utility in fluid combat situations. Only after the front stabilized somewhat during late 1942 did headquarters and force formations and units tend to rely more heavily on wire communications, and then only when the Red Army was not on the offensive.

In short, reliable radio and wire communications linked virtually all Red Army headquarters and their subordinate operating forces by the end of 1943. By this time, most mobile forces were also equipped with an adequate quantity of radios. Thereafter the NKO eventually extended this capability down to all tactical units and even individual fighting vehicles such as tanks as the war progressed.

Finally, the Red Army employed messengers on foot and on skis, message collection points within formations, units, and subunits, liaison officers, messenger dogs, single light Po-2 and U-2 aircraft, vehicles, motorcycles, and BA-10 and BA-64 armored cars to supplement its radio and wire communications. Each of these mobile means had specific associated indices regarding level of command, speed of movement and delivery, range, and density of employment at each force level.

Chemical and Flame Weapons

Ever suspicious of German intentions, the Red Army was prepared to conduct chemical warfare defensively, by employing forces and equipment to shield its forces against German chemical attacks and decontaminate its forces and equipment in the wake of these attacks, and offensively, by employing a variety of flame and smoke weapons both prior to and during the entire war. Even though the *Wehrmacht* abstained from conducting chemical warfare, the Red Army maintained defensive chemical forces at a constant high state of readiness until war's end. At the same time, it developed, fielded, and employed an imposing array of flamethrower and incendiary weapons and smoke-generating equipment to mask its forces' movements and operations.

The Red Army's wartime chemical weapons ranged in sophistication from simple, crude, ubiquitous, and inexpensive self-igniting flame bottles, which the Finns christened Molotov cocktails during 1939 and 1940 and the Red Army's soldiers used massively in the war, to more elaborate flamethrowers and incendiaries manufactured in great quantities by Soviet industry. In addition to "Molotov cocktails," which contained flammable KS fuel mixtures, the Red Army's inventory of flamethrower incendiary weapons when war began included man-packed ROKS-2 flamethrowers, which had a fuel capacity of 10 liters and a range of 30–35 meters, and heavier FOG-1 flamethrowers, which had a capacity of 25 liters and a range of 60–140 meters.

To supplement its backpack flamethrowers, the NKO also developed and fielded ampule (fuel shell)-throwing carriage-mounted mortars *(ampulemety)* during the late fall of 1941 to engage enemy tanks at ranges of 250–300 meters and, at roughly the same time, a rifled mortar capable of "throwing" KS incendiary bottles. In addition, it also fielded great numbers of new FOG-2 and ROK-3 flamethrowers during 1943. The former had a capacity of 25 liters, a range of up to 100 meters, and a shortened directional barrel that permitted more extensive terrain coverage than previous models. Lighter than the FOG-3, the man-packed ROKS-3 flamethrowers had a capacity of 10 liters contained in a back-mounted reservoir and a range of 30–35 meters.

Tank-mounted flamethrowers available in the Red Army's weapons inventory on the eve of war included high-capacity 360–liter model OT-26, 130, and 133 flamethrowers, which were mounted on chassis of T-26 tanks, and 100-liter ATO-41 model flamethrowers, which were mounted on T-34 tanks. However, since both of these models proved quite difficult to employ in combat and were largely ineffective, the NKO fielded modernized models, including automatic model ATO-42 flamethrowers, which were mounted on both T-34 and KV tanks, later during the war. These tank-mounted models had fuel capacities of 200–570 liters and ranges of 100–120 meters.

The NKO began deploying smoke-generating equipment into the Red Army's operating *fronts,* primarily for the purposes of camouflage and deception, during August 1941. It had delayed doing so because it believed smoke weapons were only useful in offensive operation, Red Army troops were inexperienced in their use, and these weapons were in extremely short supply. As a result, during the first few months of the war, commanders required special permission before they could employ smoke-generating equipment.

Thereafter, the Red Army's primary smoke-generating weapons were smoke charges and smoke grenades. The model PDM and PDG-2 smoke grenades, which the NKO fielded during late 1941, released white and black smoke, respectively, the former to create smokescreens and the latter to simulate burning tanks, vehicles, buildings, and other installations. The PDG-2 smoke grenade weighed 0.5 kilograms and released smoke for five to six minutes. The more modern and larger model DM-II, DM-B, and DSh-2 smoke charges, which the NKO fielded during 1942 and 1943, economized on the use of metal but were generally ineffective. Model DM-II-3 smoke charges, which it introduced in late 1943, had a far greater smoke-generating capability and were far more effective.

Finally, during early 1944 the NKO introduced tank-mounted model TDP-MDSh smoke generators, which served successfully for the remainder of the war.

Table 9.1 Formation, Composition, Missions, and Ultimate Disposition of Sapper Armies, 1941–1942

	Formation	Composition (Brigades)	Missions	Ultimate Disposition
2nd	Arkhangel'sk MD (Vologda): 27.10.41–27.2.42	1st–3rd SB (6th, 7th, and 8th Army UVPS)	2nd–3rd SB: Vytegra, Cherepovets, Poshekhovo, and Vologda defenses; 1st SB (10 bns): Medvezh'egorsk, Pudozh, Vyterga obstacle line (Karelia)	Disbanded
3rd	Moscow MD (Iaroslavl'): 29.10.41–12.9.42	4th–7th SB, less 5th SB (Apr) and 7th SB (May)	Poshekhovo, Rybinsk, Gor'kii, Cheboksary, Ivanovo defense line and Vladimir defense line (Dec 41), Mozhaisk defense line (1942)	34th UOS
4th	Volga MD (Kuibyshev): 10.41–18.5.42	8th–11th SB, less 9th SB (Apr) and 8th SB (May)	8th–9th SB: Cheboksary, Kazan', Ul'ianovsk, Syzran', Khvalynsk defense line and Kazan', Kuibyshev defenses. 10th–11th SB: Kuibyshev factories	Disbanded
5th	Stalingrad, North Caucasus MDs (Stalingrad): 15.10.41–1.3.42	12th–15th SB (5th NKVD UOBR, 5th, 16th, 18th–19th Army UVPS)	Khalynsk, Saratov, Kamyshin, Stalingrad defense lines, Stalingrad defenses, Zamost'e, Chernyshevskaia, Boguchar sector, Astrakhan defense line, Astrakhan defenses; Rostov defenses (Jan 42)	Disbanded
6th	Volga MD (Penza), Briansk Front: 10.41–13.9.42	16th–19th SB less 16th SB (May)	Vasil'sursk, Saransk, Penza, Petrovskoe sector, Volga-Sursk defense line (1941), Don River, Voronezh, Stalingrad defenses, combat support (1942)	35th UOS
7th	Volga and Stalingrad MDs (Saratov), Southwestern and Southern Fronts: 10.41–15.9.42	20th–22nd SB (2nd, 15th, 17th, 19th UVPS), 12th, 14th, 15th, 20th, 21st SB (Mar)	Petrovskoe, Atkarsk, Frolovo sector, Volga-Sursk defense line (1941), Oskol, Don River, Stalingrad, Rostov defenses, combat support (1942)	36th UOS
8th	North Caucasus MD (Sal'sk), Southern, Caucasus, Trans-Caucasus Fronts: 30.10.41–15.10.42	23rd–26th SB, 8th U Oboronstroia (special directorate, Commissariat of the Coal Industry), 23rd–30th SB (Mar), 11th, 23rd–26th, 28th–30th (Jun), 10th, 23rd–26th, 28th–30th (Aug)	Stalingrad, Rostov defenses (1941), Voroshilovgrad, Rostov, Stalingrad, North Caucasus, Ordzhonikidze, Groznyi, Aksai Mineral'nye Vody, Terek defenses, combat support (1942)	24th UOS
9th	North Caucasus MD (Krasnodar): 10.41–1.3.42	27th–28th SB	Piatigorsk, Krasnodar, Kerch Straits defense line	Disbanded
10th	North Caucasus MD (Groznyi): 26.10.41–5.3.42	29th–30th SB	Piatigorsk, Groznyi, Caspian Sea defense line	Disbanded
1st	Western Front: 25.12.41–1.9.42	31st–40th SB (5th *Front* UVPS, 2nd, 4th, 6th, 11th–13th, 20th–22nd, 24th, 26th Army UVPS), less 35th SB (Mar), 33rd SB (May)	Road, mine, and obstacle clearing (Dec 41), Mozhaisk defense line, combat (1942)	33rd UOS

Abbreviations: UVPS: Directorate for Military-Field Construction; U Oboronstroia: Directorate for Defensive Construction; UOBR: Directorate of Defensive Work (NKVD)

Source: G. V. Malinovsky, "Sapernye armii i ikh rol' v pervyi period Velikoi Otechestvennoi voiny [Sapper armies and their role in the initial period of the Great Patriotic War], in *Voenno-istoricheskii arkhiv* [Military-historical archives], no. 2 (17) (Moscow: Tserera, 2001), 153–65.

PART III

THE LEADERS AND THE LED

CHAPTER 10

Strategic Leadership and Control Organs

STRATEGIC LEADERSHIP

At the heart of the Soviet state were those persons, organs, and apparatuses, loosely termed the Center *(tsentr)*, that controlled the levers of power within the Soviet Union and, individually or collectively, planned and directed virtually every state function, including planning for and waging war and ensuring the population and armed forces remained loyal to the state. Although the term "Center" was used most frequently to describe the central apparatuses of state intelligence, it applied equally well to all other persons and organizations exercising total authority within their jurisdictions at the center of state power, beginning with Iosif (Joseph) Stalin.

Stalin

Iosif Vissarionovich Stalin, dictator of all Russia, stood like a colossus over the Soviet Union's war effort. Elected to the relatively obscure post of general secretary of the Communist (Bolshevik) Party's Central Committee during 1922 at Lenin's recommendation, during the late 1920s Stalin exploited the many hitherto untapped powers of that post in a singular pursuit of power and became the undisputed leader of the Soviet Union during the early 1930s by ruthlessly purging and destroying all of his potential political challengers, real or perceived. After becoming a Hero of Labor in 1939, Stalin had himself appointed chairman of the Council of People's Commissars of the Soviet Union (*Sovet narodnykh komissarov*, or SNK) in May 1941.

Immediately after the *Wehrmacht* invaded the Soviet Union Stalin assumed, in rapid succession, the posts of chairman of the State Defense Committee (GKO) and people's commissar of defense in late June 1941, head of the *Stavka* of the Supreme High Command (*Stavka* VGK) in July, supreme high commander of the Soviet Armed Forces in August, and later in the war, marshal of the Soviet Union on 6 February 1943 and generalissimo of the Soviet Union on 27 July 1945. Despite the paralyzing shock and devastating effects of the German surprise attack and the immense carnage and damage the *Wehrmacht* inflicted on his country and its armed forces during the remainder of Operation Barbarossa, Stalin never once relinquished his iron grip on the levers of power within the Soviet Union.

Like his German counterpart, Adolph Hitler, in addition to bearing full and final responsibility for directing the Soviet war effort, Stalin involved himself in virtually every key political and military decision associated with the conduct of the war and military operations. However, unlike Hitler, whose increasingly arbitrary and petty involvement in military decision-making often rejected sound military advice, stifled initiative on the part of his military commanders, and hindered the conduct of effective military operations, as the war progressed, although never relinquishing his tight grip on the reigns of power, more prudently, Stalin tended to heed and act on the counsel of his most trusted military advisers. Therefore, unlike Hitler, Stalin emerged from the war unscathed as the unchallenged *vozhd'* (leader) of the Soviet Union and, in the eyes of his countrymen, the sole architect of victory.

State Defense Committee (GKO)

Officially, Stalin exercised virtually unlimited powers throughout the war by serving as chairman of the USSR's State Defense Committee (GKO), which functioned as a virtual war cabinet:

> War required mobilizing all of the nation's strength and resources, employing them in concentrated fashion in the interests of achieving victory in war, centralizing the leadership of the state to a maximum, and concentrating all power in the hands of one all-powerful organ. Under the chairmanship of General Secretary of the Party, I. V. Stalin, the State Committee of Defense (GKO), which was organized on 30 June 1941 by decision of the Communist Party Central Committee, the Presidium of the USSR Supreme Soviet [Council], and the Council of Ministers of the USSR [SNK], was such an organ. The direction of all aspects of national life and the work of all governmental and societal organs were concentrated within the GKO. Its directives on all matters became law.[1]

In addition to its chairman, Stalin, the initial members of this "extraordinary highest state organ of the USSR during the Great Patriotic War, in whose hands absolute power was always concentrated," were People's Commissar for Foreign Affairs V. M. Molotov, who served as its deputy chairman; Marshal of the Soviet Union K. E. Voroshilov, Stalin's crony general, former people's commissar of defense, and future Main Direction commander; L. E. Beriia, the chief of the People's Commissariat of Internal Affairs (NKVD); and G. M. Malenkov, a senior Party leader.[2] Later in the war, Stalin added N. A. Voznesensky, L. M. Kaganovich, and A. I. Mikoian to the committee in 1942 and N. A. Bulganin to the committee in 1944.

Acting collectively, but with Stalin making the final decision on all matters, the GKO directed, supervised, and supported the work of the Council of People's Commissars and its respective commissariats, in particular, the People's Commissariat of Defense (NKO), the *Stavka* of the Supreme High Command, and all other governmental and military organs and institutions involved in the war effort. In addition, each GKO member became a specialist in specific matters "within the sphere of his own competency."[3] The GKO's directives had the "full force of law during wartime, and all State, Party, economic, all-union, and military organs were bound to fulfill GKO decisions and orders unquestionably."[4] After war's end, on 4 September 1945, the Presidium of the USSR's Supreme Soviet disbanded the GKO.

Stavka of the Supreme High Command (SVGK)

The GKO provided strategic direction for the Soviet war effort through the *Stavka,* which was the "highest organ of strategic leadership for the Armed Forces of the USSR during the Great Patriotic War."[5] Formed by the GKO on 23 June 1941 as the *Stavka* of the Main Command (*Stavka Glavnogo Komandovaniia,* or *Stavka* GK), its initial members included Marshal of the Soviet Union S. K. Timoshenko, the people's commissar of defense who served as its chairman; Marshal of the Soviet Union K. E. Voroshilov, former people's commissar of defense; People's Commissar of Foreign Affairs V. M. Molotov; G. K. Zhukov, chief of the Red Army General Staff; Marshal of the Soviet Union S. M. Budenny, Stalin's former cavalry crony from the Civil War years and future main direction commander; N. G. Kuznetsov, people's commissar of the navy and navy commander; and Stalin himself.[6]

The GKO also created a permanent "Institute" of advisers to provide the *Stavka* with necessary counsel. Initially, the members of this "Institute" included Marshal G. I. Kulik, deputy people's commissar of defense and chief of the People's Commissariat of Defense's Main Artillery Directorate; B. M. Shaposhnikov, former and future chief of the Red Army General Staff; K. A. Meretskov, former chief of the Red Army General Staff; P. F. Zhigarev, chief of the People's Commissariat of Defense's Main Air Force (VVS) Directorate; N. F. Vatutin, chief of the Red Army General Staff's Operations Directorate and future *front* commander; N. N. Voronov, chief of the People's Commissariat of Defense's National Air Defense Directorate (PVO Strany) and future chief of Red Army artillery; L. I. Beriia, chief of the NKVD; L. Z. Mekhlis, people's commissar of state control and chief of the Red Army's Main Political Directorate; A. A. Zhdanov, first secretary of the Leningrad Communist Party; and Party leaders A. I. Mikoian, L. M. Kaganovich, and N. A. Vosnesensky.[7]

Within three weeks after Operation Barbarossa began, on 10 July, Stalin reorganized the *Stavka* of the Main Command into the *Stavka* of the High Command (*Stavka Verkhovnogo Komandovaniia,* or *Stavka* VK), with himself as chairman, and added Shaposhnikov as a new member.[8] Later still, on 8 August, Stalin accepted, or more properly accorded himself, the title of supreme high commander of the Soviet Armed Forces and renamed the *Stavka* VK as the *Stavka* of the Supreme High Command (*Stavka* VGK). The composition of the *Stavka* and its "Institute" of advisers changed throughout the war, but at various times included N. A. Bulganin, Party leader and future commissar; General A. I. Antonov, the future chief of the Red Army General Staff; and General and later Marshal of the Soviet Union A. M. Vasilevsky, also a future chief of the Red Army General Staff and deputy commissar of defense.[9]

After receiving strategic guidance from Stalin, the Politburo of the Communist Party's Central Committee, and the GKO and concrete proposals from its representatives in the field and its *front* commanders, the *Stavka* was responsible for making all decisions concerning the planning, preparation, conduct, and support of military campaigns and strategic operations and the creation and employment of strategic reserves.[10] Although the Red Army General Staff, the *Stavka's* principal working organ, prepared all strategic and operational plans for the conduct of specific military campaigns and operations, the *Stavka* coordinated, amended, and approved these plans in close consultation with its representatives and its operating *fronts,* and all involved people's commissariats and the approval of Stalin and the GKO. After these plans were approved, the *Stavka,* its representatives, and its operating *fronts* coordinated, conducted, and provided necessary materiel and logistical support for all military campaigns and operations under the constant direction of Stalin, the Party, and the GKO.

Within these parameters, the *Stavka* directly supervised all of the Red Army's operating and nonoperating *fronts* and military districts, the Soviet Navy (*Voenno-morskoi flot,* or VMF), and long-range aviation, in addition, also created, developed, and directed an extensive partisan movement in German-occupied territories through its Moscow-based Central Headquarters of the Partisan Movement.

The *Stavka* usually maintained close communications with the General Staff and its operating *fronts,* fleets and other naval forces, and long-range aviation by employing normal signal means such as teletype, radio, and land lines, but early in the war it also communicated with its main direction or *front* commanders by means of close personal contact either in Moscow or at the front. For example, it frequently summoned main command, *front,* and fleet commanders to meetings in Moscow, and after mid-1942 it routinely dispatched its representatives to specific *fronts* and fleets to control and coordinate the organization and conduct of operations by groups of *fronts, fronts,* and fleets.

Among the many generals who served as "*Stavka* representatives" throughout the war, the most prominent were G. K. Zhukov, A. M. Vasilevsky, K. E. Voroshilov, S. K. Timoshenko, B. M. Shaposhnikov, A. I. Antonov, A. A. Novikov (for air matters), N. G. Kuznetsov (for naval matters), L. A. Govorov, and N. N. Voronov (for artillery matters). Others, such as L. Z. Mekhlis, whose oversight role was essentially political in nature and for intimidation's sake, served with considerably less distinction.[11]

People's Commissariat of Defense (NKO)

The highest-level military organ at the center of the Soviet state when war began was the People's Commissariat of Defense (NKO), which was headed by the people's commissar of defense and was responsible for the direction and command and control of the entire Soviet Armed Forces, including military districts and separate armies in peacetime plus all *fronts* in wartime.[12] In addition, the NKO was assisted by a political-military consultative organ called the Military Council, which was chaired by the people's commissar of defense, who approved all of its decisions, and consisted of members appointed by the Council of People's Commissars of the USSR.

The NKO itself consisted of central and lesser directorates and other organs including the Main Political Directorate of the Red Army (*Glavnoe politicheskoe upravlenie Krasnoi Armii,* or GlavPU RKKA) (before June 1940 the Political Directorate of the Red Army); the Directorate for Combat Preparation (Training) of the Red Army; the Directorate of the Air Forces of the Red Army; the Directorate of Naval Forces of the Red Army; an Administrative Directorate; the Directorate for Red Army Cadre; a Mobilization Directorate; the Red Army Inspectorate; other directorates, and the Red Army General Staff.[13]

The NKO functioned through not only its organs at the center but also an extensive network of local military organs, including military commissariats and administrations in the Soviet Union's union and autonomous republics, districts *(oblasti),* cities, and regions *(raiony)* throughout the country. Also subordinate to the military councils in each military district, these organs were responsible for performing such NKO missions as pre-induction and conscript training by employing periodic call-ups, military exercises, and the training of militarily obligated reservists.

After the Politburo created the *Stavka* GK on 23 June 1941 and assigned it responsibility for the strategic leadership of the armed forces under the GKO's direct supervision, the NKO, with the people's commissar of defense and his several deputies, and the People's Commissariat of the Navy and the

General Staff served as the *Stavka's* working organs and supported it in a wide variety of functional areas. The first wartime people's commissar of defense was Marshal of the Soviet Union S. K. Timoshenko, who replaced K. E. Voroshilov in May 1940 after the Red Army's debacle in the Soviet-Finnish War. Stalin assumed the post himself in July 1941 and retained it until March 1947, appointing himself as a marshal of the Soviet Union in 1943 and generalissimo of the Soviet Union in 1945.[14]

After war began, the GKO formed several new directorates within the NKO to handle critical functions hitherto performed by the Red Army's central organs (see Chapter 11). For example, on 29 July it converted the Red Army's Cadre Directorate into the NKO's Main Cadre Directorate and assigned it responsibility for selecting, registering, and assigning the Red Army's command cadre.[15] Soon after, on 1 August, it formed a Main Directorate for the Red Army Rear within the NKO to supervise and coordinate the complex matter of providing logistical support for the Red Army's operating *fronts* and armies.[16]

Red Army General Staff (GShKA)

The Red Army General Staff (*General'nyi shtab Krasnoi Armii,* or GShKA), or simply the General Staff, was directly subordinate to the *Stavka* and responsible to Stalin alone for all strategic planning and the direction of all Soviet Armed Forces operating at the front during wartime.[17] When war began, the General Staff consisted of 12 directorates, which were upgraded from departments in 1939, and three separate departments, which, both individually and collectively, were responsible for all matters pertaining to the mobilization, organization, and operations of the armed forces during wartime. These included the Operations, Intelligence, Organizational, Mobilization, Manning and Constructing Forces, Military Communications (Routes), Auto-Road, Organization of the Rear and Supply, Military-Topographical, Organization of the Operational Rear, Construction of Fortified Regions, and Cipher directorates and the General Matters, Cadre, and Military Historical departments.[18]

The GKO spelled out the General Staff's specific wartime responsibilities more precisely in a 10 August directive, which declared that the General Staff was the "central control organ of the NKO for training and employing the armed forces for the defense of the country." Specifically, the directive charged the General Staff with preparing *Stavka* VGK war plans, directives, and orders concerning the operational employment of the armed forces in theaters of military operations, organizing and supervising all intelligence activities, developing air defense (PVO), planning and directing the construction of fortified regions, directing the Red Army's military-topographical service and supplying topographical maps to all forces, supervising operational training in all forces, staffs, services, and rear service organs, organizing and supervising the operational rear of operating armies, collecting, analyzing, and exploiting war experience materials and procedures for its use, organizing and supervising the Red Army's cipher service, and ensuring secrecy in force command and control.[19]

The GKO and NKO reorganized the General Staff's internal structure substantially after war began, primarily to remove from it all organizations not directly associated with the planning and conduct of military operations.[20] After these piecemeal changes during 1941 and early 1942, on 25 April 1942, they reorganized the General Staff into seven directorates, three departments, and a group of General Staff officers on mission to the Red Army's field forces, a structure it retained with few changes to war's end. Under this reorganization, the General Staff consisted of Operations (First), Main Intelligence (Second), and Organizational (Third) directorates, Directorates for the Formation of the Operational Rear and for the Construction of Fortified Regions, Military-Topographical and Cipher directorates, Military-Historical, Cadre, and General Matters departments, and Groups of Officers of the Red Army General Staff.[21]

To supplement the work of special representatives the General Staff was already using to assist *front* commanders and staffs in their operational planning, during 1942 the General Staff also began dispatching small groups of officers directly to the headquarters of its operating *fronts,* armies, and corps for extended periods of time on the basis of two per corps, three per army, and three per operating *front* and even to some divisions. Once assigned, these groups of officers verified the combat situation and conditions within these operating forces, reported back to the General Staff on how well they were fulfilling their assigned combat missions, and assisted these headquarters in coordinating, commanding, and controlling their forces.[22]

As the war progressed, the GKO and NKO assigned the General Staff a wide range of critical tasks not specifically spelled out in its 10 August 1941 charter. These included such operational tasks as planning, organizing, and supervising operational transport (movements) of forces and coordinating the activities of all of the armed force's service commands and their headquarters with the NKO's main and central directorates. In the logistical realm, it coordinated with the NKO, the Red Army's Main Rear Services Directorate, and the Soviet Fleet in the formulation of production requirements of weapons and equipment on the part of Soviet defense industries, presented these requirements to the GKO and *Stavka* for approval and implementation, and maintained close contacts with GOSPLAN (the state production planning organization) and other governmental organs responsible for logistically supporting the Soviet war effort in accordance with the *Stavka's* strategic plans.

In addition, the General Staff was also directly responsible for monitoring the state of Red Army forces, particularly the adequacy of their material support and their combat capabilities, it provided the NKO with guidance on force structuring, and it controlled the formation and training of reserve forces and their timely employment within the context of the *Stavka's* decisions and plans. Finally, at the highest state level, the General Staff prepared proposals, reports, and other materials concerning military issues to be discussed at meetings between heads of state and Allied power conferences, particularly regarding military cooperation between Red Army and Allied forces.[23]

Intellectually but practically as well, one of the most important tasks the General Staff performed during wartime was to collect, analyze, and exploit (generalize) the military experiences of its forces and use that experience to prepare orders, instructions, regulations, and other materials designed to improve the Red Army's combat performance. The General Staff circulated this processed experience throughout the armed forces by means of published studies, informational bulletins, collections of materials *(sborniki materialov)* for the exploitation of war experience, and collections of combat documents and combat examples. This vast amount of processed war experience data also provided the rationale and practical basis for testing and fielding new and more effective types of combat forces and force structures and for developing new operational and tactical combat techniques.[24]

The wartime chiefs of Red Army General Staff were Marshal of the Soviet Union B. M. Shaposhnikov, who replaced Zhukov during July 1941 but resigned due to ill health during May 1942, Colonel General (Army General on 18 January 1943 and Marshal of the Soviet Union on 16 February 1943) A. M. Vasilevsky, who replaced Shaposhnikov in May 1942 and served as chief to February 1945, and Army General A. I. Antonov, who succeeded Vasilevsky and then served as chief until 1946.[25] The chiefs of the critical Operations Directorate included Vasilevsky until April 1942, when he began first deputy chief of the General Staff; his successor, Lieutenant General P. I. Bodin, who was directorate chief from April through December 1942; Antonov until he was appointed first deputy chief of the General Staff during May 1943; and finally, Lieutenant General S. M. Shtemenko, Antonov's deputy, who headed the directorate until war's end.

Central Staff of the Partisan Movement (TsShPD)

When the *Wehrmacht* swept across the western Soviet Union during the first six months of 1941 and once again across the southern Soviet Union during 1942, it left in its wake millions of Red Army soldiers isolated and literally abandoned by the retreating Red Army. The Russians admit that over

2.3 million of these leaderless soldiers fell into captivity or simply went missing in 1941 and another 1.5 million did the same in 1942, but many of those who escaped *Wehrmacht* capture continued resisting the German occupation, forming the nucleus of what would ultimately become a formidable partisan force. Although at first only poorly organized and capable of only symbolic acts of resistance, in time these partisan forces became larger and better organized. Arming themselves with weapons from abandoned Red Army supply dumps or weapons captured from German soldiers, partisan bands were conducting more effective diversionary and sabotage activity against German rear-area facilities and communications routes by early 1942.

In time, thousands of civilians alienated by harsh German occupation policies, which often treated their newly conquered subjects as little more than chattel at best and as subhumans destined to serve their German masters at worse, either joined the partisans' ranks or formed underground resistance cells to resist the German occupation authorities. This partisan and underground activity swelled to include both passive resistance to Nazi rule and armed resistance in the form of sabotage and armed attacks on German rear-area installations by mid-1942.[26]

Stalin and the *Stavka* were slow to appreciate the potential negative impact partisan actions could have on the *Wehrmacht's* ability to wage war. However, the *Stavka* finally took measures, albeit belatedly, during late 1941 and early 1942 to assist partisan activities, supply partisans with more effective weapons, and provide better leadership within and centralized command and control over partisan forces so that they could support the Red Army's combat operations more effectively.[27] The most important step in this process was the GKO's creation of the Central Headquarters of the Partisan Movement (*Tsentral'nyi shtab partizanskogo dvizheniia,* or TsShPD) on 30 March 1942.

Directly subordinate to the *Stavka,* the new headquarters mission was "to establish communications with partisan formations, direct and coordinate their activity, generalize and disseminate the experiences of the partisan struggle, supply partisans with weapons, ammunition, and medicine, train cadre, and facilitate the cooperation of partisan formations with the operating armies."[28] Once formed, the headquarters performed all of these missions in close cooperation with underground Party organizations in the Soviet Union's republics and regions and the military councils of the Red Army operating *fronts* and armies. The first and only chief of the partisan headquarters and partisan movement was Lieutenant General P. K. Ponomarenko, chief of the Belorussian Communist Party.

By October 1942, the TsShPD had been organized into operational, intelligence-informational, political, and supply directorates and separate departments for communications, diversionary weapons and tactics, cadre, ciphers, finance, secrecy (operational security), and administration. To ensure that its operations were well coordinated with those of the Red Army's operating *fronts,* the TsShPD dispatched its special representatives to operating *fronts* to effect close liaison. Conversely, the fronts also often sent senior staff officers from their headquarters to key partisan forces, particularly prior to its offensive operations.[29]

The TsShPD had a checkered history throughout the war, in part because Stalin often questioned the partisans' political reliability and, in part, because he anticipated difficulties in reestablishing Soviet authority over regions where they operated after the Red Army liberated these regions. For example, the GKO disbanded the TsShPD during March 1943, only to reestablish it once again during May. Thereafter, the TsShPD directed the partisan movement and supervised the partisan war until 13 January 1944, when Stalin ordered it abolished once and for all.[30] Throughout its existence, the TsShPD succeeded in creating a more far more effective and reliable partisan movement and thus created an unconventional force that would have a significantly adverse impact on the *Wehrmacht's* military fortunes during 1944.

CONTROL ORGANS

In wartime as in peacetime, one of the most characteristic features of Stalin's dictatorship was the utter dominance and frequent interference of the Communist Party and state security organs in the daily operations of the Red Army and other branches of the armed forces from *front* level down to battalion and even company level. In addition to packing the GKO with Party cronies and maintaining a strong Party representation within the *Stavka,* Stalin actively and often ruthlessly employed several people's commissariats to enforce pervasive Party discipline and ensure absolute loyalty to the state within all levels of the military.

State Security

Stalin assigned the function of ensuring state security within the Soviet Union and its armed forces to several commissariats. First, the People's Commissariat of State Control (Narkom Goskontrolia SSSR), which was formed in 1940 and headed in June 1941 by L. Z. Mekhlis, functioned as a general inspectorate with extraordinary powers to enforce discipline within the Communist Party and state and, when necessary, within the military as well.[31] Second, and even more important, the People's Commissariat of Internal Affairs (NKVD), whose chief in June 1941 was L. P. Beriia, wielded virtually unlimited powers over the entire structure of the Soviet state, including the military. Responsible for "carrying out the organization of local organs of Soviet authority and protecting social order and state security, socialist property, border defense, and registering civil acts," the NKVD's Third Directorate served specifically as a "watchdog" over the military by virtue of the activities of its special departments (see "Military Security" below).[32]

As described in Chapter 4, in addition to its security function, the NKVD also controlled border and internal troops, workers and peasants militias, fire commands, and the penal and work camp system through its Main (Labor) Camp Directorate (*Glavnoe upravlenie lagerei,* or GULAG). Fearful lest too much power fall into Beriia's hands, Stalin deprived the NKVD of a portion of its growing power on 3 February 1941 by ordering it to transfer its state security functions, hitherto performed by its Main Directorate for State Security *(Glavnoe upravlenie gosudarstvennoi bezopasnosti),* to the newly formed People's Commissariat of State Security (*Narodnyi komissariat gosudarstvennoi bezopasnosti,* or NKGB). At the same time, he transferred the NKVD's 3rd Directorate, which controlled the special departments in the military, to the People's Commissariat of Defense. To soften the blow, Stalin appointed Beriia as deputy chairman of the Council of People's Commissars and commissar for general state security. V. N. Merkulov, Beriia's close associate, became commissar of the NKGB, with I. E. Serov as his deputy.[33]

The NKGB and its regional and territorial branches were responsible for state security and counterintelligence operations against enemy agents and enemy intelligence collection from 3 February to 20 July 1941. After the outbreak of war, on 20 July Stalin once again merged the NKGB and NKVD, with Beriia as its commissar and Serov as his deputy. The NKGB reemerged as a separate and full-fledged security and counterintelligence arm in April 1943.[34] Finally, after war's end, Stalin combined the NKGB with the NKVD to form the Ministry of State Security (*Ministerstvo gosudarstvennoi bezopasnosti,* or MGB) during 1946.[35] Within their separate realms, the working organs of the NKGB and NKVD worked closely with the armed forces' special departments and counterintelligence departments throughout the entire war to effectively and often ruthlessly root out disloyalty and enforce state authority in the military, the Party, and the country as a whole.

Political

Two powerful organizations were responsible for maintaining strict Party discipline in the armed forces when war began. The first was the Main Directorate for Political Propaganda in the Red Army (*Glavnoe upravlenie politicheskoi propagandy Krasnoi Armii),* which was headed by A. O. Zaporozhets, and the second was its companion Directorate for Political

Propaganda in the Navy. To make both of them more effective, shortly after the outbreak of war, Stalin reorganized the former into the Main Political Directorate of the Red Army (GlavPU RKKA) on 16 July, with A. S. Shcherbakov, as its head and the latter into the Main Political Directorate of the Fleet (*Glavnoe politicheskoe upravlenie Voenno-Morskogo Flota,* or GlavPU VMF) on 21 July.

Stalin tasked the two new main directorates with responsibility for "directing Party-political and Komsomol (Communist youth) organizations in the army and navy; protecting Party influence on all aspects of soldiers' [and sailors'] lives; working out the most important issues of Party construction, ideological work, and the structure of political organs, Party and Komsomol organizations appropriate to the requirements of war, . . . and implementing resolutions of the Communist Party Central Committee and the GKO and orders of the *Stavka* and NKO."[36] They did so by forming intricate networks of military councils *(sovety)*, other political organs, and Party and Komsomol organizations and committees at virtually every level of command.

At the highest level, the GlavPU RKKA and GlavPU VMF appointed military commissars as "members" of the military councils at main direction headquarters and *front,* fleet, and army headquarters. These members were ostensibly responsible for "helping" commanders and their chiefs of staffs, who were also council members, reach appropriate decisions, but in reality they "checked" the propriety of those decisions. Below *front* level, the two main directorates appointed military commissars or political officers at army, corps, division, regiment, and battalion level and in military schools and other army installations and political workers *(politruki)* in companies, batteries, and squadrons to perform the same functions as the "members" of the *fronts'* military councils.[37]

Officially, military councils *(voennye sovety)* were "collegial organs of the military and political leadership created to discuss and sometimes to decide important questions of military construction, the organization of military operations, command and control, and the training and support of forces."[38] Once established, military councils consisted of a leadership *troika* made up of three commanders (or chiefs in force branches or services), who served as chairmen, "members" of the military councils (or commissars or political workers), who were often the Party secretary of the union republic or *oblast'* Party committee; and chiefs of staff or the first deputy commanders. Collectively, the council members were responsible to the Communist Party Central Committee and the Soviet government for literally everything that occurred within their forces.

Political members of the military councils shared full responsibility with their respective commanders for the condition and combat activities of the troops and assisted the commanders in the formulation of operational plans and orders. In addition to assume responsibility for distinct specific functional areas within the forces to which they were assigned, they managed their own "commissar" chain of command within subordinate headquarters, and they received and dispatched orders, instructions, reports, and messages to both higher and subordinate headquarters by means of a separate communications network controlled and managed by their respective main political directorates in Moscow.

Members of the military councils and the councils as a whole also answered to the Communist Party's Central Committee regarding the political, physical, morale, and disciplinary condition of their troops, troop combat readiness and performance, and Party and political training, and, when necessary, they represented the power and authority of the Soviet state itself. In addition, military councils also provided technical and material support to the troops, supervised the development of the partisan movement in occupied territories, and coordinated partisan and Red Army operations. Ultimately, however, the respective commander issued orders implementing all military council decisions.

In general, the powers and responsibilities of the main political directorates and their military councils at *front* and army level increased steadily throughout the war. For example, as evidence of the GlavPU RKKA's unquestioned authority, Stalin appointed its chief, A. S. Shcherbakov, a candidate member of the Communist Party's Politburo and a full Party secretary in June 1942.[39] In addition, many prestigious party leaders served as members of military councils throughout the war, including such future political leaders of the Soviet Union as N. S. Khrushchev and L. I. Brezhnev.

Although this dual command and commissar (political officer) system was designed to improve decisionmaking and command effectiveness, in reality it functioned as a system of checks and balances designed to guarantee strict Party discipline, reliability, and loyalty to Stalin and the country on the part of all persons serving in the military, officers and soldiers alike. In practice, however, in addition to creating some dissension in the ranks, the commissar system often complicated decisionmaking and led to less effective command and control, particularly below army level.

Within the context of the Red Army's defeat in Operation *Blau* during the summer and fall of 1942, Stalin decided to alter the more onerous aspects of the commissar system to improve command and control in the Red Army and to raise the morale and fighting spirit of its officers and troops. By this time Stalin and the Communist Party had also concluded that the armed forces' command cadre was sufficiently reliable politically and that its military commissars and political workers were experienced enough militarily to dispense with the commissar system and return to the principle of unified command *(edinonachalie)*. Consequently, the Presidium of the Supreme

Soviet of the USSR abolished the military commissar system on 9 October, replacing it with a new system marking the return to the principle of unified command.[40]

After this decision was implemented, commanders alone became responsible for their soldiers' lives and activities, and commissars at all levels of command beneath armies became deputy commanders for political affairs (political units) responsible primarily for their soldiers' morale and welfare.[41] However, although the commissar system was officially abolished in late 1942, the main political directorates never relinquished their tight control over the Red Army.

Judicial

In addition to maintaining strict command and control over the armed forces through the dual but distinct command and political ("commissar") channels, Stalin, the Party, the GKO, and the *Stavka* employed other state, Party, and military organs to ensure their control remained absolute. All of these control organs were an outgrowth and utterly reflective of the Communist totalitarian system they served.

The primary instruments of judicial control were the military prosecutor system, headed by a chief military prosecutor, and an extensive and pervasive network of military tribunals. Ostensibly, the purpose of all institutions and organs in the Soviet military judicial system was "to supervise observance of the rule of law and the struggle with crime."[42] In wartime, however, this included such new missions as "the responsibility to provide the strictest supervision over the exact observance and unconditional fulfillment of wartime laws and to assist the military authorities in the use of forces and means [weapons] for the requirements of defense."[43] In short, within the limits of his authority, the chief military prosecutor had to ensure "social order and state security" and, additionally, "undertake urgent measures for the rebirth of law and order in the territories liberated from the occupiers by the reestablishment of law and order."[44]

The Presidium of the USSR's Supreme Soviet broadened the jurisdiction of its military tribunals and, accordingly, the investigative authority of its military prosecutors as early as 22 June 1941.[45] Henceforth, military prosecutors and their investigators were responsible for "matters of state crime, banditry, premeditated murder and violent liberation of prisoners from confinement and arrest, evasions of military service, unlawful misappropriation of goods and the maintenance of weapons, all aspects of crimes committed by servicemen, and some other matters in regions declared to be in a military situation."[46]

The military prosecutor system and its associated tribunals paralleled the command organization of the Soviet Armed Forces during wartime. As before, the Chief Prosecutor of the USSR, the main military prosecutor, and chief prosecutors of the Red Army and Fleets formed the highest level of the judicial structure. Beneath them were military prosecutors at *front,* army, and corps level, and, in addition, a chief military prosecutor for transport forces appointed during January 1942, whose duties were to supervise the prosecutors within rail transport and mobile construction forces. The lowest level of this judicial system consisted of divisional prosecutors assigned to the field forces and separate prosecutors at aviation bases and in sapper and reserve formations, reserve and training divisions and brigades, and fortified regions. Additionally, the main military prosecutor militarized all prosecutors serving in regions behind the immediate front and in transport regions.

Throughout the war, military prosecutors were responsible for ensuring the absolute fulfillment of all GKO, Council of People's Commissars, NKO, and military orders and directives, conducting preliminary legal (and often extralegal) investigations and inquiries, supervising investigations by counterintelligence organs, and monitoring the work of military tribunals and prisons and disciplinary and penal units.

The military tribunal (court) system, which served this pervasive network of prosecutors, worked under the immediate supervision of respective prosecutors in military districts, *fronts,* fleets, armies, corps, some separate formations, and other military institutions. Normally consisting of three members and sometimes a people's jurist selected from appropriate councils of workers' deputies, the jurisdiction and responsibilities of these tribunals generally corresponded to those of the military prosecutors. For example, military tribunals had the right to award all sentences, including death sentences (euphemistically, "deprivation of life"). However, *front* and army commanders had the right to suspend death sentences if they disagreed with the tribunals' judgment by immediately sending a telegram to either a representative of the Military Collegium of the USSR's Supreme Court or the main military prosecutors of the Red Army and Fleet. In this case, the sentence was carried out only if the responsible governing authority failed to suspend the sentence within 72 hours after receipt of the telegram (see Chapter 13).

Beginning in October 1942, however, officers and soldiers who were convicted of crimes could have their sentence remitted or reversed if they served honorably (and survived) in penal *(shtrafnye)* units. Soviet commanders employed these units and subunits for the most perilous missions in the most dangerous sectors of the front (see Chapter 13).[47]

Military Security (Intelligence and Counterintelligence)

In addition to these state, Party, and judicial organs, Stalin employed two organs controlled at various times by the NKVD, NKO, and General Staff whose functions were normally strictly military in nature to perform a secondary but ultimately vital role in maintaining control, good order, and discipline in the wartime Red Army and armed forces as a whole. These were the Main Intelligence Directorate (GRU) and, later, the Main Directorate for Counterintelligence (GUK and later SMERSH).

The Main Intelligence Directorate (GRU), or Second Directorate, began the war subordinate to the General Staff but was transferred to NKO control on 23 October 1942. After its transfer, the GRU became responsible only for agent operations, and the GKO created a new Directorate for Force Intelligence (*Upravlenie voiskovoi razvedki,* or UVR) in the General Staff, assigning it responsibility for conducting force intelligence (see Chapter 11). However, while the GRU and UVR and their subordinate intelligence departments and sections (*razvedivatel'nye otdely* and *otdelenie,* or ROs) at *front,* army, and division level were primarily responsible for the collection, processing, and analysis of intelligence, they also played a control and intimidation role akin to that played by comparable NKVD and NKO counterintelligence organs, in particular their special departments and counterintelligence departments.[48]

The second of these control organs were the special departments (*osobye otdely,* or OOs), which worked under the NKVD's and NKO's joint control until April 1943, and the counterintelligence departments (*otdely kontrrazvedki,* OKRs), which functioned under the NKO's Main Directorate for Counterintelligence's control from April 1943 until war's end. Formed at every level from *front* through division, in addition to performing their primary function of conducting counterintelligence operations *(kontrrazvedka),* the OKRs proved instrumental in ensuring the maintenance of state and Party control over the Soviet Armed Forces.[49]

During their existence, the OOs were subordinate to the NKO's Third Directorate but under the operational control of the NKVD's Third Directorate and its chiefs, A. N. Mikheev and V. S. Abakumov.[50] Assigned to *fronts* and armies to perform duties similar to the normal intelligence collection and assessment functions of the *fronts'* and armies' ROs, the OOs were responsible for maintaining security within the Red Army's and Navy's forces against German intelligence collection, agent recruiting, and diversionary work. Like the ROs, however, they also suppressed real or perceived disloyalty, discontent, and sabotage by senior officers, officer cadre, or common soldiers within the military.

The GKO formally recognized the increased importance of counterintelligence work on 14 April 1943, by transforming the OOs into OKRs and by subordinating the new OKRs to the NKO's new Main Directorate for Counterintelligence *(Glavnoe upravlenie kontrrazvedki).* Popularly known as SMERSH (*"smert' shpionam,"* or "Death to Spies"), the new directorate was headed by now Commissar of Security Services 2nd Rank Abakumov.[51]

Present at every level of the Red Army from *front* down to division, the influence of SMERSH and its OKRs permeated the military across the entire front, from the shores of the Barents Sea to the Black Sea and throughout the depths of the Soviet Union. While performing routine counterintelligence, SMERSH also investigated frequent charges of sabotage, treason, and malfeasance by Red Army officers and soldiers, particularly those who failed to accomplish their assigned missions, retreated without orders, or surrendered to the enemy.[52] More important still, from the standpoint of Party and state control over the armed forces, the NKVD's and NKO's OOs and SMERSH's OKRs employed repressive measures on a massive scale against the Red Army's officer cadre and soldiers to stifle criticism, dissent, and real or perceived disloyalty. This included the outright repression of at least 35 general officers and a host of lesser figures.[53]

As repressive and pervasive as they were, these state, Party, judicial, and military control organs performed legitimate missions and functions associated with protecting the security and vital interests of the Soviet Union and its Red Army, and did so quite effectively. In the process, however, they also performed the entirely different role of ensuring that the Soviet state remain totalitarian in nature and under Stalin's absolute control. In this sense, these organs were active and effective instruments of a repressive system that transcended the war and employed intimidation, terror, and force liberally, ruthlessly, and efficiently against officers and soldiers alike to achieve Stalin's and the Communist Party's purposes. Just as their wartime activities merely continued the repression of the prewar decades, this repression would not cease at war's end.

PERSONALITIES

Stalin's Cronies

As with all totalitarian states, the capabilities, competence, and character of those who provided strategic military leadership for the Soviet Union's war effort varied considerably. Since the cardinal prerequisite for service in Stalin's strategic leadership was unqualified and proven personal loyalty to the dictator and to the Communist Party and the Soviet state, such qualities as professional military competence and good character were clearly of secondary importance. Understandably, then, those who filled key leadership positions in the vital centers of political and military power in the wartime Soviet Union displayed a curious mixture of these qualities.

Stalin's immediate entourage, specifically, his closest political and military associates and advisers who occupied positions in the Politburo, GKO, *Stavka,* NKO, NVKD, the Red Army's higher commands, and other key organs of power, reflected this reality. From early in the war to war's end,

Stalin relied most heavily on close friends and colleagues who had served him loyally during the Russian Civil War. First and foremost, this group comprised the "cavalry clique," men who had served with or under Stalin while he was serving as political commissar in S. M. Budenny's famous 1st Cavalry Army and had assisted him in the famous defense of Tsaritsyn (later Stalingrad) during 1918 and 1919. In addition to Marshals Budenny, Voroshilov, and Timoshenko, the "cavalry clique" also included more junior officers who entered Stalin's cavalry circle in the post–Civil War years, such as Zhukov, K. K. Rokossovsky, I. Kh. Bagramian, A. I. Eremenko, R. Ia. Malinovsky, P. S. Rybalko, K. S. Moskalenko, and K. A. Meretskov.

Since Stalin's GKO was essentially a political organ, it had only one military member throughout the war. This military man, one of Stalin's most loyal cronies, was Marshal of the Soviet Union Kliment Efremovich Voroshilov, whom one of the dictator's biographers has described as "mediocre, faceless," and "intellectually dim," and a "product of a system which valued obedience, assiduity, ruthlessness, and obsession," particularly during the military purges of the late 1930s.[54] Voroshilov demonstrated his thorough incompetence while serving as people's commissar of defense during the Soviet-Finnish War of 1939–1940. Although Stalin tacitly recognized his incompetence by replacing him with S. K. Timoshenko in May 1940, Voroshilov continued to perform ineptly as a GKO member, commander of the Northwestern Main Direction and Leningrad Front during 1941, and *Stavka* representative on several occasions during 1943 before Stalin finally relegated him to lesser posts for the remainder of the war.

Unlike his appointments to the GKO, Stalin appointed seven military men to serve on his *Stavka* during various periods of the war, including Timoshenko, Voroshilov, Budenny, Zhukov, Vasilevsky, and Antonov from the army and Kuznetsov from the navy, the first four of whom were closely associated with his "cavalry clique." In addition, during the early stages of Operation Barbarossa, on 10 July, Stalin appointed his three most trusted cronies, Voroshilov, Timoshenko, and Budenny, to command his three new strategic main direction commands (see Chapter 12 for their biographies).[55] Because all three men proved their ineptitude commanding large forces during the Red Army's many defeats during 1941 and 1942, Stalin relieved all three of them of their commands and abolished main direction commands.

Stalin generally ceased turning to his old cronies after the summer of 1942, instead relying more heavily on a relatively new generation of military men for strategic and operational advice. In addition to including them in the *Stavka,* he frequently used them as special *Stavka* representatives to plan, direct, and coordinate strategic operations conducted by *fronts* or groups of *fronts*. Among others, this new and generally younger generation of officers included Zhukov, Vasilevsky, and Antonov, who served within as *Stavka* members, Zhukov, Vasilevsky, Novikov, Govorov, Voronov, and others, who served as *Stavka* representatives in the field, and Shaposhnikov, Vasilevsky, and Antonov, who served in the General Staff. All proved far more capable and, hence, more successful than their predecessors.

The *Stavka* and General Staff

After serving in the Red Army's cavalry during the Russian Civil War and the 1920s and 1930s, Georgii Konstantinovich Zhukov earned Stalin's favor by commanding the 57th Special Rifle Corps in its stunning victory over two infantry divisions of the vaunted Japanese Kwantung Army at Khalkhin Gol during August 1939. In recognition of this accomplishment, Stalin elevated this junior member of his "cavalry clique" to command the Kiev Special Military District in June 1940, and to chief of the Red Army General Staff and deputy defense commissar in January 1941.[56]

Stalin appointed Zhukov to the *Stavka* immediately after war began and, during August 1942, elevated him to the twin posts of first deputy commissar of defense and deputy supreme high commander, which he occupied until war's end. Shortly after war began, Zhukov served from 22 to 26 June as *Stavka* representative to the Southwestern Front, where he organized a futile mechanized counterstroke against advancing *Wehrmacht* forces. After commanding the Reserve Front at Smolensk during August and September 1941 and the Leningrad Front from September and October 1941, Zhukov commanded the Western Front from October 1941 through August 1942 and, simultaneously, the Western Main Direction from February through May 1942.

During the first year of the war, Zhukov earned lasting fame for his successful defense of Leningrad during September 1941 and of Moscow during October and November 1941, and for organizing the Moscow counteroffensive and ensuing winter offensive of 1941–42. Although he failed to achieve all of the *Stavka's* campaign objectives, his single-minded but frequently ruthless conduct of operations inflicted an unprecedented defeat on the *Wehrmacht* and spelled doom for Operation Barbarossa. During the summer and fall of the following year, when the *Wehrmacht's* forces were advancing dramatically across southern Russia, Zhukov's Western Front conducted partially successful offensive operations in the Zhizdra and Bolkhov regions during July and August 1942 and in the Rzhev region during August and September, which materially assisted the Red Army's Stalingrad defense.

When the Red Army resumed offensive operations during late November 1942, Zhukov planned and coordinated operations by the Kalinin and Western Fronts against German defenses in the Velikie Luki and Rzhev regions. Although this offensive failed, it so weakened Army Group Center that the Germans abandoned their Rzhev defenses two months later.[57] After organizing operations to crack the Leningrad blockade and being promoted to marshal of the Soviet Union during January 1943, Zhukov planned and directed the aborted Operation Polar Star against Army Group North in February and, as *Stavka* representative, helped plan and conduct the Red Army's victory at Kursk during July and August, its pursuit to the Dnepr River during September, and its struggle to seize bridgeheads over the river during November and December.

Thereafter, Zhukov coordinated the Red Army's victory in the Korsun'-Shevchenkovskii offensive during January 1944, commanded the 1st Ukrainian Front from March to May 1944, and helped coordinate the Red Army's successful Belorussian and L'vov-Sandomierz offensives from late June through September 1944. During this period, his *fronts* won signal victories in the western Ukraine and in Poland. Perhaps because he wished to curb the burgeoning power and fame of his leading *Stavka* representative, Stalin appointed Zhukov to command the 1st Belorussian Front during November 1944, a post Zhukov occupied through June 1945. During this period Zhukov burnished his fame with his spectacular but costly assault on Berlin.[58] In addition to his stints in command or as *Stavka* representative, while serving in his capacity as deputy supreme commander Zhukov also helped plan and conduct many major and minor operations, the most notable being the Stalingrad offensive.

Zhukov was an energetic but stubborn commander who conducted military operations with dogged determination. His sheer force of will, tempered by occasional ruthlessness and utter disregard for casualties, sustained the Red Army during its costly trial by fire during the initial period of war, steeled its defense of Leningrad and Moscow, inspired it as it embarked on its offensive path from late 1942 through 1944, and ultimately helped propel it to victory in 1945. Like the American Civil War general, U. S. Grant, Zhukov understood the terrible nature of modern war and was psychologically prepared to wage it. He demanded and received absolute obedience to his orders, he identified and protected key subordinates, and, at times, he stood up to and incurred Stalin's wrath.

Although there was little finesse in his operations, Zhukov skillfully employed the Red Army as the club it was and to its full operational effect. His temperament was ideally suited to the nature of the warfare on the Soviet-German front, and Stalin knew it. For this reason alone, Stalin and the Red Army emerged victorious, despite immense casualties. Thus, Zhukov's fame as a "Russian" great captain derived, first and foremost, from his reputation as a proven tenacious fighter. This reputation, plus his membership in the "cavalry clique," protected him from criticism for his obvious failures and made him one of Stalin's most trusted generals.

Arguably the most skilled member of the *Stavka* and the second of Stalin's two most trusted generals was Aleksandr Mikhailovich Vasilevsky. An infantryman who did not enjoy the benefits of belonging to the "cavalry clique," Vasilevsky nevertheless rose through merit alone and joined the General Staff after his graduation from the General Staff Academy in the truncated "purge" class of 1937. Rising from the rank of colonel to colonel general in just four years, Vasilevsky was a favorite of Marshal B. M. Shaposhnikov and his heir apparent as chief of the Red Army General Staff.

Largely due to Shaposhnikov's favor, Vasilevsky became deputy chief of the General Staff's Operations Directorate during May 1940, where he was instrumental in developing Soviet defense and mobilization plans during the months preceding the war. After war began, Stalin appointed Vasilevsky as chief of the General Staff's Operations Directorate and deputy chief of the General Staff during August 1941. Thereafter, Vasilevsky replaced Shaposhnikov as chief of the General Staff during June 1942 and, simultaneously, became a deputy people's commissar of defense during October 1942.[59]

While he participated in planning most of the Red Army's most important wartime operations, Vasilevsky also served as *Stavka* representative to operating *fronts* conducting many of these operations. For example, he helped restore the Red Army's defenses west of Moscow after its disastrous encirclements at Viaz'ma and Briansk during October 1941, and, just prior to his appointment as chief of the General Staff, he coordinated the failed Northwestern Front's attempt to overcome *Wehrmacht* defenses in the Demiansk salient during April and May 1942. Although he failed to persuade Stalin not to conduct his ill-fated offensives at Khar'kov and in the Crimea during May 1942, his sage advice probably hastened his appointment to his vital General Staff post.

Vasilevsky was instrumental in formulating the *Stavka's* strategy to thwart the *Wehrmacht's* advance to Stalingrad during the summer and fall of 1942 and was one of the leading architects of the Red Army's offensive in the Stalingrad region during November and December 1942. Appropriately, as *Stavka* representative he supervised the expansion of the successful Stalingrad counteroffensive into a full-fledged winter offensive that collapsed the *Wehrmacht's* defenses in southern Russia and propelled Red Army forces westward to the Dnepr River and into the Donbas.

Having been promoted to the rank of marshal of the Soviet Union during January 1943, during early February 1943 Vasilevsky was so successful in the south that Zhukov was prompted to urge the *Stavka* to conduct a general offensive along the entire German-Soviet front, with Vasilevsky coordinating operations in the south and Zhukov in the north. Despite the ambitious aims of the offensive, which sought to collapse German defenses from Leningrad in the north southward to the Black Sea and propel Red Army forces to Pskov, Vitebsk, and the Dnepr River, it failed in virtually every sector in the face of determined and skillful *Wehrmacht* resistance, leaving Zhukov and Vasilevsky no choice but to stabilize Red Army defenses in the Kursk region during March and April 1943.

With Zhukov, Vasilevsky planned and coordinated the Red Army's defense, counteroffensive, and general offensive in the Kursk region during July and August 1943. Subsequently, while Zhukov coordinated the Red Army's advance on Kiev during September and October 1943, Vasilevsky coordinated operations to clear the *Wehrmacht's* forces from the Donbas region. Once across the Dnepr River in November 1943, Vasilevsky coordinated the 3rd and 4th Ukrainian Fronts' operations in the eastern Ukraine and supervised the liberation of the Crimea, where he was wounded during May 1944. Even while he convalesced, Vasilevsky played a significant role in planning the Red Army's June 1944 Belorussian offensive, during which he coordinated the 1st and 2nd Baltic and 3rd Belorussian Fronts' operations.

After planning and coordinating the Red Army's successful offensive in East Prussia during January and early February 1945, Stalin appointed Vasilevsky as a *Stavka* member during late February, largely in recognition of his long and distinguished service as its representative. Simultaneously, Stalin awarded him with his first wartime field command, the 3rd Belorussian Front, whose previous commander, the talented Colonel General I. D. Cherniakhovsky, had been killed in action on 18 February during the siege of Konigsberg. When Vasilevsky took over *front* command, his deputy and protégé, A. I. Antonov, replaced him as chief of the General Staff.

Vasilevsky reached the pinnacle of his career in July 1945, when Stalin demonstrated his trust in him by appointing him to lead the Soviet Far East Command during the final stages of the war against Japan.[60] His command's subsequent massive, complex, and spectacularly successful Manchurian offensive justified Stalin's trust in Vasilevsky and contributed materially to the Japanese government's decision to surrender unconditionally to the Allies.

Since Vasilevsky's even temperament and keen intellect balanced Zhukov's sheer power and ruthless relentlessness, the two sharply different personalities formed a superb team of effective *Stavka* troubleshooters, representatives, and commanders. As the Soviet Union's premier General Staff officer, no one contributed more than Vasilevsky to the defeat of Nazi Germany and Imperial Japan.[61]

Vasilevsky's patron, Marshal of the Soviet Union Boris Mikhailovich Shaposhnikov, was the "father" of the Red Army General Staff, a skilled General Staff officer, and a preeminent theorist and military historian in his own right. Shaposhnikov was a former tsarist officer who, as one biographer noted, "held to the officer's code of an earlier generation, something not commonly encountered among his peers."[62] As well known for his decency and independence as for his theoretical prowess, Shaposhnikov had been instrumental in creating the post–Civil War Red Army and demonstrated his honesty and candor by clashing with Tukhachevsky over the interpretation of the latter's failed Vistula campaign during 1920. This feistiness, combined with his reputation as a "top-notch military commander unequaled for erudition, professional skill and intellectual development" and his love for cavalry, conditioned his survival and rise to prominence as chief of the Red Army General Staff during the spring of 1937.[63]

Shaposhnikov occupied this vital post with brief interruptions until August 1940, when Stalin appointed him as deputy people's commissar of defense. Shaposhnikov's massive, erudite, and insightful work, *The Brain of the Army,* which he wrote from 1927 to 1929, had contributed materially to the creation of the Red Army General Staff during 1935. Never ideological (he was admitted into the Party in 1939), Shaposhnikov often disagreed with Stalin regarding Soviet defense strategy, including prewar Soviet defense planning, but nevertheless survived, probably because Stalin did not fear the erudite staff officer and, in fact, respected his nonthreatening demeanor. Underscoring Shaposhnikov's strange relationship with Stalin, he was one of the few whom Stalin addressed by his *imia i otchestvo* (given name and patronymic).

After relieving him as chief of the General Staff during early 1940, ostensibly because of his association with the Red Army debacle in the Soviet-Finnish War, Stalin appointed Shaposhnikov as chief of the General Staff once again during July 1941. Thereafter, until his replacement for health reasons in May 1942, Shaposhnikov served as architect of the newly organized General Staff that helped produce wartime victory. During wartime he proved to be a moderating influence on Stalin, and, although he was associated with the Kiev disaster of September 1941, his influence ultimately prompted Stalin to defer more to General Staff advice on the war effort. More important still, Shaposhnikov was instrumental in the rapid rise of Vasilevsky, Antonov, and Vatutin to leading positions in the Red Army.

Unlike Vasilevsky, who already occupied a vital staff position when war began, Aleksei Innokentievich Antonov, the most dominant and influential figure in the wartime General Staff, began the war in relative obscurity. A veteran of the World and Civil wars, Antonov remained relatively undistinguished until he was recognized as "an excellent operations staff worker" while attending several Frunze Academy courses during the early 1930s.[64] His superb performance as chief of the Khar'kov Military District's Operations Department during the 1935 Kiev maneuvers earned Antonov praise by Defense Commissar Voroshilov and appointment to the General Staff Academy. After graduating in the class of 1937, Antonov briefly served as chief of staff of the Moscow Military District when it was commanded by Stalin's favorite, Marshal Budenny, and was then posted to the Frunze Academy to replace purged faculty members.

Promoted to major general during June 1940 (along with Vasilevsky and many others), during the wholesale command changes of January 1941, Antonov replaced Lieutenant General G. K. Malandin as deputy chief of staff of the Kiev Special Military District, where Antonov was serving when war began. After Antonov participated in the ignominious Red Army defeats around Kiev during the summer of 1941 and at Khar'kov during May 1942, Vasilevsky brought Antonov to the General Staff during December 1942, where he served simultaneously as chief of the Operations Directorate and first deputy chief of the General Staff. After relinquishing his Operations Directorate post to S. M. Shtemenko in May 1943, Antonov served as first deputy chief of the General Staff until February 1945, when he replaced Vasilevsky as its full chief.[65]

During his tenure on the General Staff, Antonov took part in planning and supervising every major operation the Red Army conducted after December 1942 and, as a reward for his excellent service, was appointed a member of the *Stavka* along with Vasilevsky during February 1945. He also served at Stalin's side while attending most major conferences of Allied powers, including the Yalta and Potsdam conferences during February and July–August 1945. Antonov's exemplary professional skill and sound strategic judgment earned Stalin's respect and the respect of all those who worked with or for him. In addition, foreigners who met with him agreed with U.S. President Truman's assessment that he was "a highly efficient staff officer and administrator."[66]

The only airman in this *Stavka* group, Aleksandr Aleksandrovich Novikov was the Soviet Union's most distinguished wartime senior air force commander.[67] A veteran of the Russian Civil War, Novikov graduated from the Vystrel Infantry School in 1922 and the Frunze Academy in 1927. While attending the Frunze Academy, Novikov studied strategy under Marshal M. N. Tukhachevsky and operational art under V. K. Triandafillov and became imbued with the twin concepts of deep battle and the deep operation conducted by massed armor, air, artillery, and airborne troops. After serving in the Belorussian Military District under the tutelage of its commander, I. P. Uborovich, Novikov transferred to Red Army aviation and received flight training.

Soon after being promoted to the rank of colonel in 1936, however, Novikov was dismissed from service and arrested, supposedly because of his association with the purged Uborovich and others. Miraculously, Novikov emerged from the incident unscathed and survived to serve as chief of staff and then commander of the Leningrad Military District's air forces, where he was serving when Operation Barbarossa began.

Novikov commanded the air forces of the Northern Front and Northwestern Main Direction during July 1941 and those of the Leningrad Front during the perilous defense of Leningrad during August and September 1941. Despite the obvious ineptitude of Marshal Voroshilov, his commander during this period, Antonov performed so well that Voroshilov's successor, Zhukov, took special note of his talent and outstanding performance. In recognition of Antonov's contributions to the successful defense of Leningrad, Zhukov selected Novikov as first deputy commander of his Western Front during February 1942 and tasked him with reorganizing and rebuilding the Western Front's air forces.

Soon, Stalin, too, began recognizing Novikov's aptitude for command by appointing him as a *Stavka* representative to supervise Red Army operations around Leningrad and Demiansk during March and April 1942. Thereafter, Stalin promoted Novikov to the rank of lieutenant general of aviation forces during April 1942 and assigned him to command of the Red Army's Air Force (VVS), a post he retained until war's end. While serving in this capacity and also as deputy commissar of defense for aviation during 1942 and 1943, Novikov supervised the transformation of hitherto fragmented Red Army *front* and army aviation into a powerful new tool capable of effectively supporting modern military operations.

During his tenure as air force chief, Novikov fashioned the modern air army structure and supporting reserve aviation armies and oversaw the development and fielding of an entire new generation of modern aircraft. Simultaneously, he also served as *Stavka* representative in many major operations, including the Battle of Stalingrad, Operation Polar Star, the Battle of Kursk, and the Smolensk offensive during 1943, the Korsun'-Shevchenkovskii offensive, operations in the Ukraine and Karelia, and the Belorussian offensive during 1944, and the Vistula-Oder offensive and the Battle for Berlin during 1945. To cap his wartime career, Novikov served as Marshal Vasilevsky's air commander in the Far Eastern High Command during its Manchurian offensive in August and September 1945.

Within a year after the war ended, Novikov was caught up in L. I. Beriia's "purge of the victors." Arrested along with many of the most competent senior Red Army commanders, Novikov was subjected to unspeakable physical and psychological cruelties at the hands of Beriia's henchman, V. S. Abakumov. After six years in Stalin's prisons, Novikov was released and rehabilitated during 1953, only months after Stalin's death. Novikov had performed superbly as the Red Army's Air Force commander, but like many of his illustrious colleagues of the 1930s, he also suffered dearly for his competency.[68]

The *Stavka's* premier artillery specialist, Nikolai Nikolaevich Voronov, was the artillery's equivalent of the airman Novikov. His rise to fame in the artillery and the *Stavka's* frequent reliance on him as one of its representatives during major military operations underscored both Voronov's own skills and expertise as an artilleryman and the high regard Stalin and the Red Army's senior leadership had for the importance of artillery as a vital element of the combined-arms team.[69]

A Red Army member since 1918 and veteran of the Russian Civil War, Voronov graduated from the Higher Artillery Command School in 1924 and the Frunze Academy in 1930. During the 1920s he commanded artillery batteries and battalions, finally rising to command the Moscow Proletarian Rifle Division's artillery regiment. After Voronov had served as the division's chief of artillery during 1933 and 1934, the NKO posted him to the Leningrad Military District, where he served as chief and military commissar of the Leningrad Artillery School.

When the Spanish Civil War broke out, the Soviet government sent Voronov to Spain, where he served as adviser to the Republican government's forces during 1936 and 1937. Since Voronov was equipped with fresh war experiences but unblemished by the dangerous political entanglements associated with his assignment, Stalin appointed him as chief of Red Army Artillery during 1937, a post that he held until 1940.

As artillery chief, Voronov supervised the reorganization and technical re-equipping of the Red Army's artillery forces during its stormy period of pre–World War II expansion. In close cooperation with Zhukov, he also participated in the August 1939 battles against Japanese forces at Khalkhin Gol, where he amassed extensive experience in the planning and employment of artillery on an army group scale. During late 1939 and 1940, he performed the same function for Red Army forces when they invaded eastern Poland and Bessarabia, and during the Soviet-Finnish War he directed artillery operations during the penetration of the Finns' powerful Mannerheim Defense Line. After the war ended, the NKO appointed Voronov deputy chief of the Red Army's Main Artillery Directorate, where he was serving when Operation Barbarossa began.

Shortly after war broke out, the *Stavka* appointed Voronov to the two most prestigious artillery positions in the Red Army, chief of the Main Directorate of National Air Defense (PVO Strany) in late June, and chief of Red Army Artillery in July. At the same time, Voronov became a deputy commissar of defense of the USSR and a member of the *Stavka's* advisory board. Subsequently, he served as commander of Red Army Artillery continuously from March 1943 through March 1950. During this period he was instrumental in developing the theoretical and practical basis for the employment of artillery in large-scale combat operations, specifically, concepts for conducting the artillery offensive and systematic antitank warfare. At the same time, he supervised the creation of large artillery formations such as artillery divisions and corps and was responsible for the development of

RVGK artillery as the key component for conducting penetration operations and operational exploitations.

In addition to his strictly artillery role, Voronov served extensively as *Stavka* representative in many operations both as senior artillery adviser and as a combined-arms coordinator. As such, he helped plan and coordinate operations by the Leningrad, Volkhov, Southwestern, Don, Voronezh, Briansk, Northwestern, Western, Kalinin, 3rd Ukrainian, and 1st Belorussian Fronts, including the Stalingrad offensive, the liquidation of the German Sixth Army at Stalingrad, and the Orel offensive during July and August 1943, and he supervised the employment of artillery in the Belorussian and Berlin offensives during 1944 and 1945.

Although far less well known than his illustrious colleagues, Leonid Aleksandrovich Govorov established a substantial record both as a *Stavka* representative and as a *front* commander, primarily in the northwestern theater of military operations. A veteran of the World and Civil wars and an artilleryman like Voronov, Govorov graduated from the Red Army's Artillery Course in 1927, the Higher Academy Course in 1930, the Frunze Academy in 1933, and the General Staff Academy in 1938, where he was a member of the first full class to graduate after the beginning of the military purges. During the 1920s and 1930s, Govorov commanded an artillery battalion, the famous 51st Perekop Rifle Division's artillery regiment, the artillery assigned to a fortified region, and the 14th and 15th Rifle Corps' artillery.[70]

Govorov began his long relationship with the northwestern theater of operations by serving as chief of staff of the 7th Army's artillery during the Soviet-Finnish War, where his superiors, particularly Voronov, praised him for the instrumental role he played in penetrating the Mannerheim Defense Line. After war's end in early 1940, he served as deputy inspector general of Red Army artillery and chief of artillery at the Red Army's Dzerzhinsky Political Academy, earning promotion to the rank of major general of artillery.

During Operation Barbarossa, Govorov commanded the Western Main Direction's artillery during the chaotic initial period of the war and the Reserve Front's artillery during its victory at El'nia in September and its subsequent tragic encirclement and destruction at Viaz'ma in October. After he miraculously survived this ordeal, and in recognition of his role in the El'nia victory, the *Stavka* appointed him as deputy commander of the important Mozhaisk Defense Zone in mid-October and the Western Front's 5th Army in late October 1941, which he led with distinction throughout the Battle for Moscow. Based on his success at Moscow, the *Stavka* dispatched him to Leningrad in April 1942, first to command the Leningrad Front's groups of forces and, in June 1942, the full Leningrad Front, which he successfully commanded to war's end.

During his tenure as Leningrad Front commander, Govorov planned and conducted the January 1943 Siniavino offensive, which partially lifted the German blockade, and participated in Zhukov's unsuccessful Operation Polar Star in February. Thereafter, he planned and coordinated all subsequent multi-*front* operations in the Leningrad region, including the Leningrad-Novgorod offensive during January 1944, which drove *Wehrmacht* forces from the Leningrad region, the Vyborg and Karelian offensives during June and July 1944, which drove Finnish forces away from Leningrad, and operations to expel *Wehrmacht* forces from the Baltic region and Courland during late 1944 and 1945.

Stalin chose Govorov as a *front* commander and *Stavka* representative because of his consistently sound judgment and remarkable skill as a planner and a motivator of his troops. A colleague in the General Staff noted, "[H]e enjoyed great and well-deserved prestige among the troops. . . . Govorov was too reticent and somber to make a very favorable impression on first acquaintance, but all those who had served under him knew that a generous and kindly Russian character was hidden beneath this grim exterior."[71] Govorov was one of only 11 Red Army generals awarded the USSR's highest military order, the Order of Victory.[72]

The sole *Stavka* member and representative from the Soviet Navy was Nikolai Gerasimovich Kuznetsov, who began his service during the Russian Civil War as a sailor in the Northern Dvina Flotilla in the Arkhangel'sk region. Commissioned as a naval officer during 1926, his first command assignment was on board the cruiser *Chervona Ukraina* (Red Ukraine) in the Black Sea Fleet. After studying at the Leningrad Naval Academy from 1929 through 1932, he served once again in the Black Sea Fleet and commanded the *Chervona Ukraina* during 1935, when his ship was awarded the designation "best ship in the navy."

This feat and the attrition among naval officers during the military purges launched Kuznetsov on a meteoric career. After serving as military attaché to the Spanish Republican government during 1937, Kuznetsov became first deputy commander of the Pacific Fleet in August 1937, and, after purging its commander, Kireev, Stalin appointed Kuznetsov to command the entire fleet in November 1938. Thereafter, Stalin appointed Kuznetsov as first deputy commander-in-chief of the navy in February 1939 and, at the age of 36, to commander-in-chief and people's commissar of the navy in April 1939, posts he occupied continuously until 1946. In accordance with those responsibilities, Stalin promoted Kuznetsov to the rank of admiral in June 1941.[73]

During the war, Kuznetsov directed all Soviet fleet operations, served as *Stavka* representative during the seizure of Bulgaria in September 1944 and the Manchurian offensive in August 1945, and participated in the Yalta and Potsdam conferences in 1945. However, he also frequently provoked controversies that threatened to end his career. Although an extremely competent commander in the Soviet Armed Forces' junior service, the strong-willed Kuznetsov constantly defended naval interests against those of the army. This brought him into direct conflict with several leading Red Army generals, the shipbuilding commissariat, and even Stalin himself. For example, on the eve of Operation Barbarossa, in direct violation of Stalin's orders, Kuznetsov ordered the Baltic and Black Sea fleets to take precautionary measures against a surprise German invasion. Although these actions saved the two fleets, Stalin rebuked Kuznetsov but still included him in his newly created *Stavka.*

Kuznetsov proved to be an extremely effective leader throughout the war. Unlike the situation that prevailed in the Red Army, where many generals were cashiered or shot for incompetence or worse, Kuznetsov selected most of his subordinates well, and those that he selected served with him until war's end.[74]

Kuznetsov's bluntness and candor with superiors and colleagues alike finally caught up with him after war's end. Perhaps in delayed retribution, Stalin arrested Kuznetsov and several of his associates during 1946 on the trumped up charge of passing Soviet military secrets to the British. Many of his colleagues received long prison sentences, and Kuznetsov was dismissed from the service and demoted to the rank of rear admiral. Like Novikov, however, he was rehabilitated after Stalin's death, only to be dismissed and retired in 1956 at age 51 after running afoul of Khrushchev.

Predators and Watchdogs

Among the many men who served Stalin as *Stavka* members or representatives and leaders of other key Party or state control organs were those whose cunning, ruthlessness, and outright cruelty ideally suited them to serve as predators and watchdogs for a tyrant ruling a thoroughly totalitarian state. The very existence of these men acted as the "glue" that held the regime together and preserved autocracy during trying wartime conditions. These predators and watchdogs produced and sustained the intimidating sense of fear necessary to maintain strict Party and state discipline and loyalty, even though that fear often inhibited the war effort.

No man characterized this class of men better than Lev Zakharovich Mekhlis, who earned a well-deserved reputation as a scourge of Stalin's generals. Mekhlis was conscripted into the tsarist Army in 1911 and served as an artilleryman during the First World War. After joining the Red Army during the Russian Civil War, he served in the Ukraine, primarily as a military commissar at the brigade and division level, where he developed a close working relationship with Stalin. After war's end, Mekhlis began his long career as a Party activist in the army, ultimately rising to the rank of colonel general in

1944. A 1930 graduate of the Institute of Red Professors, he was a member of the Communist Party's Department of Writers (propagandists) and, simultaneously, a member of the editorial board of the Party newspaper, *Pravda.*

Mekhlis served as chief of the Red Army's powerful Main Political Directorate, as army commissar 1st rank from 1937 through 1940. During this period he and his directorate were directly responsible for conducting the military purges in the Red Army, a task that Mekhlis performed with characteristic efficiency and ruthlessness. After serving as people's commissar of state control of the USSR during 1940 and 1941, completing Stalin's purge of the military, he was appointed once again by the dictator as chief of the Red Army's Main Political Directorate and, in addition, deputy people's commissar of defense, a position he used to continue his role as political watchdog over the Soviet officer's corps.[75]

Mekhlis served as *Stavka* representative and Stalin's personnel envoy to many *fronts* throughout the duration of the war, always displaying his complete military incompetence in the process. For example, while serving as *Stavka* representative to the Crimean Front during May 1942, he presided over the *front's* catastrophic defeat in spring 1942. Even though Stalin recalled, reprimanded, and relieved him from his posts as *Stavka* representative and chief of the Main Political Directorate, he continued to employ Mekhlis as his chief political intimidator.

Despite his role in the Crimean debacle, Mekhlis continued to serve Stalin from July 1942 to war's end as commissar of the 6th Army and, later, as commissar in the Voronezh, Volkhov, Briansk, 2nd Baltic, Western, 2nd Belorussian, and 4th Ukrainian Fronts. Mekhlis' survival and prolonged career proved that his absolute and unquestioned loyalty to Stalin and ruthless effectiveness in rooting out real or potential threats to Stalin's rule and authority more than outweighed his clear military incompetence. In short, his mere presence produced an obedient and subservient Red Army officer corps. Even though Stalin reinstated Mekhlis to the post of people's commissar of state control after war's end, Mekhlis died in mysterious circumstances shortly before his master, three years after Stalin removed him from all of his official posts in 1950, suggesting that Mekhlis finally became too dangerous even for his master.

Although few senior Red Army commanders felt confident or secure enough to criticize Mekhlis, certainly during the war and even during the immediate postwar years, this situation changed abruptly after Stalin's death. Zhukov had few kind words about him in his memoirs, and Shtemenko later caustically wrote:

> His reports often passed through my hands and always left a bitter aftertaste; they were as black as night. Taking advantage of the great powers that had been granted to him, he would dismiss dozens of people from

> positions of command and at once replace them with people he had brought with him. He demanded that Division Commander Vinogradov be shot for losing control of his division [in 9th Army during the Finnish War]. Later on, I came into contact with Mekhlis more than once and formed the conclusion that this man was always predisposed to adopt the most extreme measures.[76]

The fact that Shtemenko could address this and other instances of Mekhlis's machinations so candidly at a time when Soviet censorship was still severe underscored the scorn and unbridled hatred many Red Army commanders harbored toward their tormentors such as Mekhlis. It also attested to Mekhlis's effectiveness as Stalin's watchdog over the Red Army.

Just as Mekhlis and his ilk ruthlessly rooted out officers' suspected disloyalty to Stalin, Aleksandr Sergeevich Shcherbakov enforced Party discipline with equal vigor after he replaced Mekhlis as chief of the Red Army's Main Political Directorate during May 1942. Like Mekhlis, Shcherbakov began his long career as Party leader and political officer during the Russian Civil War, when he served in the Red Guards, organized workers in the city of Rybinsk, and fought in combat in Iaroslavl' province *(guberniia).* After joining the Communist Party in 1918, Shcherbakov worked in Komsomol and Party organizations in Turkestan, studied at Sverdlov Communist University from 1921 to 1924, served as secretary of the Regional Communist Party Committee in Nizhegorod province, where he also edited the provincial Party newspaper from 1924 to 1930, and attended the Institute of Red Professors from 1930 to 1932.

Rising precipitously through the Party's ranks from 1937 through 1940, Shcherbakov served as first secretary of Party committees in the Leningrad, Irkutsk, and Donetsk regions and, finally, as first secretary of the Moscow Party Committee during 1941. He reached the pinnacle of his power in June 1941, when Stalin appointed him chief of the Red Army's Main Political Directorate to replace Mekhlis, and also deputy people's commissar of defense and chief of the SOVINFORMBURO (Soviet Information Bureau), the Party's premier propaganda organ.

Shcherbakov's official biography states that, while playing a significant role in the defense of Moscow during late 1941, he "accomplished immense work in implementing the resolutions of the Communist Party Central Committee and the GKO and the orders of the *Stavka* and the NKO concerning the mobilization of Soviet soldiers for the selfless struggle with the enemy and destruction of the German-fascist invaders."[77] Shtemenko added:

> Shcherbakov handled the SOVINFORMBURO, a very large and troublesome organization. I often had dealings with him, and, every time, I found myself wondering how this very sick man could cope with such an enormous

> amount of work, where he found the energy, and how he managed at the same time to be so humane and considerate in his relations with the people around him. . . .
>
> Principled, energetic, and very strict about work, Shcherbakov was at the same time an unaffected and warm-hearted person. . . . But his days were numbered. He died on May 10, 1945, at the age of 44. His death was illuminated by the dawn of our great victory, for which he had given so much of his strength and health.[78]

Shtemenko failed to note, however, that, together with other state, Party, judicial, and military control organs, Shcherbakov's directorate also led the struggle to maintain Party purity in the Red Army and to ensure Stalin's total control over its officer corps and rank-and-file soldiers. Thus, Shcherbakov and his directorate remained an important instrument of what was, in essence, a permanent purge.

One of the Stalin's most sinister predators and watchdogs was Viktor Sergeevich Abakumov, an NKVD leader who served as the wartime head of the People's Commissariat of Defense's Main Directorate for Counterintelligence (SMERSH).[79] Abakumov, whose still shadowy career paralleled that of his NKVD mentor, L. P. Beriia, was the most notorious of Beriia's creatures. Beginning his career as a common "blue collar" worker in Moscow before 1925, Abakumov rose steadily through the ranks of the factory workers' protection services and the Komsomol organization and become an operative in the NKVD's State Political Directorate (OGPU) during 1933, where he provided technical support for security service operations.

Impressed by the young Chekist's work in the NKVD's labor camp (GULAG) directorate during 1935 and 1936, Beriia appointed Abakumov as a branch chief in the NKVD's Security Department in 1937. After Beriia replaced N. I. Ezhov as people's commissar of internal affairs in 1938, the following year he appointed Abakumov as NKVD chief in the Rostov region with the rank of NKVD captain. Abakumov excelled in his new duties. In reward for Abakumov's effective completion of Beriia's purges in the Rostov region, Beriia promoted him to the rank of major in 1940 and appointed him as deputy people's commissar for internal affairs in February 1941, with the responsibility for raising and organizing people's militia and fire protection forces.[80]

Three months after war began, when A. N. Mikheev, chief of the Red Army's Special Departments (OOs), was killed in the fighting around Kiev during September 1941, Beriia appointed Abakumov, with Stalin's approval, as chief of the OOs and also as deputy commissar of defense. Finally, when the GKO transformed the OOs into OKRs under the NKO's Main Directorate for Counterintelligence (SMERSH) in April 1943, Stalin appointed Abakumov as chief of SMERSH, with I. I. Moskalenko as his deputy.[81] Abakumov excelled in both posts. In addition to performing its statutory counterintelligence functions, Abakumov's new organization and its subordinate OKRs in the Red Army's *fronts* and armies ensured Party and state control over the military and quelled any and all suspected dissent and sabotage by continuing, in essence, a permanent purge of the Soviet officer corps with characteristic ruthlessness.

SMERSH's infamous work included identifying and prosecuting Red Army generals and other officers associated with General A. A. Vlasov, capturing and executing Vlasov and his accomplices, prosecuting other senior Red Army officers who surrendered to the Germans or displayed other examples of "malfeasance" in combat, and massively repressing the officer corps as a whole, generally on trumped up charges. Senior officers caught up in Abakumov's web during the war included at least 35 generals, all charged with treason, most groundlessly.[82] At one point, Abakumov also began pursuing Zhukov relentlessly because he believed he had become a replica of the infamous Tukhachevsky and a danger to Stalin and the Soviet state. However, Zhukov managed to elude Abakumov's grasp, although his former chief of staff, General V. S. Golushkovich, fell victim to the grand inquisitor.

Nor did Abakumov cease his grisly work after war's end. For example, during late 1945 and 1946 Abakumov and his accomplices investigated, arrested, tried, and convicted a host of former Red Army generals who had just been released from German prisoner-of-war camps and another group of serving generals whom Abakumov considered a potential threat to Stalin's leadership.[83] The latter included Chief Marshal of Aviation A. A. Novikov, through whom Abakumov also hoped to get at Zhukov. Between 1941 and 1952, a total of 101 generals and admirals fell victim to Abakumov's repression.

In May 1946 Stalin appointed Abakumov, then a colonel general, to head the newly formed Ministry of State Security (MGB), which combined the former NKGB and NKVD, in place of the infamous V. S. Merkulov, one of Beriia's most reliable henchmen. Abakumov quickly staffed the new ministry with his many of his creatures from SMERSH and dramatically increased the security organization's power. Abakumov's actions also raised concerns on Beriia's part that the new ministry actually posed a genuine threat to his power.[84]

However, powerful men often make equally powerful enemies, and, in this respect, Abakumov was no exception. After alienating both Beriia and Serov, the chief of the Ministry of Internal Affairs (MVD), the two persuaded Stalin to arrest and execute Abakumov as an enemy to the state, and he was tried, found guilty, and executed during December 1954. In the end, the very same permanent purge that he unleashed also consumed Abakumov, who by this time had earned the questionable honor of being Stalin's longest-serving security watchdog.[85]

Hundreds of other notorious but shadowy figures, whose stories are only now emerging from obscurity, occupied key positions in Stalin's political, state, judicial, and military control organs. Chief among these were three men, I. E. Serov, V. S. Merkulov, and V. V. Ul'rich, who personified this class of predators. During his checkered career, I. E. Serov occupied the posts of deputy chief and chief of the NKVD's militia, NKVD chief in the Ukraine, deputy commissar and 1st deputy commissar of the NKGB/NKVD, deputy minister and minister of the NKVD/MVD, first chief of the postwar KGB, and chief of the GRU.[86] While serving as a virtual *Stavka* representative for the NKVD during the war, Serov was involved in deporting the Volga Germans in August 1941, assisting in the organization of the Moscow defense in October and November 1941, the "de-Islamization" of the Trans-Caucasus region during 1943 and 1944, a program that included the famous forced mass deportation of the Chechen and Kalmyk peoples, and the "Sovietization" of Poland during 1944 and 1945.

After war's end, Serov was responsible for "processing" Soviet citizens interned in German labor camps and crushing German resistance to Soviet rule. During the spring of 1946, now a colonel general, Serov returned to Moscow, where he served as deputy and then first deputy minister of the MVD and, after Stalin's death, as deputy MVD minister. After helping suppress the East German uprising during 1953, Serov became first head of the new independent KGB, only to be replaced by A. N. Shelepin in 1958, after which he became head of the GRU. Serov, whose career went into sharp decline after 1960, died in July 1990.

V. S. Merkulov served as people's commissar of the newly formed NKGB during 1941 and as the first wartime deputy to NKVD chief Beriia. His subsequent career in the security services included service as *Stavka* representative for the NKGB in the Leningrad region during the dangerous summer of 1941 and participation in the "de-Islamization" of the Trans-Caucasus region during 1943 and 1944. As a reward for his valuable services, Stalin promoted Merkulov to the rank of army general in 1945, to the post of chief minister of the MGB in 1946, and, soon after, to the position of chairman of the Council of Ministers. Ultimately, Merkulov's star also began to fade because Beriia was suspicions of him as well. However, after Abakumov replaced him as MGB chief in May 1946, Merkulov replaced Mekhlis as minister of state control in October of the same year.[87]

V. V. Ul'rikh, who served as the chairman of the Military Collegium of the USSR Supreme Soviet, the organization that served as Stalin's "chief instrument of legal terror" during the war, was also the organizer of the infamous Katyn massacre of former Polish officers during the summer of 1941. Although little more is known about his career, an expert on the Soviet security services and their role in the permanent purge notes, "During the first two years of the war, the military courts of the Red Army passed more than 150,000 death sentences, a far higher number than the NKVD."[88]

I. V. Stalin

G. K. Zhukov

A. M. Vasilevsky

B. M. Shaposhnikov

A. I. Antonov

A. A. Novikov

N. N. Voronov (center)

L. A. Govorov

N. G. Kuznetsov

L. Z. Mekhlis

CHAPTER 11

Central Military Administration

PEOPLE'S COMMISSARIAT OF DEFENSE (NKO)

The principal working organs of the People's Commissariat of Defense (NKO) were its main and central directorates, commonly referred to as the "Center," which performed specific functions necessary for the Red Army to wage war, and branch main directorates, which served the commanders of specific Red Army branches, such as the artillery, air forces, armored (tank) and mechanized forces, and engineers, most of which were formed during the first six months of the war (see Table 11.1). The commanders of force branches supervised all matters related to their branches through their directorates and in close coordination with the chiefs of other main and central directorates, subdirectorates, and departments. In addition, the State Defense Committee (GKO) established the position of deputy supreme commander of the Soviet Armed Forces in August 1942 to assist Stalin and help coordinate the work of the branch chiefs with the *Stavka* and General Staff and appointed Zhukov to that prestigious post.

Together with the General Staff's directorates and departments, the NKO's main and central directorates functioned individually and collectively as the *Stavka's* principal working organs. During the war the NKO included branch-specific directorates for artillery, armor-mechanized, engineer, airborne, air force, and national air defense (PVO Strany) forces and functional directorates for mobilization, force manning, cadres, military education and training, signal communications, military communications routes (rail, road, riverine, and air), rear service support (quartermaster, medical, and veterinary), and, most important of all, for political affairs, intelligence, and counterintelligence.

As their designations indicated, the primary wartime missions of the NKO's main and central directorates were to support the Red Army and its force branches in terms of mobilization, force manning, military education and training, testing and fielding weaponry and other equipment, development of operational and tactical techniques, and other specific force branch activities, and in terms of such vital functional areas as communications, force movements, intelligence, counterintelligence, and logistics.[1]

Headed by chiefs and several deputies who supervised their work, the NKO's main and central directorates consisted of elaborate networks of subdirectorates and departments, base facilities, and military-scientific (research) organizations, and, in the case of many, military academies and schools responsible for educating and training branch-specific officer and staff cadre, noncommissioned officers, and soldier specialists. Many of these main and central directorates worked through corresponding directorates and departments within the Red Army's operating *fronts* and armies.[2] In addition, the NKO's main or central directorates associated with such critical war-fighting functions such as operations, intelligence, and counterintelligence also worked under the close supervision of the General Staff.

Artillery

Driven by necessity, the NKO attempted to improve the combat performance of the Red Army's artillery, armor, engineer, and signal forces during the first few months of the war, first and foremost, by appointing commanders to lead these forces and supervise their respective NKO directorates. It began this effort on 19 July 1941 by reestablishing the position of chief of Red Army artillery, which it had abolished in 1940, and appointing Colonel General of Artillery N. N. Voronov to this post.[3] Voronov had served as chief of Red Army artillery from 1937 to 1940, and when Stalin abolished this position in the wake of the Soviet-Finnish War, Voronov served as deputy to Marshal G. I. Kulik, chief of the NKO's Main Artillery Directorate, and was promoted to colonel general of artillery in 1941. Stalin appointed Voronov as chief of the Main Directorate for National Air Defense (PVO Strany) soon after war began and as chief of Red Army artillery on 19 July.

Voronov's principal operating organ was the NKO's Main Artillery Directorate (GAU), one of the oldest directorates in the Red Army, which was headed by Lieutenant General N. D. Iakovlev, who replaced its incompetent former chief, Marshal (and Hero) of the Soviet Union G. I. Kulik, shortly after war began.[4] A veteran of the World and Civil Wars and a graduate of the artillery course and the Course for the Improvement of Command Cadre, Iakovlev commanded an artillery battery, battalion, and regiment, and served as chief of artillery for the Polotsk Fortified Region and the Belorussian, North Caucasus, and Kiev Special Military Districts during the 1930s. After taking part in the invasion of eastern Poland during September 1939 and the Soviet-Finnish War during 1939 and 1940, Stalin promoted Iakovlev to the rank of lieutenant general in June 1941 and to chief of GAU shortly after war began.

Voronov and the GAU faced many problems during the first few months of the war. When the Red Army began its precipitous retreat, the Red Army's weapons and ammunition supply system utterly collapsed and the army lost most of its supply bases and dumps. Worse still, the subsequent forced evacuation of Soviet military industrial facilities to safer regions in the central and eastern Soviet Union seriously complicated the GAU's ability to supply its forces adequately.[5] As a result, the Red Army's field forces lacked sufficient artillery weapons and ammunition by late summer of 1941, which, in part, prompted the NKO to truncate the army's force structure and reduce supply norms (consumption requirements) for all classes (types) of supplies.

Voronov addressed these problems vigorously, first by reorganizing the GAU into subdirectorates for ammunition production, weapons development and supply, ammunition supply, and organization and planning, and, later, by organizing an intricate and increasingly effective network of supply and support organs within the field forces, all of which were subordinate to the GAU. Ultimately, this network consisted of artillery directorates and repair and reconstruction battalions within *fronts,* artillery department within armies, lesser artillery supply organizations within corps, divisions, and regiments, and a vast network of warehouses (depots), bases, workshops, and ammunition points spread throughout all levels of the Red Army from *fronts* down to battalions.[6]

Under Voronov's leadership the GAU overcame all of its supply problems by early 1943, and, at the same time, improve the effectiveness of the Red Army's artillery in many other respects. For example, during this period, the GAU nearly tripled ammunition production from 44,346 to 114,057 wagonloads and established an elaborate and effective system of ammunition supply bases in spite of the country's deplorable road conditions.[7] It also developed and fielded an sufficient array of new artillery weapons by mid-1943 to ensure Soviet artillery superiority for the remainder of the war, and it established an Artillery Committee (Board), supported by a formidable array of artillery weapons designers, to conduct scientific research and design new weapons. In addition, the GAU supervised weapons production at over 1,000 arms factories, established an elaborate system of *front* and army field warehouses to ensure these weapons reached the operating *fronts* and armies, and organized central and field workshops to maintain and repair these weapons.[8] Finally the GAU also prepared and distributed numerous technical manuals, instructions, firing tables, repair instructions, and other written materials pertaining to all Soviet and many foreign artillery weapons systems.

Arguably, the GAU's most important directorates were the Directorate for Ammunition Supply (*Upravlenie snabzheniia boepripasami,* or USB) and the Directorate for Artillery Weapons Supply (*Upravlenie snabzheniia artilleriiskim vooruzheniem,* or USAV), both of which the NKO formed on 29 July 1941. These directorates maintained a vast array of central artillery bases, warehouses (depots), repair facilities, factories, and arsenals, which distributed hundreds of millions of artillery and mortar rounds from Soviet industry down to operating *fronts* and armies according to General Staff plans.[9]

As was the case with other NKO directorates, GAU also administered an elaborate network of academies and schools to educate and train artillery officers. The highest-level artillery school was the Dzerzhinsky Military-Technical Academy, which was located in Moscow and Samarkand during the war. Its most important and distinguished graduates were future Marshals of the Soviet Union L. A. Govorov and K. S. Moskalenko, Main Marshal of Artillery M. I. Nedelin, and Marshals of Artillery Iu. P. Bazhanov, V. I. Kazakov, P. N. Kuleshov, G. F. Odintsev, and M. H. Chistiakov.[10]

Underscoring the growing importance of guards-mortar (multiple-rocket launcher) weapons and their unique differences from conventional artillery, the GKO created the separate position of commander of guards-mortar units and appointed Military Engineer 1st Rank V. V. Aborenkov to that post on 9 September 1941.[11] At the same time, it also formed the Main Directorate for Guards-Mortar Units (*Glavnoe upravlenie gvardeiskikh minometnykh chastei*, or GUGMCh) and corresponding operational groups of guards-mortar forces in the Red Army's operating *fronts* and armies. Parallel to but separate from Voronov's artillery command and control structure, Aborenkov's new guards-mortar structure was responsible for raising, fielding, and supervising these forces throughout the Red Army.

Subsequently, Aborenkov and the GUGMCh expanded the Red Army's guards-mortar force structure and formulated operational and tactical concepts for the combat employment of guards-mortar forces. Once this expansion program was complete, however, in May 1943 the NKO began reducing the size of the GUGMCh and subordinated all guards-mortar units directly to Voronov, the chief of Red Army artillery, a process it completed by August 1944. Thereafter, Voronov's deputy for guards-mortar units managed guards-mortar forces operating at *front* level.[12]

Armor and Mechanized Forces

When war began, the Main Auto-Armored Directorate of the Red Army (*Glavnoe avtobronetankovoe upravlenie Krasnoi Armii*, or GABTU KA) was responsible for the development and support of all tank, mechanized, and automotive forces in the Red Army.[13] Its chief, Lieutenant General of Tank Forces Ia. N. Fedorenko, had joined the Red Army during 1918 and graduated from the Higher Artillery Commanders School, Officers Cadre Improvement Courses, the Commanders Party-Political Training Course at the Lenin Military-Political Academy, and the Frunze Academy during the 1920s and 1930s. Beginning his career as a seaman in the Black Sea Fleet, Fedorenko served as a sailors representative in a revolutionary committee during the February Revolution and led the detachment of Red Guards sailors that seized the city of Odessa for the Bolsheviks during the October Revolution.[14]

After embellishing his career by serving as an army commissar and as commissar and commander of an armored train during the Civil War and as a commander of an armored train battalion and regiment during the 1920s, quite naturally, Fedorenko transferred to the fledgling tank forces in the early 1930s and commanded a tank regiment and mechanized brigade in the Moscow Military District during 1934 and 1935. Fedorenko's fortunes soared during the late 1930s, probably as a result of Stalin's military purge. After Stalin appointed him chief of the Kiev Special Military District's Armored and Mechanized Forces in 1937, he appointed him as chief of the NKO's Auto-Armored Directorate in 1940 and chief of GABTU in 1941. Stalin elevated Fedorenko to the position of commander of the Red Army's armored and mechanized forces in December 1942 and, at the same time, appointed him as a deputy commissar of defense. Thereafter, Fedorenko played a vital role in reforming the Red Army's tank and mechanized force structure and developing techniques for its operational and tactical employment. All the while, he also served as special *Stavka* representative during the Battles of Moscow, Stalingrad, and Kursk and many other operations and was elevated to the rank of chief marshal of armored forces in 1944.[15]

GABTU's principal wartime missions were to supervise the mobilization of the tank and mechanized forces' officer cadre, raise and field tank and mechanized forces, and "handle all questions related to the employment, repair, and evacuation of armored and auto-tractor equipment, the calculation and supply of forces with armored and auto-tractor material, and the specialized training of personnel."[16] Although Fedorenko's directorate increased the size of the Red Army's tank fleet to more than 23,000 tanks, including 892 new model T-34 medium tanks and 504 heavy KV tanks, when war began, unfortunately, the army lost more than 11,000 tanks during the first two weeks of the war, a total of 20,500 by 31 December 1941, and another 15,000 during 1942.[17] Therefore, Fedorenko and his GABTU had to rebuild the army's tank and mechanized forces virtually from scratch during late 1941 and 1942, a daunting task that Fedorenko performed with extraordinary effectiveness.

The drastic expansion of the Red Army's tank and mechanized force structure and its inventory of wheeled and tracked vehicles during 1942 forced the NKO to reorganize and enlarge GABTU. As a result, the GKO and NKO reorganized GABTU into the Directorate of the Commander of Armored and Mechanized Forces of the Red Army *(Upravlenie komanduiushchego bronetankovymi i mekhanizirovannymi voiskami KA)* and promoted Fedorenko to the rank of colonel general in December 1942. Fedorenko's expanded directorate consisted of the Main Armored Directorate *(Glavnoe bronetankovoe upravlenie, or GBTU),* whose chief was Lieutenant General of Tank Forces V. G. Vershinin, and the Main Directorate for Formation and Combat Training, both of which were subordinate to Fedorenko's command directorate.[18] Later still, on 15 January 1943 the NKO removed the automotive portion of Vershinin's directorate from Fedorenko's jurisdiction by forming a separate Main Automobile Directorate (*Glavnoe avtomobil'noe upravlenie,* or GLAVTU), which became responsible for all matters related to auto-tractor equipment.[19]

Fedorenko's command and subordinate directorates supervised an extensive network of associated armored directorates and armored supply and repair departments within the Red Army's *fronts* and armies. These directorates and department in turn controlled a vast array of supporting units and subunits, including technical support companies and platoons, mobile tank repair bases, separate tank repair battalions, mobile tank assembly and tank repair factories, evacuation battalions and companies, and armored equipment warehouses, all echeloned to provide effective support at virtually every level of command level. In addition, assistant (deputy in 1944) commanders for technical affairs in all brigades, regiments, and battalions directly supervised tank forces at those levels of command.[20]

The tank and mechanized forces highest-level educational institution was the Military Academy of Armored and Mechanized Forces, which was located in Moscow and Uzbekistan during the war. The academy's graduates included many distinguished tank officers, such as future Marshal of the Soviet Union V. I. Chuikov, Marshals of Tank Forces S. I. Bogdanov, P. P. Poluboiarov, and M. E. Katukov, and Army Generals P. A. Belik, A. L. Getman, A. A. Epishev, S. K. Kurkotkin, V. F. Tolubko, I. D. Cherniakhovsky, S. M. Shtemenko, and I. E. Shavrov.[21]

Engineer Forces

When war began, the Main Military-Engineer Directorate of the Red Army (*Glavnoe voenno-inzhernernoe upravlenie Krasnoi Armii,* or GVIU KA), whose chief was Major General of Engineer Forces L. Z. Kotliar, supervised all engineer and sapper forces in the Red Army.[22] Kotliar had joined the Red Army during 1920 and, after serving in engineer units during the 1920s, graduated from the Dzerzhinsky Military-Technical Academy in 1930. After Stalin appointed him chief of GVIU in 1940, Kotliar was promoted to the rank of major general of engineer forces in June 1941.[23]

The primary mission of Kotliar's GVIU and its subordinate and associated organs was to provide general engineer support to the Red Army, which included advising combat forces on the employment of engineer forces, organizing and conducting engineer cadre and force training, preparing prospective theaters of military operations (TVDs), constructing defense lines and positions, and supplying and repairing engineer weaponry and equipment to the Red Army's field armies.

To do so, GVIU was organized into three subdirectorates. The first, which included a special department tasked with engineer preparation of the TVD, was responsible for engineer training, combat training, mine laying and mine clearing, and camouflage; the second was responsible for all defensive construction, construction training, and the formation and employment of fortified regions; and the third, named the Directorate for Engineer Supply, developed and procured engineer weaponry and equipment and distributed it to the Red Army's field forces.[24] In addition, an advisory organ called the Technical Council, which was created in 1940 and worked under the chairmanship of the GVIU chief, provided advice and technical assistance to the GVIU, and a Military-Engineer Inspectorate, which was embedded within the GVIU, worked closely with the Main Inspectorate of the Red Army to monitor the quality of engineer training. Major General M. P. Vorob'ev served as Stalin's first general-inspector of engineer forces.

Like the other main directorates, the GVIU cooperated closely with the chiefs of engineer directorates in the military districts and the chiefs of engineer departments and sections in other levels of the Red Army from corps down to regiment. In addition, the engineer chiefs and their directorates in the military districts were also responsible for the operations of separate departments engaged in defensive construction, and logistics.

This GVIU structure proved markedly deficient in several respects during the first few months of the war. Because it lacked any capability for commanding and controlling engineer forces in combat or conducting engineer reconnaissance, engineer support for operating *fronts* and armies was wholly inadequate during the initial period of war. Worse still, as was the case with its artillery, the NKO's decision to abolish the position of chief of military district engineer forces during the first few days of war proved foolish and exacerbated the parlous situation regarding engineer support. By the fall of 1941 the NKO realized it could not correct these serious problems without fundamentally reorganizing its entire engineer force command structure.

The *Stavka* set the stage for this reorganization on 28 November 1941, when Stalin and Shaposhnikov signed a report severely criticizing field commanders for their failure to organize effective engineer support. In addition to directing *front* and army commanders to employ engineer forces massively along the most important axes and only for the purposes for which they were trained, it ordered the NKO to create a new command and control structure for engineer forces that could effectively plan operations, maneuver engineer forces, form, manage, and protect engineer reserves, and better serve the engineer requirements of the ground forces.[25]

At the same time, Stalin created the position of chief of Red Army engineer forces with a small headquarters staff, assigned General Kotliar to the post, and placed at Kotliar's disposal the full resources of the GVIU, the NKO's

Main Directorate for Construction Work, new sapper armies as they were formed, and the Military-Engineer Academy and all engineer schools and courses. To assist Kotliar, the order re-established the positions of chiefs of engineers in the military districts, which, it noted, "had been incorrectly eliminated at the beginning of the war."[26]

The GKO and NKO continued improving its engineer command and control structure during 1942. First, Stalin promoted Vorob'ev to marshal of engineer forces and appointed him as commander of Red Army engineer forces in April 1942 and a deputy commissar of defense in early May. Kotliar, the former GVIU chief, became the general-inspector of engineer forces and, later, chief of engineers in the Voronezh, Southwestern, and 3rd Ukrainian Fronts until war's end.

Vorob'ev, who was responsible for most of the improvements in engineer forces thereafter, had begun his military career as a noncommissioned officer in the tsar's army during World War I. After being elected to a regimental revolutionary committee during 1917, he served as a brigade and division engineer in the Southern, Western, and Caucasus Fronts during the Civil War, graduated from the Dzerzhinsky Academy in 1929, joined the faculty of the Engineer Academy in March 1932, and became the academy's commandant in July 1932, where he wrote extensively on the combat employment of engineer forces. In recognition of his accomplishments, the NKO assigned Vorob'ev as commandant of the Leningrad Military-Engineer School during 1936 and, four years later, as general inspector of the Red Army's Engineer Forces.[27]

The NKO assigned Vorob'ev to field duty as chief of the Western Front's Engineer Directorate only days after war began and, a few months later, as chief of the Western Front's Engineer Forces and, simultaneously, commander of the *front's* 1st Sapper Army. Vorob'ev's decisive role in constructing Moscow's formidable defenses during October and November 1941 and providing effective engineer support for the Western Front's December counteroffensive and winter offensive prompted Stalin to appoint him as commander of the Red Army's engineer forces in April 1942.

Thereafter, Vorob'ev contributed significantly to the effective coordination of engineer support for Red Army forces during the Battle of Stalingrad, in operations to raise the Leningrad blockade during early 1943, and in preparing engineer defenses during the Battle of Kursk and several other major wartime operations. Promoted to marshal of engineer forces in 1944, Vorob'ev continued to serve as chief of the Red Army's engineer forces well into the postwar years.[28]

The effectiveness of the GVIU, its three subdirectorates, and its associated military councils and engineer forces in the Red Army's *fronts* and armies improved dramatically under Vorob'ev's direction. For example, by the summer of 1942, the GVIU's three subdirectorates included separate departments responsible for information collection, training engineer officer cadre, staffing and manning engineer forces, employing engineer forces in combat, planning engineer support of combat forces with new equipment, and developing and producing new engineer equipment. In addition, Vorob'ev elevated the Directorate for Construction Work, which was responsible for all large-scale defensive construction work, into a main directorate in its own right.

Vorob'ev created an elaborate and effective engineer command and control structure within the Red Army's *fronts* and armies in the field by 1943. At *front* level, this system consisted of engineer directorates with operational, technical, obstacle, and supply departments and cadre sections, which operated under the direction of assistant chiefs of staff for engineer affairs, who were also responsible for all engineer reconnaissance within their respective *fronts.* At army level, this system consisted of engineer departments responsible for road and bridge construction and repair, field fortifications, and obstacle emplacement and removal, which functioned under assistant chiefs of staff for operational engineer matters and two assistants who were responsible for all aspects of engineer supply. The thoroughness of Red Army engineer support during the Battle of Kursk clearly demonstrated the scope and effectiveness of Vorob'ev's reforms.

The engineer forces' highest-level educational institution was the Kuibyshev Military-Engineering Academy, which was located in Moscow and Frunze during the war.

Airborne (Air Assault) Forces

When war began, the Directorate of Airborne Forces (UVDV) controlled the Red Army's fledgling airborne forces (*vozdushno-desantnye voiska,* or VDV), which were organized as a separate branch of the Red Army.[29] After having its airborne forces fight primarily as infantry under the control of *fronts* during the first few months of the war, the NKO began reorganizing those forces in late summer so that they could operate in their specialized role. After withdrawing their shattered remnants from *front* control, on 29 August 1941 it subordinated them to the new Directorate of the Commander of the Red Army's Airborne Forces (*Upravlenie komanduiushchego vozdushno-desantnykh voisk Krasnoi Armii,* or UKVDV KA), and appointed Major General V. A. Glazunov as the first commander of the Red Army's airborne forces, a post he occupied until 1943.[30]

Less than a week later, on 4 September 1941, the NKO ordered the UKVDV to form ten new airborne corps, five airborne brigades, and two reserve airborne regiments, as well as a new training system for VDV forces.[31] A month later the NKO made this force genuinely mobile by forming ten separate aviation transport squadrons and five separate aviation detachments, which it later combined into two aviation glider and two aviation transport regiments equipped with U-2, R-5, DB-3, TB-3, PS-84, and, later, Li-2 aircraft and assigning them to transport its reformed airborne forces into combat.[32]

The *Stavka* began employing its airborne forces in an air assault role during its Moscow counteroffensive in December 1941 and its subsequent winter offensive. For example, after conducting smaller air assaults west of Moscow in December 1941, airborne forces conducted brigade- and corps-scale operations in the Viaz'ma region in February 1942 and along the Dnepr River in September 1943, joint air-ground operations near Demiansk in March and April 1942, and smaller-scale tactical assaults near Iukhnov and Rzhev in February and March 1942. Later still, the *Stavka* planned but ultimately canceled two large-scale airborne assaults in support of the 1st Baltic Front's advance into northern Belorussia in November 1943. Throughout this period, VDV forces conducted hundreds of tactical and reconnaissance and diversionary assaults in small groups of 20–500 men.

The frequent reorganization of VDV forces throughout the war reflected the *Stavka's* divided attitude toward its employment of airborne forces, specifically, its confusion over whether they should be employed in an airborne role or as elite ground troops. Reflecting this attitude and VDV forces' wartime experiences, by war's end the *Stavka* subordinated the remainder of its airborne forces as well as the Directorate of Airborne Forces to the commander of the Red Army Air Force.

Air Force

The Red Army Air Force (VVS) was an integral part of the Red Army when war began and remained so for the war's duration, although with substantial reorganizations. The Main Directorate of the Air Force (*Glavnoe upravlenie voenno-vozdushnykh sil,* or GUVVS), whose chief was Lieutenant General of Aviation P. F. Zhigarev, controlled and supervised the Red Army Air Force on 22 June 1941. Zhigarev, who had replaced Lieutenant General of Aviation P. V. Rychagov on 12 April 1941, was a 1927 graduate of pilot school and a 1932 graduate of the Zhukovsky Air Force Academy and had commanded a squadron, an aviation brigade, and the air forces of the 2nd Separate Red Banner Army in the Far East during the 1930s. Stalin's appointment of Zhigarev as deputy commander of the Main Air Force Directorate in December 1940 and commander of the Main Air Force Directorate in April 1941 brought to an end a period of prolonged command turbulence in the VVS caused largely by the purges.[33]

The GUVVS consisted of several functional subdirectorates and separate departments and the VVS headquarters with its own subordinate departments, the most important of which was the operations department, which was responsible for the preparation of operational and tactical techniques and personnel training. However, neither Zhigarev's GUVVS nor the VVS headquarters had any dedicated rear services organs of its own. The VVS's combat forces included long-range bomber aviation (DBA) subordinate to the High Command, *front* aviation subordinate to military districts, and army and corps aviation.[34]

The *Wehrmacht* devastated and crippled the VVS during the initial few weeks of Operation Barbarossa, destroying much of its aircraft, killing many of its pilots and crews, shaking the VVS's force structure to its foundations, and, worse still, depriving the Red Army's operating forces of any meaningful air support. Engulfed by the Barbarossa disasters, the *Stavka* and NKO struggled to rebuild, reorganize, and reequip the VVS, train new VVS commanders, staffs, and aircraft crews, and, simultaneously, increase flagging Soviet aircraft production, all under the worst possible conditions.

The day after war began, the Council of People's Commissars transferred the Soviet Civil Air Fleet to NKO and VVS control, and less than a week later, on 29 June, the *Stavka* created the position of commander of the VVS complete with a military council and headquarters staff and appointed Zhigarev as commander as well as a deputy commissar of defense.[35] By appointing Zhigarev as VVS commander with his own dedicated military council and staff, the *Stavka* made him responsible for both the VVS and the UVVS, Stalin broadened his administrative and operational responsibilities, improved VVS command and control, particularly regarding its operational and strategic employment, increased the combat readiness and logistical support of VVS aviation forces, and streamlined and accelerated aircraft production.

Zhigarev and his staff coordinated VVS air operations during the Battle of Moscow and the subsequent winter campaign far more effectively than it had during its previous defensive operations. Nevertheless, when the *Wehrmacht* threatened Moscow during mid-October 1941, the *Stavka* divided the General Staff and Zhigarev's VVS into two echelons, keeping the latter's first echelon and military council in Moscow, while dispatching its second echelon to safety in the city of Kuibyshev.[36] After the Battle of Moscow ended, the *Stavka* reassigned Zhigarev on 26 April 1942 to command the Far Eastern Front's VVS and appointed Lieutenant General A. A. Novikov to replace Zhigarev as VVS commander, a post that Novikov occupied with increasing distinction until war's end (see Chapter 10 for Novikov's biography).

At Novikov's recommendation, the NKO continued reorganizing its VVS during March 1942 by removing long-ranger bomber aviation (DBA) from the *fronts'* control, renaming it long-range action aviation (ADD), and placing it under direct *Stavka* control, with Lieutenant General of Aviation A. E. Golovanov as its chief.[37] The 38-year-old Golovanov had built a formidable record in long-range aviation by commanding the 212th Long-Range Aviation Regiment from February to August 1941 and the newly formed 81st Long-Range Aviation Division from August until his appointment as long-range aviation chief. Golovanov's dizzying rise from the rank of lieutenant colonel in June 1941 to chief marshal of aviation in 1944 culminated with his assignment to command the 18th Air Army in December 1944.[38]

Under Novikov's leadership, the VVS's organizational structure and combat performance improved rapidly and dramatically throughout 1942 and 1943. For example, at Novikov's recommendation, in May 1942 the NKO began forming and fielding air armies to support its operating *fronts* and separate aviation corps for the RVGK, fielding 17 of the former and 13 of the latter by year's end. During the same period, Novikov also developed and implemented the concept of the air offensive. These and other organizational and operational measures permitted the VVS to gain strategic air superiority over the *Luftwaffe* by mid-summer 1943.

Although the VVS maintained a formidable network of educational and training institutions, the highest-level air force academy during the war was the Air Force Academy For Command and Navigator Cadre of the Red Army Air Force, which was located in Moscow and Orenburg. The academy's wartime graduates included more than 70 percent of the VVS's pilots and navigators and the majority of its senior commanders.[39]

Air Defense of the Country (PVO Strany)

The Main Directorate for PVO Strany of the Red Army (GUPVO Strany KA) controlled and directed all of the Red Army's air defense forces and early warning systems on the eve of war. Its chief was Colonel General G. N. Shtern, who had replaced its first chief, Major General D. T. Kozlov, in March 1941.[40] Although PVO forces were controlled operationally by the General Staff, GUPVO Strany was responsible for planning the country's air defense system, directing the combat preparation and combat employment of all PVO forces, and, in the event of war, preparing the theater of military operations for air defense.[41]

When war began, the NKO was in the midst of reorganizing the Red Army's Forces for the Air Defense of the Country (PVO Strany) in response to the *Luftwaffe's* devastating effectiveness during the German conquest of Western Europe and the poor performance of their own air defense forces during the Soviet-Finnish War.[42] Consequently, the Communist Party and Council of People's Commissars issued a directive on 14 February 1941 ordering the NKO to reorganize the country's air defense and early warning system.[43]

During the next four months, the NKO reorganized PVO Strany into PVO zones, which corresponded to the military districts and were defended by newly formed PVO corps and divisions, and subdivided these zones into PVO regions and PVO points, in which new separate PVO brigades provided air defense for large cities and important political and economic objectives. Although assigned to PVO Strany, all PVO air and ground forces operating within these zones were subordinate to the deputy commanders for PVO in the military districts, except for fighter aviation units, which were directly subordinate to the VVS, and antiaircraft forces organic to Red Army field forces stationed in these military districts.[44] Under this arrangement, the commanders of the PVO zones were responsible for protecting all potential objectives within their zones, and the commanders of the PVO corps, divisions, and brigades subordinate to each military district commander were responsible for defending PVO regions.[45]

In addition to reorganizing PVO Strany as a whole, the 1941 directive also reorganized the associated Air Observation, Warning, and Communication System (VNOS), which was manned by specially designated VNOS regiments, battalions, and companies and VNOS radio battalions, most operating under the control of PVO Strany but some subordinate to Red Army field forces (wartime *fronts* and peacetime armies, corps, and divisions).[46] Operationally, these VNOS forces were responsible for observing, detecting, and warning of the approach of enemy aircraft by employing an elaborate system of observation posts and radio location stations (*radiolokatsionnye stantsii,* or RLS). In June 1941 the VNOS system included a dense network of visual air observation posts deployed to a depth of 150–250 kilometers within the country's borders and 60–120 kilometers around major key objectives in the country's depths. This system was manned by six VNOS regiments, 35 separate VNOS battalions, five VNOS companies, and four separate VNOS radio battalions, of which one VNOS regiment, 19 separate battalions, and three companies manned VNOS posts in the western military districts.[47]

Exclusive of its VNOS forces, in June 1941 PVO Strany included 13 PVO zones, three PVO corps, two PVO divisions, nine separate PVO brigades, 28 separate antiaircraft artillery regiments, 109 antiaircraft artillery battalions, and other smaller units.[48] Including its VNOS forces, PVO forces fielded 182,000 men, 3,329 medium-caliber and 330 small-caliber antiaircraft guns, 650 antiaircraft machine guns, 1,500 searchlights, 850 aerostatic obstacles, and up to 45 radio detection stations and were supported by 40 fighter aviation regiments equipped with around 1,500 combat aircraft.[49] Although the 1941 reorganization did indeed improve the PVO system's overall effectiveness and made it easier to command and control, command and control problems, persistent equipment shortages, and severe training problems plagued PVO Strany and its associated VNOS forces on the eve of war and particularly after war began.

These problems became apparent immediately after the German invasion. First and foremost, since PVO Strany's zones were subordinate to *front* commanders, it was impossible to maneuver PVO forces to provide necessary air defense for the most threatened regions. Worse still, PVO air forces and their aircraft were subordinate to both the *front* VVS commanders and the PVO zone commanders. Complicating this command and control dilemma, Stalin produced unnecessary command turbulence within PVO Strany's command structure by arresting its commander, General Shtern, on 14 June, replacing him with Voronov, and then replacing Voronov less than a month later.[50] Because of these and other problems and the virtual collapse of air defenses in the western Soviet Union, the GKO concentrated PVO Strany's forces and weaponry throughout Operation Barbarossa to defend the most vital regions, including Leningrad, Moscow, the Iaroslavl' and Gor'kii industrial regions, the Donbas, and key bridges across the Volga River.[51]

The GKO finally resolved PVO Strany's most serious problems on 9 November 1941 by issuing a decree reorganizing the country's entire air defense system. This decree established the position of commander of PVO Strany forces, appointed Major General M. S. Gromadin as commander and as a deputy commissar of defense, and placed at Gromadin's disposal a military council, a complete staff, and a new Directorate of the Commander of PVO Strany Forces (*Upravlenie komanduiushchego voiskami PVO Strany, or* UKVPVO Strany), which included subordinate separate directorates for PVO fighter aviation and antiaircraft artillery forces. Most important, the decree also subordinated all PVO forces in military districts and operating *fronts* (except those in the Leningrad region) to Gromadin.[52]

Organizationally, this decree disbanded the PVO zones in the European USSR, replacing them with PVO corps regions at Moscow and Leningrad and 13 PVO division regions spread across the country but retained PVO zones in the Trans-Caucasus region, Central Asia, Siberia, and the Far East.[53] Shortly thereafter, on 24 November, the GKO improved PVO Strany's operational effectiveness by subdividing air defense forces—principally its antiaircraft forces—into two separate elements: PVO Strany, responsible for air defense of the country; and Force PVO, responsible for air defense within the Red Army's field forces.

The GKO and NKO continued to rationalize and strengthen PVO Strany's organization during 1942, first, on 22 January by subordinating all fighter aviation corps, divisions, and regiments actively engaged in the defense of key objectives throughout the country to the commander of PVO Strany.[54] In addition to centralizing and improving PVO Strany's command and control, this measure also fostered better cooperation between different PVO defense systems. Soon afterward, the NKO assigned 56 airfield support battalions to fighter aviation corps, division, and separate regiments supporting PVO Strany. As a result, by 1 April 1942, PVO Strany's antiaircraft force consisted of two PVO corps, two PVO divisions, and two PVO brigades, and one

PVO corps region, 15 divisional regions, and 14 brigade regions. At the same time, its air forces consisted of three fighter aviation corps, 13 fighter aviation divisions, and nine separate PVO fighter aviation regiments.[55] Finally, on 5 April the GKO increased the size of PVO Strany formations by upgrading the Moscow PVO Corps Region into the Moscow PVO Front, the Leningrad and Baku Corps Regions into PVO armies, and a few other PVO division regions into full PVO corps regions.[56]

The GKO also began replacing a significant number of male soldiers in PVO Strany with female soldiers during 1942, in part to create a manpower reserve to man combat formations at the front. For example, a 25 March 1942 GKO decree ordered the NKO to raise 100,000 female soldiers, "girl-Komsomol members," for assignment to PVO Strany by 10 April 1942.[57] This included 45,000 women assigned to antiaircraft artillery forces as observers, radio operators, telephone operators, rangefinders, and instrument operators, 3,000 to antiaircraft machine-gun forces as scouts, gunners, and communicators, 7,000 to searchlight units as communicators and crew members, 5,000 to aerostatic obstacle balloon units as communicators and crew, and 40,000 to VNOS as observers and telephone operators.

Although the comprehensive reorganization of PVO Strany's command and control and organizational structure during 1941 and early 1942 centralized PVO resources and improved air defense within operating *fronts* and the rear area, the growth and proliferation of PVO forces complicated command and control, particularly in the defense of vital industrial and administrative objectives. As a result, on 31 May 1942, the NKO disbanded the Directorate for PVO Strany, reassigning all of its directorates and departments to Gromadin, the commander of PVO Strany, and created two deputy commanders of PVO Strany force to serve Gromadin, the first responsible for training and training institutions and the second for weaponry and material support.[58]

Only days later, on 2 June, the NKO placed all PVO and VNOS forces located within operating *fronts* and armies under the control of the commander of Red Army artillery, Voronov, and his artillery directorate (GAU). Thereafter, the GAU included its own PVO department, which was upgraded to a full directorate in November 1942.[59] Voronov also established a new Central Headquarters of PVO Forces, a Central Headquarters for Fighter Aviation, a Central VNOS (air warning) Post, a main inspectorate, and a combat training directorate subordinate to GAU. In effect, the June reform created two separate and distinct air defense forces, Force PVO (PVO *voisk*) and PVO Strany, within the Red Army. Finally, the NKO also directed Gromadin to provide command cadre for all Force PVO units.[60] Later still, in October ordered NKO's PVO Strany and the NKVD's MPVO (local PVO) to cooperate more closely in the country's air defense.[61]

When the Red Army intensified its offensive operations during the winter of 1942–43 and the front moved steadily westward, it became apparent that more changes were required in the organization of the country's air defenses. As a result, on 10 June 1943, the GKO subdivided PVO Strany forces in the European Soviet Union into Western and Eastern PVO Fronts, the former commanded by Gromadin in Moscow and the latter by General G. S. Zashikhin in Kuibyshev.[62] At the same time, the Far Eastern, Trans-Baikal, and Central Asian PVO Zones reverted to control of their respective *fronts* and military districts and the Leningrad PVO Army and the Ladoga PVO Region remained under the Leningrad Front's operational control.[63]

Soon after, the GKO abolished the directorate of the commander of PVO Strany and assigned all of its functions to PVO Strany central headquarters (PVO Strany "Central") in Moscow. While both PVO *fronts* and all Force PVO formations and units remained directly subordinate to the commander of Red Army artillery, PVO Strany Central was responsible for coordinating the operations of both PVO *fronts,* which were separated by a line extending from Arkhangel'sk on the White Sea through Kostroma and Krasnodar to Sochi on the Black Sea.

Because it faced the greater threat, the Western PVO Front included the Special Moscow PVO Army, 11 PVO corps and division regions, and 14 PVO fighter aviation formations and fielded 1,012 fighter crews, 3,106 mid-caliber and 1,066 small caliber antiaircraft guns, 2,280 antiaircraft machine guns, 1,573 searchlights, and 1,834 aerostatic obstacles by June 1943.[64] The smaller Eastern PVO Front, which provided air defense for vital objectives in the Ural, middle and lower Volga, Caucasus, and Trans-Caucasus regions, consisted of the Trans-Caucasus PVO Zone, seven PVO corps and brigade regions, and eight fighter aviation formations and fielded 447 fighter crews, 2,459 mid-caliber and 800 small caliber antiaircraft guns, 1,142 searchlights, 1,814 anti-aircraft machine guns, and 491 aerostatic obstacles.[65]

To improve command and control over PVO forces during strategic operations, such as during the Kursk defense, PVO Strany Central often established special groupings of PVO forces. At Kursk, for example, it established an operational group of PVO forces led by Colonel V. S. Gavrilov, chief of staff of the Voronezh PVO Corps Region, which centralized the control and employment of all PVO forces, protected Kursk and its adjacent rail lines, coordinated all PVO Strany and Force PVO forces in the region, and maintained close contact with the staffs of the defending Central and Voronezh Fronts. Gavrilov's operational group fielded 761 antiaircraft guns, over 200 fighter aircraft, 558 antiaircraft machine guns, and 125 search lights.[66]

Combined with the vast amounts of new weaponry and equipment PVO forces received during 1943, these improvements in command and control significantly increased PVO's capabilities for detecting and destroying enemy air targets. However, the abolition of a single commander for all PVO forces was a mistake because it increased the workload for the commander of Red Army artillery's and made it difficult for him to coordinate the operations of the vast air defense structure. The lack of a single PVO commander also necessitated further changes in the PVO structure during 1944 and 1945.

The NKO also made dramatic improvements to PVO Strany's VNOS system structurally during the first 30 months of the war by forming new VNOS divisions and separate radio companies and operationally by increasing the number of VNOS radio detection stations. By mid-1943, these stations had become the primary means of early warning, and the PVO was using its visual observation posts to an increasing extent to form dense observation networks along the immediate approaches to vital air objectives.[67]

In addition to exploiting the air forces' and artillery's educational system, the NKO created the Higher Military School of the Red Army PVO on the base of the Frunze Academy's PVO faculty during 1941. In addition, many PVO officers were trained by *front* and army PVO command organs and staffs and at their PVO assignment.

Mobilization, Force Manning, and Cadre

Although the GKO bore overall responsibility for mobilizing Soviet citizens subject to military service under the Universal Military Service Law of 1939, the Main Directorate for the Formation of Red Army Reserves (*Glavnoe upravlenie formirovaniia reservov Krasnoi Armii*, or Glavupraform), which was created on 29 July 1941 from the NKO's Mobilization Directorate and the General Staff's Directorate for Force Manning, handled all conscription (call-ups) and the enlistment of all civilians for other duties associated with the defense of the country, in addition to a host of other manpower matters.[68] Its first chief, Marshal G. M. Kulik, who also served as deputy people's commissar of defense and was one of Stalin's cronies, was replaced by Army Commissar 1st Rank (soon after, Lieutenant General) E. A. Shchadenko, who also served as a deputy commissar of defense, on 6 August 1941.

Shchadenko's long career dated back to the revolution and Civil War, when he organized and led Red Guards detachments and served as a member of the Don Military-Revolutionary Committee in the Donbas region, worked for Stalin during the defense of Tsaritsyn, and later became a commissar in the 10th, Budenny's 1st Cavalry, and the 2nd Cavalry Armies. Shchadenko graduated from the Military Academy of the RKKA, commanded a cavalry division, and served as assistant commandant of the Frunze Academy for political affairs and chief of the Kiev Military District's political directorate during the 1920s and 1930s. As a result of the purges, he became commissar of the Kiev Military District in May 1937 and deputy commissar of defense and chief of the NKO's Directorate of Red Army Command Cadre in November 1937. After war began, he continued to serve as deputy commissar of defense and chief of Glavupraform (later, called GUFUKA, until September 1943, when he was appointed as commissar of the Southern (later 4th Ukrainian) Front.[69]

In addition to its mobilization and manning responsibilities, Glavupraform was responsible for training, equipping, feeding, and housing officers and conscripted soldiers, for forming all infantry and airborne formations and units (tank, aviation, and artillery forces were formed by other main directorates), for preparing and determining the weapons requirements of strategic reserves and reinforcements and organizing their dispatch to the Red Army's field forces, for developing manpower requirements of the Red Army's force structure in accordance with operational and tactical requirements and General Staff guidance, and for "registering" or otherwise keeping track of the Red Army's personnel losses during the war.[70] To perform these functions, Glavupraform was organized into organizational, force manning and employment, unit formation, reserve and security units, combat training directorates, and weapons and supply, cadre, and general departments.

Even though a new order the NKO issued on 9 August 1941 changed Glavupraform's name to the Main Directorate for the Formation and Manning of the Red Army (*Glavnoe upravlenie formirovaniia i ukompletovaniia voisk Krasnoi Armii,* or GUFUKA) and drastically expanded the new directorate's size and missions, the names "Glavupraform" and "GUFUKA" coexisted to war's end. The August order expanded GUFUKA's Directorate for the Formation of Units (regiments and brigades) into a Directorate for the Formation of Formations (divisions and corps) and Units, established an Inspectorate for New Formations, a Political Department, a Department for Registering Personnel Losses, and a correspondence (administration) bureau within GUFUKA. In addition, the order made GUFUKA responsible for creating all types of formations and units except aviation, tank and mechanized, and motorcycle and motorized forces, allocating them to operating *fronts* and armies, and inspecting them once they reached the front.

Since, in practice, these responsibilities conflicted sharply with the General Staff's responsibility for ensuring the combat effectiveness of Red Army forces, considerable tension arose between the two organs.[71] To resolve this tension, on 20 June 1942, the NKO ordered Shchadenko to coordinate the work of his main directorate with the General Staff. Ultimately, on 29 April 1943, the NKO assigned GUFUKA specific responsibility for creating formations and units and the General Staff responsibility for employing them operationally.[72]

Complementing the work of GUFUKA, the NKO formed the Main Cadre Directorate (*Glavnoe upravlenie kadrov NKO USSR,* or GUK) from the

General Staff's former Directorate of Cadre on 29 July 1941. Responsible for "directing matters of selecting, registering, and placing command cadre of the Red Army," GUK performed the critical function of controlling the assignment of command cadre to the Red Army's entire force structure under its chief, Major General A. D. Rumiantsev.[73] In addition, on 20 September 1941, the NKO formed parallel cadre directorates and departments within all other NKO main directorates, ordered the GUK to coordinate closely with these organs in selecting, registering, and placing officer cadre, and subordinated all military educational facilities and schools to appropriate directorates and departments.

Military Education and Training

The Directorate for Military-Educational Institutions (*Upravlenie voenno-uchebnykh zavedenii,* or GUVUZ) was responsible for universal military education, in particular for officers and soldiers, and supervision of all military-educational institutions, when war began.[74] As such, it was responsible for directing the work of 19 military academies, ten military faculties at civilian educational institutions, seven higher naval schools, and 203 military academies and schools. The chief of GUVUZ after war broke out was Lieutenant General I. K. Smirnov, who had been appointed to his post in 1940 and relinquished it in August 1941 to assume command of an army.[75] Under his direction, the various academies and schools altered their curriculum to meet wartime needs, dispatched experienced command and staff cadre from these faculties to the front, and began the arduous process of educating and training a new generation of Red Army officers. Throughout the war, GUVUZ worked closely with the other directorates, each of which assumed responsibility for the faculties and curricula within its specific functional area.

Among the NKO's central administrative organs most responsible for the training and education of officers and soldiers, the most important was the Main Directorate for Universal Military Education (*Glavnoe upravlenie vseobshchego voennogo obucheniia,* or GUVVO), which administered universal military education (VSEVOBUCH-all Union Education) after the GKO reintroduced that principle on 17 September 1941. The principle itself called for mandatory universal military education among all citizens of the USSR.[76] Once formed, GUVVO worked directly for Army Commissar 1st Rank E. A. Shchadenko, who was a deputy Commissar of Defense as well as the wartime chief of Glavupraform and GUFUKA.

Once formed, GUVVO controlled all universal military education at the national level (the center) and created parallel departments to perform the same function in the military commissariats within military districts, regions *(oblasti),* districts *(krai),* and the union republics.[77] To do so effectively, it formed small teams of military instructors in all subunits from squad to battalion level in these regional military commissariats, and they conducted 110-hour training programs for all men between the ages of 16 and 50 years. The VSEVOBUCH program provided minimal military training for about 9.8 million men during the war, who were then dispatched to fill out army forces. The first chief of GUVVO was Lieutenant General N. N. Pronin.[78]

Closely associated with the Glavupraform (GUFUKA) was a unique organization called OSOAVIAKHIM (*Obshchestvo sodeistviia oborone, aviatsionnomu i khimicheskomu stroitel'stvu SSSR*), or the Society for Assistance to Defense, Aviation and Chemical Structuring of the USSR, which was instrumental in the military education of the Soviet population, particularly its youth, and in the training of potential wartime reserves during the prewar years and wartime.[79] OSOAVIAKHIM numbered 14 million trained members formed into 329 primary organizations, 156,000 groups, 26,680 commands, and 350 detachments, including 2.6 million military specialists, on 22 June 1941.[80] More than half of OSOAVIAKHIM's members either joined the Red Army or helped form people's militia forces, NKVD (People's Commissariat of Internal Affairs) destruction units, and partisan units and detachments during the first few months of the war.

Thereafter, its organs at the national level and its local branches provided the population with universal military education and air and chemical defense training and assisted in the collection of funds, equipment, and other materials required for defense production.[81] Finally, in addition to general military education and training conducted at the military academies at the national level, each separate service branch created and supervised its own elaborate network of military educational and training institutions.

Signal Communications

When war began, the Communications Directorate (*Upravlenie sviazi Krasnoi Armii*, or USKA), led by Major General of Signals N. I. Gapich, chief of Red Army Communications, was responsible for all aspects of communications, in particularly, developing, supplying, and repairing signal equipment. With this limited mission, Gapich's directorate had little or no control over communications procedures and techniques within the Red Army.[82] The only signal resources under Gapich's direct control when war began were High Command radio communications units, which were supposedly capable of linking the General Staff with its military districts and wartime *fronts*.

Because the Red Army was short of its required signal equipment, particularly radios, and Soviet industry was producing and distributing new models of radios at an alarmingly slow pace, USKA's strategic and operational communications network consisted primarily of a civilian network of wire and cable land lines operated by the People's Commissariat of Communications. In addition, because the USKA possessed no reserve signal units or subunits of its own that it could assign to the Red Army's operating *fronts* and armies, the combat forces were deprived of signal equipment necessary to conduct the sort of mobile warfare that characterized operations during the initial period of war. Exacerbating this problem was the nearly congenital inability of commanders and staffs at all levels to either appreciate, understand, or employ available communications resources effectively. So parlous was the situation that the NKO issued an order on 23 July 1941 describing these rampant deficiencies and demanding commanders take corrective actions to centralize, standardize, and improve their command and control system communications.[83]

The same day, the GKO appointed Colonel I. T. Peresypkin as chief of Red Army communications to replace Gapich. The 37-year-old Peresypkin was an experienced signal officer who had fought in the Red Army during the Civil War and, after a short absence, had rejoined the Red Army in 1923 and graduated from the Military-Political School in 1942 and the Military Electro-Technical Academy in 1937. Stalin appointed Peresypkin as deputy chief of the Red Army's Communications Directorate in March 1939 and people's commissar for communications of the USSR in May 1939, a post he held until November 1944.[84]

Peresypkin's control over both military and civilian communications positions eliminated the artificial distinctions between military and civil communications, broke down institutional barriers, and paved the way for improved communications between operating *fronts* and armies. Soon Stalin also appointed Peresypkin to the post of deputy people's commissar of defense for communications and accelerated his promotion to the rank of lieutenant general of communications in December 1941.[85] These measures paved the way for the ultimate correction of the communications problems that had plagued the Red Army during the initial period of war.

Shortly after Peresypkin's appointment as communications chief, on 28 July, the NKO reorganized the weak Communications Directorate into the more formidable Main Directorate of Communications of the Red Army (*Glavnoe upravlenie sviazi Krasnoi Armii,* or GUSKA) with Colonel Peresypkin at its head. GUSKA consisted of a headquarters staff, operational-technical, equipment, and equipment supply directorates, the NKO's communications center, mobilization, finance, cadre, and defensive construction departments, a communications inspectorate, and "general" and secret units.[86] In addition, he immediately established closer cooperation between GUSKA and the communications departments of the People's Commissariat of Communications Routes (NKPS) and the NKVD, and coordinated communications with other key state commissariats.[87]

Peresypkin's new main directorate was responsible for organizing and ensuring "continuous" *Stavka* communications, organizing secure and reliable communications to and between all Red Army formations and units, preparing and fully exploiting all civil communications for the needs of the military, preparing and processing orders for signal equipment from Soviet industry, maintaining and repairing signal equipment, supplying signal equipment to Red Army forces and training signal personnel in its use, inspecting the combat readiness of signal forces, and selecting, training, and assigning higher-level signal cadre to Red Army forces.[88]

Peresypkin's reorganization of the Red Army's communications system produced significant results. By 1 December 1941, for example, the NKO and NKPS had jointly formed many new communications organs and units to provide basic civil and military communications, some of which were assigned to the RVGK so that the *Stavka* could create backup communications centers and build or restore communications between the General Staff and the Red Army's operating *fronts* and armies.[89] These improvements continued during 1942 and 1943, spurred on by an NKO order of 29 April 1942, "Concerning the Improvement in the Employment of Radio Communications for Supporting Command and Control of Forces," which required greater reliance on organized radio communications within *fronts* and armies.[90]

The GKO improved coordination of communications between GUSKA and the NKVD in January 1943, when it issued a decree defining their respective responsibilities and working relationship. Henceforth, NKVD communications units had the mission of employing only high-frequency (HF) communications, the General Staff's Operations Directorate was responsible for providing internal communications in the General Staff and its subordinate forces for operational planning, and the GUSKA was responsibility for managing communications between the General Staff and operating *fronts*.

In addition, the decree established *shtats* for the *fronts'* communications directorates and the armies' signal departments that further improved their capabilities. It created chiefs of communications in the *fronts* who were responsible for communications with their subordinate armies, deputies to these chiefs who were responsible for establishing and directing the *fronts'* auxiliary command posts, and separate divisions for radio, wire, and other communications within the armies' signal departments.[91]

GUSKA also worked to create effective air-ground communications within the Red Army. After the single aircraft allocated by the VVS headquarters and the Main Directorate of the Civil Air Fleet to provide liaison between the General Staff and *front* and army staffs turned out to be ineffective, in December 1941 the *Stavka* formed the 233rd Separate Aviation Liaison Squadron and assigned it to GUSKA to perform the liaison function. Later still, the *Stavka* also assigned the Moscow Special Designation Air Group's 2nd Air Squadron to support the General Staff's liaison requirements.[92]

However, when these forces failed to satisfy the General Staff's liaison requirements, on 3 December 1942, the NKO formed the 3rd Separate Air Liaison Division from the GVF (Civil Air Fleet's) Special Air Liaison Group, which consisted of two aviation regiments, a separate airlift detachment, and an air base maintenance battalion, and subordinated it to Peresypkin to provide air communications between the General Staff and its operating *fronts* and armies. At the same time, the NKO assigned one or two squadrons with 19–20 U-2 and R-5 aircraft to operating *fronts* and small air liaison squadrons of 6 U-2 aircraft to all armies to provide internal and external air communications, and in October 1943 it upgraded these squadrons to regiments.[93]

All of these measures materially increased the quantity and quality of communications forces at every level of command. Communications forces grew fourfold during the war to comprise 10 percent of the Red Army's total force structure in 1945. The effectiveness of strategic and operational communications also improved dramatically, due largely to the institution of unified management of state and military communications and the work of Peresypkin and his Main Communications Directorate.

Finally, the Communications Directorate also ran its own system of military academies, military schools and schools, and courses for command and technical cadre. Its highest-level educational institution was the S. M. Budenny Military Electro-Technical Communications Academy, which was located in Leningrad and Tomsk during the war. During the war, over 30 officer graduates from the academy served as chiefs of *front* communications directorates, and 40 more served in the same capacity at army level.

Military Communications (Rail, Road, Water, and Air Routes)

On the eve of war, responsibility for controlling ground, water, and air communications routes in the Soviet Union and using them to move and transport troops and equipment in peacetime and wartime by train, automobile, boat and barge, and aircraft was shared by civilian governmental organs that controlled, maintained, and supervised the use of these routes, military organs that used them to transport troops and material, and security organs that protected them.

For example, the People's Commissariat of Communications Routes (NKPS) controlled and administered the Soviet Union's well-developed railroad network, which was the primary means for transporting troops, weapons and other combat equipment, ammunition, supplies, food, and other cargo to the army's field forces and for regrouping forces during the war.[94] In addition, railroad troops assigned to the NKPS's Special Railroad Corps were responsible for reconstructing railroads behind advancing forces, building and operating forward railroad sectors, increasing railroad capacity, blocking railroads during defensive operations, and, in theory, also protecting railroads within the frontal zone. However, other railroad troops subordinate to the NKO shared some of the maintenance responsibilities, and railroad security forces subordinate to the NKVD were responsible for defending the railroads.

On the other hand, since the road system in the Soviet Union was crude, underdeveloped, and in bad condition on the eve of war, automotive road transport played a far less significant role than did the railroads in moving troops and materiel, particularly bulky military items. However, tactical road transport along the country's few macadamized main highways *(shosse)* and along dirt roads leading from the operational rear to the tactical forward area was important for moving forces, equipment, and supplies to the forward edge. Unlike the railroads, no single organ controlled motor transport along the USSR's road system. For example, both the Road Department in the General Staff's Directorate for the Organization of the Rear and Supply of Forces and the Red Army's Motor-Armored Directorate were responsible for supplying and repairing automobiles and automotive equipment, and both the NKO and the NKVD's Main Directorate of Main Highways fielded only cadre road units, which they maintained at reduced strength in peacetime but planned to expand to full-strength road exploitation regiments, road and brigade construction battalions, and forward road bases in wartime.[95]

The wartime exploitation of waterways for military transport, including navigable rivers, lakes and canals, and operations in coastal regions, was the responsibility of the People's Commissariat of the River Fleet (*Narodnyi komissariat rechnogo flota,* or NKRF). However, the NKRF had to coordinate the employment of water transport with rail and road movement, and this movement was often intermittent due to seasonal conditions, in particular, freezing and thaws. Finally, no special military air transport directorate or units existed within the NKO and the Red Army's VVS, and most transport aircraft belonged to civil aviation organs.

Militarily, two NKO organs were responsible for the movement and transport of military forces, weapons, equipment, and other cargo along these communications routes. The first was the Red Army's Military Communications Service (VOSO), whose specially trained automobile and railroad forces were subordinate to and supervised by a network of military communications and military commandants, directorates, and departments in the NKO's military districts and field armies and were responsible for preparing military forces and equipment for rail, road, and air transport and conducting their actual movement. The second organ was the Red Army General Staff's Central Directorate for Military Communications (*Tsentral'noe upravlenie voennogo soobshcheniia,* or TsUVS), whose first wartime chief was Major

General P. A. Ermolin and which was responsible for organizing and directing the military communications service in support of its strategic and operational plans.[96]

The TsUVS's principal operating organs were UVSs subordinate to the chiefs of military communications and military rail and water transport in the military districts *(fronts)* and military commandants in charge of railroad sectors and stations and water regions. Collectively, the TsUVS and its subordinate UVSs were responsible for assessing the communications and transport routes in the USSR and potential enemy countries, planning their use for large-scale troop movements, coordinating these plans with other transportation organs, and submitting these plans for approval. Once the plans were approved, the TsUVS ensured they were fulfilled by supervising troop movements and providing material, financial, technical, and medical support in coordination with field commands and other transport organs.

After war began, the TsUVS deployed military transport field organizations to its operating *fronts* and armies and to its vast network of administrative and supply stations and was assisted by PVO units, the NKO's railroad forces (to January 1942), military food supply points, and road control points. However, the war generated a whole range of new communications missions for the TsUVS, such as converting Western-gauge railroad tracks to Russian gauge, constructing and organizing reloading and transshipment regions and stations, and organizing antiaircraft defenses for trains that lacked their own defenses.

In addition, to facilitate rail transport, on 30 June the Communist Party Politburo ordered the NKPS to assign special representatives to operating *fronts* to coordinate with their UVS organizations. Although directly subordinate to NKPS's organizations, these representatives helped coordinate railroad reconstruction, construction, and repair so that they would be more responsive to the *front* commanders' needs. The NKPS also allocated construction organizations to its representatives in the *fronts* to do repair and blocking work and help evacuate industrial enterprises to the east.[97] Finally, to improve air transport, the GKO subordinated the Main Directorate of the Civil Air Fleet (*Grazhdanskii vozdushnyi flot,* or GVF) and its chief, Major General of Aviation R. N. Morgunov, to the NKO on 23 June.[98] Morgunov's directorate transferred transport aviation units from the Civil Air Fleet and reorganized them into separate aviation groups and detachments to support the *Stavka, fronts,* and fleets.[99]

Despite the well-defined theoretical division of transport responsibilities between the NKO and General Staff and the vast array of transportation resources at its disposal, because it was fragmented the Red Army's transport communications system functioned very poorly during the first few weeks of the war. For example, the mobilization of railroad forces during the initial period of war was truly chaotic. Although ostensibly complete by the end of July, most railroad formations comprised only untrained recruits. Therefore, they were not able to implement their required destruction plans and suffered huge losses during the rapid German advance.

This wholesale confusion in the command and control of transportation forces and the immense losses the railroad and road services suffered during the first month of the war prompted the GKO to implement a series of corrective measures to improve command and control. For example, on 16 July it created a new Automobile-Road Directorate (*Avtomobil'no-dorozhnoe upravlenie*, or GADU) within the General Staff's UVS with Major General Z. I. Kondrat'ev as its chief, and it formed automobile–road departments in operating *fronts* to supervise automobile subunits, units, and formations within them and their operating armies.[100]

Two weeks later, on 1 August, the GKO created the position of chief of the Red Army Rear (Services), appointed Lieutenant General of the Quartermaster Services A. V. Khrulev as chief of rear services, and formed the Main Directorate of Rear Services (GUTA KA) as Khrulev's principal working organ. At the same time, the GKO reorganized the General Staff's TsUVS into the new Directorate for Military Communications (UPVOSO), appointed Military Engineer 1st Rank I. V. Kovalev as its chief in place of Ermolin, and subordinated UPVOSO and its former communications directorates, such as GADU, to Khrulev. By virtue of this reorganization, UPVOSO became NKO's principal agent for coordinating military transport communications.

In addition to transferring GADU from the General Staff to UPVOSO, the GKO established subordinate automobile transport and road services departments within *fronts* and armies. Kondrat'ev remained GADU's chief with Brigade Commander A. A. Slavin, the former chief of the General Staff's Auto-Road Department, as his deputy.[101] During the remainder of 1941, GADU supervised the wholesale mobilization of military and civilian vehicles, formed numerous motor transport brigades, regiments, battalions, and companies, and began the construction of a network of military automotive roads (VADs) (see Chapter 9).[102]

However, these attempts to solve the Red Army's transport problems by centralizing command and control failed, largely because the responsibility for transporting military troops and material was still scattered among a wide variety of supply services and directorates, and the Red Army's branches and the NKO's directorates still planned all auto-transport work separately.[103] In addition to wasting time and resources, their work was largely ineffective. As a result, the NKO began restructuring UPVOSO to better satisfy wartime requirements. For example, on 19 August the NKO formed a special department within it to plan and direct operational and supply transport by types of materials, and, in September, a special department for medical evacuation.

At the same time, UPVOSO created special sections to manage supply cargoes in the operating *fronts* and armies.[104]

At the same time, the GKO attempted to improve railroad transport and communications. For example, on 16 September it ordered the NKPS to reorganize the Reconstruction Department in its Military Mobilization Directorate into a full directorate and create 19 military reconstruction services with their own mobile reconstruction formations in the *fronts* and the *fronts'* rear zones.[105] However, when the Red Army went over to the offense during the winter of 1941–42, railroad troops were too weak and unskilled to meet reconstruction requirements and UPVOSO's rail transport structure proved equally inadequate.[106]

The GKO sought to solve this problem on 3 January 1942 by assigning the NKPS responsibility for reconstructing and clearing damaged and destroyed rail lines and transferring all of the NKO railroad troops to NKPS control.[107] The GKO decree also established the Main Directorate for Military Reconstruction Work (*Glavnoe upravlenie voenno-vosstanovitel'nykh rabot,* or GUVVR) within the NKPS and a Directorate for Railroad Troops *(Upravlenie zheleznodorozhnykh voisk)* within the GUVVR. Major General (Lieutenant General in February 1944) N. A. Prosvirov served as chief of the NKPS's railroad troops from February 1942 until war's end.[108]

In addition to its Directorate for Railroad Troops, the GUVVR also included subdirectorates for military reconstruction and obstacle work known as UVVRs, which were supervised by NKPS representatives and were responsible for performing all railroad reconstruction and obstruction work in operating *fronts,* and forward bases, which maintained and secured necessary supplies.[109] While the chiefs of the UVVRs were normally subordinate to the *fronts,* in the case of special operations, they were subordinate to the chief of the GUVVR. In turn, forward reconstruction departments subordinate to the *fronts'* UVVRs supervised reconstruction work and troops at army level.

In effect, although *front* commanders and their NKPS counterparts were jointly responsible for all railroad reconstruction work, the *fronts'* operations directorates controlled the NKPS's railroad regiments working in the operating *fronts* instead of the GUVVR or UVVR, while the NKPS representatives supervised all railroad reconstruction and railroad operations. Thus, the NKPS's railroad troops became regular Red Army troop units subject to normal Red Army regulations.[110] Finally, the GKO forbade *front* commanders from employing the NKPS's railroad forces and special formations from performing any task other than railroad reconstruction.[111]

The GKO acted to clarify command and control over railroad reconstruction work in February 1942 by abolishing the NKPS's representatives in the *fronts.* Thereafter, even though the chiefs of the *fronts'* UVVRs were officially subordinate to the chief of the NKPS's GUVVR, they were actually subordinate to the *fronts*. However, the NKPS still determined the resources required by the *fronts*, established quotas for the UVVRs' reconstruction work, and adjusted the assignment of NKPS resources according to the *front* commanders' plans. This measure improved command and control and the technical quality of railroad reconstruction work and led to a gradual increase in the rate and quality of railroad reconstruction.[112]

To further improve the organization and coordination of transport in the wake of the winter campaign of 1941–42, on 14 February the Politburo established a special Transport Committee within the GKO made up of key government and military figures involved in transport communications. Chaired by Stalin, the committee's mission was to coordinate the operations of all types of transport, ensure more effective planning, and regulate both military and national economic transport by mobilizing and rationalizing all types of transport, streamlining command and control of transport resources, and altering the UPVOSO's work to strengthen its links with the General Staff.[113] Thereafter, in addition to planning and controlling all military transport, the UPVOSO became the working organ of the GKO's Transport Committee with responsibility for organizing and conducting military transport, developing transport communications, and responding to the transport requirements of other people's commissariats. As a representative of the GKO, Kovalev, the UPVOSO chief, could now organize military transport more effectively.

The GKO also rationalized its road transport system during early 1942 by ending the dual responsibility of the NKO and NKVD for road security and repair. It did so on 8 May by reorganizing UPVOSO's Auto-Road Directorate (GADU) into the Main Directorate of Auto-Transport and Road Services of the Red Army (*Glavnoe upravlenie avtotransportnoi i dorozhnoi sluzhby Krasnoi Armii*, or GUADSKA), assigning the new main directorate complete responsibility for supervising all road transport and road services, evacuation, and technical support in operating *fronts* and armies, and subordinating all of the NKVD's road security forces to it.[114] In addition, GUADSKA also inherited its associated directorates and departments within *fronts* and armies and many of the NKVD's road service directorates and bases in operating *fronts*.[115] To complete this process, on 22 May the NKO subordinated GUADSKA's auto-road directorates and departments in *fronts* and armies to the chiefs of the *fronts'* and armies' rear services and their respective directorates and converted these chiefs into deputy commanders for rear services in their respective *fronts* and armies.[116]

The GKO and *Stavka* continued rationalizing Red Army transport communications during 1943. The most important step in this process occurred on 31 January, when the *Stavka* reorganized the UPVOSO into the Central Directorate for Military Communications (*Tsentral'noe upravlenie voennykh soobshchenii*, or TsUPVOSO), transferred it from the control of the chief of Rear Services to the General Staff, and created military transport communications departments in *fronts*, military districts, and armies directly responsive to the fronts', military districts', and armies' chief of staff.[117] However, since this command and control structure for military transport communications did not work, on 7 March the NKO transferred TsUPVOSO and its associated departments in *fronts* and armies from General Staff control and placed them under the control of the chief of the Red Army Rear and deputy commanders of rear services in *fronts* and armies. In addition, the NKO strengthened TsUPVOSO and reorganized it into specific departments responsible for general planning, operational transport, material transport (ammunition, arms and equipment, fuel and lubricants, quartermaster material, and food), medical evacuation, and other less vital functions.

After this reorganization, TsUPVOSO was responsible for preparing military transport plans for the NKPS corresponding to the General Staff's and the chief of the Red Army Rear's plans and implementing those plans once they were approved. Additionally, when the GKO's Transport Committee anticipated problems in force movements, TsUPVOSO prepared proposals to correct the problems.

In general, this new command and control structure vastly improved the Red Army's military transport system. The TsUPVOSO performed the vital task of planning and regulating military transport and ensuring precise and successful fulfillment of operational transport plans, and the GKO and NKO constantly supervised its work and provided it with assistance by obliging all transport organs to fulfill all of the TsUPVOSO's troop transportation requirements quickly and unconditionally. The GKO also prohibited the chiefs of the rail services in the *fronts'* zones from interfering with control of the dispatch sequence of military trains.[118]

Since rail transport played the most significant role in supporting Red Army operations during 1943, UPVOSO and TsUPVOSO had to cooperate closely with the NKPS, which controlled all railroads and rail traffic. Consequently, TsUPVOSO and NKPS representatives formed joint operational groups, usually headed by the chief of TsUPVOSO or his deputies and comparable leaders from the NKPS, to provide on-the-spot and general assistance to the *fronts*' railroads that were supporting major operations.[119] Their joint efforts also significantly improved the effectiveness of military troop movements of material shipments.

In addition, the TsUPVOSO had its own military forces with which to provide air defense for the rail lines and important rail installations. By 1 January 1944, these included 10 antiaircraft artillery regiments equipped with 40 antiaircraft machine guns each and 14 separate antiaircraft artillery battalions with 20 antiaircraft machine guns, each centrally organized under an air defense department. These units escorted military trains and the most important rail cars.[120]

Other improvements occurred within the realm of railroad communications during this period. For example, the NKO eliminated the NKPS's forward reconstruction sectors during early 1943 because they were no longer necessary. Thereafter, as the scope of rail reconstruction increased throughout the year, the role of the *fronts* in determining transport and reconstruction requirements increased, while the importance of the NKPS's UVVRs decreased significantly. By mid-1943, for example, the GUVVR directly tasked railroad forces only in the event of a major strategic offensive operation involving more than a single *front*. By this time, *front* commanders normally approved plans for railroad reconstruction after their approval by the *front* VOSO chief.

The organizational structure of railroad forces also improved during 1943 when the NKPS established a service to supply construction materials and technical equipment to its UVVRs and strengthened their logistical support departments. In February, for example, the GKO approved a new *shtat* for a standard railroad brigade and converted all of the brigades of the former Special Railroad Corps to the new *shtat*.[121] For the remainder of the year, the NKO added a variety of new types of forces to railroad brigades and battalions that markedly improved their capabilities.[122] While the railroad service performed its reconstruction work, it placed special emphasis on restoring and increasing the rail throughput capacity at vital railroad junctions, primarily by constructing nearby connecting spurs that enabled trains to bypass junctions whenever necessary and increased the overall forward traffic flow. Another vital task performed by railroad reconstruction forces was the construction of trans-loading regions to bypass portions of the rail lines that were blocked, destroyed, or under reconstruction.[123]

One of the most important considerations in the maintenance of continuous rail traffic was the skillful employment of locomotives, particularly during the planning and conduct of offensive operations. To do so, the NKPS organized steam locomotive columns and steam locomotive repair trains (*parovozoremontnye poezda*, or PRP). The former, which consisted of 15–30 locomotives and were employed both at the front and in the rear, were quite mobile and were not tied down to any specific railroad depot or station. So successful was this measure that the NKPS established a separate reserve of steam locomotive columns (ORPKs) in 1942. The ORPKs were self-sufficient entities whose crews were housed in the railroad cars. For example, the NKPS employed an ORPK equipped with over 500 locomotives to support troop combat operations during the Battle for Stalingrad and used another 600 during the Battle of Kursk.[124]

The rationalization of the Red Army's road transport and road services continued in 1943. For example, after assigning GUADSKA responsibility for supervising, reconstructing, and maintaining all military roads, on 15 January the NKO reorganized GUADSKA's former auto-road directorate into the Main Automobile Directorate of Automobile and Road Service (*Glavnoe avtomobil'noe upravlenie,* or GAVTU) to improve the organization of repair and technical maintenance of the Red Army's motor vehicle park by charging it with repairing and supplying motor vehicle and tractor equipment.

Still later, the GKO took its final step to improve the effectiveness of both auto-transport and road services by abolishing the Main Directorate for Rear Services on 9 June and subordinating its main directorates and directorates, including GUADSKA and GAVTU, directly to the chief of Red Army Rear Services. In essence, this measure formed two new main directorates, the Main Automobile Directorate of the Red Army (*Glavnoe avtomobil'noe upravlenie Krasnoi Armii,* or GAVTU KA) and the Main Road Directorate of the Red Army (*Glavnoe dorozhnoe upravlenie Krasnoi Armii,* or GRU KA), each with its own organs, facilities, and units at the center and the road directorates and departments in the operating *fronts* and armies.[125] Thereafter, both main directorates continued to coordinate closely with one another for the remainder of the war, in particular in the creation, employment, and maintenance of military automotive roads (VADs).[126] This reorganization of the road automobile transport service centralized road preparation, reconstruction, and maintenance in the same organs at the center and in the *fronts* and armies and operated effectively until war's end. The road troops themselves eventually became a special branch of Red Army forces, and the structure operated effectively until war's end.

As far as water transport was concerned, the People's Commissariat of the River Fleet (NKRF) formed military reconstruction directorates and detachments to restore traffic in river basins liberated from German forces began during late 1942 and accelerated this activity during 1943. However, the GKO entrusted this task to the navy during the summer of 1943, and it, in turn, assigned it to its newly organized Directorate for Ship-Raising and Salvage Work in the River Basins.[127] In the meantime, the NKRF also organized a reconstruction service for river transport consisting of the Central Military-Reconstruction Directorate (*Tsentral'noe voenno-vosstanovitel'noe upravlenie*) of the NKRF and separate military-reconstruction directorates in each river basin during November 1942.[128]

Finally, in the realm of air transport, the Directorate for Military Communications (UPVOSO) reorganized its special aviation groups into regiments and the detachments into squadrons during November 1942. The Moscow Special Air Group became the 1st Aviation Transport Division. Thereafter, the reorganization of aviation groups into divisions rationalized the military air transport structure and improved its efficiency. The principal missions of air transport organizations throughout the war were to drop or air-land airborne forces, deliver equipment and supplies to the troops, transport troops, sick, and wounded, and support partisan combat operations, primarily to those encircled or otherwise operating in the German rear area. In addition, air transport forces delivered emergency freight to Leningrad, Stalingrad, Sevastopol', and Odessa and shipments of various scarce instruments and parts on behalf of the defense industry.[129]

UPVOSO and TsUPVOSO and their associated communications services performed prodigious feats when transporting troops and material throughout the war. For example, these directorates moved more than 19.7 million rail cars, 2.7 million more by water and air, and 45,000 rail cars with troops and troop combat equipment from 1941 through 1945.[130] Transport activity was heaviest during preparations for the Battles of Moscow, Stalingrad, and Kursk, when 1,500–1,700 railroad trains were moving simultaneously under centrally planned control, not counting intra-*front* trains and up to 10,000–12,000 other vehicles. Railroad troop and supply movement in support of multi-*front* operations reached a tempo of 450–500 trains per day by war's end.[131]

During the same period, the NKO's 35 brigades of railroad and other special NKPS formations built or rebuilt about 120,000 kilometers of railroad track and 2,756 large and medium railroad bridges, laid about 71,000 kilometers of communications routes, rebuilt 2,345 water supply stations, 182 steam locomotive depots, and 7,990 railroad stations and sidings, and deactivated and destroyed more than 2 million mines throughout the war.[132] Finally, the Red Army's road service built, rebuilt, or strengthened approximately 100,000 kilometers of roads and more than 1,000 kilometers of bridges throughout the war.[133]

The highest-level educational institution charged with educating and training Red Army transportation officers throughout the war was the Military-Transport Academy, which was located in Leningrad and Kostroma. The transport academy's graduates included I. V. Kovalev, people's commissar of communications, S. M. Baev, deputy people's commissar of the Soviet river fleet, and Z. I. Kondrat'ev and A. V. Skliarov, deputy chiefs of the Red Army's VOSO. The chief of the academy throughout the entire war was Major General of Technical Forces (Lieutenant General in December 1943) V. M. Filichkin.[134]

The Rear (Rear Service Support)

On the eve of the war, the Directorate for the Organization of the Rear [Rear Services], Weapons, and Supply *(Upravlenie ustroistva tyla, vooruzheniia i snabzheniia)* loosely controlled all of the Soviet Armed Forces' rear service organizations, including a dizzying array of rear service forces and installations organic to army and navy forces in the military districts, bases, depots, and warehouses containing reserve military stocks, railroad, automobile, and road repair forces, and engineer, airfield, medical, veterinary, and other rear service forces and installations subordinate to the NKO.[135] The directorate's first wartime chief was Major General P. A. Ermolin.

In addition to its own quartermaster, medical, and veterinary directorates, lesser supply organs, and a separate but associated directorate for fuel supply, Ermolin's directorate coordinated closely with the Red Army's Military Communications Service (VOSO), whose forces were responsible for organizing rail and water transport and evacuating, restoring, and demolishing railroads, and the General Staff's Central Directorate for Military Communications (Transport) (TsUVS), which controlled and supervised the rail and waterways network through UVSs and departments in military districts (wartime *fronts*) and armies.

The most powerful and prestigious organ within Ermolin's directorate was the Main Quartermaster Directorate (*Glavnoe intendantskoe upravlenie,* or GIU), which was formed during 1940 as the principal organ responsible for supplying the Red Army's forces with military uniforms, personnel equipment and kit, and foodstuffs, and for troop billeting. The GIU, which was headed by Lieutenant General of the Quartermaster Service A. V. Khrulev, who had been appointed chief quartermaster *(intendant)* of the Red Army in early 1941, contained subdirectorates for each type of supply and supervised an analogous structure of directorates and departments in military districts, fleets, and armies.[136]

The GIU's Directorate for Clothing Supply (*Upravlenie veshchevogo snabzheniia.* or UVS), whose chief was Brigade Quartermaster N. N. Karpinsky, was responsible for the acquisition, storage, and distribution of military uniforms and clothing in accordance with GKO requirements and plans.[137] As such, Karpinsky's directorate supervised clothing supply departments in military districts *(fronts),* clothing supply sections in armies, and chiefs of clothing supply in regiments and brigades, who operated an elaborate system of warehouses, clothing and footwear repair facilities, and supply organs at each level. In addition, Karpinsky's UVS coordinated closely with industrial enterprises on the manufacture and distribution of required uniforms and clothing. In addition to collecting and maintaining reserve clothing stocks in the theaters of military operations, it also exploited local resources to support operating forces and collected captured (trophy) equipment from the battlefield and from the enemy.

The crucial task of feeding the many-million-man Red Army was the responsibility of the GIU's Directorate for Food Supply of the Red Army *(Upravlenie prodovol'stvennogo snabzheniia Krasnoi Armii, or UPS KA),* whose chief on the eve of war was Major General of the Quartermaster Service V. F. Belousov, who served as chief until February 1942.[138] Beneath the directorate were food supply departments subordinate to the quartermaster directorates in the military districts and armies, food and forage supply sections in corps and divisions, and food and forage supply chiefs in regiments. When war began, the food supply chain extended from the "center" through *fronts,* armies, divisions (brigades), regiments, battalions, and companies to the individual soldier. The food supply service and its governing directorate also maintained field installations that included a vast array of *front,* army, divisional, and regimental warehouses, bread factories, and bread bakeries and livestock points and even complete livestock herds.

No less vital was the Directorate for Fuel Supply (*Upravlenie snabzheniia goriuchim,* or USG), which was separate from but worked closely with the Directorate for Rear Services Organization and Supply, whose chief through 1942 was Major General of Tank Forces P. V. Kotov. Kotov's directorate was responsible for procuring, transporting, maintaining, and distributing all required fuel and lubricants to all Red Army forces.[139]

In addition to the GIU, the Directorate for Rear Services Organization and Supply contained two directorates responsible for providing medical support for men and animals assigned to and working for the Red Army. The first of these was the Medical Directorate (*Sanitarnoe upravlenie,* or SU), whose chief throughout the entire war was Lieutenant General of the Medical Service E. I. Smirnov, who was promoted to the rank of colonel general in 1943. Smirnov, only 37 years old in 1941, had graduated in 1932 from the Military-Medical Academy and from the Frunze Academy in 1938.[140] Smirnov's SU also controlled and managed the Red Army's Military-Medical Service *(Voenno-sanitarnaia sluzhba, or VSS),* which was customarily referred to simply as the Medical Service and included all medical units, subunits, and facilities responsible for the protection of the health of military personnel. On the eve of the war, the Medical Service was in the process of reorganizing on the basis of lessons learned in combat at Lake Khasan (1938), Khalkhin Gol (1939), and the Soviet-Finnish War (1939–1940).

The second medical support directorate was the Veterinary Directorate of the Red Army (*Veterinarnoe upravlenie Krasnoi Armii,* or VUKA), whose head throughout the war was Lieutenant General of the Veterinary Service V. M. Lekarev.[141] VUKA was particularly important because of the key role horses played in the Red Army's cavalry and artillery forces and its logistical transport system. VUKA also controlled and managed the Red Army's Military-Veterinary Service *(Voenno-veterinarnaia sluzhba),* which consisted of command and control organs, veterinary subunits, and veterinary installations and was responsible for acquiring, handling, and caring for horses and other animals and allocating them to the combat and supporting forces.[142] When it shifted to a war footing, VUKA operated through veterinary directorates and department in *fronts* and armies, which included all veterinary organs within their domains and the veterinarians who worked in them. Corps, divisions, and regiments also had assigned veterinarians, as did all other units and facilities possessing horses.[143]

During peacetime the Directorate for Rear Services Organization and Supply and its subordinate and associated directorates and department controlled logistical forces and facilities in the Red Army through deputy chiefs of staff for rear services and deputy and assistant commanders for rear services who headed departments and sections in military districts (wartime *fronts*), armies, corps, divisions, and regiments. The Red Army General Staff planned for the employment of these forces and facilities during wartime.[144]

However, some key logistical functions were outside the purview of the Directorate for Rear Services Organization and Supply on the eve of war. For example, the NKPS was responsible for running and manning the railroads with its Special Railroad Corps, and the NKVD was responsible for providing railroad security and performing local reconstruction and repair with its forces, which were to become subordinate to *front* commanders in wartime.[145] This lack of centralized control of logistics proved to one of the Red Army's many Achilles' heels when war began.

Another key shortcoming of the Red Army's logistical system on the eve of war was the lack of continuity between supply organs at the "center" and the recipients of those supplies in the field. For example, the chiefs of services and branches subordinate to military districts and armies and their supply organs were responsible for providing their forces with artillery, engineer, chemical defense, and communications (signal) equipment, quartermaster (food, forage, clothing, and other) supplies, fuel and lubricants, and pay through deputy chiefs of staff for rear services at all levels of command. However, since these chiefs were involved in other matters, few of them had time to plan rear service support. Worse still, the commanders at these levels also lacked direct responsibility for supply since the supply services were not subordinate to them.[146] Therefore, although a logistical structure existed within the NKO, unified command and control of logistical support did not exist throughout the military chain of command.

Other problems the Red Army faced on the eve of war were the inadequacy of uniform and clothing norms and inefficiencies in the system for distributing fuel and lubricants. Although the NKO issued new instructions concerning wartime clothing requirements during June 1941 and established new clothing production norms for Soviet industry, supply organs could not meet these norms during the first few months of war (see Chapter 13).[147] Likewise, the delivery of fuel and lubricants to the field forces was chaotic and inadequate, and this led to immediate and acute shortages when war began.

Just before war began, the NKO tried to solve its logistical problems by assigning Zhukov, the chief of the General Staff, responsibility for directing the Directorates for Rear Service Organization and Supply, Military Communications, and Fuel Supply and Marshal S. M. Budenny, the deputy people's commissar of defense, responsibility for coordinating the Main Quartermaster Directorate, Medical and Veterinary Directorate, and Department of Material Stocks. However, this measure neither unified nor increased the effectiveness of the NKO's logistical system.[148]

Therefore, the operating *fronts* and armies lacked any logistical support whatsoever after war and mobilization began, in part because the NKO failed to anticipate wartime logistical requirements and in part because their rear services simply collapsed under the weight and ferocity of the German assault. What little logistical support existed ended abruptly when the Red Army was routed and it lost most of its supply depots and bases to the advancing *Wehrmacht.* For example, during the first two months of the war, the *Wehrmacht's* rapid advance produced havoc in food, uniforms, and fuel supply and distribution when it captured most of the Red Army's forward supply bases and those in the immediate rear. At the same time, mobilization and massive troop movements paralyzed the distribution of supplies. Massive shortages resulted throughout the army, forcing units and troops to resort to "local" procurement (confiscation and theft).

Faced with these titanic logistical problems, in late June the *Stavka* simply improvised by assigning members of the newly created GKO individual responsibility for fulfilling specific supply functions.[149] A month after war began, in response to a GKO decree dated 28 July, the NKO fundamentally reorganized the army's rear service support structure on 1 August by creating the position of chief of Rear Services of the Red Army and a subordinate Main Directorate for Rear Services of the Red Army (*Glavnoe upravlenie tyla Krasnoi Armii,* or GUTA KA). GUTA KA included the NKO's Directorates for the Organization of the Rear and Military Communications, the General Staff's Automobile-Road Directorate, and the Inspectorate for Rear Services to GUTA KA and the Main Quartermaster, Fuel Supply, Main Military-Medical, and Veterinary directorates were directly subordinate to the new chief of the rear, Lieutenant General of the Quartermaster Service A. V. Khrulev, whom Stalin appointed to this key position.[150] Henceforth, Khrulev and GUTA KA were responsible for organizing all Red Army rear services, supplying all types of supplies and equipment to operating *fronts,* and evacuating casualties and equipment to the rear.[151]

In addition to creating this unified logistical structure within the NKO, the August order replaced the rear service hierarchy within *fronts* and armies with rear service directorates and departments headed by the chiefs of rear services in *fronts* and armies, who also served as the *fronts'* and armies' deputy commanders for rear services, and established the position of chief of rear services in the VVS. For example, the USG worked directly under Khrulev and supplied fuel and lubricants to the field forces through departments for fuel supply established in the operating *fronts* and corresponding chiefs of rear services in subordinate and separate armies, corps, divisions, brigades, and regiments. Distribution of fuel and lubricant occurred from distribution bases at the center (which were renamed *front* bases during 1942), through *front* and army depots, to a growing number of field depots at division and unit level. As this system developed, the distance between field depots and operating units decreased, thus facilitating greater continuity and better-sustained operations.[152]

Finally, the GKO capped these reforms on 19 August by upgrading the Medical Directorate to the Main Military-Medical Directorate (*Glavnoe voenno-sanitarnoe upravlenie*, or GVSU) to solve serious problems it encountered in treating and evacuating casualties, which only exacerbated the Red Army's already catastrophic manpower losses (see Chapter 13). The rapid German advance during Operation Barbarossa destroyed up to 50 percent of the Red Army's hospital base in the western military districts, forced it to evacuate the other half into the country's interior, and disrupted mobilization. As a result, the Red Army's operating *fronts* lacked almost half of their resources by August 1941 and had to rely solely on a limited number of regimental medical points, medical battalions, and field and garrison hospitals for medical support.[153]

Smirnov's new GVSU and associated Medical Service were responsible for medical treatment and evacuation, anti-epidemiological and medical-sanitary procedures, curing the sick, and preventing mass illness in the army's ranks. It performed these duties by establishing and supervising an elaborate network of medical agencies, units, and facilities throughout the entire force structure extending from *front* down to company level.[154]

Symptomatic of the supply problems the Red Army wrestled with during the first four months of war was the inadequacy of ration norms and the food distribution system, which the NKO tried to remedy by establishing more austere but timelier distribution of food to its field forces in September 1941.[155] The NKO directive established new monthly norms for the allocation of 14 categories of foodstuffs and forage to the forces based on their actual rather than theoretical strength and the combat missions they actually performed (see Chapter 13).[156] The GKO also formed the Committee for Food and Clothing Supply of the Red Army, chaired by Party leader A. I. Mikoian, in the fall of 1941 to implement GKO supply directives and restore order and centralized direction to the entire supply system. This committee accomplished its work effectively, albeit slowly.

As evidence of the Communist Party's keen interest in rear service affairs, on 20 November 1941, an NKO order made the members of military councils in *fronts* and armies responsible for rear service work by ensuring military council orders were fulfilled and by coordinating rear service efforts with local Party organs and councils in the *fronts'* and armies' zones.[157]

The GKO and NKO reorganized and reformed the Red Army's rear service support slowly but steadily during 1941 and early 1942. As its directorates and departments in the center and the operating *fronts* and armies decreased in size but increased in efficiency, command and control became more stable and reliable and rear service units and installations became more mobile, flexible, and effective. At the same time, the depths of the *fronts* and armies' rear service areas shrank and rear service installations deployed ever closer to the forces they supported. Helpful to this effort was the introduction of a new supply system based on the principle of "pushing" supplies "from the top down," meaning that higher organs were responsible for providing supplies to their subordinate forces. Increased quantities of vehicular transport, much of it provided by Lend-Lease, permitted increased centralization of supply distribution.

All the while, the GKO and NKO continued reorganizing the armed forces logistical structure during 1942, improving in particular its command and control. For example, the GKO removed the food supply service from the Main Quartermaster Directorate on 27 January, reorganized it into an independent Main Directorate for Food Supply of the Red Army (*Glavnoe upravlenie prodovol'stvennogo snabzheniia Krasnoi Armii*, or GUPS), and assigned D. V. Pavlov, the former people's commissar for trade, as its chief. At the same time, it transformed departments responsible for food supply in *fronts* and armies into full directorates and subordinated them directly to their respective chiefs of rear services, and appointed General P. I. Drachev as chief quartermaster of the Red Army.[158]

Soon after, on 19 April, the NKO abolished the Main Directorate for Rear Services of the Red Army and subordinated its former headquarters, directorates, and departments to the chief of the Red Army's Rear Services.[159] Thus, GUPS and the other logistical directorates became directly subordinate to Khrulev.[160]

This reorganization continued on 22 May, when the GKO appointed Khrulev as deputy commissar of defense and created the position of chief of Naval Rear Services, appointing Lieutenant General of Coastal Services S. I. Vorob'ev to that post. On the same day it also reorganized the Red Army's rear services structure by streamlining and strengthening the duties of chiefs of rear services in operating *fronts* and armies by designating them as deputy commanders and established similar positions in all corps and divisions. It charged these chiefs (deputy commanders) with responsibility for all aspects of rear service support within their jurisdiction, including weapons, equipment, and material supply, evacuation, and logistical support of their subordinate rear services.[161] Finally, the GKO established a medical hierarchy analogous to its centralized rear service system and appointed Academician N. N. Burdenko as chief surgeon of the Red Army and a broad array of chiefs for other medical specialties at the NKO level and within the *fronts* and armies.[162]

Continuing this reorganization during 1943, the GKO elevated the food directorate (UPS) to the status of a main directorate in its own right in January but reorganized it into a subdirectorate under the chief of Red Army Rear Services' Main Quartermaster Directorate in June.[163] As a result, a new ration supply system emerged by mid-1943 that persisted until war's end and was directly responsive to the UPS and the chief of the Red Army's Rear Services through his quartermaster general. This system included dedicated food supply organs at every level down to battalion.[164] Finally, when the NKO formed air armies during 1943, it also created an army rear in each air army, and rear service units, facilities, and organs in all large PVO formations. Khrulev, who was promoted to the rank of colonel general in November 1942 and army general in November 1943, remained the Red Army's chief of rear services and supervised this reformed logistical system throughout the entire war.[165]

By every standard of measurement, the scope of logistical support the chief of the Red Army's Rear Services and associated NKO's directorates provided to the Red Army's operating *fronts* and armies during the war was staggering. In addition to the 100,000 kilometers of roads constructed and repaired by the Road Directorate and the 117,000 kilometers of railroad constructed and repaired by the NKPS, other rear service forces constructed over 6,000 airfields and supplied Soviet partisan and underground forces.[166]

At the same time, the chief of rear services' main and subordinate directorates acquired, stored, and distributed to the field more than 10 million tons of ammunition and vast quantities of foodstuffs, forage, and other supplies. Truck transport alone carried more than 145 million tons of cargo and rail another 19 million railroad car loads. Although it obtained most of the Red Army's uniforms and other clothing from Soviet light industry, the clothing directorate also collected clothing voluntarily or on a requisition basis from workers in Soviet industry and civilians. For example, the UVS provided more than 38 million military greatcoats, 70 million sets of uniforms, 117 million sets of underwear, 64 million pairs of leather boots, 20 million padded jackets and quilted trousers, and 2 million sheepskin coats to the Red Army's troops during the war.[167]

By mid-1942 the food directorate had managed to accumulate food reserves amounting to 20 days of supply in military districts; 30 days in operating *fronts;* five days in divisions, mobile corps, and brigades; one and one-half to three days in battalions and weapons' crews; and one day in the backpacks of individual soldiers.[168] Overall, the Red Army's troops and animals consumed about 40 million tons of food and forage, much of this grain, other agricultural products, and unprocessed meat, throughout the war. Lend-Lease supplied 4.3 million tons of this total quantity, primarily critical foodstuffs such as 610,000 metric tons of sugar and 664,900 metric tons of vital canned meat (including the ubiquitous Spam). While constituting only 10 percent of Soviet food production, Lend-Lease supplies included high-quality foodstuffs necessary to sustain the army in its military operations. For example, sugar deliveries amounted to 41.8 percent of Soviet production, and canned meat amounted to more than 18 percent of Soviet meat deliveries.[169]

Fuel supply was one of the most important aspects of logistical support throughout the war, because the success of the Red Army as a whole depended on successful operations by its tank and mechanized forces, and the highly mobile offensive operations the Red Army conducted after November 1942 created an immense demand for fuel and lubricants. For example, the Red Army's average monthly fuel expenditure increased from 222,000 tons during 1942 to 320,000 tons during 1944 and reached the staggering total of 420,000 tons during the summer of 1944. By war's end, the Red Army had consumed 16.3 million tons of fuel.[170] Overall, the fuel directorate supplied 20 million tons of fuel and lubricants to the Red Army throughout the war.[171]

In the realm of medical support, the medical directorate increased the number of doctors in the Red Army from 44,729 in July 1942 to almost 61,000 in July 1944 and increased the total of all medical personnel in the Red Army from just over 93,000 to almost 122,000 during the same period.[172] However, when all was said and done, the medical support and health care provided to Red Army soldiers remained weak throughout the war. As a result, out of the total number of just over 22 million Red Army and Fleet medical cases treated by the GVSU's agencies, 7.6 million resulted from various diseases.[173] This grim toll from sickness was clearly excessive and was a direct result of poor field sanitary conditions, mediocre medical treatment, and the general shortage of medicines and other medical equipment.

Finally, the veterinary directorate's (VUKA) veterinarians and veterinary assistants *(fel'dshers)*, 62.5 and 97.2 percent of whom were conscripted from the civilian sector, respectively, and its associated Military-Veterinary Service assisted wounded and sick horses, arranged for their evacuation to veterinary hospitals, and treated them at every stage of the evacuation.[174] This included 46.9 percent of the Red Army's horses during 1941 and 1942, 44.3 percent during 1943, and 27.4 percent during 1944. These organizations treated and returned to service over 2.1 million horses and achieved a recovery rate of 86.9 percent throughout the war.[175]

The chief of the Red Army's Rear Services and its subordinate directorates also managed an extensive system of military academies, schools, and training courses. The most important of these included the Quartermaster

Academy of the Red Army, which was renamed the Military Academy of the Rear and Supply in September 1942, which was located at Moscow and Kalinin; the Kirov Military-Medical Academy in Leningrad and Samarkand; the Kuibyshev Military-Medical Academy in Kuibyshev; and the Military-Veterinary Academy in Moscow, Aral'sk, and Samarkand.

Political Affairs

The GKO organ most responsible for ensuring ideological purity and enforcing Communist Party discipline in the Red Army was the Main Political Directorate of the Red Army (*Glavnoe politicheskoe upravlenie Krasnoi Armii*)–GlavPU, *for short.* Formed on 16 July 1941 with Army Commissar 1st Rank L. Z. Mekhlis as its chief, GlavPU was the direct descendant of the Political Department of the Revolutionary Military Council (REVOENSOVET) of the union republics, which was formed in 1919 and became the Political Directorate of the RKKA in 1921 and the Main Directorate for Political Propaganda in the Red Army (*Glavnoe upravlenie politicheskoi propagandy Krasnoi Armii,* or GUPP KA) in June 1940.[176]

The Communist Party's Politburo and the GKO assigned GlavPU a host of responsibilities, which ranged from establishing and supervising political organs in the Red Army's forces structure and conducting constant political education and indoctrination to ensuring the loyalty and morale of the Red Army's officers and soldiers.[177] In short, as the political watchdog of the Party, the GlavPU was involved in virtually every aspect of the lives of Red Army officers and soldiers.

Working through the GKO, the Communist Party's Central Committee determined and improved GlavPU's organization throughout the war. Initially, it consisted of subdirectorates and departments responsible for organizational work, political instruction, propaganda and agitation, political cadres, Komsomol, and other Party-political work. However, the GKO added a department responsible for political work among partisans and the civilian populations in occupied territories to GlavPU in late 1941 and a directorate for special propaganda in 1944. In addition, the GKO also organized a special Council for Military-Political Propaganda within GlavPU in 1942. Consisting of A. S. Shcherbakov, who was GlavPU's chief and a Party secretary, Party Secretary A. A. Zhdanov, and Central Committee members D. Z. Mangul'sky and E. M. Iaroslavsky, this council was responsible for gathering and processing war experiences to improve the directorate's overall effectiveness.

The GlavPU also formed and fielded special groups of permanent and nonpermanent agitators (lecturers), which often included notable Party, state, social, and cultural leaders, whose mission was to conduct agitation throughout the entire Red Army chain of command.[178] Stalin appointed

A. S. Shcherbakov, who was a Party secretary and a candidate member of the Politburo, as chief of GlavPU in June 1942. Promoted to the rank of colonel general in 1943, Shcherbakov remained as the directorate's chief to war's end.[179]

Intelligence

In terms of its vital function, arguably one of the NKO's most important directorates was the Main Intelligence Directorate (GRU), which it did not directly control until October 1942. Prior to the war, the NKO had formed the Intelligence Directorate (RU) (the Fifth Directorate) on 22 November 1934, as the "central organ for organizing and supervising the Red Army's intelligence service." However, on 26 July 1940 the NKO transferred the RU to the General Staff, where it was performing the same critical function when war began.[180]

Because intelligence collection and processing was increasing in importance and complexity, on 16 February 1942, without removing it from the General Staff's control, the NKO reorganized the RU into the Main Intelligence Directorate, tasked it with conducting strategic, operational, and force intelligence, and strengthened its organizational structure substantially. However, since this reorganization did not improve the GRU's effectiveness, the NKO reorganized the GRU once again on 23 October 1942, this time removing it from the General Staff and placing it under its own direct control. Specifically, the NKO stripped the GRU of all responsibility for force intelligence *(voiskovaia razvedka)*, which became the responsibility of the General Staff's Directorate of Force Intelligence (*Upravlenie voiskovoi razvedki*, or UVR), and, instead, made the GRU responsible for "the conduct of agent intelligence of foreign armies both abroad and within the territory of the USSR under temporary enemy occupation" under its own control.[181]

The new GRU was organized into a First Directorate, which was responsible for agent operations abroad, and a Second Directorate, which was responsible for agent operations in territories temporarily occupied by enemy forces. At the same time, the NKO also transferred the deciphering department of the GRU's Second Directorate to the NKVD and converted the GRU's former Main Department for Military Censorship into a separate and independent department within its structure.

Since even this reorganization failed to improve intelligence collection and processing to the degree the *Stavka* desired, the NKO once again reorganized the country's central military intelligence organs on 19 April 1943, by transforming the General Staff's UVR into the Intelligence Directorate and assigning it responsibility for "direction of force and agent intelligence of the *fronts* and regular information about enemy actions and intentions, and the conduct of disinformation of the enemy."[182]

Therefore, the April 1943 reorganization assigned responsibility for conducting agent intelligence and diversionary work in territories of the Soviet Union temporarily occupied by the enemy to the General Staff's RU and the subordinate ROs within the Red Army's *fronts.* At the same time, it disbanded the 2nd Directorate of the NKO's GRU, which controlled agent operations in territories of the Soviet Union temporarily occupied by enemy forces, and transferred the GRU's agent network in these regions to the General Staff's RU. Thereafter, the GRU was responsible only for conducting agent intelligence abroad. This structure for intelligence collection and processing then endured to war's end.[183]

Counterintelligence

Just as the GlavPU protected the Soviet Union against political and ideological subversion from within, military counterintelligence organs performed the equally vital function of protecting state security against subversion from enemies outside the Soviet Union's borders in close cooperation with state security organs controlled by the NKVD. When war began, the GKO detached all counterintelligence organs from the NKO and NKVMF (navy) and reorganized them into so-called special departments (OOs) in operating *fronts,* fleets, and armies, which functioned under the operational control of the NKVD's Third Directorate, the Directorate for Special Departments. Despite this command and control arrangement, the GKO still considered the OOs as elements of the NKO.

Soviet sources described the OOs' responsibilities as follows:

> Relying on the keen awareness of the Soviet people and the soldiers of the Soviet Army and Navy and their devotion to the Homeland, in cooperation with the commands and political organs, military counterintelligence agents *[kontrarazvechiki]* created an effective system of measures for revealing and interrupting enemy subversive acts and for unmasking his agents. The intelligence services of fascist Germany strove to conduct extensive subversive activity against the USSR. They created more than 130 reconnaissance-diversionary organs and about 60 special reconnaissance-diversionary schools on the Soviet-German front. In fact, the Soviet Army repelled these diversionary detachments and terrorists. Soviet military counterintelligence organs actively sought out enemy agents in areas of combat operations and where military objectives were located, provided timely information concerning the dispatch of enemy spies and diversionary agents, and penetrated enemy intelligence and counterintelligence organs.[184]

To increase the responsiveness of counterintelligence to the *Stavka* and political authorities, the GKO converted the NKVD's Directorate for Special Departments into the Main Directorate for Counterintelligence (*Glavnoe upravlenie kontrrazvedki*, or GUK) on 14 April 1943, and placed it under the nominal control of the NKO. However, as before, although supervised by the NKO, the NKVD controlled it operationally.[185] Known by its pseudonym SMERSH, meaning "Death to Spies," this directorate coordinated closely with the NKVD and MVD for the remainder of the war.[186] The GKO appointed the long-term security operative, V. S. Abakumov, as SMERSH's chief and a deputy commissar of defense on 21 April, posts that he occupied until war's end.

Under Abakumov's efficient and often ruthless direction, together with the NKVD and MVD, SMERSH

> developed and implemented operational plans for the struggle with enemy intelligence at the front, in the Soviet rear area, and in temporarily occupied territory. Relying on the vigilance of soldiers, together with the [Red Army's] commands, the SMERSH's organs protected formations and units against penetration by enemy agents, battled the underground activities of enemy intelligence organs in the Soviet rear, and organized intelligence and counterintelligence work beyond the front lines and in the German rear. They neutralized thousands of enemy agents and made a significant contribution to the achievement of victory.[187]

No less important from the standpoint of ensuring Stalin's iron grip over the beleaguered country and its struggling armed forces, SMERSH also directed the activities of all political organs in the Red Army and the Navy and served as the premier instrument for maintaining discipline in the military, often by means of outright terror and intimidation.[188]

INTERNAL SECURITY FORCES (NKVD)

Just as the NKO was responsible for protecting the Soviet Union against foreign aggression, the People's Commissariat of Internal Affairs (NKVD) was responsible for maintaining internal security within the country. Therefore, it was quite natural that the missions of the two commissariats overlapped in some respects and complemented one another in others. For example, the NKVD fielded various types of internal forces *(vnutrennie voiska)*, which, as an integral part of the Soviet Armed Forces, were responsible for protecting "vital state objectives" such as government facilities, industrial enterprises, key communications centers, rail lines, and the country's borders; securing and administering the Soviet Union's extensive labor and penal camp system (GULAG), combating enemy diversionary forces and agents operating on Soviet territory, and conducting counterintelligence operations in support of the armed forces as a whole (see Chapter 5).

Depending on their specific mission, these internal forces were subordinate to six NKVD functional directorates, specifically, the Main Directorate of Border Troops, the Main Directorate of NKVD Forces for the Protection of Important Industrial Enterprises, the Main Directorate for NKVD Escort Troops, the Main Directorate of NKVD Forces for Protecting Railroad Facilities, the Main Directorate for NKVD Supply, and the Main Military-Construction Directorate of NKVD Forces of the USSR.[189] A deputy commissar of internal affairs for forces supervised and coordinated the work of these directorates and exercised operational control over the internal forces assigned to them.[190]

When *Wehrmacht* forces invaded the Soviet Union, the Politburo and Council of People's Commissars (SNK) quickly committed the NKVD's internal forces to the struggle both along the borders and in the depth of the Soviet Union. On 23 June, the day after Operation Barbarossa began, the SNK assigned responsibility for protecting the rear areas of the Red Army's operating *fronts* and armies to the NKVD's Main Directorate for Border Troops (*Glavnoe upravlenie pogranichnykh voisk*, or GUPV) and also established the Main Directorate for Internal Forces (*Glavnoe upravlenie vnutrennikh voisk*, or GUVV) within the NKVD and made it responsible for protecting the "deep rear areas" of the Red Army's operating *fronts*.

At the same time, the SNK ordered the Red Army's operating *fronts* to create subordinate directorates for front rear area security (*Upravleniia okhrany tyla fronta*, or UOTFs) around the nucleus of border guards directorates operating within the prewar military districts from which they were formed. The chiefs of these UOTFs were responsible for ensuring general security in the *fronts'* rear areas and protecting all rail lines, installations, and facilities, communications centers and routes, and critical industrial facilities within their *fronts'* zones of operations. To do so, the GKO gave them operational control over all NKVD internal troops, border guards, and police units and subunits operating in their *fronts'* zones.[191]

However, this was easier said than done since the *Wehrmacht* had already destroyed many of the NKVD's border guards detachments along the country's western borders by 23 June, and within weeks the collapse of the Red Army's forward defenses had produced utter chaos in its rear area. Consequently, many of the NKVD internal forces that survived the initial German onslaught ended up fighting alongside Red Army forces as infantry and others were swallowed up in the Red Army during its subsequent mobilization. All the while, however, the NKVD conducted a mobilization of its own to field forces to accomplish its assigned security missions.

The organizational structure of the NKVD's rear-area security forces evolved in tandem with the quantity of Red Army operating *fronts* and the enemy's capability for operating in each *front's* rear area during the first six months of the war. As a rule, however, from four to nine NKVD regiments performed security tasks in each *front's* rear area, and a single regiment or separate battalion did so for individual armies.[192] Although these forces remained subordinate to their respective NKVD organs administratively, they actually functioned under the operational control of *front* and army commanders, and many actively took part in combat operations.

As the size and strength of the NKVD's rear-area security forces increased dramatically during late 1941 and early 1942, the GKO also increased their assigned missions. For example, in addition to providing security in the *fronts'* zones in cooperation with Red Army forces and protecting vital lines of communications and other objectives, on 4 January 1942, the GKO assigned the NKVD's rear-area security forces responsibility for garrisoning cities and large towns liberated from German control and assisting other NKVD organs in rooting out enemy agents and collaborators in formerly occupied territory.[193] Therefore, on 4 April the GKO ordered the NKVD to form a Directorate of NKVD Forces for Protecting the Rear of Operating Soviet Armies *(Upravlenie voisk NKVD po okhrane tyla deistvuiushchei Sovetskoi Armii)* within its Main Directorate of Internal Forces to improve command and control of its forces.

When the Red Army went over to a general offensive during the winter of 1942–43, the GKO expanded the role of NKVD's rear-area security forces regarding the struggle with German reconnaissance and diversionary groups and assigned them the new missions of supervising the construction of defense lines and positions and the evacuation of industrial enterprises and securing and controlling prisoners of war as well as Red Army officers and soldiers accused of treason by the Soviet state. So that it could do so effectively, the GKO reorganized the Directorate of NKVD Forces for Protecting the Rear of the Soviet Field Armies into a main directorate in its own right in May 1943.

The responsibilities of the NKVD's internal forces expanded dramatically during late 1943 and 1944, when, in addition to their already extensive missions, the GKO assigned them responsibility for maintaining order and combating "counterrevolutionary" and "antisocialist" elements in the increasingly vast liberated territories liberated by the Red Army, in particular, Belorussia, the Ukraine, Crimea, and Galicia. Finally, in addition to the 53 NKVD divisions, 20 NKVD brigades, and 30 NKVD armored trains that supported the Red Army throughout the war (see Chapter 5), the NKVD also formed special sniper commands from its internal forces and assigned them to key *fronts* and armies.[194] As a result, together with the GRU and SMERSH, this "army within an army" ensured the maintenance of security and iron discipline within the Soviet Union, its Red Army, and the vast territories liberated by the Red Army outside the Soviet Union's prewar frontiers.

RED ARMY GENERAL STAFF (GSHKA)

As Stalin's chief war-planning and fighting organizations, the 12 directorates and three departments subordinate to the Red Army General Staff on the eve of war were responsible to the *Stavka* for all strategic planning and the direction of the Soviet Armed Forces operating at the front during wartime. Collectively, these directorates and departments were responsible for all operational, mobilization, and organizational matters in the Soviet Armed Forces, except military education and training, which was the responsibility of the NKO (see Table 11.2).[195]

Since the General Staff was the *Stavka's* main organ responsible for planning and conducting military operations, the GKO began stripping it of many of its nonoperating directorates after war began so that it could focus its attentions on operational matters. For example, the GKO transferred the General Staff's organizational and mobilization directorates and its Directorates for Manning and Constructing Forces, Military Communications Routes, Auto-Road, and Formation of the Rear and Supply of Forces, as well as its communications center, to the NKO or other commissariats on 28 June.[196] This left the General Staff with Operations, Intelligence, Organization of the Operational Rear, Construction of Fortified Regions, Military-Topographical, and Cipher directorates and the General Matters, Military-Historical, and Cadre departments.

However, as the war progressed and the GKO determined what organizations were actually necessary to supervise and support military operations, it formed new directorates within the General Staff. For example, the General Staff's involvement in organizational matters was so significant that the GKO formed a new organizational directorate in the General Staff during April 1942. In addition, the GKO created a directorate for automobile-road transport in the General Staff briefly during late July 1941 and, later, new departments for secret command and control, the exploitation of war experience, and special missions.[197] Some of these departments, such as the Departments for the Exploitation of War Experience and Special Missions became full directorates before war's end; other directorates, such as the Directorate for the Operational Rear, reverted to departmental status.

Needless to say, since the General Staff and NKO contained directorates and departments whose functions were quite similar, these organs closely cooperated with one another while fulfilling their shared tasks. For example, in the realm of force organization, the General Staff routinely coordinated with Glavupraform (GUFUKA) to determine the Red Army's most effective organizational structure.

Immediately after war began, the large-scale destruction of Red Army forces and the chaotic mobilization caused extreme personnel turbulence within the General Staff that seriously disrupted its operations and reduced its effectiveness. For example, the NKO transferred 393 senior and mid-grade staff officers from the General Staff to positions in the Red Army's operating *fronts* and armies during late June and early July and another 449 officers on 18 August 1941. As a result, the General Staff suffered a chronic shortage of fully qualified general staff officers ranging from 78 percent during 1941 and 29 percent during late 1942 to 100 percent from mid-1943 through war's end. Thus, although the General Staff was fully manned during the last two years of the war, its average fill throughout the duration of the war was about 85 percent.[198]

Finally, like other commissariats and key governmental organs, the General Staff displaced several times during the war in response to the changing military situation. For example, the German air offensive against Moscow during June and July 1941 forced the General Staff to relocate several times within the city of Moscow, and, when the *Wehrmacht's* forces approached the city during October, the General Staff relocated the General Staff to safety in the city of Kuibyshev. During its absence, an operational group of the staff headed by A. M. Vasilevsky remained in Moscow to provide continuous support for the *Stavka*.

Operations

The Main Operations Directorate (*Glavnoe operativnoe upravlenie*, or GOU), or First Directorate, was the most important directorate in the General Staff, and its chief, who also served as the General Staff's first deputy chief, was its most important senior staff officer. Based on guidance it received from the *Stavka* and the chief of the General Staff, the GOU was responsible for all operational planning, collecting and analyzing all information related to the situation at the front, and ensuring the *Stavka's* directives were properly carried out.

In accordance with the *Stavka's* directives and together with its members and the chief of the General Staff, the GOU planned, prepared, and conducted Red Army strategic operations by sketching out the general outline of these operations, establishing suitable force objectives and missions, and determining the most effective methods for these forces to conduct these operations. Once the *Stavka* approved these operational plans and issued appropriate directives, the GOU helped the operating *fronts* plan and prepare their operations, and, later, supervised the actual conduct of the operations by assisting responsible *Stavka* representatives or by dispatching its own representatives to provide advice to the participating *fronts* and armies. Since its chief and his two deputies were the only General Staff officers who accompanied the chief of the General Staff when he briefed Stalin and the *Stavka* and, therefore, had to be aware of virtually everything going on within the General Staff, all other General Staff directorates cooperated closely with the GOU.[199]

Although the GOU consisted of 12 separate departments organized on a functional, branch, or service basis when war began, in August 1941 the GKO reorganized it into 8 departments consisting of a chief, a deputy chief, and five to ten operations officers each, and assigned these departments responsibility for handling all operational matters within the Red Army's eight operating *fronts*. In addition, the GKO also defined the tasks the GOU and its departments were to perform with far greater specificity, in essence, assigning them responsibility for every conceivable operational matter along the northern, northwestern, western, central, southwestern, southern, near eastern, and far eastern strategic axes.[200]

Thereafter, as the number of operating *fronts* changed from eight in the fall of 1941 to ten in May 1942, 14 in November 1942, 13 in the summer of 1943, and 26 from the fall of 1943 through war's end, the number of departments in the GOU changed accordingly.[201] Finally, the GOU also established two departments to coordinate the Red Army's operations with allied Polish and Romanian forces by war's end. In addition, the GOU also included numerous departments organized along functional lines, such as the Organization-Registration, Operational-Training, Operational Transportation, Auto-Armored, Communications, and War Experience departments, many of which the GKO transferred to other NKO directorates or elevated to full directorates in their own right during the war.

As with other directorates, staff officers assigned to the GOU worked in around-the-clock shifts to ensure continuous fulfillment of their specific responsibilities and to match Stalin's unique work habits, which required the chief of the General Staff and/or the chief of the GOU to report to the supreme commander, Stalin, at 1000–1100 hours, 1600–1700 hours, and 2100–0300 hours daily.[202] With only slight variations, this same work regime characterized the work of virtually every other General Staff directorate, particularly those working directly with operating *fronts*.[203]

This rigorous and unorthodox work schedule meant that sleep was at a premium in the General Staff. For example, the deputy chief of the General Staff had to be present on the job for 17–18 hours per day and was able to rest only between 0500–0600 and 1200 hours daily, and the chief of the GOU had to catch his rest between 1400 and 1800–1900 hours daily.[204] At least in part, the deputy chief of the General Staff and the chief of the GOU bore such a severe workload because the chiefs of the General Staff spent a total of 22 months working at the front throughout the entire war.[205]

The nine wartime chiefs of the GOU were Lieutenant General G. K. Malandin (February–June 1941), Lieutenant General V. M. Zhlobin (July 1941), Major General (Lieutenant General in October 1941 and Colonel General in May 1942) A. M. Vasilevsky (August 1941 to 26 June 1942), Lieutenant General P. I. Bodin (June–July 1942), Lieutenant General N. F. Vatutin (July 1942), Lieutenant General V. D. Ivanov (July to 10 December 1942), Lieutenant General S. M. Teteshkin, Lieutenant General (Colonel General in April 1943) A. I. Antonov (11 December 1942 to May 1943), and Lieutenant General (Colonel General in November 1943) S. M. Shtemenko (May 1943 to war's end).[206]

Intelligence

Since accurate intelligence was a prerequisite for the successful conduct of military operations, the second most important wartime directorate in the General Staff when war began was its Intelligence Directorate (RU), or Second Directorate, which was responsible for collecting, processing, and analyzing intelligence information in support of the Red Army's operations. To improve intelligence support for the Red Army, on 16 February 1942, the NKO transformed the RU into the General Staff's Main Intelligence Directorate (GRU), substantially beefed up its organizational structure, and tasked it with conducting strategic, operational, and force intelligence. Specifically, the new GRU consisted of agent (the First) and information directorates (the Second), and eight new main departments tasked with handling functional matters (see Table 11.3).

However, because intelligence collection and processing problems persisted, the GKO reorganized its intelligence organs on 23 October 1942 by removing the GRU from the General Staff and assigning it directly to the NKO. The GRU became responsible for the conduct of agent operations at home and abroad under NKO control, and the GKO assigned the responsibility for conducting force intelligence *(voiskovaia razvedka)* to a new Directorate for Force Intelligence (UVR) it created within the General Staff.

The new UVR, whose chief also served as a deputy chief of the General Staff, was responsible for directing all intelligence departments (*razvedivatel'nye otdely*, or ROs) in the Red Army's operating *fronts* and armies and was categorically forbidden from conducting any agent intelligence. In addition, the NKO's October order transferred the deciphering department, which had formerly been in the GRU's Second Directorate, to the NKVD and converted the GRU's Main Department of Military Censorship into an independent department in the NKO.

The GKO rationalized the intelligence support for its operating *fronts* and armies once again on 19 April 1943 by reorganizing the UVR into an Intelligence Directorate (RU) and assigning it responsibility for "directing the *fronts'* force and agent intelligence, [the collection] of regular information about enemy actions and intentions, and conducting disinformation of the enemy."[207] In essence, this reform tasked the General Staff's new RU and its subordinate ROs within operating *fronts* to conduct agent intelligence and diversionary work in territory of the USSR temporarily occupied by the enemy, but forbade the armies' ROs from performing the same functions (see Table 11.4). It also disbanded the Second Directorate of the NKO's GRU, which had been responsible for conducting agent operations in Soviet territory temporarily occupied by enemy forces, and transferred its agent network to the General Staff's RU. Thereafter, the GRU was responsible only for conducting agent intelligence abroad.

This reform also defined the relationship between the NKO's GRU, the General Staff's RU, and the new counterintelligence directorate, called SMERSH, which the NKO had established on 14 April 1943. Specifically, it ordered the chief of the General Staff to "form a group of commanders headed by Colonel General Comrade Golikov with the mission of generalizing and analyzing information about the enemy received from all intelligence and counterintelligence organs (NKO, NKVD, NKVMF, the Main Directorate SMERSH, and the partisan headquarters)."[208] While SMERSH was to provide the RU and the *fronts'* and armies' ROs with specialists qualified in securing and debriefing prisoners of war and coordinate closely with the RU on matters regarding enemy employment of agents, including their organization, operating techniques, and communications, the RU was to pass all relevant information on enemy agent operations to SMERSH. The only substantive change to the RU's structure after April 1943 occurred when the NKO transferred its Department of Military Censorship to it on 18 September 1943.[209]

From May 1943 through war's end, the RU and its subordinate ROs dispatched more than 1,200 special designation (SPETSNAZ) reconnaissance-diversionary groups, totaling more than 10,000 men, into the enemy's rear area and enlisted the efforts of more than 15,000 local inhabitants as agents and other types of operatives in their intelligence collection efforts. These groups and agents provided invaluable information concerning German military intentions and plans, the strength and dispositions of German forces and reserves, and the timing of the *Wehrmacht's* military operations and troop movements.[210] The wartime chiefs of the RU (and GRU) were Major General of Tank Forces A. P. Panfilov, Lieutenant General I. I. Il'ichev, and Colonel General F. F. Kuznetsov.[211]

Organization, Mobilization, and Force Manning

When war began, the General Staff's Organizational, Mobilization, and Manning and Constructing Forces directorates, which were responsible for supervising the organization, mobilization, conscription, and manning of the Red Army's forces, prepared many of the GKO's decrees regarding these matters jointly with the NKO.[212] However, the General Staff's preoccupation with these matters distracted from and hindered its control over military operations.[213] Therefore, the GKO abolished these three directorates on 28 July 1941, turning their functions first over to the NKO's Glavupraform and, later, GUFUKA.[214]

Although Glavupraform and GUFUKA remained responsible for all aspects of organizing and manning the Red Army's force structure, its departments for military training and operational movements cooperated closely with the General Staff's Operations Directorate in terms of assigning missions to VOSO (Directorate for Military Communications Routes) for troop transport prior to or during military operations. The only organizational functions remaining under General Staff control were concerned with statistics, manpower registration, and troop deployments, which its Organizational-Registration Department performed.[215]

However, as the General Staff's involvement with Red Army organization and manning grew, the General Staff formed an Organizational Directorate (*Organizatsionnoe upravlenie,* or OU) of its own on 25 April 1942, which was responsible for working on force structure matters jointly with GUFUKA (Glavupraform). While GUFUKA worked on Red Army tables of organization *(shtats),* the OU prepared organizational directives, monitored their implementation, and kept track of the number of troops at the front. The OU also took custody of the Operations Directorate's Organization and Registration Department and assumed some of the organizational responsibilities of the GUFUKA, even though the latter retained control over the Red Army's Personnel Department.[216]

Since the existence of two parallel organizational directorates within the NKO and General Staff inevitably caused significant friction and confusion, Stalin intervened in June 1942 by redefining the specific functions of each competing organ.[217] When this measure failed to smooth out organizational work, between 29 April and 4 May 1943, Stalin abolished GUFUKA's Organizational and Personnel Department and established in its stead a full-fledged Main Organizational Directorate (GOU) in the General Staff, which consisted of separate functional departments responsible for branch-specific matters and specialized General Staff organizational missions.[218] In effect, this order accorded GUFUKA responsibility for creating Red Army formations and units and the General Staff responsibility for assigning these forces and employing them operationally. Lieutenant General A. G. Karponosov, who had served as chief of the Organizational Directorate since April 1942, continued to serve as new main directorate's chief until 1946.[219]

Military Communications (Routes)

On the eve of war, the Central Directorate for Military Communications Routes (TsUVS), whose chief was Major General P. A. Ermolin, was responsible for supervising all military communications along road and water routes in the Soviet Union through UVSs subordinate to the chiefs of military communications in the military districts *(fronts)* and armies, who were responsible for all communications within the Red Army's field forces. However, these UVSs shared overlapping responsibilities with the NKPS, which controlled and managed the railroads, and the NKO and the NKVD, whose Military Communications Service and security forces repaired and provided security for the railroads.

After war began, the GKO attempted to resolve military communications problems on 1 August 1941 by reorganizing the TsUVS into the Directorate for Military Communications (VOSO) and by subordinating both it and the General Staff's Automobile-Road Directorate (GADU), which it had created on 16 July, to the new chief of the Red Army's Rear Services, Khrulev, and his new Main Directorate for the Red Army Rear Services (GUTA KA) in the NKO. Even after this reorganization, however, the General Staff's Organizational Directorate still played an advisory role in the organization of transport units.

Despite numerous organizational changes, rail, road, and water transport remained shared responsibilities of the NKO and NKPS for the remainder of 1941 and 1942. However, the *Stavka* acted to make the communications system more efficient and responsive to its needs on 31 January 1943 by reorganizing VOSO into the Central Directorate for Military Communications (TsUPVOSO) and by transferring the new directorate from the Main Directorate of Rear Services to the General Staff. At the same time, it also formed military communications departments within all of the Red Army's *fronts*, military districts, and armies that, while directly responsible to the *fronts'* and armies' chiefs of staff, also worked closely with the new central directorate.[220]

However, this attempt to establish a more expedient structure to control military communications organs also failed to live up to expectations. Therefore, on 7 March 1943, the NKO removed TsUPVOSO and its associated departments in the *fronts* and armies from the jurisdiction of the General Staff and *front* and army staffs and subordinated them to the chief of the Red Army's Rear Services and his respective *front* and army chiefs of the rear, where it remained until war's end.[221]

Rear Services and Supply and the Operational Rear

Prior to the outbreak of war, the provision of rear service (logistical) support for the Red Army was principally the responsibility of command and control organs in its military chain of command, in particular, the headquarters and staffs of its *fronts* and armies. Coordinated by the General Staff, these staffs were responsible for logistical planning, supervising rear service work, and organizing necessary troops and supply transport under the deputy chiefs of staff for the rear at these levels. This principle applied to material-technical support and artillery, engineer, chemical defense, signal, quartermaster (food, forage, clothing), administrative, and fuel and lubricants supplies and pay.

Although this entire logistical system was controlled by the NKO's Directorate for Rear Services Organization and Supply, the General Staff's Directorate for the Rear and Supply Planning *(Upravlenie tyla i planirovaniia material'nykh sredstv)* handled all rear service matters within the General Staff, and rear service departments subordinate to the deputy chiefs of staff for the rear did the same in military districts *(fronts),* armies, and corps.[222] Cooperating closely with the NKO's Directorate for Rear Services Organization and Supply, this directorate's primary responsibility during wartime was to keep the Red Army's forces at the front supplied with weapons and equipment, estimate mobilization resources and requirements, and collate information regarding wartime weapons equipment and supply production.[223] In addition, on the eve of war, the General Staff also included a Directorate of the Formation of the Operational Rear *(Upravlenie ustroistva operativnogo tyla),* which was directly responsible for the creation of a supply system to sustain the Red Army's operating *fronts* and armies.

When the GKO created the post of chief of Red Army Rear Services on 1 August 1941, it assigned the General Staff's Directorate for the Rear and Supply Planning and Automobile-Road Directorate to the chief of the Rear Services' new main directorate (GUTA KA). Although this measure stripped the General Staff of its main logistical directorates, of necessity other General Staff directorates and departments coordinated closely with the new NKO organs, in particular, the Directorate for the Formation of the Operational Rear, which remained a part of the General Staff.

Thereafter in the war, the organization of the General Staff's logistical organs fluctuated depending on military requirements. For example, it truncated its Directorate for the Formation of the Operational Rear into a department during June 1943 but once again elevated it to the status of a full directorate during December 1944. Throughout the war, this directorate (department) prepared directives and determined the basic organizational structure of rear services in operating *fronts* and armies, and its representative controlled the work of *front* and army rear services, primarily in the realm of military supply transport. This amounted to about 12 million wagonloads of supplies and 145 millions tons of cargo carried on automobile transport over the course of the war.[224]

Military Topography

The Military-Topographical Directorate (*Voenno-topograficheskoe upravlenie,* or VTU) was responsible for preparing, maintaining, and distributing all maps for the Red Army at every level of command by means of survey and aerial observation prior to and throughout the war.[225] These included strategic-scale maps for *Stavka* and General Staff use, operational maps of 1:200,000 scale for *fronts* and armies, and tactical maps of 1:100,000 and 1:50,000 scale for corps, divisions, and regiments.

VTU's work during the first six months of the war was complicated by the fact that the *Wehrmacht's* advancing forces seized about 96 million military-topographical maps stored in warehouses in the western Soviet Union, creating acute shortages of accurate operational and tactical maps that the VTU was not able to overcome until early 1942. Thereafter, the directorate routinely assigned topographers to rifle and cavalry divisions to help prepare new maps and amend existing maps.

Throughout the war the VTU's cartographers and topographical specialists reconnoitered, photographed, and prepared maps of an area encompassing 5.2 million square kilometers, arranged and produced 16,500 new map series, and printed 800 million topographical and special maps, as well as other documents related to military aspects of terrain.[226] The only identifiable chief of the VTU during wartime was Lieutenant General M. K. Kudriavtsev.

Fortified Regions

The Directorate for the Construction of Fortified Regions (*Upravlenie ustroistva ukreplennykh raionov,* or UUUR) was responsible for all matters related to the construction and employment of fortified regions and field defense lines and positions prior to and throughout the war. In addition to supervising the construction and maintenance of fortified regions in the Stalin Line, which was built along the Soviet Union's western border in 1939, the UUUR was in the process of constructing a new line of fortified regions along the country's new western borders when war broke out in June 1941. Although the *Wehrmacht* overran these defenses in a matter of days, during the first three months of war the UUUR planned and organized the construction of about 25,000 kilometers of new defense lines in the depth of the country, which were anchored on fortified regions placed along likely axes of German advance, and planned the construction of a like number of defense lines in 1942.

In addition to its defensive construction work, the UUUR prepared and published new instructions and regulations regarding the selection and construction of field fortified positions and defense lines in 1943. *Front* and army commanders remained responsible for fortifying their own sectors, but the General Staff was responsible for creating deeply echeloned positional defenses in the depths. Under the UUUR's supervision, the Red Army's operating *fronts* and armies and other construction forces built about 80,000 kilometers of field defensive lines and formed 36 standard and field fortified regions by war's end. Since defense lines became less important when the Red Army was almost constantly on the offensive after the summer of 1943, the GKO converted the UUUR into a department within the Operations Directorate.

Cipher and Secret Command and Control

One of the more obscure yet most important directorates in the General Staff throughout the war was the Directorate for the Cipher Service (*Upravlenie shifroval'noi sluzhby*, or UShS) (the Eighth Directorate), known simply as the Cipher Directorate, whose wartime chief was Lieutenant General P. N. Beliusov. The UShS, whose wartime workload was immense, was ultimately responsible for "organizing enciphered communications for the *Stavka*, the General Staff, and the Red Army's operating forces, training cadre for the encoding of communications transmissions, and controlling the organization of secret command and control of forces."[227] Structurally, the UShS consisted of several separate special departments, organized on a functional basis, which supervised cipher departments and sections in the military districts *(fronts)*, and separate armies.

In addition to its cipher work, the GKO had assigned Beliusov's directorate responsibility for managing the secret command and control of forces *(skrytnyi upravlenie voiskami)* by 1942. This entailed ensuring the secrecy of strategic and operational force regroupings and associated command and control arrangements prior to the conduct of large-scale offensives and concealing the identity of *Stavka* representatives and General Staff officers who were planning and coordinating these operations.[228] The UShS was also responsible for all troop control security measures and the employment of associated codes, ciphers, and other security techniques. This, in turn, required the directorate to work closely with the NKPS, the General Staff's

Operations Directorate, and the NKO's Central Directorate for Military Communication.[229]

The UShS also provided secure communications support for Red Army airborne, raiding units, reconnaissance-diversionary (SPETSNAZ) groups and teams, and partisan detachments operating in the enemy rear, since communications with these forces were subject to near constant monitoring by German counterintelligence organs. The volume of enciphered traffic handled by the cipher directorate grew steadily throughout the war, averaging up to 1,500 messages per day, for a total of more than 1.6 million messages.[230]

In addition to its routine duties, the UShS supervised the production of all secret written materials in the Red Army, developed procedures and published regulations and instructions for the conduct and maintenance of operational security, and controlled the conduct of operational security at all command levels during the planning and conduct of military operations. In this regard, one of its most important contributions to the war effort was its publication of new comprehensive regulations governing the operation of the Red Army's cipher staff service during May 1943.

War Experience

One of the less tangible but most vital functions the General Staff performed during wartime was the collection, analysis, generalization, and exploitation of war experiences. During late 1941 and early 1942, several operating *fronts*, but in particular Zhukov's Western Front, established organizations under their chiefs of staff whose specific missions were to collect and analyze combat experience to learn lessons that would improve their forces' combat performance.[231] The success of these efforts soon attracted high-level attention.

Convinced of the utility if not necessity of learning how to fight more effectively, on 25 April 1942, the GKO directed the General Staff to establish a Department for the Exploitation of War Experience (*Otdel' po izpol'zovaniiu opyta voiny*, or OPIOV) formed around the nucleus of its existing operational training section. Appointing Major General P. P. Vechnyi as its first chief, the chief of the General Staff charged OPIOV with responsibility for "studying and generalizing war experience, preparing combined-arms regulations and instructions regarding the conduct of combat and operations, and preparing directive orders for the NKO's main and central directorates regarding the exploitation of war experiences."[232] Ultimately, Vechnyi's department disseminated this processed war experience to Red Army forces by means of orders, directives, instructions, field manuals, and full-fledged combat studies.[233] In addition, this processed war experience provided the basis for numerous articles published in the General Staff's own house organ, *Voennaia mysl'* (Military thought).

The OPIOV published its first two collections of war experiences during August 1942 and distributed them to all commanders in the Red Army's chain of command down to regimental level. The twin volumes proved of immediate utility to the forces. For example, the first volume provided the basis for the famous Order No. 325, which related to the more effective combat employment of tank and mechanized forces, and the second volume contained the full order. Stalin and the General Staff were so impressed with the OPIOV's efforts that they ordered it to accelerate the production of subsequent volumes.[234] In addition, by early 1943 the OPIOV began preparing and publishing an extensive series of collections of tactical examples and informational bulletins addressing in detail virtually all aspects of tactical combat and the tactical employment of all types of weaponry.

In recognition of the important role the OPIOV was playing, the NKO reorganized it into the Directorate for the Generalization and Exploitation of Military Experience (*Upravlenie po obobshcheniiu i ispol'zovaniiu opyta voiny*, or UPOIIOV) in March 1944, with Vechnyi still functioning as its chief. Subsequently, by May 1945, the directorate had produced 17 volumes of collected war experiences, 10 book-length collections of tactical combat examples, and 33 informational bulletins.[235]

While accomplishing their work, the OPIOV and its successor UPOIIOV cooperated closely with the Operations Directorate and frequently visited the operating *fronts*, whose chiefs of staff supervised similar organs at *front* and army level. At the same time, they worked in tandem with the General Staff's Military History Department, which produced numerous detailed operational studies in its own right, most of which appeared after war's end.

Among the most prolific military analysts preparing war experience volumes were Major Generals N. A. Talensky, P. D. Korkodinov, and N. M. Zamiatin, Colonels F. D. Vorob'ev, P. G. Esaulov, and P. S. Boldyrev, and Lieutenant Colonels I. P. Marievsky, N. G. Pavlenko, and I. V. Parotkin. Others, such as Lieutenant General Ia. A. Shilovsky and Lieutenant General of Artillery F. A. Samsonov, who edited even larger studies, became distinguished military historians after war's end.[236]

Special Missions Department (Foreign Relations)

Another vital and delicate aspect of the General Staff's work, particularly during the later stages of the war, involved managing the Soviet Armed Force's relations with foreign nations, in particular, the armed forces of its allies. Since the Operations Directorate was barely able to cope with its normally heavy workload and could not keep track of and analyze the consequences of its allies' actions, the chief of the General Staff established a separate department, the Department of Special Missions (*Otdel' spetsial'nykh zadanii,* or OSZ), to monitor its allies' operations and handle foreign relations.

These contacts were quite limited early in the war and included only the exchange of information on military operations, war experiences, some intelligence data, and technical information. However, as Soviet-Allied cooperation expanded during 1942 and 1943 to include an increasing number of conferences, such as those held at Moscow in 1942, at Teheran in late 1943, and at Yalta in early 1945, and expanded Lend-Lease cooperation, the OSZ was overwhelmed with work. When a modest expansion of the department failed to solve its problems, the NKO transformed the OSZ into a full directorate on 23 September 1944, adding the NKO's Department of External Relations to it and tasking it with the dual missions of carrying out special assignments related to the Soviet Union's allies and handling all questions related to the General Staff's activities regarding Soviet foreign policy.[237] The new directorate's primary responsibilities were to maintain contact and coordination with the military missions of the United States and Great Britain, representatives of the Free French government, the governments-in-exile of Norway and Czechoslovakia, and the National Liberation Committee in Yugoslavia.

In addition, the OSZ and its successor directorate coordinated the work of Soviet military missions, which were assigned to the headquarters of major Allied commands and worked in direct subordination to the *Stavka.* Lieutenant General N. V. Slavin, who had worked extensively in this arena as the chief of the OSZ, became chief of the new directorate with Major General M. N. Kutuzov as his deputy.[238]

The General Staff also shared information concerning the *Stavka's* strategic intentions and intelligence on Germany and Japan with its allies through the OSZ beginning in 1943. This applied in particular to the coordination of Allied air activity over regions close to advancing Red Army forces, Allied use of Soviet air bases in the Ukraine to conduct bombing raids against German-held territory, and the touchy issue of no-bombing lines between Red Army and Allied forces, primarily in the Balkans region.

Officer Corps of the General Staff

During late 1941 the General Staff formed a special group of staff officers from its Operations Directorate to serve as its representatives and conduct a variety of liaison duties in major subordinate Red Army field commands such as *fronts* and separate armies. These officers were responsible for assisting *front* and army commanders in fulfilling *Stavka,* NKO, and General Staff directives, orders, and instructions, monitoring the implementation of these directives, orders, and instructions, verifying the operational situation and the combat readiness of these forces and their troops, ensuring their material support, assisting in the conduct of combat operations, and reporting to the General Staff on all matters regarding the combat situation, prospective and ongoing military operations, and logistical support.[239]

The GKO separated this special group of staff officers from the Operations Directorate in late 1942, renamed it the Separate Officer Corps of the General Staff, and appointed, first, Major General N. I. Dubinin and, later, Major General S. N. Geniatullin, as chief of this corps with Major General F. T. Peregudin as their deputy for political affairs.[240] The *Stavka* assigned officers from this corps to *fronts*, armies, and even corps and divisions on a semi-permanent basis. In addition, officers from this corps helped train Allied forces, such as Czech and Polish brigades, divisions, corps, and even armies, which were integrated into the Red Army's force structure during the war. The GKO transferred the Officer Corps of the General Staff back to the General Staff's Main Operational Directorate in mid-1943 to make it more responsive to General Staff planning.[241]

Table 11.1 Deputy Supreme Commander and Red Army Branch Chiefs during the War

Branch	Date Formed	Commanders
Deputy supreme commander	28 Aug 1942	Army General G. K. Zhukov
Commanders		
Air force	29 Jul 1941	Lieutenant General P. F. Zhigulev, Lieutenant General A. A. Novikov (May 1942)
Artillery	19 Jul 1941	Colonel General N. N. Voronov
Armored and mechanized forces	14 Dec 1942	Lieutenant General (Colonel General in December 1942) Ia. N. Fedorenko
Guards-mortar units	Sep 1941	Major General (Lieutenant General in March 1943) V. V. Aborenkov, Major General of Artillery (Lieutenant General of Artillery in September 1943) P. A. Degtiarev
Airborne forces	29 Aug 1941	Major General V. A. Glazunov
Engineer forces	28 Nov 1941	Major General L. Z. Kotliar, Lieutenant General M. P. Vorob'ev (April 1942)
Air defense forces	9 Nov 1941	Lieutenant General M. S. Gromadin
Rear service forces	1 Aug 1941	Lieutenant General A. V. Khrulev

Source: V. A. Zolotarev, ed., "Prikazy narodnogo komissara oborony SSSR 22 iiuia 1941 g.–1942" [Orders of the People's Commissar of Defense, 22 June 1941–1942], in *Russkii arkhiv: Velikaia Otechestvennaia* [The Russian archives: The Great Patriotic (War)], 13, 2(2) (Moscow: Terra, 1997), 29–30, 41–43, 75, 287, 379–80.

Table 11.2 Organization of the Red Army General Staff, 22 June 1941 to 1 January 1944

1939	July 1941
Directorates	**Directorates**
Operations	Main Operations
Intelligence	Intelligence (RU)
Organization	Organization of the Operational Rear
Mobilization	Construction of Fortified Regions
Manning and Constructing Forces	Military-Topographical
Military Communications Routes	Cipher
Auto-Road	**Departments**
Organization of the Rear and Supply of Forces	General Matters
Military-Topographical	Military-Historical
Organization of the Operational Rear	Cadre
Construction of Fortified Regions	
Cipher	
Departments	
General Matters	
Fortified Regions	
Military History	

April 1942	January 1943
Directorates	**Directorates**
Main Operations	Main Operations
Main Intelligence (GRU)	Force Intelligence (UVR)
Organizational	Military Communications Routes (31 Jan to May 1943)
Formation of the Operational Rear	Organizational
Construction of Fortified Regions	Formation of the Operational Rear
Military-Topographical	Construction of Fortified Regions
Cipher and Secret Command and Control	Military-Topographical
Departments	Cipher and Secret Command and Control
General Matters	**Departments**
Military-Historical	General Matters
Cadre	Military-Historical
Exploitation of War Experience	Cadre
	Exploitation of War Experience
	Special Missions

July 1943	January 1944
Directorates	**Directorates**
Main Operations	Main Operations
Intelligence (RU)	Intelligence (RU)
Main Organizational	Main Organizational
Construction of Fortified Regions	Military-Topographical
Military-Topographical	Cipher and Secret Command and Control
Cipher and Secret Command and Control	**Departments**
Departments	General Matters
General Matters	Military-Historical
Military-Historical	Cadre
Cadre	Exploitation of War Experience
Exploitation of War Experience	Formation of the Operational Rear
Formation of the Operational Rear	Special Missions
Special Missions	

Table 11.3 Organization of the General Staff's Main Intelligence Directorate (GRU), 20 February 1942

Departments	Area of Responsibility
First Directorate	**Agent operations**
First	German
Second	European
Third	Far Eastern
fourth	Near Eastern
Fifth	Diversionary
Sixth	*Front,* army, and military district intelligence
Seventh	Operational equipment
Eighth	Agent communications and radio-intelligence *(radiorazvedka)*
Second Directorate	**Information**
First	German
Second	European
Third	Far Eastern
Fourth	Near Eastern
Fifth	Editorial-publishing
Sixth	Force information
Seventh	Deciphering (decryption)
Main departments	
Political	
External Relations	
Special Communications	
Special Missions	
Cadre	
Military Censorship	
Control-Finance	
Material-Technical Support	

Source: V. A. Zolotarev, ed., "Prikazy narodnogo komissara oborony SSSR 22 iiuia 1941 g.–1942 g." [Orders of the People's Commissar of Defense of the USSR 22 June 1941–1942], in *Russkii arkhiv:Velikaia Otechestvennaia* [The Russian archives: The Great Patriotic (War)], 13, 2(2) (Moscow: Terra, 1997), 154.

Table 11.4 Structure of the General Staff's Intelligence Directorate (RU) and Subordinate Intelligence Departments (ROs), 1 May 1943

Level and Principal Intelligence Organ	Subordinate Departments and Sections	Responsibility
General Staff: Intelligence Directorate (RU)	First Department	Force intelligence
	Second Department	Agent intelligence
	Third Department	Control of *front* agent intelligence
	Fourth Department	Operational information
	Fifth Department	Radio-intelligence and blocking enemy radio stations
	Sixth Department	Radio and communications
	Seventh Department	Cadre
	Eighth Department	Ciphers
	Administrative Department	

—*Continued*

Table 11.4 continued

Level and Principal Intelligence Organ	Subordinate Departments and Sections	Responsibility
	Special Section (Disinformation)	
	Section for Operational Equipment	
	Finance Section	
	Investigative Section	
	Secretariat	
	Aviation Detachment	
	Communications Center	
	Agent Training School	
Front: Intelligence Department (RO)	First Section	Force intelligence
	Second Section	Agent intelligence
	Third Section	Diversionary actions
	Fourth Section	Information
	Fifth Section	Aviation intelligence
	Sixth Section	Radio intelligence
	Seventh Section	Agent equipment
	Eighth Section	Ciphers
	Investigative unit	
	Administrative unit	
	Cadre section	
	Finance unit	
	Secret unit	
	Radio center	
	Motorized intelligence company	
Army: Intelligence Department (RO)	First Section	Force intelligence
	Second Section	Information
	Investigative unit	
	Recordkeeping unit	
Corps: Intelligence Department (RO)	Chief of Corps Intelligence (Assistant Chief of Staff for Intelligence)	
	Senior Deputy Chief of the RO for Force Intelligence	
	Senior Deputy Chief of the RO for Information	
	Two translators	
Division: Intelligence Section	Chief of the Division Intelligence Section	
	Assistant Chief of the Division Intelligence Section	
	Translator	
	Reconnaissance company	
Regiment: Intelligence organ	Assistant Chief of Staff for Reconnaissance	
	Translator	
	Foot reconnaissance platoon	
	Horse reconnaissance platoon	

Source: V. A. Zolotarev, ed., "Prikazy Narodnogo komissara oborony SSSR (1943–1945 gg)" [Orders of the People's Commissar of Defense of the USSR (1943–1945)], in *Russkii arkhiv Velikaia Otechestvennaia* [The Russian archives: The Great Patriotic (War)], 13, 2(3) (Moscow: Terra, 1997), 125–27.

CHAPTER 12

The Officer Corps and Command Cadre

FROM CRISIS TO RECOVERY

The Purges and Expansion of the Red Army on the Eve of War

The Red Army's dismal combat performance in its invasion of eastern Poland during September 1939 and the Soviet-Finnish War during late 1939 and early 1940 indicated it was struggling to overcome many serious problems that had been adversely affecting its combat readiness even before Operation Barbarossa began. The army's most serious problems were the acute shortages of trained, experienced, and competent command cadre and staff officers at virtually every level of command, the natural consequences of Stalin's deliberate and devastating purges of both the Red Army's officer corps from 1937 through 1941 and his dramatic expansion of the Red Army from 1938 through June 1941. Regardless of cause, these shortages placed impossible demands on the Red Army's officer corps that were catastrophic for the army and the country after 22 June 1941.

In addition to liquidating about 50,000 of the Red Army's finest and most accomplished commanders and military theorists, Stalin's purges, which were still under way when war began, had a paralyzing impact on surviving officers:[1]

> The wave of repression, which touched the entire people, inflicted irreparable damage. The matter was not only the guiltless death of hundreds of thousands of people, among whom were the most valuable specialists in all spheres of activity, including the military. Moreover, to a great extent, the command cadre that survived the terror proved to be paralyzed by fear and lost its ability to reach independent decisions in the face of higher authorities. Many commanders became afraid to display initiative and take reasonable risks.[2]

Thus, while having to weather disaster after military disaster during the first 18 months of its war with Germany, the Red Army's officer corps and command cadre also had to endure a continuing purge and associated terror and intimidation. Instigated by an ever-suspicious Stalin and conducted by his ruthless henchman such as V. I. Beriia and V. S. Abakumov, these purges engulfed many senior Red Army officers during the war and even after war's end.

The officers Stalin and his political and state security operatives purged during wartime fell into five categories.[3] The first, the "scapegoat" officers, included *front* and army commanders Stalin blamed for the disasters that befell the Western Front as the *Wehrmacht* virtually destroyed it during the desperate first few weeks of war; and the second, the "wreckers," were army and corps commanders whom he accused of failing to conduct counterstrokes or counterattacks with sufficient vigor.[4] No less guilty in Stalin's eyes were those in the third category, which included the "traitor-generals" whom the *Wehrmacht's* forces either killed or captured after defeating their armies in combat, and a fourth, which included A. A. Vlasov, the ill-fated commander of the Volkhov Front's 2nd Shock Army, who fell captive when the *Wehrmacht's* forces destroyed his army near Liuban' during June 1942, and those officers who joined his Russian Liberation Army (ROA) in German captivity.[5]

Finally, the sixth, and by far the largest category of purged officers, included those whose personnel records contained any hint whatsoever of hostility to Stalin, his regime, or its policies. This catch-all category included tens of senior officers assigned to military forces, military-educational institutions, and even the NKO (People's Commissariat of Defense) central directorates who, in one way or another, raised the ire of Stalin's henchmen in state security and counterintelligence organs. All told, in addition to the tens of thousands of army officers purged before war began, at least 100 senior officers suffered the same fate prior to Stalin's death in 1953, most of them as unwitting and wholly tangential victims of Stalin's Great Patriotic War.[6]

In addition to yawning gaps in the officer corps' ranks caused by the bloody purges, the rapid expansion of the Red Army during the three years prior to the war and the massive mobilization of millions of reserve officers after the war forced the NKO to assign relatively inexperienced officers to command positions they were not prepared to occupy. For example, while the Red Army's size increased from 930,000 men during 1935 to 1,513,000 men by the end of 1938, and to 4,200,000 men, including internal security forces, on 1 January 1941, graduates of the Red Army's military academies and training satisfied only 40–45 percent of the Army's requirements for trained officers, and few if any of these had any combat experience at the command levels to which they were being assigned.[7]

As a result, the army lacked 35 percent of its required officers by May 1940, and about 70 percent of its command cadre had served in their current duty positions for six months or less. Worse still, 50 percent of the army's battalion commanders and up to 68 percent of its company and platoon commanders had received only six months of training at various branch training schools and courses, and only a few regimental and just over 26 percent of its division commanders were combat experienced. Nor was the situation much better at corps and army level. For example, in 1940 only 30 percent of army commanders, deputy commanders, chiefs of staff, and chiefs of force branches were veterans of the World and Civil wars, although about 70 percent had served in command or staff positions during the Soviet-Finnish War, the Spanish Civil War, or the conflict with the Japanese at Khalkhin Gol.[8]

In an attempt to solve this problem, Stalin reestablished the military ranks of marshal of the Soviet Union and general on 7 May 1940 and appointed G. I. Kulik, B. M. Shaposhnikov, and S. K. Timoshenko as marshals and another 982 officers as generals on 4 June.[9] Although some of these officers were Stalin's cronies, many others were selected solely on the basis of their loyalty to the Party, and most lacked significant combat experience. Almost miraculously, many of these relatively young officers ultimately emerged as competent and even famous senior field commanders during the ensuing war.[10]

As the clouds of war darkened across Europe, Stalin once again shuffled the Red Army's command structure in January 1941 by appointing Army General G. K. Zhukov as chief of the General Staff, K. A. Meretskov as deputy people's commissar of defense for military training, I. P. Apanasenko, M. P. Kirponos, M. M. Popov, A. I. Eremenko, S. G. Trofimenko, and P. L. Romanenko as military district or army commanders, and many other generals in the "class of 1940" as army, corps, and division commanders or chiefs of staff. As their subsequent careers indicated, many of these 982 generals would survive to play prominent roles during the war (see Appendix 4 in companion volume for data on the careers of key Red Army command cadre).[11] However, when all was said and done, these measures proved more cosmetic than genuine by concealing rather than solving the serious problem of senior officer shortages at all levels of command.

While Stalin resorted to his advanced promotion program during 1940 and early 1941, the NKO accelerated its officers' professional training program by doubling the number of military schools and by drastically increasing the quantities of graduates from existing academies, military schools, and officers training courses. Nevertheless, the Red Army's demand for trained officers was so great in the summer of 1940 that S. K. Timoshenko, the people's commissar of defense, petitioned for the re-examination of over 300 senior officers who had been caught up in the terror and been repressed. As a result, the NKO returned 250 half-purged officers to active service, including K. K. Rokossovsky, A. V. Gorbatov, A. I. Todorsky, A. V. Golubev, N. A. Ern'st, and V. A. Shtal'. In addition, by 1 January 1941, the NKO and state security organs rehabilitated and returned to service more than 12,000 commanders and political officers who had been arrested as unreliable "politicals."[12]

Despite these strenuous efforts to remedy the officer shortage, the Red Army still lacked 80,000 of its required command cadre in early 1941. Therefore, the NKO ordered the Frunze Academy, the Artillery Academy, the "Vystrel" Course, and other infantry schools to graduate their class of 1941 in May rather than late June. In addition, it directed 75,000 officers to participate in special training exercises during May and June 1941 and ordered Red Army forces to conduct special local training exercises and classes.[13]

These measures did ease the quantitative shortage of command cadre somewhat by 1 June 1941, but the Red Army's officer corps, in particular its senior command cadre, remained seriously depleted–somewhat deficient numerically, but woefully deficient qualitatively–when war began in June 1941. For example, the Red Army and Red Fleet included about 600,000 officers with another 916,000 officers in the reserves on 22 June 1941. However, its ground and air forces still lacked 36,000, or 14 percent, of its required officer cadre, and the reserves also lacked 55,000 officer specialists in critical combat and technical fields when mobilization began.

Another adverse effect of the purges and the Red Army's tumultuous prewar expansion was the severe age imbalance it produced within the army's officer corps. For example, 28.6 percent of the Red Army's command cadre were 25 years old or younger on 22 June 1941, 1.4 percent were 45 years old or older, and 12.4 percent lacked any formal military education whatsoever. Worse still, 57.6 percent of its senior commanders were 45 years old or younger, 52.6 percent had received a higher military education, 47.2 percent had only a mid-level military education, and fully 91 percent had served in the army for less than 20 years. In addition, 39 percent of all reserve officers were 40 years of age or younger.

Therefore, many, if not most, of the Red Army's command cadre lacked enough experience on the eve of war to perform competently in the command positions to which they were assigned. Although this characterized officers serving at virtually every level of command, this situation was most prevalent at military district *(front)* and army level. For example, Colonel General F. I. Kuznetsov, who commanded the Baltic Special Military District on 22 June 1941, had served in his post for about one year, Colonel General D. G. Pavlov, who commanded the Western Special Military District, had occupied his post since December 1940, and Colonel General M. P. Kirponos, who commanded the Kiev Special Military District, had replaced Zhukov as commander in January 1941, when Stalin appointed Zhukov as chief of the General Staff.[14] At the bottom of the chain of command, on 22 June almost 70 percent of the Red Army's division and regiment commanders and 80 percent of its battalion commanders had commanded their forces for less than one year.

In short, although some officers, primarily mid-grade, did survive the terrible initial period of the war and emerged as effective senior commanders later in the war, soon it would be quite apparent that many others simply could not cope with the immensity of the task they faced.

The Challenges of War

The *Wehrmacht's* sudden and devastating invasion of the Soviet Union and the catastrophic damage it inflicted on the Red Army and its officer corps presented the NKO with two immediate but enduring challenges related to the Red Army's command cadre and its capacity for conducting effective military operations. First, the NKO had to select and train new commanders either from the army's ranks or from its reserves to make up for prewar shortages and to replace the many commanders who perished during the initial months of the war. Second and no less daunting, it had to improve the quality of serving command cadre and staff officers.

The NKO encountered several imposing obstacles as it attempted to accomplish this, the most daunting of which were systemic inefficiencies in its mobilization system. Poor and incomplete mobilization planning and the severe disruptions caused by the German invasion prevented the NKO and General Staff from providing newly mobilized armies and divisions with requisite command cadre, to say nothing of generating new command cadre and staff officers for the Red Army's formations already fighting in the field. For example, the *Wehrmacht's* surprise invasion and subsequent rapid advance prevented 44–56 percent of reserve officers living in the western military districts during peacetime from reporting to their duty stations during the mobilization. Only in the Leningrad and Odessa Military Districts were a majority of reserve officers able to report for duty. Mobilization elsewhere occurred hastily and in haphazard fashion.[15]

Despite the chaotic mobilization and disastrous military situation, the *Stavka* managed to improvise and crudely fashion a new command and control structure for its operating *fronts* and armies adequate enough for them to continue fighting through the remainder of 1941. For example, the *Stavka* formed three main direction commands, 11 *fronts*, and 29 armies manned by approximately 30,000 officers from June through September 1941. In addition, by 31 December 1941, the NKO had raised 286 new divisions, reformed 22 others, and disbanded 124, most of which the *Wehrmacht* had destroyed in combat, and formed hundreds of brigades, regiments, and battalions, including 250 ski battalions. Including forces already in the army's force structure on 22 June 1941, the Red Army fielded a total of 821 divisional equivalents during 1941.[16] By 31 December the NKO had called to active duty roughly 75 percent of the total number of officers assigned to its pool of reserve officers on 22 June 1941.[17]

The NKO continued to mobilize forces at a frenetic pace throughout 1942 and most of 1943. For example, it formed 16 new armies, four tank armies, 28 tank corps, eight mechanized corps, 50 rifle and cavalry divisions, and hundreds of specialized tank, artillery, engineer, and air formations and units and refitted 67 rifle and cavalry divisions between 1 January and 1 November 1942, and it raised two more combined-arms armies, three tank armies, 42 rifle divisions, and 44 brigades of various types between 1 November 1942 and 31 December 1943.[18] Understandably, this process placed immense demands on the NKO to identify, recruit, and train command cadre for these forces.

Worse still, once war began, the casualty rate among officers, in particular mid-level and junior command cadre, was extremely high, and this too placed an enormous strain on the NKO's officer procurement and training systems. For example, the Red Army lost more than 2 million officers throughout the entire war, including 631,000 killed, 392,000 missing in action, and over 1 million severely wounded. This gruesome toll included 316,000 officers in 1941, 544,000 in 1942, 577,000 in 1943, 450,000 in 1944, and 166,000 in 1945, the vast majority of whom (80.2 percent) were serving as command cadre (see Table 12.1 for the number of killed or missing in action).[19]

Rebuilding the Officer Corps: Education and Training

Ultimately, the NKO overcame its formidable problem of officer and command cadre procurement by calling up reserve officers, transferring officers from noncombat to combat positions, elevating officers from the enlisted ranks, and reorganizing, reforming, and expanding its military education system:

Source	*Quantity of Officers, 1941–1945*
Called-up reservists	722,586
Trained in military schools	882,790
Trained in military academies	80,860
Trained in officers' courses	322,327
Transferred from political to command positions	122,310
Transferred from other people's commissariats	21,473
Returned wounded	721,511
Elevated from the ranks (soldiers and sergeants)	266,891[20]

At the same time, it implemented measures designed to increase the authority, material condition, and morale of its officer corps.

The NKO procured the bulk of its officer and command cadre replacements throughout the war either from its reserves and its military academies, schools, and other officers' courses or from those returning to field duty from its hospitals or from convalescent leave. For a variety of reasons, the number of officers in each of these categories varied considerably from year to year. For example, while the NKO was still reforming and expanding its military education system during 1941 and 1942, it obtained most of its officer replacements from staff and teaching positions in military academies and schools, headquarters and staff positions in rear service units and installations, duty positions in military commissariats and administrative services, and political officer positions scattered throughout the Red Army. In addition, the NKO and NKVMF (People's Commissariat of the Navy) had conscripted 80,000 female officers for service in the army and navy by 1943.[21]

After instituting universal military training throughout the entire country on 17 September 1941, the NKO intensified its officer procurement efforts by increasing the quantity of officer command cadre and by improving their quality, since failure to do so meant continued high officer attrition rates and certain battlefield defeat. To accomplish this, the *Stavka* and NKO reorganized, reformed, and drastically expanded its military education structure by increasing the quantity, strength, and officer output of its educational and training institutions by 67 percent from 22 June 1941 to mid-summer 1943.

When war began, the Red Army and Navy were educating their senior command cadre at 19 higher military academies, seven higher naval schools, and ten military faculties in civilian institutions of higher education and training their mid-level command cadre at 203 military academies *(voennye uchilishcha)*, hundreds of other military schools *(voennye shkoly)*, and 68 "courses for the improvement of officer cadre" *(kursy usovershenstvovaniia ofitserskogo sostava)* in these and other educational and training institutions.[22] The duration of instruction at these institutions ranged from three to five years at the higher military academies, two to four years at the military academies, 4–9 months at military schools, and 2–12 months at the improvement courses. About 240,000 officer-students, most of whom had received some secondary normal or technical education, attended the 203 military academies and graduated as platoon leaders with the rank of junior lieutenant.[23]

Although the NKO's Main Directorate for Military-Educational Institutions (GUVUZ) was responsible for administering these military education institutions, after 20 September 1941, it shared responsibility for doing so with the NKO's branch main directorates and directorates. The NKO educated most of its senior command cadre at the Voroshilov Academy of the General Staff, the Frunze Military Academy, and the "Vystrel" School (the Field Academy), which remained under GUVUZ control, and at higher military academies administered by the Red Army's services and branches. The principal missions of these academies were to overcome the Red Army's shortage of senior command cadre and improve the quality of their instruction and graduates by reforming and modernizing their curricula and streamlining their courses, which was no mean task during the first 18 months of the war.

The Voroshilov Academy of the General Staff, which became the Voroshilov Higher Military Academy in early 1942 and was located at Moscow and Ufa during the war, ultimately graduated 1,178 officers from its main course and 176 from its Course for the Improvement of Higher Command Cadres.[24] In addition to the critical role it played in preparing senior command cadre, the Higher Military Academy also served as a "think tank," responsible for thoroughly analyzing combat operations and developing new operational and tactical theory. In addition to preparing revised combat regulations for all types of forces, it produced numerous in-depth studies of all types of wartime operations, particularly at the strategic and operational level. For example, it prepared more than 1,700 detailed military-scientific and historical studies throughout the war, including massive analytical critiques of the Battles of Moscow, Stalingrad, Kursk, Belorussia, and Berlin.[25]

The Frunze Military Academy, whose proper name was the Military Academy in the name of M. V. Frunze and which was located at Moscow and Tashkent during the war, had dispatched more than 6,000 graduates to the front by December 1943 and 11,000 more by war's end.[26] Like the Higher Military Academy, it too worked on generalizing war experience and incorporating lessons learned from that experience into its course of study.[27]

Unlike the Voroshilov and Frunze academies, which offered combined-arms instruction, the Red Army's Higher Officers Courses, which were known collectively as the "Vystrel" School or Courses and were located at Solnechnogorsk, west of Moscow, and at Kyshtym in the Cheliabinsk region, provided their graduates primarily with infantry refresher (rifle) training. Since rifle forces predominated in the Red Army, the "Vystrel'" courses provided mid-level and senior military and political command cadre and instructors at other Red Army military-educational institutions with their initial training.[28] In addition, "Vystrel's" faculty helped prepare the Red Army's *Infantry Combat Regulations of 1942* and other tactical branch handbooks and instructions based on the study of war experiences. The "Vystrel" courses had prepared more than 20,000 junior command cadre for the Red Army by war's end.[29]

In addition to these combined-arms and infantry academies, schools, and courses, the NKO's education and training system also included branch-specific military academies, schools, and courses that operated under the direct control of its branch directorates (artillery, tank and mechanized, engineer, etc.). Even though all of these institutions evacuated their facilities eastward in late 1941, they graduated more than 564,000 officers during 1942.

Both the quantity and quality of officer cadre training improved dramatically during 1943. While the officer corps amassed greater combat experience as the Red Army embarked on ever more ambitious and extensive offensive operations, the total number of military academies, schools, and courses rose to 250 by 31 December 1943, including more than 30 higher military schools and more than 200 different officers courses. Throughout the year, these institutions graduated about 360,000 young officers, commanders, and political workers and sent them to the front, while the branch academies trained more than 12,500 officers.[30] Another 250,000 officers returned to the field forces from hospitals and convalescent leave during 1943 and another 7,000 officers entered service from the reserves.[31]

The NKO's strenuous officer procurement efforts and its military education system had produced enough officers to meet all of the Red Army's current command cadre requirements by July 1943. By this time it had also formed a reserve pool of 93,500 experienced and well-trained officers in all branches, 41,000 of which it assigned to its Main Directorate for the Formation and Manning of the Red Army (GUFUKA) and the military districts and the remainder to its operating *fronts* and armies.[32] After further changes during the last six months of 1943, by year's end the NKO's military education and training system, which consisted of 17 higher and branch military academies, two military institutes, eight military faculties at civilian educational institutions, 184 military academies and schools, and more than 200 separate courses, was operating at full efficiency and was educating and training officer cadre for the Red Army's branches and specialized forces at all levels of command.[33]

In addition, working under the auspices of the General Staff's Department (and later Directorate) for the Generalization and Exploitation of Military Experience, the NKO's military-educational institutions were also preparing hundreds of studies on all types of combat and support operations based on the analysis of wartime combat experiences. These studies provided the essential basis for subsequent General Staff, NKO, *Stavka,* and GKO orders, directives, and instructions designed to improve the organizational structure and operational and tactical effectiveness of the Red Army's officer corps, command cadre, and forces.

Finally, in addition to overcoming its shortages of officers and command cadre, beginning in the first few months of the war, Stalin, the Communist Party's Central Committee, the GKO, and the NKO issued a series of decrees designed to improve the stature and status of the officers' corps and increase officer morale by decentralizing the award of military ranks to lower levels of command and by openly recognizing the feats of officers who distinguished themselves in combat. For example, during August and September 1941, the GKO authorized the military councils of *fronts* and armies to award officers with ranks of up to major and the chiefs of the NKO's main directorates to appoint commanders up to regimental level.[34]

Similarly, in October 1941 the GKO began recognizing individual feats of bravery performed by individual Red Army soldiers by authorizing the military councils of *fronts* and fleets to award medals and decorations in the name of the Presidium of the Supreme Soviet of the USSR to soldiers who distinguished themselves in battle. It extended this right to the military councils of armies and fleets and the commanders of corps, division, and regiments during 1942.[35] Collectively, these measures speeded up promotion, fostered upward mobility in the officer corps, and improved the officer corps' stature and quality. Of course, the war's bloody toll also helped shape the officer cadre by ensuring that only the most fit and effective officers survived.[36]

The Presidium of the Supreme Soviet took another major step in increasing the stature and quality of the officer corps when it abolished the formal commissar system (the institute of military commissars) and restored the principle of single (unified) command *(edinonachalie)* within the Red Army on 9 October 1942, and did the same within the navy and NKVD on 13 October.[37] Under the new principle of *edinonachalie,* which meant the commander had full authority over his force, deputy commanders for political affairs replaced the former commissars at every level of command. Therefore, although this measure evidenced increased Party faith in the reliability of the Red Army's command cadre, political education continued unabated.

The GKO accelerated its introduction of the principle of *edinonachalie* throughout the army during late May 1943, when it abolished the duty position of deputy commander for political affairs at company and battery levels. At the same time, it reduced the number of deputy chiefs of staff for political affairs in corps, divisions, brigades, PVO (air defense) regions, and fortified regions, and it replaced the deputy commanders and deputy chiefs for political affairs in formations and military-educational institutions with the chiefs of the political departments. In addition to lessening the stifling presence of commissars and political officers, these measures freed up more than 122,000 political officers and workers who had considerable combat experience for service in line combat command positions.[38]

To further "strengthen the moral spirit" of its soldiers, the GKO published new "Regulations Concerning Force Honorifics" during late 1942, which authorized the award of specified honorifics in the name of the Presidium of the USSR Supreme Soviet to Red Army formations and units as well as officers and soldiers that distinguished themselves in combat. Over time these included, among others, the Order of the Patriotic War, and the Orders of Suvorov, Kutuzov, and Aleksandr Nevsky.[39]

Finally, the Presidium of the Supreme Soviet of the USSR instituted new symbols of officer ranks, the distinctive rank shoulder strap, in early 1943, and created a new rank and grade structure to "increase the authority of the command-leadership cadre and their responsibility for fulfilling their military duty" in July.[40] Thereafter, it recognized all commanders and leaders from junior lieutenant to colonel as officers. The Presidium reinforced this reform in January and October 1943, when it created new ranks for the chiefs of the main force branches, including marshals and main (chief) marshals of aviation, artillery, tank and mechanized, engineer, and signal forces.[41]

COMMAND CADRE

For several reasons it remains difficult if not impossible to evaluate comprehensively the capabilities and combat effectiveness of those marshals and generals who constituted the Red Army's senior command cadre during the first 30 months of the war, if not the war as a whole. Soviet and Russian military histories reveal little about the character traits and behavior of these commanders, and, to a lesser extent, they also routinely obscure portions of their wartime careers. Second, although many of these commanders wrote memoirs and have been the subject of one or several biographies, state censors carefully removed from these works any and all information of potential embarrassment to the Soviet Union, its armed forces, or the reputations of the commanders themselves, in particular, if they rose to occupy positions of prominence after war's end.

Finally, the contents of these postwar memoirs and biographies in terms of how they portray the officers' careers also reflected the political situation and power relationships within the Soviet Union at the time they were written. For example, prior to his death in 1953, Stalin prohibited senior officers from writing memoirs, at least in part, to perpetuate what Khrushchev later termed Stalin's "cult of personality" and to protect the dictator's carefully orchestrated reputation as the sole architect of the Red Army's victory. After Stalin's death, the trickle of memoirs and biographies published between 1953 and 1958 turned into a flood between 1958 and 1964. Although far more accurate and candid than their predecessors, these books represented efforts by the new Soviet leader, N. S. Khrushchev, to "de-Stalinize" the Soviet Union by emphasizing Stalin's failures, such as Operation Barbarossa, and by denigrating the reputations of Stalin's favorite commanders, such as Zhukov, while excluding information damaging to the reputations of Khrushchev and his wartime colleagues.

Soviet memoirs, biographies, and other historical works continued to reflect the political realities of the time long after Khrushchev's enemies removed him from power during 1964. For example, Zhukov's reputation soon soared, at least in part because he opposed Khrushchev and supported the new Kremlin leadership; during the 1970s historians lionized L. I. Brezhnev, the new Soviet leader, for his wartime accomplishments; and during the late 1980s Gorbachev exposed new and often unflattering information about the wartime Red Army and its senior commanders in the spirit of his new *glasnost'* program. However, although the "de-Stalinization" and *glasnost'* programs revealed new and more accurate information about the Red Army, the political motivations surrounding this new candor continued to cast doubt on the accuracy of these books.

Even today, over ten years after all fetters on historical research and accuracy seemed to have disappeared in the wake of the Soviet Union's collapse in 1991, older inhibitions restricting accuracy persist, now reinforced by a tendency to protect the traditional grandeur of the Red Army's victory in the war as well as the reputations of those "great captains," whom previous histories have anointed as the real architects of victory. In a nation with precious few heroes, keeping these figures as modern "icons " has required further manipulation of historical fact.[42]

Another reason why it has been so difficult to ascertain the real character and talents of senior Red Army wartime commanders is that they have been victimized by stereotypes produced by a generation of *Wehrmacht* officers who wrote their own memoirs in the postwar years. Driven either by self-justification or an obsession to blame Hitler for all of the *Wehrmacht's* defeats, with some notable exceptions, most of these officers heaped scorn on the military prowess of their Red Army opponents. Here is a gentler version of this stereotype:

> To some extent, the good military qualities of the Russians are offset by dullness, mental rigidity, and a natural tendency towards indolence. But during the war they were improving all the time, and the higher commanders and staffs learned much from the Germans and their own experience. They became adaptable, energetic, and ready to take decisions. Certainly in men like Zhukov, Koniev, Vatutin, and Vassilevsky, Russia possessed army and army group commanders of a very high order. The junior officers, and many among the middle command group, were still clumsy and unable to take decisions; because of draconian discipline they were afraid of shouldering responsibility. Purely rigid training squeezed the lower commanders into the vice of manuals and regulations, and robbed them of initiative and originality which are vital to a good tactician. Among the rank and file the gregarious instinct is so strong that an individual fighter is always submerged in the "crowd." Russian soldiers and junior commanders realized that if left on their own they were lost, and in this herd instinct one can trace the roots of panic as well as deeds of extraordinary heroism and self-sacrifice.[43]

Finally, during certain periods of the war, such as Operations Barbarossa and *Blau*, the wholesale chaos coincident to military operations was so extraordinary that it has been difficult if not impossible to assess accurately the real capabilities of the Red Army's commanders, particularly because Stalin's political blunders placed them in utterly untenable situations. For example, is it reasonable to assume that any Red Army commander such as the illustrious but purged prewar leaders like Tukhachevsky, Uborovich, Gamarnik, Iakir, and Kork could have coped more effectively with the *Wehrmacht* during June 1941 than their Polish, French, and British counterparts had during 1939 and 1940? No one will ever know, but we do know that the extraordinary circumstances surrounding Operation Barbarossa confounded the Red Army's entire command cadre, capable and incapable alike.

Given these realities, in the absence of complete biographical information, the best if not the only way to judge the capabilities of the senior Red Army commanders is on the basis of their accomplishments while in command and the impressions they made on their subordinate officers and soldiers.

Main Direction Commanders

Shortly after the war began, in July 1941, Stalin appointed three of his cronies, Marshals of the Soviet Union Voroshilov, Timoshenko, and Budenny, to command new Main Commands of Forces along the Northwestern, Western, and Southwestern Directions (axes), which were responsible for controlling Red Army forces fighting along these three vital axes. Although Stalin's most trusted, experienced, and, presumably, most competent senior commanders, to a man, none of the three was able to cope with the *Wehrmacht's* offensive. Acting woodenly and even fatalistically, and never in control of the situation, they tried to implement defense plans that German blitzkrieg tactics rendered utterly irrelevant.

Marshal of the Soviet Union Semen Mikhailovich Budenny had earned his fame commanding the famous 1st Cavalry Army during the Russian Civil War and after war's end had served as Stalin's inspector of cavalry from 1924 to 1937, commander of the Moscow Military District from 1937 to 1939, and first deputy commissar of defense in 1940 and 1941.[44] Although Stalin's favorite cavalryman, Budenny was entirely out of his element trying to cope with the modern mobile warfare that characterized operations during the summer and fall of 1941. As a result, although he commanded the Southwestern Direction from July through September and the Reserve Front from September through October, Budenny was a largely passive and almost coincidental observer of the disasters that befell his forces in the western Ukraine during July, at Uman' and Kiev during August, and at Viaz'ma and Briansk during October.

Undismayed by Budenny's mediocre performance in 1941, Stalin appointed him to command the new Main Command of Forces along the North Caucasus Direction in early 1942, only to watch him preside over the infamous Crimean debacle of May 1942. Despite his catastrophic failures in command, Budenny commanded the North Caucasus Front from May through August 1942, after which Stalin relegated him to the largely ceremonial positions of chief of the Red Army's Cavalry Forces and a member of the People's Commissariat of Defense's Higher Military Council to war's end. Although Budenny had been a skilled, daring, and spectacularly successful cavalry commander during the Civil War, by 1941 time had clearly passed him by. As his record indicated, he was simply incapable of commanding large forces effectively in modern mechanized warfare.[45]

Like Budenny, Marshal of the Soviet Union Kliment Efremovich Voroshilov became famous during the Russian Civil War, during which he assisted Stalin in the defense of Tsaritsyn and later organized and served as commissar of Budenny's 1st Cavalry Army.[46] After helping suppress the Kronshtadt mutiny in 1921, Voroshilov commanded the North Caucasus and Moscow Military Districts from 1921 to 1924, helped M. V. Frunze reorganize and reform the Red Army in 1925, and, as people's commissar for military and naval affairs from 1925 through 1934, helped Stalin consolidate his position as absolute dictator of the Soviet Union. As a reward for his loyalty, Voroshilov served as Stalin's people's commissar of defense from 1934 to early 1940, but during the Soviet-Finnish War was largely responsible for the Red Army's embarrassing performance. Although he replaced Voroshilov with Timoshenko after war's end, Stalin retained Voroshilov as deputy chairman of the Council of People's Commissars (SNK) and chairman of the SNK's defense committee, posts he occupied when Operation Barbarossa began.

Voroshilov performed no more effectively than the hapless Budenny once Operation Barbarossa began. As commander of the Main Command of Forces along the Northwestern Direction during July, August, and early September 1941, he presided over his forces' ignominious and costly retreat to the outskirts of Leningrad. After being replaced by Zhukov, who saved the city during September, Stalin employed Voroshilov to organize the partisan movement during 1942, as *Stavka* representative (with Zhukov) to coordinate operations to crack the German siege of Leningrad during January 1943, and to coordinate operations to clear *Wehrmacht* forces from the Crimea during December 1943.

After realizing Voroshilov had outlived his usefulness at the front, Stalin employed him in largely ceremonial positions until war's end, such as including him in his entourage at the "Big Three" Conference at Teheran during 1943. Voroshilov's ruthlessness in service to Stalin, his obsequious attitude toward the Generalissimo, and his manifest professional military incompetence accorded him the dubious distinction of being Stalin's model crony. This quality alone saved him from liquidation.[47]

Marshal of the Soviet Union Semen Konstantinovich Timoshenko, the most competent of the three main direction commanders militarily, fared little better during the war than his colleagues. A veteran of both the World and Civil wars as a cavalryman, Timoshenko also participated with Stalin in the defense of Tsaritsyn and commanded a division in Budenny's 1st Cavalry Army.[48] After war's end, he commanded the 3rd Cavalry Corps from 1925 through 1933, served as deputy commander of the Belorussian and Kiev Military Districts from 1933 to 1937, and commanded the Khar'kov and Kiev Special Military Districts from 1937 through 1939, during which time he led the Ukrainian Front in its September 1939 invasion of eastern Poland. After pulling Voroshilov's chestnuts out of the fire by commanding the Northwestern Front's successful offensive during the Soviet-Finnish War, Stalin appointed Timoshenko as commissar of defense in May 1940 in place of Voroshilov. Timoshenko then carried out a massive but failed effort to reform the Red Army on the eve of war.

When Operation Barbarossa began, Stalin appointed Timoshenko as chief of the new *Stavka* on 23 June 1941, Western Front commander on 30 June, and Western Direction commander on 10 July, while retaining him as deputy commissar of defense. The stoic and unflappable Timoshenko watched helplessly throughout this period as the *Wehrmacht's* forces utterly destroyed his Western Front. Although matters were clearly beyond his control, Timoshenko organized defenses in the Smolensk region during July and coordinated the Red Army's first concerted counterstrokes and counteroffensive against German forces around Smolensk during August and early September, which prompted Hitler to abandon his offensive against Moscow temporarily and instead attack toward Kiev. Too late, and despite warnings from Zhukov, Stalin then assigned Timoshenko command of the Southwestern Direction in place of Budenny, where Timoshenko watched helplessly as *Wehrmacht* forces encircled and destroyed his forces at Kiev.

Despite these disasters during 1941, Timoshenko continued to command the Southwestern Direction and Southwestern Front until its catastrophic defeat at Khar'kov in May 1942. Despite Timoshenko's many failures, most of which were beyond his control to avoid, Stalin assigned him to command the Northwestern Front from October 1942 through March 1943 and to represent the *Stavka* in several major military operations prior to war's end.

Unlike Voroshilov, Timoshenko, to his credit, played no apparent part in the vicious repression of the Red Army officers' corps during the 1930s and avoided adopting the fawning attitude to Stalin so characteristic of Voroshilov, Budenny, and many other senior officers. Despite his many defeats, militarily, Timoshenko proved to be the most competent member of Stalin's immediate circle.[49] As one of his colleagues later wrote, "While possessing superior and strong qualities, irreproachable personal bravery, and a sensible critical mind, [Timoshenko] was not prepared to fulfill the high position of people's commissar of defense, and Stalin knew it."[50] To a lesser extent, the same applied to Timoshenko's service as main direction commander.

Front Commanders

The largest and most important formations in the Red Army's wartime force structure were its operating and nonoperating *fronts,* which the *Stavka* considered capable of performing missions of operational-strategic significance. Operating separately or in groups, first under the loose control of main direction commands and later under the tighter control of *Stavka* representatives, *fronts* played the most vital role in the Red Army's strategic defensive and offensive operations. As a result, their commanders were the most important senior command cadre in the Red Army at the strategic and operational levels. However, as their combat performance indicated, few if any Red Army *front* commanders were prepared to cope with German blitzkrieg tactics during the initial period of the war.

As with any army confronting sudden and multiple military catastrophes, a brutal process of "natural selection" by combat during the first 18 months of the war soon separated the competent from the incompetent. Although many Red Army *front* commanders were unable to cope with the cascading military defeats of 1941 and 1942 and failed as effective leaders, a surprisingly large number managed to overcome their deficiencies and remain in command, although not always at *front* level. Those who failed to meet the *Stavka's* expectations did so either because they were incapable of waging modern mobile warfare or because the war simply wore them out. With few exceptions, Stalin dealt with those in both categories quickly, firmly, and often ruthlessly. Curiously, however, at times extraordinary political reliability displayed by less than fully competent *front* commanders was justification enough for Stalin to retain them in command long after their poor combat performance clearly indicated that change was necessary.

1941. With notable exceptions, a surprisingly high percentage of Red Army *front* commanders who served during the disastrous six months from June through December 1941 survived their ordeal and continued in command, although sometimes at lower command level. The Red Army began the war with three *fronts* (the Northwestern, Western, and Southwestern), added two more (the Northern and Southern) during the first two days of war, and created five more over the ensuing two months (the Front of Reserve Armies on 14 July, the Central Front on 24 July; the Briansk Front on 16 August; the Trans-Caucasus Front on 23 August, and the Karelian and Leningrad Fronts formed from the Northern Front on 23 August). After the Red Army's defeat at Smolensk and Viaz'ma from August into early October, the *Stavka* disbanded the Central and Reserve Fronts but formed the Kalinin Front on 16 October and the Volkhov and Caucasus Fronts on 17 and 30 December, the latter from the Trans-Caucasus Front.

Although the *Stavka* doubled the number of operating *fronts* in the Red Army from five to ten during the first six months of war, a total of 25 generals served as *front* commanders. Of these 25 *front* commanders, 4–K. A. Meretskov, G. K. Zhukov, I. S. Konev, and S. K. Timoshenko–served continuously in *front* command or as *Stavka* representatives until war's end and another 4–A. I. Eremenko, G. F. Zakharov, I. V. Tiulenev, and R. Ia. Malinovsky–ended the war commanding *fronts* after serving successfully as army commanders. Therefore, eight (32 percent) of the Red Army's generals who served as *front* commanders during the harrowing first six months of war performed well enough to end the war in command of *fronts*.

In addition, 15 (60 percent) of the Red Army generals who served as *front* commanders during the first six months of war later served shorter stints in command of *fronts* before perishing in combat or ending the war in lower-level command or staff positions. These included I. I. Fediuninsky, P. A. Kurochkin, and M. G. Efremov (army commanders), I. A. Bogdanov (tank army commander), P. A. Artem'ev, V. A. Frolov, M. S. Khozin, and F. I. Kuznetsov (military district commanders), Ia. T. Cherevichenko and D. I. Riabyshev (rifle corps commanders), M. M. Popov (*front* chief of staff), D. T. Kozlov and F. Ia. Kostenko (deputy *front* commanders), P. P. Sobennikov (deputy army commander), and S. M. Budenny (chief of Red Army Cavalry).

Finally, two (8 percent) of the generals who served as *front* commanders during the first six months of the war perished during 1941 and two died in 1942, either at the Germans' or Stalin's hands: M. P. Kirponos, who died when the *Wehrmacht* encircled and destroyed his entire Southwestern Front near Kiev during September 1941; M. G. Efremov, the 33rd Army's successful commander who committed suicide near Viaz'ma during April 1942 to avoid falling into German hands; F. Ia. Kostenko, who perished during the Khar'kov encirclement in May 1942 while serving as deputy commander of the Southwestern Front; and D. G. Pavlov, whom Stalin executed for dereliction of duty when his Western Front was encircled and destroyed west of Minsk in late June 1941.

Since command turbulence, meaning frequent changes in command, tends to undermine a military force's effectiveness, as the Red Army's combat performance clearly indicated, turbulence in the command of its operating *fronts* was exceptionally high during the summer and fall campaigns of 1941 and 1942, when the Red Army was trying frantically to halt successful *Wehrmacht* offensives. For example, while the quantity of operating *fronts* in the Red Army doubled from five to ten during the last six months of 1941, these *fronts* experienced 28 assumptions of or changes in command, for an average of 2.8 commanders per *front* or 5.6 commanders on an annualized basis.[51]

The most accurate way to assess the capabilities of the 25 generals who served as *front* commander during the first six months of the war is to examine how well they performed in the defensive and offensive operations the Red Army conducted during the first six months of the war within the context of their previous military experience. First, 24 of these 25 generals—I. P. Apanasenko, P. A. Artem'ev, I. A. Bogdanov, Ia. T. Cherevichenko, M. G. Efremov, A. I. Eremenko, V. A. Frolov, M. S. Khozin, M. P. Kirponos, I. S. Konev, F. Ia. Kostenko, M. P. Kovalev, D. T. Kozlov, P. A. Kurochkin, F. I. Kuznetsov, R. Ia. Malinovsky, K. A. Meretskov, D. G. Pavlov, M. M. Popov, D. I. Riabyshev, P. P. Sobennikov, I. V. Tiulenev, G. F. Zakharov, and G. K. Zhukov—were members of the famous "class of 1940," who had been promoted in June 1940 to the rank they wore when war began.

Of these 24 officers, 15 had served as general officers prior to June 1940. These included Zhukov, Meretskov, and Tiulenev, who were promoted to the rank of army general in June 1940, Apanasenko and Pavlov, who were promoted to the ranks of colonel general and colonel general of tank forces, respectively, in June 1940, and Eremenko, Efremov, Kirponos, Konev, Kostenko, Kovalev, Kozlov, Kuznetsov, Popov, and Riabyshev, who were promoted to the rank of lieutenant general in June 1940. Therefore, all of these generals possessed at least a modicum of military experience when war began. However, the remaining nine officers—Artem'ev, Bogdanov, Cherevichenko, Frolov, Khozin, Kurochkin, Malinovsky, Sobennikov, and Zakharov—who were promoted to the rank of major general during June 1940, were colonels only a year before war began and, hence, lacked significant experience as senior command cadre.

The woeful lack of experience of most generals in the "class of 1940" became abundantly clear from their performance once war began. Although some *front* commanders were competent enough to avoid outright disaster during the border battles, the Battle for Smolensk, and the defense of Kiev, as well as during the Red Army's subsequent summer–fall defensive campaign, only the feats of Zhukov, Meretskov, Cherevichenko, and future *front* commander N. F. Vatutin stood out above the others. Overall, 11 of the 24 (46 percent) members of the "class of 1940" who served as *front* commanders during 1941 survived the year in *front* command.

Zhukov displayed his unique talents in his stubborn, successful, but bloody defenses of Leningrad during September and Moscow during November and December, Meretskov defeated *Wehrmacht* forces at Tikhvin in November and December while commanding the 4th Army, and Cherevichenko won his signal victory at Rostov in November and December while commanding the Southern Front. At the same time, Vatutin burnished his already sound reputation as a superbly competent General Staff officer by orchestrating failed but otherwise significant counterattacks and counterstrokes at Sol'tsy and Staraia Russa in July and August and at Kalinin in October. Likewise, Konev, Kostenko, Kurochkin, Malinovsky, and, to a lesser extent, Meretskov, helped lead the Red Army to victory during its Moscow counteroffensive and subsequent winter campaign.[52]

Typical of *front* commanders who successfully weathered the storm of 1941 and went on to command competently later in the war was Colonel General Markian Mikhailovich Popov, who had already built a reputation as an audacious fighter before the war and had served alongside Zhukov earlier in his military career.[53] After war began, the 41-year-old Popov faced the awesome challenge of defending Leningrad with his Northern Front, whose original mission had been to defend only the northern land approaches to the city from Finland. However, the rapid collapse of the Northwestern Front, which was supposed to defend Leningrad's southern approaches, ultimately forced Popov to defend Leningrad against assaults from both north and south. Despite constant meddling by his incompetent superior, Voroshilov, and with Zhukov's help, Popov accomplished this challenging task in credible fashion.

After commanding the Leningrad Front and the 61st and 40th Armies in late 1941 and 1942 and serving as chief of staff of the Stalingrad and Southwestern Fronts during the Battle of Stalingrad, Popov went on to command the newly formed 5th Shock Army in late 1942 and an experimental mobile group bearing his name during an audacious but unsuccessful offensive into the Donbas region in February 1943. In recognition of his prowess, Stalin appointed Popov to command the Reserve Front and Steppe Military District prior to the Battle of Kursk and, after the Red Army emerged victorious at Kursk, to command the Briansk Front, which he led in the successful offensive to liberate Briansk during August and September 1943. Thereafter, Popov commanded the Baltic and 2nd Baltic Fronts and later served as chief of staff of the Leningrad and 2nd Baltic Fronts until war's end.

Although sparing of praise for the Red Army's generals, one colleague noted:

> Popov . . . was yet another distinctive individual. Popov was tall, with good posture, blond hair, and fine features. He was young-looking, communicative, and jolly, and an ardent sportsman. Popular with both officers and enlisted men, he had a quick, logical mind; yet he was unlucky in the war. Yes, he met with success on the battlefield, extraordinary success at times, but he was not liked by those close to Stalin. Perhaps Stalin himself did not like him. Popov was twice removed from command over a front and

> for the rest of his life he served under the most talentless, tactless, and crude of the commanders, Chuikov. I encountered Popov more than once after service in the Far East. During the war I served for a time in the armies of the Second Baltic Front, which he commanded. . . . I retain the greatest respect for this man.[54]

While Zhukov studiously avoided mentioning Popov in his memoirs, Shtemenko praised Popov as "one of our most outstanding generals."[55]

The general who best typified the *Stavka's* unrealistically high expectations of its *front* commanders during the first six months of war was Lieutenant General Andrei Ivanovich Eremenko, who was an experienced 49-year-old officer when he began the war as the commander of the Red Army's prestigious 1st Red Banner Far Eastern Army. Based on his previous service as commander of a mechanized corps during the invasion of eastern Poland, Eremenko had earned the sobriquet, the "Russian Guderian."[56]

The *Stavka* recalled Eremenko from his posting in the Far East in July 1941 and assigned him as deputy commander of the Western Front. After Eremenko served in this capacity during the early stages of the Battle for Smolensk, in late August Stalin appointed him to command the Briansk Front and assigned him the utterly unrealistic mission of halting the *Wehrmacht's* advance on Kiev. Guderian's Second Panzer Group then shattered Eremenko's thoroughly outnumbered and outgunned *front* in heavy fighting in September and later encircled and largely destroyed it in the Briansk region in October, wounding Eremenko in the process.

After Eremenko recovered from his wounds, Stalin gave him command of the newly formed 4th Shock Army in December 1941, and in January 1942 Eremenko led this army on a spectacular offensive toward Smolensk deep in the *Wehrmacht's* rear area. In recognition of his accomplishments during the winter of 1941–42, Stalin appointed Eremenko to command the Southeastern (later, the Stalingrad) Front in July 1942 and ordered him to halt the *Wehrmacht's* advance on Stalingrad. Steeled by their commander's tenacity, Eremenko's forces fought the German Sixth Army to a standstill in the ruins of Stalingrad during September and October.

After Eremenko played an instrumental role in planning and conducting the Red Army's offensives in the Stalingrad region during November and December 1942, as a reward for his accomplishments, Stalin assigned him command of the Southern Front during January and February 1943, the Kalinin Front from April through October 1943, the 1st Baltic Front during October and November 1943, the Separate Coastal Army from February to April 1944, the 2nd Baltic Front from April 1944 to March 1945, and the 4th Ukrainian Front from March 1945 to war's end.[57] In addition to achieving his signal victory at Stalingrad, Eremenko planned the successful offensive at Nevel' in October 1943 and defeated *Wehrmacht* forces in difficult fighting in the Baltic region in 1944 and 1945.

The illustrious record Eremenko compiled from late 1942 through war's end largely erased most of the unpleasant memories associated with the embarrassing defeats he suffered during 1941. Zhukov says virtually nothing in his memoirs about Eremenko's qualities as a commander, probably because of the latter's close association with Khrushchev at Stalingrad; however, Shtemenko notes that Eremenko "had commanded six Fronts before this [his assignment to command the 2nd Baltic Front], and his name was closely associated with the magnificent achievement of Soviet troops at Stalingrad."[58] Eremenko's combat record indicates that, against whatever odds, above all, he remained a skilled and tenacious fighter.

Despite the disastrous defeats he presided over as army and *front* commander during the first six months of the war, Army General Ivan Stepanovich Konev first achieved fame during the Battle for Moscow, when his Kalinin Front helped spearhead the Red Army's victory. Thereafter, Konev grew in reputation to become one of the Red Army's finest and most accomplished *front* commanders by war's end and a clear counterweight to Zhukov.[59]

After war began, the 56-year-old Konev commanded the 19th Army during its unsuccessful defense of Smolensk and the Western Front, when the *Wehrmacht* destroyed it in the battles around Viaz'ma in October 1941.[60] In part because Zhukov interceded on his behalf, Konev survived Stalin's wrath to become commander of the Kalinin Front during the defense of Moscow and the subsequent Moscow offensive. Again serving under Zhukov's direction, Konev commanded the Kalinin and Western Fronts during the summer and fall of 1942 and, with Zhukov, suffered serious defeat in the ill-fated Operation Mars during November and December 1942, when, once again, Zhukov intervened to save Konev from disgrace.

After briefly commanding the Northwestern Front in the spring of 1943 and, on Zhukov's recommendation, the Steppe Military District in June, Konev's fortunes changed for the better. In addition to commanding the Steppe Front during its victory at Kursk in July and August, Konev led his *front* (renamed the 2nd Ukrainian) on its spectacular pursuit of *Wehrmacht* forces to the Dnepr River in September and seized sizable bridgeheads across the river in October, although his forces failed to clear *Wehrmacht* forces from the Krivoi Rog region as ordered later in the year. After his spectacular successes in 1943, Konev led the 2nd and, later, the 1st Ukrainian Front with distinction to war's end.

Although his colleagues described Konev as "emotional and hot tempered," one also noted, "Personal courage and energetic initiative in difficult circumstances were characteristic of Konev as a military leader throughout the war. . . . Konev was particularly taken with military history, and, throughout his life, he regarded it as an integral component of success." Another claimed that Konev was often harsh with his subordinates, vain, and prone to jealousy of his peers.[61] Still another praised him, noting he "was swift in his decisions and actions and unrestrained with his subordinates." Although "his behavior was acceptable," at times it was "somewhat frightening for the target of his wrath. . . . However, those who fought under him all commented on his temper. Still, they did not accuse him, as they did Chuikov, of being insulting."[62]

1942. The Red Army had to weather yet another trying ordeal in 1942; however, this one was far less harrowing than what it had endured in 1941. As a result, by year's end the *Stavka* was able to identify most of the senior command cadre who would lead the Red Army to ultimate victory. In 1942 the *Stavka* supplemented its nucleus of five *front* commanders who survived the ordeal of 1941 with another five *front* commanders who would retain their commands until war's end.

After beginning military operations on 1 January 1942 with ten operating *fronts* (Karelian, Leningrad, Volkhov, Northwestern, Kalinin, Western, Briansk, Southwestern, Southern, and Caucasus), the *Stavka* divided the Caucasus Front into the Crimean Front and Trans-Caucasus Military District during the winter campaign of 1942. After the Crimean Front suffered ignominious defeat at Kerch in April and May 1942, on 20 May the *Stavka* transformed the decimated *front's* remnants into the North Caucasus Front and elevated the Trans-Caucasus Military District to the status of a full-fledged *front.*

When the *Wehrmacht* shattered and destroyed major portions of the Southwestern Front in the initial stages of Operation *Blau* in late June and early July 1942, the *Stavka* abolished this *front*, replaced it with the Voronezh and Stalingrad Fronts on 7 and 14 July, and ordered the two new *fronts* to defend the Don River line and Stalingrad axis. After the Southern Front buckled under unrelenting *Wehrmacht* pressure, the *Stavka* also disbanded this *front* on 28 July, assigned its forces to a new North Caucasus Front, and ordered the new *front* to defend the approaches into the Caucasus region. In a final attempt to parry the *Wehrmacht's* rapid advance toward Stalingrad, on 7 August the *Stavka* formed the Southeastern Front from the armies deployed on the Stalingrad Front's left wing and ordered it to defend the southeastern approaches to Stalingrad.

As the situation in southern Russia deteriorated and *Wehrmacht* forces reached Stalingrad and lunged into the Caucasus region, the *Stavka* transformed the North Caucasus Front into the Trans-Caucasus Front's Black Sea Group of Forces on 1 September. Later still, on 28 September, when German forces penetrated into Stalingrad proper, the *Stavka* redesignated the

Stalingrad Front, which was actually defending the Don River line, as the Don Front and the Southeastern Front, which was defending Stalingrad city proper, as the Stalingrad Front. Finally, as the momentum of the *Wehrmacht's* offensive ebbed, the *Stavka* established a new Southwestern Front on 22 October and deployed it at the junction of the Don and Voronezh Fronts to prepare for future offensive operations in the Stalingrad region.

Therefore, in spite of the frequent changes in designation, the *Stavka* actually increased the quantity of Red Army operating *fronts* from ten on 1 January 1942 to 12 on 31 December 1942.[63] Including the four holdovers from 1941, a total of 21 generals served as *front* commanders during 1942. Of these 21 generals, nine—L. A. Govorov, K. A. Meretskov, G. K. Zhukov, I. S. Konev, M. A. Purkaev, K. K. Rokossovsky, S. K. Timoshenko, N. F. Vatutin, and I. V. Tiulenev—served continuously in *front* command or as *Stavka* representatives until their death or until war's end, and another two—A. I. Eremenko and R. Ia. Malinovsky—ended the war in *front* command after serving successfully as army commanders. As a result, 11 (52 percent) of the Red Army's generals who served as *front* commanders during 1942 performed well enough to end the war in *front* command, in contrast to the 32 percent who did so in 1941.

In addition, 10 (48 percent) of the Red Army generals who served as *front* commanders in 1942 later served shorter stints in command of *fronts* before perishing in combat or ending the war in lower-level command or staff positions, as opposed to 60 percent in 1941. These included P. A. Kurochkin and V. N. Gordov (army commanders), V. A. Frolov, M. S. Khozin, and M. A. Reiter (military district commanders), F. I. Golikov (NKO directorate chief), D. T. Kozlov and F. Ia. Kostenko (deputy *front* commanders), and Ia. A. Cherevichenko (rifle corps commander). Finally, Stalin relegated Budenny to the figurehead position of chief of Red Army Cavalry until war's end. The two *front* commanders of 1942 who perished during the war were F. Ia. Kostenko, who was killed in action in May 1942 during the Battle of Khar'kov, and N. F. Vatutin, who was mortally wounded by Ukrainian partisans in late February 1944, while serving as commander of the 1st Ukrainian Front.

Although command turbulence within the *fronts* decreased somewhat during 1942, it remained rather high because of the rapid changes in the *fronts'* organization to counter Operation *Blau*. As a result, although the quantity of operating *fronts* in the Red Army increased modestly from ten to 12 in 1942, these *fronts* experienced 21 assumptions of command or changes in command, for an average of two commanders per *front* as opposed to 2.8 per *front* in the six months in 1941 or 5.8 on an annualized basis.[64] Many of the Red Army's most accomplished wartime *front* commanders emerged in command during this period, particularly during the victory at Stalingrad and the ensuing winter offensive of 1942–43.

In 1942, seven more graduates of the generals' class of 1940 (L. A. Govorov, F. I. Golikov, V. N. Gordov, M. A. Purkaev, M. A. Reiter, K. K. Rokossovsky, and N. F. Vatutin) had joined the ranks of the 12 class members (I. P. Apanasenko, Ia. T. Cherevichenko, A. I. Eremenko, V. A. Frolov, M. S. Khozin, M. P. Kovalev, D. T. Kozlov, I. S. Konev, P. A. Kurochkin, R. Ia. Malinovsky, K. A. Meretskov, and I. V. Tiulenev) who had begun the year as *front* commanders. By year's end, 13 (Apanasenko, Eremenko, Frolov, Govorov, Kovalev, Konev, Malinovsky, Meretskov, Purkaev, Reiter, Rokossovsky, Vatutin, and Tiulenev) of these 19 generals of 1940 were still serving in *front* command. The remaining six class members (Cherevichenko, Golikov, Gordov, Khozin, Kurochkin, and Kozlov) were relegated to army command by year's end because their performances as *front* commanders did not live up to Stalin's expectations.

Based on their combat records and personal qualities, the most capable and accomplished Red Army generals to become *front* commander during 1942 were K. K. Rokossovsky, N. F. Vatutin, R. Ia. Malinovsky, and L. A. Govorov.

Army General Konstantin Konstantinovich Rokossovsky, who was appointed to *front* command in July 1942 at age 45, had already built a reputation as an effective and unusually humane commander.[65] Rokossovsky first demonstrated his combat skill and bravery by leading his woefully understrength 9th Mechanized Corps in a well-organized but fruitless counterattack against German panzer spearheads in the Dubno region of the Ukraine during late June 1941. After being transferred from the southwestern to the western axis, Rokossovsky's skillful leadership of the Iartsevo Operational Group (Group Rokossovsky) during early July was instrumental in thwarting German attempts to encircle Red Army forces around Smolensk and helped persuade Hitler to delay his advance on Moscow and, instead, eliminate Red Army forces in the Kiev region.

While commanding the Western Front's 16th Army in late 1941 and the first six months of 1942, Rokossovsky played a vital role in the defense of Moscow in November 1941, the Moscow offensive in December, the ensuing general offensive during the winter of 1941–42, and in spoiling attacks to slow the *Wehrmacht's* advance toward Stalingrad in the summer of 1942. As Zhukov's most reliable and effective army commander during this period, Rokossovsky often challenged Zhukov's judgments and later criticized his harshness and callous disregard for casualties.[66] However, despite his reservations about Zhukov's command style, Rokossovsky's star continued to rise. Assigned to command the Briansk Front in July 1942, he orchestrated several offensives against *Wehrmacht* forces in the Voronezh region, which, although unsuccessful, contributed significantly to the Red Army's subsequent successful defense at Stalingrad. In recognition of his achievements, Stalin assigned Rokossovsky command of the new Don Front in September 1942, which he led with distinction during the Battle of Stalingrad.

After destroying the vaunted German Sixth Army at Stalingrad, Rokossovsky led the newly formed Central Front during the Orel-Briansk-Smolensk offensive in February and March 1943 in an attempt to collapse *Wehrmacht* defenses and reach the Dnepr River. Despite severe winter weather conditions, Rokossovsky recorded dramatic gains until the bad weather and von Manstein's counteroffensive in the Donbas and Khar'kov regions halted Rokossovsky's offensive in mid-March 1943, leaving the infamous Kursk bulge as stark evidence of his audacity and ability to take maximum advantage of limited forces.

Rokossovsky burnished his reputation as an effective *front* commander in July 1943 at Kursk, where his skillful defense defeated the cream of the *Wehrmacht's* panzer forces before they penetrated his tactical defenses. Although his *front* was severely weakened during the fierce fighting at Kursk, Rokossovsky's forces participated in the offensive to eliminate the Germans' Orel salient in August and September. Exploiting the victory at Orel, Rokossovsky then unhinged the *Wehrmacht's* defenses near Sevsk in early September and launched a deep thrust, which, by early October, had totally ruptured the *Wehrmacht's* defenses in the East and propelled his forces to and beyond the Dnepr River.

Rokossovsky performed equally imposing feats in the Red Army's failed attempt to liberate Belorussia in the fall of 1943 by recording remarkable successes while neighboring *front* commanders such as Sokolovsky registered only repeated failures.[67] Rokossovsky later capped his illustrious wartime career by commanding the 1st and 3rd Belorussian Fronts to repeated victories until war's end. Curiously enough, although accustomed to covering up combat failures, Soviet and Russian historians have also avoided mentioning some of Rokossovsky's most notable operational successes.[68]

Rokossovsky had a fine reputation among other Red Army's generals, and many German generals regarded him as "the Russian Army's best general."[69] Most important, unlike many Red Army senior officers, his soldiers respected him. For example, I. M. Chistiakov, commander of the 21st (later 6th Guards) Army, wrote: "In general, one must say that every time I met with Rokossovsky, I felt a sense of enthusiasm. Konstantin Konstantinovich always listened to his colleagues with great attentiveness and was demanding but just. He never demeaned the dignity of his subordinates and never raised his voice. It is understandable that not all people possessed that quality."[70]

Another more recent biographer added: "Rokossovsky combined outstanding professional ability with self-effacing modesty and a sense of traditional military values. There were times during the war when, amid the destructive urge for bestial vengeance on both sides, Rokossovsky displayed humanity and compassion for the suffering of the once powerful adversary and the hapless German population."[71]

Army General Nikolai Fedorovich Vatutin, known early in the war as the "boy wonder" of the *Stavka,* rose rapidly through key staff positions to command the Southwestern Front at Stalingrad in November 1942. An army general at the age of 42, Vatutin had a well-deserved reputation as the Red Army's most audacious general.[72] While serving in the General Staff prior to the war, he figured prominently in war and mobilization planning under Zhukov's and Shaposhnikov's direction, and, over Vatutin's objections, Stalin began employing him as his personal representative in key operational sectors after war began.

Vatutin first displayed his innate audacity after Stalin appointed him as the Northwestern Front's chief of staff in late June 1941. In that capacity, Vatutin orchestrated the Red Army's fierce counterattacks at Sol'tsy and Staraia Russa during July and August, which, although costly in terms of losses, delayed the *Wehrmacht's* advance on Leningrad and helped save the city. Likewise, during the defense of Moscow in October, Vatutin formed and led a special operational group that halted the *Wehrmacht's* advance at Kalinin and prevented them from severing the vital Moscow-Leningrad rail line.

Vatutin served as *Stavka* representative to the Northwestern Front during the Red Army's winter offensive of 1941–42, when its forces encircled two German corps in the Demiansk region but failed to destroy the encircled forces. Recalled to Moscow in May 1942, Vatutin served as Vasilevsky's deputy in the General Staff until, at Vatutin's own request, Stalin appointed him to command the Voronezh Front during July 1942. After Vatutin conducted several punishing although unsuccessful counterstrokes against *Wehrmacht* forces in the Voronezh region during the late summer of 1942, Stalin chose him to command the new Southwestern Front, which was to spearhead the Red Army's November counteroffensive at Stalingrad. With characteristic skill and audacity, Vatutin's forces routed Romanian forces along the Don River and encircled the German Sixth Army in Stalingrad in November, and, after a short respite, crushed the Italian Eighth Army along the Middle Don River in December, ending any German hopes of rescuing its beleaguered Sixth Army. After his victories in the Stalingrad region, Vatutin led the Southwestern Front's spectacular but impetuous advance into the Donbas during February 1943. Although von Manstein ultimately defeated Vatutin's overextended forces, the latter's offensive subjected the defending Germans to a rare fright.

Many of Vatutin's colleagues credited him as the principal architect of the victory at Stalingrad. His subordinate, I. M. Chistiakov, commander of the 21st (later the 6th Guards) Army, later wrote:

> Those associated with him already understood what a great military culture and broad operational horizon he possessed! N. F. Vatutin was able to state the situation, foresee the development of events, and, no less important, inspire confidence in the success of what was intended with amazingly simplicity and clarity. . . . [Vatutin] had one other notable quality. He could listen to others without losing rank or authority. We, his subordinates, felt free with him, and that, understandably, unleashed initiative.[73]

Because they appreciated his keen organizational skills and audacity as a fighter, Zhukov and Vasilevsky selected Vatutin's *front* to defend the most vulnerable sector of the front during the defensive stage of the Battle for Kursk in July 1943 and to spearhead the offensive toward Khar'kov in August. After fulfilling both missions brilliantly, Vatutin led the ensuing advance to the Dnepr River in September and captured Kiev in an equally brilliant coup de main in early November 1943. By year's end Vatutin was rightly considered the Red Army's most pugnacious and tenacious *front* commander.

Vatutin's hallmarks as a *front* commander were his keen appreciation for the value of careful staff work and an audacious enthusiasm for command. His opponent, German armored specialist von Mellenthin, once noted, "Certainly in men like Zhukov, Konev, Vatutin, and Vasilevsky, the Russians possessed army and army group commanders of a very high order." Unlike many other Red Army *front* commanders, Vatutin was well respected by his subordinates and soldiers alike.

Army General Rodion Iakovlich Malinovsky, whose wartime career was marred by frequent defeats during 1941 and early 1942, overcame his previous failures by late 1942 to emerge as one of the Red Army's most reliable *front* commanders throughout the remainder of the war.[74] Also a veteran of the World and Russian Civil wars, Malinovsky began the war as commander of the Odessa Military District's 48th Rifle Corps. Although his forces withdrew before the *Wehrmacht's* onslaught during the summer and fall of 1941, Malinovsky performed credibly enough as a corps commander and as commander of the 6th Army for Stalin to appoint him commander of the Southern Front in December 1941.

After playing a leading role in the partially successful Barvenkovo-Lozovaia offensive in the winter of 1941–42, however, Malinovsky shared blame for the Red Army's disastrous defeat at Khar'kov in May 1942. Nonetheless, Stalin retained him in *front* command throughout the summer of 1942 and assigned him command of the Don Operational Group and 66th Army during the early stages of the Battle for Stalingrad, where his tenacious defense of the Don River line earned the 45-year-old Malinovsky command of the powerful new 2nd Guards Army, the *Stavka's* premier operational reserve during its Stalingrad offensive.

During the latter stages of this offensive, Malinovsky's army blocked and defeated the *Wehrmacht's* attempts to rescue the Sixth Army encircled in Stalingrad and then led the spectacular advance through Rostov to the Mius River. As reward for his outstanding performance during these offensive, Stalin assigned Malinovsky command of the Southern Front in February 1943 and the Southwestern Front in March. Although Malinovsky failed to overcome the *Wehrmacht's* formidable defenses along the Mius River in February, his front (renamed the 3rd Ukrainian Front) did so in the late summer of 1943, subsequently liberating the Donbas in August and September and capturing the key city of Dnepropetrovsk and seizing bridgeheads over the Dnepr River in October. Thereafter, Malinovsky commanded the 3rd and later 2nd Ukrainian Fronts to war's end.

Malinovsky, who rose to become Soviet defense minister in the 1960s, was a competent but not a flashy commander. Steady and thoughtful, he rose to *front* command based on his reputation as a tenacious fighter in the mold of Zhukov. In the words of one biographer, Malinovsky, "while unusually able, courageous and keenly intelligent, was also headstrong, ambitious, prone to vanity, and, at times, ruthless when the occasion warranted. Once his mind was made up, nothing could shake his determination to do things his way."[75]

Although frequently overlooked by historians because he served in a region they considered secondary in importance, Leonid Aleksandrovich Govorov's career as a *front* commander was no less illustrious than the careers of his more famous counterparts. A veteran of the Russian Civil War and an artilleryman by trade, Govorov commanded the 7th Army's artillery with distinction during the Soviet-Finnish War and was rewarded for his service by his appointment as deputy inspector general of Red Army artillery in 1940 and chief of the Dzerzhinsky Artillery Academy in May 1941, where he was serving when war began.[76]

Govorov left the schoolhouse in July 1941 to become chief of the Western Direction's and Reserve Front's artillery during the Battle for Smolensk. He performed superbly in this otherwise lackluster operation, so the NKO appointed him deputy commander of the Mozhaisk Defense Line and chief of the Western Front's artillery in late August to exploit his artillery knowledge during the defense of the capital. After *Wehrmacht* forces destroyed the Western and Reserve Fronts at Viaz'ma in October, the *Stavka* appointed Govorov to command the new 5th Army, which had just been raised to defend Moscow. The veteran artilleryman's effective performance during the defense of Moscow and the ensuing Moscow offensive prompted Stalin to appoint Govorov as commander of the Leningrad Group of Forces in April 1942 and the Leningrad Front in June 1942, a command he retained until war's end.

While commander of the Leningrad Front, Govorov cracked the *Wehrmacht's* siege of Leningrad in January 1943, planned and conducted the massive offensives that raised the siege of Leningrad entirely and liberated the southern portion of the Leningrad region in January and February 1944, and orchestrated the offensive on the Karelian Isthmus, which liberated the region from Finnish control and ultimately drove Finland from the war, in June and July 1944.

A patient and methodical officer, Govorov was a master at employing artillery, both independently and as an integral part of a modern combined-arms team. Like Rokossovsky and Vatutin, he too earned the respect of his subordinate officers and soldiers:

> Govorov enjoyed great and well-deserved prestige among the troops. He had played an outstanding part in the Battle of Moscow as commander of the 5th Army, which had straddled the Minsk road. In 1943, the troops of the Leningrad Front under his command, in co-operation with other Fronts, had broken the enemy's death grip on the city of Leningrad. Govorov was too reticent and somber to make a very favourable impression on first acquaintance, but all those who had served under him knew that a generous and kindly Russian character was hidden beneath this grim exterior.[77]

Echoing this judgment, Zhukov later noted: "I noticed that out of all of the Front commanders, Stalin had the greatest regard for Marshals of the Soviet Union Rokossovsky, Govorov, and Konev, and for General of the Army Vatutin. . . . [Govorov was] a military expert of high class [who] had an excellent knowledge of artillery. And not only artillery, he was also well versed in operational-tactical problems."[78]

1943. After the Red Army regained the strategic initiative with its victory at Stalingrad in November 1942 and embarked on its new winter campaign, the Red Army's structure of operating *fronts* stabilized somewhat and command turbulence at *front* level diminished significantly. This trend continued throughout the summer of 1943, particularly after the Battle of Kursk, as Stalin identified and selected a new team of thoroughly competent *front* commanders who would lead the Red Army to victory in 1945.

The Red Army began operations in January 1943 with 12 operating *fronts* (Karelian, Leningrad, Volkhov, Northwestern, Kalinin, Western, Briansk, Don, Voronezh, Southwestern, Southern [the Stalingrad Front to 1 January 1943], and Trans-Caucasus). During the winter campaign of 1942–43, the *Stavka* transformed the Trans-Caucasus Front's Northern Group of Forces into the North Caucasus Front on 24 January 1943 and created the Central Front from the former Don Front on 15 February.[79]

In the wake of its winter offensive, the *Stavka* hastily erected new strategic defenses as it prepared to resume offensive operations in the summer of 1943. During this period, it briefly transformed the Briansk Front into first the Kursk and then the Orel Fronts in mid-March, it created new Briansk and Reserve Fronts on 28 and 6 April, respectively, and it converted the latter into the Steppe Military District on 15 April as the nucleus of its new strategic reserve. Finally, during the Battle of Kursk, the *Stavka* transformed the Steppe Military District into the Steppe Front on 9 July and ordered it to halt the *Wehrmacht's* offensive at Kursk and spearhead its subsequent strategic offensive.

As the *Stavka* expanded its offensive operations during the fall of 1943, it reorganized and renamed many of its operating *fronts* to match their changing missions and geographical responsibilities. Accordingly, it abolished the Briansk Front on 10 October, assigning its forces to the Western and Central Fronts and using its headquarters to serve as a nucleus for the new Baltic Front. Subsequently, the *Stavka* renamed the Baltic Front the 2nd Baltic Front, the Kalinin Front the 1st Baltic Front, the Central Front the Belorussian Front, and the Voronezh, Steppe, Southwestern, and Southern Fronts the 1st, 2nd, 3rd, and 4th Ukrainian Fronts on 20 October. Finally, the *Stavka* disbanded the Northwestern Front and converted the North Caucasus Front into the Separate Coastal Army on 20 November. In addition, although it continued functioning as a *front*, the *Stavka* designated the Trans-Caucasus Front as a nonoperating *front* in February.

Despite the frequent changes in designation and the *Stavka's* frenetic attempts to restructure its *fronts* in the Kursk region in March and April, the quantity of Red Army operating *fronts* decreased from 12 on 1 January 1943 to 11 on 31 December.[80] Including the 12 holdovers from 1942, a total of 19 generals served as *front* commanders during 1943. Of these 19 generals, 11—L. A. Govorov, K. A. Meretskov, S. K. Timoshenko, I. S. Konev, M. A. Purkaev, I. Kh. Bagramian, K. K. Rokossovsky, N. F. Vatutin, R. Ia. Malinovsky, F. I. Tolbukhin, and I. V. Tiulenev—served continuously in *front* command or as *Stavka* representatives until their death or war's end, and another two—A. I. Eremenko and I. I. Maslennikov—ended the war in *front* command after serving successfully as army commanders. As a result, 13 (68 percent) of the Red Army marshals or generals who served as *front* commanders during 1943 performed well enough to end the war in *front* command, in contrast to the 32 percent who did so during 1941 and the 52 percent who did so during 1942.

In addition, six (32 percent) of the Red Army marshals or generals who served as *front* commanders in 1943 later served shorter stints in command of *fronts* before perishing in combat or ending the war in lower-level command or staff positions, as opposed to 60 percent in 1941 and 48 percent in

1942. These included P. A. Kurochkin (an army commander), V. A. Frolov and M. A. Reiter (military district commanders), V. D. Sokolovsky (a deputy *front* commander), and M. M. Popov and I. I. Petrov (*front* chiefs of staff). Finally, N. F. Vatutin perished in early April 1944 after being severally wounded by hostile partisans. Therefore, Stalin had identified the nucleus of his winning team of *front* commanders by the summer of 1943, most of whom joined that select team of "Marshals of Victory" in May 1945.

Because Stalin formed most of his winning team of *front* commanders during 1943, command turbulence within the *fronts* diminished significantly throughout the year. As a result, although the quantity of operating *fronts* in the Red Army decreased from 12 to 11 in 1942, these *fronts* experienced only nine assumptions of command or changes in command, for an average of 1.7 commanders per *front*, as opposed to 2.8 per *front* in 1941 (5.8 percent on an annualized basis) and 2.0 per *front* in 1942.[81]

Throughout the year, seven more graduates of the generals' "class of 1940" (I. Kh. Bagramian, I. I. Maslennikov, I. E. Petrov, V. D. Sokolovsky, F. I. Tolbukhin, and P. A. Kurochkin and M. M. Popov for a second time) joined the ranks of the 13 class members (Apanasenko, Eremenko, Frolov, Govorov, Kovalev, Konev, Malinovsky, Meretskov, Purkaev, Reiter, Rokossovsky, Vatutin, and Tiulenev) who began the year as *front* commanders. By year's end 14 (Bagramian, Frolov, Govorov, Kovalev, Konev, Kurochkin, Malinovsky, Meretskov, Petrov, Purkaev, Rokossovsky, Sokolovsky, Vatutin, and Tiulenev) of these 20 generals of 1940 were still serving in *front* command. Of the remaining six class-member generals relieved of *front* command during 1943, four (Eremenko, Kurochkin, Popov, Maslennikov) commanded armies by year's end, and the other two (Apanasenko and Reiter) became deputy *front* and military district commanders.

Although most of these new *front* commanders performed up to Stalin's expectations, two warrant special mention, the first, I. Kh. Bagramian, because he typified the stolid sort of *front* commander who emerged at midwar, and the second, V. D. Sokolovsky, who illustrated why an effective *front* chief of staff did not automatically make an effective *front* commander.

Major General Ivan Khristoforovich Bagramian, who was 45 years old when war began and an experienced cavalryman, was one of the two most famous ethnic Armenians who achieved high rank and considerable distinction in the wartime Red Army (the other was tank corps commander A. Kh. Babadzhanian).[82] Bagramian was serving as the deputy chief of operations of the Kiev Special Military District on 22 June 1941. After surviving the harrowing first few months of war, Bagramian earned notoriety in September 1941 when Timoshenko, the newly appointed commander of the Southwestern Direction, dispatched him to the Southwestern Front's commander Kirponos with orders to withdraw his forces eastward from Kiev to avoid certain encirclement by the Germans. Although Kirponos refused to withdraw without written orders to do so and later perished along with his entire front, Bagramian managed to escape the cauldron with his staff.

While serving as chief of operations and, later, chief of staff of Timoshenko's Southwestern Direction and the Southwestern Front during the winter campaign of 1941–42, Bagramian helped plan the marginally successful Barvenkovo-Lozovaia offensive in January 1942. However, during the spring he also played an instrumental role in planning the ambitious but futile and utterly disastrous offensive at Khar'kov in May. Since Bagramian shared responsibility for the Khar'kov debacle, Stalin relieved him from his post in June, assigning him first as deputy commander of the 61st Army and later as commander of the Western Front's 16th (later 11th Guards) Army in July, after which Bagramian reclaimed his shattered reputation.

Bagramian's army helped thwart the *Wehrmacht's* offensive to liquidate the Viaz'ma-Sukhinichi salient (Operation *Wirbelwind*) in July 1942 and helped plan the Western Front's offensive at Bolkhov, which drove German forces back across the Zhizdra River, in August 1942. During 1943 Bagramian's army conducted violent but bloody and failed assaults against the *Wehrmacht's* defenses north of Orel during February and March in support of the Central and Briansk Fronts' Orel-Briansk-Smolensk offensive and later spearheaded the Western Front's successful offensive against the Orel salient in July and August. As a reward for his success, Stalin appointed Bagramian command of the 1st Baltic Front in November 1943.

Subsequently, Bagramian's forces nearly encircled the *Wehrmacht's* fortress city of Vitebsk during the Red Army's failed Belorussian offensive against Army Group Center from October 1943 through March 1944 and played a leading role in the Red Army's spectacularly successful Belorussian, Riga, Memel', and East Prussian offensives in 1944 and early 1945. Bagramian commanded the Zemland Group of Forces and the 3rd Belorussian Front and defeated *Wehrmacht* forces in the Konigsberg region from February 1945 until war's end.

Twice a Hero of the Soviet Union, the Armenian Bagramian was the only non-Slavic general to rise to *front* command. As one biographer later wrote:

> His intellectual capacity was recognized in 1935, when the General Staff Academy appointed him direct from pupil to lecturer, and his later sponsorship by Zhukov, Timoshenko, and Stalin was obviously based on high regard for his abilities. . . .
>
> His performance in command of [the 16th Army, already one of the best in the Red Army] was undoubtedly well above average. He was again fortunate in that by the time he became a Front commander the war

was clearly won and both human and materials resources were abundant, but he made good use of them and achieved impressive results.[83]

At the other extreme, the military career of Colonel General Vasilii Danilovich Sokolovsky, who was 44 years old when war began and was a close associate of Zhukov, spanned two wars and extended well into the Cold War.[84] Sokolovsky was serving as Zhukov's deputy chief of the General Staff when war began and soon after served as Zhukov's chief of staff in the Western Front and Western Direction and, once again, as his chief of staff during the Battle of Moscow.

On Zhukov's recommendation, Stalin assigned Sokolovsky to command the Western Front in February 1943, replacing I. S. Konev, who was assigned command of the Steppe Military District in June 1943. Sokolovsky's reputation as a superb organizer was tempered considerably by his *front's* poor performance in Operation Mars in November and December 1942 and by his relief from *front* command in April 1944 after his forces performed poorly and suffered heavy losses during the many unsuccessful offensives he conducted against *Wehrmacht* forces defending Belorussia in the fall of 1943 and winter of 1944.[85] Despite his weaknesses as a *front* commander, Sokolovsky continued to serve in senior staff positions for the remainder of the war. More important still, well after war's end, he became chief of the General Staff and Soviet minister of defense under Khrushchev and wrote a famous book, *Military Strategy,* which articulated Soviet military strategy in the nuclear age. Historians concealed Sokolovsky's poor wartime performance as a *front* commander primarily because of his close association and friendship with Zhukov and the prestigious posts he filled during the postwar years.

Although they still languish in the shadows of Zhukov, Konev, Rokossovsky, and other more famous Red Army wartime "great captains," many less famous but nevertheless equally competent generals commanded the Red Army's *fronts* during 1943 and the remainder of the war. These generals included F. I. Tolbukhin, I. V. Tiulenev, E. I. Petrov, F. I. Golikov, M. A. Purkaev, K. A. Meretskov, V. A. Frolov, and P. A. Kurochkin, two of whom (Meretskov and Tolbukhin) Stalin had promoted to the rank of marshal of the Soviet Union by war's end and another (Golikov) to marshal after war's end.

A veteran of the World and Russian Civil wars, Fedor Ivanovich Tolbukhin was a 51-year-old major general serving as chief of staff of the Trans-Caucasus Military District when war began. After Tolbukhin had served as chief of staff of the Trans-Caucasus, Caucasus, and Crimean Fronts in 1941 and 1942, Stalin demoted him to deputy commander of the Stalingrad Military District in late May 1942, largely because of his association with the military disaster in the Crimea. However, Tolbukhin's star rose once again when he commanded the 57th Army with distinction during Operation *Blau,* the defense of Stalingrad, and the Red Army's Stalingrad offensive. The *Stavka* was so impressed with Tolbukhin's tenacity and fighting spirit that it appointed him to command the new 68th Army in February 1943, which it designated to spearhead Zhukov's Operation Polar Star. Thereafter, Tolbukhin commanded the Southern and 4th and 3rd Ukrainian Fronts to war's end, in the process becoming one of eight *front* commanders to be awarded the Order of Victory.

More senior than many of his counterparts and considered by Stalin as one of his most politically reliable senior officers, Ivan Vladimirovich Tiulenev was a 49-year-old army general when war began. After Tiulenev had commanded the Southern Front from its creation in early July through August 1941, Stalin relieved him from command after two of his armies were encircled and destroyed in the Uman' region.[86] Despite this failure in command, Stalin appointed the reliable Tiulenev to command the 28th Army in November 1941 and, thereafter, the Trans-Caucasus Military District and Trans-Caucasus Front in March 1942, a post he held through war's end. A favorite of Stalin, Tiulenev played a critical role in the defense of the Caucasus region during late 1942. Thereafter, and to war's end, Tiulenev also presided over the ruthless liquidation of "disloyal" minorities in the region, including the forced exile of Chechens, Kalmuks and many other groups.

As fascinating as it is depressing, the fate as *front* commander of Ivan Efimovich Petrov remains a classic case study in how the Red Army's harsh system of political control thwarted the military careers of many promising military officers. Also a Civil War veteran, Petrov was a 45-year-old major general commanding the Central Asian Military District's 27th Mechanized Corps when war began. After 22 June he commanded, in succession, the 2nd Cavalry and 25th Rifle Divisions and the Separate Coastal Army from October 1941 through July 1942, while doing so distinguishing himself in the famous defenses of Odessa and Sevastopol'. Subsequently, he commanded the 44th Army, the Trans-Caucasus Front's Black Sea Group of Forces, the North Caucasus Front, the 33rd Army, and the 2nd and 4th Ukrainian Fronts from July 1942 to April 1945.[87] His frequent rise and fall from *front* to army command reflected Stalin's mistrust of Petrov and the near constant meddling in his affairs of Stalin's hated henchman and crony Mekhlis. A critic of Stalin later noted:

> Perhaps my admiration [of Petrov] was due to his fame as organizer of the defense of Odessa and subsequently of Sevastopol.
>
> But though Petrov was one of our most talented military leaders, he also had a large number of failures in his career. Stalin did not like him. More than once Petrov had been demoted. Later he was removed as commander of the Fourth Ukrainian Front, just before the end of the

war. His replacement, Yeremenko, was present at the victory parade as the "Hero of Carpathia," though he had commanded the front for only eighteen days. Petrov, who had led his forces through the entire Carpathian chain under the most difficult conditions, was never mentioned at the parade.[88]

Although his tenure as *front* commander was relatively brief, Filipp Ivanovich Golikov warrants mention, if only because he served in such a wide variety of posts throughout the war. Only 41 years old when war began, Golikov was also a Russian Civil War veteran and a 1933 graduate of the Frunze Academy. In July 1940 he was assigned as deputy chief of the General Staff and chief of the General Staff's Intelligence Directorate (RU). Although Golikov revitalized Soviet military intelligence on the eve of war, he shared some responsibility for the intelligence failure in June 1941 because, although he detected Hitler's preparations for war, he failed to press his case on Stalin. After the war began, as Stalin's emissary Golikov was instrumental in preparing the way for the emergence of the future Allied wartime alliance.[89]

When Moscow was threatened in late 1941, Stalin appointed Golikov to command the 10th Reserve Army, which he led with distinction during the ensuing Moscow offensive. Stalin rewarded Golikov for his accomplishments by assigning him to command the Briansk Front in April 1942, which he was commanding when the *Wehrmacht* began Operation *Blau*. Golikov then commanded the Voronezh Front in July and once again from October 1942 through March 1943, and, in the interim, commanded the 1st Guards Army and served as deputy commander of the Southeastern (Stalingrad) Front from July to October. Although Golikov performed competently during the Battle for Stalingrad, Stalin made him the scapegoat for many of his own failures during the summer of 1942.

Golikov's tenure in field command ended in April 1943 after *Wehrmacht* forces defeated his Voronezh Front in the Khar'kov region in February and March. Thereafter, Golikov headed the NKO's Main Cadre Directorate until war's end, managing the often grisly and sordid task of repatriating Soviet citizens from abroad, many of whom ended up in the GULAG. His role in the intelligence failures of 1941 and the Red Army's failures in the spring and summer of 1942 have since been at the focal point of many wartime controversies.

One of the most faceless of the Red Army wartime *front* commanders was Maksim Alekseevich Purkaev, who nevertheless remained in *front* command until war's end. A Russian Civil War veteran and a 1936 graduate of the Frunze Academy, Purkaev was serving as chief of staff of the Kiev Special Military District when war began. Unlike his Southwestern Front, which perished at Kiev in September 1941, Purkaev survived to command the newly formed 60th (3rd Shock) Army during the Moscow offensive and the winter campaign of 1941–42, and the Kalinin and Far Eastern (1st Far Eastern) Fronts to war's end. Although his forces failed to achieve victory in Operation Mars, the determination he evidenced in the capture of Velikie Luki assured his reputation as a fighter and earned him command of the 2nd Far Eastern Front during the Red Army's Manchurian offensive of August 1945.[90]

No Red Army *front* commander had a more varied or checkered career than Pavel Aleksandrovich Kurochkin, who commanded at both army and *front* levels throughout the war and, during the postwar years, authored the most detailed and thorough analysis of Red Army wartime operations.[91] The 41-year-old Kurochkin was commanding the Orel Military District when war began. During the war he served successively as the commander of the 20th and 43rd Armies in July and August 1941, representative of the *Stavka* to the Northwestern Front, commander and deputy commander of the Northwestern Front from August 1941 through October 1942 and from June through November 1943, respectively, commander of the 11th and 34th Armies from November 1942 through March 1943 and from March through June 1943, respectively, deputy commander of the 1st Ukrainian Front from December 1943 through February 1944, commander of the 2nd Belorussian Front from February through April 1944, and commander of the 60th Army from April 1944 through May 1945.[92]

Kurochkin's failure to retain *front* command until war's end resulted largely from his inability to defeat and destroy German forces at Demiansk during 1942 and 1943 and his unsuccessful stint as 2nd Belorussian Front commander in early 1944, when his forces were unable to defeat *Wehrmacht* forces encircled at Kovel'.

No less fascinating was the wartime career of Kirill Afanas'evich Meretskov, who soared to prominence as Zhukov's predecessor as chief of the General Staff before the war and languished in NKVD imprisonment early in the war only to emerge as a full-fledged marshal of the Soviet Union, *front* commander, and recipient of the Order of Victory by war's end.

Meretskov began his wartime career as deputy people's commissar of defense for training from January through September 1941 and also served as *Stavka* representative to the Northwestern and Karelian Fronts before being arrested and imprisoned (and severely beaten) in September 1941 for either malfeasance or presumed disloyalty to Stalin. Suddenly exonerated in October, a chastened Meretskov found himself in command of the 7th Separate Army in Karelia in October and the 4th Army in November and December, where his forces won a rare but significant victory at Tikhvin. Elevated to command the Volkhov Front from December 1941 through May 1942, Meretskov planned and conducted the ill-fated Liuban' offensive, during which his *front's* 2nd Shock Army was encircled. Removed from command for this failure, after Meretskov served a short stint in command of the Western Front's 33rd Army in May and June, Stalin assigned him to command the Volkhov Front once again in June, after his successor, Khozin, presided over the destruction of the 2nd Shock Army.

Meretskov's fortunes changed for the better while he commanded the Volkhov Front through January 1944 and the Karelian Front from February 1944 through August 1945. During this period his *front* helped crack the Leningrad blockade in January 1943, defeated Army Group North in the Leningrad-Novgorod offensive in January–February 1944, and liberated the Karelian Isthmus from Finnish control in June and July 1944. By then an expert in conducting operations in heavily forested regions, Meretskov was chosen by Stalin to command the 1st Far Eastern Front in its offensive into eastern Manchuria in August 1945.[93]

Meretskov was a competent *front* commander, and his imprisonment ensured his loyalty if not obsequious subservience to Stalin; Meretskov followed Stalin's orders to the letter regardless of cost. A colleague described Meretskov as "by nature a very sociable and energetic man" who "easily grasped the matter in hand."[94]

Finally, Valerian Aleksandrovich Frolov, who set the longevity record for his tenure of command, led the Karelian Front from September 1941 through February 1944, spending virtually his entire career serving in Karelia and the far north. Few biographies of Frolov exist, and comments on his character and capabilities are as rare as the region where he served was barren. Frolov began the war as a 46-year-old lieutenant general commanding the Northern Front's 14th Army in the far north.[95] He assumed command of the Karelian Front after serving as its deputy commander in August and September 1941 and, later, served as deputy *front* commander from February to November 1944, while Meretskov was commanding the *front*. Thereafter, Frolov remained in the north as commander of the White Sea Military District until after war's end.[96]

Army Commanders

Operationally and tactically, the Red Army's combat performance during the first 30 months of the war depended directly on the effectiveness of its command cadre at army, mobile corps, and tank army levels. Although the *Wehrmacht's* ferocious and devastating Barbarossa invasion taxed these generals to and often beyond their limits and many perished during their ordeal, a combination of sheer attrition and the will to survive ultimately produced a remarkably competent cadre of army commanders by the end of the first 18 months of the war.

High attrition rates and severe turbulence at every command level, but particularly at the army level, characterized the situation in the Red Army during the first 18 months of the war. During the summer and fall of 1941, for example, the *Wehrmacht* destroyed multiple Soviet armies and many of their unfortunate commanders in massive encirclement operations west of Minsk in June, at Uman' and Kiev in August and September, at Viaz'ma and Briansk in October, and on lesser scales in other sectors of the front. However, as this gruesome process unfolded, the *Stavka* managed to raise and field new armies even more rapidly than the *Wehrmacht* could destroy them.

Although this pattern of destruction and regeneration ceased almost entirely while the Red Army was on the offensive during the winter of 1941–42, it resumed once again when the *Wehrmacht* launched Operation *Blau* during the summer of 1942. In the interim, however, the *Stavka* identified a new generation of army commanders, who, in addition to being blooded during the first six months of war, had demonstrated both the skills and the will to win. As a result, when the *Wehrmacht's* "wrecking ball" decimated many more Soviet armies during the summer of 1942, despite the command turbulence that continued to plague the Red Army, it was in a far better state regarding the capabilities its army commanders than it had been during 1941. In short, in the Stalingrad region in November and December 1942, Stalin's team of army commanders who had survived the tests of Operations Barbarossa and *Blau* demonstrated to the *Wehrmacht*, if not the world as a whole, that they were capable of besting it at its own game, at least for brief periods of time and in limited sectors of the front.

As the Red Army's offensive operations during the winter of 1942–43 indicated, the army's ability to expand and sustain its Stalingrad victories was an entirely different matter, however. These victories proved that its army commanders could crush Romanian and Italian armies and, by doing so, outflank, encircle, and defeat a German army in the process, but its subsequent defeats in the Donbas and at Khar'kov proved that these commanders were not yet capable of sustaining successful offensives for an entire campaign. Thus, when the Red Army's first genuinely strategic offensive bogged down in the late winter of 1942–43 it demonstrated that the Red Army's senior command cadre, especially its army commanders, still had much to learn.

Beginning early in the winter campaign of 1942–43, and to an increasing degree after the Battle of Kursk in July and August 1943, the *Stavka* was able to identify and assign generals to army command who would serve in that capacity to war's end. As it did so, with a few exceptions, it created a degree of command stability at the army level that would also endure to war's end.

1941. The Red Army began the war with 21 armies in its field forces and strategic reserves, 15 of which were subordinate to its four operating *fronts*.[97]

Even though the *Wehrmacht* encircled and destroyed three armies (the 3rd, 10th, and 13th) west of Minsk and decimated four more (the 16th, 19th, 20th, and 28th) in the Vitebsk, Smolensk, and Roslavl' regions, through mobilization the *Stavka* was able to increase its quantity of field armies to 29 by 1 August. Likewise, although the Red Army lost two armies (the 6th and 12th) in the Uman' encirclement in August, four more (the 5th, 37th, 26th, and 21st) in the Kiev encirclement in September, and the bulk of seven more (the 19th, 20th, 24th, 32nd, 3rd, 13th, and 50th) in the Viaz'ma and Briansk encirclements in October, the *Stavka* increased its quantity of field armies to 37 on 1 October, 48 on 1 December, and 50 on 31 December 1941.

Therefore, including those destroyed and newly mobilized, the *Stavka* fielded a total of 76 armies during the first six months of war. During this period a total of 101 generals served as army commanders, for an average of 1.3 commanders per army or 2.6 commanders per army on an annualized basis. Although this figure appears quite low given the ferocity of the fighting and the damage the Red Army suffered, command turbulence was extremely high at army level because the *Wehrmacht* destroyed or decimated over one-third of the armies the *Stavka* fielded. For example, the 76 armies existing when war began or formed during the first six months of the war experienced 119 assumptions of command or changes in command, for an average of 1.6 commanders per army or 3.2 per army on an annualized basis.[98]

Regarding the individual fate of the 101 generals who served as army commanders during 1941, 18 (18 percent) were killed in action, captured, repressed, or relieved of their commands, 69 (68 percent) were still serving as *front*, army, or military district commanders on 1 January 1942, and the remaining 14 (14 percent) were serving in staff assignments or commanding at lower levels. The 18 losses included seven who were killed in action or fatally wounded (M. I. Potapov, F. M. Filatov, A. K. Smirnov, V. Ia. Kachalov, K. I. Rakutin, M. P. Petrov, and P. S. Pshennikov), one who died from unknown causes (I. D. Akimov), five who were captured (I. N. Muzychenko, P. G. Ponedelin, M. F. Lukin, F. A. Ershakov, and S. V. Vyshnevsky), four who were repressed (A. A. Korobkov, F. S. Ivanov, K. M. Kachanov, and P. P. Sobennikov), and one who was relieved of command (N. I. Pronin).

The 69 generals who continued to command at army level or above at year's end included eight who were promoted to *front* command (K. A. Meretskov, R. Ia. Malinovsky, Ia. T. Cherevichenko, V. A. Frolov, I. S. Konev, P. A. Kurochkin, F. Ia. Kostenko, and M. S. Khozin), 58 who remained army commanders, and three who ended up commanding military districts. Finally, the 14 generals who were relieved from army command included seven who became rifle division or brigade commanders and seven who were assigned as *front*, army, or NKO staff officers or deputy commanders.

Since these army commanders faced extraordinarily harsh combat situations during the first six months of war, many in circumstances largely beyond their control, the only valid basis for assessing their command qualities or performance in combat is to examine the role they played in defensive and offensive operations and the way Stalin and the *Stavka* treated them in terms of promotion and their future assignments.

Within the context of the *Wehrmacht's* rapid advance along the northwestern and western axis and the total collapse of Red Army forces defending these axes, even though their actions proved futile, several army commanders distinguished themselves during the border battles and the Red Army's defense of the Dnepr River line. For example, despite the catastrophic circumstances they faced, P. P. Sobennikov and V. I. Morozov, the commanders of the Northwestern Front's 8th and 11th Armies, and V. I. Kuznetsov, the commander of the Western Front's 3rd Army, managed to conduct counterstrokes at Kelme, Raseiniai, and Grodno, respectively. Although all of these counterstrokes failed, their performance was forceful enough for Stalin to permit them to remain in army command and, in the case of Kuznetsov and Sobennikov, to promote them to *front* command. On the other hand, Stalin vindictively arrested and executed A. A. Korobkov, the commander of the Western Front's 4th Army, for losing control of his forces in circumstances where no commander could have maintained control.

Likewise, along the southwestern axis, where Zhukov and Kirponos orchestrated counterstrokes that slowed the *Wehrmacht's* advance, the vigorous if futile resistance of M. I. Potapov's and I. N. Muzichenko's 5th and 6th Armies significantly slowed the *Wehrmacht's* advance by days by stoutly defending the Rovno, Lutsk, and Brody regions before their armies were forced to fall back eastward under unrelenting German pressure. Later, however, Muzichenko was captured when his army was encircled and destroyed at Uman' in August, and Potapov, whose army remained the thorn in the *Wehrmacht's* flesh throughout the summer, was killed in September during the Kiev encirclement.

After the *Wehrmacht* smashed the Red Army's forward defenses, army commanders such as V. A. Khomenko (30th Army), S. A. Kalinin (24th Army), I. S. Konev (19th Army), K. K. Rokossovsky (Iartsevo Group and 16th Army), V. A. Kachalov (28th Army), P. A. Kurochkin (20th Army), M. F. Lukin (16th Army), and K. A. Rakutin (24th Army) performed vigorously and often successfully during combat in the Smolensk region from early July through early September. For example, Lukin managed to extract his army from encirclement at Smolensk, only to fall captive to the *Wehrmacht* when it destroyed his army at Viaz'ma in October. Similarly, Rokossovsky, who had already led the understrength 9th Mechanized Corps with considerable skill in the fighting near Dubno in late June, conducted a spirited defense at Iartsevo in July and August, materially assisting the escape of Red Army forces from the Smolensk pocket. Somewhat later, Rakutin achieved the Red Army's first significant victory in the war at El'nia in early September, although he perished in the Viaz'ma encirclement in October.

During the same period, Kachalov died while leading his army in a heroic but suicidal counterstroke south of Smolensk, and although he lost the bulk of his army in combat west of Smolensk and later commanded the Western Front during its ensuing disaster at Viaz'ma, Konev survived these ordeals to command the Kalinin Front in late October. Finally, Khomenko, Rokossovsky, and Kurochkin survived the Battle of Smolensk as army commanders, and Stalin appointed Kalinin as deputy commander of the Western Front.

Generals commanding armies operating along the northwestern and southwestern axes in the wake of the border battles also experienced mixed fates. For example, after the Northwestern Front's counterstroke at Staraia Russa in August, Stalin relieved N. I. Pronin, the commander of the 34th Army, from further command but retained V. I. Morozov and N. E. Berzarin, the commanders of the 11th and 27th Armies, in command of their armies. Along the southwestern axes, after the disastrous encirclements at Uman' and Kiev in August and September, R. Ia. Malinovsky's 6th Army, I. V. Galinin's 12th Army, V. Ia. Kolpakchi's 18th Army, and Ia. T. Cherevichenko's 9th Army conducted skillful withdrawals eastward through the Ukraine in late September and October. Stalin rewarded all four commanders by appointing Malinovsky and, later, Cherevichenko to command the Southern Front and by retaining Galanin and Kolpakchi in army command for the remainder of the war.

Later still, the Red Army's successful defense of Leningrad, Tikhvin, Moscow, and Rostov in October and November and its subsequent offensives in these regions in November and December significantly increased the prestige of many army commanders. These included I. I. Fediuninsky (54th Army) and K. A. Meretskov (4th Army), whom Stalin appointed to command *fronts* after they won victories at Leningrad and Tikhvin, and V. Ia. Kolpakchi (18th Army), A. I. Lopatin (37th Army), and F. M. Kharitonov (9th Army), who retained command of their armies after defeating *Wehrmacht* forces at Rostov.

At the same time, many army commanders, including D. D. Leliushenko (30th Army), V. I. Kuznetsov (1st Shock Army), A. A. Vlasov (20th Army), K. K. Rokossovsky (16th Army), L. A. Govorov (5th Army), M. G. Efremov (33rd Army), D. K. Golubev (43rd Army), I. G. Zakharkin (49th Army), I. V. Boldin (50th Army), and F. I. Golikov (10th Army) either earned or burnished their reputations during the Battle for Moscow. While Rokossovsky, Govorov, and Golikov later became successful *front* commanders, Leliushenko, Kuznetsov, Golubev, Zakharkin, and Boldin continued to command effectively at the army level for the remainder of the war. In addition, three generals commanding armies in the Briansk Front, which won a signal victory at Elets, south of Moscow, in December, significantly added to their reputations as effective army commanders. The first, F. Ia. Kostenko, who commanded a special operational group that spearheaded the offensive, became a *front* commander only to perish at Khar'kov in May 1942; the second, Ia. G. Kreizer (3rd Army), remained in army command until war's end; and the third, A. M. Gorodniansky (13th Army), served as an army commander until his death at Khar'kov in May 1942.

On the other hand, Efremov's promising career ended with his death when his army was encircled east of Viaz'ma in February 1942, and Vlasov, who was captured shortly after taking command of the 2nd Shock Army, which was encircled and destroyed near Liuban' in June 1942, later cooperated with his captors, earning fame as the Red Army's most famous wartime traitor.

1942. After the Red Army began military operations in January 1942 with 50 armies, including 48 subordinate to its operating *fronts* and two in the RVGK, the *Wehrmacht* destroyed or decimated the 6th and 57th Armies at Khar'kov and the 44th and 51st Armies in the Crimea in May, the 2nd Shock Army at Liuban' in June, the 39th Army west of Rzhev in August, and the 2nd Shock Army for a second time at Siniavino in September. Despite these losses, by mobilizing new armies, the *Stavka* was able to increase its quantity of field armies to 63 on 1 June 1942, 66 on 1 October, and 67 on 31 December.[99]

Therefore, including those destroyed or newly mobilized, the *Stavka* fielded a total of 83 armies during 1942. During this period a total of 133 generals served as army commanders, for an average of 1.6 commanders per army as opposed to 2.6 commanders on an annualized basis during 1941. Even though the average tenure in command of army commanders increased somewhat during 1942, command turbulence continued to plague the army until after the Stalingrad offensive in November. For example, the 83 armies existing when the year began or mobilized during the year experienced 117 assumptions of command or changes in command, for an average of 1.4 commanders per army in contrast to 3.2 commanders on an annualized basis in 1941.[100]

Regarding the individual fate of the 133 generals who served as army commanders in 1942, ten (8 percent) were killed in action, captured, repressed, or relieved from command, 88 (66 percent) were still serving as *front*, army, or military district commanders on 1 January 1943, and, excluding eight generals (6 percent) (P. A. Ivanov, M. A. Parsegov, A. N. Pervushkin, A. A. Khriashchev, A. M. Kuznetsov, A. G. Batiunia, D. N. Nikishev, and N. A. Moskvin) whose ultimate fate remains obscure, the remaining 27 (20 percent) were serving in staff assignments or commanding at lower levels. The ten losses included five who were killed in action or fatally wounded (A. M.

Gorodniansky, M. M. Ivanov, Ia. I. Broud, K. P. Podlas, and L. N. L'vov), one who was captured (A. A. Vlasov), one who committed suicide to avoid capture (M. G. Efremov), one repressed (I. F. Dashichev), and two who were relieved of command (M. A. Antoniuk and G. G. Sokolov).

The 88 generals who continued to command at army level or above at year's end included seven who were promoted to *front* command (L. A. Govorov, F. I. Golikov, K. K. Rokossovsky, M. A. Reiter, I. V. Tiulenev, M.A. Purkaev, A. I. Eremenko), 78 who remained army commanders, and three who commanded military districts. Finally, the 27 generals who were relieved from army command included 11 who became corps commanders, three who became rifle division or brigade commanders, and 13 who were assigned as *front,* army, or NKO staff officers or deputy commanders.

As was the case during 1941, the most accurate basis for assessing the command qualities and combat effectiveness of these army commanders is to examine their combat record and the way Stalin and the *Stavka* treated them in terms of promotion and their future assignments.

In addition to those army commanders who achieved fame during the Battle for Moscow, many others distinguished themselves during the ensuing winter campaign. For example, because they led their 3rd and 4th Shock Armies effectively in the successful Toropets-Kholm offensive in January, Stalin promoted A. I. Eremenko and M. A. Purkaev to command the Southeastern and Kalinin Fronts in August. Similarly, M. M. Popov (61st Army), P. I. Batov (3rd Army), and N. P. Pukhov (13th Army) increased their reputations as effective army commanders in the Orel-Bolkhov offensive in January and February, and K. P. Podlas (40th Army) and V. N. Gordov (21st Army) added luster to their reputations in the Oboian-Kursk offensive during the same period. While Stalin appointed Gordov to command the Stalingrad Front in July and retained Popov, Batov, and Pukhov in army command, Podlas perished in the disaster at Khar'kov in May.

In addition, A. G. Maslov (38th Army), A. M. Gorodniansky (6th Army), D. I. Riabyshev (57th Army), A. I. Lopatin (37th Army), F. M. Kharitonov (9th Army), and K. A. Koroteev (12th Army) operated effectively in the Lozovaia-Barvenkovo offensive in January and February. Because they performed well in this offensive, the *Stavka* assigned Maslov to command of one of its new tank corps in the spring of 1942 and retained the other generals in army command.

On the other hand, the twin disasters that occurred at Khar'kov and in the Crimea in May took a grim toll on the reputations, if not the lives, of many participating army commanders. For example, although Gorodniansky (6th Army) and Podlas (57th Army) perished in the battle, Riabyshev's (28th Army) reputation never recovered from the defeat, and, after serving brief stints in army command, he ended the war as a corps commander. On the positive side of the ledger, K. S. Moskalenko (38th Army) performed well enough during and after the Khar'kov disaster to remain a successful army commander to war's end. Meanwhile, in the Crimea L. N. L'vov (51st Army) died in the May disaster, and, after Stalin demoted them to the rank of colonel, L'vov's counterpart army commanders, S. I. Cherniak (44th Army) and K. S. Kolganov (47th Army), ended the war as rifle division and corps commanders, respectively.

The Red Army's prolonged defense during Operation *Blau* proved to be a graveyard for some army commanders' reputations, but it propelled others to lasting prominence. For example, although Stalin relieved A. I. Parsegov (40th Army), D. I. Riabyshev (28th Army), F. A. Parkhomenko (9th Army), V. S. Tsyganov (56th Army), and M. A. Antoniuk (60th Army) from army command during this trying period, others like K. S. Moskalenko (38th and 40th Armies) emerged from this ordeal with vastly improved reputations. On the other hand, the Red Army's successful defense during Operation *Blau* and its spectacular victory at Stalingrad also provided context for the emergence of a new generation of effective army commanders, many of whom would command their armies to war's end. These included I. M. Chistiakov (21st Army), V. F. Gerasimenko (28th Army), former *front* commander P. M. Kozlov (37th Army), A. A. Grechko (12th Army), F. M. Kamkov (18th Army), A. I. Ryshov (56th Army), V. I. Chuikov (64th and 62nd Armies), and M. S. Shumilov (64th Army).

While the Operation *Blau* and the struggle for Stalingrad were taking place, other army commanders added to their already good reputations during combat in other sectors of the front. These included I. D. Cherniakhovsky (60th Army) and N. E. Chibisov (38th Army), whose armies conducted incessant counterstrokes near Voronezh in July and August, and K. K. Rokossovsky (16th Army), P. A. Belov (61st Army), and I. Kh. Bagramian (16th Army), whose armies hammered away at the *Wehrmacht's* defenses in the Orel and Zhizdra sectors with varying degrees of success during the same period. Meanwhile, in the Moscow region to the north, armies commanded by D. D. Leliushenko (30th Army), V. S. Polenov (31st Army), M. A. Reiter (20th Army), I. I. Fediuninsky (5th Army), and former *front* commander M. M. Khozin (33rd Army) also achieved notable if limited success in the Kalinin and Western Fronts' offensives against the *Wehrmacht's* Rzhev-Viaz'ma salient in August. As a result, Stalin appointed Rokossovsky to command the Briansk and Don Fronts in July and September and Reiter to command the Briansk Front in September. Finally, F. I. Starikov (8th Army), N. I. Gusev (Neva Operational Group), and V. P. Sviridov (55th Army) performed effectively enough in the Leningrad Front's Siniavino offensive in August and September to remain in command of armies until war's end.

The twin strategic offensives the *Stavka* conducted in the Rzhev and Stalingrad regions in November and December solidified the reputations of most but not all of the army commanders who participated in them. With the exception of N. I. Kiriukhin, whose 20th Army spearheaded the Western Front's failed attempt to penetrate the *Wehrmacht's* defenses during Operation Mars and who never again commanded at army level, most of the participating army commanders continued in command or were promoted to command guards armies or *fronts* in early 1943.

For example, D. D. Leliushenko (1st and 3rd Guards Armies), I. M. Chistiakov (21st Army), P. I. Batov (65th Army), I. V. Galanin (24th Army), A. S. Zhadov (66th Army), V. I. Chuikov (62nd Army), M. S. Shumilov (64th Army), F. I. Tolbukhin (57th Army), N. I. Trufanov (51st Army), V. F. Gerasimenko (28th Army), F. M. Kharitonov (6th Army), M. M. Popov and V. D. Tsvetaev (5th Shock Army), V. I. Kuznetsov (1st Guards Army), and R. Ia. Malinovsky (2nd Guards Army) all distinguished themselves during the Stalingrad and ensuing Middle Don and Kotel'nikovskii offensives. As rewards for their accomplishments, Stalin appointed Tolbukhin to command the Southern Front in March 1943, Popov the Reserve Front in April, and Malinovsky the Southwestern Front in March.

At the same time, while K. N. Galitsky (3rd Shock Army) improved his reputation as a fighter in his victory at Velikie Luki, G. F. Tarasov (41st Army), V. A. Iushkevich (22nd Army), A. I. Zygin (39th Army), V. Ia. Kolpakchi (30th Army), V. S. Polenov (30th Army), and E. P. Zhuravlev (29th Army) performed credibly enough in Operation Mars to retain army command at least for a time, although their subsequent careers never matched those of their colleagues who fought in the Stalingrad region.

1943. The Red Army began military operations on 1 January 1943 with 67 armies, including 65 in its operating *fronts* and two in the RVGK reserve. Unlike previous years, however, the *Wehrmacht* destroyed only one army during 1943, the 6th Army in the Donbas region in March, but the *Stavka* quickly reestablished this army by the summer. Even though the *Stavka* renumbered, reorganized, and disbanded several armies during the year, it increased its quantity of field armies to 69 on 1 June and then decreased it to 61 by 31 December.

Therefore, including those destroyed or mobilized, the *Stavka* fielded a total of 75 armies in 1943. During this period a total of 106 generals served as army commanders, for an average of 1.4 commanders per army as opposed to 1.6 commanders in 1942 and 2.6 commanders in 1941. Command turbulence remained fairly high during the winter of 1943, but it decreased significantly after the Battle of Kursk in July and August. For example, the 75 armies existing when the year began or mobilized or redesignated during the year experienced only 82 assumptions of command or changes in command, for an average of 1.1 commanders per army in contrast to 1.4 commanders per army in 1942 and 3.2 in 1941.[101]

Regarding the individual fate of the 106 generals who served as army commanders during 1943, four (4 percent) were killed in action, 76 (71 percent) were still serving as *front*, army, or military district commanders on 1 January 1944, and, excluding two generals (2 percent), G. A. Khaziulin and V. M. Sharapov, whose ultimate fate remains obscure, the remaining 24 (23 percent) were serving in staff assignments or commanding at lower levels. The four losses included P. P. Korzun, F. M. Kharitonov, A. I. Zygin, and V. A. Khomenko, who were killed in combat or fatally wounded during the year.

The 76 generals who continued to command at army level or above at year's end included three who were promoted to *front* command (I. Kh. Bagramian, F. I. Tolbukhin, and R. Ia. Malinovsky), 70 who remained army commanders, and three who commanded military districts. Finally, the 24 who were relieved from command included seven who became corps commanders, one who became a rifle division commander, and 16 who were assigned as *front,* army, or NKO staff officers or deputy commanders.

In addition, of the 70 generals who were still serving as army commanders on 1 January 1944, five (K. N. Leselidze, I. F. Nikolaev, I. G. Zakharkin, and G. F. Tarasov) were killed in combat in 1944, one (I. D. Cherniakhovsky) was killed in 1945, two (I. D. Cherniakhovsky and I. I. Maslennikov) rose to command *fronts* and one (D. D. Leliushenko) rose to command a tank army prior to war's end, and 52 remained army commanders until war's end.

As before, the performance of these army commanders in 1943 and their subsequent careers provide the most accurate measure of their effectiveness. Unlike the previous two years, Stalin did not relieve any of the commanders whose armies suffered defeat in the Donbas, Khar'kov, and Orel regions in February and March, primarily because they were carrying out his orders to apply maximum pressure on the retreating *Wehrmacht* to the letter. On the contrary, despite these defeats Stalin appointed three of his most successful army commanders during this period—Tolbukhin (57th and 68th Armies), Malinovsky (2nd Guards Army), and Popov (5th Shock Army and Operational Group Popov)—to command the Southern, Southwestern, and Reserve Fronts in March and April and I. Kh. Bagramian (16th Army) to command the 1st Baltic Front in November.

After the winter campaign ended, Stalin redesignated the 24th, 66th, 21st, 64th, 62nd, 30th, and 16th Armies as guards armies on 16 April, renumbering them as the 5th through 8th and 10th and 11th Guards Armies, respectively, and either retained or assigned his most accomplished generals to command these armies. Five of these seven new guards armies and one of the four guards armies previously formed (the 1st through 4th) had only a single commander from 1943 throughout the remainder of the war. These commanders included A. A. Grechko (1st Guards Army, from December 1943), A. S. Zhadov (5th Guards Army, from April 1943), I. M. Chistiakov

(6th Guards Army, from April 1943), M. S. Shumilov (7th Guards Army, from April 1943), V. I. Chuikov (8th Guards Army, from April 1943), and K. N. Galitsky (11th Guards Army, from November 1943).

As further evidence of improved command stability at army level in 1943, the 34 generals appointed to army command during the year commanded their armies until war's end or until their armies were disbanded (some with short absences). As a result, 39 (64 percent) of the 61 field armies in the Red Army's force structure on 31 December 1943 were led by a single commander until (or close to) war's end. Finally, after year's end, the *Stavka* elevated I. I. Maslennikov, P. A. Kurochkin, and I. D. Cherniakhovsky to *front* command, Maslennikov and Kurochkin to command the 3rd Baltic and 2nd Belorussian Fronts in 1944, and Cherniakhovsky to command the 3rd Belorussian Front in 1944 and 1945.

The Red Army produced many competent army commanders throughout the war, based on their combat records, but the most distinguished of these were I. Batov, A. S. Zhadov, V. I. Chuikov, I. M. Chistiakov, M. S. Shumilov, N. P. Pukhov, K. N. Galitsky, K. S. Moskalenko, I. M. Managarov, N. I. Krylov, A. V. Gorbatov, A. A. Grechko, V. Ia. Kolpakchi, S. G. Trofimenko, F. I. Starikov, I. I. Fediuninsky, K. A. Koroteev, P. A. Belov, and, at least in terms of his longevity in command, I. V. Boldin.

Mobile Corps Commanders

Besides its *front* and army commanders, the Red Army's most important command cadre were the generals and colonels who commanded its mechanized corps, tank divisions, and cavalry corps in June 1941 and its cavalry, tank, and mechanized corps and tank armies from 1942 through 1945.[102] The success of the Red Army as a whole in both offensive and defensive operations depended directly on the combat performance of its mobile force commanders.

Although the Red Army's mechanized corps and separate tank divisions formed the nucleus of its mobile shock and maneuver forces at the outset of war, after their destruction in the summer of 1941, only fragile cavalry corps remained to perform this vital function later in the year.

1941. When war began, the Red Army's mobile force consisted of a total of 30 mechanized and four cavalry corps, including 25 mechanized and three cavalry corps subordinate to its operating *fronts* and strategic reserves, and five mechanized and one cavalry corps assigned to its military districts and nonoperating *fronts*.[103] This force included 61 tank divisions, 58 of which were organic to the 29 mechanized corps and two more loosely affiliated with the partially formed 30th Mechanized Corps in the Far East.

After the initial stages of Operation Barbarossa, during which the *Wehrmacht* destroyed or decimated most of the Red Army's mechanized and cavalry corps and tank divisions, on 1 September, the Red Army's operating *fronts* contained only four surviving mobile corps, including two mechanized and two cavalry corps and a total of 21 tank and 25 cavalry divisions. However, attrition associated with heavy fighting during the fall reduced this force further to five cavalry corps, 48 cavalry divisions, and three tank divisions on 31 December.

A total of 32 generals commanded the Red Army's 30 mechanized corps during the first three months of the war (see Appendix 4 in the companion volume). However, since most of these mechanized corps perished quickly in the fierce fighting along with their commanders, command turbulence had no effect on their operations, and, with the exception of one mechanized corps (the 22nd), which had three commanders, all of the corps had only one commander each.

Regarding the individual fate of the 32 generals who served as mechanized corps commanders during 1941, nine (28 percent) were killed in action or "repressed" by Stalin for dereliction of duty, 16 (50 percent) were still serving in command positions at army, corps, or division level on 1 January 1942, and, excluding four generals (13 percent) (M. L. Cherniavsky, I. I. Karpezo, A. D. Sokolov, and M. A. Miasnikov) whose ultimate fate remains obscure, the remaining three (9 percent) were serving in staff assignments. The nine losses included seven who were killed in action or fatally wounded (I. P. Alekseenko, M. G. Khatskilovich, N. M. Shestapalov, P. N. Akhliustin, S. M. Kondrusov, V. N. Simvolokov, and V. I. Chistiakov) and two who were repressed by Stalin (S. O. Oborin and V. S. Tamruchi).

The 16 generals who continued to command at army, corps, or division level at year's end included seven who were promoted to army command (A. A. Vlasov, D. I. Riabyshev, A. A. Rokossovsky, M. P. Petrov, D. D. Leliushenko, I. E. Petrov, and V. V. Novikov), seven who were selected to command tank, mechanized, or cavalry corps (A. V. Kurkin, I. G. Lazarov, D. K. Mostovenko, N. V. Feklenko, S. M. Krivoshein, N. Ia. Kirichenko, and M. I. Pavelkin), one who commanded a rifle corps (V. S. Golubovsky), and one who commanded a rifle division (Iu. V. Novosel'sky). Finally, the remaining three generals became *front* or army chiefs of staff (V. I. Vinogradov, P. V. Volokh, and A. G. Nikitin).

In addition, a total of 67 colonels commanded the 71 tank divisions the Red Army fielded between 22 June 1941 and year's end subordinate to its mechanized corps or as separate divisions.[104] Of these 67 officers, ten (15 percent) were killed or captured and 45 (67 percent) were still serving in command positions at various levels in 1942. However, the ultimate fate of the other 12 (18 percent) (M. I. Myndro, P. S. Fotchenko, F. U. Grachev,

L. V. Bunin, O. A. Akhmanov, S. Z. Miroshnikov, V. P. Krymov, M. V. Shirobokov, S. I. Kapustin, D. A. Iakovlev, K. F. Shvetsov, and A. A. Kotliarov) remains obscure. The ten losses included six who were killed or fatally wounded in combat (E. N. Soliankin, A. G. Potachurchev, S. V. Borzilov, T. A. Mishanin, I. V. Vasil'ev, and V. P. Puganov), three who were killed or possibly captured (F. F. Fedorov, N. P. Studnev, and N. M. Nikoforov), and one who was captured (S. Ia. Ogurtsov).

The 57 colonels who were still serving in command positions at various levels in 1942 included 29 who commanded tank brigades and later tank or mechanized corps (A. I. Liziukov, G. I. Kuz'min, E. G. Pushkin, I. P. Korchagin, I. D. Vasil'ev, F. T. Remizov, M. E. Katukov, M. I. Chesnokov, M. F. Panov, I. D. Cherniakhovsky, S. I. Bogdanov, F. G. Anukushkin, V. I. Polozkov, G. S. Rodin, V. T. Obukhov, N. I. Voeikov, V. A. Koptsov, K. A. Semenchenko, P. P. Pavlov, M. D. Solomatin, B. S. Bakharov, V. M. Badanov, V. G. Burkov, V. M. Alekseev, M. D. Sinenko, B. M. Skvortsov, A. F. Popov, S. A. Ivanov, and V. A. Mishulin), seven who commanded tank brigades (V. I. Baranov, N. A. Novikov, G. G. Kuznetsov, S. A. Kalikhovich, N. V. Starkov, I. G. Tsibin, and P. G. Chernov), seven who commanded tank or motorized rifle divisions (G. M. Mikhailov, I. D. Illarionov, A. S. Beloglazov, S. P. Chernobai, P. N. Domrachev, I. V. Shevnikov, and A. L. Getman), and two who commanded rifle divisions (K. Iu. Andreev and T. S. Orlenko).

Many of these mobile corps and division commanders performed bravely and, in some cases, even skillfully during the disastrous first six months of war. For example, A. V. Kurkin conducted a spirited if wholly unsuccessful counterattack with his 3rd Mechanized Corps near Raseiniai in Lithuania during the first week of the war, D. K. Mostovenko did the same with his 11th Mechanized Corps near Grodno in Belorussia, and D. I. Riabyshev, K. K. Rokossovsky, and N. F. Feklenko led their 8th, 9th, and 19th Mechanized Corps during the first large-scale tank battle of the war near Dubno in the western Ukraine. As a result, Stalin elevated Riabyshev and Rokossovsky to army command soon after and Feklenko to tank corps command in early 1942.

A surprisingly high percentage of those who commanded tank divisions during 1941 achieved even greater notoriety and higher rank later in the war. For example, after successfully commanding the 2nd Rifle Corps during the Battle for Moscow, I. I. Liziukov commanded the 5th Tank Army and the 2nd Tank Corps before perishing in combat near Voronezh in July 1942. Seven others, including G. I. Kuz'min, E. G. Pushkin, F. G. Anukushkin, V. I. Polozkov, P. P. Pavlov, V. A. Koptsov, B. S. Bakharov, and V. M. Alekseev, served successfully as tank brigade commanders in late 1941 and tank or mechanized corps commanders later in the war. However, the first six were killed in action later in the war and the seventh, P. P. Pavlov, was captured in late February 1943.

Several other colonels who commanded tank divisions in this "class of 1941" fared even better. For example, I. D. Cherniakhovsky commanded the 60th Army and 3rd Belorussian Front effectively until he was killed in action in February 1945, M. E. Katukov, S. I. Bogdanov, M. D. Solomatin, V. M. Badanov, and M. D. Sinenko commanded tank armies prior to war's end, and I. P. Korchagin, I. D. Vasil'ev, M. F. Panov, G. S. Rodin, V. T. Obukhov, N. I. Voeikov, V. G. Burkov, V. A. Mishulin, B. M. Skvortsov, A. F. Popov, S. A. Ivanov, and A. L. Getman later performed well as tank or mechanized corps commanders. Most of these officers also cut their teeth in the Red Army's fledgling tank force by commanding tank brigades during the Battle for Moscow and in other offensive operations in late 1941.[105]

Although the three cavalry corps (2nd, 5th, and 6th) subordinate to the Red Army's operating *fronts* on 22 June 1941 were mere auxiliaries to the army's more powerful tank and mechanized forces, the *front* commanders employed them to conduct raids in the *Wehrmacht's* rear area throughout the summer and to exploit whatever success their attacking forces achieved at the end of the year. Although the 2nd and 5th Cavalry Corps survived Operation Barbarossa, the *Wehrmacht* swallowed up and destroyed the 6th Cavalry Corps in the Belostok pocket during the first few days of war.

After conducting operations with only two cavalry corps and two ad hoc cavalry groups during the summer and fall of 1941, in November the *Stavka* formed the 3rd Cavalry Corps and later converted the 2nd and 3rd Cavalry Corps into the 1st and 2nd Guards Cavalry Corps. The Red Army expanded its fledgling cavalry force in December by converting the 5th Cavalry Corps into the 3rd Guards Cavalry Corps and by forming new 6th and 1st (formerly Separate) Cavalry Corps, increasing its total quantity of cavalry corps to five by year's end.

A total of seven generals commanded the six cavalry corps the Red Army fielded during 1941.[106] Two of these commanders were either killed in action or captured, including L. M. Dovator, the commander of the 2nd Guards Cavalry Corps, who was killed in action while defending Moscow in November, and I. S. Nikitin, who perished with his 6th Cavalry Corps in the Belostok region in June. All of the five cavalry corps commanders who survived (F. A. Parkhomenko, P. A. Belov, I. A. Pliev, F. V. Kamkov, and A. F. Bychkovsky) were still commanding their corps on 1 January 1942.

Several commanders of cavalry corps or ad hoc cavalry groups led their forces audaciously and with considerable success amid the Red Army's many operational disasters in the summer and fall of 1941. For example, Dovator's ad hoc cavalry group, which consisted of the 50th and 53rd Cavalry Divisions, conducted a spectacular but only partially successful raid deep into Army Group Center's rear during the Smolensk offensive in late August and protected the Western Front's right flank after its defeat at Viaz'ma in October.

As a reward, the *Stavka* transformed Dovator's group into the 3rd Cavalry Corps and, later, the 2nd Guards Cavalry Corps by November.

Belov's 1st and Dovator's 2nd Guards Cavalry Corps conducted incessant spoiling attacks against the advancing Germans in the defense of Moscow in November and early December, and both spearheaded the Red Army's successful counterstrokes north and south of Moscow in early December. After Dovator was killed in action on 11 December, Pliev, the former commander of the 50th (3rd Guards) Cavalry Division, succeeded him in command. Meanwhile, V. D. Kriuchenkin's 5th (later 3rd Guards) Cavalry Corps, which formed the nucleus of Operational Group Kostenko, spearheaded the Red Army's successful offensive at Elets.

Nor did the reputations of many of these cavalry officers diminish later in the war. For example, after Belov commanded the 1st Guards Cavalry Corps on its deep raid into the Viaz'ma region during the winter campaign of 1941–42, Stalin assigned him to command the 61st Army, a position he occupied until war's end. Likewise, after commanding the 2nd, 3rd, and 4th Guards Cavalry Corps in succession through November 1944, Pliev successfully commanded a cavalry-mechanized group during offensive operations in the Balkans, Hungary, and Manchuria in late 1944 and 1945, and capped his long career by commanding Soviet rocket forces in Cuba in the early 1960s. In addition, Parkhomenko commanded cavalry and rifle corps to war's end, Kriuchenkin commanded several armies and a tank army, and F. V. Kamkov commanded the 4th Guards Cavalry Corps through May 1945. Finally, after serving as inspector of cavalry forces in the Southwestern Front and deputy commander of the 31st Army, the less fortunate A. F. Bychkovsky was repressed on Stalin's orders in 1943, for either malfeasance or disloyalty. Excepting Bychkovsky, every cavalry corps commander from the "class of 1941" who survived the war served with distinction to war's end.

1942. After beginning military operations in 1942 with five cavalry corps, 48 cavalry divisions, and three tank divisions in its operating *fronts,* in the first half of 1942 the *Stavka* beefed up its mobile forces by forming new but smaller cavalry corps in January and February and new tank corps in the spring and early summer. Although it soon disbanded many of its new cavalry corps, the quantity of mobile corps in its operating *fronts* and RVGK increased to 28, including ten cavalry and 18 tank corps by 1 June, and to 30, including six cavalry corps and 24 tank corps, by 1 September.[107] Finally, after creating new mechanized corps beginning in September and converting some tank corps into mechanized corps during the fall, the quantity of mobile corps rose steadily to 34, including eight cavalry, 18 tank, and eight mechanized on 31 December.[108]

Therefore, including those formed but later disbanded, the *Stavka* fielded a total of 19 cavalry corps in 1942. A total of 35 generals served as cavalry corps commanders during this period, for an average of 1.8 commanders per corps, and these corps experienced 42 assumptions of command or changes in command, for an average of 2.2 commanders per corps.

Regarding the individual fate of the 35 generals who served as cavalry corps commanders in 1942, three (8 percent) were killed in action or captured, 23 (66 percent) were still serving as army or corps commanders on 1 January 1943, and, excluding eight generals (23 percent) (S. T. Shmuilo, I. F. Lunev, G. T. Timofeev, N. I. Gusev, V. F. Trantin, A. I. Dudkin, A. I. Khvostov, and L. D. Il'in), most of whom commanded the short-lived cavalry corps but whose ultimate fate remains obscure, one (3 percent) was serving in a staff assignment. The three losses included V. A. Pogrebov and G. A. Kovalev, who were killed in action in March and May, and A. A. Noskov, who fell captive to the Germans in May.

The 23 generals who continued to command at army or corps level at year's end include nine who were promoted to army command (P. A. Belov, V. D. Kriuchenkin, A. A. Grechko, K. S. Moskalenko, I. M. Managarov, P. P. Korzun, A. S. Zhadov, K. S. Mel'nik, and M. F. Maleev), 10 who remained cavalry corps commanders (V. K. Baranov, V. A. Gaidukov, M. D. Borisov, I. A. Pliev, V. V. Kriukov, T. T. Shapkin, F. V. Kamkov, S. V. Sokolov, N. Ia. Kirichenko, and A. G. Selivanov), and two who commanded rifle corps (F. A. Parkhomenko and V. F. Damberg). Finally, the two who were demoted included M. A. Usenko, who became a rifle division commander and A. F. Bychkovsky, who was assigned to a *front* staff.

Several cavalry corps commanders earned lasting fame while conducting raids into the *Wehrmacht's* rear area during the winter campaign of 1942. For example, Belov's reinforced 1st Guards Cavalry Corps raided from Kaluga to the Viaz'ma region during late January and early February in cooperation with airborne forces. Although he failed to capture his objective, Viaz'ma, and fought in encirclement until his force escaped during June 1942, Belov's cavalrymen disrupted *Wehrmacht* communications for over four months. During the same period, the 11th Cavalry Corps, commanded by G. F. Timofeev and S. V. Sokolov, raided into the *Wehrmacht's* rear area northwest of Smolensk for more than a month, and K. S. Moskalenko's 6th, F. A. Parkhomenko's 1st, and A. A. Grechko's 5th Cavalry Corps spearheaded the partially successful Barvenkovo-Lozovaia offensive south of Khar'kov. The *Stavka* later rewarded Belov, Moskalenko, and Grechko, as well as A. S. Zhadov and I. M. Managarov and several others who commanded cavalry corps briefly during early 1942, by promoting them to army command. However, after penetrating the *Wehrmacht's* defenses along the Volkhov River during the same period, N. I. Gusev's 13th Cavalry Corps was encircled and destroyed in June along with Vlasov's 2nd Shock Army, and Gusev perished in the fighting.

Later in the year, V. V. Kriukov's 2nd Guards Cavalry Corps operated as the Western Front's mobile group in the Rzhev-Sychevka offensive in August, but was severely damaged in the same region in Operation Mars in November and December.[109] Also in November M. D. Borisov's 8th, I. A. Pliev's 3rd Guards, and T. T. Shapkin's 4th Cavalry Corps played important roles encircling the *Wehrmacht's* Sixth Army at Stalingrad.

Including those destroyed or converted to mechanized corps, the *Stavka* fielded a total of 28 tank corps during 1942, converted five of these tank corps to mechanized corps, and formed three other mechanized corps by year's end for a total of 31 tank and mechanized corps.[110] During this period a total of 46 generals or colonels served as tank or mechanized corps commanders, for an average of 1.5 commanders per corps. However, command turbulence within these corps was extremely high during Operation *Blau* as the *Stavka* struggled to identify commanders who could employ their mobile corps effectively. For example, the 31 tank and mechanized corps experienced 58 assumptions of command or changes in command, for an average of 1.9 commanders per corps.[111]

Of the 46 generals or colonels who served as tank or mechanized corps commanders during 1942, four (9 percent) were killed in action or relieved from command, 32 (69 percent) were still serving as army or corps commanders on 1 January 1943, and the ultimate fate of ten (22 percent) (S. P. Maltsev, D. K. Mostovenko, K. A. Semenchenko, V. V. Butkov, A. V. Kurkin, M. I. Chesnokov, N. N. Radkevich, M. I. Pavelkin, V. V. Koshelev, and F. T. Remizov) remains obscure, although they held no further command at corps or division level.

The four losses included three who were killed in action or fatally wounded (G. I. Kuz'min, I. A. Liziukov, and P. E. Shurov) and one who was relieved from command (N. V. Feklenko). Kuz'min died when his 21st Tank Corps was destroyed at Khar'kov in May, Liziukov perished leading his 2nd Tank Corps near Voronezh in July, Shurov was killed when his 13th Tank Corps was crushed during the first few days of Operation *Blau*, and Stalin relieved Feklenko from command of the 17th Tank Corps for his ineffectiveness in combat west of Voronezh in early July.

The 32 generals or colonels who continued to command at the army and corps levels at year's end included one who was promoted to army command (I. D. Cherniakhovsky), 24 who remained tank corps commanders (V. V. Burkov, I. G. Lazarov, A. G. Kravchenko, A. M. Khasin, M. D. Sinenko, V. A. Mishulin, A. L. Getman, P. A. Rotmistrov, A. A. Shamshin, A. F. Popov, S. I. Bogdanov, T. I. Tanaschishin, V. A. Koptsov, A. G. Maslov, B. S. Bakharov, P. P. Poluboiarov, S. A. Vershkovich, D. M. Gritsenko, M. M. Volkov, E. G. Pushkin, V. M. Badanov, P. P. Pavlov, A. G. Rodin, and G. S. Rodin), and six who commanded mechanized corps (M. E.

Katukov, M. D. Solomatin, I. P. Korchagin, V. T. Vol'sky, I. N. Russiianov, and K. Z. Sviridov).

Most of the officers the *Stavka* selected to command tank and mechanized corps in 1942 were experienced tank division or brigade commanders. Nevertheless, their generally poor performance during the first eight months of 1942 demonstrated they had much to learn before they could command, control, and employ larger tank and mechanized forces effectively. In short, as the heavy combat at Khar'kov, Voronezh, Zhizdra, Bolkhov, and on the approaches to Stalingrad indicated, prior to November, *Wehrmacht* panzer divisions thoroughly outclassed and outfought the Red Army's tank and mechanized corps.[112]

However, these tank and mechanized corps commanders performed far more effectively in offensive operations in the Stalingrad region in November and December. For example, Butkov's 1st and Rodin's 26th Tank Corps (of the 5th Tank Army), Kravchenko's 4th, Maslov's 16th, and Tanaschishin's 13th Tank Corps, and Vol'sky's 4th Mechanized Corps spearheaded the Red Army's successful Stalingrad offensive in November; Poluboiarov's 17th, Bakharov's 18th, Badanov's 24th, and Pavlov's 25th Tank Corps and Russiianov's 1st Guards Mechanized Corps did the same along the Middle Don in December; and Rotmistrov's 7th and Tanaschishin's 13th Tank Corps and Sviridov's 2nd Guards, Vol'sky's 3rd Guards, and Bogdanov's 6th Mechanized Corps led the successful Kotel'nikovskii offensive in December.

Despite these overall successes, however, when required to operate singly during exploitations into the depths of the *Wehrmacht's* defenses, these tank and mechanized corps were decimated by a combination of mechanical "wear and tear" and skillful *Wehrmacht* resistance. For example, the 11th Panzer Division virtually destroyed Butkov's 1st Tank Corps along the Chir River in early December, and the 6th and 11th Panzer Divisions did the same to Badanov's 24th Tank Corps at Tatsinskaia in late December. Therefore, although many of the Red Army's tank and mechanized corps commanders performed effectively in offensive operations around Rzhev and Stalingrad, they would face even more rigorous trials during the winter campaign of 1943.

1943. After beginning military operations in 1943 with 34 mobile corps, including eight cavalry, 18 tank, and eight mechanized corps, in its operating *fronts* and RVGK, the *Stavka* increased the quantity of mobile corps in its operating *fronts* and RVGK during the first half of 1943 to 37 mobile corps, including seven cavalry, 21 tank, and nine mechanized corps, on 1 June, and to 43 mobile corps, including seven cavalry, 24 tank, and 12 mechanized corps, on 31 December.[113] This meant the *Stavka* had sufficient mobile corps at its disposal by mid-summer 1943 to assign multiple separate tank, mechanized, and cavalry corps to each *front* conducting offensive operations along key strategic axes and at least one mobile corps to each army operating along main attack axes.

Therefore, including two corps (the 4th and 19th) that existed for only part of the year, the *Stavka* fielded a total of nine cavalry corps during 1943. During this period a total of 13 generals served as cavalry corps commanders, for an average of 1.4 commanders per corps as opposed to 1.8 commanders per corps during 1942, and these corps experienced only seven assumptions of command or changes in command, for an average of less than 1.3 commander per corps in contrast to 2.2 per corps in 1942.[114]

Regarding the individual fate of the 13 generals who served as cavalry corps commanders during 1943, two (15 percent) died or were captured, seven (54 percent) were still commanding cavalry corps on 1 January 1944, and the ultimate fate of four (31 percent) (R. I. Golovanovsky, Ia. S. Sharaburko, M. F. Maleev, and N. Ia. Kirichenko) remains obscure, although they held no further command at corps or division level. The two losses included T. T. Shapkin, commander of the Southern Front's 4th Cavalry Corps, who died from unknown causes in March, and M. D. Borisov, commander of the 8th [7th Guards] Cavalry Corps, who was captured by the Germans when his corps was encircled and largely destroyed near Debal'tsevo in the Donbas region in February 1943.

The seven generals who continued to command cavalry corps at year's end were S. K. Sokolov, M. P. Konstantinov, V. K. Baranov, V. V. Kriukov, N. S. Oslikovsky, I. A. Pliev, and A. G. Selivanov. Sokolov, Baranov, Oslikovsky, and Pliev achieved even greater fame later in the war as successful cavalry-mechanized group commanders in strategic offensives during 1944 and 1945.

Many of these cavalry corps commanders distinguished themselves in 1943. For example, Kirichenko's 4th Guards and Selevanov's 5th Guards Cavalry Corps led the Red Army's successful offensives in the northern Caucasus and Rostov regions during the winter of 1943, and Sokolov's 7th (6th Guards) Cavalry Corps spearheaded the Voronezh Front's Ostrogozhsk-Rossosh' and Khar'kov offensives in January and February until being defeated in the Donbas and Khar'kov regions in late February and March. At the same time, Kriukov's 2nd Guards Cavalry Corps led the Central Front's offensive to the Desna River before being driven back to the Kursk region in March.

Once again, these cavalry corps commanders played a leading role in the Red Army's advance to and beyond the Dnepr River after weather conditions deteriorated during the fall. For example, Oslikovsky's and Sokolov's 3rd and 6th Guards Cavalry Corps spearheaded the Kalinin and Western Fronts' advance through Smolensk in August and September, and Oslikovsky's corps supported the Kalinin (1st Baltic) Front's offensives in the Vitebsk regions in October and November. During the same period, Kriukov's 2nd Guards Cavalry Corps was instrumental in the Briansk Front's victory at

Briansk in September and, with Maleev's 7th Guards Cavalry Corps, effectively spearheaded the Central (Belorussian) Front's advance across the Dnepr River into eastern Belorussia in October and November.

Farther south, Baranov's 1st Guards and Kirichenko's 4th Guards Cavalry Corps skillfully supported the Southwestern and Southern Front's offensive into the Donbas region in August and September, and Baranov's corps supported the Voronezh (1st Ukrainian) Front's fierce two-month long struggle for possession of Kiev in October and November. Finally, Kirichenko's 4th Guards and Selivanov's 5th Guards Cavalry Corps contributed significantly in the Southern (4th Ukrainian) Front's victory at Melitopol' in October and November 1943. Because these cavalry corps commanders performed so effectively in the fall of 1943, the *Stavka* began employing combinations of cavalry and tank or mechanized corps under their command to conduct exploitation operations as cavalry-mechanized groups in early 1944.

After beginning operations during 1943 with 18 tank corps and eight mechanized corps in its operating *fronts* and RVGK, the *Stavka* formed seven more tank and four more mechanized corps and converted one tank corps (the 13th) into a mechanized corps during the year, for a total of 37 tank and mechanized corps by year's end. During this period a total of 68 generals or colonels served as tank or mechanized corps commanders, for an average of 1.8 commanders per corps as opposed to 1.5 per corps in 1942. However, in contrast to other forces, the Red Army's tank and mechanized force was characterized by a remarkably high degree of command stability. For example, the 37 tank and mechanized corps experienced only 42 assumptions of command or changes of command, most of those during the winter of 1943, for an average of 1.1 commanders per corps in contrast to 1.9 per corps during 1942.[115]

Of the 68 generals or colonels who served as tank or mechanized corps commanders in 1943, 15 (22 percent) were killed in action, fatally wounded, or captured, 42 (62 percent) were still serving as army or corps commanders on 1 January 1944, and, excluding nine generals (13 percent) (N. N. Parkevich, I. P. Sukhov, A. V. Lozovsky, K. F. Suleikov, K. V. Skorniakov, A. V. Egorov, S. A. Vershkovich, N. A. Iuplin, and A. K. Pogosov) whose ultimate fate remains obscure, two (3 percent) were serving in division command or as deputy commanders.

Vividly underscoring the intense nature of armored fighting during 1943 and thereafter, the 15 combat losses included six who were killed in action or fatally wounded in 1943 (G. S. Rudenko, M. I. Zin'kovich, V. A. Koptsov, D. Kh. Chernienko, A. V. Kukushkin, and A. P. Sharogin), five who were killed in action or fatally wounded in 1944 (V. M. Alekseev, T. I. Tanaschishin, B. S. Bakharov, V. I. Polozkov, and E. G. Pushkin), three who were wounded in action who did not return to corps command (V. G. Burkov, K. G. Trufanov, and P. K. Zhidkov), and one who was captured (P. P. Pavlov).

Koptsov and Kukushkin perished in the fighting in the Donbas and Khar'kov regions in February and March, Chernienko was killed and Burkov was wounded in the Battle of Kursk in July and August 1943, and Rudchenko, Zin'kovich, Trufanov, and Sharogin died during the Red Army's subsequent pursuit to and across the Dnepr River. The following year, Tanaschishin and Pushkin were killed during heavy fighting in the Ukraine in March 1944, Bakharov and Polozkov died in the Belorussian offensive in July and August, and Alekseev perished during the Iassy-Kishinev offensive in August 1944.

The 42 generals or colonels who continued to command at army or corps levels included nine who were promoted to tank army command (M. D. Sinenko, A. G. Kravchenko, S. I. Bogdanov, A. G. Rodin, V. M. Badanov, P. A. Rotmistrov, M. D. Solomatin, M. E. Katukov, and V. T. Vol'sky), 21 who remained tank corps commanders (V. V. Butkov, A. F. Popov, N. M. Teliakov, M. G. Sakhno, A. A. Shamshin, A. N. Panfilov, I. G. Lazarov, D. M. Gritsenko, V. A. Mitrofanov, F. N. Rudkin, S. A. Ivanov, V. E. Grigor'ev, P. P. Poluboiarov, I. D. Vasil'ev, F. G. Anukushkin, I. F. Kirichenko, G. S. Rodin, M. F. Panov, A. S. Burdeiny, I. A. Vovchenko, and I. V. Dubovoi), and 12 who remained mechanized corps commanders (A. N. Fursovich, I. P. Korchagin, S. M. Krivoshein, M. V. Volkhov, B. M. Skvortsov, F. G. Katkov, A. M. Khasin, K. A. Malygin, I. N. Russiianov, K. Z. Sviridov, V. T. Obukhov, and A. I. Akimov).[116] The remaining 2 included A. L. Getman, who became a deputy tank army commander, and A. G. Maslov, who ended the year commanding a rifle division.

The fact that many other tank and mechanized corps commanders in the "class of 1943" would have made excellent tank army commanders had the Red Army chosen to field more tank armies than it did vividly underscores the fact that these mobile corps commanders developed qualities necessary for them to defeat the experienced, but increasingly threadbare *Wehrmacht*.

Tank Army Commanders

While the Red Army's mobile corps contributed most to the victories it achieved during 1941 and 1942, its tank armies did so from November 1942 through war's end. As was the case with its tank and mechanized corps, by late 1942 and thereafter, the success of the Red Army as a whole depended directly on the combat performance of its tank armies and their commanders.

1942. The *Stavka* fielded its first four "first formation, mixed composition" tank armies (the 1st, 3rd, 4th, and 5th) on an experimental basis in the summer of 1942, employing them to spearhead offensives in the most critical sectors of the front during Operation *Blau*. The 1st, 4th, and 5th Tank Armies went into action near Voronezh and along the Don River west of Stalingrad in July 1942, but performed atrociously and suffered terrible losses, while the 3rd Tank Army conducted the failed offensive near Bolkhov in August with scarcely better results. However, after being completely reorganized, the 5th Tank Army achieved lasting fame by spearheading the successful Stalingrad offensive in November.

A total of six generals commanded the Red Army's four tank armies during the last six months of 1942, for an average of 1.5 commanders per army or three commanders on an annualized basis. During the same period, the four armies experienced eight assumptions of command or changes in command, for an average of two commanders per army or four commanders on an annualized basis.[117] Although one tank army commander was killed in action during the year, five were still commanding armies on 1 January 1943. A. I. Liziukov, the 5th Tank Army's first commander, was killed in action near Voronezh in late July after being relieved from command and assigned to command the 2nd Tank Corps. On the other hand, K. S. Moskalenko and V. D. Kriuchenkin, who commanded the 1st and 4th Tank Armies from July through October 1942, were commanding field armies by year's end, and P. L. Romanenko, P. S. Rybalko, and M. M. Popov commanded their 2nd, 3rd, and 5th Tank Armies with considerable success to year's end.[118]

1943 Since the mixed composition tank armies the *Stavka* fielded during the final six months of 1942 failed to perform up to its expectations, it began developing new and more effective model tank armies beginning in January 1943, in the interim employing its old-style 2nd, 3rd and 5th Tank Armies to conduct exploitation operations for the remainder of the winter campaign. However, as had been the case during late 1942, these older tank armies achieved only limited success. For example, after leading the successful Ostrogozhsk-Rossosh' and Khar'kov offensives, Rybalko's 3rd Tank Army was annihilated near Khar'kov in March and reorganized into the 57th Army soon after, and, during the same period, the *Stavka* stripped Popov's 5th Tank Army of its mobile corps in January and February and converted it into the 12th Army in April. After spearheading the Central Front's offensive west of Kursk in mid-February, although defeated in early March, Rodin's 2nd Tank Army withdrew to the Kursk region virtually intact. Thereafter, the *Stavka* formed four new tank armies, the 1st, 3rd Guards, 4th, and 5th Guards, and converted the old-style 2nd Tank Army to the new organization in the late spring and early summer of 1943.

Therefore, including Mobile Group Popov, which the *Stavka* formed and employed as a virtual tank army before it was destroyed in the Donbas in February 1943, the *Stavka* formed a total of nine tank armies in 1943. During this period a total of nine generals served as tank army (or mobile group) commanders, for an average of one commander per tank army as opposed to three in 1942. Although the three old-style tank armies experienced considerable command turbulence, the new tank armies experienced none.[119]

Regarding the fate of the nine generals who commanded tank armies (or mobile groups) during 1943, none were killed in action or captured before war's end, eight were still serving as *front* or army commanders on 1 January 1944, and one ended the year serving on *front* staff. The eight generals who continued to command at army level or above by year's end included M. M. Popov, who was promoted to *front* command, M. E. Katukov, S. I. Bogdanov, P. S. Rybalko, V. M. Badanov, and P. A. Rotmistrov, who remained tank army commanders, and P. L. Romanenko and I. T. Shlemin, who became army commanders. Finally, A. G. Rodin became chief of armored and mechanized forces at *front* level by year's end.

Nor did the luster of most of these tank army commanders of 1943 fade by war's end. For example, Katukov, Bogdanov, and Rybalko were still commanding the 1st, 2nd, and 3rd Guards Tank Armies in May 1945, and Rotmistrov, who commanded the 5th Guards Tank Army with distinction during most of 1944, ended the war serving as deputy chief of the Red Army's tank and mechanized forces. As for the remaining five, Romanenko ended the war as a military district commander, Shlemin as an army commander, Popov as a *front* chief of staff, Rodin as a chief of armored forces in several *fronts,* and Badanov as chief of Red Army armored and mechanized force training.

Individually and collectively, these tank army commanders, who underwent their baptism by fire and combat education while commanding tank divisions, brigades, and corps in 1941 and 1942, were the finest and most capable generals in the Red Army:

> Only the most gifted, daring and resolute generals, who were ready to take full responsibility for their actions without looking back for support, were selected as commanders of the tank armies. Only such men could cope with the tasks that tank armies had to carry out, since these armies were usually thrown into the gaps that had been forced in the enemy's defences and would operate in operational depth, isolated from the main forces of the Front, smashing the enemy's reserves and rear services, upsetting their control system and seizing advantageous lines and vital objectives.[120]

The Red Army's most capable tank army commanders during 1943, and arguably the war as a whole, were P. S. Rybalko, M. G. Katukov, P. A. Rotmistrov, and S. I. Bogdanov.[121]

Pavel Semenovich Rybalko, who commanded the 3rd Tank Army from October 1942 through April 1943 and the 3rd Guards Tank Army for the final two years of war, contributed significantly to many of the Red Army's most important wartime victories. For example, in 1943 Rybalko's tank army smashed the *Wehrmacht's* defenses around Orel in July and August, spearheaded the Voronezh Front's race to the Dnepr River in September, captured Kiev in November, and advanced deep into the Ukraine in December. Building his reputation further, Rybalko's tank army led the 1st Ukrainian Front's Proskurov-Chernovtsy and L'vov-Sandomierz offensives in March and April and then in July and August of 1944, and served the same *front* even more effectively in the Vistula-Oder, Berlin, and Prague offensives in January, April, and May of 1945. For these and other accomplishments, Rybalko emerged from the war twice a Hero of the Soviet Union and received a baton as marshal of armored forces soon after war ended.

In short, Rybalko "commanded a tank army longer than anyone else. He was an extremely erudite and strong-willed person. In the years immediately after the war he commanded all our armoured forces and made a tremendous contribution of work and energy to their reorganizing and rearming."[122]

> Hard driving, demanding Rybalko, the hammer, imposed his resourceful and direct style on all aspects of his command. Impatient, graceless, at times, in dealing with his subordinates, he could be inspirational with a judicious, satiric humor. He was always fair. He operated with a swift, surprising style of warfare that made him a kindred spirit of the American General George S. Patton. Rybalko understood the character and potential of large tank units, appreciating the technical capabilities and limitations of tanks–his distinguishing mark as a tank commander. Adaptable, cunning, Rybalko's nerves of steel allowed him to fight close to the edge of disaster. . . . Rybalko finished the war as the premier tank commander eclipsing the other tank commanders in the swift race across Poland and the bold capture of Berlin.[123]

Close behind Rybalko in terms of his longevity in tank army command and his many combat accomplishments was Mikhail Efimovich Katukov, the commander of the 1st (1st Guards) Tank Army from its formation in January 1943 to its storming of Berlin in May 1945. Along the way, Katukov's tank army helped defeat the *Wehrmacht's* southern panzer fist at Kursk in July 1943, defeated von Manstein's panzer west of Kiev in December 1943, and earned lasting fame by its dramatic 500–kilometer thrust into the *Wehrmacht's* rear in the 1st Ukrainian Front's Proskurov-Chernovtsy offensive in March and April 1944, in the process cutting off and almost destroying the German First Panzer Army. Katukov capped his illustrious career by skillfully outflanking *Wehrmacht* forces defending L'vov in July 1944 and seizing bridgeheads over the Vistula River in August, by conducting a spectacular exploitation across Poland to the Oder River in January 1945, and by unhinging *Wehrmacht* defenses along the Neisse River to help encircle and capture Berlin in April and May.

By war's end Katukov, too, had become a double recipient of the title Hero of the Soviet Union and, somewhat belatedly, a marshal of armored forces in 1959. As one colleague noted, "Mikhail Katukov is a real soldier and a great expert on the combat training and tactics of armored forces. The tank brigade which he commanded in the Battle of Moscow was the first in the Soviet Army to receive the Guards title. Katukov was on the battlefield from the first to the last day of the Great Patriotic War."[124]

> A conservative risk-taker, Katukov earned the reputation of being a careful, cautious commander who always worked out plans, weighing the consequences of an operation trying to see the practical results before committing a single tank from his reserve. This cautiousness was particularly true in the early days, as he developed his skills in combat. He preferred the enemy coming after him on his terms and known ground. Katukov liked controlling events, and enjoyed stabilizing situations. He quickly grasped that Soviet tanks were able to concentrate their tactical advantage due to the superior mobility of their tanks. Later, as a corps and army commander, he sought ways to avoid the massed and mindless direct approach to tactical and operational problems. He would rather pick the lock than wield a sledgehammer. Katukov liked the use of forward detachments in raids to predetermine situations and preempt enemy actions.
>
> Katukov's leadership style and the use of his staff makes him a good example of the collective approach encouraged by the Soviet military's ideal for command. In the war from the first to the last days, Katukov often at the spearhead of an operation expertly led the armored guards against the masters of armored warfare and won [*sic*].[125]

Although his field service ended in late summer of 1944, perhaps because his performance failed to satisfy Stalin's standards, by year's end 1943, Pavel Alekseevich Rotmistrov was the Red Army's most famous tank army commander, primarily because his 5th Guards Tank Army was victorious in the fields outside of Prokhorovka during the Battle for Kursk. After supporting the Steppe Front in its capture of Khar'kov in August 1943, Rotmistrov's tank army led the Steppe (2nd Ukrainian) Front's pursuit to the Dnepr River in September, its bloody struggle to seize Krivoi Rog and the "great bend" of the Dnepr River in late 1943 and early 1944, and its encirclement and partial destruction of two *Wehrmacht* army corps at Korsun'-Shevchenkovskii in January and February 1944. After leading the 2nd Ukrainian Front's spectacular offensive across the

Ukraine to the Romanian borders in March and April 1944, Rotmistrov's tank army was defeated at Tirgu-Frumos in the 2nd and 3rd Ukrainian Front's unsuccessful invasion of Romania in late April and May 1944.

After Rotmistrov's tank army was transferred in late May 1944 to Belorussia, where it led the Red Army's massive offensive in late June and July, Stalin relieved Rotmistrov of command, probably due to the heavy losses his army suffered in the offensive, particularly in the struggle for Vilnius. Despite his relief and subsequent assignment as deputy commander of Red Army armored and mechanized forces under Fedorenko, Rotmistrov nevertheless earned high grades for his performance in command, at least until his relief:

> Rotmistrov possessed an uncanny ability to quickly assess a situation and devise a creative approach for decisions. Decisions came easily to Rotmistrov, in a word, he was a builder. As an authoritative theorist and practitioner, he took an active part in the reorganizing and structure of the Soviet tank army. This, at times, put him at odds with senior commanders–especially when he believed that he had a better idea. Rotmistrov was conscious of the credentials of his critics and was not impressed by rank or title. He was the supreme pragmatist.
>
> Rotmistrov's fighting style of a hard, direct, and swift blow upset the enemy. Using in full measure the tank unit's agility, he broke up the enemy's main forces, encircled them, and destroyed them in detail. His rapid rise was a combination of his demonstrated erudition and his bold, decisive initiative on the battlefield. In its struggle for survival, the Red Army tolerated such an eccentric nature in its top armored guards theoretician and architect.[126]

Carefully skirting any mention of his specific wartime contributions, a colleague of Rotmistrov added, "Pavel Rotmistrov is also undoubtedly one of our outstanding tank generals. Commanding rich practical experience acquired on the battlefield and a fund of theoretical knowledge, he, too, contributed notably to the postwar development of tank engineering and the training of tank commanders."[127] After his removal from tank army command in 1944, but also belatedly, Rotmistrov became a marshal of armored forces in 1962 and a Hero of the Soviet Union in 1965.

The final general in this famed foursome of wartime tank army commanders was Semen Il'ich Bogdanov, who commanded the 2nd (2nd Guards) Tank Army from September 1943 through war's end. Bogdanov and his tank army first became famous for their stubborn defense of the northern flank of the Kursk Bulge in July 1943 and the offensive at Sevsk in September, which unhinged the *Wehrmacht's* defenses, helping force their precipitous withdrawal to the Dnepr River. After refitting for several months, Bogdanov's tank army took part in the bloody struggle at Korsun'-Shevchenkovskii in January and February 1944 and then spearheaded the 2nd Ukrainian Front's offensive across the Ukraine in March and April 1944, only to suffer defeat at Tirgu-Frumos in northern Romania in April and May 1944.

After convalescing from wounds received during the battle for Lublin in July 1944, Bogdanov led his army on a dramatic advance across Poland to the Oder River in January 1945 and fought alongside Katukov's 1st Guards Tank Army in the final assault on Berlin.[128] Like his counterpart Rybalko, Bogdanov became twice a hero of the Soviet Union during the war and a marshal of armored forces in 1945. As regards his performance as a commander, according to one colleague, "Semyon Bogdanov, the commander of the 2nd Guards Tank Army, was a man of astonishing audacity. From September 1943 onwards his army took part in nearly all of the decisive battles of the war. He displayed outstanding abilities after the war, too, as head of an academy, and for nearly five years he held the post of commander of Armoured Troops of the Soviet Armed Forces."[129]

As regards his command style, a biographer noted:

> General Bogdanov, as a good organizer and personally brave, was respected by German commanders as one of the best Red Army tank commanders. . . . Bogdanov was a very paladin of courage and efficiency when fighting began, moved forward on the battlefield to ensure his subordinate commanders understood their tasks and missions. Using his physical presence to motivate and inspire, he could correct problems on the spot with the ability to clearly and precisely set the mission. His presence on the battlefield from the first to the last days added an unwearied tenacity and vigor. Bogdanov exemplified the universal, great combat leader who must be up front with sword in hand. Capitalizing on enemy mistakes, Bogdanov looked for an opponent backing up on the battlefield and that is where he poured his armored force.[130]

Excepting its most famous *Stavka* representatives and *front* commanders, no senior officers contributed more to the Red Army's ultimate victory than this distinguished group of tank army commanders.

Engineer, Artillery, and Air Defense (PVO) Commanders

Since the most visible and stirring combat forces in battle are infantry, tanks, and cavalry, it is understandable that they and their commanders–the Red Army's *front*, field army, and tank, mechanized, and cavalry corps commanders–achieved far greater fame and notoriety during and after the war than their counterparts in less glamorous supporting arms. However, although these "great captains" who planned and conducted the war's most famous battles and operations received most of the public acclaim for the Red Army's victories, to a great extent, their combat successes depended directly on the scale and effectiveness of their air, artillery, engineer, antiaircraft, and other types of combat support. In short, throughout most of the war, the Red Army's "great captains" relied heavily on artillery, engineers, and, to a lesser extent, the air force and other supporting arms to overcome the inherently superior tactical and operational skills of the *Wehrmacht's* commanders and troops.

Engineers. The ferocity of the *Wehrmacht's* advance during Operation Barbarossa and the Red Army's inability to contend with its more experienced foe during most of the first 18 months of the war, in part because it lacked tank and mechanized forces capable of fighting on equal terms with the *Wehrmacht*'s formidable panzer armies, groups, corps, and divisions, placed a premium on the construction of strategic, operational, and tactical defenses to slow and halt the invading forces. Therefore, such famous defensive works as the Stalin, Luga, and Mozhaisk defense lines, Leningrad's defensive rings, and the comparable defenses around Moscow played a significant role in the Red Army's successful defense during Operation Barbarossa. Similarly, defense lines in southern Russia, particularly in and around Stalingrad, helped the Red Army defeat Axis forces the following year during Operation *Blau*.

Much of the credit for the construction of these defense lines and associated fortifications belongs to those senior and, in some cases, surprisingly less senior officers who erected them, specifically, the commanders of the ten sapper armies the Red Army fielded between October and December 1941 and employed for varying periods from October 1941 through October 1942. Although the NKO replaced these armies with other defensive construction forces in 1942 because they proved less than fully effective, while they existed they served a useful if not vital function during that most critical and dangerous period of the war. While they existed, these armies were commanded by a diverse lot of officers selected from the army's engineer forces, the state security services, and even the civilian economy.

During the 12-month period from October 1941 to October 1942, four of these sapper armies (the 2nd, 5th, 9th, and 10th) operated for four months before being disbanded, one (the 4th) operated for six months, one (the 1st) operated for eight months, two (the 3rd and 7th) operated for ten months, and two (the 6th and 8th) operated for 11 and 12 months, respectively. During this period a total of 24 officers served as sapper army commanders, for an average of 2.4 commanders per army or more than five commanders per army on an annualized basis. At the same time, the sapper armies experienced 28 assumptions of command or changes in command, for a relatively high average of 2.8 commanders per army or almost six commanders on an annualized basis. Compared with other Red Army formations, then, command turbulence in the sapper armies was a severe problem.[131]

On the other hand, most of the officers the NKO appointed to command its sapper armies were quite experienced in constructing defensive lines and positions. For example, 12 of the 24 had previously served as chiefs of engineer forces or chiefs of construction directorates (UOSs) at *front* or NKO level (or their NKVD equivalents, the UORs), another five had served as deputy chiefs of UOSs, and four were assigned to command directly from the Main Engineering Academy. Furthermore, after completing their stints in command, most of these officers continued to perform critical roles in the Red Army's engineer construction effort for the remainder of the war.

For example, M. P. Vorob'ev, who commanded the 1st Sapper Army from December 1941 through March 1942, became the chief of the Red Army's engineer forces, and N. P. Baranov, who commanded the 1st Sapper Army from June through August 1942, became the inspector-general of the Red Army's engineer forces. In addition, V. V. Kosarev and A. S. Gundorov became chiefs of engineer forces at *front* and military district level, five more headed *front* defensive construction directorates (UOSs), and several others headed a variety of NKO and NKVD engineer directorates.

Artillery. No supporting arm proved more important to the Red Army's war effort than its artillery. Particularly on the offense, no Red Army infantry, tank, mechanized, or cavalry force could penetrate the *Wehrmacht's* defenses and wreak havoc in its operational rear until artillery paved the way by pulverizing its tactical defenses. The Red Army was routinely employing its vastly expanded artillery force to perform this vital function with brutal efficiency by mid-1943.

Even though the Red Army fielded an immense force of various types of artillery regiments, brigades, and divisions in late 1942 and early 1943, its most important and effective large artillery formations were the six artillery penetration corps it fielded in 1943. After it formed its first artillery penetration corps (the 3rd) in March 1943, the NKO fielded five more of these corps in April 1943 and assigned its most accomplished artillery officers to command these corps.

As expected in so important a force, the NKO kept command turbulence within its artillery penetration corps to a minimum for the remainder of the war. For example, discounting three commanders who trained the 4th and 5th Artillery Corps while they were forming in April and May, the six artillery penetration corps had only a single commander each throughout 1943. Furthermore, two of these generals, specifically, N. V. Ignatov and P. M. Korol'kov, commanded the 4th and 5th Artillery Penetration Corps until war's end, and M. M. Barsukov commanded the 2nd Artillery Penetration Corps until it was disbanded in April 1944.

Air Defense (PVO). As in the case of field artillery, considerable command stability also characterized the Red Army's national air defense (PVO Strany) force structure. After beginning the war with three PVO corps, the NKO formed the Moscow PVO Front and the Baku and Leningrad PVO Armies in April and May 1942 and later reorganized its PVO forces into Western and Eastern PVO Fronts and a subordinate Special Moscow PVO Army in June and July 1943. Therefore, including the PVO corps existing on 22 June 1941, the Red Army included a total of nine PVO *fronts,* armies, or corps from June 1941 through July 1943. During this period seven senior artillery officers served as PVO *front,* army, or corps commanders, for an average of less than one commander per force and even fewer on an annualized basis. Furthermore, since these forces experienced only nine assumptions of command or changes in command, command turbulence was similarly quite low.

More impressive still was the continuity in command within key PVO forces from 1941 through 1943 as well as the war as a whole. For example, D. A. Zhuravlev, who began the war as commander of the 1st PVO Corps in Moscow, was appointed to command the Moscow PVO Corps Region on 19 November 1941, the Moscow PVO Front on 5 April 1942, and the Special Moscow PVO Army in July 1943, and commanded the Western PVO Front from December 1944 to war's end. His counterpart, G. S. Zashikhin, who was commanding the 2nd PVO Corps in Leningrad when war began, was assigned command of the Leningrad PVO Army in April 1942, the Eastern PVO Front on 29 June 1943, the Southern PVO Front on 29 March 1944, and the Southwestern PVO Front on 24 December 1944, and commanded the latter to war's end.

Likewise, P. E. Gudymenko, who commanded the 3rd PVO Corps at Baku from June 1941 through early 1944, commanded the Trans-Caucasus PVO Front in 1944 and 1945, and M. S. Gromadin, who commanded the 1st PVO Corps in 1940 and became deputy people's commissar of defense for PVO and commander of PVO forces in 1941 and 1942, later commanded the Western, Northern, and Central PVO Fronts from June 1943 through war's end. In addition, P. M. Beskrovnov, who commanded the 3rd PVO Corps at Baku in late 1941 and early 1942, rose to command the Baku PVO Army from 1942 to early 1944 and the 8th PVO Corps thereafter to war's end. Beskrovnov's counterpart, M. M. Protsvetkin, who commanded the 2nd PVO Corps at Leningrad in mid-1941, went on to command the 79th PVO Division and the 13th PVO Corps to war's end. Overall, six of the seven generals who commanded the Red Army's most important air defense forces in 1943 ended the war in similarly important command posts and continued to serve in these posts after war's end.[132]

Aviation (Air Army and Corps) Commanders

Even before the war began, Stalin's purge of several senior air force (VVS) commanders produced extreme and damaging turbulence within the Red Army Air Forces' command structure.[133] Stalin continued this vendetta against senior VVS officers after war began by purging several more VVS commanders as scapegoats for the Red Army's early defeats.[134] Compounding the devastating effects of these purges, the invading *Wehrmacht* utterly demolished the VVS's already fragile and largely decentralized force structure during the first few months of the war, producing utter chaos in its command and control.

After beginning the war with a VVS force consisting of five bomber aviation corps in the RGK's long-range aviation, 58 aviation divisions of various types in *frontal* aviation, and three mixed aviation divisions in army aviation, the *Stavka* abolished two of its aviation corps and reduced the number and size of its aviation divisions and their component regiments during Operation Barbarossa. As it searched for a new VVS organizational structure to better support its operating *fronts,* the *Stavka* experimented with reserve aviation groups in late 1941 and early 1942 and shock aviation groups from March to June 1942, before deciding to support its operating *fronts* with new air armies in May 1942.

1942. The *Stavka* formed its first five air armies (the 1st, 2nd, 3rd, 4th, and 8th) in May 1942, four more (the 5th, 6th, 14th, and 15th) in June and July, five (the 16th, 12th, 9th, 10th, and 11th) in August, and its final three (the 7th, 13th, and 17th) in November. In addition, it also formed its 1st and 2nd Fighter Armies and the 1st Bomber Army under direct RVGK control in July, although these armies were short-lived.[135]

Therefore, discounting the fighter and bomber aviation armies, the *Stavka* fielded a total of 17 air armies in 1942. During this period, a total of 19 generals of aviation served as air army commanders, for an average of 1.1 commanders per army or slightly higher on an annualized basis, and, also indicative of the greater command stability in these forces as opposed to others, these armies experienced only 21 assumptions of command or changes in command, for an average of just 1.2 per army (see Appendix 4 in the companion volume).[136]

Unlike the senior command cadre in other arms, several generals of aviation, such as M. M. Gromov, T. T. Khriukhin, T. F. Kutsevalov, and I. G. Piatykhin, the commanders of the 3rd, 8th, 12th, and 15th Air Armies, had already become Heroes of the Soviet Union before the war began.[137] Even more astonishing, none of the 19 generals who commanded air armies in 1942 perished during the war, and, as if underscoring the high degree of command stability, 11 air army commanders (65 percent), including S. A. Krasovsky (the 2nd), N. F. Naumenko (the 4th), S. K. Goriunov (the 5th), I. M. Sokolov (the 7th), T. T. Khriukhin (the 8th), V. A. Vinogradov (the 10th), V. N. Bibikov (the 11th), T. F. Kutsevalov (the 12th), S. D. Rybal'chenko (the 13th), I. P. Zhuravlev (the 14th), and S. I. Rudenko (the 16th), were still commanding either their original air army or another air army at war's end or before it was disbanded or reverted to *Stavka* control in late 1944.

Longevity in command and relative command stability also characterized the careers of generals who served as commanders of the VVS's aviation corps. For example, including the 4 long-range bomber aviation corps (but excluding the partially formed 5th in the Far East) operational on 22 June 1941 but disbanded in August 1941, the VVS included a total of 20 aviation corps in 1941 and 1942. During this period of about 18 months, a total of 22 generals served as aviation corps commanders, for an average of 1.1 commanders per corps, or roughly 0.7 commanders on an annualized basis, and these corps experienced 19 assumptions of command or changes in command, for an average of less than 1 per corps on an annualized basis.[138]

Even more significantly, eight (36 percent) of these 22 aviation corps commanders commanded their corps through war's end and two others, K. N. Smirnov and V. A. Sudets, were promoted to command air armies, the former the 2nd Air Army in 1942 and 1943 and the latter the 17th Air Army until war's end.

1943. The same pattern of command stability persisted in the VVS's air armies during 1943, when, for example, a total of 21 generals served as commanders of 17 air armies, for an average of 1.2 commanders per army, and the armies experienced 24 assumptions of command or changes in command, for an average of just 1.4 per army.[139] Furthermore, although none of these air army commanders perished during the war, 16 (94 percent), including S. A. Khudiakov (the 1st), S. A. Krasovsky (the 2nd and 17th), N. F. Papivin (the 3rd), K. A. Vershinin (the 4th), N. F. Naumenko (the 4th and 15th), S. K. Goriunov (the 5th), F. P. Polynin (the 6th), I. M. Sokolov (the 7th), T. T. Khriukhin (the 8th), V. A. Vinogradov (the 10th), V. N. Bibikov (the 11th), T. F. Kutsevalov (the 12th), S. D. Rybal'chenko (the 13th), I. P. Zhuravlev (the 14th), S. I. Rudenko (the 16th), and V. A. Sudets (the 17th), were still commanding their original or another air army at war's end.

In addition, Vershinin, Zhuravlev, and Rudenko became Heroes of the Soviet Union in 1944, and Krasovsky, Goriunov, Sudets, and Khriukhin became Heroes in 1945, Khriukhin for the second time.[140] Stalin also promoted Khudiakov and Rudenko to air marshals by war's end, and Sudets, Krasovsky, and Vershinin became air marshals in the 1950s.

Discounting frequent changes in aviation corps designations, the *Stavka* increased the quantity of aviation corps in the VVS from 16 on 1 January 1943 to a total of 40 by year's end. Altogether, 48 generals served as aviation corps commanders during this period, for an average of 1.2 commanders per corps as opposed to less than 1 during 1942, and these corps experienced a total of 32 assumptions of command or changes in command, for an average of only 0.8 per corps, which was about the same as 1942.[141] Regarding the individual fates of the 48 generals who served as aviation corps commanders during 1943, 28 (58 percent) were commanding aviation corps at war's end, and Sudets, who was promoted to command the 17th Air Army in March 1943, commanded that army to war's end.

As their extraordinary longevity in command indicated, Stalin had found his cadre of effective air army and aviation corps commanders by 1943, and most would perform with distinction for the remainder of the war.

In conclusion, contrary to popular belief, with the exception of its main direction commands, some of its field armies, and its sapper armies, command stability was far greater in the Red Army and command turbulence was significantly less damaging than has previously been assumed, not only after November 1942 but also during the first 18 months of the war. Furthermore, command was most stable in the Red Army's *fronts,* key armies, tank and mechanized forces and in its largest supporting air, artillery, and air defense formations, which formed the most important part of its force structure.

More important still, when command instability was the greatest during 1941 and 1942, Stalin was still able to identify and develop the key commanders who would lead the Red Army to victory during the last two years of war. For example, the Red Army's "greatest captains" such as Zhukov, Konev, Malinovsky, Meretskov, Rokossovsky, Tolbukhin, Govorov, Timoshenko, and Vasilevsky, who survived the war to become "Marshals of Victory" during 1945, were already serving in key command or staff positions during 1941. In the same fashion, the Red Army's most famous tank army commanders such as Katukov, Bogdanov, Rybalko, Leliushenko, Rotmistrov, and Kravchenko all served apprenticeships as tank brigade or tank and mechanized corps commanders during 1941 and 1942, rose to tank army command during 1942, 1943, or early 1944, and commanded their tank armies until late 1944 or war's end. The same general pattern also characterized the careers of the Red Army's most illustrious cavalry, engineer, artillery, PVO, and aviation commanders.

In short, most of the marshals and generals who led the Red Army to victory during May 1945 were already serving as generals or colonels in responsible command positions when war began on 22 June 1941. What is surprising is the relatively high percentage of these officers who survived their education at the hands of the *Wehrmacht* during 1941 and 1942 to emerge as successful commanders in the victorious Red Army of 1945.

Table 12.1 Red Army Officers Killed or Missing in Action, 1941–1945

	Killed	Missing	Total
1941	50,884	182,432	233,316
1942	161,857	124,488	286,345
1943	173,584	43,423	217,007
1944	169,553	36,704	206,257
1945	75,130	5,038	80,168
Total	631,008	392,085	1,023,093

Source: A. A. Shabaev, "Poteri ofitserskogo sostava Krasnoi Armii v Velikoi Otechstvennoi voine" [Red Army officer cadre losses in the Great Patriotic War], *Voenno-istoricheskii arkhiv* [Military-historical archives], no. 3 (1998); 183.

CHAPTER 13

The Red Army Soldier

CONSCRIPTION

On the Eve of War

As the clouds of war gathered in Europe and Asia during the mid- and late 1930s, the growing military threats to the Soviet Union convinced Stalin that the Red Army could not expand fast enough or produce sufficient forces to guarantee the future security of the Soviet state in the event of war.[1] As a result, Stalin decided to alter the Red Army's peacetime configuration and force generation system significantly during early 1935 so that it could make the transition from peace to war more effectively. When further crises erupted later in the decade, Stalin began increasing the Red Army's size and strength in early 1937.

In early 1935 the Red Army was organized on the basis of the so-called territorial (militia)-cadre (regular) system, a system that M. V. Frunze had instituted ten years before while serving as the Soviet Union's people's commissar of military and naval affairs. Within the context of this system, the army consisted of 100 divisions, including a cadre (regular) force of 26 rifle and 16 cavalry divisions, which the People's Commissariat of Defense (NKO) maintained at several levels of cadre strength during peacetime, and a territorial force of 58 rifle, mountain, and cavalry divisions, which were stationed throughout the Soviet Union on a regional basis and were manned by partially trained conscripts and local reservists. At least in theory, the NKO intended to expand the Red Army's size several fold by mobilizing territorial divisions once war approached or began.[2]

By this time, however, Stalin had lost faith in the ability of this system to protect the Soviet state adequately:

> It is important to note that the mixed territorial-cadre system for forming and organizing our forces was already bankrupt by the mid-1930s and had become a brake on the progress of their combat improvement. It became urgently necessary to shift our formation of forces to a unified cadre principle. One of the main reasons was that the temporary manpower within the territorial units and formations were not able to master the new com-

> plex technology and learn how to employ it in ever-changing conditions during their short training exercises. . . . To a considerable degree, the transformation to a cadre system was dictated by growing requirements for increased combat and mobilization readiness because the danger of a war with Fascist Germany was increasing.[3]

As a result, in May 1935 Stalin ordered the NKO to convert the Red Army's organization from the territorial (militia) system to a regular (cadre) system by 1 January 1939.[4] It did so in stages over the next four years, nearly simultaneously with Stalin's purge of the army's officer corps, by disbanding or converting territorial divisions to regular division and by increasing the quantity of cadre forces from 49 divisions to 98 divisions and five separate brigades.[5] Although this conversion process did not significantly increase the quantity of divisions in the Red Army as a whole, it did fundamentally alter its peacetime composition and configuration and the manner in which it was to expand during the period of transition from peace to war.[6]

As if to validate Stalin's concerns, the Soviet Union became involved tangentially in several international crises in 1937 and early 1938, and then more actively, first, by invading Poland in concert with Hitler's *Wehrmacht* in September 1939 and, second, by provoking war with Finland in late 1939, during which, to Stalin's consternation, the Red Army performed quite poorly. Thereafter, however, Stalin stood on the sidelines in 1940 and the first half of 1941 while Hitler's *Wehrmacht* conquered most of Western Europe, satisfying himself only by forcibly annexing the Baltic states and Romanian Bessarabia.[7]

Considered within the context of the Red Army's dismal combat performance in Poland and during the Soviet-Finnish War, the *Wehrmacht's* spectacular victories in Poland in September 1939 and in Western Europe and Scandinavia during the spring and summer of 1940 frightened and chagrined Stalin. Fearing for the security of his regime, Stalin responded by vastly expanding the Red Army's size and strength, and, simultaneously, ordering his new defense commissar, Marshal of the Soviet Union S. K. Timoshenko, to reform its organizational structure and combat techniques and reequip it with new weaponry. In reality, therefore, in September 1939 Stalin began implementing a policy of "creeping up to war," which he hoped would improve the country's security posture. This policy and Timoshenko's associated reforms were to be complete by the summer of 1942.

To provide the manpower necessary for this expansion program, the Supreme Soviet of the USSR issued a new Law on Universal Military Service on 1 September 1939 whose provisions significantly increased the number of males subject to military conscription by expanding the pool of manpower available to the Red Army and by increasing the term of military service for enlisted men and junior (noncommissioned) officers to three years and, supposedly, provided more extensive training to prospective Red Army soldiers. As a result, the Red Army's size and strength increased dramatically from one army, 38 corps, 138 divisions, and 1.5 million men on 1 January 1938 to 20 armies, 34 corps, 206 divisions, and 4.2 million men in December 1940, and, finally to 27 armies, 95 corps, 303 division, and over 5 million men on 22 June 1941 (see Table 13.1).

Despite Timoshenko's best attempts to reorganize, reform, and reequip the Red Army during 1940 and 1941, its conversion from a territorial-cadre to a regular-cadre force and its rapid expansion had an extremely deleterious impact on individual and unit training. For example, in June 1941 most reservists supposedly fully trained by the territorial-cadre system remained largely untrained, and excessive turbulence caused by the Red Army's rapid expansion inhibited the training of the new soldiers. In short, as its subsequent combat performance indicated, even though the army could mobilize a vast force of up to 14 million partially trained reservists and conscripts, on 22 June 1941, the Red Army was a colossal force with feet of clay.

Even before Hitler began Operation Barbarossa on 22 June, Stalin had set the Soviet Union's cumbersome military mobilization system into motion as a precautionary measure. For example, Stalin mobilized several armies stationed in internal military districts during April and May 1941, moving them forward into reserve positions along the Dnepr River in the rear of his western military districts. In addition, Stalin began shifting the Red Army from a peacetime to a wartime footing in May by ordering the call-up of 805,264 reservists under the guise of large-scale training exercises (*bol'shie uchebnye sbory,* or BUS). However, although the BUS increased the armed forces' strength to 5,707,116 men, the NKO failed to allocate most of these troops to its field forces prior to 22 June 1941. Worse still, when it finally did so shortly after war began, most of the new soldiers lacked much of their required weapons and other equipment.[8]

After Operation Barbarossa began and the initial phases of mobilization were complete, by 1 July 1941 the Soviet Armed Forces had fielded 9,638,000 men, including 3,533,000 in its operating armies, 5,562,000 in its military districts, and 532,000 in the navy.[9] Thereafter throughout the war, further mobilization brought another 28,769,636 personnel into the Red Army's ranks, including 490,000 women soldiers and 80,000 women officers.[10]

The Initial Period of War

Once Operation Barbarossa began, the rapidly deteriorating military situation forced Stalin to engage in a dangerous game of catch-up with the Germans. While the *Wehrmacht's* war machine was savaging the Red Army, Stalin and his colleagues worked feverishly to mobilize the army to its fully authorized wartime strength and, simultaneously, replace the staggering losses it was suffering. At Stalin's direction, the State Defense Committee (GKO) and *Stavka* issued tens of special mobilization decrees and directives during the first eight months of the war. This process began on 24 June, when Stalin authorized the formation of destroyer *(istrebitel'nye)* battalions in all regions to combat German diversionary and airborne forces, a decree that resulted in the formation of 1,755 destroyer battalions with 100–200 men for a total of 328,000 men by 31 July and, ultimately, 400,000 men by year's end. Then, on 28 June, the GKO approved a request by the Leningrad city committee (*gorodskoi sovet,* or GORKOM) to form seven people's militia divisions (DNOs), which ultimately resulted in the formation in Leningrad of ten DNOs and 16 separate people's militia machine-gun artillery battalions with a total of 135,400 men.

After the Red Army's border defenses collapsed in late June, on 4 July the GKO authorized the formation of 25 more DNOs totaling 270,000 men in the Moscow region, 12 of which formed by 7 July, and similar militia forces in other regions, districts, and cities.[11] Four days later, on 8 July, the GKO ordered the NKO to reinforce the Red Army by raising 50 new rifle and 10 new cavalry division with a total of 600,000 men "as soon as possible." However, the NKO was able to field only 34 (28 rifle and 6 cavalry) of these divisions by 23 July.[12] Finally, on 15 July, the *Stavka* disbanded all of the Red Army's mechanized corps except the two stationed in the Moscow Military District and ordered the NKO to use the mechanized corps' surviving tank division to form ten new 100-series tank divisions.[13]

This nearly frantic force generation process accelerated in the late summer and fall. For example, on 11 August the GKO ordered the NKO to form 85 new rifle and 25 new cavalry divisions totaling 1,100,000 men by late fall, and on 24 August it ordered the NKO to disband most of the new 100-series tank divisions and use their tanks to form 65 new smaller tank brigades and several separate tank regiments and battalions.[14] On 15 October, even before these new divisions reached the Red Army, the GKO ordered the NKO to form 50 new rifle divisions with 500,000 men drawn primarily from Siberia, Central Asia, and the Caucasus and Volga Military Districts, and three days later, 25 rifle brigades with a total of 150,000 men to serve as the nuclei for future rifle divisions.[15] Finally, because of the immense losses the Red Army suffered during October, on 26 November the GKO ordered the NKO to strip men from "non-ground force elements" of the Red Army to reinforce its operating *fronts* with an additional 70 rifle divisions and 50 rifle brigades totaling 700,000 and 300,000 men, respectively.[16] Capping this force expansion effort, on 16 February 1942, the GKO ordered the NKO to form 120 new smaller tank brigades.[17]

Thus, after the Red Army began the war with a line-combat strength of roughly 3,734,000 men assigned to its 303 divisions (198 rifle, 61 tank, 31 motorized, and 13 cavalry divisions) and 22 brigades of various types, the GKO mobilized over 6 million men between 22 June and 31 December 1941. These included at least 4.02 million riflemen and cavalrymen assigned directly to the Red Army and another 2.67 million militiamen raised by military commissariats and other local authorities throughout the country, many of which ultimately joined the Red Army's ranks in the 36 DNOs assigned to it in 1941.[18] In addition, Politburo decrees authorized the People's Commissariat of Internal Affairs (NKVD) to raise numerous destroyer battalions totaling another 328,000 men in 1941.[19]

Combined with the enormous personnel losses the Red Army suffered during the first six months of the war, this incessant mobilization of fresh rifle, cavalry, and tank forces to replace these staggering losses strained the Soviet Union's manpower resources to the breaking point. Indicative of this problem, not only did it dig deeply into the Soviet Union's immense pool of manpower legally subject to conscription, but the mobilization also engulfed many soldiers who were originally not subject to conscription. As a result, beginning only days after war began and to an increasing extent throughout the late summer and fall, the necessity of replacing the Red Army's combat losses forced the NKO to abandon precipitously many of its prewar assumptions and restrictions regarding the conscription of Soviet citizens it hitherto regarded as unfit for military service, in particular, those pertaining to the conscription of older reservists, ethnic minorities, and women in military service (see below).

For example, as early as 4 July, when it ordered the formation of DNOs in Moscow and elsewhere, the GKO directed the military districts, "to form the people's militia divisions by mobilizing workers between the ages of 17 and 55 years."[20] Later still, on 20 August, the NKO ordered its operating *fronts*, armies, and military districts to transfer all soldiers under the age of 35 years from rear service units, subunits, and installations to combat formations and units by 1 September and to replace them with lower-quality troops over the age of 35 (see Appendix 5 in companion volume, which contains documents regarding the wartime Red Army).[21] Soon the NKO extended this waiver in age limitations to regular army forces as well. For example, one Red Army soldier who ultimately reached the rank of sergeant major recalled: I was drafted in October 1941 from the 10th grade, during the days of widespread ruin, robbery, and panic in Moscow. I was drafted despite the fact that I had just recently celebrated my seventeenth birthday–probably, so that a potential soldier wouldn't be left to the Germans."[22]

Thereafter and through 1943, the NKO steadily eased the age restrictions on combat and noncombat military service in the Red Army to include younger, older, and less fit reservists and conscripts, ultimately, conscripting men well under the age of 18 years and exceeding the age of 55 years into the Red Army's operating forces (see Table 13.2). Despite the new legal age limits on service, many soldiers exceeded these limits by the end of 1943. According to a former regimental chief of staff:

> Based on my experience, I know that, in some operations, the ages [of the soldiers] differed greatly, from 18 to 20 [years] and up to 50 years, and there were also some 60 year olds. The sorting process was as follows. The old men went to the rear area, to supply, logistical, [and] medical units. The selection was usually like this. Replacements arrived, and the first thing done was asking the questions, 'Who is a gunner? Take off. Who can drive a vehicle? Take off.' They first selected the specialists, and, when all of the specialists had been selected, those who remained were looked at from the standpoint of age. If someone was very old, he didn't go to the front lines. One time into an attack, and he is tired out. He will be very weak. There were unique situations when the old ones did not withdraw. They left their positions and went forward. But usually those who returned after being wounded became commanders [noncommissioned officers] because a soldier who has fought in combat already can become a section [squad] commander. We took good care of our soldiers and we used them, as they put it, rationally and effectively.[23]

Impressment

The Red Army began resorting to impressments, in reality, forced conscription, to fill its ranks during its winter offensive of 1941–42, when Stalin first recognized the potential of raising fresh manpower for the Red Army from liberated territories. On 9 February 1942, the *Stavka* ordered its operating *fronts* to conscript "citizens in the liberated territories between the ages of 17 to 45 who are subject to conscription and have not been conscripted into the Red Army during the previous months of the war" and assign them to "reserve rifle regiments in all armies, which, in practice, must select, conscript, and combat train these contingents within their armies' operational sectors."[24] However, the Red Army's failure to drive *Wehrmacht's* forces back to the Smolensk region during its winter offensive and the *Wehrmacht's* advance in Operation *Blau* in the summer and fall of 1942 rendered Stalin's February 1942 order largely irrelevant.

The NKO resumed impressing soldiers into the Red Army's rank during the winter of 1942–43, after its victory at Stalingrad, and accelerated this policy during the late summer and fall of 1943, when the front lines began moving inexorably westward after the Battle of Kursk, primarily to obtain fresh manpower the Red

Army desperately needed to sustain its massive offensive operations. During this period it forcibly conscripted large numbers of military-age men, Russians as well as non-Russians, who were living in territory liberated from German control. By this time, NKVD internal forces accompanying the advancing Red Army were responsible for fulfilling this important mission.

For example, a rifle division participating in the Central Front's Orel-Briansk-Smolensk offensive in February and March 1943, reported:

> The division [the 60th Army's 121st Rifle Division] took part in the battles for Voronezh, Kursk, and L'gov. The division suffered heavy losses in the battles for the Lukashevka and Soldatskoe line because of unskillful leadership by the division's former commander, [Colonel M. A.] Bushin, for which he was relieved from his duties. The division's strength on 25 March 1943 was of 7,025 men, of which 5,573 joined us as replacements by virtue of a mobilization [conscription] in the territory of the Kursk region, which we had just liberated from the German invaders.[25]

At roughly the same time, the 60th Army's 248th Student Rifle Brigade reported:

> [The brigade] joined the 60th Army on 30 January 1943. It took part in the battles for Kursk and L'gov. The brigade operated particularly skillfully and energetically during the L'gov operation. After being sent far forward to the Nizhne Chupakhino and Konoprianovka line (along the western bank of the Svapa River) on the army's flank, the brigade threatened Ryl'sk from the north, by doing so helping to capture L'gov. U-2 [bomber] aircraft supplied the brigade with ammunition and the division obtained its foodstuffs from local resources during this period. The brigade's strength on 25 March 1943 was 2,389 men, including 774 replacements, which we mobilized in the Kursk region after we liberated it from the Fascist invaders, and from the disbanded Drozdov Partisan Detachment.[26]

Despite the apparent effectiveness of these conscription procedures, combat reports indicate that these "recruits" were not always happy to serve. For example, on 16 March 1943, the Briansk Front's 13th Army ordered its blocking detachments, which were used to prevent desertions, particularly by new conscripts, to ensure these conscripts remained in the ranks:

> Replacements are joining the ranks of the Red Army from regions liberated from the enemy's forces. In the struggle against possible instances of desertion and the avoidance of military service, the army commander orders:

1. Strengthen the blocking duties of army blocking detachments;
2. Systematically conduct universal inspections of the entire male population in all populated points;
3. Comb all forests and orchards thoroughly and examine all haystacks, uninhabited buildings, and especially dugouts situated along the lines of the old defenses; and
4. Strengthen the inspection of documents of those passing through the populated points and [other] suspicious persons.

Report on all implemented measures by 25 March 1943.

Major General Petrushevsky, chief of staff, 13th Army[27]

After the Red Army expanded its offensive operations to encompass the entire front from Velikie Luki to the Black Sea later in the year, on 15 October the *Stavka* issued specific instructions signed by Stalin regarding the conscription of manpower from reoccupied territories in eastern Belorussia and the central Ukraine:

1. Only army military councils can conscript soldiers from regions liberated from the German occupiers into [its] reserve regiments, and division and regiment commanders are prohibited from conducting this conscription [mobilization].
2. The chief of Glavupraform will determine the quantity [of men] subject to conscription [mobilization] for each *front* in accordance with my plan for providing reinforcements to each *front*.
3. Dispatch all soldiers mobilized above and beyond the planned norms for each *front* to reserve units subordinate to the chief of Glavupraform.[28]

As the Red Army's westward advance continued, on 16 November the *Stavka* further defined what it described as "centralized control over local conscription," at the same time providing clear evidence of the massive scope of its mobilization efforts in liberated regions.

During November the *fronts* listed below are authorized to mobilize the following quantities of soldiers in territories liberated from German occupation to reinforce their forces: 1st Baltic Front 15,000 men, Western Front 30,000 men, Belorussian Front 30,000 men, 1st Ukrainian Front 30,000 men, 2nd Ukrainian Front 30,000 men, 3rd Ukrainian Front 20,000 men, and 4th Ukrainian Front 30,000 men, for a total of 185,000 men.

The *fronts'* military councils will assign those who are conscripted above the established norms to reserve brigades subordinate to the military districts' commanders to be trained in accordance with Glavupraform's

> instructions. The chief of the Red Army's Rear Services will distribute clothing [uniforms] to the *fronts* for those conscripted based on the established quantities of conscripted for each *front.*[29]

Orders such as this, which the *Stavka* issued on a monthly basis, underscored the immense scale of the Red Army's mobilization effort while it was "on the march" westward. Although most of these orders have yet to be declassified, the Red Army conscripted at least 200,000 soldiers and perhaps more per month from the regions it liberated. As vividly described in their official histories, some Red Army divisions combed haystacks and cellars for potential recruits, who, when detected, were immediately assigned to training battalions. Based on this pattern, the Red Army probably conscripted as many as 2.8 million soldiers into its ranks during the remainder of 1943 and 1944, primarily from the Ukraine, Belorussia, the Baltic region, and Moldavia, and up to 1 million more soldiers in the same fashion during 1945.

As an additional benefit, the Red Army's ability to tap into this fresh and ever-expanding pool of manpower lessened its reliance on non-Slavic ethnic minorities and women as a source of conscripts later in the war. Therefore, as the quantity of Ukrainians, Belorussians, and Moldavians conscripted in territories liberated by the Red Army increased dramatically during 1944 and 1945, the number of non-Slavic soldiers conscripted into the Red Army during the same period fell precipitously (see Table 13.2).

Convicts and Political Prisoners

Indicative of the critical manpower shortages the Red Army experienced during the first six months of the war, particularly in its operating *fronts,* during the summer of 1941 and accelerating during early 1942, the GKO began ordering the conscription of what ultimately became hundreds of thousands of men from "the condemned of the last reserve of the Empire," specifically, the over 2 million men and women exiled to Soviet labor camps for a variety of political and criminal offenses.[30] Most of these prisoners were kulaks (landed peasants) who had been arrested and exiled prior to the war.[31]

Discounting the number of prisoners who perished in captivity, it is likely that as many as 420,000 of these prisoners were impressed into the Red Army in 1941 and even more in 1942. In addition, the GKO and Presidium of the Supreme Soviet of the USSR freed more than 157,000 more "politicals" by special resolutions during 1941 and early 1942 and sent them to the Red Army. The most recent estimate is that 975,000 of these prisoners were "freed" and ultimately served in the Red Army before war's end.[32] However, how many of these prisoners returned to captivity in the GULAG after war's end remains unknown.

The first recorded large-scale combat employment of these prisoners in the Red Army occurred in the late summer of 1941, when the "Polar" Rifle Division, which "was, on the whole, made up of prisoners, including its command cadre," helped defend Murmansk in the far north. These troops "wore the numerical designations of the Vorkuta camps instead of swords and diamonds" and "even now they basically remain anonymous."[33] Although Stalin's initial motive in employing these camp prisoners as Red Army soldiers, or more properly as cannon fodder, was to replace the 2.8 million troops the Red Army lost during the first six months of the war, after the victory at Moscow, he needed them to fill in the Red Army's depleted ranks so that it could conduct and sustain offensive operations. Therefore, on 11 April 1942, the GKO ordered the NKVD to "draft 500,000 men who were fit for line service from its work settlements," and on 26 July ordered the conscription for an additional 500,000 men from the same category of prisoners.[34]

Originally, the GKO intended to remove the names of labor deportees who were impressed into the army and the names of their family members from the official lists of NKVD deportees once they completed a full year of service in the army. To improve their morale, however, on 22 October 1942, the NKVD ordered "all labor deportees conscripted into the Red Army and their immediate family members (wives, children) to be removed from the lists of labor exiles, issued passports without restrictions, and released from the 5 percent deduction from their salary that is being collected to cover the costs of maintaining the administrative apparatus for labor exiles."[35]

Because it failed to anticipate this program, the GKO's removal of the names of labor deportees who served in the Red Army and their families from these prisoner lists progressed very slowly. As a result, only 47,116 labor deportees serving in the Red Army had been "de-listed" by 10 December 1942 (including 17,775 draftees and 29,341 family members) and another 102,250 draftees and family members were de-listed in 1943. Nevertheless, as a result of this conscription and de-listing, the number of labor deportees still in camps and at various work projects fell from 911,716 on 1 January 1942 to 69,687 on 1 January 1944.[36]

The formation of Red Army forces in the Siberia Military District provided an accurate indicator of the scope and impact of this prisoner conscription program. For example, the NKO, the Siberian Communist Party, and the Siberian Military District jointly formed the 6th Volunteer Rifle Corps, which adopted the name "Stalin," in July 1942. The Novosibirsk Regional Communist Party Committee and the Siberian Military District began forming the new rifle corps on 8 July, when it formed the 1st Siberian Volunteer Rifle Division, which the NKO later renumbered as the 150th Rifle Division, as its nucleus.

During the next six weeks, the military district formed the Separate Stalin Siberian Rifle Brigade, which the NKO later designated as the 75th Rifle Brigade, at Omsk on 17 July, and the 1st Special Siberian Altai Volunteer Brigade, which the NKO later designated as the 74th Separate "Stalin" Altai Siberian Brigade, on 24 August, and assigned both to the 6th Volunteer Rifle Corps.[37] The Siberian Military District completed filling out the corps by adding the 78th Krasnoiarsk Siberian Volunteer Rifle Brigade and the 91st "Stalin" Special Siberian Volunteer Rifle Brigade to it during September and October 1942.[38] Although a large percentage of the rifle corps' soldiers were former labor deportees, the NKO made sure that most of its command cadre were members of the Communist Party or Komsomol to ensure the corps remained reliable.[39]

In addition to conscripting labor camp prisoners into the Red Army, the NKO broadened conscription on 6 April 1943 by including all civilians of military age who had not been conscripted before because of legal problems or criminal activity.[40] This order authorized NKVD organs, military commissariats, and other local organs to conscript "all males of up to 50 years of age who have not yet been conscripted into the army because of their loss of rights, excluding those persons who have been serving sentences for counterrevolutionary crimes (those who have actually carried out the crimes) and banditry" and "register all males of up to 55 years of age who have lost their rights while serving the full measure of their sentence (for other than counterrevolutionary crimes and banditry) and who have been designated by medical certification as unfit for military service but fit for physical work."[41]

Clearing out prisons and labor camps by dispatching their inmates to fill out the Red Army's ranks could not have had a salutary effect on discipline. The best evidence that it did not was an NKO order issued on 21 August 1943 and signed by Stalin to stiffen discipline in the Red Army. Drastically expanding the quantity of officers who could be sentenced to penal units, this order granted

> the commanders of regiments (separate units) in the operating armies and the commanders of divisions (separate brigades) and their equivalents in the military districts and nonoperating *fronts* . . . the right to send sergeants and rank-and-file soldiers who are guilty of absence without leave, desertion, disobedience to orders, squandering and theft of property, violation of regulations of the guards service, and other military crimes to penal units of the operating army, in those instances when normal disciplinary measures for these misdemeanors have proved inadequate . . . without trial.[42]

Later still the NKO surfaced another problem with regard to conscripting criminals and "politicals" into the Red Army in an order it issued on 26 January 1944, which demanded military tribunals be more careful when screening convicts for military service:

> In a number of cases, judicial organs are groundlessly employing delayed execution of the sentence with assignment of the convicted to the operating army for persons convicted of counterrevolutionary crimes, banditry, brigandage, robbery, and recidivist theft, for persons who have already been convicted in the past for multiple crimes, and also for recidivist deserters from the Red Army. In addition, the required order is lacking in the dispatch to the operating army of those who have been convicted but the execution of whose sentence has been delayed. [As a result], many of those convicted have the opportunity to desert and commit crimes once again.[43]

To rid the judicial system of these shortcomings, the NKO forbade "the courts and military tribunals from applying Note 2 to Article 28 of the RSFSR Law Code [entry into Red Army service] to those convicted of counterrevolutionary crimes, banditry, brigandage, robbery, and recidivist theft, to those persons who have already had many convictions in the past for multiple crimes, and also to recidivist deserters from the Red Army."[44]

Individually and collectively, these decrees and orders decrees provided the legal basis for conscripting thousands if not millions of former criminals and political prisoners into the Red Army from both prisons and the infamous GULAG. Dictated by the Red Army's immense and often unrequited manpower requirements, these conscription measures formed but a small portion of an immense mosaic of massive call-ups to military service of numerous ethic and religious minorities, many citizens above the normal age of military service, and millions of women.

ETHNICITY (NON-SLAVIC SOLDIERS)

Prewar

By law and custom, the Soviet Union's political and military leaders severely restricted the inclusion of non-Slavic ethnic minorities, religious minorities, and women in its armed forces prior to 22 June 1941. This was a practice the GKO intended to adhere to after war began. Although the Red Army included many distinctive national formations when it was organized on the basis of the territorial-militia system prior to 1935, when the NKO began converting the army to the regular cadre system, it restructured it into an all-union cadre force under firm Russian (Slavic control). It did so at least in part because, like many of his tsarist predecessors, Stalin questioned the reliability of national (ethnic) formations in the military, particularly in time of war.

When it adopted the regular-cadre manning system, the NKO thoroughly integrated those non-Slavic minorities who were permitted to serve in the army into largely Slavic-based (Russian, Belorussian, and Ukrainian) military formations and units, and, while fulfilling their military obligations, most non-Slavic soldiers served in noncombat forces such as construction or railroad troops. The same general restrictions applied to women serving in the military, their role being limited to serving as nurses in the medical service or as clerks and chauffeurs (see below).

Even though the NKO began transforming the army to the regular-cadre system in 1935, nationality formations continued to exist in the Red Army until 7 March 1938, when the NKO decreed the abolition of "extraterritorial" recruitment and soon after disbanded national formations, incorporating them into the Red Army as a whole.[45] At the time, the Red Army included 13 divisions, one brigade, and ten regiments made up primarily of national minorities, most of which were specialized mountain rifle or cavalry forces (see Table 13.3).

As the Red Army "crept up to war" during the period 1939–41, the increasing demand for military manpower to fill out the expanding Red Army forced the Presidium of the Supreme Soviet to enact new laws regarding the military service of Slavs and non-Slavs alike. For example, the Law on Universal Military Service enacted on 1 September 1939 increased the number of soldiers conscripted into the Red Army from ethnic minorities and lengthened their terms of service: "On 1 September 1939, a new law concerning universal military service was issued, which revoked the class limits on military service and established a new order for military service. The interests of state security urgently required the creation of a multi-million-man cadre army based on a unified extraterritorial principal of formation independent of ethnic nationality."[46]

Wartime

Within months after Operation Barbarossa began, the demands of war swept away many of these restrictions on the conscription of non-Slavic national minorities into the military, as well as similar restrictions on the conscription of religious minorities, such as Jews and fundamentalist Muslims. In short, by 1943 the Red Army's insatiable appetite for additional manpower transformed the Red Army into a thoroughly multi-ethnic force manned by both men and women.

The process of conscripting non-Slavic minorities and integrating them into the Red Army during war occurred in two closely related ways: first, outright formation of new national military formations; and, second, the integration of soldiers from non-Slavic minorities into military formations and units on an individual or collective basis. The Politburo of the Communist Party's Central Committee decided to adopt both approaches in November 1941, when *Wehrmacht* forces were advancing on Moscow. The rationale for doing so and the consequences of this decision were quite clear:

> Often one encounters the opinion that the Soviet people defended their own Fatherland, Russia, against foreign invasion–which is correct, but not completely so. This desire belongs to all peoples. However, historically in the USSR, it turns out that the patriotism of separate peoples became inseparable from the recognition of the Russian "elder brother" and "a feeling of family unity." By saving themselves from enslavement, every people together with other peoples defended a single Homeland–the Soviet Union, in which Uzbeks and Kazakhs, Tartars and Chuvash, and many other peoples found their government, created their industry, and received the opportunity to develop their language and national culture, to train national cadres, and so on.
>
> Active combat against the invaders went on in all of the union republics subjected to occupation. Regions located in the deep rear accepted evacuated enterprises. The citizens of Central Asia and Kazakhstan, who were called up by the military commissariats, joined the "workers army," but, for various reasons, were not sent to the front. They worked on construction and in industrial enterprises in the Urals and Siberia. National military formations were created during the most dangerous time of the war. The first of these, the 201st Latvian Rifle Division, entered combat at Moscow in December 1941. On 13 November 1941, the GKO decided to create national military units and formations in the republics of Central Asia, Kazakhstan, Bashkiria, Kabardino-Balkaria, Kalmykia, and Chechnia-Ingushetia. On the whole, the soldiers of these national formations and the soldiers of these nationalities who fought in the Red Army made their contributions to the defeat of the enemy.[47]

After November 1941 but particularly during 1941 and 1942, the NKO formed numerous national military formations in the Red Army and, throughout the war as a whole, mobilized as many as 8 million non-Slavic soldiers to fight in the Red Army's ranks out of a total of more than 34 million mobilized soldiers (see Tables 13.2, 13.4, 13.5, and 13.6).

The greatest influx of non-Slavic minority soldiers into the Red Army occurred in late 1941 and 1942 and, to a lesser extent, in early 1943. As a result, by the end of 1943, the Red Army was a multi-ethnic army manned by soldiers ranging in age from 17 to 55 years who represented virtually every ethnic and religious group in the Soviet Union. In fact, when the need arose later in the war, the Red Army also conscripted soldiers from other ethnic groups, such as Galicians, who had been living outside the Soviet Union when war began. As a result, the description of the composition of one officer's rifle division typified the Red Army as a whole:

> Our regiment and division [the 343rd Rifle Division] was formed in Stavropol' [in the North Caucasus Military District in August 1941]. It was formed in the second echelon after the war had already begun. The cadre army had already begun to fight, and it received a portion of its replacements through conscription and mobilization while our division was forming in Stavropol'. And the ages [of the soldiers], I would say, were stable: 40 years old, 38 years old, *kolkhoz* [collective farm] chairmen, *raiispolkom* [district executive committee] chairmen, *raikom* [district committee] secretaries, and so forth, but they were not young.
>
> Later the composition changed. I must tell you that our regiment traveled through 7,500 kilometers of combat during the entire war, and only 16 veterans who had joined up in Stavropol' remained. And, I must tell you that I preserved them as "relics." I simply did not send them into battle. Thus, the regiment's personnel changed quite often. The losses were quite significant, and we suffered tens of thousands killed and several thousands wounded; for that reason, the ages differed.
>
> What were the ages? There were guys 40 and 45 [years old]. When I became a company commander at Zaporozh'e [in October 1943], I was the "old man." Here I was, 22 years old, and I had fathers who were 45 years old. Of course, I showed concern for them by making sure they were clothed and fed. The composition also varied by nationality. There were all kinds–Kazakhs, Uzbeks, Tatars, Armenians, Georgians, and Azerbaijanis; it was a varied group.
>
> There were up to 25 nationalities in the regiment, but no questions arose during that period. It was an international regiment. They fought, and they all accomplished the mission with which we had been tasked: to rout the enemy as rapidly as possible. No problems arose. It was one big friendly family—a regimental family.
>
> There were also [women] in the regiment. There was Mariia Bukharskaia, she is famous throughout the entire world. She was a nurse and was awarded

> the Order of Florence, but I forget what it was for. She was a medic and the commander of the medical platoon. She removed 500 people from the battlefield. And, there were other nurses. They were also [women] communicators, doctors, and medics, not many, but, at any rate, there were always 10–15 women in the regiment.[48]

While underscoring the remarkable degree of ethnic diversity within the ranks of this and other Red Army divisions, this description also surfaces another issue Soviet officials and historians have long avoided: the role women played in the Red Army's ultimate victory.

WOMEN IN THE RED ARMY

One of the most obscure and controversial issues regarding the composition of the wartime Red Army is the extent to which the GKO and NKO conscripted and employed women as soldiers in either combat or in more traditional, noncombat roles. Until very recently most Soviet and Russian accounts of the war have generally ignored the combat contributions of women during the war, focusing instead on their contributions as nurses and vehicle drivers and emphasizing the role they played in keeping the Soviet economy afloat, primarily by replacing men in industrial or agricultural pursuits.[49]

For example, when asked whether women served in his unit, one veteran responded typically, "Not in our unit. Some signaler girls appeared, but eventually the officers married all of them. Later, I saw these old signalers, who came as our regiment's officers' wives of many years, to a reunion of the regiment's veterans in Moscow. Back then I had thought they were simply whores; but it turned out that these relationships lasted for the rest of their lives."[50] On the other hand, the most recent Russian official history of the war offers a fairer but rather perfunctory description of the contributions of Russian women to the war effort. This history mentions "more than 550,000 women" conscripted into PVO, the medical service, signal forces, the road service, as snipers, and other noncombat specialties, the three women's aviation regiments, and women in partisan and underground organizations.[51]

It is now abundantly clear that the severe manpower shortages the Red Army experienced during late 1941 and 1942 compelled Stalin to grant women a more active role in the war effort. For example, shortly before the defense of Moscow, an NKO order signed by Stalin on 8 October 1941 ordered the VVS (air force) to form the 586th Fighter and 588th Night Bomber Aviation Regiments at Engels airfield and the 587th Close Bomber Aviation Regiment at Kamenka by 1 December 1941, "for the purpose of employing women flight-technical cadre."[52] Staffed completely by women officers and soldiers, these aviation regiments went on to establish a formidable combat record throughout the war.

Faced with continuing severe manpower shortages, after authorizing the Red Army to conscript manpower locally from liberated regions, during the spring of 1942, Stalin directed the GKO and NKO to replace men in noncombat forces with conscripted women so that these men could reinforce combat forces fighting in the operating *fronts.* Taken together, these measures drastically increased the number of women in military uniform. The first step in this process took place on 25 March 1942, when the GKO ordered the NKO to mobilize 100,000 "girl-Komsomol members" to replace Red Army male soldiers in PVO and VNOS (early warning) units. While assigning many of these women to such noncombat duties as telephone and radio operators, scouts, observers, clerks, cooks, chauffeurs, and medical orderlies, this order also specifically designated others as actual antiaircraft machine gunners and directed the NKO to "use the freed up Red Army male soldiers to fill out those rifle divisions and rifle brigades that have been withdrawn from the front in accordance with the Glavupraform's plans."[53]

About a week later, on 3 April, the GKO ordered the NKO to continue this process by systematically replacing many male soldiers in rear service units and facilities with female personnel. This decree ordered the commanders of *fronts,* separate armies, and reserve armies, the commanders of military district forces, and the chiefs of the Red Army's main and central directorates to "withdraw a total of 80,828 men, who are exclusively fit for line service, from rear service units and facilities by no later than 15 April 1942, and replace them with women."[54]

The respective commanders and chiefs of directorates were to accomplish this by disbanding some units and reducing the authorized strength of others and, in the case of military-medical facilities, which were to generate 20,352 men for the combat duties, by replacing them with either women or with men who were unfit for front-line duty. The order required these commanders and chiefs to "dispatch the replaced personnel to the military councils of the appropriate military districts no later than 20 April to form artillery, tank, aviation, and mortar units as well as fill out rifle divisions that had been withdrawn from the front in accordance with the Glavupraform's plans."[55]

The process of replacing men with women continued on 13 April, when the GKO ordered the NKO to conscript 30,000 women into the signal services to replace male soldiers. Specifically, this order assigned women soldiers as BODO (encoded telegraph), ST-35, Morse code, telephone, radio, and telegraph operators and technicians, field postal workers, warehouse clerks, draftsman, secretaries, cooks, medical assistants, librarians, tailors, metalworkers, and lathe operators.[56] By way of justification, the order added, "first and foremost, use the replaced Red Army signalmen from the *fronts'* and armies' signal units to fill out and replace signalmen losses in rifle divisions and rifle brigades, and in artillery, tank, and mortar units situated at the front. Use the remaining excess specialist-signalmen to fill out communications units in rifle divisions and rifle brigades that have been withdrawn from the front in accordance with the Glavupraform's plans."[57]

This insertion of women into the Red Army's ranks accelerated on 19 April, when the NKO issued two more orders regarding the use of female soldiers "to free up personnel resources to fill out combat units." The first order severely truncated or abolished outright a whole range of rear service units and facilities, which *front* and army military councils had formed "without specific NKO authorization," and listed additional specific duty positions to be manned exclusively by women soldiers.[58] All of these changes were to take effect by 15 May, and, as before, the NKO directed that "the freed up personnel be used to fill out rifle divisions, rifle brigades, tank brigades, and artillery regiments."[59]

In the second NKO order, Stalin ordered the mobilization of 40,000 more female soldiers to replace male soldiers who were serving in the VVS in stages by 1 September. In addition to filling such noncombat positions as BODO, ST-35, Morse, telephone, radio, and telegraph operators, warehouse managers and assistant managers, warehouse men, product managers, office workers, cooks, mess hall managers, firemen, librarians, bookkeepers, accountants, "other specialists in administrative-housekeeping services," clerks, and chauffeurs, these women also became tractor operators and "weapons gunners." Once again, Stalin added, "Use the freed up Red Army soldiers and noncommissioned officers from the air force units located at the front to fill out *front* ground and air units at the direction of the *front* commanders and in the military districts under the overall supervision of the Glavupraform."[60]

The NKO completed this round of replacing Red Army male soldiers with females on 25 April, when it ordered its main and central directorates and the headquarters of military districts to truncate their *shtats* and replace command and management cadre fit for line service with older soldiers less fit or unfit for line service and women. Although it did not specify the exact number of personnel affected by this order, the NKO formed a special commission to scour the Red Army's ranks to determine which additional positions women soldiers might occupy. Chaired by Major General A. D. Rumiantsev, the chief of its Main Cadre Directorate, and consisting of all chiefs of related NKO directorates, the commission's mission was to screen all personnel covered by the order and provide a list of all replacements to Stalin by 5 May 1942.[61] Although no documentary evidence exists regarding the commission's work, no doubt it added thousands more women soldiers to the Red Army's administrative structure.

When the Red Army went over to the offense in the late fall of 1942 and the winter of 1942–43, the GKO increased its use of women to release manpower for the Red Army's combat forces, in particular, its tank and mechanized forces, which were spearheading these offensives. As a result, on 3 January 1943, the NKO ordered a truncation in the size of its tank brigades, tank training regiments, and field army automotive-tank warehouses by 15 January and replaced many of the male soldiers assigned to these units with older soldiers and women to the specific end of using "the freed up personnel to fill out tank and mechanized units and formations at the direction of the commander of the Red Army's tank and mechanized forces."[62] Although the attachment to this order, which listed the number of women and the precise duty positions they were to occupy, has yet to be published, and most of these positions were noncombat in nature, some were probably combat related.

Recently released archival documents also reveal a tangential but nonetheless interesting consequence of the increased number of women serving in the Red Army, specifically, the increased requirement, and perhaps demand, for improved sanitary conditions in the forward area. For example, on 11 April 1943, the NKO increased the soap ration for women by 50 percent in an order that read, "In accordance with GKO Decree No. 3113ss dated 3 April 1943, a ration of 100 grams of soap per month is established effective 1 April 1943 for women soldiers in addition to the ration norm set forth in accordance with NKO Order No. 312 of 1941."[63]

Collectively, while decrees and orders the GKO and NKO issued between March 1942 and January 1943 conscripted a total of over 250,000 women into the Red Army, additional unpublished orders probably added tens of thousands more women to the Red Army's ranks. For example, official Russian sources claim a total of 490,000 women soldiers and 80,000 women officers served in the Red Army and Navy during wartime, and 463,503 women were serving in the Red Army and Navy on 1 January 1945.[64] Although the roughly 300,000 women soldiers who served in the MPVO (local air defense) made up the bulk of women in uniform, more than 150,000 other women served in noncombat positions in the rear services, the VVS, and the signal forces, and fewer in aviation, tank, and mechanized forces, some in combat positions. However, this figure of over 500,000 women soldiers does not include the many who served as nurses, medical assistants, and medical helpers in medical facilities and organizations supporting MPVO. Counting these auxiliaries, it is likely that more than 1 million women served their country in uniform throughout the war.[65]

THE SOLDIER'S LIFE

Like that of his predecessors in tsarist times, whether male or female, Slav or non-Slav, Orthodox, Jewish, Muslim, or simply atheist, by any standard of measurement, the daily life of the Red Army soldier was distinctly Spartan.[66] Despite the Communist Party's strenuous attempts to transform the Red Army into a socially conscious and reliable instrument for the defense of socialism and the new Soviet state, during the 1930s the Red Army was still largely a peasant force made up of soldiers whose material living conditions barely surpassed those of their tsarist predecessors.[67] Worse still, in the wake of the purges and the Red Army's drastic expansion in the late 1930s, Stalin remained suspicious of its political reliability as massive numbers of fresh conscripts, many whose families had suffered through Stalin's bitter collectivization and industrialization programs, swelled its ranks.[68]

Although there are many ways to measure the quality of life of Red Army soldiers, the most obvious regard how they were fed and clothed, and, as separate subjects, how the army maintained order and discipline among its soldiers, the state of their morale, and the motives that impelled them to serve, fight, and, in the process, often die.

Food

Since "armies travel on their stomachs," the most accurate measure of the quality of soldiers' lives is how well they are fed. Since the Soviet Union as a whole experienced severe food shortages throughout the war, particularly during the first two years, and the Red Army's logistical system collapsed in the wake of Operation Barbarossa, thereafter, its soldiers suffered from severe and persistent food deprivation.

When war began, the NKO allocated Red Army soldiers daily food rations based on an order it issued on 24 May 1941, which specified the precise quantity of foodstuffs to be issued daily to soldiers performing various types of military duties based on their perceived needs in terms of the foods' caloric, protein, fat, carbohydrate, and vitamin content.[69] As had been the case for years, if not centuries, the bulk of this food consisted of bread, potatoes, cabbage, and groats (to make the cereal-like *kasha*) and, to a lesser extent, meat, fish, and small amounts of condiments such as salt, pepper, mustard, bay leaves, and other seasonings.

However, because of severe food shortages, the NKO established new ration standards on 22 September 1941, which, while continuing to allocate food to soldiers based on their specific duty assignments, sharply reduced their daily rations (see Table 13.1). According to this new and stricter ration regime, combat soldiers were to subsist on 3,450 calories per day and soldiers assigned to rear service organizations in operating armies, 2,954 calories per day. Depending on the duties they performed, soldiers assigned to reserve, rear area, construction, and security units were to receive 2,659–2,722 calories per day, which usually proved wholly inadequate to sustain their health:

> According to their caloric content, protein, fat, carbohydrates, and vitamins, and also the assortment of products, norms nos. 1 and 2 [for soldiers in the operating armies] fully corresponded to the energy expended by personnel in the operating armies. At the same time, according to their food value, the foodstuff norms for personnel serving in rear units (nos. 3 and 4) were minimal and did not always correspond to the work rear service units performed. When feeding personnel on the basis of the rear service norm (for example, in the Trans-Baikal Front), there were instances of feeding disorders and illness from emaciation. During the war several of the daily food norms were increased and improved.[70]

With only minor modifications, the NKO left this ration system largely unaltered to war's end, with combat soldiers receiving the largest daily food allocation. However, as in most armies, forward-based aircraft crews and air crews in garrisons to the rear received the most ample and varied rations, and soldiers convalescing in hospitals received special types of foodstuffs necessary to help them recover from their wounds or illnesses.

Since daily rations established by the NKO during September 1941 only represented an ideal, in reality, soldiers' lacked adequate rations for prolonged periods, particularly when the Red Army was retreating in the summer and early fall of 1941 and 1942, and when it was operating at the end of a long and tenuous logistical umbilical while on the offensive in 1943. In short, with the exception of relatively static periods, the soldiers were expected to fend for themselves by foraging, eating whatever substitute was available, or simply going without. As one soldiers recalled:

> We kept falling back with the ground forces until the front stabilized along the river Don at the end of the summer [in 1942], on whose bank we were deployed right up to the beginning of the counteroffensive. It was a difficult time. Ammunition was scarce, and we were poorly fed. For our first and second courses we had soup or porridge made from whole grain wheat or peas, which were freshly cooked with Uzbek cotton oil that looked like rust. And one time we didn't even have salt, which was real torture. We were fed this way for about a month.[71]

Red Army soldiers quickly learned how to survive on their own by developing the practice of scavenging to a high art, and also valued the foodstuffs provided by the Allies under the auspices of Lend-Lease enough to add the word "spam" to their daily vocabulary. Nor did this situation change significantly prior to war's end:

When it came to food, we lived mostly off trophies [captured goods] during the last period of war. Even bread was different all the time; sometimes it was dark and sometimes white and either coarse ground or fine ground, depending on what was present in trophy stockpiles and bases. Sometimes we received dried bread, real bread and not the devilish invention I encountered at the home front's food distribution points, which was dried dough. They explained its [the dried dough's] appearance by their desire to prevent it from crumbling and breaking up in the soldier's knapsack. I can testify to the fact that there wouldn't be any crumbs, even if you carried the knapsack with the dried dough through the entirety of Europe. It was impossible to break up and bite such boulders. Perhaps you could suck on it, but it didn't fit in your mouth. . . . Even now I want to find out who came up with that idea.

We were very tired of meat, which was either salted or canned. Our supply troops, as well as the soldiers in the combat formations, acquired abandoned and ownerless cattle. While there could be no talk of vegetables before and during the spring, we often found large quantities of preserved fruit and vegetables remaining in the cellars of settlements abandoned by the Germans and from which the local German population had fled with their retreating forces, or from which the Poles had been driven out by the Germans. Of course, we put these to good use.

Trophy [captured] stockpiles in southern Poland were overflowing with sugar. My scouts prepared an extremely strong syrup by pouring hot tea over half of a flask of sugar. Such a concentrated solution fortified us very well during the required shifts at the FOP [forward observation post]. This situation with the food supply was understandable: first of all, our transport was barely able to supply us with ammunition and fuel, and, secondly, they weren't overeating on the home front either. Everything was like Tvardovsky [a Russian poet] described it [when he wrote], "In the defense one way or another, in the offense we go hungry!"[72]

To compensate for the chronic shortages of food and help the soldiers endure the other deprivations associated with life in the field, in particular, the ever-present specter of sudden violent death, the NKO also instituted a daily ration of spirits, in this case Russian vodka, in much the same fashion the British Royal Navy relied on grog to inspire its seamen afloat. The NKO introduced the concept of a daily vodka ration to its soldiers on 25 August 1941, when it ordered its *fronts* and armies to "issue 100 grams of 40-proof vodka per day to Red Army soldiers and command cadre in the forward line of the operating armies beginning on 1 September 1941," and "issue vodka equal to that of the forward line units to Red Army VVS flight crews that are carrying out combat missions, and to engineer-technical personnel who are serving at the operating armies' field airfields."[73] This order made the *fronts'* and armies' military councils responsible for organizing and delivering the vodka and for assigning "special individuals" to secure, distribute, and account for vodka distribution based on the *fronts'* overall requests.

Apparently the military authorities had second thoughts about the wisdom of issuing vodka to its troops on such an indiscriminate basis. On 11 May 1942, the GKO directed the NKO to cease the wholesale distribution of vodka by establishing new criteria for its distribution only on an incentive and celebratory basis. Signed by Stalin and effective on 15 May, the order directed *fronts* to "cease the massive daily issue of vodka to personnel in the operating armies' forces" and issue daily vodka rations "only to forward line soldiers" in units that distinguished themselves in combat," although it increased the ration to these soldiers to 200 grams per day. In addition, *front* armies were to issue 100 grams of vodka daily to front-line soldiers on specific holidays.[74]

Since vodka soon became virtual currency among Red Army soldiers, quite naturally abuses began occurring and commanders frequently failed to follow the NKO's guidance regarding its proper distribution. In fact, these the abuses became so widespread that, on 12 June 1942, the NKO sent a caustic warning to responsible commanders:

> Despite repeated instructions and categorical demands regarding distribution of vodka to the operating army exactly as prescribed by established norms, lately instances of unlawful distribution of vodka have not ceased. Vodka is being issued to headquarters, command cadre, and subunits that do not deserve to receive it. By exploiting their duty positions, the commanders of some units and formations and the command personnel in headquarters and directorates are taking vodka from warehouses without due regard to orders or established procedures. The *fronts'* and armies' military councils are controlling the distribution of vodka poorly and inventory control of vodka is unsatisfactory in units and warehouses.[75]

Perhaps concerned about the adverse impact of its previous orders on the soldiers' morale, only days before the Red Army began a major offensive operation, the NKO once again revised its rules for distributing vodka on 13 November 1942, this time by increasing the ration. Specifically, field armies were to issue:

> 100 grams per person per day to subunits of units that are conducting direct combat operations and are located in trenches in the forward positions, subunits conducting reconnaissance, artillery and mortar units that are attached to and supporting the infantry and are located in firing positions,

and combat aircraft crews upon the fulfillment of their combat missions, and 50 grams per person per day to regimental and division reserves, to combat security subunits and units that are working in the forward positions, to units that are fulfilling responsible missions in special cases (constructing and repairing bridges and roads, and others in special working conditions under enemy fire), and, on the instructions of doctors, to the wounded who are located in medical service field installations. . . .

In the Trans-Caucasus Front, issue 200 grams of "strong" [fortified] wine or 300 grams of table wine instead of the 100 grams of vodka, and, in place of the 50 grams of vodka, 100 grams of strong wine or 150 grams of table wine.[76]

This order also designated the total vodka allocation to operating *fronts* during the period from 25 November through 31 December 1942:

Front and Separate Army	*Consumption Limit (in liters) (% of total)*
Karelian	364,000 (6.4)
7th Separate Army	99,000 (1.7)
[MCL]Leningrad	533,000 (9.4)
Volkhov	407,000 (7.2)
Northwestern	394,000 (6.9)
Kalinin	690,000 (12.1)
Western	980,000 (17.2)
Briansk	414,000 (7.3)
Voronezh	381,000 (6.7)
Southwestern	478,000 (8.4)
Don	544,000 (9.6)
Stalingrad	407,000 (7.1)
Total (vodka)	5,691,000 (100)
Tran-Caucasus (strong wine)	1,200,000

If vodka distribution was any indication of the importance of forthcoming offensive operations, the Western and Kalinin Fronts' allocation was the largest, followed by the Don, Leningrad, and Southwestern Fronts.[77]

As the Red Army expanded its offensive operations during the winter of 1942–43, the NKO also expanded the parameters of its vodka distribution policy. For example, presumably after receiving complaints from Red Army aviators, on 13 January it granted "personnel and technical personnel in VVS units of the operating armies and VVS units based on military district territory but equal to units in the Red Army" a vodka ration of 50 grams per day, although it restricted distribution to "only on the days of flights on combat missions."[78] Finally, after the winter offensive ended, on 2 May, the NKO increased the vodka ration for troops engaged in offensive combat at the front lines and all troops on recognized holidays to 100 grams per day.[79]

Despite the NKO's stringent controls over vodka distribution, abuses continued. For example, a 7 December 1942 report by a commissar in the

20th Army's 8th Guards Rifle Corps, which was spearheading the Western Front's offensive in the Sychevka region, lamented that "the soldiers received the agreed upon norm of vodka extremely irregularly."[80] In addition, although the NKO seemed to consider the vodka ration a critical ingredient in maintaining soldier's morale, on occasion it had a distinctly adverse impact on discipline and the course and outcome of some military operations, as described in a report prepared on 31 March by the 60th Army's 121st Rifle Division:

> Recently we have observed many incidents in the division's units that are unacceptable for Red Army soldiers and commanders, including drinking binges, which have spread among the command personnel to a considerable extent. Instead of ceasing this unnecessary phenomenon, in some instances, unit and subunit commanders have encouraged these persons and often participated in these brawls themselves, which leads to a loss of a soldierly state of mind in some Red Army soldiers and, in other instances, the divulging of military secrets. Inebriated persons have employed weapons while drunk, and, as a result, unnecessary and completely unwarranted losses have occurred. While in an inebriated state and without cause, on 27 March 1943, Senior Lieutenant Remizov, the commander of an automatic weapons company in the 383rd Rifle Regiment, shot two Red Army soldiers in a burst of submachine-gun fire.
>
> The 121st Rifle Division's commander, Major General Ladygin
> The 121st Rifle Division's chief of staff,
> Lieutenant Colonel Generalov[81]

In addition to these reports, the German archives also document many instances of assaults by Russian troops fortified by vodka or other alcoholic means. For example, while capturing the city of Zhitomir in November 1943, the 1st Ukrainian Front's 1st Guards Cavalry Corps also liberated the German Fourth Panzer Army's wine, brandy, and schnapps warehouses. Within days, a German counterattack against what Germans described as "thoroughly inebriated cavalrymen" recaptured the city.

Clothing

Its enormous expansion from 1939 through 1941, its chaotic mobilization after war began, and the damage the advancing *Wehrmacht* inflicted on it during Operation Barbarossa combined to create massive shortages of uniforms and military kit in the Red Army. For example, during the first week of the war, *Wehrmacht* forces captured 60 logistical warehouses and more than 400,000 sets of uniforms in the Western Front's sector alone. As a result, the army experienced huge shortages of uniforms and other military kit throughout the summer and fall of 1941, forcing newly mobilized armies and divisions to assemble and deploy into combat partially uniformed and lacking much of their weapons and other items of equipment.

As early as 25 June, for example, the Western Front's 2nd Rifle Corps reported, "The corps' units . . . have no auto transport, and many soldiers lack uniforms."[82] Less than a month later, on 26 July, Lieutenant General P. A. Kurochkin, commander of the 20th Army, reported that his army, which was still mobilizing, "was considerably understrength in personnel and logistical units. . . . Attempts to fill out the army with soldiers and NCOs who have straggled from their units has had no effect since the majority of these [soldiers] are not armed and uniformed, and the army has no reserves of weapons and uniforms."[83] On 31 July, Marshal Budenny, commander of the Southwestern Direction, complained to Stalin, "All divisions completely lack kit bags, towels, foot bindings, steel helmets, raincoats, mess tins (except the 301st Division, which is short 3,729 pieces), waist belts, and provision satchels" and "sabers, automatic weapons, artillery, ammunition, engineer equipment, signal gear, cavalry trousers, soldiers blouses, steel helmets, raincoats . . . are completely absent in the cavalry divisions." He went on to report, "The formation of the Odessa Military District's divisions is unsatisfactory. The 273rd Rifle Division . . . has . . . no weapons, engineer gear, equipment, and clothing." Budenny concluded by informing Stalin, "The period the General Staff allocated for formation has turned out to be unrealistic, and the central supply administrations have done nothing to provide forming divisions with equipment and gear called for by organizational tables."[84]

A soldier assigned to a people's militia division recalled that the situation did not change for the better in the fall:

> In October 1941 I found myself in the Moscow *narodnoe opolchenie* (people's militia). I was in the eighth grade and lived in the Arbat. One day our entire middle school at Potylikha, the one near Mosfilm Street, was assembled in the schoolyard. They issued us small caliber hunting rifles, one for every five men, and also gave us five sabers. That was it! There were no uniforms; everyone wore whatever they arrived in and went off to fight in the same clothes. The literature teacher, a handsome man who was good to students, became our commander.[85]

As a result, throughout the summer and fall, the GKO and NKO instituted extraordinary measures to supply adequate uniforms, in particular warm clothing, to mobilizing soldiers so they could survive the impending winter. For example, on 3 July, the GKO ordered the Far Eastern Front and Trans-Baikal Military District to transfer 500,000 sets of winter uniforms and underwear and 1,030,000 foot bindings and warm winter gloves from their emergency supply warehouses to warehouses in Omsk, Cheliabinsk, Sverdlovsk, and Chkalov.[86] Later, on 11 August, the NKO ordered its military commissariats to "temporarily cease issuing uniforms and kit to personnel in Red Army rear service facilities, organs of local military directorates, and district and central apparatuses, hospitals, warehouses, military academies, military schools, and others" and "provide all of [these] new uniforms and kit . . . to the nearest central or district clothing warehouse by 25 August to support units being sent to the front."[87]

After the State Control Commission inspected army warehouses in September and discovered numerous deficiencies in the maintenance and distribution of uniforms and other kit, on 11 October the NKO relieved the responsible officers and ordered Division Quartermaster N. I. Kuznetsov, chief of the Clothing Supply Directorate, and other responsible commanders to establish firmer control over the warehouse system. At the same time, it ordered the commanders of the Ural and Volga Military Districts to confiscate uniforms from rear service personnel and turn them in to central and district warehouses for distribution to soldiers in the operating *fronts*.[88]

Even after solving many of these initial clothing supply problems, the NKO issued an order, on 3 March 1942, highlighting "disgraceful incidents of misappropriation and squandering of military uniforms and kit" in operating *fronts* and frontal regions. Claiming that "the people's property is often being stolen by persons who are directly responsible for its safety and storage" and "a considerable amount of military clothing is also being wasted from neglect at storehouses and during transport and cart transport" by "various sorts of hostile elements who have entered the Red Army," Stalin blamed this phenomenon on "commanders, military commissars, political workers, and chiefs of services" who "have lost their sense of obligation to the Motherland for the people's property entrusted to them."

Since "criminal elements and all sorts of direct or indirect enemy stooges are revealing and will continue to reveal themselves in the multi-million-man Red Army," Stalin declared, "the primary mission of commanders, military commissars, political workers, and suppliers is to prevent theft and bad management, expose thieves, swindlers, and ne'er-do-wells in timely fashion, and punish them mercilessly to the full extent of Soviet law."[89]

In response to Stalin's harsh criticism, on 4 April the GKO issued new regulations concerning the distribution of uniforms and military kit, establishing stringent controls over the storage and distribution of all military goods and making commanders and chiefs at all levels responsible for implementing the regulations. For example, the regulations required commanders of units and formations to "conduct an investigation in all instances of loss, waste, or misappropriation of goods and combat losses. The persons found guilty of deliberate wastage of goods will be answerable in criminal proceedings, and the goods will be eliminated from the books by a certificate of investigation."[90]

Despite these warnings and the new regulations, shortages of some types of warm winter uniforms continued to plague the Red Army. As evidence of this fact, the NKO ordered military districts, *fronts,* and armies, on 4 April 1942, "to cease issuing greatcoats to soldiers and noncommissioned officers in rear service units and facilities and to some categories of soldiers and, instead, issue them [two-sided] quilted jackets."[91] Once again, it threatened that "persons found guilty of violating this requirement will be strictly answerable in accordance with the law 'Concerning the Protection of Red Army Property in Wartime.'"[92] Although supply problems persisted, these and other measures ensured that Red Army soldiers were better protected than their *Wehrmacht* counterparts against the rigorous assault of the brutal winter of 1941–42.

The shortages in uniforms eased considerably in 1942, in part because Soviet industry began producing uniforms and other items of kit in sufficient quantities and in part because the volume of Lend-Lease deliveries increased.[93] Many former Red Army soldiers still recall the improving supply situation. For example, a soldier assigned to the 77th Naval Rifle Brigade, which was operating in northern Karelia in December 1943, recalled his living conditions:

> It was cold, scary, and difficult. Just try to survive for almost three weeks in 20–30 degrees of frost! [Centigrade]. That's right! We were pretty well dressed in *valenki* [felt boots], quilted pants, and winter camouflage coveralls; then padded jackets, our uniforms, warm flannel underwear, and even regular linen underwear under it all. They gave us vodka and fed us 100 grams of bread per man per day. We had American canned meat. Tasty bitch! A large can had pork fat inside, which you could spread on top of a slice of bread and, in the middle, a piece of meat the size of a fist. All in all, we didn't starve. . . . [We also had] *salo,* a dried bread. We even had oil lamps, of the so-called "push-press" variety. It was a small tin, like one for preserves, which contained stearin [oil] diluted with alcohol. If you ignited this mixture, it burned with a colorless flame. You could warm food or boil water. But why would you burn alcohol–you should drink it! That's why we dragged a rag through it and wrung it out. Perhaps you could get 50 grams of alcohol, and, since we received several of these tins, you could drink a decent amount, although it was, of course, disgusting; however, the remaining candle wax also burns.[94]

Another young officer recalled:

Junior officers, NCOs, and privates received the same uniform until war's end, soldiers' greatcoats with hooks instead of buttons and tarpaulin boots, which, contrary to common opinion, were not at all heavy at all, but instead were lighter than regular leather boots. However, their tops quickly became frayed at the creases, and, after two months of use, if not earlier, started letting water in. Many people had shoulder boards (with stars on the officers' shoulder boards), hats, and pilot caps that were self-made. Skilled workmen cut the stars and emblems from tin cans that came from the "second front" (tins of American pork called *tushonka*), and sewed them on with threads. Those who could use needles embroidered the stars on their shoulder boards with white thread, although the white thread soon became indistinguishable from the shoulder boards' color.

Few wore their peak caps near the forward positions. We all lived in the same conditions as one big family, and officers, NCOs, and privates literally ate from the same mess tin, drank from the same flask, and covered ourselves with the same greatcoat in pairs, by using the second one as a common bed. And our exterior differences weren't great, visible only up close. That closeness, determined by our comradeship-in-arms, corresponded completely to the requirements of camouflage and security.

Before war's end, when they provided our division, and perhaps other divisions as well, with our last issue of uniforms [before war's end], the officers received trousers and tunics made of a light silky sand colored fabric, which differed sharply from the usual khaki cotton fabric received by the NCOs and privates.[95]

ORDER AND DISCIPLINE

Political Control

One of the most perplexing questions associated with the Soviet-German War is why Stalin's Red Army, which suffered even more devastating defeats and grievous losses than its tsarist predecessor suffered during World War I, emerged victorious over Hitler's *Wehrmacht* instead of collapsing like the tsar's army did in late 1917. For example, the tsar lost two armies and 245,000 men in the Battles of Tannenberg and the Masurian Lakes in the late summer of 1914, while Stalin lost three armies and 748,850 men during the first two weeks of Operation Barbarossa. Furthermore, while the tsar lost 2,254,369 men during the entire war and fielded an army of 6,752,700 men on 1 May 1917, Stalin lost at least 6,155,000 soldiers from 22 June 1941 through 18 November 1942, and another 2,553,400 soldiers from 19 November 1942 through 31 December 1943, for a total of 8,708,400 soldiers out of the 29 million soldier his army fielded by war's end.[96]

At least in part, the answer to this question is political. The tsar's army collapsed in 1917 because it was waging an increasingly unpopular war and because skillful and relentless political agitation undermined the will and morale of its soldiers, producing mutinies, wholesale desertion, and finally the army's utter collapse under the hammer blows of the enemy and a welter of revolutionary agitation. In contrast, Stalin's army remained a coherent, viable, and reliable military force throughout its war in spite of even greater defeats and losses because an armada of commissars and political workers exercised stringent political control and military tribunals and other security organs used harsh punitive measures ruthlessly and effectively to enforce discipline within its ranks. Equally important, Stalin's soldiers also fought on both because they were defending their fatherland against foreign invaders and because they had no other choice but to do so.

Stalin established and maintained political control over the Red Army through an elaborate system of commissars and political workers *(politruki)* at virtually every level of command. Similar to political apparatuses within every sector of Soviet government, industry, agriculture, and society, these ubiquitous Party representatives constantly monitored troops' political reliability and morale and, whenever necessary, acted forcefully to ensure strict discipline. The Presidium of the Supreme Soviet of the USSR formed this pervasive system of political watchdogs on 16 July 1941, when it ordered the established of the so-called Institute of Military Commissars, which consisted of a complex network of political commissars and political workers responsible for monitoring the loyalty of soldiers and officers, their fulfillment of assigned orders, and maintaining absolute military discipline within every level of command.[97]

This system of political control remained in effect until 9 October 1942, when the Party felt secure enough to replace it with the principle of unitary (single) command *(edinonachalie)*. By doing so, the NKO ordered "all commissars in units, formations, headquarters, military-educational institutions, and the NKO's central and main directorates and political workers in subunits be freed up from their assigned duty positions and assigned as these commanders' (chiefs') deputies for political affairs," and *front* and army commanders were to "confer military command ranks on these political workers within their assigned rights within one month."[98]

While disbanding the Institute of Military Commissars, this order actually did not significantly alter the Red Army's structure for political control since military councils continued to control the Red Army's *fronts* and armies and deputy commanders for political affairs performed many of the same functions as their commissar predecessors at every other level of command. However, it did tacitly underscore Stalin's confidence that senior commanders had attained a satisfactory level of political reliability.

Disciplinary Regulations

Symbolic of the striking differences between the tsars' armies and Stalin's army, when the Germans destroyed Tsar Alexander II's 2nd Army at the Battle of Tannenberg in September 1914, its commander, General Samsonov, committed suicide on the battlefield amid his defeated army. In contrast, when the *Wehrmacht* destroyed the Red Army's Western Front during July 1941, Stalin simply executed its commander, General Pavlov, on charges of treason. Unlike Alexander II, Stalin ruthlessly enforced iron discipline in the Red Army initially and throughout the entire because he had to if he was to avoid suffering Alexander's fate.

Stalin had good reason to fear such an eventuality. First, the staggering defeats and combat losses the Red Army incurred in 1941 and 1942 naturally undermined the morale of its soldiers. Second, as indicated by countless instances of individual and even collective desertion, frequent disobedience to seemingly unreasonable orders, routine exploitation of self-inflicted wounds to escape combat, and a host of lesser violations of regulations and outright crimes, the high probability of perishing in combat, the privations they had to endure, and latent hostility toward Stalin's regime by the sons and daughters of millions of repressed kulaks and collectivized peasants, undermined the morale and loyalty of many Red Army soldiers.

A directive the *Stavka* sent to the Northwestern Front on 10 July 1941 vividly underscored this problem:

> The *Stavka* of the High Command and the GKO are completely dissatisfied with the Northwestern Front's work.
>
> First, to date you have not punished commanders who have failed to fulfill our orders and who, like criminals, have abandoned their positions and have withdrawn from their defensive positions without orders. With such a liberal attitude towards cowardice, you cannot defend.
>
> Your destroyer detachments have not worked to date, and the fruits of their labors are not apparent. The Northwestern Front's units are constantly recoiling to the rear because its division, corps, and army commanders and its *front* commander are inactive. It is time this shameful matter ceases. Begin active operations immediately, in the first place, using destroyer operations at night with small detachments.

> The commander and the member [commissar] of the military council, the [military] prosecutor, and the chief of the 3rd Directorate [OO] will immediately go to forward units to deal with cowards and criminals on the spot. Organize active operations on the spot to destroy the Germans and to attack and destroy them at night.
>
> G. K. Zhukov, chief of the General Staff[99]

After Marshal Timoshenko's Western Front lost the city of Smolensk on 16 July and a sizable number of his forces in encirclement, on behalf of the GKO Stalin accused him and his subordinate commanders of displaying an "evacuation attitude" by surrendering the city too easily. Declaring such commanders as "criminals who committed treason against the motherland," Stalin demanded they "nip such an attitude, which disgraced the honor of the Red Army, in the bud with an iron hand," and "hold on to Smolensk at all cost."[100] A recent Russian historian confirmed this problem:

> In reality, after the enemy's panzer groups penetrated our defenses, some commanders lost their heads and did not know what to do. Finding themselves in this situation, they either abandoned their positions without orders or moved in an eastern direction, trying to conceal themselves in the forests. NKVD reports to the GKO indicate that, from the beginning of military operations up to 20 July, the NKVD's Special Departments in *fronts* and the armies halted 103,876 soldiers who had lost their units and were withdrawing along the roads in disorder. The majority of those who were detained were then used to form new military units and sent back to the front in those units.[101]

Rokossovsky, whose Iartsevo Group prevented the Western Front from collapsing during the Battle for Smolensk and helped countless Red Army soldiers escape from the Smolensk encirclement, later described the general breakdown in discipline:

> To my great regret, about which I have no right to be silent, I encountered a great number of instances of cowardice, panic, desertion, and self-mutilation to evade combat among the soldiers. At first, this so-called "left-handedness" appeared when [they] shot themselves in the palms of their left hands or shot off one or several of their fingers. Then we noted "right-handedness" began to appear, which was done in the same way, only with the right hand. Self-mutilation occurred by agreement; a pair of soldiers would mutually shoot one another in the hands. Soon a law was issued that mandated the highest penalties (execution) for desertion,

> evasion of combat, "shooting oneself," and insubordination to superiors in combat conditions.[102]

After General Kachalov, the commander of the 28th Army, perished courageously while leading his army in a counterstroke south of Smolensk, on 16 July a vindictive Stalin issued his infamous Order No. 270, which declared, "Lieutenant-General Kachalov, the commander of the 28th Army, displayed cowardice and fell captive to the German Fascists while encircled with a group from his force's staff."[103] Nor was the situation much different in other fronts. For example, on 29 July, Major General I. I. Alekseev, the commander of the 6th Rifle Corps in the Southwestern Front's 6th Army, castigated his forces for lack of discipline in the face of enemy attacks, declaring, "Make it known to all personnel that no one has the right to withdraw a single step from his occupied defensive position without orders from above."[104] Only weeks before, on 3 July, the Southwestern Front's Political-Propaganda Directorate had complained about the excessive number of desertions in Alekseev's rifle corps to Army Commissar 1st Rank Lev Mekhlis, chief of the Red Army's Main Political Propaganda Directorate, stating, "During the period from 29 June through 1 July 1941, the Southwestern Front's Third Section [OO] arrested 697 deserters, including 6 command cadre. We have arrested as many as 5,000 deserters from the 6th Rifle Corps during military operations."[105]

Later still, Stalin and Zhukov indicated their attitude to the problem in a telephone conversation on 4 September during the heavy fighting around Smolensk:

> Zhukov: I will employ it [the 211th Rifle Division] as a reserve and not let it sleep. I request you allow me to arrest and condemn [execute] all scaremongers to which you refer. Over.
>
> Stalin: The 7th [as the date of the attack] will be better than the 8th. We welcome and permit you to judge all of them with full severity. Over and goodbye.
>
> Zhukov: Good health.[106]

Stalin clearly articulated the standards he expected his officers and soldiers to adhere to in a GKO decree dated 16 July. Although he declared that, "in a majority of instances Red Army units are holding the great banner of Soviet power high and are behaving satisfactorily and sometimes openly heroically while fighting for their motherland against the fascist plunderers," he claimed that "some commanders and soldiers are displaying unsteadiness, panic, and disgraceful cowardice, and, by throwing down their weapons and forgetting about their debt to the motherland, they are crudely violating their oath, transforming themselves into herds of sheep, and running away in panic before the impudent enemy." As a result, Stalin announced the GKO would "employ severe measures against cowards, panic-mongers, and deserters . . . to protect unsullied the great profession of the Red Army soldier." "Henceforth," he declared, we "will stop any appearance of cowardice and disorganization in the ranks of the Red Army with an iron hand, remembering that iron discipline in the Red Army is the most important condition for victory over the enemy."[107]

By listing by name nine senior officers who would be executed for committing these crimes, Stalin's 16 July was a clear message to all Red Army soldiers and officers that he would enforce discipline at all cost. Thereafter, Stalin quickly condemned and executed all senior officers who failed to live up to his expectations along with their key subordinates, in particular, those who permitted themselves to be captured.[108]

Military Tribunals

Stalin's chief instrument for administering military justice was an elaborate system of military tribunals, all functioning under military procurators, the Soviet equivalent of public prosecutors. Established by the GKO and NKO on 23 June 1941 immediately after the two organs placed the Soviet Union on a wartime footing, this military tribunal system was responsible for dispensing justice and enforcing military discipline. The accompanying NKO regulations provided legal justification for the military tribunal system, established its organizational, territorial, and jurisdictional parameters, and described the specific procedures it was to follow:[109]

> On the basis of paragraph 57 of the Law Concerning the Judicial System of the USSR and those of the union and autonomous republics, military tribunals will function: a) in military districts, *fronts,* and naval fleets; and b) in armies, corps, and other force formations and militarized facilities. The People's Commissariat of Justice of the USSR will reorganize line courts of rail and water transport into military tribunals corresponding to the railroads and water routes of communications.[110]

As far as their authority was concerned, military tribunals were to "examine matters related to their jurisdiction under Article 27 of the Criminal-Legal Codex of the RSFSR and corresponding articles of the criminal-legal codes of the other union republics," and those in military districts, *fronts,* fleets, armies, and flotillas were to "examine matters related to their jurisdiction under the Regulation of the Central Executive Committee (TsIK) of the USSR of 10 July 1943." After detailing the specific jurisdictions of tribunals from front down to division level, the regulations described the precise rights, composition, and procedures the tribunals were to employ.[111]

In short, the regulations empowered military tribunals, which consisted of three permanent members, "to investigate matters beginning 24 hours after the accused is handed over for confinement" and "to inform the military councils of the districts, *fronts,* and armies and the commanders of corps and divisions about the work of military tribunals in the struggle with crime in appropriate military formations." Although sentences of military tribunals were "not subject to appeal," the military districts', *fronts'*, and armies' military councils, and the military districts', *fronts'*, and armies' commanders could "exercise the right of suspending death sentences (by shooting) by simultaneously notifying the chairman of the Military Collegium of the Supreme Court of the USSR and both the chief military prosecutor of the Red Army and the chief prosecutor of the navy by telegraph through proper channels of his opinion concerning the matter for further resolution."[112]

In addition to enforcing military order and discipline by employing quick, harsh, and often summary justice to identify and root out criminals and "shirkers," military tribunals also enforced discipline without wasting precious manpower by employing a pervasive system of penal or disciplinary units throughout the Red Army.

Penal (Disciplinary) Units

When war began, the Red Army maintained a fairly well-developed system of disciplinary battalions to which it assigned soldiers found guilty of a wide range of crimes. As defined by a 6 July 1940 order of the Presidium of the Supreme Soviet of the USSR, a disciplinary battalion was a "special" military unit consisting of fixed-term soldiers who were serving sentences for various crimes committed while serving in the armed forces, in particular, multiple absences without leave.[113]

However, in light of the severe losses the Red Army suffered during the first few months of the war, in August Stalin decided to abolish these disciplinary battalions to generate fresh manpower to reinforce the Red Army's operating *fronts.* At his direction, the Presidium of the Supreme Soviet of the USSR published a decree on 12 August that declared, "*Fronts'*, [military] districts,' and fleets' military councils are authorized to free all servicemen from disciplinary battalions and send those freed [soldiers] to operating units of the Red Army and the VMF [navy], with the exception of those whom the military councils recognize as unreliable and injurious for the front."[114]

This order, which did not apply to the Soviet Union's eastern regions, required the NKO to assign convict-soldiers released from the disbanded disciplinary battalions to either regular Red Army military formations or so-called penal *(shtrafnye)* units in the operating *fronts.* However, since the order did not formally define the actual composition or functions of penal units, during the fall of 1941 and the first six months of 1942, individual *front* commanders formed and employed penal units made up of soldiers and officers sentenced for breeches of the disciplinary codes on an ad hoc basis. Although many of these penal units existed, there is little documentation about their activities, and the NKO did not systematize their formation or employment throughout the Red Army.

However, when the Red Army once again experienced heavy casualties and decaying discipline during Operation *Blau* in the summer of 1942, Stalin concluded drastic measures were needed to restore discipline and, at the same time, provide new manpower for the Red Army. As a result, in addition to easing the age restrictions on military service, on 28 July 1942 Stalin issued his infamous Order No. 227, since known as the "Not a Step Back" order, which, while addressing the apparent breakdown in discipline, also helped solve the critical shortage in manpower by authorizing the employment of criminals, both common and political, in the Red Army's ranks.

Underscoring the gravity of the situation, Stalin acknowledged, "The enemy is throwing new forces forward to the front and, despite increasing losses, is thrusting forward, bursting into the depths of the Soviet Union, capturing new regions, devastating and smashing our cities and villages, and raping, robbing, and murdering our population."[115] Convinced that "some foolish people at the front are consoling themselves with discussions that we can retreat further to the east since we have great territories, much land, and a large population, and that we will always have an abundance of bread [grain]," Stalin accused these soldiers of wishing, "to justify their shameful behavior at the front," but added, "such talk is spurious and false through and through, and it is advantageous only for our enemy."[116]

Therefore, he declared, "We must radically nip in the bud the talk that we have an opportunity to retreat without end and that our great territory, our great and rich country, and our large population and bread will always be in abundance" because "such talk is false and harmful, and it weakens us and strengthens the enemy because, if the retreat does not cease, we will be left without bread, without oil, without metal, without raw materials, without mills and factories, and without railroads." Concluding that the time had come "to end the retreat," Stalin announced the slogan, "Not a step back!" declaring, "We must stubbornly defend every position and every meter of Soviet territory to the last drop of our blood and cling to every shred of Soviet land and fight for it to the utmost."[117]

Striking at the very heart of the problem, Stalin asked, "What are we short of?" and answered rhetorically, "We are short of order and discipline in our companies, battalions, regiments, and divisions, in our tank units, and in our aviation squadrons. This is now our main shortcoming. We must institute the strictest of order and iron discipline in our army if we wish to save the situation and defend our Homeland." Therefore, since "we can no longer tolerate commanders, commissars, and political workers whose units and formations willfully abandon their positions," and "we can no longer tolerate it when commanders, commissars, and political workers permit a few panic-mongers to determine the situation on the field of battle so that they entice other soldiers to retreat and open up the front to the enemy," these "panic-mongers and cowards must be exterminated on the spot."[118]

Declaring that "company, battalion, regimental, and division commanders, and associated commissars and political workers who retreat from their combat positions without orders from higher commands are enemies of the Homeland" who must be treated as " enemies of the Homeland," Stalin demanded all commanders and commissars implement a series of stringent measures designed to restore "iron discipline" within the Red Army's ranks "to defend our land, to save the Motherland, and to exterminate and conquer the hated enemy."[119]

Specifically, Stalin ordered all *front*, army, corps, and division commanders to "unconditionally eliminate the mood of retreat in the forces and halt the propaganda that we must and can supposedly retreat farther to the east and that such a retreat will supposedly not be harmful," and "relieve from their posts army [corps, division, regiment, and battalion] commanders and their commissars who permit unauthorized retreats by their forces from occupied positions without an order from [their senior commanders] and send them to the *Stavka* [or *fronts*] for trial by military court."[120]

In addition, Stalin ordered the creation of new generations of penal battalions and so-called blocking detachments within each of the Red Army's operating *fronts* and armies, the former "to redeem themselves with their blood for their crimes against the homeland," and the latter "to shoot panic-mongers and cowards on the spot in the event of panic and unauthorized retreat" (see below). Specifically, depending on the situation, Stalin ordered *fronts* to form "one to three penal battalions (of 800 men each), assign all junior and senior commanders and corresponding political workers from all types of forces who have been guilty of violating discipline by their cowardice or unsteadiness to them, and place them in the most dangerous sectors of the front," and armies to form "from five to ten penal companies (of 150–200 men each), assign common soldiers and noncommissioned officers who have been guilty of violating discipline by cowardice and unsteadiness to them, and place them in dangerous army sectors."[121]

Three days after issuing Order No. 227, on 1 August, Stalin ordered the commanders of the Moscow, Volga, and Stalingrad Military Districts and the NKVD to begin forming penal battalions in the form of "assault rifle battalions," each consisting of 929 former command cadre (company commanders and higher) who were imprisoned in special NKVD camps. Stalin ordered them to be employed "in the most active sectors of the front," where they would have an opportunity "to demonstrate their devotion to their motherland with weapons in hand." As a recent Russian historian has noted, "These former commanders released from the special camps were immensely fortunate that they somehow reached the front" because "they knew that the majority of them would lay down their lives, but this death provided hope for freeing themselves and their families from the dishonor and retribution that threatened them during their sojourn as prisoners or in their surroundings."[122]

In the wake of Stalin's initial orders regarding penal service, on 28 September, the NKO issued but did not openly publish yet another order formally creating penal battalions and companies in all operating armies and also issued three official *shtats* detailing their precise composition.[123] According to these instructions, which precisely defined their purpose, subordination, and employment, these penal subunits were to "provide an opportunity to individual mid-level and senior command, political, and command cadre personnel who have violated discipline by cowardice or unsteadiness, to redeem their honor before the motherland with their blood by virtue of courageous struggle with the enemy in the most difficult sectors of combat operations."[124] Under the direct supervision of their military councils, *fronts* were to form one to three penal battalions and armies five to ten penal companies, the former attached to subordinate rifle divisions and separate rifle brigades and the latter to rifle regiments.

The military councils were also responsible for specifying precisely where each penal battalion and company would operate within their operational sectors and for providing them with reliable command and political cadre. Specifically, they were to assign "commanders and *politruki* who have distinguished themselves the most in combat," as penal battalion and company commissars, platoon commanders and *politruki*, and other permanent command cadre.[125] Those assigned to these positions were authorized to "use every measure of action up to and including execution [shooting] on the spot for disobedience to an order, self-mutilation, and fleeing from the field of battle or an attempt to desert to the enemy."[126] In compensation for performing this service, which was often dangerous, officers assigned to penal subunits served only half as long as their counterparts in regular rifle battalions and companies, and each month of their service in penal subunits qualified them for six months' regular pension. As far as their authority was concerned, these commanders and political commissars enjoyed "disciplinary authority" equivalent to officers commanding two full levels above their command levels.[127]

As far as the convict-soldiers, or *shtrafniki,* themselves were concerned, they had to serve from one to three months in either penal battalions or companies before they earned release–if they were fortunate enough to survive their ordeal. On the other hand, *shtrafniki* could be appointed as corporals, junior sergeants, or sergeants by their battalion or company commanders, and fortunate *shtrafniki* could also receive combat awards or even be freed ahead of time if they distinguished themselves in combat.[128] In addition to those who served their full term in penal subunits, *shtrafniki* who were wounded in combat were judged to have served their sentences, were restored in rank and all rights, and, after recovering, were sent back to regular combat units, while those invalided out of the army received pensions commensurate to the pay they received before entering the penal subunits. Finally, the families of *shtrafniki* who perished in combat received pensions similar to the families of other serving soldiers.[129]

Within a month after authorizing the wholesale formation of penal subunits, on 16 October, the NKO extended the scope of penal service to encompass all soldiers serving in the Soviet Union's internal military district, in particular deserters. Repeating the original justification Stalin provided in Order No. 227, the NKO applied virtually the same criteria to all soldiers throughout the Soviet Union, particularly those soldiers who were convicted by military tribunals but whose sentences were deferred until war's end. To move the convicts forward to the front, the NKO required specific military districts to create march companies (commands) made up of convicted soldiers to reinforce specific operating *fronts* on a one-to-one basis.[130] Ten days later, on 20 October, the NKO expanded the legal basis for forming and employing penal forces by ordering forces garrisoned and deployed along communications routes in the rear area to send its "problem" soldiers to penal subunits. As justification it noted:

> Recently, numerous instances of violations of military discipline have been noticed in a number of rear-area garrisons and, in particular, at railroad stations. Soldiers are drinking heavily, crudely violating dress codes and regulation requirements when addressing chiefs and seniors, and wandering in groups along the streets and bazaars. Instances have been noted where soldiers have sold clothing and products in the market as well as instances of begging, despite the fact that all sorts of rascals and dubious elements often engage in begging under the guise of soldiers. . . . The wounded and sick who have been discharged from hospitals and soldiers who have deserted from the front are responsible for a considerable portion of the violations of military discipline and these instances of disgraceful conduct.
>
> This situation exists because of the low expectations of commanders with regard to their subordinates, their weak attentiveness to disciplinary matters, and the failure by command cadre and NKO organs to properly struggle with these unsatisfactory phenomena.[131]

To resolve this problem, the NKO established strict order and discipline in garrisons, along communications routes, and in market places and bazaars, "to struggle decisively with desertion," primarily by creating "halting point-blocking commands *[komendatura]*" along the railroads and sending patrols into towns and villages to catch and arrest a vast array of violators, which included:

> [D]eserters; those absent without leave from trains and commands; malicious violators of military discipline who discredit the Red Army, namely, hooligans, drunkards, and those who begin to argue with commanders; soldiers who, when following orders given by the commands, clearly violate the established regulations of the command; . . . soldiers who do not salute their chiefs and seniors as well as the slovenly and those dressed not according to form; . . . soldiers who are guilty of begging; civilians who are engaged in begging under the guise of soldiers; militarily-obligated civilians who are detained for evading military registration or summons for military service; and soldiers found guilty of selling items of military clothing.[132]

Vividly illustrating how it applied these disciplinary orders, on 30 January 1943, the NKO sent a junior officer assigned to the 310th Rifle Division of the Volkhov Front's 4th Army to a penal battalion for "slandering" his commanders. In this case, a certain junior lieutenant, S. O. Karamal'kin, had sent a letter to the army newspaper *Red Star* requesting he be summoned to Moscow to report "serious facts that expose great people." While in Moscow, Karamal'kin "subjected the actions of all of his commanders to criticism, beginning with his company commander and ending with his army and *front* commanders," and "without presenting any proof whatsoever, claimed many commanders groped their way through their command duties, only to exploit their great authority and save their skin." Therefore, the NKO accused Karamal'kin, who "received a barely perceptible scratch on his hand," before "hastily beating it from the front," and who "was not an immediate participant in the battle," of trying "to bring false accusations against his command," and sentenced "Semen Osipovich Karamal'nik to be sent to a penal battalion for three months with reduction in rank to private for fault-finding and an attempt to slander his commanders and undermine discipline in his subunit."[133]

Although these and other severe punitive measures did indeed tighten up military discipline, combined with other measures, such as the continued use of draconian forced recruitment, they also tended to undermine discipline. For example, during its unsuccessful attempt to capture Ryl'sk, on 12 March 1943, the 60th Army's 121st Rifle Division reported that "discipline among its personnel fell precipitously during the period of offensive combat operations" since "soldiers and their commanders no longer maintain their required military bearing and neither tucked in [their boots] nor saluted their superiors." As a result, the division commander ordered the organization "of one hour of military training daily for all personnel in all of the division's units to focus first and foremost on the troops' external appearance (such as the correct wearing of headgear, the tucking in of greatcoats, waist belts, equipment, leg-wrappings, etc.)"[134]

While these disciplinary violations bordered on the petty, other reports spoke of more serious instances of drunkenness and self-mutilation among soldiers and even officers. For example, after taking part in the unsuccessful Orel-Briansk-Smolensk offensive, on 25 March 1943, General Batov, the commander of the Central Front's 65th Army, reported the presence of "unstable elements in our army's units who, motivated by cowardice, have carried out various crimes, including especially widespread self-mutilation." Batov asserted "22 men have been exposed and identified as self-mutilators just in the 246th Rifle Division" during the first half of March, "most of which occurred in the 908th Rifle Regiment." "Self-mutilation," he added, "is most prevalent in the 37th Guards, 246th, and 354th Rifle Divisions."[135]

Within the context of these decrees and orders, the NKO formed and employed a total of well over 200 penal battalions subordinate to its operating *fronts* and probably as many as 400 penal battalions and companies subordinate to its operating armies from 1 August 1942 to war's end. Allowing for some local variations, on average penal battalions were organized into two or three rifle companies, heavy and light machine-gun companies, an antitank rifle company, and antitank, mortar, sapper, and signal platoons, for a strength of about 800 men. Separate penal companies were organized into three to six rifle platoons and supporting machine-gun, mortar, and antitank platoons, for a strength of 150–200 men and, on occasion, as many as 700 men.

As was the case with regular Red Army forces, as the war progressed, *fronts* and armies reinforced their penal subunits with additional antitank and submachine guns and improved their reconnaissance capability by reinforcing them with reconnaissance platoons. These reinforcements increased the average penal company's strength to over 200 men by mid-1943. Quite naturally, these "holding areas" for the condemned experienced appallingly high attrition rates while fulfilling their routinely hazardous missions.

Archival records now indicate that, excluding their permanent nonconvict cadre, the total number of *shtrafniki* serving in penal subunits increased from 24,993 in 1942, to 177,694 in 1943, and then decreased to 143,457 in 1944 and 81,766 in 1945, for a wartime total of 427,910 men.[136] However, these grim figures do not include thousands of convict-soldiers who served in "unofficial" penal units prior to 1 August 1942.

Accurate data do not exist for other wartime years; however, Russian archival documents indicate the total number of penal battalions subordinate to operating *fronts* in 1944 fluctuated from a high of 15 in January to a low of eight in May, for a monthly average of 11, and the average strength of a penal battalion during the year was 227 *shtrafniki.* That same year, the total number of penal companies assigned to field armies ranged from a high of 199 during April to a low of 301 in September, for a monthly average of 243, and the strength of penal companies during the year was 102 *shtrafniki.*

With regard to their casualties, the same records indicate that a cumulative total of 170,298 *shtrafniki* serving in penal subunits were killed, fatally wounded, wounded, or fell ill during 1944. On a monthly basis, the average losses of permanent cadre and *shtrafniki* in all penal units during the year was 14,191 soldiers or 52 percent of their average monthly strength of 27,326 men. This grim toll was three to six times greater than the overall average monthly personnel losses suffered by regular Red Army units in offensive operations in 1944.[137]

With regard to their combat employment, as Stalin demanded, most *fronts* and armies employed their penal subunits to perform the most harrowing missions in their "most dangerous" sectors. This involved conducting assaults against fortified positions (a Red Army version of the concept of the "Forlorn Hope," which the British Army employed during the Napoleonic wars), attacking bypassed strong points, and "manually" clearing minefields before and during offensive operations. For obvious reasons, few *front* and army commanders employed penal units during the exploitation phase of offensive operations, when opportunities for individual or collective desertion arose. In return for performing these hazardous tasks, the NKO returned *shtrafniki* who were fortunate enough to survive penal service to regular Red Army units and annotated, "Expiated his guilt with his own blood" on their service records.[138]

Many archival records now document the Red Army's employment of penal subunits, although not always with positive results. For example, on 18 March 1943 General Rokossovsky, the commander of the Central Front, complained about the poor performance of penal companies during offensive operations his *front* was conducting west of Kursk:

> An investigation of instances of treachery against the Homeland that took place in the 13th, 70th, 65th, and 48th Armies has established weak discipline and unsatisfactory organizational work in training and educating personnel in penal companies and battalions and flagrant violations of NKO Order No. 227 regarding the employment of penal subunits. The desertion to the Germans by 19 men from the 179th Penal Company of

> the 13th Army's 148th Rifle Division, which Major General Mishchenko, the division commander, had sent on reconnaissance, was especially intolerable. The commander of the 148th Rifle Division grossly violated the NKO's Order No. 227, which required penal subunits be employed for particularly difficult missions with mandatory blocking detachments following after them. This was not done in the 148th Rifle Division. The penal troops displayed cowardice; a portion of them fled from the field of battle, and 19 men surrendered to the enemy. This company's command personnel did not train their personnel satisfactorily, and it is apparent that special department [OO] representatives functioned ineffectively because they were unaware in advance of the squad's planned treachery.[139]

Rokossovsky concluded his report by ordering his army commanders "to employ penal subunits only in situations that permit blocking detachments to be deployed immediately following them."[140]

In addition, many former *shtrafniki* now recall their service in penal subunits with varying degrees of fondness. For example, V. V. Karpov, a soldier in the 134th Rifle Division who became a Hero of the Soviet Union in 1944, recalled:

> I went on an attack many times after I arrived in the penal battalion. I was lucky since I was never even wounded. In the first company, out of the 198 soldiers who were assigned, only six survived. I then served in the second company, but once again I escaped injury. They threw us into the most dangerous sectors, sending us to almost certain death, at first even without artillery cover. Later it became better. The penal companies went into action together with everyone else, but they were still in the forefront.[141]

Another soldier, this time a sergeant, also recalled his service in a penal unit:

> I was put into a penal company where there were about 150 of us. We were armed only with rifles. We had neither SMG's [submachine guns] nor machine guns. All of the officers were regular commanders, not prisoners; but the soldiers and noncommissioned officers were prisoners. You could get out of the penal battalion alive either by being wounded or if you gained the commander's approval in combat and he recommended that your conviction be removed. Yes, [my conviction was removed]. It was at Taganrog in the Southern Front. I participated in a reconnaissance-in-force. Since the situation was do-or-die, I performed my combat task diligently and it worked. Right after that they recommended that my con-

viction be removed, and, several days later, I was called to the military tribunal at division HQ where they removed my conviction. After that, I was sent to a regular unit. [I was in the penal unit] for three weeks.

The most terrible thing was an attack–that's the hardest test. You know that you might get hit, but you have to keep moving forward–that's horrible! It was difficult to get up and most felt that they would never come back. That was also difficult. The mortar shelling was terrifying as well as the machine gun fire. There was enough of everything. Tracer fire, when it starts from above, and you only see the luminescent line lower, lower, falling toward you, now it will reach your level and cut you in half. Well, in short, war is war, what is there to talk about?[142]

Finally, a veteran of the 73rd Rifle Corps' 213th Rifle Division in the 1st Ukrainian Front's 52nd Army recalled his experiences with a subordinate penal company:

We received one penal company around Görlitz during April 1945. What did that mean? While they were primarily criminals, bandits, thieves, and also demoted officers, most were soldiers who failed to follow orders. The situation was such that every penal company member had to buy his life with his blood. After being wounded he was absolved of his crime. The company took a position on a hill near Görlitz, lay down, and exposed their arms and legs to German fire hoping to be wounded and therefore free.

The commander of the penal company fulfilled the orders of the battalion commander. His first concern was to see to it that none of the people would desert to the Germans. And he had the right, as did any regular officer, to shoot the man right on the spot for such an attempt (no such right existed in a regular unit). The company fought next to us for two weeks, and I know of four cases where the company commander shot his own men (four men).[143]

Although no comprehensive "order of battle" exists showing the number of penal subunits the Red Army employed during the war, fragmentary Russian and German archival materials indicate that operating *fronts* and armies employed as many as 600 penal battalions and companies during wartime (see Table 13.3).

Blocking Detachments

In addition to employing penal units to enforce discipline in the Red Army's ranks, the NKO also authorized the formation and employment of so-called blocking detachments *(zagraditel'nye otriady)* to prevent Red Army soldiers or entire units from deserting in the face of enemy fire and to round up deserters and potential conscripts. For example, Stalin's Order No. 227 required each army to form three to five blocking detachments with up to 200 men each and employ them in the immediate rear of "unsteady" divisions to "shoot panic-mongers and cowards on the spot," in the event they panicked or retreated without orders to do so.[144]

Actually, Red Army field commanders had begun employing blocking detachments on an ad hoc basis as early as the fall of 1941 to prevent desertion under fire and restore stability within their forces. For example, on 24 September 1941, Major General A. Z. Akimenko, commander of the famous 2nd Guards Rifle Division, reported employing similarly harsh measures to prevent a portion of his division from deserting while it was defending the city of Glukhov against Guderian's advancing panzers:

> The 395th Rifle Regiment stubbornly held on to its position and assisted the 875th Rifle Regiment with its fire. However, a large group of 70–80 enemy tanks attacked the junction of the 535th and 395th Rifle Regiments from the railroad station north of the village of Kholopkovo. Although they wedged into and burst through both regiments' combat formations, the units defended stubbornly. However, unexpected confusion and an extraordinary incident occurred in our combat formations.
>
> When the tanks attacked our positions and burst into the 2 regiments' combat formations, about 900 replacement troops from Kursk committed treachery against our Homeland. As if by command, this group rose up, threw their rifles away, and proceeded toward the enemy tanks with their hands raised. The enemy tanks quickly edged up to the traitors and began to take the traitors away under protection of the tanks. This event seriously affected the morale of our troops. Although I saw this situation occur while I was at my observation post, I lacked the forces and means necessary to remedy the situation and seize control of the traitors so that our Soviet organs could punish them. But a traitor is a traitor, and he deserved immediate punishment on the spot. Therefore, I ordered two artillery battalions to open fire on the traitors and the enemy tanks. As a result, a considerable number of the traitors were killed and wounded, and the enemy tanks were scattered. I reported this extraordinary incident to the *Stavka* of the Supreme High Command by ciphered message.
>
> The division had received the group of traitors from a reserve brigade in the city of Kursk. At that time, the 2nd Guards Rifle Division received 5,000 men, who were poorly trained and even more badly prepared in an ideological sense. The Kursk *oblast'* party committee was informed about

> the treachery. The party *obkom* [*oblast'* committee] bore the responsibility for political training and ideological preparation of the population.[145]

Several weeks before, on 5 September, B. M. Shaposhnikov, who had just been appointed as chief of the General Staff, specifically authorized General Eremenko, the commander of the Briansk Front, to employ blocking detachments during his offensive in the Roslavl' region: "The *Stavka* has familiarized itself with your report and will permit you to create blocking detachments in those divisions that show themselves to be unreliable," Shaposhnikov stated. "The purpose of these blocking detachments is to prevent unauthorized withdrawal by units and, in instances of flight, to halt them using all necessary weaponry." However, he added, "The question of assigning one rifle company to each artillery battalion," which Eremenko had apparently requested by done to ensure they remained reliable, "is under discussion, and we will report the *Stavka's* decision to you later.[146]

Therefore, Stalin's Order No. 227, which required blocking detachments be employed routinely, only confirmed a practice the army was already employing on a widespread basis. Furthermore, Stalin also assigned the mission of creating blocking detachments to the NKVD as well as to regular Red Army troops. One Red Army veteran recalled:

> The soldiers knew well that, while on the offensive, there were MVD troops three kilometers to the rear of the advancing infantry and all who lagged behind would be shot. On one occasion during March 1945, we were approaching an elevated railroad embankment through which there were passages blocked by heavy barriers. The battalion commander ordered me to remove the barriers so that the rear services could move through. By that time the MVD troops had arrived. If a representative of the division's operations section who knew me had not been present, I would have been shot. They would have only been concerned with why I lagged behind.[147]

A report prepared on 16 March 1943 by Major General Petrushevsky, chief of staff of the Central Front's 13th Army, underscored the need for blocking detachments by claiming that unreliable "replacements are joining the ranks of the Red Army from regions liberated from the enemy's forces." Noting the increased need to "struggle against possible instances of desertion and avoidance of military service," on behalf of the army commander, Petrushevsky ordered subordinate commanders to "strengthen the blocking duties of the army's blocking detachments, systematically conduct universal inspections of the entire male population in all population points, comb all forests and orchards thoroughly and examine all haystacks, uninhabited buildings, and especially dugouts situated along the lines of the old defenses, and strengthen the inspection of documents of those passing through the populated points and suspicious persons."[148]

Officially at least, the NKO appeared to abolish the practice of employing blocking detachments in regular Red Army forces in late 1944.[149] However, as archival evidence and numerous eyewitness accounts now confirm, some commanders continued to use blocking detachments to enforce Red Army discipline until war's end, although, by this time, NKVD and MVD forces performed most of these grisly tasks.

MOTIVATION AND MORALE

It is now abundantly clear that the iron discipline demanded and administered by Stalin and his senior political and military henchmen served as the essential "glue" that bound the Red Army together as a coherent fighting force and permitted it to survive and, ultimately, prevail despite the appalling combat conditions its soldiers had to endure. As one Russian soldier recorded, "Shoot, kill, bury, go on the attack, reconnoiter–war. And hungry, barefoot women wandering God knows where with their knapsacks and hungry children; old men, refugees, those who have lost everything in the conflagration–this is the horror of war."[150]

Constant fear and the ever-present brutality of the war motivated Red Army soldiers in distinct but varied ways. On the one hand, fear and dread of the ruthless enemy often fostered panic and desertion in the Red Army's ranks. One conscript, a soldier who was drafted in August 1941 and sent straight into combat in one of the Red Army's most famous rifle divisions, poignantly described this fear and dread:

> I received my notice right in the middle of my workday. They called me to the office, I arrived, and they said, "Get your things packed, Shelepov, tomorrow morning go to the address mentioned on the slip." That was in August 1941, but I do not remember the date, and it was quite a surprise. At that time, I lived in Kineshma, a small town near Ivanovo. What a landscape! The Volga region! They collected us all up and took us to the [infantry] school in Ivanovo. They told us first the course would last three months. However, since the Germans apparently broke through, after two weeks we were all armed and sent to the railway station on trucks. Then we went directly from the railroad station to the front near Smolensk.
>
> Our 161st Rifle Division was incorporated into the [Western Front's] 2nd Rifle Corps.[151] We received our first dry tack [food] by nightfall, and our regiment assaulted the German's positions without any artillery support

the next morning. It seemed as if the whole division took part. It was quite a feeling. Just an hour ago I was a civilian and now I had a rifle in my hands. I knew war was scary, but I could never imagine such an all-embracing horror. I am wasting my time telling you about it because it is impossible to describe. The feeling was that you lived your whole life without any past or future. For some time thereafter, I swear that I could not even move because of shock! Of course, the company commanders walked around and warned us that we would attack at dawn. However, it all happened in a very strange way. I do not know why I do not remember that fight in detail. While some fights still stand out in my memory as if they happened only yesterday, my first combat experiences are very vague. I will always confuse them.

The squads stayed huddled together in shallow trenches, and we covered ourselves with branches so that the Germans would not spot us. Although I thought that someone would cry, "Forward!," that we would all shout, "Hurra!," and we would attack, everything turned out quite different. Our company commander said quietly, "Let's go, guys!" and climbed out on the parapet, and I did the same. I followed him automatically, without realizing what I was doing. We quietly stood up and just walked forward. We did not even run. We just walked. There were no "Hurras!," no noise, and no shouting. We just stood up and went ahead. It was still dark, and there was fog over the fields. There was dead silence all around and just the quiet rattling of our weapons. I do not remember how, but suddenly the scene changed. It turned out that they were firing like crazy at us, first rifles and then two machine guns. Or was it machine guns right away? Damn it–I don't remember. Then we all ran forward, bending. I ran behind a guy, but I don't know his name. Throughout the entire assault, all I only remember was his back with a bag-pack. I don't remember anything else.

I ran as fast as I could, but where I ran, I do not know. A cry, "Forward," rang out in my head, but I don't think I really shouted it. I do not know how long I ran, perhaps a second or even an hour, because time stopped for me. Suddenly something hit me from the side. I thought I even flew through the air and then fell to the ground. I jumped up and fell again, this time from pain. My foot!!! My foot was twisted with pain. I tried to turn and see what happened to my foot, but I couldn't see. As I crept forward, I then thought, "Wait! Why am I creeping forward? I need to go back to the medical unit." However, for a long time, I could not understand where "back" and "forward" were. Smoke was all around with constant explosions, shooting, and crashing sounds. The whole battlefield was littered with people convulsing from pain and other debris.

I found my bearings and crept back. In desperation I thought I would never make it back to our lines. Then someone grabbed my foot and pulled. I think I even blacked out from pain. I do not know how I ended up in the trench. The commissar was right there! And he said, 'What the hell are you doing here, Coward!' I said that I was not a coward but was wounded in my foot. 'Where is the wound?' he shouted. Although I could not find the wound myself, a medic rushed on stage, touched my foot, and laughed loudly, saying, "It is a dislocation, now I am now going to pull on your foot and heal you!" Before I could say "Mama," he grabbed my foot and pulled it! The commissar just shook his head, my cursing was so strong. I didn't know myself I could curse so strongly.

Oh no!, the commissar didn't order an investigation. Since he needed me, why would he do so? He just asked which unit I came from and then left me alone. After he learned that I was from the 3rd Company that had unloaded the night before, the medic thawed and said that the companies were returning. "Again, it all came to nothing, damn it! So many people are lost in vain." "You creep over to your friends," he said, "and look out, because the Germans are going to send their air force now." He added, "You were really lucky today. Remember this day! All of your friends are going to be dead now."

We didn't attack again because there was nobody left to attack with. Together with the lieutenant, the company was reduced to 10–12 soldiers. The sergeant major, I still remember his last name, Chumilin, was killed. I feel so sorry for him now, I don't know why I should, but I do. Although he was only 20 years old, his hair was already gray, and he was missing a finger. But I don't know anything more about him.

Of course, we took part in more attacks, actually twice. Those who survived the war were lucky because their fate was unusual. Those whose fate was usual died without even firing a shot and without even seeing the Germans.[152]

In the words of another soldier-survivor:

We were afraid of death. Death was around us every day, every hour, and on all sides. You could sit quietly, drink tea, and a stray shell would fall on you. It was impossible to get used to that. It doesn't mean that we were all constantly jittery and that everyone sat and walked expecting death at any moment. Death simply came or it didn't. It was scary during the massed air raids. People lost their minds from fear. The feeling was as if every bomb was falling straight at your head. It was horrible! This armada floats in the sky, two or three hundred aircraft, and bombs fall like hail, and all of them howl. Terror! I remember, there was one Nekrasov–he almost went mad. When the air raid was over, he couldn't be found anywhere. Then we found him in some trench. And he refused to come out! And what terror was in his eyes!

Those who returned from the war either became fatalists or found faith in God. Nowhere could the hand of fate be found so clearly, so rigidly and unavoidably, like there. I experienced this myself, and not just once.[153]

Perhaps the aspect of the soldier's existence that generated the greatest fear was his realization of the utter anonymity associated with death in combat:

We bury our dead comrades in the evening. The bodies wrapped in ground sheets are placed in a half filled and slightly straightened trench. These were comrades-in-arms with whom we did not even have time to become acquainted. Two short speeches. The earth falls with a dull sound. Flashes from the officer's handguns punctuate the darkness. I salute with everyone else. Although the grave is marked on the commander's map, there is no marker. Who knows who will control this land tomorrow.[154]

On the other hand, this same constant fear and dread of the enemy that tormented Red Army soldiers also strengthened their resolve never to fall captive to the Germans. Incessant reports of German brutality, such as one recorded on 27 November 1942 by the commissar of the 8th Guards Rifle Corps during the fighting near Rzhev, only reinforced their resolve: "The soldiers of the 148th Rifle Brigade witnessed the brutal execution of three wounded Red Army soldiers by Hitlerite scoundrels. An examination of the bodies indicated that the soldiers, who had been wounded by fire, were then burned while still alive. The Fascist monsters wound rags and towels soaked in flammable liquid around the wounded and threw them into a bonfire."[155]

Fear, however, was a two-way street, since many Red Army soldiers feared, and sometimes hated, their own commanders and commissars as well. In the words of one veteran:

If you attack, you should run until its end and never duck for cover! If you lie down, you will never lift your ass from the ground again. You could also get a bullet from the company commander, since he had this right. It was his duty to make you attack, and neither the battalion nor the regiment commander would have charged him if he had shot someone. Right away, our company commander warned us that, if we lay down, he would shoot all of us, and he really did shoot some. After that, we never tried to lie down again.[156]

Although naked fear of the enemy and their own officers and commissars, pervasive and constant propaganda and political agitation, and threats of severe disciplinary measures and outright intimidation motivated Red Army soldiers to fight, they also fought and endured because they were patriotic. Whether or not they despised Stalin's regime, like their ancestors before them, they understood that foreigners were invading their motherland *(rodina).* Even those who welcomed the Germans as liberators came to realize that, instead of freeing the Soviet population from Bolshevik bondage, the Germans were conducting an Aryan crusade to enslave the "Slavic subhumans *(untermenschen).*" Nor did the Germans' brutal treatment of the populations in the territories they occupied disabuse the population of this truth.

Therefore, as their ancestors had resisted Mongol Tartars, Teutonic Knights, Lithuanians, Swedes, French, Poles, and Germans, Russians rose up against the invaders, this time under the red rather than the imperial banner. Understanding this feeling, and perhaps also motivated by a degree of desperation, Stalin himself resurrected the names of Russia's "great captains" of the past, its traditional military ranks, orders, and awards, and, to a lesser extent, even the despised banner of Russian Orthodoxy, and mobilized them all in the service of achieving victory. More extraordinary still was the apparent willingness of other ethnic nationalities living within the Soviet Union to share in Stalin's crusade against Nazism, which, at least in part, validated the Bolsheviks' attempt to overcome ethnic divisions and produce a genuine Soviet people.

For whatever reason, crude patriotism, whether rooted in pan-Slavism, traditional Russian nationalism, some sort of loyalty to the Soviet state, or sheer hatred of the German invaders, proved a powerful bond and motive force within the ranks of the Red Army. As expressed by one woman soldier:

> I became a Party member when I was 17 years old. It was easy; you were a candidate member for three months and then became a full member. I must say that most Communists behaved with dignity during the war. A person had to fill out a tricky questionnaire before being enrolled in the Party. One of the questions was, "What class did you come from?" I was very smart and wrote honestly, "From the nobility."[157] Out of the blue, I received an order to report to the chief of our division's political department. As I stood before his piercing eyes, he asked me, "Girl, do you understand what you have written? Are you out of your mind?" I was highly educated and answered that Lenin was a nobleman himself. In any case, he did not make me rewrite that questionnaire.
>
> Patriotism was a real thing and that is no exaggeration. Every one of us fought for our motherland. I never heard that anybody cried out, "Long live Stalin!" or even "Hurrah!" during battle. Many people carried a cross.

> Some people wore icons in pouches around their necks. The army consisted mostly of peasants. People tried to find ways to escape enlisting, maybe not the youth, but their parents who understood that the front meant death.[158]

When asked what motivated her to fight, a young woman defender of Leningrad added:

> Despite the immense human suffering, being young and a small part of the people as a whole, I believed in victory and gave no thought whatsoever to the surrender of Leningrad. All those who surrounded me at home, at work, and in military service maintained a high moral spirit. All of our exertions and thoughts during the war years were only of victory. We believed in Stalin and our military leaders and also in the motto, "Our victory is just, victory will be ours."
>
> Many years later there is talk that we should have surrendered Leningrad in order to avoid such loss of human life. But if you ask me about this, I will answer, "No!" It was better to die than to live under the Germans. We heard much about the death camps and gas chambers. The Germans were a brutal enemy for us all and for me as well. I simply hated the Germans for a long time. Now, at the age of 77, the emotion has become blunted, and, yes, Germany has become quite different and repentant for what occurred. But God forbid such a war ever again occur.[159]

Trying to explain what impelled him to fight, a young lieutenant later wrote, "Perhaps these notes will help someone understand certain details and the general environment of those years, and, if I was successful, the whole optimistic, tragic, and heroic spirit of that time, when most people knew and believed, 'Our cause is just. Victory will be ours.'"[160]

Finally, if fear, harsh discipline, and the all-consuming fire of patriotism failed to motivate soldiers to fight on, there was also a certain inertia associated with the numbing effects of war that impelled them to do so. Like anesthesia administered to a patient before painful medical surgery, the sounds, sights, and pains of war consumed and mesmerized soldiers, rendering them incapable of recoiling against its horrors. In essence, the war itself hardened many of the soldiers and made them its own creatures until they were consumed by the conflagration or returned to society as survivors. In the poignant words of another veteran, "During war everything is from the perspective of war. Is there anything other than the savage dictates of war? At times, feelings of compassion are also remolded into something more in line with war. Although I am not higher, wiser, more ignoble, or cleaner than war, I belong to it."[161]

CONCLUSIONS

Collectively, the soldiers who made up the Red Army during wartime formed a complex mosaic of warriors, some reluctant, some enthusiastic, but many not, representing men and women, peasants, blue and white collar workers, nomadic herdsmen, bureaucrats, criminals, misfits, ne'er-do-wells, and even the sons and daughters of the Soviet *nomenklatura* (ruling class). Whether volunteers, conscripts, or impressed civilians, these soldiers came from every ethnic and religious group inhabiting the Soviet Union's vast territories, and even groups living outside of the country's prewar borders.

Ranging in age from under 17 to over 55 years, dedicated Communists and Komsomol members served and fought alongside the apolitical, sons and daughters of former nobles and kulaks, members of exiled if not almost exterminated ethnic groups, and "politicals" both pardoned and condemned. Together, the educated and the illiterate, the cultured and the uncultured, the skilled and the unskilled, and the healthy and not so healthy shared and endured the privations of a war that exacted a deadly toll on them all.

Ultimately, about 35 million souls manned a Red Army that expanded in size from a force of 5.4 million soldiers serving in 27 armies, 95 corps, and 303 divisions on 22 June 1941 to a force of roughly 10 million soldiers assigned to 94 armies, 253 corps, and 838 divisions on 31 December 1943.[162] During this period the army suffered 8.7 million irreplaceable combat or noncombat losses and roughly 19.7 million wounded or ill and lost over 250 divisions or division equivalents destroyed in combat.

Of the 35 million soldiers who served in the Red Army during wartime, over 21 million (67 percent) came from the Russian Federation, including roughly 19 million (90 percent) who were ethnic Russians and another 6.4 million soldiers (19 percent) who were primarily Slavs conscripted in the Ukraine and Belorussia. The remaining 6.9 million soldiers raised in the Soviet Union's other union and autonomous republics included as many as 3.5 million non-Slavic soldiers, bringing the number of non-Slavic soldiers to as many as 8 million. In addition, roughly 1 million women soldiers served in the Red Army, at least 500,000 of these in combat forces, principally in PVO, MPVO, and aviation forces, and another 500,000 women performed uniformed service in traditional noncombat duties or supporting forces.

Although the Red Army's soldiers varied widely with regard to their ethnicity, social origin, education, ideology, and temperament, they all had many experiences in common. First and foremost, they fought in a massive army that suffered equally immense casualties regardless of when, where, or how it fought, largely because its senior leaders frequently, if not routinely, exploited the country's seemingly inexhaustible supply of manpower and senselessly disregarded the value of human life by callously squandering soldiers' lives in the defense of their homeland. After fighting hungry during the first 18 months of the war, thereafter, they relied on foraging and "scrounging" to compensate for the inadequacy of their daily rations. For most of these soldiers, luxury was defined as a loaf of bread, one or two potatoes, and a crude piece of fat each day. Worse still, in addition to their perpetual hunger, they shared in shortages of weapons, uniforms, and proper kit, at least during the first six months of the war, although their German counterparts fared little better in this respect.

In short, all of the Red Army's soldiers endured a Spartan existence and learned to survive on a subsistence basis. Although their daily vodka rations alleviated their suffering to a degree, improved their morale, and stiffened their soldierly resolve, too often it also undermined their discipline and dulled the combat skills they needed to survive.

All of the Red Army's soldiers also lived, fought, and frequently died within a military system controlled by an elaborate and extensive network of political commissars and political workers *(politruki),* and later deputy commanders for political affairs, who permeated the army's entire force structure from *front* down to company level and exercised absolute and pervasive political control over their lives. Through incessant political education, agitation, encouragement, and often intimidation and with their own separate chain of command and military reporting system, these "watchdogs" of the Communist Party ensured that discipline and order prevailed and detected and ruthlessly stamped out any and all dissension in the ranks. At the same time, together with soulless representatives of the internal security services, the watchdogs and tribunals of the prosecutor's justice system enforced arbitrary and harsh discipline and administered swift summary retribution and punishment against soldiers, often by gruesomely imaginative means.

Commander and commissar alike exploited the Soviet Union's draconian legal code and the Red Army's simple but efficient military tribunal system to enforce order and discipline within their forces, at the same time skillfully exploiting the sinister instrument of penal subunits to restore their authority when order and discipline flagged. Finally, commanders also relied on intimidation by blocking detachments to prevent disobedience of orders or desertion, at first as a last resort and later more routinely.

In the end, those Red Army soldiers who survived the war while enduring this harsh discipline, near constant fear, and outright intimidation, did so, first and foremost, because they were conditioned to do so. Unlike their counterparts in Western armies, the Red Army's soldiers were products of a political system and society whose innate harshness replicated life in the military in many ways. It was but a short step from the internal passports, arbitrary arrests and confinement, punishment by imprisonment, death, or internal exile, and other restrictions many civilians experienced during the peacetime years to the political controls, disciplinary measures, and individual or collective punishments soldiers experienced during wartime. In short, just as many civilians became accustomed to surviving in Soviet society, the Red Army's soldiers became accustomed to coping with and surviving in the military. The principal difference in this regard was that, during wartime, Red Army soldiers had to survive the *Wehrmacht* as well.

Whether worker, peasant, or bureaucrat, Slav or non-Slav, man or woman, Orthodox, Muslim, Jew, or atheist, and whether motivated by "Soviet" patriotism, "Great Russian nationalism," sheer love of the motherland, or simple hatred of the German invaders, most Red Army soldiers managed to endure unprecedented and unimaginable deprivation and still survive the most terrible war mankind has experienced. By doing so they accomplished the remarkable feat of vanquishing Europe's most formidable military machine in an astonishingly brief period of just under four years, albeit at tremendous human cost.

Table 13.1 Expansion of the Red Army, 1939–1941

Formations and Units	1 Jan 1938	1 Sep 1939	Dec 1940	22 Jun.1941
Armies	1	2	20	27
Rifle corps	27	25	30	62
Rifle divisions	71 regular, 35 territorial	96	152	198
Motorized (mechanized) divisions	0	1	10	31
Cavalry corps	7	7	4	4
Cavalry divisions	32	30	26	13
Rifle brigades	0	5	5	5
Mechanized (tank) corps	4	4	9	29
Tank divisions	0	0	18	61
Fortified regions	13	21	21	57
Airborne corps	0	0	0	5
Airborne brigades	6	6	12	16
Strength	1,513,000	1,520,000	4,207,000	5,373,000

Sources: I. Kh. Bagramian, ed., *Istoriia voin i voennogo iskusstva* [A history of wars and military art] (Moscow: Voenizdat, 1970); A. Ryzhakov, "K voprusu o stroitel'tsve bronetankovykh voisk Krasnoi Armii v 30–e gody" [Concerning the question of the formation of the Red Army's armored forces in the 1930s], *VIZh*, no. 8 (August 1968); and *Boevoi sostav Sovetskoi Armii, chast' 1 (iiun'–dekabr' 1941 goda)* [The combat composition of the Soviet Army, part 1 (June–December 1941)] (Moscow: Voroshilov General Staff Academy, 1963).

Table 13.2 Age (Year Group) of Serving Soldiers and Ethnic Composition of Selected Red Army Divisions, 1941–1945

Division	Date	Composition
1 RD, 63 A	Jul 1942	40% penal troops (58th GRD Dec 1942)
4 RD, 69 A (2nd)	Jul 1944	50% young Russians, 50% older Ukrainians
7 RD, 3 SA (2nd)	May 1943	81% Estonian
8 RD	Jun 1941	Many Kazakh
8 RD, 18 A (2nd)	Mar 1944	80% Russian, 10% Ukrainian, 10% Asians
16 RD (2nd)	Feb–Jun 1943	36.5% Lithuanian, 75% Jewish (Oct 1943: 10% before year group 1908, 40% year groups 1908–1924, 50% 1925).
23 RD	Feb 1943	50% Russian, 50% Asian (year groups 1903–1925) (71 GRD Mar 1943)
29 RD, 64 A (2nd)	Aug 1942	50% Russian, 30% Ukrainian, 20% Kazakh (72nd GRD Mar 1943)
38 RD, 40A (3rd)	May 1944	70% Russian, 20% Ukrainian, 10% non-Slavic
45 RD, 62 A	Jun 1941	95% Uzbek (Oct 1942 50% Uzbek, 20% Kazakh, 15% Tartar, 15% Russian (90% year groups 1897–1922, 10% 1923–1924)(74th GRD Mar 1943)
58 MnRD, 38 A	Nov 1943	95% Russian (90% year group 1925) (50% Ukrainian in Aug 1944)
63 RD	Nov 1942	30–40% Russian, 60%–70% Turkmen (Sep 1943 20% Russian, 80% Turkmen) (52 GRD Nov 1942)
70 RD, 13 A (2nd)	Sep 1944	80% Asian (80% year group 1900–1909)
76 RD	Nov 1942	70% Russian, 30% Azerbaijani (51 GRD Nov 1942)
77 RD, 58 A	Sep 1942	66% Azerbaijani (216 RD Oct 1942)
81 RD, 13 A (2nd)	Feb 1943	60% Turkmen, 40% Russian (most from year groups 1900–1924)
83 MtnRD	Jun 1941	95% Turkmen (128 GRD Oct 1943)
89 RD (2nd)	Dec 1941	95% Armenian
91 RD, 51 A (2nd)	Apr 1942	95% Russian and Ukrainian in year group 1924
91 RD, 21 A (2nd)	Jul 1943	70%–80% Turkmen
92 RD, 59 A (2nd)	Jan 1945	67% Russian, 33% Ukrainian
93 RD, 41 A (2nd)	Sep 1942	50% Kazakh (year groups 1902–1912), many penal troops and GULAG inmates
95 RD	Mar 1943	60% Turkmen, 40% Russian (75 GRD Mar 1943)
96 RD	Jan 1942	70% Russian, 30% Asian (14 GRD Jan 1942)
96 RD, 21 A (2nd)	Jul 1942	All Siberian (68th GRD Feb 1943)
98 RD, Far East	Aug 1941	70% Siberians (year groups 1902–1922) (disbanded Sep 1941)
99 RD	Apr 1943	70% Russian, 30% Asian (88 GRD Apr 1943)
100 RD, 40 A (2nd)	Mar 1942	80% Russian, 20% Tartars and Lapps (Apr 1942 75% Russian, year groups 1898–1923)
102 RD, FE (3rd)	Nov 1942	70% Russian, 10% Ukrainian NKVD (70% year groups 1918–1923, 30% 1903–1917)
103 RD, 6 A (2nd)	May 1942	50%–60% Russian, 20%–30% Kirghiz, 20% Uzbek (90% year groups 1901–1905, 10% 1920–1923) (destroyed in May 1942)
109 RD, Sep. CA	Mar 1942	2,534 Russians (43%), 1,613 Ukrainians (28%), 459 Georgians (8%), 309 Azerbaijanis (5%), 301 Armenians (5%), 249 Jews (4%), 141 Tartars (2%), 63 Lezgins, 58 Ossetians, 50 Belorussians, 23 Moldavians, 21 Kalmuks, 20 Uzbeks (5,841) (destroyed in May 1942)

—*Continued*

Table 13.2 Continued

Division	Date	Composition
110 RD	Sep 1941	90% workers, 60% Communists (DNO) (destroyed in Sep 1941)
111 RD	Mar 1943	40% Asian (24 GRD Mar 1943)
112 RD, 1 RA (2nd)	Apr 1942	Mostly Siberian Russian (year group 1923), many penal troops (Feb 1943 60% Turkmen, 30% Russian, 10% Ukrainian, year groups 1925–1927)
118 RD, 2 GA (3rd)	May 1943	50% Russian, 20% Ukrainian, 30% non-Slavic (Mar 1944 50% Russian, 20% Ukrainian, 30% non-Slavic)
119 RD (2nd)	Nov 1942	50% Russian, 50% Asian and Ukrainian (54 GRD Dec 1942)
121 RD, 38 A	May 1944	80% conscripted Ukrainians
124 RD (2nd)	Nov 1942	80% Russian, 20% Asian (50 GRD Nov 1942)
126 RD, 16 A	Sep 1941	Russian and Uzbek (disbanded Dec 1941)
126 RD (2nd)	May 1943	75% Uzbek, Tartar, and Kazakh
127 RD (2nd)	Jan 1943	60% Russian, 40% Asian (62 GRD Jan 1943)
127 RD (3rd)	May 1943	90% Russian, 8% Ukrainian, 1% Belorussian and Jewish (Apr 1944 60% Ukrainian, 30% Russian)
129 RD (2nd)	Nov 1943	70% year group 1924–1925
131 RD, Ural (2nd)	Jan 1942	90% Russian
132 RD, 60 A	Apr 1944	50% Russian, 50% Ukrainian (Jul 1944 50% Russian, 50% Ukrainian, most year groups 1924–1925)
136 RD (3rd)	Apr 1944	70% Uzbek, 15% Russian, 15% Ukrainian (60% year group 1904 or older)
137 RD, 48 A	Nov 1944	90% Belorussian, 10% Ukrainian
140 RD (4th)	Feb 1943	50% Russian, 15% Ukrainian, 35% mixed non-Slavic (NKVD)
147 RD, 1 GA (2nd)	Mar 1944	90% conscripted Ukrainian
148 RD, 60 A	Sep 1944	65% Russian (year groups 1904–1924), 35% Ukrainians (year group 1924)
149 RD, 13 A (2nd)	Dec 1943	80% Ukrainian
152 RD, 28 A (2nd)	Dec 1944	60% Bukovinian, 30% Ukrainian, 10% Russian
153 RD, 63 A (2nd)	Jul 1942	40% penal troops (57 GRD Dec 1942)
155 RD, 27 A (2nd)	Jan 1944	60% conscripted Ukrainian
157 RD, 44 A	Dec 1941	77% Russian, Belorussian, and Ukrainian, 23% Armenian and Georgian (replaced by Russians and Ukrainians, Jan–Mar 1942) (76 GRD)
162 RD, Ural (2nd)	Jan 1942	70% Russian, 20% Ukrainian (20% penal troop) (disbanded Jul 1942)
162 RD, 65 A (3rd)	Feb 1944	35% Ukrainian, 35% Kazakh, 20% Russian, 10% mixed (50% year group 1923) (Jul 1944 80% Ukrainian (mostly year group 1904)
172 RD, 13 A (2nd)	Jul 1944	65% Ukrainian, 35% Russian (70% year groups 1900–1914, 30% 1914–1925)
175 RD, Siberia (2nd)	Mar 1942	95% Siberian, Bashkir, and Tartar (mostly year groups 1900–1909), 30% penal troops (disbanded Sep 1942)
175 RD, Ural (3rd)	Nov 1942	70% Russian, 25% Ukrainian (mostly year groups 1913–1923) (Oct 1944 90% conscripted Ukrainian and Belorussian)
180 RD, 38 A (2nd)	Sep 1943	50% conscripted Ukrainian (year groups 1894–1926)
181 RD, 27 A	Jul 1941	50% Latvians (disbanded Sep 1941)

—Continued

Table 13.2 Continued

Division	Date	Composition
181 RD, 7 RA (2nd)	Jul 1942	(12,719) 2,271 Communists (18%), 297 veterans (2%), 1,530 kulak penal troops (12%), 8,864 Russians (70%), 2,616 Ukrainians (21%), 298 Jews (2%), 182 Belorussians (1%), 168 Kazakhs (1%), 139 Tartars (1%), 89 Armenians (2,602 under 20 years, 1,515 20–25 years, 2,043 26–30 years, 2,178 31–35 years, 2,280 36–40 years, 2,043 1941–45 years, 81 over 45 years) (destroyed Aug 1942)
183 RD, 11 A	Aug 1941	50% Latvian (Jul 1943 60% Turkmen, 15% Russian, 25% mixed)
193 RD, 62 A (2nd)	May 1942	50% Russian, 50% Azerbaijani, Kirghiz, Siberian, and Cossack (Sep 1942 50% Russian, 30% Uzbek and Kazakh, 20% Communist (NKVD)
195 RD, Volga	Oct 1941	50% Kazakh (disbanded Dec 1941)
196 RD, Ural (2nd)	Jan 1942	80% Kazakh, 20% Russian
202 RD, 70 A	Jul 1943	30% year group 1925
204 RD, FE	Nov 1941	95% Kazakh and Uzbek (78 GRD Mar 1943)
206 RD, 27 A (2nd)	Jul 1944	80% Kazakh, 20% Russian
208 RD, FE	Oct 1941	60% Azerbaijani, 40% Russian and Far Easterner (disbanded Aug 1942)
211 RD, 13 A (2nd)	Nov 1943	70% year groups 1893–1902
212 RD, Ural	Aug 1942	Kazakh, Uzbek, Tartar, and Ukrainian (year groups 1899–1923) (disbanded Dec 1942)
213 RD, 7 GA	Sep 1943	50% Russian and Ukrainian, 50% Central Asian
214 RD, 69 A (2nd)	Sep 1944	50% Ukrainian, 25% Russian, 25% Uzbek
216 RD, 58 A	Nov 1942	60% Azerbaijani (77 RD)
219 RD, 57 A (2nd)	Jun 1943	30% Russian, 30% Ukrainian, 40% Asian
221 RD, Ural	Mar 1942	75% Uzbek, Kazakh, and Kirghiz, 25% Russian (disbanded Nov 1942)
223 RD, 44 A	Sep 1941	95% Azerbaijani (year groups 1905–1921) (destroyed Aug 1941)
226 RD, 66 A	Sep 1942	80% Uzbek, Bashkir, Tajik, and Ukrainian, 20% Russian (95 GRD May 1943)
226 RD, 60 A (2nd)	Jul 1943	90% Russian (Jun 1944 85% Ukrainian, 5% Russian, 5% Tartar, 5% Uzbek (60% year groups 1893–1904, 40% 1905–1916)
232 RD, 60 A (2nd)	May 1942	60% Russian, 30% Cossack, 10% Azerbaijani
233 RD (2nd)	Apr 1942	75% Azerbaijani, 25% Russian (Apr 1943 60% Uzbek and Kazakh (about 10% penal troops)
236 RD, 44 A	Jan 1942	40% Russian, 20% Belorussian and Ukrainian, 40% non-Slavic (disbanded Feb 1942)
238 RD, 11 A (2nd)	Aug 1943	70% year group 1924
244 RD, 28 A	Jan 1942	90% year group 1900 (disbanded in Jun 1942)
244 RD, 6 A (2nd)	Oct 1942	33% year groups 1905–1923, the rest older
248 RD, 28 A (2nd)	May 1942	60% Russian, 40% Kirghiz and Kalmuk (destroyed in Jun 1942)
248 RD, 28 A (3rd)	Aug 1942	80% Russian (year groups 1923–1925)
249 RD, 3 SA (2nd)	Jun 1943	63% Estonian
252 RD, 24 A	Aug 1942	60% Yakut, 40% Russian (Jan 1943 50% Kazakh and Uzbek, 50% Yakut and Russian)
258 RD, 24 A (2nd)	Dec 1942	50% Russian, 50% Turkmen, 20% penal troops (96 GRD May 1943)

—Continued

Table 13.2 Continued

Division	Date	Composition
260 RD, 47 A (2nd)	Mar 1944	70% Russian, 30% Asian and Turkmen
266 RD, Volga (3rd)	Aug 1942	30% penal troops
273 RD, 11 A (2nd)	Apr 1944	70% Ukrainian, 20% Russian, 10% non-Slavic
276 RD, 9 A	Oct 1942	70% Georgian
279 RD, 3 GA (2nd)	Feb 1943	50% Russian, 50% Turkmen
294 RD, 52 A	Apr 1944	65% conscripted Ukrainians
297 RD, 53 A (2nd)	May 1944	80% Ukrainian (year groups 1888–1924)
299 RD, 53 A (2nd)	Aug 1943	60% Uzbek, 40% Russian
303 RD, 60 A (2nd)	Mar 1942	40% Russian, 60% Siberian and others
308 RD, 67 A (3rd)	Jul 1944	Mostly Latvian
310 RD	Jun 1941	Mostly Kazakh
312 RD	Jul 1941	Mostly Kazakh
316 RD, 16 A	Oct 1941	90% Kazakh and Kirgiz, 10% Russian
316 RD, 66 A (2nd)	Jul 1942	95% Kirghiz and Kazakh, few spoke Russian, most were age 35–50 (disbanded Nov 1942)
319 RD, 58 A (2nd)	Aug 1942	70% Caucasian (disbanded Dec 1942)
321 RD, FE (2nd)	Mar 1942	85% Yakut and Buriat (82 GRD Mar 1943)
322 RD, 10 RA	Oct 1941	90% Russian, 8% Communist
324 RD, 10 A	Oct 1941	90% Russian
325 RD, 10 A	Oct 1941	90% Russian (90 GRD May 1943)
326 RD, 10 A	Oct 1941	60% Russian, 40% Tartar
328 RD, 10 A	Oct 1941	90% Russian (31 GRD May 1942)
328 RD, 45 A (2nd)	Jul 1942	50–60% Caucasian (mostly Armenian) (Nov 1944 75% Belorussian, 20% Ukrainian, 5% Russian)
330 RD, 10 A	Oct 1941	90% Russian
332 RD, 10 A	Aug 1941	100% Russian (DNO)
345 RD, 44 A	Dec 1941	38% Russian, 62% Central Asian and Caucasian (disbanded Jul 1942)
349 RD, 3 TA	Feb 1943	70% Russian, 30% Turkmen and Caucasian
352 RD, 60 A	Aug 1941	High percentage of Tartars
353 RD, 46h A	Nov 1943	40% Russian, 60% Tajik, Uzbek, and Turkmen
367 RD, LMD	Dec 1941	Mostly 35–1941 year olds
368 RD, SMD	Sep 1941	Mostly Siberians
370 RD, 69 A	Feb 1945	50% Belorussian, 25% Russian, 25% Ukrainian and Moldavian
372 RD, 59 A	Sep 1941	90% Siberians
385 RD	Nov 1941	Mostly Kirghiz
387 RD, 61 A	Nov 1941	Mostly Kazakh
389 RD, 3 GA	May 1944	50% Russian, 40% Ukrainian, 10% non-Slavic
390 RD	Aug 1941	50% Russian, 50% Armenian (disbanded Apr 1942)
391 RD, 61 A	Sep 1941	Mostly Kazakh
392 RD, 46 A	Aug 1941	Mostly Georgian (Jan 1944 90% Georgian)
394 RD, TCF	Aug 1941	Mostly Georgian
396 RD, 51 A	Sep 1941	70% Caucasian (disbanded Jan 1942)
396 RD, 44 A (2nd)	Nov 1942	10% Russian, 20% Ukrainian and Belorussian, 30% Azerbaijani, 40% Georgian
399 RD, TBMD	Mar 1942	Mostly Siberian (disbanded Jul 1942)
402 RD, 45 A	Sep 1941	90% Azerbaijani (Jan 1944 50% Azerbaijani)
404 RD, 44 A	Dec 1941	Mostly Caucasian (disbanded Jun 1942)
406 RD, 46 A	Sep 1941	Mostly Georgian
408 RD, 45 A	Aug 1941	31% Russian and Ukrainian, 25% Georgian, 23% Azerbaijani, 21% Armenian (disbanded Nov 1942)

—*Continued*

Table 13.2 Continued

Division	Date	Composition
409 RD, 45 A	Aug 1941	95% Armenian
413 RD, FEMD	Sep 1941	Mostly Siberian and Kazakh
414 RD, 44 A	Feb 1942	95% Georgian (disbanded Feb 1942)
414 RD, 44 A (2nd)	Apr 1942	95% Georgian
415 RD	Jan 1942	70% Georgian
416 RD, 44 A (2nd)	Mar 1942	95% Azerbaijani
446 RD, TCMD	Jan 1942	95% Armenian (328th RD 2nd formation)
2 GAbnD, 13 A	Sep 1943	60% Russian, 40% Turkmen (year groups 1923–1925) (Mar 1945 33% Russian, 33% Bessarabian, 33% Lithuanian)
4 GAbnD, 13 A	Aug 1943	60% Russian, 40% Turkmen (80% year group 1925)
5 GAbnD	May 1943	50% Russian, Belorussian, Ukrainian, 50% non-Slavic (50% year groups less than 1903, 20% 1903–1913, 30% 1914–1925)
6 GAbnD, 5 GA	Oct 1943	40% Russian, 35% Ukrainian, 25% non-Slavic (May 1944 60% conscripted Ukrainian, 40% Russian, plus 300 penal troops)
6 GRD, 13 A	Feb 1944	40% Russian, 50% Ukrainian, 10% Asian (25% year group 1925, 40% 1904–1924, 35% before 1904) (120 RD)
7 GAbnD, 4 GA	Sep 1943	50% Ukrainian, 40% Russian, 10% Uzbek (70% year groups 1918–1932, 20% 1901–1913, 10% 1910–1913) (Jan 1944 80% Ukrainian)
8 GRD, 16 A	Dec 1941	95% Kirghiz and Kazakh (Jun 1942 70% Kirghiz and Kazakh, 30% Uzbek) (316 RD)
9 GAbnD, 5 GA	Mar 1945	70% Russian and east Ukrainian, 30% west Ukrainian (year groups 1896–1926)
10 GAbnD	Dec 1943	Mostly year groups 1925–1926 (Feb 1944 mostly year group 1926)
14 GRD, 53 A	Jan 1944	50% Russian, 50% Asian (Aug 1944 25% Russian, 50% Ukrainian, 15% Moldavian, 10% Asian (50% year group 1914) (96 MtnRD)
15 GRD, 7 GA	Apr 1943	50% Russian, 50% Tajik and Central Asian (Nov 1944 90% Ukrainian) (Jan 1945 66% Russian, 33% Ukrainian)
24 GRD, 28 A	Sep 1943	50% Asian (111 RD)
25 GRD, 7 GA	Jan 1945	60% Bessarabian and Moldavian
27 GRD, 1 GA	Jul 1943	50% Russian, 50% mixed
31 GRD	May 1942	90% Russian
33 GRD, 2 GA	Dec 1942	95% Russian and Ukrainian (year groups 1922–1928) (Aug 1943 30% Bashkir)
35 GRD, 8 GA	Nov 1943	70% Ukrainian (Dec 1943 mostly year groups 1925–1926)
39 GRD, 8 GA	Jan 1945	40% Russian, 50% Ukrainian, 10% Uzbek
40 GRD, 5 SA	Apr 1943	10% Kirghiz and Turkmen penal troops
41 GRD, 4 GA	Jul 1944	20% Russian, 80% conscripted Ukrainian
1942 GRD, 40 A	Jan 1944	80% Ukrainian, 20% Turkmen (80% year groups 1893–1913, 20% 1914–1923)
47 GRD, 6 A	Oct 1943	60% Russian (Dec 1943 30% Tartar) (Nov 1944 50% Russian, 30% Ukrainian, 20% mixed)
48 GRD, 57 A	Jun 1943	80% Asian (Jul 1943 40% Russian, 30% Ukrainian, 30% Turkmen)
50 GRD, 51 A	May 1943	70% Russian, 30% Asian (124 RD 2nd)

—*Continued*

Table 13.2 Continued

Division	Date	Composition
51 GRD, 6 GA	Jul 1943	50% Russian, 50% Asian (76 RD)
52 GRD, 6 GA	Jul 1943	30–40% Russian, 60–70% Turkmen (Sep 1943 20% Russian, 80% Turkmen) (63 RD)
54 GRD, 3 GA	Mar 1943	50% Russian, 50% Asian and Ukrainian (May 1944–70% Russian, 30% mixed) (119 RD 2nd)
61 GRD, 3 GA	Jun 1943	95% Kazakh, 5% Russian
62 GRD, 37 A	Oct 1943	40% Russian, 60% Asian (60% year groups 1923–1924) (127 RD 2nd)
66 GRD, 5 GA	Oct 1943	80% Ukrainian (year groups 1895–1926) (Feb 1944 90% conscripted Ukrainian, year groups 1897–1907, 10% 1925)
68 GRD, 4 GA	Jun 1942	Siberian and Turkmen (50% year groups 1918–1924) (96 RD)
70 RD, 38 A	Sep 1944	50% Russian (year groups 1894–1927), 50% Asian
71 GRD, 6 GA	Apr 1943	50% Russian, 50% Asian (year groups 1903–1925) (Jul 1944 90% Ukrainian) (23 RD)
72 GRD, 6 GA	Apr 1943	50% Russian, 30% Ukrainian, 20% Kazakh
73 GRD, 57 A	Apr 1944	95% Ukrainian
74 GRD	Mar 1943	50% Uzbek, 20% Kazakh, 15% Tartar, 15% Russian (45 RD)
75 GRD, 13 A	Sep 1943	80% Turkmen, 20% Russian (year groups 1924–1925) (95 RD, 2nd)
76 GRD, 61 A	Mar 1943	10% penal troops
77 GRD, 69 A	Jun 1944	50% Russian
78[h] GRD, 7 GA	May 1943	80% Asian, 20% Russian (Jul 1943 60% Russian, 40% Asian) (204 RD)
79 GRD, 8 GA	Oct 1943	60% Russian, 20% Ukrainian, 20% mixed (year groups 1903–1926)
80 GRD, 4 GA	Aug 1943	50% Russian (year groups 1898–1925) (Dec 1943 50% Russian, 25% Ukrainian, 25% mixed)
82 GRD	Apr 1943	70% Yakut and Buriat (321 RD)
87 GRD, 2 GA	Jul 1943	50% Russian, 50% Kazakh and Asian (year groups 1924–1925)
88 GRD, 8 GA	Jul 1943	70% Russian, 30% Asian (99 RD)
90 GRD	May 1943	90% Russian (325 RD)
92 GRD, 37 A	Sep 1943	70% Russian, 30% Asian (year group 1925)
93 GRD, 69 A	Jul 1943	60% Russian, 40% Asian (year groups 1924–1927)
94 GRD, 69 A	Jul 1943	30% Russian, 70% Asian
95 GRD, 5 GA	Jul 1944	60% Ukrainian, 40% Russian
96 GRD, 2 GA	May 1943	50% Russian, 50% Turkmen (Sep 1943 50% year group 1925) (258 RD)
97 GRD, 5 GA	Aug 1943	75% Russian and Ukrainian, 25% Turkmen (Nov 1944 67% Ukrainian, 50% year groups 1900–1914)
110 GRD, 37 A	Sep 1943	70% Asian, 30% Russian (Jun 1944 85% conscripted Ukrainian) (Mar 1945 67% Russian year groups 1926–1937, 33% Ukrainian)
117 GRD, 18 A	Jan 1944	20% Russian, 45% Ukrainian, 35% Armenian (40% year groups 1924–1925, 35% 1903–1908, 35% older)
121 GRD, 13 A	Aug 1944	70% west Ukrainian, 30% Russian
128 GRD, 4 UF	Jun 1941	95% Turkmen (Sep 1944 30% Russian, 30% Ukrainian, 40% Caucasian and Turkmen (83 MtnRD)

—Continued

Table 13.2 Continued

Division	Date	Composition
129 GRD, 38 A	Dec 1943	60% Caucasian, 40% Russian (45% year group 1926) (Apr 1945 50% Russian, 30% Ukrainian, 20% Bessarabian)
1 MtnCD, 45 A	Jul 1941	95% Kuban Cossack
2 CD, 9 A	Jun 1941	95% Kuban Cossack
3 CD, 5 CC	Jun 1941	95% Bessarabian (5 GCD Dec 1941)
4 CD, 6 CC	Jun 1941	95% Kuban-Terek Cossack
4 CD, 9 CC	Apr 1942	95% Kuban Cossack (formed 7 CC Apr 1942)
5 CD, 2 CC	Aug 1941	95% Caucasian (1 GCD Nov 1941)
6 CD, 6 CC	Jun 1941	95% Don (Chongar) Cossack (destroyed Aug 1941)
8 CD	Aug 1941	95% Kazakh (to war's end)
9 CD, 2 CC	Jun 1941	95 % Crimean (2 GCD Nov 1941)
10 CD, NCMD	Jan 1942	95% Kuban Cossack (integrated into 12, 13 CD Apr 1942)
11 CD, VMD	Sep 1941	95% Kazakh (8 GCD Jan 1943)
12 CD, NCMD	Feb 1941	95% Kuban Cossack (9 GCD Aug 1942)
13 CD, 17 CC	Feb 1942	95% Kuban Cossack (10 GCD Aug 1942)
14 CD	Jun 1941	95% Asian (6 GCD Dec 1941)
15 CD, 17 CC	Feb 1942	95% Kuban Cossack (11 GCD Aug 1942)
17 MTnCD	Jul 1941	95% Caucasian and Uzbek (disbanded Jul 1942)
18 MtnCD	Nov 1941	95% Turkmen (disbanded Jul 1942)
19 MtnCD	Jul 1941	95% Uzbek (destroyed Jul 1941)
20 MtnCD	Nov 1941	95% Tajik (17 GCD Aug 1943)
21 MtnCD, 8 CC	Jan 1942	95% Uzbek (14 GCD Feb 1943)
29 CD, 6 CC	Jun 1941	95% Cossack (disbanded Mar 1942)
31 CD	Jul 1941	95% Russian (7 GCD Jan 1942)
44 CD	Jul 1941	95% Uzbek (merged into 17 CD Apr 1942)
50 CD	Jul 1941	95% Don Cossack (3 GCD Nov 1941)
53 CD	Jul 1941	95% Don Cossack (4 GCD Nov 1941)
55 CD (2nd form)	Jul 1942	95% Turkmen (15 GCD Feb 1943)
57 CD	Aug 1941	95% Asian (integrated into 1 GCD Feb 1942)
83 MtnCD	Dec 1941	95% Central Asian (13 GCD Jan 1943)
97 CD	Dec 1942	95% Turkmen (disbanded Apr 1943)
98 CD	Dec 1941	95% Turkmen (disbanded Apr 1942)
99 CD	Jan 1942	95% Uzbek (disbanded Jul 1942)
100 CD	Jan 1942	95% Uzbek (disbanded Jul 1942)
101 CD	Jan 1942	95% Uzbek (disbanded Jul 1942)
102 CD	Jan 1942	95% Uzbek (disbanded Jun 1942)
103 CD	Jan 1942	95% Uzbek (disbanded Mar 1942)
104 CD	Dec 1941	95% Tajik (disbanded Jul 1942)
105 CD	Jan 1942	95% Kazakh (disbanded Jul 1942)
106 CD	Jan 1942	95% Kazakh (disbanded Mar 1942)
107 CD	Jan 1942	95% Kirghiz (disbanded Aug 1942)
108 CD	Jan 1942	95% Kirghiz (disbanded Mar 1942)
109 CD	Jan 1942	95% Kirghiz (disbanded May 1942)
110 CD	May 1942	95% Kalmuk (disbanded Jan 1943)
111 CD	Mar 1942	95% Kalmuk (disbanded Apr 1942)
112 CD	Apr 1942	95% Bashkir (16 GCD Feb 1943)
113 CD	Dec 1941	95% Bashkir (disbanded Mar 1942)
114 CD	Jan 1942	95% Chechen-Ingush (255 RR Mar 1942)
115 CD	Mar 1942	95% Kabarino-Balkar (disbanded Oct 1942)
116 CD, 17 CC	Mar 1942	95% Don Cossack (12 GCD Aug 1942)
1 GCD, 1 GCC	Oct 1943	Mostly Russian (Feb 1944 60% Russian, 30% Ukrainian, 10% mixed) (Aug 1944 50% Ukrainian)

—*Continued*

Table 13.2 Continued

Division	Date	Composition
2 GCD, 1 GCC	Nov 1941	95% Crimean (9 CD)
3 GCD, 2 GCC	Nov 1941	95% Don Cossack (50 CD)
4 GCD, 2 GCC	Nov 1941	95% Kuban Cossack (53 CD)
5 GCD	May 1942	95% Caucasian, Don and Kuban Cossacks (3 CD)
6 GCD	Dec 1941	95% Asian (14 CD)
7 GCD, 13 A	Feb 1944	50% Russian, 50% non-Slavic (70% year groups 1918–1926, 30% 1913–1917) (Jan 1945 60% Russian, 20% Asian, 15% Ukrainian, 5% mixed of year groups 1920–1924) (31 CD)
8 GCD, 13 A	Feb 1944	(90% Russian, 30% year groups 1914–1924, 40% 1904–1913, 30% 1896–1903)
9 GCD	Aug 1942	95% Kuban Cossacks (12 CD)
10 GCD	Aug 1942	95% Kuban Cossacks (Apr 1945 mostly Russian, 50% year groups 1920–1926) (13 CD)
11 GCD, 5 GCC	May 1943	30% Kalmyk, 30% Cossack, 40% Russian (year groups 1898–1923) (15 CD)
12 GCD	Aug 1942	95% Don Cossack (116 CD)
13 GCD	Jan 1943	90% Central Asian (83 MtnCD)
14 GCD	Feb 1943	95% Uzbek (21 MtnCD)
15 GCD	Feb 1943	95% Turkmen (55 CD 2nd form)
16 GCD	Mar 1943	95% Bashkir (112 CD)
17 GCD	Aug 1943	95% Tajik (20 MtnCD)

Note: Year group means soldiers who reached 18 years of age in the given year.
Sources: Robert G. Poirier and Albert Z. Conner, Red Army Order of Battle in the Great Patriotic War, Unpublished manuscript, 2nd ed., 1985. These data are derived from German *Fremde Heere Ost* (Foreign Army's East) reports, 1941–1945, and Aleksander Maslov, *Captured Soviet Generals: The Fate of Soviet Generals Captured by the Germans 1941–1945* (London: Frank Cass, 2001).

Table 13.3 Red Army National Military Formation Strength, 1 January 1938

Force	Officers	Men	Ethnic	Origins
Georgian				
47th Stalin Georgian Mountain Rifle Division	413	3,739	3,693	Georgian RD (1922), 1st Georgian RD (1924), Stalin (1930), Mtn RD (1931), 47th RD (1936)
63rd Frunze Georgian Rifle Division	566	3,516	1,664	1st Georgian RD (Apr 1924), Territorial (Nov 1924), Frunze (1927), 63rd Mtn. RD (1936), 63rd RD (Jun 1940)
24th Georgian Cavalry Regiment	41	561	336	(May 1922), renamed in 1929
1st Caucasus Rifle Division	603	3,491	1,715	(1921)
7th Georgian Rifle Regiment	35	411	320	(1919), renamed in 1940
16th Caucasus Rifle Regiment	52	539	341	(1920), renamed in 1939
1st Caucasus Rifle Regiment	47	491	397	(1922), renamed in 1939

—*Continued*

Table 13.3 Continued

Force	Officers	Men	Ethnic	Origins
Armenian				
76th Voroshilov Mountain Rifle Division	433	3,575	3,284	Armenian RD (1931), 76th RD (1936)
22nd Cavalry Regiment	51	366	337	(1920), renamed in 1939
Azerbaijani				
77th Ordzhonikidze Azerbaijani Mountain Rifle Division	392	3,711	3,192	1st Mixed Azerb RD (1920), Azerb RD (1922), Mtn RD (1929) Ordzhonikidze (1930), 77th Ordzhonikidze RD (1936)
34th Azerbaijani Mountain Rifle Division	401	2,989	2,071	(1920), Orzhonikidze (1930)
3rd Baku Worker-Peasant Regiment	51	601	19423	(1920), renamed in 1940
Uzbek and Kazakh				
19th Uzbek Mountain Cavalry Division	110	1,137	847	6th Uzbek Mtn RD (1922), 19th Uzbek Mtn RD (1936), 19th Mtn RD (1940)
48th Kazakh Cavalry Regiment	60	573	415	(1920), renamed in 1940
Turkmen				
18th Turkmen Mountain Cavalry Division	87	1,145	735	4th Turkmen Mtn CD (1932), 18th Turkmen Mtn CD (1936)
21st Turkmen Mountain Cavalry Division	47	603	367	8th Turkestan Mtn CD (1932), 21st Turkmen Mtn CD (1936)
72nd Turkmen Mountain Rifle Division	450	3,011	2,719	4th Sep Turkestan RB (1922), 4th Turkmen RD (1922), 72nd Turkmen Mtn RD (1936)
1st Turkestan Mountain Rifle Division	307	2,906	2,112	(1922), 83rd Turkestan Mtn RD (1936)
3rd Cavalry Regiment	41	517	406	(1923), Turkestan Mtn CR (1931), 81st Mtn CR (1935), renamed in 1938
Kirghiz				
53rd Kirgiz Territorial Cavalry Regiment	53	386	197	(1922), renamed in 1939
Tajik				
20th Tajik Mountain Cavalry Division	246	2,580	1,548	(1935)
Gori				
127th Cavalry Regiment	52	397	321	(1921), renamed in 1939
Buriat-Mongol				
Buriat-Mongol Cavalry Brigade	166	1,664	872	(1929)

Source: V. V. Gradosel'sky, "Natsional'nye voinskie formirovaniia v Krasnoi Armii (1918–1938 gg.)" [National military formations in the Red Army (1918–1938)], *Voenno-istoricheskii zhurnal* {Military-historical journal], no. 10 (October 2001); 4.

Table 13.4 Red Army National Military Formation Strength, 22 June 1941 to 1943

Designation	Date Formed	Combat Record
Azerbaijani		
77th Mtn RD (1st formation)	1920, renamed 77th RD (25 May 1942)	In combat Dec 1941 to Mar 1942
77th RD (2nd formation)	19 Oct 1942	In combat to war's end
402nd RD	15 Aug 1941	In combat 1 Oct 1942 to 30 Mar 1943 (Trans-Caucasus Front) and *front* reserve to war's end
416th RD (2nd formation)	15 Mar 1942	In combat 15 May to war's end (44, 58, 28A, 3GA, 4S, and 3SA)
223rd RD (2nd formation)	18 Oct 1941	In combat to war's end (44, 58, 37A, and 7GA)
Armenian		
76th MtnRD	1922, renamed 76th RD (7 Dec 1941) and 51st GRD (23 Nov 1942)	In combat to war's end
409th RD	19 Aug 1941	In combat Dec 1942 to war's end (44, 37, 46, 57A)
408th RD	1 Sep 1941	In combat to 25 Nov 1942 with heavy losses and disbanded
89th RD	15 Dec 1941	In combat to war's end
Georgian		
47th Stalin Mtn RD	1922	In combat Sep 1941 to Jun 1942, encircled and destroyed with 6A (25 May 1942) (Khar'kov)
63rd Frunze Mtn RD	1924	In combat Sep–Jun 1942, encircled and destroyed with 44A (13 May 1942) (Crimea)
414th RD (2nd formation)	18 Apr 1942 (Trans-Caucasus Front)	In combat Apr 1942 to war's end (44, 37, 58, 46A)
406th RD	1 Sep 1941 (Trans-Caucasus Front)	In combat 17–28 Jan 1942, May–Dec 1942 (46A), in *front* reserve to war's end
296th RD (2nd formation)	16 Jul 1943 (Trans-Caucasus Front)	In *front* reserve to war's end
392nd RD (1st formation)	18 Aug 1941 (Tran-Caucasus Front)	In combat Dec 1941 to Jan 1942 (44A), May–Sep 1942 (37A) with heavy losses
392nd RD (2nd formation)	7 Dec 1942 (Trans-Caucasus Front)	In *front* reserve to war's end
276th RD (2nd formation)	11 Sep 1942 (Trans-Caucasus Front)	In combat to war's end
349th RD (2nd formation)	Sep 1942	In *front* reserve to war's end
9th Mtn RD	1st Cauc RD (1921), 9th Mtn RD (4 May 1939), 9th Plastun RD (5 Sep 1943)1939), 9th Plastun RD (5 Sep 1943)	In combat Sep 1943 to war's end
306th Caucasus Rifle Regiment	1st Cauc. RR (1939), 25th RR (1936), 306th RR (1939), 36th MRR (9th MRD) (1943)	In combat to war's end

—Continued

Table 13.4 Continued

Designation	Date Formed	Combat Record
Tajik		
20th Mtn CD	1935, 17th GCD (18 Sep 1943)	In combat to war's end
104th CD	13 Nov 1941	Disbanded 15 Jul 1942
98th, 99th RBs	Dec 1941	Disbanded Mar 1942
Turkmen		
18th CD	1932	In combat Nov 1941 to 7 Aug 1942 with heavy losses and disbanded
83rd Mtn RD	1st Turk Mtn RD (1922), 83rd Mtn RD (1936), 13th GRD (19 Jan 1943)	In combat to war's end
128th Gds. Mtn RD	9 Oct 1943	In combat to war's end
97th CD	7 Dec 1942	Disbanded 4 Mar 1943
98th CD	27 Nov 1941	Disbanded 27 Apr 1942
87th Sep RBn	Dec 1941, 76th RD (2nd formation) (20 Apr 1943)	In combat Oct 1942 to 9 Apr 1943 (27, 11A); 76th RD (Apr 1943) to war's end
88th Sep RBn	Dec 1941	Disbanded Apr 1942
72nd Mtn RD	1922	In combat to 19 Sep 1941 with heavy losses and disbanded
Uzbek		
19th CD	1936	In combat to Jul 1941, encircled, destroyed, and disbanded
90th Sep RBn	Dec 1941	In combat Oct 1942 to Jan 1943 (3A) with heavy losses and disbanded
94th Sep RBn	Dec 1941	In combat Oct 1942 to Jan 1943 (3A) with heavy losses and disbanded
89th, 91st, 92nd, 93rd, 95th, 96th, 97th Sep RBns	Dec 1941	Disbanded early 1942
99th CD	22 Dec 1941	Disbanded 27 Apr 1942
100th CD	22 Dec 1941	Disbanded 7 Jul 1942
101st CD	22 Dec 1941	Disbanded 9 Jul 1942
102nd CD	25 Dec 1941	Disbanded 10 Jun 1942
103rd CD	19 Dec 1941	Disbanded 10 Mar 1942
Kazakh		
100th Sep RBn	Dec 1941, 1st RD (2nd formation) on 8 Dec 1943	In combat Oct 1942 to Sep 1943, 1st RD (2nd formation) to war's end
105th CD	13 Dec 1941	Disbanded 15 Jul 1942
106th CD	25 Dec 1941	Disbanded 16 Mar 1942
101st Sep RB	Dec 1941	In combat Oct 1942 Jul 1944 (4SA) and disbanded
102nd Sep. RB	Dec 1941	In combat Oct 1942 Jul 1944 and disbanded
Kirghiz		
107th CD	8 Dec 1941	Disbanded 15 Aug 1942
108th CD	25 Dec 1941	Disbanded 16 Mar 1942
109th CD	19 Dec 1941	Disbanded 11 May 1942

—Continued

Table 13.4 Continued

Designation	Date Formed	Combat Record
Estonian		
8th RC (headquarters)	25 Sep 1942, 41st GRC (May 1945)	In combat Dec 1942 to war's end
249th RD (2nd formation)	6 May 1942, 122nd GRD (May 1945)	In combat Jun 1942 to war's end (1942A, 1SA)
7th RD (2nd formation)	27 Dec 1941, 118th GRD (May 1945)	In combat to war's end (3SA, 1SA, 8, 1942A)
Lithuanian		
16th RD	3 Apr 1942	In combat Dec 1942 to war's end (2TA, 48, 10A, 6GA, 4SA)
Latvian		
130th RC (headquarters)	5 Jun 1944	In combat to war's end
201st RD	13 Aug 1941, 43rd GRD (5 Oct 1942)	In combat Dec 1941 to war's end (33A, 1SA)
308th RD (3rd formation)	1 Jul 1944	In combat to war's end
Kalmyk		
110th CD	20 May 1942	In combat May 1942 with heavy losses and disbanded
111th CD	31 Mar 1942	Disbanded 19 Apr 1942
Bashkir		
112th CD	28 Apr 1942, 16th GCD (14 Feb 43)	In combat to war's end
113th CD	13 Nov 1941	Disbanded 3 Mar 1942
Chechen-Ingush		
114th CD	1 Jan 1942	255th Sep CR (3 Mar 1942)
Kabardino-Balkar		
115th CD	2 Feb 1942	In combat May–Oct 1942 (51A) with heavy losses and disbanded 19 Oct 1942
Chinese		
88th Sep RBn	Aug 1942 (Far Eastern Front)	In combat 9 Aug to 2 Sep 1945 (2nd Far Eastern Front)

Sources: *Boevoi sostav Sovetskoi armii, 1941–1945 gg. v piatikh chastiakh* [The combat composition of the Soviet Army 1941–1945 in five parts] (Voroshilov General Staff Academy and Voenizdat, 1963–1990); and V. V. Gradosel'sky, "Natsional'nye voinskie formirovaniia v Velikoi Otechestvennoi voine" [National military formations in the Great Patriotic War], *Voenno-istoricheskii zhurnal* [Military-historical journal], no. 1 (January 2001); 18–24.

Table 13.5 Red Army National Military Formation Strength, 1941–1945

Nationality	Rifle (Mtn Rifle) Divisions	Cavalry Divisions	Regiments, Brigades, and Battalions	Total
Azerbaijani	5	0	0	5
Armenian	4	0	0	4
Georgian	10	0	1	11
Tajik	0	2	2	4
Turkmen	2	4	2	8
Uzbek	0	6	9	15
Kazakh	0	2	3	5
Kirghiz	0	3	0	3
Estonian	2	0	0	2
Lithuanian	1	0	0	1
Latvian	2	0	0	2
Kalmuk	0	2	0	2
Bashkir	0	2	0	2
Chechen-Ingush	0	1	0	1
Kabardino-Balkar	0	1	0	1
Chinese	0	0	1	1
Total	26	23	18	67

Source: V. V. Gradosel'sky, "Natsional'nye voinskie formirovaniia v Velikoi Otechestvennoi voine" [National military formations in the Great Patriotic War], *Voenno-istoricheskii zhurnal* [Military-historical journal], no. 1 (January 2001); 18–24.

Table 13.6 The Wartime Red Army's Ethnic Composition and Death Rate (by Nationality)

	Soldiers		Dead
Mobilized	29,574,900		NA
Total served	34,476,700		8,668,400
Russian Republic	21,187,600	(67%)(1)	5,756,000
Tartar			187,700
Mordovian			63,300
Chuvash			63,300
Bashkir			31,700
Udmurt			23,200
Mariitsy			20,900
Buriat			13,000
Komi			11,600
Dagestani			11,100
Ossetian			10,700
Polish			10,100
Karelian			9,500
Kalmyk			4,000
Kabardino/Balkar			3,400
Greeks			2,400
Chechen/Ingush			2,300
Finns			1,600
Bulgars			1,100
Czechs/Slovaks			400
Chinese			400
Yugoslavians			100
Others			33,700
Ukrainian	5,300,000		1,376,500
Belorussian	1,100,000		252,900
Kazakh	1,000,000		125,500
Uzbek	1,200,000	(6,000 women)	117,900
Armenian	600,000		83,700
Georgian	800,000	(16,000 women)	79,500
Azerbaijani	600,000		58,400
Moldavian	300,000		53,900
Kirghiz	400,000		26,600
Tajik	400,000		22,900
Turkmen	400,000		21,300
Estonian	270,000		21,200
Latvian	90,000		11,600
Lithuanian	70,000		11,600
Jews	800,000		142,500
Union republics	13,289,100	(total)	
Total			8,668,400

Sources: *Liudskie poteri SSSR v Velikoi Otechestvennoi voine* [Personnel losses of the USSR in the Great Patriotic War] (Saint-Petersberg: Insititut Rossiiskoi Istorii, 1995), 75–81; G. F. Krivosheev, ed., *Rossiia i SSSR v voinakh XX veka, poteri vooruzhennykh sil: Statisticheskoe issledovanie* [Russia and the USSR in twentieth-century wars, the losses of the armed forces: A statistical investigation] (Moscow: Olma-Press, 2001), 238; V. A. Zolotarev, ed., *Velikoi Otechestvennaia voina 1941–1945 v chetyrekh knigakh* [The Great Patriotic War 1941–1945 in four books] (Moscow: Nauka, 1999), IV: 13–14, 290; and S. Enders Windbush and Alexander Alexiev, *Ethnic Minorities in the Red Army: Asset or Liability* (Boulder, CO: Westview Press, 1988), 55.

Table 13.7 The Red Army Soldier's Authorized Daily Food Ration, 22 September 1941
Daily Ration in Grams (ounces) for Soldiers Assigned to:

	Operating Armies						
Foodstuff	Combat Units	Rear Units	Reserve Units	Security and Rear Units	Aircraft Combat Crews	Aircraft Crews (Garrison)	Hospitals
Bread							
Winter (Oct–Mar)	900 (31.7)	800 (28.2)	750 (26.5)	700 (24.7)	400 (14.1)	400 (14.1)	300 (10.6)
Summer (Apr–Sep)	800 (28.2)	700 (24.7)	650 (22.9)	600 (21.1)	400 (14.1)	300 (10.6)	300 (10.6)
Flour, wheat, 2nd Cl.	20 (0.7)	10 (0.35)	10 (0.35)	10 (0.35)	40 (1.4)	20 (0.7)	20 (0.7)
Flour, wheat, 1st Cl.	—	—	—	—	—	—	10 (0.35)
Potato flour	—	—	—	—	5 (.18)	5 (.18)	5 (.18)
Groats	140 (4.9)	120 (4.2)	100 (3.5)	100 (3.5)	90 (3.2)	80 (2.8)	60 (2.1)
Semolina	—	—	—	—	—	—	20 (0.7)
Rice	—	—	—	—	50 (1.76)	30 (1.1)	20 (0.7)
Macaroni	30 (1.1)	20 (0.7)	20 (0.7)	100 (3.5)	50 (1.76)	20 (0.7)	30 (1.1)
Meat	150 (5.3)	120 (4.2)	75 (2.6)	75 (2.6)	350 (12.3)	300 (10.6)	120 (4.2)
Chicken	—	—	—	—	40 (1.4)	—	—
Fish	100 (3.5)	80 (2.8)	120 (4.2)	100 (3.5)	90 (3.2)	70 (24.7)	50 (1.8)
Cottage cheese	—	—	—	—	20 (0.7)	20 (0.7)	25 (0.88)
Sour cream	—	—	—	—	10 (0.35)	10 (0.35)	10 (0.35)
Fresh milk	—	—	—	—	200 (7))	100 (3.5)	200 (7)
Condensed milk, coffee, or cocoa	—	—	—	—	20 (0.7)	—	—
Eggs (single)	—	—	—	—	0.5 (0.02)	0.5 (0.02)	—
Soy flour	15 (0.5)	—	—	—	—	—	—
Butter	—	—	—	—	90 (3.2)	60 (2.1)	—
Cheese	—	—	—	—	20 (0.7)	20 (0.7)	—
Fat	30 (1.1)	25 (0.88)	20 (0.7)	20 (0.7)	—	—	10 (0.35)
Beef fat	—	—	—	—	—	—	40 (1.4)
Vegetable oil	20 (0.7)	20 (0.7)	20 (0.7)	20 (0.7)	5 (0.18)	5 (0.18)	5 (0.18)
Sugar	35 (1.2)	25 (0.88)	25 (0.88)	20 (0.7)	80 (2.8)	60 (2.1)	50 (1.77)
Tea	1 (0.04)	1 (0.04)	1 (0.04)	1 (0.04)	40 (1.4) (month)	1 (0.04)	1 (0.04)
Coffee (natural or ersatz)	—	—	—	—	—	—	0.3 (.01) 3 (0.1)

—*Continued*

Table 13.7 Continued

Foodstuff	*Operating Armies* Combat Units	Rear Units	Reserve Units	Security and Rear Units	Aircraft Combat Crews	Aircraft Crews (Garrison)	Hospitals
Salt	30 (1.1)	30 (1.1)	30 (1.1)	30 (1.1)	30 (1.1)	30 (1.1)	30 (1.1)
Vegetables	820 (28.9)	820 (28.9)	920 (32.4)	920 (32.4)	885 (31.2)	835 (29.5)	735 (25.9)
Potatoes	500 (17.6)	500 (17.6)	600 (21.1)	600 (21.1)	500 (28.9)	500 (28.9)	450 (15.9)
Cabbage	170 (6)	170 (6)	170 (6)	170 (6)	200 (7)	200 (7)	150 (5.3)
Carrots	45 (1.6)	45 (1.6)	40 (1.4)	40 (1.4)	55 (1.9)	40 (1.4)	40 (1.4)
Beets	40 (1.4)	40 (1.4)	45 (1.6)	45 (1.6)	40 (1.4)	30 (1.1)	30 (1.1)
Onions	30 (1.1)	30 (1.1)	30 (1.1)	30 (1.1)	40 (1.4)	30 (1.1)	30 (1.1)
Roots, greens, cucumbers	35 (1.2)	35 (1.2)	35 (1.2)	35 (1.2)	45 (1.6)	35 (1.2)	35 (1.2)
Dried fruit	—	—	—	—	20 (0.7)	20 (0.7)	—
Fruit juice	—	—	—	—	3 (0.10)	3 (0.10)	—
Fruit juice or berry extract	—	—	—	—	—	—	10 (0.35)
Dried fruit or preserves	—	—	—	—	—	—	0.5 (0.02) 20 (0.7) 75 (2.6)
Tomato paste	6 (0.2)	6 (0.2)	6 (0.2)	6 (0.2)	8 (.28)	6 (0.2)	6 (0.2)
Bay leaves	0.2 (.007)	0.2 (.007)	0.2 (.007)	0.2 (.007)	0.2 (.007)	0.2 (.007)	0.2 (.007)
Pepper	0.3 (.01)	0.3 (.01)	0.3 (.01)	0.3 (.01)	0.3 (.01)	0.3 (.01)	0.3 (.01)
Vinegar	2 (.07)	2 (.07)	2 (.07)	2 (.07)	2 (.07)	2 (.07)	2 (.07)
Mustard	0.3 (.01)	0.3 (.01)	0.3 (.01)	0.3 (.01)	0.3 (.01)	0.3 (.01)	0.3 (.01)
Cigarettes or tobacco (box)	—	—	—	—	25 (.88)	—	—
Tobacco (crude)	20 (0.7)	20 (0.7)	—	—	—	—	—
Matches (per month)	3 packs	3 packs	—	—	10 packs	—	—
Cigarette paper (per month)	7 books	7 books	—	—	—	—	—
Soap (per month)	200 (7)	200 (7)	200 (7)	200 (7)	300 (10.6)	300 (10.6)	200 (7)

Notes:
Dashes indicate not authorized at that time.
1. A daily ration of 800 grams of bread per day, including 400 grams of rye bread and 400 grams of wheat flour bread, is established for recovering Red Army soldiers and commanders.
2. Issue 25 cigarettes *(papirosy)*, 3rd class, per man per day and three boxes of matches per month or 15 grams of tobacco to the wounded or sick who arrive from the operating armies for medical treatment in hospitals.
Source: V. A. Zolotarev, ed., "Prikazy narodnogo komissara oborony SSSR 22 iiunia 1941 g.–1942" [The orders of the People's Commissar of Defense of the USSR 22 June 1941–1942] in *Russkii arkhiv: Velikaia Otechestvennaia* [The Russian archives: The Great Patriotic (War)], 13, 2(2) (Moscow: Terra, 1997), 97–102.

Table 13.8 Identified Red Army Penal Subunits and Their Subordination, 1942–1945

Unit	Subordination	Date Identified
5th Penal Battalion	Northwestern Front	August 1942
8th Penal Battalion	Don, Central Front	October 1942
9th Penal Battalion	*Stavka* reserve	1942
12th Penal Battalion	Leningrad Front	1942
20th Penal Battalion	Western, 1st Belorussian Front	1942
22nd Penal Battalion	Kalinin, 1st Baltic Front	1942
34th Penal Battalion	Voronezh Front	mid-1943
38th Penal Battalion	Central Front	June 1943
76th Penal Battalion	Southern Front	June 1943
123rd Penal Battalion	5th Shock Army, 3rd Ukrainian, 1st Belorussian Front	1944
156th Penal Battalion	Central or Western Front	mid-1943
216th Penal Battalion	Southwestern Front	mid-1943
3rd Penal Company	31st Army, Western Front	late 1942
7th Penal Company	24th Army	late 1942
10th Penal Company	60th Army, Central Front	May 1943
67th Penal Company	Don Front	late 1942
100th Penal Company	1st Guards Army, Southwestern Front	late 1942
131st Penal Company	3rd Army	1943
138th Penal Company	31st Army	1943
179th Penal Company	13th Army	1943
186th Penal Company	48th Army	1944
259th Penal Company	65th Army	1944
275th Penal Company	22nd Army	1944

Main Direction Commanders

S. M. Budenny

K. E. Voroshilov

S. K. Timoshenko

Front Commanders

F. I. Kuznetsov

D. G. Pavlov

M. P. Kirponis

M. M. Popov

A. I. Eremenko

I. S. Konev (right)

K. K. Rokossovsky

N. F. Vatutin

R. Ia. Malinovsky

I. Kh. Bagramian

V. D. Sokolovsky

I. V. Tiulenev

F. I. Tolbukhin

I. E. Petrov (far left)

F. I. Golikov

M. A. Purkaev

P. A. Kurochkin

K. A. Meretskov

V. A. Frolov

P. S. Rybalko

M. E. Katukov

S. I. Bogdanov

P. A. Rotmistrov (center)

CHAPTER 14

Conclusions

THE COURSE OF WAR

The Red Army underwent a severe test and costly education at the hands of the *Wehrmacht* during the first 30 months of the war. Within three months after war began, Hitler's invading force virtually destroyed the peacetime Red Army, shattering its force structure, killing, capturing, or maiming almost 3 million of its soldiers, destroying or damaging most of its weapons and equipment, and seriously undermining its political and military leaders' faith that they could ever achieve victory. Within the first six months of war, the Red Army lost almost 5 million men, including most of its peacetime forces and a sizable proportion of the millions of soldiers it had mobilized since Operation Barbarossa began. Worse still, by this time the Soviet Union had lost up to one-half of its industry's productive capacity and most valuable agricultural heartland, rendering it incapable of producing the military weaponry and equipment necessary to pursue the war successfully and even feed its soldiers and population adequately.

In the face of these grim realities, the victories the Red Army achieved at Leningrad in September and November and at Rostov and Moscow in December were nothing short of miraculous. Driven by Stalin's indomitable will tempered by outright desperation and its soldiers' own stoic determination, the Red Army won these victories by employing masses of hastily mobilized and poorly trained and equipped reserves who paid for these victories with staggering losses. While inflicting an unprecedented defeat on Hitler's hitherto invincible *Wehrmacht* and preventing him from achieving the ambitious aims of Operation Barbarossa, at the same time the Red Army paid a hefty price in blood for victories that proved only transitory.

After Stalin attempted to capitalize on his army's victory at Moscow by ordering it to resume offensive operations in the spring of 1942, its disastrous defeats at Khar'kov and in the Crimea shocked Stalin and demonstrated to him that the army's education in modern warfare was still far from complete. More sobering still, the *Wehrmacht's* subsequent dramatic advance during Operation *Blau,* which savaged the Red Army once again, indicated that, although the *Wehrmacht* was vulnerable during the winter, it remained virtually invincible during the summer. The Red Army's brutal bludgeoning at the hands of the *Wehrmacht* in the summer and fall of 1942 cost it 6 million more casualties and forced Stalin to revert to nearly the same defensive strategy he had employed during 1941, although with a bit less desperation.

After the beleaguered Red Army conducted a prolonged, painful, and costly fighting withdrawal, it finally contained the *Wehrmacht's* advance in the ruins of Stalingrad and the rugged foothills of the Caucasus Mountains in late October 1942, but only after raising and fielding a massive new wave of reserve armies. A month later and at considerable risk, Stalin unleashed his reinforced Red Army in massive twin offensives against *Wehrmacht* forces in the Rzhev and Stalingrad regions. Although the former failed, for the first time in the war, in its victory at Stalingrad, the Red Army managed to encircle and completely destroy three Axis armies, an unprecedented feat, demonstrating to the world that Hitler could no longer win the war on any terms.

Inspired and emboldened by his victory at Stalingrad, Stalin unleashed the Red Army on relentless attacks during the winter of 1942–43. Advancing with ever-increasing abandon toward Millerovo and Rostov in December, into the Khar'kov and Donbas regions in January and early February, and toward Staraia Russa, Orel, Briansk, and the Desna and Dnepr rivers in late February and March, the Red Army spread the conflagration to the entire front from Leningrad to the Caucasus. Once again, however, in spite of its desperate wounds, the *Wehrmacht* demonstrated its enduring military prowess by inflicting sharp reverses on the overextended Red Army in the Donbas, at Khar'kov, and south of Orel in late February and March. Despite its impressive territorial gains, the sobering setbacks the Red Army suffered in early spring demonstrated that its education was far from over.

The *Stavka* and NKO exploited the combat lull that embraced the front from early March through late June 1943 to study the Red Army's experiences during the previous winter and shape it into a more effective mobile fighting force capable of conducting sustained offensives in any season of the year against a *Wehrmacht* whose strength was clearly flagging. The fruits of their efforts became apparent in July 1943 on the hilly plains north and south of the city of Kursk, where a thoroughly restructured, reorganized, and reequipped Red Army vanquished the most powerful and best-equipped armada Hitler could raise against it. At Kursk, for the first time during the war, the Red Army proved capable of defeating a deliberate *Wehrmacht* offensive before its panzers could reach even the operational depths.

Capping this unprecedented feat, on 12 July, even before Hitler abandoned his Kursk offensive, the Red Army struck back violently at its tormentors with massive offensives of its own against *Wehrmacht* defenses in the Orel and Khar'kov regions, smashed these defenses, and forced the defenders to begin retreating back to safety along the Dnepr River. Adding insult to injury, after a month more of heavy fighting, the Red Army breached the *Wehrmacht's* formidable "Eastern Wall" along the Dnepr in late October and November, seized the cities of Gomel', Kiev, Kremenchug, and Dnepropetrovsk, and, with them, vital strategic bridgeheads in Belorussia and the Ukraine on the Dnepr's western and southern banks. While the Red Army's victory at Kursk guaranteed that Hitler's defeat would ultimately be total, as if to underscore this reality, in late November the Red Army finally accomplished those missions Stalin had assigned to it in February. Thereafter, the Red Army's westward advance remained inexorable to war's end.

Having barely weathered its harrowing education during the first 18 months of war, in 1943 the Red Army exploited what it had learned to graduate with honors on the battlefields around Kursk in July and August. Nor did the Red Army fail to exploit its education as it marched to victory in May 1945.

THE FORGOTTEN WAR

Despite the fact that hundreds of presses worldwide have published thousands if not tens of thousands of books about the Soviet-German war during the more than 50 years since its end, the historical record of the war and the Red Army's role in it remains appallingly incomplete. While recording the war's general pulse and describing most of its famous battles and military operations with fair accuracy, for a variety of motives, most historians have overlooked, obscured, or deliberately neglected many events or subjects. Many of these historians simply did not realize that these events had occurred or that the subjects existed because governments denied them access to relevant archival documents, but others deliberately skirted them either because they proved unpleasant or offensive to their national psyches and traditions or they perceived them as harmful to their country's or army's reputations. Finally, in the case of many Russian historians, state censors simply expunged offending information from their books to avoid sullying the reputations of the Red Army or of key national leaders, past or present.

At one end of this spectrum, German historians and those who have described the war from the German perspective or relied almost exclusively on German sources preferred to focus on the stunning victories the *Wehrmacht* achieved during the first 30 months of the war to the exclusion of more embarrassing topics such as German war guilt and the specter of the *Wehrmacht's* humiliating defeats during 1943, 1944, and 1945.[1] At the other extreme, Russian historians have focused almost exclusively on the Red Army's remarkable victories at Moscow, Stalingrad, and Kursk, and its triumphal march to victory in 1944 and 1945, and have avoided detailing the Red Army's humiliating performance during the first 18 months of the war, the persistent unflattering Western stereotypes of Soviet officers and soldiers, Western portrayals of Stalin's inept, devious, and often brutal conduct of the war, and the perception that the war on the German Eastern Front was only a bloody backwater of war unworthy of serious analysis.

Both historical "schools" have described the war as a prolonged and brutal struggle between Europe's most formidable armies fought on an unprecedented scale over vast expanses of territories whose sheer size, geographical complexity, and seasonal climatic extremes made the conflict episodic in nature. As they have described it, the war took the form of a series of alternating German and Soviet offensives or campaigns, such as the *Wehrmacht's* Operations Barbarossa, *Blau,* and Citadel in 1941, 1942, and 1943 and the Red Army's winter campaigns in 1941–42 and 1942–43, its summer–fall campaigns in 1943 and 1944, and its winter–spring campaign of 1945, which, while punctuated by periods of relative quiet, began with major battles such as the *Wehrmacht's* surprise attacks in June 1941 and June 1942 and the Red Army's victories in the Battles of Moscow, Stalingrad, Kursk, Belorussia, and along the Vistula River and culminated in the titanic Battle of Berlin.

Although the historians in both these "schools" agree regarding the war's general course and nature, they offer wildly differing interpretations as to exactly what occurred and why. More tragic still, since their histories are "selective," collectively, they ignore as much as 40 percent of the combat action on the Soviet-German front. Even more damaging from the standpoint of objectivity, by obscuring the real nature of the war, these sharply differing accounts and interpretations reinforce the natural penchant for Westerners to view the war in the East as nothing more than a bloody backdrop for far more dramatic and significant battles in Western theaters of operations, such as the Battle at El Alamein, Operation Torch, the battles at Salerno and Anzio, Operation Overlord in Normandy, and the Battle of the Bulge. Finally, these "selective" histories have contributed to the wholly mistaken impression that the Soviet Union's Western allies actually won the war over Nazi Germany.

Regardless of their perspective, most of these histories are woefully incomplete in two important respects. First, although they accurately describe the Soviet-German war's general ebb and flow, these histories offer incomplete, warped, or otherwise distorted descriptions of the war's most famous operations, battles, and campaigns, such as Operations Barbarossa and *Blau,* and the Battles of Smolensk, Leningrad, Moscow, Stalingrad, Kursk, Belorussia, and Berlin, masking the real nature, course, and significance of these famous events. Second, and even more damaging, these histories discount, overlook, or deliberately ignore many other battles and operations, large and small, whose existence, potential significance, and ultimate outcome would fundamentally alter traditional descriptions of what actually took place during the war and why.

For example, although they frequently question Hitler's wisdom in altering his line of advance during Operation Barbarossa, German and, to a slightly lesser extent, Russian historians have minimized or totally overlooked the many counterattacks, counterstrokes, and counteroffensives the Red Army conducted during this period, instead portraying Operation Barbarossa as a virtually seamless *Wehrmacht* march from the Soviet Union's western frontiers to Leningrad, Moscow, and Rostov. While seriously understating the Red Army's resistance during Operation Barbarossa, these accounts have also presented a perverted view of the *Stavka's* strategic planning and intent during this period as well as an inadequate context in which to assess the reasons for and nature of the Red Army's subsequent victory at Moscow. Likewise, by obscuring or otherwise overlooking key aspects of the Red Army's Moscow offensive and other offensives it conducted during the winter of 1941–42, Russian historians have obscured the *Stavka's* strategic intent and overstated the Red Army's achievements during this period.

Similarly, by long concealing the scope and scale of the Red Army's twin defeats at Khar'kov and in the Crimea in the spring of 1942 and in the initial stages of Operation *Blau* in July and August 1942, Russian historians have concealed the scope of the disaster that befell their Red Army during these periods, obscured the *Stavka's* strategic planning and intent during these periods, and denied adequate context for the subsequent Battle for Stalingrad. Worse still, within the context of the Red Army's successful November offensive at Stalingrad, Russian historians have totally ignored its strategic defeat near Rzhev in late November and less significant operational failures coincident to its successful Stalingrad offensive, such as its setback along the Chir River in December 1942.

Continuing this pattern of obfuscation, Russian historians have belatedly and only grudgingly described the Red Army's setbacks in the Donbas and Khar'kov regions in February and March of 1943, while studiously concealing every aspect of its defeats west of Kursk and in the Leningrad and Demiansk regions during this same period. Even in the wake of the Red Army's spectacular victory at Kursk in July and August 1943 and its dramatic advance to and across the Dnepr River from September through December 1943, Russian historians have obfuscated or totally ignored numerous Red Army combat failures, in particular, the prolonged and costly struggle for possession of eastern Belorussia and Kiev in October, and, to a lesser extent, for possession of Krivoi Rog and Nikopol' farther south along the Don River in November and December.

Regardless of motive, the unintentional or deliberate omission of these and other "forgotten battles" from the annals of the war—or their obfuscation—has perverted the history of the war by preventing accurate analysis of why and how many military operations occurred and an understanding of these operations' real or potential significance. In addition to denying us an adequate understanding of the nature and accomplishments of the Red Army during wartime, tangentially it has also thwarted a valid assessment of the leadership qualities of the Red Army's "great captains" and the army's overall contributions to the overall war effort.

THE FORCE

Although the Red Army was indeed colossal in terms of size, force structure, and perceived capabilities on the eve of war, the *Wehrmacht's* spectacular accomplishments during Operation Barbarossa proved without any doubt that it was a colossus with feet of clay. After Hitler's experienced and blooded *Wehrmacht* exploited the Red Army's inability to either control or employ its forces in high-intensity maneuver war by shattering this colossus during the first six months of war, Stalin and his *Stavka* had no choice but to reconstruct the Red Army from scratch in 1942. In short, combat during the first six months of the war demonstrated that the Red Army's inexperienced command cadre could not effectively command and control its forces in combat.

Therefore, as a stopgap measure, during late 1941 and early 1942, the *Stavka* replaced the unwieldy colossus the *Wehrmacht* had destroyed in the summer and fall of 1941 with a smaller force its officers could employ more effectively. This dramatic transformation replaced the Red Army's demolished massive mechanized and rifle corps and large rifle and tank divisions with an almost skeletal force of shrunken rifle divisions, demi-divisions called rifle brigades, and pathetically weak tank brigades and battalions. As combat during the winter of 1941–42 indicated, however, the new Red Army was ideal for training new commanders in the art and science of modern war, but it was not capable of conducting sustained offensive operations.

Therefore, beginning in the spring of 1942 and thereafter throughout the summer, the *Stavka* and NKO slowly and painstakingly rebuilt the army so that it could achieve these critical aims. After fielding sapper, tank, and air armies, new tank and mechanized corps, destroyer divisions and brigades, and an impressive array of other supporting forces, the Red Army recorded its first decisive strategic victory in November 1942 at Stalingrad, where, for the first time during the war, its forces were able to penetrate Axis defenses and sustain offensive operations well enough to encircle a large Axis force.

Exploiting its Stalingrad victory and the victories and defeats they experienced during the ensuing winter campaign, the *Stavka* and NKO were able to field a new and far more capable Red Army by July 1943, one that was finally able to fulfill the promises of "deep battle" and "deep operations" theories as articulated by Soviet military theorists during the 1930s and to implement its new concepts of "artillery" and "air offensives." The Red Army demonstrated these capabilities at Kursk in July and August, when, for first time in the war, it halted a *Wehrmacht* offensive in its tracks well short of the operational depths and, later, conducted sustained exploitation operations into the *Wehrmacht's* deep operational rear and fought its panzer reserves to a standstill.

Under Stalin's constant watchful supervision, the *Stavka's* and NKO's strenuous efforts to reform, restructure, and reequip the Red Army had culminated by July 1943 in the formation of a new and more modern army formed around the nucleus of an imposing tank and mechanized force and supported by a formidable array of supporting artillery, air, and engineer forces. This force soon vindicated the hard work of its creators by triumphing on numerous battlefields, from the rolling plains around Kursk and Orel to the banks of the Dnepr River.

Although scarcely mentioned by any histories of the war, a formidable force of over 500,000 NKVD border guards, field forces, convoy, railroad, and construction forces fought side by side with the new Red Army, contributing significantly to its victory against Hitler's *Wehrmacht.* This "shadow army's" border guards felt the full brunt impact of invading *Wehrmacht* forces in June 1941, its field combat divisions and brigades assisted the Red Army's combat forces during the first two years of war, and its brigades and regiments helped steel iron discipline within the Red Army's ranks during war by manning blocking detachments, guaranteeing strict security in its rear areas, and conscripting manpower in liberated territories to fill its depleted ranks. At the same time, its railroad and construction forces protected the Red Army's vital communications network and, when necessary, mobilized labor to construct the Red Army's formidable defensive lines and positions.

THE LEADERS

As first secretary of the Communist Party and chairman of the Council of People's Commissars (SNK), Stalin exercised absolute power and absolute authority over the Soviet Union and its Red Army on the eve of war. But since the People's Commissariat of Defense (NKO) and the Red Army General Staff shared responsibility with Stalin for directing and supervising the Red Army, the army lacked the centralized direction necessary to conduct war successfully. Stalin solved this problem immediately after the war began by forming the State Defense Committee (GKO) and the *Stavka,* granting the former full power in the country and the latter responsibility for directing the war effort together with the General Staff. Despite the changes, as chairmen of the GKO and *Stavka,* Stalin never once relinquished his firm grip on the levers of power either politically or militarily through war's end.

While the *Stavka* and its working organs, the NKO and General Staff, ensured centralized direction of the war effort at the national level, soon after war began, Stalin created main direction commands under the *Stavka's* direct control to direct and coordinate operations by the Red Army's operating *fronts,* which were incapable of doing so on their own. Since these main direction command headquarters functioned poorly, too, Stalin abolished them by late 1942, gradually replacing them with *Stavka* representatives dispatched directly to operating *fronts* to control and coordinate their operations. Working in close coordination with an ever-increasing network of directorates and departments within the NKO and General Staff, by 1943 and for the remainder of the war, the *Stavka* and its field representatives formed an effective centralized command and control system for planning, directing, and coordinating military operations.

The Red Army fought the war under tight *Stavka* control, but other state commissariats and NKO directorates played a vital role in enforcing strict discipline, unit cohesion, and loyalty within the Red Army's ranks and the country as a whole. For example, the People's Commissariat of Internal Affairs (NKVD) troops and special departments (OOs) maintained order and security within the country and the army, the NKO's Main Political Directorate (GlavPu) employed a ubiquitous system of military councils, commissars, *politruki,* and, later, deputy commanders for political affairs at every level of command to ensure strict political control over the army and navy, and the NKO's General Prosecutor's Office managed an equally elaborate system of military prosecutors, military tribunals, and associated penal subunits, which ruthlessly exploited the Soviet legal code to maintain strict order and discipline in the army. Finally, the NKO's and General Staff's Main Intelligence Directorate (GRU) and, after April 1943, its Main Directorate for Counterintelligence (SMERSH) struggled against espionage and dissention, both foreign and domestic, within the ranks of the military.

Although this centralized system controlled Red Army operations effectively, it was also flawed in that it concentrated too much decisionmaking power in Stalin's hands. As a result, particularly during the first year of war but to a lesser extent thereafter as well, Stalin often intimidated or overruled his GKO and *Stavka* colleagues by requiring the Red Army to operate as he saw fit, often to its detriment. Thus, in addition to bearing responsibility for the catastrophe that befell the Red Army in Operation Barbarossa, Stalin was also directly responsible for other major Red Army debacles during 1941 and most of 1942, including its failed counterstrokes and counteroffensives in the summer of 1941, the disastrous Uman', Kiev, Viaz'ma, and Briansk encirclements from August through October 1941, the Khar'kov and Crimean failures in May 1942, and the catastrophic intelligence failure on the eve of Operation *Blau.*

In mitigation, however, although Stalin's iron will and grim determination contributed to the Red Army's victory at Moscow in late 1941, the dictator's increased willingness to heed the counsel of his most senior advisers in late 1942 contributed significantly to the Red Army's victory at Stalingrad and the impressive string of victories it achieved during and after 1943.

Regardless of the effectiveness of Stalin's military command and control system, the Red Army could not hope to defeat the *Wehrmacht* on the battlefield unless and until Stalin, the *Stavka,* and the NKO were able to identify competent command cadre and assign them to command its forces. This was the most daunting challenge the leaders faced during the first 18 months of the war, and detailed examination of the Red Army's command cadre demonstrates that they mastered this challenge in spades. Despite the Red Army's uniformly dismal performance during most of Operation Barbarossa and Stalin's initial penchant for assigning incompetent cronies to high command positions during the initial period of the war, a remarkable number of Red Army generals and colonels survived the carnage of 1941 to emerge with enough experience to perform credibly until their death or war's end.

For example, all of Stalin's cronies who served as main direction commanders in 1941 rightfully disappeared into obscurity, whereas 23 of the 25 generals who served Stalin as *front* commanders during 1941 remained in *front* command later in the war, eight until war's end. Likewise, 19 of the 21 generals who served as *front* commanders during 1942 remained *front* commanders later in the war, nine until war's end, and 18 of the 19 generals who served as *front* commanders during 1943 retained their commands in 1944, including 11 who ended the war in *front* command. Nor was this phenomenon limited to *front* level. For example, 65 of the 101 generals who commanded Stalin's armies during 1941 survived the year in either *front* or army command, as did 86 of the 133 generals who served as army commanders in 1942 and 74 of the 106 generals who commanded armies in 1943.

Command stability was even more apparent within the Red Army's vital mobile forces, especially its separate tank and mechanized corps and its tank armies, which operated continuously from mid-1942 to war's end but also even in the mechanized corps it fielded on the eve of war. For example, 15 of the 32 generals who commanded the Red Army's ill-fated mechanized corps in June and July 1941 survived to command armies or corps in 1942, and 36 of the 67 colonels who commanded tank divisions in 1941 continued to command at tank brigade or tank corps in 1942. More impressive still, five of the seven generals who commanded cavalry corps in 1941 retained their commands in 1942, 22 of the 35 generals who commanded cavalry corps in 1942 commanded either armies or cavalry or rifle corps in 1943, and seven of the

11 generals who commanded cavalry corps in 1943 commanded cavalry corps or cavalry-mechanized groups in 1944.

In addition, 32 of the 46 generals who commanded tank or mechanized corps in 1942 commanded tank armies or tank or mechanized corps in 1943, and 43 of the 68 generals who commanded tank and mechanized corps in 1943 commanded either tank armies or tank or mechanized corps in 1944, many of these to war's end. Finally, five of the six generals who commanded tank armies in 1942 retained command of either tank or combined-arms armies until war's end, and eight of the nine generals who commanded tank armies in 1943 commanded either *fronts,* tank armies, or combined-arms armies until war's end, three of these their original tank armies.

With a few notable exceptions, these command patterns clearly indicate that the wartime Red Army evidenced far greater command stability and far less command turbulence than has previously been assumed. More important still, this stability was most apparent in the most vital elements of its force structure—at *front* level, within key armies, and within the Red Army's tank, mechanized, and cavalry forces. In short, beginning as early as late 1941 and early 1942, the *Stavka* and NKO were able to identify and nurture those key officers who would lead the Red Army to victory in 1945. Arduous and costly though this education process was, it ultimately proved quite effective.

Despite enduring stereotypes of the Red Army as a monolithic and rigid force that employed artless steamroller tactics to achieve victory regardless of cost, as early as 1942, but certainly by 1943, the Red Army actually consisted of two distinct armies distinguished from one another by uniquely differing natures, characteristics, and command cadres. On the one hand, the 80 percent of the Red Army comprising the infantry, artillery, and engineer forces assigned to its rifle (combined-arms) armies, corps, divisions, brigades, and regiments, conformed in many ways to this unflattering stereotype. This massive force constituted the Red Army's imposing bludgeon, which blunted the *Wehrmacht's* panzer spearheads while on the defense and penetrated the *Wehrmacht's* defenses in painstakingly rigid fashion while on the offense, often artlessly and regardless of cost.

In mitigation, however, the imposing challenge of penetrating deep and well-prepared defenses, without which operational exploitations could not occur, compelled army, corps, division, and regimental commanders to fulfill their missions precisely in conformance with detailed plans, like cogs in an immensely complex mechanism, lest the penetration operation fail. Understanding that success in operations as a whole depended on effective penetrations, these forces defended or attacked within rigidly defined boundaries to secure objectives along linear phase lines with little or no deviation.

Side by side with this army, however, the Red Army also contained a sizable mobile force consisting of its tank armies, tank, mechanized, and cavalry corps, cavalry-mechanized groups, and separate tank, self-propelled, and antitank artillery brigades, which, although constituting only about 20 percent of its strength, formed the swift sword imparting sustained offensive momentum to its forces as a whole. Since it was responsible for halting or containing the *Wehrmacht's* panzer thrusts and exploiting the Red Army's successful penetration operations, usually during fluid combat situations, this force had to operate flexibly and with considerable initiative both tactically and operationally if it was to achieve success.

Since the Red Army's success as a whole depended directly on how well these forces operated, the commanders of mobile forces operated with far greater latitude regarding when, where, and how to employ their forces. As a result, their forces routinely operated within broad and frequently flexible boundaries against area and point objectives, and, when the situation required it, their commanders were expected to show initiative when confronted by unanticipated operational and tactical opportunities. In short, while serving as the Red Army's critical and indispensable spearhead, its mobile forces ultimately determined the pace and scope of Soviet battlefield victories, thereby defying all stereotypes.

This explains the contradiction inherent in the claim that, on the one hand, "junior officers, and many among the [Red Army's] middle command group, were clumsy and unable to take decisions . . . and were afraid of shouldering responsibility," and, on the other, "higher commanders and staffs . . . became adaptable, energetic, and ready to take decisions. . . . Certainly in men like Zhukov, Koniev, Vatutin, and Vassilevsky, Russia possessed army and army group commanders of a very high order." As these contradictory claims and their wartime success indicate, contrary to the overarching stereotype, many Red Army *front,* army, and corps commanders possessed command capabilities and military skills enabling them to best the *Wehrmacht* on the battlefield. Furthermore, the combat success these "great captains" achieved depended directly on the combat performance of equally competent and imaginative officers commanding their subordinate divisions, brigades, regiments, and battalions.

THE LED

Tragically, history has often overlooked, obscured, and, in some instances, totally forgotten the contributions of the over 35 million servicemen and servicewomen who fought, died, survived, or otherwise endured the harsh rigors of service in the Red Army during the war. While memorializing the contributions of many of its "great captains" and a few of its army's most illustrious heroes, for a variety of reasons, Russian historians have generally shied away from candidly relating the experiences of the vast majority of its officer corps and its millions of individual soldiers. Just as political and ideological imperatives required the protection or preservation of some reputations and the sullying of others, this reticence to speak openly about the life and fate of individual Red Army soldiers reflects many motives, including acute embarrassment over their appallingly high casualty rates, the base conditions they had to endure during wartime, and their diverse ethnicities, religions, and genders.

The Red Army was indeed a multi-ethnic and religiously diverse force made up of male—and a surprisingly large contingent of female—soldiers who volunteered, were conscripted, or were dragooned into its forces from every walk of life. Of the over 35 million soldiers who ultimately served, roughly 26 million were Slavs, roughly 8 million were not, and about 1 million were female. At least 8.7 million and perhaps as many as 14.7 million of these soldiers perished, and at least 10 million more suffered wounds or illness, often multiple times.

Regardless of their ethnicity, economic status, or social characteristics, most of the Red Army's soldiers shared a wide range of experiences. As indicated by their immense losses, they fought in a massive army whose *Stavka* and senior command cadre often displayed a callous if not ruthless disregard for the value of human life. In addition to fighting hungry, particularly during the first 18 months of the war, and thereafter developing the practice of foraging and "scavenging" to an art, they also often fought without adequate uniforms or kit, at least during the first six months of the war, and, while living a Spartan existence, they nonetheless learned to survive on a subsistence basis. Although it helped them endure their suffering and bolstered their morale and resolve, their daily vodka ration also often undermined their discipline and dulled the combat skills they needed to survive.

The Red Army's soldiers lived and fought within a ubiquitous system of near absolute political control, continuous political agitation, arbitrary and often brutal military discipline, and swift retribution for real or imagined crimes. The elaborate network of political "watchdogs" monitored their every action to prevent or stamp out any dissension in their ranks, and a regime of draconian laws and military tribunals administered swift and harsh punishments to those committing any and every crime or indiscretion, real or perceived. Even if threats of assignment to penal subunits for their crimes failed to ensure order and discipline within their ranks, equally ubiquitous blocking detachments prevented their disobedience to orders or outright desertion. In short, despite the ever-present specter of death at the hands of the enemy, harsh discipline, constant political education, and pervasive intimidation, most of the Red Army's soldiers endured their service, fought, and either perished or survived because, as products of an effective totalitarian system, they were accustomed to obeying their masters' orders.

In the final analysis, regardless of economic status, social origin, ethnicity, religion, or sex, whether motivated by fear of the Germans or their own commissars, whether inspired by "Soviet" patriotism, innate "Great Russian nationalism," sheer love of the motherland, or an innate hatred of foreign invaders, most of the Red Army's soldiers endured unimaginable deprivations, and many survived their terrible ordeal, helping to vanquish Europe's most formidable military machine within the relatively brief period of just under four years.

THE COSTS OF WAR

The costs incurred by the Red Army during its Great Patriotic War were indeed dear, in terms of both military personnel and weaponry. Truly catastrophic in proportion during the first two years of war, these losses remained appallingly high virtually to war's end, explaining in part why manpower shortages and disciplinary problems plagued the Red Army until war's end. These high casualty rates applied, first and foremost, to the army's front-line rifle forces, particularly those condemned to penal subunits forming the army's sacrificial shock force in virtually every offensive operation it conducted. In the words of a veteran machine-gun company commander, "After every operation, we were immediately without half of our people. Towards the end, there were 60–70 men in the companies. We did not have large companies. We used to have large companies of 150 men, but there now were simply 60–70 men and there were 7,000–8,000 [men] in the divisions."[2] This officer and others assert that their regiments routinely suffered about 50 percent casualties in each and every penetration operation they participated in, regardless of the year of the war. As a result, the Red Army and Navy suffered a total of over 19 million casualties during the first 30 months of the war, including almost 9 million dead, missing-in-action, and prisoners of war (see Table 14.1).

When analyzed on a quarterly basis, most of the Red Army's combat losses occurred during offensive operations and at a fairly constant daily rate, regardless of the year of war. For example, after losing roughly 460,000 soldiers killed in action during its winter offensive in first quarter of 1942, the Red Army lost about 550,000 soldiers killed in action during its winter offensive in the first quarter of 1943, another 670,000 soldiers killed in action during the Battle of Kursk and its associated counteroffensives in the late summer of 1943, and roughly 490,000 soldiers killed in action while conducting offensive operations along the Dnepr River line in the final quarter of 1943. Nor did these losses decrease substantially in 1944 and 1945. For example, the Red Army lost roughly 450,000 soldiers killed in action during its major offensives in the third quarter of 1944 and another 488,000 killed in action during the offensive operations it conducted during the first quarter of 1945.[3]

Understandably, the Red Army suffered its greatest prisoner-of-war and missing-in-action losses while retreating in the face of successful *Wehrmacht* offensives. For example, after losing almost 1.7 million men captured or missing in action during the disastrous encirclements battles in the third quarter of 1941, it lost roughly 636,000 captured and missing in the Viaz'ma and Briansk encirclements in October and November 1941, another 530,000 during the Khar'kov and Crimean disasters in May 1942, and another 685,000 men in encirclements in the Donbas during the *Wehrmacht's* advance toward Stalingrad. Despite these heavy losses of captured and missing in action, the total quantity of Red Army soldiers captured or missing in action decreased significantly from over 2.3 million in 1941 and about 1.5 million in 1942 to nearly 370,000 in 1943, 170,000 in 1944, and under 69,000 in 1945.

In regard to its soldiers taken captive, Russian sources claim 2,335,482 Red Army soldiers were captured, missing in action, or otherwise unaccounted for in 1941 and another 1,515,221 in 1942 and 367,806 in 1943, for a total of 4,218,509 soldiers lost over a period of 30 months. Many of these soldiers actually perished in combat or deserted, but the bulk of these captives ended up in German prisoner-of-war or labor camps if they were fortunate enough to survive their harrowing initial days in captivity. From the reverse perspective, German archival records indicate that the number of Red Army prisoners in German captivity at any given time varied from a low of roughly 800,000 to a maximum of over 2 million former soldiers (see Table 14.2).

It is impossible to determine exactly how many captured Red Army soldiers died en route to prisoner-of-war camps; however, fragmentary evidence indicates this gruesome toll ranged from a minimum of 250,000 soldiers to as many as 1 million. For example, OKW (German High Command) documents dated 1 May 1944 claim 3,291,157 Red Army prisoners of war had already perished in captivity, including 1,981,000 who died in prisoner-of-war camps, 1,030,157 who were shot and killed during escape attempts, and 280,000 who died while in transport to the camps.[4] On the other hand, Russian documents claim that, out of the almost 4.5 million Red Army soldiers who were held in captivity in Germany or elsewhere during the war, 1,836,562 ultimately returned to the Soviet Union after war's end, 339,000 of then tragically ending up in NKVD labor camps, primarily on the charge of "compromising" themselves while in captivity.[5]

Indicative of the harsh service conditions they had to endure and the inadequacy of Red Army medical support, the quantity of soldiers lost to illness and infectious disease also rose dramatically during wartime, from just over 66,000 in the second half of 1941 (130,000 on an annualized basis) and about 577,000 in 1942, to over 915,000 in 1943 and over 1.1 million in 1944. On the other hand, improved discipline and training reduced frostbite casualties significantly from about 13,500 in 1941 (27,000 on an annualized basis) and 58,268 in 1942 to 14,742 in 1943 and 3,227 in 1944, numbers indicative of the NKO's improved ability to clothe its soldiers properly.

In addition to the heavy personnel losses, the Red Army also lost immense quantities of weaponry, particularly in 1941 and 1942 (see Table 14.3). Understandably, the Red Army suffered its heaviest losses in weaponry and other equipment in 1941, when, depending on category of weaponry, losses ranged up to 56 percent of its rifle weaponry, 34–70 percent of its artillery, 73 percent of its tanks, and well over half of its combat aircraft. For obvious reasons, these losses were highest among the weapons employed by front-line troops, such as almost 60 percent of the Red Army's rifles, 62–65 percent of its light and medium machine guns, 56 percent of its field and almost 70 percent of its antitank guns, over 60 percent of its mortars, 73 percent of its tanks, and almost 60 percent of its combat aircraft, although the *Luftwaffe* destroyed more than half of the latter while they were still on the ground.

The Red Army's weapons losses decreased significantly and steadily during 1942 and 1943; calculated on an annualized basis, though, the loss rates in certain weapons categories remained high during the two years—for example, as high as over 40 percent for antitank guns (in 1942), 42–50 percent for tanks, and over 40 percent for fighters and assault aircraft.

Virtually unprecedented by any standard, when these losses are added to the equally massive toll of civilian casualties, they underscore the immense price the Soviet Union had to pay to achieve victory over Nazi Germany. It is no wonder, therefore, that the slogan, "Никто не забыт ничто не забыто" ("No one is forgotten, nothing is forgotten") remains a watchword among Russians to this very day.

With tremendous exertions and at terrible cost, the Soviet Union's political and military leadership was able to transform the Red Army from a colossus with feet of clay to a colossus reborn during the first 30 months of its Great Patriotic War. It did so by transforming the Red Army from a military instrument scarcely able to satisfy the Soviet Union's most rudimentary defensive requirements into a military tool capable of vanquishing the most formidable military force Europe had ever produced, Hitler's *Wehrmacht*. It would continue doing so with ruthless, willful, and lethal abandon for the remaining 16 months of war.

Table 14.1 Red Army and Navy Personnel Losses, 1941–1943

	Irreplaceable				*Medical*				
	Dead								
	Combat	Noncombat	MIA/ POW	Total	Wounded in action	Sick	Frostbitten	Total	Grand Total
1941									
3rd qtr	277,052	153,526	1,699,099	2,129,677	665,961	21,665	0	687,626	2,817,303
4th qtr	289,800	81,813	636,383	1,007,996	590,460	44,504	13,557	648,521	1,656,517
Total	566,852	235,339	2,335,482	3,137,673	1,256,421	66,169	13,557	1,336,147	4,473,820
1942									
1st qtr	459,332	34,328	181,655	675,315	1,011,040	117,007	51,410	1,179,457	1,854,772
2nd qtr	288,149	26,294	528,455	842,898	552,237	154,210	0	706,647	1,549,545
3rd qtr	486,039	53,689	685,767	1,224,495	1,146,667	136,395	0	1,283,062	2,507,557
4th qtr	360,322	38,842	120,344	515,508	765,577	169,461	6,858	941,896	1,457,404
Total	1,593,842	149,153	1,515,221	3,258,216	3,475,721	577,073	58,268	4,111,062	7,369,278
1943									
1st qtr	552,386	30,200	144,128	726,714	1,181,338	230,055	14,299	1,425,692	2,152,406
2nd qtr	154,221	15,231	22,452	191,904	252,954	237,683	0	490,637	682,541
3rd qtr	673,729	14,413	115,714	803,856	1,829,666	231,139	0	2,060,805	2,864,661
4th qtr	489,128	15,315	85,512	589,955	1,349,890	217,607	443	1,567,940	2,157,895
Total	1,869,464	75,159	367,806	2,312,429	4,613,848	916,484	14,742	5,545,074	7,857,503
Total to 1943	2,160,694	459,651	4,218,509	8,708,318	9,345,990	1,625,895	86,567	10,992,283	9,700,601

Source: G. F. Krivosheev, ed., *Grif sekretnosti sniat: Poteri vooruzhennykh sil SSSR v voinakh, boevykh deistviiakh i voennykh konfliktakh* [The secret classification is removed: Losses of the Soviet Armed Forces in wars, combat operations, and military conflicts] (Moscow: Voenizdat, 1993), 146.

Table 14.2 German High Command (OKW) Records of Red Army Soldiers in Captivity, 1942–1944

	POW Camps *(Lager)*	German Industries	Total
1 Feb 1942	1,020,531	147,736	1,168,267
1 Mar 1942	976,458	153,674	1,130,132
1 Apr 1942	643,237	166,881	810,118
1 Jun 1942	734,544	242,146	976,690
1 Sep 1942	1,675,626	375,451	2,051,077
1 Oct 1942	1,118,011	455,054	1,573,065
1 Nov 1942	766,314	487,535	1,253,849
1 Jan 1943	1,045,609	NA	NA
1 Feb 1943	1,038,512	493,761	1,532,273
1 Jul 1943	647,545	505,975	1,153,520
1 Aug 1943	807,609	496,106	1,303,709
1 Dec 1943	766,314	564,692	1,331,006
1 Mar 1944	861,052	594,279	1,455,331

Source: G. F. Krivosheev, ed., *Rossiia i SSSR v voinakh XX veka, poteri vooruzhennykh sil: Statisticheskoe issledovanie* [Russia and the USSR in twentieth-century wars and the losses of the armed forces: A statistical investigation] (Moscow: Olma-Press, 2001), 460.

Table 14.3 Red Army Weapons Losses in Combat, 1941–1943

	1941		1942		1943	
	Total on hand	Lost (%)	Total on hand	Lost (%)	Total on hand	Lost (%)
Rifle weapons						
Revolvers	1,370,000	440,000 (32.1)	1,100,000	390,000 (35.5)	1,080,000	80,000 (7.4)
Rifles	9,310,000	5,550,000 (59.6)	7,800,000	2,180,000 (27.9)	9,470,000	1,260,000 (13.3)
Submachine guns	200,000	100,000 (50)	1,660,000	550,000 (33.1)	3,170,000	530,000 (16.7)
Light machine guns	215,700	134,700 (62.4)	253,800	76,700 (30.2)	427,300	82,800 (19.4)
Medium machine guns	84,700	54,700 (64.6)	88,000	24,500 (27.8)	154,000	21,000 (13.6)
Heavy machine guns	3,600	1,400 (38.9)	9,600	4,900 (51)	19,100	900 (4.7)
Antitank rifles	17,700	8,800 (49.7)	257,900	86,900 (33.7)	335,500	46,600 (13.9)
Total	11,200,000	6,290,000 (56.2)	11,170,000	3,310,000 (29.6)	14,060,000	2,020,000 (14.4)
Artillery, mortars, and rocket artillery						
Antiaircraft guns	12,000	4,100 (34.2)	14,700	1,600 (10.9)	25,300	800 (3.2)
25mm	300	100 (33.3)	400	0	0	0
37, 40mm	2,800	1,200 (42.8)	5,400	600 (11.1)	11,700	400 (3.4)
76, 85, 90mm	8,900	2,800 (31.5)	8,900	900 (10.1)	11,800	300 (2.5)

Antitank guns	17,400	12,100 (69.5)	25,800	11,500 (44.6)	37,700	5,500 (14.6)
45mm	17,000	12,000 (70.6)	25,500	11,300 (44.3)	35,700	5,200 (14.6)
57mm	400	100 (25)	300	200 (66.7)	2,000	300 (15)
Field guns	43,300	24,400 (56.3)	49,000	12,300 (25.1)	58,800	5,700 (9.7)
76mm	21,800	12,300 (56.4)	33,100	10,100 (30.5)	39,600	5,000 (12.6)
100, 107mm	1,000	400 (40)	600	100 (16.7)	500	0
122mm howitzers	10,000	6,000 (60)	8,500	1,500 (17.6)	10,800	600 (5.6)
122mm guns	1,600	900 (56.2)	1,000	0	1,500	0
152mm howitzers	4,100	2,600 (63.4)	1,500	200 (13.3)	1,400	0
152mm gun/howitzers	3,700	2,100 (56.8)	3,300	400 (12.1)	4,000	100 (2.5)
203mm +	1,100	100 (9.1)	1,000	0	1,000	0
Mortars	98,500	60,500 (60.5)	268,300	82,200 (30.6)	254,000	26,700 (10.5)
50mm	59,500	38,000 (63.9)	125,900	37,300 (29.6)	106,100	13,300 (12.5)
82mm	31,100	18,500 (59.5)	113,100	34,800 (30.8)	111,900	10,300 (9.2)
107, 120mm	7,900	4,000 (50.6)	29,300	10,100 (34.5)	36,000	3,100 (8.6)

—Continued

Table 14.3 Continued

	1941		1942		1943	
	Total on hand	Lost (%)	Total on hand	Lost (%)	Total on hand	Lost (%)
Rocket artillery	1,000	0	4,300	700	6,900	2,100
		(16.3)		(30.4)		
BM-8	400	0	1,300	300	1,400	500
		(23.1)		(35.7)		
BM-13	600	0	3,000	400	5,500	1,600
		(13.3)		(29.1)		
Tanks and self-propelled guns						
Tanks	28,200	20,500	35,600	15,000	43,500	22,400
		(72.7)		(42.1)		(51.5)
Heavy (KV-1, 2)	1,500	900	3,200	1,200	2,900	1,300
		(60)		(37.5)		(44.8)
Medium (T-34)	3,100	2,300	14,200	6,600	23,900	14,700
		(74.2)		(46.5)		(61.5)
Light (T-60, 70)	23,600	17,300	18,200	7,200	16,700	6,400
		(73.3)		(39.5)		(38.3)
Self-propelled guns	0	0	100	100	4,400	1,100
			(100)		(25)	
Heavy	0	0	30	30	1,300	500
				(100)		(38.5)
Medium	0	0	0	0	800	100
						(12.5)
Light	0	0	70	70	2,300	500
			(100)		(21.7)	

Armored cars	23,900	300 (12.5)	31,100	9,000 (28.9)	32,700	12,500 (38.2)
Aircraft						
Bombers	10,900	7,200/4,600 (66/42.2)	7,800	2,500/1,600 (32/20.5)	10,400	3,600/1,700 (34.6/16.3)
Assault aircraft	1,500	1,100/600 (73.3/40)	7,600	2,600/1,800 (34.2/23.7)	16,000	7,200/3,900 (45/24.4)
Fighters	17,500	9,600/5,100 (54.9/29.1)	18,600	7,000/4,400 (37.6/23.7)	28,600	11,700/5,600 (40.9/19.6)
Total combat	29,900	17,900/10,300 (59.9/34.4)	34,000	12,100/7,800 (35.6/22.9)	55,000	22,500/11,200 (40.9/20.4)
Others	13,200	3,300/300 (25/2.3)	15,600	2,600/1,300 (16.7/8.3)	18,100	4,200/500 (23.2/2.8)
Grand total	43,100	21,200/10,600 (49.2/24.6)	49,600	14,700/9,100 (29.6/18.3)	73,100	26,700/11,700 (36.5/16)
Vehicles and radios						
Vehicles	477,500	159,000 (33.3)	470,000	66,200 (14.1)	563,000	67,000 (11.9)
Radios	43,000	23,700 (55.1)	46,800	7,000 (15)	89,300	17,700 (19.8)

[a]The numerator in these fractions denotes total aircraft losses, and the denominator, losses in air combat.

Source: G. F. Krivosheev, ed., *Rossiia i SSSR v voinakh XX veka, poteri vooruzhennykh sil: Statisticheskoe issledovanie* [Russia and the USSR in twentieth-century wars and the losses of the armed forces: A statistical investigation] (Moscow: Olma-Press, 2001), 473–81.

Notes

1. The First Period of the War, 22 June 1941 to 18 November 1942

1. Convinced of the scientific nature of war, Soviet and Russian military theorists have viewed the study and exploitation of military experience as a valuable tool for improving the current and future combat performance of their military forces. To do so, they have established within the General Staff and operating headquarters an extensive system for collecting, processing, and exploiting the military experiences of their military forces and those of foreign countries.

2. For example, see Earl F. Ziemke and Magna E. Bauer, *Moscow to Stalingrad: Decision in the East* (Washington, DC: Office of the Chief of Military History United States Army, 1987); Albert Seaton, *The Russo-German War 1941–1945* (New York: Praeger, 1971); John Erickson, *The Road to Stalingrad* (New York: Harper & Row, 1975); P. N. Pospelov, ed. *Istoriia Velikoi Otechestvennoi voiny Sovetskogo Soiuza 1941–1945 v shesti tomakh* [A history of the Great Patriotic War of the Soviet Union 1941–1945 in six volumes] (Moscow: Voenizdat, 1960–1965); A. A. Grechko, ed., *Istoriia Vtoroi Mirovoi voiny 1939–1945 v dvenadtsati tomakh* [A history of World War II 1939–1945 in twelve volumes] (Moscow: Voenizdat, 1973–1982); and V. A. Zolotarev, ed., *Velikaia Otechestvennaia voina 1941–1945: Voenno-istoricheskie ocherki v chetyrekh tomakh* [The Great Patriotic War 1941–1945: Military-historical essays in four volumes] (Moscow: Nauka, 1998–1999). For a survey of the war that includes most but not all of the of the missing operations, see David M. Glantz and Jonathan M. House, *When Titans Clashed: How the Red Army Stopped Hitler* (Lawrence: University Press of Kansas, 1995).

3. While the Germans employed army groups as their premier strategic force, the Red Army employed *fronts*, which, initially, were roughly equivalent in size and mission to army groups. After the 1941 campaign, the Red Army reduced the size and increased the number of *fronts*, making them roughly equivalent in strength to German field armies.

4. Although Stalin and his *Stavka* were different if overlapping entities, they were essentially one and the same.

5. For a sample of the newly released documents that support this contention, see V. A. Zolotarev, ed., "Stavka VGK: Dokumenty i materialy 1941 goda" [The *Stavka* VGK: Documents and materials of 1941], in *Russkii arkhiv: Velikaia Otechestvennaia* [The Russian archives: The Great Patriotic (War)], 16, 5 (1) (Moscow: Terra, 1996), and "Dokumenty po ispol'zovaniiu bronetankovykh i mekhanizirovannykh voisk Sovetskoi Armii v period s 22 iiunia po sentiabr' 1941 g. vkliuchitel'no" [Documents on the employment of armored and mechanized forces of the Soviet Army in the

period from 22 June to September 1941, inclusively], in *Sbornik boevykh dokumentov Velikoi Otechestvennoi voiny* [A collection of combat documents of the Great Patriotic War], no. 33 (Moscow: Voenizdat, 1957), classified secret.

6. David M. Glantz, *The Initial Period of War on the Eastern Front* (London: Frank Cass, 1993).

7. David M. Glantz, *Forgotten Battles of the Soviet-German War (1941–1945), volume 1: The Summer–Fall Campaign (22 June–4 December 1941)* (Carlisle, PA: Self-published, 1999), 19–44; and David M. Glantz, *The Battle for Leningrad, 1941–1944* (Lawrence: University Press of Kansas, 2002), 37–50.

8. Glantz, *Forgotten Battles,* I: 47–51; Glantz, *The Initial Period of War;* and David M. Glantz, *The Battle for Smolensk (7 July–10 September 1941)* (Carlisle, PA: Self-published, 2001), 11–23.

9. Glantz, *Forgotten Battles,* I: 44–47.

10. Ibid., 51–71; and Glantz, *The Battle for Leningrad,* 54–59.

11. Glantz, *The Initial Period of War;* and Glantz, *The Battle for Smolensk,* 43–56.

12. Glantz, *Forgotten Battles,* I: 71–74.

13. Glantz, *The Battle for Smolensk,* 56–92; and David M. Glantz, *Barbarossa: Hitler's Invasion of Russia 1941* (Charleston, SC: Tempus, 2001), 75–115. The latter also covers the other "forgotten battles" of the 1941 campaign.

14. Glantz, *Barbarossa,* 154; and "Boevye deistviia Sovetskikh voisk na Kalininskom napravlenii v 1941 gody (s oktiabria 1941 po 7 ianvaria 1942 g.)" [Combat operations of Soviet forces on the Kalinin axis (from October 1941 through 7 January 1942)], in *Sbornik voenno-istoricheskikh materialov Velikoi Otechestvennoi voiny* [Collection of military-historical materials of the Great Patriotic War], no. 7 (Moscow: Voenizdat, 1952), classified secret.

15. The crux of this argument is advanced in Viktor Suvorov, *Icebreaker: Who Started the Second World War?* (London: Hamish Hamilton, 1990), and its sequel, Viktor Suvorov, *Den'-M, 6 iiulia 1941: Kogda nachalas' Vtoraia Mirovaia voina?* [M-Day, 6 July 1941: When did World War II begin?] (Moscow: Vse dlia Vas, 1994).

16. For a refutation of Suvorov's arguments from a military standpoint, see David M. Glantz, *Stumbling Colossus: The Red Army on the Eve of War* (Lawrence: University Press of Kansas, 1998); and Harold C. Deutsch and Dennis E. Showalter, eds., *What If? Strategic Alternatives of WWII* (Chicago: Emperor's Press, 1997), 56–60.

17. For counterarguments, see Deutsch and Showalter, *What If?,* 67–73.

18. This claim is refuted in ibid., 73–77; and Glantz, *Barbarossa,* 96, 157–58, 211–14.

19. For a refutation of this argument, see Deutsch and Showalter, *What If?,* 73–81.

20. Among the many traditional accounts of the Battle of Moscow and combat elsewhere along the German Eastern Front during the winter campaign, see Col. Albert Seaton, *The Battle for Moscow* (Edison, NJ: Castle Books, 2001) (reprinted from 1971); P. A. Zhilin, ed., *Besprimernyi podvig* [An unprecedented deed] (Moscow: Nauka, 1968); A. M. Samsonov, ed., *Proval gitlerovskogo nastupleniia na Moskvu* [The defeat of Hitler's offensive on Moscow] (Moscow: Nauka, 1966); and M. I. Khametov, *Bitva pod Moskvoi* [The Battle at Moscow] (Moscow: Voenizdat, 1989).

21. For further details, see David M. Glantz, *Forgotten Battles of the Soviet-German War (1941–1945), volume 2: The Winter Campaign (5 December 1941–27 April 1942)* (Carlisle, PA: Self-published, 1999), 11–47.

22. Ibid., 63–118; and Glantz, *The Battle for Leningrad,* 149–83.

23. For further details on both operations, see Glantz, *Forgotten Battles,* II: 67–62, 118–55.

24. For example, in the spring of 1943, the *Stavka* ordered the Red Army to conduct offensive operations along a broad front from the Leningrad region to the Black Sea. While the Voronezh, Southwestern, and Southern Fronts pounded German Army Group South in the Donbas region, the Central, Western, and later the Kalinin Fronts conducted offensive operations against German Army Group South aimed at liberating Orel, Briansk, and Smolensk. Simultaneously, the Northwestern, Volkhov, and Leningrad Fronts, all operating under Zhukov's supervision, conducted Operation Polar Star, an unsuccessful attempt to destroy Army Group North at Leningrad and in the Leningrad *oblast'* (region).

Once again, in the fall of 1943, the *Stavka* ordered the Kalinin (1st Baltic), Western, Briansk, and Central (Belorussian) Fronts to capture Minsk and clear German Army Group Center's forces from Belorussia and the Voronezh (1st Ukrainian), Southwestern (2nd Ukrainian), Steppe (3rd Ukrainian), and Southern (4th Ukrainian) Fronts to capture Vinnitsa and drive the forces of German Army Groups South and "A" from the Ukraine.

Nor did this broad front strategy end thereafter. During the winter of 1944, the Leningrad, Volkhov, and 2nd Baltic Fronts assaulted German Army Group North, drove it from the Leningrad region, and attempted to penetrate into the Baltic region. Simultaneously, the 1st Baltic, Western, and Belorussian Fronts attacked Army Group Center in a failed attempt to capture Vitebsk, Bobruisk, and Minsk, and the four Ukrainian Fronts savaged German Army Groups South and "A" in the Ukraine and the Crimea.

For information on these offensive operations, see key *Stavka* orders found in V. A. Zolotarev, ed., "Stavka Verkhovnogo Glavnokomandovaniia: Dokumenty i materialy 1943 goda" [The *Stavka* VGK: Documents and materials of 1943], in *Russkii arkhiv: Velikaia Otechestvennaia* [The Russian archives: The Great Patriotic (War)], 16, 5 (3) (Moscow: Terra, 1999); V. A. Zolotarev, ed., "Stavka VGK: Dokumenty i materialy 1944–1945" [The *Stavka* VGK: Documents and materials of 1944], in *Russkii arkhiv: Velikaia Otechestvennaia* [The Russian archives: The Great Patriotic (War)], 16, 5 (4) (Moscow: Terra, 1999); and written accounts found in David M. Glantz, *Forgotten Battles of the Soviet-German War (1941–1945), volume 4: The Winter Campaign (19 November 1942–21 March 1943)* (Carlisle, PA: Self-published, 1999); and David M. Glantz, *Forgotten Battles of the Soviet-German War (1941–1945), volume 5, parts 1 and 2: The Summer–Fall Campaign (1 July–31 December 1943)* (Carlisle, PA: Self-published, 2000).

25. For an elaboration on this argument see Glantz, *Barbarossa,* 208–9.

26. Ibid., 211–13.

27. Among the many traditional accounts of the Battle of Stalingrad and combat elsewhere along the German Eastern Front during the summer campaign of 1942, see William Craig, *Enemy at the Gates: The Battle for Stalingrad* (New York: Dutton,

1973); Heinz Schröter, *Stalingrad: The Battle That Changed the World* (New York: Ballantine, 1958); V. E. Tarrant, *Stalingrad* (New York: Hippocrene, 1992); Antony Beevor, *Stalingrad, the Fateful Siege: 1942–1943* (New York: Viking, 1998); A. M. Samsonov, *Stalingradskaia bitva* [The Battle of Stalingrad] (Moscow: Nauka, 1960); K. K. Rokossovsky, ed., *Velikaia bitva na Volge* [The great battle on the Volga] (Moscow: Voenizdat, 1965); and A. M. Samsonov, ed., *Stalingradskaia epopeia* [The Stalingrad epic] (Moscow: Nauka, 1968).

28. For details on the strategic debate within the *Stavka* during the late winter and spring of 1942, see David M. Glantz, *Kharkov 1942: Anatomy of a Military Disaster* (London: Ian Allen, 1998), 21–59.

29. Ibid., 59–248.

30. David M. Glantz, *Forgotten Battles of the Soviet-German War (1941–1945), volume 3: The Summer Campaign (12 May–18 November 1942)* (Carlisle, PA: Self-published, 1999), 86–101.

31. Ibid., 6–86.

32. Ibid., 101–29.

33. For details, see Glantz, *The Battle for Leningrad,* 213–31.

34. For example, see I. Kh. Bagramian, *Tak shli my k Pobede* [As we went on to victory] (Moscow: Voenizdat, 1977); K. S. Moskalenko, *Na iugo-zapadnom napravlenii* [Along the southwestern axis], vol. 1 (Moscow: Nauka, 1969); A. M. Vasilevsky, *Delo vsei zhizni* [Life's work] (Moscow: Politizdat, 1971); and G. Zhukov, *Reminiscences and Reflections,* vol. 2 (Moscow: Progress, 1985). A detailed account of this debate together with fresh conclusions is found in Glantz, *Kharkov 1942.*

35. Virtually every German-based general history of the war and work on the Battle of Stalingrad has raised this issue. The most cogent discussion of this issue is found in Gotthardt Heinrici, "The Campaign in Russia," trans. Joseph Welch, vol. 1, National Archives manuscript in German (Washington, DC: United States Army G-2, 1954).

36. For a detailed discussion of this issue, see Deutsch and Showalter, *What If?,* 77–78.

37. See, for example, Heinrici, "The Campaign in Russia."

38. See Glantz, *The Battle for Leningrad,* 213–31.

2. *The Second Period of the War, 1943*

1. For studies of combat during the second period of the war and, particularly, the Battle of Stalingrad, see Chapter 1, note 27.

2. The most thorough accounts of these operations are V. P. Morozov, *Zapadnee Voronezha* [West of Voronezh] (Moscow: Voenizdat, 1956); Friedrich Schulz, *Reverses on the Southern Wing (1942–1943), MS #T-15* (Headquarters, United States Army, Europe, Historical Division, n.d.); and H. Scheibert, *Panzer Zwischen Don und Donez: Die Winterkampfe 1942/1943* [Panzers between the Don and Donets: The Winter Battle of 1942–1943] (Freidberg: Podzun-Pallas-Verlag, 1979).

3. The only detailed Soviet account of Red Army operations at Khar'kov and in the Donbas is A. G. Ershov, *Osvobozhdenie Donbassa* [The liberation of the Donbas] (Moscow: Voenizdat, 1973). See also the more recent study, David M. Glantz, *From*

the Don to the Dnepr: Soviet Offensive Operations December 1942–August 1943 (London: Frank Cass, 1991), which, while providing unprecedented detail on the Red Army's Khar'kov and Donbas offensive operations, also misses many of the "forgotten" dimensions of the Red Army's winter offensive.

4. For details on Operation Mars, see David M. Glantz, *Zhukov's Greatest Defeat: The Red Army's Epic Defeat in Operation Mars, 1942* (Lawrence: University Press of Kansas, 1999); and Glantz, *Forgotten Battles,* IV: 17–67. For the Russian counterargument, see A. S. Orlov, "Operatsiia 'Mars': Razlichnye traktov" [Operation Mars: Different roads], in *Mir istorii* [World of history], no. 4 (April 2000): 1–4; and V. V. Gurkin, "'Mars' v orbite 'Urana' i 'Saturna': O vtoroi Rzhevsko-Sychevskoi nastupatel'noi operatsii 1942 goda" ["Mars" in the orbit of "Uranus" and "Saturn": On the second Rzhev-Sychevka offensive operation], *Voenno-istoricheskii zhurnal* [Military-historical journal], no. 4 (July–August 2000), 14–19. Hereafter cited as *VIZh,* with appropriate article, number, and date. These are the first and only articles ever to appear in the Russian military press concerning Operation Mars.

5. Prior to Stalin's death in 1953, Soviet historians avoided writing about any Red Army failures. Thereafter, during Khrushchev's de-Stalinization program (1958–1964), when Zhukov and Khrushchev were at odds, most histories credited Vasilevsky and Eremenko with the Stalingrad victory but still avoided any mention of Operation Mars. After Khrushchev's removal as Party first secretary and Soviet leader in 1964, in part with the military's acquiescence if not full support, histories began according Zhukov virtually full credit for orchestrating the Stalingrad victory, while maintaining utter silence about Operation Mars.

6. The *Stavka* formed the Central Front in early February 1943 from the Don Front's 65th and 21st Armies, which had just completed liquidating German forces encircled at Stalingrad, and the 2nd Tank and 70th Armies from the *Stavka's* reserve. Its commander was Army General K. K. Rokossovsky, the former commander of the Don Front. For details on the Orel-Briansk-Smolensk offensive see Glantz, *Forgotten Battles,* IV: 213–311; David M. Glantz, "Prelude to Kursk: Soviet Strategic Operations, February–March 1943," *Journal of Slavic Military Studies* 8, no. 1 (March 1995): 1–35; and V. A. Zolotarev, ed., "Preludiia Kurskoi bitvy" [Prelude to the Battle of Kursk], in *Russkii arkhiv: Velikaia Otechestvennaia* [The Russian archives: The Great Patriotic (War)], 15, 4 (3) (Moscow: Terra, 1997).

7. For details see, Glantz, *Forgotten Battles,* IV; 381–430; and Glantz, *The Battle for Leningrad,* 286–98.

8. For details on the Southern Front's role in the 1st Donbas (Mariupol') offensive, see Glantz, *Forgotten Battles,* IV: 83–183.

9. Soviet military histories claim that heavy fighting occurred throughout the planned German withdrawal, when, in fact, the heavy fighting occurred only when Red Army forces attempted to penetrate new defenses German forces erected after their withdrawal. See ibid., 311–81.

10. I. Kh. Bagramian, ed., *Istoriia voin i voennogo iskusstva* [A history of wars and military art] (Moscow: Voenizdat, 1970), 207–8.

11. Specifically, in Belorussia, Red Army forces assaulted Mozyr', Kalinkovichi, Ptich', and Vitebsk in an attempt to reach Bobruisk and Minsk.

12. The Red Army conducted these successive offensives against Army Group Center in Belorussia (23 June 1944), Army Group North Ukraine in Poland (16 July 1944), and Army Group South Ukraine in Romania (20 August 1944).

13. For details, see Glantz, *From the Don to the Dnepr,* 10–82.

14. Ibid.

15. German-based accounts of the Battle of Kursk include Geoffrey Jukes, *Kursk: Clash of Armour,* Battle Book no. 7 (London: Purnell's History of the Second World War, 1968); Janusz Pielkalkiewicz, *Operation "Citadel": Kursk and Orel: The Greatest Tank Battle in the Second World War* (Novato, CA: Presidio, 1987); and Mark Healy, *Kursk 1943: The Tide Turns in the East* (London: Osprey, 1992). The most thorough analysis of the battle from the German point of view is Gotthardt Heinrici, "Citadel: The Attack on the Russian Kursk Salient," Manuscript (Washington, DC: U.S. National Archives, n.d).

16. The most substantial accounts of the Battle of Kursk from the Russian perspective are G. A. Koltunov and B. G. Solov'ev, *Kurskaia bitva* [The Battle of Kursk] (Moscow: Voenizdat, 1983); and David M. Glantz and Harold S. Orenstein, *The Battle for Kursk 1943: The Soviet General Staff Study* (London: Frank Cass, 1999).

17. More recent accounts of the Battle of Kursk include David M. Glantz and Jonathan M. House, *The Battle of Kursk* (Lawrence: University Press of Kansas, 1999), a balanced reassessment of the battle based on both German and Soviet archival materials; and Niklas Zetterling and Anders Frankson, *Kursk 1943: A Statistical Analysis* (London: Frank Cass, 2000), which focuses on hitherto unattainable statistical data on the battle.

18. Virtually all general histories and accounts of specific battles that took place during the fall of 1943, whether written from the German or Russian point of view, claim that the only important operations that took place during this period occurred along the southwestern and southern axes, that is, into the Ukraine.

19. For details see, and Glantz, *Forgotten Battles,* V (1): 107–59.

20. Ibid., 19–61.

21. Ibid., 159–70.

22. Ibid., 171–407; and ibid., pt. 2, 408–563.

23. Ibid., pt. 2, 564–673.

24. Ibid., 674–818.

25. For example, the Red Army's 2nd and 3rd Ukrainian Fronts conducted the 1st Iasi-Kishinev offensive in April and May 1944, fully four months prior to the same *fronts'* successful 2nd Iasi-Kishinev offensive of August–September 1944. Likewise, the Red Army attempted to penetrate deep into East Prussia in October 1944, three months prior to its successful East Prussian offensive of January 1945. Finally, in early February 1945, the Red Army began its final drive on Berlin, only to halt the offensive after roughly one week of heavy fighting. In this case, however, Stalin seems to have halted the offensive in order to shift reserves into Hungary and mount offensives in that region aimed at securing Vienna and a foothold in the Danube basin. He did so, at least in part, because Roosevelt and Churchill had provided him assurances during the Yalta Conference (4–11 February 1945) that the Red Army could seize Berlin and eastern Germany. Subsequently, the Red

Army began its Berlin offensive on 16 April 1945, the day after its forces occupied Vienna. See David M. Glantz, "The Failures of Historiography: Forgotten Battles of the German-Soviet War (1941–1945)," *Journal of Slavic Military Studies* 8, no. 1 (December 1995): 768–808.

26. See the sources highlighted in chapter 1, note 19.

27. These included the 21st (6th Guards in April), 24th (4th Guards in April), 62nd (8th Guards in April), 63rd, 64th (7th Guards in April), 1st Tank, 27th, 53rd, and 47th Armies. See Glantz, "Prelude to Kursk," 1–35; and David M. Glantz, *Soviet Military Intelligence in War* (London: Frank Cass, 1990), 172–283.

28. See Glantz and House, *The Battle of Kursk.*

29. See also David M. Glantz, "Soviet Military Strategy during the Second Period of War (November 1942–December 1943): A Reappraisal," *Journal of Military History* 60 (January 1996): 115–50.

30. The *Wehrmacht* conducted numerous counterstrokes of operational significance after the summer of 1943. These included a counterstroke southeast of Bobruisk in Belorussia in December 1943, at Krivoi Rog in the Ukraine in October 1943, at Tirgu-Frumos, along the Dnestr River, and at Iasi in northern Romania in May 1944, at Buchach in the western Ukraine in April 1944 (the relief of encircled First Panzer Army), at Siauliai in Lithuania in August 1944, at Gumbinnen in East Prussia in October 1944, and around Budapest in Hungary in January 1945. However, Hitler attempted his only strategic counteroffensive in the East at Lake Balaton in Hungary in March 1945.

31. For example, based upon this study of war experience, by early 1943 the Red Army General Staff had begun fundamentally altering its force structure (e.g., the directives creating new rifle corps and tank and air armies) and improving its operational and tactical techniques (e.g., directives and orders on proper concentration, the creation of the concepts of the artillery and air offensive, and the concerted employment of armor and mechanized forces).

3. *Soviet Military Art*

1. R. A. Savushkin, ed., *Razvitie Sovetskikh vooruzhennykh sil i voennogo iskusstva v Velikoi Otechestvennoi voine 1941–1945 gg.* [The development of the Soviet Armed Forces and military art in the Great Patriotic War 1941–1945] (Moscow: Lenin Political-Military Academy, 1988), 48–49.

2. N. V. Ogarkov, ed., "Strategiia voennaia" [Military strategy], in *Sovetskaia voennaia entsiklopediia* [Soviet military encyclopedia], 8 vols. (Moscow: Voenizdat, 1976–1980), VII: 562. Hereafter cited as *SVE* with appropriate entry and page(s).

3. Ibid.

4. *Stavka* directives specified the location, objectives, timing, and duration of military operations; the specific forces and weaponry to be employed; concentration areas and key operational axes; precise instructions pertaining to cooperation with adjacent *fronts*, fleets, flotillas, and supporting aviation; and specific time constraints for all phases of *front* planning and conduct of the operation. They also indicated the *fronts'* immediate and subsequent missions, the width of designated penetration

sectors, force densities, recommended operational formations, and instructions concerning the employment of mobile groups and second echelons.

5. Fragmentary or warning orders often related to subsequent phases of ongoing operations.

6. The Soviets defined campaigns as multiple defensive or offensive operations conducted successively or simultaneously within a single or multiple seasons of a given year.

7. For example, its *fronts* operating along the Moscow and Stalingrad axes were conducting Operations Mars and Uranus to capture Rzhev and Stalingrad and then subsequent code-named operations to capture Viaz'ma and Rostov. In these cases, however, the failure of Operation Mars forced the *Stavka* to postpone the subsequent offensive against Viaz'ma, while German resistance prompted it to truncate its offensive toward Rostov.

8. Ibid.

9. In 1941 these offensives included the Northwestern Front's counterstrokes at Sol'tsy and Staraia Russa in July and August, the Leningrad Front's counterattacks south of Leningrad in August and September and at Tikhvin in November 1941, and the Southern Front's counterstroke at Rostov in November. In 1942 these included the Western and Kalinin Fronts' counterstrokes at Bolkhov, Zhizdra, and in the Rzhev and Sychevka regions in July, August, and September 1942. For details, see Glantz, *Forgotten Battles,* vols. I–III.

10. For example, during Operation Barbarossa, the *Stavka's* forward *fronts* conducted counterstrokes in late June and, after these actions proved ineffective, major offensives near Smolensk in August and early September. During German Operation *Blau,* the *Stavka's fronts* defending along the main axis conducted major offensives near Voronezh and along the Chir River in July and August and, later, in the Serafimovich and Kletskaia regions south of the Don River and in the Stalingrad region proper in August and September. These offensives forced the Germans to redeploy portions of their Sixth Army and the Romanian Third and Italian Eighth Armies to the threatened Don River front, in doing so significantly weakening the *Wehrmacht's* forces struggling in and around Stalingrad proper.

11. These included offensives by the Kalinin, Western, Southwestern, Don, and Stalingrad Fronts in November 1942 by the Leningrad, Volkhov, Briansk, Voronezh, Southwestern, Don, Southern, and North Caucasus Fronts in January 1943 and by the Leningrad, Volkhov, Northwestern, Kalinin, Western, Briansk, Central, Voronezh, Southwestern, Southern, and North Caucasus Fronts in February and March 1943.

12. For example, the Central, Voronezh, and Steppe Fronts conducted the Kursk defense, the Voronezh and Steppe Fronts conducted the Belgorod-Khar'kov offensive, the Western, Briansk, and Central Fronts conducted the Orel offensive, the Kalinin and Western Fronts conducted the Smolensk offensive, and the Southwestern and Southern Fronts conducted the Donbas offensive.

13. "Deistviia aviatsii v Kurskom srazhenii" [Aviation operations during the Battle of Kursk], in *Sbornik materialov po izucheniiu opyta voiny* [Collections of materials for the study of war experience], no. 11 (March–April 1944) (Moscow: Voenizdat, 1944), 160–87, classified secret. Hereafter cited as *SMPIOV,* with appropriate article, number, and date.

14. Savushkin, *Razvitie,* 82. These partisan operations included operations "Railroad War" and "Concert."

15. These included the Kalinin (1st Baltic), Western, and Central (Belorussian) Fronts operating against Belorussia, the Voronezh (1st Ukrainian) and part of the Central Fronts operating against Kiev, and the Steppe (2nd Ukrainian), Southwestern (3rd Ukrainian), and Southern (4th Ukrainian) Fronts operating against Krivoi Rog.

16. Throughout the entire first period of the war, the *Stavka* compensated for its lack of experience by engaging in a single-minded effort to amass strategic reserves and employ them at the point of most acute danger. In doing so, the *Stavka* consciously capitalized on what it recognized as the innate strength of the Soviet state—its large population—and exploited the most obvious German weaknesses, a limited supply of manpower and an inability to establish sound strategic priorities. By playing this Soviet strength against these German weaknesses, and despite the Red Army's numerous disasters, the *Stavka* was able to maintain a reasonable correlation of forces and, ultimately, achieve its preeminent strategic aim of conducting a viable strategic defense and halting the German drive, albeit just short of its initial strategic objectives.

The *Stavka's* often ruthless and careless exploitation of the Soviet Union's seemingly inexhaustible supply of fresh manpower enabled the Red Army to survive a series of unprecedented strategic defeats and compensated for a host of other obvious Red Army weaknesses. All the while, *Stavka* members and those Red Army command cadre at *front* and army level who survived the Red Army's numerous failures steadily amassed the combat experience necessary to withstand the German onslaught and, ultimately, embark on strategic offensive operations of their own.

17. N. Pavlenko, "Na pervom etape voiny" [During the first stage of the war], *Kommunist* [Communist], no. 9 (June 1988): 92.

18. For example, see "Archives Document the Torture of Marshal Meretskov," *JPRS-UMA 88-019* (19 August 1988), 21, quoting from an article in *Literaturnaia gazeta* [Literary gazette], 20 April 1989, 13.

19. For the most recent Soviet discussion identifying wartime strategic defensive operations, see V. V. Gurkin and M. I. Golovnin, "K voprosu o strategicheskikh operatsiiakh Velikoi Otechestvennoi voiny 1941–1945 gg" [Concerning the question of strategic operations of the Great Patriotic War 1941–1945], *VIZh,* no. 10 (October 1985): 10–23; V. S. Shlomin, "K voprosu o strategicheskikh operatsiiakh Velikoi Otechestvennoi voiny 1941–1945 gg" [Concerning the question of strategic operations of the Great Patriotic War 1941–1945], *VIZh,* no. 4 (April 1986): 49–52; A. I. Mikhalev and V. I. Kudriashov, "K voprosu o strategicheskikh operatsiiakh Velikoi Otechestvennoi voiny 1941–1945 gg" [Concerning the question of strategic operations of the Great Patriotic War 1941–1945], *VIZh,* no. 5 (May 1986): 48–51; Kh. M. Dzhelaukhov and B. N. Petrov, "K voprosu o strategicheskikh operatsiiakh Velikoi Otechestvennoi voiny 1941–1945 gg" [Concerning the question of strategic operations of the Great Patriotic War 1941–1945], *VIZh,* no. 7 (July 1986): 46–48; P. T. Kunitsky, "O vybore napravleniia glavnogo udara v kampaniiakh i strategicheskikh operatsiiakh" [On the selection of the main attack axis in campaigns and strategic

operations], *VIZh*, no. 7 (July 1986): 29–40; and "Itogi diskussii o strategicheskikh operatsiiakh Velikoi Otechestvennoi voiny 1941–1945 gg" [Results of the discussion on strategic operations of the Great Patriotic War 1941–1945], *VIZh*, no. 10 (October 1987): 8–24.

20. These figures count destroyer divisions, three separate destroyer brigades, and fortified regions as equivalent to rifle divisions.

21. Savushkin, *Razvitie*, 112.

22. Ibid., 112.

23. Iu. A. Gor'kov and Iu. N. Semin, "Lzhi: Kogda Kiev eshche ne bombili: Operativnye plany zapadnykh prigranichnykh voennykh okrugov 1941 goda svidetel'stvuiut: SSSR ne gotovilsia k napadeniiu na Germaniiu" [Lies: When Kiev had still not been bombed: The operational plans of the western military districts in 1941 bear witness: The USSR did not prepare for an attack on Germany], *VIZh*, no. 4 (July–August 1996): 3.

24. Savushkin, *Razvitie*, 102. For example, during its defense of Moscow in October and November, the *Stavka* partially or completely rested and refitted 23 Western Front rifle divisions and 27 Southwestern Front rifle divisions. During the same period, it reinforced its Mozhaisk Defense Line west of Moscow with 14 rifle divisions, 16 tank brigades, and over 40 artillery regiments, which it regrouped primarily from its Northwestern and Southwestern Fronts.

25. Later still, as it prepared for its strategic defense during the summer, the *Stavka* renamed the Reserve Front the Steppe Military District and assigned it the mission of backing up its forward *fronts* in the Kursk region.

26. Savushkin, *Razvitie*, 102.

27. The best examples of *front* defensive operations later in the war are the 1st Baltic Front's defense at Siauliai in Lithuania during August 1944 and the 3rd Ukrainian Front's defense at Lake Balaton in Hungary during March 1945.

28. "Boevoi opyt ukreplennykh raionov (UR)" [Combat experiences of fortified regions (FR)], in *SMPIOV*, no. 3 (November–December 1942) (Moscow: Voenizdat, 1942), 122–32; and "Oborona" [Defense], in *Sbornik boevykh dokumentov Velikoi Otechestvennoi voiny* [Collection of combat documents of the Great Patriotic War], no. 1 (Moscow: Voenizdat, 1947), 54–61, classified secret. Hereafter cited as *SBDVOV*, with appropriate article, number, and date.

29. Between 27 June and 10 July 1941, the *Stavka* ordered the Red Army to build and man a defense line extending from Pskov and Ostrov southward along the Western Dvina and Dnepr rivers with portions of five armies allocated from its strategic reserve. By doing so, the *Stavka* managed to restore briefly a contiguous defensive front along the northwestern axis by 20 July. Although *Wehrmacht* forces ultimately penetrated this defensive line, their battle to do so and subsequent Red Army counterstrokes in the Sol'tsy and Staraia Russa regions during mid-July and mid-August delayed the German advance for at least two weeks, thereby disrupting German plans to seize Leningrad by a coup de main from the march. For details, see Glantz, *Forgotten Battles*, I: 19–44, 51–70.

30. The principal defense line the *Stavka* constructed in early 1942 extended from northeast of Moscow through Vladimir and Tambov east and southeast of Moscow

southward to the Stalingrad region. Other lines extended from north to south along the Oskol' and Don rivers, and along the Terek River to protect the Caucasus region.

31. Savushkin, *Razvitie*, 99.

32. Since war's end, many Russian military theorists and historians have asserted that the numerous strategic encirclements the Red Army endured in 1941, such as those at Minsk, Uman', Kiev, Viaz'ma, and Briansk, actually assisted the *Stavka's* strategic defense by delaying the *Wehrmacht's* advance. However, these claims are largely disingenuous rationalizations.

33. Soviet (Russian) historians ignored or simply covered up these failed counteractions either because the defeats were embarrassing or to protect the reputation of the Red Army and its senior commanders who planned and conducted these counterattacks, counterstrokes, or counteroffensives. German historians overlooked them because they seemed insignificant incidents within the context of their far more important offensive operations. See, Glantz, *Forgotten Battles*, vol. 1.

34. Ibid.

35. Ibid., 101–6; V. A. Anfilov, *Krushenie pokhoda Gitlera na Moskvu 1941* [The ruin of Hitler's advance on Moscow 1941] (Moscow: Nauka, 1989), 196–270; Glantz, *The Battle for Smolensk;* and David M. Glantz, *Atlas of the Battle of Smolensk, 7 July–10 September 1941* (Carlisle, PA: Self-published, 2001).

36. For details regarding these forgotten Red Army offensive operations, see Glantz, *Forgotten Battles*, vol. 3.

37. For details, see Glantz and House, *The Battle of Kursk.*

38. Savushkin, *Razvitie*, 64.

39. Ibid., 68.

40. Glantz, *The Battle for Smolensk.*

41. Zhukov coordinated the Kalinin and Western Fronts' offensives in the Rzhev region during Operation Mars, and Vasilevsky coordinated the Southwestern, Don, and Stalingrad Fronts' operations in the Stalingrad region during Operations Uranus and Little Saturn.

42. These mobile groups consisted either of tank and cavalry corps operating as a cavalry-mechanized group as at Rzhev or of tank, mechanized, and cavalry corps operating singly as at both Rzhev and Stalingrad.

43. For further details, see Glantz, *Forgotten Battles*, vol. 4.

44. For example, the *Stavka* formed a special shock group consisting of the 1st Tank and 68th Armies in the Northwestern Front's second echelon and ordered it to exploit rapidly toward Pskov and a cavalry-rifle group within the Central Front and ordered it to cooperate with the *front's* 2nd Tank Army and exploit toward Briansk and Vitebsk. At the same time, it also formed new mobile groups to lead the Southwestern Front's exploitation into the Donbas region. These included, first, Group Popov with four understrength tank corps, and, later, the full-strength 1st Guards and 25th Tank Corps and the 1st Guards Cavalry Corps.

45. For further details, see Glantz, *Forgotten Battles*, vol. 5.

46. See Glantz, *The Battle for Smolensk;* and Glantz, *Barbarossa*, 137–59.

47. At Stalingrad, the *Stavka* formed the Southwestern Front covertly and regrouped the 5th Tank Army and many other forces into their attack positions without

German detection. During the defensive stage of the Battle of Kursk, the *Stavka* secretly regrouped five armies (the 27th, 53rd, 5th Guards, 47th, and 5th Guards Tank) into its strategic reserves east of Kursk and concealed much of their immense defensive preparation. During the offensive stage of the Battle of Kursk, it conducted diversionary operations along the Northern Donets and Mius rivers while its *fronts* attacking the Belgorod region employed extensive offensive simulations to confuse the Germans. For further details on the *Stavka's* and Red Army's employment of deception and achievement of surprise during the war, see David M. Glantz, *Soviet Military Deception in the Second World War* (London: Frank Cass, 1989); M. M. Kir'ian, *Vnezapnost' v nastupatel'nykh operatsiiakh Velikoi Otechestvennoi voiny* [Surprise in offensive operations in the Great Patriotic War] (Moscow: Nauka, 1986); V. A. Matsulenko, *Operativnaia maskirovka voisk* [Operational concealment (deception) of forces] (Moscow: Voenizdat, 1975); and V. N. Lobov, *Voennaia khitrost' v istorii voin* [Military stratagems in the history of wars] (Moscow: Voenizdat, 1988).

48. Savushkin, *Razvitie,* 85–86.

49. For example, the Western Front employed five special operational shock groups to conduct its July offensive at Smolensk, and the Western, Reserve, and Briansk Fronts employed groups of divisions under army control and a small cavalry group to do so in August. Likewise, special groups from the 4th Separate Army operating under direct *Stavka* control conducted the Tikhvin offensive during November, and the Western Front employed two cavalry corps (the 1st and 2nd Guards), reinforced by tank units, to conduct more sustained maneuver during the initial stages of the Battle for Moscow. Although its attacking *fronts* concentrated their forces more effectively during the strategic offensives the Red Army conducted during the winter campaign of 1941–42 and employed multiple cavalry corps to conduct deep operations, their attack formations remained essentially linear, and they were unable to sustain the maneuver to significant depths.

50. For example, during their offensives at Stalingrad in November, the Southwestern Front conducted its main attack with the 5th Tank Army's two tank and one cavalry corps, and the Southwestern, Don, and Stalingrad Fronts assigned the armies delivering their main attacks either a tank or a mechanized corps to conduct their exploitation. During Operation Little Saturn in December, the attacking Voronezh and Southwestern Fronts employed four tank and two mechanized corps to both complete their penetration operation and conduct their exploitations. Since the strength of these corps eroded significantly (80 percent) during this operation, in February the *Stavka* ordered the Southwestern Front to spearhead its advance into the Donbas with four tank corps combined into a single operational group (Group Popov).

Otherwise, the Voronezh Front employed the fresh 3rd Tank Army in first echelon in its offensives to Rossosh' in late January and Khar'kov in February, and the Southern Front employed several mechanized corps during its advance into the eastern Donbas region in February. In general, all of these tank armies and mobile corps were unable to sustain deep operations and, at one stage or another, ultimately fell victim to *Wehrmacht* counterattacks or counterstrokes and were essentially destroyed.

51. For example, the Voronezh and Steppe Fronts employed deep cutting blows

in their Belgorod-Khar'kov offensive during August 1943. Initially, they employed five armies to smash German defenses west of Belgorod and immediately exploited the resulting penetration with the 1st and 5th Guards Tank Armies and one tank and one mechanized corps and, later, committed four fresh armies and two more tank corps into combat along the flanks of the penetration and, ultimately, two more armies and two more mobile corps to reinforce the exploitation. By doing so, the attacking *fronts* established overwhelming superiorities of eight to one tactically and over three to one operationally, quickly penetrated the Germans' defenses, and subsequently exploited to a depth of 120 kilometers into the German's defenses in a period of only seven days. See David M. Glantz, *From the Don to the Dnepr* (London: Frank Cass, 1991), 215–365.

Similarly, during its offensive to capture Kiev in November 1943, the Voronezh Front initially employed two armies, one tank corps, and elements of one tank army to penetrate German defenses north of Kiev and conducted its initial exploitation with the tank army and a cavalry corps. Subsequently, it reinforced its offensive with three more armies before the offensive ended, when it encountered counterattacking German forces about 80 kilometers deep into the Germans' defenses ten days into the offensive. Finally, the Southern Front employed, first, mechanized, tank, and cavalry corps separately and, later, cavalry-mechanized groups to spearhead its offensive in the Donbas region.

52. The *Stavka* attempted to conduct its offensive into Belorussia during the fall of 1943 in the form of a massive strategic envelopment of Army Group Center by the Kalinin and Central Fronts attacking toward Minsk from the northeast and southeast and the Western Front pressuring the German army group from the east. However, none of the three attacking *fronts* possessed mobile forces capable of conducting deep enough operations for the offensive to succeed. See Glantz, *Forgotten Battles,* vol. 5.

53. *Boevoi sostav Sovetskoi armii, chast' 1 (iiun'–dekabr' 1941 goda)* [The combat composition of the Soviet Army, part 1 (June–December 1941)] (Moscow: Voroshilov Academy of the General Staff, 1963).

54. Savushkin, *Razvitie,* 104–6; V. Zemskov, "Nekotorye voprosy sozdaniia i ispol'zovaniia strategicheskikh reservov" [Some questions on the creation and employment of strategic reserves], *VIZh,* no. 10 (October 1971): 14; and A. G. Khor'kov, "Nekotorye voprosy strategicheskogo razvertyvaniia Sovetskikh vooruzhennykh sil v nachale Velikoi Otechestvennoi voiny" [Some questions on the strategic deployment of the Soviet Armed Forces at the beginning of the Great Patriotic War], *VIZh,* no. 1 (January 1986): 13. The 291 formations the *Stavka* allocated to its *fronts* included 194 newly formed rifle divisions and 94 newly formed rifle brigades, 70 rifle divisions transferred from the internal military districts and 27 from the Far East, the Trans-Baikal region, and Central Asia.

55. These included the 28th–30th Armies, which reinforced the Western Front's defenses east of Smolensk, the 24th, 31st–34th, and 43rd Armies, which formed the Reserve Front, the 44th, 45th, 47th, and 48th Armies, which reinforced the Trans-Caucasus Military District in July, and the 48th–50th Armies, which reinforced the Northern, Reserve, and Briansk Fronts, respectively, during August. In addition to

these armies, the *Stavka* also formed the 51st and 52nd Armies as separate reserve armies, assigning the former to defend the Crimea and the latter the northwestern axis. Finally, the *Stavka* reassigned its 34th Army to the Northwestern Front in mid-August. See, Savushkin, *Razvitie,* 105; "Dokumenty Stavki Verkhovnogo Komandovaniia i General'nogo shtaba Krasnoi Armii" [Documents of the *Stavka* of the High Command and the General Staff of the Red Army], *SBDVOV,* no. 37 (Moscow: Voenizdat, 1947), 11–13; and "Stavka VGK 1941." This volume includes the orders that formed the 29th through 33rd Armies, largely from NKVD units, regular forces, and people's militia forces from the Moscow Military District.

56. For example, the *Stavka* employed the 4th Separate Army in its November offensive at Tikhvin, its 5th and new 33rd Armies to defend Moscow, and its 5th, 33rd, 1st Shock, 10th, and 20th Armies to initiate and expand its counterstroke and offensive at Moscow.

57. Savushkin, *Razvitie,* 105. The Western Front's strength increased as follows:

Type Force	*1 October 1941*	*5 December 1941*
Rifle divisions	30	50
Rifle brigades	1	16
Aviation divisions	5	8
Cavalry divisions	3	16
Tank brigades	3	22
Artillery regiments (RVGK)	28	53
Guards-mortar battalions	1	30
Separate antiaircraft battalions	11	16

In addition, prior to and during its defense of Moscow, the *Stavka* raised and employed a complete reserve *front,* as well as forces assigned to the Moscow Defense Zone, which formed a *front* in its own right, to back up the first echelons of its forward defending *fronts.*

58. For example, the size of the RVGK during the winter of 1941–42 varied on a monthly basis from two to three armies, eight to 27 rifle and cavalry divisions, and four to 23 brigades.

59. Savushkin, *Razvitie,* 104–6; Zemskov, "Nekotorye voprosy," 14; and Khor'kov, "Nekotorye voprosy," 13.

60. Savushkin, *Razvitie,* 107.

61. Zemskov, "Nekotorye voprosy," 16.

62. Ibid. In addition, from April to July 1943, the *Stavka* reinforced its Central and Voronezh Fronts, which were to conduct the Kursk defense, with 14 rifle divisions, five tank destroyer brigades, 24 separate tank destroyer regiments, 30 artillery and mortar regiments, four artillery brigades, 12 tank brigades, and seven separate tank regiments from its reserve. See Savushkin, *Razvitie,* 107.

63. V. Golubovich, "Sozdanie strategicheskikh reservov [The creation of strategic reserves], *VIZh,* no. 4 (April 1977): 13–14.

64. *Boevoi sostav Sovetskoi armii, chast' 3 (ianvar'–dekabr' 1943 goda)* [The combat composition of the Soviet Army, part 3 (January–December 1941)] (Moscow: Voenizdat, 1972).

65. Savushkin, *Razvitie,* 78.

66. For example, prior to the Battle of Kursk, the *Stavka* covertly regrouped nine armies from its Northwestern and North Caucasus Fronts and deployed them in strategic defense in the region between Moscow and Voroshilovgrad, seven of which German intelligence failed to detect. In addition, it regrouped and refitted the 3rd Guards, 4th, and 5th Guards Tank Armies, employing the 5th Guards Tank Army during the later stages of its Kursk defense, and all three to spearhead its subsequent offensives side by side with its 1st and 2nd Tank Armies, which had taken part in the Kursk defense. Finally, it transferred the 5th Guards and 5th Guards Tank Armies from the Steppe Front to the Voronezh Front while the defensive operation was under way, and it committed the Steppe Front into combat, first, to blunt the *Wehrmacht's* offensive during the latter stages of its strategic defense and in early August to spearhead its Belgorod-Khar'kov offensive.

After the Belgorod-Khar'kov offensive was under way, the *Stavka* reinforced its attacking *fronts* with the 47th and 4th Guards Armies from the RVGK to strengthen the attack, protect its flanks, and repel German counterattacks. In addition, during the fall of 1943, the *Stavka* reinforced its *fronts* operating along and across the Dnepr River with nine combined-arms armies, two tank armies, one cavalry and two tank corps, and three cavalry divisions from the RVGK. For further details on the Battle of Kursk, see Glantz, *Soviet Military Intelligence in War,* 172–284; and Glantz and House, *The Battle of Kursk.*

67. N. V. Ogarkov, ed., *Voennyi entsiklopedicheskii slovar'* [Military-encyclopedic dictionary] (Moscow: Voenizdat, 1983), 514, defines operational art as, "Conducting combined-arms, joint, and independent operations (combat actions) with formations of various types of armed forces." Although this definition is of more recent vintage, Alexander Svechin and other Soviet military theorists developed this concept as early as the late 1920s, and others refined it significantly prior to the war. See Harold S. Orenstein, ed. and trans., *The Evolution of Soviet Operational Art, 1927–1991: The Documentary Basis, volume 1: Operational Art, 1927, 1964* (London: Frank Cass, 1995).

68. These included operations such as the Northwestern Front's counterstrokes at Sol'tsy and Staraia Russa in July and August 1941, the Kalinin Front counterstroke at Kalinin in October 1942, and the Western Front's offensives near Rzhev and Zhizdra in July and August 1942.

69. For example, the *Wehrmacht* destroyed the Southwestern Front during the Kiev defensive operation in September and the Reserve Front and the bulk of the Western and Briansk Fronts during the Viaz'ma and Briansk defensive operations in October. In addition, it destroyed the Western Front's 3rd, 4th, and 10th Armies during the initial border battles in Belorussia in late June and early July, and the Southwestern and Southern Fronts' 6th and 12th Armies perished during the Uman' defensive operation in August.

70. Soviet and, more recently, Russian historians have claimed that the Red Army lost no armies during the summer of 1942, but the Southwestern Front's 28th, 38th, 40th, and several other armies were essentially destroyed or badly damaged during the July retreat in the face of Operation *Blau,* and the Kalinin Front's 39th Army was destroyed southwest of Rzhev in August. See Glantz, *Forgotten Battles,* vol. 3.

71. For example, during their Staraia Russa offensive in August, the Northern and Northwestern Fronts attacked on frontages of 90 and 130 kilometers, respectively, and although the attack by the former immediately stalled, the latter advanced up to 50 kilometers before being repulsed by German counterattacks. At Smolensk in August, the Western, Reserve, and Briansk Fronts advanced on frontages of 250, 100, and about 150 kilometers, respectively, to more limited depths before being driven back. During the Smolensk offensive, however, the Reserve Front's 24th Army captured El'nia after advancing about 25 kilometers and held it until early October.

72. Strokov, *Istoriia voennogo iskusstva,* 391.

73. The Western Front's right wing north of Moscow advanced 38–90 kilometers during December before being halted, and its left wing south of Moscow from 30 to almost 200 kilometers. During January the entire Western Front advanced 60–120 kilometers.

74. For the full contents of *Stavka* Directive Letter No. 03 dated 10 January 1942, see V. A. Zolotarev, ed., "Stavka VGK: Dokumenty i materialy 1942" [The *Stavka* VGK: Documents and materials of 1942], in *Russkii arkhiv: Velikaia Otechestvennaia* [The Russian archives: The Great Patriotic (War)], 16, 5 (1) (Moscow: Terra, 1996), 33–35 (hereafter cited as Zolotarev, "Stavka VGK 1942," with appropriate pages); and A. Radzievsky, "Proryv oborony v pervom periode voiny" [The penetration of a defense in the first period of the war], *VIZh,* no. 3 (March 1972): 17–18.

75. A. A. Strokov, ed., *Istoriia voennogo isskustva* [A history of military art] (Moscow: Voenizdat, 1966), 390–91.

76. Ibid., 110.

77. Savushkin, *Razvitie,* 159–60; and Bagramian, *Istoriia voin i voennogo iskusstva,* 187.

78. Bagramian, *Istoriia voin i voennogo iskusstva,* 187–88. Strokov, *Istoriia voennogo isskustva,* 390, cites slightly different indices, such as army average depths of 20 kilometers, one division per 20 kilometers of front, and weapons densities of 15–25 guns per kilometer of front.

79. See "Podgotovka k oborone Kurskogo platsdarma" [Preparations to defend the Kursk bridgehead], *SMPIOV* 11 (March–April 1944): 24–37; David M. Glantz, *Soviet Defensive Tactics at Kursk (July 1943)* (Carlisle, PA: Self-published, 1998); and Glantz and House, *The Battle of Kursk.* The Red Army's success at Kursk was due to the nature of its defenses and its careful and skillful employment of superior forces, in particular, operational and strategic reserves. At Kursk, for the first time in the war, the *Stavka* and its defending *fronts* were able to plan and construct all of their defensive belts completely and man their first two defensive belts fully before the *Wehrmacht* offensive. The defending Central and Voronezh Fronts' first-echelon armies constructed five to six defensive belts, which included two tactical belts manned by their first-echelon rifle corps, one army belt manned by their second-echelon rifle corps, and three *front* belts occupied by *front* reserves and mobile forces. Stretching far to the rear, the armies of the RVGK's Steppe Front formed additional defensive belts backed up by a "state defensive belt" extending along the western bank of the Don River. While the tactical defensive zone in this defense extended to a depth of 15–20 kilometers, the depth of the entire strategic defense was 300 kilometers, more

than twice as deep as the best-prepared Red Army defense in 1941 or 1942. The defense also included three belts, each up to 70 kilometers deep, consisting of strong fortified positions deployed in depth along expected German main attack axes, which were manned by unprecedented densities of forces and weaponry. The densities of up to 2,000 mines per kilometer of front were two to three times higher than in the best-prepared Red Army defenses in 1941 and 1942. As a result, the *Wehrmacht's* panzer spearheads against the flanks of the Kursk bulge penetrated to depths of only 12 and 35 kilometers, respectively. Furthermore, this was the first time in the war that Red Army forces were able to contain a concerted *Wehrmacht* offensive short of the operational and strategic depths.

80. Bagramian, *Istoriia voin i voennogo iskusstva,* 245.

81. Ibid., 246.

82. For example, the Southwestern Front employed the 21st and 23rd Tank Corps to exploit its Khar'kov offensive in May 1942, the Briansk Fronts and Stalingrad Fronts employed the 5th, 1st, and 4th Tank Armies and several separate tank corps to lead and exploit their offensives west of Voronezh along the Don River in July 1942, the Western Front used its 3rd Tank Army to lead its offensive at Zhizdra in August, and the Southwestern Front employed the 5th Tank Army to lead its attack from first echelon during its Stalingrad offensive in November.

83. S. Lotosky, "Iz opyta vedeniia armeiskikh nastupatel'nykh operatsii v gody Velikoi Otechestvennoi voiny" [From the experience of the conduct of army offensive operations during the Great Patriotic War], *VIZh,* no. 12 (December 1965): 3–14.

84. For example, during their November offensive at Rzhev, the Kalinin Front employed two mechanized corps as mobile groups in two army attack sectors, and the Western Front initially employed one tank and one cavalry corps as a cavalry mechanized group in one army sector and, later, two tank corps as mobile groups in the same sector. At Stalingrad, the Southwestern Front used the 5th Tank Army to lead its offensive and the 8th Cavalry Corps and the tank armies' two tank corps to conduct its exploitation, and both it and the Stalingrad Front used separate tank, mechanized, and cavalry corps to serve as mobile groups for their subordinate armies.

85. For details on the Red Army's wartime employment of operational maneuver, see David M. Glantz, *Deep Attack: The Soviet Conduct of Operational Maneuver* (Carlisle, PA: Self-published, 1998).

86. These early attempts to conduct defensive operational maneuver included the Northwestern and Western Fronts' failed counterstrokes in the Kelme, Raseinai, and Grodno regions with elements of four mechanized corps (the 3rd, 12th, 6th, and 11th) and the Southwestern Front's attempt to orchestrate a counteroffensive in the Dubno and Brody regions relying on coordinated operational maneuver by six mechanized corps (the 4th, 8th, 15th, 22nd, 9th, and 19th).

87. This instance of attempted defensive operational maneuver involved the Briansk Front's counterstroke with its 5th Tank Army near Voronezh coordinated with the Stalingrad Front's counterstrokes with its 1st and 4th Tank Armies along the Don River west of Stalingrad.

88. In this case, the Voronezh Front used its 1st Tank Army in positional defense and its 2nd and 5th Guards and 2nd and 10th Tank Corps to conduct defensive

operational maneuver, and the *Stavka* employed the Steppe Front's 5th Guards Tank Army to conduct defensive operational maneuver at Prokhorovka.

89. The 1st Ukrainian Front employed the mobile corps of its 3rd Guards Tank Army and its 4th and 5th Guards Tank and 1st Guards Cavalry Corps to conduct defensive operational maneuver west of Kiev, and the 2nd Ukrainian Front employed the mobile corps of its 5th Guards Tank Army and its 1st Guards Mechanized and 7th Mechanized Corps to conduct defensive operational maneuver north of Krivoi Rog.

90. These instances included the defeat of the 21st and 23rd Tank Corps at Khar'kov, the 5th, 1st, and 4th Tank Armies and other separate tank corps at Voronezh and along the Don River, and the 3rd Tank Army and several separate tank corps at Zhizdra, all of which were functioning as *front* or army mobile groups. See, for example, Glantz, *Kharkov 1942;* and Glantz, *Forgotten Battles,* III: 11–66.

91. "Prikaz NKO no. 325 ot 16 oktiabria 1942 g." [People's Commissariat of Defense order no. 325 of 16 October 1942], *VIZh,* no. 10 (October 1974): 68–73; and V. A. Zolotarev, ed., "Prikazy narodnogo komissara oborony SSSR 22 iiunia 1941 g.–1942 g." [Orders of the People's Commissar of Defense of the USSR 22 June 1941–1942], in *Russkii arkhiv: Velikaia Otechestvennaia* [The Russian archives: The Great Patriotic (War)], 13, 2 (2) (Moscow: Terra, 1997), 334–38, for the complete contents of Order No. 325. Hereafter cited as Zolotarev, "NKO 1941," with appropriate page(s).

92. Prior to the war, the Soviets called the mobile group the "echelon to develop [exploit] success" *(eshelon razvitiia uspekha).* Mobile groups were the precursors of operational maneuver groups, which the Soviet Army developed during the late 1970s.

93. For example, the Voronezh and Southern Fronts used the 3rd and 5th Tank Armies as mobile groups to spearhead their offensives in January, and the Southwestern Front employed ad hoc Group Popov to spearhead its offensive during February. During the same period, other *fronts* and armies relied on separate tank, mechanized, or cavalry corps as mobile groups to lead their exploitation operations. Finally, the Central Front used the new 2nd Tank Army to spearhead its unsuccessful offensive toward Orel, Briansk, and Smolensk in late February and March. The results of the General Staff's analysis of mobile group, particularly tank and mechanized corps, operations during the winter of 1942–43, as summarized in David M. Glantz, *Soviet War Experiences: Tank Operations* (Carlisle, PA: Self-published, 1998). For details on the Central Front's largely forgotten Orel, Briansk, Smolensk offensive, see Glantz, *Forgotten Battles,* IV: 213–381.

94. Field regulations required *fronts* and armies to commit their mobile groups into combat only after their combined-arms armies had completely penetrated the *Wehrmacht's* tactical defenses so as to conserve the mobile group's strength for the vital exploitation phase of the operation. More often than not, however, during most of 1943, the strength of German defenses compelled *front* and army commanders to use part or all of their mobile groups to complete the tactical penetration, thus making the exploitation phase far more difficult.

95. For details on the evolution and function of the forward detachment, see David M. Glantz, *The Soviet Conduct of Tactical Maneuver: Spearhead of the Offensive* (London: Frank Cass, 1991).

96. Strokov, *Istoriia voennogo iskusstva,* 390–91. The 189 rifle divisions included 72 that the *Stavka* withdrew from its operating *fronts,* 67 that it reconstructed, and 50 that it formed from scratch.

97. To understand these improvements in antitank capabilities, compare the course and outcome of the Central, Southwestern, and Voronezh Fronts' offensive and defensive operations in February and March 1943 with the 1st Ukrainian Front's operations west of Kiev in November and December 1943.

98. Ibid.

99. Savushkin, *Razvitie,* 140. See also "Stavka VGK 1942," for the details of *Stavka* Directive Letter No. 03, which formulated the concept of the artillery offensive.

100. Savushkin, *Razvitie,* 142–43.

101. The most notable exceptions were the Southern Front's Rostov offensive in December 1941, the Kalinin Front's Toropets-Kholm offensive in January 1942, and the Southwestern and Southern Fronts' Barvenkovo-Lozovaia offensive south of Khar'kov in January 1942. Curiously enough, the Southwestern Front's effective operational deception plan to conceal preparations for its Khar'kov offensive in May 1942 fell victim to an even more successful German strategic deception plan code-named Operation *Kreml'.* For more details on Soviet operational deception throughout the war, see Glantz, *Soviet Military Deception,* 105–292.

102. For example, the Southwestern and Southern Fronts conducted diversionary offensives along the Northern Donets and Mius rivers in July 1943 to distract the Germans from a planned Red Army offensive in early August along the Belgorod-Khar'kov axis.

103. David M. Glantz, *Soviet Military Operational Art: In Pursuit of Deep Battle* (London: Frank Cass, 1991), 23, quoting Alexander Svechin, the "father" of Soviet operational art.

104. Strokov, *Istoriia voennogo iskusstva,* 192; and Bagramian, *Istoriia voin i voennogo iskusstva,* 391–92.

105. Strokov, *Istoriia voennogo iskusstva,* 192–93; and Bagramian, *Istoriia voin i voennogo iskusstva,* 391.

106. Strokov, *Istoriia voennogo iskusstva,* 429.

107. Bagramian, *Istoriia voin i voennogo iskusstva,* 245–46; and Lotosky, "Iz opyta," 4–8.

108. See Zolotarev, "NKO 1941," 323–26, for the complete contents of Order No. 306; and "Prikaz NKO no. 306 ot 8 oktiabria 1942 g." [People's Commissariat of Defense order no. 306 of 16 October 1942], *VIZh,* no. 9 (September 1974): 62–66.

109. Zolotarev, "NKO 1941," 334–38.

110. Strokov, *Istoriia voennogo iskusstva,* 427.

111. Ibid.; and V. Matsulenko, "Razvitie taktiki nastupatel'nogo boia" [The development of offensive battle tactics], *VIZh,* no. 2 (February 1968): 28–30.

112. For example, army and rifle corps commanders began assigning separate tank brigades and regiments and, if available, self-propelled artillery regiments as well, echeloned in depth, to provide direct fire support and protective fires for their attacking rifle corps and divisions.

113. For example, during the Battle for Berlin in April 1945, the forces under Marshal Zhukov's 1st Belorussian Front suffered casualty rates as high as his Western Front had suffered during Operation Mars in November and December 1942 and during the Battle for Moscow in late 1941 and early 1942. It is also now clear that, on at least a few occasions, the *Stavka* did indeed censor some of its *front* commanders for permitting excessive casualties. For example, the *Stavka* relieved Colonel General V. D. Sokolovsky, the commander of the Western Front in 1943 and early 1944 and a future Marshal of the Soviet Union in the 1960s, from his *front* command in February 1944. It did so because Sokolovsky's *front* suffered over 100,000 casualties during its often crude and futile offensives in the Orsha and Vitebsk region of eastern Belorussia during the fall of 1943 and winter of 1943–44. For details on the Western Front's unsuccessful offensive in the fall of 1943 and winter of 1944 and the *Stavka* directive relieving Sokolovsky of command, see M. A. Gareev, "O neudachnykh nastupatel'nykh operatsiiakh Sovetskikh voisk v Velikoi Otechestvennoi voine. Po neopublikovannym dokumentam GKO" [On the unsuccessful offensive operations by Soviet forces in the Great Patriotic War. Based on unpublished GKO documents], *Novaia i noveishshaia istoriia* [New and recent history], no. 1 (January 1994): 2–28. It is also likely that the *Stavka* removed Colonel General P. A. Rotmistrov from command of his 5th Guards Tank Army during the late summer of 1944 because of the excessive losses his tank army suffered during the Belorussian offensive, particularly during its struggle with the German 5th Panzer Division along the Berezina River and the subsequent intense fighting for possession of the city of Vilnius.

114. Interview with Colonel K. A. Borisov, Moscow, 1989. For further details, see David M. Glantz, *Red Army Officers Speak: Interviews with Veterans of the Vistula-Oder Operation (January–February 1945)* (Carlisle, PA: Self-published, 1997).

115. See for example, V. E. Korol', "The Price of Victory," *Journal of Slavic Military Studies* 9, no. 2 (June 1996): 417–26. Korol' states: "A considerable number of senior commanders, including the well known G. K. Zhukov, I. S. Konev, N. F. Vatutin, F. I. Golikov, A. I. Eremenko, G. I. Kulik, S. M. Budenny, K. E. Voroshilov, S. K. Timoshenko, R. Ia. Malinovsky, V. D. Sokolovsky, V. I. Chuikov, and some of lower ranks, who considered soldiers as 'cannon fodder,' fought with maximum losses. On the other hand, K. K. Rokossovsky, A. A. Grechko, A. V. Gorbatov, I. E. Petrov, I. D. Cherniakhovsky, and several others fought with minimum casualties, but still at the required professional level. Unfortunately, the latter were in the minority."

4. Strength and Major Components

1. Nonrecoverable losses included killed-in-action, missing-in-action, or those wounded or ill enough to be rendered hors de combat. The strength figures are from "GKO Decrees" dated 2 February 1943 and 9 July 1943, in *TsPA UML* [Central Party Archives of the Institute of Marxism and Leninism], f. 644, op. 1, d. 100, l. 95, and f. 644, op. 1, d. 125, ll. 35–36. These figures do not include those who were hospitalized: 659,000 men on 2 February, 446,445 on 9 July, and roughly 900,000 on 31 December 1943.

2. *TsPA UML,* f. 644, op. 1, d. 85, ll. 95–96. This document is a State Defense Committee (GKO) decree dated 2 February 1943 contained in the files of the Central Party Archives of the Institute of Marxism and Leninism.

3. *TsPA UML,* f. 644, op. 1, d. 125, ll. 35–36.

4. B. G. Solov'ev, ed., *Istoriia vtoroi mirovoi voiny 1939–1945* [A History of the Second World War 1939–1945] (Moscow: Voenizdat, 1976), VI: 31–35, 76, 93, and VII: 120.

5. For further details on the structure, composition, and combat employment of wartime Red Army *fronts,* see M. M. Kir'ian, ed., *Fronty nastupali: po opytu Velikoi Otechestvennoi voiny* [The *fronts* were attacking: Based on the experience of the Great Patriotic War] (Moscow: Nauka, 1987).

6. Solov'ev, *Istoriia vtoroi mirovoi voiny,* VII: 114, 120, 140, 159, 172, 194, 221, 241.

7. For further details on the structure, composition, and combat employment of Red Army armies, see P. A. Kurochkin, ed., *Obshchevoiskovaia armiia na nastuplenii: po opytu Velikoi Otechestvennoi voiny 1941–1945 gg.* [The combined-arms army in the offensive: Based on the experience of the Great Patriotic War 1941–1945] (Moscow: Voenizdat, 1966); A. I. Radzievsky, ed., *Armeiskie operatsii (Primery iz opyta Velikoi Otechestvennoi)* [Army operations (Examples from the experience of the Great Patriotic War)] (Moscow: Voenizdat, 1977); and *Armeiskie operatsii (Boevye deistviia obshchevoiskovoi armii v gody Velikoi Otechestvennoi voiny)* [Army operations (Combat operations of the combined-arms army during the Great Patriotic War)] (Moscow: Frunze Academy, 1989), classified for faculty use only.

8. See *Boevoi sostav Sovetskoi armii, chast' 3,* 46.

9. Glantz, *Forgotten Battles,* IV: 345–48. See also Zolotarev, "Preludiia Kurskoi bitvy," for the complete orders mandating these changes.

10. Ibid., 362–64.

11. Ibid., 365–66.

12. See V. A. Zolotarev, ed., "Stavka Verkhovnogo Glavnokomandovaniia: Dokumenty i materialy 1943 god" [The *Stavka* of the Supreme High Command: Documents and materials of 1943], in *Russkii arkhiv: Velikaia Otechestvennaia* [The Russian archives: The Great Patriotic (War)], 15, 4 (3) (Moscow: Terra, 1999), 114–15, for the complete orders mandating these changes.

13. Ibid., 116.

14. Ibid., 127–28.

15. *Boevoi sostav Sovetskoi armii, chast' 3,* 50–53. For personnel strength, see *TsPA UML,* f. 644, op. 1, d. 85, ll. 95–96. This document is a State Defense Committee (GKO) decree dated 2 February 1943 contained in the files of the Central Party Archives of the Institute of Marxism and Leninism.

16. *TsPA UML,* f. 644, op. 1, d. 125, ll. 35–36.

17. *TsPA UML,* f. 644, op. 1, d. 85, ll. 95–96; and *TsPA UML,* f. 644, op. 1, d. 125, ll. 35–36. These documents are State Defense Committee (GKO) decrees, dated 2 February and 9 July 1943 contained in the files of the Central Party Archives of the Institute of Marxism and Leninism.

18. See David M. Glantz, *The Soviet Strategic Offensive in Manchuria 1945: "August Storm"* (London: Frank Cass, 2003), 8–9.

5. The Shadow Army: NKVD Forces

1. See K. A. Kalashnikov, V. I. Fes'kov, A. Iu. Chmykhalo, and V. I. Golikov, *Krasnaia Armiia v iiune 1941 goda* [The Red Army in June 1941] (Tomsk: Tomsk University Press, 2001), 19.

2. *TsPA UML,* f. 664, op. 1, d. 23, ll. 127–29, d. 1, l. 85, ll., and d. 218, ll. 103–4. For NKVD strength on 22 June 1941, see A. G. Lensky, *Sukhoputnye sily RKKA v predvoennye gody* [The RKKA's ground forces in the prewar years] (Saint Petersburg: 2000), 185. This figure includes approximately 3,000 men in border guards aviation units.

3. V. F. Nekrasov, "Vklad vnutrennikh voisk v delo pobedy sovetskogo naroda v Velikoi Otechestvennoi voine" [The internal forces' contribution to the victory of the Soviet people in the Great Patriotic War], *VIZh,* no. 9 (September 1985): 35.

4. "Vnutrennie voiska" [Internal forces], in *SVE,* II: 165.

5. Lensky, *Sukhoputnye sily RKKA,* 185.

6. Ibid. When border guards detachments were originally formed in the mid- and late 1930s, there were 108 detachments numbered from one through 107. When the Soviet border shifted westward in September 1939, however, 12 border guards detachments, including the 14th, 15th, 19th, 21st, 31st, 84th, 85th, 104th, and several other detachments, were disbanded, leaving 96 existing on the eve of the war. See also S. V. Stepashin, ed., *Organy gosudarstvennoi bezopasnosti SSSR v Velikoi Otechestvennoi voine: Sbornik dokumentov, tom 1: Nakanune, kniga vtoraia (1 ianvaria–21 iiunia 1941 g.)* [Organs of state security of the USSR in the Great Patriotic War: A collection of documents, volume 1: On the eve, book 2 (1 January–21 June 1941)] (Moscow: Kniga i Biznes, 1995), 270–71; and Kalashnikov, *Krasnaia Armiia v iiune 1941 goda,* 19.

7. Kalashnikov, *Krasnaia Armiia v iiune 1941 goda,* 21.

8. Lensky, *Sukhoputnye sily RKKA,* 185.

9. Ibid., 187. See also Kalashnikov, *Krasnaia Armiia v iiune 1941 goda,* 21.

10. Lensky, *Sukhoputnye sily RKKA,* 185

11. Ibid.

12. Ibid.

13. This was Commissariat of Defense Order No. 1756–762 cc, dated 23 June 1941. See Kalashnikov, *Krasnaia Armiia v iiune 1941 goda,* 21; Lensky, *Sukhoputnye sily RKKA,* 187–88; and A. I. Chugunov, *Granitsy srazhaetsia* [Border guards battle] (Moscow: Voenizdat, 1989), 1–284.

14. Lensky, *Sukhoputnye sily RKKA,* 185.

15. Ibid., 188.

16. Ibid., 189.

17. Ibid.

18. Ibid., 190.

19. Ibid.

20. Ibid., 189.

21. *Vnutrennie voiska v gody mirnogo sotsialisticheskogo stroitel'stva, 1922–1941 gg.* [The internal forces in the years of peaceful Socialist construction, 1922–1941] (Moscow: Iuridicheskaia Literatura, 1977), 507–8; and N. Ramanichev, "The Red

Army, 1940–1941: Myths and Realities" (Moscow, 1966), 106. This draft manuscript is being translated and prepared for future publication.

22. The *Stavka's* Group of Reserve Armies consisted initially of the 19th, 21st, and 22nd Armies and was commanded by Marshal of the Soviet Union S. M. Budenny.

23. Zolotarev, "*Stavka* VGK 1941," 31. This was *Stavka* Order No. 0097.

24. Ibid., 32. This was *Stavka* Order No. 0098. Designated formally as chiefs of the *front's* rear, these NKVD generals were Lieutenant General Stepanov for the Northern Front and Major Generals K. I. Rakutin, V. A. Khomenko, and Nikol'sky for the Northwestern, Southwestern, and Southern Fronts, and Major General Liuby for the Armies of the Second Line (the initials of some of these generals remain unknown). At the same time, the *Stavka* appointed Lieutenant General of NKVD Forces P. A. Artem'ev to command the Moscow Military District.

25. Ramanichev, "The Red Army," 177–78.

26. Zolotarev, "Stavka VGK 1941," 32–33. This was *Stavka* Order No. 00100.

27. "Prikaz NKVD SSSR o formirovanie narkomatom piatnadtsati strelkovykh divizii dlia peredachi v deistvuiushchuiu armiiu" [Order of the NKVD of the USSR about the formation by the People's Commissariat of 15 rifle divisions for assignment to the operating army], in V. V. Dushen'kin, ed., *Vnutrennie voiska v Velikoi Otechestvennoi voine 1941–1945 gg.: Dokumenty i materialy* [Internal forces in the Great Patriotic War 1941–1945: Documents and materials] (Moscow: Iuridicheskaia Literatura, 1975), 544; and G. P. Sechkin, *Pogranichnye voiska v Velikoi Otechestvennoi voine* [Border guards forces in the Great Patriotic War] (Moscow: Order of Lenin Red Banner Higher Border Guards Command Courses of the KGB USSR, 1990), 86–87.

28. For example, the 1st NKVD Rifle Division, commanded by Colonel S. I. Donskov, was formed from the 3rd, 7th, 33rd, and 102nd Border Guards Detachments and internal troops from the Leningrad garrison. See Sechkin, *Pogranichnye voiska,* 100.

29. Ibid., 78–84. See also Glantz, *Forgotten Battles,* II: 11–21. The 57th NKVD Rifle Brigade also took part in fighting east of Orel under 3rd Army control.

30. This was NKVD Directive No. 24/9829.

31. Dushen'kin, *Vnutrennie voiska v Velikoi Otechestvennoi voine,* 704.

32. Nekrasov, "Vklad vnutrennikh voisk," 29.

33. A. Alekseenkov, "Vnutrennie voiska: Pravda i vymysel—na trekh frontakh" [Internal forces: Truth and fantasy—on three fronts], *Voennaia znaniia* [Military knowledge], no. 1 (January 1991): 4.

34. These were the 2nd, 12th, 20th, 32nd, 83rd, 86th, 88th, 94th, 95th, 97th, 105th, 106th, and 107th Border Guards Detachments, the 42nd and 43rd Reserve Regiments, and the 2nd, 3rd, 4th, and 5th Separate Border Guards Commands. For documents concerning the combat record of border guards detachments and commands during the war, see A. I. Chugunov, ed., *Pogranichnye voiska v gody Velikoi Otechestvennoi voiny 1941–1945: Sbornik dokumentov* [Border guards forces in the Great Patriotic War 1941–1945: A collection of documents] (Moscow: Nauka, 1968).

35. Sechkin, *Pogranichnye voiska,* 97.

36. V. S. Vinogradov, ed., *Krasnoznamennyi pribaltiiskii pogranichnyi* [Red Banner Baltic border guards] (Riga: Abots, 1988), 141.

37. For details, see "Tyly deistvuiushchei armii okhraniali voiska NKVD" [NKVD forces protected the rear areas of the operating army], *VIZh*, no. 6 (November–December 1998): 16–25.

38. Ibid., 145. For example, in mid-1944 the 218th NKVD Border Guards Regiment, which was protecting the 3rd Belorussian Front's rear area during operations in northern Belorussia, absorbed the 99th NKVD Regiment into its structure.

39. For further details concerning the wartime organization and function of the brigade, see, "Iz otcheta o boevoi deiatel'nosti otdel'noi motostrelkovoi brigady osobogo naznacheniia za period 27 iiunia 1941 g.–27 iiunia 1945 g." [From a summary of the combat activities of the special designation motorized rifle brigade for the period 27 June 1941–27 June 1945], in Dushen'kin, ed., *Vnutrennie voiska v Velikoi Otechestvennoi voine,* 517–25.

40. Ibid., 518.

41. Ibid., 517–18.

42. Ibid., 518.

43. See S. I. Vilenko, *Na okhrane tyla strany: Istrebitel'nye batal'ony i polki v Velikoi Otechestvennoi voine 1941–1945* [Guarding the country's rear area: Destruction battalions and regiments in the Great Patriotic War 1941–1945] (Moscow: Nauka, 1988).

6. Rifle and Airborne Forces

1. Iu. P. Babich and A. G. Baier, *Razvitie vooruzheniia i organizatsii sovetskikh sukhoputnykh voisk v gody Velikoi Otechestvennoi voiny* [The development of the weaponry and organization of Soviet ground forces in the years of the Great Patriotic War] (Moscow: Izdanie Akademii, 1990), 34–35.

2. Ibid., 35–40.

3. Steven J. Zaloga and Leland S. Ness, *Red Army Handbook, 1939–1945* (Gloucestershire, UK: Sutton, 1998), 44–45.

4. Kh. Kh. Kamalov, *Morskaia pekhota v boiakh za rodinu* [Naval infantry in battles for the homeland] (Moscow: Voenizdat, 1966), 7–19.

5. V. Shlomin, "Dvadtsat' piat' morskikh strelkovykh" [25th Naval Infantry], *VIZh,* no. 7 (July 1970): 96–99.

6. Kamalov, *Morskaia pekhota v boiakh za rodinu,* 7–19.

7. Zaloga and Ness, *Red Army Handbook,* 50–52.

8. This organization reflected *shtat* (table of organization and equipment) no. 04/270. For more details on destroyer forces, see A. N. Ianchinsky, *Boevoe ispol'zovanie istrebitel'no-protivotankovoi artillerii RVGK v Velikoi Otechestvennoi voine* [The combat employment of destroyer antitank artillery of the *Stavka* Reserve in the Great Patriotic War] (Moscow: Voroshilov Academy of the General Staff, 1951), 18–22, classified secret.

9. Zaloga and Ness, *Red Army Handbook,* 55–56.

10. Ibid.

11. David M. Glantz, *A History of Soviet Airborne Forces* (London: Frank Cass, 1994), 44–45.

12. Ibid., 104–228.

13. Ibid., 228–62.

14. *Boevoi sostav Sovetskoi armii, chast' 2 (ianvar'–dekabr' 1942 g.)* [The combat composition of the Soviet Army, part 2 (January–December 1943)] (Moscow, Voenizdat, 1966), 181.

15. *Boevoi sostav Sovetskoi armii, chast' 3,* 122, 176.

16. Ibid., 242–69.

17. Ibid., 290–98.

18. The NKO disbanded its 3rd and 8th Guards Airborne Brigades in February 1944 and integrated them into the Red Army's guards airborne divisions. The number of guards airborne divisions in the Red Army decreased to 14 in July 1944, and in August the NKO combined 9 of these divisions into 3 guards airborne corps, the 37th, 38th, and 39th, which formed the nucleus of the future Separate Airborne Army in October 1944 and the elite 9th Guards Army in January 1945. In recognition of the elite nature of this force, the *Stavka* ordered that it be employed only as a shock force in a major ground offensive. Thus, the Red Army fielded three guards airborne corps and 18 guards airborne divisions in December 1944.

19. Glantz, *Soviet Airborne Forces,* 62; and Zaloga and Ness, *Red Army Handbook,* 148–51.

20. Average division strengths were highest in the Leningrad Military District (11,985, or 83 percent), but significantly lower in the Baltic Special, Western Special, and Kiev Special Military Districts (8,712 or 60 percent; 9,327 or 64 percent; and 8,712 or 60 percent, respectively), primarily because the German invasion produced chaos in the planned Soviet mobilization. These divisions fielded 80–90 percent of their weaponry and 25–30 percent of their auto-transport vehicles. See Strokov, *Istoriia voennogo iskusstva,* 356.

21. Exceptions to this rule were the series of people's militia divisions (DNO) raised at Leningrad, Moscow, and elsewhere, whose strength in largely untrained personnel was high but whose weaponry was very weak. In addition, the regular divisions the *Stavka* transferred from the Far East, including the crack 32nd and 78th Rifle Divisions, and the divisions and rifle brigades the NKO mobilized in late fall and assigned to its 1st Shock, 10th, and other reserve armies, were far closer to full strength. The Red Army was able to achieve significant victories in its Moscow counteroffensive and subsequent winter campaign despite its severely understrength forces because *Wehrmacht's* forces also suffered from severe attrition.

22. Zaloga and Ness, *Red Army Handbook,* 189; and A. B. Zhuk, *Strelkovoe oruzhie* [Rifle weapons] (Moscow: Voenizdat, 1992), 51, 255.

23. Zhuk, *Strelkovoe oruzhie,* 544.

24. Babich and Baier, *Razvitie vooruzheniia,* 84.

25. Ibid., 9.

7. Tank, Mechanized, and Cavalry Forces

1. For further details regarding the formation, organization, and deployment of these mechanized corps, see Glantz, *Stumbling Colossus,* 116–45. During the first stage of forming its mechanized corps, the NKO retained about 25 tank brigades

in the force structure to provide tank support to infantry, but during the second stage in 1941, it disbanded all tank brigades and battalions to equip new mechanized corps, leaving no armor whatsoever in rifle corps and rifle and cavalry divisions. Of the 37,895 tanks authorized in the new mechanized, rifle, cavalry, and airborne formation in June 1941, only 23,100 old model tanks were on hand and only 18,700 of these were combat ready. In addition, 3,600 of the tanks were T-37, T-38, and T-40 models, which were equipped with only machine guns. For further details, see Ramanichev, "The Red Army, 1940–1941: Myths and Realities," 92, quoting archival materials in *TsAMO,* f. 38, op. 11353, d. 909, ll. 2–18, 924, and ll. 135–38.

2. Among many sources on the composition of the mechanized corps, see *Nachal'nyi period Velikoi Otechestvennoi voiny* [The initial period of the Great Patriotic War] (Moscow: Voroshilov Academy of the General Staff, 1989), 45–47; and O. A. Losik, ed., *Stroitel'stvo i boevoe primenenie sovetskikh tankovykh voisk v gody Velikoi Otechestvennoi voiny* [The formation and combat use of Soviet tank forces during the Great Patriotic War] (Moscow: Voenizdat, 1979), 44.

3. See Zolotarev, "NKO 1941," 29.

4. Zaloga and Ness, *Red Army Handbook,* 70–71.

5. Ibid., 71.

6. For the complete order, see Zolotarev, "NKO 1941," 51–53.

7. A. I. Radzievsky, ed., *Taktika v boevykh primerakh, polk* [Tactics in combat examples, the regiment] (Moscow: Voenizdat, 1974), figure 2.

8. Kurochkin, *Obshchevoiskovaia armiia na nastuplenii,* 206.

9. Ibid., 49.

10. Ibid., 53.

11. I. M. Anan'ev, *Tankovye armii v nastuplenii* [Tank armies in the offensive] (Moscow: Voenizdat, 1988), 79.

12. Zaloga and Ness, *Red Army Handbook,* 82–83.

13. Losik, *Stroitel'stvo i boevoe primenenie Sovetskikh tankovykh voisk,* 48–49.

14. Anan'ev, *Tankovye armii v nastuplenii,* 79.

15. Ibid.

16. Ibid. The NKO revised the organization of these regiments in February 1944 by adding to them a 94-man submachine-gun company and sapper and logistical support platoons and by substituting new Iosif Stalin-2 (IS-2) model heavy tanks for the older KV models. By February 1944 the heavy tank regiment's strength was 374 men and 21 IS-2 tanks.

17. Anan'ev, *Tankovye armii v nastuplenii,* 81.

18. Ibid., 81–82. Nor did this steady improvement in the tank corps' structure cease at the end of 1943. Throughout 1944 the NKO further improved the corps' structure by adding three self-propelled artillery regiments with 21 self-propelled guns each in February, a full medical battalion in May, an artillery command platoon in June, a light artillery regiment equipped with twenty-four 76mm guns in August, and a corps vehicle exchange point in September. Finally, in November the NKO added mobile tank and mobile automotive repair bases to the corps, which significantly improved the volume and quality of in-corps repair work.

19. Losik, *Stroitel'stvo i boevoe primenenie Sovetskikh tankovykh voisk,* 56–57; and Anan'ev, *Tankovye armii v nastuplenie,* 82.

20. Losik, *Stroitel'stvo i boevoe primenenie Sovetskikh tankovykh voisk,* 57; and V. F. Tolubko and N. I. Baryshev, *Na iuzhnom flange: Boevoi put' 4-go gvardeiskogo mekhanizirovannogo korpusa (1942–1945 gg.)* [On the southern flank: The combat path of the 4th Guards Mechanized Corps (1942–1945)] (Moscow: Nauka, 1973), 47. The 13th Tank Corps consisted of the 17th, 61st, and 62nd Mechanized Brigades, the 35th and 166th Separate Tank Regiments, the 398th Antiaircraft and 565th Antitank Artillery Regiments, the 348th Separate Guards-Mortar Battalion (M-13), the 214th Separate Sapper Battalion, a separate reconnaissance battalion, the 34th Separate Engineer-Mine Company, and the 84th Field Repair Base.

21. Losik, *Stroitel'stvo i boevoe primenenie Sovetskikh tankovykh voisk,* 79.

22. Ibid.; and Zaloga and Ness, *Red Army Handbook,* 85–86.

23. Anan'ev, *Tankovye armii v nastuplenii,* 82–83.

24. While the 5th Tank Army's 2nd, 7th, and 11th Tank Corps attacked west of Voronezh under the Briansk Front's control, the 1st and 4th Tank Armies attacked along the Don River west of Stalingrad under the Stalingrad Front's control. However, all three tank armies performed dismally in these operations, the *Stavka* subsequently relieved the commander of the 5th Tank Army, and the 4th Tank Army lost so many of its tanks that its men subsequently referred to it as "the four-tank army."

25. *Boevoi sostav Sovetskoi armii, chast' 3,* 16.

26. Anan'ev, *Tankovye armii v nastuplenii,* 55–60.

27. The *Stavka* used the 3rd Reserve Army's headquarters as the nucleus for the 2nd Tank Army.

28. Ibid., 64. This was GKO Directive No. 2791.

29. Ibid., 75. Later still, in early 1944 the NKO added a light self-propelled artillery brigade with 60 SU-76 self-propelled guns and five T-70 tanks and a light artillery brigade with forty-eight 76mm and twenty 100mm guns to each tank army.

30. Each engineer brigade consisted of two motorized engineer battalions and one pontoon-bridge battalion. However, even this brigade proved inadequate, and each tank army's parent *front* had to provide additional engineer and pontoon-bridge support for the tank armies until war's end.

31. The 2nd Tank Army, which fielded an aviation liaison squadron, was an exception to this rule. See Anan'ev, *Tankovye armii v nastuplenii,* 76–77.

32. Ibid., 77.

33. Ibid., 78.

34. Zaloga and Ness, *Red Army Handbook,* 97–98.

35. Ibid., 97.

36. *Boevoi sostav Sovetskoi armii, chast' 3,* 31–169.

37. Zaloga and Ness, *Red Army Handbook,* 97.

38. Ogarkov, *SVE,* V: 438.

39. M. A. Moiseev, ed., *Sovetskaia voennaia entsiklopediia v vos'mi tomakh* [Soviet military encyclopedia] (Moscow: Voenizdat, 1990), I: 505.

40. See Babich and Baier, *Razvitie vooruzheniia,* 61; and *Nachal'nyi period*

Velikoi Otechestvennoi voiny, 53. In wartime, cavalry corps were to consist of three cavalry divisions.

41. *Nachal'nyi period Velikoi Otechestvennoi voiny,* 53; and K. Malan'in, "Razvitie organizatsionnykh form sukhoputnykh voisk v Velikoi Otechestvennoi voine" [The development of ground forces' organizational forms in the Great Patriotic War], *VIZh,* no. 8 (August 1967): 31.

42. See also Zaloga and Ness, *Red Army Handbook,* 109–10.

43. For example, a cavalry group made up of the 32nd, 43rd, and 47th Cavalry Divisions conducted a spectacular if ultimately futile raid into the German's rear area southwest of Bobruisk during mid-July 1941, and another cavalry group consisting of the 50th and 53rd Cavalry Divisions did the same in the region northwest of Smolensk during August. In the same fashion, the 2nd, 3rd, and 5th Cavalry Corps proved their worth during the Battle of Moscow and in the Donbas region and, as a reward for their achievements, were reorganized in December 1941 as the 1st, 2nd, and 3rd Guards Cavalry Corps, respectively.

44. Zaloga and Ness, *Red Army Handbook,* 112–13.

45. Babich and Baier, *Razvitie vooruzheniia,* 63; and Zaloga and Ness, *The Red Army Handbook,* 113–14.

46. Babich and Baier, *Razvitie vooruzheniia,* 62; and Zaloga and Ness, *The Red Army Handbook,* 115–16.

47. Exceptions to this general rule include the Trans-Caucasus Military District's 28th Mechanized Corps and the Far Eastern Front's 30th Mechanized Corps, both of which were stronger largely because of their vital strategic location along the Soviet Union's most threatened borders.

48. For example, the 6th Mechanized Corps with its 99 percent fill was the strongest in the Western Special Military District, followed in order of their strength by the 11th, 14th, 13th, 20th, and 17th Mechanized Corps. Likewise, the 4th and 8th Mechanized Corps were the strongest corps in the Kiev Special Military District, followed by the 8th, 15th, 22nd, 16th, 19th, 9th, and 24th Mechanized Corps. In this case, the 9th Mechanized Corps was among the weakest because it was assigned to the military district's reserve. The same pattern held true in the Leningrad Military District, where the 1st Mechanized Corps was twice as strong as the 10th, and in the Baltic Special Military District, where the 3rd Mechanized Corps was stronger than the 12th.

49. These included, for example, the Baltic Special Military District's 3rd Mechanized Corps, the Western Special Military District's 6th and 11th Mechanized Corps, the Kiev Special Military District's 4th, 8th, 15th, and 16th Mechanized Corps, and the Odessa Military District's 2nd Mechanized Corps. In general, mechanized corps in the border military districts' reserves and those stationed in the internal military districts fielded few if any new model tanks.

50. Glantz, *The Battle for Leningrad,* 32–33.

51. Glantz, *The Initial Period of War on the Eastern Front,* 212–16, 260–61.

52. Ibid., 276–79.

53. Glantz, *Soviet War Experiences: Tank Operations.*

54. After the Battle of Kursk, the *Stavka* withdrew its 1st, 3rd Guards, 4th, and 5th Guards Tank Armies into reserve for rest and reconstitution in late August and

early September, but employed its 2nd Tank Army in offensive operations around Sevsk and Chernigov. Thereafter, its 3rd Guards Tank Army led the Voronezh Front's dash to the Dnepr River in late September and early October, the 5th Guards Tank Army spearheaded the Steppe Front's advance to and across the Dnepr in October, and the 1st Tank Army joined battle west of Kiev in mid-December.

55. For example, the 112th Tank Division, which was later reorganized as the 112th Tank Brigade, supported Group Belov's 1st Guards Cavalry Corps in December 1941, and a separate tank brigade accompanied Group Belov on its January 1942 raid until harsh winter and rough terrain forced Belov to leave the brigade behind. Likewise, several tank brigades supported Cavalry Group Bobkin's 6th Cavalry Corps during its ill-fated Khar'kov operation in May 1942.

56. See Kalashnikov, Fes'kov, Chmykhalo, and Golikov, *Krasnaia Armiia v iiune 1941 goda,* 144, for additional details.

57. I. G. Pavlovsky, *Sukhoputnye voiska SSSR* [The ground forces of the USSR] (Moscow: Voenizdat, 1985), 105–7. See Zaloga and Ness, *Red Army Handbook,* 180–81, for additional tank production figures.

58. See Zaloga and Ness, *Red Army Handbook,* 162–65, for further details about this modification process.

59. Ibid., 176–79; and G. L. Kholiavsky, ed., *Entsiklopediia tankov: Polnaia entsiklopediia tankov mira 1915–2000 gg.* [An encyclopedia of tanks: A complete encyclopedia of the world's tanks, 1915–2000] (Moscow: n.p., 1998), 268–78.

60. Proposed by U.S. President Franklin D. Roosevelt in December 1940, approved by the U.S. Congress on 11 March 1941, and extended to the Soviet Union in late July 1941, Lend-Lease military aid from the United States and Great Britain included a dizzying array of weaponry and material, including trucks, tanks, and aircraft, as well as raw materials, foodstuffs, and other supplies critical to the Soviet war effort.

61. Zaloga and Ness, *Red Army Handbook,* 180. See Kholiavsky, *Entsiklopediia tankov,* 289–93, for further detailed information from the Russian perspective concerning the balance between Soviet tank production and tanks provided by Lend-Lease. According to Kholiavsky, the Red Army's operating forces fielded a total of 1,731 Soviet-produced tanks in December 1941, of which 1,214 were light T-26, BT, T-40, and T-60 models. During the period from September through December 1941, the Allies provided the Red Army with 750 British and 180 U.S. model tanks, that is, fully half of the Red Army's total tank strength.

62. Zaloga and Ness, *Red Army Handbook,* 174.

63. Kholiavsky, *Entsiklopediia tankov,* 293.

64. Zaloga and Ness, *Red Army Handbook,* 186–87.

65. Ibid., 187.

66. Ibid.

8. *Artillery and Air Forces*

1. Babich and Baier, *Razvitie vooruzheniia,* 50; and B. I. Nevzorov, *Razvitie sposobov boevogo primeneniia artillerii v Velikoi Otechestvennoi voine* [The development of the means of the combat employment of artillery in the Great Patriotic War] (Moscow:

Frunze Academy, 1984), table 3. As distinct from the terms *diviziia* (division), which referred to rifle, tank, motorized, artillery, and aviation divisions, and *batal'on* (battalion), which referred to rifle, tank, and other types of battalions, the Red Army used the term *divizion* (also battalion) to describe artillery battalions of all types.

2. Zaloga and Ness, *Red Army Handbook*, 132. Some confusion exists regarding the strength of the revised standard corps artillery regiment. Zaloga and Ness claim the regiment consisted of four battalions with a total of 48 guns, but Lensky, *Sukhoputnye sily RKKA v predvoennye gody*, 52, claims that the third type of corps artillery regiment consisted of two battalions of 152mm gun-howitzers with 12 guns each, for a total of 24 guns. Nevzorov, *Razvitie sposobov boevogo primeneniia artillerii,* fails to mention the third type of regiment altogether. The NKO planned to employ 1 standard corps artillery regiment to support each rifle corps and either 2 standard regiments or a second or third type of regiment to support each rifle corps stationed in the western military districts. However, when war began only 32 rifle corps fielded two corps artillery regiments and the remaining corps had only one. For details, see Kalashnikov, Fes'kov, Chmykhalo, and Golikov, *Krasnaia Armiia v iiune 1941 goda,* 16.

3. A. V. Vladimirsky, *Na kievskom napravlenii* [On the Kiev axis] (Moscow: Voenizdat, 1989), 31.

4. Babich and Baier, *Razvitie vooruzheniia,* 34; and A. I. Radzievsky, ed., *Taktika v boevykh primerakh (diviziia)* [Tactics in combat examples (the division)] (Moscow: Voenizdat, 1976), figure 1. At the same time, the number of 76mm guns assigned to the division's three rifle regiments fell from 18 to 12.

5. Zaloga and Ness, *Red Army Handbook,* 12; Babich and Baier, *Razvitie vooruzheniia,* 34, 52; and Radzievsky, *Taktika v boevykh primerakh (diviziia),* figure 1. At the same time, the March table of organization added five tractors to each rifle division to replace horses as the prime movers for the division's 122mm howitzers.

6. Babich and Baier, *Razvitie vooruzheniia,* 52. Regimental artillery strength remained at twelve 76m guns.

7. Radzievsky, *Taktika v boevykh primerakh (diviziia),* figure 1.

8. Zaloga and Ness, *Red Army Handbook,* 132–33.

9. Lensky, *Sukhoputnye sily RKKA v predvoennye gody,* 53.

10. Ibid.

11. Depending on their subordination, some of these new RVGK artillery regiments were designated simply as artillery regiments, while others were named army artillery regiments.

12. Lensky, *Sukhoputnye sily RKKA v predvoennye gody,* 53–54. This source states that there were a total of 215 RVGK artillery regiments on 31 December 1941. The 159 artillery regiments and 26 separate artillery battalions of RVGK artillery included eight corps artillery, 57 artillery, 34 gun artillery, 52 howitzer artillery, and seven high-power howitzer artillery regiments and seven artillery and 18 special-power artillery battalions and one high-power artillery battalion.

13. The total of 323 artillery regiments and 22 artillery battalions in RVGK artillery on 1 July 1942 included eight corps artillery, 74 army artillery, three artillery, 98 gun artillery, 86 howitzer artillery, and 54 high-power howitzer artillery regiments and 12 special-power and ten artillery battalions. The 301 artillery regiments and 23 artil-

lery battalions on 1 February include 61 army artillery, 15 corps artillery, 87 gun artillery, 59 howitzer artillery, and 51 high-power howitzer artillery regiments and 13 special-power artillery, one gun artillery, one heavy gun artillery, two high-power gun artillery, and six heavy artillery battalions. Beginning in the fall of 1942, the quantity of artillery regiments and separate artillery battalions in RVGK artillery decreased sharply because the NKO began fielding artillery divisions, brigades, and, later, artillery corps.

14. Zolotarev, "NKO 1941," 353–57. See also Babich and Baier, *Razvitie vooruzheniia,* 53.

15. Zaloga and Ness, *The Red Army Handbook,* 140; Babich and Baier, *Razvitie vooruzheniia,* 53–54; and N. E. Medvedev, "Artilleriia RVGK v pervom periode voiny" [Artillery of the *Stavka* Reserve in the initial period of the war], *VIZh,* no. 11 (November 1987): 81–87.

16. Zaloga and Ness, *Red Army Handbook,* 139. This division, which fought at Stalingrad, converted into a standard artillery division in April 1943.

17. Babich and Baier, *Razvitie vooruzheniia,* 53–54; and Zaloga and Ness, *Red Army Handbook,* 137–38.

18. Zaloga and Ness, *Red Army Handbook,* 136–37.

19. Babich and Baier, *Razvitie vooruzheniia,* 57; and Zaloga and Ness, *Red Army Handbook.*

20. Zaloga and Ness, *Red Army Handbook,* 140.

21. Babich and Baier, *Razvitie vooruzheniia,* 53.

22. Zaloga and Ness, *Red Army Handbook,* 130.

23. Ibid., 131.

24. Ibid.

25. Ianchinsky, *Boevoe ispol'zovanie istrebitel'no-protivotankovoi artillerii RVGK,* 7. The eleventh antitank brigade formed in the Northwestern Front.

26. Ibid. This brigade's *shtat* (table of organization) was numbered 04/132.

27. Ibid, 10. This regiment's *shtat* was numbered 04/133.

28. Zaloga and Ness, *Red Army Handbook,* 119.

29. Ianchinsky, *Boevoe ispol'zovanie istrebitel'no-protivotankovoi artillerii RVGK,* 11. According to its *shtat,* which was numbered 08/56, this regiment fielded 30 tractors, ten trailers, ten submachine guns, and 66 trucks and other vehicles.

30. Ibid. The *shtats* of these regiments were numbered 08/55 and 08/70, respectively. The heavy regiments included five batteries with four 76mm guns each and one battery with four 25mm or 37mm guns for a total strength of 545 men, twenty 76mm guns, four 25mm or 37mm antiaircraft guns, ten light machine guns, 57 vehicles, 30 tractors, and ten trailers, the light regiments consisted of four batteries, including two batteries with four 37mm or 45mm guns each and two batteries with four 85mm antiaircraft guns for a total strength of 364 men, eight 37mm or 45mm guns, eight 85mm antiaircraft guns, four light machine guns, 46 vehicles, 12 tractors, and four trailers.

31. Ibid., 13.

32. Most of these regiments were destroyed during the border battles of late June and early July and the Battle for Moscow in October and November, and most were armed with 37mm and 85mm guns.

33. Ianchinsky, *Boevoe ispol'zovanie istrebitel'no-protivotankovoi artillerii RVGK*, 16. The 1,360 guns on 22 June 1941 included 24 of the 107mm, 480 of the 85mm, 480 of the 76mm, and 160 of the 37mm guns; the 1,188 guns on 31 December included 48 of the 107mm, 660 of the 85mm, 236 of the 76mm, 48 of the 45mm, and 196 of the 37mm guns.

34. Ibid., 17. *Shtat* 08/107 dated 15 April organized antitank regiments consisting of five batteries with four 76mm guns each for a total strength of 489 men, twenty 76mm guns, 20 antitank rifles, ten light machine guns, 47 vehicles, and 25 tractors; and *shtat* 08/100 dated 15 May organized regiments containing five batteries with four 45mm guns each for a total strength of 260 men, twenty 45mm guns, 20 antitank rifles, ten light machine guns, and 39 vehicles.

35. Modified *shtat* 08/107 added the sixth battery.

36. Zolotarev, "NKO 1941," 264–65. NKO Order No. 0528, dated 1 July 1942, renamed all RVGK light artillery and antitank artillery regiments and antitank battalions and batteries organic to rifle divisions and rifle regiments as antitank destroyer (tank destroyer) artillery. In addition, the order established monetary and other rewards for the commander and crew of gun batteries that destroyed a German tank (500 and 200 rubles, respectively).

37. Ianchinsky, *Boevoe ispol'zovanie istrebitel'no-protivotankovoi artillerii RVGK*, 22. These regiments, which were organized under *shtat* 08/84, consisted of four battalions, three made up of three batteries with four 76mm guns each, and one made up of three batteries with six 45mm guns each for a regimental strength of 964 men, 54 guns (36 of the 76mm and 18 of the 45mm), 19 light machine guns, six motorcycles, and 125 trucks and other vehicles.

38. Ibid. These regiments, organized under *shtat* 08/166, consisted of four 45mm gun batteries, one antitank rifle company, and an automatic weapons company. The gun batteries in these regiments fielded three 45mm guns, eight DShK machine guns (in two platoons), and 16 antitank rifles; the antitank rifle companies consisted of three platoons with 12 antitank rifles each; and the automatic weapons companies consisted of two platoons for a regimental strength of 484 men, twelve 45mm guns, 36 large caliber machine guns, 100 antitank rifles, 50 pistols, 25 vehicles, and 18 armored transporters.

39. Ibid., 43. The heavy regiments, organized under *shtat* 08/135, consisted of five batteries, each equipped with three 107mm guns and ten antitank rifles for a total strength of 551 men, 15 guns, 50 antitank rifles, ten light machine guns, and 62 trucks, and the rifle support antitank battalions, organized under *shtat* 08/148, consisted of three batteries with four 76mm guns each, a mortar company with three platoons of three 82mm mortars each, and an antitank rifle company with three platoons of nine antitank rifle each, for a total battalion strength of 585 men, twelve 76mm guns, nine 82mm mortars, 27 antitank rifles, 109 machine pistols, three light machine guns, 48 trucks, and three tractors.

40. Ibid., 44. Each of the tank destroyer regiments assigned to artillery divisions fielded 24 of the 76mm guns, 24 antitank rifles, 12 light machine guns, 46 trucks, and 30 motorized tractors manned by 557 men. See also, Zolotarev, "NKO 1941," 355–56, for details regarding NKO Order No. 00226.

41. For details on losses during 1942, see Ianchinsky, *Boevoe ispol'zovanie istrebitel'no-protivotankovoi artillerii RVGK*, 25–26. The Red Army suffered its heaviest losses in tank destroyer regiments during July and August 1942, when *Wehrmacht* forces were advancing toward Stalingrad. For example, during this period the Southwestern, Stalingrad, and North Caucasus Front lost four, 13, and eight regiments, respectively.

42. Ibid., 25. The antitank rifle battalions with three companies, organized under *shtat* 08/102, had a strength of 193 men and 72 antitank rifles, while those organized with four companies under *shtat* 08/140, had a strength of 332 men, 108 antitank rifles, and 61 machine pistols.

43. Ibid., 50. These included regiments organized under *shtats* 08/135, 08/84, 08/107, 08/107, 08/100, and 08/166.

44. Ibid., 50–51. These included tank destroyer battalions organized under *shtat* 08/148 and antitank rifle battalions organized under *shtats* 08/102 and 08/140.

45. Ibid., 51. Antitank artillery regiments assigned to field armies, which were formed on 1 January 1943 under *shtat* 08/115, fielded six batteries with a total of 24 ZIS-3 76mm antitank guns.

46. See V. A. Zolotarev, ed., "Prikazy narodnogo komissara oborony SSSR (1943–1945 gg.) [The orders of the People's Commissar of Defense of the USSR (1943–1945)], in *Russkii arkhiv: Velikaia Otechestvennaia* [The Russian archives: The Great Patriotic (War)], 13, 2 (3) (Moscow: Terra, 1997), 114–15. Hereafter cited as Zolotarev, "NKO 1943," with appropriate page(s). This NKO order was numbered 0063 and the new *shtat* was numbered 08/115. The heavy tank destroyer regiments had a strength of 496 men, twenty-four 76mm antitank guns, 24 antitank rifles, 12 light machine guns, 39 trucks, and 30 tractors, and the lighter version had a strength of 274 men, twenty 45mm guns, 18 trucks, and 22 tractors.

47. Ibid., 115. The *shtat* for these tank destroyer brigades was numbered 08/530. The strength of the 1943 brigades contrasted sharply to the 1941 brigades, whose strength was 5,309 men and 136 guns.

48. Ianchinsky, *Boevoe ispol'zovanie istrebitel'no-protivotankovoi artillerii RVGK*, 54. By the time the NKO completed this process in September, all RVGK tank destroyer artillery brigades were organized under *shtat* 08/595 and fielded forty 76mm and twenty 57mm guns.

49. Ibid., 55, 87. The strength of reinforced tank destroyer artillery brigades organized under *shtat* 08/596 with six-battery regiments was 1,492 men, 72 antitank guns including forty-eight 76mm and twenty-four 57mm guns, 36 light machine guns, 72 antitank rifles, 133 trucks, and 90 tractors. Brigades organized under *shtat* 08/586 with five-battery regiments had a strength of sixty 76mm guns, and those organized under *shtat* 08/580 with five-battery regiments had 60 antitank guns, including forty 67mm and twenty 57mm guns.

50. See Zolotarev, "NKO 1941," 381–82, for the 21 December order forming this new directorate.

51. Ianchinsky, *Boevoe ispol'zovanie istrebitel'no-protivotankovoi artillerii RVGK*, 24. The self-propelled artillery regiments *shtat* was numbered 08/158.

52. N. Popov, "Razvitie samokhodnoi artillerii" [The development of self-propelled artillery], *VIZh*, no. 1 (January 1977): 27–31.

53. See Zolotarev, "NKO 1943," 136–37, for the order resubordinating this directorate.

54. Popov, "Razvitie samokhodnoi artillerii," 28–29.

55. Ibid., 29.

56. Ibid., 29–30. The NKO accepted these new self-propelled artillery systems, which were named SU-100 self-propelled guns and were dedicated tank killers armed with 100mm guns, in June 1944 and began fielding them in September 1944.

57. Ibid.; and Zaloga and Ness, *Red Army Handbook*, 92–93. The NKO completed this streamlining process in February 1944 by converting all of its self-propelled artillery regiments to uniform organizations consisting of four batteries with five guns each, plus an additional gun in the regimental headquarters, for a total strength of 21 self-propelled guns.

58. For details, see M. Tur, "Razvitie protivovozdushnoi oborony voisk v Velikoi Otechestvennoi voine" [The development of antiaircraft defense for forces in the Great Patriotic War], *VIZh*, no. 1 (January 1962): 15; and Zaloga and Ness, *Red Army Handbook*, 9–10.

59. Tur, "Razvitie," 15.

60. Ibid., 17.

61. Zaloga and Ness, *Red Army Handbook*, 18. These changes eliminated the unwieldy 76mm guns from the rifle division and the four-barreled 13.7mm machine guns from the rifle regiment.

62. Ibid., 127; and K. Lavrent'ev, "Voiskovaia PVO v gody voiny" [Force air defense in the war years], *Voennyi vestnik* [Military herald], no. 10 (October 1989): 49.

63. See Zolotarev, "NKO 1941," 247–48, for details regarding NKO Order No. 0442, which assigned PVO regiments to the Southwestern Front on the basis of two per four of its armies.

64. Ibid., 248.

65. Zaloga and Ness, *Red Army Handbook*, 128.

66. See Zolotarev, "NKO 1941," 347–48, for details regarding NKO Order No. 0841.

67. Ibid. The *Stavka* assigned the 1st through 13th Antiaircraft Artillery Divisions to the Force Antiaircraft Artillery Training Center, the 14th and 17th to the Western Front, the 16th to the Briansk Front, and the 15th and 18th to the Don Front. Eight of these divisions were to be prepared for action by 20 November 1942, that is, the date of anticipated major Red Army offensive operations, and the remainder were to complete their formation by the end of the year. See also Zaloga and Ness, *Red Army Handbook*, 128.

68. Tur, "Razvitie," 19; and Babich and Baier, *Razvitie vooruzheniia*, 60–61.

69. Tur, "Razvitie," 20.

70. Zaloga and Ness, *Red Army Handbook*, 129; and Lavrent'ev, "Voiskovaia PVO v gody voiny," 49.

71. Zaloga and Ness, *Red Army Handbook*, 129.

72. N. Kornienko, "Boevoe primenenie bronepoezda PVO" [The combat employment of PVO armored trains], *VIZh*, no. 4 (April 1979): 31–32. By this time the standard antiaircraft armored train battalions consisted of two trains, each armed with three 76mm and two 37mm antiaircraft guns, three 12.7mm DShK heavy machine

guns, an antiaircraft detector, and a stereoscopic rangefinder. The trains themselves consisted of a base element made up of a locomotive and supporting boxcars for housing and supplies and a combat element made up of seven armored platforms mounted on 20–ton double-axle railroad flatcars with side armor 12–15 mm thick and 1 meter high and an armor-plate floor. Organizationally, the combat element of each train consisted of a command element, a headquarters platoon, two weapons platoons, one with three medium 76mm guns and the other with light 37mm guns, a machine-gun platoon, and small service elements. The guns were mounted on the armored platforms, with one 76mm gun on each of five flatcars, and one 37mm gun and one DShK machine gun each on the other two flatcars.

73. See P. A. Degtiarev and P. P. Ionov, *"Katiushi" na pole boia"* [Katiushas on the field of battle] (Moscow: Voenizdat, 1991), for the most detailed coverage of the development and fielding of guards-mortar forces.

74. Ibid., 10–11. The first rocket launcher battery went into action on 14 July 1941, west of Smolensk in support of the Western Front's 20th Army. On 22 June the Western Front assigned a second rocket battery, this one equipped with nine launchers, to support the 19th Army and, a few days later, a third battery with three launchers to support Group Rokossovsky east of Smolensk. The fourth, fifth, and sixth batteries, three with four launchers and one with five, joined the first battery in the fighting at El'nia in early August. The seventh and eighth batteries, with four and six launchers, respectively, went into action in the Leningrad region and Southwestern Front also in August.

75. Ibid., 8.

76. Ibid., 14.

77. Ibid.

78. Ibid. The first and second rocket launcher regiments reached the front on 12 and 19 August, the first eight completed deploying by 12 September, and the ninth reached the field in late September.

79. Ibid., 17–18. This removed responsibility for raising guards-mortar units from the chief of Red Army Artillery and the NKO's Main Artillery Directorate (GAU).

80. See Zolotarev, "NKO 1941," 137, for this full order, which was numbered 008. The *Stavka* began this process by ordering the 30th and 1st Shock Armies and 2nd Cavalry Corps to consolidate their guards-mortars into operational groups in November and December to improve their performance in its offensive at Moscow.

81. Degtiarev and Ionov, *"Katiushi" na pole boia,* 19. See also Babich and Baier, *Razvitie,* 50–51; and Zaloga and Ness, *Red Army Handbook,* 141.

82. Zolotarev, "Stavka VGK 1942," 33–35.

83. Degtiarev and Ionov, *"Katiushi" na pole boia,* 46. These regiments also included two antiaircraft platoons, one equipped with two DShK machine guns and the other with two 37mm antiaircraft guns, and the batteries in their battalions fielded four rocket launchers each.

84. Ibid., 51. The 300mm M-30 launcher entered production with new launch vehicles in May. In addition, the GKO also formed the 1st Guards-Mortar Training Brigade, which trained over 18,000 officers, sergeants, and drivers for service in guards-mortar units by year's end. Ultimately, Soviet industry managed to produce a total of 648 M-8 and 1,542 M-13 systems by year's end.

85. Ibid., 52.

86. Ibid.

87. Ibid., 53. Eight of the initial type of M-30 battalions supported the 61st Army's offensive near Bolkhov and Zhizdra in early July. Ultimately, the NKO deployed 74 M-30 battalions to the front by 20 August 1942, and based another six battalions in Moscow in the RVGK.

88. Ibid., 54.

89. Ibid.

90. Ibid., 79. The NKO used 15 M-13 guards-mortar regiments, 14 separate M-30 guards-mortar battalions, 5,000 men from other guards-mortar units, 5,000 sailors, and the personnel from the 1st and 2nd Guards-Mortar Training Brigades to form these three divisions. The *Stavka* assigned the 1st Guards-Mortar Division to the Northwestern Front to participate in the reduction of the German Demiansk salient and Operation Polar Star, the 2nd and 3rd to the Don Front to destroy the German Sixth Army encircled at Stalingrad, and the 4th to the Voronezh Front to support its advance toward Khar'kov.

91. See Zolotarev, "NKO 1941," 370–71, for this full order, which was numbered 00244.

92. Degtiarev and Ionov, *"Katiushi" na pole boia,* 78.

93. Ibid., 79–80.

94. Ibid., 93. See the NKO order mandating this organizational change in Zolotarev, "NKO 1943," 152. This was NKO Order No. 0082.

95. Ibid.,106.

96. Guards-mortar regiments consisted of a headquarters; three battalions with two batteries of four launchers each for a total of eight launchers, and a DShK machine-gun platoon with two machine guns for a total of 191 men; and an antiaircraft battery with four 37mm AA guns, for a regimental strength of about 620 men and 24 BM-8 or BM-13 launchers.

97. Ibid., 18–56; Babich and Baier, *Razvitie,* 50–51; and Zaloga and Ness, *Red Army Handbook,* 142.

98. For organizational details, see M. P. Pevnevets, *Boevoe primenenie Sovetskikh voenno-vozdushnykh sil v gody Velikoi Otechestvennoi voiny* [The combat employment of the Soviet Air Force during the Great Patriotic War] (Moscow: Frunze Academy, 1984), 7–9.

99. See Zolotarev, "NKO 1941," 25, for the contents of NKO Order No. 0052, dated 15 July, which organized the 81st Long-Range Aviation Division on the basis of the same *shtat* (015/140) as previous bomber-aviation divisions. The 81st Division was the first division to conduct a raid on Berlin, which it did on the night of 10–11 August 1941. Aircraft from the Baltic Fleet had conducted the first raid on the city on the night of 7–8 August. See also Zolotarev, "NKO 1941," 48, 61–62.

100. Pevnevets, *Boevoe primenenie Sovetskikh voenno-vozdushnykh sil,* 10.

101. Ibid., 11. Major General of Aviation A. E. Golovanov commanded ADD.

102. M. N. Kozhevnikov, *Komandovanie i shtab VVS Sovetskoi Armii v Velikoi Otechestvennoi voine 1941–1945 gg.* [The command and staff of the Air Force of the Soviet Army in the Great Patriotic War 1941–1945] (Moscow: Nauka, 1977), 120.

103. Pevnevets, *Boevoe primenenie Sovetskikh voenno-vozdushnykh sil,* 10–11. ADD was reorganized into the 18th Air Army in late 1944 and subordinated to the VVS commander, and its organic corps were strengthened from two to four aviation divisions. By May 1945 the 18th Air Army consisted of four aviation corps and three separate aviation divisions.

104. Pevnevets, *Boevoe primenenie Sovetskikh voenno-vozdushnykh sil,* 8.

105. For further details, see Kalashnikov, Fes'kov, Chmykhalo, and Golikov, *Krasnaia Armiia v iiune 1941 goda,* 18. The most serious problem faced by the VVS on the eve of war was the mismatch between assigned aircraft and crews in regiments assigned to the western military districts, where, in general, there were almost twice as many assigned aircraft as crews. Making matters worse, many of these aircraft were obsolete. For example, the 149th Fighter Aviation Regiment, which was assigned to the 12th Army's 64th Fighter Aviation Regiment, had 67 old I-16 and I-153 aircraft and 64 new MiG-3 aircraft, and the 55th Fighter Aviation Regiment of the 9th Separate Army's 20th Mixed Aviation Division had 54 I-16 and I-153 aircraft and 62 MiG-3 aircraft.

106. Pevnevets, *Boevoe primenenie Sovetskikh voenno-vozdushnykh sil,* 8. See Zolotarev, "NKO 1941," 70–71, for the complete NKO order, no. 0305.

107. See Zolotarev, "NKO 1941," 112–13, for this full order, no. 0099. Formed at Engels and Kamenka airfields, the command cadre and navigators for these regiments were trained locally or at the 2nd Ivanovo Higher Navigators School. Organized as standard regiments without any special designation, these three regiments would fly thousands of sorties, and two of them, the 587th and 588th, ultimately earned the respective guards designations of the 125th Guards Dive-Bomber Aviation Regiment and the 46th Guards Night Bomber Aviation Regiment. For further details about the combat record of these regiments, see Reina Pennington, *Wings, Women, and War: Soviet Airwomen in World War II Combat* (Lawrence: University Press of Kansas, 2001), 2; and Kazimiera J. Cottam, *Women in War and Resistance: Selected Biographies of Soviet Women Soldiers* (Nepean, Canada: New Military, 1998).

108. See Zolotarev, "NKO 1941," 107–8 for this full order, no. 0090.

109. Pevnevets, *Boevoe primenenie Sovetskikh voenno-vozdushnykh sil,* 8.

110. See Zolotarev, "NKO 1941," 138, for this full order, no. 030. This measure was a logical extension of a 23 June 1941 GKO order subordinating the Civil Air Fleet to the NKO and a subsequent 9 July NKO order on the operational employment of Civil Air Fleet resources in wartime. See also Pevnevets, *Boevoe primenenie Sovetskikh voenno-vozdushnykh sil,* 19–20.

111. Kozhevnikov, *Komandovanie i shtab VVS Sovetskoi Armii v Velikoi Otechestvennoi voine,* 83.

112. Ibid., 82–83. Ultimately, aircraft availability determined the exact composition of each group. For example the 1st Shock Group consisted initially of two bomber aviation regiments equipped with Pe-2 aircraft, two assault aviation regiments with Il-2 ground attack aircraft, two fighter aviation regiments with LaGG-3 and IaK-1 fighters, and two heavy bomber regiments with DB-3f bombers.

113. See Zolotarev, "NKO 1941," 224–25, for the complete order forming the 1st Air Army, no. 0081.

114. Kozhevnikov, *Komandovanie i shtab VVS Sovetskoi Armii v Velikoi Otechestvennoi voine,* 82–83.

115. Ibid., 85. Elsewhere along the front, a portion of the 1st Bomber Aviation Army attacked German communications lines along the Western axis in July, but in August the *Stavka* ordered the VVS to disband the army and subordinate its divisions to the Western Front's 1st Air Army and long-range aviation. In the midst of this formation, the VVS redistributed the incomplete divisions of the 2nd Fighter Army to the 1st and 3rd Air Armies on 27 July 1942.

116. Ibid.

117. The United States and Great Britain transferred Lend-Lease aircraft to the Soviet Union either through the Persian corridor from Abadan on the coast of Iran to the southern Soviet Union or along the air ferry route from Alaska to Siberia (the ALSIB). Earlier, smaller Lend-Lease shipments had reached the Soviet Union via the far more treacherous sea route to Murmansk, but this had resulted in heavy losses because of German air attacks. Thereafter, most shipments arrived via Iran or the Soviet Far East.

To support this effort and ensure that these precious aircraft reached the VVS's forces, the NKO formed special aviation brigades responsible for ferrying the aircraft along the vital Persian corridor and ALSIB routes. For example, on 3 August 1942, the NKO ordered the VVS to form the Headquarters of the Krasnoiarsk Air Route and the 1st Aviation Brigade, which was subordinate to it, by 15 August. The new headquarters was located in Iakutsk, in eastern Siberia, and its subordinate aviation brigade was stationed in Krasnoiarsk, in western Siberia. The two organizations were responsible for transporting aircraft along the ALSIB to airfields belonging to the VVS's 6th Reserve Aviation Brigade based at Ivanovo, 150 miles northeast of Moscow, which, in turn, would convey them to operating VVS forces.

The new 1st Aviation Brigade, which formed in mid-September, consisted of six fighter and bomber aviation regiments from the Volkhov, Voronezh, and Stalingrad Fronts and the Arkhangel'sk Military District and over 320 flight crews from the VVS's Cadre Directorate, the Far Eastern Front, and personnel from the southern (Iranian) ferry route, which was already operating. Once formed, the brigade was organized into one squadron of "Boston-3" aircraft consisting of six groups with two aircraft each, one mixed aviation regiment consisting of one squadron of B-25 aircraft and one squadron of "Boston-3" aircraft, one aviation regiment of "Boston-3" with six squadrons, and two aviation regiments with "Airacobra" and R-40E aircraft consisting of eight squadrons each. This and similar ferrying brigades deployed in the southern Soviet Union performed their work well, flying over new 10,000 aircraft to assist the VVS by war's end. For further details, see Evgenii Altunin, "ALSIB: On the History of the Alaska-Siberian Ferrying Route," *Journal of Slavic Military Studies* 10, no. 2 (June 1997): 85–97; and Zolotarev, "NKO 1942," 279–80. Hereafter cited as *JSMS* with appropriate issue and pages. For details on the aircraft provided to the Soviet Union under Lend-Lease and the experiences of Soviet pilots who flew the U.S. "Airacobra" aircraft, see Dmitriy Loza, *Attack of the Airacobras: Soviet Aces, American P-39s, and the Air War against Germany* (Lawrence: University Press of Kansas, 2002).

118. Small air armies, such as the 7th supporting the Karelian Front and the 13th supporting the Leningrad Front, consisted of four aviation divisions and two to three separate aviation regiments or squadrons, while larger air armies, such as the Kalinin Front's 3rd Air Army, consisted of three aviation corps, eight separate aviation divisions, and 11 separate aviation regiments or squadrons.

119. Loza, *Attack of the Airacobras*, 9.

120. Kozhevnikov, *Komandovanie i shtab VVS Sovetskoi Armii v Velikoi Otechestvennoi voine*, 143.

121. Zolotarev, "NKO 1943," 111–12. NKO Order No. 0062, dated 8 April 1943, formed 28 night bomber aviation regiments, each consisting of 896 U-2 aircraft by 5 June, to be formed in three stages (seven by 15 April, seven by 25 April, ten by 15 May, and four by 5 June). The NKO also ordered the VVS to create three aviation division headquarters by 1 May to control the 28 regiments.

122. Ibid.

123. Finally, after assessing both the 85mm and 100mm guns in an antitank role, in 1944 the NKO selected the 100mm BS-3 antitank gun for serial production. It also fielded specialized antitank weapons such as the 37mm ChK-M1 Model 1944 gun for use primarily in airborne units.

124. The NKO also modernized the 85mm antiaircraft gun in 1944 as the KS-12A Model 1944.

125. Zaloga and Ness, *Red Army Handbook*, 214–15.

126. The NKO began this phase of the experimentation on 15 April 1942, when it ordered the Main Artillery Directorate (GAU), the People's Commissariat of Armaments, and weapons constructors to jointly develop a self-propelled assault gun that could better accompany and support the infantry. For further details, see Kholiavsky, *Entsiklopediia tankov*.

127. Zaloga and Ness, *Red Army Handbook*, 174. See also Popov, "Razvitie samokhodnoi artillerii," 27–31.

128. Zaloga and Ness, *Red Army Handbook*, 174.

129. In 1944 the NKO also fielded heavy ISU-122C D-25 self-propelled guns, which mounted A-19 122mm guns, and ISU-152 Model ML-20C guns, which were armed with a version of the ML-20 152mm gun-howitzers, both mounted on the chassis of Iosif Stalin (IS) heavy tanks.

130. Babich and Baier, *Razvitie vooruzheniia*, 20. See also Pevnevets, *Boevoe primenenie Sovetskikh voenno-vozdushnykh sil.* Soviet industry produced 40,241 aircraft in 1944 and 15,317 more by 10 May 1945, for a total of 125,655 aircraft produced during the entire war. By the end of 1945, this total reached the staggering figure of over 134,000 aircraft. By war's end Soviet wartime production included roughly 54,000 fighters, 35,000 assault, and 16,000 bomber aircraft.

9. *Engineer, Signal, Chemical, Railroad, Auto-Transport and Road, and Construction Forces*

1. For a general survey of the evolution of engineer forces during wartime, see S. Kh. Aganov, ed., *Inzhenernye voiska Sovetskoi armii 1918–1945* [Engineer forces

of the Soviet Army 1918–1945] (Moscow: Voenizdat, 1985), 254–76; and A. A. Soskov, "Sovershenstvovanie organizatsionnoi struktury inzhenernykh voisk v gody Velikoi Otechestvennoi voiny" [Improvement in the organizational structure of engineer forces during the Great Patriotic War], *VIZh,* no. 12 (December 1985): 66–70.

2. A. D. Tsirlin, et al., eds., *Inzhenernye voiska v boiakh za sovetskuiu rodinu* [Engineer forces in battles for the Soviet homeland] (Moscow: Voenizdat, 1970, 1976), 72–73.

3. Kalashnikov, Fes'kov, Chmykhalo, and Golikov, *Krasnaia Armiia v iiune 1941 goda,* attachment 3.2.

4. Ibid.

5. Tsirlin, *Inzhenernye voiska,* 72. This source claims that there were 18 engineer and 16 pontoon-bridge regiments in the Red Army on 22 June, but official orders of battle place the number at 19 and 9, respectively.

6. Ibid., 17.

7. Ibid., 77.

8. Ibid., 78.

9. Babich and Baier, *Razvitie vooruzheniia,* 69.

10. G. V. Malinovsky, "Sapernye armii i ikh rol' v pervyi period Velikoi Otechestvennoi voiny [Sapper armies and their role in the initial period of the Great Patriotic War], in *Voenno-istoricheskii arkhiv* [Military-historical archives], no. 2 (17) (Moscow: Tserera, 2001), 147, which states: "One of the principal tasks of engineer support for Soviet Army combat operations during the course of the summer–fall campaign of 1941 was the construction of force and rear defense lines and the erection of various barriers. The rapid advance of the German-fascist forces' shock group at that time made it necessary to create strategically significant rear defense lines erected in accordance with the General Staff plans along the main likely enemy attack axes. All of these lines were created to somehow halt the fascist forces along them for as long as possible and win time for the gathering of forces from the depths of the country and creating reserves that could be deployed along the most important axes."

11. Ibid., 148.

12. Ibid., 149.

13. Ibid., 150.

14. Ibid., 149–50, which provides the complete GKO orders, which were numbered 782cc and 782cc.

15. Ibid.

16. Ibid., 153.

17. Ibid., 157. Of the 570 sapper battalions, two had the identical numerical designation, the 1485th. As of October 1941, the first nine sapper armies had only about 5 percent of their required equipment. In addition, throughout their existence, the sapper armies were poorly outfitted with uniforms, other necessary winter gear, weapons, and construction equipment.

18. Ibid., 151. The *shtats* of the sapper armies, sapper brigades, and sapper battalions were numbered 012/91, 012/92, and 012/93, respectively.

19. Ibid.

20. Ibid., 159–60. The NKO ordered the formation of a 1st Sapper Army to work on fortifications in the Medvezh'egorsk region of Karelia on 7 November 1941. However, a subsequent NKO order dated 19 November scaled down the effort, instead sending a separate operational-engineer group (the 1st) to the region. Less than a month later, on 21 December, when the Western Front realized that its 80 separate sapper battalions lacked sufficient command and control and resources to erect necessary defense lines west of Moscow, Major General M. P. Vorob'ev, the *front* chief of engineers, requested that the NKO form another 1st Sapper Army. Once formed, this army consisted of ten sapper brigades with eight sapper battalions each, for a grand total of 80 sapper battalions and 45,160 men. Unlike the other nine sapper armies, the 1st performed defensive and offensive work in support of the Western Front, primarily by clearing access to the *front's* rear-area communications routes.

21. Ibid., 153. Specifically, the GKO decree, "Concerning the Shortening of Defensive Lines," halted work on the Volga defense line from Rybinsk to Astrakhan and the defenses around Ivanovo and Penza but continued work on fortifications around Astrakhan and Rostov, on the Vladimir defense line from Vytegra through Cherepovets to Rybinsk, and on local defenses along key strategic axes.

22. Ibid., 166. GKO Decree No. 1229ss, dated 1 February and entitled "Concerning the Formation of 50 New Rifle Divisions and 1000 Student Rifle Brigades," required the NKO to disband the 2nd, 3rd, 4th, 5th, 6th, 7th, and 9th Sapper Armies and employ their 164,150 men, numerous horses, and vehicles to form 50 new rifle divisions and 100 student rifle brigades. However, GKO Order No. 1239ss, dated 4 February, countermanded the previous order by requiring the NKO to disband the 2nd, 4th, 5th, 9th, and 10th Sapper Armies and the 5th, 7th–11th, 13th, 16th, and 22nd Sapper Brigades and assign the 1st, 2nd, and 3rd Sapper Brigades to the Karelian, Leningrad, and Volkhov Fronts and the 14th, 15th, and 27th–30th Sapper Brigades to the 7th and 8th Sapper Armies. The same order assigned the 7th and 8th Sapper Armies to the Southwestern and Southern Fronts, the 6th Sapper Army's 17th, 18th, and 19th Sapper Brigades to the Briansk Front, and the 3rd Sapper Army's 4th and 6th Sapper Brigades to the Moscow Defense Zone with instructions to improve the Mozhaisk Defense Line. In addition, the 3rd and 17th–19th Sapper Brigades formed one pontoon-bridge battalion each, which were transferred to operating *fronts* in March, and during April and May the NKO converted the 27th and 33rd Sapper Brigades into special designation engineer brigades. The five remaining sapper armies dispatched 67 specialized battalions to the Karelian, Leningrad, Volkhov, Northwestern, Kalinin, Briansk, Southwestern, and Crimean Fronts by 21 May.

23. Ibid., 167. For example, the 2nd, 3rd, and 12th Sapper Brigades decreased in size to six sapper battalions each and the 21st Sapper Brigade to three battalions, while the 8th Sapper Army's 23rd–26th Sapper Brigades dispatched 9,625 men to form reserve rifle regiments.

24. Ibid. See NKO Order No. 0294, dated 19 April 1942, which adopted *shtats* nos. 012/155, 012/156, and other new *shtats* for sapper forces.

25. Ibid., 171.

26. Ibid. This was NKO Order No. 00176.

27. Ibid., 172–73. The NKO reorganized the 1st Sapper Army into the 33rd UOS on 1 September, disbanded the army's 38th, 39th, and 40th Sapper Brigades, assigned its 36th and 37th Sapper Brigades to the RVGK, transferred 8,000 men from its 32nd, 34th, 38th, 39th, and 40th Sapper Brigades to the Moscow Military District, and assigned its remaining sappers to the 32nd and 34th Sapper Brigades, which, together with the 31st Sapper Brigade, remained under Western Front control. Soon after, it reorganized the 34th Brigade into three battalions.

On 12 September the NKO reorganized the 3rd Sapper Army into the 34th UOS and assigned the army's 4th and 6th Sapper Brigades to the RVGK, where they were disbanded, and it reorganized the 6th Sapper Army into the 35th UOS and assigned its 10th and 18th Sapper Brigades to the Voronezh and Briansk Fronts the next day. On 15 September the NKO converted the 7th Sapper Army into the 36th UOS, disbanded the army's 14th and 15th Sapper Brigades, assigned 6,000 men from its 12th, 14th, 15th, and 20th Sapper Brigades to the Volga Military District, and assigned its remaining sappers to the 12th and 20th Sapper Brigades, which it subordinated to the Stalingrad Front.

Finally, on 15 October the NKO converted the 8th Sapper Army into the 24th UOS, disbanded the 28th, 29th, and 30th Sapper Brigades, transferred 16,000 men from the 11th, 23rd, 25th, 26th, 28th, 29th, and 30th Sapper Brigades to the Trans-Caucasus Front, and assigned its remaining sappers to the 11th, 23rd, 25th, and 26th Sapper Brigades, which it assigned to the Trans-Caucasus Front (the 24th Sapper Brigade was already assigned to this *front*).

28. Ibid., 173–74. The remaining 18 sapper brigades still in the force structure on 15 October included the 2nd, 7th, 9th–12th, 17th, 18th, 20th, 23rd–26th, 31st, 32nd, 34th, 36th, and 37th. In addition, the NKO reorganized the 36th Sapper Brigade's seven battalions into army engineer battalions on 29–30 September and assigned them to the Western Front's armies during October, at the same time forming seven more battalions in the 36th Brigade with newly assigned personnel.

29. Ibid., 177–79. The five brigades whose descendents still exist are the 1st Guards Assault Engineer Sapper Brigade, the 1st Engineer-Sapper Brigade, and the 12th Engineer Sapper Brigade in the Russian Army, the 2nd Guards Motorized Assault Engineer-Sapper Brigade in the Belorussian Army, and the 15th Assault Engineer-Sapper Brigade in the Ukrainian Army.

30. Ibid., 174.

31. Ibid., 168–69.

32. Ibid., 175.

33. Soskov, "Sovershenstvovanie," 66.

34. Initially, the NKO assigned two guards-miner battalions to the Karelian Front.

35. "Brigada" [Brigade], in I. I. Rodionov, ed., *Voennaia entsiklopediia v vos'mi tomakh* [Military encyclopedia in eight volumes] (Moscow: Voenizdat, 1997), I: 580. This was NKO Order No. 0634.

36. Ibid.

37. Malinovsky, "Sapernye armii," 176. This was NKO Order No. 00232, "Concerning the Reorganization of Sapper Brigades into RVGK Engineer-Mine Brigades." It reorganized the 3rd, 10th, 12th, 18th, 19th, 20th, 21st, 31st, 32nd, 35th, and 36th

and the 2nd formation 7th, 9th, 17th, and 34th Sapper Brigades into the 1st through 15th RVGK Engineer-Mine Brigades.

38. Ibid., 175–76.

39. Soskov, "Sovershenstvovanie," 66. The five sapper brigades converted into mountain engineer-mine brigades were the 11th, 23rd, 24th, 25th, and 26th Sapper Brigades.

40. Malinovsky, "Sapernye armii," 177.

41. Soskov, "Sovershenstvovanie," 67.

42. Babich and Baier, *Razvitie vooruzheniia,* 71.

43. Ibid.; and Malinovsky, "Sapernye armii," 175.

44. Soskov, "Sovershenstvovanie," 67.

45. Ibid., 67; and "Brigada," 580.

46. Soskov, "Sovershenstvovanie," 67.

47. Ibid.

48. Babich and Baier, *Razvitie vooruzheniia,* 72–73.

49. Kalashnikov, Fes'kov, Chmykhalo, and Golikov, *Krasnaia Armiia v iiune 1941 goda,* 17.

50. Ibid., appendix 3.2.

51. A. I. Leonov, ed., *Voennye sviazisty v dni voiny i mira* [Military signalmen during war and peace] (Moscow: Voenizdat, 1968), 140. Leonov's study is the most thorough work on Red Army wartime communications.

52. See Zolotarev, "NKO 1941," 34–35, for the complete text of Order No. 0243, "Concerning the Improvement of Communications Work in the Red Army."

53. Ibid.

54. For details on this NKO Order No. 0251, see ibid., 38–39.

55. Ibid., 72–73. This was NKO Order No. 0316.

56. Ibid., 74; and Leonov, *Voennye sviazisty v dni voiny i mira,* 140–41.

57. For periodic NKO critiques of poor Red Army communication (in April and May 1942), see Zolotarev, "NKO 1941," 221–24, 245–46.

58. For the full text of this order, which was numbered 0284, see ibid., 212–13.

59. Rifle divisions would not field full signal battalions until 1944.

60. Leonov, *Voennye sviazisty v dni voiny i mira,* 177.

61. V. Sokolov, "Razvitie organizatsionnoi struktury voisk sviazi v gody voiny" [The development of the organizational structure of signal forces in the war years], *VIZh,* no. 4 (April 1981): 25. In addition, the RVGK included seven complete separate signal brigades by January 1945.

62. Babich and Baier, *Razvitie vooruzheniia,* 75–76.

63. Ibid., 76.

64. The NKO orders were numbered 0065, 0066, and 0285. See Zolotarev, "NKO 1941," 53–57.

65. Babich and Baier, *Razvitie vooruzheniia,* 77.

66. Ibid.

67. Although the NKO decreased the number of flamethrowers in its flamethrower companies to 135 in January 1942, it did assign five vehicles to each company.

68. Babich and Baier, *Razvitie vooruzheniia,* 77–78.

69. "Ampulemet," in Moiseev, *Sovetskaia voennaia entsiklopediia,* I: 125.

70. Babich and Baier, *Razvitie vooruzheniia,* 78. The NKO added a machine-gun company to each horse-drawn battalion in December 1943.

71. Ibid., 79. The NKO did add backpack flamethrower battalions to its engineer-sapper brigades in May 1944. These new flame battalions consisted of two flamethrower companies equipped with 120 ROKS-2 flamethrowers each and 35 vehicles. At the same time, the NKO also assigned flamethrower tank regiments with 20 tanks each to some of its assault engineer-brigades. By this time, the *Stavka* had already disbanded the Red Army's separate flamethrower tank battalions.

72. See Zolotarev, "NKO 1941," 41–44. This was NKO Order No. 0257.

73. A. M. Kriukov, "Zheleznodorozhnye voiska" [Railroad forces], in *SVE,* III: 321–23.

74. For example, the 28th Railroad Brigade consisted of the 11th, 12th, and 27th Separate Railroad Battalions, the 20th Separate Railroad Bridge Battalion, and the 13th Separate Railroad Exploitation Company. The 5th Bridge Battalion was added during early 1943. The brigade added the 2nd Signal Battalion, and the 13th Separate Railroad Exploitation Company became the 21st Separate Battalion of Mechanized Work during April 1944. See K. P. Terekhin and A. S. Taralov, *Gvardeitsy zheleznodorozhniki* [Guards railroad men] (Moscow: Voenizdat, 1966), 10, 80, 105.

75. See Kalashnikov, Fes'kov, Chmykhalo, and Golikov, *Krasnaia Armiia v iiune 1941 goda,* 17, 22, 162–63. This enumeration of railroad brigades differs slightly from other sources, probably due to differences in defining the western military districts. The most reliable sources place the 1st Railroad Brigade in the Moscow Military District, the 6th, 9th, and 17th in the Western Special Military District, the 4th, 5th, 13th, 19th, and 27th in the Kiev Special Military District, the 11th in the Leningrad Military District, the 28th in the Khar'kov Military District, the 29th in the Odessa Military District, and the 3rd in an unidentified internal military district. See also A. Ia. Ponomarev and B. G. Smirnov, "Zagrazhdenie zheleznykh dorog v pervom perioda voiny" [The obstruction of railroads in the initial period of the war], *VIZh,* no. 3 (March 1986): 77–81.

76. Kalashnikov, Fes'kov, Chmykhalo, and Golikov, *Krasnaia Armiia v iiune 1941 goda,* 22. For example, the respective load capacities on opposing sides of the border were as follows: Leningrad MD, 77 pair of trains per day vice 127; Baltic Special MD, 87 vice 192; Western Special MD, 120 vice 216; Kiev Special MD, 132 vice 366; and Odessa MD, 28 vice 91.

77. F. F. Gusarev and L. A. Butakov, "Tekhnicheskoe prikrytie zheleznykh dorog" [Technical protection of the railroads], *VIZh,* no. 4 (April 1988): 52–53.

78. See Zolotarev, "NKO 1941," 135–37, for the contents of this order, which was numbered 018.

79. Kalashnikov, Fes'kov, Chmykhalo, and Golikov, *Krasnaia Armiia v iiune 1941 goda,* 22.

80. Ibid., 21.

81. Vysotsky, *Tyl Sovetskoi Armii,* 92.

82. See Zolotarev, "NKO 1941," 26–27, for the contents of this order, which was numbered 163ss, and the associated NKO order, which was numbered 0055.

83. Ibid. These new VADs included roads extending from Leningrad to Pskov, from Moscow to Iaroslavl', from Moscow through Tula, Orel, and Briansk to Gomel', from Kursk through Glukhov to Kozelets, from Khar'kov through Poltava and Lubny to Kiev, and from Kiev to Odessa.

84. Ibid., 41–44.

85. N. Popov, "Sovershenstvovanie sistemy transportnogo obespecheniia v gody voiny" [Improvement of the transport support system in the war years], *VIZh*, no. 8 (August 1982): 22.

86. This system consisted of three types of VADs including *Stavka* VADs within one or several *fronts* and also connecting multiple *fronts*; *front* VADs extending from the *Stavka's* VADs to the *fronts* and from distribution stations and regions located near or at the *fronts'* rear boundaries, which was where the *fronts'* main supply dumps were located, down to field army depots; and army VADs extending from the *fronts'* VADs and the forward elements of field armies' supply depots down to divisional supply dumps.

87. Ibid.

88. See Zolotarev, "NKO 1941," 227–28, for the contents of this order, which was numbered 0370.

89. N. Maliugin, "Avtomobil'nyi transport frontov i armii v gody voiny" [Automobile transport of *fronts* and armies in the war years], *VIZh*, no. 2 (February 1971): 87.

90. I. V. Kovalev, *Transport v Velikoi Otechestvennoi voine* [Transport in the Great Patriotic War] (Moscow: Nauka, 1981), 381. Subsequently, the NKO formed literally hundreds of these auto-transport and road formations, units, and subunits throughout the remainder of the war, assisted by the steady flow of Lend-Lease trucks and other vehicles. For example, in the Red Army's Manchurian offensive during August 1945, the three attacking Red Army *fronts* fielded one complete road directorate, one road exploitation regiment, and 17 road exploitation, 26 road construction, and 12 bridge construction battalions. Auto-transport forces available to the *fronts* and their subordinate armies included three automobile brigades, five automobile regiments, and 35 separate auto-transport battalions.

91. Tsirlin, *Inzhenernye voiska,* 77; and Aganov, *Inzhenernye voiska Sovetskoi armii,* 186.

92. A. Tsirlin, "Voennye stroiteli v Velikoi Otechestvennoi voine" [Military constructors in the Great Patriotic War], *VIZh*, no. 5 (May 1968): 107. For example, the NKO reorganized the 16th and 23rd UNSs into UVPSs, two others into the 8th Front UVPS, and disbanded five other UNSs.

93. Aganov, *Inzhenernye voiska Sovetskoi armii,* 277.

94. Soskov, "Sovershenstvovanie," 66–70.

95. Aganov, *Inzhenernye voiska Sovetskoi armii,* 278.

96. Ibid., 279.

97. Babich and Baier, *Razvitie vooruzheniia,* 23, 99.

98. Ibid., 23–24.

99. See ibid., 23–25, for further information on Red Army bridging means.

100. For details on all of these communications means, see I. P. Grishin, ed., *Voennye sviazisty v dni voiny i mira* [Military signalmen in war and peace] (Moscow: Voenizdat, 1968), 123, 128–29, 168–70.

101. In addition, the NKO began fielding radios in the model A7 series radio in early 1944, for employment at the battalion, regiment, division, and corps level and throughout the artillery chain of command. Although the initial A-7 and A-7a series radios operated effectively at ranges of up to 20 kilometers, the A-7b, which entered field forces in 1944, extended the radio's operating range up to 50 kilometers.

102. Ibid., 180.

103. Ibid., 179.

10. Strategic Leadership and Control Organs

1. Savushkin, *Razvitie,* 50.

2. Zolotarev, "NKO 1941," 387.

3. "Gosudarstvennyi komitet oborony" [The State Defense Committee], in *SVE,* III: 621–27; and *Krasnaia zvezda* [Red Star], 5 May 1975. For details on the GKO's organization and wartime functions, see Iuriy Gor'kov, *Gosudarstvennyi Komitet Oborony postanovliaet (1941–1945): Tsifry, dokumenty* [The State Defense Committee decrees (1941–1945): Numbers and documents] (Moscow: Olma-Press, 2002).

4. Zolotarev, "NKO 1941," 387.

5. Ibid., 386.

6. For more details, see V. D. Danilov, "Stavka VGK, 1941–1945," in *Zashchita otechestva* [Defense of the fatherland], no. 12 (December 1991): 1–39; V. D. Danilov, "Razvitie sistemy organov strategicheskogo rukovodstva v nachale Velikoi Otechestvennoi voiny" [The development of a system of strategic leadership organs in the beginning of the Great Patriotic War], *VIZh,* no. 6 (June 1987): 25–30; A. M. Mairov, "Strategicheskoe rukovodstvo v Velikoi Otechestvennoi voine" [Strategic leadership in the Great Patriotic War], *VIZh,* no. 5 (May 1985): 28–40; M. Zakharov, "Strategicheskoe rukovodstvo vooruzhennymi silami" [Strategic leadership of the armed forces], *VIZh,* no. 5 (May 1970): 23–34; and V. Kulakov, "Strategicheskoe rukovodstvo vooruzhennymi silami" [Strategic leadership of the armed forces], *VIZh,* no. 6 (June 1975): 12–24.

7. See also Zolotarev, "Stavka VGK 1941," 20, for the contents of the SNK order establishing the *Stavka* GK.

8. See ibid., 62–63, for the contents of GKO Decree No. 83, which formed the SVK.

9. S. M. Shtemenko, *The Soviet General Staff at War 1941–1945,* vols. 1–2 (Moscow: Progress, 1985), I: 37.

10. The *Stavka's* specific duties included evaluating political-military and strategic conditions, reaching strategic and operational-strategic decisions, creating force groupings, and organizing cooperation between and coordinating the operations of groups of *fronts, fronts,* separate armies, field armies, and partisan forces, raising and training strategic reserves and allocating them to operating *fronts* and armies, ensuring material and technical support of the armed forces, and resolving all other issues relating directly or indirectly to the conduct of military operations.

11. Among the many articles on *Stavka* representatives, see I. Vyrodov, "Rol' predstavitelei Stavki VGK v gody voiny. Organizatsiia i metody ikh raboty" [The role of *Stavka* VGK representatives in the war years: Their organization and work meth-

ods], *VIZh*, no. 8 (August 1980): 25–33; and M. Petrov, "Predstavitel' Stavki" [*Stavka* representative], *VIZh*, no. 2 (February 1981): 50–56.

12. The NKO was formed in June 1934 by a decree of the Communist Party's Central Committee and the Council of People's Commissars and replaced the former People's Commissariat for Military and Naval Affairs.

13. For details, see M. M. Kozlov, ed., "Narodnyi komissariat oborony" [People's Commissariat of Defense], in *Velikaia Otechestvennaia voina 1941–1945: Entsiklopediia* [The Great Patriotic War 1941–1945: An encyclopedia] (Moscow: Sovetskaia Entsiklopediia, 1985), 480. Hereafter cited as *VOV*, with appropriate article and page. Prior to 30 December 1937, the NKO included a separate Directorate for Naval Forces of the Red Army. However, on that date, the Council of People's Commissars formed the People's Commissariat of Naval Forces as a separate commissariat and placed the Directorate for Naval Forces with its subordinate fleets and flotillas under the new commissariat's jurisdiction.

14. Stalin combined the People's Commissariats of Defense and the Navy into a single all-union People's Commissariat of Defense on 25 February 1946. Later still, when the Soviet Union shifted to a ministerial system during March 1946, the Politburo renamed the Defense Commissariat the Ministry of the Armed Forces of the USSR with Stalin continuing on as minister of defense until he appointed Marshal N. A. Bulganin to the post in 1947.

15. Zolotarev, "NKO 1941," 40–41.

16. Ibid., 41–45.

17. The Red Army General Staff (GShKA) was created in 1935 to replace the former Red Army Staff *(Shtab RKKA)*.

18. For details, see Shtemenko, *The Soviet General Staff at War*, I: 180–211, II: 15–19.

19. V. A. Zolotarev, ed., "General'nyi shtab v gody Velikoi Otechestvennoi voiny: Dokumenty i materialy 1942 goda" [The General Staff in the Great Patriotic War: Documents and materials, 1942], in *Russkii arkhiv: Velikaia Otechestvennaia* [The Russian archives: The Great Patriotic (War)], 23, 12 (1) (Moscow: Terra, 1997), 8 (hereafter cited as Zolotarev, "General'nyi shtab 1942," with appropriate volume and pages); and Zolotarev, "NKO 1941," 389–90. Among many other sources, see N. Lomov and V. Golubovich, "Ob organizatsii i metodakh raboty General'nogo shtaba" [About the organization and work methods of the General Staff], *VIZh*, no. 2 (February 1981): 12–19; and G. Mikhailovsky and I. Vyrodov, "Vysshie organy rukovodstva voinoi" [The higher organs for directing the war], *VIZh*, no. 4 (April 1978): 16–26. This GKO directive was entitled "The Position of the General Staff."

20. For example, on 28 July the GKO transferred the General Staff's Organizational and Mobilization directorates to the NKO and renamed them the Main Directorate for the Formation and Manning of the Red Army (*Glavnoe upravlenie formirovaniia i ukomplektovaniia Krasnoi Armii*, or GUFUKA). When this measure proved unworkable, in April 1942 the GKO formed a new Organizational Directorate within the General Staff and assigned it responsibility for tracking troop distribution and losses and training officer cadres in the vast military school system throughout the Soviet Union.

21. Zolotarev, "NKO 1941," 216–17. This reorganization also stripped three departments, the Organization-Registration, Operational-Training, and Operational Transportation departments, from the General Staff's Operations Directorate, reassigning the first to the Organizational Directorate, transforming the second into the Department for the Exploitation of War Experience, and reorganizing the third into an independent General Staff department. At the same time, the order abolished the Operations Directorate's Auto-Armored and Communications departments and transferred their functions and personnel to the Organizational Directorate and the Department for the Exploitation of War Experience.

22. See N. Saltykov, "Predstaviteli General'nogo shtaba" [Representatives of the General Staff], *VIZh,* no. 9 (September 1971): 56–59; N. D. Saltykov, "Podvig (Korpus ofitserov—predstavitelei General'nogo shtaba v Velikoi Otechestvennoi voine)" [Victory (Officers corps—General Staff representatives in the Great Patriotic War)], *VIZh,* no. 12 (December 1988): 23–28; and "Polozhenie i instruktsiia po rabote korpusa ofitserov—predstavitelei General'nogo shtaba Krasnoi Armii" [Regulation and instruction on the work of officers corps—Red Army General Staff representatives], *VIZh,* no. 2 (February 1975): 62–66.

23. Shtemenko, *The Soviet General Staff at War,* II: 26–31.

24. For an analysis of General Staff war experience studies and other materials, see David M. Glantz, "Newly Published Works on the Red Army, 1918–1991," *JSMS* 8, no. 2 (June 1995): 319–32.

25. B. M. Shaposhnikov served as chief of the General Staff from July 1941, when he replaced the first wartime chief of staff, Army General G. K. Zhukov. Shaposhnikov, who resigned because of ill health, died in 1945.

26. For the best source on the partisan movement, see Leonid Grenkevich, *The Soviet Partisan Movement 1941–1944* (London: Frank Cass, 1999).

27. The *Stavka* developed an appreciation of partisan warfare during the Battle of Moscow and ensuing winter campaign, when partisan groups and regiments assisted exploiting Red Army cavalry and airborne forces, in particular, the operations of Cavalry Group Below and the 11th Cavalry Corps near Viaz'ma.

28. Zolotarev, "NKO 1943," 403.

29. "Tsentral'nyi shtab partizanskogo dvizheniia" [Central headquarters of the partisan movement], in *VOV,* 776.

30. Despite the abolition of the TShPD, partisan forces continued operations effectively in 1944, now under the control of the central committees of the republics and regions *(oblasti)* but with continued NKVD influence and increasingly close coordination with the Red Army's operating *fronts.*

31. "Mekhlis, Lev Zakharovich," in Ogarkov, *SVE,* V: 273.

32. "Narodnyi komissariat vnutrennikh del" [People's Commissariat of Internal Affairs], in Ogarkov, *VES,* 475. For more details on the operations and subordinate organs of the NKVD, see Michael Parrish, *The Lesser Terror: Soviet State Security, 1939–1953* (Westport, CT: Praeger, 1996); and Michael Parrish, "The Last Relic: Army General I. E. Serov," *JSMS* 10, no. 3 (September 1997): 109–29.

33. Parrish, "The Last Relic," 112–13; and I. I. Kuznetsov, "Stalin's Minister V. S. Abakumov 1908–54," *JSMS* 12, no. 1 (March 1999): 149–65.

34. For details, see A. I. Kolpakidi and D. P. Prokhorov, *Vneshniaia razvedka Rossii* [Russia's external intelligence] (Moscow: Olma-Press, 2001), 39–50. For the complete order combining the two security organs, see "Nachalo, 22 iiunia–31 avgusta 1941 goda" [The beginning, 22 June to 31 August 1941], vol. 2, book 1, in *Organy gosudarstvennoi bezopasnosti SSSR v Velikoi Otechestvennoi voine* [The organs of state security of the USSR in the Great Patriotic War] (Moscow: Rus', 2000), 373.

35. "Narodnyi komissariat gosudarstvennoi bezopasnosti" [People's Commissariat of State Security], in Ogarkov, *VES,* 475.

36. "Glavnoe politicheskoe upravlenie raboche-krest'ianskoi Krasnoi armii" [Main Political Directorate of the Red Army], and "Glavnoe politicheskoe upravlenie Voenno-morskogo flota" [Main Political Directorate of the Navy], both in *VOV,* 208–9.

37. The GKO also established military councils in the Red Army Air Force, the Air Defense Forces, and armored and mechanized forces.

38. "Voennyi sovet" [The military council], in *VOV,* 164; and A. A. Epishev, "Voennyi sovet" [The military council], in *SVE,* II: 272–74. On the eve of war, main military councils existed in the Red Army and Navy as well as in every military district, army, fleet, and flotilla. After war began and the *Stavka* was formed, on 23 June 1941, the GKO abolished the main military councils for the army and navy but replaced them with separate military councils formed in all operating *fronts.*

39. "Shcherbakov, Dmitrii Ivanovich," in *VOV,* 800.

40. See Zolotarev, "NKO 1941," 326–27, for the contents of this decree, which was numbered 307.

41. M. N. Timofeevich, "Edinonachalie" [Unified command], in *SVE,* III: 301–2.

42. "Voennaia prokuratura" [Military prosecutor's office], in *VOV,* 145.

43. Ibid.

44. Ibid.

45. For details contained in this order, whose number was 218, see Zolotarev, "NKO 1941," 14–16.

46. "Voennaia prokuratura," 145.

47. "Voennye tribunaly" [Military tribunals], in *VOV,* 162–63.

48. Details on GRU organization and functions are sketchy at best. See Shtemenko, *The Soviet General Staff at War,* I: 194; and Glantz, *Soviet Military Intelligence in War,* 114–15, 210–14, 215–16.

49. V. I. Lenin, the founder of the Bolshevik state, and F. E. Dzerzhinsky, his first security chief, formed the first special departments (OOs) during the Russian Civil War. Initially, these departments constituted a part of the infamous Cheka, the All-Russian Extraordinary Commission (*Vserossiiskaia chrezvychainaia komissiia,* or VChK) for the Struggle with Counterrevolutionaries, Speculators, and Malfeasance (and, up to 1918, for the Struggle with Counterrevolutionaries and Saboteurs). After 1923, and particularly in the 1930s, when they were subordinated to the dreaded Combined State Political Directorate (*Ob"edinennoe gosudarstvennoe politicheskoe upravlenie,* or OGPU), special departments throughout every level of the army and navy ruthlessly rooted out real or perceived internal subversion against the Soviet state and the military, in the process repressing many figures within the Soviet Union's military leadership. For scant details on the OOs and OKRs, see "Glavnoe upravlenie

kontrrazvedki" [Main Counterintelligence Directorate], in Ogarkov, *VES,* 195; "Sovetskaia voennaia kontrrazvedka" [Soviet military counterintelligence], in *VOV,* 662; Glantz, *Soviet Military Intelligence in War,* 91, 94, 115, 117, 125, 202, 266; and Parrish, *The Lesser Terror.*

50. Parrish, *The Lesser Terror,* 111–13; and I. I. Kuznetsov, "Stalin's Minister V. S. Abakumov 1908–54," *JSMS* 12, no. 1 (March 1999): 149–65. After Mikheev perished during the Kiev encirclement of September 1941, Commissar of Security Services V. S. Abakumov became chief of the OOs.

51. "Sovetskaia voennaia kontrrazvedka," 662.

52. For example, SMERSH was instrumental in unearthing those who sympathized with the famous General A. A. Vlasov, whose encircled 2nd Shock Army surrendered to the Germans during June and July 1942 near Liuban' (southeast of Leningrad) and who later entered German service. In addition, it investigated and prosecuted (often in absentia) senior Red Army officers whom the Germans (or Finns) had taken captive during the war, usually on the trumped up charge of treason. See Aleksander A. Maslov, *Captured Soviet Generals: The Fate of Soviet Generals Captured by the Germans, 1941–1945* (London: Frank Cass, 2001).

53. Kuznetsov, "Stalin's Minister."

54. Dmitri Volkogonov, "Kliment Yefremovich Voroshilov," in Harold Shukman, ed., *Stalin's Generals* (London: Weidenfeld & Nicolson, 1993), 313. Details on Voroshilov's life are also contained in "Voroshilov, Klement Efremovich," in *SVE,* II: 362–63.

55. These commands, which were officially termed main commands of directions *(glavnye komandovaniia napravlenii),* were designed to provide unity of control for all *fronts* or other forces operating along a single strategic direction (axis), in this case, northwestern, western, and southwestern axes. In addition, three of Stalin's favorite political cronies, A. A. Zhdanov, N. A. Bulganin, and N. S. Khrushchev, served as members of these directions' military councils and would rise to further political prominence during the postwar years. For details, see V. D. Danilov, "Glavnye komandovaniia napravlenii v Velikoi Otechestvennoi voine" [Main Direction commands in the Great Patriotic War], *VIZh,* no. 9 (September 1987): 17–23; S. P. Ivanov and N. Shekhovtsov, "Opyt raboty glavnykh komandovanii na teatrakh voennykh deistvii" [Experience in the work of Main Commands in theaters of military operations], *VIZh,* no. 9 (September 1981): 11–18; and M. N. Tereshchenko, "Na zapadnom napravlenii: Kak sozdavalis' i deistvovali glavnye komandovaniia napravlenii [On the Western Direction: How Main Direction commands were created and functioned], *VIZh,* no. 5 (May 1993): 17.

56. Zhukov replaced K. A. Meretskov as chief of the General Staff.

57. Most Soviet sources written after 1964 credit Zhukov with planning the Stalingrad offensive, although many sources prior to that date accord credit for doing so to Vasilevsky and Eremenko. Certainly, as deputy supreme commander, Zhukov indeed played a considerable role in all *Stavka* strategic planning.

58. In addition to his memoir, Zhukov, *Reminiscences and Reflections,* see Viktor Anfilov, "Georgy Konstantinovich Zhukov," in Shukman, *Stalin's Generals,* 343–60; and M. A. Gareev, *Marshal Zhukov: Velichie i unikal'nost' polkovodcheskogo iskusstva* [Marshal Zhukov: The greatness and uniqueness of a commander's art] (Moscow and Ufa: Eastern University, 1996).

59. In addition to his memoir, Vasilevsky, *Delo vsei zhizni;* see also Geoffrey Jukes, "Alexander Mikhailovich Vasilevsky," in Shukman, *Stalin's Generals,* 275–85.

60. The Far East Command was the first full-fledged theater of military operations headquarters the Soviet Union created during the war. As such, Vasilevsky commanded all ground, air, and naval forces in the extensive Far East region.

61. Vasilevsky's most important protégés were Vatutin and Antonov.

62. Oleg Rzheshevsky, "Boris Mikhailovich Shaposhnikov," in Shukman, *Stalin's Generals,* 229.

63. Ibid., 221.

64. Richard Woff, "Alexei Innokentievich Antonov," in Shukman, *Stalin's Generals,* 14.

65. Ibid., 11–23.

66. For more details, see Woff, "Alexei Innokentievich Antonov," 11–24; and I. I. Gaglov, *General Antonov* (Moscow: Voenizdat, 1978).

67. For more details, see John Erickson, "Alexander Alexandrovich Novikov," in Shukman, *Stalin's Generals,* 155–74; and A. M. Khorobrykh, *Glavnyi marshal aviatsii A. A. Novikov* [Chief Marshal of Aviation A. A. Novikov] (Moscow: Voenizdat, 1989).

68. Erickson, "Alexander Alexandrovich Novikov," 173–74; and Parrish, "The Last Relic," 121–22.

69. For further details, see "Voronov, Nikolai Nikolaevich," in *SVE,* II: 363–63.

70. "Govorov, Leonid Aleksandrovich," in *SVE,* II: 582–83.

71. Shtemenko, *The Soviet General Staff at War,* I: 368.

72. Ibid., 448.

73. "Kuznetsov, Nikolai Gerasimovich," in *SVE,* IV: 511. See also Kuznetsov's now unexpurgated autobiography, N. G. Kuznetsov, *Kursom k pobede* [The path to victory] (Moscow: Golos, 2000).

74. See also Geoffrey Jukes, "Nikolai Gerasimovich Kuznetsov," in Shukman, *Stalin's Generals,* 109–15.

75. "Lev Zakharovich Mekhlis," in *SVE,* V: 273. Although his official biography avoids any criticism, Mekhlis remains one of the very few wartime leaders bitterly criticized by his fellow senior officers in their memoirs.

76. Shtemenko, *The Soviet General Staff at War,* I: 24–25.

77. "Shcherbakov, Aleksandr Sergeevich," in *SVE,* VIII: 551–52.

78. Shtemenko, *The Soviet General Staff at War,* I: 199, 214.

79. Understandably, given his position and role, little was written about Abakumov in official Soviet historical literature prior to 1991. That has changed recently thanks to a few authors who have reconstructed Abakumov's gruesome career. For further details on this foremost of Stalin's "creatures," see Parrish, *The Lesser Terror;* and Kuznetsov, "Stalin's Minister."

80. Parrish, *The Lesser Terror,* 26; and Kuznetsov, "Stalin's Minister," 150–51.

81. Kuznetsov, "Stalin's Minister," 151.

82. Abakumov's victims included Major General K. M. Kachanov, commander of the Northwestern Front's 34th Army, who was executed for dereliction of duty after the defeat at Staraia Russa; Lieutenant General F. S. Ivanov, commander of the Leningrad Front's 42nd Army, who was executed for dereliction of duty during the

defense of Leningrad; Major General A. N. Ermakov, commander of the Briansk Front's 50th Army, who was executed for dereliction of duty during the Briansk encirclement; and Major General P. P. Sobennikov, commander of the Western Front's 43rd Army (and former commander of the Northwestern Front), who was executed for dereliction of duty during the Viaz'ma encirclement; Lieutenant General D. T. Kozlov, commander of the Crimean Front, who was reduced in rank for his incompetent conduct of operations in the Crimea; Lieutenant General S. I. Cherniak, commander of the Crimean Front's 44th Army, who was reduced to the rank of colonel for his poor performance in the Crimea; Major General K. S. Kolganov, commander of the Crimean Front's 47th Army, who was reduced to the rank of colonel for his poor performance in the Crimea; Major General V. S. Golushkevich, chief of the Operations Section of Zhukov's Western Front, who was arrested for treasonous activities during early 1942 but released in 1952; Lieutenant General V. A. Khomenko, commander of the 4th Ukrainian Front's 44th Army, who was wounded and captured by the Germans and died of his wounds but was accused of treachery and desertion; and Major Generals G. A. Armaderov, F. S. Burlachko, G. S. Diakov, F. S. Kuz'min, N. I. Plushnin, A. Ia. Sokolov, and A. G. Shirmakher, all professors at the Frunze Academy, who were sentenced to prison for 10–25 years for treason. See Kuznetsov, "Stalin's Minister," 155.

83. For details on the fate of Red Army generals who either perished or returned from captivity, see Maslov, *Captured Soviet Generals.*

84. Kuznetsov, "Stalin's Minister," 158–59.

85. Ibid., 163–65. By 1950 Abakumov had already alienated General I. Serov, chief of the MVD, and the always suspicious Beriia himself, who began to fear the growing power of his effective protégé. Consequently, at Beriia's instigation, Stalin ordered Abakumov's arrest on 12 July 1951, ironically on trumped up charges of malfeasance in prosecuting the supposed ongoing "Zionist conspiracy" against Stalin, a conspiracy Beriia had recently "discovered." The next day Abakumov's wife and two-month-old son joined him under arrest. Suffering terrible tortures, Abakumov remained in prison even after Stalin's death in 1953, a testament to the legacy of fear he left behind him. Tried and judged guilty on 19 December 1954, Abakumov was shot the same day.

86. For more details on Serov, see Parrish, "The Last Relic."

87. For details, see Parrish, *The Last Terror.*

88. Parrish, "The Last Relic," 123. Parrish provides the only existing credible description of both Merkulov's and Ul'rikh's role in the permanent purge. For more thorough details on their sordid careers, see Parrish, *The Lesser Terror.*

11. Central Military Administration

1. "Narodnyi komissariat oborony" [People's Commissariat of Defense], in *VOV,* 480.

2. "Ministerstvo oborony SSSR" [Ministry of Defense of the USSR], in *SVE,* V: 294–96; "Ministerstvo oborony SSSR" [Ministry of Defense of the USSR], in I. D. Sergeev, ed., *Voennaia entsiklopediia v vos'mi tomakh* [Military encyclopedia in eight volumes] (Moscow: Voenizdat, 2001), V: 133–35; and "Narodnyi komissariat oborony SSSR," in *VOV,* 480.

3. Zolotarev, "NKO 1941," 29–30. For more information on Voronov, see "Voronov, Nikolai Nikolaevich," in *SVE,* II: 262–63.

4. For further details regarding GAU, see P. N. Kuleshov, "Glavnoe artilleriiskoe upravlenie" [Main Artillery Directorate], in *SVE,* II: 561–62; and M. E. Pemkin, "Glavnoe raketno-artilleriiskoe upravlenie" [Main Rocket-Artillery Directorate], in *VE,* II: 421–22. One of Stalin's cronies since the Tsaritsyn days of the Russian Civil War, while serving as chief of the Main Artillery Directorate from 1937 to shortly after war began, Kulik was instrumental in convincing Stalin to abolish the post of artillery chief in 1940, largely out of his jealously of Voronov. For more details on Kulik's and Iakovlev's careers, see "Kulik, Grigorii Ivanovich," in *SVE,* IV: 517; "Iakovlev, Nikolai Dmitrievich," in *SVE,* VIII: 658; and "Iakovlev," in *VOV,* 824. See also Erickson, *The Road to Stalingrad,* 15–17. Promoted to marshal of artillery in 1944, Iakovlev continued to serve as the chief of the GAU and as the member of the Military Council of Red Army Artillery Forces until war's end.

5. The NKO normally supplied its field forces with weapons and ammunition prior to the war by sending them from its central bases and warehouses directly to army supply centers, and the armies then distributed them to division ammunition dumps and points. However, the failure of rational mobilization, dismal accounting procedures, and the chaos caused by the *Wehrmacht's* rapid advance resulted in the complete breakdown of the system and the loss of many bases and dumps.

6. The Main Artillery Directorate's functional organs with the Red Army's force structure included the following:

Level of Command	*GAU Organizations*
Front	Directorate of Artillery Supply
	Artillery weapons and ammunition warehouses (depots)
	Mobile artillery workshops
	Field tractor repair bases
	Separate repair and reconstruction battalions
Army	Artillery Supply Department
	Field army artillery weapons and ammunition depots
	Army artillery and tractor repair workshops
Rifle corps	Artillery equipment registration and distribution organizations
Rifle division	Artillery supply organization
	Mobile artillery workshop (truck-mounted)
Rifle regiment	Chief of artillery supply
	Regimental artillery warehouse and workshop
Rifle battalion and company	Ammunition point

From "Sluzhba artilleriiskogo snabzheniia" [The artillery supply service], in *VOV,* 654.

7. Glavnoe artilleriiskoe upravlenie" [Main Artillery Directorate], in *SVE,* II: 561. The new system for artillery supply involved the creation of new artillery weapons supply depots and artillery ammunition supply depots at *front* level and new combined

field depots at army level that fed into the existing supply organs at division and below. The resulting supply chain ran from the GAU's main supply bases to *front* distribution centers, and then on to *front* depots or directly to army depots. Motor transport units then carried the supplies from *front* depots to army depots and on to division dump, regiments, and firing batteries. The entire process was severely complicated by the lack of serviceable all-weather roads.

8. Ibid. Army workshops alone repaired more than 5.5 million small arms, 620,000 machine guns, and 312,000 guns and mortars in the course of the war.

9. Ibid. Throughout the war this amounted to more than 430,000 wagonloads of ammunition.

10. For further details on the NKO's education and training system during wartime, see David M. Glantz, *The Red Army's Education and Training System during the Soviet-German War, 1941–1945* (Carlisle, PA: Self-published, 2004).

11. Aborenkov was promoted to the rank of major general on 19 January 1942 and lieutenant general on 25 March 1943. Major General of Artillery P. A. Degtiarev, who was promoted to the rank of lieutenant general in September 1943, succeeded Aborenkov in April 1943.

12. "Artilleriia reaktivnaia" [Rocket artillery], in *VOV*, 68; "Gvardeiskie minometnye chasti" [Guards-mortar units], in *SVE*, II: 492–93; and V. G. Kriukov, "Gvardeiskie minometnye chasti" [Guards-mortar units], in *VE*, II: 361–62.

13. "Bronetankovye i mekhanizirovannye voiska" [Armored and mechanized forces], in *VOV*, 68. The GABTU KA was formed in July 1940 from the NKO's former Auto-Armored Directorate, which had been created in December 1934 from the Directorate for Mechanization and Motorization of the RKKA, which had been formed during 1929, shortly after the Red Army began experimenting with armored and mechanized forces.

14. "Fedorenko, Iakov Nikolaevich," in *SVE*, VIII: 263.

15. Ibid.

16. "Bronetankovaia sluzhba" [The armored service], in *VOV*, 112.

17. N. I. Vakalov, "Glavnoe bronetankovoe upravlenie" [The main armored directorate], in *VE*, II: 417.

18. The GKO added a Main Directorate for the Repair of Tanks to Fedorenko's directorate during March 1944 and the Directorate for Self-Propelled Artillery during January 1945.

19. "Bronetankovaia sluzhba," 112; and I. V. Balobai, "Glavnoe avtomobil'noe upravlenia" [Main Automobile Directorate], in *VE*, II: 416.

20. See "Bronetankovaia sluzhba," in *VOV*, 112. These support forces included the following:

Command Level	*Repair Unit/Subunit*
Tank battalion	Technical support platoon (servicing and routine repair)
Tank brigade	Technical support company (servicing and routine repair)
Tank corps	Mobile tank repair bases (mid-level and routine repair)
Tank armies	Separate tank repair battalion (mid-level repair)
Fronts	Mobile tank assembly and repair factory (mid-level and capital repair)

21. O. A. Losik, "Voennaia akademiia bronetankovykh voisk" [The Military Academy of the Armored Forces], in *SVE,* II: 172.

22. "Inzhenernaia sluzhba" [The engineer service], in *VOV,* 299. Formed in July 1940 from the Engineer Directorate of the Red Army, the GVIU's first chief was Brigade Commander A. F. Krenov, who was succeeded by General Kotliar in March 1941. After being replaced, Krenov continued to serve with distinction as the chief of engineer forces for several key *fronts* during the duration of the war.

23. "Kotliar, Leonid Zakharovich," in *VOV,* 373.

24. Aganov, *Inzhenernye voiska Sovetskoi Armii 1918–1945,* 175.

25. A. D. Tsirlin, P. I. Biriukov, V. P. Istomin, and E. N. Fedoseev, eds., *Inzhenernye voiska v boiakh za Sovetskuiu rodinu* [Engineer forces in combat for the Soviet homeland] (Moscow: Voenizdat, 1970), 384. The report was entitled "Concerning the Underestimation of the Engineer Service and the Incorrect Use of Engineer Forces and Equipment."

26. Zolotarev, "NKO 1942," 126–27.

27. "Vorob'ev, Mikhail Petrovich," in *SVE,* II: 354–55.

28. Ibid., 354.

29. Based on extensive experimentation during the 1930s, the NKO created a large airborne (VDV) force of corps and separate brigades to perform vertical maneuver in support of the operational maneuver conducted on the ground by tank, mechanized, and cavalry forces. However, since these forces were hastily formed and lacked most of their air delivery aircraft and other specialized equipment, none were fully combat ready. Consequently, *front* and army commanders generally employed these forces as simple rifle forces. For details on the organization and employment of Soviet airborne forces in the initial and subsequent periods of war, see Glantz, *A History of Soviet Airborne Forces,* 47–60.

30. See Zolotarev, "NKO 1941," 75, for the contents of this order, which was numbered 0329.

31. Ibid., 80–82, contains the contents of the order, which was numbered 0083.

32. "Vozdushno-desantnye voiska" [Air-assault forces], in *VOV,* 165.

33. Kozhevnikov, *Komandovanie i shtab VVS Sovetskoi Armii,* 26. To a far greater degree than other services, the VVS experienced extreme command turbulence on the eve of war, when several of its commanders, including Colonel General A. D. Loktionov, the Air Force commander from 1937 to 1939, and Lieutenant General Ia. V. Smushkevich, its commander from 1939 to 1940, fell victim to Stalin's purges. In addition, Rychagov, who was chief of the GUVVS until April and thereafter chief of the VVS's headquarters, was tried and shot in summer 1941 as a scapegoat for the disaster the air force suffered in the first few weeks of war. See also Richard Woff, "Stalin's Ghosts," in Shukman, *Stalin's Generals,* 362.

34. The NKO separated naval aviation from the VVS in 1935, converted it into a branch of the Red Navy, and by June 1941 also subordinated 40 of the VVS's aviation regiments to PVO Strany (National Air Defense) to protect vital rear-area objectives. For more details on air force development, see P. S. Kumakhov, "Voenno-vozdushnye sily (VVS)" [The Air Force (VVS)], in *SVE,* II: 203–8.

35. P. S. Deinekin, "Voenno-vozdushnye sily" [The Air Forces], in *VE,* II: 144; and Kumakhov, "Voenno-vozdushnye sily," 204.

36. Kozhevnikov, *Komandovanie i shtab VVS,* 64.

37. Ibid., 77.

38. "Golovanov, Aleksandr Evgen'evich," in *VOV,* 210.

39. N. M. Skomorokhov, "Voenno-vozdushnaia akademiia" [The Air Force Academy], in *SVE,* II: 200.

40. The GUPVO was formed in December 1940 from the PVO Directorate of the RKKA. After his replacement, Kozlov was appointed commander of the Trans-Caucasus Military District.

41. N. Svetlishin, "Primenenie Voisk protivovozdushnoi oborony v letne-osennei kampanii 1941 goda" [The employment of air defense forces in the summer–fall campaign of 1941], *VIZh,* no. 3 (March 1968): 27; and A. Koldunov, "Organizatsiia i vedenie protivovozdushnoi oborony po opytu nachal'nogo perioda Velikoi Otechestvennoi voiny" [The organization and conduct of antiaircraft defense based on the experience of the initial period of the Great Patriotic War], *VIZh,* no. 4 (April 1984): 13.

42. The USSR's political leadership was concerned that, in the event of war, the country might be subjected to massive damaging air attacks against its most vital political and economic centers.

43. The February directive was entitled "Concerning the Strengthening of the USSR's Air Defenses."

44. See V. D. Sozinov, "Protivovozdushnaia oborona strany" [The country's air defense], in *SVE,* VI: 588–89; P. F. Batitsky, "Voiska protivovozdushnoi oborony strany" [Forces for the country's air defense], in *SVE,* II: 316–21; "Protivovozdushnaia oborona strany" [The country's air defense], in *VOV,* 589–90; and Koldunov, "Organizatsiia i vedenie protivovozdushnoi oborony," 12–13. The commanders of the PVO zones along the Soviet Union's borders during June 1941 were as follows: Northern Zone, Major General of Artillery F. Ia. Kriukov; Northwestern, Colonel M. M. Karlin; Western, Major General of Artillery S. S. Sazanov; Kiev, Major General A. I. Danilov; Southern, Division Commander G. A. Burichenkov; and Trans-Caucasus, Colonel I. F. Korolenko. See Svetlishin, "Primenenie voisk protivovozdushnoi oborony," 27.

45. Ibid.

46. "Voiska VNOS (vozdushnogo nabliudeniia, opoveshcheniia i sviazi)" [VNOS (air observation, warning, and communications) forces], in *VOV,* 167.

47. Koldunov, "Organizatsiia i vedenie protivovozdushnoi oborony," 15; and "Voiska VNOS," 167.

48. Svetlishin, "Primenenie voisk protivovozdushnoi oborony," 28–30. On 22 June 1941, PVO forces included the 1st, 2nd, and 3rd PVO Corps protecting Moscow, Leningrad, and Baku, the 3rd PVO Division at Kiev, and the 4th PVO Division at L'vov, and PVO brigades at Riga (10th), Vilnius (12th), Kaunus (14th), Minsk (7th), Belostok (13th), Drogobich (11th), Odessa (15th), and Batumi (8th). For comparison's sake, Colonel M. Z. Kotikov's 7th PVO Brigade, which fought at Minsk and Smolensk in summer 1941, and later at Viaz'ma and Moscow, consisted of the 188th and 741st Antiaircraft Artillery Regiments, the 30th Separate Antiaircraft Artillery Battalion, the 191st Separate Antiaircraft Artillery Battalion, and the 5th VNOS Regiment.

49. "Voiska VNOS," 167; and Svetlishin, "Primenenie voisk protivovozdushnoi oborony," 30.

50. Stalin had Shtern executed on 28 October 1941.

51. "Voiska VNOS," 167.

52. See S. A. Tiushkevich, ed., *Sovetskie vooruzhennye sily* [Soviet Armed Forces] (Moscow: Voenizdat, 1978), 289; and Koldunov, "Organizatsiia i vedenie protivovozdushnoi oborony," 17–18. This decree was entitled, "Concerning the Reinforcement and Strengthening of PVO on the Territory of the Soviet Union." Later the directorate was renamed the Main Directorate for PVO Strany (*Glavnoe upravlenie protivovozdushnoi oborony*, or GUPVO).

53. The NKO created three more PVO division regions in early 1942.

54. See Zolotarev, "NKO 1941," 141, for the contents of this order, which was numbered 056.

55. Ibid., 290.

56. Tiushkevich, *Sovetskie vooruzhennye sily,* 289. See also Zolotarev, "NKO 1943," 408, 165, for the subsequent order 00087, which converted the Moscow PVO Front into the Special Moscow PVO Army.

57. See Zolotarev, "NKO 1941," 184–85, for the contents of this order, which was numbered 0058.

58. Ibid., 247, contains the contents of this NKO order, which was numbered 0439. The deputy commander of PVO forces for training and training institutions controlled the combat training directorate, the education department, and the rifle-tactical committee, and the deputy commander of PVO forces for weaponry and material support controlled the weapons directorate, the supply and construction directorates, and the supply, engineer, transport, and scientific research departments.

59. Ibid., 369, contains the contents of this NKO order, which was numbered 0894.

60. Ibid., 248, contains the contents of this NKO order, which was numbered 0443. See also I. M. Mal'tsev, "Sovershenstvovanie sistemy upravleniia Voiskami protivovozdushnoi oborony v gody Velikoi Otechestvennoi voiny" [The improvement of the command and control systems of air defense forces during the Great Patriotic War], *VIZh,* no. 4 (April 1986): 24–25.

61. See Zolotarev, "NKO 1941," 330.

62. N. Svetlishin, "Voiska PVO Strany v letne-osennei kampanii 1943 goda" [The forces of PVO Strany in the summer–fall campaign of 1943], *VIZh,* no. 9 (September 1971): 24. See Zolotarev, "NKO 1943," 408, for the full contents of this order.

63. Ibid.

64. Tiushkevich, *Sovetskie vooruzhennye sily,* 325.

65. Ibid.

66. Svetlishin, "Voiska PVO strany v letne-osennei kampanii 1943 goda," 25.

67. N. Svetlishin, "Nekotorye voprosy primeneniia voisk PVO strany" [Some questions on the employment of PVO Strany forces], *VIZh,* no. 12 (December 1969): 17–18.

68. Zolotarev, "NKO 1941," 40–41. This NKO order was numbered 245.

69. "Shchadenko Efim Afanas'evich," in *SVE,* VIII: 550.

70. For further details, see *VE,* II: 423. P. S. Grachev edited this volume. See also S. A. Il'enkov, "Concerning the Registration of Soviet Armed Forces' Wartime

Irrevocable Losses, 1941–1945," *JSMS* 9, no. 2 (June 1996): 440–41; and Aleksander A. Maslov, *Fallen Soviet Generals: Soviet General Officers Killed in Battle, 1941–1945* (London: Frank Cass, 1998), xvi–xvii.

71. Ibid.

72. Zolotarev, "NKO 1943," 141–43, 405, for the complete NKO orders, which were numbered 00126 and 0317.

73. Zolotarev, "NKO 1941," 40–41.

74. *VE,* II: 423. The GUVUZ was organized as a main directorate on 19 January 1919, a directorate under the Red Army Inspectorate during 1924, and an NKO directorate during 1936. Thereafter, it continued to perform its duties until 1968.

75. *SVE,* II: 257.

76. Zolotarev, "NKO 1941," 88–89. First created in 1918 as a means for training Red Army reserves, the VSEVOBUCH program was abandoned in 1923.

77. "VSEVOBUCH" [Universal military education], in *VOV,* 182; and P. N. Dmitriev, "VSEVOBUCH," in *SVE,* II: 395.

78. Tiushkevich, *Sovetskie vooruzhennye sily,* 278.

79. "OSOAVIAKHIM," in Ogarkov, *VES,* 525; and "OSOAVIAKHIM," in *SVE,* VI: 141. This "massive, voluntary, social-military-patriotic organization" was formed in 1927 as an expansion of the existing Military-Scientific Society *(Voenno-nauchnoe obshchestvo),* which had been formed in 1920 at the instigation of Frunze, Voroshilov, Tukhachevsky, and others. Over time, the original society grew from an all-army organ into a far broader mass organization that was renamed the Society for the Assistance of the USSR's Defense (*Obshchestvo sodeistviia oborone SSSR,* or OSO) in 1925. The OSO merged with other similar groups in 1927 to form OSOAVIAKHIM, whose principal missions included developing mass defense work among the workers to strengthen the defense capabilities of the Soviet Union, assisting the development of the aviation and chemical industry, spreading military knowledge among the population, and educating the population in the spirit of Soviet patriotism.

80. Ibid.

81. After war's end, OSOAVIAKHIM was subdivided into three separate organs supporting the army, air force and navy, combined into a single support organization, the Voluntary Society for Assistance to the Army, Air Force, and Navy *(Dobrovol'noe obshchestvo sodeistviia armii, aviatsii, i flot, DOSAAF)* in 1951.

82. Leonov, *Voennye sviazisty v dni voiny i mira,* 121–23.

83. Ibid.,136. See also Zolotarev, "NKO 1941," 34–35, for the contents of this NKO Order No. 0243, "Concerning the Improvement of Red Army Communications."

84. "Peresypkin, Ivan Terent'evich," in *SVE,* VI: 291.

85. Ibid.

86. See Zolotarev, "NKO 1941," 38–39, for the NKO order, which was numbered 0251.

87. Leonov, *Voennye sviazisty,* 140–41.

88. Ibid.

89. For details, see Sokolov, "Razvitie organizatsionnoi struktury voisk sviazi v gody voiny," 20–27. In January 1942, in his capacity as chief of the NKPS, Peresypkin cre-

ated a Military Reconstruction Directorate within the NKPS, which helped as a backup communications center for the *Stavka* and General Staff.

90. "Voiska sviazi" [Signal Forces], in *VOV,* 168. See the contents of NKO Order No. 0338, in Zolotarev, "NKO 1941," 221–22. The *Stavka* issued a similar order (no. 00107) dated 30 May 1942. For its contents, see Zolotarev, "Stavka VGK 1942," 227–28.

91. Sokolov, "Razvitie organizatsionnoi struktury voisk," 24–25.

92. This squadron was later reorganized into a special liaison group of the Civil Air Fleet (*Grazhdanskii vozdushnyi flot,* or GVF).

93. Leonov, *Voennye sviazisty,* 126–27.

94. In 1940 rail transport carried 85.1 percent of the Soviet Union's total transport cargo. See F. F. Gusarov and L. A. Butakov, "Tekhnicheskoe prikrytie zheleznykh dorog" [Technical protection of the railroads], *VIZh,* no. 4 (April 1988): 51.

95. Sokolov, "Razvitie organizatsionnoi struktury voisk," 21.

96. "Sluzhba voennykh soobshchenii" [The military communications service], in *VOV,* 655. Ermolin's successors as UVS (and VOSO) chief were Lieutenant General of Technical Forces N. I. Trubetskoi, who became chief when the directorate was transferred to NKO control in August 1941, Military Engineer 1st Rank I. V. Kovalev, who replaced Trubetskoi in late 1941 and was promoted to the ranks of major general of technical forces in December 1942 and lieutenant general of technical forces in September 1943, and Major General of Tank Forces V. I. Dmitriev, who replaced Kovalev in 1944. Trubetskoi, Kovalev, and Dmitriev also headed the VOSO during their tenures as chiefs of the UVS, although Army General A. V. Khrulev also headed VOSO briefly in 1944 while he was serving as chief of the Rear.

97. For examples, see Gusarov and Butakov, "Tekhnicheskoe prikrytie zheleznykh dorog," 52.

98. See Zolotarev, "NKO 1941," 19–20, for the complete NKO order, which was numbered 0047. The name "Morgunov" was crossed out on the order and replaced by the name "Vol'sky" by Stalin himself, for unknown reasons.

99. See, for example, ibid., 20–21, for the formation and role of special aviation groups formed by the 9 July NKO order.

100. See Zolotarev, "NKO 1941," 26–27, for the complete NKO order, which was numbered 0055.

101. N. Strakhov, "Na voenno-avtomobil'nykh dorogakh" [On military automobile roads], *VIZh,* no. 3 (November 1964): 67.

102. Popov, "Sovershenstvovanie sistemy transportnogo obespecheniia," 22. For example, in September 1941 vehicles belonging to the Western Front's 15th Automobile Regiment were distributed among 17 different directorates and services, and the subunits subordinate to the Western Front's 106th and 65th Automobile Regiments worked at 24 separate points, located hundreds of kilometers apart.

103. Maliugin, "Avtomobil'nyi transport frontov i armii," 88.

104. A. S. Klemin, "Voennye soobshcheniia v gody Velikoi Otechestvennoi voiny" [Military communications during the Great Patriotic War], *VIZh,* no. 3 (March 1985): 70.

105. Ibid., 52–53.

106. Ibid. For example, during the Battle for Moscow, the 1st, 4th, 6th, and 26th Railroad Brigades supported the Western Front, and, during the same period, the 5th, 13th, 19th, 25th, 27th, 28th, and 29th Railroad Brigades supported the Southwestern Front. As a result, the actual restoration rate of 2.5–3.5 kilometers of rail lines per day proved wholly inadequate to support the army's offensive operations. See also M. K. Makartsev, "Sovershenstvovanie organizatsii zheleznodorozhnykh voisk v gody Velikoi Otechestvennoi voiny" [The improvement of the organization of railroad forces during the Great Patriotic War], *VIZh,* no. 9 (September 1985): 81.

107. See Zolotarev, "NKO 1941," 135–36, for the complete GKO and NKO (10 January) orders, which were numbered 1095c and 018, respectively. This GKO decree was entitled, "On the Reconstruction of the Railroads."

108. "Zheleznodorozhnye voiska" [Railroad forces], in *VOV,* 267.

109. Gusarov and Butakov, "Tekhnicheskoe prikrytie zheleznykh dorog," 54.

110. Popov, "Sovershenstvovanie sistemy transportnogo obespecheniia," 25.

111. Makartsev, "Sovershenstvovanie organizatsii zheleznodorozhnykh voisk," 82.

112. Ibid., 83.

113. Ibid., 69. The Transport Committee's members were A. A. Andreev, its deputy chairman, A. I. Mikoian, deputy chairman of the Council of People's Commissars, L. M. Kaganovich, people's commissar of communications, A. V. Khrulev, deputy commissar of defense and chief of the Red Army's Rear Services, I. V. Kovalev, VOSO chief, P. P. Shirshov, people's commissar of the navy, Z. A. Shashkov, people's commissar of the river fleet, G. B. Kovalev, deputy people's commissar for communications, and A. G. Karposonov, deputy chief of the General Staff's Operations Directorate.

114. See Maliugin, "Avtomobil'nyi transport frontov i armii," 88; and V. K. Vysotsky, ed., *Tyl Sovetskoi Armii* [The rear of the Soviet Army] (Moscow: Voenizdat, 1968), 152–54.

115. See Zolotarev, "NKO 1941," 227–28, for the complete NKO order, which was numbered 0370.

116. Ibid., 237–39.

117. See Zolotarev, "NKO 1943," 50, for the complete NKO order, which was numbered 076.

118. Klemin, "Voennye soobshcheniia," 71.

119. The deputy chiefs of the TsUPVOSO included P. A.Bakulin, V. I. Dmitriev, I. G. Kashcheev-Semin, S. A. Stepanov, and V. V. Stoliarov.

120. Klemin, "Voennye soobshcheniia," 72.

121. The new railroad brigades comprised a headquarters, four track, one bridge, and one mechanized battalion, and one service company. All track battalions had teams for reconnoitering rail lines.

122. These additions included a communications reconstruction company and, then, a full battalion to each brigade so that it could cope with the formidable task of rebuilding line communications and a water company for it to reconstruct a water supply. See Makartsev, "Sovershenstvovanie organizatsii zheleznodorozhnykh voisk," 84. These additions enabled a railroad brigade to carry out all reconstruction work in a railroad sector independently. During the same period, the NKO added a bridge reconstruction unit to each railroad restoration battalion and separate carpenter

battalions and heavy lift companies to handle repair of heavy bridges. The carpenter battalions consisted of four carpenter companies and a heavy lift crane company. Once these changes were made, the structure of railroad forces remained constant until war's end.

123. Popov, "Sovershenstvovanie sistemy transportnogo obespecheniia," 25. This work included building trans-loading areas in such regions as Aleksin in 1941 and 1942, Barvenkovo-Lozovaia in 1942, Kremenchug in 1943, Mogilev-Podol'sk in 1944, and Torun', Warsaw, and Baia in 1945. In addition to this extensive reconstruction work, the rail reconstruction forces employed various lesser expedients to increase rail-carrying capacity within a short period. These measures included the use of uneven and packet train traffic schedules, "live" block signaling, and the organization of one-way or "caravan" train traffic.

124. Ibid., 26.

125. Ibid., 22. See also Zolotarev, "NKO 1943," 172–75, for the complete GKO order, which was numbered 300c.

126. Strakhov, "Na voenno-avtomobil'nykh dorogakh," 50.

127. Popov, "Sovershenstvovanie sistemy transportnogo obespecheniia," 22.

128. Ibid., 25.

129. Strakhov, "Na voenno-avtomobil'nykh dorogakh," 23.

130. "Sluzhba voennykh soobshchenii," in *VOV,* 655.

131. Ibid.

132. Makartsev, "Sovershenstvovanie organizatsii zheleznodorozhnykh voisk," 85; and Popov, "Sovershenstvovanie sistemy transportnogo obespecheniia," 25.

133. Popov, "Sovershenstvovanie sistemy transportnogo obespecheniia," 25.

134. Ibid.

135. "Tyl vooruzhennykh sil" [The armed forces' rear], in *VOV,* 735. For more detail, see also Vysotsky, *Tyl Sovetskoi Armii,* 83–110.

136. Vysotsky, *Tyl Sovetskoi Armii,* 89–91.

137. Karpinsky was promoted to the rank of major general in the quartermaster service in May 1942.

138. "Sluzhba prodovol'stvennogo snabzheniia" [The food supply service], in *VOV,* 655. Brigade Engineer D. V. Pavlov, who was promoted to major general of the Quartermaster Service in January 1943, succeeded Belousov in February 1942.

139. For more details about the work of the USG, see I. N. Bazanov, "Obespechenie frontov goriuchim v tret'em periode Velikoi Otechestvennoi voiny" [The provision of fuel to the *fronts* during the third period of the Great Patriotic War], *VIZh,* no. 3 (March 1987): 50–56; and V. Nikitin, "Obespechenie voisk goriuchim v kontrnastuplenii pod Kurskom" [The provision of forces with fuel during the counteroffensive at Kursk], *VIZh,* no. 8 (August 1979): 25–30. Kotov was succeeded as chief of the USG in 1942 by Brigade Engineer M. I. Kormilitsyn, who was later promoted to major general of technical forces in January 1943 and directed the USG to war's end. See "Sluzhba snabzheniia goriuchim" [Fuel supply service], in *VOV,* 655–56.

140. "Smirnov, Efim Ivanovich," in *VOV,* 656.

141. "Voenno-veterinarnaia sluzhba" [The military-veterinary service], in *VOV,* 146–47.

142. VUKA's structure in operating forces included:

Command Level	*Organization*
Front	Several veterinary hospitals
	Veterinary laboratories
	Veterinary depots
Army	Veterinary evacuation hospitals
	Field marching (mobile) veterinary laboratories
	Field veterinary depots
Division and regiment	Veterinary laboratories

143. Ibid.

144. Ibid., 89.

145. Ibid., 108.

146. Ibid., 90.

147. "Sluzhba veshchevogo snabzheniia" [The clothing supply service], in *VOV,* 654–55.

148. Ibid. The NKO's June 1941 instructions established a new supply system extending from the "center" (NKO and industrial organs), through *front,* army, and division (brigade), to regiment, company, and individual soldier and established priorities in clothing distribution.

149. Ibid. See also A. Khrulev, "Stanovlenie strategicheskogo tyla v Velikoi Otechestvennoi voine" [The establishment of a strategic rear in the Great Patriotic War], *VIZh,* no. 6 (June 1961): 66–67. For example, A. I. Mikoian became responsible for fuel, food, and material supply, Party Secretary A. A. Andreev for rail transport, GOSPLAN chief N. A. Voznesensky for ammunition production and supply, and many other Party leaders for mobilizing other aspects of the economy.

150. See Zolotarev, "NKO 1941," 41–45, for the full NKO order, which was numbered 0257. See also, Khrulev, "Stanovlenie strategicheskogo tyla," 68–69. Major Generals M. V. Zakharov and P. A. Ermolin were Khrulev's deputies and Major General of the Quartermaster Service P. V. Utkin was Khrulev's chief of staff, with Major General M. P. Milovsky and Lieutenant General of the Quartermaster Service P. I. Drachev as his deputies.

151. Vysotsky, *Tyl Sovetskoi Armii,* 114.

152. In addition, the USG fielded a growing network of field laboratories to ensure greater quality control over fuel, particularly fuel used by aviation forces, and USG representatives supervised an extensive system of fuel production facilities deep in the country.

153. "Voenno-meditsinskaia sluzhba" [The military medical service], in *VOV,* 152. The operating *fronts* were short 40.1 percent of their required field hospitals, 48.8 percent of their automobile medical companies, and 44.8 percent of their evacuation points as envisioned in the General Staff's wartime mobilization plan. Although the SU began mobilizing hospitals in mid-July 1941, their number of beds did not come close to satisfying the army's burgeoning requirements. To help solve its catastrophic problems with medical support, on 7 July the GKO ordered additional evacuation hospitals be mobilized. The capacity of these hospitals reached 1 million beds

by 1 October 1941, and improved steadily thereafter. Clearly, however, the Red Army's appallingly poor medical support contributed to its extraordinarily high casualty rates during 1941 and 1942. Although the NKO was not able to establish an adequate medical support structure until early 1942, the new system improved markedly in the later war years.

154. The GVSU controlled medical services within the Red Army's operating *fronts* by means of subordinate *front* military-medical directorates. The most important *front* facilities were the *front,* local, and field evacuation points (FEPs, MEPs, and PEPs). Each of the evacuation points had its own attached hospital and military-medical transport forces, which included automobile medical companies, mobile medical detachments, military-medical trains, and medical aviation units. In addition, the *fronts* contained other medical agencies, including *front* medical depots and other sanitary equipment and anti-epidemiological facilities such as medical laboratories, infectious disease field mobile hospitals, medical anti-epidemiological detachments, bathing and disinfecting companies, and medical control points.

Once the new medical support system was established during 1942, *front* evacuation points (FEPs), each of which consisted of *front* evacuation hospitals and field mobile hospitals, deployed so-called advanced (or forward) hospitals, which coordinated directly with army hospital bases. Local evacuation points (MEPs) deployed their evacuation hospitals in the *front* rear close to the army hospital bases. Collectively, this complex of FEPs, MEPs, and PEPs, as well as their associated hospitals, formed the *front* hospital base (GBF), which was responsible for up to 90 days of medical treatment. Those among the wounded and ill who required longer-duration treatment were evacuated to hospitals in the rear area. The capacity of *front* hospital bases grew dramatically between 1941 and 1943. For example, on the eve of the Moscow counteroffensive (5 December 1941), the Western and Kalinin Fronts had 75,000 and 26,200 hospital beds, respectively. On the eve of the Stalingrad counteroffensive, the Stalingrad Front had 62,400 hospital beds, while the Western Front had 157,750 beds prior to the beginning of the August 1943 Smolensk operation. Soviet data indicated that the medical service returned 72 percent of Red Army wounded and 90 percent of the sick to active service.

Below *front* level, medical departments provided medical support to armies. Each army's medical department controlled field evacuation points (PEPs) with associated hospitals, separate medical companies, medical depots, and anti-epidemiological facilities, which, collectively, formed the army's hospital base (GBA). The GBA usually maintained a capacity of 5,000–6,000 beds. Medical support at division level usually consisted of a divisional doctor, who commanded the division's military-medical battalion, senior regimental doctors, and medical workers (medics) in subunits. At regimental level, a senior regimental doctor commanded a medical company as well as medical platoons within battalions and squads within companies. Company and battalion medical subunits in tank and artillery regiments were somewhat smaller than their counterparts in rifle regiments.

At lower levels, medical companies fielded regimental medical points, which were responsible for basic treatment and timely evacuation of the wounded during combat and hygienic and anti-epidemiological measures. At the battalion level, a medical platoon under the command of a doctor's assistant *(fel'dsher)* provided immediate medical assistance to wounded or ill soldiers and then dispatched them to regimental medical points for further treatment. Medical squads at company level, which were led by medical instructors, performed essentially the same functions.

The quantity and sophistication of Red Army military hospitals had also improved by 1942. Armies fielded single-type mobile field hospitals at the beginning of the war. However, their staffing and quality varied greatly, and many were lost in the fluid combat conditions. By the end of 1942, new hospitals had replaced those that were either destroyed or abandoned, and the Main Medical Directorate began fielding new types of specialized installations, including therapeutic and surgical field mobile hospitals to take care of the increasing numbers of maimed and wounded soldiers. In addition, the main directorate began fielding new hospitals for the treatment of the lightly wounded, which permitted rapid treatment and return to combat units of soldiers without prolonged stays in the *front* and army hospital bases. In addition, this also underscored the shortage of manpower that began to plague the Red Army. See also V. I. Selivanov and N. A. Vishnevsky, "Organizatsiia meditsinskogo obespecheniia voisk v kontrnastuplenii pod Moskvoi" [The organization of medical support of forces during the counteroffensive at Moscow], *Voenno-meditsinskii zhurnal* [Military-medical journal], no. 1 (January 1992): 47–49; and Dmitriy Loza, ed., *Fighting for the Soviet Motherland: Recollections from the Eastern Front,* trans. James F. Gebhardt (Lincoln: University of Nebraska Press, 1998), 189–203.

155. For example, see Zolotarev, "NKO 1941," 95–103, for NKO orders numbered 312 and 313, which established food norms in the Red Army.

156. Although extremely austere, the new food standards and norms satisfied minimal force requirements. The 14 categories included perishable food prepared by field kitchens, including potatoes, groats *(kasha),* meat (usually dried meat or sausage), macaroni, and vegetables, usually used to prepare porridges and stews, the all-important and ubiquitous black bread, and dried milk and canned items, much of which was ultimately supplied through Lend-Lease. For an excellent description of food supply and preparation by a serving junior officer, see Loza, *Fighting for the Soviet Motherland,* 176–88.

157. See Vysotsky, *Tyl Sovetskoi Armii,* 114; and Zolotarev, "NKO 1941," 124, for the full NKO order, which was numbered 0437.

158. Ibid., 148–49 contains the full NKO (and GKO order) order, which was numbered 080.

159. "Tyl vooruzhennykh sil," 735.

160. Zolotarev, "NKO 1941," 215.

161. "Tyl vooruzhennykh sil," 735. See also Zolotarev, "NKO 1941," 236–39, for the full NKO order, which was numbered 0409.

162. Khrulev, "Stanovlenie strategicheskogo tyla," 73.

163. Tiushkevich, *Sovetskie vooruzhennye sily,* 292.

164. "Sluzhba prodovol'stvennogo snabzheniia" [The food supply service], in *VOV,* 655. For example, operating *fronts* had their own dedicated food supply departments in their quartermaster directorates; armies had their own food supply sections in their quartermaster departments; tank and mechanized corps, divisions, and brigades had

food and forage sections in their rear services; regiments had chiefs of food and forage supply; and battalions, the lowest distribution level, had food and forage supply squads in their supply platoons.

165. Ibid.

166. "Tyl vooruzhennykh sil," 735.

167. "Sluzhba prodovol'stvennogo snabzheniia," 655.

168. Ibid.; and Loza, *Fighting for the Soviet Motherland,* 177.

169. Among many sources, see Boris V. Sokolov, "Lend-Lease in Soviet Military Efforts," *JSMS* 7, no. 3 (September 1994): 579–80; and V. Vorsin, "Pomoshch' po Lend-Lizu" [Assistance by Lend-Lease], *Tyl vooruzhennykh sil* [Rear of the armed forces], no. 10 (October 1991): 29–30.

170. "Sluzhba prodovol'stvennogo snabzheniia," 655.

171. Ibid., 656.

172. Red Army medical personnel in the Red Army from 1942 to 1945 included the following:

	Jul 42	*Jul 43*	*Jul 44*	*Jan 45*	*May 45*
Doctors	44,729	49,939	60,988	65,632	67,507
Feld'shers and nurses	37,435	39,715	49,477	45,814	48,186
Dentists	3,001	2,552	3,036	2,835	2,857
Pharmacists	7,979	7,491	8,437	8,316	8,505
Total	93,114	99,697	121,938	122,597	127,055

From F. I. Komarov and O. S. Lobastov, "Osnovnye itogi i uroki meditsinskogo obespecheniia Sovetskoi armii v gody Velikoi Otechestvennoi voiny" [The main conclusions and lessons of Soviet Army medical support during the Great Patriotic War], *Voenno-meditsinskii zhurnal* [Military-medical journal], no. 5 (May 1990): 10.

173. Equally tellingly, the percentage of sick constituted about one-third of the Red Army's total medical casualties, which the GVSU registered as having been treated during wartime, and about 25 percent of the total 29 million combat losses recorded by the operating *fronts.* The latter constituted irrevocable (irreplaceable) losses, which included those assessed as killed, captured, or missing in action. These figures also indicate that the percentage of sick among the casualties treated overall increased to over 40 percent in 1944 before declining somewhat by 1945. The average duration of hospitalization of the sick was 34.5 days. Red Army and Navy casualties treated at GVSU medical facilities included the following (by category and year):

	Total	*Wounded, Shell-shocked, Burned, and Frostbitten*	*Sick*	*Sick (%)*
1941	2,118,666	1,712,981	405,685	(19.1)
1942	5,573,484	3,625,351	1,948,133	(35.0)
1943	6,299,955	4,124,093	2,175,862	(34.5)
1944	5,901,524	3,520,203	2,381,321	(40.4)
1945	2,433,276	1,702,965	730,311	(30.0)
Total	22,326,905	14,685,593	7,641,311	(34.2)

From G. F. Krivosheev, ed., *Grif sekretnosti sniat: Poteri vooruzhennykh sil SSSR v voinakh, boevykh deistviakh i voennykh konfliktakh* [The seal of secrecy has been removed: The Soviet armed forces losses in wars, combat operations, and military conflicts] (Moscow: Voenizdat, 1993), 134.

174. "Veterinariia" [Veterinary medicine], in *VOV,* 126.

175. Ibid. In addition to horses, the VUKA and its veterinary service also treated service dogs and hundreds of thousands of head of livestock in herds designated to feed the troops. Intense and careful wartime veterinary work prevented large-scale outbreaks of disease and epidemics among the horses and herds alike and protected soldiers from infectious diseases spread by animals. The navy and the NKVD had their own independent veterinary services.

176. G. V. Sredin, "Glavnoe politicheskoe upravlenie" [Main Political Directorate], in *SVE,* II: 562. A. I. Zaporozhets headed the GUPP KA until July 1941.

177. The GlavPU's specific missions included organizing and supervising an extensive array of political work throughout the Red Army and other specific missions, including directing political, Party, and Komsomol' organizations in the Army, promoting Party influence in all aspects of the soldiers' lives; working out all important issues associated with Party construction, ideological work, and the structure of political, Party, and Komsomol organizations in conformity with the requirements of war, controlling the fulfillment of Party and governmental decisions and the NKO's and its orders and directives, organizing ideological work in the army and partisan detachments, developing and approving individual plans and programs in the social sciences for military-educational institutions, conducting propaganda among the enemy's forces and populations, generalizing and introducing advanced experience in political and Party work, ascertaining and responding in timely fashion to the spiritual needs and morale of army personnel, ensuring material support and cultural "servicing" of soldiers, examining, selecting, and assigning cadres of Party and political workers, directing military-political educational institutions and training and retraining political cadre, developing and modifying organizations *(shtats)* in the Party-political apparatus, and organizing and conducting the registration of Communists and Komsomol members on the army's rolls.

178. Sredin, "Glavnoe politicheskoe upravlenie," 562–63.

179. "Glavnoe politicheskoe upravlenie Raboche-Krest'ianskoi Krasnoi Armii (GlavPU RKKA)" [The Main Political Directorate of the Workers' and Peasants' Red Army (GlavPU RKKA)], in *VOV,* 208.

180. Zolotarev, "NKO 1941," 394.

181. Ibid., 348–49. This NKO order was numbered 00222.

182. See Zolotarev, "NKO 1942," 124–27. This NKO order was numbered 0071.

183. Ibid. After war's end in May 1945, the GKO combined the NKO's GRU and the General Staff's RU into a new organization, the GRU, which it once again subordinated to the General Staff.

184. "Sovetskaia voennaia kontrrazvedka" [Soviet military counterintelligence], in *VOV,* 662.

185. Ibid. At the same time, the GKO formed an analogous directorate within the People's Commissariat of the Navy.

186. For a detailed description of the wartime organization and actions of Red Army counterintelligence organs, see Robert W. Stephan, *Stalin's Secret War: Soviet Counterintelligence against the Nazis, 1941–1945* (Lawrence: University Press of Kansas, 2004).

187. Zolotarev, "NKO 1942," 405.

188. For another detailed description of SMERSH's role and activities, see Parrish, *The Lesser Terror,* 111–45. Parrish also acknowledges the wholesale lack of credible detail on this organ and the companion GRU.

189. V. F. Nekrasov, "Osnovnye etapy stroitel'stva vnutrennikh voisk" [Basic stages in the formation of internal forces], *VIZh,* no. 11 (November 1986): 83. At the time of its organization on 10 July 1934, the NKVD (All-Union NKVD) contained a Main Directorate for Border and Internal Security *(Glavnoe upravlenie pogranichnoi i vnutrennei okhrany),* which later became the Main Directorate for the NKVD's Border Guards and Internal Forces. However, the tense international environment in the late 1930s and the increasing complexity of required security tasks forced the Party and government to reorganize the NKVD force structure. A Politburo directive dated 2 February 1939, which took effect in March, subdivided the Main Directorate for Border and Internal Security into six separate main directorates, each of which performed a specific NKVD mission.

190. Ibid., 83. Generals I. I. Maslennikov, A. N. Apollonov, and S. N. Perevertkin served in this post before war began. The 1 September 1939 Law Concerning Universal Military Service recognized the NKVD's forces as a component part of the USSR's Armed Forces.

191. Iu. Piliugin, "Okhrana sukhoputnykh kommunikatsii v khode voiny" [The protection of ground communications during the war], *VIZh,* no. 9 (September 1983): 31.

192. For example, in June 1941 the Southern Front fielded nine regiments of NKVD border guards and internal troops, one border guard detachment, and one separate battalion. In the fall of 1941, the Western Front had six regiments, and, in August 1944 the 2nd Ukrainian Front had four border guards regiments, three regiments, and one battalion of internal troops, while the 3rd Ukrainian Front had four border guards regiments. See Piliugin, "Okhrana," 31' and Tiushkevich, *Sovetskie vooruzhennye sily,* 293.

193. I. K. Iakovlev, "Vnutrennie voiska" [Internal forces], in *SVE,* II: 164–65; and "Vnutrenniaia sluzhba" [Internal service], in *SVE,* II: 165.

194. In peacetime, each platoon of NKVD troops had two trained snipers, and after the outbreak of war, the training and assignment of snipers expanded significantly, particularly after May 1942. The NKVD trained 27,604 snipers between May 1942 and May 1943, 14,989 of whom served in Red Army forces, and these snipers recorded a reported 182,445 enemy kills. See Nekrasov, "Vklad vnutrennikh voisk," 33.

195. V. Danilov, "General'nyi shtab RKKA v predvoennye gody (1936–iiun' 1941 g.)" [The RKKA General Staff in the prewar years (1936–June 1941)], *VIZh,* no. 3 (March 1980): 70. The Directorate for Military Training, which had been part of the General Staff in the early 1930s, was removed from the General Staff in April 1936 and reorganized into a separate NKO Directorate of Combat Training of the Red Army. The last prewar reorganization of the General Staff occurred in March 1940,

when a plenum of the Communist Party Central Committee redefined the precise functions of each General Staff directorate, placing greater emphasis on the General Staff's role in war planning.

196. Zolotarev, "General'nyi shtab 1941," 7. This General Staff order was numbered 300.

197. On 16 July 1941, for example, the NKO created a new Automobile-Road Directorate within the General Staff with Major General Z. I. Kondrat'ev as its chief and corresponding automobile-road departments within each operating *front* to supervise automobile subunits, units, and formations within the Red Army's operating *fronts* and armies. Less than three weeks later, however, on 1 August, the GKO reassigned the GADU to the newly formed Main Directorate for Rear Services. See Zolotarev, "NKO 1941," 26, for the complete NKO order, which was numbered 0055.

198. See also Zolotarev, "General'nyi shtab 1941," 11.

199. For additional details, see A. P. Antonov, "Operativnoe upravlenie General'nogo shtaba v gody Velikoi Otechestvennoi voiny" [The General Staff's Operational Directorate during the Great Patriotic War], *VIZh*, no. 5 (May 1988): 12–18.

200. Ibid. Henceforth, the GOU was responsible for collecting information about the combat situation, the condition and combat capabilities of Red Army forces, and their logistical support, supervising the timely preparation of *Stavka*, General Staff, and Operations Directorate orders, directives, and instructions to the *fronts*, receiving and analyzing operational summaries, final battle reports, and other information from the *fronts*, preparing proposals for the chief of the Operations Directorate regarding the employment of large force formations, maintaining maps on the operational situation within each *front* and the strategic situation as a whole for Stalin and the *Stavka*, and coordinating all matters regarding cooperation with adjacent *fronts* or naval forces and with other appropriate General Staff directorates and departments. In addition to its responsibilities in the western and southern theaters of military operations, the GOU was also responsible for ensuring the security of the Far East and the Soviet Union's internal military districts. To do so, it received daily reports from the chiefs of staff of the Far Eastern and Trans-Baikal Fronts, and beginning in October 1941 the General Staff's communications center established direct wire communications links between the two *front* headquarters and the GOU from 1400 to 1630 hours and from 1330 to 1830 daily. Later still, the staff of the directorate's Far Eastern Department moved to Kuibyshev. Beginning on 25 October 1941, all correspondence from the headquarters of the two *fronts* that dealt with operational matters went directly to the Operations Directorate in Moscow, and those concerning supply, organization, and weaponry went to the department in Kuibyshev.

201. Antonov, "Operativnoe upravlenie," 12–13; and Lomov and Golubovich, "Ob organizatsii i metodakh raboty General'nogo shtaba," 5.

202. Antonov, "Operativnoe upravlenie," 18.

203. Ibid. The chief of operations routinely presented his first report to Stalin between 1000 and 1100 hours daily, usually by telephone. Between 1600 and 1700 hours, the deputy chief of the General Staff delivered his report to Stalin either in person or by telephone. Finally, after midnight the deputy chief of the General Staff and his chief of operations briefed Stalin personally in his quarters, using 1:200,000

scale *front* situation maps as the basis for their detailed briefings. The General Staff's workday ended in the early hours of each morning, only after Stalin had received this final daily combat report, which covered the full 24 hours of action at the front. After the briefings were complete, Stalin would approve, amend, or reject orders, directives, instructions, or other documents prepared for his signature. If Stalin rejected the proposals, responsible officers would then have to revise the materials according to Stalin's desires before ending their workday.

204. Shtemenko, *The Soviet General Staff at War 1941–1945,* I: 182.

205. Lomov and Golubovich, "Ob organizatsii i metodakh raboty General'nogo shtaba," 18–19.

206. The generals who served as deputy chiefs of the General Staff's Operations Directorate included Lieutenant Generals A. A. Gryzov and N. A. Lomov and Major General I. N. Ryzhkov, who served as deputy chief of staff for political affairs. The most notable department chiefs were Majors General M. A. Kraskovets, S. I. Gruneev, G. M. Chumakov, V. D. Utkin, V. F. Mernov, S. M. Eniukov, N. E. Sokolov, K. V. Postnikov, K. F. Vasil'chenko, Iu. A. Kutsev (later deputy chief of the Operations Directorate), M. N. Korchagin (Far Eastern expert), S. A. Petrovsky (Middle Eastern expert), Lieutenant General S. P. Platonov for reports, Rear Admirals V. I. Sumin and V. A. Kasatonov for the Navy, Major General N. M. Maslennikov for artillery and PVO, Majors General of Tank Forces P. I. Kalinichenko (later a tank army chief of staff), V. N. Baskakov, and L. M. Kitaev for tank forces, Majors General N. G. Kolesnikov and N. V. Voronov for air forces, Major General K. I. Nikolaev for signal forces, Major General V. A. Boliatko for engineer forces, and Lieutenant General L. V. Onianov for GRU liaison. See Shtemenko, *The Soviet General Staff at War,* I: 197.

207. See Zolotarev, "NKO 1942," 124–27. This NKO order was numbered 0071.

208. Ibid., 125.

209. Ibid., 206. The NKO order was numbered 0420.

210. Zolotarev, "General'nyi shtab 1941," 8.

211. Shtemenko, *The Soviet General Staff at War,* I: 194. Kuznetsov had been the political commissar of the 60th Army and the Voronezh Front before taking over the GRU from General Il'ichev on 19 April 1943. The volume of required intelligence work decreased significantly after the war in the Western Theater ended in May 1945. Therefore, the GKO combined the NKO's GRU and General Staff's RU into a new organization, the GRU, which was once again subordinate to the General Staff. See Parrish, *The Lesser Terror,* 238.

212. These included decrees mobilizing draftees, reducing the number of rear service units, facilities, and installations, forming 120 rifle divisions, 17 cavalry divisions, 50 separate rifle brigades, and numerous tank brigades and battalions, and manning existing formations both at the front and in the reserves.

213. Lomov and Golubovich, "Ob organizatsii i metodakh raboty General'nogo shtaba," 19.

214. Ibid., 14, states that Glavupraform was created on 28 July.

215. Shtemenko, *The Soviet General Staff at War,* II: 13.

216. Lomov and Golubovich, "Ob organizatsii i metodakh raboty General'nogo shtaba," 14.

217. Shtemenko, *The Soviet General Staff at War,* II: 15.

218. The most important departments in the General Staff's Organizational Directorate and their chiefs were:

Department	*Chief*
Rifle and airborne units	Colonel A. N. Nyrkov
	Colonel F. F. Trishin (1944)
Cavalry and tank forces	Major General S. V. Sretensky
Artillery and mortar units	Major General P. I. Kaniukov
Technical units (engineer, signal, communications, etc)	Colonel V. V. Vishniakov
	Colonel P. A. Polityko (1944)
Air forces	Colonel I. S. Alekseev
	Colonel N. K. Ermakov (1944)
Troop control	Colonel F. M. Arkhipov
	Major General A. I. Sychev (1945)
Training centers and military training institutions	Colonel I. O. Skvortsov
	Colonel A. V. Goldenkov (1944)
Rear service units	Colonel I. M. Eshchenko
Organizational planning	Colonel I. A. Kiselov
	Colonel S. N. Riabokoilko
	Colonel P. V. Dudoladov
	Colonel I. I. Il'chenko
	Colonel A. A. Bochkov
	Colonel M. N. Kostin
Force strength	Colonel (Major General) S. M. Podolsky
Registration and issuing of banners (honorifics)	Colonel I. V. Smirnov
Force manning	Colonel I. I. Zotkin
	Colonel P. V. Dudoladov (1944)
Priority transportation	Colonel I. K. Tkachenko
Force dispositions	Colonel A. K. Nemchinov
Inspectorate	Colonel A. N. Shumilov
Supervisory staff	Major V. N. Khrustaliov
	Captain I. I. Zubkov

See Shtemenko, *The Soviet General Staff at War,* I: 197.

219. Ibid., 16–17. Karponosov's deputy from May 1943 to war's end was Lieutenant General N. I. Chertverikov, who had amassed 25 years of experience working on organizational matters. Chertverikov also headed the directorate's Organizational Department. Shtemenko's description of Karposonov's career and subsequent fate vividly underscores the difficulties of working in the General Staff given Stalin's often fickle and arbitrary manner:

> From April 1942 to October 1946, Lieutenant-General A. G. Karposonov headed the bodies that dealt with organizational questions. He was a real General Staff officer: intelligent, industrious, and efficient, polite, although mild and somewhat diffident. He knew the work entrusted to him perfectly well, conducted it skillfully and with care, and always told the truth. And still,

for some reason, he failed to make a successful career. Some people are simply ""unlucky"; their every slip is noted, and, even when they are not at fault, they are blamed for the mistakes of others and cannot defend themselves. If reserves were not brought up to the front in time, Karposonov was blamed, although the transport organizations had committed the oversight. If the Glavupraform failed to supply reinforcements for divisions when they were needed, Karposonov would be blamed yet again, for not asking them at the proper time. A. I. Antonov and I heard unflattering remarks about him from Stalin on several occasions, even though the Supreme Commander realized that Karposonov knew his job and did it well. And over and over again, Antonov defended him when Stalin suggested replacing him with another general.

Shortly after the end of the war in the Far East, Stalin brought up this subject once again. "The experience gained in the General Staff should be passed on to the Military Districts," he said, pacing deliberately back and forth behind his desk, as was his habit. "The General Staff should reduce its personnel now, and all the officers it lets go should be sent to the Military Districts. That goes for your favourite, too–Karposonov. Let him share his experience too. Where do you suggest sending him?" he asked, turning suddenly to Antonov.

For a moment Antonov was at a loss. He was about to defend Karposonov, but Stalin with his question had cut off the possibility of objections. He often did this when he did not want to discuss things.

"Allow me to give it some thought," relied Antonov.

"Good. Pick out a place for him as Deputy Chief of Staff in one of the military districts."

On October 20, 1946, Karposonov was appointed Deputy Chief of Staff for the Volga Military District. He held this post for the rest of his life.

220. See Zolotarev, "NKO 1943," 50, for the complete NKO order, which was numbered 076.

221. Shtemenko, *The Soviet General Staff at War,* I: 194. After war's end, the communications directorate once again reverted to General Staff control. However, throughout this entire process of continuous change in subordination, of military necessity the General Staff maintained close contact with the various communications directorates.

222. The NKO had established the Directorate for the Formation of the Rear and Supply *(Upravlenie ustroistva tyla i snabzheniia)* within the General Staff during the summer of 1940 and converted this directorate into the Directorate for the Rear and Supply during early 1941 to underscore the General Staff's premier role in planning.

223. Ibid., 195. The Directorate for the Rear and Supply Planning's only identified chiefs were A. I. Shimonaev and N. P. Mikhailov.

224. Zolotarev, "General'nyi shtab 1941," 10.

225. "Voenno-topograficheskaia sluzhba" [The military-topographical service], in *VOV,* 158.

226. Zolotarev, "General'nyi shtab 1941," 10.

227. Shtemenko, *The Soviet General Staff at War,* I: 194.

228. Ibid., 196.

229. Ibid., II: 38–40. The UShS's tasks became even more complicated in late 1944, when the *Stavka* dispensed with its practice of using its representatives to coordinate *front* operations along the most vital strategic axes. This required that the General Staff maintain uninterrupted communications and control directly from Moscow in these vital sectors where there was no *Stavka* representative, for example, in the 1st Belorussian and 1st Ukrainian Fronts, which were operating along the Warsaw-Berlin axis. Elsewhere, *Stavka* representatives continued to coordinate operations,

for example, Marshal S. K. Timoshenko in the 2nd and 3rd Ukrainian Fronts, Marshal Vasilevsky in the 1st and 2nd Baltic Fronts, and Marshal I. A. Govorov in the 1st and 2nd Baltic Fronts and Leningrad Front.

230. Ibid., 11.

231. The Red Army General Staff had systematically studied war experiences throughout the late 1920s and 1930s, for example, during the Spanish Civil War, but apparently ceased doing so or did so much less thoroughly during the late 1930s.

232. Zolotarev, "NKO 1941, "216–17, which includes the complete NKO order, which was numbered 0324. See also Zolotarev, "NKO 1943," 228–31, for NKO Order No. 0443, dated 11 December 1943, which established a detailed working relationship between this department and the Red Army's operating *fronts* and armies on the matter of exploiting war experiences.

233. Shtemenko, *The Soviet General Staff at War,* II: 20–24. Among many other sources, see S. A. Gladysh, "Obobshchenie i ispol'zovanie boevogo opyta v pervom periode Velikoi Otechestvennoi voiny" [The Exploitation and use of war experience in the first period of the Great Patriotic War], *VIZh,* no. 7 (July 1987), 14–20.

234. Coincidentally, this department's effective work also benefited its head, General Vechnyi, by helping to erase the memory of his direct involvement in the Red Army's debacle in the Crimea in May 1942.

235. The UPOIIOV produced a total of 26 volumes of collected war experiences, 22 book-length collections of tactical examples, and 70 informational bulletins by 1948. See, for example, *Sbornik materialov po izucheniiu opyta voiny* [Collections of materials on the study of war experience], nos. 1–26 (Moscow: Voenizdat, 1942–1948), and *Sbornik takticheskikh primerov po opytu Otechestvennoi voiny* [Collection of tactical examples on the experience of the Patriotic War], vols. 1–23 (Moscow: Voenizdat, 1943–1947). Nor did the UPOIIOV's work cease after 1948. Beginning in 1947, for example, and thereafter to 1960, the UPOIIOV and its successor, the Military-Scientific Directorate, compiled and published a 43–volume collection of combat documents related to the Great Patriotic War. See *Sbornik boevykh dokumentov Velikoi Otechestvennoi voiny* [Collection of combat documents of the Great Patriotic War], vols. 1–43 (Moscow: Voenizdat, 1949–1960). In addition to covering military issues topically (offense, defense, pursuit, etc.), this series included an ambitious effort to assemble combat orders and reports, chronologically by main direction and *front.* Unfortunately, the General Staff abandoned this effort in the early 1960s, when it turned historical matters over to the Military History Institute, which subsequently ceased compiling these collections. After war's end, the General Staff's Military-Historical Directorate, which became a subordinate directorate of the General Staff's new Main Military-Scientific Directorate in 1951, and reverted to the status of a department of the General Staff's Military-Scientific Directorate in 1953, produced 19 detailed military operational studies in its series entitled *Collection of Military-Historical Materials of the Great Patriotic War (1949–1968).* See *Sbornik voenno-istoricheskikh materialov Velikoi Otechestvennoi voiny* [Collection of military-historical materials of the Great Patriotic War], vols. 1–19 (Moscow: Voenizdat, 1949–1968).

236. Shtemenko, *The Soviet General Staff at War,* II: 22–23.

237. See Zolotarev, "NKO 1943," 315, for the full contents of NKO Order No. 0318, which converted the department into a full directorate.

238. The OSZ established its first contacts with Allied military missions in Moscow in November 1942 and expanded these contacts significantly as Allied forces expanded their operations in North Africa, Sicily, and Italy during 1943 and, in particular, after the Allies finally opened the second front in France in June 1944. Ultimately, the OSZ and the new directorate worked closely with Allied military missions accredited to the General Staff, including the U.S. Military Mission headed by Brigadier General J. R. Deane, the British Military Mission under General Burrows, the French Military Mission of General Jean de Lattre de Tassigny, and similar smaller missions from Norway, the Czechoslovak Republic, and the National Liberation Committee of Yugoslavia.

Slavin's directorate also served Soviet military missions sent to the General Staffs of Allied countries, which worked directly with the GHQ in those countries rather than the ambassadors. The first chief of the Soviet Military Mission to Great Britain, which reached London in July 1941, was Lieutenant General F. I. Golikov. However, Rear Admiral N. M. Kharlamov replaced Golikov after a very few days and occupied the post until November 1944 when he was replaced by General A. F. Vasil'ev, who served to war's end.

In the summer of 1944, the General Staff assigned Major General I. A. Susloparov, the former chief of artillery in the Western Front's 10th Army, as its representative to the Allied Supreme Headquarters in France. Susloparov occupied this sensitive position until the German surrender in May 1945. His counterparts in the Mediterranean and Pacific Theaters were Major General A. A. Kislenko and Rear Admiral Ivanovsky. For further details, see Shtemenko, *The Soviet General Staff at War,* II: 26, 27–36.

239. Lomov and Golubovich, "Ob organizatsii i metodakh raboty General'nogo shtaba," 17.

240. Shtemenko, *The Soviet General Staff at War,* I: 205.

241. For additional detail on the Officer Corps of the General Staff, see "Polozhenie i instruktsiia po rabote korpusa ofitserov—predstavitelei General'nogo shtaba Krasnoi Armii," 62–66; Saltykov, "Podvig," 23–28; Saltykov, "Predstaviteli General'nogo shtaba," 54–59; and I. Kulikov, "Ofitsery—predstaviteli General'nogo shtaba v oboronitel'nom srazhenii pod Kurskom" [Officers—representatives of the General Staff in the defensive battle at Kursk], *VIZh,* no. 8 (August 1976): 79–84.

12. The Officer Corps and Command Cadre

1. For details on the purges, see O. A. Suvenirov, *Tragediia RKKA 1937–1938* [The tragedy of the RKKA 1937–1941] (Moscow: Terra, 1998).

2. R. M. Portugal'sky, *Komandnye kadry Sovetskikh vooruzhennykh sil v gody Velikoi Otechestvennoi voiny* [The command cadre of the Soviet Armed Forces in the Great Patriotic War] (Moscow: VAF, 1991), 8, classified "For official use only."

3. For further details, see Maslov, *Fallen Soviet Generals;* and Maslov, *Captured Soviet Generals.*

4. The scapegoats included D. G. Pavlov, the hapless commander of the Western Front, A. A. Korobkov, commander of the Western Front's 4th Army, several of Pavlov's senior staff officers, and other "wreckers," including K. M. Kachanov, commander of the Northwestern Front's 34th Army, whose forces participated in the Northwestern Front's failed counterstroke at Staraia Russa during August 1941, and K. P. Piadyshev, commander of the Luga Defense Line, whose defenses the *Wehrmacht* bloodily penetrated as they advanced toward Leningrad during August. Stalin had both Kachanov and Piadyshev executed for dereliction of duty.

5. "Traitor-generals" included I. M. Muzychenko and P. G. Ponedelin, commanders of the Southwestern Front's 6th and 12th Armies, whose forces the *Wehrmacht* encircled and destroyed during August 1941. Stalin branded both as traitors and executed them after their return from German captivity at war's end. Another member of this group was V. Ia. Kachalov, commander of the Western Front's 28th Army, which the *Wehrmacht* destroyed during the Battle for Smolensk. Although the unfortunate Kachalov died in the fighting, Stalin nevertheless condemned him to death for treason. Nor did this sordid process end in 1941. For example, when V. A. Khomenko, commander of the 4th Ukrainian Front's 44th Army, was killed in action while his army was pursuing retreating *Wehrmacht* during November 1943, Stalin accused him of desertion, arrested many of his subordinates, disbanded his army, and never assigned the designation "44th" to any other army.

6. For further details, see Parrish, *The Lesser Terror,* 69–95.

7. Portugal'sky, *Komandnye kadry Sovetskikh vooruzhennykh sil,* 8–9.

8. Ibid., 7, citing archival reference *TsAMO,* f. 4, op. 14, d. 2371, l. 37.

9. These included G. K. Zhukov, K. A. Meretskov, and I. V. Tiulenev, Colonel Generals I. P. Ananesenko, O. I. Gorodovikov, A. D. Loktionov, G. M. Shtern, D. G. Pavlov, N. N. Voronov, and V. D. Grendal', who became army generals, 120 others (including six NKVD officers), who became lieutenant generals, and 852 who became major generals.

10. For a detailed analysis of the "Generals of 1940," see I. I. Kuznetsov, *Marshaly, generaly i admiraly 1940 goda* [Marshals, generals and admirals of 1940] (Irkutsk: n.p., 2000).

11. Ibid., 10–14. Regarding the fate of the 982 officers who were promoted to general in the Red Army's "class of 1940," ten were repressed, 100 were killed in action, and 80 were captured during the war. The 792 who survived the war included eight wartime marshals of the Soviet Union (G. K. Zhukov, A. M. Vasilevsky, L. A. Govorov, I. S. Konev, R. Ia. Malinovsky, K. A. Meretskov, K. K. Rokossovsky, and F. I. Tolbukhin), seven postwar marshals of the Soviet Union (S. S. Biriuzov, F. I. Golikov, M. V. Zakharov, A. I. Eremenko, K. S. Moskalenko, V. D. Sokolovsky, and V. I. Chuikov), ten wartime marshals of forces (F. A. Astakhov, M. P. Vorob'ev, N. N. Voronov, S. F. Zhavoronkov, A. A. Novikov, P. S. Rybalko, F. Ia. Falaleev, Ia. N. Fedorenko, M. I. Chistiakov, and N. D. Iakovlev), three postwar marshals of forces (P. F. Zhigarev, V. I. Kazakov, and S. A. Krasovsky), 16 wartime army generals (P. I. Batov, N. F. Vatutin, G. K. Malandin, I. I. Maslennikov, P. A. Kurochkin, M. M. Popov, M. A. Purkaev, A. N. Antonov, K. N. Galitsky, A. S. Zhadov, F. G. Zakharov, V. D. Ivanov, M. I. Kazakov, D. D. Leliushenko, I. E. Petrov, and A. V. Khrulev), 36 wartime *front* commanders (I. P. Apanasenko, P. A. Artem'ev, A. I. Bogdanov, Ia. T. Cherevichenko, A. I. Eremenko, M. G. Efremov,

V. A. Frolov, L. A. Govorov, F. I. Golikov, V. N. Gordov, M. S. Khozin, M. P. Kirponos, M. P. Kovalev, D. T. Kozlov, I. S. Konev, F. Ia. Kostenko, P. A. Kurochkin, F. I. Kuznetsov, R. Ia. Malinovsky, I. I. Maslennikov, K. A. Meretskov, D. G. Pavlov, I. E. Petrov, M. M. Popov, M. A. Purkaev, M. A. Reiter, K. K. Rokossovsky, D. I. Riabyshev, P. P. Sobennikov, V. D. Sokolovsky, F. I. Tolbukhin, I. V. Tiulenev, A. M. Vasilevsky, N. F. Vatutin, G. F. Zakharov, and G. K. Zhukov), 50 wartime deputy army commanders or chiefs of staff, 130 wartime rifle division commanders, five wartime tank army commanders (V. T. Vol'sky, D. D. Leliushenko, K. S. Moskalenko, V. V. Novikov, P. L. Romanenko, and P. S. Rybalko), 18 wartime air army commanders, two wartime chiefs of the General Staff (A. M. Vasilevsky and A. I. Antonov), nine wartime recipients of the Order of Victory (A. I. Antonov, L. A. Govorov, I. S. Konev, R. Ia. Malinovsky, K. A. Meretskov, K. K. Rokossovsky, F. I. Tolbukhin once, and G. K. Zhukov and A. M. Vasilevsky twice), and 80 wartime recipients of Hero of the Soviet Union (13 twice and G. K. Zhukov fourfold).

12. Portugal'sky, *Komandnye kadry Sovetskikh vooruzhennykh sil,* 9–10.

13. Ibid., 10–11, citing archival reference *TsGASA,* f. 4, op. 14, d. 2781, l. 119.

14. Kuznetsov replaced the purged Colonel General A. D. Lokionov, who was shot during October 1941, in June 1940. The Baltic Military District itself was rather new, having been established on 11 July 1940 and transformed into the Baltic Special Military District on 17 August of the same year.

15. Portugal'sky, *Komandnye kadry Sovetskikh vooruzhennykh sil,* 12.

16. This calculation counts two brigades as equivalent to one division.

17. Portugal'sky, *Komandnye kadry Sovetskikh vooruzhennykh sil,* 13; and S. A. Tiushkevich, ed., *Sovetskie vooruzhennye sily* [The Soviet Armed Forces] (Moscow: Voenizdat, 1978), 296.

18. These included the 1st through the 10th Reserve Armies, the 1st, 3rd, 4th, and 5th Tank Armies, the 27th and 53rd Armies, the 70th NKVD Army, and the 1st, 2nd, and 3rd Guards Armies. For further details, see David M. Glantz, *Soviet Mobilization in Peace and War, 1924–1942: A Survey* (Carlisle, PA: Self-published, 1998), 48–54.

19. Portugal'sky, *Komandnye kadry Sovetskikh vooruzhennykh sil,* 12. For overall losses, see Krivosheev, *Grif sekretnosti sniat,* 128–325.

20. Portugal'sky, *Komandnye kadry Sovetskikh vooruzhennykh sil,* 14.

21. Ibid.

22. V. K. Provorov and A. P. Porokhin, "Voenno-uchebnye zavedeniia" [Military training institutions], in *SVE,* 255–56; and "Voenno-uchebnye zavedeniia" [Military training institutions], in *VOV,* 159.

23. "Voennye uchilishcha" [Military schools], in *VOV,* 159. For further details on the Red Army's officer education and training system, see David M. Glantz, *The Red Army's Education and Training System during the Soviet-German War, 1941–45* (Carlisle, PA: Self-published, 2004).

24. "Akademiia General'nogo shtaba," in *VOV,* 44.

25. The Voroshilov Academy's wartime commandants included Lieutenant General V. K. Mordvinov, Lieutenant General E. A. Shilovsky on 3 August 1941, Colonel General F. I. Kuznetsov on 30 April 1942, and Marshal of the Soviet Union B. M. Shaposhnikov from 25 June 1943 to war's end.

26. Portugal'sky, *Komandnye kadry Sovetskikh vooruzhennykh sil,* 20.
27. Ibid., 18–19.
28. D. A. Dragunsky, ed., Polevaia akademiia: Istoriia vysshikh ofitserskikh ordena Lenina i Oktiabr'skoi Revoliutsii Krasnoznamenykh kursov "Vystrel" imeni Marshala Sovetskogo Soiuza B. M. Shaposhnikova [Field academy: A history of the "Vystrel" Order of Lenin and October Revolution, Red Banner higher officers courses in the name of Marshal of the Soviet Union B. M. Shaposhnikov] (Moscow: Voenizdat, 1983), 137. The chief of the "Vystrel'" courses from 1941 through 1945 was Major General S. A. Smirnov, who replaced the school's last prewar commandant, Major General V. V. Kosiakhin, in 1941 and was promoted to lieutenant general in 1944.
29. Ibid.
30. Ibid., 331.
31. Ibid. For example, the period of study in all ground force military schools (except the topographical and quartermaster schools) increased from one to two years, as did the courses for training new junior lieutenants. Education and training also became longer and more effective in the higher military-educational institutions. Specialist education shifted from an accelerated to a full program during late 1942, and the combined-arms academies did likewise during May 1943. At the same time, both faculty members and students were far more experienced than their predecessors.
32. Ibid. This, in turn, permitted the NKO to lengthen many of the courses in its military education and training system.
33. In addition, the navy had two military academies, five higher naval schools, two naval faculties at civilian schools, eight naval schools, and seven courses for the improvement and retraining of command cadre.
34. Tiushkevich, *Sovetskie vooruzhennye sily,* 297. For example, an order of the Presidium of the Supreme Soviet dated 18 August 1941 authorized *front* military councils to award military ranks from captain up to major, battalion commissar, and its equivalent. Army councils could do likewise for lieutenants, *politruki* (political workers), and the equivalent. The GKO authorized the chiefs of the NKO's main directorates to appoint commanders up to regimental level inclusive during September 1941. Subsequently, the GKO extended this right to promote subordinates *front* military councils, and army, corps, division, and regimental commanders. GKO orders issued during late 1941 and early 1942 established shorter periods of service before commanders and chiefs in the field forces could be promoted to higher rank. The orders granted the military councils the right, in certain instances, to award accelerated promotions to those who earned it within the limits of their jurisdiction.
35. Zolotarev, "NKO 1941," 342.
36. Tiushkevich, *Sovetskie vooruzhennye sily,* 298.
37. Ibid., 302–7. See also M. N. Timofeechev, "Edinonachalie" [Unified command], in *SVE,* III: 301–2; and Zolotarev, "NKO 1941," 326. The Presidium abolished the commissar system based on the assumption that political education conducted by the NKO's Main Political Directorate had achieved its ends and command cadre were as reliable as the army's and navy's commissars.
38. Tiushkevich, *Sovetskie vooruzhennye sily,* 330.

39. Ibid., 308.

40. See Zolotarev, "NKO 1943," 24, 30, 191–92, for the contents of these NKO orders, which were numbered 24, 25, and 258.

41. Tiushkevich, *Sovetskie vooruzhennye sily*, 311; and Zolotarev, "NKO 1943," 32–35, 57, for these NKO orders, which were numbered 32, 38, and 39. These orders awarded the rank of marshal of the Soviet Union to G. K. Zhukov, N. N. Voronov, and S. M. Budenny.

42. Since 1991, for example, the Russians have published unexpurgated versions of many memoirs originally published in the 1960s and 1970s (such as K. K. Rokossovsky's), that starkly underscore what was left unsaid in their earlier editions. In addition, they have released documents collections related to military operations, primarily unsuccessful, that their histories had long ignored. They have slowed this effort since about 1998, however, apparently because the truth became too unpleasant. See K. K. Rokossovsky, *Soldatskii dolg* [A soldier's duty] (Moscow: Golos, 2000), and compare with the original expurgated edition published in 1970.

43. W. F. Mellenthin, *Panzer Battles: A Study of the Employment of Armor in the Second World War*, trans. H. Betzler (Norman: University of Oklahoma Press, 1955), 295.

44. Among many biographies of Budenny, see his official biography in "Semen Mikhailovich Budenny," in *SVE*, I: 615–17.

45. Viktor Anfilov, "Semen Mikhailovich Budenny" in Shukman, *Stalin's Generals*, 57–65; and "Budenny, Semen Mikhailovich," in *VOV*, 117.

46. See Voroshilov's official biography in "Voroshilov Kliment Efrimovich" in *SVE*, II: 363–65.

47. D. Volkogonov, "Kliment Yefremovich Voroshilov," in Shukman, *Stalin's Generals*, 313–24.

48. See Timoshenko's official biography in "Timoshenko, Semen, Konstantinovich," *SVE*, VIII: 43–44.

49. See Viktor Anfilov, "Semen Konstantinovich Timoshenko," in Shukman, *Stalin's Generals*, 239–53.

50. Kuznetsov, *Marshaly*, 6.

51. Command turbulence varied considerably from *front* to *front*, ranging from one commander each in the Karelian and Kalinin Fronts, two each in the Kalinin, Briansk, Central, and Southwestern Fronts, three each in the Northwestern, Western, and Reserve Fronts, and a total of four in the Leningrad Front.

52. At the same time, however, the Red Army's many defeats during the spring and summer of 1942 tarnished the luster of many of these *front* commanders, specifically, Meretskov's involvement in the tragic annihilation of his *front's* 2nd Shock Army at Liuban', the failure of Kurochkin's Northwestern Front to destroy the two German corps encircled at Demiansk, and Kostenko's and Malinovsky's involvement in the Red Army's major defeat at Khar'kov in May 1942.

53. Popov entered the Red Army in 1920 and fought as a private during the Civil War. During the interwar years, he attended the "Vystrel'" command course and the Frunze Academy and rose to command in the Red Army's fledgling mechanized forces during the late 1930s as chief of staff of a mechanized brigade and the 5th Mechanized

Corps. He joined Zhukov in the Far East as commander of the 1st Separate Red Banner Army in 1939, and when Zhukov became chief of the General Staff in January 1941, Stalin appointed Popov to command the Leningrad Military District. See "Markian Mikhailovich Popov," in *SVE,* VI: 453–54.

54. Petro G. Grigorenko, *Memoirs* (New York: Norton, 1982), 113.

55. Shtemenko, *The Soviet General Staff at War,* I: 233.

56. Eremenko had joined the tsarist army during 1913 and the Red Army during 1918. He served as chief of staff of a cavalry brigade and as deputy commander of a cavalry regiment during the Russian Civil War, and, after war's end, he graduated from the Higher Cavalry School in 1923, the Command Cadre Course in 1925, and the Frunze Academy in 1935. In between his schooling, he commanded a cavalry regiment in December 1929, a cavalry division in August 1937, and the 6th Cavalry Corps in 1938, which he led in the offensive into eastern Poland in September 1939. The NKO assigned Eremenko to command one of the Red Army's new mechanized corps in June 1940 and to command the 1st Red Banner Far Eastern Army in December 1940, where he was serving when the war began. Eremenko was promoted to the rank of lieutenant general in June 1941. See *VE,* 165.

57. *VOV,* 260.

58. Shtemenko, *The Soviet General Staff at War,* I: 361.

59. A veteran of the World War, after joining the Red Army in 1918, Konev served as a commissar in an armored train, a rifle brigade, and a rifle division, and in the People's Revolutionary Army in the Far East during the Russian Civil War. At war's end he took part in suppressing anti-Bolshevik uprisings in Moscow and at the naval base at Kronstadt. After serving as commissar in the 17th Coastal Rifle Corps and 17th Rifle Division during the 1920s, he attended the Course for Improving Red Army Command Cadre (KUVNAS) and was then assigned as a regimental and deputy division commander. During the following decade, Konev attended the Frunze Academy and rose to command a rifle division, a rifle corps, and the 2nd Red Banner Far Eastern Army. Although accused of disloyalty during the purges, he avoided the fate of many of his colleagues, and he was assigned to command, first, the Trans-Baikal and, later, the North Caucasus Military District during 1940 and 1941. Unfortunately, Konev's memoirs, I. S. Konev, *Zapiski komanduiushchego frontom* [Notes of a *front* commander] (Moscow: Voenizdat, 1981), begin only in January 1943. See also P. M. Portugal'sky, *Marshal I. S. Konev* (Moscow: Voenizdat, 1985). Both of these works and others studiously ignore Konev's role in Operation Mars and provide scant information on Konev's activities and performance in 1941 and 1942.

60. The NKO secretly deployed Konev's 19th Army from the North Caucasus Military District to the Kiev region before war began with orders to attack the flank of any German force advancing on Kiev. However, the successful German advance toward Smolensk prompted the *Stavka* to redeploy Konev's army northward, where German forces literally ground it up during the early stages of the Battle for Smolensk.

61. See Oleg Rzheshevsky, "Konev," in Shukman, *Stalin's Generals,* 91–107, for these positive and negative comments on Konev's personality. Rzheshevsky is the first to surface Konev's problems during the purges.

62. Grigorenko, *Memoirs,* 112–13.

63. On 31 December the Red Army included the Karelian, Leningrad, Volkhov, Northwestern, Kalinin, Western, Briansk, Voronezh, Southwestern, Don, Stalingrad, and Trans-Caucasus Fronts.

64. As in 1941, command turbulence varied widely from *front* to *front,* ranging from one commander each in the Karelian, Volkhov, Don, Southern, Caucasus, Crimean, North Caucasus, and Trans-Caucasus Fronts to two each in the Leningrad, Northwestern, Kalinin, and Western Fronts, three in the Voronezh Front, and four each in the Briansk, Southwestern (1st and 2nd formation), and Southeastern (Stalingrad) Fronts.

65. See K. K. Rokossovsky, *A Soldier's Duty* (Moscow: Progress, 1970) and his unexpurgated biography, Rokossovsky, *Soldatskii dolg.* Rokossovsky fought as a common soldier and junior officer during the World War and served as a cavalry squadron, battalion, and regimental commander during the Russian Civil War. During the 1920s he commanded cavalry regiments and brigades, graduated from the Frunze Academy, and participated in the 1929 Sino-Soviet conflict in Manchuria. Continuing his cavalry service, after 1930 Rokossovsky commanded the 7th and 15th Cavalry Divisions (Zhukov was a regimental commander in the former) and the Leningrad Military District's 5th Cavalry Corps. Rokossovsky was accused of "sabotage" and "impairing combat effectiveness" in 1937 and was arrested. Despite being imprisoned and tortured for three years on the trumped up charges, he was released from confinement in March 1940 and soon reassigned to command the 5th Cavalry Corps. Promoted to major general, Rokossovsky participated in the 1940 invasion of Bessarabia and took command of the Kiev Special Military District's newly formed 9th Mechanized Corps in October 1940, which he was commanding when war broke out in June.

66. For example, Rokossovsky was extremely critical of Zhukov's role in ordering his 16th Army to conduct what turned out to be an unsuccessful attack on German defenses near Zhizdra in July 1942.

67. While Bagramian's Kalinin (1st Baltic) Front recorded modest gains in the Vitebsk region and Sokolovsky's Western Front pounded in vain against German defenses in eastern Belorussia, Rokossovsky recorded signal successes with limited tank and mechanized resources. Employing effective deception, his forces (renamed the Belorussian Front on 20 October 1943) breeched German defenses along the Dnepr River at Gomel' in October, broadened the bridgehead into strategic proportions in November, and defeated a determined German counterstroke in December. After the turn of the year, Rokossovsky's forces captured Mozyr' and Kalinkovichi, turning Army Group Center's left flank and severing communications between Army Groups Center and South, and drove threatening wedges into German Second Army's defenses north of the Pripiat Marshes. With more effective support from his neighboring *front* commanders to the north, it is likely that Rokossovsky's fall offensive would have collapsed German defenses in Belorussia. That, however, would have to wait another six months.

68. For example, these historians have studiously avoided mention of Rokossovsky's successful offensives west of the Dnepr River in southern Belorussia in the fall of 1943 and, in particular, in the winter of 1944, probably to avoid damaging the

reputation of V. D. Sokolovsky, the Western Front commander, who although relieved of command in late winter of 1944, rose to prominence after war's end. For details on these successes, see Glantz, *Forgotten Battles*, vols. 5–6.

69. Richard Woff, "Konstantin Konstantinovich Rokossovsky," in Shukman, *Stalin's Generals*, 177.

70. I. M. Chistiakov, *Sluzhim otchizne* [We serve the fatherland] (Moscow: Voenizdat, 1975), 83.

71. Woff, "Konstantin Konstantinovich Rokossovsky," 177.

72. Iu. D. Zakharov, *General armii Vatutin* (Moscow: Voenizdat, 1985); and David M. Glantz, "Nikolai Fedorovich Vatutin," in Shukman, *Stalin's Generals*, 287–98. Vatutin joined the Red Army in 1920 and saw only minimal service during the Russian Civil War. After serving in staff, school, and infantry assignments during the 1920s, he graduated from the Frunze Academy, where he attracted the attention of Shaposhnikov, the academy's director. After graduating from the General Staff Academy's shortened class of 1937, Vatutin served as chief of staff of the Kiev Special Military District, chief of the General Staff's Operations Directorate, and first deputy chief of the General Staff. Described by his contemporaries as a penultimate staff officer, Vatutin long cherished a desire to command. The energetic Vatutin planned the incursion into Poland in September 1939 and into Romanian Belorussia in June 1940.

73. Chistiakov, *Sluzhim otchizne*, 89.

74. Malinovsky fought with and deserted from a Russian expeditionary force in France during the World War. Returning to Russia through Vladivostok, Malinovsky rose through the Red Army ranks during fighting in the Far East, commanded at subunit level in the 1920s, and attended the Frunze Academy in 1930. Thereafter, he served in cavalry staff and command assignments until "volunteering" for service in the International Brigade fighting in the Spanish Civil War. After his return from Spain in 1938, he miraculously escaped the purges and taught at the Frunze Academy. See V. S. Golubovich, *Marshal Malinovsky* (Moscow: Voenizdat, 1984); and John Erickson, "Rodion Iakovlevich Malinovsky," in Shukman, *Stalin's Generals*, 117–24.

75. Woff, "Rokossovsky," 187.

76. Govorov graduated from an artillery course in 1926, the Higher Academy Course in 1930, the Frunze Academy in 1933, and the General Staff Academy in 1938. During the World War he was drafted into the tsarist army in December 1916, attended the Konstantinovskoe Artillery Academy, and served as a junior officer in a mortar battery in Tomsk. After being drafted into Admiral Kolchak's White Army in October 1918, he deserted along with his battery, joined the Red Guard, and, later, the Red Army in 1920. Thereafter, he fought with the Eastern and Southern Fronts, rising to command an artillery battalion. After war's end, he served as an artillery battalion commander and as commander of the famous 51st Perekop Rifle Division's artillery regiment in 1924. When not in school during the 1930s, Govorov served as chief of artillery in the 14th and 15th Rifle Corps and the Rybnitsa Fortified Region and taught at the Dzerzhinsky Artillery Academy. See *VE*, II: 438.

77. Shtemenko, *The Soviet General Staff at War*, I: 368.

78. Zhukov, *Reminiscences and Reflections*, I: 371, 381, 385.

79. The Central Front, which was formed around a nucleus of the Don Front's headquarters and its 65th and 21st Armies and was reinforced by the 2nd Tank and 70th Armies from the RVGK, was formed to spearhead the Orel-Briansk-Smolensk offensive west of Kursk.

80. On 31 December 1943, the Red Army included the Karelian, Leningrad, Volkhov, 2nd Baltic, 1st Baltic, Western, Belorussian, and 1st, 2nd, 3rd, and 4th Ukrainian Fronts.

81. Throughout the year the Karelian, Leningrad, Volkhov, Western, Don (Central and Belorussian), Voronezh (1st Ukrainian), Steppe (2nd Ukrainian), and Southwestern (3rd Ukrainian) Fronts had only one commander each, the Briansk (Baltic and 1st Baltic), North Caucasus, and Southern (4th Ukrainian) had two each, and the Northwestern and Kalinin (1st Baltic) Fronts had a total of three each.

82. See *VOV,* 73; and *VE,* I: 337–38. After serving as a junior officer in the tsarist army during the World War, Bagramian joined the Red Army in 1920 and helped solidify Bolshevik power in Armenia and Georgia during the Russian Civil War. A cavalry officer during the 1920s and 1930s, he graduated from the Frunze Academy in 1934 and the General Staff Academy in 1938, after which he lectured at the academy for four more years. Although initially eclipsed by such famous cavalry luminaries as Zhukov and Eremenko, with Zhukov's assistance Bagramian was appointed, first, as chief of operations in the 12th Army in Zhukov's Kiev Special Military District in early 1940 and then as deputy chief of operations in the same military district three months later, a post that then Colonel Bagramian occupied when war broke out in June 1941.

83. Geoffrey Jukes, "Ivan Khristoforovich Bagramian," in Shukman, *Stalin's Generals,* 32.

84. "Vasilii Danilovich Sokolovsky," in *SVE,* VII: 436–37. A veteran of the Russian Civil War and a 1921 graduate of the RKKA Military Academy, Sokolovsky fought the Basmachi (guerrillas) in Central Asia and served in key staff and command positions in several rifle divisions, a rifle corps, and in the Volga, Ural, and Moscow Military Districts during the interwar years. Zhukov appointed him as his deputy chief of the General Staff in February 1941.

85. For the censorship regarding Sokolovsky's wartime career, see Gareev, "O neudachnykh nastupatel'nykh operatsiiakh sovetskikh voisk," 3–27. Although Gareev was the first to detail hidden aspects of the failed Belorussian operation in the fall of 1943 and winter of 1943–44, he failed to mention the Kalinin (1st Baltic) Front's participation in the offensive.

86. Also a veteran of the World and Civil wars, Tiulenev had graduated from the Military Academy of the RKKA in 1922 and a Higher Command Cadre Course in 1929 and was serving as commander of the Moscow Military District by 1940.

87. *SVE,* VI: 312–13.

88. Grigorenko, *Memoirs,* 151. See also, Shtemenko, *The Soviet General Staff at War,* I: 319, for verification of Grigorenko's judgments.

89. See *VOV,* 210; and Gabriel Gorodetsky, "Filip Ivanovich Golikov," in Shukman, *Stalin's Generals,* 77–88.

90. See *VOV,* 594–95.

91. Kurochkin, who fought during the Russian Civil War, graduated from the Frunze Academy in 1932 and the General Staff Academy in 1940 and commanded the 28th Rifle Corps during the Soviet-Finnish War.

92. Ibid., 393.

93. Ibid., 444; and Geoffrey Jukes, "Kiril Afanasievich Meretskov," in Shukman, *Stalin's Generals*, 127–34.

94. Shtemenko, *The General Staff at War*, II: 373.

95. A Russian Civil War veteran, Frolov graduated from the "Vystrel'" Course in 1924 and the Frunze Academy in 1932 and commanded the 14th Army during the Soviet-Finnish War.

96. *VOV*, 763.

97. In addition, one army was subordinate to the Khar'kov Military District and five armies were subordinate to the Trans-Baikal Military District and Far Eastern Front, bringing the total of armies to 27.

98. For example, counting armies that were destroyed or decimated, the *Stavka* formed or reformed four armies (the 10th, 16th, 19th, and 26th) three times and 12 armies (the 3rd–6th, 12th, 13th, 20th, 21st, 24th, 28th, 31st, and 37th) twice. Worse still from the standpoint of command turbulence, one army (the 8th) had six commanders, for an average of one per month, five armies (the 4th, 13th, 21st, 42nd, and 43rd) had five commanders each, two armies (the 34th and 38th) had four commanders each, and 14 armies (the 3rd, 5th, 10th, 12th, 18th, 19th, 22nd, 23rd, 24th, 31st, 32nd, 50th, 51st, and 54th) had three commanders each. Only nine armies (the 11th, 27th, 40th, 49th, 57th, 59th, 60th, and the 1st and 2nd Shock) had only a single commander each, although the *Stavka* formed most of these armies late in the year.

99. The Red Army also included eight armies stationed in its internal military districts or assigned to its nonoperating *fronts* by 31 December 1942.

100. For example, considering outright destruction or decimation, one army (the 2nd Shock) experienced three formations or reorganizations, and ten armies (6th, 24th, 28th, 38th, 39th, 44th, 51st, 57th, 58th, and 1st Guards) were formed or reformed twice. Throughout the year, one army (the 44th) had eight commanders, two armies (the 24th and 47th) had six commanders each, three armies (the 9th, 51st and 57th) had five commanders each, six armies (the 28th, 38th, 40th, 58th, 66th, and 2nd Shock) had four commanders each, and 13 armies (the 3rd, 4th, 5th, 8th, 18th, 21st, 31st, 33rd, 46th, 62nd, the 1st and 4th Shock, and the 1st Guards [1st formation]) had three commanders each. Only 14 armies (the 19th, 23rd, 26th, 27th, 42nd, 43rd, 48th, 49th, 55th, 63rd [2nd formation], 67th, 70th, the 1st Guards [3rd formation], and the Separate Coastal) had just one commander each.

101. For example, only the 6th and 37th Armies went through two formations in 1943, and the remaining armies experienced considerable stability throughout the year. Overall during 1943, one army (the 47th) had six commanders, two (the 9th and 20th) had five commanders each, six (the 18th, 24th [4th Guards], 46th, 53rd, 70th, and 4th Shock) had four commanders each, and ten (the 5th, 11th, 16th [11th Guards], 30th [10th Guards], 34th, 37th, 51st, 56th, and the 2nd and 3rd Guards) had three commanders each. On the other hand, 25 armies (the 4th, 8th, 10th, 13th, 14th, 21st [6th Guards], 23rd, 29th, 32nd, 33rd, 41st, 43rd, 44th, 45th, 50th, 55th,

58th, 60th, 61st, 62nd [8th Guards], 64th [7th Guards], 65th, 66th [5th Guards], 5th Shock, and Separate Coastal) had just a single commander each.

102. For a comprehensive listing of all officers who commanded at the corps and division (and tank brigade) level during the war and their tenure in command, see *Komandovanie korpusnogo i divizionnogo zvena Sovetskikh vooruzhennykh sil perioda VOV 1941–1945* [Commanders at the corps and division levels of the Soviet Armed Forces during the Great Patriotic War 1941–1945] (Moscow: Frunze Academy, 1964), which provides all the data used to analyze command at these levels during the war.

103. In addition, the 30th Mechanized Corps, which was stationed in the Far East, never functioned in combat as a complete corps.

104. These tank divisions included the 61 divisions assigned to its mechanized corps when war began and ten so-called 100–series tank divisions, which the *Stavka* formed in August 1941, primarily on the base of older tank divisions. By year's end, however, the *Stavka* had either disbanded most of these divisions or converted them into new-model smaller tank brigades.

105. Among the most illustrious Red Army tank division commanders was A. L. Getman, whose 112th Tank Division accompanied P. A. Belov's renowned 1st Cavalry Corps on its famous deep operations against Guderian's Second Panzer Group south of Moscow in December 1941.

106. This number includes two commanders for the 3rd (2nd Guards) Cavalry Corps and one each for the five other corps.

107. On 1 June 1942, the Red Army also included three cavalry and three tank corps in its military districts and nonoperating *fronts,* for a grand total of 13 cavalry and 19 tank corps in the Red Army. On 1 September the Red Army also included three cavalry corps in its military districts and nonoperating *fronts,* for a grand total of 33 mobile corps.

108. On 31 December the Red Army also included two cavalry and two tank corps in its military districts and nonoperating *fronts,* for a grand total of 38 mobile corps.

109. One of the 2nd Guards Cavalry Corps' divisions broke through German defenses and spent a month in the *Wehrmacht's* rear area before making its way back to the Red Army's lines.

110. The NKO converted the 8th, 14th, 22nd, 27th, and 28th Tank Corps into the 3rd, 6th, 5th, 1st, and 4th Mechanized Corps, respectively, and formed the 4th, 3rd Guards, and 2nd Guards Mechanized Corps during the second half of 1942.

111. During this period, one tank corps (the 2nd) had six commanders, two (the 17th and 23rd) had four commanders each, and two (the 8th [3rd Mechanized] and 18th) had three commanders each. At the other extreme, 11 tank and mechanized corps (the 5th, 6th, 10th, 15th, 19th, 20th, 21st, and 25th Tank and the 2nd and the 1st and 2nd Guards Mechanized Corps) had only a single commander, although one of these tank corps (the 21st) was destroyed in its first offensive action shortly after its creation.

112. The only exceptions to this rule occurred during the Western Front's Rzhev-Sychevka offensive of July and August, when Getmans' 6th and Solomatin's 8th Tank Corps, both operating with the 2nd Guards Cavalry Corps in a mobile group commanded by I. V. Galanin, the deputy commander of the Western Front, successfully

penetrated *Wehrmacht* defenses until halted by fierce counterattacks along the Vazuza River. In addition, in Operation Mars in November, Solomatin's and Katukov's 1st and 3rd Mechanized Corps operated effectively under Kalinin Front control, although in this instance the Western Front's failure to achieve success in its offensive sector spoiled Katukov's and Solomatin's efforts and led to the destruction of the latter's corps.

113. On 1 June the Red Army also included two cavalry, three tank, and three mechanized corps in its military districts and nonoperating *fronts,* for a grand total of 45 mobile corps, and on 31 December it also included one cavalry and one mechanized corps in its military districts and nonoperating *fronts,* for a grand total of 45 mobile corps.

114. One cavalry corps (the 8th [7th Guards]) had five commanders, two (the 4th and 4th Guards) had two commanders each, but the remaining six had only a single commander each.

115. For example, 2 corps (the 15th [7th Guards] and 18th Tank) had five commanders each, four corps (the 9th, 12th [6th Guards], 16th and 20th Tank) had four commanders each, and five corps (the 3rd, 10th, 11th, 19th, and 1st Guards Tank) had three commanders. At the other extreme, 14 corps (the 1st, 2nd [8th Guards], 4th [5th Guards], 5th, 6th [11th Guards], 13th [4th Guards Mechanized], 23rd, and 30th [10th Guards] Tank and the 1st, 2nd [7th Guards], 5th [9th Guards], and 1st, 2nd, and 6th Guards Mechanized Corps) had only a single commander each.

116. Katukov commanded the 1st [Guards] Tank Army; Rodin and Bogdanov, the 2nd and 2nd Guards Tank Army; Badanov, the 4th Tank Army; Rotmistrov, Sinenko, and Vol'sky, the 5th Guards Tank Army; and Kravchenko, the 6th [Guards] Tank Army.

117. During this period, the 5th Tank Army had four commanders, the 3rd Tank Army two, and the 1st and 4th Tank Armies one each.

118. Thereafter, Moskalenko commanded the 1st Guards, 40th, and 38th Armies to war's end, Rybalko commanded the 3rd Guards Tank Army from the Battle of Kursk through the Battle for Berlin, Romanenko commanded the 48th Army and the Eastern Siberian Military District to war's end, Kriuchenkin commanded the 69th and 33rd Armies before ending the war as deputy *front* commander, and Popov commanded the Reserve, Briansk, Baltic and 2nd Baltic Fronts before ending the war as a *front* chief of staff.

119. For example, the old-style 2nd Tank Army had three commanders, the first formation 5th Tank Army had two commanders, and Mobile Group Popov and the 3rd Tank Army had one commander each. On the other hand, all five of the new-model tank armies (the 1st, 3rd [3rd Guards], 4th, and 5th Guards) each had only one commander each during 1943.

120. Shtemenko, *The General Staff at War,* I: 479.

121. D. D. Leliushenko, A. G. Kravchenko, and V. T. Vol'sky emerged as equally effective tank army commanders in 1944.

122. Shtemenko, *The Soviet General Staff at War,* I: 479.

123. For further details, see Richard N. Armstrong, *Red Army Tank Commanders: The Armored Guards* (Atglen, PA: Schiffer, 1994), 332.

124. Shtemenko, *The General Staff at War,* I: 479.

125. Armstrong, *Red Army Tank Commanders,* 94–95.

126. Ibid., 376–77.

127. Shtemenko, *The General Staff at War,* I: 479.

128. Bogdanov's deputy commander, A. I. Radzievsky, commanded the 2nd Tank Army during its controversial advance exploitation from Lublin to the gates of Warsaw in July and August 1944, where heavy *Wehrmacht* counterstrokes thwarted the tank army's efforts to rescue the Polish underground, which had seized part of the inner city, in the process badly damaging the tank army.

129. Shtemenko, *The General Staff at War,* I: 479.

130. Armstrong, *Red Army Tank Commanders,* 155.

131. For example, one sapper army (the 8th) had five commanders in 12 months; two armies (the 3rd and 6th) had four commanders each in 12 and 11 months, respectively; three armies (the 1st, 4th, and 7th) had three commanders each in eight, six, and ten months, respectively; two armies (the 5th and 9th) had two commanders each in four months; and only two sapper armies (the 2nd and 10th) had one commander each during the four months each existed.

132. For example, D. A. Zhuravlev commanded the Western and Northwestern PVO Districts from war's end to 1954 and later served as deputy commander of PVO Strany and chief of VNOS radio-technical forces and services within PVO Strany. His counterpart, M. S. Gromadin, became chief of PVO Strany from 1950 to 1954, G. S. Zashikhin became a district and regional PVO commander until his death in 1950, and P. E. Gudymenko commanded the Northwestern PVO District from 1946 to 1948 and, thereafter, served as deputy commander of other PVO districts and regions before his death in 1953.

133. For example, shortly before war began, Stalin ordered Beriia, his state security chief, to arrest Lieutenant Generals of Aviation Ia. Smushkevich and P. V. Rychagov and Colonel General A. D. Loktionov, all former VVS commanders, and both were shot for treason on 28 October 1941. Worse still, the same fate befell Lieutenant General of Aviation P. I. Pumpur, the commander of the Moscow Military District's Air Forces, who was arrested on 31 May 1941 on trumped up charges of treason and was shot in February or March 1942.

134. For example, when the Western Front collapsed during the first few days of war, Beriia arrested Major General of Aviation A. I. Taursky, deputy commander of the Western Front's air forces, and executed him on 22 July 1941, along with the unfortunate *front* commander, D. G. Pavlov. Taursky suffered this ignominious fate simply because the Western Front's air force commander, Major General of Aviation I. I. Kopets, had anticipated Stalin's reaction and committed suicide on the third day of the war. For details, see Parrish, *The Lesser Terror,* 76–81.

135. The *Stavka* formed the first group of five air armies specifically to support the Red Army's offensive operations in the spring of 1942, the second group of nine air armies to stiffen its defense in the summer, and the final group of three air armies to support its offensive operations in November and December.

136. For example, in 1942 the 1st, 2nd, 4th, and 16th Air Armies had two commanders each and the remainder had only one.

137. Khriukhin became a "Hero" in February 1938 for his role in defeating Japanese forces at Lake Khasan in 1938, and Kutsevalov became a Hero in November 1939 for flying 59 sorties and shooting down nine Japanese aircraft while commanding the 56th Fighter Aviation Regiment during the battle at Khalkhin Gol. Piatykhin was honored as a Hero in April 1940 after he distinguished himself as commander of the Northwestern Front's 15th Bomber Aviation Brigade during the Russo-Finnish War. Finally, Gromov became a Hero in 1934 for establishing a nonstop flight record of 12,000 kilometers. See I. N. Shkadov, ed., *Geroi Sovetskogo soiuza v dvukh tomakh* [Heroes of the Soviet Union in two volumes] (Moscow: Voenizdat, 1987).

138. While the 6th, 7th, and 8th Fighter Aviation Corps PVO had two commanders each, the remaining 17 had only one, although many of the corps either disbanded in August 1941 or formed in late 1942.

139. During this period, the 1st, 2nd, 3rd, 4th, 6th, 15th, and 17th Air Armies had two commanders each, and the remainder had only one each.

140. Khriukhin earned his Hero award in April 1945 for his courageous leadership of the 3rd Belorussian Front's 1st Air Army during the Battle for Berlin.

141. Seven aviation corps (the 1st and 2nd Bomber Aviation, the 2nd and 5th Mixed Aviation, the 5th and 6th Fighter Aviation, and the 7th Fighter Aviation PVO Corps) had two commanders each and the remaining 33 corps had only one commander each.

13. The Red Army Soldier

1. In the wake of M. V. Frunze's reforms, the Red Army in 1928 consisted of a nucleus of 28 regular (cadre) rifle and 11 cavalry divisions formed on a national (all-union) basis and manned at two levels of fill in peacetime, which were to be assigned to 20 rifle corps in the army's operating forces during wartime, and 45 territorial (militia) divisions formed on a regional basis and manned at three strength levels during peacetime, which were to fill out the army's 20 regular rifle corps and form additional rifle corps if necessary during wartime. First-line regular (cadre) divisions consisted of 6,300 permanent cadre and 12,300 mobilization personnel, and the second line consisted of 604 permanent personnel and 11,750 mobilization personnel. First-, second-, and third-line territorial divisions consisted of 2,400, 604 or 622, and 190 cadre and 10,681, 11,734 or 11,750, and over 12,000 reservists, respectively. In some instances, some territorial division formed the nucleus of up to three new divisions. See I. Berkhin, "O territorial'no-militsionnom stroitel'stve v Sovetskoi Armii" [On territorial-militia construction in the Soviet army], *VIZh*, no. 12 (December 1960): 15–16.

2. See S. V. Lipitsky, "Voennaia reforma 1924–1925 godov" [The military reforms of 1924–1925], *Kommunist* [Communist], no. 4 (March 1990): 69, 105: "The territorial [militia] formations were deployed in the internal military districts, primarily in economically developed regions with adequate population densities. As a rule, the boundaries of the districts where the divisions, regiments, and battalions were staffed and deployed corresponded to the boundaries of provinces *[gubernii]*, regions *[uezdy]*, and districts *[volosti]*. This made possible the close rapprochement and merger of the armed forces with the masses of toiling people and the Soviets [councils]."

Frunze's reforms also included a Law on Universal Military Service, which required all male citizens between the ages of 19 and 40 to undergo two years of pre-induction military training at local military commissariats and serve two to five years in the Red Army before entering the reserves. Up to 90 percent of the personnel assigned to territorial (militia) formations were draftees living in that region who received three months of combat and political training in their units and subunits during their first year of service and one to two months during their next four years of service. The territorial soldiers lived at home and worked at their civilian jobs between training periods during their five years of service.

3. Pavlovsky, *Sukhoputnye voiska SSSR,* 65–68.

4. N. A. Mal'tsev, "Kadrovaia ili militsionnaia" [Cadre or militia], *VIZh,* no. 11 (November 1989): 38. According to this plan, the Red Army was to consist of 106 divisions by 1 January 1938, including 71 regular (cadre) division, and complete transforming all divisions to a regular (cadre) organization by early 1939.

5. See Pavlovsky, *Sukhoputnye voiska SSSR,* 65. The Red Army consisted of 49 cadre rifle, four cadre mountain rifle, 35 territorial, and four mixed rifle divisions and two separate territorial regiments on 1 January 1937 and 85 cadre rifle and 14 cadre cavalry divisions and five separate brigades on 1 January 1939.

6. Ibid.

7. For example, during the Spanish Civil War (1937–1939), the Soviet Union actively supported the Republican government's struggle against Franco's Nationalists with a significant amount of military weaponry and supplies at a time when Hitler and his ally Mussolini were supporting Franco in similar fashion. Later, after World War II began, Red Army forces invaded eastern Poland in September 1939 in conjunction with *Wehrmacht* forces after Stalin negotiated a cynical nonaggression pact with Hitler, and, on the other side of the world, a Red Army corps under Zhukov's command defeated two Japanese divisions at Khalkhin Gol in eastern Mongolia in August and September 1939. Finally, the Red Army fought a bloody and embarrassingly unsuccessful war with Finland in late 1939 and early 1940 and, later, occupied the Baltic region and Romanian Bessarabia.

8. Pavlovsky, *Sukhoputnye voiska SSSR,* 65–68; G. F. Krivosheev, ed., *Rossiia i SSSR v voinakh XX veka, poteri vooruzhennykh sil: Statisticheskoe issledovanie* [Russia and the USSR in twentieth-century wars and the losses of the armed forces: A statistical investigation] (Moscow: Olma-Press, 2001), 220; and, for a definition of the BUS, Glantz, *Stumbling Colossus,* 101. On 22 June 1941, the Soviet Armed Forces consisted of 4,826,907 men in the Red Army and Navy, 74,945 men assigned to NKO duties, and 805,264 men involved in large training exercises (BUS) who were awaiting assignment to mobilized units, for a total of 5,707,116 men.

9. Lensky, *Sukhoputnye sily RKKA v predvoennye gody,* 59.

10. Krivosheev, *Rossiia i SSSR v voinakh XX veka,* 247.

11. The 4 July decree was numbered 10ss and entitled "Concerning the Volunteer Mobilization of Workers in Moscow and the Moscow Region in People's Militia Divisions (DNO)." The other decrees formed the 1st, 2nd, and 3rd Kuban Cossack Cavalry Divisions (later designated the 10th, 12th, and 13th) in the Krasnodar region; four rifle divisions with 48,000 men in the Crimea; one rifle (unnumbered) and

the 15th Cavalry Division in the Stalingrad region; the 116th Don Cossack Cavalry Division in the Rostov region; the 49th and 332nd Rifle Divisions in Ivanovo; 234th Rifle Division in Iaroslavl', the 186th Rifle Division in Murmansk; two mixed rifle corps in Khar'kov and Dnepropetrovsk; eight rifle divisions in Voroshilovgrad, the Stalinsk and Sumy region, Kremenchug, and Kirovograd; and one rifle division in Vitebsk—for a total of 60 divisions, 36 of which ultimately joined the Red Army. On 16 July GKO Decree No. 172ss organized ten of its DNOs with 100,000 men into two armies with five divisions each and dispatched them to the Mozhaisk Defense Line. For this and subsequent GKO decrees, see Gor'kov, *Gosudarstvennyi komitet oborony postanovliaet,* 117–21.

12. Ibid., 118. This GKO decree was numbered 48ss and entitled "Concerning the Formation of Additional Rifle Divisions."

13. The 100-series tank divisions were supposed to field 217 tanks each.

14. Gor'kov, *Gosudarstvennyi komitet oborony postanovliaet,* 118. These GKO decrees were numbered 459ss and 570ss, and the latter was entitled, "Concerning Tank Units." The rifle divisions were to be prepared for combat duty by 15 November and the cavalry divisions by 15 December; to speed up the formation process, the GKO ordered them to form in major cities instead of union republics. The new tank brigades were supposed to field 93 tanks each.

15. Ibid. This GKO decree pertaining to the rifle divisions was numbered 796ss and ordered the NKO to concentrate these divisions in the Moscow region "as soon as possible." The second GKO decree was numbered 810ss and entitled "Concerning the Formation of Separate Rifle Brigades."

16. Ibid., 120. This GKO decree was numbered 966ss and entitled "Concerning the Reduction of [the Size] of the Army."

17. Ibid., 122. This GKO decree was numbered 1295ss and entitled "Concerning the Formation of Tank Brigades in February–March 1942." These new brigades were supposed to field 46 tanks each.

18. A. D. Kolesnik, *Opolchenskie formirovaniia Rossiiskoi Federatsii v gody Velikoi Otechestvennoi voiny* [Militia formations of the Russian Federation during the Great Patriotic War] (Moscow: Nauka, 1988), 7–38.

19. These calculations are based on 10,000 men per DNO. Although the DNOs entered the army with their own unique numerical designations, 36 later received new Red Army numerical designations. The GKO and NKO formed 661 divisions of various types by war's end, including 490 rifle, 18 airborne, 91 cavalry, one motorized, 13 NKVD, and 11 tank divisions, and 37 DNOs with a total strength of about 6,610,000 men. On an annualized basis, the GKO fielded 419 divisions in 1941, 126 in 1942, 92 in 1943, 22 in 1944, and two in 1945. In addition, the GKO formed 666 brigades in 1941 and 1942, including 313 rifle, 22 airborne, 48 motorized, 32 mechanized, and 251 tank, plus 128 brigades whose troops it assigned to other units before their formation was complete, with a total strength of 3,330,000 men (calculated on the basis of 5,000 men per brigade and 12,000 men per division). Therefore, considering two brigades equivalent to one division, the GKO began the war with a force of 303 divisions and formed another 981 division equivalents by war's end. However, during the war, but particularly during its first 18 months, the *Wehrmacht* destroyed

297 Red Army divisions and 85 brigades, including 215 rifle, 45 cavalry, 12 motorized, and 25 tank divisions and 51 rifle, two airborne, six motorized rifle, two mechanized, and 24 tank brigades. See Gor'kov, *Gosudarstvennyi komitet oborony postanovliaet,* 117; and *Liudskie poteri SSSR v period Vtoroi Mirovoi voiny: Sbornik statei* [Personnel losses of the USSR in the Second World War: A collection of articles] (Saint Petersburg: Russian Academy of Sciences, 1995), 72.

20. "GKO postanovliaet" [The GKO decrees], *VIZh,* no. 2 (February 1992): 34.

21. See Zolotarev, "NKO 1941," 71. This was NKO Directive No. 55, "Concerning the Replacement of Junior Command Cadre and Young Soldiers in Rear Service Units and Installations."

22. Iuri Koriakhin, "Memories of War," in *Memories of War: The Experiences of Red Army Veterans of the Great Patriotic War,* vol. 8 (Carlisle, PA: Self-published, 2001), 1.

23. *Red Army Officers Speak,* 60. This interview is with V. A. Dontsov, chief of staff of the 107th Rifle Division's 504th Rifle Regiment, which was assigned to the 60th Army's 15th Rifle Corps.

24. The was *Stavka* Order No. 089. See Zolotarev, "Stavka VGK 1942," 88–89.

25. "Boevaia kharakteristika na 121 sd" [Combat characteristics of the 121st Rifle Division], from "Boevye rasporiazheniia shtaba Voronezhskogo fronta" [Combat orders of the Voronezh Front], *TsAMO,* f. 417, op. 10564, d. 252, l. 12.

26. "Boevaia kharakteristika na 248 otdel'nuiu kursantskuiu strelkovuiu brigadu" [Combat characteristics of the 248th Student Rifle Brigade], from "Boevye rasporiazheniia shtaba Voronezhskogo fronta," l. 13.

27. "Komandiram 1, 2, 3 armeiskikh zagradotriadov. 16.3.43g. No. 0224" [Order No. 0224, dated 16 March 1943, to the commanders of the 1st, 2nd, and 3rd Army Blocking Detachments], from "Direktivy SVGK, GSh, KA voiskam Brianskogo fronta, 13A, 2.1–20.7.43" [Directives of the *Stavka* of the Supreme High Command to the Briansk Front and the 13th Army, 2 January to 20 July 1943], *TsAMO,* f. 361, op. 6079, d. 173, l. 105.

28. See Zolotarev, "NKO 1943," 216. This was Order No. 0430.

29. Ibid., 219.

30. Igor Mangazeev, "A 'Penal' Corps on the Kalinin Front," *JSMS* 15, no. 3 (September 2002): 123. In March 1940 the NKVD's GULAG system consisted of 53 separate labor camps and work projects manned by 1,668,200 prisoners and 107,000 guards, and the number of prisoners rose to between 2 million and 2.3 million by 22 June 1941. Many of these prisoners were products of either outright political repression or the mass resettlement of "unreliable elements" of Soviet society, meaning ethnic or religious groups that Soviet authorities perceived as threats to the Soviet state.

In addition to peasants who resisted Stalin's forced collectivization program during the late 1920s and 1930s, prisoners included Germans transported from the Volga region and other localities and, later, Crimean Tartars, Chechens, and other nationalities transported because they demonstrated the slightest receptivity to German propaganda or disloyalty to Stalin and the Soviet authorities. Between 1941 and 1944, the Soviet authorities forcibly exiled tens of thousands of these peoples to camps in remote regions of the Soviet Union such as Kazakhstan and Siberia. However, the number of prisoners lodged in GULAG labor camps and other work projects decreased significantly to about 1.2 million persons on 1 June 1944.

31. Ibid., 123. Kulaks were termed "special migrants" *(spetspereselentsy)* prior to 1934, "labor deportees" *(trudposelentsy)* from 1934 to March 1944, and "special migrants from the former kulak contingent" *(spetspereselentsy kontingenta 'byvshie kulaki')* after March 1944.

32. Ibid., 120–21.

33. Ibid., 120.

34. Ibid., 123. This was GKO Order No. 1575ss.

35. Ibid., 124. This was NKVD Order No. 002303, "On Removing Labor Deportees Conscripted into the Red Army and Their Family Members from the Lists of Labor Exiles."

36. Ibid.

37. Ibid., 124–25. The 75th Omsk Rifle Brigade included 1,200 Siberian labor deportees.

38. The 74th Rifle Brigade, which formed in the Kuznets Basin (Kuzbas) region in July 1942, consisted primarily of so-called special volunteers, who were actually prisoners from NKVD camps and labor colonies.

39. Ibid., 126, 136. For example, every third man in the 6,720-man 91st Rifle Brigade was a Party or Komsomol member. Local records also indicate that, of the 6th Rifle Corps' total strength of 37,500 men, 44 percent were industrial workers or miners, 26.6 percent were peasants, and 29.4 percent were white collar workers, while 38.6 percent of the corps were Party or Komsomol members and up to 40 percent special volunteers from former labor deportees. Attesting to this fact, Colonel Mikhail Ivanovich Rybkin, who was serving in 2002 as military commissioner of the Altai Republic, reported that. during the war, "Everyone—the young and old, the sick and healthy, men and women, and volunteers and those unwilling to fight—was drafted. In all, 42,268 men were drafted from the Oirota Autonomous Oblast' [district]."

40. This decree, which responded to a GKO decree dated 7 January, was entitled "Concerning Procedures for the Early Removal of Loss of Rights [Disenfranchisement] Regarding Persons Who Have Served Most of Their Punishment and Whose Age Subjects Them to Conscription or Mobilization."

41. Ibid., 109–10.

42. Zolotarev, "NKO 1943," 198. This was Order No. 0413, "Concerning the Granting of Rights to Unit and Formation Commanders to Send Sergeants and Rank and File Soldiers Judged Guilty of Some Types of Crimes to Penal Companies on Their Own Authority and without Trial."

43. Ibid., 214–42. This was NKO Order No. 004/0073/006/23ss, "Concerning the Order of Employing Note 2 to Article 28 of the USSR's Legal Code (and the Corresponding Articles in the Legal Codes of the Union Republics) and Sending the Condemned to the Operating Army."

44. Ibid.

45. For additional details, see V. V. Gradosel'sky, "Natsional'nye voinskie formirovaniia v Krasnoi Armii (1918–1938 gg.) [National military formation in the Red

Army (1918–1938)], *VIZh*, no. 10 (October 2001): 4. The 7 March 1938 decree of the Communist Party's Central Committee, "Concerning the RKKA's National Units and Formations," reorganized all formations, military academies, and schools as all-union, based on the principle of "extraterritoriality."

46. Ibid., 4.

47. Zolotarev, *Velikaia Otechestvennaia voina 1941–1945,* IV: 13–14.

48. *Red Army Officers Speak,* 116–17. The interview is with Iu. A. Naumenko, commander of the 97th Guards Rifle Division's 289th Guards Rifle Regiment, which was assigned to the 5th Guards Army's 32nd Guards Rifle Corps.

49. Historians are just beginning to lift the veil of secrecy cloaking this subject. Among these are Kazimiera J. Cottam, who has written several books, including *Women in War and Resistance: Selected Biographies of Soviet Women Soldiers;* and Reina Pennington, who wrote the recent study, *Wings, Women, and War: Soviet Airwomen in World War II Combat.* Both relied heavily on oral history to document the combat and noncombat achievements of Russian women during the war.

50. Simeon Aria, "From Tanks to Katiushas," in *Memories of War,* V: 21.

51. See *VOV,* 269–70:

> Women entered the ranks of the Soviet Army from the first days of the war, voluntarily, in the people's militia divisions. A massive mobilization of women began on the basis of GKO decrees dated 25 March and 13 and 23 April 1942. On the basis of the conscription of Komsomol members alone, more than 550,000 patriots–representatives of all nationalities in the country–became soldiers. More than 300,000 women were called up into the PVO forces (more than one quarter of all of the soldiers in that branch), and hundreds of thousands entered service in the military-medical facilities of the Soviet Army's medical service, in the signal forces, in road units, and in other services.
>
> In May 1942 the GKO issued a decree concerning the mobilization of 25,000 women into the navy. Communist women conducted five mobilizations. Along the line of the Red Cross, 300,000 women received the specialty of nurse, 300,000 as medical orderlies, and more than 500,000 as medical helpers in MPVO. 220,000 young girl-snipers, communicators, and others were trained in youth subunits of Vsevobuch.
>
> Three aviation regiments, one of which was commanded by Hero of the Soviet Union M. M. Raskova, were formed from women. Hero of the Soviet Union V. S. Grizodubova commanded the 101st Long-Range Aviation Regiment. The 1st Separate Women's Volunteer Rifle Brigade [based in Moscow], the 1st Women's Reserve Rifle Regiment, and the Central Women's School for Sniper Training were formed, and other women participated in decisive operations of the Red Army. In addition, more than 100,000 women fought in the partisan movement and in the Party and Komsomol underground.
>
> More than 150,000 women were awarded with combat orders and medals for bravery in the struggle against the German-fascist invaders. More than 200 persons received the Order of Glory 2nd and 3rd degree, and N. A. Zhirkina, N. P. Petrova, D. Iu. Staniliene, and M. S. Necheporchukova became full cavaliers of the Order of Glory. Eighty-six Soviet women were awarded with the rank of Hero of the Soviet Union, including 29 pilots, 26 partisans, and 17 medical service workers, 18 of whom received the reward posthumously.

According to Cottam, *Women in War and Resistance,* xx, recently published Russian statistics indicate a total of about 220,000 women received military training through VSEVOBUCH, including at a minimum 6,097 mortar operators, 4,522 heavy machine gunners, 7,796 light machine gunners, 15,290 submachine gunners, 102,333 snipers, and 49,509 communications specialists, for a total of 185,547 women soldiers.

52. See Zolotarev, "NKO 1941," 112–13. This was NKO Order No. 0099, "Concerning the Formation of Women's Aviation Regiments in the Red Army's VVS."

53. Ibid., 184–85. This was NKO Order No. 0058, "Concerning the Conscription of Women-Komsomol Members into PVO Forces."

54. Ibid., 195–96. This was NKO Order No. 0065, "Concerning the Allocation of Servicemen Fit for Field Duty from Red Army Rear Service Units and Installations," and the GKO decree upon which it was based was numbered 1562ss.

55. Ibid.

56. Ibid., 212–13. This was NKO Order No. 0284, "Concerning the Mobilization of Women to Replace Red Army Men in the Signal Services."

57. Ibid.

58. These "excess personnel" included all personnel excess to approved *shtats*, male personnel assigned to specific quartermaster and goods warehouses (which were listed in an appendix to the order), and much of the extra medical support previously provided to guards rifle corps.

59. Zolotarev, "NKO 1941," 213–14, and 396, note 40. This was NKO Order No. 0296, "Concerning the Truncation of the *Shtats* of Rear Services Units and Installations and the Replacement of Red Army Men Serving Separate Duties in Military Units and Facilities with Women."

60. Ibid., 214–15. This NKO order, which responded to GKO decree no. 1618ss, dated 18 April 1942, was numbered 0297 and entitled "Concerning the Mobilization of 40,000 Women into the VVS to Replace Red Army Male Soldiers."

61. Ibid., 217–18. This was NKO Order No. 0325, "An Order Concerning the Truncation of the *Shtats* of the NKO's Main and Central Directorates and Military District Headquarters and Also Concerning the Replacement of Command and Management Cadre Fit for Line service with Older Soldiers Who Are Limited in Fitness or Unfit for Line Service and Women."

62. Zolotarev, "NKO 1943," 13–14. This was NKO Order No. 002, "Concerning a Reduction in the Number and the Replacement of Servicemen in Units and Formations in the Red Army's Tank and Mechanized Forces with Older Age [Men] and Women." The GKO decree upon which it was based was no. 2640ss dated 20 December 1942. This order required the armored and mechanized chief to report the precise number of freed up personnel to Stalin every three days beginning on 10 January 1943.

63. Ibid., 115.

64. *Liudskie poteri,* 74.

65. Numerous sources, some anecdotal but others archival, including unit reports and wartime photographs, indicate that an as yet undetermined number of women soldiers performed combat duties in combat units. However, greater access to archival materials is essential before the questions, "How many women served in combat?" and "How long did they serve?" can be adequately answered.

66. This tradition was rooted in Ivan I's (the Great) postfeudal army of the late fourteenth century and Ivan IV's (the Terrible) army of the mid-fifteenth Century. Unlike soldiers in Western armies, who evolved from serfs to freemen during this century, Russian soldiers slowly but inexorably lapsed into serfdom. Thereafter, con-

scripted peasant serfs remained the backbone of the Russian army under the rule of the early Romanov tsars and Tsars Peter I (the Great) and Catherine II (the Great) during the seventeenth and eighteenth centuries and even under the rule of Alexander I and his successors well into epoch of mass armies of the nineteenth century. Throughout this prolonged period, soldiers' living conditions and treatment during their extended tours of military service reflected their base social, economic, and political status.

Despite the military reforms of the mid-nineteenth century associated with the Russian army's defeat in the Crimean War, the liberation of the serfs in 1861, and the economic reforms at the turn of the twentieth century, which resulted in the emergence of a bourgeoisie and worker class in Russia, soldiers' lives remained particularly harsh compared with Western standards. At least in part, the crudeness and brutality that characterized soldiers' lives in Imperial Russian Army service, combined with the army's defeats and immense casualty tolls during the Russo-Japanese War (1904–1905) and the World War that followed, produced political unrest in 1905 and revolution and ultimate dissolution of the army in 1917, when the Bolsheviks seized the reins of power.

Nor did the tsarist army's collapse in 1917 and replacement in 1918 and 1919 with a new Red Army born of the Bolshevik Red Guards materially change soldiers' lives. Even though the Bolsheviks loudly proclaimed the formation of a new social and economic order in Russia and a new Red Army imbued with the consciousness of workers and peasants, the Red Army remained a mass army tightly controlled by a Communist Party perceived as besieged by capitalism from without and threatened by dangerous bourgeois influences from within.

67. See, for example, Roger R. Reese, *Stalin's Reluctant Soldiers: A Social History of the Red Army, 1925–1941* (Lawrence: University Press of Kansas, 1996).

68. Some have argued that the Red Army was an inherently Asiatic force in which human life and the human condition were of little consequence, while others have claimed the harsh conditions soldiers endured in the Red Army merely reflected the totalitarian state they served. The truth, if it can be determined at all, probably rests somewhere in between.

69. This was NKO Order No. 208.

70. Zolotarev, "NKO 1941," 393.

71. G. V. Shutz, "Memories of War," in *The Experiences of Red Army Veterans of the Great Patriotic War*, vol. 4 (Carlisle, PA: Self-published, 2001), 17–18.

72. Evgenii Moniushko, "Memoirs of the Soviet-German War, Part 4, Red Army Service in Silesia and Czechoslovakia during 1945," *JSMS* 15, no. 3 (September 2002): 193.

73. Zolotarev, "NKO 1941," 73. This was NKO Order No. 0320, "Concerning the Issuing of 100 Grams of Vodka per Day to Servicemen in the Red Army's Forward Lines."

74. Ibid., 228–29. This was NKO Order No. 0373, "Concerning the Order of Issuing Vodka to the Red Army's Operating Forces." "Vodka" holidays included the Anniversary of the Great October Socialist Revolution (7 and 8 November), Constitution Day (5 February), New Years Day, Red Army Day (23 February), International

Workers Day (1 and 2 May), All-Union Physical Culture Day (19 July), All-Union Aviation Day (16 August), International Youth Day (6 September), and the day of the unit's formation.

75. Ibid., 252–53. This was NKO Order No. 0470, "Concerning Order in the Securing and Issuing of Vodka to the Operating Army's Forces." This order reiterated the rules for distributing vodka, demanded responsible commanders assign guards to secure their vodka stores against unauthorized requisitions, and assigned specific responsibilities to key commanders and staff officers regarding implementation of the order.

76. Ibid., 365–66. This was NKO Order No. 0883, "Concerning the Issuing of Vodka to the Army's Operating Forces as of 25 November 1942."

77. This may have been indicative of the relative importance of Operations Mars (the Rzhev-Sychevka offensive), which the Western and Kalinin Fronts were to conduct during this period, and Operation Uranus (the Stalingrad offensive), which the Southwestern, Don, and Stalingrad Fronts were to conduct during this period.

78. Zolotarev, "NKO 1943," 28. This was NKO Order No. 031, "Concerning the Announcement of Norms and the Order of Issuing Vodka to Technical Personnel in the Operating Army's VVS."

79. Although no further documentation on vodka consumption is available, presumably the quantity issued corresponded to increases in Red Army offensive operations.

80. "Politdoneseniia 8Gv SK" [Political reports of the 8th Guards Rifle Corps], *TsAMO,* f. 825, op. 1, d. 411, ll. 185–86.

81. "Prikaz chastiam 121 sd No. 074. 31. 3. 43g. [Order no. 074 to the 121st Rifle Division's units, dated 31 March 1943], from "Boevye prikazy soedinenii 60A (1943g.)" [Combat orders to the 60th Army's formations (1943)], *TsAMO,* f. 417, op. 10564, d. 251, l. 6.

82. Glantz, *Stumbling Colossus,* 114.

83. Ibid., 209.

84. Ibid., 214.

85. Vladimir Dolmatov, "Memories of War," in *Memories of War,* IV: 1.

86. "GKO postanovliaet," 33.

87. Zolotarev, "NKO 1941," 49.

88. Ibid., 114–16. The was NKO Order No. 0404, "Concerning the Results of an Inspection of the Securing, Economizing, Repairing, and Accounting for Clothing [Uniform] Supplies in NKO Central and District Warehouses and Force Units in the Moscow, Orel, Khar'kov, and Volga Military Districts."

89. Ibid., 165–67. This was NKO Order No. 0169, dated 3 March 1942, "Concerning the Improving of Security and Measures to Halt the Misappropriation and Squandering of Military Uniforms."

90. Zolotarev, "NKO 1941," 191–93. This was NKO Order No. 0240, "Concerning the Order of Distributing Clothing Supplies to the Red Army during Wartime."

91. Ibid., 193–94. The GKO order upon which this NKO order was based was numbered 1490s.

92. Ibid., 194.

93. For example, countless wartime photographs of Soviet general officers, other commanders (usually standing by their 'willies' jeeps), tank crews, and aviators show them wearing the leather tanker or flight jackets so ubiquitous in the United States Army and its Air Force.

94. Koriakhin, "Memories of War," 3.

95. Moniushko, "Memoirs , part 4," 192–93.

96. See Krivosheev, *Rossiia i SSSR v voinakh XX veka,* 96–100, 263; and *Liudskie poteri,* 74. The tsar's army lost 1,890,369 men due to combat action out of a force whose total strength ranged from 2,711,253 on 1 October 1914 to 6,752,700 on 1 May 1917.

97. This order was entitled, "Concerning the Reorganization of the Organs of Political Propaganda and the Introduction of the Institute of Military Commissars in the RKKA."

98. See Zolotarev, "NKO 1941," 326–27. This was NKO Order No. 307, "Concerning the Establishment of Full Single Command and the Abolition of the Institute of Military Commissars in the Red Army."

99. See Zolotarev, "Stavka VGK 1941," 62. This directive was entitled "*Stavka* GK Directive to the Northwestern Front Commander Concerning the Conduct of Active Military Operations."

100. Zolotarev, *Velikaia Otechestvennaia voina,* I: 174.

101. Ibid.

102. K. K. Rokossovsky, "Soldatskii dolg" [A soldier's duty], *VIZh,* no. 6 (June 1989): 52.

103. Zolotarev, *Velikaia Otechestvennaia voina,* I: 179. Although his memory was disgraced and dishonored, Kachalov was exonerated of these charges and rehabilitated well after war's end.

104. Maslov, *Captured Soviet Generals,* 57.

105. Mangazeev, "A 'Penal' Corps on the Kalinin Front," 132.

106. Zolotarev, "Stavka VGK 1941," 162–63. This document is entitled "Notes of a Conversation by Direct Line between the Supreme High Commander, the Chief of the General Staff, and the Reserve Front Commander." This reference to the 211th Rifle Division related to an earlier *Stavka* message that mentioned the division abandoning the field of battle in a panic, leaving the adjacent 149th Rifle Division in a precarious position. Zhukov reported that he was "personally taking the situation in hand."

107. Ibid., 388. For the full text of this decree, which was numbered 169ss, see N. S. Gishko, "GKO postanovliaet" [The GKO decrees], *VIZh,* no. 4–5 (April–May 1992): 19–20.

108. For details, see Maslov, *Captured Soviet Generals.*

109. The Presidium of the Supreme Soviet of the SSSR issued a decree placing the Soviet Union in a "military state" *(voennoe polozhenie)* on 23 June 1941. See Zolotarev, "NKO 1941," 11–13, for the NKO order, which was numbered 219 and was entitled "Regulations Concerning Military Tribunals in Localities Where a Military State [Condition] Has Been Declared and in Regions of Combat Operations."

110. Ibid., 15. This was NKO Order No. 218, that is, one number below Order No. 219, which established the wartime state by specifying mechanisms for the country

to function in a military state, and was entitled "Regarding the Announcement of Decrees by the Presidium of the USSR's Supreme Soviet 'Concerning the Situation Regarding Military Tribunals in Regions Where a Military State Has Been Declared and in Regions of Combat Operations' and 'The Situation Regarding Military Tribunals.'"

111. Ibid., 15–16.

112. Ibid., 16.

113. Ibid., 390. According to the 6 July 1940 order, all soldiers and junior command cadre "who had been sentenced for a period of from six months to two years for absence without leave more than one time up to two hours or continuously over two hours (up to a day), even if only once," were subject to assignment to these battalions. On 13 July 1940, the Council of People's Commissars of the USSR issued "Regulations Concerning Disciplinary Battalions in the Red Army," which mandated disciplinary battalions be used for fixed-service soldiers and noncommissioned officers who were serving sentences assigned by military tribunal as well as those called up from the reserves for a period from six months to two years. According to these regulations, the duration of stay in the disciplinary battalion of those convicted did not take into consideration the period of service in the army, and those who were convicted and sent to serve sentences in disciplinary battalions were not removed from the rolls of their original units. These orders required soldiers sent to disciplinary battalions to work 12-hour days, including nine hours on menial tasks and construction work and three hours in political training. Those serving sentences in these battalions and their families were deprived of all rights and privileges established for servicemen and their families from the moment they were sentenced by military tribunals until their release from the disciplinary battalion. Finally, the disciplinary battalions themselves were organized under a special *shtat* and were directly subordinate to military district or army commanders.

114. Ibid., 50. This was NKO Order No. 265, "An Order Announcing the Presidium of the USSR's Supreme Soviet's Decree 'Concerning the Freeing of Military Servicemen from Disciplinary Battalions.'" President M. Kalinin and Presidium Secretary A. Gorkin signed the GKO decree.

115. Ibid., 276–78. This order, which was signed by Stalin, was entitled "Order No. 227 Concerning Measures for Strengthening Discipline and Order in the Red Army and Preventing Unauthorized Retreat from Combat Positions."

116. Ibid.

117. Ibid.

118. Ibid., 278–79.

119. Ibid.

120. Ibid.

121. Ibid.

122. Zolotarev, *Velikaia Otechestvennaia voina,* I: 356.

123. Ibid., 312–15. This was Order No. 298, "An Announcement about the Situation Concerning Penal Battalions and Companies, the Headquarters of Penal Battalions and Companies, and Blocking Detachments of the Red Army." The NKO also promulgated three official *shtats* for penal units, which were numbered 04/393, 04/392, and 04/391 but whose exact contents have not been released.

124. Ibid., 312–13.

125. Ibid.

126. Ibid.

127. Ibid. For example, battalion, company, and platoon commanders serving in penal subunits exercised authority equivalent to that of division, battalion, and company commanders, respectively, and deputy battalion commanders the authority of regimental commanders.

128. *Shtrafniki* were paid 8 rubles, 50 kopeks per month. Early release required a written statement by the penal battalion [company] commander approved by the *front* military council.

129. See Zolotarev, "NKO 1941," 313–14.

130. Ibid., 332–33. This was NKO Order No. 323, "Concerning the Sending of Soldiers Convicted by Military Tribunals with Deferred Execution of Their Sentences until War's End to Penal Units."

131. Ibid., 351–53 This NKO order, which was essentially identical to Order No. 323, was numbered 0860 and entitled "Concerning the Strengthening of Force Discipline in Garrisons and along Communications Routes."

132. Ibid.

133. Zolotarev, "NKO 1943," 45–46. This was Order No. 47, "Concerning the Reduction in Rank to Private and the Sending to a Penal Battalion of Junior Lieutenant S. O. Karamal'nik for Criticizing His Chiefs."

134. See "Prikaz chastiam 121sd no. 0045. 12. 3. 43." [Order No. 0044 to the 121st Rifle Division's units, dated 12 March 1943], from "Boevye prikazy i pazporiazheniia soedinenii 60A (1942–1943 gg.)" [Combat orders and instructions of the 60th Army's formations (1942–1943)], *TsAMO,* f. 417, op. 10564, d. 215, l. 67.

135. From "Prikaz 65A. 25. 3. 43g." [65th Army order no. 4, dated 25 March 1943], from "Dokumenty iz fondov 65A" [Documents from the archives of the 65th Army], *TsAMO,* f. 422, op. 10496, d. 81, l. 12.

136. Krivosheev, *Rossiia i SSSR v voinakh XX veka,* 441.

137. Ibid.

138. For further details concerning the 123rd Penal Company, see S. Khomenko, "A Disciplinary Battalion Joins Battle," *Soviet Soldier,* no. 11 (November 1990): 36–38.

139. Direktiva voennogo soveta Tsentral'nogo fronta no. 027 ot 18.4.43g. [Directive No. 027 of the Central Front's military council dated 18 April 1943], l. 166.

140. Ibid.

141. Mangazeev, "A 'Penal' Corps on the Kalinin Front," 122.

142. Aria, "From Tanks to Katiushas," 22–24.

143. *1986 Art of War Symposium: From the Vistula to the Oder: Soviet Offensive Operations, October 1944–March 1945* (Carlisle, PA: U.S. Army War College, 1986), 70.

144. Zolotarev, "NKO 1941," 279.

145. A. A. Maslov, "How Were Soviet Blocking Detachments Employed?" *JSMS* 9, no. 2 (June 1996): 430–31, quoting *TsAMO,* f. 1047, op. 1, d. 12, ll. 11–12. The observation post of the division commander was situated on the left bank of the Kleven' River on the western outskirts of Shalygino village.

146. Zolotarev, "Stavka VGK 1941," 164. This was "*Stavka* VGK Directive No. 001650 to the Briansk Front Commander Permitting the Creation of Blocking Detachments."

147. *1986 Art of War Symposium: From the Vistula to the Oder,* 72.

148. "Komandiram 1, 2, 3 armeiskikh zagradotriadov. 16. 3. 43g. no. 0224" [no. 0224, dated 16 March 1943 to the commanders of the 1st, 2nd, and 3rd Army Blocking Detachments], in "Direktivy SVGK, GSh, KA voiskam Brianskogo fronta, 13A, 2.–20.7. 43" [Directives of the *Stavka* of the Supreme High Command to the Briansk Front and the 13th Army, 2 January to 20 July 1943], *TsAMO,* f. 361, op. 6079, d. 173, l. 105.

149. For example, on 29 October 1944, NKO Order No. 0349, which was signed by Stalin, stated, "In connection with the changing overall situation at the front, the necessity for the further maintenance of blocking detachments at the front has passed." Therefore, it ordered all *front* and army commanders "to disband separate blocking detachments effective 15 November of this year" and "use personnel from the disbanded detachments to reinforce rifle divisions." Commanders were to report the dissolution of their blocking detachments to the NKO by 20 November 1944. See Zolotarev, "NKO 1943," 326.

150. Rzhevskaia, "Roads and Days," 57.

151. On 18 September 1941, the 2nd Rifle Corps' 161st and the 100th Rifle Divisions became the first guards units in the Red Army for their exemplary bravery, courage, and stoicism under fire in July and August 1941.

152. Ivan Ignatievich Shepelov, "To War as in War," in *Memories of War,* VII: 28–31. Shepelov was a sergeant in the 161st Rifle Division.

153. Aria, "Memories of War," 1, 20.

154. Evgenii Moniushko, "Memoirs of the Soviet-German War, part 2: Siberia, the Front and Hospital, 1942–1944," *JSMS* 15, no. 2 (June 2002): 155–56.

155. "Iz politdoneseniia Mikhailova Pasha, ot 27.11.42" [From a political report of Mikhailov Pasha, dated 27 November 1942], in "Papka iskhodiashchikh politdonesenii 8GvSK v vyshestoiashchie politorgany" [Folder of outgoing political reports of the 8th Guards Rifle Corps to higher-level political organs], *TsAMO,* f. 825, op. 1, d. 411, l. 187.

156. Ibid., 33.

157. This women veteran was a member of the Assembly of Nobles, a registry of the older aristocracy.

158. Ibid., 11–12.

159. From an interview with Valentina Fedorovna Kozlova, in Glantz, *Battle for Leningrad,* 138–39.

160. Moniushko, "Memoirs of the Soviet-German War," 180.

161. Rzhevskaia, "Roads and Days," 63. Elena Rzhevskaia served as a translator in the 4th Airborne Corps and the 30th Army to war's end.

162. On 31 December 1941, the Red Army consisted of 94 armies (70 field, five tank, 18 air, and three PVO), 253 corps (161 rifle, eight cavalry, 24 tank, 13 mechanized, six artillery, seven PVO, and 34 aviation), and 838 divisions (489 rifle, 16 airborne, 26 cavalry, two tank, 26 artillery, seven guards-mortar, 78 antiaircraft, 14 PVO, and 180 aviation).

14. Conclusions

1. Other themes emphasized by the "German school" include the prolonged, tragic but ill-fated struggle by German generals against Hitler's irrational, arbitrary, and ultimately flawed conduct of the war, the bravery and honor of the German soldier in a struggle not of their own making, and, more recently, Stalin's share of guilt for the war.

2. *Red Army Officers Speak*, 22. As recalled by K. A. Borisov, commander of a machine-gun company in the 172nd Rifle Division, which was assigned to the 13th Army's 102nd Rifle Corps.

3. Krivosheev, *Grif sekretnosti sniat*, 146.

4. Krivosheev, *Rossiia i SSSR v voinakh XX veka*, 457.

5. Ibid., 463.

Selected Bibliography

Abbreviations

JSMS	*The Journal of Slavic Military Studies*
TsAMO	*Tsentral'nyi arkhiv Ministerstva Oborony* [Central Archives of the Ministry of Defense]
TsPA UML	*Tsentral'nyi partiinyi arkhiv Instituta Marksizma-Leninizma* [Central Party Archives of the Institute of Marxism and Leninism]
VIZh	*Voenno-istoricheskii zhurnal* [Military-historical journal]

Primary Sources

Armeiskie operatsii (Boevye deistviia obshchevoiskovoi armii v gody Velikoi Otechestvennoi voiny) [Army operations (Combat operations of the combined-arms army in the Great Patriotic War)]. Moscow: Frunze Academy, 1989. Classified for faculty use only.

Barvenkovo-Lozovaia operatsiia (18–31 ianvaria 1942 g.) [The Barvenkovo-Lozovaia operation (18–31 January 1942)]. Moscow: Voenizdat, 1943. Classified secret.

"Boevoi opyt ukreplennykh raionov (UR)" [Combat experiences of fortified regions]. In *Sbornik materialov po izucheniiu opyta voiny* [Collection of materials for the study of war experience], no. 3 (November–December 1942), pp. 122–32. Moscow: Voenizdat, 1942. Classified secret.

Boevoi i chislennyi sostav vooruzhennykh sil SSSR v period Velikoi Otechestvennoi voiny (1941–1945 gg.): Statisticheskii sbornik no. 1 (22 iiunia 1941 g.) [The combat and numerical composition of the USSR's armed forces in the Great Patriotic War (1941–1945): Statistical collection no. 1 (22 June 1941)]. Moscow: Institute of Military History, 1994.

Boevoi sostav Sovetskoi armii, chast' 1 (iiun'–dekabr' 1941 goda) [The combat composition of the Soviet Army, part 1 (June–December 1941)]. Moscow: Voroshilov Academy of the General Staff, 1963. Classified secret.

Boevoi sostav Sovetskoi armii, chast' 2 (ianvar'–dekabr' 1942 goda) [The combat composition of the Soviet Army, part 2 (January–December 1941)]. Moscow: Voenizdat, 1966. Classified secret.

Boevoi sostav Sovetskoi armii, chast' 3 (ianvar'–dekabr' 1943 goda) [The combat composition of the Soviet Army, part 3 (January–December 1943)]. Moscow: Voenizdat, 1972. Classified secret.

Boevoi sostav Sovetskoi armii, chast' 4 (ianvar'–dekabr' 1944 goda) [The combat composition of the Soviet Army, part 4 (January–December 1944)]. Moscow: Voenizdat, 1988. Classified secret.

"Boevye deistviia Sovetskikh voisk na Kalininskom napravlenii v 1941 gody (s oktiabria 1941 po 7 ianvaria 1942 g.)" [Combat operations of Soviet forces on the Kalinin axis (from October 1941 through 7 January 1942)]. In *Sbornik voenno-istoricheskikh materialov Velikoi Otechestvennoi voiny* [Collection of military-historical materials of the Great Patriotic War], no. 7. Moscow: Voenizdat, 1952. Classified secret.

Chugunov, A. I., ed. *Pogranichnye voiska v gody Velikoi Otechestvennoi voiny 1941–1945: Sbornik dokumentov* [Border guards forces in the Great Patriotic War 1941–1945: A collection of documents]. Moscow: Nauka, 1968.

"Dokumenty po ispol'zovaniiu bronetankovykh i mekhanizirovannykh voisk Sovetskoi Armii v period s 22 iiunia po sentiabr' 1941 g. vkliuchitel'no" [Documents on the employment of armored and mechanized forces of the Soviet Army in the period from 22 June to September 1941, inclusively]. In *Sbornik boevykh dokumentov Velikoi Otechestvennoi voiny* [A collection of combat documents of the Great Patriotic War], no. 33. Moscow: Voenizdat, 1957. Classified secret.

"Dokumenty nemetskogo komandovaniia po voprosam podgotovki voiny" [Documents of the German command on issues of preparing for war] and "Dokumenty nemetskogo komandovaniia po voprosam vedeniia voiny" [Documents of the German command on issues of the conduct of the war]. In *Sbornik voenno-istoricheskikh materialov Velikoi Otechestvennoi voiny*[Collection of military-historical materials of the Great Patriotic War], no. 18. Moscow: Voenizdat, 1960. Classified secret.

Dushen'kin, V. V., ed. *Vnutrennie voiska v Velikoi Otechestvennoi voine 1941–1945 gg.: Dokumenty i materialy* [Internal forces in the Great Patriotic War 1941–1945: Documents and materials]. Moscow: Iuridicheskaia Literatura, 1975.

Eletskaia operatsiia (6–16 dekabria 1941 g.) [The Elets operation (6–16 December 1941)]. Moscow: Voenizdat, 1943. Classified secret.

Gishko, N. S. "GKO postanovliaet" [The GKO decrees]. *VIZh*, no. 2 (February 1992): 31–34; *VIZh*, no. 3 (March 1992): 17–20; and *VIZh*, no. 4–5 (April–May 1992): 19–23.

Gor'kov, Iurii. *Gosudarstvennyi Komitet Oborony postanovliaet (1941–1945): Tsifry, dokumenty* [The State Defense Committee decrees (1941–1945): Numbers and documents]. Moscow: Olma-Press, 2002.

Guide to Foreign Military Studies 1945–54. Historical Division, United States Army, Europe.

Guide to German Archival Records Microfilmed at Alexandria, Va. Washington, DC: National Archives and Records Administration, 1974–1979.

Ianchinsky, A. N. *Boevoe ispol'zovanie istrebitel'no-protivotankovoi artillerii RVGK v Velikoi Otechestvennoi voine* [The combat employment of destroyer antitank artillery of the *Stavka* Reserve in the Great Patriotic War]. Moscow: Voroshilov Academy of the General Staff, 1951. Classified secret.

Komandovanie korpusnogo i divizionnogo zvena Sovetskikh vooruzhennykh sil perioda Velikoi Otechestvennoi voiny, 1941–1945 gg. [Commanders at the corps and division level in the Soviet armed forces during the Great Patriotic War, 1941–1945]. Moscow: Frunze Academy, 1964. Classified secret.

"Oborona" [Defense]. In *Sbornik boevykh dokumentov Velikoi Otechestvennoi voiny* [Collection of combat documents of the Great Patriotic War], no. 1. Moscow: Voenizdat, 1947: 54–61. Classified secret.

Rostovskaia operatsiia, noiabr'–dekabr' 1941 g. [The Rostov operation, November–December 1941]. Moscow: Voenizdat, 1943. Classified secret.

Sbornik boevykh dokumentov Velikoi Otechestvennoi voiny [Collection of combat documents of the Great Patriotic War], vols. 1–43. Moscow: Voenizdat, 1949–1960. Classified secret.

Sbornik materialov po izucheniiu opyta voiny, no. 5 (mart 1943 g.) [Collection of materials for the study of war experience, no. 5 (March 1943)]. Moscow: Voenizdat, 1943. Classified secret.

Sbornik materialov po izucheniiu opyta voiny, no. 6 (aprel'–mai 1943 g.) [Collection of materials for the study of war experience, no. 6 (April–May 1943)]. Moscow: Voenizdat, 1943. Classified secret.

Sbornik materialov po izucheniiu opyta voiny, no. 7 (iiun'–iiul' 1943 g.) [Collection of materials for the study of war experience, no. 7 (June–July 1943)]. Moscow: Voenizdat, 1943. Classified secret.

Sbornik materialov po izucheniiu opyta voiny, no. 10 (ianvar'–fevral' 1944 g.) [Collection of materials for the study of war experience, no. 10 (January–February 1944)]. Moscow: Voenizdat, 1944. Classified secret.

Sbornik materialov po izucheniiu opyta voiny, no. 14 (sentiabr'–oktiabr' 1944 g.) [Collection of materials for the study of war experience, no. 14 (September–October 1944)]. Moscow: Voenizdat, 1945. Classified secret.

Sbornik takticheskykh primerov po opytu Otechestvennoi voiny [Collection of tactical examples based on the experience of the Patriotic War], nos. 1–23. Moscow: Voenizdat, 1943–1947. Classified secret.

Sbornik voenno-istoricheskikh materialov Velikoi Otechestvennoi voiny [Collection of military-historical materials of the Great Patriotic War], no. 1. Moscow: Voenizdat, 1949. Classified secret.

Sbornik voenno-istoricheskikh materialov Velikoi Otechestvennoi voiny [Collection of military-historical materials of the Great Patriotic War], no. 2. Moscow: Voenizdat, 1949. Classified secret.

Sbornik voenno-istoricheskikh materialov Velikoi Otechestvennoi voiny [Collection of military-historical materials of the Great Patriotic War], no. 7. Moscow: Voenizdat, 1952. Classified secret.

Sbornik voenno-istoricheskikh materialov Velikoi Otechestvennoi voiny [Collection of military-historical materials of the Great Patriotic War], no. 9. Moscow: Voenizdat, 1953. Classified secret.

Sbornik voenno-istoricheskikh materialov Velikoi Otechestvennoi voiny [Collection of military-historical materials of the Great Patriotic War], no. 12. Moscow: Voenizdat, 1953. Classified secret.

Sbornik voenno-istoricheskikh materialov Velikoi Otechestvennoi voiny [Collection of military-historical materials of the Great Patriotic War], no. 13. Moscow: Voenizdat, 1954. Classified secret.

Sbornik voenno-istoricheskikh materialov Velikoi Otechestvennoi voiny [Collection of military-historical materials of the Great Patriotic War], no. 14. Moscow: Voenizdat, 1954. Classified secret.

Scherff, Walter. *OKW, WFST, Kriegsgeschichtlichen Abteilung, Kriegstagebuch.* Nurnberg: International Military Tribunal Document 1809 PS.

Schramm, Percy E. *Kriegstagebuch des Oberkommandos der Wehrmacht (Wehrmachtfuehrungsstab).* 2 vols. Frankfurt: Bernard and Graefe, 1961–1965.

Shaposhnikov, B. M., ed. *Razgrom nemetskikh voisk pod Moskvoi* [The defeat of German forces at Moscow]. Parts 1, 2, and 3. Moscow: Voenizdat, 1943. Classified secret.

"State Defense Committee Decree of 11 September 1941." *TsPA UML.* F. 644, op. 1, d. 9.

Stepashin, S. V., ed. *Organy gosudarstvennoi bezopasnosti SSSR v Velikoi Otechestvennoi voine: Sbornik dokumentov, tom 1: Nakanune, kniga vtoraia (1 ianvaria–21 iiunia 1941 g.)* [Organs of state security of the USSR in the Great Patriotic War: A collection of documents, volume 1: On the eve, book 2 (1 January to 21 June 1941)]. Moscow: Kniga i Biznes, 1995.

Truppen-Übersicht und Kriegsgliederungen Rote Armee: Stand August 1944 [Troop summary and order of battle of the Red Army: August 1944]. Ic-Unterlagen Ost, Merkblatt geh. 11/6, Pruf.-Nr.: 0157. National Archives Microfilm (NAM) T-78, roll 495. Classified secret.

Vasil'ev, A. V. *Rzhevsko-Viazemskaia operatsiia Kalininskogo i Zapadnogo frontov (ianvar'–fevral' 1942 g.)* [The Kalinin and Western Fronts' Rzhev-Viaz'ma operation (January–February 1942)]. Moscow: Voroshilov Academy, 1949. Classified secret.

Zabaluev, A. A., and S. G. Goriachev. *Kalininskaia nastupatel'naia operatsiia* [The Kalinin offensive operation]. Moscow: Voroshilov Academy, 1942. Classified secret.

Zolotarev, V. A., ed. "General'nyi shtab v gody Velikoi Otechestvennoi voiny: Dokumenty i materialy 1941 goda" [The General Staff in the Great Patriotic War: Documents and materials from 1941]. In *Russkii arkhiv: Velikaia Otechestvennaia* [The Russian archives: The Great Patriotic (War)], 23, 12 (1). Moscow: Terra, 1997.

———. "General'nyi shtab v gody Velikoi Otechestvennoi voiny: Dokumenty i materialy 1942 goda" [The General Staff in the Great Patriotic War: Documents and materials from 1942]. In *Russkii arkhiv: Velikaia Otechestvennaia* [The Russian archives: The Great Patriotic (War)], 23, 12 (2). Moscow: Terra, 1999.

———. "General'nyi shtab v gody Velikoi Otechestvennoi voiny: Dokumenty i materialy 1943 goda" [The General Staff in the Great Patriotic War: Documents and materials from 1943]. In *Russkii arkhiv: Velikaia Otechestvennaia* [The Russian archives: The Great Patriotic (War)], 23, 12 (3). Moscow: Terra, 1999.

———. "Preludiia Kurskoi bitvy" [Prelude to the Battle of Kursk]. In *Russkii arkhiv: Velikaia Otechestvennaia* [The Russian archives: The Great Patriotic (War)], 15 (4–3). Moscow: Terra, 1997.

———. "Stavka VGK: Dokumenty i materialy 1941 goda" [The *Stavka* VGK: Documents and materials of 1941]. In *Russkii arkhiv: Velikaia Otechestvennaia* [The Russian archives: The Great Patriotic (War)], 16, 5 (1). Moscow: Terra, 1996.

———. "Stavka VGK: Dokumenty i materialy 1942" [The *Stavka* VGK: Documents and materials of 1942]. In *Russkii arkhiv: Velikaia Otechestvennaia* [The Russian archives: The Great Patriotic (War)], 16, 5 (2). Moscow: Terra, 1996.

———. "Stavka Verkhovnogo Glavnokomandovaniia: Dokumenty i materialy 1943 goda" [The *Stavka* VGK: Documents and materials of 1943]. In *Russkii arkhiv: Velikaia Otechestvennaia* [The Russian archives: The Great Patriotic (War)], 16, 5 (3). Moscow: Terra, 1999.

———. "Stavka VGK: Dokumenty i materialy 1944–1945" [The *Stavka* VGK: Documents and materials of 1944–1945]. In *Russkii arkhiv: Velikaia Otechestvennaia* [The Russian archives: The Great Patriotic (War)], 16, 5 (4). Moscow: Terra, 1999.

Secondary Sources: Books

Aganov, S. Kh., ed. *Inzhenernye voiska Sovetskoi armii 1918–1945* [Engineer forces of the Soviet Army 1918–1945]. Moscow: Voenizdat, 1985.

Alekseev, P. D., and V. B. Makovsky. *Pervaia oboronitel'naia operatsiia 4–i armii v nachale Velikoi Otechestvennoi voiny* [The initial defensive operation of the 4th Army in the beginning of the Great Patriotic War]. Moscow: Frunze Academy, 1992.

Allen, W.E.D., and Paul Muratoff. *The Russian Campaign of 1944–1945*. Harmondsworth, England: Penguin, 1946.

Altukhov, P. K., ed. *Nezabyvaemye dorogy: Boevoi put' 10–i gvardeiskoi armii* [Unforgettable roads: The combat path of the 10th Guards Army]. Moscow: Voenizdat, 1974.

Anan'ev, I. M. *Tankovye armii v nastuplenii* [Tank armies in the offensive]. Moscow: Voenizdat, 1988.

Anfilov, V. A. *Krushenie pokhoda Gitlera na Moskvu 1941* [The ruin of Hitler's march on Moscow 1941]. Moscow: Nauka, 1989.

Armstrong, Richard N. *Red Army Tank Commanders: The Armored Guards*. Atglen, PA: Schiffer, 1994.

Armstrong, Richard N., ed. *Red Army Combat Orders: Combat Regulations for Tank and Mechanized Forces 1944*. Trans. Joseph G. Welsh. London: Frank Cass, 1991.

Babich, Iu. P. *Podgotovka oborony 62-i armii vne soprikosnoveniia s protivnikom i vedenie oboronitel'noi operatsii v usloviiakh prevoskhodstva protivnika v manevrennosti (po opytu Stalingradskoi bitvy)* [The preparation of the 62nd Army's defense outside contact with the enemy and the conduct of a defensive operation with a more maneuverable enemy (based on the experience of the Battle of Stalingrad)]. Moscow: Frunze Academy, 1991.

———. *Vstrechnye boi soedinenii 3-go mekhanizirovannogo korpusa v raione Akhtyrki 19–20 avgusta 1943 g. v kontrnastuplenii pod Kurskom* [Meeting engagements of the 3rd Mechanized Corps' formations in the Akhtyrka region on 19–20 August 1943 in the Kursk counteroffensive]. Moscow: Frunze Academy, 1990.

Babich, Iu. P., and A. G. Baier. *Razvitie vooruzheniia i organizatsii sovetskikh sukhoputnykh voisk v gody Velikoi Otechestvennoi voiny* [The development of

Soviet ground forces' weaponry and organization during the Great Patriotic War]. Moscow: Izdanie Akademii, 1990).

Bagramian, I. Kh., ed. *Istoriia voin i voennogo iskusstva* [A history of war and military art]. Moscow: Voenizdat, 1970.

———. *Tak shli my k Pobede* [As we went on to victory]. Moscow: Voenizdat, 1977.

Bartov, Omer. *The Eastern Front, 1941–45: German Troops and the Barbarisation of Warfare*. New York: St. Martin's Press, 1986.

Baryshev, N. I. *Na iuzhnom flange* [On the southern flank]. Moscow: Nauka, 1973.

Beevor, Antony. *Stalingrad: The Fateful Siege: 1942–1943.* New York: Viking, 1998.

Bellamy, Chris. *Red God of War: Soviet Artillery and Rocket Forces.* London: Brassey's, 1986.

Berdnikov, G. I. *Pervaia udarnaia* [The First Shock (Army)]. Moscow: Voenizdat, 1985.

Bialar, Seweryn, ed. *Stalin's Generals.* New York: Pegasus, 1969.

Blau, George. *The German Campaign in Russia: Planning and Operations, 1940–1942.* Department of the Army Pamphlet 20–261a. Washington, DC: Government Printing Office, 1955.

Burdick, Charles, and Hans-Adolf Jacobsen. *The Halder War Diary, 1939–1942.* Novato, CA: Presidio, 1988.

Carell, Paul. *Hitler's War on Russia 1941–1943.* London: Harrap, 1964.

———. *Scorched Earth: The Russian-German War 1943–44.* London: Harrap, 1970.

Chaney, Otto P. *Zhukov.* Norman: University of Oklahoma Press, 1971.

Chistiakov, I. M. *Sluzhim otchizne* [We serve the fatherland]. Moscow: Voenizdat, 1975.

Chuikov, V. I. *The Battle for Stalingrad.* New York: Holt, Rinehart and Winston, 1964.

Clark, Alan. *Barbarossa: The Russian-German Conflict 1941–45.* New York: William Morrow, 1966.

Cottam, Kazimiera J. *Women in War and Resistance: Selected Biographies of Soviet Women Soldiers.* Nepean, Canada: New Military, 1998.

Craig, William. *Enemy at the Gates: The Battle for Stalingrad.* New York: Dutton, 1973.

Dallin, Alexander. *German Rule in Russia, 1941–1945.* New York: St. Martin's, 1957.

Das Deutsche Reich und der Zweite Weltkreig. 10 vols. Stuttgart: Deutsche Verlags-Anstadt, 1981–1995.

Degtiarev, P. A., and P. P. Ionov. *"Katiushi" na pole boia* [*Katiushas* on the field of battle]. Moscow: Voenizdat, 1991.

Demin, A. A., and R. M. Portugal'sky. *Tanki vkhodiat v proryv: Boevoi put' 25-go tankovogo korpusa* [Tanks enter the penetration: The combat path of the 25th Tank Corps]. Moscow: Voenizdat, 1988.

Deutsch, Harold C., and Dennis E. Showalter, eds. *What If? Strategic Alternatives of WWII.* Chicago: Emperor's Press, 1997.

Dragunsky, D. A., ed. *Polevaia akademiia: Istoriia vysshikh ofitserskikh ordena Lenina i Oktiabr'skoi Revoliutsii Krasnoznamenykh kursov "Vystrel" imeni Marshala Sovetskogo Soiuza B. M. Shaposhnikova* [Field academy: A history of the "Vystrel" Order of Lenin and October Revolution, Red Banner higher officers courses in the name of Marshal of the Soviet Union B. M. Shaposhnikov]. Moscow: Voenizdat, 1983.

Dunn, Walter S., Jr. *Hitler's Nemesis: The Red Army, 1930–1945.* New York: Praeger, 1994.

Egorov, P. A., I. V. Krivoborsky, I. K. Ivlev, and A. I. Rogalevich. *Dorogami pobed: Boevoi put' 5-i gvardeiskoi tankovoi armii* [Roads to victory: The combat path of the 5th Guards Tank Army]. Moscow: Voenizdat, 1969.

Eremenko, A. I. *The Arduous Beginning.* Moscow: Progress, 1966.

Erickson, John. *The Road to Berlin.* Boulder, CO: Westview Press, 1983.

———. *The Road to Stalingrad.* New York: Harper & Row, 1975.

———. *The Soviet High Command 1918–1941.* London: Frank Cass, 2001.

Erickson, John, and Ljubica Erickson. *The Soviet Armed Forces, 1918–1992: A Research Guide to Soviet Sources.* Westport, CT: Greenwood Press, 1996.

Ershov, A. G. *Osvobozhdenie Donbassa* [The liberation of the Donbas]. Moscow: Voenizdat, 1973.

Frolov, B. P. *Forsirovanie rek Desny i Dnepra, osvobozhdenie Chernigov voiskami 13-i armii v Chernigovsko-Pripiatskoi operatsii (sentiabr' 1943 g.)* [The forcing of the Dena and Dnepr rivers and the liberation of Chernigov by the 13th Army in the Chernigov-Pripiat' operation]. Moscow: Frunze Academy, 1989.

Gaglov, I. I. *General Antonov.* Moscow: Voenizdat, 1978.

Gan'shin, V. I. *Tankovye voiska v moskovskoi operatsii* [Tank forces in the Moscow operation]. Moscow: Voroshilov Academy, 1948. Classified secret.

Gareev, M. A. *Marshal Zhukov: Velichie i unikal'nost' polkovodicheskogo iskusstva* [Marshal Zhukov: The greatness and uniqueness of a commander's art]. Moscow and Ufa: Eastern University, 1996.

Glantz. David M. *Atlas of the Battle of Smolensk, 7 July–10 September 1941.* Carlisle, PA: Self-published, 2001.

———. *Barbarossa: Hitler's Invasion of Russia in 1941.* Charleston, SC: Tempus, 2001.

———. *The Battle for Leningrad 1941–1944.* Lawrence: University Press of Kansas, 2002.

———. *The Battle for Smolensk, 7 July–10 September 1941.* Carlisle, PA: Self-published, 2001.

———. *Deep Attack: The Soviet Conduct of Operational Maneuver.* Carlisle, PA: Self-published, 1998.

———. *Forgotten Battles of the German-Soviet War (1941–1945), volume 1: The Summer–Fall Campaign (22 June–4 December 1941).* Carlisle, PA: Self-published, 1999.

———. *Forgotten Battles of the German-Soviet War (1941–1945), volume 2: The Winter Campaign (5 December 1941–April 1942).* Carlisle, PA: Self-published, 1999.

———. *Forgotten Battles of the German-Soviet War (1941–1945), volume 3: The Summer Campaign (12 May–18 November 1942).* Carlisle, PA: Self-published, 1999.

———. *Forgotten Battles of the German-Soviet War (1941–1945), volume 4: The*

Winter Campaign (19 November 1942–21 March 1943). Carlisle, PA: Self-published, 1999.

———. *Forgotten Battles of the German-Soviet War (1941–1945), volume 5, parts 1 and 2: The Summer–Fall Campaign (1 July–31 December 1943).* Carlisle, PA: Self-published, 2000.

———. *From the Don to the Dnepr: Soviet Offensive Operations, December 1942–August 1943.* London: Frank Cass, 1991.

———. *A History of Soviet Airborne Forces.* London: Frank Cass, 1994.

———. *Kharkov 1942: The Anatomy of a Military Disaster.* London: Ian Allen, 1998.

———. *The Military Strategy of the Soviet Union: A History.* London: Frank Cass, 1992.

———. *Red Army Officers Speak: Interviews with Veterans of the Vistula-Oder Operation (January–February 1945).* Carlisle, PA: Self-published, 1997.

———. *The Siege of Leningrad 1941–1945: 900 Days of Terror.* London: Brown Partworks, 2001.

———. *The Soviet Conduct of Tactical Maneuver: Spearhead of the Offensive.* London: Frank Cass, 1991.

———. *Soviet Defensive Tactics at Kursk (July 1943).* Carlisle, PA: Self-published, 1998.

———. *The Soviet-German War 1941–1945: Myths and Realities: A Survey Essay.* Carlisle, PA: Self-published, 2001.

———. *Soviet Military Deception in the Second World War.* London: Frank Cass, 1989.

———. *Soviet Military Intelligence in War.* London: Frank Cass, 1990.

———. *Soviet Military Operational Art: In Pursuit of Deep Battle.* London: Frank Cass, 1991.

———. *Soviet Mobilization in Peace and War, 1924–1942: A Survey.* Carlisle, PA: Self-published, 1998.

———. *Soviet War Experiences: Tank Operations.* Carlisle, PA: Self-published, 1998.

———. *Stumbling Colossus: The Red Army on the Eve of War.* Lawrence: University Press of Kansas, 1998.

———. *Zhukov's Greatest Defeat: The Red Army's Epic Disaster in Operation Mars.* Lawrence: University Press of Kansas, 1999.

———, ed. *1984 Art of War Symposium: From the Don to the Dnepr: Soviet Offensive Operations, December 1942–August 1943.* Carlisle, PA: U.S. Army War College, 1984.

———. *1985 Art of War Symposium: From the Dnepr to the Vistula: Soviet Offensive Operations, November 1943–August 1944.* Carlisle, PA: U.S. Army War College, 1985.

———. *1986 Art of War Symposium: From the Vistula to the Oder: Soviet Offensive Operations, October 1944–March 1945.* Carlisle, PA: U.S. Army War College, 1986.

———. *The Initial Period of War on the Eastern Front, 22 June–August 1941.* London: Frank Cass, 1993.

Glantz, David M., and Jonathan House. *The Battle of Kursk.* Lawrence: University Press of Kansas, 1999.

———. *When Titans Clashed: How the Red Army Stopped Hitler.* Lawrence: University Press of Kansas, 1995.

Glantz, David M., and Harold S. Orenstein. *The Battle for Kursk: The Soviet General Staff Study.* London: Frank Cass, 1999.

Golubovich, V. S. *Marshal Malinovsky.* Moscow: Voenizdat, 1984.

Grachev, P. S., ed. *Voennaia entsiklopediia v vos'mi tomakh* [Military encyclopedia in eight volumes]. Vols. 2–3. Moscow: Voenizdat, 1994–1995.

Great Patriotic War of the Soviet Union 1941–1945. Moscow: Progress, 1974.

Grechko, A. A. *Battle for the Caucasus.* Moscow: Progress, 1971.

———, ed. *Istoriia Vtoroi Mirovoi voiny 1939–1945 v dvenadtsati tomakh* [A history of World War II 1939–1945 in twelve volumes]. Moscow: Voenizdat, 1973–1982.

———. *Sovetskaia voennaia entsiklopediia v vos'mi tomakh* [Soviet military encyclopedia in eight volumes]. Moscow: Voenizdat, 1976–1980.

Grenkevich, Leonid. *The Soviet Partisan Movement 1941–1944.* London: Frank Cass, 1999.

Grigorenko, Petro G. *Memoirs.* New York: Norton, 1982.

Hardesty, Von. *The Red Phoenix: The Rise of Soviet Air Power 1941–1945.* Washington, DC: Smithsonian Institute Press, 1982.

Heiber, Helmut, and David M. Glantz. *Hitler and His Generals: Military Conferences 1942–1945.* New York: Enigma Books, 2003.

Heinrici, Gotthardt. "The Campaign in Russia." Vol. 1. Trans. Joseph Welch. National Archives manuscript in German. Washington, DC: United States Army G-2, 1954.

———. "Citadel: The Attack on the Russian Kursk Salient." Manuscript. Washington, DC: U.S. National Archives, n.d.

Istomin, V. P. *Smolenskaia nastupatel'naia operatsiia (1943 g.)* [The Smolensk offensive operation (1943)]. Moscow: Voenizdat, 1975.

Ivanov, S. B., ed. *Voennaia entsiklopediia v vos'mi tomakh* [Military encyclopedia in eight volumes]. Vol. 6. Moscow: Voenizdat, 2002.

Jones, Robert H. *The Roads to Russia: United States Lend-Lease to the Soviet Union.* Norman: University of Oklahoma Press, 1969.

Kalashnikov, K. A., V. I. Fes'kov, A. Iu. Chmykhalo, and V. I. Golikov. *Krasnaia Armiia v iiune 1941 goda* [The Red Army in June 1941]. Tomsk: Tomsk University Press, 2001.

Kamalov, Kh. Kh. *Morskaia pekhota v boiakh za rodinu* [Naval infantry in battles for the homeland]. Moscow: Voenizdat, 1966.

Khametov, M. I. *Bitva pod Moskvoi* [Battle at Moscow]. Moscow: Voenizdat, 1989.

Kholiavsky, G. L., ed. *Entsiklopediia tankov: Polnaia entsiklopediia tankov mira 1915–2000 gg.* [An encyclopedia of tanks: A complete encyclopedia of the world's tanks, 1915–2000]. Moscow: n.p., 1998.

Khorobrykh, A. M. *Glavnyi marshal aviatsii A. A. Novikov* [Chief Marshal of Aviation A. A. Novikov]. Moscow: Voenizdat, 1989.

Kir'ian, M. M., ed. *Fronty nastupali: Po opytu Velikoi Otechestvennoi voiny* [The *fronts* were attacking: Based on the experience of the Great Patriotic War]. Moscow: Nauka, 1987.

Kirpichnikov, Lieutenant General [initials unknown]. *Osnovy boevykh deistvii krupnykh kavaleriiskikh soedinenii v tylu protivnika* [The bases of combat operations by large cavalry formations in the enemy's rear]. Moscow: Voroshilov Academy, 1944. Classified secret.

Kolesnik, A. D. *Opolchenskie formirovaniia Rossiiskoi Federatsii v gody Velikoi Otechestvennoi voiny* [Militia formations of the Russian Federation during the Great Patriotic War]. Moscow: Nauka, 1988.

Kolpakidi, A. I., and D. P. Prokhorov. *Vneshniaia razvedka Rossii* [Russia's foreign intelligence]. Moscow: Olma-Press, 2001.

Koltunov, G. A., and B. G. Solov'ev. *Kurskaia bitva* [The Battle of Kursk]. Moscow: Voenizdat, 1983.

Kondrat'ev, Z. I. *Dorogi voiny* [Roads of war]. Moscow: Voenizdat, 1968.

Konev, I. S. *Zapiski komanduiushchego frontom* [Notes of a *front* commander]. Moscow: Voenizdat, 1981.

Kovalev, I. V. *Transport v Velikoi Otechestvennoi voine* [Transport in the Great Patriotic War]. Moscow: Nauka, 1981.

Kozhevnikov, M. N. *Komandovanie i shtab VVS Sovetskoi Armii v Velikoi Otechestvennoi voine 1941–1945 gg.* [The command and staff of the Air Force of the Soviet Army in the Great Patriotic War 1941–1945]. Moscow: Nauka, 1977.

Kozlov, M. M., ed. *Akademiia General'nogo shtaba* [The General Staff Academy]. Moscow: Voenizdat, 1987.

———. *Velikaia Otechestvennaia voina 1941–1945: Entsiklopediia* [The Great Patriotic War 1941–1945: An encyclopedia]. Moscow: Soviet Encyclopedia, 1985.

Kravchenko, I. M., and V. V. Burkov. *Desiatyi tankovyi dneprovskii: Boevoi put' 10-go tankovogo Dneprovskogo ordena Suvorova korpusa* [The 10th Dnepr Tank: The combat path of the 10th Tank Dnepr, Order of Suvorov Corps]. Moscow: Voenizdat, 1986.

Krivosheev, G. F., ed. *Grif sekretnosti sniat: Poteri Vooruzhennykh sil SSSR v voinakh, boevykh deistviiakh i boevykh konfliktakh, statisticheskoe issledovanie* [The secret classification has been removed: Losses of the Soviet Armed Forces in wars, combat operations, and military conflicts, a statistical study]. Moscow: Voenizdat, 1993.

———. *Rossiia i SSSR v voinakh XX veka, poteri vooruzhennykh sil: Statisticheskoe issledovanie* [Russia and the USSR in twentieth-century wars and the losses of the armed forces: A statistical investigation]. Moscow: Olma-Press, 2001.

Kudriashov, O. N. *Proryv oborony protivnika i razvitie uspekha v operativnoi glubine soedineniiami 5-i tankovoi armii. Sryv popytok protivnika deblokirovat' okruzhennuiu gruppirovku* [Penetration of the enemy defense and development of success in operational depth by the formations of the 5th Tank Army: The disruption of the enemy's attempt to relieve the encircled grouping]. Moscow: Frunze Academy, 1987.

Kudriashov, O. N., and N. M. Ramanichev. *Boevye deistviia Sovetskikh voisk v nachal'nom periode Velikoi Otechestvennoi voiny* [Combat operations of Soviet forces in the initial period of the Great Patriotic War]. Moscow: Frunze Academy, 1989.

Kumanov, G. A. *Sovetskii tyl v pervyi period Velikoi Otechestvennoi voiny* [The Soviet rear in the first period of the Great Patriotic War]. Moscow: Nauka, 1988.

———. *Voina i zheleznodorozhnyi transport SSSR* [War and railroad transport of the USSR]. Moscow: Nauka, 1988.

Kurochkin, P. A., ed. *Obshchevoiskovaia armiia na nastuplenii: Po opytu Velikoi Otechestvennoi voiny 1941–1945 gg.* [The combined-arms army in the offensive: Based on the experience of the Great Patriotic War 1941–1945]. Moscow: Voenizdat, 1966.

Kuz'min, A. V., and I. I. Krasnov. *Kantemirovtsy: Boevoi put' 4-go gvardeiskogo tankovogo Kantemirovskogo ordena Lenina Krasnoznamennogo korpusa* [The men of Kantemirovka: The combat path of the 4th Guards Kantemirovka, Order of Lenin, Red Banner Tank Corps]. Moscow: Voenizdat, 1971.

Kuznetsov, I. I. *Marshaly, generaly i admiraly 1940 goda* [Marshals, generals, and admirals of 1940]. Irkutsk: n.p., 2000.

Kuznetsov, N. G. *Kursom k pobede* [The path to victory]. Moscow: Golos, 2000.

Lensky, A. G. *Sukhoputnye sily RKKA v predvoennye gody* [RKKA ground forces in the prewar years]. Saint Petersburg: n.p., 2000.

Leonov, A. I., ed. *Voennye sviazisty v dni voiny i mira* [Military signalmen during war and peace]. Moscow: Voenizdat, 1968.

Liudskie poteri SSSR v Velikoi Otechestvennoi voine [Personnel losses of the USSR in the Great Patriotic War]. Saint Petersberg: Insititut Rossiiskoi Istorii, 1995.

Losik, O. A., ed. *Stroitel'stvo i boevoe primenenie Sovetskikh tankovykh voisk v gody Velikoi Otechestvennoi voiny* [The formation and combat use of Soviet tank forces during the Great Patriotic War]. Moscow: Voenizdat, 1979.

Loza, Dmitry. *Attack of the Airacobras: Soviet Aces, American P-39s, and the Air War against Germany.* Lawrence: University Press of Kansas, 2002.

———, ed. *Fighting for the Soviet Motherland: Recollections from the Eastern Front.* Trans. James F. Gebhardt. Lincoln: University of Nebraska Press, 1998.

Lukashev, E. K., and V. I. Kuznetsov. *Podgotovka i vedenie nastupleniia 5-i gvardeiskoi armii vo vzaimodeistvii s podvizhnoi gruppoi fronta v kontrnastuplenii pod Kurskom* [The preparation and conduct of the offensive by the 5th Guards Army in cooperation with the *front* mobile group in the counteroffensive at Kursk]. Moscow: Frunze Academy, 1991.

Luttichau, Charles V. P. von. *The Road to Moscow: The Campaign in Russia 1941.* Center for Military History Project 26–P. Currently being prepared in two volumes by David M. Glantz.Washington, DC: Office of the Chief of Military History, 1985. Now being prepared for publication in two volumes by David M. Glantz.

Mackintosh, Malcolm. *Juggernaut: A History of the Soviet Armed Forces.* London: Secker and Warburg, 1967.

Malygin, K. A. *V tsentre boevogo poriadka* [In the center of the combat formation]. Moscow: Voenizdat, 1986.

Manstein, Erich von. *Lost Victories.* Chicago: Henry Regnery, 1958.

Maslov, Aleksander. *Captured Soviet Generals: The Fate of Soviet Generals Captured by the Germans, 1941–1945.* London: Frank Cass, 2001.

———. *Fallen Soviet Generals: Soviet General Officers Killed in Battle, 1941–1945.* London: Frank Cass, 1998.

Mellenthin, F. W. von. *Panzer Battles: A Study of the Employment of Armor in the Second World War.* Norman: University of Oklahoma Press, 1956.

Memories of War: The Experiences of Red Army Veterans of the Great Patriotic War. 8 vols. Carlisle, PA: Self-published, 2001.

Meretskov, K. A. *Serving the People.* Moscow: Progress, 1971.

Moiseev, M. A., ed. *Sovetskaia voennaia entsiklopediia v vos'mi tomakh* [Soviet military encyclopedia in eight volumes]. Vol. 1. Moscow: Voenizdat, 1990.

Morozov, V. P. *Zapadnee Voronezha* [West of Voronezh]. Moscow: Voenizdat, 1956.

Moskalenko, K. S. *Na iugo-zapadnom napravlenii* [Along the southwestern axis]. Vols. 1–2. Moscow: Nauka, 1969.

Motter, T. Vail. *The Persian Corridor and Aid to Russia.* Washington, DC: Government Printing Office, 1952.

Muriev, D. Z. *Proval operatsii 'Taifun'* [The defeat of Operation Typhoon]. Moscow: Voenizdat, 1966.

"Nachalo, 22 iiunia–31 avgusta 1941 goda" [The beginning, 22 June to 31 August 1941], vol. 2, book 1. In *Organy gosudarstvennoi bezopasnosti SSSR v Velikoi Otechestvennoi voine* [The organs of state security of the USSR in the Great Patriotic War]. Moscow: Rus', 2000.

Nachal'nyi period Velikoi Otechestvennoi voiny [The initial period of the Great Patriotic War]. Moscow: Voroshilov Academy of the General Staff, 1989.

Nersesian, N. G. *Kievsko-Berlinskii: Boevoi put' 6-go gvardeiskogo tankovogo korpusa* [Kiev-Berlin: The combat path of the 6th Guards Tank Corps]. Moscow: Voenizdat, 1974.

Nevzorov, B. I. *Vozrastanie ustoichivosti oborony i osobennosti nastupleniia s khody v bitve pod Moskvoi (noiabr'–dekabr' 1941 g.)* [Growth in the durability of the defense and characteristics of the offensive from the march in the battle at Moscow]. Moscow: Frunze Academy, 1982.

Ogarkov, N. V. ed. *Sovetskaia voennaia entsiklopediia, v vos'mi tomakh* [Soviet military encyclopedia, in eight volumes]. Moscow: Voenizdat, 1976–1989.

———. *Voennyi entsiklopedicheskii slovar'* [Military-encyclopedic dictionary]. Moscow: Voenizdat, 1983.

Orekhov, O. A. "Maloizvestnye stranitsy Velikoi Otechestvennoi voiny: Velikolukskaia nastupatel'naia operatsiia" [Little-known pages from the Great Patriotic War: The Velikie Luki offensive operation]. Unpublished study based on archival materials. Moscow, n.d.

Orenstein, Harold S., ed. and trans. *The Evolution of Soviet Operational Art, 1927–1991: The Documentary Basis, volume 1: Operational Art, 1927, 1964.* London: Frank Cass, 1995.

———. *Soviet Documents of the Use of War Experience, volume 1: The Initial Period of War; volume II: The Winter Campaign; and volume III: Military Operations 1941 and 1942.* London: Frank Cass, 1991–1993.

Pan'kin, V. E. *1941 god—opyt planirovaniia i primenenie voenno-vozdushnykh sil, uroki i vyvody* [1941: The experience of planning and employing the air force, lessons and conclusions]. Moscow: Center for the Operational-Tactical Employment of the VVS, USSR Ministry of Defense, 1989.

Pankov, F. D. *Ognennye rubezhi: Boevoi put' 50-i armii v Velikoi Otechestvennoi voine* [Fiery lines: The combat path of the 50th Army in the Great Patriotic War]. Moscow: Voenizdat, 1984.

Panov, M. F. *Na napravlenii glavnogo udara* [On the main attack axis]. Moscow: n.p., 1995.

Parotkin, I., ed. *The Battle of Kursk*. Moscow: Progress, 1974.

Parrish, Michael. *Battle for Moscow: The 1942 Soviet General Staff Study*. London: Brassey's, 1989.

———. *The Lesser Terror: Soviet State Security, 1939–1953.* Westport, CT: Praeger, 1996.

———. *The USSR in World War II: An Annotated Bibliography of Books Published in the Soviet Union, 1945–1975, with an Addendum for the Years 1975–1980.* 2 vols. New York: Garland, 1981.

Pavlovsky, I. G. *Sukhoputnye voiska SSSR* [Ground forces of the USSR]. Moscow: Voenizdat, 1985.

Pennington, Reina. *Wings, Women, and War: Soviet Airwomen in World War II Combat.* Lawrence: University Press of Kansas, 2001.

Petrov, Iu. P., ed. *Istoriia Velikoi Otechestvennoi voiny Sovetskogo Soiuza 1941–1942 v shesti tomakh* [A History of the Great Patriotic War of the Soviet Union 1941–1945 in six volumes]. Vol. 3. Moscow: Voenizdat, 1961.

Pevnevets, M. P. *Boevoe primenenie Sovetskikh voenno-vozdushnykh sil v gody Velikoi Otechestvennoi voiny* [The combat employment of the Soviet Air Force during the Great Patriotic War]. Moscow: Frunze Academy, 1984.

Platonov, S. P., ed. *Vtoraia mirovaia voina 1939–1945 gg.* [The Second World War 1939–1945]. Moscow: Voenizdat, 1958.

Pogrebnoi, S. A. *Lavinoi stali i ognia: Boevoi put' 7-go mekhanizirovannogo Novoukrainsko-Khinganskogo ordena Lenina, Krasnoznamennogo, ordena Suvorova korpusa* [In an avalanche of steel and fire: The combat path of the 7th Novoukraine-Khingan Order of Lenin, Red Banner, Order of Suvorov Mechanized Corps]. Moscow: Voenizdat, 1980.

Poirier, Robert G., and Albert Z. Conner. "Red Army Order of Battle in the Great Patriotic War." 2d ed. Unpublished manuscript, 1985.

Portugal'sky, R. M. *Komandnye kadry Sovetskikh vooruzhennykh sil v gody Velikoi Otechestvennoi voiny* [The command cadre of the Soviet Armed Forces during the Great Patriotic War]. Moscow: VAF, 1991.

———. *Marshal I. S. Konev.* Moscow: Voenizdat, 1985.

Portugal'sky, R. M., and P. Ia. Tsygankov. *Voennoe iskusstvo Sovetskikh voisk v boiakh za Stalingrad* [The military art of Soviet forces in the battles for Stalingrad]. Moscow: Frunze Academy, 1983.

Portugal'sky, R. M., and L. A. Zaitsev. *Voennoe iskusstvo Sovietskikh voisk v bitve za Leningrad* [Military art of Soviet forces in the battle for Leningrad]. Moscow: Frunze Academy, 1989.

Pospelov, P. N., ed. *Istoriia Velikoi Otechestvennoi voiny Sovetskogo Soiuza 1941–1945 v shesti tomakh* [A history of the Great Patriotic War of the Soviet Union 1941–1945 in six volumes]. Moscow: Voenizdat, 1960–1965.

Radzievsky, A. I., ed. *Armeiskie operatsii (Primery iz opyta Velikoi Otechestvennoi)* [Army operations (Examples from the experience of the Great Patriotic [War])]. Moscow: Voenizdat, 1977.

———. *Taktika v boevykh primerakh (diviziia)* [Tactics in combat examples (the division)]. Moscow: Voenizdat, 1976.

———. *Taktika v boevykh primerakh, polk* [Tactics in combat examples, the regiment]. Moscow: Voenizdat, 1974.

Ramanichev, N. "The Red Army, 1940–1941: Myths and Realities." Unpublished draft manuscript. Moscow, 1996.

Reese, Roger R. *Stalin's Reluctant Soldiers: A Social History of the Red Army, 1925–1941*. Lawrence: University Press of Kansas, 1996.

Reinhardt, Klaus. *Moscow—The Turning Point: Failure of Hitler's Strategy in the Winter of 1941–42.* Oxford: Berg, 1992.

Riazansky, A. P. *V ogne tankovykh srazhenii* [In the fire of tank battles]. Moscow: Nauka, 1975.

Rodionov, I. N., ed. *Voennaia entsiklopediia v vos'mi tomakh* [Military encyclopedia in eight volumes]. Vol. 1. Rev. ed. Moscow: Voenizdat, 1997.

Rokossovsky, K. *A Soldier's Duty.* Moscow: Progress, 1970.

———. *Soldatskii dolg* [A soldier's duty]. Moscow: Golos, 2000.

———, ed. *Velikaia bitva na Volge* [The great battle on the Volga]. Moscow: Voenizdat, 1965.

Salisbury, Harrison E. *The 900 Days: The Siege of Leningrad.* New York: Harper & Row, 1969.

Samsonov, A. M. *Ot Volgi do Baltiki: Ocherk istorii 3-go gvardeiskogo mekhanizirovannogo korpusa 1942–1945 gg.* [From the Volga to the Baltic: Study in the history of the 3rd Guards Mechanized Corps 1942–1945]. Moscow: Nauka, 1973.

———. *Stalingradskaia bitva* [The Battle of Stalingrad]. Moscow: Nauka, 1960.

———, ed. *Proval gitlerovskogo nastupleniia na Moskvu* [The defeat of Hitler's offensive on Moscow]. Moscow: Nauka, 1966.

———. *Stalingradskaia epopeia* [The Stalingrad epic]. Moscow: Nauka, 1968.

Sandalov, L. M. *Pogorelo-Gorodishchenskaia operatsiia* [The Pogoreloe-Gorodishche operation]. Moscow: Voenizdat, 1960.

Sarkis'ian, S. M. *51-aia armiia* [The 51st Army]. Moscow: Voenizdat, 1983.

Savushkin, R. A., ed. *Razvitie Sovetskikh vooruzhennykh sil i voennogo iskusstva v Velikoi Otechestvennoi voine 1941–1945 gg.* [The development of the Soviet Armed Forces and military art in the Great Patriotic War 1941–1945]. Moscow: Lenin Political-Military Academy, 1988.

Scheibert, H. *Panzer Zwischen Don und Donez: Die Winterkampfe 1942/1943* [Panzers between the Don and Donets: The winter battle of 1942–1943]. Freidberg: Podzun-Pallas-Verlag, 1979.

Schroter, Heinz. *Stalingrad.* London: Michael Joseph, 1958.

Schulz, Friedrich. *Reverses on the Southern Wing (1942–1943). MS #T-15.* Headquarters, United States Army, Europe, Historical Division, n.d.
Seaton, Albert. *The Battle for Moscow 1941–1942.* London: Rupert Hart-Davis, 1971.
———. *The Russo-German War 1941–1945.* New York: Praeger, 1971.
Sechkin, G. P. *Pogranichnye voiska v Velikoi Otechestvennoi voine* [Border guards forces in the Great Patriotic War]. Moscow: Order of Lenin Red Banner Higher Border Guards Command Courses of the KGB USSR, 1990.
Sekretov, A. N. *Gvardeiskaia postup'* [Guards gait]. Dushanbe: Donish, 1985.
Semonov, G. G. *Nastupaet udarnaia* [The shock army attacks]. Moscow: Voenizdat, 1988.
Sergeev, I. D., ed. *Voennaia entsiklopediia v vos'mi tomakh* [Military encyclopedia in eight volumes]. Vols. 4–5. Moscow: Voenizdat, 1999–2001.
Shirokorad, A. B. *Entsiklopediia Otechestvennoi artillerii* [An encyclopedia of national artillery]. Minsk: Kharvest, 2000.
Shkadov, I. N., ed. *Geroi Sovetskogo soiuza v dvukh tomakh* [Heroes of the Soviet Union in two volumes]. Moscow: Voenizdat, 1987.
Shtemenko, S. M. *The General Staff at War, 1941–1945.* Moscow: Progress, 1970.
———. *The Last Six Months.* Garden City, NY: Doubleday, 1977.
———. *The Soviet General Staff at War 1941–1945.* 2 vols. Moscow: Progress, 1985.
Shukman, Harold, ed. *Stalin's Generals.* London: Weidenfeld and Nicolson, 1993.
Shutov, Z. A. *Puti dostizheniia ustoichivosti i aktivnosti oborony v gody Velikoi Otechestvennoi voiny* [Paths to the achievement of durability and dynamism in the defense during the Great Patriotic War]. Moscow: Frunze Academy, 1990.
Skomorokhov, N. M. *Voenno-vozdushnaia akademiia imeni Iu. A. Gagarina* [The Iu. A. Gagarin Air Force Academy]. Moscow: Voenizdat, 1984.
Smirov, A. F., and K. S. Ogloblin. *Tanki za Vislou: Boevoi put' 31-go tankovogo korpusa* [Tanks beyond the Vistula: The combat path of the 31st Tank Corps]. Moscow: Voenizdat, 1991.
Smirnov, E. I. *Voina i voennaia meditsina* [War and military medicine]. Moscow: Meditsina, 1979.
Stephan, Robert W. *Stalin's Secret War: Soviet Counterintelligence against the Nazis, 1941–1945.* Lawrence: University Press of Kansas, 2004.
Strokov, A. A., ed. *Istoriia voennogo isskustva* [A history of military art]. Moscow: Voenizdat, 1966.
Sukhinin, Iu. M., and Iu. N. Iarovenko. *Oborona 1-i Tankovoi armii pod Kurskom (6–11 iiulia 1943 g.)* [The 1st Tank Army's defense at Kursk (6–11 July 1943)]. Moscow: Frunze Academy, 1989.
Suvenirov, O. A. *Tragediia RKKA 1937–1938* [The tragedy of the RKKA 1937–1941]. Moscow: Terra, 1998.
Sychev, K. V., and M. M. Malakhov. *Nastuplenie strelkogo korpusa* [Rifle corps offensive]. Moscow: Voenizdat, 1958.
Tarrant, V. E. *Stalingrad.* New York: Hippocrene Books, 1992.
Terekhin, K. P., and A. S. Taralov. *Gvardeitsy zheleznodorozhniki* [Guards railroad men]. Moscow: Voenizdat, 1966.

Tiushkevich, S. A., ed. *Sovetskie vooruzhennye sily* [Soviet Armed Forces]. Moscow: Voenizdat, 1978.

Tolubko, V. F., and N. I. Baryshev. *Na iuzhnom flange: Boevoi put' 4-go gvardeiskogo mekhanizirovannogo korpusa (1942–1945 gg.)* [On the southern flank: The combat path of the 4th Guards Mechanized Corps (1942–1945)]. Moscow: Nauka, 1973.

Tsirlin, A. D., P. I. Biriukov, V. P. Istomin, and E. N. Fedoseev, eds. *Inzhenernye voiska v boiakh za sovetskuiu rodinu* [Engineer forces in combat for the Soviet homeland]. Moscow: Voenizdat, 1970, 1976.

Ustinov, D. F., ed. *Istoriia Vtoroi Mirovoi voiny 1939–1945 v dvenadtsati tomakh* [A history of the World War II in twelve volumes]. Vol. 8. Moscow: Voenizdat, 1977.

Vasilevsky, A. M. *Delo vsei zhizni* [Life's work]. Moscow: Politizdat, 1971. Translated as *A Lifelong Cause*. Moscow: Progress, 1976.

Vilenko, S. I. *Na okhrane tyla strany: Istrebitel'nye batal'ony i polki v Velikoi Otechestvennoi voine 1941–1945* [In protection of the country's rear area: Destruction battalions and regiments in the Great Patriotic War 1941–1945]. Moscow: Nauka, 1988.

Vinogradov, V. S., ed. *Krasnoznamennyi pribaltiiskii pogranichnyi* [Red Banner Baltic border guards]. Riga: Abots, 1988.

Vladimirsky, A. V. *Na kievskom napravelenii* [On the Kiev axis]. Moscow: Voenizdat, 1989.

Vnutrennie voiska v gody mirnogo sotsialisticheskogo stroitel'stva, 1922–1941 gg. [The internal forces in the years of peaceful Socialist construction 1922–1941]. Moscow: Iuridicheskaia Literatura, 1977.

Voennoe isskustvo vo Vtoroi Mirovoi voine [Military art in World War II]. Moscow: Voroshilov Academy, 1973.

Volkogonov, Dmitri. *Stalin: Triumph and Tragedy.* Rocklin, CA: Prima, 1992.

Volkov, A. A. *Kriticheskii prolog: Nezavershennye frontovye nastupatel'nye operatsii pervykh kampanii Velikoi Otechestvennoi voiny* [Critical prologue: Incomplete *front* offensive operations in the initial campaigns of the Great Patriotic War]. Moscow: Aviar, 1992.

Vysotsky, V. K., ed. *Tyl Sovetskoi Armii* [The rear of the Soviet Army]. Moscow: Voenizdat, 1968.

Wagner, Roy, ed. *The Soviet Air Forces in World War II: The Official History.* Trans. Leland Fetzer. Garden City, NY: Doubleday, 1973.

Warlimont, Walter. *Inside Hitler's Headquarters.* New York: Praeger, 1961.

Whaley, Barton. *Codeword Barbarossa.* Cambridge, MA: MIT Press, 1973.

Windbush, S. Enders, and Alexander Alexiev. *Ethnic Minorities in the Red Army: Asset or Liability.* Boulder, CO: Westview Press, 1988.

Zakharov, Iu. D. *General armii Vatutin* [Army General Vatutin]. Moscow: Voenizdat, 1985.

Zaloga, Steven J., and Leland S. Ness. *Red Army Handbook 1939–1945.* Gloucestershire, UK: Sutton, 1998.

Zetterling, Niklas, and Anders Frankson. *Kursk 1943: A Statistical Analysis.* London: Frank Cass, 2000.

Zhilin, P. A., ed. *Besprimernyi podvig* [An unprecedented deed]. Moscow: Nauka, 1968.

Zhuk, A. B. *Strelkovoe oruzhie* [Rifle weapons]. Moscow: Voenizdat, 1992.

Zhukov, G. *Reminiscences and Reflections.* 2 vols. Moscow: Progress, 1985.

Ziemke, Earl F. *The German Northern Theater of Operations, 1940–1945.* Washington, DC: Government Printing Office, 1959.

———. *Stalingrad to Berlin: The German Defeat in the East.* Washington, DC: Office of the Chief of Military History United States Army, 1968.

Ziemke, Earl F., and Magna E. Bauer. *Moscow to Stalingrad: Decision in the East.* Washington, DC: Office of the Chief of Military History United States Army, 1987.

Zolotarev, V. A., ed. *Velikaia Otechestvennaia voina 1941–1945: Voenno-istoricheskie ocherki v chetyrekh tomakh* [The Great Patriotic War 1941–1945: Military-historical essays in four volumes]. Moscow: Nauka, 1998–1999.

Zvartsev, A. M. *3-ia gvardeiskaia tankovaia: Boevoi put' 3-i gvardeiskoi tankovoi armii* [The 3rd Guards Tank Army: The combat path of the 3rd Guards Tank Army]. Moscow: Voenizdat, 1982.

Secondary Sources: Articles

Alekseenkov, A. "Vnutrennie voiska: Pravda i vymysel—Na trekh frontakh" [Internal forces: Truth and fantasy—on three fronts]. *Voennye znaniia* [Military knowledge], no. 1 (January 1991): 3–4.

Altunin, Evgenii. "ALSIB: On the History of the Alaska-Siberian Ferrying Route." *JSMS* 10, no. 2 (June 1997): 85–97.

Antonov, A. P. "Operativnoe upravlenie General'nogo shtaba v gody Velikoi Otechestvennoi voiny" [The General Staff's Operational Directorate during the Great Patriotic War]. *VIZh,* no. 5 (May 1988): 12–18.

Bazanov, I. N. "Obespechenie frontov goriuchim v tret'em periode Velikoi Otechestvennoi voiny" [Fuel provision to the *fronts* in the third period of the Great Patriotic War]. *VIZh,* no. 3 (March 1987): 50–56.

Berkhin, I. "O territorial'no-militsionnom stroitel'stve v Sovetskoi Armii" [On territorial-militia construction in the Soviet army]. *VIZh,* no. 12 (December 1960): 1–20.

Cheremnykh, A. "Razvitie voenno-uchebnykh zavedenii v predvoennyi period (1937–1941) [The development of military-educational institutions in the prewar period (1937–1941)], *VIZh,* no. 8 (August 1982): 75–80.

Danilov, V. D. "General'nyi shtab RKKA v predvoennye gody (1936–iiun' 1941 g.)" [The RKKA General Staff in the prewar years (1936 to June 1941)]. *VIZh,* no. 3 (March 1980): 68–73.

———. "Glavnye komandovaniia napravlenii v Velikoi Otechestvennoi voine" [Main direction commands in the Great Patriotic War]. *VIZh,* no. 9 (September 1987): 17–23.

———. "Razvitie sistemy organov strategicheskogo rukovodstva v nachale Velikoi Otechestvennoi voiny" [The development of a system of strategic leadership organs in the beginning of the Great Patriotic War]. *VIZh,* no. 6 (June 1987): 25–30.

———. "Stavka VGK, 1941–1945." *Zashchita otechestva* [Defense of the fatherland], no. 12 (December 1991): 1–39.

Dzhelaukhov, Kh. M., and B. M. Petrov. "K voprosu o strategicheskikh operatsiiakh Velikoi Otechestvennoi voiny 1941–1945 gg." [Concerning the question of strategic operations of the Great Patriotic War 1941–1945]. *VIZh*, no. 7 (July 1986): 46–48.

Gareev, M. A. "O neudachnykh nastupatel'nykh operatsiiakh Sovetskikh voisk v Velikoi Otechestvennoi voine. Po neopublikovannym dokumentam GKO" [On the unsuccessful offensive operations of Soviet forces in the Great Patriotic War: Based on unpublished GKO documents]. *Novaia i noveishshaia istoriia* [New and recent history], no. 1 (January 1994): 2–28.

Gladysh, S. A. "Obobshchenie i ispol'zovanie boevogo opyta v pervom periode Velikoi Otechestvennoi voiny" [The exploitation and use of war experience in the first period of the Great Patriotic War]. *VIZh*, no. 7 (July 1987): 14–20.

Glantz, David M. "The Failures of Historiography: Forgotten Battles of the German-Soviet War (1941–1945)." *JSMS* 8, no. 4 (December 1995): 768–808.

———. "Newly Published Works on the Red Army, 1918–1991." *JSMS* 8, no. 2 (June 1995): 319–32.

———. "Prelude to Kursk: Soviet Strategic Operations, February–March 1943." *JSMS* 8, no. 1 (March 1995): 1–35.

———. "Soviet Military Strategy during the Second Period of War (November 1942–December 1943): A Reappraisal." *Journal of Military History*, no. 60 (January 1996): 115–50.

Gradosel'sky, V. V. "Natsional'nye voinskie formirovaniia v Krasnoi Armii (1918–1938 gg.) [National military formations in the Red Army (1918–1938)]. *VIZh*, no. 10 (October 2001): 2–6.

———. "Natsional'nye voinskie formirovaniia v Velikoi Otechestvennoi voine" [National military formations in the Great Patriotic War], *VIZh*, no. 1 (January 2002): 18–24.

Gurkin, V. V. "Liudskie poteri Sovetskikh vooruzhennykh sil v 1941–1945: Novye aspekty" [Personnel losses of the Soviet Armed Forces in 1941–1945: New aspects]. *VIZh*, no. 2 (March–April 1999): 2–13.

———. "'Mars' v orbite 'Urana' i 'Saturna': O vtoroi Rzhevsko-Sychevskoi nastupatel'noi operatsii 1942 goda" ["Mars" in the orbit of "Uranus" and "Saturn": On the second Rzhev-Sychevka offensive operation]. *VIZh*, no. 4 (July–August 2000): 14–19.

Gurkin, V. V., and M. I. Golovnin. "K voprosu o strategicheskikh operatsiiakh Velikoi Otechestvennoi voiny 1941–1945 gg" [Concerning the question of strategic operations of the Great Patriotic War 1941–1945]. *VIZh*, no. 10 (October 1985): 10–23.

Gusarev, F. F., and L. A. Butakov. "Tekhnicheskoe prikrytie zheleznykh dorog" [Technical protection of the railroads]. *VIZh*, no. 4 (April 1988): 51–58.

Il'enkov, S. A. "Concerning the Registration of Soviet Armed Forces' Wartime Irrevocable Losses, 1941–1945." *JSMS* 9, no. 2 (June 1996): 440–42.

"Itogi diskussii o strategicheskikh operatsiiakh Velikoi Otechestvennoi voiny 1941–1945 gg." [Results of the discussion on strategic operations of the Great Patriotic War 1941–1945]. *VIZh*, no. 10 (October 1987): 14–20.

Ivanov, S. P., and N. Shekhovtsov. "Opyt raboty glavnykh komandovanii na teatrakh voennykh deistvii" [Experience in the work of main commands in theaters of military operations]. *VIZh*, no. 9 (September 1981): 11–18.

Khomenko, S. "A Disciplinary Battalion Joins Battle." *Soviet Soldier*, no. 11 (November 1990): 36–38.

Khor'kov, A. G. "Nekotorye voprosy strategicheskogo razvertyvaniia Sovetskikh vooruzhennykh sil v nachale Velikoi Otechestvennoi voiny" [Some questions concerning the strategic deployment of the Soviet Armed Forces at the beginning of the Great Patriotic War]. *VIZh*, no. 1 (January 1986): 9–15.

Khrulev, A. "Stanovlenie strategicheskogo tyla v Velikoi Otechestvennoi voine" [The establishment of a strategic rear in the Great Patriotic War]. *VIZh*, no. 6 (June 1961): 64–86.

Klemin, A. S. "Voennye soobshcheniia v gody Velikoi Otechestvennoi voiny" [Military communications during the Great Patriotic War]. *VIZh*, no. 3 (March 1985): 66–74.

Koldunov, A. "Organizatsiia i vedenie protivovozdushnoi oborony po opytu nachal'nogo perioda Velikoi Otechestvennoi voiny" [The organization and conduct of antiaircraft defense based on the experience of the initial period of the Great Patriotic War]. *VIZh*, no. 4 (April 1984): 12–19.

Komarov, F. I., and O. S. Lobastov. "Osnovnye itogi i uroki meditsinskogo obespecheniia Sovetskoi armii v gody Velikoi Otechestvennoi voiny" [The main conclusions and lessons of Soviet Army medical support during the Great Patriotic War]. *Voenno-meditsinskii zhurnal* [Military-medical journal], no. 5 (May 1990): 3–20.

Kornienko, N. "Boevoe primenenie bronepoezda PVO" [The combat employment of the PVO armored train], *VIZh*, no. 4 (April 1979): 31–34.

Korol', V. E. "The Price of Victory." *JSMS* 9, no. 2 (June 1996): 417–26.

Kulikov, V. "Strategicheskoe rukovodstvo vooruzhennymi silami" [The strategic leadership of the armed forces]. *VIZh*, no. 6 (June 1975): 12–24.

Kunitsky, P. T. "O vybore napravleniia glavnogo udara v kampaniiakh i strategicheskikh operatsiiakh" [On the selection of the main attack axis in campaigns and strategic operations]. *VIZh*, no. 7 (July 1986): 29–40.

Kuznetsov, I. I. "Stalin's Minister V. S. Abakumov 1908–54." *JSMS* 12, no. 1 (March 1999): 149–65.

Lavrent'ev, K. "Voiskovaia PVO v gody voiny" [Force air defense in the war years], *Voennyi vestnik* [Military herald], no. 10 (October 1989): 48–51.

Lipitsky, S. V. "Voennaia reforma 1924–1925 godov" [The military reforms of 1924–1925]. *Kommunist* [Communist], no. 4 (March 1990): 104–6.

Lomov, N., and V. Golubovich. "Ob organizatsii i metodakh raboty General'nogo shtaba" [About the organization and work methods of the General Staff]. *VIZh*, no. 2 (February 1981): 12–19.

Lotosky, S. "Iz opyta vedeniia armeiskikh nastupatel'nykh operatsii v gody Velikoi Otechestvennoi voiny" [From the experience of the conduct of army offensive operations during the Great Patriotic War]. *VIZh*, no. 12 (December 1965): 3–14.

Mairov, A. M. "Strategicheskoe rukovodstvo v Velikoi Otechestvennoi voine" [Strategic leadership in the Great Patriotic War]. *VIZh*, no. 5 (May 1985): 28–40.

Makartsev, M. K. "Sovershenstvovanie organizatsii zheleznodorozhnykh voisk v gody Velikoi Otechestvennoi voiny" [Improvement of the organization of railroad forces during the Great Patriotic War]. *VIZh,* no. 9 (September 1985): 80–85.

Malan'in, K. "Razvitie organizatsionnykh form sukhoputnykh voisk v Velikoi Otechestvennoi voine" [The development of ground forces' organizational forms in the Great Patriotic War]. *VIZh,* no. 8 (August 1967): 28–39.

Malinovsky, G. V. "Sapernye armii i ikh rol' v pervyi period Velikoi Otechestvennoi voiny [Sapper armies and their role in the initial period of the Great Patriotic War]. In *Voenno-istoricheskii arkhiv* [Military-historical archives], vol. 2 (17), pp. 146–79. Moscow: Tserera, 2001.

Maliugin, N. "Avtomobil'nyi transport frontov i armii v gody voiny" [Automobile transport of *fronts* and armies in the war years]. *VIZh,* no. 2 (February 1971): 87–91.

———. "Nekotorye voprosy tylovogo obespecheniia stalingradskogo fronta v kontranastuplenii" [Some questions about the rear support of the Stalingrad Front during the counteroffensive]. *VIZh,* no. 8 (August 1977): 98–104.

Mal'tsev, I. M. "Sovershenstvovanie sistemy upravleniia voiskami protivovozdushnoi oborony v gody Velikoi Otechestvennoi voiny" [The improvement of the command and control systems of air defense forces during the Great Patriotic War]. *VIZh,* no. 4 (April 1986): 22–31.

Mal'tsev, N. A. "Kadrovaia ili militsionnaia" [Cadre or militia]. *VIZh,* no. 11 (November 1989): 30–40.

Mangazeev, Igor. "A 'Penal' Corps on the Kalinin Front." *JSMS* 15, no. 3 (September 2002): 115–45.

Maslov, A. A. "How Were Soviet Blocking Detachments Employed?" *JSMS* 9, no. 2 (June 1996): 427–35.

Matsulenko, V. "Razvitie taktiki nastupatel'nogo boia" [The development of offensive battle tactics]. *VIZh,* no. 2 (February 1968): 28–46.

Medvedev, N. E. "Artilleriia RVGK v pervom periode voiny" [Artillery of the *Stavka* Reserve in the initial period of the war], *VIZh,* no. 11 (November 1987): 81–87.

Mikhailovsky, G., and I. Vyrodov. "Vysshie organy rukovodstva voinoi" [The higher organs for directing the war]. *VIZh,* no. 4 (April 1978): 16–26.

Mikhalev, A. I., and V. I. Kudriashov. "K voprosu o strategicheskikh operatsiiakh Velikoi Otechestvennoi voiny 1941–1945 gg" [Concerning the question of strategic operations of the Great Patriotic War 1941–1945]. *VIZh,* no. 5 (May 1986): 48–51.

Moniushko, Evgenii. "Memoirs of the Soviet-German War, part 2: Siberia, the Front and Hospital, 1942–1944." *JSMS* 15, no. 2 (June 2002): 100–80.

———. "Memoirs of the Soviet-German War, part 4: Red Army Service in Silesia and Czechoslovakia during 1945." *JSMS* 15, no. 3 (September 2002): 146–202.

Nekrasov, V. F. "Osnovnye etapy stroitel'stva vnutrennikh voisk" [Basic stages in the formation of internal forces]. *VIZh,* no. 11 (November 1986): 81–84.

———. "Vklad vnutrennikh voisk v delo pobedy sovetskogo naroda v Velikoi Otechestvennoi voine" [The internal forces' contribution to the victory of the

Soviet people in the Great Patriotic War]. *VIZh,* no. 9 (September 1985): 29–35.

Nikitin, V. "Obespechenie voisk goriuchim v kontrnastuplenii pod Kurskom" [Fuel provision for forces during the counteroffensive at Kursk]. *VIZh,* no. 8 (August 1979): 25–30.

Orlov, A. S. "Operatsiia 'Mars': Razlichnye traktov," [Operation Mars: Different roads]. *Mir istorii* [World of history], no. 4 (April 2000): 1–4. On the Internet at http://www.tellur.ru/~historia/orlov.htm.

Parrish, Michael. "The Last Relic: Army General I. E. Serov." *JSMS* 10, no. 3 (September 1997): 109–29.

Pavlenko, N. "Na pervom etape voiny" [During the first stage of the war]. *Kommunist* [Communist], no. 9 (June 1988): 90–96.

Peresypkin, I. "Sviaz' General'nogo shtaba" [General Staff communications]. *VIZh,* no. 4 (April 1971): 19–25.

Petrov, M. "Predstavitel' Stavki" [*Stavka* representative]. *VIZh,* no. 2 (February 1981): 50–56.

Piliugin, Iu. "Okhrana sukhoputnykh kommunikatsii v khode voiny" [The protection of ground communications during the war]. *VIZh,* no. 9 (September 1983): 31–36.

"Polozhenie i instruktsiia po rabote korpusa ofitserov—predstavitelei General'nogo shtaba Krasnoi Armii" [Regulation and instruction on the work of officers corps Red Army General Staff representatives]. *VIZh,* no. 2 (February 1975): 62–66.

Ponomarev, A. Ia., and V. G. Smirnov. "Zagrazhdenie zheleznykh dorog v pervom perioda voiny" [The obstruction of railroads in the initial period of the war]. *VIZh,* no. 3 (March 1986): 77–81.

Popov, N. "Razvitie samokhodnoi artillerii" [The development of self-propelled artillery]. *VIZh,* no. 1 (January 1977): 27–31.

———. "Sovershenstvovanie sistemy transportnogo obespecheniia v gody voiny" [Improvement of the transport support system in the war years]. *VIZh,* no. 8 (August 1982]: 20–26.

"Prikaz NKO No. 306 ot 8 oktiabria 1942 g." [People's Commissariat of Defense Order No. 306 of 16 October 1942]. *VIZh,* no. 9 (September 1974): 62–66.

Radzievsky, A. "Proryv oborony v pervom periode voiny" [The penetration of a defense in the initial period of the war]. *VIZh,* no. 3 (March 1972): 15–23.

Ryzhakov, A. "K voprusu o stroitel'tsve bronetankovykh voisk Krasnoi Armii v 30-e gody" [Concerning the question of the formation of the Red Army's armored forces in the 1930s]. *VIZh,* no. 8 (August 1968): 105–11.

Saltykov, N. D. "Podvig (Korpus ofitserov-predstavitelei General'nogo shtaba v Velikoi Otechestvennoi voine)" [Victory (Officers corps General Staff representatives in the Great Patriotic War)]. *VIZh,* no. 12 (December 1988): 23–28.

———. "Predstaviteli General'nogo shtaba" [General Staff representatives]. *VIZh,* no. 9 (September 1971): 56–59.

Selivanov, V. I., and N. A. Vishnevsky. "Organizatsiia meditsinskogo obespecheniia voisk v kontrnastuplenii pod Moskvoi" [The organization of medical support of forces during the counteroffensive at Moscow]. *Voenno-meditsinskii zhurnal* [Military-medical journal], no. 1 (January 1992): 47–49.

Shabaev, A. A. "Poteri ofitserskogo sostava Krasnoi Armii v Velikoi Otechestvennoi voine" [Red Army officer cadre losses in the Great Patriotic War]. *Voenno-istoricheskii arkhiv* [Military-historical archives] (Moscow) 3 (1998): 173–89.

Shlomin, V. "Dvadtsat' piat' morskikh strelkovykh" [25th Naval Infantry]. *VIZh*, no. 7 (July 1970): 96–99.

Shlomin, V. S. "K voprosu o strategicheskikh operatsiiakh Velikoi Otechestvennoi voiny 1941–1945 gg" [Concerning the question of strategic operations of the Great Patriotic War 1941–1945]. *VIZh*, no. 4 (April 1986): 49–52.

Sokolov, Boris V. "Lend-Lease in Soviet Military Efforts." *JSMS* 7, no. 3 (September 1994): 567–86.

Sokolov, V. "Razvitie organizatsionnoi struktury voisk sviazi v gody voiny" [The development of the organizational structure of signal forces in the war years]. *VIZh*, no. 4 (April 1981): 20–27.

Soskov, A. A. "Sovershenstvovanie organizatsionnoi struktury inzhenernykh voisk v gody Velikoi Otechestvennoi voiny" [Improvement in the organizational structure of engineer forces during the Great Patriotic War]. *VIZh*, no. 12 (December 1985): 66–70.

Strakhov, N. "Na avtomobil'nykh dorogakh" [Along automobile roads]. *VIZh*, no. 11 (November 1964): 63–64, and no. 8 (August 1965): 45–57.

Svetlishin, N. "Iz opyta boevoi podgotovki voisk PVO strany v gody Velikoi Otechestvennoi voiny" [From the experience of military training for PVO Strany forces during the Great Patriotic War]. *VIZh*, no. 4 (April 1982): 10–17.

———. "Nekotorye voprosy primeneniia voisk PVO strany" [Some questions on the employment of PVO Strany forces]. *VIZh*, no. 12 (December 1969): 17–28.

———. "Primenenie Voisk protivovozdushnoi oborony v letne-osennei kampanii 1941 goda" [The employment of air defense forces in the summer–fall campaign of 1941]. *VIZh*, no. 3 (March 1968): 26–39.

———. "Voiska PVO strany v letne-osennei kampanii 1943 goda" [The forces of PVO Strany in the summer–fall campaign of 1943]. *VIZh*, no. 9 (September 1971): 23–31.

Tereshchenko, M. N. "Na zapadnom napravlenii: Kak sozdavalis' i deistvovali glavnye komandovaniia napravlenii [On the Western Direction: How Main Direction commands were created and functioned]. *VIZh*, no. 5 (May 1993): 9–17.

Tsirlin, A. "Voennye stroiteli v Velikoi Otechestvennoi voine" [Military constructors in the Great Patriotic War]. *VIZh*, no. 5 (May 1968): 107–12.

Tur, M. "Razvitie protivovozdushnoi oborony voisk v Velikoi Otechestvennoi voine" [The development of antiaircraft defense for forces in the Great Patriotic War]. *VIZh*, no. 1 (January 1962): 15–24.

"Tyly deistvuiushchei armii okhraniali voiska NKVD" [NKVD forces protected the rear areas of the operating army]. *VIZh*, no. 6 (November–December 1998): 16–25.

Vorsin, V. "Pomoshch' po Lend-Lizu" [Assistance under Lend-Lease]. *Tyl vooruzhennykh sil* [Rear of the armed forces], no. 10 (October 1991): 28–31.

Vyrodov, I. "Rol' predstavitelei Stavki VGK v gody voiny. Organizatsiia i metody ikh raboty" [The role of *Stavka* VGK representatives in the war years: Their organization and work methods]. *VIZh,* no. 8 (August 1980): 25–33.

Zakharov, M. "Strategicheskoe rukovodstvo vooruzhennymi silami" [Strategic leadership of the armed forces]. *VIZh*, no. 5 (May 1970): 23–34.

Zemskov, V. "Nekotorye voprosy sozdaniia i ispol'zovaniia strategicheskikh reservov" [Some questions on the creation and employment of strategic reserves]. *VIZh*, no. 10 (October 1971): 12–19.

Index

Abadan, 668n.117
Abakumov, V. S., 384, 393, 400–402, 446, 466, 680n.50, 681–682n.82, 682n.85
Aborenkov, Lieutenant General V. V., 406, 462, 684n.11
Abwehr (counterintelligence), German, 138, 158, 166
Advanced battalions, Soviet, 119
Airborne (air assault) forces, Soviet, 186–188, 411–412, 655n.18
Air defense (PVO) forces, Soviet, 139–140, 302, 414–419
  aviation, 311, 685n.34
  commanders, 531–532
  Force (PVO *voisk*), 137, 140, 416–417
  Local (MPVO), 67, 163, 417
  National (PVO Strany), 75, 137, 147–149, 416–418
  women soldiers, 551–552, 554, 687n.58, 721n.51
Airfields, Soviet Air Force
  Engels, 551, 667n.107
  Ivanovo, 668n.117
  Kamenka, 551, 667n.107
Air Force Academy for Command and Navigator Cadre of the Red Army, 414
Air Forces (VVS), Soviet, 307, 311–319, 392–393, 412–414
  Army Aviation (AA), 311, 313–319
  Aviation of Long-range Action (ADD), 312–313, 413, 667n.103
  commanders, 532–535
  Force Aviation (VA), 311, 313–319, 413
  Frontal Aviation (FA), 311, 313–319, 413
  Long-range Bomber Aviation (Aviation of the High Command; AGK), 311–312, 413, 532
  women soldiers, 551–552, 667n.105
Air Observation, Warning, and Communications System, Soviet. *See* VNOS
"Air Offensive," Soviet concept of, 113, 414
Air support, Soviet, 112–113
Akhliustin, Major General P. N., 513
Akhmanov, Colonel O. A,, 514
Akimenko, Major General A. Z., 580
Akimov, Lieutenant General A. I., 522
Akimov, Lieutenant General I. D., 504
Aksai River, 47
Alekseenko, Major General I. P., 513
Alekseev, Lieutenant General of Tank Forces V. M., 514, 521–522
Alekseev, Major General I. I., 568
Alexander II, Tsar, 566
Algeria, 37
ALSIB (Alaska-Siberia), Lend-Lease route, 668n.117
Ampulemet antitank mortar, Soviet, 194, 350
Andreev, A. A, 690n.113, 692n.149
Andreev, Major General K. Iu., 514
Antitank defenses, Soviet, 78–79, 110–112
  antitank strong points and regions, 111, 116
Antoniuk, Lieutenant General M. A., 508–509

Antonov, Colonel General A. I., 35, 69, 372–373, 376, 386–387, 390–393, 452, 681n.61, 700n.219, 704–705n.11
Anukushkin, Major General of Tank Forces F. G., 514, 522
Apanasenko, Lieutenant General I. P., 468, 483, 489, 496, 704n.9, 704n.11
Aral'sk, 433
Arkhangel'sk, 139, 396, 418
Armaderov, Major General G. A., 682n.82
Armavir, 336
Armed Forces, Soviet, strength (on 22 June 1941), 717n.8
Armenians, in the Red Army, 496–497
Armies, German
  First Panzer, 27, 29, 53, 56, 525
  Second, 22, 27, 29, 40, 48, 51, 709n.67
  Second Panzer, 20, 22, 51
  Third Panzer, 42, 51
  Fourth, 20, 51
  Fourth Panzer, 22, 27, 29, 38, 47–48, 51, 53, 56, 560
  Sixth, 4, 17, 27, 29, 32, 36, 38, 40, 44, 46–48, 53, 81, 109, 395, 485, 490–491, 493, 518, 638n.10
  Eighth, 51, 53, 56
  Ninth, 13, 42–43, 51
  Eleventh, 27, 32, 34, 36
  Sixteenth, 42
  Seventeenth, 27, 29, 53, 55–56
  Eighteenth, 22
Armies, Hungarian, Second, 27, 35, 40, 48
Armies, Italian, Eighth, 29, 35, 40, 47–48, 491, 638n.10
Armies, Japanese, 26
  Kwantung, 5, 26, 154, 387
Armies, PVO (air defense), Soviet, 143, 148
  Baku PVO, 147, 417, 531
  Leningrad PVO, 147–148, 417–418, 531
  Special Moscow PVO, 148, 418, 531
Armies, Romanian
  Third, 27, 29, 35, 38, 48, 638n.10
  Fourth, 27, 29, 35, 38, 48
Armies, Soviet, 143–146, 178, 201–214, 259–260, 291, 298, 333–334, 342, 344–349, 355, 357, 359, 383–384, 404–405, 408–409, 411, 423–425, 428–430, 433, 435–441, 451, 453, 455–458, 462
  air, 143, 316–317: formation, composition, and subordination (May–November 1942), 331, 414, 441, 532, 669n.118, 715n.135
  bomber aviation, 316
  commanders, 470, 502
  command turbulence, 712n.98, 712n.100, 712n.101, 714n.117, 714n.119, 715n.131, 715n.136, 716n.139
  fighter aviation, 315–316
  reserve, 74, 143
  rifle (combined-arms), 60, 143: operating strength, 201–214, 298–299
  sapper (engineer), 144, 335–340, 358: formation, composition, and disposition, 366, 410, 670n.17, 671n.22
  tank, 61, 74, 108–109, 143, 178, 217–218, 230–234: average strength, 261; commanders, 522–528, 657n.29; formation and composition, 259–260; minimum and maximum strength, 261; operating strength, 265–282, 298–299; quantity of corps in offensive operations, 261
  1st Air, 316, 532, 668n.115
  1st Bomber Aviation, 532, 668n.115
  1st Cavalry, 238, 386, 419, 478–480
  1st Fighter Aviation, 316, 532, 668n.115
  1st Guards, 144–145, 190, 500, 510–511, 705n.18
  1st Guards Tank, 524–525, 528, 714n.116

1st Red Banner, 485, 708n.53
1st Reserve, 97, 705n.18
1st Sapper, 336–337, 339–341, 410, 529–530, 671n.20, 672n.27
1st Shock, 18, 88, 144–145, 184, 506, 644n.56, 655n.21, 665n.80
1st Tank (1st formation), 32, 44, 75, 230–231, 243–244, 522–523, 525, 637n.27, 641n.44, 647n.82, 647n.87, 648n90, 657n.24, 705n.18, 714n.116
1st Tank (2nd formation), 232, 244, 523, 525, 643n.51, 645n.66, 647n.88, 658–659n.54, 714n.116
2nd, 566
2nd Air, 532–533
2nd Cavalry, 419
2nd Fighter Aviation, 532, 668n.115
2nd Guards, 40, 47, 144–145, 492, 510–511, 705n.18
2nd Guards Tank, 524, 527–528, 714n.116
2nd Red Banner, 412
2nd Reserve, 97, 149–151, 705n.18
2nd Sapper, 336–338, 340, 529, 671n.22
2nd Shock, 22, 33, 36, 144–145, 467, 502, 507, 517, 680n.52, 707n.52
2nd Tank (1st formation from 3rd Reserve), 150, 231–232, 523, 635n.6, 641n.44, 648n.90, 657n.27, 657n.31, 711n.79, 714n.116
2nd Tank (2nd formation), 523, 527, 645n.66, 659n.54, 714n.116
3rd, 7, 10, 151, 504, 507–508, 645n.69, 653n.29
3rd Air, 532–533, 669n.118
3rd Guards, 144–145, 190, 510–511, 705n.18
3rd Guards Tank, 56, 98, 245, 523–524, 645n.66, 648n.89, 658–659n.54
3rd Reserve, 97, 150, 657n.27 705n.18
3rd Sapper, 336–337, 339–430, 529, 671n.22, 672n.27
3rd Shock, 42, 144–145, 501, 508, 510
3rd Tank (1st formation), 32, 89, 98, 145, 230, 243–244, 522–524, 642n.50, 648n.90, 648n.93, 705n.18
4th, 7, 145, 501, 505–506, 575, 642n.49, 644n.56, 645n.69, 704n.4
4th Air, 532–533
4th Guards, 98, 511, 637n.27, 645n.66
4th Guards Tank (1st formation), 232
4th Guards Tank (2nd formation), 59, 524
4th Reserve, 97, 705n.18
4th Sapper, 336–338, 340, 529, 671n.22
4th Shock, 22, 144–145, 485, 508
4th Tank, 32, 230–231, 243, 522–523, 645n.66, 647n.82, 647n.87, 648n.90, 657n.24, 658n.54, 705n.18, 714n.116
5th, 10, 145, 287, 395, 493–494, 504–506, 509, 644n.56
5th Air, 98, 151, 532–533
5th Guards, 59, 98, 511, 642n.47, 645n.66, 721n.48
5th Guards Tank, 59, 98, 151, 244–245, 523–524, 642n.47, 643n.51, 645n.66, 648n.88, 648n.89, 650n.113, 658–659n.54, 714n.116
5th Reserve, 97, 705n.18
5th Sapper, 336–338, 340, 529, 671n.22
5th Shock, 144, 484, 510–511
5th Tank (1st formation), 32, 98, 109, 145, 190, 230–231, 243, 316, 514, 519, 522–523, 641n.47, 642n.50, 647n.82, 647n.84, 647n.87, 648n.90, 648n.93, 657n.24, 705n.18
6th, 10, 145, 398, 492, 504–508, 510, 568, 645n.69, 704n.5
6th Air, 532

Armies, Soviet *(continued)*
6th Guards, 490–491, 511–512, 637n.27
6th Guards Tank, 714n.116
6th Reserve, 97, 705n.18
6th Sapper, 336–337, 339–340, 529, 671n.22, 672n.27
6th Tank, 232, 714n.116
7th (Separate), 293, 395, 493, 501, 559
7th Air, 532–533, 669n.118
7th Guards, 511–512, 637n.27
7th Reserve, 97, 705n.18
7th Sapper, 337–340, 529, 671n.22, 672n.27
8th, 505, 509
8th Air, 532–533
8th Guards, 511–512, 637n.27
8th Reserve, 97, 705n.18
8th Sapper, 337–340, 529, 671n.22, 671n.23, 672n.27
9th (Separate) 29, 32, 182, 398, 506, 508–509, 667n.105
9th Air, 532
9th Guards, 655n.18
9th Reserve, 97, 705n.18
9th Sapper, 337–338, 340, 529, 671n.22
10th, 7, 18, 21–22, 419, 500, 504, 506, 644n.56, 645n.69, 655n.21, 703n.238
10th Air, 532–533
10th Guards, 511
10th Reserve, 97, 500, 705n.18
10th Sapper, 337–338, 340, 529, 671n.22
11th, 12, 98, 501, 505–506
11th Air, 532–533
11th Guards, 497, 511–512
12th (1st formation), 10, 231, 645n.69, 667n.105, 704n.5
12th (from 5th Tank), 504, 506, 508–509
12th Air, 532–533
13th, 10, 150, 504, 507–508, 542–543, 577, 581, 729n.2
13th Air, 532–533, 669n.118
14th, 502
14th Air, 532–533
15th Air, 151, 532–533
16th, 10, 145, 169, 231, 489, 497, 504–506, 509, 511, 709n.66
16th Air, 532–533
17th Air, 532–534
18th, 506, 509
18th Air, 414, 667n.103
19th, 10, 486, 504–505, 653n.22, 665n.74, 708n.60
20th, 10, 42, 145, 501, 504–506, 509–510, 560–561, 644n.56, 665n.74
21st, 10, 75, 145, 165, 490–491, 504, 508–511, 635n.6, 637n.27, 653n.22, 711n.79
22nd, 42, 510, 653n.22
24th, 10, 32, 75, 149–151, 504–505, 510–511, 637n.27, 643n.55, 646n.71
26th, 10, 18, 504
27th, 12, 56, 59, 98, 151, 506, 637n.27, 642n.47, 705n.18
28th, 29, 32, 145, 499, 504–505, 508–510, 568, 643n.55, 645n.70, 704n.5
29th, 22, 42, 510, 643n.55, 644n.55
30th, 145, 505–506, 509–511, 643–644n.55, 665n.80
31st, 42, 509, 516, 643–644n.55
32nd, 10, 504, 643–644n.55
33rd, 145, 482, 499, 502, 506, 509, 643–644n.56
34th, 12, 501, 506, 643n.55, 681n.82, 704n.4
37th, 10, 145, 504, 506, 508–509
38th, 29, 32, 56, 150–151, 507–509, 645n.70
39th, 18, 22, 42, 510, 645n.70
40th, 56, 245, 484, 508–509, 645n.70
41st, 42, 145, 510
42nd, 681n.82
43rd, 501, 506, 643n.55, 682n.82

44th, 499, 507, 509, 643n.55, 682n.82, 704n.5
45th, 643n.55
46th, 151
47th, 56, 98, 151, 509, 637n.27, 642n.47, 643n.55, 645n.66, 682n.82
48th, 12, 150, 577, 643n.55
49th, 506, 643n.55
50th, 10, 22, 504, 506, 643n.55, 682n.82
51st, 145, 507, 509–510 644n.55
52nd, 98, 579, 644n.55
53rd, 59, 98, 151, 637n.27, 642n.47, 705n.18
54th, 145, 506
55th, 509
56th, 509
57th (from 3rd Tank), 32, 145, 149, 231, 499, 507–508, 510–511
60th, 18, 56, 150–151, 501, 509, 515, 542, 560, 575, 699n.211
61st, 18, 20, 150, 231, 484, 497, 508–509, 516, 666n.87
62nd, 75, 509–511, 637n.27
63rd, 75, 151, 637n.27
64th, 75, 510–511, 637n.27
65th, 145, 190, 231, 509–510, 576, 577, 635n.6, 711n.79
66th, 75, 150–151, 510–511
68th, 98, 499, 511, 641n.44
70th, 149–150, 177, 577, 705n.18, 711n.79
NKVD (future 70th) Army, 149, 177, 705n.18
Separate Airborne, 655n.18
Separate Coastal, 485, 495, 499
Special Red Banner Far Eastern, 153
Armor and Mechanized forces, Soviet, 301, 406–408
Armored trains (separate), Soviet, 237, 303, 664–665n.72
NKVD, 448
Army, United States, 25, 48–49
Army detachments *(abteilung)*, German Kempf, 51
Army groups, German
"A," 27, 29, 35, 40, 85, 633n.24
"B," 27, 29, 35, 38, 40, 85
Center, 7, 10, 12–14, 16–18, 20, 22–23, 42–43, 51, 56, 85–86, 387, 515, 633n.24, 636n.12, 643n.52, 709n.67
Don, 38, 47, 85
North, 7, 10, 12, 22, 36, 42, 44, 55,80, 502, 633n.24
North Ukraine, 636n.12
South, 7,10, 12, 27, 35, 51, 53, 55–56, 85–86, 633n.24, 709n.67
South Ukraine, 636n.12
Weichs, 27
Artem'ev, Lieutenant General P. A. (NKVD), 482–483, 653n.24, 704n.11
Artillery academies and schools, Soviet
Dzerzhinsky, 493
Higher Command, 394–395, 406
Leningrad, 394, 469
1st Moscow Red Banner, 308
Artillery Committee (Board), Soviet, 405
Artillery forces, Soviet, 112, 285–311, 393–395, 404–406
antiaircraft artillery, 302–307, 664n.67
antitank (tank destroyer), 294–300
artillery groups, 117, 119
commanders, 530–531
Force *[voiskovaia]*, 285–288
Mortars, 293–294
National Air Defense (PVO Strany), 285
rocket (guards-mortars), 307–311, 665n.74, 665n.84, 666n.87, 666n.90
self-propelled, 300–302, 664n.56, 664n.57
Stavka Reserve (RGK, RVGK), 285–286, 288–293, 324–330, 395, 660n.11
"Artillery" offensive, Soviet concept of, 310

Astakhov, Army General F. A., 704n.11
Atlantic Ocean, Battle of the, 25–26, 37, 49–50
Austria, 5, 24
Auto-transport Forces, Soviet, 353–356

Babadzhanian, Major General A. Kh., 496
Badanov, Lieutenant General of Tank Forces V. M., 514–515, 518–519, 522, 524
Baev, S. M., 434
Bagramian, Colonel General I. Kh., 35, 386, 495–498, 509, 511, 709n.67
  prewar service, 711n.82
Bakharov, Major General of Tank Forces B. S., 514, 518–519, 521–522
Balkans region, 5, 58, 461
Baltic region (states), 5, 15, 43–44, 85, 89, 167, 185, 544
Baltic Sea, 4–5, 13, 57, 66, 70
Baranov, Lieutenant General V. K., 520–521
Baranov, Major General of Engineer Forces N. P., 530
Baranov, Major General of Tank Forces V. I., 514, 517
Barbarossa, German Operation (22 June–4 December 1941), xv, 3, 7, 10–11, 13–14, 16, 25–26, 38, 49, 58, 60, 62, 64–65, 67, 69, 71, 73, 78, 80, 83, 85, 88, 90–93, 96, 100, 106–108, 111–112, 117, 120, 141, 154, 165, 182, 185, 189, 216–217, 235, 238, 241, 285, 287, 295, 303, 334–335, 344–345, 349, 352, 354, 370, 386, 392, 394–395, 397, 413, 416, 439, 447, 466, 476–480, 503, 513, 515, 529, 538, 541, 548, 555, 560, 564, 609, 612–613, 616–617, 638n.10
Barents Sea, 5, 70, 139, 160
Barsukov, Lieutenant General of Artillery M. M., 531
Baskakov, Major General V. N., 699n.206
Batiunia, Lieutenant General A. G., 507
Batov, Lieutenant General P. I., 508, 510, 512, 576, 704n.11
Battalions [*batal'on*], Soviet, 436, 441
  aerosleigh, 178, 234–235
  airfield support, 416
  antiaircraft artillery, 219, 227, 230, 232, 238–240, 286, 302–307, 415, 432
  antitank artillery, 180, 182–184, 188, 219, 227, 236, 238, 240, 286–287, 295
  antitank rifle, 184, 298–299: organization, 663n.42
  armored car, 227, 230, 233, 235–236
  armored train, 237, 303: organization, 664–665n.72
  artillery (cavalry), 239
  artillery [*divizion*], 182–183, 230, 286, 288–290: quantity and authorized strength, RVGK, 324, 660n.1
  artillery (instrumental) reconnaissance, 286, 291–292
  assault engineer-sapper, 343
  automobile, 353–354, 356
  auto-repair, 356
  auto-tractor, 336, 339
  auto-transport, 234, 355–356
  bridge construction, 354
  carpenter, 690–691n.122
  chemical armored car, 348–349
  chemical defense (antichemical defense; PkhO), 348–351
  chemical mortar, 348–349
  chemical repulse (KhO), 349
  chemical tank, 348–349
  communications reconstruction, 353
  construction (military), 357
  decontamination, 348–349
  destruction (NKVD), 170, 539
  disciplinary, 570–571, 726n.113
  electro-technical, 340
  engineer, 333–335, 338, 340, 342
  engineer-mine, 184, 340–341

engineer obstacle, 340
engineer-sapper, 227, 295, 334, 341
flamethrower, 348, 351, 674n.71
flamethrower tank, 348, 350, 674n.71
guards-miners, 170, 341–342
gun artillery, 289
heavy multiple-rocket launcher (guards-mortar; "*Katiusha*"), 308–310
heavy gun artillery, 293
high-power [*bol'shoi moshnosti*] artillery, 290, 292
howitzer artillery (light and medium), 286, 289, 292
light engineer, 333
line (wire), 346
machine-gun-artillery, 185–186: organization and strength, 200, 538
medical (sanitary), 184, 228, 230
military construction, 336
military road and bridge, 354
mine-sapper, 342
mortar, 182–184, 227, 230, 240, 287, 293–294
motorcycle, 227–228, 230, 233, 235–237
motorized antitank flamethrower, 351
motorized engineer, 218, 232–234, 333–334
motorized pontoon-bridge, 334
motorized rifle, 226, 229–230
motor-transport, 295, 428
mountain engineer-mine, 342
mountain engineer-sapper, 341
mountain mortar, 294
multiple-rocket launcher (guards-mortar; "*Katiushas*"), 228, 230, 287, 307–311
naval infantry, 183
parachute, 186, 188
penal ("assault" rifle), 572–574,576, 727n.127
pontoon-bridge, 219, 333, 335, 338, 342–343
projector, 340
radio, 344–347
railroad, 351–353, 432, 690n.122
railroad bridge, 353
railroad mechanization, 353
railroad route, 352
railroad track, 353
reconnaissance, 219, 228, 238, 240
reconstruction exploitation (signal), 246
repair and reconstruction (maintenance), 228, 230, 232, 234
repair and reconstruction (signal), 346
rifle, 180, 182–183, 286, 347
road-bridge construction, 338, 354–355
road exploitation, 354
road service, 356
sapper, 180, 182, 228, 333–339, 342, 357, 670n.17
signal (line), 183, 188, 218, 230, 240, 344–347
ski, 183–184, 235
special designation radio (OSNZ3), 344
special-power [*osoboi moshnosti*] artillery, 288–289, 291–292
tank, 184, 186, 217–218, 220–224, 226, 242: operating strength, 265–282, 539
tank destroyer, 297–299: distribution, RVGK (31 December 1943), 329–330
technical engineer, 334
telephone-telegraph, 344, 346
training (cavalry), 240
training (rifle), 180
VNOS, 415
VNOS radio, 415
1st Railroad, 674n.75
3rd Railroad, 674n.75
4th Railroad, 674n.75
5th Railroad, 674n.75
5th Railroad Bridge, 674n.74
6th Railroad, 674n.75

Battalions [*batal'on*], Soviet (*continued*)
9th Railroad, 674n.75
11th Railroad, 674n.74, 674n.75
12th Railroad, 674n.74
13th Guards Battalion of Miners, 170
13th Railroad, 674n.75
15th Guards Battalion of Miners, 170
17th Railroad, 674n.75
19th Railroad, 674n.75
20th Railroad Bridge (Separate), 674n.74
27th Railroad, 674n.74, 674n.75
28th Railroad, 674n.75
29th Railroad, 674n.75
30th Antiaircraft Artillery, 686n.48
42nd Guards-mortar, 307
43rd Guards-mortar, 307
29th Armored Train, 162
53rd Armored Train, 162
58th Armored Train, 162
76th Armored Train, 162
78th Armored Train, 162
191st Antiaircraft Artillery, 686n.48
322nd Special-power Artillery, 289
328th Special-power Artillery, 289
330th Special-power Artillery, 289
331st Special-power Artillery, 289
Bazhanov, Marshal of Artillery Iu. P., 406
Belev, 22
Belgorod, 22, 40–41, 51
Belgrade, 5
Belik, Army General P. A., 408
Beliusov, Lieutenant General P. N., 458
Beloglazov, Colonel A. S., 514
Belorussia, 4–5, 43, 46, 49–51, 56, 67, 85, 93, 143, 151, 167, 543–544
Belostok, 238
Belousov, Major General of the Quartermaster Service V. F., 436
Belov, Lieutenant General P. A., 20, 509, 512, 515–517, 713n.105
Berdichev, 53
Berezina River, 650n.113
Beriia, L. P., 165, 370, 378–379, 393, 400–402, 466, 682n.85, 715n.133, 715n.134
Berlin, 5, 14
Berzarin, Lieutenant General N. E., 506
Beskrovnov, Major General of Artillery P. M., 531
Bibikov, Lieutenant General of Aviation V. N., 533
Biriuzov, Lieutenant General S. S., 704n.11
Black Sea, 4, 7, 13, 20, 43, 46, 57, 59, 66, 70, 75, 86, 90, 93, 139, 160, 390, 418, 543, 633n.24
Blau [Blue], German operation (28 June–18 November 1942), 3, 23, 25, 27, 29–36, 49, 58, 61–62, 67, 70–71, 74, 78, 80–81, 83, 85, 87, 90–91, 96, 98, 100, 106–107, 111, 120, 165, 187, 190, 217, 228, 243, 295, 309, 316, 339, 381, 477, 487–488, 499–500, 503, 509, 518, 522, 529, 571, 609, 612–613, 638n.10
Blocking detachments [*zagraditel'nye otriady*], Soviet (NKVD), 124, 138, 170, 542–543, 578–582, 589, 728n.149
Bobruisk, 12, 56, 246, 658n.43
Bodin, Lieutenant General P. I., 376, 452
BODO (teletype) communications, Soviet, 346
Bogdanov, Lieutenant General of NKVD Forces I. A., 164, 482–483, 704n.11
Bogdanov, Lieutenant General S. I., 408, 514–515, 518, 522, 524, 527–528, 534, 714n.116, 715n.128
Boldin, Lieutenant General I. V., 506, 512
Boldyrev, Colonel P. S., 460
Boliatko, Major General V. A., 699n.206
Bolkhov, 22

Bol'shie uchebny sbory (BUS) [large-scale training exercise], 538–539. *See also* Mobilization, Soviet
Borisov, K. A., 729n.2
Borisov, Major General M. D., 517–518, 520
Borzilov, Colonel S. V., 514
Brezhnev, L. I., 381, 476
Briansk, 10, 20, 51, 89, 165, 336
Brigade regions, PVO (air defense), Soviet, 415–416, 418
Brigades, Soviet, 146
  airborne, 178, 188, 411
  antitank, 60, 111, 288, 295–296
  artillery, 291–293
  assault engineer-sapper, 343
  automobile, 365
  destroyer, 178, 184–185, 297, 340, 640n.20
  destruction, 1941–1942, 718–719n19
  engineer, 233, 339–340
  engineer-mine (EMB), 341–343
  engineer-sapper (ESB), 341–343
  flamethrower tank, 350
  formation, 1941–1945, 718n.19
  guards-miners, 169–170, 341–342
  heavy gun artillery, 291–293
  heavy howitzer artillery, 292
  heavy multiple-rocket launcher (guards-mortar; "*Katiusha*"), 309–310
  high-power [*bol'shoi moshnosti*] howitzer artillery, 292
  howitzer artillery, 291–292
  light artillery, 291–292
  maneuver airborne, 187
  mechanized, 60, 217, 228–230, 234: composition and strength, 258; operating strength, 265–282
  mortar, 291–292, 294
  motorcycle, 236
  motorized engineer, composition, 657n.30
  motorized rifle, 222, 228: organization and strength, 253, 333
  motor transport, 428
  mountain engineer, 341
  mountain engineer-mine (MEMB), 342
  mountain engineer-sapper, 342
  multiple-rocket launcher (guards-mortar; "*Katiusha*"), 309
  naval infantry 182–183: formation and subordination, 198
  naval rifle, 182–183: formation and subordination, 199
  operating strengths, 201–215, 436, 441
  pontoon-bridge, 342
  railroad, 351–353, 432, 434, 690n.121, 690n.122
  rear area obstacle, 342–343
  rifle, 6, 60, 179–180, 182–184: organization and strength, 197, 539
  rifle (NKVD), 168, 448
  sapper, 335–343
  ski, 6, 182–184, 235
  special designation engineer (SDEB), 340, 342
  student, 183
  tank, 6, 60, 217–218, 220–223, 226, 228, 230, 233–234, 241–242: operating strength, 265–282, 333, 348, 539, 718n.14; organization and strength, 252
  tank destroyer artillery, 298: distribution, RVGK (31 December 1943), 329–330, 663n.47, 663n.48, 663n.49
  workers and peasants labor (construction), 358
  1st Aviation, 668n.117
  1st Engineer-Mine (RVGK), 673n.37
  1st Engineer-Sapper, 672n.29
  1st Guards Airborne, 188
  1st Guards Assault Engineer Sapper, 672n.29
  1st Guards Brigade of Miners, 169–170, 341
  1st Guards-Mortar (Training), 665n.84

Brigades, Soviet *(continued)*
1st Naval Infantry, 182
1st NKVD Installation Security, 163
1st Railroad, 690n.106
1st Sapper, 671n.22
1st Ski, 184
1st Special Siberian Altai Volunteer (later 74th Stalin Altai Rifle), 546
1st Women's Volunteer Rifle (Separate), 153, 721n.51
2nd Engineer-Mine (RVGK), 673n.37
2nd Guards Airborne, 188
2nd Guards Motorized Assault Engineer Sapper, 672n.29
2nd Naval infantry, 182
2nd Sapper, 671n.22, 671n.23, 672n.28
2nd Ski, 184
3rd Engineer-Mine (RVGK), 673n.37
3rd Guards Airborne, 188, 655n.18
3rd Naval Infantry, 182
3rd Reserve Aviation, 668n.117
3rd Sapper, 671n.22, 671n.23, 672n.37
3rd Ski, 183–184
4th Engineer-Mine (RVGK), 673n.37
4th Guards Airborne, 188
4th Naval Infantry, 182
4th Railroad, 690n.106
4th Sapper, 671n.22, 672n.27
4th Ski, 183
5th Engineer-Mine (RVGK), 673n.37
5th Guards Airborne, 188
5th Naval Infantry, 182
5th Railroad, 690n.106
5th Sapper, 671n.22
5th Ski, 184
6th Engineer-Mine (RVGK), 673n.37
6th Guards Airborne, 188
6th Naval Infantry, 182
6th Railroad, 690n.106
6th Sapper, 671n.22, 672n.27
6th Ski, 184
7th Engineer-Mine (RVGK), 673n.37
7th Guards Airborne, 188
7th Naval Infantry, 182
7th PVO, 686n.48
7th Sapper, 671n.22, 672n.28, 673n.37
7th Ski, 184
8th Engineer-Mine (RVGK), 673n.37
8th Guards Airborne, 188, 655n.18
8th PVO, 686n.48
8th Sapper, 671n.22
8th Ski, 184
9th Engineer-Mine (RVGK), 673n.37
9th Guards Airborne, 188
9th Sapper, 671n.22, 672n.28, 673n.37
10th Engineer-Mine (RVGK), 673n.37
10th Guards Airborne, 188
10th PVO, 686n.48
10th Sapper, 671n.22, 672n.27, 672n.28, 672n.37
11th Engineer-Mine (RVGK), 673n.37
11th Guards Airborne, 188
11th Guards Tank, 231
11th PVO, 686n.48
11th Sapper, 671n.22, 672n.27, 672n.28, 673n.39
12th Engineer-Mine (RVGK), 673n.37
12th Engineer-Sapper, 672n.29
12th Guards Airborne, 188
12th PVO, 686n.48
12th Sapper, 671n.23, 672n.27, 672n.28, 672n.37
13th Engineer-Mine (RVGK), 673n.37
13th Guards Airborne, 188
13th PVO, 686n.48
13th Railroad, 690n.106

13th Sapper, 671n.22
14th Engineer-Mine (RVGK), 673n.37
14th Guards Airborne, 188
14th PVO, 686n.48
14th Sapper, 671n.22, 672n.27
15th Assault Engineer-Sapper, 672n.29
15th Engineer-Mine (RVGK), 673n.37
15th Guards Airborne, 188
15th PVO, 686n.48
15th Sapper, 671n.22, 672n.27
16th Guards Airborne, 188
16th Sapper, 671n.22
17th Guards Airborne, 188
17th Sapper, 671n.22, 672n.28, 673n.37
18th Guards Airborne, 188
18th Sapper, 671n.22, 672n.27, 672n.28, 672n.37
19th Guards Airborne, 188
19th Railroad, 690n.106
19th Sapper, 671n.22, 672n.37
20th Guards Airborne, 188
20th Sapper, 672n.27, 672n.28, 672n.37
21st Sapper, 671n.23, 672n.37
22nd Sapper, 671n.22
23rd Sapper, 671n.23, 672n.27, 672n.28, 673n.39
24th Sapper, 671n.23, 672n.27, 672n.28, 673n.39
25th Railroad, 690n.106
25th Sapper, 671n.23, 672n.27, 672n.28, 673n.39
26th Railroad, 690n.106
26th Sapper, 671n.23, 672n.27, 672n.28, 673n.39
27th Railroad, 690n.106
27th Sapper, 671n.22
28th Railroad, 674n.74, 690n.106
28th Sapper, 671n.22, 672n.27
28th Ski, 231
29th Railroad, 690n.106
29th Sapper, 671n.22, 672n.27
30th Sapper, 671n.22, 672n.27
31st Sapper, 672n.27, 672n.28, 672n.37
32nd Sapper, 672n.27, 672n.28, 672n.37
33rd Sapper, 340
33rd Special Designation Engineer, 340
34th Sapper, 672n.27, 672n.28, 673n.37
35th Sapper, 672n.37
36th Sapper, 672n.27, 672n.28, 672n.37
37th Sapper, 341, 672n.27, 672n.28
38th Sapper, 672n.27
39th Sapper, 672n.27
39th Special Designation Engineer, 340
40th Sapper, 672n.27
41st NKVD Convoy Security, 163
42nd NKVD Convoy Security, 163
43rd NKVD Convoy Security, 163
56th NKVD Installation Security, 163
57th NKVD Installation Security, 163
57th NKVD Rifle, 653n.29
71st NKVD Installation Security, 163
74th Rifle, 720n.38
75th Omsk Rifle, 546, 720n.37
77th Naval Rifle, 563
78th Krasnoiarsk Siberian Volunteer Rifle, 546
91st "Stalin" Special Volunteer Rifle, 546, 720n.39
112th Tank, 659n.55
115th Rifle, 231
148th Rifle, 585
202nd Separate Airborne, 186, 188
248th Rifle (Student), 542
Separate Special Designation NKVD Motorized Rifle (OMSBON), 168–169
"Broad front" strategy, Stalin's, 24, 46–47, 57, 59, 633n.24

Broud, Lieutenant General Ia. I., 508
Budapest, 5
Budenny, Marshal of the Soviet Union S. M., 141, 238, 371, 386, 392, 438, 478–480, 482, 488, 561, 650n.115, 653n.22, 707n.41
Budenny Military Electro-Technical Communications Academy, 423, 425
Bukrin (Velikii Bukrin), 51, 56, 245
Bulganin, N. A., 371–372, 677n.14, 680n.55
Bulgaria, 396
Bunin, Colonel L. V., 514
Burdeiny, Major General of Tank Forces A. S., 522
Burdenko, N. N., 441
Burichenko, *Komdiv* [division commander] G. A, 686n.44
Burkov, Lieutenant General of Tank Forces V. G., 514–515, 518, 521
Burlachko, Major General F. S., 682n.82
Butkov, Major General of Tank Forces V. V., 518–519, 522
Bychkovsky, Major General A. F., 515–517

Campaigns, Soviet definition, 638n.6
Canada, 249
Casino, Mount, 49
Casualties, Red Army. *See* Red Army, losses
Caucasus (Mountain) region, 25, 27, 29–30, 33–36, 41, 51, 70, 72, 78, 81, 85, 87, 153–154, 160, 165–166, 182, 185, 224, 487, 499
Cavalry "clique," Stalin's, 386
Cavalry forces, Soviet, 237–241, 245–246
Cavalry-mechanized groups, Soviet, 516, 521, 641n.42
"Center" [*"tsentr"*], Soviet strategic leadership and control organs, 369–403
Central Asia, 137, 160
Central Committee, Communist (Bolshevik) Party of the Soviet Union (CP(b)SU), 369–370, 372, 380–381, 399, 443, 474
Central Headquarters for PVO Fighter Aviation, 417
Central Headquarters of PVO Forces (PVO "Central"), 417–418
Central Headquarters (Staff) of the Partisan Movement (TsSHPD), 372, 376–378, 678n.30
Central VNOS Post, 417
Chechens, repression of, 402, 499
Cheka (All-Russian Extraordinary Commission [*Vserossiiskaia chrezvychainaia komissiia*] for the Struggle with Counterrevolutionaries, Speculators, and Malfeasance), 679n.49
Cheliabinsk, 473, 562
chemical forces, Soviet, 348–351
force [*voiskovaia*], 348–351
Stavka Reserve (RGK, RGVK), 348–351
Cherevichenko, Lieutenant General Ia. T., 482–483, 488–489, 504, 506, 704n.11
Cherniak, Lieutenant General S. I., 509, 682n.82
Cherniakhovsky, Colonel General I. D., 390, 408, 509, 511, 514–515, 518, 650n.115
Cherniavsky, Major General M. L., 513
Chernienko, Major General of Tank Forces D. Kh., 521–522
Chernobai, Colonel S. P., 514
Chernobyl', 51, 56
Chernov, Colonel P. G., 514
Chertverikov, Lieutenant General N. I., 700n.219
Chesnokov, Colonel M. I., 514, 518
Chibisov, Lieutenant General N. E., 509

Chief Military Prosecutor, Soviet, 382–382
Chief Prosecutor of the USSR, 383
Chief Quartermaster of the Red Army, 440
Chiefs [*nachal'niki*], Soviet force branches, 285, 403
  airborne forces, 411–412, 462
  air defense, 462
  armored and mechanized forces, 301, 407, 462
  artillery, 285, 304, 371, 394, 404–406, 462, 665n.79
  cavalry, 488
  engineer forces, 337, 341, 359, 409–411, 462, 530
  guards-mortar units, 405, 462, 665n.79
  military-medical, 436
  Naval Rear (Services), 440
  PVO Strany, 416
  Rear (Services) of the Red Army, 356, 428–431, 438–439, 440–441, 456, 462, 544
  signal (communications) forces, 345–346, 422–425
  wartime branch chiefs, 462
China, 26, 37
Chir River, 40, 47, 519
Chistiakov, Lieutenant General I. M., 490–491, 509–512
Chistiakov, Major General V. I., 513
Chistiakov, Marshal of Artillery M. N., 406, 704n.11
Chkalov, 562
Chuikov, Colonel General V. I., 408, 485, 487, 509–510, 512, 650n.115, 704n.11
Chumakov, Major General G. M., 699n.206
Churchill, Winston S., 636n.25
Citadel *[Citadelle]*, German Operation (5–13 July 1943). *See* Kursk defensive *under* Operations, military
Civil Air (Aviation) Fleet (GVF), Soviet, 314–315, 413, 425, 427, 667n.110
"Class of 1940," Red Army generals and colonels, 468, 483, 489, 496
  members and their fates, 704n.11
Clothing norms (rations), Red Army, 560–564
Command cadre, Red Army, 476–535, 617–618
Commands *[komendatury]*, NKVD Border Guards, 159
  2nd, 653n.34
  3rd, 653n.34
  4th, 653n.34
  5th, 653n.34
Commissar (military) system, Soviet, 124, 380–382, 439, 475, 565–566, 589, 616, 706n.37
Committee for Food and Clothing Supply, Red Army, 439
Communist Party (Bolshevik) of the Soviet Union (CP(b)SU), 369–370, 372, 378, 382, 385, 398–399, 414, 439, 443, 546, 588, 615
Companies, Penal, Soviet, 179th, 577
Conscription, Soviet military, 536–547
Construction (labor) troops, Soviet, 356–359
Convicts and political prisoners, Soviet conscription of, 544–547. *See also* Mobilization, Soviet Corps, German
  Afrika, 17, 26, 38
  motorized (panzer), 218
  II SS Panzer, 244
  X Army, 12
  XIV Panzer, 29
  XXXXVIII Panzer, 40, 47
  LVII Panzer, 40, 47
Corps, Italian, Alpine, 40
Corps, PVO (air defense), Soviet
  1st, 531
  2nd, 531
  3rd, 531
  13th, 531

Corps, Soviet, 146, 201–215, 265–284, 288, 436, 441
  airborne, 186, 411
  artillery penetration, 292–293
  aviation, 311–313: command turbulence in, 716n.138, 716n.141
  aviation (PVO), 414, 416–417
  cavalry, 60, 238–241, 245–246: command turbulence in, 714n.114; operating strength, 283–284, 308, 333, 512, 657–658n.40; relative strength, 262
  mechanized, 60–61, 107–108, 216–219, 228–230, 232–236, 241: composition and strength, 257; distribution of tanks (on 22 June 1941), 264; formation and composition, 256; operating strength, 265–282, 308, 333, 342, 512, 539, 655–656n.1, 658n.48; relative strength, 264
  mobile corps commanders, 512–522
  PVO (air defense), 415–416
  railroad, 351, 425–426
  rifle, 60–61, 179–180: operating strengths, 201–215, 286, 288–289, 291, 303, 333, 342, 347–348; organization, 194
  tank, 61, 108, 217, 225–228, 232–236: command turbulence in, 713n.111, 714n.115; initial formation, 256; operating strength, 265–282, 308, 342, 512, 656n.18; organization and strength, 254–255
  1st Airborne, 186
  1st Cavalry, 515, 517
  1st Guards Cavalry, 246, 515–517, 521, 560, 641n.44, 642n.49, 648n.89, 658n.43, 659n.55, 713n.105
  1st Guards Mechanized, 243, 519, 648n.89
  1st Guards-mortar (training), 666n.90
  1st Guards Tank, 151, 231, 641n.44
  1st Long-range Aviation, 311–312
  1st Mechanized (former 27th Tank), 59, 151, 241, 658n.48, 713n.110, 714n.112
  1st PVO, 686n.48
  1st Tank, 225, 231, 243, 519
  2nd Airborne, 186
  2nd Artillery Penetration, 310, 530
  2nd Cavalry, 238, 515, 658n.43, 665n.80
  2nd Guards Cavalry, 150, 246, 515–516, 518, 520, 642n.49, 658n.43, 713n.106, 713n.109, 713n.112
  2nd Guards Mechanized, 519
  2nd Guards-mortar (training), 666n.90
  2nd Guards Tank, 647n.88
  2nd Long-range Aviation, 311–312
  2nd Mechanized, 241, 658n.49
  2nd PVO, 147–148, 686n.48
  2nd Rifle, 514, 561, 582
  2nd Tank, 225, 243, 514, 518, 523, 647n.88, 657n.24
  3rd Airborne, 186
  3rd Artillery Penetration, 530
  3rd Cavalry, 480, 515–516, 658n.43, 713n.106
  3rd Guards Cavalry, 515–516, 518, 520, 658n.43
  3rd Guards Mechanized, 519
  3rd Guards Tank, 151
  3rd Long-range Aviation, 311–312
  3rd Mechanized (former 8th Tank), 12, 241–242, 514, 647n.86, 658n.48, 658n.49, 713n.110, 714n.112
  3rd PVO, 147–148, 686n.48
  3rd Tank, 150–151, 225, 231, 243
  4th Airborne, 186–187
  4th Artillery Penetration, 310, 530
  4th Cavalry, 238, 518, 520
  4th Guards Cavalry, 516, 520–521
  4th Guards Mechanized, 229, 657n.20
  4th Guards Tank, 59, 150–151
  4th Long-range Aviation, 311–312

4th Mechanized (former 28th Tank), 241–242, 519, 647n.86, 658n.48, 658n.49, 713n.110
4th Tank, 225, 519
5th Airborne, 186–187
5th Artillery Penetration, 310, 530
5th Cavalry, 238, 515–517, 658n.43
5th Guards Cavalry, 246, 520
5th Guards Tank, 647n.88
5th Long-range Aviation, 311–312, 533
5th Mechanized (former 22nd Tank), 12, 151, 231, 241, 707–708n.53, 713n.110
6th Cavalry, 238, 515, 517, 659n.55
6th Guards Cavalry, 520
6th Mechanized (former 14th Tank), 12, 241–242, 519, 647n.86, 658n.49, 713n.110
6th Tank, 243, 246, 713n.112
6th "Stalin" Volunteer Rifle, 545–546, 720n.39
7th Artillery Penetration, 310
7th Cavalry, 520
7th Guards Cavalry, 520–512
7th Mechanized, 12, 181, 241, 648n.89
7th Tank, 243, 519, 657n.24
8th Cavalry, 231, 246, 518, 520, 647n.84
8th Guards Airborne (Provisional), 188
8th Guards Rifle, 560, 585
8th Mechanized, 12, 241–242, 514, 647n.86, 658n.48, 658n.49
8th Tank, 243: reformed as 3rd Mechanized, 713n.110, 713n.112
9th Mechanized, 12, 489, 505, 647n.86, 658n.48
10th Airborne, 187
10th Mechanized, 658n.48
10th Tank, 150–151, 243, 647n.88
11th Cavalry, 517, 678n.27
11th Mechanized, 12, 647n.86, 658n.48, 658n.49
11th Tank, 231, 243–244, 657n.24
12th Mechanized, 12, 647n.86, 658n.48
12th Tank, 231, 243
13th Cavalry, 22, 517
13th Mechanized, 658n.48
13th Tank, 229, 243, 518–519, 521: composition, 657n.20
14th Mechanized, 12, 658n.48
14th Rifle, 395
14th Tank, reformed as 6th Mechanized, 713n.110
15th Mechanized, 12, 647n.86, 658n.48, 658n.49
15th Rifle, 395
15th Tank, 231, 243
16th Mechanized, 658n.48, 658n.49
16th Tank, 231, 244, 519
17th Mechanized, 241, 658n.48
17th Tank, 243, 518–519
18th Tank, 151, 243, 519
19th Cavalry, 520
19th Mechanized, 12, 514, 647n.86, 658n.48
20th Mechanized, 241, 658n.48
21st Mechanized, 241
21st Tank, 518, 647n.82, 648n.90
22nd Mechanized, 12, 242, 647n.86, 658n.48
22nd Tank, reformed as 5th Mechanized, 713n.110
23rd Tank, 243, 647n.82, 648n.90
24th Mechanized, 658n.48
24th Tank, 519
25th Tank, 243, 519, 641n.44
26th Mechanized, 241
26th Tank, 519
27th Mechanized, 499
27th Tank, reformed as 1st Mechanized, 713n.110
28th Mechanized, 658n.47
28th Tank, 243: reformed as 4th Mechanized, 713n.110
30th Mechanized, 512, 658n.47, 713n.103
32nd Guards Rifle, 721n.48

Corps, Soviet *(continued)*
37th Guards Airborne, 655n.18
38th Guards Airborne, 655n.18
39th Guards Airborne, 655n.18
48th Rifle, 492
57th Special Rifle, 387
73rd Rifle, 579
102nd Rifle, 729n.2
Special Corps of Railroad Forces, 351, 425–426, 432, 437
Corps regions, PVO (air defense), Soviet, 416–419
Baku, 417
Leningrad, 416–417
Moscow, 147, 416–417, 531
Council for Military-Political Propaganda, GlavPU, 443
Council of People's Commissars (SNK), Soviet Union, 369–371, 373, 383, 413–414, 447, 479, 615
Courses for the Improvement of Command Cadre, Soviet, 404, 406, 472–475
Crimea, 5, 53, 77, 85
"Cult of personality," Stalin's, 476
Czechoslovakia, 461

Damberg, Major General V. F., 517
Danilov, Major General A. I., 686n.44
Danube River, 5
Dashichev, Major General I. F., 508
Deane, Brigadier General J. R., 703n.238
Deception [*maskirovka*], Soviet, 90–91, 113–114
"Deep battle," Soviet concept of, 216, 392, 614
"Deep operations," Soviet concept of, 216, 347, 392, 614
Defense lines (strategic), Soviet, 77–78, 128, 335, 338, 357, 640n.27, 640–641n.30
Desna River-Zhukovka, 335
Luga, 128, 335–336, 529, 704n.4
Moscow (rings), 336
Moscow (Volokolamsk-Mozhaisk-Maloiaroslavets), 128, 335, 529, 640n.24, 671n.22
Mozhaisk (Kirov-Mozhaisk), 74, 128, 335, 493
Nevel'-Vitebsk-Mogilev-Gomel'-Kremenchug-Dnepropetrovsk, 128, 335–336
Odessa-Crimea-Sevastopol', 335
Ostashkov-Olenino-Dorogobuzh-El'nia, 335
Pskov-Ostrov-Western Dvina and Dnepr Rivers, 640n.29
Rzhev-Viaz'ma, 128, 335
Stalin (1939), 457, 529
Vladimir (Vytegra-Cherepovets-Rybinsk), 671n21
Volga (Iaroslavl'-Saratov-Stalingrad-Astrakhan), 128, 671n21
Defense zones, Soviet
Moscow, 152, 169, 298, 315, 336, 338, 644n.57, 671n.22
Mozhaisk, 395
Degtiarev, Lieutenant General of Artillery P. A., 462, 684n.11
Demiansk, 22, 41–44
Departments, NKO, 403
Counterintelligence (OKRs), 384–385, 400–401
External Relations, 461
Inspectorate for New Formations (in GUFUKA), 420
Intelligence (ROs), 384
Main Military Censorship, 453
Material Stocks, 438
Organizational and Personnel, 454
Registering Personnel Loses (in GUFUKA), 420
Special [*osobye otdely;* OO] (also NKVD), 157, 379, 384, 445–446, 679n.49, 680n.50
Departments, NKPS, Military Reconstruction, 429
Departments, NKVD, Deciphering, 453
Departments, Red Army General Staff, 403–404

Auto-Armored, 451, 678n.21
Automobile-Road, 428
Cadre, 374–375, 449
Communications, 451, 678n.21
Deciphering, 452
Exploitation of War Experience (OPIOV), 449, 451, 459–460, 678n.21, 702n.232, 702n.234, 702n.235
General Matters, 374–375, 449
Intelligence (ROs) (*fronts*), 384, 445, 452, 453: organization, 464–465
Main Military Censorship, 453
Military Historical, 374–375, 449, 460
Operational Training, 451, 678n.21
Operational Transportation, 451, 678n.21
Organizational-Registration, 451, 454, 678n.21
Organization (Formation) of the Operational Rear UUOT), 449, 456
Road, 426
Secret Command and Control, 449, 558
Special Missions (Foreign Relations) (OSZ), 449, 460–461
Desna River, 43, 45
"De-Stalinization," Khrushchev's program of, 476–477, 635n.5
Detachments, NKVD Border Guards, 159, 652n.6
aviation liaison, 227
commandants (roads service and guides), 234
reserve tank, 227–228
2nd, 653n.34
3rd, 653n.28
6th, 166
7th, 653n.28
8th, 166
12th, 653n.34
14th, 652n.6
15th, 652n.6
19th, 652n.6
20th, 653n.34
21st, 652n.6
32nd, 653n.34
33rd, 653n.28
43rd, 160
48th, 160
54th, 160
58th, 160
59th, 160
67th, 160
83rd, 653n.34
84th, 652n.6
85th, 652n.6
86th, 160, 653n.34
87th, 160
88th, 160, 653n.34
90th, 160
91st, 160, 165
92nd, 160, 165
93rd, 160
94th, 160, 165, 653n.34
95th, 160
97th, 160, 653n.34
98th, 160, 165
99th, 166
102nd, 653n.28
104th, 652n.6
105th, 160, 653n.34
106th, 160, 166, 653n.34
107th, 160, 653n.34
Diakov, Major General G. S., 682n.82
Directorates, chiefs of construction (military districts) (UNS), 356–357, 675n.92
16th, 675n.92
23rd, 675n.92
Directorates, defensive construction (UOSs), Soviet, 339, 358–359, 530
24th, 672n.27
33rd, 672n.27
34th, 672n.27
35th, 672n.27
36th, 672n.27
Directorates, *front* rear area security (UOTFs), NKVD, 447–448
Directorates, military communications (UVSs), General Staff, 427, 435, 455

Directorates, military-field construction (UVPSs), 357–359
Directorates, military-field construction (reconstruction) (UVPSs), Soviet, 334, 336, 352–353, 359, 675n.92
  8th Front, 675n.92
Directorates, military reconstruction, NKRF, 433
Directorates, military reconstruction and obstacle work (UVVRs), NKPS, 429–430, 432
Directorates, military roads (VDU), Soviet, 355
Directorates, People's Commissariat of Communications (NKPS)
  Main Military Reconstruction Work (GUVVR), 352, 429, 432, 689n.89
  Military Mobilization, 429
  Railroad Forces (Troops), 429
Directorates, People's Commissariat of Defense (NKO), 403–404
  Administrative, 373
  Airborne Forces (UVDV), 187, 411–412
  Ammunition Supply (USB), 405
  Artillery Weapons Supply (USAV), 405
  Auto (Motor)-Armored (GABTU), 407, 426, 684n.13
  Cadre (Red Army Command), 373, 420
  Central Military Communications (TsUVS or TsUPVOSO), 431, 455–456, 459
  Clothing Supply (UVS), 435, 441, 562
  Combat Preparation (Training), 373: prewar organization, 697–698n.195
  Commander of Airborne Forces (UKVDV KA), 187, 411–412
  Engineer Supply, 409
  Exploitation of War Experience, 62
  Food Supply (UPSKA), 435, 441
  Formation of Formations (corps and divisions), 420
  Formation of the Rear and Supply (UUTS), 701n.222
  Formation of Units (regiments and brigades), 420
  Fuel Supply (USG), 435–436, 438–439, 442, 692n.152
  Inspectorate, 373
  Intelligence (RU) (1934–1940), 444
  Main Air Force of the Red Army (GUVVS KA), 311, 371, 373, 412–414
  Main Armored (GBTU), 407
  Main Armored Formation and Combat Training, 407
  Main Artillery (GAU), 285, 300, 371, 394, 404–406, 417, 665n.79, 669n.126: artillery and ammunition supply procedures, 683–684n.7; repair work, 684n.7; subordinate organs, 683n.6
  Main Auto-Armored (GABTU KA), 406–408, 684n.13: subordinate repair organs, 684n.20
  Main Automobile and Road Services (GLAVTU or GAVTU), 356, 408, 433
  Main Automobile of the Red Army (GAVTU KA), 433
  Main Automobile-Road (GADU), 355, 430, 455
  Main Auto-Transport and Road Services of the Red Army (GUADSKA), 355–356, 430, 433
  Main Cadre (GUK), 374, 420–421, 500, 553
  Main Civil Air Fleet (GUGVF), 424, 427
  Main Commander of Armored and Mechanized Forces (UKBMV), 407
  Main Commander of PVO Strany Forces (GUKPVO Strany), 416–417, 686n.40
  Main Counterintelligence (Third) (GUK–SMERSH), 384–385, 400–401, 446, 448, 453, 616, 680n.52

Main Defensive Construction (GUOS), 356–359, 410–411
Main Food Supply of the Red Army (GUPS KA), 440–441
Main Formation and Manning of the Red Army (GUFUKA), 338, 353, 420–421, 450, 454–455, 474, 677n.20
Main Formation of Red Army Reserves (Glavupraform, later GUFUKA), 419–420–421, 454, 543, 552–553, 616, 677n.20
Main Guards-mortar Units (GUGMCh), 308–309, 406
Main Intelligence (GRU) (from October 1942), 384, 444–445, 448, 616
Main Military-Chemical (GVKh), 349
Main Military-Engineer (GVIU KA), 169, 336–337, 358, 408–411, 685n.22
Main Military-Medical (GVSU), 438–439, 442: operating organs, 692n.154
Main Political, Fleet (GlavPU VMF), 380
Main Political, Red Army (GlavPU RKKA), 380–381, 398–399, 443–445, 568: missions, 696n.177, 706n.37
Main Political (GlavPU), 371, 373: missions, 696n.177
Main Political Propaganda in the Red Army (GUPP KA) (1940–1941), 379, 398, 443
Main PVO Strany (GUPVO KA), 285, 311, 371, 394, 404, 414–419
Main Quartermaster (GIU), 435, 438, 440–441
Main Rear (Services) of the Red Army (GUTA KA), 352, 355, 374–375, 428, 433, 438, 440, 455–456, 698n.197
Main Repair of Tanks, 684n.18
Main Road (GRU), 356
Main Road, Red Army (GRU KA), 433, 441
Main Signal (Communications) (GUSKA), 345–346, 423–425
Main Universal Military Education (GUVVO), 421–422
Mechanized Tractors and Self-propelled Artillery, 300
Medical (Sanitary) (SU), 435–436, 438: medical support (1941–1943), 692n.153
Military-Chemical Defense (UVKhZ), 348
Military Communications (UPVOSO), 352, 428, 430, 433–434, 438, 454–455, 689n.96
Military-Educational Institutions (GUVUZ), 421, 472, 668n.74
Military-Engineer Inspectorate, 409
Military Field Construction (UVPS), 357–359
Military-Historical, 62
Mobilization, 373, 419
Motor-Armored, 353–354
Naval Forces, 373
Organization of the Rear (Rear Services), Weapons and Supply (UUTVS), 434, 436–438, 456
Self-Propelled Artillery, 684n.18
Signal (Communications) (USKA), 422–423
Veterinary (VUKA), 435–438, 442: subordinate organs, 692n.142, 696n.175
Directorates, People's Commissariat of Internal Affairs (NKVD)
Airfield Construction, 157
Forces for Protecting the Rear Areas of Operating Soviet Armies (1942–1943), 448
Local Air Defense (MPVO), 157, 417
Main (NKVD Central), 166, 168–169
Main Border Guards Troops (GUPV), 157, 167, 447

Directorates, People's Commissariat of Internal Affairs (NKVD) *(continued)*
Main Camps (Labor) GULAG), 158, 162, 170, 379, 400, 447
Main Defensive Construction (GUOS), 358
Main Defensive Work (GUOBR), 336–337, 358
Main Escort (Convoy) Troops, 157, 162
Main Forces for Protecting the Rear Areas of Operating Soviet Armies (May 1943), 448
Main Forces for the Protection of Industrial Enterprises, 447
Main Forces for the Protection of Railroad Facilities, 351, 447
Main Hydro-Technical Work (Glavidrostroi), 336, 357–358
Main Internal (Operational) Forces (GUVV), 157, 165, 167, 447
Main Military Construction, 157, 447
Main NKVD Supply, 157, 447
Main Roads (Highways), 157, 426
Railroad Forces, 157
Security of Soviet Field Armies (rear areas), 158
Special Departments (Third Directorate), 384, 400, 445–446, 567, 578, 616 (*see also* Special departments, OOs)
State Political (OGPU), 400
State Security, 157, 379, 400
Directorates, People's Commissariat of State Security (NKGB), Main State Security (GUGB), 379
Directorates, People's Commissariat of the River Fleet (NKRF)
Central Military-Reconstruction, 433
Ship-Raising and Salvage Works in River Basins, 433
Directorates, Red Army General Staff, 403
Agent (First), GRU, 444, 452
Automobile-Road Transport (GADU) (1941), 449, 456, 698n.197
Cadre, 420
Central Military Communications (Routes) (TsUVS or TsUPVOSO), 351, 374–375, 434, 426–428, 431, 435, 449, 455–456, 701n.221
Cipher Service (Eighth) (UshS), 374–375, 449, 458–459, 701n.229
Communications Center, 449
Construction of Fortified Regions (UUUR), 374–375, 449, 457–458
Force Intelligence (UVR) (October 1942–April 1943), 384, 444–445, 452–453
Generalization and Exploitation of War (Military) Experience (UPOIIOV), 449, 460, 474
Information (Second), 444, 542
Intelligence (RU) (1940–1942), 374, 444, 449, 452, 500
Intelligence (RU) (from April 1943), 444–445, 453–454: organization, 464
Main Automobile-Road (GADU), 354–355, 374, 428, 438, 449
Main Intelligence (Second) (GRU) (February–October 1942)-, 169, 375, 384, 444, 452–454: organization (February 1942), 464, 699n.211
Main Operations (First) (GOU), 371, 450–452: missions, 698n.200; reporting procedures, 698n.200
Manning and Constructing Forces, 374, 419, 449, 454
Military-Topographical (VTU), 374, 449, 457
Mobilization, 374, 449, 454, 677n.20
Operations (First), 374–375, 389, 392, 424, 449, 454, 458–462, 678n.21: departments and their chiefs (deputy chiefs of staff), 699n.206; work schedule, 689–699n.203
Organizational (Third), 374–375, 449, 454–455, 677n.20, 678n.21: departments and their chiefs, 700n.218, 700n.219

Organization (Formation) of the Operational Rear (UUOT), 374–375, 449, 456
Organization of the Rear and Supply of Forces, 374, 426, 436–438, 449, 456, 701n.222
Rear and Supply Planning (UTPMS), 353, 356, 701n.223
Special Missions (Foreign Relations) (OSZ), 449, 461, 703n.238
Disciplinary regulations, Red Army, 566–569
Districts, NKVD Border Guards, 159
Division regions, PVO (air defense), Soviet, 416–418, 687n.53
79th, 531
Divisions, German
5th Panzer, 650n.113
6th Panzer, 519
8th Panzer, 12
11th Panzer, 519
Divisions, Soviet [*diviziia*], 146, 201–215, 283–284, 436, 441
age and ethnic composition, 591–498
airborne, 178
antiaircraft artillery, 233, 291, 305–306, 664n.67
artillery, 291, 293–294, 297–298
artillery penetration, 292–294
aviation, 311–319
aviation (PVO), 416–417
cavalry, 146, 238–241, 245–246: operating strength, 283–284, 333, 350, 718n.14; relative strength, 263
destroyer, 178, 184–185, 297, 640n.20
destruction (1941–1942), 718–719n19
formation (1941–1945), 718n.19
heavy gun artillery, 291, 293
heavy multiple-rocket launcher (guards-mortar; "*Katiusha*"), 309–310
light cavalry, 239: relative strength, 263
motorized, 146, 216, 219, 241, 333
motorized rifle (NKVD), 448
mountain cavalry, 238
mountain rifle, 182
multiple-rocket launcher (guards-mortar; "*Katiusha*"), 292, 309–310
people's militia (DNO), 538
PVO (air defense), 415–416
railroad (NKVD), 351–352, 448
rifle, 146, 179–182: average strength (on 22 June 1941), 655n.20, 718n.14; operating strength, 201–215, 286–287, 289, 302–304, 333, 335, 347–350, 640n.20; organization and strength, 195–196
rifle (NKVD), 167–168, 291, 448
tank, 146, 216–220, 241–242: operating strength, 265–282, 333, 348, 539, 713n.104, 718n.13
1st Aviation Transport, 433
1st Guards Airborne, 188
1st Guards Motorized Rifle (from 1st Tank), 181–182
1st Guards Rifle (former 100th Rifle), 181
1st Heavy Guards-Mortar, 309–310, 666n.90
1st Moscow Motorized Rifle, 181
1st NKVD Rifle, 165, 653n.28
1st Siberian Volunteer (late 150th Rifle), 545
1st Tank (former 1st Moscow Motorized Rifle), 181
2nd Cavalry, 499
2nd Guards Airborne, 188
2nd Guards Rifle (former 127th Rifle), 165, 580
2nd Heavy Guards-Mortar, 309–310, 666n.90
2nd NKVD Motorized Rifle, 160
2nd NKVD Railroad, 162
2nd Tank, 242
3rd (Separate) Air Liaison, 425
3rd Guards Airborne, 188
3rd Guards Cavalry, 516

Divisions, Soviet [*diviziia*] *(continued)*
3rd Guards Rifle (former 153rd Rifle), 181
3rd Heavy Guards-Mortar, 309–310, 666n.90
3rd NKVD Railroad, 162
3rd PVO, 686n.48
4th Guards Airborne, 188
4th Guards Gun Artillery (heavy), 293
4th Guards Rifle (former 161st Rifle), 181
4th Heavy Guards-Mortar, 309–310, 666n.90
4th NKVD Railroad, 162
4th PVO, 686n.48
5th Guards Airborne, 188
5th Guards Rifle (former 107th Rifle), 181
5th Heavy Guards-Mortar, 309–310
5th NKVD Railroad, 162
5th NKVD Rifle, 165
6th Guards Airborne, 188
6th Guards Gun Artillery (heavy), 293
6th Guards Rifle (former 64th Rifle), 181
6th Heavy Guards-Mortar, 310
6th NKVD Railroad, 162
6th NKVD Rifle, 165
7th Guards Airborne, 188
7th Guards Rifle (former 316th Rifle), 181
7th Heavy Guards-Mortar, 310
7th NKVD Motorized Rifle, 165
7th NKVD Railroad, 162
8th Guards Airborne, 188
8th Guards Gun Artillery (heavy), 293
8th Guards Rifle (former 78th Rifle), 181
8th NKVD Motorized Rifle (63rd Rifle), 165
9th Guards Airborne, 188
9th Guards Rifle (former 52nd Rifle), 181
9th NKVD Motorized Rifle (41st Rifle), 165
9th NKVD Railroad, 162
10th Guards Airborne, 188
10th Guards Rifle (former 52nd Rifle), 181
10th NKVD Railroad, 162
10th NKVD Rifle (181st Rifle), 165
10th Stalingrad NKVD Rifle, 166
11th Guards Rifle, 188
11th NKVD Rifle (2nd Guards Rifle), 165
11th NKVD Special Installation Security, 163
12th Guards Rifle, 188
12th Mountain Rifle, 165
12th NKVD Rifle, 165
12th NKVD Special Installation Security, 163
12th Tank, 242
13th Guards Rifle, 188
13th NKVD Convoy Forces Security, 162
14th Guards Rifle, 188
14th NKVD Convoy Forces Security, 162
15th Guards Rifle, 188
15th Mountain Rifle, 165
16th Guards Rifle, 188
16th Mountain Rifle, 165
17th Mountain Rifle, 165
18th Long-Range Aviation, 311–312
19th Heavy Gun Artillery, 291
20th Mixed Aviation, 667n.105
20th NKVD Rifle, 165
20th NKVD Special Installation Security, 163
21st NKVD Motorized Rifle, 161, 164
21st NKVD Rifle, 165–166
22nd NKVD Motorized Rifle, 161, 164
23rd NKVD Motorized Rifle, 161, 164
25th Rifle, 499
26th Long-Range Aviation, 311–312
26th Mountain Rifle, 165
30th Long-Range Aviation, 311–312

32nd Guards Rifle, 187
32nd Rifle, 655n.21
33rd Guards Rifle, 187
34th Guards Rifle, 187
35th Guards Rifle, 187
36th Guards Rifle, 187
36th Motorized Rifle, 181
37th Guards Rifle, 187, 576
38th Guards Rifle, 187
39th Guards Rifle, 187
40th Guards Rifle, 187
41st Guards Rifle, 187
41st Rifle, 165
41st Tank, 242
50th Cavalry, 515–516
51st Rifle (Perekop), 395
53rd Cavalry, 515
57th Motorized Rifle, 181
60th Rifle, 231
61st Tank, 220
63rd Rifle, 165
78th Rifle, 655n.21
81st Long-Range Aviation, 314, 414, 666n.99
82nd Aviation, 314
82nd Motorized Rifle, 181
87th Aviation, 314
90th Aviation, 314
97th Guards Rifle, 721n.48
101st Tank, 219
102nd Tank, 219
103rd Aviation, 314
104th Tank, 219
105th Tank, 219
106th Motorized, 219
107th Motorized Rifle (former 108th Tank), 181
108th Tank, 181
109th Tank, 219
110th Aviation, 314
110th Tank, 219
111th Tank, 219–220
112th Rifle, 231
112th Tank, 219–220, 659n.55, 713n.105
121st Rifle, 542, 560, 575
134th Rifle, 578
148th Rifle, 578
149th Rifle, 725n.106
150th Rifle, 545
161st Rifle, 582
172nd Rifle, 729n.2
181st Rifle, 165
194th Rifle, 231
201st Fighter Aviation, 316
201st Rifle (Latvian), 549
202nd Fighter Aviation, 316
203rd Mixed Aviation, 316
204th Mixed Aviation, 316
211th Rifle, 568, 725n.106
213th Rifle, 579
243rd Rifle, 165
244th Rifle, 165
246th Rifle, 165, 576
247th Rifle, 165
249th Rifle, 165
250th Rifle, 165
251st Rifle, 165
252nd Rifle, 165
254th Rifle, 165
256th Rifle, 165
257th Rifle, 165
259th Rifle, 165
262nd Rifle, 165
265th Rifle, 165
268th Rifle, 165
273rd Rifle, 561
301st Rifle, 561
310th Rifle, 575
343rd Rifle, 550
354th Rifle, 576
F. E. Dzerzhinsky Separate Special Designation NKVD Motorized Rifle Division, 160–161
Groznyi NKVD Rifle, 166
Makhachkala NKVD Rifle, 166
Moscow Proletarian Rifle, 394
Ordzhonikidze NKVD Rifle, 166
"Polar" Rifle, 545
Sukhumi NKVD Rifle, 166
Dmitriev, Major General of Tank Forces V. I., 689n.96

Dnepropetrovsk, 51, 53, 493
Dnepr River, 4, 7, 12, 40–41, 43, 45–46, 49–51, 53–54, 56, 58, 59, 66–67, 72, 78, 85–86, 93, 96, 100, 143, 151, 190, 245, 390, 486, 490, 492, 505, 520–521, 526–527, 538, 709n.67
Domrachev, Colonel P. N., 514
Donbas (Donets Basin), 10, 32, 41, 45, 51, 55, 71, 74, 77, 85, 244, 416, 419, 633n.24
Donetsk, 399
Don River, 27, 29–30, 32, 34, 37, 40, 42, 47, 74–75, 77, 81, 151, 231, 487–488, 646n.79, 657n.24
Donskov, Colonel S. I., 653n.28
Dovator, Major General L. M., 18, 515–516
Drachev, Lieutenant General of the Quartermaster Service P. I., 440, 692n.150
Dubinin, Major General N. I., 462
Dubovoi, Major General of Tank Forces I. V., 522
Dudkin, Colonel A. I., 517
Dzerzhinsky, F. E., 679n.49
Dzerzhinsky Military-Technical Academy, 406, 408, 410
Dzerzhinsky Political Academy, 395

Eastern Wall (Panther Line), German, 49, 143, 611
East Prussia, 5, 24
Echelonment of forces, Soviet
  operational: defensive, 76–77, 88–90, 103–104; offensive, 104–106
  strategic: defensive, 72–76; offensive, 88–90
  tactical: defensive, 114–117; offensive, 117–120
Edinonachalie [unified command], Soviet principal of, 381–382, 475, 565
Efremov, Lieutenant General M. G., 482–483, 506–508, 704n.11
Egypt, 17, 26, 38
El Alamein, Battle of, 37, 612
Elets, 316
El'nia, 13, 51
Engineer (Sapper) forces, Soviet, 333–342, 408–411
  commanders, 529–530
  force [*voiskovaia*], 333–335, 342
  Stavka Reserve (RGK-RVGK), 333–342
English Channel, 6
Eniukov, Major General S. M., 699n.206
Epishev, Lieutenant General of Tank Forces A. A., 408
Eremenko, Army General A. I., 386, 468, 482–483, 485–486, 488–489, 495–496, 500, 508, 581, 650n.115, 680n.57, 704n.11, 704n.11
  prewar service,708n.56
Ermakov, Major General A. N., 682n.82
Ermolin, Major General P. A., 426–428, 435, 455, 692n.150
Ern'st, Major General N. A., 468
Ershakov, Lieutenant General F. A., 504
Esaulov, Colonel P. G., 460
Ezhov, N. I., 400

Falaeev, Colonel General of Artillery F. Ia., 704n.11
Far East, Soviet, 74, 137, 149, 154, 160, 181–182, 185–186, 485, 655n.21
Far East Command, 390, 393, 681n.60
Fastov, 53
Fediuninsky, Lieutenant General I. I., 482, 506, 509, 512
Fedorenko, Colonel General of Tank Forces Ia. N., 406–408, 462, 527, 704n.11
Fedorov, Colonel F. F., 514

Feklenko, Major General N. V., 513–514, 518
Filatov, Lieutenant General F. M., 504
Filichkin, Lieutenant General of Technical Forces V. M., 434
Finland, 185, 494
Fleets, Soviet, 427
  Baltic, 183, 397
  Black Sea, 183, 396–397, 406
  Northern, 183
  Pacific, 183, 396
Flotillas, Naval, Soviet, Northern Dvina, 396
Food (forage) supply norms (rations), Red Army, 439, 555–560
  daily ration (22 September 1941), 605–606, 694n.156
  food distribution structure, 694–695n.164
Force manning systems, Soviet, 716n.1, 717n.4, 717n.5
  cadre (regular), 536–538, 548, 716n.1
  territorial (militia), 536–538, 547, 716n.1, 716–717n.2
"Forgotten" (concealed) battles, Soviet-German War, 11–13, 21–23, 30–33, 42–44, 54–57, 611–614, 641n.33
Fortified regions (UR), Soviet, 160, 178, 185–186, 350, 357, 640n.20
  field, 186
  Korosten', 77
  Novgorod-Volynskii, 77
  Peremyshl', 77
  Polotsk, 404
  Rava-Russkaia, 77
Forward detachments *[peredovye otriady]*, 110, 119, 233
Fotchenko, Colonel P. S., 513
Free French, government in exile, 461
Frolov, Lieutenant General V. A., 482–483, 488–489, 496, 498, 502, 504, 705n.11
  prewar service, 712n.95
Fronts (operating and nonoperating), Soviet, 137, 140–143, 147–148, 153–154, 178, 230, 333–334, 339–342, 344–346, 348–349, 353–355, 357, 359, 383–384, 404–405, 408–409, 411, 414, 416–417–418, 423–425, 427–431, 433, 435, 438–441, 447–448, 450–453, 455–458, 462, 470
  Baltic, 143, 484, 495, 711n.81
  Belorussian (former Central), 51, 56, 84, 95, 143, 495, 521, 543, 633n.24, 709n.67, 711n.80, 711n.81
  Briansk, 10, 13, 16, 22, 25, 27, 30, 32, 40, 43, 51, 56, 71–75, 80, 83–84, 89, 142–143, 150–151, 169, 231, 243, 304, 395, 398, 481, 484–485, 487, 489, 494–495, 497, 507, 509, 520, 542, 559, 581, 633n.24, 638n.11, 638n.12, 642n.49, 643n.55, 645n.69, 646n.71, 647n.82, 647n.87, 671n.22, 672n.27, 682n.82, 707n.51, 709n.63, 709n.64
  Caucasus, 74, 153, 410, 482, 487, 498, 709n.64
  Central, 12, 43, 51, 56, 71–75, 84, 95, 101, 104, 142, 150–151, 169, 232, 244, 418, 481–482, 490, 494–495, 497, 520–521, 523, 542, 576–577, 581, 633n.24, 635n.6, 638n.11, 638n.12, 639n.15, 641n.44, 643n.52, 644n.62, 648n.90, 648n.97, 707n.51, 711n.79, 711n.81
  commanders, 481–502, 544, 631n.3
  command turbulence, 709n.64, 711n.81
  Crimean, 22, 27, 83, 398, 487, 498, 671n.22, 682n.82, 709n.64
  Don, 38, 40, 84, 142, 298, 309, 395, 488, 490, 494, 509, 559, 635n.6, 638n.11, 641n.41, 642n.50, 709n.63, 709n.64, 711n.79, 711n.81

Fronts (operating and nonoperating) *(continued)*
Far Eastern, 153–154, 312, 413, 501, 658n.47, 668n.117
Front of Reserve Armies, 72–73, 481
Kalinin, 20, 22, 32, 42–43, 51, 56, 71, 74–75, 83–84, 88, 95, 142–143, 183, 298, 309, 315, 337, 387, 395, 482, 485–487, 494–495, 500–501, 506, 508–509, 520, 559, 633n.24, 638n.9, 638n.11, 638n.12, 639n.15, 641n.41, 643n.52, 645n.68, 645n.79, 647n.84, 649n.101, 669n.118, 671n.22, 707n.51, 709n.63, 709n.64, 709n.67, 711n.80, 711n.81, 714n.112
Karelian, 142, 481, 487, 494, 501–502, 559, 669n.118, 671n.22, 672n.34, 707n.51, 709n.63, 709n.64, 711n.80, 711n.81
Kursk, 75, 150–151, 495
Leningrad, 22, 32, 36, 44, 55, 57, 71, 73–75, 83–84, 89, 141–142, 165, 297, 342, 386–387, 393, 395–396, 418, 481, 484, 487, 493–494, 509, 559, 633n.24, 638n.9, 638n.11, 669n.118, 671n.22, 681n.82, 702n.229, 707n.51, 709n.63, 711n.80, 711n.81
North Caucasus, 30, 51, 55, 72, 74–75, 84, 142, 151, 169, 304, 341, 479, 487, 494–495, 499, 638n.11, 646n.66, 663n.41, 709n.64, 711n.81
Northern, 7, 12, 72–73, 75, 97, 101, 164, 393, 481, 484, 502, 643n.55, 646n.71, 653n.24
Northwestern, 7, 12–13, 42–44, 71–72, 74–75, 80, 83–84, 89, 142–143, 150–151, 164, 187–188, 232, 395, 480–481, 484, 486–487, 491, 494–495, 501, 505–506, 559, 566, 633n.24, 638n.9, 638n.11, 640n.24, 641n.44, 644n.55, 645n.66, 645n.68, 646n.71, 647n.86, 653n.24, 666n.90, 671n.22, 681n.82, 682n.82, 704n.4, 707n.51, 707n.52, 709n.63, 709n.64, 711n.81
Orel, 75, 151, 495
Reserve, 10, 13, 16, 25, 71, 73–75, 80, 97, 99, 150–151, 387, 395, 478, 482, 484, 493, 495, 510–511, 640n.25, 642n.49, 643n.55, 645n.69, 646n.71, 707n.51
Southeastern, 30, 74, 231, 485, 487–488, 500, 508, 521, 709n.64
Southern, 7, 27, 30, 35, 40, 44, 51, 55–56, 71–75, 83–84, 101, 142, 164, 188, 410, 420, 481, 484–485, 487, 492–495, 499, 506, 510–511, 520–521, 578, 633n.24, 638n.9, 638n.11, 638n.12, 639n.15, 643n.51, 645n.69, 648n.93, 649n.101, 649n.101, 649n.102, 653n.24, 671n.22, 709n.64, 711n.81
Southwestern, 7, 10, 12, 16, 20, 22, 25, 27, 30, 38, 40–41, 44, 47, 51, 55–56, 71–75, 77, 80, 83–84, 88–89, 101, 109, 142–143, 164–165, 182, 231, 243–244, 287, 298, 304, 309, 387, 395, 410, 480–482, 484, 487–488, 491, 493–497, 500, 510–511, 516, 521, 559, 568, 633n.24, 638n.11, 638n.12, 639n.15, 640n.24, 641n.41, 641n.44, 641n.47, 642n.50, 645n.69, 645n.70, 647n.82, 647n.84, 647n.86, 648n.93, 649n.97, 649n.101, 649n.102, 653n.24, 663n.41, 665n.74, 671n.22, 690n.106, 704n.5, 707n.51, 709n.63, 709n.64, 711n.81
Stalingrad, 30, 32, 38, 40, 72, 74, 84, 89, 109, 230, 243, 298, 309, 342, 484–485, 487–488, 494, 500, 508, 559, 638n.11, 641n.41, 642n.50, 647n.82, 647n.84, 647n.87, 663n.41, 668n.117, 672n.27, 709n.64

Steppe, 51, 56, 72, 84, 99, 113, 143, 151, 244–245, 486, 495, 526, 633n.24, 638n.12, 639n.15, 642n.51, 645n.66, 646n.79, 648n.88, 659n.54, 709n.63, 711n.81
Trans-Baikal, 153–154, 556
Trans-Caucasus, 71, 97, 142, 151, 153–154, 169, 297, 309, 341–342, 481–482, 487, 494–495, 498–499, 559, 672n.27, 709n.63, 709n.64
Ukrainian, 480
Volkhov, 22, 32, 36, 44, 57, 74–75, 83–84, 89, 101, 142–143, 301, 340, 395, 398, 467, 482, 487, 494, 501–502, 559, 575, 633n.24, 638n.11, 668n.117, 671n.22, 709n.64, 711n.80, 711n.81
Voronezh, 30, 40–41, 47, 51, 56, 59, 72, 74–75, 84, 89, 104, 113, 141–143, 151, 188, 231, 243–245, 341, 395, 398, 410, 418, 487–488, 491, 495, 500, 520–521, 559, 633n.24, 638n.11, 638n.12, 642n.50, 642n.51, 644n.62, 645n.66, 646n.79, 647n.88, 648n.93, 649n.97, 659n.54, 666n.90, 668n.117, 672n.27, 699n.211, 709n.63, 709n.64, 711n.81
Western, 7, 10, 12–13, 16, 18, 20–21, 25, 32, 42–43, 51, 56, 71–75, 80, 83–84, 88–89, 95, 97, 101, 104, 141–143, 150–151, 164, 169, 183, 231, 243, 298, 301, 304, 309, 315, 337, 340, 387, 393, 395, 398, 410, 459, 467, 480–482, 485–487, 489, 493–495, 497–498, 502, 505–506, 509–510, 515, 518, 520, 543, 559–561, 566–567, 582, 633n.24, 638n.9, 638n.11, 638n.12, 639n.15, 641n.41, 642n.49, 643n.52, 643n.55: strength (1 October–5 December 1941), 644n.57, 645n.68, 645n.69, 646n.71, 646n.72, 647n.82, 647n.84, 647n.86, 650n.113, 665n.74, 668n.115, 671n.20, 672n.27, 672n.28, 682n.82, 689n.102, 690n.106, 703n.238, 704n.4, 704n.5, 707n.51, 709n.63, 709n.64, 709n.67, 709–710n.68, 711n.80, 711n.81, 713n.112, 714n.112, 715n.134
1st Baltic (former Kalinin), 56, 84, 95, 143, 188, 412, 485, 495, 497, 511, 520, 543, 633n.24, 639n.15, 640n.27, 702n.229, 709n.67, 711n.80, 711n.81
1st Belorussian, 167, 169, 388, 395, 490, 701n.229
1st Far Eastern, 501–502
1st Ukrainian (former Voronezh), 51, 53, 56, 84, 113, 143, 167, 245, 388, 486, 488, 495, 501, 521, 525, 543, 579, 633n.24, 639n.15, 648n.89, 649n.97, 701n.229, 711n.80, 711n.81
2nd Baltic, 390, 398, 484–485, 495, 633n.24, 702n.229, 711n.80
2nd Belorussian, 398, 501, 512
2nd Far Eastern, 501
2nd Ukrainian (former Steppe), 53, 56, 84, 143, 486, 493, 495, 499, 526–527, 543, 636n.25, 639n.15, 648n.89, 702n.229, 711n.80, 711n.81
3rd Baltic, 512, 633n.24
3rd Belorussian, 390, 490, 497, 512, 515
3rd Ukrainian (former Southwestern), 53, 56, 84, 390, 395, 410, 493, 495, 499, 527, 543, 633n.24, 636n.25, 639n.15, 640n.27, 702n.229, 711n.80, 711n.81
4th Ukrainian (former Southern), 53, 56, 84, 390, 398, 420, 485, 495, 499, 521, 543, 633n.24, 639n.15, 682n.82, 704n.5, 711n.80, 711n.81
Fronts, PVO (air defense), Soviet, 418
Central, 531
Eastern, 141, 148, 418, 531
Moscow, 141, 147–148, 417, 531
Northern, 531

Fronts, PVO (air defense), Soviet *(continued)*
Southern, 531
Southwestern, 531
Trans-Caucasus, 531
Western, 141, 148, 418, 531
Fuehrer Directives, German, No. 41 (5 April 1942), 27
Frunze, 411
Frunze, M. V., 479, 536, 716n.1
Frunze Academy, 62, 391–392, 394–395, 406, 419, 436, 469, 472, 500, 682n.82
Fursovich. Major General of Tank Forces A. N., 522

Gaidukov, Major General V. A., 517
Galanin, Lieutenant General I. V., 506, 510, 713n.112
Galitsky, Lieutenant General K. N., 510, 512, 704n.11
Gamarnik, Army Commissar 1st Rank Ia. B., 478
Gapich, Major General of Signal Forces N. I., 422–423
Gavrilov, Colonel V. S., 418
General Staff Academy, Soviet. *See* Voroshilov Academy of the General Staff
General Staff, Red Army (GshKA), 15, 34, 60, 62, 64, 66, 72, 80, 110, 118, 121, 145, 189–190, 232, 251, 287, 334, 344–346, 349, 371–372, 373–376, 383–384, 387, 389, 390–392, 403–405, 420, 422, 424–431, 438, 449–465: organization, 463, 470, 491, 498, 500–501, 561, 581, 615–616, 637n.31, 648n.93, 677n.17; work schedule, 451–452, 689–699n.203
Geniatullin, Major General S. N., 462
Gerasimenko, Lieutenant General V. F., 509–510
Getman, Lieutenant General A. L., 408, 514–515, 518, 522, 713n.105, 713n.112
GKO. *See* State Defense Committee, Soviet
"Glasnost" [openness], Khrushchev's and Gorbachev's programs of, 476–477
Glazunov, Major General V. A., 411
Glukhov, 580
Golikov, Colonel General F. I., 453, 488–489, 498, 500, 508, 650n.115, 703n.238, 704–705n.11
Golovanov, Lieutenant General of Aviation A. E., 413–414
Golovanovsky, Major General R. I., 520
Golubev, Lieutenant General A. V., 468
Golubev, Lieutenant General D. K., 506
Golubovsky, Major General V. S., 513
Golushkovich, Lieutenant General V. S., 401, 682n.82
Gomel', 51, 53, 56
Gorbatov, Lieutenant General A. V., 468, 512, 650n.115
Gordov, Lieutenant General V. N., 488–489, 508, 705n.11
Goriunov, Lieutenant General of Aviation S. K., 533
Gor'kii, 336, 416
Gornostaipol', 56
Gorodniansky, Lieutenant General A. M., 507–508
Gorodok, 53
Gorodovikov, Colonel General O. I., 704n.9
GOSPLAN (State production planning organ), Soviet, 375, 692n.149
Govorov, Army General L. A., 373, 387, 395–396, 406, 488–489, 493–496, 506, 508, 534, 702n.229, 704–705n.11
prewar service, 710n.76
Grachev, Colonel F. U., 513
Grand Alliance, 6
Great Britain, 6, 16–18, 26, 249, 461
Grechko, Lieutenant General A. A., 509, 511–512, 517, 650n.115

Greece, 15
Grendal', Colonel General V. D., 704n.9
Grigor'ev, Major General of Tank forces V. E., 522
Gritsenko, Colonel D. M., 518. 522
Gromadin, Colonel General M. S., 416–418, 462, 531
  postwar service, 715n.132
Gromov, Lieutenant General of Aviation M. M., 532, 716n.137
Groups, Soviet
  Black Sea Group of Forces, 487, 499
  Cavalry Group Belov, 21–22, 516, 659n.55, 678n.27, 713n.105
  Cavalry Group Bobkin, 659n.55
  Cavalry Group Dovator, 516
  Cavalry Group Pliev, 658n.43
  Don Operational, 492
  Group of Reserve Armies, 165, 653n.22
  Iartsevo (Group Rokossovsky), 489, 505, 567, 665n.74
  Leningrad Group of Forces, 395, 493
  Mobile Group Popov, 94, 244, 511, 523, 641n.44, 642n.50, 648n.93
  Neva Operational, 509
  Northern Group of Forces (Trans-Caucasus Front), 494
  Operational Group Khozin, 150, 641n.44
  Operational Group Kostenko, 516
  Operational Group Vatutin (Kalinin), 491
  Reserve Aviation, 315–316,532
  Shock aviation (UAG), 315–316, 532, 667n.112
  Special Designation Aviation Group (Moscow), 315, 425, 433
  Zemland Group of Forces, 497
Groups of *fronts,* Soviet, 67, 75, 90–92, 95, 141, 373, 386, 481
Groups of Officers, Red Army General Staff, 374–375
Gruneev, Major General S. I., 699n.206
Gryzov, Lieutenant General A. A., 699n.206
"Guards," designation, Soviet, 144, 179, 181, 183, 287, 728n.151
Guderian, Colonel General Heinz, 16, 20, 25, 580, 713n.105
Gudymenko, Lieutenant General of Artillery P. E., 531, 715n.132
GULAG (Main Directorate of Camps), NKVD, 158, 162, 170, 447, 500, 544–547, 622
  scope of system, 719–720n.30
Gundorov, Lieutenant General of Engineer Forces A. S., 530
Gusev, Major General N. I., 509, 517

High Command, German Armed Forces (OKW), 136, 622
High Command, German Army (OKH), 18, 23, 26–27, 30, 33, 36, 40, 49, 136
Higher Military School of the PVO, 419
Historical debates (controversies), Soviet-German War, 14–17, 24–25, 34–36, 45–48, 58–59
Hitler, Adolf, xv, 3, 5–6, 10–11, 13–17, 20, 25–27, 29, 34–36, 38, 43, 47–50, 55, 58–61, 63, 75, 90, 120, 370, 477, 489, 500, 537–538, 564, 609–611, 613–614, 622, 729n.1
Honorifics (orders), force, Soviet, 475
  Order of Aleksandr Nevsky, 475
  Order of Kutuzov, 475
  Order of Suvorov, 475
  Order of the Patriotic War, 475
Hungary, 5, 24

Iakir, *Komandarm* [army commander] 1st Rank I. E., 478
Iakovlev, Colonel D. A., 514
Iakovlev, Lieutenant General N. D., 404, 704n.11
Iakutsk, 668n.117
Iaroslavl', 416
Iaroslavsky, E. M., 433

Ignatov, Major General of Artillery N. V., 530
Il'ichev, Lieutenant General I. I., 454, 699n.211
Il'in, Major General L. D., 517
Impressment, Soviet. *See* Mobilization, Soviet
Infantry Combat Regulations of 1942, Soviet, 473
Inner Mongolia, 153
"Institute" of Advisers, *Stavka*, 372, 394
Institute of Military Commissars, Soviet, 565–566
Institute of Red Professors, 398–399
Internal (Security) Forces. *See* NKVD forces
Iran, 153
Irkutsk, 399
Italy, 48–49
Iuplin, Colonel N. A., 521
Iushkevich, Lieutenant General V. A., 510
Ivanov, Lieutenant General F. S., 504, 681n.82
Ivanov, Lieutenant General P. A., 507
Ivanov, Lieutenant General V. D., 452, 704n.11
Ivanov, Major General of Tank Forces S. A., 515, 522
Ivanovsky, Rear Admiral, 703n.238

Japan, 6, 17, 154
Jews, Service in the Red Army, 548

Kachalov, Lieutenant General V. Ia., 504–506, 568, 704n.5, 725n.103
Kachanov, Lieutenant General K. M., 504, 681n.82, 704n.4
Kaganovich, L. M., 371, 690n.113
Kalach, 29
Kalinichenko, Major General of Tank Forces P. I., 699n.206
Kalinin, 165, 443
Kalinin, Lieutenant General S. A., 505–506
Kalinkovichi, 709n.67
Kalmyks, repression of, 402, 499
Kaluga, 20
Kamkov, Lieutenant General F. M., 509, 515–517, 534
Kapustin, Colonel S. I., 514
Karelia, 139, 224, 501
Karlin, Colonel M. M., 686n.44
Karpezo, Lieutenant General I. I., 513
Karpinsky, Brigade Quartermaster N. N., 435
Karponosov, Lieutenant General A. G., 455, 690n.113, 700–701n.219
Kasatonov, Rear Admiral V. A., 699n.206
"*Katiusha*" multiple rocket launchers, Soviet, 61, 111–112, 233, 307–311. *See also* Multiple-rocket launcher
Katkov, Major General of Tank Forces F.G., 522
Katukov, Lieutenant General of Tank Forces M. E., 408, 515, 518, 522, 526, 714n.112, 714n.116
Katyn massacre, 402
Kazakhstan, 160
Kazakov, Lieutenant General M. I., 704n.11
Kazakov, Lieutenant General V. I., 406, 704n.11
Khalikhovich, Major General of Tank Forces S. A., 514
Khalkhin-Gol, 154, 387, 394, 436, 468, 716n.137, 717n.7
Kharitonov, Lieutenant General F. M., 506, 508, 510
Khar'kov, 10, 20, 40–41, 51, 71, 74, 85, 143, 165, 169, 231, 244–245
Kharlamov, Rear Admiral N. M., 703n.238
Khasin, Major General of Tank Forces A. M., 518, 522
Khatskilovich, Major General M. G., 513
Khaziulin, Lieutenant General G. A., 511

Kholm, 139
Khomenko, Lieutenant General V. A. (NKVD), 505–506, 511, 653n.24, 682n.82, 704n.5
Khozin, Lieutenant General M. S., 482–483, 488–489, 502, 504, 509, 705n.11
Khriashchev, Major General A. A., 507
Khriukhin, Lieutenant General of Aviation T. T., 532–534, 716n.137, 716n.140
Khrulev, Army General of the Quartermaster Services, A. V., 428, 435, 438, 440–441, 455, 462, 689n.96, 690n.113, 692n.150, 704n.11
Khrushchev, N. S., 35, 381, 476, 486, 498, 635n.5, 680n.55
Khudiakov, Lieutenant General of Aviation S. A., 533–534
Khvostov, Colonel A. I., 517
Kiev, 6–7, 10, 12–13, 16, 25, 49, 51, 53, 56, 67, 69, 73, 77–78, 80, 185
Kirichenko, Major General N. Ia., 513, 517, 520–522
Kiriukhin, Lieutenant General N. I., 510
Kirov, 22
Kirov Military-Medical Academy, 436, 443
Kirponos, Colonel General M. P., 468–469, 482–483, 496–497, 505, 705n.11
Kislenko, Major General A. A., 703n.238
Kitaev, Major General L. M., 699n.206
Klin, 20
Kola Peninsular, 139
Kolesnikov, Major General N. G., 699n.206
Kolganov, Lieutenant General K. S., 509, 682n.82
Kolpakchi, Lieutenant General V. Ia., 506, 510, 512
Komsomol (Communist youth organization), Soviet, 380, 399, 400, 443, 546, 552, 588, 721n.51
Kondrat'ev, Major General Z. I., 354–355, 428, 434, 698n.197
Kondrusev, Major General S. M., 513
Konev, Colonel General I. S., 20, 22, 477, 482–484, 486–489, 492, 494–496, 498, 504–506, 534, 619, 650n.115, 704–705n.11
  prewar service, 708n.59, 708n.60
Konigsberg, 390
Konstantinov, Major General M. P., 520
Kopets, Major General of Aviation I. I., 715n.134
Koptsov, Major General of Tank Forces V. A., 514, 518, 521–522
Korchagin, Lieutenant General of Tank Forces I. P., 515, 519, 522
Korchagin, Major General M. N., 699n.206
Korea, 154
Kork, *Komandarm* [army commander] 2nd Rank A. I., 478
Korkodinov, Major General P. D., 460
Korobkov, Lieutenant General A. A., 504–505, 704n.4
Korolenko, Colonel I. F., 686n.44
Korol'kov, Lieutenant General of Artillery, P. M., 530
Korosten', 12
Koroteev, Lieutenant General K. A., 508, 512
Korzun, Lieutenant General P. P., 511, 517
Kosarev, General of Engineer Forces V. V., 530
Koshelev, Major General V. V., 518
Kosiakhin, Major General V. V., 706n.28
Kostenko, Lieutenant General F. Ia., 482–484, 488, 504, 507, 705n.11, 707n.52
Kostroma, 418, 434
Kotikov, Colonel M. Z., 686n.48
Kotliar, Major General of Engineer Forces L. Z., 408–410, 462, 685n.22

Kotliarov, Colonel A. A., 514
Kotov, Major General of Tank Forces P. V., 436
Kovalev, Colonel G. A., 517
Kovalev, G. B., 690n.113
Kovalev, Lieutenant General M. P., 489, 496, 705n.11
Kovalev, Military Engineer 1st Rank I. V., 352, 428, 430, 434, 483, 689n.96, 690n.113
Kozlov, Lieutenant General P. M., 509
Kozlov, Major General D. T., 414, 483, 488–489, 682n.82, 686n.40, 705n.11
Kozlova, Valentina Fedorovna, 728n.159
Kraskovets, Major General M. A., 699n.206
Krasnodar, 51, 165, 418
Krasnoiarsk, 668n.117
Krasovsky, Lieutenant General of Aviation S. A., 533–534, 704n.11
Kravchenko, Lieutenant General of Tank Forces A. G., 518–519, 522, 534, 714n.116, 714n.121
Kreizer, Lieutenant General Ia. G., 507
Kremenchug, 46, 51, 53, 56
"Kremlin" [*Kreml'*], German deception operation, 649n.101
Krenov, *Kombrig* [brigade commander] A. F., 685n.22
Kriuchenkin, Lieutenant General V. D., 516–517, 523
Kriukov, Lieutenant General V. V., 517–518, 520
Kriukov, Major General of Artillery F. Ia., 686n.44
Krivoi Rog, 53, 56, 67
Krivoshein, Lieutenant General S. M., 513, 522
Kronshtadt mutiny (1921), 479
Kruglov, Commissar of State Security 3rd Rank S. N., 164
Krylov, Lieutenant General N. I., 512
Krymov, Colonel V. P., 514
Krymskaia, 55
Kudriavtsev, Lieutenant General M. K., 457
Kuibyshev, 6, 413, 418, 443, 450
Kuibyshev Military-Engineering Academy, 411
Kuibyshev Military-Medical Academy, 443
Kukushkin, Major General of Tank Forces A. V., 521–522
Kulaks, landed peasants, 566, 588, 720n.31
Kuleshov, Marshal of Artillery P. N., 406
Kulik, Marshal of the Soviet Union G. I., 371, 404, 419, 468, 640n.115
Kuril Islands, 154
Kurkin, Major General of Tank Forces A. V., 513–514, 518
Kurkotkin, Lieutenant General of Tank Forces S. K., 408
Kurochkin, Lieutenant General P. A., 482–484, 488–489, 496, 498, 501, 504–506, 512, 561, 704–705n.11, 707n.52
  prewar service, 712n.91
Kursk, 22, 27, 40–41, 43, 48, 55, 58, 69–71, 75, 139, 142–143, 151, 169, 244
Kutsev, Major General Iu. A., 699n.206
Kutsevalov, Lieutenant General of Aviation T. F., 532–533, 716n.137
Kuz'min, Major General F. S., 682n.82
Kuz'min, Major General G. I., 514, 518
Kuznets Basin (Kuzbas), 720n.38
Kuznetsov, Admiral N. G., 371, 373, 386, 396–397
Kuznetsov, Colonel General F. F., 454, 483, 699n.211
Kuznetsov, Colonel General F. I., 469, 482, 705n.11, 705n.14, 705n.25
Kuznetsov, Colonel G. G., 514
Kuznetsov, Division Quartermaster N. I., 562
Kuznetsov, Lieutenant General V. I., 505–506, 510
Kuznetsov, Major General A. M., 507

Kuznetsov, Major General M. N., 461
Kyshtym, 473

Labor camps, Soviet. *See* GULAG (Main Directorate of Camps), NKVD
Lake Il'men', 12
Lake Khasan, 154, 436, 716n.137
Lake Ladoga, 139, 142
Lazarov, Lieutenant General of Tank Forces I. G., 513, 518, 522
Lekarev, Lieutenant General of the Veterinary Service V. M., 436
Leliushenko, Lieutenant General D. D., 506, 509, 511, 513, 534, 704–705n.11, 714n.121
Lend-Lease Program, Allied, 6, 38, 122, 153, 192, 236, 247, 249–251, 317, 321, 323, 356, 440–441, 461, 556, 563–564, 659n.60, 659n.61, 668n.117, 668n.117, 675n.90, 694n.156, 725n.93
Lenin, V. I., 369, 679n.49
Leningrad, 5–7, 10, 12, 15, 20, 27, 30, 32, 34, 36, 44, 47, 67, 69–70, 73–74, 77–78, 85, 185, 224, 301, 399, 416, 425, 434, 529, 587, 613, 633n.24
Leningrad Military-Engineer School, 410
Leningrad Naval Academy, 396
Lenin Military-Political Academy, 406
Lepel', 12
Leselidze, Lieutenant General K. N., 511
Lithuania, 12
Little Saturn. *See* Middle Don offensive *under* Operations, military
Liutezh, 51, 53, 56
Livny, 151
Liziukov, Lieutenant General A. I., 514, 518, 523
Locomotive columns (steam) (ORPKs), 432
Locomotive repair trains (PRPs), 432
Loktionov, Colonel General of Aviation A. D., 685n.33, 704n.9, 705n.14, 715n.133
Lomov, Lieutenant General N. A., 699n.206
Long-Range Bomber Aviation. *See* Air forces, Soviet
Lopatin, Lieutenant General A. I., 506, 508
Lozovsky, Lieutenant Colonel A. V., 521
Luftwaffe, German Air Force, 312, 318–319, 345, 414
Luga, 7
Lukin, Lieutenant General M. F., 504–505
Lunev, Colonel I. F., 517
L'vov, Lieutenant General L. N., 508–509

Main Direction Commands [*glavnye komandovanniia voisk upravlenia*], Soviet, 141, 470, 478–481, 493, 617, 680n.55
  North Caucasus, 141, 478
  Northwestern, 141, 386, 393, 478–479
  Southwestern, 35, 141, 478, 480, 496–497, 561
  Western, 141, 387, 395, 478, 480, 497
Malandin, Lieutenant General G. K., 392, 452, 704n.11
Maleev, Major General M. F., 517, 520–521
Malenkov, G. M., 370
Malinovsky, Colonel General R. Ia., 35, 386, 482–484, 488–489, 492–493, 495–496, 504, 506, 510–511, 534, 650n.115, 704–705n.11, 707n.52
  prewar service, 710n.74
Mal'tsev, Major General S. P., 518
Malygin, Major General of Tank Forces K. A., 522
Managarov, Lieutenant General I. M., 512, 517

Manchuria (Manchukuo), 26, 153–154, 160
Maneuvers, Soviet military, 1935 Kiev, 391
Mangul'sky, D. Z., 443
Mannerheim Defense Line, Finnish, 394–395
Manstein, Field Marshal Erich von, 27, 34, 36, 38, 40–41, 43–48, 53, 58–59, 151, 231, 244, 490–491
Marievsky, Lieutenant Colonel I. P., 460
"Marshals of Victory," Red Army, 496, 534
Maslennikov, Lieutenant General I. I., 495–496, 511–512, 704–705n.11
Maslennikov, Major General M. N., 699n.206
Maslov, Lieutenant General of Tank Forces A. G., 508, 518, 522
Medical support, Red Army, 693n.154
  field evacuation points (PEPs), 692n.154
  front evacuation points (FEPs), 692n.154
  hospitalized casualties, 1941–1945, 695n.173
  hospital system, *front* evacuation points (FEPs), 692–693n.154
  local evacuation points (MEPs), 692n.154
  personnel strength, 695n.172
Medvezh'egorsk, 671n.20
Mekhlis, I. Z., 371, 373, 378, 397–399, 402, 443, 499, 568, 680n.75
Melitopol', 51, 53
Mellenthin, General F. W. von, 492
Mel'nik, Major General K. S., 517
Mel'nikov, Major General of Technical Forces P. G., 349
Meretskov, Marshal of the Soviet Union K. A., 371, 386, 468, 482–484, 488–489, 495–496, 498, 501–502, 504, 506, 534, 704n.9, 704–705n.11, 707n.52
Merkulov, V. N., 379, 401–402
Mernov, Major General V. F., 699n.206
Miasnikov, Major General M. A., 513
Midway, Battle of, 25
Mikhneev, A. N., 384, 400, 680n.50
Mikoian, A. I., 371, 439, 690n.113, 692n.149
Military academies and schools, Soviet, 472–475
  Central Women's Sniper Training, 721n.51
  period of study in, 706n.31
Military Academy of Armored and Mechanized Forces, 408
Military Academy of the Rear and Supply, 443
Military Academy of the RKKA, 419
Military-automobile roads (VAD), Soviet, 354–356, 428, 433, 675n.83, 675n.86
Military commissariats, Soviet KNO, 422
Military councils [*voennye sovety*], Soviet, 380–381, 679n.37, 679n.38
Military counterintelligence, Soviet, 384–385
Military districts [*voennye okrugy*], Soviet, 137, 152–153, 333, 337, 344, 348, 356, 415–416, 418, 427, 436–437, 441, 455
  Baltic, 705n.14
  Baltic Special, 152, 186, 469, 655n.20, 658n.48, 658n.49, 674n.76, 705n.14
  Belorussian, 153, 392, 404, 480
  Caucasus, 539
  Central Asian, 148, 154, 182, 238, 499, 539
  Far Eastern, 182, 561
  Khar'kov, 153, 186, 312, 343, 391, 480, 674n.75
  Kiev, 480
  Kiev Special, 152, 186, 312, 387, 392, 404, 407, 419, 469, 480, 496, 500, 655n.20, 658n.48, 658n.49, 674n.75, 674n.76

Leningrad, 312–313, 392, 394, 470, 655n.20, 658n.48, 674n.75, 674n.76, 708n.53
Moscow, 153, 164, 169, 187, 338, 341, 343, 392, 407, 478–479, 539, 572, 644n.55, 653n.24, 672n.27, 674n.75, 715n.133
North Caucasus, 153, 182, 338, 343, 404, 479, 550, 708n.60
Odessa, 186, 312, 470, 492, 561, 658n.49, 674n.75, 674n.76
Orel, 153, 501
Siberian, 545–546
Stalingrad, 153, 338, 498, 572
Steppe, 72, 75, 99, 143, 151, 486, 495, 498, 640n.25
Trans-Baikal, 153, 181, 312, 561
Trans-Caucasus, 153, 182, 312, 487, 498, 658n.47, 686n.40
Ural, 148, 343, 562
Volga, 153, 338, 539, 562, 572, 672n.27
Western Special, 152, 186, 312, 469, 655n.20, 658n.48, 658n.49, 674n.75, 674n.76
White Sea, 502
Military education and training, 421–422
Military-Engineer Academy, 410
Military intelligence, Soviet, 384
Military Missions, Allied in Moscow
British, 703n.238
French, 703n.238
United States, 703n.238
Military Missions, Soviet
Great Britain, 703n.238
Mediterranean Theater, 703n.238
Pacific Theater, 703n.238
Supreme Allied Headquarters, France, 703n.238
Military prosecutor system, Soviet, 382–383, 570–571
Military strategy, Soviet, 63–100
Military Transport Academy, 434
Military tribunal system, Soviet, 382–383, 547, 569–570, 589
Military Veterinary Academy, 433
Millerovo, 29, 40, 151
Milovsky, Major General M. P., 692n.150
Ministry of Defense (MO), 677n.14
Ministry of Internal Affairs (MVD), 401–402
Ministry of State Security (MGB), 379, 401
Minsk, 7, 56, 66
Miroshnikov, Colonel S. Z., 514
Mishanin, Colonel T. A., 514
Mishchenko, Major General A. A., 578
Mishulin, Major General of Tank Forces V. A., 514–515, 518
Mitrofanov, Major General of Tank Forces V. A., 522
Mius River, 40, 55, 59, 231
Mobile groups [*podvizhnye gruppy*], 89, 94–95, 105–106, 108–110, 184, 218, 518, 641n.42, 648n.92, 648n.93, 648n.94
Mobilization, Soviet, 537–541
convicts and political prisoners, 544–547
"creeping up to war," Stalin's concept of, 537, 548
impressments, 541–544
large-scale training exercise [*bol'shie uchebny sbory*–BUS], 538–539
non-Slavic nationalities, 547–551, 588
Red Army ethnic composition and death rates, 604, 620
total strength mobilized, 550, 619–620, 716n.1
women, 554, 620
Mogilev, 78, 86
Moldavanskoe, 55
Moldavia, 7, 544
Molotov, V. M., 370
Mordvinov, Lieutenant General V. K., 705n.25
Morgunov, Major General of Aviation R. N., 427
Morocco, 37
Morozov, Lieutenant General V. I., 505–506
Mosal'sk, 20

Moscow, 6–7, 10, 13, 15–16, 18, 20, 30, 67, 69–70, 73–74, 77–78, 80, 163, 399, 406, 408, 411, 413–414, 416, 418, 443, 450, 473, 529, 614
Moscow Conference (1942), Allied, 461
Moskalenko, I. I., 400
Moskalenko, Lieutenant General K. S., 386, 406, 509, 512, 517, 523, 704–705n.11
Moskvin, Lieutenant General N. A., 507
Mostovenko, Major General of Tank Forces D. K., 513–514, 518
Mozyr', 709n.67
Murmansk, 70, 139, 142, 545, 668n.117
Mussolini, Benito, 49
Muzychenko, Lieutenant General I. N., 504–505, 704n.5
Myndro, Colonel M. I., 513

Napoleon Bonaparte, 17
Narva. 44, 46
National Liberation Committee, Yugoslavia, 461
National military formations, Red Army, 547–551
  composition (1941–1943), 600–602
  composition and strength (1 January 1938), 598–599
  strength (1941–1945), 603
Naumenko, Iu. A., 721n.48
Naumenko, Lieutenant General of Aviation N. F., 533
Navy (VMF), Soviet, 137, 182, 372, 396–397
  strength, 138–139, 155
Nedelin. Marshal of Artillery M. I., 406
Neva River, 22
Nevel', 53, 56
Nikishev, Major General D. N., 507
Nikitin, Major General A. G., 513
Nikitin, Major General I. S., 515
Nikoforov, Colonel N. M., 514
Nikolaev, Lieutenant General I. F., 511
Nikolaev, Major General K. I., 699n.206
Nikopol', 53, 56
NKO. *See* People's Commissariat of Defense
NKVD forces, 138, 149, 157–177, 446–447, 615, 644n.55
  border guards, 157, 159–161: organization (on 22 June 1941), 171–173, 652n.6
  composition (on 22 June 1941), 697n.192
  convoy security, 159, 162–163: organization (on 22 June 1941), 176
  installation security, 159, 161: organization (on 22 June 1941), 176, 446–447
  internal security (operational), 157–161, 163–164: organization (on 22 June 1941), 174; planned deployment (in June 1941), 177, 542; subordination to Red Army *fronts* (on 23 June 1941), 175
  railroad, 159, 161–162: organization (on 22 June 1941), 176
  snipers, 697n.194
  state communications security, 159
  strength, 138–139, 155, 157–158, 160–163, 167
North Africa, 25–26, 37, 50
Northern Donets River, 27, 40–41, 55, 59, 143
Norway, 6, 461
Noskov, Major General A. A., 517
"Not a Step Back" Order (Order 227; 28 July 1942), 571–572, 574, 577–578, 580–581
Novgorod, 7
Novikov, Colonel N. A., 514
Novikov, Lieutenant General A. A., 316, 373, 387, 392–393, 397, 401, 413–414, 462, 704n.11
Novikov, Lieutenant General V. V., 513, 705n.11
Novosel'sky, Lieutenant General Iu. V., 513

Oborin, Major General S. O., 513
Obukhov, Lieutenant General of Tank Forces V. T., 514–515, 522
Occupation of Bessarabia (June 1940), Soviet, 394, 537, 717n.7
Occupation of eastern Poland (September 1939), Soviet, 394, 404, 466, 537, 717n.7
Occupation of the Baltic states, Soviet, 537, 717n.7
Oder River, 5, 528
Odessa, 7, 10, 67, 77, 406, 434, 499
Odintsev, Marshal of Artillery G. F., 406
Officer corps, Red Army, 466–535
  killed or missing in action, 535
Officer Corps of the General Staff, 461–462
OGPU (Combined State Political Directorate [*Ob'edinennoe gosudarstvennoe politicheskoe upravlenie*]), 679n.49
Ogurtsov, Colonel S. Ia., 514
Omsk, 562
Onianov, Lieutenant General L. V., 699n.206
OO's. *See* Special departments, NKVD
Operational art, Soviet, 100–114, 645n.67
Operational formations. *See* *Echelonment* of forces, Soviet
Operational maneuver, 89, 106–110
  airborne dimension, 685n.29
Operations, Military (Red Army by Soviet classification)
  Arctic and Karelian defensive (29 June–10 October 1941), 125
  Balaton (Lake) defensive (March 1945), 637n.30, 640n.27
  Baltic defensive (22 June–9 July 1941), 125
  Barvenkovo-Lozovaia offensive (18–31 January 1942), 21, 23, 101, 145, 246, 492, 497, 508, 517, 649n.101, 658n.43
  Belgorod-Khar'kov offensive (Operation Rumiantsev; 3–23 August 1943), 51, 53, 84, 86, 89, 93, 101, 113, 129–130, 143, 244, 390, 486, 492, 522, 525–526, 610, 613, 638n.12, 642n.47, 643n.51, 645n.66, 649n.102
  Belorussian defensive (22 June–9 July 1941), 125
  Belorussian (1st) offensive (Vitebsk, Orsha, Gomel', and Bobruisk; 3 October–31 December 1943), 55–57, 83, 86, 95, 129, 188, 412, 490, 497–498, 520–521, 613, 33n.24, 635n.11, 637n.30, 639n.15, 643n.52, 650n.113, 709n.67, 709–710n.68
  Belorussian (2nd) offensive (Operation Bagration; June–August 1944), 57, 388, 390, 393, 395, 497, 527, 612, 650n.113
  Berlin (April–May 1945), 388, 393, 395, 525–526, 528, 612, 636n.25, 650n.113
  Bolkhov offensive (24 March–3 April 1942), 21–22, 489, 519
  Bolkhov offensive (23–29 August 1942), 32–33, 81, 231, 243, 489, 497, 519, 523, 638n.9, 647n.82
  Border (Frontier) Battles (22 June–9 July 1941), 7, 11, 482–483, 503–504, 515, 622, 641n.32, 645n.69
  Briansk offensive (1 September–3 October 1943), 51, 54, 484, 520–521
  Budapest defensive (January–February 1945), 637n.30
  Caucasus defensive (August–November 1942), 499, 610
  Chernigov-Poltava offensive (Chernigov-Pripiat', Sumy-Priluki, and Poltavaf; 26 August–30 September 1943), 51, 54, 129
  Crimean defensive (8–19 May 1942), 23, 33–34, 36, 68, 398, 479, 498, 507–509, 682n.82

Operations, Military (Red Army by Soviet classification) *(continued)*
Crimean offensive (27 February–15 April 1942), 21, 23, 26, 30–31, 97, 389, 398, 487, 498, 609, 613, 616, 622
Demiansk offensive (7 January–25 February 1942), 21–22, 491, 707n.52
Demiansk (1st) offensive (1 March–30 April 1942), 21, 187, 389, 393, 412, 491, 501
Demiansk (2nd) offensive (17–24 July 1942), 32, 81, 501, 707n.52
Demiansk (3rd) offensive (10–21 August 1942), 32, 81, 501, 707n.52
Demiansk (4th) offensive (15–16 September 1942), 32, 81, 501, 707n.52
Demiansk (5th) offensive (15 February–1 March 1943), 42, 501, 613, 666n.90
Donbas defensive (7–24 July 1942), 31
Donbas defensive (20 February–6 March 1943), 42–43, 47, 101, 491, 511, 520, 522–523, 610, 613
Donbas (1st) (Voroshilovgrad) offensive (29 January–23 February 1943), 41–46, 244, 246, 485, 490–491, 493, 503, 511, 520, 610, 641n.44, 642n.50
Donbas (2nd) offensive (Izium-Barvenkovo and Mius River; 17 July–2 August 1943), 55, 57, 93, 493, 521, 642n.47, 649n.102
Donbas (3rd) offensive, 13 August-22 September 1943, 51, 54, 129, 390, 493, 638n.12, 643n.51
Donbas-Rostov defensive (29 September–16 November 1941), 125
Donbas, Khar'kov, and Sevsk-Kursk defensive (21 February–28 March 1943), 127, 613
East Prussian (1st) (October 1944), 636n.25, 637n.30
East Prussian (2nd) (January–February 1945), 497, 636n.25
Gomel-Rechitsa offensive (10–30 November 1943), 54, 56, 611, 709n.67
Iassy-Kishinev (1st) offensive (April–May 1944), 527–528, 636n.25, 637n.30
Iassy-Kishinev (2nd) (August 1944), 636n.25
Kalinin defensive (October 1941), 12–13, 484, 491, 645n.68
Karelian (July 1944), 396, 494, 502
Kelme, Raseinai, Grodno, and Dubno offensives (24–29 June 1941), 12, 80, 90, 242, 387, 489, 505, 514, 647n.86
Kerch-Feodosiia offensive (25 December 1941–2 January 1942), 21, 128
Khar'kov defensive (5–23 March 1943), 42–43, 231, 244, 503, 511, 520, 522–523, 610, 613
Khar'kov offensive (12–29 May 1942), 26–27, 30–31, 33–35, 61, 68, 97, 108, 145, 228, 243, 389, 392, 480, 482, 488, 492, 497, 507–509, 518–519, 609, 613, 616, 622, 647n.82, 648n.90, 649n.101, 659n.55, 707n.52
Khar'kov offensive (2–23 February 1943), 42, 45–47, 101, 231, 244, 490, 500, 520, 523, 610, 642n.50, 666n.90
Kiev defensive (7 July–26 September 1941), 7, 10–11, 16, 68, 125, 391–392, 478, 480, 482–483, 503–506, 616, 641n.32, 645n.69
Kiev defensive (13 November–22 December 1943), 54
Kiev (1st) offensive (Chernobyl', Gornostaipol', Liutezh, and Bukrin; 1–24 October 1943), 55–57, 83, 86, 129, 521, 525, 611, 613, 639n.15

Kiev (2nd) offensive (3–13 November 1943), 54, 57, 91, 108, 113, 129, 492, 525, 611, 643n.51, 648n.89
Korsun'-Shevchenkovskii (January-February 1944), 388, 393, 526, 528
Kotel'nikovskii defensive (12–December 1942), 40–41, 47, 493, 510, 519
Kotel'nikovskii offensive (30 December 1942), 41, 47, 493, 510, 519
Kovel' offensive (February 1944), 501
Krasnodar-Novorossiisk offensive (11 January–24 May 1943), 41, 46, 51, 129
Krivoi-Rog-Nikopol' offensive (Krivoi Rog, Aleksandriia-Znamenka, Apostolovo, and Nikopol'; 14 November–31 December 1943), 55–57, 86, 108, 245, 486, 526, 611, 613, 639n.15, 648n.89
Kursk defensive (Operation Citadel; 5–23 July 1943), 4, 25, 38, 44, 48–51, 53–54, 57–59, 62–63, 66, 69, 71–72, 76–77, 80, 83, 87, 91, 96, 98–101, 104, 107, 116, 122, 127–128, 140, 190, 244–245, 390, 393, 407, 410, 418, 432, 434, 484, 486, 490, 494–495, 503, 510, 525–527, 541, 610–613, 638n.12, 642n.47, 645n.66, 646–647n.79, 647–648n.88, 658n.54
Leningrad defensive (10 July–30 September 1941), 7, 11, 68, 80, 125, 387, 393, 479, 483, 484, 506, 609, 682n.82
Leningrad offensive (Operation Spark; January 1943), 44, 89, 129, 301, 340, 388, 410, 479, 494, 502
Leningrad-Novgorod (Liuban') offensive (7 January–30 April 1942), 21, 101, 144–145, 393, 501–502, 507, 517, 680n.52, 707n.52
Leningrad-Novgorod (January–February 1944), 396, 494
Lepel' (Timoshenko "Offensive"; July 1941), 12
Liuban' (Miasnoi Bor) defensive (13 May–10 July 1942), 31, 33
Lower Dnepr offensive (26 September–20 December 1943), 54, 56, 129
Lublin-Brest offensive (July–August 1944), 528, 715n.128
L'vov-Sandomierz (July–August 1944), 388, 525
Manchurian (August 1945), 390, 393, 396, 501–502
Melitopol' offensive, 26 September–5 November 1943, 54, 521
Middle Don offensive (Operation Little Saturn; 16–30 December 1942), 40–41, 47, 94, 129, 243, 309, 491, 510, 519, 610, 641n.41, 642n.50
Moscow defensive (Operation Typhoon; 30 September–5 December 1941), 7, 10–11, 13, 16, 18, 21, 68, 80–81, 125, 128, 154, 242, 387, 395, 399, 407, 413, 434, 486, 489, 493, 498, 506, 508, 515–516, 526, 640n.24, 658n.43
Moscow offensive (5 December 1941–7 January 1942), 10–11, 18, 21, 24–25, 83, 85, 87–88, 91, 97, 101–102, 108, 128, 144–145, 149, 242, 246, 296, 308, 350, 387, 412–413, 434, 486, 489, 493, 498, 500–501, 506–508, 526, 609, 611–613, 642n.49, 644n.55, 650n.113, 678n.27, 713n.105
Moscow offensive (8 January–20 April 1942), 14, 18, 20, 23–25, 38, 63, 82–83, 85, 87–88, 97, 101–102, 108, 128, 130, 145, 149, 239, 246, 296, 308, 387, 412–413, 434, 486, 489, 493, 498, 500–501, 506–508, 516, 526, 611–613, 642n.49, 644n.55, 650n.113, 678n.27, 713n.105

Operations, Military (Red Army by Soviet classification) *(continued)*
Nevel'-Gorodok offensive (6 October–31 December 1943), 54, 56, 486
North Caucasus offensive (1 January–4 February 1943), 129, 520
Northern Caucasus defensive (25 July–31 December 1942), 126
Novorossiisk-Taman' offensive (10 September–9 October 1943), 54, 129
Oboian'-Kursk offensive (3–26 January 1942), 21–22, 508
Orel offensive (Operation Kutuzov; 12 July–18 August 1943), 51, 53, 82, 84, 86, 89, 93, 101, 129–130, 395, 484, 490, 497, 525, 610, 613, 638n.12
Orel-Bolkhov offensive (7 January–18 February 1942), 21, 508, 527
Orel-Briansk-Smolensk offensive (5 February–28 March 1943), 42–43, 45, 61, 83, 89, 101, 129, 143, 232, 244, 246, 490, 497, 509, 511, 520, 523, 542, 576, 610, 633n.24, 635n.6, 641n.44, 648n.93, 711n.79
Ostrogozhsk-Rossosh' offensive (13–27 January 1943), 40–41, 231, 243, 520, 523, 642n.50
Prague (May 1945), 525
Proskurov-Chernovtsy (March-April 1944), 525, 637n.30
Riga (1944), 497
Rostov defensive (18 October–16 November 1941), 7, 23, 506
Rostov (1st) offensive (17 November–2 December 1941), 11, 68, 83, 87, 90–92, 97, 128, 145, 483, 506, 520, 638n.9, 649n.101
Rostov (2nd) offensive (1 January–18 February 1943), 40–41, 46, 493, 610
Rzhev defensive (encirclement of 39th Army; 2–27 July 1942), 31, 507, 645n.70
Rzhev-Sychevka (1st) offensive (30 July–23 August 1942), 30, 32, 81, 145, 387, 486, 509, 518, 638n.9, 645n.68
Rzhev-Sychevka (2nd) offensive (Operation Mars; 25 November–20 December 1942), 4, 32, 36–38, 42–43, 46, 57, 82–85, 89–90, 92, 98, 113, 118, 129–130, 145, 243, 246, 298, 309, 351, 387, 486, 498, 501, 509–510, 518–519, 585, 610, 613, 635n.4, 635n.5, 638n.7, 641n.41, 641n42, 647n.84, 650n.113, 713–714n.112
Rzhev-Viaz'ma (1st) offensive (15 February–1 March 1942), 21–22, 85, 412, 486, 517
Rzhev-Viaz'ma (2nd) offensive (2 March–1 April 1943), 42, 486
Sevastopol' siege (5 October 1941–4 July 1942), 125
Siauliai defensive (August 1944), 637n.30, 640n.27
Siniavino (1st) offensive (10–26 September 1941), 638n.9
Siniavino (2nd) offensive (19 August–10 October 1942), 30, 33, 36, 81, 507, 509
Siniavino (3rd) offensive (Operation Spark; 12–30 January 1943), 41, 396
Siniavino (6th) offensive (15–18 September 1943), 55
Smolensk defensive (10 July–10 September 1941), 7, 10–12, 73, 80–81, 91, 97, 125, 480, 483, 485–486, 489, 493, 504–506, 515, 567, 612, 658n.43, 708n.60
Smolensk offensive (21 July–7 August 1941), 13, 16, 80, 83, 85, 87–88, 90–91, 97, 101, 128, 387, 480, 383, 486, 506, 612, 642n.49, 646n.71, 704n.5

Smolensk offensive (Operation Suvorov; 7 August–2 October 1943), 51, 54, 89, 93, 95, 129, 520, 638n.12
Smolensk, El'nia, and Roslavl' offensive (17 August–12 September 1941), 13, 80, 83, 91, 97, 101, 128, 130, 395, 480, 485, 489, 506, 642n.49, 646n.71
Sol'tsy, Lepel', Bobruisk, and Kiev offensive (July 1941), 12, 80, 101, 484, 491, 638n.9, 640n.29, 645n.68
Stalingrad (Volga) defensive (Operation *Blau* [Blue]; 17 July–18 November 1942), 23, 25–27, 29–35, 61–62, 69–71, 74, 80–81, 85, 87, 90, 96, 98, 100, 106, 120, 126, 128, 149, 217, 228, 231, 243, 298, 316, 339, 389, 407, 410, 432, 434, 484–485, 487, 490, 492, 499–500, 503, 509, 518, 609–610, 613, 616, 638n.10, 645n.70
Stalingrad offensive (Operation Uranus; 19 November 1942–2 February 1943), 4, 25, 36–38, 41, 43–48, 57, 59, 61, 63, 67, 81–85, 89, 91–94, 98, 106, 108–109, 113, 118, 122, 129–130, 144–145, 149, 217, 227, 231, 243, 298, 309, 342, 351, 388–389, 393, 395, 407, 410, 432, 434, 484–485, 489, 491–494, 499–500, 503, 509–510, 518–519, 523, 541, 610–613, 638n.7, 641n.41, 641n.42, 641n.47, 642n.50, 647n.82, 647n.84, 666n.90
Staraia Russa-Pskov offensive (Operation Polar Star; 15–28 February and 4–19 March 1943), 42–46, 83, 89, 129, 150, 388, 393, 396, 499, 610, 613, 633n.24, 641n.44, 666n.90
Staraia Russa, Smolensk, and Kiev offensive (August 1941), 12, 80, 484, 491, 506, 638n.9, 640n.29, 645n.68, 646n.71, 681n.82, 704n.4
Taman' offensives (4 April–10 May, 26 May–22 August 1943), 55, 57, 83, 129
Tikhvin defensive (16 October–10 November 1941), 7, 125, 483, 501, 506
Tikhvin offensive (10 November–30 December 1941), 11, 21, 23, 83, 87, 90–92, 97, 128, 145, 483, 501, 506, 609, 638n.9, 642n.49, 644n.55
Toropets-Kholm offensive (9 January–6 February 1942), 21–22, 145, 485, 508, 649n.101
Uman' defensive (July 1941), 7, 10–11, 68, 73, 478, 499, 503–506, 616, 641n.32, 645n.69, 704n.5
Viaz'ma and Briansk defensive (30 September–5 November 1941), 10–11, 13, 68, 165, 242, 389, 395, 478, 482, 485–486, 493, 403, 504–506, 515, 616, 622, 641n.32, 645n.69, 682n.82
Viaz'ma defensive (Operation Hannover; 24 May–21 June 1942), 31
Vistula-Oder (January 1945), 393, 525–526, 612
Voronezh (1st) offensive (5–23 July 1942), 30–33, 61,81, 90, 108, 231, 243, 316, 491, 509, 514, 518–519, 523, 657n.24
Voronezh (2nd) offensive (12–15 August 1942), 30, 32–33, 61, 81, 231, 489, 491, 509, 519
Voronezh (3rd) offensive (15–28 September 1942), 30, 33, 491, 519
Voronezh-Don offensive (4–26 July 1942), 32–33, 81, 83, 90, 231, 243, 316, 519, 522, 647n.82, 647n.87, 648n.90, 657n.24
Voronezh-Kastornoe offensive (24 January–5 February 1943), 40–41
Voronezh-Khar'kov offensive (Ostrogozhsk-Rossosh', Voronezh-Kastornoe, Khar'kov; 13 January–3 March 1943), 129

Operations, Military (Red Army by Soviet classification) *(continued)*
Voronezh-Voroshilovgrad defensive (28 June–24 July 1942), 126, 491, 518, 622, 645n.70
Vyborg (June–July 1944), 396
Western Ukraine defensive (22 June–6 July 1941), 125
Zhitomir-Berdichev offensive (24 December 1943–14 January 1944), 54, 108, 129, 525, 560
Zhizdra-Bolkhov offensive (5–14 July 1942), 31–33, 61, 81, 108, 145, 231, 243, 387, 489, 497, 509, 519, 638n.9, 645n.68, 647n.82, 648n.90, 666n.87, 709n.66
Operations, Military, by Soviet Partisans
"Concert," 639n.14
"Railroad War," 639n.14
Order and discipline, Red Army, 564–582
Orders, People's Commissariat of Defense (NKO)
No. 227 (28 July 1942) (*see* "Not a Step Back Order")
No. 306 (8 October 1942), 118
No. 325 (16 October 1942), 108, 118
Orel, 20, 43, 51, 59, 139, 169, 231
Orenburg, 414
Orlenko, Major General T. S., 514
Orsha, 56
Oslikovsky, Lieutenant General N. S., 520
OSOAVIAKHIM (Society for the Assistance to Defense, Aviation and Chemical Structuring of the USSR), Soviet, 314, 422, 688n.79, 688n.81
Overlord, Allied operation, 612

Pacific Ocean, 17–18, 25–26, 37, 49
Panfilov, Major General of Tank Forces A. P., 454, 522
Panov, Major General of Tank Forces M. F., 514–515, 522
Panzer groups, German
Second, 12, 16, 713n.105
Third, 18
Fourth, 18
Papivin, Lieutenant General of Aviation N. F., 533
Park, Pontoon-bridge, Soviet, 334, 341–342
N2P, 334
NPL, 334, 341
Parkevich, N. N., 521
Parkhomenko, Lieutenant General F. A., 509, 515–517
Parotkin, Lieutenant Colonel I. V., 460
Parsegov, Major General A. I., 507, 509
Partisan Movement. *See* Central Headquarters (Staff) of the (TsSHPD)
Patten, General George S., 525
Paulus, Field Marshal Friedrich, 47
Pavelenko, Lieutenant Colonel N. G., 460
Pavelkin, Major General of Tank Forces M. I., 513, 518
Pavlov, Colonel General D. G., 469, 482–483, 566, 704n.4, 704n.9, 705n.11, 715n.134
Pavlov, D. V., 440
Pavlov, Major General of Tank Forces P. P., 514, 518–519, 521
Pearl Harbor, 6, 17
Penal camps, 573. *See also* GULAG (Main Directorate of Camps), NKVD Vorkuta
Penal (disciplinary) [*shtrafnye*] units (battalions and companies), Soviet, 124, 383, 570–579
identified (1942–1945), 607, 726n.113, 727n.127
pay, 727n.128
strength of, 576–577, 589
People's Commissariat of Communications (NKS), 345–346, 423

People's Commissariat of Communications Routes (NKPS), 351–353, 423–434, 437, 458, 688–689n.88
People's Commissariat of Defense (NKO), 61, 64, 76–77, 79, 108–110, 118–121, 137–139, 153, 155, 157, 165, 180, 184–190, 216–241, 243, 247–251, 285–323, 333–340, 344–359, 371, 373–376, 380, 383, 394, 399, 403–446, 449, 452, 454–455, 461, 468, 470–475, 493, 504, 508, 529–531, 536–541, 545–548, 551–563, 565, 569–579, 610, 614–618, 656n.16, 656n.18, 660n.2, 666n.87, 667n.110, 668n.117, 669n.123, 669n.126, 671n.20, 672n.27, 674n.71, 677n.12, 677n.13, 677n.14
  weapons and ammunition supply procedures, 683n.5
People's Commissariat of Foreign Affairs (NKID), 370
People's Commissariat of Internal Affairs (NKVD), 124, 137–138, 157, 378–379, 383, 400–402, 422–424, 426, 430, 437, 446–449, 455, 475, 501, 530, 540, 545–546, 567, 572–573, 581–582, 616
  prewar chiefs, 697n.190
  prewar organization, 697n.189
People's Commissariat of Justice, 569–570
People's Commissariat of State Control (Narkom Gostkontrolia SSSR), 371, 378–379, 398
People's Commissariat of State Security (NKGB), 157, 168, 379, 402
People's Commissariat of the Navy (NKVMF), 137–138, 157, 159, 373, 396, 472
People's Commissariat of the River Fleet (NKRF), 426, 433
People's militia, Soviet, 400, 402, 422, 538, 540, 561, 655n.21
  mobilization of (in 1941), 717–718n.11
Peredugin, Major General F. T., 462
Peresypkin, Colonel General I. T., 345, 423–424, 688–689n.89
Pervushin, Major General A. N., 507
Petrov, Colonel General I. I., 496, 498–500
Petrov, Lieutenant General I. E., 513, 650n.115, 705n.11
Petrov, Lieutenant General M. P., 504, 513
Petrovsky, Major General S. A., 699n.206
Piadyshev, Major General K. P., 704n.4
Piatykhin, Lieutenant General of Aviation I. G., 532, 716n.137
Platonov, Lieutenant General S. P., 699n.206
Pliev, Lieutenant General I. A., 515–518, 520
Plushnin, Major General N. I., 682n.82
Podlas, Lieutenant General K. P., 508
Pogosov, Major General of Tank Forces A. K., 521
Pogrebov, Colonel V. A., 517
Point blocking commands *[komendatura]*, NKVD, 475
Points, PVO (air defense), 415
Poland, 5, 24, 185
Polar Star. *See* Demiansk-Pskov offensive *under* Operations, military
Polenov, Lieutenant General V. S., 509–510
Politburo, Communist Party Central Committee, 372–373, 381, 427, 430, 443–444, 447, 540, 549
Political Directorate of the RKKA (1921–1940), 443
Politruk(i) [political worker(s)], Communist Party of the Soviet Union, 380–382, 565, 573, 589, 616
Polotsk, 188
Polozkov, Major General of Tank Forces V. I., 514, 521–522
Poluboiarov, Major General of Tank Forces P. P., 408, 518–519, 522

Polynin, Lieutenant General of Aviation F. P., 533
Ponedelin, Lieutenant General P. G., 504, 704n.5
Ponomarenko, Lieutenant General P. K., 377
Popov, Lieutenant General M. M., 268, 482–485, 496, 508, 510–511, 523–524, 704–705n.11
  prewar service, 707–708n.53
Popov, Major General of Tank Forces A. F., 514–515, 518, 522
Postnikov, Major General K. V., 699n.206
Potapov, Lieutenant General M. I., 504–505
Potsdam Conference, July-August 1945, 392, 396
Prague, 5
Pravda, Communist Party newspaper, 398
Pripiat' Marshes, 709n.67
Prisoners-of-war, Red Army. *See* Red Army, losses
Prokhorovka, 82, 107, 244–245, 526, 648n.88
Pronin, Lieutenant General N. I., 504, 506
Pronin, Lieutenant General N. N., 422
Prosvirov, Major General N. A., 429
Protsvetkin, Major General of Artillery M. M., 531
Potachurchev, Colonel A. G., 514
Presidium. *See* Supreme Soviet, USSR's
Pshennikov, Lieutenant General P. S., 504
Pskov, 7, 44, 46, 390
Puganov, Colonel V. P., 514
Pukhov, Lieutenant General N. P., 508, 512
Pumpur, Lieutenant General of Aviation P. I., 715n.133
"Purge of the victors" (Stalin's 1945), 393, 401
Purges, Soviet military (Stalin's), 466–470, 537, 685n.33
Purkaev, Colonel General M. A., 488–489, 495–496, 498, 500–501, 508, 704–705n.11
Pushkin, Major General of Tank Forces G. I., 514, 518, 521–522

Quartermaster Academy of the Red Army, 443

Radio location stations (RLS), PVO VNOS system, 415
Radkevich, Major General N. N., 518
Radzievsky, Lieutenant General A. I., 715n.128
Railroad forces (troops), Soviet, 351–353, 427, 429
Rakutin, Lieutenant General K. I. (NKVD), 504–506, 653n.24
Rasputitsa [rainy season), 48
Rations, Red Army. *See* Food (forage) supply norms, Red Army
Rechitsa, 53, 56
Reconnaissance-in-force *[razvedka boem],* 119
Red Army (RKKA)
  air defense forces (*see* Air defense forces, Soviet)
  expansion (1939–1941), 590
  losses (personnel), 564–565, 588, 609, 620–623: by quarter, year, and cause 624; prisoners-of-war per month by OKW count, 625, 650n.1
  losses (weaponry), by type and year, 626–629
  military districts and non-operating *fronts* (*see* Military Districts and *Fronts*)
  operating army [*deistvuiushchaia armia*] (field forces), 137, 139–147
  strength and composition, 135, 138–140, 155–156, 538–540, 588, 619–620, 717n.8, 728n.162
Red Guards, 406, 419

Regiments, Soviet, 146, 288, 436, 660n.2
airborne, 411
antiaircraft artillery (light and medium), 228, 230, 233, 240, 291, 304–307, 415
antiaircraft machine-gun, 431: organization, 665n.83
antitank artillery, 184, 227–228, 230, 232–233, 240, 291, 295–297: quantity and location, RVGK, 325, 661n.30, 661n.32, 662n.33, 662n.34, 662n.36, 662n.37, 662n.38, 662n.39
army artillery, 290, 660n.2
artillery, 180, 219, 233, 286–291: quantity and authorized strength, RVGK, 324
artillery-mortar (cavalry), 240
automobile, 353, 356, 689n.102
auto (motor)-transport, 234, 428
aviation, 312–319, 669n.121
aviation (PVO), 415–417
aviation glider, 412
aviation liaison (PO-2), 232–233
aviation signal, 347
aviation transport, 412
cavalry, 238–241, 333
corps artillery, 286–288, 290, 292, 333, 660n.2
destroyer, 297
destruction (NKVD), 170
engineer, 333–334
engineer tank, 225: organization and strength, 253, 343
flamethrower (flame) tank, 348, 674n.71
gun artillery, 288–292
heavy antitank artillery, 296
heavy multiple-rocket launcher (guards-mortar; "*Katiusha*"), 308
heavy tank, 224: organization and strength, 253
high-power *[bol'shoi moshnosti]* howitzer artillery, 290–292
howitzer artillery, 232, 286–292
light artillery (antitank), 296–297
light cavalry, 239
mortar, 227–228, 292, 294
motorcycle, 218, 232–233, 235–236
motorized mountain mortar, 294
motorized rifle, 219, 333
mountain artillery, 182
mountain cavalry, 238
mountain mortar, 294
mountain rifle, 182
multiple-rocket launcher (guards-mortar; "*Katiusha*"), 232–233, 240, 308,-311, 665n.78: organization, 666n.96
naval infantry, 183
night bomber aviation, 669n.121
pontoon-bridge, 333–334, 342–343
railroad, 351–353, 429
rifle, 180, 302–304, 333, 347–350
rifle (NKVD), 168, 448
road (service) exploitation, 354–356
self-propelled artillery (mixed), 227–228, 230, 233, 240, 300–301
self-propelled artillery (SU-76 light), 227, 230, 233, 300–302
self-propelled artillery (SU-85, SU-100 medium), 230, 240, 301–302
self-propelled artillery (SU-122 medium), 227, 233, 300–302
self-propelled artillery (SU-152, ISU-122 heavy), 227, 230, 301–302
signal, 232–233, 344–347
special-power [*osoboi moshnosti*] artillery, 289, 292
tank, 217–219, 224–225, 228, 230, 233, 240: organization and strength, 253, 333, 539, 656n.16
tank (light) (cavalry), 238–239
tank destroyer artillery, 230, 233, 297–299: distribution, RVGK (15 November 1942), 326–327; distribution, RVGK (1 January 1943), 328; distribution, RVGK (31 December 1943), 329–330, 662n.40, 663n.41, 663n.46
tank penetration, 224

Regiments, Soviet *(continued)*
VNOS, 415
1st Belostok NKVD Motorized Rifle, 161
1st Women's Reserve Rifle, 721n.51
3rd Training Aviation (Separate), 316
4th Kiev NKVD Motorized Rifle, 160–161
5th Rostov NKVD Motorized Rifle, 160
6th L'vov NKVD Motorized Rifle, 161, 165
6th NKVD Border Guards, 166
13th Alma Ata NKVD Motorized Rifle, 160–161
14th NKVD Motorized Rifle, 161
15th Automobile, 689n.102
16th NKVD Border Guards, 167
16th NKVD Motorized Rifle, 165
18th NKVD Border Guards, 167
28th NKVD Motorized Rifle, 165
42nd NKVD Reserve, 653n.34
43rd NKVD Reserve, 653n.34
46th Guards Dive-Bomber Aviation (former 588th Night Bomber Aviation), 667n.107
55th Fighter Aviation, 667n.105
64th Fighter Aviation, 667n.105
65th Automobile, 689n.102
83rd NKVD Border Guards, 167
99th NKVD Border Guards, 166, 654n.38
101st Long-Range Aviation, 721n.51
104th NKVD Border Guards, 166
106th Automobile, 689n.102
106th NKVD Border Guards, 166
125th Guards Dive-Bomber Aviation (former 587th Night Bomber Aviation), 667n.107
127th NKVD Border Guards, 167
149th Fighter Aviation, 667n.105
157th NKVD Border Guards, 167
212th Long-range Aviation, 414
218th NKVD Border Guards, 654n.38
281st Special-power Artillery, 289
289th Guards Rifle, 721n.48
586th Fighter Aviation, 314, 551, 667n.107
587th Bomber Aviation, 314, 551, 667n.107
588th Night Bomber Aviation, 314, 551, 667n.107
Regions, PVO (air defense), 415
Ladoga, 418
Voronezh, 418
Reiter, Lieutenant General M. A., 488–489, 496, 508–509, 705n.11
Remizov, Major General F. T., 518
Revolution, Russian (February and October1917), 406
Revolutionary Military Council (REVOENSOVIET), 443
RGK. *See Stavka* Reserve
Riabyshev, Lieutenant General D. I., 482–483, 508–509, 513–514, 705n.11
Riga, 7
Road Construction and Repair Forces, Soviet, 353–365
Rodin, Lieutenant General of Tank Forces A. G., 518, 522–524, 714n.116
Rodin, Lieutenant General of Tank Forces G. S., 514–515, 518–519, 522
Rokossovsky, Colonel General K. K., 43, 150–151, 386, 468, 488–491, 494–496, 498, 505–506, 508–509, 513–514, 534, 577, 635n.6, 650n.115, 704–705n.11, 707n.42
prewar service, 709n.65, 709n.66, 709n.67, 709–710n.68
Romania, 5, 47, 58, 185, 527
Romanenko, Lieutenant General P. L., 468, 523–524, 705n.11
Rommel, Field Marshal Erin, 26, 38
Roosevelt, President Franklin D., 363n.25, 659n.60
Roslavl', 51, 581
Rostov (Rostov-on-the-Don), 13, 27, 29–30, 40, 42, 47, 66, 70, 73–74, 77–78, 85, 165, 400, 613

Rotmistrov, Lieutenant General of Tank Forces P. A., 518–519, 522, 524, 526–527, 534, 650n.113, 714n.116
Rudenko, Lieutenant General of Aviation S. I., 533–534
Rudenko, Major General of Tank Forces G. S., 521–522
Rudkin, Major General of Tank Forces F. N., 522
Rumiantsev, Major General A. D., 421, 553
Russian Civil War, 237, 386–387, 390–392, 394–397, 399, 404, 407, 411, 419, 423, 468, 478–480, 493–494, 498–500, 707n.53
Russian Liberation Army (ROA), 22, 467
Russiianov, Lieutenant General of Tank Forces I. N., 519, 522
RVGK. *See Stavka* Reserve
Rybal'chenko, Lieutenant General of Aviation S. D., 533
Rybalko, Colonel General P. S., 386, 523–525, 528, 534, 704–705n.11
Rybinsk, 399
Rychagov, Lieutenant General of Aviation P. V., 412, 685n.33, 715n.133
Ryshov, Lieutenant General A. I., 509
Ryzhov, Major General I. N., 699n.206
Rzhev, 20, 22, 36, 41, 43, 66
Rzhevskaia, Elena, 728n.161

Sakhalin Island, 154
Sakhno, Major General of Tank Forces M. G., 522
Samarkand, 405, 443
Samsonov, Lieutenant General of Artillery A. M., 460
Sapper forces, Soviet. *See* Engineer forces, Soviet
Saratov, 165, 336
Sazanov, Major General of Artillery S. S., 686n.44
"Second front" dispute, 50, 63
Sectors, (military) construction work (UVSRs), Soviet, 356–357, 359
Selivanov, Major General A. G., 517, 520–521
Semenchenko, Major General K. A., 514, 518
Serov, Lieutenant General I. E. (NKVD), 379, 401–402, 682n.85
Services, NKO
  Military Communications (VOSO), 351–352, 426, 430, 435, 455
  Military-Medical (VSS), 436, 439
  Military-Reconstruction, 352
  Military-Veterinary, 436, 442
  Railroad, NKPS, 432
  Road Construction, 353
Sevastopol', 23, 36, 67, 434, 499
Sevsk, 71, 74
Shamshin, Major General of Tank Forces A. A., 518, 522
Shapkin, Major General T. T., 517–518, 520
Shaposhnikov, Marshal of the Soviet Union B. M., 371–373, 376, 387, 389–391, 409, 468, 491, 581, 678n.25, 705n.25
Sharaburko, Major General Ia. S., 520
Sharapov, Lieutenant General V. M., 511
Sharogin, Major General A. P. 522
Shashkov, Z. A., 690n.113
Shavrov, Lieutenant General I. E., 408
Shchadenko, Lieutenant General E. A., 419, 421
Shcherbakov, A. S., 381, 399–400, 443–444
Shelepin, A. N., 402
Shestapalov, Major General N. M., 513
Shevnikov, Major General I. V., 514
Shilovsky, Lieutenant General E. A., 705n.25
Shilovsky, Lieutenant General Ia. A., 460
Shirmakher, Major General A. G., 682n.82
Shirobokov, Colonel M. V., 514
Shirshov, P. P., 690n.113
Shlemin, Lieutenant General I. T., 524
Shmuilo, Colonel S. T., 517
Shtal', Major General V. A., 468

Shtemenko, Lieutenant General S. M., 376, 392, 399–400, 408, 452, 485–486
Shtern, Colonel General G. N., 414, 416, 704n.9
Shumilov, Lieutenant General M. S., 509–510, 512
Shurov, Major General P. E., 518
Shvetsov, Colonel K. F., 514
Siberia, 154
Sicily, 48–49
Signal (Communication) Forces, Soviet, 343–347, 422–425
Simvolokov, Major General V. N., 513
Sinenko, Lieutenant General of Tank Forces M. D., 514–515, 518, 522, 714n.116
Siniavino Heights, 56
Skiarov, Lieutenant General A. V., 434
Skorniakov, Major General of Tank Forces K. V., 521
Skvortsov, Major General of Tank Forces B. M., 514–515, 522
Slavin, *Kombrig* [Brigade Commander] A. A., 428
Slavin, Lieutenant General N. V., 461, 703n.238
SMERSH [Death to spies] (Soviet Counterintelligence Directorate), 124
Smirnov, Colonel General of the Medical Services E. I., 436, 439
Smirnov, Lieutenant General A. K., 504
Smirnov, Lieutenant General I. K., 421
Smirnov, Lieutenant General of Aviation K. N., 533
Smirnov, Major General S. A., 706n.28
Smolensk, 7, 10, 20, 22, 51, 85–86, 88–89, 246
Smushkevich, Lieutenant General of Aviation Ia. V., 685n.33, 715n.133
Sobennikov, Lieutenant General P. P., 482–483, 504–505, 682n.82, 705n.11
Sochi, 418
Sokolov, Lieutenant General A. D., 513
Sokolov, Lieutenant General G. G., 508
Sokolov, Lieutenant General of Aviation I. M., 533
Sokolov, Major General A. Ia., 682n.82
Sokolov, Major General N. E., 699n.206
Sokolov, Lieutenant General S. V., 517, 520
Sokolovsky, Colonel General V. D., 496, 498, 650n.113, 650n.115, 704–705n.11, 709n.67, 709–710n.68
  prewar service, 711n.84
Soliankin, Colonel E. N., 514
Solnechnogorsk, 473
Solomatin, Lieutenant General of Tank Forces M. D., 514–515, 519, 522, 714n.112
Soviet-Finnish War, 1939–40, 216, 374, 386, 391, 394–395, 399, 404, 414, 436, 466, 479–480, 494, 537, 716n.137
SOVINFROMBURO (Soviet Information Bureau), 399
Sozh River, 12, 66, 96, 143, 151
Spanish Civil War, 216, 394, 468, 702n.231, 717n.7
Spas-Demensk, 51
SPETSNAZ (special designation reconnaissance and diversionary teams), 169, 453–454, 459
Squadrons, Soviet
  ammunition (cavalry), 239
  aviation, 312, 313–319
  aviation transport, 412
  cavalry (sabre), 238–240
  corrective aviation, 317
  chemical (cavalry), 239
  machine-gun (cavalry), 238–239
  medical (cavalry), 239
  sapper (cavalry), 238–239, 333
  signal (cavalry), 238–240, 344
  supply (cavalry), 239
  tank (light) (cavalry), 238–239

2nd Special Designation Aviation, 425
233rd Separate Aviation Liaison, 424
Stalin, I. (Joseph) S., 4, 6, 11, 13–17, 20, 22–24, 26–27, 30–31, 33–35, 41–42, 45–47, 49–50, 54, 58–60, 63–64, 67–68, 78, 122–124, 136, 148, 154, 157, 189, 216, 238, 304–305, 369–372, 374–375, 377–383, 385–387, 389–394, 396–404, 407–410, 412, 416, 419, 423, 430, 443, 449, 451, 460
purges, 466–470, 474, 476, 478–482, 488–490, 492–493, 496–497, 500–502, 505–506, 508–511, 513–514, 516, 526–527, 532, 534, 536, 541, 543, 546, 551–552, 558, 561–562, 564–571, 577, 582, 586, 609–611, 614–617, 631n. 4, 636n.25, 677n.14, 682n.85, 685n.33, 689–699n.203, 700–701n.219, 704n.5, 715n.133, 715n.134, 719–720n.30, 728n.149, 729n.1
Stalin (GKO) disciplinary decree, 16 July 1942, 568–569
Stalingrad, 17, 25, 27, 29–30, 34–35, 66, 69–70, 72, 74, 77–78, 163, 165, 231, 336, 434, 487–488
Staraia Russa, 44
Starikov, Lieutenant General F. I., 509, 512
Starkov, Colonel N. V., 514
State Control Commission, Soviet, 562
State Defense Committee (GKO), Soviet, 63–64, 124, 138, 148, 158, 163, 165, 300, 308, 310, 312, 314, 318, 335–339, 344–345, 353–359, 369–375, 378, 380, 382–383–384, 386, 399–400, 403–404, 410, 416–419, 421, 423, 427–430, 438, 441, 443, 448–449, 451, 453–456, 458–459, 462, 474, 539–540, 544–545, 547, 551–554, 558, 561–562, 566–569, 615–616, 665n.84, 677n.20, 679n.37, 679n.38
State Defense Plan 1941 (DP-41), Soviet, 11, 72–73
Stavka, Soviet, 10–11, 13, 16, 18, 22–24, 26, 30–31, 33–34, 36, 40–46, 48, 50, 53–54, 57, 59–63, 66, 68, 70–73, 75–100, 107–108, 110, 113–114, 118, 121–123, 136–137, 139–146, 151–152, 169, 178–179, 187–189, 225, 231–232, 240–246, 250, 285, 288, 290–291, 296–298, 309, 312, 315–317, 330, 335–337, 339, 341–343, 345–346, 351–352, 355, 369, 371
Stavka GK (Main Command), 372
Stavka VGK (Supreme High Command), 372, 373–375, 377, 380, 382, 386, 389–390, 392–397, 399, 403, 409, 413, 424–425, 427, 438, 449–451, 455, 457–458, 461–462, 470, 472, 474, 479–482, 485, 487, 491–492, 495, 499, 503–505, 508, 510, 512, 515–523, 532, 534, 541, 543–544, 566, 581, 610, 613–614, 616–618, 620, 631n.3, 633n.24, 635n.6, 637–638n.4, 638n.7, 638n.10, 639n.16, 640n. 24, 640n.25, 640n.29, 640–641n.30, 641n.32, 641–642n.47, 642n.50, 643n.52, 643n.54, 644n.55, 644n.56, 644n.57, 644n.62, 645n.66, 648n.88, 648n.96, 650n.113, 653n.22, 653n.24, 655n.18, 655n.21, 665n.80, 666n.90, 674n.71: specific duties, 676n.10, 678n.27, 701n.229
Stavka VK (High Command), 371
Stavka representatives, 60, 65, 89, 92, 123, 310, 372–373, 386, 388–390, 393, 396, 398, 402, 495, 501, 616, 641n.41, 701–702n.229
Stavka Reserve(s) (RGK, RVGK), 36, 70, 72, 91–92, 96–100, 135, 137, 140, 143–144, 149–152, 188, 230, 235, 285–294, 304–306, 310–312, 315–316, 372, 414, 507, 516, 519, 521, 635n.6, 639n.16, 643n.54, 644n.58, 645n.66, 646n.79, 649n.96, 653n.22, 660n.12, 660n.13, 666n.87

Strategic cooperation [*vzaimodeistvie*], 66–68
Strategic operations, Soviet, 69–96, 125–131, 450
  defensive, 69–82, 125–128
  offensive, 82–96, 128–131
Studnev, Colonel N. P., 514
Sudets, Lieutenant General of Aviation V. A., 533–534
Sukhinichi, 20
Sukhov, Major General of Tank Forces, I. P., 521
Suleikov, Major General of Tank Forces K. F., 521
Sumin, Rear Admiral V. I., 699n.206
Supreme Court of the USSR (Military Collegium), 383, 570
Supreme Soviet, (Presidium) USSR's, 371, 381, 383, 402, 475, 544, 548, 565, 570
Susloparov, Major General I. A., 703n.238
Svechin, Alexander, 645n.67
Sverdlovsk, 562
Sverdlovsk Communist University, 399
Sviridov, Lieutenant General K. Z., 519, 522
Sviridov, Lieutenant General V. P., 509

Tactics, Soviet
  defensive, 113–117
  offensive, 117–120
Taganrog, 70
Talensky, Major General N. A., 460
Taman' peninsular, 51, 55
Tamruchi, Major General V. S., 513
Tanaschishin, Major General of Tank Forces T. I., 518–519, 522
Tannenberg and the Masurian Lakes, Battle of (August–September 1914), 564, 566
Tarasov, Lieutenant General G. F., 510–511
Tashkent, 473
Tassigny, General Jean de Lattre de, 703n.238
Tatsinskaia, 519
Taursky, Major General of Aviation A. I., 715n.134
Teheran Conference (1943), Allied, 461, 479
Teliakov, Major General of Tank Forces N. M., 522
Teteshkin, Lieutenant General S. M., 452
Tikhvin, 165
Timofeev, Major General G. T., 517
Timoshenko, Marshal of the Soviet Union S. K., 15, 27, 35, 141, 371, 373–374, 386, 468, 478–482, 488, 495–497, 534, 537–538, 567, 650n.15, 702n.229
Tiulenev, Army General I. V., 482–483, 488–489, 495–496, 498–500, 508, 704n.9, 705n.11
  prewar service, 711n.86
Todorsky, Major General A. I., 468
Tolbukhin, Colonel General F.I., 495–496, 498–499, 510–511, 534, 704–705n.11
Tolubko, Lieutenant General of Tank Forces V. F., 408
Tomsk, 425
Torch, Allied operation, 37, 612
Training centers, artillery, Soviet
  Gor'kii, 298
  Moscow, 298
Training centers, guards-mortar, Soviet
  Moscow, 308
  Tatar, 308
Trans-Baikal region, 149, 154, 160
Trans-Caucasus region, 160, 166
Transport Committee, GKO, 430–431, 690n.113
Triandafillov, V. K., 392
Trofimenko, Lieutenant General S. G., 468
Trubetskoi, Lieutenant General of Technical Forces N. I., 352, 689n.96

Trufanov, Lieutenant General N. I., 510
Trufanov, Major General of Tank Forces K. G., 521–522
Truman, President Harry S., 392
Tsaritsyn (Stalingrad), 386, 419, 479–480
Tsibin, Colonel I. G., 514
Tsvetaev, Lieutenant General V. D., 510
Tsyganov, Lieutenant General V. S., 509
Tukhachevsky, Marshal of the Soviet Union, M. N., 391–392, 401, 478
Tula, 20, 165
Tunisia, 37–38
Turkestan, 399
Turkey, 153
"Turning points," in the Soviet-German War, 25, 38, 48, 59

Uborovich, *Komandarm* [army commander] 1st Rank I. P., 392, 478
Ufa, 473
Ukraine, 4–5, 10, 20, 46–47, 50–51, 53, 55, 58, 67, 143, 151, 163, 167, 461, 543–544, 633n.24
Ul'ianovsk, 336
Ul'rich, V. V., 402
United States of America, 6, 16–18, 25–26, 63, 249–250, 461
Universal Military Service Law (1925), Soviet, 717n.2
Universal Military Service Law (1 September 1939), Soviet, 419, 537, 548
Usenko, Major General M. A., 517
Utkin, Major General of the Quartermaster Service P. V., 692n.150
Utkin, Major General V. D., 699n.206
Uzbekistan, 408

Vasil'chenko, Major General K. F., 699n.206
Vasil'ev, Lieutenant General A. F., 703n.238
Vasil'ev, Lieutenant General of Tank Forces I. D., 522
Vasil'ev, Major General I. V., 514–515
Vasilevsky, Marshal of the Soviet Union A. M., 34, 69, 372–373, 376, 386–387, 389–393, 450, 452, 477, 491–492, 534, 619, 635n5, 641n.41, 680n.57, 681n.60, 681n.61, 702n.229, 704–705n.11
Vatutin, Lieutenant General N. F., 13, 371, 391, 452, 477, 483–484, 488–489, 491–492, 494–496, 619, 650n.115, 681n.61, 704–705n.11
  prewar service, 710n.72
Vazuza River, 714n.112
Vechnyi, Army General P. P., 459
Velikie Luki, 42–43, 57, 59, 66, 86, 501, 510, 543
Vershinin, Lieutenant General of Aviation K. A., 533–534
Vershinin, Lieutenant General of Tank Forces V. G., 407
Vershkovich, Lieutenant Colonel S. A., 518, 521
Viaz'ma, 10, 20, 22, 66, 336, 678n.27
Vienna, 5, 636n.25
Vilnius, 527, 650n.113
Vinnitsa, 53, 66–67
Vinogradov, Lieutenant General of Aviation V. A., 533
Vistula River, 525
Vitebsk, 4, 20, 46, 56, 66, 86, 90, 188, 390
Vlasov, Lieutenant General A. A., 22, 144, 401, 467, 506–508, 513, 517, 680n.52
VNOS (Air Observation, Warning, and Communications System), Soviet PVO (air defense), 148–149, 415–419
  women soldiers, 552

Vodka, Red Army rations, 557–560
by *front* on 25 November 1942, 559
as an offensive indicator, 724n.77, 724n.79
"vodka" holidays, 723–724n.74, 724n.75
Voeikov, Major General N. I., 514–515
Voennia mysl' [Military thought], Red Army General Staff journal, 459
Volga Germans, deportation of, 402
Volga River, 29–30, 32, 36, 74, 416
Volkhov River, 22, 224
Volkov, Lieutenant General of Tank Forces M. M., 518, 522
Vologda, 336
Volokolamsk, 20
Vol'sky, Major General of Tank Forces V. T., 519, 522, 705n.11, 714n.116, 714n.121
Volturno River, 49
Vorkuta, 545
Vorob'ev, Colonel F. D., 460
Vorob'ev, Lieutenant General of Coastal Services S. I., 440
Vorob'ev, Lieutenant General of Engineer Forces M. P. 341, 409–411, 462, 530, 671n.20, 704n.11
Voronezh, 29–30, 34, 40, 58, 70, 72, 74–75, 81, 139, 151, 165, 169, 231
Voronov, Colonel General N. N., 69, 371, 373, 387, 393–394, 404–406, 416–417, 462, 704n.9, 704n.11, 707n.41
Voronov, Major General of Aviation N. V., 699n.206
Voroshilov, Marshal of the Soviet Union K. E., 141, 370–371, 373–374, 386, 391, 478–480, 484, 650n.115
Voroshilov Academy of the General Staff (Higher Military Academy–1943), 62, 389, 391, 395, 472–473, 497
commandants, 705n.25
Voroshilovgrad, 29, 40
Vovchenko, Major General of Tank Forces I. A., 522
Voznesensky, N. A., 371, 692n.149
VSEVOBUCH (universal military education), Soviet system, 421–422, 688n.77
women trained by, 721n.51
"Vystrel" Infantry School (Courses), 392, 469, 472–473
chiefs, 706n.28, 707n.53

War experiences, collection and analysis of, Red Army General Staff, 376, 459–460, 473, 631n.1, 637n.31, 702n.231
Warsaw, 715n.128
Weapons and equipment, Soviet
aircraft, 312–319, 323, 668n.117: Soviet production, 669n.130
antiaircraft guns, 304–306, 321, 669n.123
antitank artillery, 320, 669n.123
antitank dogs, 194
antitank grenades, 194
antitank rifles, 193
armored cars, 250
armored personnel carriers, 250
artillery, 319–322
chemical (flame), 348, 364–365
engineer, 360–362
machine guns, 193
mortars, 319
multiple-rocket launchers (guards-mortars; "*Katiushas*"), 307–310, 321–322
pictures of, *following 332*
pistols, 191
rifles, 191–192
self-propelled (assault) guns, 300–302, 322, 669n.129
signal, 362–364, 676n.101
submachine guns, 192
tanks, 61, 246–250
trucks, 250–251
Western Dvina River, 7

White Sea, 418
Women, Service in the Red Army, 314, 347, 417, 538, 540, 551–554, 588, 721n.51, 722n.65

Yalta Conference (4–11 February 1945), Allied, 392, 396, 461, 636n.25
Yugoslavia, 15

Zakharkin, Lieutenant General I. G., 506, 511
Zakharov, Lieutenant General G. F., 482–483, 705n.11
Zakharov, Major General M. V., 692n.150, 704n.11
Zamiatkin, Major General N. M., 460
Zaporozh'e, 40, 51, 53
Zaporozhets, A. O., 379
Zashikhin, Lieutenant General of Artillery G. S., 418, 531, 715n.132
Zhadov, Lieutenant General A. S., 510–512, 517, 704n.11
Zhavoronkov, Colonel General, of Aviation S. F., 704n.11
Zhdanov, A. A., 371, 443, 680n.55
Zhidkov, Colonel P. K., 521
Zhigarev, Lieutenant General of Aviation P. F., 371, 412–413, 462, 704n.11
Zhitomir, 53, 560
Zhizdra River, 231
Zhlobin, Lieutenant General V. M., 452
Zhukov, Marshal of the Soviet Union G. K., 12, 15, 18, 21, 23–24, 32, 34, 42–44, 55, 69, 231, 371, 373, 376, 386–390, 393–394, 396, 398, 401, 403, 438, 459, 462, 468–469, 476–477, 479–480, 482–483, 485–486, 488–489, 491–494, 497–499, 501, 505, 534, 566–568, 633n.24, 635n.5, 641n.41, 650n.113, 650n.115, 678n.25, 680n.57, 704n.9, 704–705n.11, 707n.41, 708n.53, 709n.66, 717n.7, 725n.106
Zhukovsky Air Force Academy, 412
Zhuravlev, Lieutenant General E. P., 510
Zhuravlev, Lieutenant General of Artillery D. A., 531
  postwar service, 715n.132
Zhuravlev, Lieutenant General of Aviation I. P., 533
Zin'kovich, Major General of Tank Forces M. I., 521
Zones, PVO (air defense), Soviet, 148, 414–416, 418, 686n.44
  Central Asian, 416, 418
  Far Eastern, 416, 418
  Northern, 686n.44
  Northwestern, 686n.44
  Siberian, 416
  Southern, 686n.44
  Trans-Baikal, 418
  Trans-Caucasus, 416, 418, 686n.44
  Western, 686n.44
Zygin, Lieutenant General A. I., 511